Business and Law

Fifth Edition

Robert T. Cheng
B.Sc., J.D., M.Sc., LL.M., J.S.D.
Professor of Law and
Chairman of the Department of Law and Administration of Justice
at the Los Angeles City College

Robert D. Upp
B.S.J., M.A., M.S., J.D.
Professor of Law Emeritus, Los Angeles City College
Attorney at Law
Member of the California Bar

IN MEMORIAM
JORDAN L. PAUST (1915–1985)

who, through years of caring and devotion to his students, the law, democratic values and human dignity, continues to teach.

WEST PUBLISHING COMPANY
St. Paul   New York   Los Angeles   San Francisco

Composition: Parkwood Composition Services, Inc.
Copy editor: Deborah Cady
Interior design: Roslyn M. Stendahl, Dapper Design

COPYRIGHT © 1969, 1974, 1979, 1984 By WEST PUBLISHING COMPANY
COPYRIGHT © 1990 By WEST PUBLISHING COMPANY
50 W. Kellogg Boulevard
P.O. Box 64526
St. Paul, MN 55164-1003

All rights reserved

Printed in the United States of America

97 96 95 94 93 92 91 90   8 7 6 5 4 3 2 1 0

Library of Congress Cataloging-in-Publication Data
Cheng, Robert T.
    Business and law.—5th ed. / Robert T. Cheng, Robert D. Upp.
      p.   cm.
    Rev. ed. of: Business law / Jordan L. Paust, Robert D. Upp, John E.H. Sherry. 4th ed. c1984.
      ISBN 0-314-66495-5
    1. Commercial law—United States. 2. Trade regulation—United States. 3. Business enterprises—United States. 4. Law—United States. I. Upp, Robert D. II. Paust, Jordan L. Business law. III. Title.
KF889.C435   1990
346.73'07347.3067—dc20
                                                    89-39463
                                                    CIP

> **DEDICATION**
>
> Robert T. Cheng dedicates this book to his wife, Jennifer, who assisted him in this revised edition.

About The Authors

Dr. ROBERT T. CHENG is a lawyer and a businessman. He obtained his political science and law education in Europe, Asia, and subsequently in the United States, where he attended the University of Southern California and Yale Law School. In 1966, Yale University conferred on him its highest law degree of Doctor of the Science of Law (J.S.D.). Dr. Cheng practiced law for almost a decade and has been teaching law for an aggregate of eighteen years. He is presently Professor of Law and Chairman of the Law and Administration of Justice Department at Los Angeles City College, which department provides business law, paralegal, and police science courses. Dr. Cheng's business experience includes banking and finance, foreign trade, and real estate. He owned and presided over a real property holding company in Southern California that dealt with multi-unit commercial and residential properties.

ROBERT D. UPP received a B.S. in journalism from the University of Illinois and his J.D., M.S. in education, and M.A. in social science from the University of Southern California. He taught in the law department at Los Angeles City College for thirty years and is now Professor Emeritus at L.A.C.C. Professor Upp was named an outstanding educator of America for 1972. Licensed to practice law since 1949, he is a member of the California State Bar Association, the San Diego Bar Association, the Inter-American Bar Association, and the Judge Advocates Association. He is a long-time member of the American Business Law Association and of its Western Regional.

Professor Upp served with the Judge Advocate General's Corps of the U.S. Army, both on active duty and as an active reservist. During the Korean War he was War Crimes Historian and Legal Officer of the United Nations Command. His mobilization assignments included Chief of Foreign Law, Assistant Commandant of the JAG School, and Assistant to The Judge Advocate General of the Army. He retired with the rank of Brigadier General.

Contents in Brief

PART ONE
Law and the Courts 1

Chapter 1
Introduction to the Law 3

Chapter 2
United States Legal System 9

Chapter 3
Wrongful Acts in Business 37

Chapter 4
Government Regulation of Business 69

PART TWO
Contracts 95

Chapter 5
Making Contracts 97

Chapter 6
Other Basic Requirements 127

Chapter 7
Reality of Consent 149

Chapter 8
Formalities 167

Chapter 9
Interpretation and Third Parties 187

Chapter 10
Discharging the Contract 203

PART THREE
Agency 227

Chapter 11
Introduction to Agency Law 229

Chapter 12
Principal and Agent Relationship 249

Chapter 13
Agency and Third Parties 261

PART FOUR
Property 279

Chapter 14
Personal Property 281

Chapter 15
Multiple Ownership and Real Property 309

Chapter 16
Landlord and Tenant 331

PART FIVE
Law of Sales 349

Chapter 17
Sales (I) 351

Chapter 18
Sales (II) 373

CONTENTS IN BRIEF

Chapter 19
Product Liability 397

Chapter 20
Consumer Protection 423

PART SIX
Business Organizations 449

Chapter 21
Forms of Business Organizations and Partnership (I) 451

Chapter 22
Partnership (II) 475

Chapter 23
Corporation (I) 503

Chapter 24
Corporation (II) 531

PART SEVEN
Commercial Papers 561

Chapter 25
Negotiable Money Instruments 563

Chapter 26
Transfer of Money Instruments 597

Chapter 27
Presentment, Discharge, and Banking Procedures 623

Chapter 28
Payment Assurances and Documents of Title 649

PART EIGHT
Secured Transactions, Insurance, Bankruptcy, Estates and Trusts 675

Chapter 29
Secured Transactions 677

Chapter 30
Insurance 709

Chapter 31
Bankruptcy 733

Chapter 32
Estates and Trusts 757

Appendix A
The Constitution of The United States of America A-1

Appendix B
The Uniform Commercial Code A-11

Appendix C
Spanish Equivalents for Important Legal Terms in English A-155

Glossary G-1

Index I-1

Contents

Preface   xxi

PART ONE
Law and the Courts   1

CHAPTER 1
Introduction to the Law   3
Law Defined   4
Rules of Law   4
J*Middle Georgia Livestock Sales*itations   5
West Reporter System   6
Justice   7
Questions   7
Problems   7

CHAPTER 2
United States Legal System   9
2.1 Sources of Law   10
   The Constutition   10
   State Powers   10
   Judicial Case Law   11
      Stare Decisis   11
   Legislative Law   12
   The Uniform Commercial Code   12
   Executive Orders and Administrative Regulations   12
2.2 Court Systems   13
   U.S. Courts   13
      District Courts   13
      Appellate Courts   15
      U.S. Supreme Court   15
   State Courts   17
      State Trial Courts   17
      State Appeals Court   18
      State Supreme Courts   18
   Characteristics of U.S. Courts   18
      Parties   18
      Complaint   19
      Statute of Limitations   19
      Summons   19
      Answer   19
      Pretrial   19
      Depositions   20
      Interrogatories   20
      Admissions   20
      Pretrial Conference   20
      Subpoena   20
      Stipulation   21
      Evidence   21
      Direct Examination   21
      Final Argument   21
      Motions   22
      Appeal   22
      Mediation   23
      Arbitration   23
      Hearings   25
2.3 Administrative Agencies   26
   Powers   27
   Independent Agencies   28
   Rules   28
   Notice   29
   Due Process   29
      Hearings   29
      Findings   31
   Judicial Review   31
      Exhaustion of Administrative Remedies   32
      Final Order   33
   Freedom of Information   34
   Sunshine Act   34
   Privacy Act   35
   Questions   13, 26, 35
   Problems   35

CHAPTER 3

Wrongful Acts in Business   37

3.1 Ethics in Business and Law   38
   Ethics Defined   38
   Ethical Conduct in Business   38
   Lying   39
      White Lies   39
   Codes of Ethics   40
   Cost-Benefit Considerations   41
   Rules of Ethics   42
   Ethical Issues   42

3.2 Business-Related Torts   44
   Tort Defined   44
   Negligence   44
      Proximate Cause   45
      Contributory and Comparative Negligence   45
      Assumption of Risk   45
      Res Ipsa Loquitor   46
   Common Business Torts   46
      Malpractice   46
      Fraud   46
      Defamation   47
      Trade Libel   49
      Emotional Distress   49
      Invasion of Privacy   50
      False Imprisonment   51
      Assault and Battery   51
      Nuisance   51
      Conversion   52
      Trespass   52
      Interference with Contract   52
      Unfair Competition   53

3.3 Crime in Business   54
   Crime Defined   54
   Types of Crime   54
   Safeguards   55
      Fair Trial   55
      Presumption of Innocence   56
      Intent   56
      Criminal Negligence   56
      Illegal Evidence   56
      Corpus Delecti   57
   Defenses to Crimes   57
      Ignorance of the Law   57
      Mistake   57
      Infancy   58
      Insanity   58
      Intoxication   58
      Self-Defense   58
   Entrapment   58
   Double Jeopardy   59
   Statute of Limitations   59
   Immunity   59
   Common Business Crime   59
      White-Collar Crime   60
      Theft   60
      Robbery   61
      Burglary   61
      Receiving Stolen Property   61
      Assault and Battery   61
      Arson   61
      Misuse of Documents   61
      Forgery   62
      Counterfeiting   62
      Bad Checks   62
      Credit Cards   62
      Bribery   62
      Extortion   62
      Antitrust   63
      Income Tax Evasion   63
      Fraud   64
   Political Crimes   63
   Computer Crimes   64
   Organized Crime   64
   Conspiracy   65
   Solicitation   65
   Questions   44, 53, 66
   Problems   67

CHAPTER 4

Government Regulation of Business   69

4.1 Federal Regulation   70
   Commerce Clause   70
   National and State Regulations   70
   Taxation   70
   Antitrust Laws   71
      Sherman Act   71
      Clayton Act   74
      Federal Trade Commission   74
      Robinson-Patman Act   75

4.2 Environmental Protection   75
   Environmental Control Act   75
   EPA   76
   NEPA   76
   Clean Air Act   76
   Energy Act   77
   Clean Water Act   77
   Toxic Substances Control Act   77
   RCRA   78
   Superfund   78
   Marine Protection Act   78
   Nuclear Regulatory Commission   78
   Pesticide Control Act   79
   Endangered Species Act   79
   Noise Control Act   79

Surface Mining Act 79
Antiquities Preservation 80
4.3 **Employment Regulation** 81
Labor Relations 81
Norris-LaGuardia Act 81
Wagner Act 81
NLRB 82
Fair Labor Standards Act 82
Taft-Hartley Act 82
Landrum-Griffin Act 83
Employee Protection 83
Workers' Compensation 83
OSHA 84
Social Security 86
Medicare 86
ERISA 86
Unemployment Compensation 86
Employment Discrimination 87
Equal Pay Act 87
Equal Employment Opportunities Act 87
BFOQ 87
Sexual Harassment 88
Racial Discrimination 89
Age Discrimination 90
Pregnancy Act 90
Wrongful Discharge 90
Rehabilitation Act 91
Affirmative Action 91
Questions 75, 81, 92
Problems 93

PART TWO

Contracts 95

CHAPTER 5

Making Contracts 97

5.1 **Introduction to Contract Law** 98
Contract Defined 98
Elements of a Contract 98
Types of Contracts 98
5.2 **Reaching the Agreement** 101
Intent 101
Offer 103
Offer In Jest 104
Ads as Offers 104
Preliminary Negotiations 105
Offer Certainty 105
Rewards 106
Auctions 106
Sealed Bids 106
Sales of Personal Property 107

Duration of Offer 107
Illegality 108
Death and Insanity 108
Revocation by Offeror 108
Counteroffer 109
Rejection 110
Acceptance 110
5.3 **Consideration** 114
Benefit or Detriment 114
Gift 115
Unilateral Consideration 115
Bilateral Consideration 116
Illusory Offer 117
"Needs" Contract 117
Inadequacy of Consideration 117
Duty to Perform 118
Past Consideration 118
Moral Obligation 118
Liquidated Debt 119
Unliquidated Debt 119
"Paid In Full" as Accord and Satisfaction 120
Partial Payment 121
Promissory Estoppel 121
Justifiable Reliance 123
Executed Contracts 123
UCC Consideration Exceptions 123
Promise to Pay Debt of Another 124
Questions 101, 114, 124
Problems 125

CHAPTER 6

Other Basic Requirements 127

6.1 **Contractual Capacity** 128
Competency 128
Incompetence 128
Minors 128
Intoxication 132
Mental Incapacity 132
Aliens 133
Convicts 134
6.2 **Illegal Agreements** 134
Illegal Contracts 134
Divisible Contracts 134
Pari Delicto 135
Exceptions 135
Protected Classes 135
Simple Knowledge 136
Agreement to Commit a Crime 136
Torts 136
Sunday Laws 137
Repentance 137
Usury 138
Usury Exceptions 138

6.3 Public Policy   139
Gambling   140
Lottery   140
Insurance Contracts   141
Agreement Not to Prosecute   141
Suppression of Justice   141
Public Interest   141
Lobbying   142
Licenses   142
   Regulatory   142
   Revenue   142
   Substantial Compliance   144
Exculpatory Clauses   144
Promise Not to Compete   145
   Blue-Pencil Rule   146
Employment Restriction   146
Marriage Contracts   147
Questions   134, 139, 147
Problems   147

CHAPTER 7

Reality of Consent   149

7.1 Fraud and Misrepresentation   150
Fraud   150
   Material Fact   150
   Knowledge of Falsity   151
   Innocent Misrepresentation   151
   Intent   151
   Deceit   151
   Damages   151
   Fraud in Inducement   152
   Fraud in Execution   152
   Silence as Fraud   152
   Stipulation   153

7.2 Mistake, Duress, and Undue Influence   154
Mutual Mistake of Fact   154
Mistake of Value   154
Unilateral Mistake   154
Exceptions   156
Mistake of Law   156
   Mistake of Law Exceptions   156
Duress   156
   Economic Compulsion   157
   Threat of Criminal Prosecution   157
Undue Influence   158

7.3 Unconscionability   159
Definition   159
Element   160
Unequal Bargain Power   160
Disclaimer   160
Adhesion Contracts   161
Standard Clauses   161
Flexibility   162
Questions   153, 159, 163
Problems   163

CHAPTER 8

Formalities   167

8.1 Conditions   168
Condition Defined   168
Condition Precedent   168
   Express and Implied Conditions   169
   Promise to Pay   169
Condition Concurrent   169
Condition Subsequent   169
Covenants   170
   Good Faith   170

8.2 Statute of Frauds   171
Purpose of Statute   171
Writing   171
   Sale of Goods over $500   172
   Exceptions to Writing   172
   Minerals   174
   Timber   174
   Securities   174
   $5,000 Property   174
   Sale of Land   175
   Contracts of More Than One Year   175
   Contracts Performed Within One Year   176
   Employment Contracts   176
   Exceptions for Oral Contracts   176
Wills   177
Promise to Pay Another's Debt   177
Marriage as Consideration   179
Contract Modification   179

8.3 Parol Evidence Rule   180
Oral Negotiations and the Written Contract   181
The Rule as a Warning   181
Exceptions to the Rule   181
   Mistake of Fact   182
   Fraud   182
   Lack of Capacity   182
   Incomplete Contract   182
   Condition Precedent   182
   Conditional Clauses   182
Later Changes   183
Consideration   184
UCC Provisions   184
Questions   171, 180, 185
Problems   185

CHAPTER 9

Interpretation and Third Parties   187

9.1 Judicial Interpretation   188
  Court Interpretation   188
  Intent of the Parties   188
    Reasonable Interpretation   188
    Contract as a Whole   188
    Conflicts Within a Contract   189
    Usage and Custom   189
    Subsequent Conduct   190
  Party Causing Uncertainty   190
  Insurance Contracts   190
  Conflict of Laws   191

9.2 Third-Party Beneficiaries   192
  Donee Beneficiary   193
  Creditor Beneficiary   193
  Incidental Beneficiary   194
  Intended Beneficiary   194
  Change of Insurance Beneficiary   194

9.3 Assignments   195
  Assignable Contracts   195
  Delegation of Duty   195
  Express Provisions   198
  Employment Contracts   198
  Judgment   198
  Prohibited Contracts
  Effect of Assignment   199
    Liability of Assignor   199
    Liability of Assignee   199
  Acceptance by Assignee   199
  Right to Assurances   199
  Rights of Assignee   200
  Defense Waivers   200
  Priorities Among Successive Assignees   201
  Questions   192, 195, 201
  Problems   201

CHAPTER 10

Discharging the Contract   203

10.1 Termination   204
    Performance   204
    Payment   204
    Time of Performance   204
    Substantial Performance   205
    Personal Satisfaction   206
  Actions of the Parties   207
    Conditions   207
    Mutual Release   208
    Notivation   208
    Accord and Satisfaction   208
    Account Stated   208
    Material Alteration   209
    Prevention of Performance   209
  Impossibility   210
    Act of God   212
    Strikes and Other Hazards   212
    Act of an Enemy   212
    Destruction of Subject Matter   212
    Unforeseen Difficulty   212
    Commercial Frustration   213
    Disability or Death   213
  Operation of Law   214
    Bankruptcy   214
    Insolvency   214
    Statute of Limitations   214

10.2 Damages   215
  Compensatory Damages   215
    Construction Contracts   216
    Attorney's Fees   216
    Emotional Reactions   217
    Computer Error   218
    Loss of Profits   218
  Punitive Damages
  Liquidated Damages   219
  Late Payments   220
  Mitigation of Damages   220
    Goods and Services   220
  Interest   220

10.3 Equitable Relief   221
  Specific Performance   221
    Real Estate and Personal Property   221
    Personal Services   222
  Rescission   223
    Restitution   223
  Reformation   224
  Questions   215, 220, 225
  Problems   225

PART THREE

Agency   227

CHAPTER 11

Introduction to Agency Law   229

11.1 Nature of Agency   230
  Agency Defined   230
    Servants and Employees   230
    Independent Contractor   230
    Liability   230

11.2 Creation and Termination   234
  Capacity to Act as Agent   234

Creation 235
 Agreement 235
 Estoppel 235
 Implied Agency 236
 Ratification 237
 Operation of Law 238
Termination 238
 Agreement 238
 Contract Expiration 238
 Revocation 238
 Renunciation by Agent 238
 Option 239
 Operation of Law 239
 Death 239
 Insanity 239
 Bankruptcy 239
 Impossibility 240
 War 240
 Change in Business Conditions 240
Irrevocable Agency 240

11.3 Franchises 241
Definition 241
Legal Implications 242
Disclosure Acts 242
Control 242
 Lanham Act 242
 Determining Amount of Control 243
 Independent Contractor versus Agent 243
 Absence of Control 245
Franchise Contracts 246
Questions 234, 241, 246
Problems 246

CHAPTER 12

Principal and Agent Relationship 249

12.1 General Rules 250
General Agent 250
Special Agent 250
Power of Attorney 251
Durable Power 251

12.2 Duties of Agent 251
Duty of Care 251
Good Conduct 252
Duty to Inform 252
Accounting 252
Duty to Be Practicable 252
Obedience 253
Loyalty 253
 Dual Agency 254
Termination 254
Remedies of Principal 255
Defenses of Agent 255

12.3 Duties of Principal 256
Performance 256
No Interference 256
Duty to Inform 256
Accounting 256
Good Conduct 256
Duty to Indemnify 257
Compensation 258
Duty Not to Terminate 258
Agent Actions 258
Defenses of Principal 258
Questions 251, 255, 258
Problems 259

CHAPTER 13

Agency and Third Parties 261

13.1 Principal's Liability for Agent's Contracts 262
Types of Authority 262
 Express Authority 262
 Implied Authority 262
 Customary Authority 263
 Apparent Authority 264
 Ostensible Authority 264
Equal Dignities Rule 264
Delegation of Authority 265
Undisclosed Principal 265
 Election Rule 265

13.2 Principal's Liability for Agent's Torts 266
Scope of Employment 266
 Personal Business 267
 Substantial Deviation 268
 Business Disputes and Property Protection 270
 Fraud 271
Auto Statutes 272

13.3 Other Liabilities 272
Agent Liability 272
 Tort Liability 272
 Contract Liability 272
 Incompetency Nondisclosure 274
 Wrongful Receipt of Money 274
Third-Party Liability to Principal 275
 Contract Liability 275
 Tort Liability 275
Third-Party Liability to Agent 275
 Undisclosed Principal 275
 Intention to Bind Agent 276
 Agent as Assignee 276
 Wrongful Acts 276
 Agent as Bailee 276
Questions 266, 272, 276
Problems 276

PART FOUR

Property   279

CHAPTER 14

Personal Property   281

14.1 Acquisition of Title   282
- Property Defined   282
  - Tangible Property   282
  - Intangible Property   282
- Acquisition of Property Rights   282
  - Gift   282
  - Creation   284
  - Accession   287
  - Confusion   287
  - Possession   288
  - Operation of Law   290
- Fixtures   290
  - Trade Fixtures   291

14.2 Bailments   292
- Bailment Defined   292
  - Essential Elements   292
  - Distinguished from Sale   293
  - Distinguished from Pledge or Pawn   293
  - Distinguished from Lease or License   294
- Bailee's Duty of Care   294
- Sole Benefit of Bailor   294
- Mutual Benefit   294
- Sole Benefit of Bailee   294
- Liability Limitations   295
- Bailee's Lien   295
- Duty to Return Property   295
- Termination of Bailment   296
  - Performance   296
  - Agreement of Parties   296
  - Breach   296
  - Destruction of Property   296
  - Operation of Law   296

14.3 Special Bailments   297
- Liability of Hotel Keepers   297
  - Negligence   298
  - Theft   298
  - Baggage Lien   298
- Liability of Common Carriers   298
  - Exceptions to Absolute Liability   298
  - Termination of Strict Liability   299
  - Limited Liability   299
  - Passenger Safety   300
- Liability of Warehousepersons   301
  - Duty under UCC   301
  - Personal Property Lessor   301
  - Bailee Liability   302
- Liability of Parking Lot Operators   302
- Checkrooms   303
- Liability of Safe Deposit Box Lessors   304
- Container Contents   304
- Constructive Bailment   304
- Questions   292, 297, 306
- Problems   306

CHAPTER 15

Multiple Ownership and Real Property   309

15.1 Multiple Ownership of Property   310
- Types of Ownership   310
  - Tenants in Common   310
  - Joint Tenancy   310
  - Community Property   311
  - Tenants by the Entirety   311
  - Condominium Ownership   312
  - Cooperative   313

15.2 Real Property   313
- Real Property Defined   313
- Estates   313
  - Freehold Estates   314
  - Dower and Curtesy   315
- Easement   315
  - Appurtenant   316
  - Easement in Gross   316
  - Prescriptive Easement   316
  - Implied Easement   317
- License   317
- Operation of Law   318
  - Rights to Space   318
  - Riparian Rights   318
  - Lateral Support   318
  - Percolating Water   319
  - Zoning   319
  - Nuisances   321

15.3 Title Acquisition   321
- Government Ownership   321
  - Eminent Domain   322
  - Police Power   322
  - Zoning   322
  - Escheat   322
  - Homestead Laws   322
- Transfer of Title   323
- The Deed   323
  - Deed Elements   323
  - Quitclaim Deed   324
  - Warranty or Grant Deed   324
  - Delivery of Deed   324
  - Recordation   324
  - Title Insurance   325
- Transfer through Operation of Law   325

Forced Sale   325
  Adverse Possession   326
      License   326
  Transfer of Property by Death   326
      Will   326
      Intestate Succession   327
      Administration of Estate   327
  Transfer by Action of Nature   327
      Questions   313, 321, 328
      Problems   328

CHAPTER 16

Landlord and Tenant   331

16.1 Leasehold Tenancies   332
  Terminology   332
  Types of Leasehold Tenancies   332
      Estate for Years   332
      Periodic Tenancy   332
      Tenancy at Will   333
      Tenancy at Sufferance   334
  Termination of Lease   334
      Lease Terms   334
      Destructions or Loss of Premises   334
      Breach of Covenants   335

16.2 Covenants   335
  Common Covenants   335
      Rent   336
      Security or Cleaning Deposit   336
      Use of Premises   336
      Assignment or Sublease   337
      Quiet Enjoyment   338
      Full Enjoyment   339
  Exculpatory Clause   339
  Retaliatory Eviction   339
  Landlord's Remedy to Tenant's Breach   339
  Tenant's Remedy to Landlord's Breach   340
      Constructive Eviction   340
  Rent Control   340

16.3 Liabilities   341
  Modern Liability Laws   341
  Common Law Rule   341
      Landlord's Responsibility   341
  Tort Liability   344
      Due Care Test   344
      Tenant Liability   344
      Lessor Liability   344
      Duty to Repair   344
      Building Code Violations   345
      Latent Defects   345
      Maintenance   346
  Questions   335, 341, 346
  Problems   346

PART FIVE

Law of Sales   349

CHAPTER 17

Sales (I)   351

17.1 Concept of Sales   352
  Sale   352
      Definition   352
      Present Sale, Contract to Sell   352
      Bailment, Gift   352
      Option   352
      Bulk Sale   353
      Auction   353
      Conditional Sale   355
  Fungible Goods   355
  Merchant   355
  Contracts for Labor or Services   356

17.2 Title and Risk of Loss (1)   357
  Title Transfer   357
  Risk Transfer   358
  Parties' Own Rules   359
  Role of UCC   359
  Identification   360
      When Identification Occurs   360
      Identification and Buyer's Rights   361
      Identification and Seller's Rights   362
  Sale by Nonowner   362
  Resale by Fraudulent Buyer   363

17.3 Title and Risk of Loss (2)   363
  With Movement of Goods   363
      Shipment Contracts   363
      Destination Contracts   365
      C.O.D.   365
      Sale on Approval   366
      Sale or Return   366
      Consignment   367
      Auction   367
      Automobiles   367
  Without Movement of Goods   368
      With Document of Title   368
      Without Document of Title   368
  Questions   357, 363, 370
  Problems   370

CHAPTER 18

Sales (II)   373

18.1 Shipping Terms and Buyer's Performance   374
  Shipping Terms   374
      F.O.B.   374

F.A.S.   375
C. & F.   375
C.I.F.   375
No Arrival, No Sale   376
Ex Ship   376
Buyer's Payment   376
Tender of Payment   376
Installment Contract Payments   377
Payment and Inspection   379
18.2 Seller's Performance   380
Seller's Delivery   380
Duty to Ship   380
Tender of Delivery   381
Inspection, Acceptance, or Rejection   381
Perfect Tender Versus Substantial Performance   383
Seller's Right to Cure   383
Duties Upon Rejection   384
Substitution   385
Uncertainty of Performance   385
Goods in Possession of Seller   386
Goods with Bailee   386
Installment Contracts   386
Shipment with Reservation   387
18.3 UCC Remedies in Sales   388
Seller's Remedies   388
Withholding of Goods   388
Stop Carrier's Delivery   388
Identify Goods to Contract   389
Cancel the Contract   389
Reclaim the Goods   389
Resell the Goods   389
Recover Damages   390
Recover Contract Price   391
Buyer's Remedies   391
Recover Identified Goods   391
Replevin the Goods   392
Specific Performance   392
Cancel the Contract   392
Revoke Acceptance   393
Coverage   394
Price Reduction   394
Damages   395
Retain Security Interest   395
Questions   380, 387, 395
Problems   395

CHAPTER 19

Product Liability   397

19.1 Warranty (1)   398
Bases of a Claim   398
Injury   398
Negligence   399

Statutory Duty   400
Warranty Defined   400
Privity   400
Express Warranties   401
Affirmation or Promise   401
Description   403
Sample or Model   403
19.2 Warranty (2)   404
Implied Warranties   404
Title   404
Merchantability   405
Fitness for Particular Purpose   408
Exclusion, Modification, and Disclaimer   408
By Inspection: Express Warranties   409
By Inspection: Implied Warranties   409
Description Warranty   409
Trade Usage Warranty   409
Automobile Warranty   410
Family Use of Goods   410
Title Warranty   410
Merchantability Warranty   411
Particular Purpose Warranty   411
Other Ways of Excluding Implied Warranties   411
Notice of Defect   411
Contributory Negligence   412
Assumption of Risk   412
Statute of Limitations   412
Federal Consumer Protection   413
19.3 Strict Liability in Tort   414
Definition   414
Buyer's Advantages   414
Concept Elements   415
Unreasonably Dangerous   415
Defective Product   416
Liable Parties   417
Wholesaler   417
Suppliers of Parts   418
Secondhand Dealers   418
Lessor or Bailor   418
Seller of Real Estate   419
Services   419
Contributory Negligence   420
Assumption of Risk   420
Damages   420
Intentional Torts   421
Questions   404, 414, 421
Problems   421

CHAPTER 20

Consumer Protection   423

20.1 Advertising and Sales Practice   424
Advertising   424

CONTENTS

Advertising 424
    Deceptive Product Advertising 424
    Bait and Switch 426
Sales Practice 428
    Door-to-Door 428
    Referral Sales and Leases 430

20.2 Consumer Credit (1) 431
Credit Advertising 431
Equal Credit Opportunity 432
Credit Reporting 434
Disclosure of Credit Terms 436

20.3 Consumer Credit (2) and Other Consumer Legislations 439
Credit Cards 439
Balloon Payments 440
Credit Billing 441
Collection Practices 442
Consumer Defenses 444
Other Federal Legislation 445
State Legislation 447
Questions 431, 438, 447
Problems 447

PART SIX

Business Organizations 449

CHAPTER 21

Forms of Business Organizations and Partnership (I) 451

21.1 Business Structures 452
Basic Considerations 452
    Capital 452
    Creation and Duration 452
    Taxes 452
    Control 452
    Liability 453
    Transferability 453
Forms of Business 453
    Sole Proprietorship 453
    Partnership 454
    Corporation 455
    Joint Venture 455
    Cooperative 456
    Syndicate 456
    Joint Stock Company 457
    Business Trust 457
    Franchise 457
    Unincorporated Association 458

21.2 Partnership Formation 459
Partnership versus Corporation 459
Partnership Defined 460

Creation 460
    By Agreement 460
    By Estoppel 464
    Determining the Existence 464
Fictitious Name 465

21.3 Limited Partnership and Partnership Property 466
Limited Partnership 466
Partnership Property 470
    Capital 471
    Title 471
    Possessory Rights 472
    Assignability 472
    Execution, Charging Order 472
    Death of a Partner 473
Questions 458, 466, 473
Problems 473

CHAPTER 22

Partnership (II) 475

22.1 Powers, Rights, and Duties 476
Powers 476
    Management 476
    Agency Authority 477
Rights 479
    Capital Contributions 479
    Profits and Losses 479
    Reimbursement and Indemnification 479
    Bookkeeping and Accounting 479
    Information 480
    Possession 480
Duties 481
    Fiduciary Duty 481
    Full Time, Reasonable Care, and Obedience 482
    Good Faith and Loyalty 482

22.2 Liabilities 484
In Contract 484
    In the Name of Partnership 485
    Within Authority 486
In Tort 487
In Crime 489
Extent of Partner's Liability 489
    Incoming and Outgoing Partners 491
    Upon Dissolution 491

22.3 Dissolution and Winding Up 492
Causes of Dissolution 492
    Acts of the Parties 493
    Operation of Law 493
    Court Decree 494
Effect of Dissolution 494
    On Powers 494

On Rights and Duties   494
Continuing the Business   495
Dissolution Notice   495
    To Copartners   495
    To Third Parties   496
Winding Up   497
    Rules of Distribution   497
    Partnership Assets   499
    Capital Contribution   499
    Distribution in Kind   499
    Insolvency and Bankruptcy   500
Questions   484, 491, 500
Problems   500

CHAPTER 23

Corporation (I)   503

23.1 Nature and Types of Corporations   504
Nature   504
    Personality   504
    Legal Entity   505
Types   507
    De Jure   507
    De Facto   508
    By Estoppel   508
    Private versus Public   509
    Nonprofit   509
    Domestic versus Foreign   509
    Close Corporation   510
    Professional Corporation   510

23.2 Promoters, Formation, and Termination   511
Promoters   511
    Disclosure   511
    Promoter's Contracts   512
    Preincorporation Stock Subscription   512
Formation   513
    Articles and Certificate of
        Incorporation   513
    Bylaws   515
Termination   515
    Dissolution: Voluntary, Involuntary, Merger
       and Consolidation   515
    Winding Up   519

23.3 Corporate Powers and Shareholders   519
Powers of the Corporation   520
    Express   520
    Implied   521
    Ultra Vires   521
Shareholders   523
    Meetings   523
    Election and Removal of Directors   525
    Bylaws and Resolutions   525
    Unusual Matters   526
    Inspection of Books   526
    Shareholders' Actions   527
    Other Rights   528
    Shareholder Liability   528
Questions   510, 519, 528
Problems   528

CHAPTER 24

Corporation (II)   531

24.1 Corporate Management   532
Directors   534
    Qualifcations   534
    Term and Removal   534
    Compensation   534
    Functions and Powers   534
    Meetings   535
    Fiduciary Duty   536
    Liability   536
Officers   537
    Qualifications   537
    Term and Removal   537
    Compensation   537
    Functions and Powers   537
    Fiduciary Duty   538
    Liability   538

24.2 Corporate Finance   540
Stock   540
    Par and No Par Value   541
    Stockholders' Equity   541
    Kinds of Stock   541
    Market Value   545
    Book Value   545
    Liability for Shares   546
Bonds   546
Retained Earnings   546
Dividends   547
    Sources   547
    Declaration by Board   547
    Persons Entitled to Dividend   548
    Stock Dividend   549
    Stock Split   549

24.3 Stock Acquisition and Securities Regulation   550
Subscription and Transfer   550
    Negotiability   550
    Restrictions   551
Government Regulatory Policies   552
    Securities Defined   552
    Securities and Exchange Commission   553
The Securities Act of 1933   553
    Registration Statement   553
    Liabilities and Defenses   554
    Exemptions   555
The Securities Exchange Act of 1934   555

Prior Payment or Cancellation 619
Unauthorized Completion 619
Fraud in the Inducement 620
Relative Duress 620
Circumstantial Incapacity 621
Illegality as to Public Policy 621
Adverse Claims 621
Questions 605, 613, 621
Problems 621

CHAPTER 27

Presentment, Discharge, and Banking Procedures 623

27.1 Presentment and Notice of Dishonor 624
Presentment 624
  Who Presents 624
  To Whom Presentment Is Made 625
  Manner of Presentment 625
  Time of Presentment 625
  Place of Presentment 626
  When Presentment Is Excused 626
  Nonpayment 626
Notice of Dishonor 626
  Who Gives Notice 627
  To Whom Notice Is Given 627
  Form of Notice 628
  Time of Notice 628
  Protest 630

27.2 Discharge 631
Grounds for Discharge 631
  Payment or Satisfaction 631
  Tender of Payment 632
  Cancellation or Renunciation 632
  Impairment 634
  Reacquisition 635
  Material Alteration 635
  Certification 635
  Acceptance 636
  Unexcused Delay 636
Effect of Discharge 636

27.3 Banking Procedures 636
The Depositary Bank 637
  Endorsements 638
  Depositor's Warranties 638
  Presentment 639
  Notice of Dishonor and Charge-Back 639
  Bank as H.D.C. and Its Security Interest 641
The Payor Bank 641
  Promptness and Due Care 641
  Signature Card 642
  Overdraft 642

Stop Payment 642
Termination of Bank's Authority 644
Customer's Duty 644
Bank's Recovery Rights 645
  Subrogation 645
  Other Recoveries 646
Electronic Banking 646
  Types of Transfers 646
  Procedural Provisions 646
  Liability Limitations 647
Questions 630, 636, 647
Problems 647

CHAPTER 28

Payment Assurances and Documents of Title 649

28.1 Letters of Credit (I) 650
Basic Concept 650
  Letter of Credit Defined 650
  Negotiability 650
  A Guaranty? 650
The Parties 653
  Account Party 653
  Issuer 653
  Advising Bank 653
  Confirming Bank 654
  Paying Bank and Negotiating Bank 654
  A Beneficiary 654
Contractual Bases 654
Governing Law 655
Form 656
  Self-Containing Document 656
  Duration 656
Types of Letters of Credit 656

28.2 Letters of Credit (II) and Bankers' Acceptances 657
Liabilities 657
  Transferability 658
  Documentary Draft 658
  Payment 659
  Reimbursement 660
Account Party's Remedies 660
Bankers' Acceptances 661
  Definition 661
  Form 662
  Liabilities 662
  Acceptance Financing 663
  Eligible Acceptances 665

28.3 Documents of Title 665
Definitions 666
  Bill of Lading 666
  Warehouse Receipt 667

Transferability 667
    Documentary Collection 667
    Duly Negotiated 668
    Unduly Negotiated 668
Liability 669
    On Warranties 669
    Bailee's Liability 669
Questions 657, 665, 672
Problems 672

PART EIGHT

Secured Transactions, Insurance, Bankruptcy, Estates and Trusts 675

CHAPTER 29

Secured Transactions 677

29.1 Security Interest in Real Estate 678
Unsecured Credit 678
Secured Credit 678
Real Estate Security Devices 679
Mortgage 679
    Form 679
    Transfer of the Property 680
    Collateral Impairment 680
    Foreclosure 680
Deed of Trust 681
    Form 684
    Property Transfer and Impairment 684
    Foreclosure 684
Land Contract 685
    Form 685
    Transfer by Vendor 687
    Transfer by Vendee 687
    Default 687

29.2 Security Interest in Personal Property (I) 689
Creation of Security Interest 690
Possession 690
Security Agreement 691
Attachment 694
    Value 694
    Debtor's Right in the Collateral 694
Perfection 695
    By Attachment 696
    By Possession 697
    By Filing a Financing Statement 697

29.3 Security Interest in Personal Property (II) 699
Priorities 699
    Between Perfected Interests 700
    Between Perfected and Unperfected Interests 700
    Between Nonperfected Interests 701
    After-acquired Property 701
    Purchase Money 701
    Future Advances 703
    Special Priorities 703
    State Regulation 704
Default of the Debtor 704
    Remedies 704
    Secured Party's Right to Possession 704
    Sale of Collateral 705
    Distribution of Proceeds 706
Questions 689, 699, 706
Problems 706

CHAPTER 30

Insurance 709

30.1 Insurance Concept (I) 710
Regulatory Authority 710
Insurance Company 710
The Insurance Contract 710
    Binder 711
    Interpretation 711
    Modification 714
Agents and Brokers 714
Premium 715

30.2 Insurance Concept (II) and Life Insurance 716
Commencement 716
Termination 718
    Lapse 718
    Cancellation 718
Claim and Coverage 718
Life Insurance 719
    Types of Policies 719
    Beneficiary 720
    Insurable Interest in Life Insurance 720
    Incontestability 722
    Surrender and Cancellation 723

30.3 Property and Liability Insurance 723
Insurable Interest in Property Insurance 724
Fire Insurance 725
    What Is Covered 725
    Who Is Covered 725
    Extent of Coverage 727
Automobile Insurance 728
    Collision Coverage 728
    Liability Coverage 729
Questions 716, 723, 731
Problems 731

CHAPTER 31

Bankruptcy   733

31.1 Chapter 7 (Part I)   734
    Legislative Policies   734
    Bankruptcy Regulation and Bankruptcy Courts   735
    Chapter 7: Liquidation   736
        Voluntary Bankruptcy   736
        Involuntary Bankruptcy   737
        Automatic Stay   739

31.2 Chapter 7 (Part II)   740
    Liquidation Continued   740
        Trustee Appointment   740
        Trustee's Duties   740
        Exemptions   741
        Voidable Transfers   742
        Provable Claims   743
        Distribution of Proceeds   743
        Discharge   744
        Reaffirmation   746

31.3 Chapters 11, 12, and 13   747
    Chapter 11   747
        Petition   747
        Proceeding   749
        The Plan   749
        Confirmation   749
        Discharge   750
    Chapter 13   751
        Petition and Proceeding   751
        The Plan   751
        Confirmation   751
        Discharge   753
    Chapter 12   753
        Who May Petition   754
        Proceeding   754
    Questions   740, 746, 754
    Problems   754

CHAPTER 32

Estates and Trusts   757

32.1 The Will   758
    Estate Planning   758
    Will Defined   758
    Validity Requirements   759
        Testamentary Capacity   759
        Testamentary Intent   760
        Proper Execution   760
    Forms of Wills   761
        Holographic Wills   761
        Nuncupative Wills   762
        Modification   762
        Revocation   762
    Testate Distribution   763
        Contesting a Will   764

32.2 Intestate Succession and Estate Administration   765
    Heirs   765
    Intestate Distribution   767
        Distribution per Stirpes   767
        Distribution per Capita   767
    Probate   768
        Admitting a Will   768
        Representation   768
        Priority of Liabilities   770

32.3 Trusts   771
    Trust Defined   771
    Express Trusts   772
        Validity Requirements   772
        Types of Trusts   773
        Form   776
        Trustee's Powers   777
        Trustee's Duties   777
        Beneficiary   778
        Remedies   778
        Termination   779
    Implied Trusts   779
        Resulting Trusts   779
        Constructive Trusts   779
    Questions   765, 771, 780
    Problems   780

Appendix A   The Constitution of the United States of America   A-1
Appendix B   The Uniform Commercial Code   A-11
Appendix C   Spanish Equivalents for Important Legal Terms in English   A-155
Table of Cases   TC-1
Glossary   G-1
Index   I-1

Preface

Law for business is of ever-increasing importance. Changing government policies and regulations, the proliferation of legislation, and the growing accumulation of reported court decisions have resulted in a vast body of legal principles and rules of law that govern our modern society in general and the business world in particular. Aware of this, the authors have sifted through the voluminous amounts of available material to extract and focus upon those points deemed most relevant to the businessperson.

Objectives

Business law is basically a conglomerate of the applicable legal tenets and rules of law. Since the field of business covers an enormous area and since the study of business consists of many segments, including management, marketing, accounting, banking, finance, personnel administration, and international trade, the variety of topics to be included in a textbook—as well as the depth to which they should be discussed—will always be subject to debate. In determining which critical areas of law to include in this work, the authors were guided by their teaching experience and law practice, by a nationwide survey of business law instructors conducted by West Publishing Company, and by the advice of numerous consultants. The end result is a compromise that caters to all students in the various areas of business. The authors realize that there may be some discussions in the book that overshoot a specific instructional need, in which event, the topic or portions thereof can be skipped at the instructor's discretion.

Since the book is essentially written for undergraduate students in four and two year colleges and universities, simplicity in presentation and language has been stressed. Indeed, it is easy to make simple things in law intricate and difficult to understand. On the other hand, it is a challenge to try to explain abstract and often illusive legal concepts in a concise and easy fashion. This fifth edition is written in such a way that the beginning college student should be able to understand it. The authors have tried to make the book interesting and one that states the important points of law in a clear and direct manner.

Organization

This revised edition has thirty-two chapters. Each chapter except the first has three subchapters, and each subchapter has subheadings for easy reference as well as marginal definitions of the legal concepts being discussed. An attempt has been made to attain some organizational uniformity throughout the text. The book can be used for a two-semester course: Law 1 to cover Chapters 1 through 16, and Law 2 to cover Chapters 17 through 32. Each half of the book, consisting of sixteen chapters, can be covered in sixteen teaching weeks, one chapter for each week of three class hours, one subchapter for each hour.

Each subchapter ends with five questions to check the reader's understanding of the material in the subchapter. At the end of each chapter there are ten situational problems to challenge the reader's grasp of the area of law being studied. These problems are practical examples of both true and hypothetical events. Answers to the questions and problems are provided in the instructor's manual, which includes the answers to the questions in the student's study guide and a test bank containing true/false and multiple-choice questions.

The student study guide is a valuable teaching aid. Not only does it provide a variety of tests to monitor the learner's knowledge of the material, it also is an effective tool to stimulate interest and motivation. Based on each chapter, the study guide has true/false, short essay, and multiple-choice questions.

Contents

All of the material of the previous edition has been completely overhauled, Chapters 1–16 by Professor Upp and Chapters 17–32 by Dr. Cheng. In addition to updating the existing text and cases, the authors have added new material. The first chapter has been rewritten to present an introductory look at the law and how the law applies to society and to business. It is tailored to fit the first class meeting for a beginning student and concludes with some controversial legal problems that demonstrate how the law may be changed by the courts. Chapter 2 combines the materials of Chapters 2, 3, 4, and 5 of the previous edition, with an updated and more detailed look at the ever-expanding field of administrative law. Chapter 3 adds a new subchapter on business ethics to the coverage of torts and crimes. Chapter 4 discusses the increasing importance of government regulation of business.

The material on contracts, which made up eleven chapters in the fourth edition, has been reorganized, updated, and condensed into six chapters. A subchapter on franchises has been added to agency law because of the many current legal issues in this area.

Chapter 24 on corporations now includes an expanded discussion of securities regulation. The information about commercial papers and money instruments in Chapters 25, 26, and 27 has been rewritten to make the subject matter more understandable. Electronic banking has been inserted in the discussion of banking procedures in Subchapter 27.3. The new coverage of bill of exchange in Subchapter 25.1, letters of credit and acceptances in Subchapters 28.1 and 2, and bill of lading in Subchapter 28.3 should be of special interest to the foreign trade student. Finally, Chapter 30 on insurance and Chapter 32 on estates and trusts are new chapters added to this edition. Chapter 31 on bankruptcy has been updated to include the Family Farmer Bankruptcy Act of 1986.

To facilitate the learning process, this revision offers an abundance of illustrative cases, explanatory diagrams, and form examples that are used in actual practice. Improvement, of course, is always possible. For this reason, the authors invite and would appreciate the reader's advice regarding any corrections or suggestions for the enhancement of future editions.

To avoid comments of sexism, the previous edition had many "his or her" and "he or she" terms to prevent gender bias. In this fifth edition, an attempt has been made to avoid gender references, but when not feasible, the singular pronoun "he" and the adjective "his" have been used. Such usage is common in statutes, legal definitions, and case opinions. The use of the masculine as a generic singular gender is not meant to offend any of our readers but rather to eliminate awkwardness that an extensive use of "he or she" often presents.

Cases

The increased number of cases selected from decisions by courts throughout the United States, are fully integrated into the text to focus at once on the legal concept discussed. Many of these cases are summarized, showing in an edited version only the facts and the court decisions. For the student to gain familiarity with the legal lingo, some cases are presented in the original court language in a compressed format.

Since the cases used are purely exemplary in function, their selection is based primarily on their suitability as a learning tool. Relevancy to the text, interesting factual situations, and ease in understanding the issues were the most important criteria used in making the selections. Such cases should leave a more lasting impression in the student's mind. As a result, on occasion, instead of using a more recent example, an earlier or classic case may be featured because of its propriety for the pertinent text.

Acknowledgments

In completing this fifth edition, the authors have received valuable contributions and indispensable assistance for which they wish to express their gratitude.

First, to all the students for whom this textbook is written and the instructors and professors who adopt it.

Second, to our editor, Susan J. Tubb, who effectively supervised the entire project, to our production editor, Stacy M. Lenzen, who very skillfully coordinated all the aspects of this work in the various production stages, to our copy editor, Deborah Cady, who provided most valuable editing and proofing services, to our promotion manager, Beth Hoeppner, who expertly handled the promotion of this book, and to the many others at West Publishing Company who helped to bring this revision into its final form.

Third, to the very able reviewers and readers of this book for their encouraging compliments and helpful comments. They include Professor Dennis Carluzzo of Georgetown University; Professor Andrew Tobia of Sacramento Community College; Professor Ken Sanford of SUNY-Binghamton; Professor Dan Van Thiel of Clatsop Community College; Professor James E. Walsh of Tidewater Community College; Professor Mary Ellen Perri of SUNY-Farmingdale; Professor Noel McKeon of Florida Junior College; Professor Alan Lawson of Ferris State University; Professor Paul D. Cummings of L.A.C.C.; Professor John C. Weaver of L.A.C.C.; Sterling Professor Emeritus Myres S. McDougal of Yale Law School; and Professor W. Michael Reisman of Yale Law School.

Fourth, to the First Interstate Bank of California for allowing us to use its bank forms in this revision.

Fifth, to our friends for their generous contribution to the popularity of this textbook: the law faculty of Los Angeles City College; Professor Mary E. Pangonis of Los Angeles Valley College; Professor Emeritus Carl Ross of Southwest College; Professor L. Edmund Kellogg, practicing attorney; Professor Jordan J. Paust of University of Houston; Judge George Kalinski; Administrative Law Judge Ben L. O'Brien; and many others.

PART ONE

Law and the Courts

CHAPTER ONE
Introduction to the Law

CHAPTER TWO
United States Legal System

CHAPTER THREE
Wrongful Acts in Business

CHAPTER FOUR
Government Regulation of Business

CHAPTER ONE

Law and the Courts

Law and the Courts may seem like a broad topic with which to introduce a course in business law, but today it is impossible to separate business from the legal environment in which it operates. Federal, state, and local laws now reach most activities, business or social. Governmental agencies and their numerous regulations impact on most transactions. Anyone serious about a career in business should realize that a knowledge of the law and its operation is an important step towards success.

In Part I we discuss the law in general and the systems under which it operates in the United States. Chapter 1 defines law and points out its flexibility to meet changing business patterns and expectations. Two cases are presented, one in the Court's language and one capsulated by the authors, to demonstrate how the Court makes such changes. Several controversial problems are posed to the student for personal judicial decisions.

Chapter 2 lists and analyzes the various sources of the law, and the available forums for the settlement of disputes. Legal procedures are explained and the modern importance of administrative law is examined. The chapter closes with a discussion of the requirements for judicial review of agency decisions and the legislative efforts to assure public disclosure of governmental records while also protecting personal privacy.

Chapter 3 takes up the problems of wrongful acts done in the conduct of business. In addition to an analysis of the most common types of crimes and civil wrongs, or torts, committed in the course of business operations, a new section has been added on ethics. Improper conduct which might not lead to criminal prosecution may still be considered unethical. Ethics is of major concern today in both business and government with efforts being made to establish codes defining proper behavior.

Chapter 4, the last one in Part I, considers the issue of government regulation of business. The proliferation of regulating agencies and the growing accumulation of regulations made to accomplish agency missions have placed a heavy burden on businessmen. Since "ignorance of the law" is not considered a valid excuse in most dealings, and the failure to file required forms or reports can lead to criminal sanctions, anyone interested in business activities needs to be aware of these restrictions.

CHAPTER ONE

Introduction to the Law

Law Defined

Rules of Law

Citations

West Reporter System

Justice

Law Defined

Law
The body of rules of conduct expected to be followed in an organized society.

Defined simply, law is the body of rules by which we are supposed to live in an organized society. In most countries, these rules are enforced through the courts, backed by the power of the government to force compliance. The threat of such power is usually enough to cause observance of the law. Laws reflect the group's idea of right and wrong.

In the United States, the law is binding on artificial persons, such as corporations, as well as on living persons. So the general laws, such as those concerning property and contracts, apply to all. Antitrust laws are examples of rules that relate only to business. Security regulations, environmental protection acts, and discrimination laws are among those created in response to changing business activities.

Antitrust Laws
Laws designed to protect commerce from unfair trade practices and monopolies.

It is an obvious fact that in the modern business environment knowledge of the pertinent law and its application is essential. Many companies employ full-time house counsel or retain lawyers for advice to avoid future problems.

Counsel
The terms counsel, counselor, attorney, and lawyer are used interchangeably to refer to a person representing another in legal matters.

Imagine the chaos in our society if each of use had complete freedom to act as we pleased. Envision the confusion that would result if anyone could drive an auto on either side of the road at any time or ignore business contracts at will. How could business be conducted if each enterprise had a different set of rules to determine whether it was bound to buy or sell materials? If there were no penal or consumer laws for the protection of the individual from illegal practices, think of the resulting unrest.

Rules of Law

Rules of law must be flexible to meet new social needs and to reflect changing business patterns and expectations. Automobiles caused the creation of an entirely new body of law, the Motor Vehicle Code. With increased power, speed, and numbers, the rules had to be changed to meet the problems. Pollution and safety concerns have resulted in even more controls. Changing patterns and goals of our society have spawned new laws relating to a number of fields, including human rights, Social Security, food and drugs, welfare, unemployment compensation, zoning, space, and computer technology.

Case Brief
An outline of a reported law case which includes the facts, issue, Court decision, and reason.

The following famous case is an example of how the U.S. Supreme Court may alter a rule of law to conform to changing social conditions and attitudes. The example is given in the words of the Court's opinion, abridged by the authors. Students should analyze cases that appear throughout the book. They should outline the cases by selecting the facts presented, the issue that the Court must decide, the Court's decision, and the reasoning to support the decision. Such an analysis is called a case brief.

Brown v. Board of Education
347 U.S. 483, 74 S.Ct. 686, 98 L.Ed. 873 (1954).

Mr. Chief Justice Warren   delivered the opinion of the Court.

In each of the cases, minors of the Negro race, through their legal representatives, seek the aid of the courts in obtaining admission to the public schools of their community on a nonsegregated basis. In each instant, they had been denied admission to schools attended by white children under laws requiring or permitting segregation according to race. This segregation was alleged to deprive the plaintiffs of the equal protection of the laws under the Fourteenth Amendment. In each of the cases other than the Delaware case, a three-judge federal district court denied relief to the plaintiffs on the so-called "separate but equal" doctrine announced by this Court in *Plessy* v. *Ferguson*, 163 U.S. 537, 16 S.Ct. 1138, 41 L.Ed. 256. . . . Under that doctrine, equality of treatment is accorded when the races are provided substantially equal facilities, even though these facilities be separate.

The plaintiffs contend that segregated public schools are not "equal" and cannot be made "equal" and that hence they are deprived of the equal protection of the laws. . . .

In approaching this problem, we cannot turn the clock back to 1868 when the amendment was adopted, or even to 1896 when *Plessy* v. *Ferguson* was written. We must consider public education in the light of its full development and its present place in American life throughout the Nation. Only in this way can it be determined if segregation in public schools deprives these plaintiffs of the equal protection of the laws.

Today, education is perhaps the most important function of state and local governments. Compulsory school attendance laws and the great expenditures for education both demonstrate our recognition of the importance of education to our democratic society. It is required in the performance of our most basic public responsibilities, even service in the armed forces. It is the very foundation of good citizenship. Today it is a principal instrument in awakening the child to cultural values, in preparing him for later professional training, and in helping him to adjust normally to his environment. In these days, it is doubtful that any child may reasonably be expected to succeed in life if he is denied the opportunity of an education. Such an opportunity, where the state has undertaken to provide it, is a right which must be made available to all on equal terms.

We come then to the question presented: Does segregation of children in public schools solely on the basis of race, even though the physical facilities and other "tangible" factors may be equal, deprive the children of the minority group of equal educational opportunities? We believe that it does. . . .

Whatever may have been the extent of the psychological knowledge at the time of *Plessy* v. *Ferguson*, this finding is amply supported by modern authority. [Footnote citing psychologists, sociologists.] Any language in *Plessy* v. *Ferguson* contrary to this finding is rejected.

Citations

All U.S. Supreme Court decisions are published, as are most of the important decisions from federal and state appellate courts. The numbers and letters found after the case names are called citations and indicate where the

Citation
As used here, it refers to the book, volume, and page where one can find the reported Court decision of a case.

decision can be found. This case, for example, can be found in volume 347 (the first number) of *United States Reports* (the letters U.S.) beginning at page 483 (the last number). It can also be found in volume 74 of *The Supreme Court Reporter* (S.Ct.) at page 686, and in volume 98 of *Lawyers Edition* (L.Ed.) at page 873. *Lawyers Edition* is now in its second series and these newer volumes are cited as L.Ed.2d.

Other Federal Court decisions are found in the *Federal Reporter* (Fed. or F.2d), *Federal Supplement* (F.Supp.), or *Federal Rules Decisions* (F.R.D.).

West Reporter System

West Reporter System
Volumes printed by West Publishing Company wherein all reported court decisions can be found.

West Publishing Company publishes the National Reporter System, which reports the state cases by geographical areas: Atlantic (A. or A.2d), Southeastern (S.E. or S.E.2d), Southwestern (S.W. or S.W.2d), Northwestern (N.W. or N.W.2d), Northeastern (N.E. or N.E.2d), Southern (So. or So.2d), and Pacific (P. or P.2d). Although New York is included in the Northeastern area and California is included in the Pacific area, cases from these two states are also reported separately and respectively in *New York Supplement* (N.Y.S.) and *California Reporter* (C.R.).

Some students are frustrated because of the confusion and uncertainty in the law. Since the law changes continually, it is often necessary to research a rule before using it to determine whether or not it has been changed or modified by legislative action, administrative regulation, or court interpretation. All contested legal issues have at least two sides, and each problem may have several answers depending upon the specific facts, time, and place of occurrence.

Most legal disputes have more than one answer, and some may have no answer at all. Different courts and states may apply varying results to similar problems. The student should remember that judges and lawmakers are human beings who possess biases, prejudices, and limitations. This uncertainty, however, should provide a challenge to one's imagination and initiative. In our adversary legal system, the forceful persuaders who convince the court or the legislative body that they have the right answer—whether or not one exists—are the individuals who shape the future trends of the law.

Facts

Girouard had been denied naturalization because he had refused to give an oath "to take up arms in defense of this country," based on his religious scruples. Three prior Supreme Court cases had required the oath as a condition to obtaining citizenship. The 1940 Naturalization Act made some changes in requirements and procedures but reenacted the oath in its preexisting form and without reference to the cases. In 1942, Congress granted naturalization to some noncombatants who would not bear arms because of their religion.

Decision

The previous Supreme Court cases do not state the correct law, and Girouard is not required to take the oath. The reenactment of the oath and the silence of Congress was negated by the 1942 affirmative recognition by Congress that one could be attached to the principles of the U.S. government and could support and defend it even though one's religious convictions prevented one from bearing arms. The oath was not designed to exact something more from one person than from another.

Girouard v. *United States,* 328 U.S. 61, 66 S.Ct. 826, 90 L.Ed. 1084 (1946). [This case has been edited and briefed by the authors to present the facts and the Court's decision with its reasoning. Many such capsulated examples will be used throughout this book to illustrate stated rules of law.]

Justice

Justice is portrayed as blind, meaning that the law is wholly objective and impartial. To judge fairly and properly, one must consider carefully the claims and arguments of both sides of a controversy together with the common interest involved. Sometimes the public concern must also be weighed. As you read the case examples, you may notice that the court seldom explains the loser's position. This is logical, since the matter has been decided the other way. There are often dissenting opinions, and there is usually some merit to the other side, since hiring an attorney to go to trial, followed by an appeal, can be a long and expensive process. Sometimes the dissent becomes the law in the future. If you disagree with a rule or decision, express yourself, but base your opinion on reason, not emotion.

At the end of this introductory chapter, the authors have posed some controversial problems based on cases decided by the courts. While most of these problems refer to social issues rather than business law controversies, they illustrate some of the factors discussed concerning changes in the law. It is realized that the student may not be aware of the legal principles involved, but the purpose is to stimulate one's ability to reason and to demonstrate that the law is flexible. As you read these problems, you be the judge and justify your decision.

Justice
The quality of being righteous, impartial and fair.

Dissent
To disagree with the majority.

QUESTIONS

1. What does the term *law* mean to you?
2. Give an example of a recent change that was made in the law and the reason for the change.
3. If you had the power to do so, what new law would you make, and why?
4. Assume that your state legislature is considering a bill that would require mandatory air bags for safety in all new autos. What arguments would you make to lobby for or against the law?
5. Give an example where, in your opinion, justice has not been totally objective and impartial.

PROBLEMS

1. Jane Roe, a single woman, asks the federal court to declare the abortion statutes of Texas, which excepted from criminality only a lifesaving procedure on behalf of the mother without regard to pregnancy stage or other factors, to be unconstitutional as a violation of her right of privacy. *Roe* v. *Wade,* 410 U.S. 113, 93 S.Ct. 705, 35 L.Ed.2d 147 (1973).
2. Four drunks and a taxpayer challenged a state law making it a crime to be drunk in a public place. The drunks argued, and presented medical evidence to support it, that they had a disease of chronic

alcoholism and were not guilty of any crime because of their affliction. The taxpayer argued that arresting drunks and treating them as criminals was a waste of money, because it would be cheaper and better to send them to detoxification centers. *Sundance* v. *Municipal Court,* 42 Cal.2d 1101, 232 Cal. Rptr. 814, 729 P.2d 80 (1986).

3. Congress directed the Secretary of Transportation to withhold a part of federal highway funds from any state in which "the purchase or public possession of any alcoholic beverage by a person under 21" is lawful. South Dakota, which permitted persons over 18 to buy 3.2 percent alcoholic beer, sued for the funds, arguing that the law was an unconstitutional interference with the state's right to regulate and control alcohol use within its borders. *South Dakota* v. *Dole,* 483 U.S. 203, 107 S.Ct. 2793, 97 L.Ed.2d 171 (1987).

4. David Mitchell registered with his Selective Service Board, was classified 1-A, and was ordered to report for induction during the Vietnam War, which he refused to do. He was found guilty of violating the law and appealed on the basis that the United States was conducting an illegal war in violation of various treaties it had signed. *United States* v. *Mitchell,* 369 F.2d 323 (2d Cir. 1966).

5. Palo Alto's city zoning laws provide that "R-1" is a single-family residential area, limited to "one person living alone, or two or more persons related by blood, marriage, or legal adoption, or a group not exceeding four persons living as a single housekeeping unit." Palo Alto Tenants' Union, representing co-op groups, argue that this is a violation of members' constitutionally protected lifestyles. *Palo Alto Tenants' Union* v. *Morgan,* 487 F.2d 883 (9th Cir. 1973).

6. A provision of the Social Security Act granted widows, but not widowers, survivors benefits while caring for their minor children. Wiesenfeld sued on the basis that this was unconstitutional discrimination. *Weinberger* v. *Wiesenfeld,* 420 U.S. 636, 95 S.Ct. 1225, 43 L.Ed.2d 514 (1975).

7. A Utah statute extended minority for males to 21 but for females to 18. Stanton, a divorced man, refused to support his daughter after she reached 18. The daughter sued on the basis that this law violated equal protection of the laws. *Stanton* v. *Stanton,* 421 U.S. 7, 95 S.Ct. 1373, 43 L.Ed.2d 688 (1975).

8. Jacksonville passed a city ordinance making it a crime and a public nuisance for a drive-in movie theatre to exhibit films containing nudity when the screen was visible from a public street or place. The theatre owner claims that the law is unconstitutional. *Erznoznik* v. *City of Jacksonville,* 422 U.S. 205, 95 S.Ct. 2268, 45 L.Ed.2d 125 (1975).

9. A Louisiana law forbade the teaching of the theory of evolution unless accompanied by instruction in the theory of "creation science." Some parents, teachers, and religious leaders challenge the constitutionality of the law. *Edwards* v. *Aguillard,* 482 U.S. 578, 107 S.Ct. 2573, 96 L.Ed.2d 510 (1987).

10. On the basis of his display of an unloaded handgun while robbing a bank, McLaughlin was convicted of assault by the use of a "dangerous weapon" during a bank robbery. He contends that an unloaded gun is not a dangerous weapon. *McLaughlin* v. *United States,* 476 U.S. 16, 106 S.Ct. 1677, 90 L.Ed.2d 15 (1986).

CHAPTER TWO

United States Legal System

2.1 Sources of Law
The Constitution
State Powers
Judicial Case Law
   Stare Decisis
Legislative Law
The Uniform Commercial Code
Executive Orders and Administrative
    Regulations

2.2 Court Systems
U.S. Courts
   District Courts
   Appellate Courts
   U.S. Supreme Court
State Courts
   State Trial Courts
   State Appeals Courts
   State Supreme Courts
Characteristics of U.S. Courts
   Parties
   Complaint
   Statute of Limitations
   Summons
   Answer
   Pretrial

   Depositions
   Interrogatories
   Admissions
   Pretrial Conference
   Subpoena
   Stipulation
   Evidence
   Direct Examination
   Final Argument
   Motions
   Appeal
   Mediation
   Arbitration
   Hearings

2.3 Administrative Agencies
Powers
Independent Agencies
Rules
Notice
Due Process
   Hearings
   Findings
Judicial Review
   Exhaustion of Administrative Remedies
   Final Order
   Freedom of Information
   Sunshine Act
   Privacy Act

2.1 Sources of Law

Constitution
The original and fundamental principles of law by which a system of government is created.

The main sources of law in this country are the Constitution of the United States, the fifty state constitutions, federal and state statutes, federal and state court decisions, the rules and regulations of federal and state administrative agencies, and the ordinances of local governments.

The Constitution

Paramount to and shaping all of our law, whether court cases, statutes, or administrative decisions, is the U.S. Constitution and the fundamental expectations of the people it protects. The document declares that the Constitution was formed by the people of the United States, so they are the ultimate source of all authority and of the law, for they will influence the law, follow it or break it, and make it effective or obsolete. Under this system, the Constitution is the supreme law of the land. No state, federal, or other law is valid if it violates the U.S. Constitution. In 1803 the U.S. Supreme Court decided that it was the final arbiter as to the constitutionality of any law and the final interpreter as to the meaning intended by the Constitution. History has demonstrated that realistically the Court is influenced by public opinion, and so by the primary source of law—the people themselves.

Arbiter
One who decides a controversy according to law.

The Constitution is a written agreement that creates a federation of the states of the United States. Seven original articles were adopted in 1787, and there have been twenty-six amendments, the last one in 1971. The document creates three separate branches of government and a system of checks and balances that defines and controls the powers of each branch. The legislative branch makes the laws, the judicial branch interprets them, and the executive branch has the responsibility to see that they are carried out and enforced. The Constitution's provisions enumerate the powers specifically delegated to the federal government, limit the powers of the separate states, and guarantee certain basic rights of the people.

Amendment
An addition to or deletion from an existing law.

State Powers

Entity
Something that exists independently.

Supremacy Clause
Article VI, Section [2] of the U.S. Constitution that makes federal acts the supreme law of the country.

Those powers not delegated to the United States are reserved for the states (Tenth Amendment) or the people themselves (Ninth Amendment). Since each state is a sovereign entity, it has the inherent power to enact its own laws. However, the Supremacy Clause of the Constitution makes state law subordinate to federal law and requires the U.S. Supreme Court to invalidate any state law that is in conflict with the federal Constitution, federal statutes, or U.S. treaties. Where federal and state laws cover the same topic, federal law will preempt the state provisions. In turn, state laws are superior to and may preempt conflicting local ordinances.

Facts

The City of Berkeley passed a municipal ordinance prohibiting the administration of any electric shock treatment to any person within its city limits. Violation carried a fine and/or six months in jail. The Northern Psychiatric Society sued to get an injunction to keep the city from enforcing the law.

Decision

A state statute defined the legal and civil rights of the mentally ill, and certain sections dealt with the administration and scope of electroconvulsive (shock) therapy. The court recognized that there were hazards associated with the administration of electric shock treatment, but the legislature had also recognized that the treatment might be lifesaving in certain circumstances. Patients were given the right to approve or veto such treatment on them. The Berkeley ordinance was in direct conflict with this scheme, was not a local matter, and was "fully occupied and preempted by general state law." Injunction granted.

Northern Psychiatric Society v. *City of Berkeley,* 178 Cal. App. 3d 90, 223 Cal.Rptr. 609 (1986).

Judicial Case Law

Stare Decisis

Before the adoption of the U.S. Constitution, the law of this country was based on the common law followed in England. This was judge-made law, or "case law." Decisions made by the courts were reported and stood as precedent for similar disputes that followed. This was called the doctrine of *stare decisis,* based on the Latin phrase meaning "to adhere to precedents and not to unsettle things established." Each judgment based on new facts set a precedent to be followed on future comparable issues. English common law courts were often inflexible and were authorized to award money damages as the only remedy. As a result of this rigidity, those cases requiring an order from the king, such as an injunction not to trespass on the land of another, were referred to an official, originally the chancellor. Eventually a separate system of equity, or chancery, courts developed to judge such matters. The courts of equity operated without a jury and provided remedies calling for court orders. In addition to ordering an injunction, they could order recission (voiding certain contracts) and specific performance (requiring parties to perform contracts). When this country's founders adopted the common law system, they also acquired the complementary equity system. Both still affect the operation of law in the United States.

Although they follow the rule of *stare decisis,* the courts today are flexible enough to meet new expectations and needs. Reasons for original decisions may change so that the judge is no longer bound to follow the precedent. Factual situations may vary enough so that the prior rule would not apply. And in some cases, the court may decide that the original rule was wrong and so refuse to follow it. These changes create conflicting laws and confusion until a higher court decides which ruling shall control and thus makes "the law" that lower courts must follow. In business law, we see a constant tension between the need for *stare decisis* so that certainty of law can guide business decisions and the need for change and flexibility

Stare Decisis
A common law rule to stand by cases already decided and to follow the decisions as precedents in similar future cases.

Equity
Established as a separate court and body of law in Common Law England to administer justice according to the principles of fairness when no common law remedy existed.

Dynamic
Relating to or tending toward change.

to meet new business expectations. It should be obvious that all law is dynamic.

Legislative Law

Legislation
The exercise of sovereign power to make laws.

Statute
An act of a legislature passed under its constitutional authority.

Legislative law, also known as statutory or code law, is law that is enacted by Congress, by the various state legislative bodies, and by local governments. Such acts, statutes, and ordinances are the primary source of new law and ordered social change in the United States today.

Statutes are compiled in official codes. All federal statutes are codified in the United States Code (U.S.C.), and federal regulations are compiled in the Code of Federal Regulations (C.F.R.).

Each state has a constitution supplemented by case law and a system of codes. California, for example, has twenty-seven different codes on a wide variety of subjects. Illinois maintains its legislative laws under "Illinois Revised Statutes," and Michigan lists its collection as "Michigan Compiled Laws."

The Uniform Commercial Code

UCC
The Uniform Commercial Code, a code of laws governing business transactions and designed to bring uniformity among state laws on these topics.

Diversity among state laws dealing with commercial law hampered the conduct of commerce on a national scale. In recent years, a great effort has thus been made to make the laws of the states uniform in certain fields. Perhaps the best example of this is the Uniform Commercial Code (UCC), which has been adopted, in whole or in part with variations, by all fifty states, the District of Columbia, and the Virgin Islands. The purpose of the Code is to simplify, clarify, and modernize the law governing commercial transactions; permit the continued expansion of commercial practices through custom, usage, and agreement of the parties; and make uniform the law among the states. Thus, the Code itself permits change in laws regulating business transactions while attempting to provide uniform guidance for business decisions.

The Code is restricted to transactions involving various aspects of the sale, financing, and security in respect to *personal* property, which generally consists of moveable things. Except for isolated instances, the Code does not apply to real property (interests in land and those things permanently attached thereto).

Under the Code, if the parties express intent to contract, some of the technical requirements for entering into a contract become unnecessary. The Code provides rules and principles that will become part of the contract if the parties have not otherwise agreed. Although the parties can tailor the contract to suit their needs, they cannot change the Code obligations of good faith, diligence, reasonableness, and due care.

Executive Orders and Administrative Regulations

Executive Order
An order issued by the executive head of a government, such as the President, and which has the force of law.

Congress and the state legislatures may from time to time delegate some of their lawmaking power to the chief executive or to a regulatory agency.

Such executive orders and administrative rules and regulations have the same effect as laws provided they do not exceed the delegated authority.

Questions

1. What is the difference between common law and legislative law? Should judges have the same authority to overrule legislative law as they have to overrule common law?
2. What does *stare decisis* mean? Once a question has been decided, can the rule be changed? How?
3. Predictability (declared in advance) and adaptability (to make suitable for a new condition) are opposites. Are they both desirable in a body of law? Why?
4. Justice is defined as "fairness" and "righteousness." What are the differences and the similarities between the meanings of *law* and of *justice*?
5. What are the differences between the sources of federal law and of state law?

2.2 Court Systems

The United States has a dual court system consisting of a broad federal structure covering all states, territories, and the District of Columbia and of the separate systems for each of the fifty states.

Court *jurisdiction* is the right to hear and make judgment in a legal dispute between parties. Original jurisdiction refers to the court in which a case is initially brought to trial and the facts presented for decision. Appellate jurisdiction rests with those courts having the right to hear appeals from original trials and to take any action deemed appropriate, including reversal.

Jurisdiction
The power to hear and decide a lawsuit.

Appeal
To go to a higher court asking for a review and reversal of a lower court decision.

U.S. Courts

Article III of the Constitution provides for a supreme court and "such inferior courts as Congress may establish." The article also authorizes the President to appoint federal judges for life, upon confirmation by the Senate.

Under this authority, Congress has created the U.S. Supreme Court, with a Chief Justice and eight Associate Justices; thirteen U.S. courts of appeals; and the U.S. district courts, with at least one in each state. Some additional special courts added to the system are the U.S. Claims Court, bankruptcy courts, the Tax Court of the U.S., U.S. Court of International Trade, and the U.S. Court of Military Appeals.

District Courts

The district courts are the courts of original jurisdiction and are the proper ones to try cases with federal questions: those arising under the Constitution; federal laws and treaties that involve personal rights; crimes under federal law; and civil matters where the controversy exceeds the sum or value of $50,000 and involves a diversity of citizenship, i.e., a case in which

Federal District Courts
Courts of original jurisdiction over all offenses against the federal laws of the United States.

the parties are citizens of different states. The question of *venue*, i.e., which of the ninety-six federal district courts is to take jurisdiction over such a dispute is answered in the following case.

Facts

Marilyn Scott was a flight attendant for PSA. Breeland, of the Oak Ridge Boys musical group, allegedly assaulted Scott while the plane was on the ground in Reno, Nevada, on its way to Los Angeles. Scott, a California resident, filed an action in federal court in California against Breeland, a Tennessee citizen, and the Oak Ridge Boys, a Tennessee corporation, on the basis of diversity of citizenship. Defendants sought dismissal of the case on the basis of lack of personal jurisdiction.

Decision

Case dismissed. The only connections between Breeland and California were that Breeland boarded the flight intending to fly to California, the group occasionally played in California, and their records and tapes were sold in California. The case should be brought in Nevada where the act took place, or in Tennessee, where the defendants are residents.

Scott v. Breeland, 792 F.2d 925 (9th Cir. 1986)

Long Arm Statutes
Laws that allow local courts to obtain jurisdiction over nonresident defendants when the cause of action occurred locally and affects local plaintiffs.

Commerce Clause
Article I, Section 8, [3] of the U.S. Constitution which gives Congress the power to regulate interstate and foreign commerce.

What happens to diversity of citizenship cases that do not go to the federal court? Most states have long-arm statutes that provide for jurisdiction over nonresidents who have committed a tort, own property, transact business, or enter into the disputed contract within the state. As pointed out in *International Shoe Co. v. State of Washington* (66 S.Ct. 154 [1945]), the nonresident defendant must have "minimum contacts" with the state that assumes personal jurisdiction over him.

The powers of the federal courts are often based on liberal interpretation of constitutional provisions, such as the Commerce Clause that concerns the federal power to regulate interstate and foreign commerce.

Russell v. United States
471 U.S. 858; 105 S.Ct. 2455, 85 L.Ed.2d 829 (1985)

Justice Stevens Petitioner owns an apartment building located at 4530 South Union, Chicago, Illinois. He earned rental income from it and treated it as business property for tax purposes. In early 1983, he made an unsuccessful attempt to set fire to the building and was consequently indicted for violating § 844(i). Following a bench trial, petitioner was convicted and sentenced to 10 years' imprisonment. . . .

Section 844(i) uses broad language to define the offense. It provides:

> "Whoever maliciously damages or destroys, or attempts to damage or destroy, by means of fire or an explosive, any building, vehicle, or other real or personal property used in interstate or foreign commerce or in any activity affecting interstate or foreign commerce shall be imprisoned for not more than ten years or fined not more than $10,000, or both. . . ."

The reference to "any building . . . used . . . in any activity affecting interstate or foreign commerce" expresses an intent by Congress to exercise its full power under the Commerce Clause. . . .

> In sum, the legislative history suggests that Congress at least intended to protect all business property, as well as some additional property that might not fit that description, but perhaps not every private home.
>
> By its terms, however, the statute only applies to property that is "used" in an "activity" that affects commerce. The rental of real estate is unquestionably such an activity. We need not rely on the connection between the market for residential units and "the interstate movement of people," to recognize that the local rental of an apartment unit is merely an element of a much broader commercial market in rental properties. The congressional power to regulate the class of activities that constitute the rental market for real estate includes the power to regulate individual activity within that class.
>
> Petitioner was renting his apartment building to tenants at the time he attempted to destroy it by fire. The property was therefore being used in an activity affecting commerce within the meaning of § 844(i).
>
> The judgment of the Court of Appeals is affirmed.

Appellate Courts

Appellate courts review matters that trial courts have already adjudicated. No new evidence is submitted, but the court examines the transcript record of trial and the legal written briefs prepared by the parties and listens to oral arguments. It may then affirm, reverse, or modify the original decision and, if deemed necessary, remand the case back to the trial court for further action.

Federal courts of appeal are situated in eleven numbered geographical circuits, the District of Columbia, and the U.S. Court of Appeals for the Federal Circuit. The numbered circuit courts take cases appealed from the district courts sited in their respective areas. The Court of Appeals for the Federal Circuit was created in 1982. It was given jurisdiction to hear appeals from the U.S. Patent and Trademark Office, the U.S. Claims Court, and the U.S. Court of International Trade (formerly the Customs Court). It was also given exclusive jurisdiction over appeals from all district courts in patent infringement cases. Most appellate court cases are heard by a panel of three judges, but in some important matters, the entire court of appeal may decide together *in banc*.

Legal Brief
A written argument based upon legal points and authorities submitted by a lawyer seeking a favorable ruling from the court.

Circuit
Judicial divisions of a state or the United States.

In Banc
The full court, all of the judges on an appeals court, considering a particular case.

U.S. Supreme Court

The U.S. Supreme Court is the final interpreter of the law under our system. Cases may be brought on appeal before the Court as a matter of right under some circumstances, including (1) when a U.S. court of appeals holds a state statute to be in violation of the Constitution, treaties, or laws of the United States; (2) when the highest court of a state declares a federal statute or treaty invalid or upholds the validity of a state statute that has been challenged as violating federal law; (3) when a federal court declares an act of Congress unconstitutional and the federal government or one of its

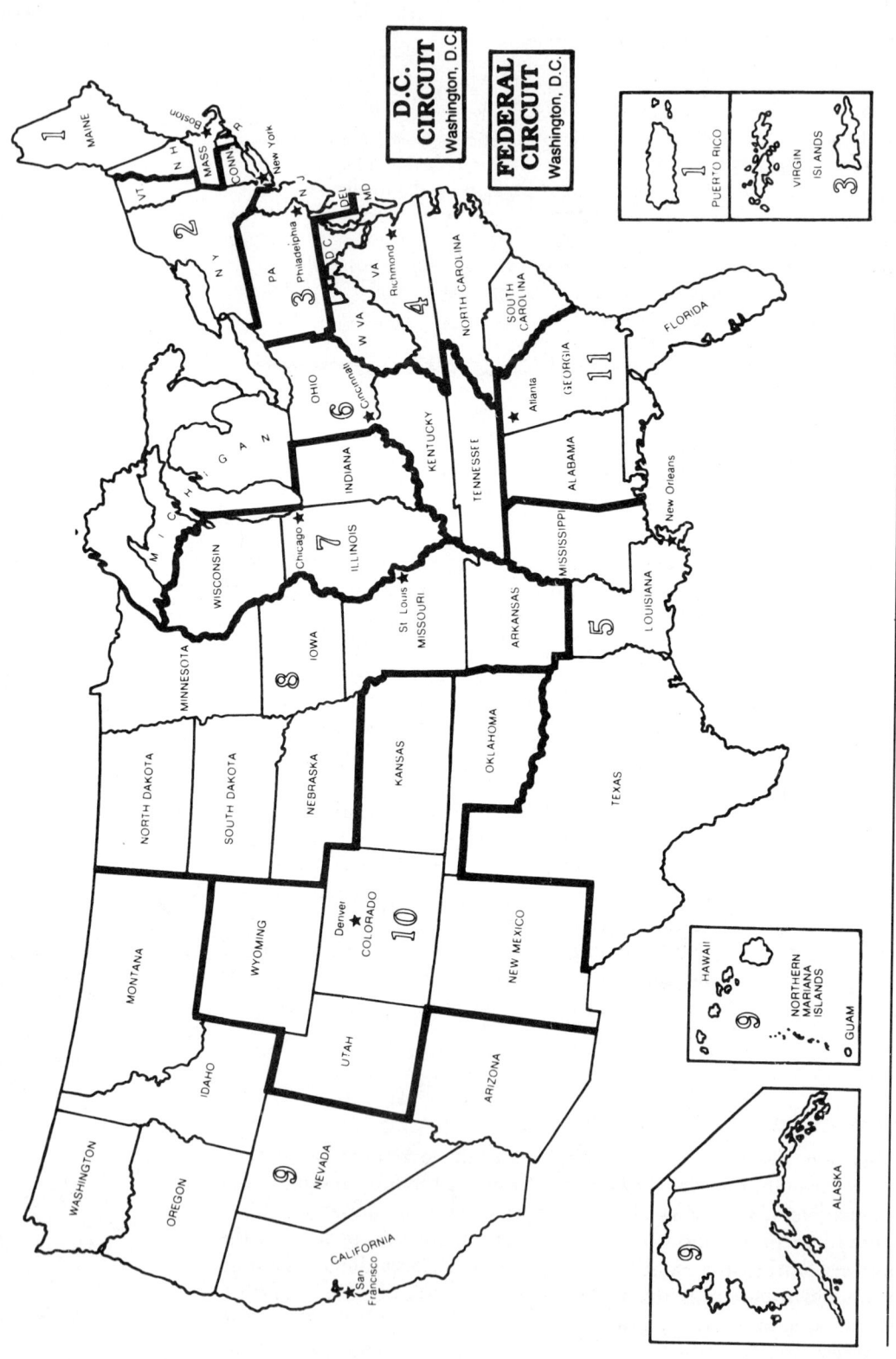

The Twelve Federal Judicial Circuits, each with a court of appeals, plus the Court of Appeals for the Federal Circuit added in 1982.

employees is a party to the case; and (4) when an appeal is from an injunction in a civil action that Congress requires a district court of three judges to determine.

Almost all cases reach the U.S. Supreme Court by petition for a *writ of certiorari*. Only a few of thousands of petitions are accepted by the court each term, and a full hearing is given only if four of the nine justices ("rule of four") vote to take the case. A Supreme Court rule specifies that the writ should be given "only when there are special and important reasons."

When issued, the *writ of certiorari* is a written order from the Supreme Court to a lower court requiring production of a certified record of the trial. Writs may be granted when there is an important federal question or a conflict between the decisions of different circuit courts of appeal.

Although primarily appellate, the U.S. Supreme Court has original trial jurisdiction in cases where a state is a party and in cases involving ambassadors, public ministers, or consuls. The Supreme Court also has the power to invalidate any federal or state statute by declaring it contrary to the U.S. Constitution. The legal principles enunciated by the Court are followed by all federal courts in similar controversies, and if a constitutional problem is involved, the ruling is followed by all courts of the United States, both federal and state.

Injunction
A court order requiring a party either to stop or to continue doing a particular act or activity.

Certiorari
An order from a higher to a lower court, commanding the latter to certify and return to the former the record of a certain case for review.

State Courts

Most states follow the federal pattern with trial courts of original jurisdiction, intermediate appellate courts, and a highest state court for final appeal. State courts have jurisdiction over all matters not made federal by law or court decision.

State Trial Courts

Some states have lower trial courts of limited jurisdiction, such as municipal courts, city courts, justice of the peace courts, or commissioner's courts, which may try misdemeanor cases and those civil actions for limited amounts of money damages.

Many states have a *small claims court* system similar to that depicted on the popular TV show, "People's Court," in which courts have a limited money jurisdiction (e.g., $2,000) and litigants handle their own cases without attorney representation. This relieves the burden on the lower courts and provides a simple, fast, inexpensive means of redressing wrongs.

All states have trial courts of unlimited jurisdiction that may decide all cases properly before them regardless of the amount of money involved or the remedy sought. These are called by various names in different states: Circuit Court (Illinois, Indiana, Michigan); Superior Court (California, Arizona, Massachusetts); Supreme Court (New York); District Court (Iowa, Minnesota, Oklahoma, Wyoming); Court of Common Pleas (Ohio, Pennsylvania).

Small Claims Court
A court of limited money jurisdiction where the parties usually represent themselves.

State Appeals Courts

Most of the larger states have created intermediate courts of appeal to relieve the highest state court of its appellate burden. Among such district courts of appeal or courts of appeal are those in Arizona, California, Illinois, Louisiana, Michigan, New York, North Carolina, Ohio, and Pennsylvania. In these states a litigant would file his initial appeal from a trial. The next appeal would be to the state's highest court.

Litigant
A party involved in a lawsuit.

State Supreme Courts

Every state has its highest court of appeals, the counterpart of the U.S. Supreme Court. Most states call it the supreme court, but Kentucky, Maryland, and New York name it the court of appeals, while Massachusetts and Maine use supreme judicial court.

Characteristics of U.S. Courts

The U.S. follows the British *adversary* system, in which a "passive" judge weighs the presentations by the opposing parties, rather than the *inquisitorial* method, in which an "active" judge conducts the examination of evidence to arrive at his judgment.

U.S. courts resolve only legal disputes, not political issues.

Facts

Spindulys, Perkonitis, and Kivikasukas are associations made up of persons from Lithuanian, Latvian, and Estonian ancestry. The Los Angeles Olympic Organizing Committee staged the Olympics in Los Angeles in 1984. Estonia, Latvia, and Lithuania are recognized by the U.S. government but not by the International Organizing Committee. The associations alleged that the committee committed acts of discrimination in violation of the Unruh Act (Calif Civil Rights Act) by refusing to permit them to participate in the ceremonies. The committee had determined that those three countries should be represented by Russia. The trial court held that this was a nonjusticiable political question, and the associations appealed.

Decision

The President has the sole power to recognize foreign governments, and such recognition is a political question that neither the U.S. Supreme Court nor any other American court may review.

Spindulys v. Los Angeles Olympic Organizing Committee, 175 Cal. App. 3d 206, 220 Cal.Rptr. 565 (1985).

Expertise
Specialized knowledge or skill.

Judicial procedures and rules vary from state to state and within the federal system. They can be complicated and do require legal expertise. The following paragraphs present a general summary of some of the common characteristics of the U.S. courts.

Parties

Plaintiff
The one who initially brings a lawsuit.

The party seeking relief, usually called the *plaintiff* or *petitioner*, initiates the lawsuit. The person or entity being sued is called the *defendant* or

UNITED STATES LEGAL SYSTEM

respondent. In the citation of cases, the plaintiff or petitioner is usually named first; however, in some states and federal cases following an appeal, the party making the appeal—the *appellant*—is named first thereafter.

Complaint

The lawsuit, or *action,* is commenced by paying the required filing fee and filing a *pleading* with the clerk of the court having jurisdiction over the matter. This first pleading is usually called a *complaint, petition,* or *declaration.* Law libraries have many volumes of suggested pleading forms, and some states are now standardizing forms to simplify this important step in the legal process.

Statute of Limitations

This first pleading alleges the facts upon which the plaintiff's cause of action is based. It must follow prescribed rules and be filed within the time period set forth in the applicable *statute of limitations* or be barred forever. In a suit against most governmental entities, rules require an initial filing of a claim against the entity itself within a specified period of time. If any administrative remedies are available for the type of grievance alleged, they must all be exhausted before filing the complaint.

Summons

A *summons* naming the parties, the court, and the time within which to respond is attached to a copy of the complaint or other pleading and is served on the defendant. Method of service varies from state to state but is usually done personally by an officer of the court or process server. In some instances, service may be by mail or by publication.

Answer

If the defendant does not respond to the summons, a default judgment may be entered for the plaintiff for whatever amount the suit demands. However, if the defendant wishes to contest the action, an *answer* or a *demurrer* must be filed with the court. An answer generally denies the allegations of the complaint and places the case in issue. The demurrer is an attack on the complaint itself as to form or substance and, if allowed, usually leads to the filing of an amended complaint.

Pretrial

When the defendant files an answer and the answer is served on the plaintiff or his attorney pursuant to local rules, the matter is ready for pretrial proceedings—procedures used to discover the basic issues and facts before the trial takes place. Search for the truth rather than surprises in court is the logic behind these rules. The main discovery devices are depositions, written interrogatories, motions for inspection, physical and mental examinations, demands for admission of facts, and exchange of expert witness information.

Defendant
One who is sued by another.

Complaint
The first pleading by a plaintiff setting out the facts on which the claim is based.

Statute of Limitations
Any law which fixes the time within which parties must bring a lawsuit or lose their right to do so.

Summons
A document notifying a defendant that he or she has been sued.

Default Judgment
Judgment entered against a defendant due to failure to answer plaintiff's complaint or appear for trial.

Answer
Pleading filed by a defendant in response to plaintiff's complaint.

Deposition
A statement by a witness under oath, taken in question and answer form as it would be in court, with the other party permitted to be present and cross-examine.

Depositions

Attorneys for the parties customarily take depositions of adverse parties and of key witnesses. The most common type of deposition consists of oral testimony given under oath in answer to questions posed by one or more attorneys, reduced to writing, and authenticated. It is normally taken in the office of one of the attorneys. The purpose is to find out what the other party intends to prove at the trial so that the facts can be disproved or disputed. Deposition testimony is very important, since the answers become a permanent written record. If any of the testimony at the time of trial is different, the deposition may be used to show that the witness does not always tell the truth.

Interrogatories

Interrogatories
Discovery tool in which written questions are asked by one party and served on the adversary, who must then answer by written replies made under oath.

Motion
An application to a court requesting an order or rule in favor of the applicant.

Depositions may also be made on written interrogatories—questions in writing submitted to the witness to answer under oath. These are not as effective as oral testimony, since the interrogator is not present to rephrase a question or to cross-examine the witness. Also, the testifier has more time to consider the answers, often with the help of an attorney.

A motion for inspection asks the court to order any party to produce and permit the inspection and copying of designated pertinent documents, papers, books, accounts, letters, photos, or other tangible items.

Where mental or physical condition or blood relationships are in controversy, the court may order a party to submit to a physical, mental, or blood examination by a physician.

Admissions
Pretrial discovery device by which one party asks another to admit or deny any important fact at issue.

Admissions

The demand for admission of facts is a request by one party against the other to admit to the genuineness of relevant documents or the truth of certain facts. The purpose is to avoid the unnecessary expense and labor involved in proving things about which the parties can agree in advance.

Expert Witness
A witness who through study, education, experience, and observation has a special knowledge of the subject about which he is to testify.

Exchange of expert trial witness information requires both parties, on demand, to list the expert witnesses they intend to use at trial, with their qualifications and the general substance of the expected testimony.

Pretrial Conference

Pretrial Conference
Conference held after pleadings filed and before trial to bring the parties together to outline discovery procedures and define the issues to be tried.

After discovery has been completed, many courts hold pretrial conferences in an effort to reach a settlement. Another purpose of such conferences is to resolve some of the facts in issue so that the trial itself might be shorter and more orderly.

Subpoena

Subpoena
A court order to compel the appearance of a witness at a trial, punishable as contempt of court for failure to comply.

On the trial date, the parties, witnesses, and attorneys appear at the proper court at the set time. An attorney of record in any court proceeding may issue a *subpoena* and have a copy of it delivered to a witness. Such personal service requires that witness to appear in court and testify at the trial.

Stipulation

Most judges will first see the attorneys in chambers (judge's private office) before trial in a final effort to settle the case or obtain *stipulations*—agreements by the parties, usually made through their respective counsel, as to some of the issues.

Jury trials may be requested by either party, or they may be waived and the trial decided by the judge alone. If the case is to be tried by jury, the attorneys and the judge examine the prospective jurors in an attempt to select those who are competent and unbiased. After the jury is selected, each attorney makes an opening statement telling what he intends to prove.

Evidence

The plaintiff has the burden of proving the facts alleged in the complaint and so goes first. The plaintiff's attorney does this by presenting *evidence* in the form of documents, testimony of witnesses, or physical objects in compliance with evidentiary rules. The purpose of such rules is to provide a systematic way of admitting into court the facts that the judge or jury as trier of fact must decide. Admissible evidence must be relevant and material; that is, it must have some important bearing on the case at hand. Evidence can also be *direct* or *circumstantial*. Testimony of what a witness has actually seen or heard is direct evidence. Circumstantial evidence is that applied indirectly or from which a principal fact may be inferred. Possession of stolen property might be circumstantial evidence that the property was stolen by the holder.

Direct Examination

When the plaintiff's attorney completes the direct examination of each witness, the defendant's attorney then has the right to cross-examine that witness to check the accuracy and value or weight that should be given the testimony. This may be followed by the plaintiff's redirect examination, usually limited to any new matter brought out by the cross-examination, and then by the defendant's recross, with the same limitations.

Plaintiff's case is rested after all of that side's evidence has been presented, and it is then the defendant's turn. Often, attorney for the defendant will first make a motion to the judge to dismiss the case on the grounds that the plaintiff has not presented sufficient evidence to prove the allegations. If the judge agrees, that ends the trial in favor of the defendant.

Final Argument

After all evidence for both sides has been presented and any motions, objections, or other technicalities have been ruled on by the judge, the plaintiff's attorney makes a final argument to the jury. In the final argument, the evidence is reviewed and related to the instructions that the judge will give to the jury. The defendant's lawyer then follows the same procedure,

---

Stipulation
An agreement made by the parties in a lawsuit or by their attorneys, relating to the business before the court.

Jury
A group of people, cross section of the community, summoned and sworn to decide facts at issue in a trial.

Evidence
The means by which an alleged fact, the truth of which is at issue in a trial, is established or disproved.

Relevant
Evidence that tends to prove or disprove a fact in issue.

Material
Evidence that is important or necessary to prove or disprove a certain fact.

Circumstantial Evidence
Indirect evidence, or secondary facts from which a primary fact may be inferred.

Direct Examination
The initial questioning of a witness by the party who called the witness.

Cross Examination
Questioning of a witness by a party or lawyer other than the one who called the witness.

Rebuttal
Time given to a party who made the first closing argument to rebut any claims made in his opponent's closing argument.

after which the plaintiff's lawyer is permitted a short rebuttal. The judge then instructs the jury on the law that is applicable to the case. The jury retires into a private room to deliberate—to decide which facts to believe, to apply the judge's instructions on the law to those facts, and to bring in a verdict to the court.

Motions

When the verdict is given, the attorney for the losing party may file a motion for a *judgment notwithstanding the verdict* on the basis that the jury verdict was not supported by the evidence. Such a motion is rarely granted, but the court has the power to do so. The attorney for either side can make a motion for a new trial on one or more of several different grounds (e.g., excessive or inadequate damages, irregularity in the proceedings, misconduct of the jury, newly discovered evidence, insufficient evidence, error in the law).

After the judgment is entered by the court and motions, if any, are resolved, any party feeling aggrieved may appeal. Some of the reasons on which an appeal may be based are that the court erred in admitting or excluding certain evidence, that it erred in the instructions given to the jury, that it should have granted a directed verdict, or that the evidence was insufficient to support the verdict.

Judgment Notwithstanding the Verdict
A judge may set aside a jury verdict that is believed to have no reasonable support in fact or is in conflict with the law.

Appeal

The appellate court hears the case without a jury and without witnesses. The attorneys for the appellant and the appellee submit written briefs to the court in which they state their reasons for appeal and support their reasons with citations of court decisions, statutes, regulations, prominent authorities, and, in some cases, legislative history. In addition, the appellate lawyers are usually permitted to make oral argument to the judges hearing the appeal. The court examines the verbatim record of the proceedings before the trial court, including the pleadings, testimony of the witnesses, documentary evidence, and instructions to the jury. It considers the appellate briefs and oral arguments as well as points prepared by the judges' own law clerks. Sometimes *amicus curiae* or *amici* (friends of the court) are allowed to file briefs to assist the court, particularly if they have a legitimate interest in the outcome. After this complete review, the appellate court makes its decision and assigns one of the judges to write the opinion. Many times the judges do not all agree, and one or more of them may opt to write a separate dissenting or concurring (agrees with the result but for a different reason) opinion. These opinions are preserved in permanently bound volumes of reports. Excerpts and briefs of some of these cases will be used throughout this book.

Under our adversary system, when a controversy ceases, it becomes *moot* and the courts no longer consider it.

Verbatim
Word for word.

Amicus Curiae
One who gives information to the court on some matter of law which is in doubt.

Moot
Controversy without legal significance.

Facts
Because of a shortage of funds, the City of Boston started laying off police officers and firefighters under a civil service rule of "last hired-first fired." The First Circuit Court of Appeals upheld a district court injunction that prohibited the laying off of people in a manner that would reduce the percentage of minority officers below the level obtained at the time the layoffs started. An appeal was taken to the U.S. Supreme Court. The state then provided more funds to the city, and all of those dismissed were reinstated.

Decision
The Supreme Court vacated the decision because the matter had become moot.

Boston Firefighters Union v. *Boston Chapter NAACP,* 461 U.S. 477, 103 S.Ct. 2076, 76 L.Ed.2d 330 (1983).

Third-party control of disputes through the adversary process in court or administrative agencies is unacceptable to many people because it is expensive, slow, and depersonalized. Also, the specific outcome has not been consented to by the parties. As a result, many businesspeople seek alternative means of dispute resolution through mediation or arbitration.

Mediation

Mediation attempts to induce disputing parties to agree upon a solution without a third party's (such as a judge or arbitrator) intervening to impose one. However, an outside party—a mediator—may actively participate in the discussion to make suggestions, offer an impartial perspective, and attempt to persuade the parties to work out arrangements on which they all agree.

Mediation
A method of settling disputes outside of a court setting.

Arbitration

Arbitration is a process whereby parties having legal obligations to each other agree to have a third, impartial party settle a dispute that has arisen or might arise in the future. This agreement is usually put in an arbitration clause in a contract or in a subsequent agreement after the parties have been unable to resolve their differences.

Arbitration
Submission of controversies, by agreement of the parties thereto, for determination by persons they have chosen.

The American Arbitration Association (AAA) provides qualified arbitrators upon request and suggests general rules to be followed. The AAA also proposes this contract clause:

> Any controversy or claim arising out of or relating to the contract, or the breach thereof, shall be settled by arbitration in accordance with the Commercial Arbitration Rules of the American Arbitration Association, and the judgment upon the award rendered may be entered by any court having jurisdiction thereof.

Federal law and most states have statutes providing for the enforcement of arbitration clauses. If a party tries to bypass arbitration by filing a lawsuit, the court may order compliance with the arbitration agreement.

AT & T Tech., Inc. v. Communications Workers
475 U.S. 643, 106 S.Ct. 1415, 89 L.Ed.2d 648 (1986).

Justice White delivered the opinion of the Court.

The issue presented in this case is whether a court asked to order arbitration of a grievance filed under a collective-bargaining agreement must first determine that the parties intended to arbitrate the dispute, or whether that determination is properly left to the arbitrator. . . .

AT & T Technologies, Inc. (AT & T or the Company) and the Communications Workers of America (the Union) are parties to a collective-bargaining agreement which covers telephone equipment installation workers. Article 8 of this agreement establishes that "differences arising with respect to the interpretation of this contract or the performance of any obligation hereunder" must be referred to a mutually agreeable arbitrator upon the written demand of either party. This Article expressly does not cover disputes "excluded from arbitration by other provisions of this contract." Article 9 provides that, "subject to the limitations contained in the provisions of this contract, but otherwise not subject to the provisions of the arbitration clause," AT & T is free to exercise certain management functions, including the hiring and placement of employees and the termination of employment. "When lack of work necessitates Layoff." . . . AT & T laid off . . . 79 workers, and soon thereafter, the Company transferred approximately the same number of installers from base locations in Indiana and Wisconsin to the Chicago base. AT & T refused to submit the grievance to arbitration on the ground that under Article 9, the Company's decision to lay off workers when it determines that a lack of work exists in a facility is not arbitrable.

The Union then sought to compel arbitration by filing suit in federal court pursuant to § 301(a) of the Labor Management Relations Act, 29 U.S.C. § 185(a). . . . Finding that "the union's interpretation . . . was at least 'arguable,'" the court held that it was "for the arbitrator, not the court to decide whether the union's interpretation has merit." . . . The Court of Appeals for the Seventh Circuit affirmed. . . .

The Court of Appeals understood the District Court to have ordered arbitration of the threshold issue of arbitrability. . . .

The principles necessary to decide this case are not new. . . . These precepts have served the industrial relations community well, and have led to continued reliance on arbitration, rather than strikes or lockouts, as the preferred method of resolving disputes arising during the term of a collective-bargaining agreement.

The first principle . . . is that "arbitration is a matter of contract and a party cannot be required to submit to arbitration any dispute which he has not agreed so to submit."

The second rule . . . is that the question of arbitrability—whether a collective-bargaining agreement creates a duty for the parties to arbitrate the particular grievance—is undeniably an issue for judicial determination. . . .

The third principle derived from our prior cases is that, in deciding whether the parties have agreed to submit a particular grievance to arbitration, a court is not to rule on the potential merits of the underlying claims. . . .

Finally, where it has been established that where the contract contains an arbitration clause, there is a presumption of arbitrability in the sense that "[a]n order to arbitrate the particular grievances should not be denied unless it may be said with positive assurance that the arbitration clause is not susceptible of an interpretation that covers the asserted dispute. Doubts should be resolved in

> favor of coverage." ... With these principles in mind, it is evident that the Seventh Circuit erred in ordering the parties to arbitrate the arbitrability question.... If the court determines that the agreement so provides, then it is for the arbitrator to determine the relative merits of the parties' substantive interpretations of the agreement. It was for the court, not the arbitrator, to decide in the first instance whether the dispute was to be resolved through arbitration. ...

The Federal Arbitration Act provides that arbitration agreements "shall be valid, irrevocable, and enforceable, save upon grounds as exist at law or in equity for revocation of any contract," and requires the court to order arbitration when the Act is applicable.

Arbitration Clause
A clause in a contract providing for arbitration of disputes arising under the contract.

Hearings

Hearings are set by the arbitrator to give both sides an opportunity to present their claims. The rules of evidence are more relaxed, and the hearings are conducted in private. This permits confidentiality, since hearings are not open to the public and there are no records available for public inspection. After all the evidence has been given, the arbitrator has up to thirty days in which to give written decision.

Generally, the arbitrator has the final say and closes the door to future litigation. However, there are limited grounds for appeal. If the loser can show corruption, bias, fraud, or an award beyond the scope of the arbitrator's authority, the award may be set aside by a court.

Hearing
A proceeding wherein evidence is taken for the purpose of determining an issue of fact and reaching a decision based on such evidence.

Facts

Misco, Inc., had a collective bargaining contract with the union that authorized arbitration of any grievance arising from interpretation of the agreement or rules made under it. One of the rules listed as cause for discharge was the possession or use of controlled substances on company property. Cooper, an employee, was apprehended by police in the back seat of someone else's car in the company parking lot with marijuana smoke in the air and a lighted marijuana cigarette in the front-seat ashtray. The police then searched Cooper's car and found traces of marijuana. Cooper was fired and filed a grievance that went to arbitration. The arbitrator found that the cigarette incident was insufficient proof that Cooper was using or possessed marijuana on company property and ordered Cooper reinstated. At the time of the firing, the company did not know of the police search of Cooper's car, so the arbitrator would not allow it in evidence. Misco took the case to the district court, which vacated the arbitration award. This was affirmed by the circuit court of appeals and then taken by the union to the U.S. Supreme Court.

Decision

Reversed. The court of appeals exceeded the limited authority possessed by a court reviewing an arbitrator's award. Absent fraud by the parties or the arbitrator's dishonesty, reviewing courts in such cases are not authorized to reconsider the merits of the award, since this would undermine the federal policy of privately settling labor disputes by arbitration without governmental intervention. No violation of public policy was clearly shown, since the assumed connection between the traces found in Cooper's car and Cooper's actual use of drugs in the workplace was tenuous at best. It was improper for the court to draw that inference, since such fact-finding is the task of the arbitrator chosen by the parties, not the reviewing court.

United Paperworkers International Union, AFL-CIO v. Misco, Inc., 484 U.S. 29, 108 S.Ct. 364, 98 L.Ed.2d 286 (1987).

Sanctions
Punishments for violations of accepted rules of social conduct.

Contempt of Court
An act or omission that interferes with the orderly administration of justice or impairs the dignity of the court or respect for its authority.

Courts make judgments and issue orders, but how are such judgments and orders enforced? The law imposes *sanctions* such as fines, imprisonment, loss of property, and required community service time for refusal or failure to comply with a court order. If the loser fails to pay a money judgment, the winner may go to the proper authority, usually the sheriff or marshall, and have nonexempt property of the debtor seized and sold at public sale with the proceeds being applied toward satisfaction of the judgment. Under some circumstances, a court may enforce its orders by holding the offender in *contempt of court* and sentencing him to jail to force compliance. Sanctions in criminal cases include fines, jail terms, and, in most states, the death penalty.

Questions

1. Most federal judges are appointed for life terms, whereas most state judges are elected for set terms or appointed to fill vacancies and then subjected to voter approval at the end of the term. In your opinion what is the best way for us to obtain the best judges? Why?

2. Countries like the United States that are based on the British system have an adversarial type of trial, where the opposing parties, almost always represented by lawyers, try to win their arguments before jury and judge. Most Western European countries follow an inquisitorial system, where impartial fact-finders conduct the investigation and present the case to a panel of expert judges. Which system best serves justice? Why?

3. Horace Hopper, an independent Iowa farmer, is self-sufficient. He raises, harvests, and consumes all of his own products. Can Congress legally regulate his activities under its commerce clause powers? Explain.

4. What is the purpose of the long-arm statute? Give some examples of its application.

5. Compare the advantages and disadvantages of settling a dispute through a court trial rather than by arbitration.

2.3 Administrative Agencies

Administrative Agency
A government body responsible for control and supervision of a particular activity or area of public interest.

If all members of our society behaved in an ethical and moral manner towards one another, there would be little need for governmental intervention. But history demonstrates that we do not, and public pressures have caused the legislative branches to implement desired changes in policy by creating new entities called *administrative agencies.*

In the industrialization of the United States following the Civil War and before the invention of the automobile, the railroads, as the only practical means of inland transport available, became quite powerful. Their alleged abuses in rate charges and other activities, combined with their political clout, caused a public outcry and led to the creation of the first large administrative agency, the Interstate Commerce Commission (ICC), in 1887.

Many more new agencies were created around the turn of the century, due partly to writings in the "muckraking" press. Upton Sinclair's 1905 novel *The Jungle* exposed the unsanitary conditions in the Chicago stockyards which aroused wide indignation followed by official investigations. Congress then created the Food and Drug Administration (FDA).

UNITED STATES LEGAL SYSTEM

Another surge of agencies occurred during the New Deal days of the Great Depression. Modern concerns over safety, hazardous wastes, the environment, discrimination, and other perceived social ills have resulted in the origination of many new agencies—federal, state, and local—along with their attendant bureaucracies.

The rules and regulations made and enforced by these many agencies affect much of our daily activity. For example, the *California Code of Regulations* lists more than 100 boards, committees, offices, authorities, divisions, departments, councils, and bureaus that license, regulate, or control many of the things done by the state's inhabitants. To list and explain all of the regulatory agencies is far beyond the scope of this book.

Some of the most important federal administrative agencies involved in business regulation and their areas of authority are listed in the following table:

Agency	Area of Authority
Consumer Product Safety Commission (CPSC)	Product safety
Environmental Protection Agency (EPA)	Pollution
Equal Employment Opportunity Commission (EEOC)	Discrimination
Federal Communications Commission (FCC)	TV, radio, etc.
Federal Deposit Insurance Corporation (FDIC)	Bank deposits
Federal Reserve Board (the Fed)	Interest rates
Federal Trade Commission (FTC)	Unfair business
Food and Drug Administration (FDA)	Food, drug safety
Internal Revenue Service (IRS)	Federal tax laws
Interstate Commerce Commission (ICC)	Transportation
National Labor Relations Board (NLRB)	Labor relations
Occupational Safety and Health Administration (OSHA)	Workplace safety
Securities and Exchange Commission (SEC)	Securities laws
Social Security Administration (SSA)	Social Security
Small Business Administration (SBA)	Small business

Powers

All administrative agencies are created by legislative action to carry out desired changes in policy. When a legislative body decides that the function of investigation, law enforcement, rule making, or adjudication in a certain area can best be performed by a separate, specialized body, if may form an agency for that purpose. The statute or law defining the agency usually sets forth the rules of law, organization, and procedure to be followed. It also specifies the powers that have been delegated, which may include executive, legislative, judicial, or any combination thereof.

Delegated Powers
Authority conferred by one (Congress) on another (Agency) to act for its (Congress) benefit.

Special training and experience are required to resolve many of today's technical problems. It is obvious that the lawmakers, judges, and executive officials do not have the full expertise needed to handle complicated problems of taxation, atomic energy, labor relations, consumer rights, transportation, and communications. Also, the merging of specialized legislative, judicial, and executive functions saves money.

Many of the agencies are set up within the executive branch. For example, the Small Business Administration (SBA) is within the Department of Commerce.

Independent Agencies

Numerous independent agencies have been formed by Congress and are considered by many to represent a "fourth branch of government." The Federal Trade Commission (FTC) and the Internal Revenue Service (IRS), for example, make rules (legislative), judge cases (judicial), and enforce the law (executive).

Although Congress retains the power to pass the laws under which an agency operates and appropriates the funds necessary for the agency's existence, the usual result is independent operation.

The President appoints the agency chief and commissioners upon advice and consent by the Senate, but he can remove them only for cause before the end of their terms. However, since the President has the absolute power to remove executive officials, he can fire without cause any such appointees from executive branch agencies.

Facts

The Federal Trade Commission Act of 1914 (FTC) fixed seven-year staggered terms for the commissioners and provided that any commissioner could be removed by the President for inefficiency, neglect of duty, or malfeasance in office. President Herbert Hoover appointed Humphrey to the commission. After he was elected, Franklin D. Roosevelt asked for Humphrey's resignation on the grounds that the commission would work better "with personnel of my own selection." Humphrey refused to resign, so FDR removed him from office. When Humphrey died, his executor sued the government for the lost salary, claiming that the deceased had been wrongfully discharged.

Decision

Independent regulatory agencies are nonpartisan and must be fair. The President's absolute power of removal is confined to executive department officers. However, those commissioners with set terms can be removed only for one or more of the causes listed in the applicable statute. Since none of these causes were used, Humphrey's estate is entitled to the salary Humphrey would have received.

Humphrey's Executor v. United States, 295 U.S. 602, 55 S.Ct. 869, 79 L.Ed. 1611 (1935).

The judiciary is often called upon to enforce, enjoin, or interpret agency rulings and to review some decisions.

Rules

Agency Rules Standards or directives by governmental agencies made in accordance with procedures authorized by Congress or as set down in the Administrative Procedure Act.

Administrative agencies are given the power to make rules and regulations which then have the force of laws. They are limited to the powers delegated by the legislative body, and once the rules are made, the agency must follow its own rules until such rules are changed. Further controls were made by

Presidents Ford, Carter, and Reagan by executive order, which required the agency to prepare a Regulatory Impact Analysis of major rules to carefully examine possible alternative approaches and to perform a cost-benefit analysis. In addition, the National Environmental Policy Act (NEPA) requires an Environmental Impact Statement, which is intended to ensure the early consideration of all alternatives that might cause less harm to the environment.

Notice

Public participation is encouraged in the rule-making process. Interested parties have a right to participate by submitting written data or arguments to the agency involved. The agency must give notice of hearing on a proposed rule, and any major rule adopted must be published in the *Federal Register* thirty days before its effective date. The final rule may be different but will be acceptable without further notice if it is a logical outgrowth of the original. The federal Administrative Procedure Act of 1946 (APA), as amended, governs most areas of administrative law and procedure.

Notice
Information concerning a fact, actually communicated to a person by an authorized person, discovered from a proper source, or presumed by law to have been acquired.

Due Process

Due process of law under the Fifth and Fourteenth Amendments to the Constitution requires that federal and state governments provide notice and a hearing before taking action that would deprive a person of liberty or property. This right is basic and is a vital protection against governmental arbitrariness, as there is no right to a jury trial under administrative law.

Due Process
Course of legal proceedings established under the U.S. Constitution, state and federal laws to protect individual rights and liberties.

Hearings

Some examples of when a hearing is *required* are the discharge of a public employee, revocation of a professional person's license to practice, right of continued employment of a tenured teacher, qualification for welfare benefits, revocation of a parole, seizure of allegedly obscene books, deportation of a resident alien, and involuntary commitment to a mental institution.

Hearings may be denied in certain cases on the grounds of national security or interest where classified material or policymaking is involved. Although a student cannot be expelled from college for disciplinary reasons without a hearing, no hearing is required when the dismissal is for failing grades.

The APA provides that persons entitled to notice of an agency hearing shall be timely informed of (1) the time, place, and nature of the hearing; (2) the legal authority and jurisdiction under which the hearing is to be held; and (3) the matters of fact and law asserted.

Another general requirement of due process is that the affected person has the right to confront any adverse witnesses and to orally present arguments and facts. The right to assistance of counsel applies only to some types of adversary proceedings.

Generally, a hearing must be provided *before* any action that would inflict serious injury on a person, but the trend is to have hearings after the fact if the need for a hearing is not urgent.

APA
The Administrative Procedure Act designed to give uniformity to the rule-making and adjudicative proceedings of federal administrative agencies.

The U.S. Supreme Court has held that a hearing was required before depriving a person of welfare benefits but that such hearing could be held after the Social Security benefits were cut off. The need for a hearing before suspending a driver's license depends upon the facts of each case. For example, the Court held that where suspension required a finding of fault, such as an uninsured motorist in an auto accident, a prior hearing was required. Such a hearing was not required in the case of an unsafe driving record or the refusal to take a breathalyzer test after being arrested for drunken driving.

Practical consequences follow an agency acting before a hearing, because the affected party then has to pay the cost and carry the burden of proof to reverse the finding. Such requirements stop most people from taking further action.

ALJ
Administrative Law Judge is the presiding officer at an administrative hearing.

ALJ Most federal agency adjudicative matters are heard by an *administrative law judge* (ALJ) (formerly called a hearing officer), who presides at the hearing and renders an initial decision, which can then be appealed to the head of the agency.

Evidence All *relevant* and *useful evidence* may be admitted at the ALJ's discretion. Common law and statutory rules of evidence do not apply in administrative hearings. Evidence cannot be excluded solely because it is hearsay. *Hearsay evidence* consists of statements made by someone out of court, not under oath, and not present for confrontation or cross-examination. Any evidence may be received in writing if it will expedite the hearing without substantial prejudice to the interest of any party.

Hearsay Evidence
Any statement other than that by a witness who is testifying at a hearing, and that is offered to prove the truth of the matter stated.

The fact-finder ordinarily may consider only the evidence presented at the hearing and not evidence from any other source. For example, the ALJ or any member of a hearing board could not go to the scene of an airplane crash, discuss the accident with the controller, and form an opinion based on that discussion, since such evidence would not be on the hearing record. However, when a physical inspection of the scene of an accident was made by an ALJ to determine whether there were adequate handholds for safety, the case was approved on the basis that this was the best evidence to prove the fact.

Statistics *Statistical data* of accepted reliability may also be a proper form of proof. Evidence that might normally be inadmissible in court may be included as part of an administrative hearing if it helps to prove the facts.

Judicial Notice
A doctrine that admits into evidence as "proved" such facts that are common knowledge to a judicial professional.

An agency may use materials in its own files if it notifies the parties so that they have an opportunity to contradict. The fact-finder may also take official notice of facts concerning special skills and judgments that are in the field in which the agency usually operates. In law courts, this is known as *judicial notice*.

Relaxation of evidence rules is allowed in agency hearings because of the expertise of the ALJ or hearing officer in the technical matters with which the agency is concerned.

Record
A precise history of a suit from its commencement to its completion.

Decisions When a hearing is required to be conducted "on the record" and the agency head does not preside, the ALJ hears the case, and his "initial decision" is final unless appealed to the agency. Some agencies require that the entire record be certified to the agency head for decision, in which case, the ALJ makes only a "recommended decision."

Influence Command influence, bias, prejudice, and a financial interest in the outcome are grounds for disqualifying the ALJ or hearing officer. Another problem is the influence used or pressure brought upon the fact-finder by members of Congress or the executive department. Congressional intervention has been held to be a violation of due process. The APA prohibits any person outside the agency from discussing the merits of a pending matter with any member of the agency, the ALJ, or any other employee who might be involved in the decision-making process.

Findings

In both federal and state courts, administrative decisions are required to be based on adequate *findings,* meaning that the record must clearly disclose and adequately support the action taken by the agency. The APA requires that all adjudicative decisions are part of the record and must include a statement of "(A) findings and conclusions, and the reasons or basis therefor, on all material issues of fact, law, or discretion presented on the record; and (B) the appropriate rule, order, sanction, relief, or denial thereof."

Findings are important because they establish the agency's jurisdiction, require the fact-finder to carefully evaluate the evidence (a check against arbitrary action), save the reviewing authority time by providing the facts for analysis, and give the parties information needed for appeal or judicial review.

Findings
Findings of fact are the factual determinations made based on the evidence presented, and findings of law are the applications of rules of law to the facts found.

Facts

Under the provisions of the Motor Carrier Act of 1980, the Interstate Commerce Commission (ICC) may grant an operating certificate to an applicant to transport goods between two points if there is a public need or demand for the services and the applying carrier is fit, willing, and able to comply with the Act. Manlowe applied to the ICC for a permit to haul goods between two California cities. At his hearing, no evidence was presented to show any public need, nor was any given to show Manlowe's fitness to serve such needs. However, the permit was granted as a matter of policy. Competing shippers who had opposed the application petitioned the federal district court for reversal.

Decision

Even though final orders of administrative agencies are usually upheld, the Administrative Procedure Act (APA) requires that such an order be set aside if it is "arbitrary, capricious, or unsupported by substantial evidence." Since there was no evidence in the record to support this order, it was set aside.

Containerfreight Corporation v. *United States,* 752 F.2d 419 (9th Cir. 1985).

Judicial Review

Most statutes creating agencies indicate the procedure for getting judicial review of the agency decisions. Appeals from the large federal agencies are usually taken to U.S. courts of appeals (often the Court of Appeals for the District of Columbia) but sometimes are taken by action in a federal district court. In many states, a single statute sets forth general procedures for

Judicial Review
The review by a court of law of some act, or failure to act, by a government official or entity.

review of state agency decisions [Model State APA (1961) in some; California Code of Civil Procedure, #1094.5; New York Civil Practice Law, Article 78.]

Where no statutory procedure is available, parties must use one of the common law writs, such as injunction, declaratory judgment, mandamus, or habeas corpus, to reach the courts. Generally, a person suffering what is considered a legal wrong because of agency action has the right of appeal, with some exceptions. Some agency laws do not permit judicial review, and many others leave such action to the discretion of the agency.

If judicial review is granted and the court disagrees with the agency on a question of *law*, the court may reverse the decision. However, if the question is one of *fact*, the court as a rule accepts the agency finding and seldom reverses. Awaiting a review, the agency may elect to withdraw or to postpone the effective date of any action it has taken.

Exhaustion of Administrative Remedies

Exhaustion of Remedies
A requirement that certain administrative or non-federal judicial remedies be pursued by a litigant before a state or federal court will hear the case.

The rule of *exhaustion of administrative remedies* applies when a person takes a case to court to block or interrupt an administrative proceeding that has not been completed. The general rule is that one cannot seek judicial review for a threatened injury until the prescribed administrative remedies have been exhausted.

Cody v. Scott
Cite as 565 F.Supp. 1031 (1983).

Owen, District Judge Plaintiff Robert F. Cody, a fourth-year cadet at the United States Military Academy, West Point, New York, commenced this action to stay his separation from the Academy as a consequence of certain events described hereafter. . . .

On March 11, 1983, a military policeman confronted plaintiff and a fellow cadet as they sat in [sic] that latter's car in a parking lot on Academy grounds. At that time the military policeman discovered certain evidence indicating that the two cadets possessed and had recently used marijuana. As a consequence, they were taken to a military police station at the Academy and defendant Scott, as their military commander, was informed. . . .

Scott elected to convene an investigative hearing to inquire into the incident, and appointed Lt. Colonel David M. McClellan as Investigating Officer ("I.O.").

In the performance of his duties as I.O., McClellan informed plaintiff of the hearing and the charges against him. He also notified plaintiff of his right to consult with legal counsel—either civilian or military—and to present evidence at the hearing as well as to cross-examine adverse witnesses, object to the introduction of evidence, and remain silent if he so desired. . . .

The investigative hearing was held over five days in April, 1983. Plaintiff, who elected to avail himself of the assistance of military counsel, participated in the hearing, cross-examined witnesses, called witnesses, and testified on his own behalf. . . .

On May 2, 1983, the I.O. issued his findings and recommendations. He concluded that plaintiff had wrongfully possessed and used marijuana in violation of the USMA regulations and he recommended that plaintiff be separated from the Academy. His recommendation was forwarded to defendant Scott together with a brief prepared by plaintiff's counsel. Scott thereupon issued . . . his recommendation that plaintiff be separated from the Academy, transferred to the Army Reserve and ordered to active duty. . . .

To avoid the anticipated consequences of the I.O.'s recommendation, plaintiff commenced this action and now seeks injunctive relief compelling, in effect, his reinstatement to the Academy. . . .

Defendants contend that plaintiff has failed to exhaust at least two avenues of administrative relief still available to him. The Secretary of the Army has not yet reviewed and approved the recommendation of separation and plaintiff has not taken his appeal to the Army Board for Correction of Military Records pursuant to 10 U.S.C. §§ 1551–54. Either of these avenues, at least facially, affords plaintiff the opportunity for full relief. . . .

It is a "long settled rule of judicial administration that no one is entitled to judicial relief for a supposed or threatened injury until the prescribed administrative remedy has been exhausted." . . .

Plaintiff has not advanced adequate justification to short-cut the normal administrative procedure. Although his chances of success before the military may be realistically assessed as slim, a disciplinary proceeding such as that before the court is particularly within the competence of the Board of Correction. Plaintiff's action is therefore barred by the administrative exhaustion doctrine.

Summary judgment granted. Case dismissed.

The U.S. Supreme Court said, "Exhaustion is generally required as a matter of preventing premature interference with agency processes, to afford the parties and the courts the benefits of agency experience and expertise, to compile a record which is adequate for judicial review, and to allow the agency to function efficiently and to have an opportunity to correct its own errors."

The rule has some exceptions. The exhaustion of administrative remedies is unnecessary when the matter is one of great public interest; when there is a constitutional issue about the legality of the administrative procedure; when the administrative remedy is useless, as in the case of a deadlocked agency vote; when administrative remedies would cause irreparable injury; or when agency appeal is required by law.

Final Order

Judicial review is usually not available until the agency has issued its *final order*. This means that the plaintiff must await the agency's final decision on the case before filing a court action. Again, some exceptions exist. Judicial review may be granted immediately when imposing the action pending a hearing would cause irreparable damage to a person, would endanger public health or safety, or would result in severe economic hardship.

Another requirement for judicial review is "ripeness." This means that the rule must have caused injury to the plaintiff before a court action can be filed. Such requirement follows the constitutional mandate that courts hear only cases or controversies and do not decide hypothetical matters.

Most administrative agencies have been given the power to make investigations and to gather information, activities that can result in the

Final Order
Despite the name, a final order from an agency is appealable, but an appeal before its issuance is premature.

Ripeness
Doctrine of the court, in accordance with a policy of self-restraint, that cases will not be decided before it is necessary to decide them.

Freedom of Information

Freedom of Information Act
A federal act that establishes a general policy of full agency disclosure unless information is clearly exempted.

Section 552 of the APA is the Freedom of Information Act, which sets forth the rights of private persons to obtain information in the possession of the government. The Act requires each agency to make available for public inspection and copying its opinions in decided cases, its statements of policy, and interpretations not previously published in the *Federal Register*. Exceptions are materials authorized by executive order to be kept secret in the interest of national defense or foreign policy; internal personnel rules and practices; information required by law to be kept from the public; trade secrets; privileged and confidential commercial or financial information; law enforcement investigatory records; and personal, medical, or similar files, the disclosure of which would clearly be an unwarranted invasion of personal privacy.

Sunshine Act

Sunshine Act
Law that requires government agencies and departments to permit the public to attend their meetings.

The Government in Sunshine Act requires generally that agencies hold their meetings open to the public. Most states have adopted similar legislation. For purposes of the law, a "meeting" means deliberation by agency members that determines or results in the conduct or disposition of official agency business. Exceptions are similar to those under the Freedom of Information Act, plus the right to close meetings where a person is accused of a crime, when an open meeting would significantly frustrate the implementation of an agency action, or when the meeting concerns the issuance of an agency subpoena.

Facts

Common Cause, a consumer activist group, challenged the Nuclear Regulatory Commission under the Government in Sunshine Act for closing its budgetary hearing meetings. The Commission said that it came under the exception of "premature disclosure" and would "be likely to significantly frustrate implementation of a proposed agency action." It added that some of the matters related "solely to the internal personnel rules and practices of an agency."

Decision

The court held that the Act establishes the policy that "the public is entitled to the fullest practicable information regarding the decision making processes of Federal Government." It concluded that increased openness would enhance citizen confidence in government, encourage higher quality work by government officials, stimulate well-informed public debate about government programs, and promote cooperation between citizens and government. It ordered the transcripts of the closed meetings to be given to Common Cause and that all future meetings be open unless the court gives prior approval for any closure.

Common Cause v. Nuclear Regulatory Commission, 674 F.2d 921 (D.C. Cir. 1982).

Privacy Act

The Privacy Act of 1974 was designed to protect the privacy of individuals by requiring governmental agencies to follow certain rules in dealing with personal information in their files. The law came as a result of the Watergate affair and reports of domestic spying by the FBI and the CIA. The protection is to citizens or aliens lawfully admitted for permanent residence and is not available to businesses. It requires notice and prior consent before the disclosure of any personal information that might identify the individual. Persons concerned also have the right of access to such records and to request amendments to correct any inaccuracies that are discovered. These rights may be enforced by court action and, in appropriate cases, an award of money damages.

Recently, as a result of criticism of administrative agencies, there have been some attempts at deregulation. Major complaints are that there are too many agencies and that the agencies have become too large. As the size and number of agencies increase, it is alleged that the ability of the people to control those in political power lessens. Some critics contend that independent agencies with legislative, executive, and judicial powers under one head violates the basic premise of constitutional separation of powers. Others claim that procedural and evidentiary rules are lax and do not provide the protection found in courts of law.

Privacy Act
Law designed to protect the privacy of individuals from disclosure of certain personal information contained in government files.

QUESTIONS

1. What are some of the advantages and disadvantages in the use of administrative agencies?
2. Name an important independent agency and explain how it uses its legislative, judicial, and executive powers.
3. What are the prerequisites for getting a judicial review of an administrative decision?
4. How do you reconcile the Freedom of Information Act with the Right of Privacy Act?
5. Can you think of a current social problem in need of regulation? What kind of agency would you create for that purpose?

PROBLEMS

1. The city council of Burbank, California, passed an ordinance making it unlawful for jet aircraft to take off from the Hollywood-Burbank Airport between 11:00 p.m. and 7:00 a.m. Lockheed Air Terminal asked for an injunction against enforcement of this ordinance, contending that the local government had no constitutional power to regulate aircraft movements. What should the U.S. Supreme Court decide? *Burbank* v. *Lockheed Air Terminal,* 411 U.S. 624, 93 S.Ct. 1854, 36 L.Ed.2d 547 (1973).
2. During the Watergate investigations, a *subpoena duces tecum* was served on President Nixon requiring production of certain tapes and papers. President Nixon made a motion to quash the subpoena on the grounds of an unqualified presidential immunity from judicial process. Because of the conflict between branches of the government, the U.S. Supreme Court took the case on direct appeal from the district trial court. What was its decision? *United States* v. *Nixon,* 418 U.S. 683, 94 S.Ct. 3090, 41 L.Ed.2d 1039 (1974).
3. Colleen Cote hired a Michigan lawyer to represent her in a medical malpractice suit in Michigan. Although she had paid him, she discovered that he had done nothing and that the case had been dismissed for want of prosecution. She then hired a Wisconsin lawyer to bring a malpractice suit against the Michigan attorney. The case was filed in a federal district court in Wisconsin as a diversity of citizenship suit. Does jurisdiction exist under a long-

arm statute? *Cote v. Wadel,* 796 F.2d 981 (7th Cir. 1986).

4. Unlike other states west of the Mississippi, Iowa prohibited by statute the use of 60-foot double-trailer trucks within its borders. Consolidated Freightways owned such trucks, and the law forbade them from hauling goods from other states through Iowa on interstate highways. Consolidated sued, claiming an unreasonable burden on interstate commerce. Iowa officials defended on the ground that it was a reasonable safety measure. Who wins the case? *Kassel v. Consolidated Freightways Corp. of Delaware,* 450 U.S. 662, 101 S.Ct. 1309, 67 L.Ed.2d 580 (1981).

5. In mediation and some arbitration hearings, witnesses often explain their evidence in story form rather than by the question-and-answer method used by attorneys in court. Direct examination and cross-examination, as such, are not followed. What are some of the advantages and disadvantages of this technique?

6. Bevles Co., Inc., was advised by its lawyers that it is unlawful in California to knowingly employ illegal aliens. After interrogating its employees suspected of being in the country illegally, Bevles fired two of them. The local union, of which the two were members, filed a grievance that the employer lacked just cause, and the matter was submitted to arbitration. The arbitrator reinstated the employees and said that one was entitled to back pay. The employer appealed the ruling to the district court on the grounds that it should be set aside, as the employees were not legally entitled to work in the United States. What decision? *Bevles Co., Inc. v. Teamsters Local 896,* 791 F.2d 1391 (9th Cir. 1986).

7. Under the Occupational Safety and Health Act of 1970 (OSHA), an employer may be ordered to end or correct an unsafe working condition. On failing to do so, a civil penalty or a fine may be assessed against the employer. Atlas Roofing was told to correct an unsafe condition and was fined for failing to do so. Atlas claimed that the administrative procedure denied to it a constitutionally guaranteed trial by jury. What do you think the U.S. Supreme Court decided? *Atlas Roofing Company Inc. v. OSH Review Commission,* 430 U.S. 442, 97 S.Ct. 1261, 51 L.Ed.2d 464 (1977).

8. Constitutional due process requires that federal and state governments provide notice and a hearing before taking action that deprives an individual of liberty or property. Robert Fain, a student of Brooklyn College, was charged with destroying copies of the campus newspaper, *Kingsman*. A notice of hearing was sent to Fain during the summer term when he was not registered but while school was in session. School bylaws require that students be given a notice of five school days preceding a hearing. Fain was found guilty by a campus committee and suspended. Is he correct in claiming that he did not receive proper notice? *Fain v. Brooklyn College of City University,* 493 N.Y.S.2d 13, 112 A.D.2d 992 (1985).

9. McGee registered for the selective service and was drafted but failed to make a personal appearance before the draft board or to appeal his classification. In the criminal proceeding against him for refusal to submit to induction, he alleges that he should have been classified as a conscientious objector and offers evidence to prove that fact. What should the court rule? *McGee v. United States,* 402 U.S. 479 91 S.Ct. 1565, 29 L.Ed.2d 47 (1971).

10. A committee of members of the Federal Communications Commission was attending an informal international conference with counterpart European agencies. The purpose was to exchange views about licensing issues but not to make decisions concerning proposals on which the agency might act. The conference was private, but the media demanded admittance under the Government in Sunshine Act. What decision? *FCC v. ITT World Communications,* 466 U.S. 463, 104 S.Ct. 1936, 80 L.Ed.2d 480 (1984).

CHAPTER THREE

Wrongful Acts in Business

3.1 **Ethics in Business and Law**
Ethics Defined
Ethical Conduct in Business
Lying
   White Lies
Codes of Ethics
Cost-Benefit Considerations
Rules of Ethics
Ethical Issues

3.2 **Business-Related Torts**
Tort Defined
Negligence
   Proximate Cause
   Contributory and Comparative Negligence
   Assumption of Risk
   Res Ipsa Loquitor
Common Business Torts
   Malpractice
   Fraud
   Defamation
   Trade Libel
   Emotional Distress
   Invasion of Privacy
   False Imprisonment
   Assault and Battery
   Nuisance
   Conversion
   Trespass
   Interference with Contract
   Unfair Competition

3.3 **Crime in Business**
Crime Defined
Types of Crimes
Safeguards
   Fair Trial
   Presumption of Innocence
   Intent
   Criminal Negligence
   Illegal Evidence
   Corpus Delecti
Defenses to Crimes
   Ignorance of the Law
   Mistake
   Infancy
   Insanity
   Intoxication
   Self-defense
Entrapment
Double Jeopardy
Statute of Limitations
Immunity
Common Business Crimes
   White-Collar Crime
   Theft
   Robbery
   Burglary
   Receiving Stolen Property
   Assault and Battery
   Arson
   Misuse of Documents
   Forgery
   Counterfeiting
   Bad Checks
   Credit Cards
   Bribery
   Extortion
   Antitrust
   Income Tax Evasion
   Fraud
Political Crimes
Computer Crimes
Organized Crime
Conspiracy
Solicitation

3.1 Ethics in Business and Law

"It's not what a lawyer tells me I may do; but what humanity, reason, and justice, tell me I ought to do." Edmund Burke.

Recent headlines make it clear that many wrongful acts take place in the business world. Some are illegal, either as civil wrongs for which the injured party may sue to recover money damages or as criminal acts for which the government punishes the violators. Some actions, such as assault and battery, may include both civil and criminal wrongs. All such improper conduct involves the issue of *ethics*.

Ethics Defined

Ethics
Standard of conduct and moral judgment.

What is ethics? A consensus of dictionary definitions as used in this context would emphasize moral conduct, or doing what is right rather than what is wrong and knowing the difference between good and evil.

How does one determine what is ethical? Different cultures have different ideas and values. It would be difficult to get a consensus on such statements as "The capitalist system of economics does the most good for the most people" or "A woman should have the right to decide for herself whether or not to have an abortion." Ethics has been a major topic of philosophical argument throughout recorded history. But since this is not a book for a course on philosophical contemplation, our concern here is with business ethics.

Esteem
Favorable opinion.

Polls and editorial comment in the media indicate that business executives, lawyers, and politicians do not rate very high in public esteem. Ethics, or the lack of it, is a major problem. Wall Street executives have been fined and sent to prison for illegal insider trading deals. Aircraft company managers have been found guilty of the crime of foreign bribery. Corporate officers of a baby food marketer were jailed for selling colored sugar water as real apple juice. Government contractors have confessed to illegally padding procurement contracts. Toxic wastes, improperly disposed of, seep through the ground or are washed up on our beaches. A federal judge was convicted of income tax evasion, impeached by the Congress, and removed from office. In 1986 the Justice Department indicted 1,193 people under the Public Corruption Act and got 1,027 convictions. Legislators have been charged with accepting illegal campaign contributions. Most of us are aware of many similar examples.

Ethical Conduct in Business

The Wall Street Journal in a 1987 survey asked 671 business managers for their views on ethics and business. Most of those surveyed contended that ethics could impede a successful career, and more than half said they would bend the rules to get ahead. The current emphasis on individualism, competition, and achieving material success that marks our society causes great pressure to cut corners. To win an election, to outsell competition, or to increase income causes some to use unethical actions they might otherwise resist. The incentives for deceit are powerful, and as yet, the controls are weak.

Through regulation, business law has tried to compel ethical conduct, but that goal obviously has not been reached. Managers have learned that it can be quite profitable to violate the law, as in the cases of illegal price fixing and the dumping of toxic wastes. If the offenders are caught, the punishment—almost always a fine—may amount to only a small portion of the vast profits made. Many regulatory laws are so complex and require so much paperwork that the average person cannot understand them.

A trend may be developing towards imposing harsher penalties. Ivan Boesky, a stock market speculator, pleaded guilty to insider trading on the stock market, was required to pay $100 million, serve a prison term, and was barred from all future market activities.

Some people see no wrong in what others may consider unethical conduct. Some authorities argue that insider trading should be legal. Although the Watergate scandal exposed much lying under oath, there was a lack of great public concern.

Insider Trading
Trading of corporate stock by a corporate officer or other *insider* who profits by his access to information not available to the public.

Lying

Lying is a major ethical problem in business. The entire basis of our system of justice rests on the assumption that everyone tells the truth under oath. Each witness in a courtroom is required to swear to "tell the truth, the whole truth, and nothing but the truth, so help me God." The ancient origin of this oath was in religious ethics and a widespread belief that God would apply horrible punishment to violators. Today the crime of perjury has replaced divine sanctions, but there are few prosecutions.

Absolutist philosophers believe that all lying is bad, whereas others argue that some types of lying may be justified or excused if the intent is to do good or to save others from harm. Since the vast majority of people would agree that lying is wrong, why do so many do it? Perhaps people lie to get out of a scrape, to save face, to avoid hurting others' feelings, to gain ascendancy for themselves, or to manipulate those around them. Lying requires a reason, whereas telling the truth does not.

Perjury
The crime of making false statements under oath.

White Lies

Most people are guilty of telling so-called little white lies. Courteous people write letters of appreciation and gratitude for unwanted gifts. Professors may inflate grades to increase their popularity. Letters of employment recommendations are usually more flattering than factual. Even President Eisenhower lied about the U-2 spy plane incident in an effort to cover up the reconnaissance mission of the pilot. Perhaps Mark Twain wasn't being cynical when he wrote, "When in doubt, tell the truth. It will confound your enemies and astound your friends."

Section 4 of the Code of Ethics of the American Medical Association requires doctors to "expose, without hesitation, illegal or unethical conduct of fellow members of their profession." In practice, however, such exposés are quite rare, and most press reports are about coverups.

Codes of Ethics

Code of Ethics
System of morals for a particular group or profession.

Lawyers, judges, and arbitrators have adopted separate codes of ethics. The U.S. House of Representatives, the U.S. Senate, and federal employees are guided by canons of ethics, and the Congress has oversight committees to check compliance. The U.S. Supreme Court has upheld the legality of the appointment of special prosecutors to investigate unethical conduct in the executive branch. CPAs, realtors, bankers, insurance people, engineers, and architects have created rules for the ethical conduct of their respective businesses. However, no such restraints have been adopted for economists and business leaders.

Some people argue that such codes may be used as a shield to protect those covered rather than as a benefit for the public. In the following case, the U.S. Supreme Court set aside some of the rules as applied to attorneys.

Zauderer v. Office of Disciplinary Counsel
471 U.S. 626, 105 S.Ct. 2265, 85 L.Ed.2d 652 (1985).

Justice White delivered the opinion of the Court. . . .

In the spring of 1982, appellant placed an advertisement in 36 Ohio newspapers publicizing his willingness to represent women who had suffered injuries resulting from their use of a contraceptive device known as the Dalkon Shield Intrauterine Device. The advertisement featured a line drawing of the Dalkon Shield accompanied by the question, "DID YOU USE THIS IUD?" The advertisement then related the following information:

> "The Dalkon Shield Interuterine [sic] Device is alleged to have caused serious pelvic infections resulting in hospitalizations, tubal damage, infertility, and hysterectomies. It is also alleged to have caused unplanned pregnancies ending in abortions, miscarriages, septic abortions, tubal or ectopic pregnancies, and full-term deliveries. If you or a friend have had a similar experience do not assume it is too late to take legal action against the Shield's manufacturer. Our law firm is presently representing women on such cases. The cases are handled on a contingent fee basis of the amount recovered. If there is no recovery, no legal fees are owed by our clients."

The ad concluded with the name of appellant's law firm, its address, and a phone number that the reader might call for "free information." . . .

The advertisement was successful in attracting clients: appellant received well over 200 inquiries regarding the advertisement, and he initiated lawsuits on behalf of 106 of the women who contacted him as a result of the advertisement. The ad, however, also aroused the interest of the Office of Disciplinary Counsel. On July 29, 1982, the Office filed a complaint against appellant charging him with a number of disciplinary violations arising out of . . . the . . . Dalkon Shield advertisement.

The State's argument proceeds from the premise that it is intrinsically difficult to distinguish advertisements containing legal advice that is false or deceptive from those that are truthful and helpful, much more so than is the case with other goods or services. This notion is belied by the facts before us: appellant's statements regarding Dalkon Shield litigation were in fact easily verifiable and completely accurate. Nor is it true that distinguishing deceptive from nondeceptive claims in advertising involving products other than legal services is a comparatively simple and straightforward process . . . Appellant's advertisement informed the public that "if there is no recovery, no legal fees are owed by our clients." The advertisement makes no mention of the distinction between "legal fees" and "costs," and to a layman not aware of the meaning of these terms of art, the advertisement would suggest that employing appellant would be a no-lose proposition in that his representation in a losing cause would come entirely free of charge. The assumption that substantial numbers of potential clients would be so misled is hardly a speculative one: it is a commonplace that members of the public are often unaware of the technical meanings of such terms as "fees" and "costs"—terms that, in ordinary usage, might well be virtually interchangeable.

. . . [T]hree separate forms of regulation Ohio has imposed on advertising by its attorneys: prohibitions on soliciting legal business through advertisements containing advice and information regarding specific legal problems; restrictions on the use of illustrations in advertising by lawyers; and disclosure requirements relating to the terms of contingent fees.

The Supreme Court of Ohio issued a public reprimand incorporating by reference its opinion finding that appellant had violated Disciplinary Rules. . . . That judgment is affirmed to the extent that it is based on appellant's advertisement involving his terms . . . on the omission of information regarding his contingent-fee arrangements in his Dalkon Shield advertisement. But insofar as the reprimand was based on appellant's use of an illustration in his advertisement . . . and his offer of legal advice in his advertisement . . . the judgment is reversed.

It is so ordered.

Cost-Benefit Considerations

Most courses in business administration are directed towards doing what is economically the most profitable. Perhaps this is why cost-benefit ratio calculations have replaced ethical considerations in the making of some important decisions. The following illustrates the application of this method.

Ford Motor Company, seeking to regain markets lost to smaller foreign cars in the 1960s, rushed production of the Pinto. Company memos showed that crash testing over twenty-five miles per hour resulted in ruptured gas tanks in every instance. Ford met existing federal safety standards and went on with production. Ford's own study concluded that the cost of design improvement ($11 per vehicle) far outweighed the social benefits. Ford's cost-benefit analysis showed that the benefit of improving the design would be the prevention of an estimated 180 burn deaths, 180 serious burn injuries, and 2,100 burned vehicles, at a unit cost to the company of $200,000 per death, $67,000 per injury, and $700 per vehicle, for a total benefit of under $50 million. The estimated cost of improving the tanks was $137 million. Ford opted for the lower figure At least fifty-three persons have died in accidents involving Pinto fires. In one of the cases, a jury returned a verdict against Ford for $128 million.

Polaroid's suit against Eastman Kodak Company also shows how costly it can be to ignore ethical considerations.

Facts

The Eastman Kodak Company was concerned about the large share of the market that Polaroid had taken with its patented instant photography system. Arguing that such should not be the perpetual domain of Polaroid, Eastman Kodak's development committee in September 1973 directed its technicians to develop a rival system, and its instructions included: "Development should not be constrained by what any individual feels is potential patent infringement." Eastman Kodak marketed a comparable camera and was then sued by Polaroid for patent infringement.

Decision

Eastman Kodak had violated several of Polaroid's patents, and it was enjoined from using them and required to recall all items distributed for sale. A further trial was ordered but only for the purpose of determining the amount of damages Polaroid should be awarded. Eastman Kodak has already paid over $400 million to compensate its own customers, and analysts believe that the final award may exceed the total value of all other Polaroid assets.

Polaroid v. *Eastman Kodak Company,* 641 F.Supp. 828 (1985), upheld on appeal, 833 F.2d 930 (Fed.Cir. 1986), and let stand by the U.S. Supreme Court.

Rules of Ethics

Corporations don't make unethical decisions, only people do. All institutions are made up of people. Ethical standards were once based on the Golden Rule, or variations thereof, such as Confucius' negative application, "Don't do unto others what you wouldn't want them to do to you."

"If it works for me" seems to be the modern rule. Even when persons believe they know what is right and wrong in business conduct, their actions don't always follow their beliefs. Peer group pressure can cause one to do something wrong that others deem right.

Sycophant
A person who seeks favor by flattering people of wealth and influence.

Young leaders usually go along with their superiors to show loyalty. One top executive stated that sycophancy (trying to win favor or get ahead by flattering those of influence) keeps America going. Another advised that the fastest way up the ladder to success was to kiss the rear of the one above you and to step on the fingers of the one below. Surrounded by such cynicism, how can honest people make ethical decisions?

Kenneth Blanchard and Norman Vincent Peale in their short book "The Power of Ethical Management," suggest some ethical guidelines. One should first ask whether the proposed action is legal and not in violation of the law or company policy. Fairness should be considered next. Is the decision fair to all concerned, both in the short term as well as in the long run? Finally, the decision maker should consider how the result will make him feel about himself. It should leave the person with a sense of pride in having done the right thing.

Ethical Issues

Following are examples of some common occurrences. Discuss the ethical problems involved in each situation.

1. You receive your monthly bank statement and notice that $1,000 has been deposited into your personal account. You know that you did not make the deposit.

2. You plan to go to your professional association's convention in Las Vegas. The Internal Revenue Service has ruled that expenses of attending such conventions are deductible for delegates only if most of the time is spent in business sessions. You go to Las Vegas, register, and check in at the opening meeting, but from then on you spend most of your time in the casinos and at shows. You deduct your expenses (not including gambling losses) from your income tax return.

3. You are a master barber, highly skilled, with many years of successful practice in Illinois. You retire and move to California. You wish to augment your retirement pay, but after checking the expense of leasing a shop and the rigid requirements to obtain a California barber's license, you decide to put a barber's chair in your garage and accommodate only a few of your personal friends for a nominal cost.

4. You are an office employee of the federal government. Your office is well stocked with U.S. government ballpoint pens and writing pads. You take some of them home for your own and your family's use. Your office also has a leased telephone line, and the cost is the same no matter how many calls are made. Since there will be no extra cost to the government, you use the phone to make many of your personal calls.

5. You are director of sales for a large corporation that deals in government contracts, and you are employing a new sales manager. Among the applicants is the sales manager of one of your leading competitors. He is by far the best of those seeking the job, and he tells you that if hired, he will bring with him some floppy discs that contain lists of customers and details of bids and specifications on government contracts involving his former employer. Such information would be a great help to you in obtaining new business, so you hire him.

6. You fall asleep while driving your car. The car drifts off the road and collides with a tree, causing vehicle body damage. The insurance adjuster estimates the damage at $900. Your policy has a $100 deductible provision. Your auto mechanic is a good friend and tells you he'll do a good job for you for $900 and as a discount to you will accept the $800 check from the insurance company as payment in full.

7. You are a skilled computer programmer looking for a steady job. A large firm wants you to program its payroll and, to get you to do it, says that it will retain you after you have completed the project. You distrust the employer, so when you set up the payroll, you program it to abort and go into a loop whenever your name fails to appear on the payroll. Shortly after you complete the work, you are dismissed. The entire system scraps the next time the payroll is run.

8. Your father is on the board of directors of a large corporation. He calls you at home one night and advises you that the company has decided on a profitable merger that won't be announced for another week. He suggests that you immediately buy as much of the company's stock as you can afford but warns you to keep it secret so that the price won't go up too soon.

9. The speed limit in your state is 55 miles per hour on freeways. You commute daily and drive at least 65, as do most others on the road.

One day an officer stops you for speeding. He advises you that the fine will be $40 but that you can pay it directly to him and be on your way.

10. You own a small dress manufacturing business. You have been advised that you are not allowed to employ illegal aliens. However, there are many such persons in your area. You feel sorry for them. You know that they work harder and do a better job for less pay. You hire ten of them.

Questions

1. Lockheed Aircraft Corporation admitted making $22 million in secret payoffs to Japanese officials to sell airplanes to Japan. Its representative said that it did not violate any American laws and that the payments were requested by the Japanese, not offered by Lockheed. It contended that if anything, the act was extortion, not a bribe. Is this a good ethical argument?

2. Adolph Coors Brewery in Golden, Colorado, required a lie-detector test be taken by all prospective employees. Questions were asked about narcotics or alcohol use, subversive activities, theft, felony convictions, and intent to do harm to the brewery or its employees. Is this requirement ethical?

3. "Ethics is a purely private matter" and "Ethics has no place in business" are statements made by some business leaders in a recent poll. What did they mean, and do you agree with them?

4. To try to cut down on the number of traffic violations, accidents, and fatalities, your state decides to use unmarked police vehicles with officers in plain clothes. Even if this accomplishes its purpose, do you believe this deception is ethical?

5. Many business leaders believe that open competition in free markets and the pursuit of profit best serve the members of society. Consumer groups argue that these policies lead to many wrongs, including uncontrolled harmful pollution, deceptive advertising, unsafe working conditions, price fixing, bribery, and fraud. Can ethical conduct resolve this conflict of views?

3.2 Business-Related Torts

Tort Defined

Tort
A private or civil wrong or injury not based on contract but resulting from the breach of a legal duty that one owes to another.

Torts are wrongs that cause harm or injury to another party (either an individual or a legal entity such as a corporation), creating the right to bring a civil action for money damages against the wrongdoer.

Negligence

A tort can result either from *negligence* (acting in an unreasonable manner) or from willful and intentional acts. Another class of tort imposes strict liability regardless of fault, such as injuries resulting from defective products. (Product liability is discussed in more detail in Chapter 19.)

The law presumes that we all act in a reasonable manner at all times and that we owe a duty of reasonable care to others. Reasonable care is that which would be used by an ordinary, sensible person acting under similar circumstances. Negligence as a tort happens when the tortfeasor acts unreasonably and such action causes damage to the injured party. Many of us have experienced the most common tort—damage and injury resulting from the negligent operation of a motor vehicle.

Negligence
Failure to exercise the care expected of an ordinary reasonable person under similar circumstances.

Proximate Cause

Traffic laws impose duties on drivers to observe speed limits and other rules of the road. If the breach of any of these rules is the *proximate cause* of injury or damage, a tort occurs. Such cause is that which, in a natural and continuous sequence unbroken by any important intervening act, results in the injury. Proximate cause would exist if a vehicle driver were to run a red light and strike a pedestrian in a crosswalk. Failing to obey the duty to stop at the red light would be the proximate cause of the harm to the pedestrian.

Proximate Cause
A cause that produces an event without which an injury would not have occurred.

Other torts might result from an automobile accident. If the drivers of vehicles in a collision should get angry at each other and get into a fight, the torts of assault and battery might occur. One of the drivers might fake an injury and claim money damages which would be a fraud against the insurance carrier. Another might be taken to a hospital where he was improperly treated, which could result in the negligent tort of medical malpractice. If the collision were due to a defective part in the auto, the maker may be liable in strict liability for a defective product.

Contributory and Comparative Negligence

Many states follow the doctrine of *contributory negligence,* which means that if the injured party were also negligent or contributed to the injuries, there can be no damage recovery regardless of the degree of fault. Other states have opted to follow a modern trend called *comparative negligence,* which apportions the damages according to the amount of negligence on either side. If the car running the red light had hit a pedestrian who was jaywalking, both would have some extent of fault. The court or a jury might decide that the driver was 90 percent wrong and the jaywalker only 10 percent. In such a case, after comparing the negligence, the injured pedestrian would receive only 90 percent of the total amount found for damages suffered.

Contributory Negligence
Conduct by the plaintiff below that reasonably needed for his own protection and that contributed to bringing about his harm.

Comparative Negligence
The allocation of responsibility for damages between the parties based upon their proportionate fault.

Assumption of Risk

Assumption of risk might be another defense in some tort actions. This refers to a situation that might be risky, but the person, knowing the risk involved, elects to assume it. Suppose a baseball fan sits in a ballpark area where he knows foul balls are hit. Even though he knows he might be hit by a ball, he decides to sit there anyway. He has assumed the risk. This rule would not apply to those who sat there unaware of the danger.

Assumption of Risk
A tort defense where the plaintiff had knowledge of a dangerous situation but voluntarily exposed himself to the hazard created by the defendant.

Facts

Rebecca Nelson, a vet's assistant, was bitten by Richard Hall's dog Amos while she was helping in the dog's treatment at the hospital at which she was employed. The dog was known to the hospital staff as one that might bite, and a notation of "careful" was written on the treatment card. Nelson sued Hall under a "dog-bite statute" imposing strict liability for keeping an animal known to be dangerous. She did not allege that Hall was negligent or had any knowledge of Amos's vicious tendencies.

Decision

Although there was strict liability on dog owners under state law, the defense of assumption of risk applied. Since Nelson assumed the risks inherent in her occupation, that was a complete defense, and the case was dismissed.

Nelson v. *Hall,* 165 Cal.App.3d 709, 211 Cal.Rptr. 668 (1985).

Res Ipsa Loquitor

Res Ipsa Loquitor
An evidence rule where negligence by the wrongdoer can be inferred from the mere fact that the accident happened. "The thing speaks for itself."

In some instances negligence and cause may be inferred from the circumstances. This is known as *res ipsa loquitor,* or "the thing speaks for itself." For example, Alice had rented a motel room and was taking a shower in the enclosed tub. When she opened the shower door, the door fell off in her hands and shattered, and she was cut badly by broken glass.

Common Business Torts

Some common business torts are negligent use of motor vehicles, defective products, professional malpractice, fraud, defamation, trade libel, infliction of mental distress, invasion of privacy, false imprisonment, assault and battery, nuisance, conversion, trespass, interference with contract, unfair competition, and antitrust violations.

Under agency law, owners of businesses are responsible for the operation of motor vehicles by their employees when using the vehicles in the scope of their employment. This is discussed in detail in Chapter 13.

Malpractice

Malpractice
A professional person's negligent performance of duties.

Doctors, lawyers, accountants, and other professional people who perform their duties in a negligent manner may be sued for malpractice. The standard of care applied to such professionals is what other persons in the same profession would be expected to do under similar circumstances.

Fraud

Fraud
Intentional deception resulting in injury to another.

Among intentional torts, fraud is one of the most common found in business activities. To prove fraud as a tort, the following essential elements are required:

1. a false representation (lie) about an important fact;
2. made with the knowledge that it was false, or with inexcusable ignorance of its truth;

3. made with the intention that it be acted upon by the party deceived;
4. that the deceived party reasonably relied upon the misrepresentation and was deceived by it; and
5. that the deceived party suffered damages as a result.

The defrauded party can recover compensatory money damages or have a fraudulent contract rescinded. If the fraud is very bad or malicious, most states allow punitive, or exemplary, damages on top of the actual loss. The purpose of such award is to punish the wrongdoer and set an example to deter others from doing similar acts. If the fraud violates a penal statute it may also be a crime. (Fraud in contracts is discussed in more detail in Chapter 6.)

Defamation

Defamation results when a party makes a false communication about another party to a third person that contains matter injurious to the defamed one's reputation. Defamation may be in writing, which is called *libel,* or oral, which is *slander.*

Proof of defamation requires the plaintiff to show that the objectionable matter was intentionally made by the defendant to someone else who understood it or that it was communicated in a negligent manner. Some lies are actionable torts even without proving damages. They may be statements that a person has a loathsome communicable disease, has committed wrongs while engaging in a profession or trade, has committed a serious crime or been in prison for one, or is unchaste.

Defamation
The publication of anything injurious to the reputation of another.

Libel
False and malicious publication printed for the purpose of defamation.

Slander
Spoken words that tend to damage the reputation of another.

Schomer v. Smidt
113 Cal.App.3d 828, 170 Cal.Rptr. 662 (1980).

Kilgarif, J. Cathleen Schomer filed a complaint . . . The principal action was for slander. The jury returned verdicts for $20,000 general damages and $16,000 punitive damages. The thrust of Schomer's slander action was that Douglas Smidt uttered false and defamatory comments to her fellow employees which caused others to infer that Schomer was a lesbian. . . .

On April 29, 1976, appellant, respondent and other members of an airline flight crew No. 217 ended their workday with an overnight layover in Long Beach, California. They were to spend the night at the Edgewater Hotel in Long Beach where the incidents which precipitated the lawsuit occurred. Appellant asked respondent on several occasions during the day to socialize with him that evening. On each occasion, respondent declined and indicated she wished to spend the evening in her room. . . . Respondent was assigned a room with Heidi Spitz. They had dinner in the hotel restaurant and returned to their room to watch television. Smidt phoned the room several times. Schomer, believing it to be Smidt calling, did not answer. Smidt approached Schomer's room and knocked on the door. Schomer testified she heard the knock but did not answer and that Smidt hit the door until it burst open with a rush. Smidt entered the room. Smidt saw respondent reclining on one of the beds and Miss Spitz standing between the two beds. Smidt testified that, at no time, did he see anything to cause him to believe there was any lesbian activity. . . . Schomer testified that Smidt was in the room for 20 to 25 minutes and as he was leaving the room he stated: "I know you Shomer. When I get through with you, your name will be mud. As far as the male crew members are concerned, you will be at the very bottom of the ladder." Smidt then returned to the bar and told Conn Thrasher and Leo Hansen that he walked in on Schomer and Spitz; that he had startled them; Spitz had her zipper down; that he was not sure what he had seen; that "they were getting it on" and "they were doing their own thing." . . .

Schomer learned of the rumors concerning her from several flight attendants. . . . Schomer testified that 50 to 75 persons, including a flight passenger, discussed the incident with her and some of these persons referred specifically to lesbian acts.

. . . The court instructions on slander, pertinent to this appeal were: "Slander is a false and unprivileged publication, orally uttered, which: (4) Imputes . . . a want of chastity; . . .

"The charge of lesbianism implies unchastity and abnormal sexual behavior. . . .

"If you find that the defendant stated, implied or gave the impression that plaintiff had engaged in lesbian sexual acts, then you are instructed as follows: The imputation of Lesbianism is slanderous per se. This means that such words are presumed by the law to cause damage and plaintiff may recover for her hurt feelings, mental suffering and humiliation without proving any out of pocket loss." . . .

The Legislature of this state has decreed that sexual conduct, of any sort, between consenting adults is legal. We are not concerned with legality but rather with chastity. To hold that *chastity* applies only to fornication borders on the ridiculous. . . . Webster's Third International Dictionary, at page 379, defines "chaste" in 2(a) as "abstaining from all sexual relations."

. . . It would appear to this court, that despite the sexual revolution and the freedom of action and expression now extant, there is a distinction which must be drawn between proper, moral and legal conduct. Based on the new thinking a homosexual or heterosexual act could be proper, legal and questionably "moral." But everyone has a right to refrain from such activity and to enjoy an unsullied reputation of restraint. To state that one carried on sexual conduct be it alone, with members of the opposite or similar sex imputes to them a "want of chastity," which in the eyes and minds of their peers might and could subject them to disgrace, ridicule, damage to reputation, lacking virtue or reliability. We find that a false imputation of the commission of a homosexual act is slanderous per se. . . .

The judgment is affirmed.

A publisher is one who is responsible for the original publication of a defamation and is liable for that defamation unless there is a valid defense. A disseminator, or distributor, merely circulates, sells, rents, or otherwise disposes of the material to others. The disseminator is liable only if he knew or reasonably should have known of the defamatory nature of the material.

Truth and Fair Comment The truth of a statement and fair comment by writers or radio and TV commentators expressing an opinion are appropriate defenses to defamation. Whether or not a comment is fair is of course largely a matter of judgment based on the way the facts are presented, the choice of words, or the tone of voice used.

Fair Comment
A defense in a libel suit that statements were not with malice but were intended to state the facts as the writer honestly understood them to be.

Facts

Mazza, a paid reporter for the University of West Virginia student newspaper, wrote a piece rating eating places near the campus. Describing a restaurant-diner called Havalunch, she wrote: "Bring a can of Raid if you plan to eat here. And paint your neck red; looks like a truck stop. You'll regret everything you eat here, especially the BLTs." When sued for libel, Mazza argued that her review was based on facts. She said that her BLT had been overcooked and dry, a roach had sauntered across the floor while she was eating, and the place did look to her like a truck stop. Havalunch recovered a judgment for $15,000, and Mazza appealed.

Decision

The West Virginia Supreme Court threw out the judgment stating that a reporter's opinion did not lose its "fair comment" protection merely because it was stated humorously or sarcastically. Ridicule in the form of humorous writings, verses, cartoons, or caricatures that carry a sting and cause adverse merriment in readers doesn't amount to defamation, as long as it's based on known or assumed facts.

Havalunch, Inc. v. Mazza, _____ W.Va. _____, 294 S.E.2d 70 (1981).

Consent In all intentional torts, including defamation, *consent* of the harmed party is good defense.

Privilege *Privilege* is also a defense to defamation. Privileges may be absolute, qualified (conditional), or constitutional. Absolute immunity under law has developed where public policy favors complete freedom of speech. Examples are statements made during a court proceeding, remarks of members of Congress on the floor of Congress and in committee meetings, statements by certain officers of the executive branch when made carrying out their governmental duties, and statements between spouses when they are alone. Qualified, or conditional, privilege is one conditioned upon its proper use. Under some circumstances, a person may publish defamatory matter to protect his own legitimate interests, such as reporting a crime believed committed against him. The U.S. Supreme Court has extended a constitutional privilege to comments regarding public officials or figures so long as such comments are made without malice. *Malice* means proof of the publisher's knowledge of falsity or reckless disregard for the truth. *Fair comment* is another type of qualified privilege.

Privilege
Benefits or exemptions from burdens available to some people because of the office they hold.

Trade Libel

Trade libel is a form of defamation against business. It has also been called slander of title or disparagement of goods. It is the intentional disparagement of the quality of another's goods that causes money damages to the plaintiff. It generally occurs when a party makes a false statement degrading the quality, character, utility, or value of a competitor's product. It is distinguished from libel in that it refers to goods rather than to reputation.

Trade Libel
Defamation against business.

Emotional Distress

Infliction of mental or emotional distress occurs when one, by outrageous conduct and without privilege, intentionally subjects another to severe mental or emotional suffering. Some courts have described it as conduct beyond all possible bounds of decency, atrocious, and utterly intolerable in a civilized community. Ordinarily, mere insults, indignities, threats, annoyances, petty oppressions, and other trivialities are not outrageous conduct. Emotional distress may consist of such mental reactions as fright, horror, grief, shame, humiliation, embarrassment, anger, chagrin, disappointment, worry, and nausea. The test is whether the plaintiff suffered a foreseeable injury that occurred in a foreseeable manner. Some examples would be wrapping a bloody, dead rat up as a loaf of bread and sending it to a sensitive person, or use of certain threatening language or conduct by a collection agency against a debtor. The defenses are similar to those for defamation.

Facts

The Reverend Jerry Falwell, a nationally prominent religious leader and political commentator, sued *Hustler* magazine and Larry Flynt, its publisher, for the intentional infliction of emotional distress caused by the publication of an outrageous parody advertisement satirizing a real advertising campaign for Campari Liqueur, in which celebrities talk about their "first time," referring to their first drink of the liqueur. The *Hustler* parody ran Falwell's picture as the celebrity along with the text of a supposed interview. It had Falwell describing his "first time" as an incestuous affair in an outhouse with his mother, who was portrayed as a promiscuous and intoxicated woman. It also depicted the Reverend Falwell as a hypocritical drunkard. Printed beneath the ad was a disclaimer: "Ad parody—not to be taken seriously." The jury found for Falwell and awarded him $200,000 for intentional infliction of emotional distress. *Hustler* appealed to the U.S. Supreme Court.

Decision

Public figures and public officials may not recover for the tort of intentional infliction of emotional distress by reason of an offensive ad parody caricature, even though without doubt, gross and repugnant in the eyes of most, unless they can also show that the publication contains a false statement of fact that was made with actual malice. Malice requires that the statement be made with the knowledge that it was false or with reckless disregard as to whether or not it was true. The trial jury had found that the ad parody "was not reasonably believable" as a fact. Reversed.

Hustler Magazine v. Falwell, 485 U.S. 46, 108 S.Ct. 876, 99 L.Ed.2d 41 (1988).

Invasion of Privacy

Invasion of Privacy
Wrongful intrusion into another's private activities by an individual or the government.

Invasion of privacy occurs when a party's right to be free from unwarranted and undesirable publicity has been invaded by another. Tort actions of privacy invasion can result from the following:

1. Intrusion upon a person's physical solitude, affairs, or seclusion.
2. Making public disclosures of private facts that the average person would find objectionable.
3. Publicity that puts a person in a false light.
4. Exploitation of a person's name, photograph, or likeness without consent.

Affirmative defenses to invasion of privacy may be the plaintiff's waiver or consent, that the matter is of public interest and newsworthy, or that the person whose privacy was invaded was a public figure. Government officials, candidates for public office, actors and actresses, and famous athletes are among those held to be public figures.

The Invasion of Privacy Act allows damages without proof of loss for eavesdropping on or electrically recording a conversation without the consent of all the parties thereto.

False Imprisonment

False imprisonment, or false arrest, is the intentional confinement of one person by another without justification. This may be a crime as well as a tort.

Confinement can consist of forcibly restraining a person within an enclosure with no reasonable means of escape. It can happen even when a person is under no physical restraint but submits to a threat of force or asserted legal authority. If a victim freely consents to the confinement, such confinement is not unlawful.

A merchant has the legal right to detain a person reasonably believed to have shoplifted merchandise. Most states require that the merchant make the detention in a reasonable manner, limited to a reasonable time, and only if there is reasonable cause.

False Imprisonment
The unjustified restraint and detention of a person.

Assault and Battery

An *assault* is the intentional action or conduct by one person directed at another that places the plaintiff in apprehension of immediate bodily harm or offensive contact. For example, if you threaten to hit someone who knows of the danger and is apprehensive of an imminent threat of injury, such a threat would be an assault. But, if you were to tell a friend that you are going to beat up someone else, it would not be an assault, since the other party is not aware of the threat.

While an assault is just the threat, *battery* is the actual harmful or offensive contact. If you threaten to hit a person and then carry out the threat, you have committed *assault and battery.* These acts are crimes as well as torts.

Assault
The attempt or threat to inflict bodily injury upon another with the apparent ability to do so.

Battery
The harmful or offensive use of any force upon the person of another.

Nuisance

Nuisance is the unreasonable interference with the possessory interest a party has in the use and enjoyment of his land. This tort may be negligent or intentional or a result of strict liability. The interference must be annoying, offensive, or inconvenient to a "normal" person in the community. Also, the harm to the plaintiff must outweigh the utility of the defendant's conduct. Some examples of nuisances are air pollution with noxious fumes, loud noises from a nearby racetrack or nightclub (particularly at night), and dangerous explosives stored in a residential area. Factors considered by the court would include the type of neighborhood, the relative value of the properties, and the existence of alternatives to reach the defendant's goals. The court may award money damages and may also order abatement of the nuisance.

Nuisance
A wrong arising from an unreasonable or unlawful use of property to the discomfort, annoyance, inconvenience, or damage of another.

Conversion

Conversion
Deprivation of another's personal property without authorization or justification.

Conversion is the unauthorized and unjustified interference with the ownership and control of another's personal property. It is a civil action for the crime of theft. Conversion may occur by taking property wrongfully or fraudulently; destroying property; using another's property without consent or authority; buying, selling, or receiving stolen property; delivering property to the wrong person; or refusing to surrender property to the rightful owner upon demand.

Trespass

Trespass
The wrongful interference with or disturbance of the possession of property of another.

Trespass against either real or personal property may be a tort. Real property is land and those things attached to it, such as minerals, trees, and buildings. Personal property generally consists of moveable things.

Landowners and possessors have a legal right to the property's exclusive use and quiet enjoyment. A party may be liable for damages in trespass if he enters land belonging to another, stays on the land, or refuses to remove from the land a thing that he has a duty to remove. Mistake is no defense even if the intruder believes he has a right to be on the land. There is no liability, however, if the trespass is not intentional. For example, a person who is thrown onto someone else's land by another person or whose garbage can is blown by a heavy gust of wind onto a neighbor's lot would not be liable for trespass.

Trespass may be committed on, beneath, or above the surface of the land. However, aviation has altered the air space rule, and airplanes are not considered trespassers when they are above the prescribed minimum altitude of flight. Aircraft that fly too low and substantially interfere with underlying landowners' use and enjoyment may be held liable.

The law protects interests in personal property such as the right to keep it, its condition and usability, and its availability for future use. Liability is usually limited to cases in which the trespasser takes another's property; substantially impairs the property's condition, quality, or value; deprives the rightful possessor of the property's use for a substantial time; or causes bodily harm to the possessor of the property. Although trespass of personal property is similar to conversion, the difference lies in the remedy. In trespass, the possessor recovers damages for the actual harm done and for loss of possession. In conversion, the possessor receives the full value of the property, which then belongs to the convertor upon payment of the judgment.

Interference with Contract

Contract Interference
Inducing a party to break a contract or interfering with a prospective contractual advantage.

Interference with contract is the tort of inducing a breach of contract or interfering with a prospective contractual advantage. For example, a third party induces another to break her contract of employment, a buyer and a seller of real estate conspire to deprive a broker of his commission, or a landlord threatens his tenant with termination unless the tenant evicts her subtenant. The plaintiff must prove the following:

1. That there was a valid and existing contract.
2. That the defendant had knowledge of the contract and intended to induce its breach.

3. That the contract was in fact broken by the other party.
4. That the breach resulted from the defendant's wrongful, unjustified conduct.
5. That the plaintiff suffered damage as result of the breach.

Facts

Gordon Getty owned 3/7 of Getty Oil Company stock and wanted to dispose of it. Pennzoil's president offered $115 a share to buy the entire company. An oral agreement was made, and a written memo was signed by a majority of Getty shareholders and approved by the board of directors. A press release was issued, and the story appeared in *The Wall Street Journal*. A formal written transaction agreement was in progress but not completed. Texaco Oil was short of oil reserves and wanted Getty's. Its president went to Gordon Getty's hotel suite in New York and offered Getty $125 a share, eventually paid $128, and bought up Getty Oil. Pennzoil sued for the tort of interference with a contract. A Texas jury awarded Pennzoil more than $11 billion in damages. Texaco appealed.

Decision

Texaco had knowingly interfered with Pennzoil's contract with Getty Oil and took an active part in persuading a party to the contract to breach the contract. The actual damages of $7.53 billion were based on expert testimony of the difference between the purchase price for Getty's reserves and the cost of exploration to find an equal amount. Punitive damages of $3 billion dollars were reduced to $1 billion. Although the jury found Texaco's actions to be intentional, willful, and in wanton disregard of Pennzoil's rights, the Court felt that $3 billion was excessive.

Texaco, Inc. v. Pennzoil Co., 729 S.W.2d 768 (Tex.App. 1987). [The case was eventually settled by Texaco's paying $3 billion to Pennzoil.]

Unfair Competition

Unfair competition is an intentional tort enabling the victim to sue for damages or for an injunction to stop the unfair practice. The tort does not attempt to prevent all competition, only that which the court deems unfair.

The use of an employer's trade secret by a former employee is an example of unfair competition, since it gives other competitors in the same business a competitive advantage.

Other examples are imitating a competitor's packaging of products, signs, advertisements, trade name, or trademarks.

Unfair Competition
Representations that tend to mislead or deceive the public and conduct that is contrary to honest commercial practice.

Trade Secret
A list, plan, process, tool, or mechanism known only to its owner and those employees to whom disclosure is necessary.

Questions

1. What factors determine whether or not a person is liable for the tort of negligence?
2. The torts of defamation and of the invasion of privacy give some protection for most of us but not much for public figures and elected officials. What protection, if any, do you believe prominent people should have from irresponsible journalists? What rules of law would you make to encourage the full discussion of public issues but still protect a person's reputation?
3. As a store manager, you have detained a suspected shoplifter, have called the police, and are holding the suspect in your office. The suspect removes a knife from his pocket and says that he cannot remain with you in the office because you have AIDS and that unless you let him go he'll cut you up with his blade. What will determine what torts, if any, have been committed in this situation?
4. What are some specific examples of what you would consider to be unfair business practices?

5. Your neighbor has a tree whose branches overhang your fence and shed dead leaves in your yard; his children cut across your lawn on the way home from school and have worn a path on your new grass; his dog uses your flower bed for its toilet; and every night he gets drunk, screams at his wife, and turns his stereo up full blast. What are your legal rights in this situation?

3.3 Crime in Business

Crime Defined

Crime
An act which the government has defined as contrary to the public good.

Felony
A serious crime, usually punishable by more than a year in prison.

Misdemeanor
A criminal offense less serious than a felony.

Infraction
A petty offense usually not classified as a crime.

Crimes are wrongs against society as defined by law. The torts section discussed civil actions in which one party sues another for money damages or to obtain a court order. The section showed that many torts can also be illegal criminal acts. However, all criminal actions are brought in the name of the people against the accused defendant. If found guilty, the criminal is then punished by the government. Sanctions include fines, imprisonment, or both. Nearly all states have specified certain capital offenses for which the death penalty can be imposed.

Most crimes have been defined by state laws and are prosecuted by the states in which they occur. However, there is a large and growing body of federal crimes that are prosecuted in federal courts. Some crimes, such as bank robbery, may be a violation of both state and federal law and may be prosecuted by both.

Types of Crimes

Serious crimes—those with a penalty of a year or more in prison—are called *felonies*. Lesser offenses with punishments of less than a year, usually served in a county jail, are called *misdemeanors*. Some states call petty offenses, such as minor traffic violations, *infractions,* which generally are not classified as crimes, thereby denying the accused certain rights, such as a trial by jury. In many states, some crimes may be either a felony or a misdemeanor, depending upon the sentence given by the court. The federal government and many states do not consider an act a crime unless there has been a law or statute passed that defines the unlawful act and provides a punishment.

United States v. Ciambrone
Cite as 750 F.2d 1416 (9th Cir. 1984).

On July 5, 1983, Agent Earl Devaney of the United States Secret Service, received a telephone call from someone identifying himself as "Becker", later found to be Ciambrone. Devaney was informed that "something of interest" was being placed in the night book return of the public library in a nearby shopping mall.

He was told that, if he was interested in more information, he should meet the caller the next day at 1:00 p.m. After the call, Devaney went to the book depository and recovered an envelope containing a xerox copy of a counterfeit $100 Federal Reserve Note, in a style not previously known to Secret Service.

The next day, Devaney met Ciambrone at the library. Ciambrone told Devaney that he knew someone who had counterfeit hundreds and twenties to trade for bearer bonds in an initial deal amount of half a million dollars. When Devaney asked Ciambrone to identify himself and the counterfeiters, Ciambrone replied, "I'm not going to tell you anything unless you give me $15,000." Devaney explained that the Secret Service pays rewards for information only after it is supplied and investigated. Ciambrone replied, "Look, this is a take it or leave it proposition. Either I get my $15,000 or I'll make that or more by joining them."

In our view, Ciambrone's partial disclosure did not result in any greater concealment of the crime than would have occurred had he stayed at home and said nothing. Indeed, in stepping forward to make at least a partial disclosure, Ciambrone provided some information and possibly valuable leads that the Secret Service would not have otherwise obtained from him.

From the Secret Service's standpoint, this partial disclosure had to be better than no disclosure at all. Rather than helping the counterfeiters conceal their criminal activity, Ciambrone's partial disclosure put them at some greater risk of detection than if he had remained silent. . . .

The way the government has argued this case suggests that it believes Ciambrone's real crime to be the conditioning of further disclosure on being paid $15,000. . . . Congress has not chosen to make it a crime to try to sell information to the government, and Ciambrone was not charged with any such crime. Analytically, this case cannot be differentiated from one where a person makes a partial disclosure of his knowledge of a crime but then decides, out of sudden fear or for some other reason, not to tell everything he knows.

In sum, Ciambrone's conduct in trying to sell information to the government may be reprehensible but it is not criminal.

The judgment of conviction [of misprision of a felony—knowing of, failing to disclose information about, *and* taking an affirmative step to conceal a felony] is REVERSED.

Safeguards

Since anyone accused of a crime faces what appears to be overwhelming odds, the plaintiff being either the United States or The People of the State of _____ , some basic safeguards are guaranteed by the federal and the state constitutions.

Fair Trial

In all criminal prosecutions, the accused has the right to a fair, speedy, and public trial by an impartial jury randomly selected from the state or district in which he is being tried. The accused must be informed of the charges and accusations made and be confronted by all witnesses against him. He is entitled to be represented by an attorney, and if the accused cannot afford to hire his own attorney, one must be provided by the government. The accused may subpoena any witnesses to appear and to present evidence on his behalf. He cannot be required to be a witness against himself, but this refers only to communications and not to physical evidence such as blood samples, hair, or fingerprints.

Presumption of Innocence

Presumption of Innocence
The principle that a person is innocent of a crime until proven guilty.

A presumption of innocence exists in all cases where the accused has denied the charges. This means that the government has the burden to prove guilt *beyond a reasonable doubt.*

Intent

Intent
A state of mind wherein the person knows and desires the consequences of the act committed.

Commission of a crime requires a criminal act or omission combined with an intent—general or specific—except where there is criminal negligence. Examples of omissions that are crimes include the failure to file income tax returns or to support one's minor children.

Criminal Negligence

Criminal Negligence
Injury or death caused by one's recklessness without regard of the consequences or with indifference to the safety and rights of others.

Criminal negligence must go beyond that needed for civil liability. It requires a "gross" or "culpable" departure from the usual standard of care. It is aggravated or reckless conduct that shows an indifference to the consequences, and with knowledge—actual or implied—that the act tends to endanger another's life.

Often, a series of acts may be only one offense, whereas there are times when one act may include several offenses. For example, possession of several articles of contraband may support only one count of possession, while selling several kinds of narcotics to one person may create multiple offenses.

Facts

Six men were playing a poker game when three or four masked men broke in and robbed them. The defendant was arrested and tried for the robbery of one of the players and acquitted. He was then tried again for the robbery of one of the other players, and this time he was convicted. The state argues that the robbery of each of the players was a separate crime. The defendant argues that it was all the same crime for which he had already been tried and found not guilty.

Decision

The Constitution bars retrial of the same facts and issues determined at a prior trial. It had been determined that the defendant was not one of the robbers, and the names or number of the victims had no bearing on whether or not he was the criminal.

Ashe v. Swenson, 397 U.S. 436, 90 S.Ct. 1189, 25 L.Ed.2d 469 (1970)

Illegally Obtained Evidence
Evidence obtained by illegal police activities that usually makes such evidence inadmissible.

Illegal Evidence

Evidence that has been obtained by an illegal search or seizure and confessions procured in an unlawful manner cannot be used against the accused. The rules regarding illegal evidence have generated much controversy. Even

Supreme Court justices do not agree as to the rules' effectiveness. The purpose of the rules is to force peace officers to comply with the law or risk the possibility that the criminal might go free. Most peace officers contend that this puts them at a disadvantage in their fight against crime and that the victims and the public suffer as a result.

Corpus Delecti

Before anyone can be found guilty of a criminal act, it must first be established that the crime was committed. This is referred to as the *corpus delecti*, or "body of the crime." Thus, a confession standing alone, without proof of the crime itself, cannot be used to obtain a conviction under our system of law.

Corpus Delecti
Objective proof that a crime has been committed.

Defenses to Crimes

Ignorance of the Law

There are many defenses available to persons accused of crime, but generally ignorance of the law is not one of them.

Ignorance of the Law
The fact that the defendant thought his illegal act was lawful does not excuse him from being punished for the crime.

Facts

A California penal statute imposes criminal penalties on second-hand and junk dealers who fail to use due diligence to learn the authority of persons seeking to sell metal parts or wire of a sort ordinarily used in public utilities. Cramblit operated a used metal business and bought twelve brass water meters from an undercover police officer without asking the officer's identity or the ownership of the items. She only asked for a signed receipt, which the officer signed with a fictitious name. When prosecuted for receiving stolen property, Cramblit said that the burden was on the state to prove that she knew that the property was stolen.

Decision

Public utility lines and fittings are scattered around the countryside, often in isolated locations, difficult to guard, and vulnerable to thievery. Utility operators often sell their surplus metal. Both thieves and honest peddlers offer the goods to junk and second-hand dealers. If willful ignorance of the metal's stolen character would be a defense to the buyer, there would be no way to deter fencing of this type of stolen goods. In the regulation of business activities, the doctrine of *ignorantia legis neminem excusat* (ignorance of the law excuses no one) applies. Conviction affirmed.

People v. *Cramblit*, 62 Cal.App.3d 475, 133 Cal. Rptr. 232 (1976).

Mistake

In some instances where a specific intent to do a certain thing is required as an element of a crime, lack of knowledge might be an excuse. A *mistake of fact*, as opposed to a mistake of law, is usually an excuse. For example, you see a car that looks like yours, your key fits, and you drive it away thinking it's yours until the police stop you for driving a stolen car.

Mistake of Fact
A mistake of fact due to ignorance or a misconception could excuse a defendant from criminal liability.

Infancy

Infancy
That period of youth wherein there is no criminal responsibility.

At common law, and in most states, children under the age of 14 are considered incapable of committing a crime because of *infancy*. They are treated as juvenile offenders rather than as criminals.

Insanity

Insanity
In criminal law, by whatever test used, it is that degree of mental disorder that relieves one of criminal responsibility for his or her actions.

Idiocy or *insanity* that amounts to a mental disease causing the defendant to lack the capacity to know the criminality of his conduct or to conform to the requirements of the law prevents the commission of a criminal act, since there is no intent. Courts have had difficulty in determining what tests to apply, and lawyers and psychiatrists have been critical of those used.

Intoxication

Intoxication
A state of drunkenness or some similar condition caused by use of drugs.

Voluntary intoxication or drug use is no defense for a criminal act but may eliminate a specific intent if the mind was too confused to form such an intent. Involuntary intoxication, as when a person puts a gun to your head and orders you to drink or die—and you do so in fear of your life—could excuse the act. Such duress, if made under fear of death to you or another, might be an excuse in itself.

Self-Defense

Self-Defense
The right to protect one's person, family, and to a lesser extent, one's property, from harm by an aggressor.

Self-defense permits a person to use as much force as is reasonably necessary to defend himself, even deadly force if it is necessary to save his own life. Other situations that permit the lawful use of violent force include protecting one's home, defending other property, and preventing a crime. In each instance, one can use only the amount of force necessary under the circumstances.

Entrapment

Entrapment
A defense that may excuse a defendant from criminal liability for crimes induced by certain types of governmental persuasion or trickery.

Entrapment occurs when an illegal plan starts with officers of the government who implant in the mind of an innocent person the idea to commit the crime. Undercover agents deal with suspected narcotics offenders, establish scam fences to catch criminals with stolen property, and engage in many similar secret operations to expose crime. The federal government and most states follow a subjective test of whether or not the accused had a predisposition to commit a crime. If so, they don't worry much about governmental participation in the criminal acts. A few states follow a minority rule of objectivity and ask whether or not the crime reasonably would have been committed without such official participation. The courts in these states see entrapment as part of the larger problem of lawless law enforcement, along with illegal search and seizure, wiretapping, false arrest, illegal detention, and third degree.

Double Jeopardy

Double jeopardy means that parties cannot be twice put in jeopardy for the same offense. It includes the guarantees that there will be no prosecution after acquittal for an offense; no second conviction for the same offense; and no multiple punishment for the same offense.

Double Jeopardy
Guarantee by the Fifth Amendment of the U.S. Constitution that a person cannot be prosecuted or punished more than once for the same offense.

Facts

Heath hired two men to kill his wife. In accordance with Heath's plan, the men kidnapped Heath's wife in her home in Alabama. Her body was found later on the side of a road in Georgia. Heath pleaded guilty in Georgia in exchange for a sentence of life imprisonment. Later, he was tried and convicted in Alabama of murder during a kidnapping and sentenced to death. He claims that under double jeopardy he cannot be tried twice for the same offense.

Decision

Under a dual sovereignty doctrine, successive prosecutions by two states or by the state and the federal government are permissible. When a single act violates the "peace and dignity" of two sovereigns by breaking the laws of each, the accused has committed two separate offenses for double jeopardy purposes.

Heath v. Alabama, 474 U.S. 82, 106 S.Ct. 433, 88 L.Ed.2d 387 (1985).

Statute of Limitations

Statutes of limitations provide that the state or federal government has a limited amount of time within which to prosecute for a crime. There is a right to a speedy trial. With the passage of time, truth is hard to determine because of the death or disappearance of witnesses and the destruction of evidence. Trials must begin within the allotted time. These time periods vary from state to state and for different offenses. There is no time limit on some serious offenses, such as murder. In most cases, the time limit begins from the time the act was committed. If the act is one difficult to discover, the time starts when the discovery is made. The time is suspended during any period that the suspect leaves the jurisdiction or cannot be found.

Statute of Limitations
Statute stating the period of time within which the government must start the prosecution of a criminal defendant.

Immunity

Immunity from prosecution can be granted by the state to obtain information from persons accused of a crime. The Fifth Amendment provides everyone the privilege against giving self-incriminating testimony. When immunity has been granted, the witness is required to testify but cannot then be prosecuted based on any of his testimony.

Immunity
Freedom from prosecution granted to a witness to compel answers to questions otherwise exempted by the privilege against self incrimination.

Common Business Crimes

Crimes include literally thousands of acts that have been made unlawful not only under penal codes but also under many other types of regulatory legislation. Some of these crimes most common to the business environment include theft, assault and battery, robbery, burglary, receiving stolen property, arson, and misuse of documents. White-collar crimes include bribery, extortion, securities violations, evasion of pure food and drug regulations, unfair and deceptive practices, income tax evasion, illegal political contributions, price fixing, bid rigging, use of the mails to defraud, bankruptcy fraud, computer crimes, conspiracy, and those acts committed under the Racketeer Influenced and Corrupt Organizations Act (RICO) of 1970.

RICO
The Racketeer Influenced and Corrupt Organizations Act was passed by Congress to aid prosecutors in apprehending and convicting persons involved in organized crime, and includes a provision for criminal forfeiture of any money or property acquired in violation of the act.

White-Collar Crime

White collar crime is a term used by the media to mean illegal acts done by an individual or a corporation using nonviolent means to obtain a business or personal advantage. Corporations are legal entities, not persons, and thus cannot form an intent. However, if the penalty is a fine and the intent may be implied or is not required, corporations have been held criminally liable for their acts or omissions. The officers and directors that run the company are individuals and may be held responsible for any of their illegal activities. When such individuals are charged with a crime, they often get off with a fine or are ordered to perform community service while a petty thief might receive a long prison term. Some writers have suggested this happens because the white-collar criminal may be from the same social class as judges who feel that trial and conviction are in themselves a serious punishment and that the offender can serve society better by remaining productive rather than by being locked up.

Theft

Theft occurs when a person intends to take and then does take property that is not his own. Crimes of theft include larceny, obtaining money under false pretenses, and embezzlement.

Theft
The intentional and unlawful taking of property that belongs to another.

Larceny *Larceny* is the wrongful taking and carrying away of another person's personal property with the intent to permanently keep it from its owner or rightful possessor. It is not larceny where the defendant takes the goods by mistake unless he had a wrongful intent at the time of acquiring the goods.

Larceny
The taking of personal property by a person not entitled to its possession and with the intent to deprive the owner of such property.

False Pretenses Obtaining money under *false pretenses,* or larceny by trick or device, is the taking of property of another by acquiring possession through fraud. Puffing statements and tricks of the trade used merely to get business rather than to defraud may be unethical, but they are not criminal false pretenses unless there is a false representation concerning the character, quality, or quantity of the merchandise involved. A false pretense can consist of any act, word, or other thing intended to deceive.

False Pretenses
Obtaining property by misrepresentation with intent to take title to such property.

Embezzlement *Embezzlement* differs from other thefts in that the offender takes possession of the property honestly and without intent to steal it in the first place. It is the wrongful appropriation of the property after a person has been entrusted with it as an agent, servant, clerk, bailee, executor, public

Embezzlement
The fraudulent appropriation to one's own use of property lawfully in his possession.

officer, or other party in lawful possession. The fact that the accused intended to restore embezzled property is no defense.

Robbery

Robbery is a form of theft but with the added element of taking the property by use of force or fear. A purse snatcher is usually guilty of larceny rather than robbery, because no force or fear is used.

Robbery
The taking of property from the person of another by violence or by causing fear.

Burglary

Burglary at common law was the breaking and entering of a dwelling at night with intent to commit a felony. Most states now have laws that expand the crime, no longer requiring that it occur at night or apply only to dwellings. Any entry without the consent of the person in possession is now sufficient, and the use of force or breaking in is not essential. The intent to commit larceny is all that is required. A typical example of modern burglary is the entering of a store or home with the intent to take and carry away personal property.

Burglary
The unlawful entry into a building with the intent to commit a crime.

Receiving Stolen Property

Receiving stolen property is the buying or receiving of property that has been stolen or obtained through any theft or extortion where the purchaser or receiver knows or reasonably should have known that the property was so stolen or obtained. For example, when a defendant buys jewelry at a price far below its value, that alone could be proof that the person had knowledge that the jewelry was stolen.

Receiving Stolen Property
Receiving property that the receiver knows or reasonably should have known was stolen by another person.

Assault and Battery

As discussed earlier under torts, *assault* is an unlawful threat, together with the actual ability, to inflict physical injury to another person, while *battery* is the actual harmful or offensive contact. Generally, an assault and battery are committed at the same time, although it is possible to commit an assault without a battery. The battery is, in fact, a completed assault. In most states, any intentional threatening conduct that places a person in reasonable fear of immediate bodily harm is an assault.

Arson

Arson occurs when a person willfully and maliciously sets fire to or burns any structure or property. If an inhabited building is involved, the crime is more serious. A frequent reason for arson is the fraudulent collection of fire insurance money.

Arson
The willful and malicious burning of a building or property.

Misuse of Documents

Illegal *misuse of documents* includes the crimes of *forgery, counterfeiting, bad checks,* and unauthorized use of *credit cards*.

Forgery

Forgery
Making or altering of a writing with an intent to defraud.

A *forgery* is a writing or a material alteration of an existing writing made by a person without the authority to do so and with an intent to defraud. The forgery must purport to be the writing of another on some sort of document that, if genuine, would establish or defeat some claim, create some liability, or harm another in his person or property. Typical documents involved in forgery are checks, deeds, mortgages, contracts, and wills. Raising the amount of a check is a forgery.

Counterfeiting

Counterfeit
Something made in imitation of something else with an intent to defraud by passing the false copy as genuine.

Counterfeiting is the unauthorized making of imitations of documents or things with the intent to defraud by passing the false copy as genuine or original. Primarily, it is a federal crime that involves counterfeiting money, but states have also enacted laws creating crimes for the making or possessing of counterfeit items and the equipment used for such purpose.

Bad Checks

Bad Check
A check that is dishonored on presentation because of insufficient funds or a closed or nonexistent bank account.

Bad check offenses occur when a person willfully and with intent to defraud makes or delivers a check for himself, as the representative of another, or as officer of a corporation when he knows that there are insufficient funds in the account to cover it. It is also a crime to issue a check on a bank where the maker has no account.

Credit Cards

Credit Card Misuse
The use of another's credit card without the cardholder's or issuer's consent.

Credit card misuse is the taking of someone else's credit card without the cardholder's or issuer's consent and with the intent to use it or pass it to another. A retailer may be guilty of a crime where, with intent to defraud, he supplies anything of value on the presentation of a credit card which he knows, or reasonably should have known, was stolen, forged, expired, or revoked.

Bribery

Bribery
The giving of something of value to influence the performance of an official duty.

Bribery is the giving of something of value or an advantage to a public official with an attempt to influence him in a way that serves a private interest. The crime occurs at the time the bribe is offered. Commercial bribery exists where kickbacks or payoffs are given by a person from one business to those who are working for another. The Foreign Corrupt Practices Act of 1977 prohibits bribes to most foreign officials where the purpose is to get business for U.S. firms.

Extortion

Extortion
Also known as blackmail, is the illegal taking of money by anyone who uses threats or fear in order to obtain the money.

Extortion is the demanding of something of value through coercion or fear but falling short of the threat to personal safety required for robbery. Whether extortion involves the taking of property or the obtaining of an official act, the thing must be obtained by the wrongful use of force or fear.

One type is commonly known as blackmail. While bribery consists of the offering or receiving of something, extortion is the demanding of something backed by coercion.

Legislatures keep creating new criminal laws in an effort to stop what they perceive to be unethical business practices. The federal government and most states regulate corporate securities and impose sanctions for violation of the acts. They regulate food, liquor, and drugs, and violators are charged with crimes. Misleading or false labeling or advertising of any food, drug, or cosmetic is illegal. Unfair and deceptive business practices, such as making false statements concerning real or personal property with the intent of getting the public to buy the items, are a crime in some states. Until recently, such actions only enabled the victims to file civil suits for money damages, but now governments have made the acts criminal as well and have imposed fines, imprisonment, or both as punishments.

Antitrust

Antitrust violations (discussed in the next chapter) include such outlawed activities as fixing prices and rigging competitive bids.

Income Tax Evasion

Income tax evasion is the crime of either failing to file a required income tax return or knowingly and willfully causing the filing of a false and fraudulent return. This may be done by intentionally understating gross income, overstating expenses, or a combination of the two.

Income Tax Evasion
The crime of failing to file an income tax return or of filing a return that is false and fraudulent.

Fraud

Other types of criminal fraud include the federal crimes of using the mails to defraud and bankruptcy fraud. Using the mail or wire services or causing someone else to use them to send out a scheme to defraud or for a contemplated or organized plan to defraud by false pretenses is illegal. When a person or company files a bankruptcy (see Chapter 31), several types of fraud could occur. False claims may be filed against the debtor's estate. Property may be transferred before the filing in an effort to defraud the creditors. Assets may be hidden and not included in the estate inventory. In some cases, there may be a true scam bankruptcy where many debts were incurred with the intention of later wiping them out in bankruptcy.

Mail Fraud
Using the mail or wire services to further a plan to defraud others.

Bankruptcy Fraud
Fraudulent use of bankruptcy laws, such as filing false claims or hiding assets to defraud creditors.

Political Crimes

As attempts are made to control the money involved in election campaigns, the media carry many stories of alleged illegal campaign contributions, and in some cases donors and donees have been prosecuted in the courts. Active and former governmental officials have been convicted of unlawful influence peddling. Every legislative session adds to the growing list of business and political crimes.

Computer Crimes

Computer Crimes
Modern unlawful computer activity such as the theft of computer programs and the manipulation of computers for private gain.

Computer crimes pose new problems that are expanding rapidly and for which detection and control are difficult. The courts have held that stealing computer programs are theft even though only magnetic impulses are involved. Many operators have manipulated computers for their own private gain, such as printing extra paychecks, transferring money between accounts, creating fictitious insurance policies to pay out dividends, and gaining access to trade secrets.

Facts

Texas National Telecommunications (TNT) is a long-distance telephone company. A customer calls TNT's toll-free phone number and punches in a personal access code. If the access code is determined to be valid by the TNT computer, the customer gets a dial tone enabling him to place a long-distance call. The call is then billed to the customer through the access number. Brewer was a "hacker," placing numerous calls to the TNT toll-free number and trying out various number combinations until he found one that the computer would accept as valid. He thereby gathered a number of personal access codes that could be used to make long-distance phone calls without identification of the user. TNT was concerned about the large number of calls charged to unassigned access codes and asked the Secret Service to investigate. Through a scam operation, an agent got Brewer to sell him some access code numbers. Brewer was convicted of knowingly—and with intent to defraud—making, using, and trafficking in counterfeit or unauthorized access devices. Brewer argues on appeal that "access device" refers to credit card types of items and not to telephone numbers.

Decision

Conviction affirmed. Although the purpose of the law was to fill cracks in the statute aimed at credit card abuse, a practical interpretation would include Brewer's action. Both the Senate and House reports on the law said that it was intended to be "broad enough to encompass technological advances." The court added that at the very least, Brewer must have known that hacking out long-distance access codes to obtain free long-distance phone service was "wrong."

United States v. *Brewer*, 835 F.2d 550 (5th Cir. 1987).

Organized Crime

RICO
The Racketeer Influenced and Corrupt Organizations Act, passed by Congress as part of the Organized Crime Control Act of 1970.

RICO, The Racketeer Influenced and Corrupt Organizations Act, was designed to eliminate, or at least reduce, the takeover of legitimate businesses by gangsters. Violations carry maximum criminal penalties of a $25,000 fine, a twenty-year prison term, and forfeiture of property. Injured persons can file civil liability suits in which they can recover treble damages, court costs, and attorney's fees.

A RICO violation is the investing in, the acquiring an interest in or control of, or the conducting of the affairs of an enterprise through racketeering money or activity or conspiring to do so. The courts have recently been flooded with RICO civil claims against big banks, accounting firms, and securities brokerages. State crimes giving rise to RICO charges are felonies relating to murder, kidnapping, gambling, arson, robbery, bribery, extortion, and drug dealing. Federal crimes that have been prosecuted under RICO include mail and wire fraud, securities fraud, bankruptcy fraud, extortion, interference with interstate commerce, union funds embezzlement, and interstate transportation of stolen property.

Most federal courts have concluded that RICO was not intended to be limited to the infiltration of legitimate business by organized crime but that it also applies to business fraud perpetrated by so-called legitimate business people. In one federal decision, the judge wrote, "It seems almost too obvious to require statement, but fraud is fraud, whether it is committed by a hit man for organized crime or by the president of a Wall Street brokerage firm."

Facts

Russello was convicted in federal district court under RICO for being involved in an arson ring that resulted in his fraudulently receiving insurance proceeds in payment for the fire loss of a building he owned. As part of the sentence, the court ordered that all of the insurance proceeds were to be forfeited to the United States as an "interest acquired" in violation of the Act. Russello argued on appeal that the insurance money was not an interest acquired.

Decision

Every property interest, including a right to profits or proceeds, may be described as an interest in something. Before profits of an illegal enterprise are divided, each participant may be said to own an "interest" in the ill-gotten gains; and after distribution, each has a possessory interest in currency or other items so distributed. The legislative history of RICO clearly demonstrates that the law was intended to provide new weapons of unprecedented scope for an assault upon organized crime and its economic roots and thus was intended to authorize forfeiture of racketeering profits. Decision affirmed.

Russello v. United States, 464 U.S. 16, 104 S.Ct. 296, 78 L.Ed.2d 17 (1983).

Conspiracy

Conspiracy is a combination of two or more persons who agree that one or more of them will commit a criminal act or a lawful act by criminal means or will make an attempt or a solicitation to commit such crime. It is not necessary that all of the conspirators meet together or agree at the same time. Each member is not required to know what part each other member is to play or that he know the identity of all of the other participants. All parties to a conspiracy assume the responsibility for all acts of the other parties done in furtherance of the conspiracy. Intent alone does not complete the conspiracy, but some steps must be taken to put it into effect.

Conspiracy
A combination of two or more persons to commit a criminal act or to commit a lawful act by unlawful means.

Solicitation

Solicitation is ordering, encouraging, or requesting another person to either commit or attempt to commit a crime. Most crimes include attempt as a part thereof. *Attempt* is an overt act, beyond mere preparation, moving directly toward the actual commission of a crime. The overt act must be near enough to completion of the actual crime to amount to the "commencement of the consummation" that would have been completed except for some intervening factor not caused by the accused.

Solicitation
Commanding, encouraging, or requesting another person to commit a crime with the intent that the crime be committed.

Attempt
An overt act, beyond mere preparation, moving directly towards the actual commission of a crime.

People v. Lorenzo
64 Cal.App.3d Supp. 47, 135 Cal.Rptr. 337 (1976).

Cole, Acting Presiding Judge Defendant appeals from his conviction of theft, . . .

Defendant was observed by the manager of a Von's market to switch price tags from one kind of glove to another kind of glove and also to switch price tags placed on chickens. The manager of the store stood five or six feet behind defendant as the latter went through the check-out counter. Defendant paid for a number of chickens, a pair of gloves and other merchandise. Defendant had no conversation with the check-out clerk. Defendant then wheeled the shopping cart into the parking lot where he was arrested by the manager. Among the merchandise in the cart was a pair of gloves which bore a price tag lower than their regular and correct price. Testimony also established that two of the chickens in the cart had price tags on them which were for less amounts than should have been the case. Two other chickens handled by defendant but left by him in the store, and not taken to the check-out counter bore loose price tags that should have been on the two chickens in question which defendant "purchased."

In other words, the evidence convincingly showed (although defendant denied it to be the case) that defendant switched price tags so as to buy merchandise for less than its correct price. . . .

"To support a conviction of theft for obtaining property by false pretenses, it must be shown that the defendant made a false pretense or representation with intent to defraud the owner of his property, and that the owner was in fact defrauded. . . . The false pretense or representation must have materially influenced the owner to part with his property. . . ."

. . . In other words, as in any other case of fraud, the injured party must have been induced to part with his property in reliance on the false representation. . . .

It is apparent to us that the crime of theft by false pretenses was not committed here. The victim of the crime was alleged to be Von's market. The manager of the market at all times was aware that defendant had switched the price labels and merely allowed defendant apparently to consummate his scheme in order to be able to arrest him in the parking lot. The manager at no time relied upon defendant's conduct.

. . . We are of the view, however, that the evidence amply establishes defendant's attempt to commit theft. Reliance is not an element of that offense. . . .

The successful consummation of the offense was prevented only by the manager's alertness. But for the manager's observations defendant would have carried the actual theft to its completion. Accordingly, pursuant to the authority vested in us . . . we hold that the verdict and judgment must be modified to show that defendant is guilty of attempted theft only and not theft. Since we do not know what punishment the trial court would assess in light of this reduced offense it will be necessary for us to remand the matter to the trial court for resentencing.

QUESTIONS

1. Under the Miranda rule, no peace officer can question a suspect in custody unless he first gives a warning of the accused's right to remain silent, the right to have his lawyer present (or one provided by the state if he cannot afford his own), and the fact that anything the accused says may be held against him.

Also, if the police obtain evidence by unlawful means, such evidence cannot be used at the time of trial. Do you approve of these rules? What are your reasons?

2. Do you believe that idiots and insane persons should be held responsible for the crimes they commit? Should a person who is so blinded by rage and emotion that he cannot stop from doing the criminal act be held responsible? Should unconscious persons or sleepwalkers be excused for any criminal acts committed under such conditions?

3. Suppose that an attractive new student enrolls in your school. She becomes friendly with many students and invites some of them to parties where illegal drugs are available. Some of her new friends ask her where they can obtain the drugs, and she replies that she'll tell them if they'll help her make distributions on the campus. Two fellow students offer to help her but only if she'll pay them well. She agrees, and when they make their first sales they are arrested. They then discover that she was an undercover police officer. What facts would determine whether or not this was entrapment?

4. What do you think would be the best way to solve the problem of ever-increasing white-collar crime?

5. In many third world countries, bribery and kickbacks seem to be an accepted way of business life. Do you think that the law making it a crime to bribe a foreign official is fair to American business people doing business in those countries? How would you deal with the problem?

PROBLEMS

1. Assume that you have bought a new compact disc of your favorite country singer and believe it to be great. You want to share it with your best friend, but you know that she does not have a CD player. However, she does have a cassette player, so you make a copy of the record on a cassette tape and send it to her as a gift. Is there an ethical problem involved in this action?

2. Ohralik, an Ohio attorney, while picking up mail at the post office was told by the postmaster's brother about an auto collision in which Carol, a casual acquaintance, was hurt. Ohralik phoned her parents, learned she was in the hospital, and asked if he could visit her. He went to the hospital and found her in traction. He convinced her that she should have him represent her in a lawsuit about the accident. The Ohio State Bar Association claims this to be a violation of the attorney's Code of Ethics. What decision? *Ohralik* v. *Ohio State Bar Association,* 436 U.S. 447, 98 S.Ct. 1912, 56 L.Ed.2d 444 (1978).

3. Gleason was driving her auto on a highway that bordered the Hillcrest Golf Course. A ball was hit out-of-bounds off the golf course, came through the window of the car, and injured her. The golf course owners denied liability, stating that Gleason had assumed the risk by driving on that highway. Are they right? What result if the person who hit the ball is not identified? *Gleason* v. *Hillcrest Golf Course,* 148 Misc. 246, 265 N.Y.S. 886 (Mun. 1933).

4. Author Blatty wrote a book entitled *Legion.* The *New York Times* (NYT) failed to include *Legion* on its best-seller list, even though Blatty's publisher, Simon and Schuster, had sent information to the NYT indicating that enough copies of *Legion* had been sold to be included on the list and had requested that the NYT include it. Blatty sued, claiming that his omission from the list was libel and that he also has a suit for unfair competition and false advertising. What should the court decide? *Blatty* v. *New York Times Company,* 42 Cal.3d 1033, 232 Cal. Rptr. 542, 728 P.2d 1177 (1986).

5. Ralph Nader wrote a book about General Motors entitled *Unsafe at Any Speed.* General Motors hired private investigators to find information to discredit Nader. The investigators followed Nader, interviewed others about his private life, wiretapped, pried into his private bank accounts, eavesdropped, made threatening phone calls, and used women to attempt to entice him. Nader sued General Motors for invasion of privacy. What result? *Nader* v. *General Motors Corp.,* 31 A.D.2d 392, 298 N.Y.S.2d 137 (1969).

6. Southard was stranded in Hawaii as the result of an airline strike called by the airline machinists' union. He had bought a round-trip ticket before leaving his home in Denver. He sued the union for the tort of interference with his contract with the airline and seeks to recover his additional expenses incurred when he had to fly back with another airline. Was the union liable to Southard? *International Assn. of Machinists* v. *Southard,* 170 Colo. 119, 459 P.2d 570 (1969).

7. Josephine Powell mailed a package containing a sawed-off shotgun 22 inches long. She was convicted of the federal offense of mailing pistols, re-

volvers, and "other firearms capable of being concealed on the person." She argues that the law refers only to small items like pistols and revolvers, not to guns this large and that she couldn't conceal on *her* person. What should the Supreme Court decide? *United States* v. *Powell,* 423 U.S. 87, 96 S.Ct. 316, 46 L.Ed.2d 228 (1975).

8. Randono and Dreyer were partners. They owned two bars and restaurants, Feliciano's and Saddleback Inn. Saddleback Inn was headed for bankruptcy. The partners decided to take advantage of the situation by ordering $20,000 worth of liquor on credit to be charged to Saddleback but to be transferred to and hidden at Feliciano's without paying for it. Randono was prosecuted for theft by false pretenses. He argued that because he had said nothing to the liquor dealers, he had made no false pretenses to them. Decide. *People* v. *Randono,* 32 Cal.App.3d 164, 108 Cal.Rptr. 326 (1973).

9. Waronek owned and operated a trucking rig, transporting goods for L.T.L. Perishables of St. Paul, Minnesota. He accepted an order to haul a trailer load of beef from Illini Beef in Illinois to Midtown Packing in New York City. After his truck was loaded with ninety-five hindquarters and ninety-five forequarters of beef in Illinois, Waronek drove to his home in Watertown, Wisconsin, and had the Royal Meat Company there butcher four of the hindquarters for him. He offered to sell ten more for a very low price, and a suspicious employee notified the authorities. When Waronek got to New York, he telephoned L.T.L. and notified the company that he was short nineteen hindquarters but that he knew where they went and he would make good on the shortage out of future settlements. He was arrested by the FBI and convicted for embezzlement of goods moving in interstate commerce. On appeal, Waronek argued that since he didn't intend to permanently deprive the owner of the property he cannot be guilty of embezzlement. Decide. *United States* v. *Waronek,* 582 F.2d 1158 (7th Cir. 1978).

10. Rusty Irons was the owner of a junkyard. One day a 12-year-old boy came in and sold Rusty four Cadillac hubcaps in almost new condition for $2 apiece. Has Rusty committed any crime?

CHAPTER FOUR

Government Regulation of Business

4.1 Federal Regulation
Commerce Clause
National and State Regulations
Taxation
Antitrust Laws
   Sherman Act
   Clayton Act
   Federal Trade Commission
   Robinson-Patman Act

4.2 Environmental Protection
Environmental Control Act
EPA
NEPA
Clean Air Act
Energy Act
Clean Water Act
Toxic Substances Control Act
RCRA
Superfund
Marine Protection Act
Nuclear Regulatory Commission
Pesticide Control Act
Endangered Species Act
Noise Control Act
Surface Mining Act
Antiquities Preservation

4.3 Employment Regulation
Labor Relations
   Norris-LaGuardia Act
   Wagner Act
   NLRB
   Fair Labor Standards Act
   Taft-Hartley Act
   Landrum-Griffin Act
Employee Protection
   Workers' Compensation
   OSHA
   Social Security
   Medicare
   ERISA
   Unemployment Compensation
Employment Discrimination
   Equal Pay Act
   Equal Employment Opportunities Act
   BFOQ
   Sexual Harassment
   Racial Discrimination
   Age Discrimination
   Pregnancy Act
   Wrongful Discharge
   Rehabilitation Act
   Affirmative Action

4.1 Federal Regulation

Practically all of today's business activities are subject to governmental regulation. New laws are continually being introduced by legislative and executive action to control and direct commercial practices. Much of this direction has been delegated to administrative agencies (refer to Chapter 2). These agencies possess rulemaking, executive, and quasi-judicial powers. The final determination of the legality of such operations is for the courts.

Commerce Clause

Commerce Clause
U.S. Constitution clause that gives the federal government the power to regulate interstate and foreign commerce.

The commerce clause (U.S. Constitution, Article I, Section 8) gives the federal government the power to regulate foreign commerce and commerce between the states. Court decisions construing this power have broadened the power considerably and extended congressional control even to businesses generally considered to be local. The states and their subdivisions obtain their authority to regulate from the Tenth Amendment, granting plenary powers to the states, and from their "police power," which is the inherent power of a governing body to control persons and property within its jurisdiction for the purposes of promoting the health, safety, and welfare of its people.

National and State Regulations

At times there may be conflict between national and local regulations that creates a priority problem. Court decisions seem to classify these issues in the following categories: those exclusively federal in nature, those where local and federal rules are deemed compatible, and those remaining solely within the state's authority. In the concurrent area, further subdivisions are made of those where Congress has preempted the field by express law, those where federal regulations exist but lack completeness to cover all areas of state interest, and those where no federal law exists and the state has legislated.

Taxation

Taxing Power
The power of the government to raise and collect taxes.

Government requires revenue to meet its expenses. Backed by the power and authority the government possesses, tax laws, not based on consent, are passed and the levies collected. Although this power can be used only for public purposes, the only real limitations are those imposed by the federal and state constitutions or the possibility of the electorate's replacing its elected representatives. Since taxes are not really debts, the constitutional prohibition against imprisonment for nonpayment is not applicable.

Taxes may be directly imposed, such as the income tax, or indirectly imposed, such as manufacturer's taxes passed on to the consumer. They may be specific on individual items, such as packs of cigarettes, or ad valorem (according to value), such as property taxes on private homes. They may be general, to benefit everybody, or special (such as street lighting assessments), benefiting only those who pay. Taxes not only are placed on the value of property but also may be placed on a privilege, commonly called excise taxes, such as paying a fee to engage in the practice of law.

The power to tax is being used to implement political, social, and economic policy as well as to obtain funds. Tax benefits that encourage investment, import duties that protect business from foreign competition, and estate taxes that break up large fortunes are a few examples. Money raised by taxes may also be spent by the federal government to encourage these ends by making grants for housing, education, roads, and other social improvements, provided certain established standards are met.

Although the validity of taxes is seldom questioned before the courts today, the interpretation and application of the rules and regulations are subject to frequent litigation. However, Congress has delegated this authority to the Internal Revenue Service, and the courts recognize that fact, generally upholding the rulings of the tax commissioner.

Internal Revenue Service
Federal agency primarily concerned with the administration of federal tax laws.

Antitrust Laws

Contracts in restraint of trade are generally against public policy. However, some are valid if they are reasonable for the parties to the contract and in the best interests of the public. For example, a promise not to compete, made in connection with the sale of a business, is enforceable as long as there is a need and the terms are reasonable both as to time and as to geographical area. During this century, many federal laws, rules, and regulations have been passed in the attempt to protect the public from monopolies. The most important of these have been the Sherman Antitrust Act, the Clayton Act, the Federal Trade Commission Act, and the Robinson-Patman Act.

Sherman Act

In response to public concern over corporate monopoly, Congress passed the Sherman Antitrust Act in 1890. Its purpose was to break up existing monopolies by making illegal any restraint of trade and by imposing criminal penalties on anyone who attempts to monopolize commerce.

However, the U.S. Supreme Court in an early decision restricted the law by applying the rule of reason, concluding that Congress intended only to prohibit "unreasonable" monopolies. Application of the rule of reason is set out in the following case.

Sherman Antitrust Act
Federal law intended to prevent unreasonable restraint of trade and monopolies in interstate or foreign commerce.

Rule of Reason
Rule made by the U.S. Supreme Court that antitrust laws applied only to "unreasonable" restraints of trade.

Facts

The National Football League (NFL) and Commissioner Pete Rozelle appealed from a district court judgment holding the "Rozelle Rule" in violation of the Sherman Act and enjoining its enforcement. The NFL operated under a reserve system whereby every player who signed a contract with an NFL club was bound to play for that club, and no other, for the term of the contract plus one additional year at the option of the club before he could become a free agent. In 1963, the Rozelle Rule was adopted which provided that if a free agent player signed a contract with a different club in the league, unless mutually satisfactory arrangements were made between the two clubs, the commissioner at his sole discretion could name and award to the former club one or more players (including future draft choices), and his decision would be final and conclusive.

Decision

The court held that the Rozelle Rule, as implemented, violated the rule of reason and was an unreasonable restraint of trade in violation of the Sherman Act, because under the Rozelle Rule, a club would sign a free agent only where there was an agreement with the player's former team as to compensation or risk the awarding of unknown compensation by the commissioner.

Mackey v. National Football League, 543 F.2d 606, (8th Cir. 1976).

Price Fixing
A combination or conspiracy formed for the purpose of fixing the price on a commodity in interstate commerce.

Boycott
As a means of protest, the refusal to work for, or to buy, use or handle the products of another.

***Per Se* Violations**
The act itself is a violation without actual proof of injury.

The Supreme Court has also held that certain activities constitute automatic, or per se, violations of the law because they are presumed to be harmful. They include price fixing, territorial restrictions, boycotts, tying arrangements, and production quotas. *Per se* means standing by itself, so that proof of the fact of occurrence is all that is required to find civil or criminal liability, and the intent of the party is irrelevant.

Price fixing is an agreement among competitors to establish the price for which they will sell their product.

Agreements among producers to divide up and keep exclusive certain sales areas are illegal territorial restrictions.

Unlawful boycott occurs when competitors agree among themselves to exclude other businesses from dealing in their products. However, some agreements, such as those creating franchise operations that give the holder the sole right to sell a certain product or service within a given territory, have been held permissible.

Production quotas are agreements that arbitrarily restrict the supply of designated items, thereby increasing prices.

Violations of the Act now carry criminal penalties of fines up to $100,000, up to three years imprisonment, or both. Corporations may be fined up to one million dollars. The Department of Justice's Antitrust Division is responsible for initiating criminal proceedings and may also get court injunctions to stop violations of the Act.

Any private person or group directly injured by violations of the antitrust law may sue for treble damages and court costs.

Principe v. McDonald's Corp.
631 F.2d 303 (4th Cir. 1980).

Phillips, Circuit Judge This suit was brought by Principe Company (plaintiff) against McDonald's Corporation (defendant) for damages under Section 1 of the Sherman Act.

McDonald's is not primarily a fast food retailer. While it does operate over a thousand stores itself, the vast majority of the stores in its system are operated by franchisees. Nor does McDonald's sell equipment or supplies to its licensees. Instead its primary business is developing and collecting royalties from limited menu fast food restaurants operated by independent business people. . . .

> Having acquired the land, begun construction of the store and selected an operator, McDonald's enters into two contracts with the franchisee. Under the first, the franchise agreement, McDonald's grants the franchisee the rights to use McDonald's food preparation system and to sell food products under the McDonald's name. The franchisee pays a $12,500 franchise fee and agrees to remit 3 percent of his gross sales as a royalty in return. Under the second contract, the lease, McDonald's grants the franchisee the right to use the particular store premises to which his franchise pertains. In return, the franchisee pays a $15,000 refundable security deposit (as evidence of which he receives a 20-year non-negotiable non-interest bearing note) and agrees to pay 8½ percent of his gross sales as rent. These payments under the franchise and lease agreements are McDonald's only sources of income from its franchised restaurants. The franchisee also assumes responsibility under the lease for building maintenance, improvements, property taxes and other costs associated with the premises. Both the franchise agreement and the lease generally have 20-year durations, both provide that termination of one terminates the other, and neither is available separately.
>
> Principe argues McDonald's is selling not one but three distinct products, the franchise, the lease and the security deposit note. The alleged antitrust violation stems from the fact that a prospective franchisee must buy all three in order to obtain the franchise.
>
> As evidence that this is an illegal tying arrangement, Principe points to the unfavorable terms on which franchisees are required to lease their stores. . . . It urges that McDonald's can protect the integrity of its trademarks by specifying how its franchisees shall operate, where they may locate their restaurants and what types of buildings they may erect. Customers do not and have no reason to connect the building's owner with the McDonald's operation conducted therein. Since company ownership of store premises is not an essential element of the trademark's goodwill, Principe argues, the franchise, lease and note are separable products tied together in violation of the antitrust laws.
>
> . . . Far from merely licensing franchisees to sell products under its trade name, a modern franchisor such as McDonald's offers its franchisees a complete method of doing business. It takes people from all walks of life, sends them to its management school, and teaches them a variety of skills ranging from hamburger grilling to financial planning. It installs them in stores whose market has been researched and whose location has been selected by experts to maximize sales potential. It inspects every facet of every store several times a year and consults with each franchisee about his operation's strengths and weaknesses. Its regime pervades all facets of the business, from the design of the menu board to the amount of catsup on the hamburgers, nothing is left to chance. This pervasive franchisor supervision and control benefits the franchisee in turn. His business is identified with a network of stores whose very uniformity and predictability attracts customers. In short, the modern franchisee pays not only for the right to use a trademark but for the right to become a part of a system whose business methods virtually guarantee his success. . . . Where the challenged aggregation is an essential ingredient of the franchised system's formula for success, there is but a single product and no tie-in exists as a matter of law. . . . Judgment for McDonald's Corporation.

When the Sherman Antitrust Act was weakened by the rule of reason, business monopolies continued to grow. Congress then tried to correct the situation by enacting the Clayton Act and the Federal Trade Commission Act.

Clayton Act

Clayton Act
Antitrust Act amending the Sherman Act and adding further restrictions to control monopolies.

The Clayton Act prohibits agreements that make as a condition of selling products a promise not to buy those of a competitor. It also forbids mergers that create potential monopolies, such as horizontal mergers among competing firms, vertical mergers among companies in a chain of distribution, and certain types of conglomerate mergers. The tests applied by the courts to determine whether a merger is to be approved include consideration of the product involved, the geographical market, and the probable future effects of the proposed combination. The Act also prohibits a person from serving on more than one board of directors of large competing industrial corporations other than banks, trust companies, and common carriers. The following case interprets the interlocking directorate prohibition rule of the Clayton Act.

Facts

The United States brought an action against three banks, their holding companies, four mutual life insurance companies, and five individuals who were directors of both a bank and an insurance company. It asserted that interlocking directorates between banks and competing insurance companies violated the Clayton Act. Section 8 of the Act bars a person from being a director of two or more large competing corporations other than banks, trust companies, and common carriers. The court of appeals held that this barred all interlocking directorates between banks and nonbanking corporations. This decision was appealed to the U.S. Supreme Court.

Decision

In a 5 to 3 decision, the Supreme Court held that the interlocking directorate rule applied only to large industrial corporations and was not intended to prohibit such activity involving banks. An individual could therefore be a director of both a bank and an insurance company even though they competed in the interstate market for mortgage and real estate loans.

BankAmerica Corp. et al. v. United States, 462 U.S. 122, 103 S.Ct. 2266, 76 L.Ed.2d 456 (1983).

Federal Trade Commission

Federal Trade Commission (FTC)
A federal agency created to protect consumers against unfair competition and fraudulent trade practices.

The Federal Trade Commission Act declares unlawful unfair methods of competition in commerce and unfair or deceptive practices in business. These methods and practices are not defined but are left up to court determination.

The Act also created the Federal Trade Commission (FTC) to investigate and enforce the laws, providing it with several different remedies:

1. The FTC may obtain a voluntary consent decree wherein the violating firm agrees to stop the challenged action and the FTC agrees not to impose penalties. Press releases may be distributed to the news media through the FTC Office of Public Information. Advisory opinions may be issued to business firms concerning the legality of a proposed activity or questionable practice.

2. The FTC may issue a cease and desist order, similar to an injunction, directing some person or entity to stop its alleged violation of the antitrust laws.

GOVERNMENT REGULATION OF BUSINESS 75

3. The FTC, through the courts, may order such drastic actions as divestiture of improper holdings, dissolution of a business, or other specific corrective action, such as requiring publication in the media of notice of errors and misrepresentations in commercial advertising. An FTC order may also be used to stop perceived antitrust violations in their early stages before they are effective.

Robinson-Patman Act

The Robinson-Patman Act, an amendment to the Clayton Act, attempts to limit the power of large purchasers by prohibiting price discrimination in interstate commerce of commodities of like grade and quality. However, price differentials are permitted if the seller can prove that a buyer received a more favorable price as a result of a specific cost savings or as a result of a good faith price reduction to meet lawful competition.

Robinson-Patman Act
A section of the Clayton Act which prohibits price discrimination between purchasers of like goods when it might tend to create a monopoly.

Questions

1. Private parties injured as a result of antitrust activities may sue the violators and, if successful, could be awarded treble damages and court costs. What are the advantages and disadvantages of such a rule?
2. The recent surge of mergers by large corporations has created many huge conglomerates. Do you think this benefits or harms the average consumer? Why?
3. The U.S. Constitution guarantees that one cannot be put in jail for nonpayment of debts. Could you be sent to jail for refusing to file an income tax return and pay your taxes? Why?
4. What is an FTC cease and desist order, and what is its purpose?
5. What is a per se violation of the antitrust laws?

4.2 Environmental Protection

Until recently, society assumed that its waste materials could all be absorbed by the existing land, air, and water. It is now obvious that modern products and practices accompanied by rapid population growth and concentration are producing emissions beyond the capacity of nature's processes to fully absorb them without irreparable harm to the environment. With newly discovered dangers such as the threat to the ozone layer that shields the earth from harmful rays, the preservation of the environment has become a matter of great concern.

Environment
One's surroundings.

Environmental Control Act
An act of Congress intended to control the pollution and degradation of the environment.

Environmental Protection Agency (EPA)
A federal agency created to coordinate governmental action for the protection of the environment and control of pollution.

Environmental Control Act

In passing the Environmental Control Act of 1970, Congress expressly found that "population increase and urban concentration contribute directly to the pollution and degradation of our environment."

EPA

In December 1970, President Nixon, in an executive reorganization plan, established the Environmental Protection Agency (EPA) to consolidate and implement legislation proposed by Congress. The agency was delegated the power to create and enforce national pollution standards. It was hoped that the new standards would be able to coordinate and control a wide range of pollutants, including air, water, and noise pollutants; toxics; solid wastes; pesticides; and radiation.

NEPA

National Environmental Policy Act (NEPA)
An Act of Congress intended to help control pollution.

Environmental Impact Statement (EIS)
Required by NEPA to be prepared before any federal action is taken that might effect the quality of the human environment.

The National Environment Policy Act (NEPA) was passed to help solve pollution problems, but it does not set pollution standards, nor does it have a veto over harmful projects. The Council on Environmental Quality (CEQ) was chartered by NEPA but merely serves as policy adviser to the President.

NEPA does require, among other things, that an Environmental Impact Statement (EIS) be prepared for all legislative or other major federal action that might significantly affect the quality of the human environment. Theoretically, NEPA should accomplish its objectives, but it must rely upon the integrity of government bureaucracies, concern of activists, and help from federal courts to get the job done. Whenever an agency undertakes a project, it must first determine if the action is one that requires an EIS, and if it decides that one is unnecessary, only a concerned citizen may take the issue to court.

Clean Air Act

Clean Air Act
Federal law that classifies air pollution but places enforcement responsibility upon the individual states.

The 1970 Clean Air Act, as amended in 1977, separates air pollution control into two categories; those dealing with mobile or transportation sources and others covering generally stationary sources (factories, utilities). The law establishes time schedules for a reduction of automobile emissions of hydrocarbons and nitrogen oxides. Primary responsibility for the improvement and enforcement of air quality was placed upon the individual states. A state cannot substantially burden interstate commerce or take an action that had been preempted by Congress.

Facts

The Clean Air Act authorized the Environmental Protection Agency (EPA) to regulate gasoline additives considered to be a hazard to the public health or welfare. The EPA issued an order that required annual reductions in the lead content of gasoline. Ethyl Corporation, a leading maker of lead-based antiknock compounds used to increase gasoline octane ratings, appealed the order, arguing that the EPA had exceeded its authority.

Decision

Under administrative law, an agency decision can be overturned by the court only if it is found to be "arbitrary, capricious, an abuse of discretion, or otherwise not in accordance with the law." In this case, there were more than 10,000 pages of evidence in the record. The EPA relied on this in making its decision, which was a reasonable result. Most agency decisions are presumed to be valid, and the court will not substitute its judgment for that of the agency.

Ethyl Corp. v. EPA, 541 F.2d 1 (D.C.Cir. 1976).

Violations of the Clean Air Act can lead to both civil and criminal actions. Civil penalties of up to $25,000 a day for the violation of emissions limits have been used most often by the EPA. Since paying these relatively small penalties can be more profitable than compliance, the Act also authorizes civil penalties equal to any economic benefits realized by the violator. Criminal prosecutions are limited to those who knowingly violate the Act or make false statements on their reports.

Energy Act

Congress passed the National Energy Act (NEA) over concern about reliance on imported oil and gas. One of the Act's provisions required power plants and other fuel-burning installations to switch from gas and oil to coal, which many say resulted in the environmental air hazard known as acid rain. So far, the EPA has not concluded that adequate scientific data exist to support a regulatory program for acid rain control.

National Energy Act (NEA)
Federal law intended to reduce reliance upon imported gas and oil.

Clean Water Act

The 1977 Clean Water Act (CWA) amends the earlier Federal Water Pollution Control Act (FWPCA). The Act classifies pollutants as conventional (sanitary waste), toxic (designated chemicals), and nonconventional (all others). The EPA must publish regulations and set effluent limitations on conventional wastes with a standard of the best conventional technology (BCT) available. The standard for toxics is stricter, requiring the best available technology (BAT) feasible. Civil and criminal enforcement sections of the Act are about the same as those for the Clean Air Act—leaving prosecution of violations primarily with the states—but federal guidelines were established with provisions for criminal penalties.

Clean Water Act (CWA)
Federal law intended to clean up water pollution.

Toxic Substances Control Act

The 1976 Toxic Substances Control Act (TSCA) attempts to set standards to control and prevent hazardous environmental and human exposure to toxic substances. Under its provisions, the federal government can regulate or stop the production or use of chemical materials deemed to cause an unreasonable risk of injury to health or the environment. Any manufacturer of new chemicals or new uses for chemicals in existence must notify the EPA ninety days before starting production. The EPA can require reports

Toxic Substances Control Act (TSCA)
An act that attempts to control and prevent hazardous exposure to toxic (poisonous) substances.

and records to be kept concerning chemicals, any adverse effects, and the number of workers exposed. Trade secrets and financial data are confidential, but any health and safety information may be made public. Records of adverse health effects must be kept for thirty years and those of environmental damage for five years.

RCRA

Resource Conservation and Recovery Act (RCRA)
An Act to control use of chemical products and hazardous waste.

Increased public awareness of the problems of hazardous waste disposal led Congress to enact the Resource Conservation and Recovery Act (RCRA) of 1976. While TSCA attempted to control the manufacture, distribution, and sale of chemical products, RCRA has a plan for the transportation and disposal of hazardous waste. Under this Act, the EPA has identified over 300 products as hazardous. Producers have to maintain records of the quantity and type of such products and comply with EPA standards for labeling, storage, and transportation. Each disposal, storage, or treatment plant operator must obtain an operating permit from the EPA. The Act also provides civil and criminal penalties for violations.

Superfund

Superfund
A fund created by Congress to help pay for cleanup costs of hazardous materials.

While the RCRA was aimed at controlling disposal of hazardous wastes, it did not permit the government to clean up those wastes already in existence. The Superfund Law was thus enacted to create a superfund to be managed by the EPA. It requires the EPA to act whenever any hazardous substances that endanger the public health or welfare are released. Cleanup costs are covered by a $1.6 billion trust fund, 86 percent of which is financed by taxes on specified chemical manufacturers and the importers of crude oil. Taxpayers make up the difference. Those identified as responsible parties can be held liable for the costs and, if cleanup orders are not strictly obeyed, can be assessed punitive damages of treble the government's costs.

Marine Protection Act

Marine Protection Act
An Act that prohibits ocean dumping of certain hazardous wastes.

The Marine Protection, Research, and Sanctuaries Act of 1972 prohibits ocean dumping of any waste or matter containing active chemical, biological, or radioactive agent.

Nuclear Regulatory Commission

Nuclear Regulatory Commission (NRC)
Formerly the Atomic Energy Commission, the federal agency responsible for civilian nuclear regulation.

Although controversial, nuclear power continues to be an important energy source. The Three Mile Island accident in Pennsylvania in 1979 and the Chernobyl disaster in the U.S.S.R. in 1986 increased public concern about the safety of nuclear power plants and radiation control. Nuclear activities are under the exclusive authority of the federal government, and the Nuclear

Regulatory Commission (NRC) (formerly the Atomic Energy Commission) is the federal agency responsible for civilian nuclear regulation. One of the major problems is that of nuclear waste control for which no permanent disposal methods are yet available. The Nuclear Waste Policy Act of 1982 requires that the federal government select and develop a site for this purpose.

Nuclear Waste Policy Act
An Act requiring the federal government to develop a site for nuclear waste disposal.

Pesticide Control Act

Agricultural productivity has been increased through the use of chemical pesticides to kill harmful insects and weeds. Recent evidence reveals that residues from these chemicals have not been absorbed by the environment. Buildups have killed animals, and long-term effects potentially harmful to the public have been identified in some areas. The Environmental Pesticide Control Act amends a former law and requires registration and labeling of such pesticides. Such toxics are classified as "general" or "restricted," and the latter may be used only by or under the supervision of state-certified and EPA-approved operators. Criminal sanctions can be imposed on farmers and private users for knowing violations of up to $1,000 in fines and thirty days in jail. Registered manufacturers, applicators, wholesalers, distributors, and retailers can face the maximum of $25,000 in fines and one year imprisonment.

Environmental Pesticide Control Act
An Act requiring registration and labeling of dangerous pesticides.

Endangered Species Act

The Endangered Species Act authorizes the Secretary of the Interior, after consulting representatives from the states, to name species of fish, wildlife, and plants threatened with extinction and those that might become endangered in the foreseeable future. Federal agencies must avoid harming such species, and fines up to $10,000 may be levied on private citizens who buy, sell, transport in interstate commerce, import, or export, in violation of the Act, any of the identified endangered species.

Endangered Species Act
An Act authorizing the Secretary of the Interior to list wildlife threatened with extinction and providing for the protection of such endangered species.

Noise Control Act

The Noise Control Acts of 1970 and 1972 require the EPA and the Federal Aviation Administration to set standards and regulations for the control of aircraft noise and sonic booms. They delegate to the EPA and the Department of Transportation the same mission for interstate railroad and motor carriers. The Acts declare a policy to have an environment free from excessive noise that jeopardizes health and welfare.

Noise Control Act
A law requiring controls to be set in order to have an environment free from excessive noise.

Surface Mining Act

Congress, using the commerce power, passed the Surface Mining and Reclamation Act of 1977, which regulates the use of privately owned land.

Surface Mining Act
An Act to control strip mining and to protect prime farmlands.

Following the lead of the Clean Air Act and the Clean Water Act, this Act provides for functions that will be carried out by states whose legislatures enact programs meeting minimum federal standards. Certain land must be designated as unsuitable for mining. On the land determined to be suitable for mining, operators are required to restore topsoil and to revegetate after mining. Any harmful minerals must be treated so that groundwater and surface water will not be contaminated. Prime farmlands cannot be mined unless the operator is able to restore the area to equivalent or higher levels of yield.

Facts

Congress passed the Surface Mining Control and Reclamation Act, which allowed surface or strip coal mining on prime farmland only if the operators could meet soil reconstruction standards and restore the surface to equivalent or higher quality. A federal district court in Indiana held the law to be unconstitutional, as it had no bearing on interstate commerce. The decision was appealed to the U.S. Supreme Court.

Decision

Congress adopted the Act to ensure that the production of coal for interstate commerce would not be at the expense of agriculture. There was a rationale for finding that surface mining on prime farmland affects interstate commerce in agricultural products. The district court had acted as a superlegislature, passing on the wisdom of congressional policy. In doing so, the court exceeded its proper role.

Hodel v. *Indiana*, 452 U.S. 314, 101 S.Ct. 2376, 69 L.Ed.2d 40 (1981).

Antiquities Preservation

Preservation of American Antiquities
An Act giving the President the right to make executive orders to preserve certain objects of historic or scientific interest.

Act for the Preservation of American Antiquities gives the President the right by executive order to declare as national monuments objects of historic or scientific interest on lands owned or controlled by the United States. A recent use of this power involved the government-owned Devil's Hole, a deep limestone cavern with a pool inhabited by a pup fish, a desert fish unlike any other in the world. The President ordered that the site be made a part of the Death Valley National Monument. Nearby ranchers were pumping groundwater from the pool to irrigate fields which lowered the water level in the pool to the extent that it endangered the spawning of the fish. Although the nearby ranch was an investment of $7 million, employed 80 people, and raised 4,000 acres of hay, wheat, and barley, the federal court granted an injunction to limit water pumping to an extent that would maintain the level of the pool.

Environmental issues pose large ethical and technological questions for business managers. Modern technology has developed effective but costly methods for pollution abatement. Most water pollutants can be removed by resorting to several processes, each one adding to the expense. Air pollution can be cleaned up by using cleaner fuels, mechanical filters, "scrubbing" processes that pass the air through liquids, and chemical treatment. Under the cost-benefit analysis system followed in many business decisions, pollution removal is difficult to measure when it involves damages to human health and loss of life.

Questions

1. Congress has passed several laws relating to the disposition of hazardous wastes. What do you think would be the best way to deal with this problem?
2. What is an Environmental Impact Statement, and when is it required?
3. The snail darter and the pup fish were considered to be endangered species. The snail darter held up completion of a large dam construction, and the pup fish put a limit on local farm production. Do you believe that the protection of such things should be an important consideration in planning the development of worthwhile projects? Why?
4. The Clean Air Act, Clean Water Act, and Noise Control Act have all been passed by Congress to ensure us all a clean and healthy environment. Do you think they have succeeded? What do you think would be the best way to accomplish this goal?
5. What is the purpose of the superfund created by the Superfund Law?

4.3 Employment Regulation

Labor Relations

The start of the twentieth century was marked by much labor strife. As workers began to organize to better their conditions, the courts looked upon such activities as illegal conspiracies. Strikes and boycotts were also held to be tortious interference with contracts.

After passage of the Sherman Antitrust Act, some courts held that many union actions were in violation of the law. Although the Clayton Act had a provision exempting unions from antitrust laws, the state and federal courts continued to rule against the emerging unions. Publicity and public pressure finally caused Congress to respond by enacting laws to protect labor movements.

Norris-LaGuardia Act

In 1932, during the Great Depression, the Norris-LaGuardia Act was passed. The Act barred the courts from issuing injunctions in nonviolent labor disputes. Peaceful refusal to work, boycotts, and picketing were free from employer or court intervention as long as there were no wildcat (not union-authorized) strikes, violence, or illegal activity. The law declared a national policy of encouraging the formation of labor unions without employer interference. The plan was to keep the courts out of the labor field and to minimize regulation.

Norris-LaGuardia Act
A 1932 law passed by Congress to protect labor movements.

Wagner Act

The Wagner Act (National Labor Relations Act) of 1935 was an affirmative effort by the federal government to support unionization and collective

National Labor Relations Act
Labor law, known as the Wagner Act, intended to support unionization and collective bargaining.

bargaining. The Act prohibited certain listed unfair labor practices by employers, including interfering with the right to unionize or bargain collectively, dominating a union, discriminating against union members, and refusing to bargain in good faith with the union.

NLRB

National Labor Relations Board (NLRB)
An independent agency created by Congress to oversee relationships between unions and employers.

The Wagner Act also created a new administrative agency, the National Labor Relations Board (NLRB), to oversee the secret elections used by employees to choose their representative for collective bargaining. The NLRB is also responsible for investigating and correcting unfair labor practices.

Fair Labor Standards Act

Fair Labor Standards Act (FLSA)
A labor law that sets pay and work standards.

The Fair Labor Standards Act (FLSA) of 1938 requires most employers to pay their employees at least a minimum hourly wage as set by the government and time and a half for hours worked in excess of forty per week. Executives, administrators, professionals, and outside salespersons are exempt from the Act. Time worked includes that which is "suffered or permitted" as well as that which is actually directed by the employer. The following case illustrates an application of the Act.

Facts

Gilbert and Wade were employed by the Old Ben Coal Corporation as mine surveyors, but they were not professionals. They placed wooden plugs into the roof of a mine as directional guides for mining machines. They determined the hours they worked as long as they had sufficient plugs in place for the next shift. Neither they nor the employer kept any records of the time they worked, and the employer considered them to be employees exempt from the FLSA. The workers claimed that they had worked about fifty hours a week and sued for overtime pay.

Decision

The court held that the employee is required to prove the actual number of hours worked overtime, and since the workers had no records to establish that fact, they could not recover.

Gilbert v. Old Ben Coal Corp., 85 Ill.App.3d 488, 40 Ill. Dec. 939, 407 N.E.2d 170 (1980).

Taft-Hartley Act

Taft-Hartley Act
An Act that contains provisions to protect employers from unfair labor practices by unions.

The Taft-Hartley (Labor-Management Relations Act) (LMRA) was passed over President Truman's veto in 1947 following a large increase in union membership and much labor unrest. The Act was intended to amend the Wagner Act and contained provisions to protect employers from unions by prohibiting certain unfair labor practices. These unfair actions included secondary boycotts (pressure upon an employer with which the union has no dispute), refusal to bargain in good faith, featherbedding (requiring pay for work not done), and strikes to force discharge of nonunion employees. The Act also reinstates the power of the courts to issue injunctions in labor disputes if requested to do so by the NLRB. A free-speech amendment

GOVERNMENT REGULATION OF BUSINESS

allowed employers to contact employees prior to union elections unless they threaten reprisals or promise benefits.

Closed shops (requiring union membership as a condition of employment) were made illegal, but union shops (requiring workers to join the union after some time on the job) were left legal. The Taft-Hartley Act allows individual states to pass their own right-to-work laws that make it illegal to require union membership for continued employment. Almost half of the states, primarily in the South, have enacted such laws.

A controversial provision of the Taft-Hartley Act provides for an eighty-day cooling-off period. This provision permits the President of the United States to obtain an injunction for eighty days where it is determined that a strike would create a national emergency. President Eisenhower used it against steelworkers in 1959, President Nixon against longshoremen in 1971, and President Carter against coal miners in 1978.

Closed Shop
A business subject to collective bargaining and that requires all workers to be union members as a condition of their employment.

Right-to-Work Law
State laws that provide for an open shop, a business that employs workers without regard to whether or not they are members of a labor union.

Landrum-Griffin Act

The Landrum-Griffin Act (the Labor Management Reporting and Disclosure Act of 1959) was passed in an effort to clean up the internal affairs of unions and eliminate corruption. It establishes an elaborate reporting system and sets forth a union member's bill of rights. Its purpose is to make the unions more democratic and assure all members of a right to participate actively in the internal affairs of the group. The Act also made it an unfair labor practice to make a "hot cargo" agreement (an agreement not to handle goods produced by a nonunion company).

Landrum-Griffin Act
An Act intended to clean up internal union affairs and eliminate corruption.

"Hot Cargo"
The unfair labor practice of refusing to handle goods produced by a nonunion company.

Employee Protection

Prior to government regulation, an injured employee could recover from the employer only by showing that the injury was caused by the negligence of the employer. The employer also had several defenses available in such suits, including the fellow servant rule (no liability if the injury was caused by another worker), contributory negligence by the employee, and the doctrine of assumption of risk by a worker who knowingly takes a dangerous job.

Workers' Compensation

All of the states have now adopted workers' compensation acts to provide a more certain and faster remedy for injured employees. These laws create commissions or boards to determine if the employee is entitled to compensation and, if so, how much. They cover practically all job-related injuries and provide for medical expenses as well as wages for time lost from work because of the incident. In most jurisdictions, claims before the commission are the sole remedy available to the worker, who is prohibited from filing a negligence lawsuit against the employer but may do so against third persons. These statutes usually permit employers to self-insure, buy insurance, or participate in a state fund. The following case illustrates the application of these laws.

Workers' Compensation Acts
Laws that establish liability of an employer for injuries or sicknesses of an employee arising out of and during the worker's employment.

Facts

Strother filed a Workers' Compensation claim against Morrison Cafeteria, her employer. She was a cashier and worked each night until 9:00 p.m. On three straight days, she observed two men in the cafeteria who were neither customers nor employees. On the third night, she drove directly home from work, and when she got out of her car, she was assaulted by one of the men who also stole her purse. She claimed that the assailant thought she was carrying the day's receipts of the cafeteria. The commission denied her claim on the basis that the injuries were not sustained in the course of her employment. She appealed.

Decision

The court held that the test for coverage was "arising out of and in the course of employment" and that the cause of her injury arose from her employment and was in the course of employment in the sense of continuity of time, space, and circumstances.

Strother v. Morrison Cafeteria, 383 So.2d 623 (Fla. 1980).

OSHA

Occupational Safety and Health Act (OSHA)
A federal law for the purpose of protecting employees from being injured or getting ill during the course of their employment.

Congress passed the Occupational Safety and Health Act (OSHA) in 1970 in an attempt to ensure that every worker would have a safe and healthful place of employment. Almost all private employers are subject to the provisions of the Act. Congress created the Occupational Safety and Health Administration (also called OSHA) in the Department of Labor and gives the administration the primary responsibility for administration and enforcement of the Act. As long as a state meets federal standards, the state can regulate its own health and safety measures in the workplace. The Act requires employers to eliminate "recognized hazards," which have been defined as dangerous conditions or activities that were known or should have been known to the employer based on what is reasonable in the particular industry.

The Secretary of Labor is required to issue regulations and set standards for specific industries. OSHA standards vary from business to business and include such things as air quality provisions, maximum noise levels, locations for machinery, and safety precautions for workers. Many business people have been critical of OSHA's voluminous regulations, strict enforcement policies, and attention to safety rather than health hazards.

American Textile Mfgrs. Inst., Inc. v. *Donovan*
452 U.S. 490, 101 S.Ct. 2478, 69 L.Ed 2d 185 (1981).

The American Textile Manufacturers Institute, Inc., a trade association representing 175 textile firms, and others (plaintiffs) challenged the validity of the cotton dust standard issued by Raymond Donovan (defendant), secretary of labor, under the Occupational Safety and Health Act.

Cotton dust—consisting of waste fibers, soil, noncotton plant matter, and other contaminants of cotton that are present in the air during the processing of cotton into cloth—causes a respiratory disease called byssinosis (brown lung disease) in a substantial proportion of the workers who are involved in that processing. It is estimated that of the currently employed and retired workers who are or have been involved in preparing the cotton and manufacturing cotton yarn, 1 in 12 suffers from the most disabling form of the disease and 25 percent are victims of the disease to some extent.

In 1976 OSHA published a proposed standard for maximum levels of the cotton dust in textile plants. After hearings had been conducted, comments from interested parties had been reviewed, and two studies estimating the costs of implementation to the industry had been reviewed, the secretary of labor in 1978 issued the final standard. This permitted exposure of textile workers to somewhat more dust than had been proposed originally and it allowed textile plants four years to reach full compliance.

Brennan, Justice— . . . The manufacturers urge not only that OSHA must show that a standard addresses a significant risk of material health impairment, but also that OSHA must demonstrate that the reduction in risk of material health impairment is significant in light of the costs of attaining that reduction. The Secretary on the other hand contends that the Act requires OSHA to promulgate standards that eliminate or reduce such risks "to the extent such protection is technologically and economically feasible."

. . . . Although their interpretations differ, all parties agree that the phrase "to the extent feasible" contains the critical language in § 6(b)(5) for purposes of this case.

The plain meaning of the word "feasible" supports the Secretary's interpretation of the statute. According to Webster's Third New International Dictionary of the English Language, "feasible" means "capable of being done, executed, or effected." Thus, § 6(b)(5) directs the Secretary to issue the standard that "most adequately assures . . . that no employee will suffer material impairment of health," limited only by the extent to which this is "capable of being done." In effect then, as the Court of Appeals held, Congress itself defined the basic relationship between costs and benefits, by placing the "benefit" of worker health above all other considerations save those making attainment of this "benefit" unachievable. Any standard based on a balancing of costs and benefits by the Secretary that strikes a different balance than that struck by Congress would be inconsistent with the command set forth in § 6(b)(5). Thus, cost-benefit analysis by OSHA is not required by the statute because feasibility analysis is. The congressional reports and debates certainly confirm that Congress meant "feasible" and nothing else in using the term. Congress was concerned that the Act might be thought to require achievement of absolute safety, an impossible standard, and therefore insisted that health and safety goals be capable of economic and technological accomplishment. Perhaps most telling is the absence of any indication whatsoever that Congress intended OSHA to conduct its own cost-benefit analysis before promulgating a toxic material or harmful physical agent standard. The legislative history demonstrates conclusively that Congress was fully aware that the Act would impose real and substantial costs of compliance on industry, and believed that such costs were part of the cost of doing business.

Affirmed for the Secretary of Labor.

State and federal laws have been passed to help protect employees and their families from the financial impact of retirement, disability, death, hospitalization, and unemployment.

Social Security

The Social Security Act of 1935 was the origin of the basic retirement plan that created Old Age, Survivors, and Disability Insurance (OASDI). Employers and employees are both required to make payments under the Federal Insurance Contributions Act (FICA) to help pay for retirement benefits. Such "contributions" are based on the maximum amount of employee wages subject to the tax. Retirement benefits are fixed by law but may get cost-of-living allowance (COLA) increases when the index rises above a certain level. However, Congress has withheld a COLA in the past and could do so again.

Medicare

Medicare is a health insurance program administered by the Social Security Administration for those over 65 years of age and some under that age who are disabled. Additional coverage is available under the plan upon payment of a monthly fee. A new provision has been added for catastrophic illness to be paid for by a limited surcharge on some income tax returns.

ERISA

The Employment Retirement Income Security Act (ERISA) of 1974 was passed to regulate private retirement plans set up by employers as a supplement to Social Security benefits. The Act empowers the Labor Management Services Administration of the Labor Department to oversee and enforce regulations governing those who operate private pension funds. ERISA requires that all pension plans be in writing and name a plan manager. All assets, except insurance, must be held in trust by a responsible plan manager. ERISA also created the Pension Benefit Guaranty Corporation to provide insurance of pension benefits in case a plan terminates. All plans are required to have such insurance. Detailed records of investments and distribution must be kept by the plan managers, and periodic reports must be submitted to the IRS, the Department of Labor, and the Pension Benefit Guaranty Corporation. ERISA is enforced by the Department of Labor and the Treasury Department. Violation of the Act can lead to both criminal punishment and civil lawsuits.

Unemployment Compensation

Federal Unemployment Tax Act (FUTA)
An act that provides for state unemployment compensation systems for eligible persons.

Qualified unemployed workers may receive payments from a fund created by the Federal Unemployment Tax Act (FUTA) and contributed to by employers. The Act provides for a state unemployment insurance system for eligible persons. The federal government maintains an Unemployment Insurance Fund built upon taxes collected by the states from employers and in which each state has an account. Requirements for eligibility vary from state to state. In some jurisdictions, payments may not be available to employees discharged for cause, to those who quit without cause, or to those who refuse to accept or seek a job for which they are qualified.

Employment Discrimination

Equal Pay Act

Following the civil rights movements of the 1950s and 1960s, several federal laws were enacted to prohibit discrimination in employment on the basis of sex, race, religion, ethnic origin, age, or handicap. One of the first of these laws was the Equal Pay Act of 1963, an amendment to the Fair Labor Standards Act. The Act declares that sex cannot be used as a basis for paying unequal pay for the same work. Seniority systems, merit systems, shift differentials, and piece rate systems are permitted as long as there is no sex discrimination. The same wages must be paid for equal work on jobs that require equal skill, effort, and responsibility for performance and that are performed under similar working conditions. An employer who violates this law must raise the pay of the worker receiving the lower wage and is not allowed to lower the wage of the higher paid employee.

Equal Pay Act
A federal law providing that sex cannot be used as a reason for unequal pay for the same work.

Equal Employment Opportunity Act

Title VII of the Civil Rights Act of 1964 as amended by the Equal Employment Opportunity Act of 1972 prohibits discrimination on the basis of race, color, sex, religion, or national origin in the hiring, firing, pay, promotion, training, or dismissal of employees. It applies to any employer engaged in industry affecting commerce who has fifteen or more employees. The Equal Employment Opportunity Act creates the Equal Employment Opportunity Commission (EEOC), which has the power and the responsibility to file actions, attempt to compromise alleged violations, investigate all charges of discrimination, set guidelines, and issue regulations.

Civil Rights Act of 1964
A federal law to amend statutes passed after the Civil War and to upgrade the rights of minorities.

Equal Employment Opportunity Act
A federal law that prohibits discrimination in employment on the basis of race, color, sex, religion, or national origin.

Equal Employment Opportunity Commission (EEOC)
An agency created to implement the equal opportunity policy.

The courts have defined two types of actions that exist under the law, one for "disparate treatment" and one for "disparate impact." Disparate treatment is an action in which an employee alleges that because of discrimination he receives less favorable treatment than his fellow workers. Disparate impact occurs when an employer uses a test or hiring method that tends to disqualify a protected class (discriminations listed in the Act) or is one that is not job related. A culture-oriented objective intelligence test that would eliminate certain minorities and height and weight requirements not essential to the position that could amount to sex discrimination are examples of disparate impact.

A plaintiff bringing an action under Title VII must first establish a prima facie case. The U.S. Supreme Court has said that a plaintiff can do this by showing that (1) he belongs to a minority class, (2) he applied for and was qualified for an open job, (3) he was rejected, and (4) the positiion remained open and the employer continued to seek applications. Another way of showing a prima facie case is by alleging harassment or retaliation. Statistical evidence may be used, as may evidence of actual incidents of discrimination.

Prima Facie Case
A case sufficient on its face, supported by at least a minimum of evidence and free from obvious defects.

BFOQ

Once the plaintiff has established a prima facie case, the burden of proof shifts to the employer, who must explain or justify the action at issue. Bona

Bona Fide Occupational Qualification (BFOQ)
Statute provision that permits discrimination based on religion, sex or national origin if it is reasonably necessary to the normal operation of a particular business.

fide occupational qualification (BFOQ) and business necessity—reasonably necessary for normal operation—may be affirmative defenses. Evidence may also be presented to show that the action was based upon a legitimate nondiscriminatory reason. If this happens, the burden shifts back to the plaintiff, who must try to prove that such defense was just a pretext. The plaintiff may also show that the same criterion was not being applied uniformly to all job applicants.

Facts

Alice LaBorde was an assistant professor at the University of California at Irvine. She was considered for promotion to full professor several times but was rejected. She brought an action under Title VII of the Civil Rights Act of 1964, alleging that the decision not to promote her was based on unlawful discrimination against her sex. She presented statistical data showing a shortage of female faculty members at the university that raised an inference of a pattern of discrimination in favor of men. The university stated that LaBorde was not promoted because of inadequate scholarship.

Decision

LaBorde established a prima facie case with the statistical evidence which then shifted the burden of proof to the university to show that she was rejected for a legitimate nondiscriminatory reason. The university then showed that she had failed to meet their standards for scholarship and research. That shifted the proof back to Laborde to show that the articulated reason was "a pretext or discriminatory in its application." Since Laborde was unable to do this to the court's satisfaction, decision was for the university.

Laborde v. Regents of the University of California, 686 F.2d 715 (9th Cir. 1982).

Sexual Harassment

Sexual Harassment
An employee policy or acceptance of the practice of exposing employees to the physical or verbal sexual advances or abuse by superiors or other co-workers.

Sexual harassment on the job has been the issue of many recent Title VII lawsuits. The EEOC guidelines state that "unwelcome sexual advances, requests for sexual favors, and other verbal or physical conduct of a sexual nature" are prohibited sexual harassments where "such conduct has the purpose or effect of unreasonably interfering with an individual's work performance or creating an intimidating, hostile, or offensive working environment." One judge wrote, "Surely, a requirement that a man or a woman run a gauntlet of sexual abuse in return for the privilege of being allowed to work and make a living can be as demeaning and disconcerting as the harshest of racial epithets." Voluntariness is not the issue, and provocative speech or dress by the plaintiff is irrelevant. The courts hold that the question to be decided is whether the alleged sexual advances were "unwelcome," not whether actual participation was voluntary.

Fletcher v. Greiner
106 Misc.2d 564, 435 N.Y.S.2d 1005 (1980).

Levitt, J. This is an action alleging charges of sexual discrimination in employment. . . . Plaintiff alleges that from July 18, 1963 to September, 1977 defendant used his "hegemonic position to importune plaintiff" into engaging in acts of sexual intercourse and deviate sexual behavior. Plaintiff asserts that compliance with defendant's requests were a condition of continuing employment and she feared that refusal of these advances would have an adverse effect.

Plaintiff, however, admits that hegemony notwithstanding, she eventually fell in love with defendant and he expressed love for her. She further alleges that they thereafter discussed a future life together and were contemplating matrimony. Indeed, she claims that at the insistence of defendant she divorced her husband in 1973 and waived alimony.

Plaintiff asserts that, four years later, in August, 1977, she refused to have any further sexual relations with defendant, whereupon defendant told her that he would not marry her and subsequently terminated her employment in September and salary payments in December.

The stated purpose of the "Human Rights Law" is to afford an equal opportunity to enjoy a full and productive life and to obtain employment without discrimination because of age, race, creed, color, national origin, sex, or marital status. It was not enacted to afford redress for breach of promise of marriage and its after-effects which, as plaintiff has cogently revealed, lies at the root of this action.

. . . The statute was not intended as a palliative for blighted love even when the lovers are employer and employee.

The primary purpose of the Civil Rights Act is to require employers to make employment-related determinations about their workers on the basis of each person's characteristics, so as to render irrelevant the employee's social, sexual, ethnic or religious background.

It was the intention of Congress to formally regulate the disparate treatment of men and women resulting from sex stereotypes. . . .

Clearly, plaintiff has, through the facts presented on the present motions, failed to come within the purview of this statute. Her action, which she has characterized as "labor lost through force," should more appropriately be designated, as did Shakespeare, "love's labour's lost."

In the instant matter, plaintiff has failed to meet the requisite criteria of a cause of action based upon sexual harassment. Plaintiff, by her own admissions, supports this finding by stating that she and defendant were lovers and that their relationship included plans for a future marriage. Clearly, during most of plaintiff's association with defendant these advances were welcome in the furtherance of their meretricious relationship. However, statutory protection is afforded only to those who repulse the sexual suggestions and advances.

Plaintiff admits that defendant "stole her life" and that relations with him are bitter. To deny defendant's motion for summary judgment of this cause of action would open the floodgates to litigation by countless employees who have emotional affairs with their superiors that subsequently turn sour.

Dismissed for defendant.

Racial Discrimination

During Reconstruction following the Civil War, Congress passed a Civil Rights Act in an attempt to prevent racial discrimination and to provide federal remedies for rights that might be denied in some states. The laws were dormant and not used until recent years but are now the basis for many civil rights suits. They are found in Title 42, Section 1981 through 1986 of the U.S. Code. Section 1981 allows private individuals to sue in federal courts for acts of racial discrimination against them, especially when

Racial Discrimination
The unequal treatment of persons because of racial ancestry.

U.S. Code, Title 42
The original Civil Rights Act, sections 1981–1986 of which allow federal lawsuits as remedies in cases of racial discrimination.

such discrimination occurs in the making or enforcing of contracts. In 1987, the U.S. Supreme Court held that Arabs and Jews, even though considered to be Caucasians, could sue under this law on the basis of racial discrimination. The Court said that the law protects identifiable classes of persons who are subjected to intentional discrimination solely because of their ancestry or ethnic characteristics.

Age Discrimination

Age Discrimination in Employment Act
A federal law that prohibits the unfair treatment of employees on the basis of age.

The Age Discrimination in Employment Act of 1967 (ADEA), as amended, prohibits both governmental and private employers from discriminating because of age against persons over 40. Compulsory retirement age for employees is allowed only if it falls under one of the exceptions in the Act, such as certain types of executives with nonforfeitable annual retirement benefits.

Age may be used as an employment criteria only if it is a bona fide occupational qualification reasonably necessary for the normal operation of the business. The Supreme Court held that an airline's BFOQ defense requiring all flight engineers to retire at age 60 was not valid. Even though safety was given as the reason, the Court said that the employer would have to show that substantially all persons over that age could not safely perform the duties of the job.

Pregnancy Act

Pregnancy Discrimination Act
An Act that adds pregnancy to the list of categories protected from discrimination.

The Pregnancy Discrimination Act of 1978 added pregnancy to the protected categories. The Act prohibits an employer from firing or refusing to hire or promote a woman just because she is pregnant. The employer cannot require the female employee to take leave at a specified time during pregnancy, but required leave policy must be based upon the individual woman's inability to continue work.

Wrongful Discharge

Wrongful Discharge
Some states hold that firing an employee without reasonable cause, for a reason against public policy, or by breach of good faith, is a wrongful discharge.

Many recent cases in some states have led to the developing law of wrongful discharge. At common law, a person hired at will could also be fired by his employer at will and without cause. Some states still follow this rule. However, about half of the jurisdictions will allow either or both of the following exceptions. These are: (1) public policy and (2) the implied contract rule, or breach of good faith. Examples of discharges that violated public policy include the firing of a worker for engaging in an activity that benefits society, such as serving on jury duty, or refusing to commit an illegal act, like price fixing. Other cases have been based on discharge for whistle blowing (revealing corrupt activities), filing a workman's compensation claim, and for refusing to violate a provision in a professional code of ethics. Many of the states also will imply a covenant of good faith and fair dealing in employment contracts which prohibits discharge except for good cause.

In 1988, the California Supreme Court in a 4–3 decision, recognized causes of action for tortious discharges against public policy; approved of cases for breach of implied-in-fact contracts requiring good cause for discharge; and authorized suits for breach of an implied covenant of good faith and fair dealing in employment contracts. However, the decision limited recovery for breach of the covenant to contract damages only, eliminating punitive awards. The court based its decision on the need for "commercial stability" and the recognition that employers would be deprived of the choice to fire an employee for fear of the possible award of excessive damages. The court added that any expansion of tort remedies in employment cases should be done, if at all, by the legislature. *Foley* v. *Interactive Data Corp.*, 47 C.3d 654, 254 Cal.Rptr. 211 (1988).

Rehabilitation Act

The Rehabilitation Act of 1973 attempts to assist the handicapped to obtain employment, rehabilitation training, and access to other facilities. Employers performing under federal contracts over $2,500 must take affirmative action to hire and advance qualified handicapped persons. Recipients of federal financial assistance are prohibited from discriminating on the basis of handicap. Regulations define a handicapped person as "any person who has a physical or mental impairment that substantially limits one or more major life activities."

Rehabilitation Act
A federal law that attempts to assist the handicapped to obtain employment, training, and access to facilities.

Affirmative Action

The EEOC strongly promotes affirmative action programs by all employers. The law requires all federal contractors to institute such programs. Wherever discrimination is found by the EEOC or a court, an affirmative action program must be put into effect. Such programs require the setting of goals to increase the proportions of minority group workers in the labor force and then seeking out members of the protected groups to fill the jobs. However, recent reverse discrimination decisions by the U.S. Supreme Court may have changed this policy.

Affirmative Action
Positive steps taken in order to correct conditions resulting from past discrimination.

United Steelworkers of America v. Weber
443 U.S. 193, 99 S.Ct. 2721, 61 L.Ed.2d 480 (1979).

Brian Weber (plaintiff) brought this class action against United Steelworkers of America (defendant) alleging discrimination on the basis of race in violation of Title VII of the Civil Rights Act of 1964.

The Steelworkers and Kaiser Aluminum & Chemical Corporation entered into a master collective bargaining contract in 1974 that contained an affirmative action plan. The contract covered 15 plants. The aim of the affirmative action plan was to eliminate racial imbalances among craft workers, who were then almost all white. The goal for each plant was to have the percentage of blacks in craft positions equal their percentage in the respective local labor forces. The plan established in each plant an on-the-job training program for craft work and reserved 50 percent of the openings in these programs for blacks.

In the first year that the affirmative action plan was in operation at the Gramercy, Louisiana, plant, 13 trainees were selected from the plant work force. Seven were black, and six were white. The most junior black in the program had less plant seniority than several white workers, including Weber, who had been rejected. Weber brought suit against both the union and the employer, claiming that giving the craft training to blacks in preference to more senior white employees was discrimination on the basis of race in violation of Title VII.

Brennan, Justice The only question before us is the narrow statutory issue of whether Title VII *forbids* private employers and unions from voluntarily agreeing upon bona fide affirmative action plans that accord racial preferences in the manner and for the purpose provided in the Kaiser-USWA plan.

. . . [I]t was clear to Congress that "the crux of the problem [was] to open employment opportunities for Negroes in occupations which have been traditionally closed to them" (remarks of Sen. Humphrey), and it was to this problem that Title VII's prohibition against racial discrimination in employment was primarily addressed.

Given this legislative history, we cannot agree with Weber that Congress intended to prohibit the private sector from taking effective steps to accomplish the goal that Congress designed Title VII to achieve. . . . It would be ironic indeed if a law triggered by a Nation's concern over centuries of racial injustice and intended to improve the lot of those who had "been excluded from the American dream for so long" (remarks of Sen. Humphrey), constituted the first legislative prohibition of all voluntary, private, race-conscious efforts to abolish traditional patterns of racial segregation and hierarchy.

We need not today define in detail the line of demarcation between permissible and impermissible affirmative action plans. It suffices to hold that the challenged Kaiser-USWA affirmative action plan falls on the permissible side of the line. The purposes of the plan mirror those of the statute. Both were designed to break down old patterns of racial segregation and hierarchy.

At the same time the plan does not necessarily trammel the interests of the white employees. The plan does not require the discharge of white workers and their replacement with new black hires. Nor does the plan create an absolute bar to the advancement of white employees; half of those trained in the program will be white. Moreover, the plan is a temporary measure; it is not intended to maintain racial balance, but simply to eliminate a manifest racial imbalance. Preferential selection of craft trainees at the Gramercy plant will end as soon as the percentage of black skilled craft workers in the Gramercy plant approximates the percentage of blacks in the local labor force.

Reversed in favor of the Steelworkers.

QUESTIONS

1. Do you think that existing laws give too much or too little protection to labor unions? What would you add or remove?

2. What are the advantages and disadvantages of a right-to-work law that prohibits mandatory union membership?

3. Should OSHA standards for health and safety in the workplace be strictly enforced regardless of the added cost to the operation of an industry?

4. Give some examples where a bona fide occupational qualification (BFOQ) would justify hiring only persons of one sex.

5. How can you tell when socializing or simple flirtation on the job becomes sexual harassment?

PROBLEMS

1. Five competitors who made and sold most of the stainless steel pipe in the country met together on several occasions to discuss their problems. At a dinner meeting, one of them stated, "I won't fix prices with any of you, but I'm going to put the price of my gidget at $50. However, you all do what you want." He then left, and competitor number two says and does the same. Following that process, all leave and all set their prices of gidgets at $50. When charged with a criminal conspiracy to fix prices in violation of the Sherman Antitrust Act, they deny that any conspiracy occurred. What result?

2. Aspen Highlands Skiing Corp. owns one of four major mountain facilities for downhill skiing at Aspen, Colorado. In earlier years, there were three competing companies, each of which offered its own tickets for daily use and an interchangeable six-day all-Aspen ticket that permitted skiers to use all of the slopes. Allocation of revenues from sale of the all-Aspen tickets was based on the number of skiers using each facility. Aspen Skiing bought out one of the competitors and started a fourth facility, now owning three of the four in business. It then said that it would continue the all-Aspen tickets only if Aspen Highlands would accept a lower fixed percentage of the revenues. When Aspen Highlands refused this arrangement, Aspen Skiing stopped selling all-Aspen tickets and sold six-day tickets for its mountains only. Aspen Highlands' business suffered, and the company sued for treble damages on the basis that Aspen Skiing had violated the Sherman Act. What result?

3. The National Commission on Egg Nutrition published advertising representing that there is no scientific evidence that eating eggs increases the risk of heart disease or heart attack. The Federal Trade Commission sought to enjoin such representations as false and violative of the Federal Trade Commission Act. What result?

4. Chicago passed an ordinance prohibiting the sale of any detergents containing phosphorus on the basis that such products polluted the city's water. Procter and Gamble sought an injunction alleging that the ordinance violated the commerce clause of the Constitution. Decide.

5. The U.S. Forest Service proposed to construct a gravel road in the Nezperce National Forest in Idaho. One purpose was to provide access to timberland to be opened for commercial development. The Forest Service prepared an environmental assessment and determined that an environmental impact statement (EIS) was not required because the road would have no significant environmental impact. The assessment discussed only the road, not the impact of the planned timber development. Landowners, ranchers, and several conservation organizations appealed the decision by the chief of the Forest Service not to prepare an EIS. Decision.

6. Illinois passed a law prohibiting movement from out of the state of any spent nuclear fuel for disposal or storage in the state. Under the Atomic Energy Act, the Nuclear Regulatory Commission has all regulatory power over such matters. However, Illinois argues that the Clean Air Act authorizes it to control and abate air pollution that includes "radioactive substance or matter which is emitted into the air." Can General Electric move spent nuclear fuel into Illinois despite this state statute?

7. Fox's widow was awarded worker's compensation death benefits by the Delaware Industrial Accident Board because of her husband's suicide. The board found that the suicide resulted from severe pain and despair due to a compensable accident at the Delaware Tire Center where Fox was employed. Should suicide be covered under worker's compensation?

8. The Duke Power Company had several operating departments but in the past had employed blacks only in the labor department, where the highest wages were lower than the lowest in the other departments. After the passage of the Civil Rights Act of 1964, the company required a high school education and a satisfactory score on two professionally prepared aptitude tests as a prerequisite for entering or transferring into the more desirable departments. Black employees sued on the basis of unlawful race discrimination. What should the U.S. Supreme Court decide?

9. Department stores in New Orleans charge for alterations made to women's clothing but not for those made to clothing sold in men's departments. A female customer claimed that this policy amounted to unlawful sex discrimination and sued under the Federal Civil Rights Act. Decision?

10. The Maryland Casualty Company was dissatisfied with the small amount of business in its Jackson, Mississippi, office. The office employed three marketing reps—Wayne, age 49; Lee, age 50; and Murray, age 56. The company decided to eliminate one of the jobs and decided that Murray was the most expendable. This decision was based on efficiency reports. Murray claims that he was fired because of age discrimination. What result?

PART TWO

Contracts

CHAPTER FIVE
Making Contracts

CHAPTER SIX
Other Basic Requirements

CHAPTER SEVEN
Reality of Consent

CHAPTER EIGHT
Formalities

CHAPTER NINE
Interpretation and Third Parties

CHAPTER TEN
Discharging the Contract

CHAPTER FIVE

Contracts

Practically all business transactions are based upon an agreement, or contract, between the parties involved. Most aspects of one's personal life are also guided by contracts. When you buy things such as food, automobiles, entertainment and clothing, you do so by agreement, express or implied. When you rent or buy a home, office, or business, the lease or sale is a contract. The insurance you purchase for protection is a contract. Contracts now reach such exotic topics as surrogate parenthood, agreeing to bear a child for another person. Contracts are voluntary agreements that create duties and obligations between two or more parties. However, the courts are often asked to settle disputes as to the existence, meaning, or legality of a contract and to enforce its provisions by granting financial or equitable relief.

Contracts are the basis for most substantive law, so the next six chapters are devoted to this subject. Chapter 5 discusses the principles involved in the making of a contract; Chapter 6 considers some of the basic requirements like capacity of parties, illegality, and public policy; Chapter 7 analyzes the problems of voluntary consent; Chapter 8 explains some of the formalities required in certain types of agreements; Chapter 9 deals with the court interpretation of contracts and third party interests; and Chapter 10 examines the termination of contracts, either through performance or by the court granting money damages or equitable relief.

CHAPTER FIVE

Making Contracts

5.1 Introduction to Contract Law
Contract Defined
Elements of a Contract
Types of Contracts

5.2 Reaching the Agreement
Intent
Offer
    Offer in Jest
    Ads as Offers
    Preliminary Negotiations
    Offer Certainty
    Rewards
    Auctions
    Sealed Bids
Sales of Personal Property
Duration of Offer
    Illegality
    Death and Insanity
    Revocation by Offeror
    Counteroffer
    Rejection
    Acceptance

5.3 Consideration
Benefit or Detriment
Gift
Unilateral Consideration
Bilateral Consideration
Illusory Offer
"Needs" Contract
Inadequacy of Consideration
Duty to Perform
Past Consideration
Moral Obligation
Liquidated Debt
Unliquidated Debt
"Paid in Full" as Accord and
    Satisfaction
Partial Payment
Promissory Estoppel
    Justifiable Reliance
Executed Contracts
UCC Consideration Exceptions
Promise to Pay Debt of Another

5.1 Introduction to Contract Law

Contract Defined

A contract is an agreement, expressly stated or implied from acts, to do or not to do something. The Restatement of the Law of Contracts, Section 1, gives the following definition: "A contract is a promise or set of promises for the breach of which the law gives a remedy, or the performance of which the law in some ways recognizes as a duty." The UCC defines contract as follows: " 'Contract' means the total legal obligation which results from the parties' agreement as affected by this Act and any other applicable rules of law."

Elements of a Contract

Generally, the following elements are required in a legal contract: (1) two or more competent parties, (2) their consent, (3) consideration, (4) a proper subject matter, and (5) mutuality of obligation. These requirements are considered in subsequent chapters.

Types of Contracts

For our purposes, we can classify contracts as follows: (1) express or implied, (2) unilateral or bilateral, (3) executed or executory, and (4) void, voidable, or unenforceable.

An express contract is one in which its terms are stated *in words,* oral or written. An implied in fact contract is one in which the existence and terms are manifested *by conduct.* The distinction between an express contract and an implied in fact contract relates only to the manner in which the consent was made evident by the parties. To illustrate: A man waves to a taxi, gets in, and gives the driver an address. No other words are spoken. This is an implied contract that the driver will receive compensation for taking the man to the address.

Contract
Voluntary agreement between two or more persons to do or not to do something.

UCC
The Uniform Commercial Code.

Consent
To approve something proposed or requested.

Express
To put into words.

Implied
Indicated but not explicitly written or stated.

Richardson v. J. C. Flood Company
190 A.2d 259 (D.C.App.1963).

Myers, Judge This is an appeal by a property owner [defendant Richardson] from a judgment against her for costs of labor and material furnished by appellee [plaintiff] plumbing company.

Appellant contends there was error in the findings of the trial court that all work done by appellee was authorized by her and that there was sufficient competent evidence to substantiate the amount of recovery.

Appellant requested appellee to correct a stoppage in the sewer line of her house. In the course of the work a "snake" used to clear the line leading to the main sewer became caught and to secure its release a portion of the sewer line

MAKING CONTRACTS 99

in the backyard was excavated. It was then discovered that the instrument was embedded in pieces of wood which had become lodged in a sewer trap from surface debris. At this time numerous leaks were found in a rusty, defective water pipe which ran parallel with the sewer line. In order to meet District regulations, the water pipe, of a type no longer approved for such service, had to be replaced then or at a later date when the yard would have to be redug for that purpose. Appellee's agent testified he so informed appellant's agent. Appellant testified she had requested appellee to clear the sewer line but denied she was told about the need for replacement of the water line and contested the total amount of the charges for all the work done by appellee.

In the absence of a written contract, but with appellant admitting she had requested correction of a sewer obstruction but denying she had agreed to replace the water pipe, the existence of an implied agreement between the parties to replace the water pipe at the same time became an issue for the trial court.

It seems clear from the record that there was evidence to support a finding that appellant and her agent through daily inspections of the repairs knew of the magnitude of the work required and made no objection to the performance of the extra work in replacing the water pipe until after the entire job was finished when appellant refused to pay any part of the total bill submitted.

Contracts for work to be done are either express or implied—*express* when their terms are stated by the parties, *implied* when arising from a mutual agreement and promise not set forth in words. Direct evidence is not essential to prove a contract which may be presumed from the acts and conduct of the parties as a reasonable man would view them under all the circumstances.

With respect to the costs of both jobs the record reveals that no testimony was offered by appellant to show that itemized amounts for labor and materials furnished by appellee were wrong or excessive and unreasonable or that the work performed was either unnecessary or unsatisfactory. Appellee produced testimony that the charges were fair and reasonable and that the work on both the sewer and the water lines was fully completed. We find no merit in appellant's claim of error that the evidence on the costs of labor and material was insufficient to support the finding on this point.

[Affirmed.]

Another type of contract is one that is implied in law, normally referred to as a quasi-contract. In this case, the law imposes an obligation on a party to prevent an unjust enrichment. That is, the law may imply a promise to pay for benefits or services rendered even though no such promise may have been made or intended. For example, a nurse furnishes beneficial services to a person who has been insane for many years. There is no contract as such. However, if the nurse rendered the services in good faith with no intention of making a gift of such services, the nurse could recover the reasonable value of the services in a quasi-contract or, as is also said, as if there were a contract. The following case is an example of a quasi-contract.

Quasi Contract
A contract created by the law for reasons of justice.

Facts

A contractor furnished labor and materials used in the construction of a bathroom in a home owned by Mr. and Mrs. Dozier. The contractor had acted upon a request by the Doziers' daughter, who lived in the home with her parents. The materials and labor were furnished with the full knowledge and consent of the homeowners. The daughter refused to pay, and the contractor sued the Doziers, who defended on the grounds that they did not have a contract with the contractor.

Decision

The court gave judgment for the contractor for the reasonable value of the improvements. A benefit was conferred on the defendants by the plaintiff, and appreciation given by the defendants of such benefit, and acceptance made of such benefit under such circumstances that it would be inequitable for the defendants to retain the benefit without payment of its value.

Actions brought upon theories of unjust enrichment, quasi-contracts, contracts implied in law, and *quantum meruit* ("as much as he deserved") are essentially the same, and courts frequently employ the various terminology interchangeably to describe that class of implied obligations where, on the basis of justice and equity, the law will impose contractual relationship between the parties, regardless of their assent thereto. [Judgment for the plaintiff.]

Paschall's, Inc. v. Dozier, 219 Tenn. 45, 407 S.W.2d 150 (1966).

Unilateral Contract
An agreement where one promises to act in return for performance instead of a promise.

Bilateral Contract
Mutual promises between the parties to a contract.

Executed Contract
An agreement that is fully performed.

Executory Contract
An agreement in which some performance remains to be done.

Void
Having no legal force, unenforceable.

Voidable
Capable of being annulled later.

Unenforceable
Something that cannot be enforced under the law.

Unconscionable
Unreasonably detrimental to the interest of a contracting party, hence unenforceable.

A unilateral contract is one in which a promise is given in exchange for an act or the forebearance of an act, with only one promisor. An example of a unilateral contract is the reward type of case. The law enforcement agency offers a reward for the capture of a criminal. The promise is the offer of the reward, and the act is the capture of the criminal.

A bilateral contract is one in which mutual promises are given. One promise is given in consideration for the other promise. Most contracts are bilateral. An attorney promises to perform certain services for a client. The client promises to pay money for the services. This is a bilateral contract.

An executed contract is one in which the object of the contract is fully performed (e.g., a cash sale). All others are executory (i.e., a contract that is wholly performed on one side but unperformed on the other side or unperformed on both sides in whole or in part). The distinction is important in certain cases such as illegality, modification of a written contract by executed oral agreement, consideration, and the statute of frauds. In such cases (discussed in detail in later chapters), the defenses normally available to performance of the contract are no longer available if the contract has been executed.

A void contract is a nullity and cannot be enforced by either party. For example, the victim of fraud in the inception did not know she was signing a legal document. A voidable contract is void or valid at the option of the parties, or of one of the parties. For example, a contract induced by fraudulent misrepresentations would be voidable at the option of the victim. (See Chapter 7.1 for a discussion of fraud.)

An unenforceable contract is one that cannot be enforced because of some legal technicality, such as the failure to satisfy the statute of frauds (failure to put the contract in writing which the statute of frauds requires of certain contracts) or because the statute of limitations has run on the contract (failure to file the lawsuit within the time prescribed by local statute). Such contracts are unenforceable rather than void or voidable.

A contract or clause therein can also be unenforceable because it is unconscionable (i.e., an absence of meaningful choice on the part of one of the parties together with unreasonable contract terms favoring the other party). (See UCC Sections 2–302 and 2–719[3], Appendix A.) The basic test is whether the clauses involved are so one-sided as to be unconscionable under the circumstances existing at the time the contract was made and in light of the general commercial needs of the particular trade or case. Examples of unconscionable contracts are those involving grossly excessive prices, particularly when the buyer is a person of limited income and education, or contracts with clauses hidden in fine print and unknown to the consumer. Most courts do not limit the test of unconscionability to the sale of goods but will apply it to any agreement. The following case is an example of an unconscionable clause in a commercial setting.

Facts

The Joneses, welfare recipients, agreed to buy a home food freezer for $900 as a result of a visit from a salesman representing the seller. With the addition of time credit charges, credit life insurance, credit property insurance, and sales tax, the total purchase price paid amounted to $1,234.80. The Joneses had already paid $619.88 and sued to have the contract reformed because of unconsionability. Star Credit Corporation, the defendant, claims that with various added charges due for a time extension there was still a balance due of $819.81. Proof at the trial established that the freezer, when bought, had a maximum retail value of $300.

Decision

The court declared the payment provision of the contract to be unconscionable under Article 2–302 of the UCC, limited it to the amount already paid, and reformed and amended the contract provision to that effect.

Jones v. Star Credit Corp., 59 Misc.2d 189, 298 N.Y.S.2d 264 (1969).

Questions

1. What is the difference between an express contract and one that is implied in fact?
2. Give an example of an implied in fact contract.
3. Why does the law impose an obligation under the theory of quasi-contract?
4. Give some examples that might cause a court to decide that a contract clause, or the entire contract, is unconscionable.
5. Do you believe that the courts should intervene to protect people who enter into contracts that are unfair to them? What are your reasons?

5.2 Reaching the Agreement

Intent

Every contract must have mutual assent or consent. Mutual assent is determined by the acts and the reasonable meaning of the words of the parties. This is referred to as the objective test for ascertaining intent. In other words, it is not necessary to have an actual meeting of the minds of the parties (subjective test) to form a valid contract. An apparent meeting of the minds is sufficient. Would a reasonable person believe that an agreement had been made? The following case illustrates the point that words and acts can be reasonably understood as an intent to make an offer rather than as a joke.

Objective
Uninfluenced by emotion or personal prejudice.

Subjective
Determined by the feelings or attitude of the person thinking rather than the quality of the thing considered.

Lucy v. Zehmer
196 Va. 493, 84 S.E.2d 516 (1954).

Buchanan, Justice This suit was instituted by W. O. Lucy and J. C. Lucy, complainants, against A. H. Zehmer and Ida S. Zehmer, his wife, defendants, to have specific performance of a contract by which it was alleged the Zehmers had sold to W. O. Lucy a tract of land owned by A. H. Zehmer in Dinwiddie county containing 471.6 acres, more or less, known as the Ferguson farm, for $50,000.

The instrument sought to be enforced was written by A. H. Zehmer on December 20, 1952, in these words: "We hereby agree to sell to W. O. Lucy the Ferguson Farm complete for $50,000.00, title satisfactory to buyer," and signed by the defendants, A. H. Zehmer and Ida S. Zehmer. . . .

The answer of A. H. Zehmer admitted that at the time mentioned W. O. Lucy offered him $50,000 cash for the farm, but that he, Zehmer, considered that the offer was made in jest; that so thinking, and both he and Lucy having had several drinks, he wrote out "the memorandum" quoted above and induced his wife to sign it; that he did not deliver the memorandum to Lucy, but that Lucy picked it up, read it, put in his pocket, attempted to offer Zehmer $5 to bind the bargain, which Zehmer refused to accept, and realizing for the first time that Lucy was serious, Zehmer assured him that he had no intention of selling the farm and that the whole matter was a joke. Lucy left the premises insisting that he had purchased the farm. . . .

The discussion leading to the signing of the agreement, said Lucy, lasted thirty or forty minutes, during which Zehmer seemed to doubt that Lucy could raise $50,000. Lucy suggested the provision for having the title examined and Zehmer made the suggestion that he would sell it "complete, everything there," and stated that all he had on the farm was three heifers. . . .

Lucy took a partly filled bottle of whiskey into the restaurant with him for the purpose of giving Zehmer a drink if he wanted it. Zehmer did, and he and Lucy had one or two drinks together. Lucy said that while he felt the drinks he took he was not intoxicated, and from the way Zehmer handled the transaction he did not think he was either. . . .

The defendants insist that the evidence was ample to support their contention that the writing sought to be enforced was prepared as a bluff or dare to force Lucy to admit that he did not have $50,000; that the whole matter was a joke; that the writing was not delivered to Lucy and no binding contract was ever made between the parties. . . .

In his testimony Zehmer claimed that he "was high as a Georgia pine," and that the transaction "was just a bunch of two doggoned drunks bluffing to see who could talk the biggest and say the most." That claim is inconsistent with his attempt to testify in great detail as to what was said and what was done. . . .

Not only did Lucy actually believe, but the evidence shows he was warranted in believing, that the contract represented a serious business transaction and a good faith sale and purchase of the farm. . . .

In the field of contracts, as generally elsewhere, "We must look to the outward expression of a person as manifesting his intention rather than to his secret and unexpressed intention. 'The law imputes to a person an intention corresponding to the reasonable meaning of his words and acts.'"

. . . The mental assent of the parties is not requisite for the formation of a contract. If the words or other acts of one of the parties have but one reasonable meaning, his undisclosed intention is immaterial except when an unreasonable meaning which he attaches to his manifestations is known to the other party. . . .

Reversed and remanded [for entry of a proper decree requiring defendants to perform the contract].

Generally, a contract that is valid on its face, when signed or accepted by a party, is deemed a binding agreement, and the party who signed or accepted it has assented to all of its terms. *Such party cannot escape liability on the grounds that he has not read the contract.* However, if fraud was used to procure the signature or if a fiduciary relationship (duty to act faithfully) existed between the parties requiring full disclosure, the signer would not be liable but still might wind up with an expensive lawsuit. A common excuse offered in a contract dispute is either "I didn't read it" or "I didn't understand it." Usually this is no defense. It is important to remember that you should never sign a legal document of any kind unless you have read it and understand it. If you do not understand the document, take it to an attorney, who can advise you of its legal consequences. The following case illustrates the point that failure to read the contract may be no defense.

Facts

In June 1940, Vargas entered into an employment contract with Esquire by which he agreed to furnish Esquire with certain art material. Vargas understood that he was signing a contract fixing the terms and compensation. There were only six paragraphs to the contract, which was written in plain and ordinary language.

Decision

In the absence of fraud, a person in possession of all his faculties who signs a contract cannot relieve himself from the obligations of the contract by saying he had not read it when he signed it or did not know or understand what it contained. It is a well-settled rule of law that a party to a contract who is able to read and has the opportunity to do so cannot thereafter claim ignorance of the terms and conditions of the contract.

Vargas v. Esquire, Inc., 166 F.2d 651, 7th Cir. (1948).

Offer

A contract results from an offer and the acceptance thereof. No particular formality is required. An offer is a proposal to enter into a contract, and it may be expressed by acts as well as by words. The person who makes the offer or proposal is the offeror; the person to whom it is made is the offeree.

To be legally sufficient, an offer must meet the following criteria:

1. The words must show a present contractual intent.
2. The terms of the offer must be sufficiently clear and complete so that a court can determine the parties' intentions.
3. The offer must be communicated to the offeree, and the offeree must have knowledge of the offer.

For example, John offers a reward for the return of his lost ring. If Bob returns the ring without knowledge of the offer, he cannot claim the reward. Or if John writes a letter offering to sell his ring to Bob but does not mail the letter, Bob has no power to accept the offer even if he learns of it from another source, since the offer was never communicated to him. If John

Offer
A proposal to enter into a contract.

Acceptance
Communication of assent with terms of an offer by the person to whom the offer was made.

Communicate
To make known.

inadvertently mails the offer to Bob, a valid offer could exist, since communication is determined *objectively* and not by what the offeror subjectively intended.

Offer in Jest

A proposal obviously made in jest, an invitation to a purely social function, or a remark made in the course of a family discussion which a reasonable person would not be justified in treating as an offer to enter into a contract is not an offer. There is a conflict of authority as to whether a proposal made under great emotional stress is a valid offer. Some courts hold that the offeree cannot take advantage of such an offer when he or she knows or should know that the offeror was unable to formulate a rational intent to contract. Other courts hold that the offeror is bound, since to do otherwise is to open the door and permit the offeror another method of escaping from the offer.

Rational
Based on reason.

Ads As Offers

When a party suggests the terms of a possible contract by a letter, circular, display, or advertisement *without making a definite proposal,* the result is a mere invitation to the other party to make an offer. For example, such language as "We can quote you" is generally considered merely a statement of terms and not an offer. However, a quotation may be sufficiently specific and promissory to constitute an offer. Thus, it may add the statement that the quotation is "For immediate wire acceptance" and could be construed as an offer.

O'Keefe v. Lee Calan Imports, Inc.
128 Ill.App.2d 410, 262 N.E.2d 758 (1970).

McNamara, Justice Christopher D. O'Brien brought suit against defendant for an alleged breach of contract. O'Brien died subsequent to the filing of the lawsuit, and the administrator of his estate was substituted in his stead. . . . Plaintiff and defendant filed cross-motions for summary judgment. The court denied plaintiff's motion for summary judgment and granted defendant's motion. . . .

On July 31, 1966, defendant advertised a 1964 Volvo Station Wagon for sale in the Chicago *Sun-Times*. Defendant had instructed the newspaper to advertise the price of the automobile at $1,795. However, through an error of the newspaper and without fault on part of defendant, the newspaper inserted a price of $1,095 for said automobile in the advertisement. O'Brien visited defendant's place of business, examined the automobile and stated that he wished to purchase it for $1,095. One of defendant's salesmen at first agreed, but then refused to sell the car for the erroneous price listed in the advertisement.

Plaintiff appeals, contending that the advertisement constituted an offer on the part of defendant, which O'Brien duly accepted and thus the parties formed a binding contract. . . .

It is elementary that in order to form a contract there must be an offer and an acceptance. A contract requires the mutual assent of the parties.

The precise issue of whether a newspaper advertisement constitutes an offer which can be accepted to form a contract or whether such an advertisement is merely an invitation to make an offer, has not been determined by the Illinois courts. Most jurisdictions which have dealt with the issue have considered such an advertisement as a mere invitation to make an offer, unless the circumstances indicate otherwise. . . .

We find that in the absence of special circumstances, a newspaper advertisement which contains an erroneous purchase price through no fault of the defendant advertiser and which contains no other terms, is not an offer which can be accepted so as to form a contract. We hold that such an advertisement amounts only to an invitation to make an offer. . . . There was no reference to several material matters relating to the purchase of an automobile, such as equipment to be furnished or warranties to be offered by defendant. Indeed the terms were so incomplete and so indefinite that they could not be regarded as a valid offer.

In *Lefkowitz* v. *Great Minneapolis Surplus Store*, 251 Minn. 188, 86 N.W.2d 689 (1957), defendant advertised a fur stole worth $139.50 for a sale at a price of $1.00, but refused to sell it to plaintiff. In affirming the judgment for plaintiff, the court found that the advertisement constituted a valid offer and, upon acceptance by plaintiff, a binding contract. However in that case, unlike the instant case, there was no error in the advertisement, but rather, defendant deliberately used misleading advertising. And in *Lefkowitz*, the court held that whether an advertisement was an offer or an invitation to make an offer depended upon the intention of the parties and the surrounding circumstances. . . .

The judgment of the Circuit Court is affirmed.

Preliminary Negotiations

An estimate usually does not suggest a binding proposal. However, where the word "estimate" is in the heading and not in the body of the document and the body contains words such as "We propose to furnish to" and "The signature herein is an authorization to install such equipment as described in the above estimate," the court can call the estimate an offer.

Offer Certainty

An offer must be sufficiently definite so that the performance required by the offeree is reasonably certain. The offer must describe the subject matter and the quantity and should state the price. However, the complete absence of any mention of the price is not necessarily fatal, as the court may interpret the contract to mean the market price or a reasonable price. The offer should state the time and place. However, failure to so state does not necessarily render the contract void if the intent of the parties is otherwise ascertainable. In determining whether a contract is sufficiently enforceable, the court will liberally interpret laypersons' agreements or nontechnical language. The court will attempt to make the contract valid if uncertainty exists by carrying into effect the reasonable intentions of the parties if they can be ascertained.

The following case is an example of an oral promise that was too uncertain to be enforceable.

Facts

Alice Sherman, niece of George Sherman, entered into an oral agreement with George whereby George would give Alice 100 acres of land if she would keep house for him until her marriage. Alice did her part, but George refused to convey the land to her. George dies and Alice sues to recover the land. George's administrator contends that it had never been made certain just what land the plaintiff was to receive, as George had many parcels of land.

Decision

A contract must be certain to be enforceable. An action brought upon an express promise lies only when a person assumes to do a certain thing, and this means a certainty to a common intent. The words must show that the understanding was certain. In this case, the action fails because the alleged contract did not state which 100 acres George was to give Alice.

Sherman v. Kitsmiller, Administrator, 17 Serg. & Rawle 45 (Penn.).

Rewards

Along with misunderstandings about price tags and ads, a few other "offer" situations can cause confusion if the wording is uncertain. Ads offering rewards for the return of lost property, for information, or for the capture of criminals are generally held to be offers for unilateral contracts. The offeree accepts by performing the requested act.

Auctions

Auction
A public or private sale to the highest bidder.

Sellers at auctions are usually held to be making invitations to offer. This makes the bidders the offerors, which the seller is then free to accept or reject. Only when the auction is advertised as "without reserve" is the seller required to accept the offer of the highest bidder.

Sealed Bids

Without Reserve
Once an auctioneer calls for a bid the article must be sold unless there is no bid within a reasonable time.

People who advertise for bids on construction projects are also generally held to be making an invitation only, and those who submit bids are treated as offerors. The following case illustrates this rule.

Facts

Korea Tungsten Mining (KTM) owned real estate in Manhattan. KTM placed newspaper ads that it would accept sealed written bids on the property and that the property would be sold to the highest bidder. Nova-Park had the highest bid of $750,000. S.S.I. Investors (SSI) had made a bid of "Five Hundred and Fifty-Six Thousand dollars ($556,000) and/or one dollar ($1.00) more than the highest bidding price you have received." KTM sold the land to Nova-Park, and SSI sued for specific performance, claiming a contract with KTM to buy the property.

Decision

For KTM. The solicitation for bids merely creates a request for an offer. Once offers are submitted, the seller has the right to accept or reject any of them. SSI's alternative bid of a dollar more than the highest bid was not an offer, because it was not "definite and certain." Allowing the use of such alternative bids "would all but eliminate sealed competitive bidding."

S.S.I. Investors Limited v. *Korea Tungsten Mining Co., Ltd.,* 80 A.D.2d 155, 438 N.Y.S.2d 96 (1981).

Sales of Personal Property

Under the Uniform Commercial Code (UCC), fundamental changes have been made in contracts involving the sale of personal property. A word of caution: These changes affect only personal property sales and not other contracts, such as contracts for personal services and real estate contracts.

The most fundamental changes relaxing the requirements of certainty in a contract for the sale of goods under the UCC can be found in the following sections set out in full in Appendix A:

1. Section 2–204, *Formation in General,* provides that a contract for sale of goods may be made in any manner sufficient to show agreement, including conduct by the parties. In other words, if the parties act as if a contract exists, there may be one. This section also provides that even though one or more of the terms of the contract are left open, the contract is still enforceable if the parties intended a contract and if the court can give an appropriate remedy.

2. Section 2–305, *Open Price Term,* supplies a price if nothing is said as to price. This usually means the market price at the time and place of delivery.

    Open Price
    When no price is stated in a contract for the sale of goods, the market price will be used.

3. Section 2–306, *Output, Requirements and Exclusive Dealings,* supplies a quantity where the parties have not stated a definite quantity, but instead the buyer agrees to buy the seller's entire output or agrees to buy all that the buyer may require. "Requirements" means actual good faith requirements. For example, the buyer cannot demand a disproportionate quantity in relation to his normal prior requirements or to his stated estimate. See Sections 1–203, 2–103(1)(b).

    Requirements
    A good faith contract to purchase all goods that a buyer may require is enforceable under the UCC.

4. Section 2–308, *Absence of Specified Place for Delivery,* supplies the place of delivery if omitted in the contract.

5. Section 2–309, *Absence of Specific Time,* supplies a time if one is omitted in the contract. For example, buyer agrees to purchase 500 crates of oranges from seller for $3,000 cash. Nothing is said regarding time for payment or delivery. In such a situation, the court would imply an agreement to perform within a commercially reasonable period of time.

6. Section 2–310, *Open Time for Payment or Running of Credit: Authority to Ship Under Reservation,* supplies payment terms and delivery terms if omitted in the contract.

7. Section 2–208, *Course of Performance or Practical Construction,* provides that repeated conduct by the parties shall be relevant to determine the meaning of the agreement.

8. Section 1–205, *Course of Dealing and Usage of Trade,* provides that a course of dealing between the parties and any usage of trade in the vocation or trade in which they are engaged shall be used to supplement or qualify the terms of the contract.

Duration of Offer

A communicated offer continues until it lapses or expires, becomes illegal or impossible by operation of law, is revoked by the offeror, is revoked by a counteroffer, is rejected by the offeree, or is accepted by the offeree. The offer is revoked if the offeree fails to accept the offer within the prescribed period of time stated in the offer. If the offer prescribes no particular time for its acceptance, it is revoked by the lapse of a reasonable time. What is a reasonable time is a question of fact depending upon the nature of the particular offer, the usages of business, and the circumstances of the case. An offer to purchase real estate would not require as prompt an acceptance as an offer to purchase personal property of a perishable nature or a fluctuating value. The Restatement of the Law of Contracts, Section 40, cites the following regarding reasonable time:

1. Whether three days is too long to accept an offer to sell land is a question of fact under the circumstances.
2. Where the buyer receives the offer at the close of business hours for the sale of ordinary goods, an acceptance by letter promptly the next morning creates a contract.
3. A telegraphic offer to sell oil, which at the time is subject to rapid fluctuation in price, received near the close of business hours is not accepted in time by a telegraphic reply sent the next day.

The following case is an example of an offer terminated by lapse of a specified time.

Facts
Plaintiff sent a letter to defendant in which he offered to sell certain lots to him for $300. The letter stated, "Let me know by return mail [the next mail pickup]." The letter was received by the defendant on September 6. On September 9, the defendant wrote a letter accepting the offer.

Decision
The offer was not accepted according to its terms. When an individual makes an offer by post stipulating that the answer must be by return mail, the offer terminates if the answer is not by return mail.

Ackerman v. Maddux, 26 N.D. 50, 143 N.W. 147 (1913).

Illegality

If the subject matter of a contract becomes illegal (e.g., the legislature passes a law making the subject illegal), the offer is revoked. Destruction of the subject matter before acceptance revokes the offer.

Death and Insanity

Death or insanity of the offeror before acceptance revokes the offer, since at the time of acceptance, there is no offeror capable of contracting. Death of the offeree also revokes the offer, since only the person to whom the offer was made can accept it.

Revocation by Offeror

The general rule is that an offer may be revoked at any time before the communication of acceptance even though the offer is stated to be good or irrevocable for a specified period. For example, seller tells his friend Richard that he will sell a rifle to him for $150 and will give him ten days to accept the offer. Three days later, seller informs Richard that he has sold the rifle to another person. Richard cannot accept the offer, as it was revoked by the seller when he sold the rifle and informed Richard of that fact.

Revocation
The cancellation of an offer by the offeror.

Exceptions Some exceptions to revocation are as follows:

1. An option where consideration is given for an agreement to keep the offer open for a stated period of time or until a certain date.
2. A unilateral contract after substantial part performance by the offeree. Normally in a unilateral contract, no acceptance is made until the offeree performs the act requested (e.g., catching the criminal in a reward type of case). However, to prevent the injustice that would occur if the offeror revoked the offer after substantial performance on the part of the offeree, most courts will protect the offeree in some way, such as making the offer irrevocable or permitting the offeree to recover in quasi-contract for the reasonable value of his or her performance up to the time of revocation. To alleviate this problem in the sale of goods, the UCC provides the following in Section 2–206(2): "Where the beginning of a requested performance is a reasonable mode of acceptance, an offeror who is not notified of acceptance within a reasonable time may treat the offer as having lapsed before acceptance."
3. Firm offers made under UCC § 2–205. A merchant's written and signed offer to buy or sell goods giving assurance by its terms that it will be held open is not revocable for the time stated and, if no time is stated, for a reasonable time (in either case, not over three months) even though there is no consideration. For definition of "merchant," see UCC Section 2–104.

Option
A contract wherein the seller agrees that the buyer has the right to buy property at a fixed price within a stated period of time.

The general rule is that a revocation must be communicated to the offeree before it is effective (i.e., received by the offeree). The minority rule, followed in California (Civil Code, Section 1587[1]), states that revocation is effective upon posting. Thus, if the offeror mails the revocation before the offeree mails the acceptance, there is no contract. In the United States, posting can be effective as early as handing the revocation to the mail carrier, since in this country the mail carrier is under a duty to accept the mail. The California rule is not favored, since the offeree does not know of the revocation until he or she receives it; and in the meantime, the offeree might have committed himself or herself to other contracts relying on a contract that never became effective. Thus, such a rule slows the economy, since the offeree cannot make other contracts until he or she is certain that the offeror has not mailed a revocation of his or her offer.

An offer made to the public may generally be revoked in the same manner in which it was made (e.g., an offer made by television may be withdrawn in the same manner).

Counteroffer

A *counteroffer* is a counterproposal by the offeree upon terms different from those contained in the offer. For example, seller offers to sell his television set for $250 to buyer. Buyer tells seller that he will give him $200

Counteroffer
Counterproposal by the offeree with different terms than were in the original offer.

for the set. This is a counteroffer, which terminates the offer. However, if seller responds to buyer's counteroffer by saying "I can't take less than $250," this impliedly renews the offer.

If the offeree's reply does not show an unwillingness to accept the original offer, no rejection or counteroffer exists. For example, in answer to the seller's offer, buyer says, "I will consider your offer. In the meantime will you consider selling the set to me for $200?" This is considered to be a mere inquiry.

Rejection

Rejection
An act or statement by the offeree conveying that the offer is not accepted.

A rejection of an offer is an act by the offeree that shows his or her unwillingness to accept the offer. It may consist of express language, or it may be implied from the language or conduct of the offeree. A rejection terminates the offeree's right to accept the offer. A rejection is not effective until it is *received* by the offeror. The right of rejection in a sales contract case must be exercised seasonably. "An act is taken 'seasonably' when it is taken at or within the time agreed or if no time is agreed at or within a reasonable time" (UCC §1–204[3]). A racehorse was purchased at a 3:00 p.m. auction one day and rejected before 1:00 p.m. the following day. The court held that the rejection came too late. *Miron* v. *Yonker's Raceway,* 400 F.2d 112 (2d Cir. 1968), 5 UCC Rep. 673 (1968)

Acceptance

An offer must be accepted before a contract exists. Acceptance is an expressed or communicated overt act by the offeree indicating that he or she assents to the terms of the offer. It may, if the offer permits, take the form of performing the act called for in the offer (unilateral contract), a promise communicated to the offeror (bilateral contract), or the formal act of both parties signing a written document. Mere words, such as "okay," can constitute an acceptance. Where the offeror signs and delivers a contract to the offeree and the latter accepts it, the offeree will be bound even though he or she does not sign it (e.g., landlord hands lease to tenant, who accepts it without objection).

The right to accept an offer cannot be assigned and therefore can be accepted only by the person to whom it was made.

It is important to remember that once an offer is accepted, a contract exists unless there is a valid defense. In the case of a fluctuating market, the offeree is in the better bargaining position, because he or she can reject or accept the offer. It is usually better procedure, therefore, to send out a quotation of prices (making it clear that it is not an offer) rather than an offer.

The following classic case concerning rewards in common law has had quite an impact on advertising.

Facts

The defendants (dealers in a device for the cure of influenza known as "The Carbolic Smoke Ball"), to induce the sale of their product, offered to pay $500 to any person who contracted influenza after having used the smoke ball in a specified manner. The plaintiff, on the faith of the advertisement containing the offer, bought one of the smoke balls and used it according to instructions but still contracted influenza. The defendants refused to pay her on the grounds that no contract existed, because the offer was not made to anybody in particular and because she did not notify them of her acceptance.

Decision
An offer of a reward is made to anybody who performs the conditions named in the advertisement, and anybody who does perform accepts the offer. No notice to the offeror is expected in the reward type of case. In a unilateral contract, it is ordinarily not necessary for the offeree to notify the offeror of his or her acceptance. Judgment for plaintiff Carlill.

Carlill v. *Carbolic Smoke Ball Co.*, Law Reports, 1 Q.B.Div. 256.

With a bilateral contract, identical offers to buy and sell goods that cross in the mail can create a contract even though the parties are each ignorant of the other's offer. Suppose the owner of an automobile sends a letter to Alice offering to sell the vehicle for $500. In the meantime, Alice had sent an offer to buy the automobile for $500. Will these crossover offers result in a contract? Under the objective theory and UCC § 2–204, a contract exists. The UCC does not demand that a person be able to pinpoint the exact moment of the contract's creation. Under the Code, the court is more interested in whether the parties intended to make a contract and whether the court can fashion a remedy.

In contracts where the UCC is not involved, the acceptance must be positive and unequivocal. It may not change any of the terms of the offer or qualify it in any way. A qualified acceptance is a new proposal and constitutes a rejection of the original offer, after which the original offer cannot be accepted by the offeree.

Additional Terms Under UCC § 2–207(1)(2), the offeree may state additional terms from those contained in the offer. The acceptance may still be valid, assuming it complies with the other requirements of a valid acceptance, as these terms are merely considered as *proposals* for additions to the contract and do not amount to a counteroffer. In other words, the offeree accepts the offer but wants the offeror to consider some additional terms (e.g., the wire of acceptance adds "Ship by Thursday" or "Rush"). A frequent example is the exchange of printed purchase order and acceptance forms. Often the seller's form contains different terms from the buyer's form. Nevertheless, the parties proceed with the transaction.

Merchants If the offeror and offeree are both merchants, the additional terms become part of the contract unless:

1. The offer expressly limits acceptance to its terms.
2. The terms materially alter the offer.
3. The offeror objects to the terms within a reasonable time.

Merchant
Under the UCC a merchant is a person who deals in the goods under contract or who by his occupation holds himself out as having knowledge or skill peculiar to such goods.

Material Alteration An example of a clause that materially alters the contract and is thus not included unless expressly agreed to by the other party is a clause negating such standard warranties as that of merchantability or fitness for a particular purpose under circumstances in which either warranty normally is attached. Arbitration clauses have been held to be material alterations of the offer. An example of a clause not material is a clause fixing a reasonable time for complaints within customary limits. An astute offeror will insert a clause in the offer incorporating (1), thus obviating the problem of (2) and (3).

In many cases, goods are shipped, accepted, and paid for before any dispute arises. In such cases, if the writings of the parties do not establish a contract, UCC § 2–207(3) establishes the contract by conduct and governs the question as to what terms are included.

Silence As Acceptance In a bilateral contract, ordinarily silence cannot constitute acceptance of an offer. This is true even though the offer states that silence will be taken as consent, for the offeror cannot force the offeree to make an express rejection. The rule has several exceptions:

1. Previous dealings between the parties place the offeree under a duty to act or be bound (e.g., failure to object to a billing statement from a creditor). Similarly, if a seller has offered lamps to a buyer on three prior occasions under identical terms, with the buyer's remaining silent and paying for the goods, the buyer must affirmatively reject any present offer.

2. Use of services or goods by the offeree when he or she had freedom to reject them amounts to an acceptance. Note that the Federal Postal Reorganization Act, Section 3009, 1970, provides that a person who receives unsolicited goods in the mail, except from a charity, has the right to retain, use, discard, or dispose of them in any manner he or she sees fit without any obligation to the sender. Some states have passed similar laws (e.g., Arizona, California, Illinois, Louisiana, Oklahoma).

3. Complete performance or tender thereof by the offeree is equivalent to a promise of acceptance resulting in a contract.

4. The terms of the offer may expressly *waive* any communication of acceptance. For example, a mail order company sends an offer that states, "Your order is only an offer and must be accepted by our home office before there is a binding contract." The order becomes a contract without notice to the customer when the home office accepts the order.

5. Under the Contracts Restatement Rule, Section 72(1)(b), if the offeror prescribes silence as the means of assent and the offeree remains silent intending to accept, a contract results; however, little authority exists approving this position.

Notification
Communication of information about a fact by an authorized person to another party.

Notification In a unilateral contract, it is ordinarily not necessary for the offeree to notify the offeror of his or her acceptance, as the offer normally requests an act rather than a promise. Even if the offeree does give one, a notification has no legal effect.

Shipment Under UCC § 2–206(1)(b), an order or offer to buy goods for prompt shipment may be accepted by a promise to ship the goods or by the prompt shipment of conforming or nonconforming goods. For example, buyer sends a telegram to seller that states, "Send me one dozen business law books. Ship on or before August 5." The order is received on August 2.

On the same day seller receives the telegram, he begins packing the order and sends the following telegram to buyer: "Your order received and promise shipment within 48 hours." On August 3, seller receives the following telegram from buyer: "Cancel business law book order." Under the UCC, seller's prompt promise to ship the goods constitutes an acceptance, which cuts off the buyer's power to revoke the offer.

A seller who ships nonconforming goods (goods that deviate from the order in quality or quantity) should notify the buyer that the shipment is an *accommodation* shipment. If the seller does not do so, he or she may be in breach of the contract that was accepted by the act of shipping.

Effective Time of Acceptance If the offer involves a bilateral contract, acceptance is effective when it is placed in the course of transmission. If the mails are used, acceptance is effected when the offeree mails the acceptance in an envelope properly addressed and stamped.

As stated, "mailing" takes place when the acceptance is placed in a U.S. mailbox or handed to the mail carrier. However, is placing the acceptance in an office out box for mailing sufficient mailing? In *Cushing* v. *Thomson* (118 N.H. 292, 386 A.2d 805 [1978]), the court held that placing the acceptance in the outbox was sufficient. The court said, "Moreover, plaintiff's counsel represented to the court that it was customary office practice for outgoing letters to be picked up from the outbox daily and put in the U.S. mail. . . . Thus the representation that it was customary office procedure for the letters to be sent out the same day that they are placed in the office outbox . . . supported the implied finding that the completed contract was mailed before the attempted revocation."

If a telegram is used, acceptance is effected when the telegram is handed to the telegraph operator. In most states, it is immaterial that the letter or telegram is delayed or not received by the offeror. Once the acceptance has been completed by posting or transmitting the telegram, it cannot be countermanded or withdrawn. If the acceptance is made too late or in an unauthorized manner, the offeror cannot waive the defect and treat the acceptance as valid. Instead, it is merely treated as a counteroffer, which would have to be accepted by the original offeror.

The *manner* in which the acceptance is to be communicated can be specified in the offer. If an unauthorized mode of acceptance is used, some courts treat the attempted acceptance as a counteroffer, while others treat it as an acceptance but delay the time of effectiveness until the offeror receives it. The risk that the acceptance will not be received in time rests with the acceptor. If the offer does not prescribe a specified manner, any reasonable manner may be used (UCC § 2–206[1]). Hence, it would be proper to answer a letter with a telegram.

An offer must be accepted within a reasonable time unless otherwise specified in the offer. An offer by telegram should be accepted by telegram rather than by letter and ordinarily sent the same day as the offer is received. If an offer by mail calls for a reply "by return mail," a letter of acceptance must be sent either by the next mail or during the day that the offer is received. If an offer states that it is "open for 10 days," the ten-day period begins on the date that appears on the offer. Thus, if the offer is delayed for ten days, it never becomes effective. However, if the offer states that the offeree has ten days in which to accept, the ten-day period does not

Accommodation Shipment
The shipment of nonconforming goods to a buyer with notice that it is for accommodation of the buyer.

Mail Box Rule
Rule that acceptance of an offer is binding at the time it is mailed.

By Return Mail
Acceptance must be by the next outgoing mail or at least during the same day in which the offer was received.

begin until the offer is received. In the latter case, if the offer is delayed and the offeree knew or had reason to know of the delay, the offeree will have ten days minus the delay to accept the offer. If an offer by mail does not specify "by return mail" or any other time, the offeree has a reasonable period of time to respond as determined by the type of offer, the type and usages of business, and all other surrounding circumstances.

The time of acceptance may be proved by the oral testimony of the offeree or his or her secretary that the acceptance was mailed at a particular time and place. A letter correctly addressed and properly mailed is presumed to have been received in the ordinary course of mail. A copy of the acceptance can be introduced in evidence to show the contents of the acceptance.

Acceptance after Rejection   A rejection is effective when it is received. An acceptance is effective when it is sent. If the offeree sends a rejection, then later changes his mind and sends an acceptance, is the acceptance valid?

The validity of the acceptance depends upon whether the acceptance or the rejection arrived first. The acceptor lost the right to have the acceptance effective when it was sent because he previously sent a rejection. Under such circumstances, an overtaking acceptance is effective upon receipt subject to the condition that the acceptance must be made timely. That is, if the offeree waits too long to send the acceptance or the acceptance takes an unreasonable time to arrive, the acceptance would be ineffective.

Questions

1. Explain the difference between objective and subjective tests in determining whether or not a contract exists.
2. Contract offers usually state the subject matter, quantity, price, and time and place of performance. Are all of these elements necessary before an offer can be accepted to make a binding contract? Which ones, if any, may be omitted? Why?
3. What is the difference between a bilateral offer and a unilateral one? Give an example of each.
4. How long does an offer last? How may it be ended?
5. What are some examples of acceptance of an offer by silence of the offeree?

5.3 Consideration

Consideration
Something of value given in return for a performance or a promise of performance by another.

Quid Pro Quo
Something for something.

Legal consideration, in addition to an intent evidenced by an offer and its acceptance, is ordinarily required to make an enforceable contract. At common law the courts decided not to enforce promises to make gifts and insisted upon a quid pro quo (something for something) as a barter or exchange in a contract.

Benefit or Detriment

Detriment
A disadvantage.

Consideration in contracts is something of value that is a benefit to one party or a loss to the other. It is the inducement to contract. It is the reason, cause, motive, or price that persuades the parties to make the agreement.

MAKING CONTRACTS

Consideration may be a benefit conferred or agreed to be conferred upon the promisor or some other person or a detriment suffered or to be suffered by the promisee or some other person. Consideration may be the giving up of a legal right, such as the right to file a lawsuit or the right to go through bankruptcy.

Facts

Fiege, a mother, sued Boehm, the alleged father, to recover on an oral contract under which Boehm agreed to pay birth expenses and support the child if the mother would not file a paternity suit against him. Boehm did not carry out his part of the agreement, and Fiege then brought a bastardy action against him. At that time, medical proof by blood test proved that Boehm was not the father. Fiege contends that giving up her right to file the suit was a detriment to her and consideration for the contract. Boehm argues that since he is not the father there was no detriment to the plaintiff and no consideration for the contract.

Decision

There was a contract. The mother's forbearance to file suit on a lawful claim in return for a promise to pay was sufficient consideration. The court held that the party giving up such right must have an honest intention to undertake legislation that is not frivolous, vexatious, or unlawful and that she believes to be well founded. It found that in this case the mother honestly believed Boehm to be the father of the child and did forego filing suit in return for the promise to make payments. This was valid, good, and sufficient consideration.

Fiege v. Boehm, 210 Md. 352, 123 A.2d 316 (1956).

Consideration must be bargained for (e.g., if you do something for me, I will do something for you). (I will wash your car if you promise to pay me $10. Washing the car is the consideration for the promise to pay $10. Promising to pay $10 is the consideration for washing the car.)

Gift

Since a promise to make a gift has no consideration, it is not enforceable. For example, if Jones promises to give Smith $100 next Tuesday, the courts would not enforce such a promise, because no consideration is given by Smith in return. However, once a gift has been made and the property delivered, it cannot be set aside for lack of consideration. So, if Jones actually gives the $100 to Smith and then asks for its return, Smith has a legal right to keep the money.

The general rule is that a contract must be supported by consideration to be valid and legally enforceable. This rule has received much criticism, however, and modern law tends to relax the requirement and to expand the exceptions.

Unilateral Consideration

In a unilateral contract, the promise by the offeror is the consideration for the act or forbearance by the offeree. For example, a sheriff promises a reward for the capture of a criminal. The consideration moving from the sheriff is the promise to pay the reward, and the consideration moving from the offeree is the act of capturing the criminal.

Hamer v. Sidway
124 N.Y. 538, 27 N.E. 256 (1891).

Action to recover the sum of $5,000 promised by an uncle to his nephew. The promisor had agreed with his nephew that if the latter would refrain from drinking liquor and using tobacco until he reached the age of twenty-one, the uncle would then pay his nephew $5,000. . . . [Hamer is the assignee of the nephew's claim, and Sidway is the executor of the uncle's estate.]

Parker, J. The trial court found as a fact that "on the 20th day of March, 1869, . . . William E. Story agreed to and with William E. Story, 2d, that if he would refrain from drinking liquor, using tobacco, swearing, and playing cards or billiards for money until he should become 21 years of age, then he, the said William E. Story, would at that time pay him, the said William E. Story, 2d, the sum of $5,000 for such refraining, to which the said William E. Story, 2d, agreed," and that he "in all things fully performed his part of said agreement."

The defendant contends that the contract was without consideration to support it and, therefore, invalid. He asserts that the promisee by refraining from the use of liquor and tobacco was not harmed but benefited; that that which he did was best for him to do independently of his uncle's promise, and insists that it follows that unless the promisor was benefited, the contract was without consideration. A contention which, if well founded, would seem to leave open for controversy in many cases whether that which the promisee did or omitted to do was, in fact, of such benefit to him as to leave no consideration to support the enforcement of the promisor's agreement. Such a rule could not be tolerated, and is without foundation in the law. . . . Courts "will not ask whether the thing which forms the consideration does in fact benefit the promisee or a third party, or is of any substantial value to anyone. It is enough that something is promised, done, forborne, or suffered by the party to whom the promise is made as consideration for the promise made to him." . . .

"In general a waiver of any legal right at the request of another party is a sufficient consideration for a promise."

. . . "Consideration means not so much that one party is profiting as that the other abandons some legal right in the present or limits his legal freedom of action in the future as an inducement for the promise of the first."

"Now, applying this rule to the facts before us, the promisee used tobacco, occasionally drank liquor, and he had a legal right to do so. That right he abandoned for a period of years upon the strength of the promise of the testator that for such forbearance he would give him $5,000. We need not speculate on the effort which may have been required to give up the use of those stimulants. It is sufficient that he restricted his lawful freedom of action within certain prescribed limits upon the faith of his uncle's agreement, and now having fully performed the conditions imposed, it is of no moment whether such performance actually proved a benefit to the promisor, and the court will not inquire into it." . . .

[Judgment for plaintiff.]

Bilateral Consideration

Bilateral Consideration
A promise as consideration for a promise.

In a bilateral contract, however, the promise of one party is the consideration for the promise of the other. Where mutual promises have been made, one of them furnishes a sufficient consideration to support an action on the other. If Jones promises to sell his car to Smith and Smith promises to pay

$500 to Jones for the car, the agreement is binding, since the promise of each to the other is the consideration. Students sometimes have difficulty with this concept but should keep in mind that *merely making the promise* is enough for consideration in bilateral (promise for a promise) contract cases.

Illusory Offer

A proposal by a buyer to purchase from a seller at a specified price all the goods of a certain kind that the buyer may *want* or *desire* during a certain period of time is an illusory (appears to be but is not) offer, which does not, upon acceptance, result in an enforceable contract. The provision in the promise itself of "want" or "desire" leaves the matter optional or entirely discretional on the part of the promisor and cannot create a valid contract. The buyer has only to say that he does not want the goods and then would not be required to buy any of them.

Illusory Offer
A promise so indefinite that it cannot be enforced.

"Needs" Contract

An offer to supply *all* goods of a certain kind that the other party *needs* in a certain business for a definite time period can be determined, and acceptance could result in a binding contract.

Needs Contract
The same as a requirements contract and enforceable if made in good faith.

Inadequacy of Consideration

As a general rule, as long as the consideration is of some value, however slight, it will be sufficient to sustain a contract in the absence of fraud or unconscionable conduct. The inadequacy is for the parties to consider at the time of making the agreement and not for the court when the agreement is sought to be enforced. For example, a promise of a nephew to name his first son after his uncle is consideration for the uncle's promise to pay the nephew $5,000.

Where the price is so inadequate as to shock the conscience of the court, inadequacy alone may furnish sufficient grounds for granting relief. For example, the seller makes a contract with the buyer to sell a parcel of real estate for $5,000. However, unknown to the seller, the land is really worth $20,000 at the time the contract is made. Before the seller delivers a deed to the buyer, he learns of the true value of the land and refuses to deliver the deed. The buyer sues the seller for specific performance (i.e., the buyer asks the court to order the seller to hand over the deed [specific performance is discussed in Chapter 10]). The seller defends on the ground that the consideration offered by the buyer is grossly inadequate. The court will examine the consideration and, finding it grossly inadequate, will not order specific performance.

Moreover, the existence of gross inadequacy of consideration may indicate fraud, misrepresentation, duress, undue influence, mistake, unconscionability, or overreaching by a dominant party in a fiduciary relationship,

Inadequate Consideration
The actual value of consideration is usually immaterial as the parties make that decision.

in which case the court will grant relief. (These items are discussed in Chapter 7.)

In some states (e.g., California Civil Code Section 3391), the courts may refuse to order specific performance on the basis of inadequacy of consideration without a showing that the inadequacy was gross. Adequacy is a question for the jury or other trier of the facts. The consideration does not necessarily have to measure up to the value of the property (e.g., eagerness to sell may explain the discrepancy).

Duty to Perform

Duty Performance
The performance of duty, doing what one is legally bound to do, is not contract consideration.

Doing or promising to do what one is already legally bound to do cannot be consideration. For example, a police officer while on duty cannot recover a reward offered for the capture of a criminal, since it is the officer's duty to capture criminals. Likewise, when an employee refuses to complete a contract unless the employer promises to pay a bonus in addition to the sum specified in the original contract and the employer promises to pay that bonus, most courts hold that the second promise of the employer is unenforceable because it lacks consideration. However, if the parties mutually rescind the first contract and enter into a new contract that includes the bonus, the second contract is enforceable. Also, if the terms of the original contract are modified so as to vary even slightly the employee's performance, the promise to make the additional payment would be enforceable.

Past Consideration

Past Consideration
Acts already completed cannot be consideration for a new promise.

Acts or forbearances previously performed are known as past consideration and are not sufficient to sustain a promise. Since such acts have already been completed, they cannot be consideration for a new promise. For example, Smith has worked for Jones for the past year at a fixed salary each week. Jones tells Smith that he is so pleased with his work that tomorrow he is going to give him a $100 bonus for his outstanding performance. Jones's promise is not enforceable, because there is no consideration from Smith. It's only a promise to make a gift. Smith's past performance has been paid for and does not support the new promise by Jones. To sustain Jones's new promise to pay the $100, Smith must have made a promise to do something extra for Jones, such as turning the lights off each day when he leaves.

Moral Obligation

Moral Obligation
A voluntary meritorious or moral act is usually treated as a gift and is not consideration.

Generally, a moral obligation is not consideration. For example, a nurse without expectation of payment cared for D, an indigent who lived in Illinois, for one month before his death. T, a friend from California, learned of the nurses's care at the funeral and the next day called the nurse and told her that he was going to give her $5,000 for her services. This promise is unenforceable, since it is based on a moral obligation. It also is merely a promise to make a gift. There are some instances, however, where a moral obligation is sufficient to sustain a promise:

1. Where a promise to pay a debt is based on a preexisting legal duty, it may be regarded as based on a moral obligation and hence enforceable (e.g., debtor owes creditor $1,000 for which there is no remedy since it is barred by the statute of limitations). Debtor, however, writes a note to the creditor stating that he will pay the debt. This promise is binding, though without new consideration (most states require that the new promise be in writing). A debt can also be revived by a mere acknowledgment in writing in most states. For example, the debtor sends a note to the creditor stating that she knows the debt is barred by the statute of limitations. However, she acknowledges that she still owes it. Also, a debt can be revived or extended by part payment in most states.

2. A few states have statutes (e.g., California Civil Code Section 1606) allowing a moral obligation originating in some benefit conferred upon the promisor or prejudice suffered by the promissee as good consideration for a promise to pay the obligation. For example, Harris, while walking along the beach, sees Segal out in deep water and in trouble. Harris, thinking he might make some money for saving Segal, swims out to Segal and brings him to shore, thereby saving him from drowning. Segal is so happy that he promises to pay Harris $5,000 the next day. The benefit conferred upon Segal by Harris is good consideration for Segal's promise to pay Harris the $5,000.

Liquidated Debt

A liquidated debt is one that is for a sum certain (e.g., a patient owes a doctor $100). There is no dispute as to the amount due. In the case of a liquidated debt, payment of a lesser sum will not discharge the balance, since there is no consideration for the release of the balance. This is true even though the creditor orally accepts the lesser sum in full payment. For example, the patient tells the doctor that he has only $75 and asks the doctor if she will accept that amount as payment in full. The doctor states that she will. Since there is no consideration for the release of the $25, the doctor's promise is not enforceable; thus, the patient still owes $25.

Some states have statutes (e.g., California Civil Code Sections 1524 and 1541) that provide that if the creditor gives the debtor a written release signed by the creditor, consideration is not necessary to discharge the balance due. In the previous example, if the doctor had given the patient a signed release of the balance due, the balance in the amount of $25 would have been discharged by such law.

Liquidated Debt
When both parties agree as to the amount owed the debt is liquidated.

Unliquidated Debt

An unliquidated debt is one in which the amount is in *good faith dispute*. In such a case, acceptance by the creditor of the lesser sum discharges the

Unliquidated Debt
When the amount owed is in dispute the debt is unliquidated.

balance. For example, the patient believes she owes the doctor $75, but the doctor believes that the patient owes him $100. This is an unliquidated debt. The patient hands the doctor $75 in cash and states that this is payment in full. The doctor takes the $75. By taking the lesser sum, the doctor discharges the balance.

"Paid in Full" as Accord and Satisfaction

Accord and Satisfaction
Payment of money or value usually less than the amount owed in exchange for cancellation of the debt.

When a debtor sends a check to his or her creditor marked "Paid in Full" and the creditor cashes the check, does that preclude the creditor from getting a judgment against the debtor for the balance that the creditor believes is still due? Has there been an "accord and satisfaction"? An *accord* is an agreement for a substituted performance in satisfaction of the original obligation. When the accord is carried out, there is an *accord* and *satisfaction,* and the original obligation is discharged. The usual purpose is to settle a claim with a different performance, such as payment of a smaller amount of money than is due.

The following two cases demonstrate the conflict in the interpretation of Section 1–207 of the UCC.

1. UCC § 1–207 is the basis for holdings in New York and in South Dakota (*Scholl* v. *Tallman* 247 N.W.2d 490 [1976]) that the creditor can maintain an action for the balance due. Note, however, in the following case that New York, unlike many states, has a special annotation to the statute upon which the court also relies to hold that accord and satisfaction has not been made and therefore the creditor can maintain an action for what he or she believes is a balance due.

Facts
Plaintiff and defendant had a dispute as to the amount due on a contract. Defendant sent a check to plaintiff on the back of which was typed: "Endorsement of this check by payee shall constitute a full accord and satisfaction of payee's invoice no. 2767 to maker hereof."

Plaintiff sent a letter to defendant stating he was not accepting the check as payment in full, that he was accepting the check as partial payment, and that he was accepting the check under protest and specifically reserving his right to collect the balance due.

Decision
The transaction between the plaintiff and the defendant is covered by UCC § 1–207. Under the New York Annotations it is stated: "This section permits a party involved in a Code-covered transaction to accept whatever he can get by way of payment, performance, etc., without losing his rights to demand the remainder of the goods, to set-off a failure to qualify, or to sue for the balance of the payment, so long as he explicitly reserves his rights." The plaintiff's reservation is more than adequate to satisfy the intent of § 1–207 of the UCC.

Kroulee Corp. v. *A. Klein & Co., Inc.,* 103 Misc.2d 441, 426 N.Y.S.2d 206 (1980). Recent cases in New York have affirmed the *Kroulee* decision.

2. The following New Jersey case holds that § 1–207 does not change the common law; therefore, there is an accord and satisfaction, and the creditor cannot maintain an action for what he or she believes is a balance due.

Facts

Plaintiff and defendant had a dispute as to the amount due on a contract. The defendant sent a check to the plaintiff with a notation on the front "Paid in Full."

Decision

Once a check is deposited by the creditor, no matter what alterations are made on the reverse side, an accord and satisfaction is reached. When a check is tendered as payment in full payment, the creditor is deemed to have accepted this condition by depositing the check for collection notwithstanding any obligation or alteration.

The New York cases are distinguishable in that the New York Annotations to the Code clearly deals with the effect of § 1–207 on the "full payment check" and concludes that the rule of accord and satisfaction has been changed. New Jersey did not adopt such an annotation. If the New York rule were followed, a convenient and informal device for the resolution of disagreements in the business community would be seriously impeded.

Chancellor, Inc. v. Hamilton Appliance Co., Inc., 175 N.J.Super 345, 418 A.2d 1326.

Courts in the following states have agreed with New Jersey: California (*Connecticut Printers, Inc. v. Gus Kroesen, Inc.*, 134 Cal.App.3d 54, 184 C.R. 436 [1982]); Illinois (*Quaintance Associates, Inc. v. PLM, Inc.*, 95 Ill.App.3d 818, 51 Ill. Dec. 153, 420 N.E.2d 567 [1981]); Florida (*Eder v. Yvette B. Gervey Interiors, Inc.*, 407 So.2d 312 [Fla.App. 1981]); North Carolina (*Brown v. Coastal Truckways, Inc.*, 44 N.C.App. 454, 261 S.E.2d 266 [1980]); and Wisconsin (*Flambeau Products Corp. v. Honeywell*, 116 Wis.2d 95, 341 N.W.2d 655 [1984]).

Relatively few states have made a direct holding one way or the other on § 1–207. A payee of a paid-in-full check who is in a state where the section is untested has the following alternatives: (1) reject the check or instrument and demand payment in full for the amount he claims is due or (2) accept the check or instrument placing a statement on the back that he accepts the check without prejudice and under protest pursuant to § 1–207, that he reserves the right to demand the balance of the amount due, and that the negotiation of the check does not effect an accord and satisfaction. The payee will then run the risk that the court will hold that there has been an accord and satisfaction.

Partial Payment

If a creditor accepts a lesser sum than is due, prior to due date, offered in full satisfaction of the debt, the balance is discharged, because the debtor incurs a legal detriment by paying before the debt is due. Similarly, if the debt is not secured and the creditor accepts a lesser amount if the debtor secures the debt with a mortgage, the balance is discharged (i.e., the giving of such security is something the debtor was not legally bound to do and therefore is sufficient consideration for the creditor's promise to accept the lesser sum).

Promissory Estoppel

Most courts hold that promissory estoppel arises when there is a clear and unambiguous promise that the promisor should reasonably expect to induce

Promissory Estoppel
When a person acts to his detriment in reliance upon a reasonable promise a court may estop the promisor from denying the existence of the contract.

action or forbearance on the part of the promisee and that does induce such action or forbearance and such promise is binding if injustice can be avoided only by enforcement of the promise. The promisor is bound when he should reasonably expect a substantial *change of position* (act or forbearance) in reliance on his promise if injustice can be avoided only by its enforcement. In such a case, the promisor is estopped from pleading a lack of consideration for his promise. In other words, promissory estoppel is a substitute for consideration (i.e., the promise is binding even though the promisor received nothing in exchange for the promise). Promissory estoppel is best defined by examples.

A common example of promissory estoppel occurs when pledges or subscriptions are made to a charity. When the charitable institution, such as a church, makes expenditures or incurs obligations in reliance on the promise of a subscriber, the promisor is estopped or prevented from using lack of consideration as a defense. As soon as the charity changes its position, such as hiring an architect or incurring other expenses in reliance upon the promise, the subscriber can be held to the agreement.

Board of Home Missions, Etc. v. Manley
129 Cal.App. 541, 19 P.2d 21 (1933).

Jamison, Justice pro tem   This action is upon a rejected claim against the estate of Martha D. Sanders, deceased. The claim is for a subscription or pledge by deceased for the benefit of plaintiff. . . . The case was tried by the court, which found . . . in her favor upon the defense of want of consideration. Judgment was thereupon rendered for defendant, and from this judgment plaintiff appeals.

The question to be determined upon this appeal is whether or not the said claim is supported by a sufficient consideration. On October 30, 1929, the said deceased executed and delivered to appellant the following subscription or pledge: "Estate Pledge. To the Board of Home Missions and Church Extension of the Methodist Episcopal Church. In consideration of my interest in Christian Missions and of the securing by the above named Board of other pledges for its work, and for value received, I hereby promise and agree to pay to The Board of Home Missions and Church Extension of the Methodist Episcopal Church, at 1701 Arch Street, Philadelphia, Pa., the sum of Five Thousand Dollars ($5,000.00) which shall become due and payable one day after my death out of my estate." . . .

A subscription is considered as a mere offer until the beneficiary has accepted it, or has acted on the faith thereof so that his conduct implies an acceptance, and until such acceptance the promisor generally has the right to revoke the subscription. The death of the subscriber before the acceptance of the subscription constitutes a revocation of the offer, and the estate of the subscriber will not be liable on the subscription. . . . An acceptance can only be shown by some act on the part of the promisee whereby some legal liability is incurred or money expended on the faith of the promise. . . . However, there is an exception to this rule, and that is that, where there is a mutual promise by several individuals to contribute to the payment of an aggregate sum for the benefit of a charitable, religious, or educational institution in which they are all interested, such mutual promise is generally held to support an adequate consideration authorizing its enforcement by the promisee. . . .

There is no evidence in the case at bar indicating that appellant performed any acts or incurred any obligations or expense in reliance upon the payment of

> the said subscription of deceased prior to her death, or that other individuals concurred with her in contributing to the payment of an aggregate sum for the benefit of appellant.... Therefore, we are of the opinion that the said estate pledge was without consideration and was revoked by the death of the said deceased....
>
> The judgment is affirmed [for defendant].

There is a modern trend to apply the doctrine of promissory estoppel as a substitute for consideration, particularly where an injustice appears, as in the following examples:

1. A debtor induces his creditor to postpone filing a lawsuit by promising not to rely on the time period in the statute of limitations. The debtor would be estopped from using this defense.
2. An insurance adjuster promises to settle a personal injury case with the injured party as soon as the doctor gives a discharge. The insurance company could not then use the statute of limitations if the time ran out before the doctor gave his release.
3. A mortgagor makes improvements on her property, relying on the mortgagee's promise not to foreclose.

Justifiable Reliance

Under the promissory estoppel theory, a promise not otherwise binding as a contract is enforced because of the promisee's justifiable reliance upon it to his detriment. An important test applies the doctrine if injustice can be avoided only by enforcement of the promise.

Executed Contracts

The requirement of consideration applies only to executory contracts. After a contract is fully executed (the obligations of the parties are completed so that nothing remains to be done), it is no longer possible to attack its validity on that particular ground.

UCC Consideration Exceptions

The UCC provides that consideration is not required in the following five situations:

1. A claim or right arising out of a breach of contract for the sale of goods can be discharged in whole or in part without consideration by a written waiver or renunciation signed and delivered by the aggrieved party (§ 1–107).
2. A written offer signed by a merchant to buy or sell goods that by its terms gives assurance that it will be held open is not revocable for lack

of consideration during the time stated that it is open and, if no time is stated, for a reasonable time, but in no event may the period of irrevocability exceed three months (§ 2–205).

3. No consideration is necessary when a check is accepted in full settlement of a disputed debt and probably has the same effect if the debt is not disputed. Official Comment number 2 of § 3–408 states in part "... an instrument given for more or less than the amount of a liquidated obligation does not fail by reason of the common law rule that an obligation for a lesser liquidated amount cannot be consideration for the surrender of the greater" (§ 3–408).

4. The holder of a promissory note or draft or check may discharge any party to the instrument without consideration by (1) intentionally cancelling the instrument, (2) striking out the signature of the party on the instrument, (3) renouncing rights on the instrument in writing signed and delivered, or (4) surrendering the instrument to the party to be discharged (§ 3–605).

5. An agreement modifying a contract for the sale of goods does not need consideration to be binding. However, the modification must meet the test of good faith (§§ 1–203, 2–103[1][b]), and a mere technical consideration cannot support a modification made in bad faith (§ 2–209[1]).

6. No consideration is necessary to establish a letter of credit (§ 5–103) or to enlarge or otherwise modify its terms (§ 5–105).

Promise to Pay Debt of Another

The guarantee to pay the debt of another is a promise made for consideration to be legally responsible for the debts of someone else (e.g., your friend promises to pay your debt if you tutor him in business law).

If the promise is made as part of a transaction in which the debt is originally incurred, no additional consideration is needed (e.g., father signs with his son to purchase a car for the son on the installment plan). The seller's reliance on the guarantee of the father as part of the debt-making transaction is sufficient consideration to hold the father liable on his promise.

QUESTIONS

1. In law, what does consideration mean?
2. What is the difference between unilateral and bilateral consideration? Give an example of each.
3. Your rich uncle promises to give you $10,000 if you stay in school all year and make straight A's in all subjects. You do, but he doesn't hold to his promise. Is this an enforceable contract? Why?
4. What are examples of some contract situations in which consideration is not a requirement?
5. You have a disagreement with a creditor as to the amount you owe her. You mail her a check for what you think is a fair settlement but less than she wants. If you make a notation on the check that acceptance of it amounts to an accord and satisfaction of payment in full, what result if she cashes the check and then sues you for the balance she claims is due?

PROBLEMS

1. Richard was seriously injured in a vehicle accident and was unconscious. A bystander called Dr. Meine while Richard was in this condition. The doctor arrived at the scene and rendered medical treatment. Later, the doctor sent Richard a bill for the reasonable value of his medical services. Richard refuses to pay on the grounds that he never intended to contract for the services. Decision?

2. The Lyle School District sent in a timely manner a copy of an unsigned contract to the plaintiff, who is a certified teacher in the district. The contract stated, "If this contract is not signed by said employee and returned to the secretary of the school district on or before June 14, 1976, the board reserves the right to withdraw this offer." In addition, the superintendent of schools personally called the plaintiff and reminded him of the time limit. The plaintiff informed the superintendent that he was considering other employment. Plaintiff did not sign and return the copy of the contract until June 16, 1976. The superintendent informed the plaintiff that the school district would not rehire him. Plaintiff sues. Decision?

3. Seyler, a resident of Chicago, owned a building lot located in Milwaukee that the seller thought was worth $10,000. The buyer, who lived near the lot, knew that it was worth $50,000. Buyer went to the seller in Chicago and offered him $10,000 for the lot. In the discussion, the buyer did not make any misstatements; he merely remained silent as to the true value of the lot. The parties then prepared a written contract for the sale of the real estate. Later, when the buyer tendered the $10,000 purchase price, the seller refused the money and refused to deliver a deed. Buyer sues seller for specific performance. Decision?

4. John and Mary are brother and sister. Upon the death of their mother, it was discovered that the mother's will left the bulk of the estate to Mary. John threatened to contest the will. Mary told him that if he would tell the truth when he was a witness at the court hearing, she would give him $10,000. John accepted and told the truth in court; the will was upheld. John now demands the $10,000. Decision?

5. Seller sends a signed written offer to buyer in which seller offers to sell 1,000 number 51 J coats to buyer at a certain price. The offer states that it will be kept open for a period of sixty days. Buyer sends an acceptance ten days before the sixty-day period is up. Thinking the buyer was not going to accept, the seller had sold the coats to another retailer. Buyer sues seller for damages. Seller contends he could revoke the offer at any time. Decision?

6. S mailed an offer to sell certain land to B for $15,000. S mailed the letter on June 4, and B received the letter on June 5. On June 5, B mailed a letter to S that contained the following language: "Will you take less?" S replied in the negative. B then mailed a letter on June 7 that stated, "I accept your offer of June 4." Is there a contract? Explain.

7. On January 15, buyer mailed an offer from Los Angeles to seller in New York for the purchase of 500 dresses at a certain price. On January 18, the buyer mailed a revocation of the offer. On January 19, the seller received the offer and mailed an acceptance. Seller immediately purchased sufficient yardage to make the special dresses. On January 22, the seller received the revocation. Is there a contract?

8. Defendant owed plaintiff $10,000, evidenced by an unsecured note. The parties agreed that a new note in the amount of $8,000 secured by a mortgage on the defendant's property would be executed in place of the note for $10,000. Defendant signed the new note and mortgage, but the plaintiff now claims the defendant owes the entire $10,000, as there was no consideration for the release of the $2,000. Decision?

9. In February, defendant signed a pledge to his favorite college in the amount of $50,000. In March, the college signed a contract to have an addition built onto the law school for the amount of the pledge. In April, defendant rescinded the pledge. The college sues for the $50,000. Decision?

10. Red Owl promised plaintiffs that it would build a store building in Chilton, Wisconsin, and stock it with merchandise for plaintiffs to operate. Later, plaintiffs would pay Red Owl the sum of $18,000 for a franchise agreement. In reliance on the promise of Red Owl, plaintiffs sold their bakery building and business in Wautoma, Wisconsin, purchased a building site in Chilton, and rented a residence there. When plaintiffs wanted to enter into the franchise agreement, Red Owl refused. Plaintiffs sue for damages. Red Owl defends on the grounds that there was no consideration for the promise to grant a franchise. Decision?

CHAPTER SIX

Other Basic Requirements

6.1 Contractual Capacity
Competency
Incompetence
   Minors
   Intoxication
   Mental Incapacity
   Aliens
   Convicts

6.2 Illegal Agreements
Illegal Contracts
   Divisible Contracts
   Pari Delicto
   Exceptions
   Protected Classes
   Simple Knowledge
Agreement to Commit a Crime
Torts
Sunday Laws
Repentance

Usury
   Usury Exceptions

6.3 Public Policy
Gambling
Lottery
Insurance Contracts
Agreement Not to Prosecute
Suppression of Justice
Public Interest
Lobbying
Licenses
   Regulatory
   Revenue
   Substantial Compliance
Exculpatory Clauses
Promise Not To Compete
   Blue-Pencil Rule
Employment Restriction
Marriage Contracts

6.1 Contractual Capacity

Competency

Competent
The capacity to understand and to act reasonably.

An essential requirement for a binding contract is that the parties thereto have the legal capacity to enter into such agreements. In other words, they must be legally competent.

Incompetence

Many contracts involve persons under some legal disability such as minors, intoxicated persons, those of unsound mind, aliens, convicts, and some business organizations. The limitations on partnerships and corporations are found in later chapters on those topics. This subchapter considers the limitations on individuals.

Minors

Minor
One who is not of legal age.

Rescind
To cancel a contract.

Under common law, a person who had not reached age 21 was considered to be a minor. Today, by statute in most states, people are given adult status at the age of 18 for most purposes, such as the right to make contracts, to will property, to vote, and to marry without parental consent.

Generally, a contract made by a minor can be rescinded by such minor at any time during the period of minority and for a reasonable time thereafter. What constitutes a reasonable time depends upon the circumstances, such as the intelligence of the minor, the access to knowledge, the nature and kind of agreement involved, and the purpose intended. One case has held that seven months after reaching majority was an unreasonable time, whereas another held that fourteen years was reasonable. In an average situation, several months would be considered reasonable. Although minors can avoid contracts, any adult party to the agreement is bound by it.

Facts
The plaintiff Adams, while a minor, purchased an automobile from the defendant Barcomb. The plaintiff operated the car for approximately two weeks and was dissatisfied with it. She disaffirmed the contract and requested her money back. The defendant refused to return her money. The plaintiff sued for the return of the money.

Decision
The law in Vermont has always been that a minor can disaffirm a contract, if not for necessities, while a minor or within a reasonable time after arriving at adult age. After disaffirmance, the plaintiff is entitled to the return of the consideration paid for the automobile.
Adams v. *Barcomb*, 125 Vt. 380, 216 A.2d 648 (1966).

Disaffirm
To refuse to honor a contract.

Disaffirmation When a minor disaffirms a contract by notice to the other party, must the consideration be returned? Under the rule followed in most states, the minor does not have to return the consideration if the contract was for a luxury and he no longer has the item. For example, a minor buys an automobile from a dealer and then disaffirms the contract. Must the automobile be returned? The majority rule is that it must be returned if the minor still has it. If the car has been wrecked, it may be returned in that condition. If it has been sold but the minor no longer has the money, most courts will not require that it be returned. The policy behind these rules is to discourage adults from making contracts with minors. This right to avoid contracts is for the minor's protection against his own inexperience, indiscretion, and immaturity and the designs and manipulations of others.

The disaffirmance by the minor may be made by any act or declaration disclosing an intent to repudiate the contract. Express notice to the other party is not required.

By statutes and by court decisions in some states, the minor must account for the property's value if he or she cannot return the consideration. Suppose a minor trades in his Ford automobile and purchases a new Chevrolet from a dealer and the dealer sells the Ford to an innocent third party. Upon disaffirmance, can the minor get the Ford back from the third party? Under UCC § 2–403, the minor cannot.

Necessities A minor is liable for the reasonable value of necessities actually furnished to him by another person at the minor's request. The minor is not bound by the terms of the contract but is required to pay the reasonable value of the necessities on the theory of unjust enrichment under a quasi-contract. What is a necessity depends on the surrounding circumstances of the minor, such as age, actual need, and financial or social status. Necessities include food, clothing, shelter, medical care, tools of a trade, vocational education, and possibly a college education.

There has been a tendency to expand the concept of necessities to include property and services necessary for the minor to make a living (e.g., farm implements, employment agency fee). It is likely the trend will continue to include as necessities items that under modern living standards are associated with necessities of life. Of course, as the courts expand the concept of necessities, the minor becomes liable for more types of contracts.

Necessities
Food, clothing, shelter, medical care and other things reasonably necessary to maintain a person's status in life.

Gastonia Personnel Corp. v. Rogers
276 N.C. 279, 172 S.E.2d 19 (1970).

On May 29, 1968, defendant was [a minor] emancipated and married. He needed only "one quarter or 22 hours" for completion of the courses required at Gaston Tech for an A.S. degree in civil engineering. His wife was employed as a computer programmer at First Federal Savings and Loan. He and she were living in a rented apartment. They were expecting a baby in September. Defendant had to quit school and go to work.

For assistance in obtaining suitable employment, defendant went to the office of plaintiff, an employment agency, on May 29, 1968. After talking with Maurine Finley, a personnel counselor, defendant signed a contract containing, *inter alia*, the following: "If I ACCEPT employment offered me by an employer as a result of a lead (verbal or otherwise) from you within twelve (12) months of such lead even though it may not be the position originally discussed with you, I will be obligated to pay you as per the terms of the contract."

After making several telephone calls to employers who might need defendant's services as a draftsman, Mrs. Finley called Spratt-Seaver, Inc., in Charlotte, North Carolina. It was stipulated that defendant, as a result of his conversation with Mrs. Finley, went to Charlotte, was interviewed by Spratt-Seaver, Inc., and was employed by that company on June 6, 1968, at an annual salary of $4,784.00. The contract provided that defendant would pay plaintiff a service charge of $295.00 if the starting annual salary of accepted employment was as much as $4,680.00.

. . . Plaintiff sued to recover a service charge of $295.00. In his answer, defendant admitted he had paid nothing to plaintiff; alleged he was not indebted to plaintiff in any amount; and, as a further answer and defense, pleaded his infancy. . . .

Bobbitt, Chief Justice. . . . In general, our prior decisions are to the effect that the "necessaries" of an infant, his wife and child, include only such necessities of life as food, clothing, shelter, medical attention, etc. In our view, the concept of "necessaries" should be enlarged to include such articles of property and such services as are reasonably necessary to enable the infant to earn the money required to provide the necessities of life for himself and those who are legally dependent upon him.

. . . To hold, as a matter of law, that such a person cannot obligate himself to pay for services rendered him in obtaining employment suitable to his ability, education and specialized training, enabling him to provide the necessities of life for himself, his wife and his expected child, would place him and others similarly situated under a serious economic handicap.

In the effort to protect "older minors" from improvident or unfair contracts, the law should not deny to them the opportunity and right to obligate themselves for articles of property or services which are reasonably necessary to enable them to provide for the proper support of themselves and their dependents. The minor should be held liable for the reasonable value of articles of property or services received pursuant to such contract. . . .

To establish liability, plaintiff must satisfy the jury by the greater weight of the evidence that defendant's contract with plaintiff was an appropriate and reasonable means for defendant to obtain suitable employment. If this issue is answered in plaintiff's favor, plaintiff must then establish by the greater weight of the evidence the reasonable value of the services received by defendant pursuant to the contract. Thus, plaintiff's recovery, if any, cannot exceed the reasonable value of its services to defendant.

Accordingly, the judgment of the Court of Appeals is reversed and the cause is remanded to that Court with direction to award a new trial to be conducted in accordance with the legal principles stated herein.

Error and remanded.

Ratification
Approval of something already done.

Ratification A minor can no longer avoid a contract that he or she ratifies after becoming an adult. A ratification may be made expressly by the minor or by his or her conduct. For example, a minor purchases an automobile and after becoming an adult sells it; the act of selling is a ratification by conduct.

By statutes and court decisions in many states, minors cannot avoid certain types of contracts (e.g., contracts for legal or medical services; loans by a governmental agency made to obtain a higher education; life insurance contracts; credit union, bank, or building and loan association contracts; contracts that involve the transfer of shares of stock; contracts for the purchase of homes and farms with the Veterans' Welfare Board; and contracts arising from a business the minor operates). The U.S. Supreme Court has held that a minor's enlistment in the armed forces may be binding subject to statutory qualifications as to age.

In some states, minors making large incomes from creative or artistic services or from professional sports may have contracts approved by the court. Such agreements may not be disaffirmed.

Emancipation Some states treat emancipated minors as adults for contract purposes. Emancipation depends on state laws but usually requires either a valid marriage, active duty in the armed forces, or a person over the age of 14 who is living separately by consent and who manages his or her own financial affairs with no income from crime.

Emancipation
A parent's giving up authority and control over a minor child.

Age Misrepresentation Under the majority rule, the fact that a minor misrepresents his age will not preclude him from disaffirming the contract. This rule has been changed by statute in some states. The general rule is that even though the minor can disaffirm the contract, he is still liable in damages for the tort (civil wrong or injury not arising out of the contract) of deceit on the theory that the tort is independent of the contract and that minors generally should be held liable for their torts.

Breach of Duty By the majority view, a minor is not liable for a tort that involves a breach of a duty flowing from the contractual status. For example, a minor rents an automobile under a contract that requires him to use reasonable care in the operation of the automobile. Through negligence, the minor damages the car, thus breaching the contract. His contractual immunity absolves him from liability on the contract. Can the adult recover in a suit for damages based on the minor's tort (negligence in damaging the automobile)? In most states, the adult cannot. However, if the minor goes beyond the contract (by making an unauthorized use, for example) and during this unauthorized use negligently damages the automobile, most courts would hold that the tort was independent of the contract and would allow recovery.

Parental Liability Ordinarily, a parent is not liable for the contracts of a minor child. The parent is liable, however, if the child acted as the parent's agent. If a parent has not provided the child with necessities, the parent is liable to third persons for the reasonable value of the necessities furnished to the minor. If a parent joins in a contract with a minor (e.g., to purchase an automobile), the parent is liable even though the minor may be able to disaffirm.

Parental Liability
Responsibility of parents for torts committed by their minor children.

Exceptions Generally, a parent is not liable for the tortious acts of the minor child even though the child may be liable. The following are exceptions:

1. A parent is liable for the torts of the child when the child is acting as an agent or servant of the parent.

2. Where the negligence of the parent made the injury possible, the parent is liable on the basis of the ordinary rules of negligence but not on the parent-child relationship.
3. Where the parent directs, consents to, or sanctions the tort, the parent is liable.
4. In most states, by statute the parents are liable for willful, malicious, intentional, or unlawful acts of the minor child.
5. In some states, the parent is liable by special statute (e.g., limited amount associated with a driver's license).

Intoxication

If a person is so intoxicated or under the influence of drugs at the time of entering into a contract that he cannot comprehend the nature and effect of the transaction, the contract is voidable at that person's option.

Mental Incapacity

Mental Incapacity
A mental condition under which a party to a contract does not understand the nature of the act or the extent of the property involved.

If a person is so deranged mentally that he does not know that he is making a contract or does not understand the consequences of the transaction, the contract is voidable. Rescission of such voidable contracts requires the party to return whatever consideration was received.

Most states by special statute (e.g., California Civil Code Section 38–40) provide that if a person had been *judicially* declared insane, the contract is void. If a person is incompetent but not judicially declared insane, the contract is voidable.

By case law in California, it has been held that where a person in a hospital signed an insurance release while in a dazed and semiconscious condition as a result of injuries sustained in an automobile accident, the release was wholly void.

The test used by the courts is whether the party was mentally competent to deal with the subject before him with a full understanding of his rights and whether he understood the nature, purpose, and effect of the contract. One may be incompetent to some extent and yet have sufficient mentality to comprehend the nature and effect of a particular transaction and thus to execute a valid contract.

Hanks v. McNeil Coal Corp.
114 Colo. 578, 168 P.2d 256 (1946).

Stone, Justice Lee A. Hanks, who was a prosperous farmer and business man in Nebraska, came to Colorado with his family in 1918, at first settling on a farm in Weld county, which included the coal lands involved in this proceeding; then, in 1920 moving to Boulder where he purchased a home, engaged in the retail coal business, and thereafter resided. His son, J. L. Hanks, continued to operate and live on the farm as a tenant. . . . Shortly after 1922 Lee Hanks discovered that he was afflicted with diabetes, and members of his family noticed a progressive change in his physical and mental condition thereafter. He became irritable and easily upset, very critical of his son's work, and increasingly interested in the emotional type of religion. He began to speculate in oil and other doubtful ventures with money needed for payment of debts and taxes. About 1934 he sent his son what he denominated a secret formula for the manufacture of medicine to cure fistula in horses, which was compounded principally of ground china, brick dust, burnt shoe leather and amber-colored glass. If the infection was in the horse's right shoulder, the mixture was to be poured in the animal's left ear, and if on the left shoulder then in the right ear. In 1937 Mr. Hanks started to advertise this medicine through the press under the name of Crown King Remedy. Thereafter he increasingly devoted his efforts and money to the compounding and attempted sale of this concoction, his business judgment became poor and he finally deteriorated mentally to the point that on May 25, 1940, he was adjudicated insane and his son was appointed conservator of his estate.

... Hanks learned that the defendant coal company, which had leased other lands lying to the north of his property, was extracting coal from their other leased lands and conveying it by means of the open haulage way through his lands to its shaft located to the south thereof. Hanks made demand for payment of royalty on the coal so transported across his land and there was extended argument and controversy which finally led to discussion of outright purchase of the Hanks property and the ultimate signing of the contract here involved on July 21, 1937, between Hanks and the defendant companies. . . .

The present action was brought by the conservator seeking to have the court set aside this contract. . . . The record is voluminous; the case was carefully considered by the court below and judgment of dismissal entered on findings against plaintiff on the question of insanity.

There is always in civil, as well as in criminal, actions a presumption of sanity. . . . Insanity and incompetence are words of vague and varying import. Often the definition of the psychiatrist is at variance with that of the law. The legal test of Hanks' insanity is whether "he was incapable of understanding and appreciating the extent and effect of business transactions in which he engaged." . . .

The legal rule does not recognize degrees of insanity. It does not presume to make a distinction between much and little intellect. . . . One may have insane delusions regarding some matters and be insane on some subjects, yet capable of transacting business concerning matters wherein such subjects are not concerned, and such insanity does not make one incompetent to contract unless the subject matter of the contract is so connected with an insane delusion as to render the afflicted party incapable of understanding the nature and effect of the agreement or of acting rationally in the transaction.

... Patently Hanks was suffering from insane delusion in 1937 with reference to the efficacy of the horse medicine, but there is no evidence of delusions or hallucinations in connection with this transaction or with his transaction of much of his other business at that time; there is no basis for holding voidable his sale here involved on the ground of his insanity, and the trial court correctly so held. . . .

Accordingly, the judgment is affirmed.

Aliens

Generally, aliens who are legally in this country have the same right to contract as citizens. Thus, they can contract for the transfer of land, be admitted to the practice of law (which involves entering into contracts),

Alien
One not a citizen of the country in which he resides.

receive state educational and welfare benefits, and be employed in non-policymaking civil service jobs.

Laws generally provide that aliens cannot vote, hold high public office, act as jurors, or be employed in sensitive areas with broad discretionary powers (e.g., as police officers). The U.S. Supreme Court has given the states wide latitude in excluding all aliens from public employment.

Convicts

Convict
One who has been determined by a court to be guilty of the crime charged.

Generally, convicts are accorded full contractual capacity. The law varies from state to state. In some states, a convict under a life sentence cannot contract except to sell real property he or she may own. The trend is to liberalize the contract rights of prisoners and convicts. California Penal Code § 2600 states that prisoners may be deprived of only such rights as are necessary to provide for reasonable security of the institution and for protection of the public.

Questions

1. Do you believe that competent, intelligent teenage minors should be permitted to avoid their contracts? Discuss.
2. Under what circumstances should a college education be deemed a necessity?
3. Why should minors be responsible for their torts when they are allowed to rescind their contracts?
4. Give some examples of situations in which parents may be liable for the torts of their minor child?
5. How drunk does a person have to be to get out of a contract he has made? How insane does the person have to be to set aside contracts?

6.2 Illegal Agreements

Illegal Contracts

Contracts that call for a violation of the law or are contrary to public policy are unenforceable. Some examples of illegal contracts include restraints of trade, bribery of public officials, usury, violations of regulatory or licensing laws, an agreement to injure or defraud another party, and gambling.

Divisible Contracts

Divisible Contract
An agreement that can be divided up into separate independent provisions.

If part of the consideration for a contract is illegal, the entire contract fails unless the contract can be divided into separate provisions, in which case the legal part will be upheld. For example, an employee is to receive $200 a week for sweeping the floor and serving beer in a bar, but the latter act is illegal because the employer has no license. The employee cannot recover money, because part of the consideration is illegal and the contract is not divisible. If the employee were to be paid $100 a week for sweeping the floor and $100 a week for serving the beer, the parts of the contract could be separated and the employee would be able to recover the $100 for the legal part, sweeping the floor.

Pari Delicto

When both parties to a contract are aware of the contract's illegality (are in *pari delicto*) but are not equally at fault, the court will not help the more innocent party but will leave the parties where it finds them. For example, Joe agrees to drive a getaway car for Mike and Jim, bank robbers, if they pay him $1,000. Joe merely sits in the car at the curb while the other two complete the robbery. He then drives the robbers away from the scene. The courts would not permit Joe to recover the $1,000 if he were to bring an action for it.

Some courts make a somewhat artificial distinction between contracts *malum in se* (bad in themselves, or against good morals) and those that are *malum prohibitum* (bad because they are prohibited by statute). In either case, the contract is void if the parties are in *pari delicto*. However, in some cases that are in violation of statutes, the court may make exceptions. The contract will not be enforced, but the relatively innocent party may obtain restitution under quasi-contract theory to prevent unjust enrichment.

In *Pari Delicto*
Equally at fault.

Malum in Se
Naturally evil, as judged by civilized standards.

Malum Prohibitum
Wrong because it is prohibited by statute.

Facts
A baseball team owner hired an off-duty fireman to do part-time announcing for ballgames. Both knew about a fire department regulation prohibiting firefighters from moonlighting. When the team owner refused to pay because of an illegal contract, the fireman sued.

Decision
The fireman could recover a reasonable value for the services performed under a quasi-contract. The contract violated an internal administrative rule that did not affect public morality. That rule may be enforced by disciplinary action, but the violation was not so serious as to call for voiding the contract and the resulting unjust enrichment of the defendant.

Vick v. *Patterson,* 158 Cal.App.2d 414, 322 P.2d 548 (1958).

Exceptions

Where public policy is not involved, courts have allowed parties to bring suit where they were not in *pari delicto,* no serious wrong was involved, the adverse party was unjustly enriched, and the forfeiture involved was disproportionately harsh in relation to the extent of the illegality.

When the illegality is due to facts of which the defendant is aware but the plaintiff is excusably ignorant, courts will permit the innocent party to rescind the contract.

Protected Classes

Where a statute has been passed to protect a certain class of people, a member of that class may enforce an illegal contract even though the other party cannot. For example, a borrower or buyer who pays usurious interest is not as guilty as the lender. An employer who pays an employee less than the legal minimum wage or works people in excess of the maximum number of hours permitted by law is another example. These laws were passed to protect those who have been taken advantage of so the courts will allow such people to recover.

Simple Knowledge

Mere knowledge of wrongful use will not preclude recovery. For example, a seller can recover for the price of sugar sold even though she knew the buyer was going to use the sugar to make illegal whiskey, or a lender can recover money loaned even though he knew the borrower was going to use it for illegal gambling. Of course, the seller or lender must not do anything in furtherance of the unlawful design or participate in the unlawful venture.

Agreement to Commit a Crime

Any agreement between parties to commit a crime that is morally wrong (*malum in se*) is illegal. If a man hires a hit man to murder his spouse or an arsonist to burn down his place of business, the courts will not assist the criminal to collect the fee.

Torts

Agreements to commit torts (civil wrongs or injuries, Chapter 3.2) or to cause torts to be done are also illegal. For example, if a politician promises a newspaper editor that he will pay the editor $10,000 to print a false story that his opposing candidate is a communist, such agreement is not enforceable. If the editor were to publish the story, he would also be guilty of the tort of libel (which may also be a crime).

Atkins v. Johnson
43 Vt. 78 (1870).

The defendant had written a defamatory article about one Gregory, and to induce the plaintiff, a publisher, to print it in his newspaper, the defendant had agreed to protect him against any action for damages brought by Gregory, or any other liability that might arise from the publication. The plaintiff, having been sued successfully by Gregory, brings this action upon the defendant's promise to indemnify him.
Pierpoint, C.J. . . . The plaintiff is here seeking to compel the defendant to indemnify him for the damage which he has sustained in consequence of publishing a libel, at the request of the defendant, and from the consequences of which the defendant agreed to save him harmless. The question is whether such an agreement as the plaintiff sets out in his declaration can be legally enforced.

> In this case, these parties in the outset conspired to do a wrong to one of their neighbors, by publishing a libel upon his character. The publication of a libel is an illegal act upon its face. This both parties are presumed to have known. The publication not only subjects the party publishing to a prosecution by the person injured for damages, but also to a public prosecution by indictment. . . .
>
> Both these parties knew that they were arranging for and consummating an illegal act, one that subjects them to legal liability, hoping, to be sure, that they might defend it; but the plaintiff, fearing they might not be able to do so, sought to protect himself from the consequences by taking a contract of indemnity from the defendant. To say under such circumstances that these parties were not joint wrongdoers, within the full spirit and meaning of the general rule, would be an entire perversion of the plainest and simplest proposition. This being so, the law will not interfere in aid of either. It will not inquire which of the two are most in the wrong, with a view of adjusting the equities between them, but regarding both as having been understandingly engaged in a violation of the law, it will leave them as it finds them, to adjust their differences between themselves as they best may. . . .
>
> [Case dismissed.]

Other tortious agreements that are unenforceable include those that promise to wrongfully interfere with a contract of a third person or to break a contract, those by a fiduciary to violate his duty, and (in some states) those by an attorney to sell the goodwill of his law practice.

Fiduciary
One who has a legal duty to act primarily for the benefit of another.

Sunday Laws

Most states have Sunday or Sabbath laws that hold some agreements made on Sunday to be illegal or unenforceable. A few states make all Sunday contracts illegal. Others have so-called blue laws that make the sale of certain merchandise, particularly alcoholic beverages, unlawful on Sunday. These laws vary widely among the states and even in local communities within some of them. Excluded from these laws, however, are acts that must be done on Sunday to protect health, life, or property. Some contracts that may be illegal on Sunday are proper if ratified on a weekday. Many states do not enforce their Sunday laws, and a few have held the laws to be unconstitutional.

Illegal contracts in violation of the antitrust laws were discussed in Chapter 4.1, and unlawful discrimination contracts were covered in Chapter 4.3.

Blue Laws
Any state or local law that for religious or moral purposes restricts activities on Sunday. Some early such laws in Connecticut were printed on blue paper.

Repentance

Courts want to encourage repentance, so even when parties to an illegal contract are equally guilty, the law assists any party who wants to get out of the unlawful agreement by having the agreement rescinded before it is carried out. For example, Bill pays John $500 to beat up his neighbor, Joe, when Joe comes home from work on Saturday. Bill changes his mind on

Repentance
To feel sorrow or regret for what has been done or left undone by oneself.

Friday and tells John the deal is off and he wants his $500 back. If John refuses to return the $500 because the contract was illegal, Bill can sue to get it.

Usury

Usury
An illegal excessive rate of interest.

Usury means an illegal contract for a loan in which illegal interest is charged (i.e., a rate of interest greater than allowed by statute). Intent to violate the law is not necessary.

Most states strictly regulate by statute the interest rates on loans. The maximum chargeable annual interest rate allowable varies from 6 percent to 30 percent in the various jurisdictions. If the lender charges interest over the permitted maximum rate, the contract is illegal. Although most states deny the lender any interest at all if he charges an illegal amount, a few states permit the lender to recover the maximum legal amount that has been established by statute. In a few states, the lender forfeits the entire amount of the principal and the interest. If the interest has been paid by the borrower, jurisdictions differ as to whether the borrower recovers merely the amount of the interest paid or whether he or she recovers two or three times that amount as a penalty.

Usury Exceptions

Most states have statutes that provide for so many exceptions to the general rule of usury that the purpose of the law (i.e., to protect debtors from excessive interest) has been largely nullified.

A few of the many exceptions to the usury laws are as follows:

Installment Sales
Contracts by which goods are bought now but paid for over a period of time by a number of installments.

1. Installment sales (i.e., sales on credit) generally do not come within the usury statutes. The theory is that in such cases the seller does not lend money to the buyer but agrees that he or she is to be paid by the buyer later. Since no loan is made, the usury law does not apply. The seller is free to sell for cash at one price and on credit at a different price that is much higher. However, many states (e.g., California) have adopted statutes that regulate the differential between cash and time prices that may be charged by the seller. If the sale is going to be financed by a bank and the credit sale contract provides that the buyer is to make payments directly to the bank, it is considered a loan, and the unpaid balance is subject to the usury law.

2. Reasonable expenses or service fees incidental to the loan may be charged in addition to the maximum rate of interest (e.g., inspecting of property, investigating the credit of the borrower, and drawing necessary documents). However, points (the fee or charge a lender sometimes makes for the privilege of making a loan and which is one or more of the percentages of the principal amount of the loan) are considered interest and are prorated over the term of the loan to determine if the points added to the regular interest is usurious. Finance or carrying charges on long-term loans are also allowable. There is a conflict in the court de-

cisions as to late charges. Some courts hold that late charges are not interest and therefore not subject to usury laws, while others hold they are interest, on the theory that they are payments due because the money was not repaid on time.

3. Most statutes provide that collecting interest in advance, compound interest, or accelerated maturity for nonpayment of installments is not usury as long as the total interest does not exceed the maximum rate per annum for the full period of the loan.
4. The purchase of a note at a discount greater than the maximum interest with no intent to evade the law is not usury.
5. Where the borrower has the option to pay the principal of the debt before the due date, together with some months' unearned interest, there is no usury.
6. Most states have enacted statutes that permit licensed money lenders, such as banks, to charge more interest than is permissible in ordinary business transactions.

Questions

1. As a judge, how would you determine whether an illegal contract was divisible so that part of it could be enforced?
2. What is the difference between a contract that is *malum in se* and one that is *malum prohibitum*? Give an example of each.
3. What are some of the exceptions when a court will enforce a contract that is otherwise illegal?
4. If you have paid out money as consideration for an illegal contract, is it possible for you to get your money back legally? How?
5. Joe Green approaches you and says that he is starting a new business and already has good government contracts. However, he needs machine tools that cost $2,000. He tells you that if you will loan him the $2,000, he'll pay you back in six months when he gets his first check and will add $1,000 interest for its use. What would you do, and what would you advise him to do?

6.3 Public Policy

Anything that has a tendency to injure the public welfare is, in principle, against public policy. Some courts make the decision, but most leave the decision up to the legislative bodies to define the acts that are illegal because they are against public policy.

A police chief had arrested Jones on a felony charge. While Jones was still in custody without legal counsel, the chief made a contract with him to buy his land at a low price and had the deed signed, notarized, and recorded. Jones sued to rescind the sale, and although the court found nothing actually illegal, it held that any contract made by an officer that might interfere with the unbiased discharge of his public duty was against public policy and unenforceable. The deal was rescinded.

Public Policy
The general attitude of the public toward good conduct and behavior required of the community members.

Chapter Six

Gambling

Gambling
Wagering value against an uncertain event in the hope of gaining something of value.

Gambling is a typical activity that most states hold to be either illegal or against public policy. Even in states like Nevada where gambling is legal, the courts hold that enforcement of gambling debts is against public policy. However, recent statutes in New Jersey (1977) and Nevada (1983) now provide methods for the collection of certain gambling debts evidenced by credit instruments.

What happens if a person cashes a check in a casino, uses the money there for gambling, and then stops payment on the check?

Facts

Harvey's Wagon Wheel in Nevada offered Gibbs free airfare on a private plane, lodging, meals, and drinks. Gibbs lost $1,100 gambling. During one night, he cashed five checks at two different clubs at the cashier's cage and lost the proceeds of each check in the place where he cashed them. Gibbs stopped payment on the checks and was sued in California.

Decision

The owner of a gambling house who honors a check for the purpose of providing prospective customers with funds for gambling and then participates in the transaction cannot recover on the check. If the check is made in a gambling establishment in full operation while the games are still in progress, as in this case, the purpose is clear, and enforcement would be against public policy. However, if the check is cashed at a place different from the gambling establishment or is not made when the party has been recently playing or is made for some other legitimate purpose by the recipient, there would be no presumption that it has been made for gambling purposes, and recovery might be allowed.

Lane & Pyron v. *Gibbs,* 266 Cal.App.2d 61, 71 Cal.Rptr. 817 (1968).

In a recent case, the defendant passed bad checks in a casino in England for chips that he lost gambling. The casino got a judgment in England and tried to enforce it in California. The court allowed the suit, saying that gambling was legal in England and that current developments, including the California state lottery, indicated that gambling was not "so antagonistic to public policy" that the contract shouldn't be enforced. (*Crockford's* v. *Si-Ahmed,* 203 Cal.App.3d 1402, 250 Cal.Rptr. 728 [1988]).

Lottery

A lottery is a scheme for the distribution of property by chance to a person who paid for the chance of winning a prize, or "a chance for a prize for a price." Lotteries are prohibited by statute in most states. Many states, however, now run official state lotteries for the purpose of augmenting tax revenues. Many other exceptions are granted. California leaves it up to local cities and counties whether or not to permit legal bingo games for charitable purposes. An illegal lottery is such no matter what is is called or how it is programmed, because the court will look through the form to substance. However, if participation in the game does not require the party

OTHER BASIC REQUIREMENTS

to buy anything or to pay anything of value, it is not a lottery but may be a giveaway deal or an advertising plan.

Insurance Contracts

Insurance contracts are not lotteries, as they share existing risks of loss from a possible future event, such as a fire, and therefore promote public policy. But the buyer of an insurance policy must have an insurable interest in the subject matter. To insure somebody else's property against fire or a stranger's life would be wagering that the event would happen.

Insurance
An agreement by an insurer to give to the insured money or some other benefit in the event of destruction, loss or injury to a specified person or thing in which the insured has a legal interest.

Agreement Not To Prosecute

An agreement not to prosecute a crime in return for the payment of something of value is in itself a crime. It has been referred to as blackmail or extortion. Someone who is injured by a felony and refuses to prosecute the felon in exchange for a bribe or reparations, may be guilty of the crime of compounding a felony.

Compounding a Felony
The crime of a victim's refusal to prosecute a felon in return for a bribe or other favor.

Suppression of Justice

Contracts made to suppress justice are illegal. An example would be a contract with a witness to withhold evidence. An agreement with someone, such as a private investigator, to procure evidence of a certain character only or to establish those facts necessary for success in a trial would be against public policy. Justice requires obtaining all facts, not just those favorable to one side.

Public Interest

Any agreement that tends to be against the public interest is unenforceable. Public officials must avoid conflict of interests when they make contracts in their official capacity.

Facts

Taxpayers filed an action against Hubert Call, his wife, and a corporation to set aside a contract for the sale of land. The corporation, as a go-between, bought a parcel of land from the Calls for $258,000 and then conveyed it to the City of Albany while Call was a member of the Albany city council.

Decision

Under California law, and as a matter of public policy, no public officer shall be financially interested in any contract made by that person with any body or board of which he is a member. The court found the Calls liable to the city for the $258,000 paid as consideration and let the city keep the land. The city (or other contracting agency) under such circumstance is entitled to recover any consideration paid without restoring the benefits received. The law will not permit a person who acts in a fiduciary capacity to deal with himself in his individual capacity. The goals of eliminating temptation, avoiding the appearance of impropriety, and assuring the city of officers undivided and uncompromised in their allegiance make the question of actual fraud or dishonesty immaterial. Whether the contract was fair, just, equitable, or more advantageous to the public had no bearing on the question of its validity.

Thomson v. Call, 38 Cal.3d 633, 214 Cal.Rptr. 139, 699 P.2d 316 (1985). *Certiorari* denied by the U.S. Supreme Court.

Lobbying

Lobbyists
Those who are in the business of persuading legislators to pass laws that are favorable and to defeat those that are unfavorable to the lobbyists' clients.

Attempts to corrupt a public official to influence legislation or to obtain government contracts are also unlawful. Open advocacy to influence legislative bodies is widely practiced and is legal as long as no improper methods are used in the process. Some improper methods of lobbying are using secret personal influence, bribery, threat of loss of votes, and contingency fees based upon success.

Contingency Fee
A charge made by an attorney depending upon the successful outcome of the case and often agreed to be a percentage of the recovery.

Licenses

License
A right granted which gives one permission to do something that could not legally be done without such permit.

Every state has laws requiring persons engaged in many types of occupations and professions, such as doctors, lawyers, brokers, accountants, architects, and contractors, to be licensed. Such laws either are regulatory in nature or are merely for the purpose of raising revenue.

Regulatory

Regulatory License
A license required for one to engage in a business or profession and granted only when set standards of expertise have been demonstrated.

Regulatory licenses require individuals to meet certain standards of education, experience, and expertise demonstrating proficiency in their occupation or profession before they are issued a license. The purpose is to protect the public. Revenue licenses are issued for payment of a fee and then permit the licensee to conduct his business or profession in the area.

Revenue

Revenue License
A license issued for the primary purpose of raising tax money.

If the law is regulatory in nature, contracts made by an unlicensed person are not enforceable. However, if the license is only to raise revenue, failure to obtain one may lead to fines or other sanctions but does not affect the making of contracts.

If a painting contractor does not have the required regulatory license and she paints your house pursuant to a contract, can she enforce the contract? The answer is no, since the license was required so that the state could regulate the particular business. However, suppose that you pay the painter for her work and then you discover that she did not have a license. Can you recover the money paid? The answer is no, since there can be no recovery of money paid on an executed contract involving an unlicensed person. The typical city business license is one for revenue purposes only, since the city does not attempt to regulate the particular business. Thus, if the painter had her state regulatory license, she would be able to enforce the contract even though she did not have the revenue license.

Elephant Lumber Co. v. Johnson
120 Ohio App. 266, 202 N.E.2d 189 (1964).

Collier, Presiding Judge The Elephant Lumber Company, a corporation, . . . herein designated the plaintiff, brought this action on June 10, 1963, in the Chillicothe Municipal Court to recover for services rendered . . . Helen Johnson, herein referred to as the defendant, in preparing and drawing plans, specifications and material lists for the erection of a building to be used as a nursing home. . . .

No answer or other pleading was filed by the defendant and, on July 15, 1963, a default judgment was entered in favor of plaintiff for the full amount claimed in the petition. . . . The defendant now seeks a reversal of that judgment. . . .

The defendant's contentions are that the petition does not state a cause of action for the reason it is not alleged in the petition that the plaintiff is an architect or has as its employee an architect authorized to draw and furnish plans and specifications and to charge for such services; that the alleged contract is in violation of statute and therefore void; that a valid default judgment may not be rendered upon such defective petition. Section 4703.18, Revised Code, provides:

> No person shall enter upon the practice of architecture, or hold himself forth as an architect or registered architect, unless he . . . is the holder of a certificate of qualification to practice architecture issued or renewed and registered under such sections.

. . . Ohio is one of the many states that have enacted statutes regulating architects in the practice of their profession. It is generally held that designing a building for another, or furnishing the plans and specifications for such a building for another, constitutes architectural services. It is also well settled that such legislation is a proper exercise of the police power.

. . . The general rule is that a contract entered into by a person engaged in a business without taking out a license as required by law is void and unenforceable and that where a license or certificate is required by statute as a requisite to one practicing a particular profession, an agreement of a professional character without such license or certificate is illegal and void. . . .

It is also a well established rule that a contract which cannot be performed without a violation of a statute is void. . . .

Our conclusions are that the plaintiff's claim is for services rendered as an architect; that to practice the profession of architecture in Ohio and to recover in an action for such services, it is necessary to obtain a license as prescribed by law; that a contract for such services entered into by one who is not so licensed and registered is void; that a default judgment, rendered on a petition to recover for such services in which it is not alleged that the plaintiff is a licensed and registered architect, is void. The judgment will be reversed and final judgment rendered for the defendant.

Although most courts say that such contracts are void, where the violation of the regulatory statute is a technicality and the public interest is not harmed, the agreement may be enforced.

Facts

Plaintiff, a sole proprietor, had a valid contractor's license in the name of "ARTKO Remodeling and Construction" (ARTKO). Using his own name (Asdourian), plaintiff made a written contract with the defendants to do some remodeling work. A permit was obtained, and when the job was practically completed, the defendants stopped making payments, claiming that Asdourian was not a licensed contractor and could not sue for compensation.

Decision

The purpose of the licensing law to protect the public from the perils of contracting with incompetent or untrustworthy contractors had been met, since Asdourian as a sole proprietor was the same person as ARTKO and had personally qualified for the regulatory license. Substantial compliance with the law is all that is required. To allow the defendants to prevail on such a technicality would be to use the statute as a "shield for avoidance of a just obligation."

Asdourian v. Araj, 38 Cal.3d 276, 211 Cal.Rptr. 703, 696 P.2d 95 (1985).

Substantial Compliance

Substantial Compliance
Performance of the essential terms of a contract so that the purpose has been accomplished even though unimportant omissions or technical defects may exist.

Some examples wherein the court has applied the substantial compliance doctrine are where the contractor's license expired before the job was completed and where the business entity and name were changed when two licensed contractors formed a partnership.

Exculpatory Clauses

Exculpatory Clause
A clause in a contract which excuses a party from liability for negligent acts.

A provision in a contract that relieves a party from his or her ordinary negligence (exculpatory clause) is not favored by the law and is strictly construed against the party relying on it. Statutes and court decisions in many states have declared such provisions as illegal, since they are contrary to public policy. For example, California Civil Code Section 1668 provides that all contracts that have as their object, directly or indirectly, to exempt anyone from responsibility for his or her own fraud or willful injury to the person or property of another or violation of law, whether willful or negligent, are against the policy of the law. The California supreme court has ruled that an exculpatory clause in a residential lease violates public policy and therefore does not relieve an owner from liability for injuries caused to his or her tenants while on a common stairway in an apartment building.

Where such clauses are declared illegal, it is usually because the public interest is involved. For example, if a public parking lot attempts to avoid liability for the negligence of one of its attendants, the attempt will generally fail. Courts have held that a reasonable person would not be aware of the condition and would not understand that a parking lot claim check was a contract that limited liability. Many states have statutes that prohibit such clauses where a duty is owed to protect the public. Some of these agreements have been held to be unconscionable because of the unequal bargaining power of the parties. However, where the public interest is not involved and there is no statutory limitation, many courts hold that such a clause in private agreements is valid.

Ciofalo v. Vic Tanney Gyms, Inc.
10 N.Y.2d 294, 220 N.Y.S.2d 962, 177 N.E.2d 925 (1961).

Froessel, Judge This action by plaintiff wife for personal injuries, and by plaintiff husband for medical expenses and loss of services, stems from injuries which the wife sustained as a result of a fall at or near the edge of a swimming pool located on defendant's premises. Plaintiff claimed that because of excessive slipperiness and lack of sufficient and competent personnel she was caused to fall and fractured her left wrist. . . .

At the time of the injury, plaintiff wife was a "member" or patron of the gymnasium operated by defendant, and in her membership contract she had agreed to assume full responsibility for any injuries which might occur to her in or about defendant's premises, "including but without limitation, any claims for personal injuries resulting from or arising out of the negligence of" the defendant.

Although exculpatory clauses in a contract, intended to insulate one of the parties from liability resulting from his own negligence, are closely scrutinized, they are enforced, but with a number of qualifications. Whether or not such provisions, when properly expressed, will be given effect depends upon the legal relationship between the contracting parties and the interest of the public therein. . . . [W]here the intention of the parties is expressed in sufficiently clear and unequivocal language . . . and it does not come within any of the . . . categories where the public interest is directly involved, a provision absolving a party from his own negligent acts will be given effect.

. . . Here there is no special legal relationship and no overriding public interest which demand that this contract provision, voluntarily entered into by competent parties, should be rendered ineffectual. Defendant, a private corporation, was under no obligation or legal duty to accept plaintiff as a "member" or patron. Having consented to do so, it had the right to insist upon such terms as it deemed appropriate. Plaintiff, on the other hand, was not required to assent to unacceptable terms, or to give up a valuable legal right, as a condition precedent to obtaining employment or being able to make use of the services rendered by a public carrier or utility. She voluntarily applied for membership in a private organization, and agreed to the terms upon which this membership was bestowed. She may not repudiate them now. . . .

The judgment appealed from should be affirmed, without costs.

Several exceptions apply to such nonpublic contracts. For example, exculpatory clauses cannot be used to exempt a person from *gross* negligence; relieve an employer from liability for injuries to his employees; or excuse anyone from fraud, willful injury, or violation of the law.

Promise Not To Compete

Many states have laws providing that any contract by which anyone is restrained from engaging in a lawful profession, trade, or business of any kind is void. However, a major exception is recognized where an agreement not to compete is made in connection with the sale of the goodwill of a business. Such a contract is enforceable if it is reasonable as to time and area. Thus, if a contract for the sale of a grocery store in the city of New

Good Will
An intangible business asset that reflects the value of good will relationship with customers and suppliers, and the standing of the business in its community.

York contains a clause that prohibits the seller from entering into the grocery business in that city for a period of one year, the clause would be enforceable by an injunction against the seller. However, if the clause provides for a time that is too long or an area that is too great, a problem can arise.

Blue-Pencil Rule

Blue Pencil Rule
The practice of some courts when ruling on a divisible contract not to compete in a business to edit out any unreasonable part and then enforce the amended agreement.

Many courts blue-pencil the unreasonable part and leave the rest of the clause if it is divisible. For example, if the sale of the grocery store had a covenant that provided that the seller would not enter into a competing business for a period of one year in the cities of New York, Albany, Syracuse, and Rochester, a court could blue-pencil out all of the cities except New York and hold the contract valid.

Many courts (e.g., California, Delaware, Florida, Massachusetts, Mississippi, New Jersey, New York, Texas, Washington, and Wisconsin) redo the clause by inserting *reasonable* restrictions. For example, if the clause prohibited the seller from engaging in the grocery business for thirty years in the entire state of New York, such courts would insert a reasonable time and a reasonable area. This is the modern tendency. Many object that the rule tends to encourage employers and purchasers possessing superior bargaining power over that of their employees and vendors to insist upon unreasonable and excessive restrictions, secure in the knowledge that the promise may be upheld in part, if not in full. At least these contractors could get reasonable restrictions inserted by the court.

Employment Restriction

A clause incident to a contract of *employment* that restricts an employee from discussing trade secrets or engaging in competition after employment has terminated has been a prolific source of litigation. Some of the criteria generally considered by the courts in determining whether or not such a clause is valid are as follows:

1. Is the restraint reasonable in the sense that it is no greater than necessary to protect the employer in some legitimate interest?

2. Is the restraint reasonable in the sense that it is not unduly harsh and oppressive on the employee?

3. Does the employee's work for the rival party irreparably injure the employer or threaten to injure him or her irreparably?

In *Washington Capitols Basketball Club, Inc. v. Barry* (304 F.Supp. 1193, N.D.Cal. [1969]), a star basketball player signed one contract too many, and his original employer sought a restraining order to prevent him from playing for his new employer. The court, in granting the temporary injunction, held that the contract was not unconscionable, unenforceable, or otherwise void and stated, "The precedents for granting injunctive relief against 'star' athletes 'jumping' their contracts—and certainly defendants do not deny that Barry is a unique, a 'star' athlete—are numerous."

OTHER BASIC REQUIREMENTS

By statute in a few states, an employer cannot restrict an ordinary employee from engaging in competition after the employment ends. For example, California B. & P. C. Section 16600, provides that a covenant not to compete between an employer and an employee after termination of employment is void.

Covenant Not To Compete
A clause in a contract by which one party agrees not to conduct business or professional activities similar to those of another party.

Marriage Contracts

Contracts made in restraint of marriage or those having the objective of a dissolution of a marriage are void. Likewise, the consideration of the promise of a married person to marry someone else is void, because it contemplates a divorce.

Antenuptial agreements that deal with property owned before the marriage and the disposal of earnings accumulated subsequent thereto are ordinarily valid. However, each party should be advised by separate counsel to assure fairness.

Antenuptial Agreement
A contract entered into by two people who intend to marry each other and which sets forth the property rights of each in the event of divorce or death.

Courts have held that an agreement to pay a wife for services incidental to the marital status is a contract against public policy, as it degrades the spouse and promotes discord in the home.

QUESTIONS

1. What is meant by public policy and its application in law?
2. Do you think that gambling contracts should be enforced by the courts in states that run public lotteries? Why?
3. What kind of legislative lobbying is illegal? What lobbying is legal? Give examples of each.
4. What are the purposes for regulatory licenses and for revenue licenses?
5. What is an exculpatory clause in a contract? Is such an agreement binding? Explain.

PROBLEMS

1. Buyer, a minor, purchased a used automobile for $1,000 from a dealer. The minor used the automobile for three months and then damaged it in an accident. The automobile is now worth $250. Buyer takes the automobile back to the dealer and demands the return of the purchase price. Decision?

2. Buyer, a minor, badly in need of an overcoat, purchases one on credit for $100. The coat is really worth only $75. The buyer wears the cost for three months during the winter season and then attempts to return the coat and disaffirm the contract. Seller sues buyer for purchase price. Decision?

3. Buyer, a minor, purchases furniture on credit. After he becomes an adult, he sells the furniture and uses the proceeds of the sale to purchase an automobile. He defaults on the furniture payments, contending that he purchased the furniture when he was a minor and therefore he can rescind the contract. Seller sues for the balance due on the contract. Decision?

4. Richie and Cody were the opposing nominees for the office of jailer of Knott County, Kentucky. Shortly before the election, Cody secretly agreed to withdraw his candidacy if Richie would agree to appoint him his deputy and divide the fees of the office. Richie agreed. To guarantee his performance of the contract, Richie deposited the sum of $500 with a third party with the understanding that the money was to be repaid when he had fully performed his agreement. Richie was elected and has fully complied with his obligations to Cody. He now seeks to recover the $500 from the third party. The third party refuses to give Richie the $500. Decision?

5. The XYZ Insurance Company contracted to insure a surgeon against personal liability for negligence in connection with his surgical work. During an operation, the surgeon carelessly injured a patient. The surgeon now sues the insurance company to compel it to protect him from loss as a result of such injury. The company's defense is that the surgeon's contract for protection against responsibility for his own negligence is illegal and void. Decision?

6. The Encino Women's Club wants to raise scholarship money for indigent college students. The club plans to have a party at which it will sell tickets for $100 each on a new automobile. The holder of the winning ticket will receive the automobile. The tickets will have the word "Donation" at the top. What is your advice as to the legality of this transaction?

7. Las Vegas Hacienda, Inc., made a public offer to pay $5,000 to any person who, having paid 50 cents for the opportunity of attempting to do so, shot a hole in one on its golf course pursuant to certain conditions. Gibson complied with the conditions, including the payment of the money, and shot a hole in one. Hacienda refuses to pay, contending the contract was a wagering contract. Gibson claims the shooting of the hole in one was a feat of skill and not a feat of chance. Decision?

8. Pancake owned a theatre and asked Jackson, who operated a plumbing shop, to give him a bid for installing some plumbing. Jackson informed Pancake that since he was neither a licensed contractor nor a union plumber he could not make a contract. He agreed, however, to do the work for the cost of the materials used plus $5 an hour for his labor. When the job was finished, Pancake refused to pay Jackson on the basis that he did not have the required license. Decision?

9. Lally sold his barbershop to Mattis "together with all good will." The contract contained a clause that provided that Lally would not engage in the barbering business for a period of two years in the city of Rockville, where the barbershop was located. Nine months after the sale, Lally set up a one-chair barbershop in his own home, which was approximately 300 yards from the shop he sold to Mattis. Mattis seeks an injunction. Decision?

10. Blackman, a real estate salesman, signed an employment contract with Abramson, a real estate broker, which provided that "The salesman shall not after the termination of this contract use to his advantage any information gained verbally or from the files of the broker." Blackman wants to leave Abramson and seeks your advice as to whether he can work for a different broker in the same area.

CHAPTER SEVEN

Reality of Consent

7.1 Fraud and Misrepresentation
Fraud
   Material Fact
   Knowledge of Falsity
   Innocent Misrepresentation
   Intent
   Deceit
   Damages
   Fraud in Inducement
   Fraud in Execution
   Silence as Fraud
   Stipulation

7.2 Mistake, Duress, and Undue Influence
Mutual Mistake of Fact
Mistake of Value
Unilateral Mistake

Exceptions
Mistake of Law
   Mistake of Law Exceptions
Duress
   Economic Compulsion
   Threat of Criminal Prosecution
Undue Influence

7.3 Unconscionability
Definition
Elements
Unequal Bargain Power
Disclaimer
Adhesion Contracts
Standard Clauses
Flexibility

7.1 Fraud and Misrepresentation

Mutual assent through an offer and its acceptance is required to create a binding contract. However, the assent must be "real," which is not the case where a party has been induced to contract through fraud, mistake, duress, or undue influence.

Fraud

Fraud
An intentional deception resulting in loss or injury to another.

Fraud has been defined as "an intentional perversion of truth for the purpose of inducing another in reliance upon it to part with some valuable thing belonging to him or to surrender a legal right; a false representation of a matter of fact, whether by words or by conduct, by false or misleading allegations, or by concealment of that which should have been disclosed, which deceives and is intended to deceive another so that he shall act upon it to his legal injury" (Black's Law Dictionary, Revised Fourth Edition).

The essentials of fraud are as follows:

1. A false representation of a *material fact*.
2. Made with knowledge of its falsity or made with inexcusable ignorance of its truth.
3. With intention that it be acted upon *by the party deceived*.
4. That the party deceived reasonably *relied* upon the representation and acted upon it.
5. That he was thereby injured.

Material Fact

Material Fact
A fact that is of legal consequence or other importance.

Puffing
A statement of opinion or belief not meant as a misrepresentation of fact.

An essential element of fraud is the misrepresentation of a material *fact*. Sales talk is not actionable fraud (e.g., "This is the best car in town," "This is a good car," "This property is worth $75,000"). It is often difficult to distinguish between sales talk, or puffing, and a statement of fact. Generally, a prediction as to what will happen in the future is treated as an opinion and is not a statement of fact (e.g., A in good faith informs B that stock in a corporation is going to rise).

Also, the misrepresentation must be of a *material* fact and must be of such a substantial nature that but for it, the person would not have entered into the contract. A false statement that a horse was not a gelding would be material.

The following case is an example of sales talk.

Facts

The plaintiff purchased a dwelling from the defendant. After living in the dwelling for six months, the plaintiff discovered the house was seriously damaged by termites. Suit was filed to rescind the sale, because the seller had stated the house to be a good house.

Decision

The representation was merely sales talk. Statements that things are "good" or "large" or "strong" necessarily involve to some extent an exercise of individual judgment, and even though such statements are made absolutely, the hearer must know that they can be only expressions of opinion.

Cannaday et ux. v. Cossey et ux., 228 Ark. 1119, 312 S.W.2d 442 (1958).

Knowledge of Falsity

The second element necessary to prove fraud consists of the statement made with knowledge of its falsity or made with inexcusable ignorance of its truth.

A statement by a used-car salesperson that a car "does not eat oil" and that "the car does not need oil added between oil changes" when the salesperson does not know this to be a fact is an example of a statement made with inexcusable ignorance.

Innocent Misrepresentation

It is unjust for a person to retain the benefits of a bargain even though the misrepresentation is innocent. Therefore, most courts will permit rescission in this type of case. However, damages in addition to rescission would not be appropriate. In most cases, it would seem unnecessary to rely on the theory of innocent misrepresentation, since the facts usually establish mutual mistake (i.e., one party mistakenly representing the facts and the other believing the representation).

Intent

Another element of fraud is that the person making the misrepresentation intends that only a certain party be deceived. A third party who overhears the misrepresentation and acts upon it cannot recover, as it was not intended that he so act.

Intent
A state of mind wherein the person knows and desires the consequences of his words and actions.

Deceit

The plaintiff is under a duty to use reasonable diligence for his own protection (i.e., he must use reasonable care to keep from being defrauded). If a buyer knows or should know that the representation of the seller is untrue, the court will not grant the buyer relief (e.g., the used-car salesperson tells the buyer that a 1988 Lincoln gets 60 miles to a gallon of gasoline).

Deceit
To be deceived one must reasonably rely upon an intentional misrepresentation and be injured as a result.

Damages

The plaintiff must suffer damages or he cannot recover money damages for fraud. Generally, the measure of damages is equal to the value the property would have been had the property been delivered as represented, less the actual price paid for the property.

Fraud in Inducement

In the usual case of fraud, the defrauded party knows what he is signing, but his consent has been induced by fraud; mutual assent is present and a contract is formed, but the contract is voidable because of the fraud. For example, seller induces buyer to purchase seller's Cadillac for $5,000, representing that the car has been driven only 25,000 miles. Before payment and delivery, buyer learns that the car was actually driven 95,000 miles. Buyer may rescind the transaction because of seller's fraud in the inducement.

Such contracts are voidable by the injured party. To avoid the contract, the defrauded person must rescind it by giving prompt notice and offering to return the consideration received, if any.

Fraud in Execution

In a fraud in the execution type of case, the defrauded party does not know what he is signing because of deceit as to the nature of the document or does not intend to enter into a contract at all. Since mutual assent is lacking, the contract is void and may be disregarded without the necessity of rescission. For example, when a party who is unable to read English signs a release relying on the representation of the insurance agent that the instrument is only a receipt, the contract is void.

Silence as Fraud

Generally, silence is not fraud, although there are several exceptions:

1. Where the parties are in a fiduciary or confidential relationship with each other, such as an attorney and client, there is a duty to speak and to make full disclosure of all facts relevant to the transaction. Failure to do so can be fraud. For example, an attorney knows that certain land owned by the client is going to increase in value because a certain corporation needs the land and plans to buy it. If the attorney wants to buy the land and later sell it to the corporation, the attorney must inform the client of the fact that the corporation is planning to buy the land.

2. Where there is a hidden defect, there is a duty to disclose (e.g., S sells cattle to B, knowing the cattle have Texas fever—which is not easily ascertainable on inspection—without informing B of the disease, or seller fails to inform buyer that a certain house is subject to flooding from the neighboring river).

3. Active concealment, or a half-truth, can be actionable fraud (e.g., auto dealer puts foreign substance in motor to conceal engine defect).

4. Important provisions that are concealed in the fine print are generally unenforceable.

Fraud in the Inducement
Fraud which is intended to and does cause one to make a contract or sign a document knowing what it contains but misled as to the true facts of the situation.

Fraud in the Execution
Fraud that occurs when the defrauded party signs one agreement believing it to be something else.

Hidden Defect
A defect not readily apparent upon a reasonable inspection.

De Joseph v. Zambelli
392 Pa. 24, 139 A.2d 644 (1958).

Dannehower, President Judge This is an action in equity by a purchaser of real estate seeking a rescission and cancellation of a deed, and the recovery of the purchase price, $18,000.00, together with costs and expenses incidental thereto, from the defendant vendors, on the grounds of false and fraudulent representations inducing the sale. . . .

The evidence discloses that the defendants' vendors had knowledge of the existence of termites in their premises as early as May, 1952, and that they persisted in attempts to check and abate them until May, 1955, when the property was sold to the plaintiff. This is established clearly by the testimony of the tenants in the second floor apartment who were disinterested parties to the controversy. . . .

It was further disclosed that the basement had been given a heavy application of paint or whitewash shortly before the plaintiff first inspected the premises in February, 1955. According to the description of one witness, the basement looked like a "white sepulcher". In addition, the joists were partially obscured by shelves laden with jars and articles of clothing, and in some areas, strips of wood had been attached with the apparent purpose of concealing the more obvious termite damage. As a result of this deception and concealment the latent defects in the joists could not be detected and were not susceptible of discovery except by expert investigation.

The inference is inescapable that the defendants knew that the dwelling was infested with termites and were aware of the serious deterioration of the joists when the property was offered for sale to the plaintiff. The reply to the plaintiff's inquiry that the joists were "as good as new" was therefore a false, material and erroneous statement of fact.

. . . Where a party is induced to enter into a transaction with another by means of the latter's fraud or material misrepresentation, such a transaction can be avoided by the innocent party. Fraud arises where the misrepresentation is knowingly false, where there is a concealment calculated to deceive, or where there is a nonprivileged failure to disclose. . . .

Applying the above principles to the case at bar, we are of the opinion that the defendants are guilty of fraud in the purposeful concealment of the termite condition in the premises, and in misrepresenting to the plaintiff that the joists in the basement were "as good as new". This being true we must conclude that the plaintiff is entitled to avoid the transaction and be returned to status quo.

Stipulation

As we saw in the last chapter, a party cannot avoid the legal effects of fraud by an exculpatory clause or stipulation in the contract that no misrepresentation has occurred in reaching the agreement or that any right based on fraud has been waived by the parties. Such provisions are against public policy and are unenforceable.

Questions

1. How can you reconcile the decision in the capsulated case, "Cannady v. *Cossey* (*et ux* means "and spouse") with the reported court case of *De Joseph* v. *Zambelli?*
2. What are essential elements that must be proved to establish fraud?
3. What is the difference between fraud in the inducement and fraud in the inception or execution? Give an example of each.
4. What is the legal effect of an innocent misrepresentation?
5. When does silence constitute fraud or misrepresentation? Give some examples.

7.2 Mistake, Duress, and Undue Influence

Mutual Mistake of Fact

Mutual Mistake
Error on the part of both parties regarding the same fact.

When both parties to a contract are mistaken and neither is at fault or both are equally at fault, such mistake prevents the creation of an enforceable agreement. Such mutual mistake may involve the nature of the contract, the identify of the person with whom it is made, or the existence of the subject matter. Such mistake must relate to a material fact.

In the famous case of *Raffles* v. *Wichelhaus* (2 H. & C. 906), there was a contract to sell cotton to be shipped to the buyer on the ship *Peerless*. Unknown to the parties, there were two ships of that name departing from the same port but at different times. The buyer had in mind the ship that sailed earlier; the seller had in mind the ship that sailed later. No contract resulted. Hence, if neither party is to blame, or both are to blame, there is no contract.

Similarly, where the subject matter, or something essential to performance, ceases to exist before the agreement is reached, there is no contract. Thus, S makes a contract to sell a horse to B. However, unknown to either party, the horse has been destroyed. There is no contract. The UCC follows the same rule if the loss is total (all the goods are destroyed). However, if the loss is partial, the buyer may accept the partial amount of goods with due allowances from the contract price but without further right against the seller (§ 2–613).

Mistake of Value

Value
The price a willing buyer would pay a willing seller in a voluntary sale where both have knowledge of the relevant facts.

While a mutual mistake as to the price can prevent the formation of a contract, a mutual mistake as to value will not permit rescission. Value is a subjective determination, and each person may have a different idea as to what a thing is worth. This is an ordinary risk in business transactions, and unless the agreement is unconscionable, the courts will not grant relief. For example, a woman in Wisconsin found a rough stone that looked like a topaz. Thinking it might be worth something, she took it to a jewelry store to sell it. The jeweler did not know the true value of the stone but nevertheless offered her one dollar for it, which the woman accepted. Later, it was discovered that the stone was an uncut diamond worth $700. The court held that the sale was valid and could not be set aside. The parties did not know what the stone was or its value. Each party assumed the risk that the value might be more or less than one dollar. There was no fraud or misrepresentation.

Unilateral Mistake

Generally, a one-sided or unilateral mistake does not justify avoidance of a contract. However, if it were caused by the defendant or the defendant had reason to know that there was a material mistake of fact, the court may void the agreement. A common example in which relief may be granted for a unilateral mistake occurs when a contractor submits a bid for a construction job and makes a material mistake in his computation that is obvious to the other party. In such cases, the courts have ruled that it would be unconscionable to hold the contractor to the bid when the other party knows of the unfairness in ample time for corrective action.

Unilateral Mistake
A mistake on the part of only one of the parties.

Beaver v. Harris' Estate
67 Wn.2d 621, 409 P.2d 143 (1965).

Bradford, Judge Plaintiff brought this action against Urban Harris and Marjorie Harris, his wife, for personal injuries received in an automobile accident. Urban Harris has since died and his estate substituted as defendant. . . .

The defendant answered and alleged . . . a settlement contract with the plaintiff wherein the plaintiff received $1,750 for a full, complete and final release of the defendant for all injuries known and unknown sustained in the accident. Plaintiff presented his case on the theory there had been a mutual mistake of a material fact and the release should be rescinded. The defendant contended the release was valid and a complete defense, and the court should have determined this as a matter of law.

The primary question raised by this appeal is, can a person who has been injured in an accident caused by another's negligence rescind or set aside a general release and bring an action for damages where there is no allegation or proof of fraud, overreaching, questionable conduct, misrepresentation or any indication of incapacity of the party signing the release?

The facts are that on May 22, 1962, plaintiff was driving his automobile in a southerly direction along Aurora Avenue in Seattle. Urban Harris, at the same time, drove his car from the east side of the street to a traffic channel in the center of Aurora, stopped, and then started on across. There is a dispute as to whether the cars actually made contact. The plaintiff swerved to avoid the defendant driver, left the road, glanced off a pole, jumped the curb and ended up against a concrete abutment. The weather was misty and the pavement was wet. The plaintiff's face was bleeding and he seemed badly shaken. The plaintiff called his doctor, Virgel Anderson, on the evening of the accident and the doctor prescribed muscle relaxants, pain killers and equanil. Plaintiff complained of headaches, painful cervical spine, and pain through his low back area. . . .

Plaintiff consulted regularly with his doctor from the date of the accident until he was discharged to return to work on June 20, 1962. Les Winder, an adjuster for defendant's insurance company, first contacted the plaintiff on May 23, 1962. He and the plaintiff had six or seven talks between this date and June 14, when plaintiff signed a settlement and release, receiving a check for $1,750. . . .

When plaintiff signed the release, he believed he had a strained back. Medical testimony, based on examinations made after August 12, indicated plaintiff had a herniated disc when he settled.

It is a well recognized principle of law that, before a plain, unambiguous instrument can be set aside on the ground of mutual mistake, the evidence must be clear and convincing. . . .

There is ample authority holding a mutual mistake must be one involving both parties, a mistake independently made by each party.

In the case now being considered, the only information of plaintiff's condition was from the plaintiff himself. Defendant had no independent knowledge and

> he accepted plaintiff's own diagnosis and opinion of his injuries. If there was a mistake, it was a unilateral mistake, rather than a mutual mistake. . . .
> The judgment is reversed and plaintiff's complaint dismissed on the merits.

Exceptions

When a party signs a contract, it is presumed that he read and understood it before signing it; thus, the general rule is that he is bound by the agreement. Ignorance through one's own negligence or through inexcusable trustfulness usually does not excuse one from his contractual obligations. The following are some exceptions to this rule:

1. Fraud or other wrongful act on the part of the other party.
2. Misrepresentation by the other party of the character of the paper (signer thinks he is signing a receipt, but it is a contract).
3. A situation in which a reasonable person would not think that the paper contained contractual provisions (e.g., a hat check stub containing provisions in fine print or an "Acknowledgment of Order" printed form that contained provisions for arbitration and the exclusion of warranties in fine print at the bottom of the form).

Mistake of Law

Mistake of Law Exceptions

Mistake of Law
One's ignorance of the legal consequences of an act.

In most states, a mistake of law will not afford grounds for rescission (e.g., buying property for a use that would violate a zoning restriction). This rule has been criticized and some of the exceptions to it include the following:

1. Fraud or undue influence.
2. The mistake's resulting in a failure of the contract to express the agreement (e.g., parties mutually agree on the terms of a contract and choose legal phrases that in legal effect express a meaning different from that agreed upon).
3. In those states where a special statute treats a mistake of law as a mistake of fact (e.g., California Civil Code Section 1578).

Duress

Duress
Unlawful threats or action by one person that compels another to do what otherwise would not have been done.

Duress consists of a wrongful act that compels assent through fear and makes the contract voidable. Duress can be of the person (i.e., unlawful confinement of the party, spouse, child, etc.) or of goods (i.e., unlawful detention of property of the party). For example, it is duress for an attorney or accountant to refuse to give a client important papers unless the client agrees to pay a higher fee than originally agreed upon (*Thompson Crane & Trucking Co.* v. *Eyman*, 123 Cal.App.2d 904, 267 P.2d 1043 [1954]).

Economic Compulsion

There is a modern trend to expand the rule of duress to include coercion in business transactions. To prove such duress by business or economic compulsion, it is generally necessary to establish that the victim would suffer irreparable loss or near financial ruin for which there could be no adequate recovery from the wrongdoer. For example, seller refuses to deliver needed goods to a buyer who cannot get the goods from any other seller unless the buyer pays a higher price than that set by the contract.

Economic Compulsion
The threat of irreparable loss or financial ruin as a form of economic duress.

Threat of Criminal Prosecution

The general rule is that the act of duress must be unlawful—either a tort or a crime. The threat of criminal prosecution can be duress. However, the threat to file a civil suit is not duress, since anyone has a right to bring civil actions to settle a dispute. For example, suppose that Robert Jones embezzles money from Kevin Smith, his employer. Smith tells Jones's father that he will not ask the district attorney to prosecute Jones if the father will make full restitution. Such threat of criminal prosecution, direct or indirect, is duress. However, a statement by Smith that he is going to sue Jones and his father for the money taken would not constitute duress.

McIntosh v. McIntosh
209 Cal.App.2d 371, 26 Cal.Rptr. 26 (1962).

Shepard, Justice. This is an appeal from a judgment . . . in regard to enforcement of a divorce decree. . . .

During the trial, sharply conflicting testimony was had regarding whether plaintiff had written and signed an alleged waiver of alimony voluntarily or involuntarily. . . .

It appears from the record that plaintiff, about November 24, 1959, gave birth to an illegitimate child by a man named Glessner. On December 2, 1959, plaintiff wrote, signed and mailed to defendant a waiver of further alimony and a promise that when the family home (which had been awarded her by the divorce decree) was sold, she would divide the proceeds with defendant. The principal controversy between the parties involves the question of validity of said waiver. Defendant's testimony, if believed, would support the conclusion that the waiver was voluntary and for a consideration. However, plaintiff testified that on November 13, 1959, defendant beat plaintiff severely, broke part of the furniture, and threatened to kill her; that thereafter defendant made further and repeated threats to kill her, that he would burn her house down, bring her into court on a charge of adultery, and take her son and daughter away from her; that she was afraid then that if she did not send defendant the written waiver defendant would kill or injure her; that immediately prior to her writing of the waiver, defendant telephoned her and dictated its contents; that when she wrote the waiver she was worried sick and didn't know what she was doing. From the foregoing we are satisfied that the trial court was justified in finding that plaintiff was coerced into writing the waiver by fear of personal injury or death at the hands of defendant; that said fear was induced by the beating of November 13, 1959, coupled with the subsequent threats of defendant; that the waiver was not the voluntary act of plaintiff and was invalid. . . .

> Under the modern doctrine there is no standard of courage or firmness with which the victim of duress must comply at the risk of being without remedy; the question is merely whether the pressure applied did in fact so far affect the individual concerned as to deprive him of contractual volition; if it did there is duress, if it did not there is none. . . .
>
> The judgment is affirmed [for plaintiff].

Undue Influence

Undue Influence
If one party unduly influences the other into an agreement they have not dealt on equal terms and the contract is voidable.

Undue influence is the unlawful control exercised by one person over another so as to substitute his will for the volition of the victim. It is a kind of mental coercion that destroys the free agency of one and constrains the person to do that which is against his will and that which he would not have done if left to his own judgment and volition so that his act becomes the act of the one exerting the influence rather than his own act. However, mere appeals to affection or understanding are not considered undue influence, nor is mere advice or fair argument and persuasion. Normally a gift occasioned by gratitude for kindness or affection is not undue influence.

In most states, undue influence makes the contract voidable and subject to ratification. However, in some states, the remedy is limited to rescission (i.e., there can be no affirmance *and* recovery of damages).

In most states where a confidential relationship exists between the parties (e.g., attorney and client, guardian and ward, trustee and beneficiary, parent and child), the confidential relationship raises a presumption of undue influence and places upon the dominant party the burden of establishing fairness of the transaction and evidence that it was the free act of the other party.

In some states, although no presumption of undue influence arises from a parent-child relationship, if dominance of the child is found to exist in fact, the burden is on the parent to establish the fairness of the transaction. In the absence of a presumption of undue influence, the person seeking to set aside the transaction must prove that by misrepresentation and deception the alleged victim was led into doing something that he would not have done but for the misrepresentation and deception. In the following case, the court held that undue influence was present and set aside the deed.

Facts
The plaintiff was an 82-year-old invalid, severely ill and completely dependent upon his son, the defendant, and his other twelve children. The plaintiff could not read or write English. The defendant was the primary person who advised the plaintiff and handled his business affairs, although the other sons helped to some degree. The plaintiff deeded his farm to the defendant for $23,500, the original purchase price. However, at the time of the transaction, the farm was worth between $145,000 and $160,000.

Decision
The court found that a confidential relationship existed between the plaintiff and the defendant that resulted in superiority and opportunity for influence, that the plain-

tiff was an invalid at the time of the conveyance, and that the plaintiff's mental acuity was impaired and he sometimes suffered from disorientation and lapse of memory. The court held that the presumption of undue influence was raised by the plaintiff's prima facie case and that the defendant failed to rebut it.

Schaneman v. Schaneman, 206 Neb. 113, 291 N.W.2d 412 (1980).

Questions

1. Explain the differences between a mutual mistake of fact, a unilateral mistake of fact, and a mistake of law.
2. Where there was no fraud or unconscionability but you are mistaken as to the value of an item you bought and want to rescind the contract, what are your legal rights?
3. What is meant by economic duress or business compulsion?
4. Considering the cost and inconvenience involved, why doesn't the threat of filing a civil action amount to duress?
5. Suppose a man's wife keeps nagging him, threatens to abandon him, refuses to sleep with him, and suggests a divorce unless he deeds some property to her. If he does so to quiet her, would a court rescind the transfer because of undue influence?

7.3 Unconscionability

In Chapter 5.1 we learned that unconscionable contracts, or unconscionable clauses in contracts, are unenforceable. UCC Article 2, Section 302, states that if a court as a matter of law finds a contract or any clause in it to have been unconscionable at the time it was made, the court may refuse to enforce the contract, or it may enforce the rest of the contract without the unconscionable clause. It may also limit the application of the unconscionable clause as to avoid any unconscionable result. Since it is made a matter of law, it is for the court, not the jury, to determine in each case what would be a just agreement. The basic test is whether, considering the business background and commercial needs in a particular case, the clauses involved are so one-sided as to be unconscionable under the circumstances existing at the time of the making of the contract.

Unconscionable
A contract that is unreasonably unfair to one of the parties is unconscionable and unenforceable.

Definition

Neither the statutes nor the courts have explicitly defined the term *unconscionable,* but an old English definition has been adopted and cited in many cases. It held that an unconscionable bargain is one "such as no man in his senses and not under delusion would make on the one hand, and no honest or fair man would accept, on the other."

Elements

The courts have held that the term *unconscionable* contains both procedural and substantive elements. Procedural unconscionability has to do with the contract formation process, which includes such things as high-pressure sales tactics, failure to disclose the terms of the agreement, misrepresentation or fraud on the part of the seller, a refusal to bargain on crucial terms, clauses hidden in the fine print, and unequal bargaining power. Substantive unconscionability involves the use of oppressive terms in the contract itself, such as inflated prices, unfair disclaimers, and cut-off clauses.

Unequal Bargain Power

Typical cases involve high-pressure salespeople and language-handicapped, uneducated, or poor persons who contract away their basic rights. Usually, the courts find that unequal bargaining power, coupled with unscrupulous dealings by one party, results in an unenforceable, unconscionable contract. Some courts use the test of the absence of meaningful choice on the part of one of the parties together with contract terms that are unreasonably favorable to the other party.

Disclaimer

Disclaimer
An express or implied denial of certain things in issue.

We discussed public policy in Subchapter 6.3, and many of the same principles are involved in unconscionability. Exculpatory or disclaimer clauses in contracts are typical. For example, California follows the modern view that a contract exempting from liability for ordinary negligence is valid where no public interest is involved or no statute expressly prohibits it. But what is the test to determine the public interest?

Facts

Gardner took his 1976 Porsche to be repaired at defendant's shop and signed a form repair order with this disclaimer: "NOT RESPONSIBLE FOR LOSS OR DAMAGE TO CARS OR ARTICLES LEFT IN CARS IN CASE OF FIRE, THEFT, OR ANY OTHER CAUSE BEYOND OUR CONTROL." While it was parked in the repair garage, the car was stolen as a result of defendant's negligence. Gardner sued and got judgment for $16,000. The defendant appealed.

Decision

Affirmed, since the disclaimer was invalid. The court applied a six-step criterion. *First*, the business was licensed and regulated; *second*, the shop performed a service of great importance to the public; *third*, defendant held itself out as willing to perform the service for anyone owning the type of auto it was equipped to repair; *fourth*, defendant had a decisive advantage of bargaining strength against a member of the public seeking its services; *fifth*, defendant confronts the public with a standardized "adhesion" contract of exculpation, incorporated in a printed form "repair order," which all customers are expected to sign; and *sixth*, plaintiff's car was placed under the control of the defendant and thereby subject to the risk of carelessness by defendant.

Gardner v. Downtown Porsche Audi, 180 Cal.App.3d 713, 225 Cal.Rptr. 757 (1986).

Adhesion Contracts

In some jurisdictions, unconscionable contracts are referred to as contracts of adhesion. This term signifies a standardized contract that, imposed and drafted by the party of superior bargaining strength, leaves the other party only the opportunity to adhere to it or reject it. The ideal concept of freedom and equality in bargaining is hardly present in such standardized contracts. Yet these contracts play a very important part in our everyday life. Our travel by rail, ship, or airplane is under standard terms. Insurance policies are made under standardized conditions. We rent houses or rooms under standardized leases. Authors and broadcasters sign standard agreements. This practice has caused a recent trend in many courts to modify or nullify harsh terms that defeat the reasonable expectations of the parties. Mass-produced agreements with boilerplate clauses permit the stronger party to dictate terms to the weaker party.

Adhesion Contract
A contract usually on a standard form and presented on a "take it or leave it" basis so that there is no true equality in bargaining power between the parties.

Boilerplate
Standard or formal language used in legal documents.

Standard Clauses

Under systems of mass production and distribution, such standardization allows forms to be tailored to office routines, simplifies operations, and reduces costs to the advantage of all parties. Most parties offering such contracts do not expect the customers to understand or even read the standard terms, and the customers usually do not. Such forms are customarily prepared by one party, and the drafters may be tempted to write them to further the interests of their employers. Such action has led to government regulation of insurance policies, bills of lading, installment contacts, loan agreements, and other specific types of contracts. Terms in such regulated contracts may be superseded by the adding or writing in of different clauses. When this has been done, the courts will interpret such changes against the drafters and subject them to the overriding obligation of good faith. The courts will then refuse to enforce any contract or term deemed unconscionable. In interpreting and applying standardized contracts, they seek to meet the reasonable expectations of the average member of the public who accepts such a contract.

Most courts in ruling on the unconscionable question take a balancing approach and require a certain amount of procedural along with some substantive unconscionability.

Facts

Chanda, a medical doctor, read that home movies would last longer if transferred to videotape, so he took his film to Fotomat for that purpose. He was given a standard warranty form to sign that said damage for negligence was limited to replacement cost of unexposed film. He read the warranty, asked the clerk about it, and signed it. The films, which were movies of his honeymoon, graduation, children growing up, and vacations he had taken, were lost and never found. Dr. Chanda sued for negligence, and a jury awarded him $9,500. Fotomat appealed.

Decision

For Fotomat. Unconscionability is the absence of meaningful choice on the part of one of the parties together with contract terms that are unreasonably favorable to the other. Two elements are required—substantive, which means the contract itself is unreasonable and unfair, and procedural, which involves the circumstances surrounding each party at the time the contract was made. This type of disclaimer was common in the industry and filled a commercial need to keep the cost reasonable. The agreement itself was not "so unconscionable that no decent, fair-minded person would view the ensuing result without being possessed of a profound sense of injustice." Dr. Chanda was made aware of the provisions, had dealt with them many times before, and consented to the terms. There was no "oppression and unfair surprise" because of a superior bargaining power, but only an allocation of risks. Dr. Chanda can recover only the replacement cost of the lost film.

Fotomat Corp. of Fla. v. *Chanda,* 464 So.2d 626 (Fla. App. 1985).

Flexibility

Flexibility
The quality of being adaptable and adjustable to change.

When General Motors marketed an automatic transmission, knowing that it was inferior and that the warranty was inadequate to protect the consumer, a New York court found such warranty clause to be an unconscionable contractual provision. It held that the concept was a flexible one to be applied to the facts in each case and that an unconscionable clause was one that no person in his right senses would make and that no honest and fair person would accept. (*State by Abrams* v. *GMC,* 120 Misc.2d 371, 466 N.Y.S.2d 124 [1983]).

D & W Cent. Station Alarm Co. v. Yep
126 Misc.2d 37, 480 N.Y.S.2d 1015 (1984).

The facts simply are that an agreement for installation and rental of certain specified burglar alarm equipment was signed by plaintiff and defendant on April 29, 1980. Paragraph 2 of the said agreement calls for defendant to pay an $80 installation fee, plus installments of $35 per month, or a total of $420 for "each year of the term . . . as rent for the use of said electrical protection apparatus." . . .

The dollar amounts, and the monthly installments filled-in spaces are occupied by handwritten letters in ink much larger than the surrounding printed agreement terms, and are easily legible. Then, in ultra-fine print, the agreement states in Paragraph 2 following the filled-in blanks that such monthly or annual payments are "terminable on the fifth anniversary of the effective date this system is operative."

Buried in the same size ultra-fine print of paragraph 3 of the agreement is the clause: "In the event of a default in the payment of the above mentioned installments . . . the entire balance for the entire term herein shall immediately become due and payable and the subscriber shall be liable therefor." This paragraph is usually known as an *"acceleration clause"*. . . .

The Court in inspecting the agreement finds that the filled-in notations in the blank spaces provided on the front page of the two-page contract were quite prominent, as compared to the almost illegible and very small fine print in which the "five-year term" of the agreement was printed. That provision blended together with all the other fine print so that the eye could not easily, without repetitive effort or patience, identify that particular, substantial, and vital element of the agreement. When the Court now looks at the agreement it notes that the eye is first led to the written fill-ins, but the "five-year term" of the agreement, not being treated in the same manner as the fill-ins, becomes a hidden trap for the unwary customer. Such customer as a result, could easily be taken advantage of by the "contractor" who is in a superior bargaining position by virtue of his knowledge of the contents of his agreement.

After the date-unspecified installation of the equipment, defendant paid all monthly installments through August 31, 1981. Prior to August 1981, defendant, the operator of a boutique in a building wherein she was a tenant, was required by Court order to vacate the premises on or before August 31, 1981, since the owner was intent upon demolishing the building. . . .

Defendant's then attorney advised plaintiff in writing by letter dated August 28, 1981, of the tenant's imminently required vacating of the premises, and further advised plaintiff to remove its rented equipment which plaintiff accomplished on the evening of August 31, 1981. Thereafter, without even billing or otherwise making demand in writing of defendant for any monthly rental amounts allegedly due on and after September 1, 1981, or for any claimed accelerated amount for a balance due under the alleged "five-year term", plaintiff commenced this suit without further ado against defendant for forty-four months' rent at $35 per month, or $1,540. . . . She thought that the agreement was "for a monthly rental, and the equipment would be removed by plaintiff" when she was required to move her business. . . .

As the sole trier of the facts in this case, the Court gives credence to defendant's testimony. Defendant is an oriental woman obviously not born in this country, who has difficulty in speaking the English language, and who testified that she cannot read English even if it is in large type; and that she did not, nor could she read the twenty-two paragraphs of finely printed clauses contained in the two-page agreement much of which printed material appeared on the back of the agreement. This Court confesses that it also finds it most difficult to read. . . .

Defendant entered into the contract without having read or having understood its contents. The crucial "five-year term" of the agreement and the *"acceleration clause"* were not specifically pointed out to her. The Court finds that there could not have been a meeting of the minds of the parties with respect to the crucial terms of the agreement. Thus, the mistake of the defendant, and the misrepresentation of the plaintiff do not spell out an enforceable contract but one that is unenforceable because of unconscionability as a matter of law. The defendant should be relieved of any further obligation under the contract.

QUESTIONS

1. What is the difference between substantive and procedural unconscionability? Give examples of each.
2. What is meant by a contract of adhesion?
3. How is a determination made as to whether or not a contract or a clause therein is unconscionable?
4. Have you read all of the provisions of your automobile insurance contract? Do you understand them?
5. Should the courts protect people who are able to understand the language but still sign foolish contracts against their own best interests?

PROBLEMS

1. Husband had an insurance policy on his life for $10,000 payable to his wife as beneficiary. Husband did not return home one day and subsequently was missing for two years. Wife was having trouble paying the premiums on the policy. After a discussion with the insurance company's agent, wife decided to take a paid-up policy for $2,500 instead of the $10,000 policy. It was discovered later that

husband had been dead before the conversion to the $2,500 paid-up policy. Wife now demands the $10,000 payment from the insurance company. The insurance company will pay her only $2,500. Decision?

2. Builder submits a written offer to homeowner to erect a building for $54,000, and homeowner accepts the offer. Builder later discovers that he made a mistake of $20,000 and that the offer should have been for $74,000. Builder now seeks to be allowed to withdraw his offer and to have the contract rescinded because of this mistake. Decision?

3. Mrs. Reed was injured in a train accident. The insurance agent had her examined by a company physician shortly after the accident and while she was en route to her destination. The physician told her that she was not seriously injured. The insurance agent requested her to sign a release for damages for the consideration of $100, which she did. After completing her journey, Mrs. Reed discovered that she sustained serious injuries requiring hospitalization. She now seeks to have the release set aside by reason of the false representations made to her by the insurance agent and the physician. She testified that she could neither read nor write and signed the release with an X mark; that she knew little about the contents of the release; that she signed it a few hours after the accident without a chance to consult with friends, a doctor, or an attorney; and that she signed at the urgent solicitation of the claims agent who was with her on the train at the time of the accident. Decision?

4. To induce buyer to purchase a tract of land, seller stated that the land was low enough to be readily irrigable from a nearby irrigation ditch. Seller knew that his statement was false. Buyer consulted an irrigation expert about the possibility of getting water upon the land from the ditch and, apparently satisfied with the expert's opinion, purchased the land. Later, buyer discovers that the land was too high for irrigation from the nearby irrigation ditch and sues seller for damages for deceit. Decision?

5. Seller built a dwelling house directly over an old cesspool and, without making any reference to the unsanitary pit beneath the cellar floor, sold the new house to buyer. The house soon became uninhabitable because of the odor from the hidden refuse. Buyer sues seller for the deceit. Seller contends that he was merely silent as to the cesspool, and silence is not fraud. Decision?

6. Debtor owed creditor $1,000. Creditor tried every friendly gesture possible to get the debtor to pay but with no result. Finally, the creditor sent the debtor a letter as follows: "I have tried to be nice about this, but you simply will not cooperate. This is to inform you that unless I receive payment in full on or before Friday at 4:00 p.m., I am going to file a civil suit against you on Monday." Debtor claims creditor is using duress to collect the money. Decision?

7. Plaintiff contracted to buy a large herd of cattle from defendant and made an initial payment of $200,000. On the day of delivery of the cattle when plaintiff was to pay the balance of the purchase price, plaintiff discovered that 460 head of cattle were missing. Plaintiff insisted on deducting the value of the missing cattle from the purchase price. Defendant refused to deliver any of the cattle unless the entire balance called for by the contract was paid. Winter was approaching, and the cattle might be exposed to great loss unless properly cared for during the winter season. To obtain the cattle and to protect his initial payment, plaintiff paid the entire sum. Plaintiff now sues for the value of the missing 460 head of cattle. Defendant claims that since plaintiff paid for all of the cattle, he has no claim. Decision?

8. Sallie Beard, 70 years of age, a widow, feeble, in ill health, and entirely without business experience, made up her mind to withdraw her extensive funds from the bank and use them elsewhere. The bank officials, close relatives of Mrs. Beard's deceased husband, and their attorney, worried that the withdrawal would injure the bank, repeatedly urged Mrs. Beard not to withdraw the money but rather to sign a deed of trust with the bank as trustee. Mrs. Beard wanted to see her attorney but was persuaded not to see him. She was told that if she withdrew the money, the bank would not survive and her father-in-law would probably be influenced to ignore her in his will if she refused to execute the deed of trust. Finally, she executed the deed of trust. Later she discovered that the deed she signed took away all control over the funds and deprived her forever of any power to revoke the trust. She brings an action to have the deed declared void on the grounds of undue influence. Decision?

9. Mrs. Friedman, 75 years old and an artist's widow, made an agreement with Egan, an art gallery owner, to permanently transfer about 300 paintings to him. Egan agreed that he would try to sell the paintings and would pay to Mrs. Friedman half of whatever money he got for each painting. Mrs. Friedman died 15 years later, during which period Egan had sold only two paintings. The Friedman estate sued to recover the paintings on the grounds that the original contract had been unconscionable. Decide.

10. Steven bought a round-trip airplane ticket from Los Angeles to Dayton, Ohio, with the return trip including a flight from Terre Haute, Indiana. He also bought from a vending machine a $62,500 Fidelity and Casualty Company insurance policy for a $2.50 premium. He mailed the policy to the beneficiary, his wife, in the envelope provided by the machine. The return flight from Terre Haute was cancelled and after exhausting other attempts to get transportation, Steven took a chartered flight on a local air-taxi, which crashed, causing his death. The insurance company denied liability because of an exclusion clause printed in the policy that excepted "travel on other than scheduled air carriers." The widow sued on the policy. Decide.

CHAPTER EIGHT

Formalities

8.1 Conditions
Condition Defined
Condition Precedent
    Express and Implied Conditions
    Promise to Pay
Condition Concurrent
Condition Subsequent
Covenants
    Good Faith

8.2 Statute of Frauds
Purpose of Statute
Writing
    Sale of Goods Over $500
    Exceptions to Writing
    Minerals
    Timber
    Securities
    $5,000 Property
    Sale of Land
    Contracts of More Than One Year
    Contracts Performed Within One Year
    Employment Contracts
    Exceptions for Oral Contracts
Wills
Promise to Pay Another's Debt
Marriage as Consideration
Contract Modification

8.3 Parol Evidence Rule
Oral Negotiations and the Written Contract
The Rule as a Warning
Exceptions to the Rule
    Mistake of Fact
    Fraud
    Lack of Capacity
    Incomplete Contract
    Condition Precedent
    Conditional Clauses
Later Changes
Consideration
UCC Provisions

8.1 Conditions

Condition Defined

Condition
Something attached to or made a part of an agreement.

In law, a *condition* is a possible future act or event, the happening or nonhappening of which creates (condition precedent) or extinguishes (condition subsequent) a duty on the part of the promisor.

Condition Precedent

Condition Precedent
An act or event that must occur before the duty to perform a promise arises.

A *condition precedent* is an act that must be performed or an uncertain event that must occur—unless its nonoccurrence is excused—before performance under a contract becomes due. A promise may be dependent upon the happening or performance of more than one condition. The most familiar example of an act as a condition is the requirement found in most installment payment contracts for the sale of real or personal property that all payments shall be made before the buyer may demand transfer of title. Also, the seller usually has a duty to clear any defects and to produce a marketable title as a condition precedent to the buyer's obligation to pay.

Insurance policies usually have several conditions precedent required of the insured before the company's obligation to pay arises. These conditions may include premium payments, filing proof of loss, examination of the insured, and appraisal of property loss.

Demand for performance may be a condition precedent before filing suit, and notice by a tenant to the landlord may be a precedent to the latter's liability under a promise to repair.

Facts

Plaintiffs leased a building for a market and other purposes. The roof started to leak, and roofers advised the plaintiffs that the roof had to be replaced. The plaintiffs obtained competitive bids and had the job done for $8,800. Under their lease, the lessors were required to repair the roof except where caused by negligence or improper use. The plaintiffs never notified the lessors before the work was done of the need to make such repairs. The plaintiffs sued to recover the costs of the new roof. The trial court said that the defendants had a contractual right to control any trial or replacement, and the contract was breached by failure to give notice; however, the plaintiffs were entitled to restitution to prevent unjust enrichment. The lessors appealed.

Decision

The defendants' duty to repair was not unconditional. The defendants had a right to determine whether the repairs were caused by the tenants' negligence or by improper use. Therefore, notice was a condition precedent and indispensable to carry out the intention of the parties. Further, there cannot be a valid express contract and an implied contract at the same time embracing the same subject matter. At best, this was a unilateral mistake by the plaintiffs, and they are not entitled to recovery.

Wal-Noon Corp. v. Hill, 45 Cal.App.3d 605, 119 Cal.Rptr. 646 (1975).

FORMALITIES

A promisor who makes an absolute or unconditional promise is bound to perform when the time arrives. However, if the promisor makes a conditional promise, he binds himself to perform only if the condition precedent occurs or he is relieved from the duty to perform if the condition subsequent occurs.

Express and Implied Conditions

Conditions can be express or implied. *Express conditions* are those that are stated in the contract as the intent of the parties. *Implied conditions* can be implied in fact, by interpretation of the contract itself, or implied by law, irrespective of intent, to avoid injustice. In the case regarding the roof repair, the requirement that the lessee give notice to the lessor to make the latter liable under his covenant to repair was an implied condition precedent.

Promise to Pay

A promise to pay money from the net profits of a business would be an example of an event as a condition precedent—the actual making of profits. Also, a promise to pay "when able" would be conditioned upon the ability to pay. Entitlements to vacation pay under many collective bargaining agreements have a condition precedent of active employment on a certain date.

Condition Concurrent

Conditions concurrent are mutually dependent conditions precedent that are to be performed at the same time. For example, in the typical sale of real property, delivery of the deed and payment of the purchase price are concurrent conditions, and there must be performance or tender by one party before the other is in default. This is usually accomplished by deposit of the money and the instruments in escrow, where a third party completes the transfer. The same principle applies to most sales of personal property, where the delivery of the goods and payment of the price are conditions concurrent.

Condition Concurrent
Mutual conditions precedent where the parties are to perform at the same time.

Condition Subsequent

A *condition subsequent* refers to a future event, upon the happening of which the obligation of the other party ceases. For example, an inventor transfers his patent rights to a corporation on condition that it manufacture and sell at least 5,000 of the items each year, and upon failure to do so, the rights revert to the inventor so that he can reassign them. An employment contract for a long period of time is made terminable upon the sale of the employer's business or if the employee is called into military service. These are valid conditions subsequent.

Condition Subsequent
A future event which ends the duty of the other party to perform the contract.

Facts

Decedent applied for life insurance and paid the first premium in full. While an additional medical examination was pending, he was killed. A clause in the policy stated that if the first premium was paid, the insurance would be in force, provided that the company was satisfied of the insured's acceptability at the date of application, and if not so satisfied, no insurance would be in force until delivery of the policy. The company argued that acceptability was a condition precedent to the existence of the contract and denied liability.

Decision

The clause was ambiguous but was really a condition subsequent, meaning that the contract of insurance arose on payment of the premium, subject to termination upon dissatisfaction with the risk. "There is an obvious advantage to the company in obtaining payment of the premium when the application is made, and it would be unconscionable to permit the company, after using language to induce payment of the premium at that time, to escape the obligation which an ordinary applicant would reasonably believe had been undertaken by the insurer."

Ransom v. Penn Mutual Life Ins. Co., 43 Cal.2d 420, 274 P.2d 633 (1954).

Although the courts are reluctant to imply conditions in contracts, they do so where the implication arises from the language of the agreement. This occurs when it would be necessary to effectuate the intent of the parties, where it was clearly within the contemplation of the parties but they deemed it unnecessary to express it, where a legal necessity exists, or where it can rightfully be assumed that had their attention been called to it the parties would have expressed the condition.

Covenants

Covenant
A promise to do or not to do something.

Covenants are merely promises to render some performance. Where a condition is required but doesn't happen, the performance is excused, and the other party cannot recover damages. However, in the case of breach of covenant, a cause of action for damages exists, and the performance may not be excused.

Good Faith

Good Faith
Honesty in fact and a sincere intention to fulfill one's obligations.

Most courts will imply in every contract a covenant by each party not to do anything that will deprive the other parties thereto of the benefits of the contract. This is often referred to as an *implied covenant of good faith and fair dealing*. For example, the defendant sold to the plaintiff his interest in a partnership and its assets, including the goodwill, and covenanted not to engage in the same business in the same city for one year. After the year was up, he began a competing business and directly solicited customers of the former partnership who were now the customers of the plaintiff. The court held that this direct solicitation of the plaintiff's customers was a violation of an implied covenant of fair dealing (*Bergum v. Weber*, 136 Cal.App.2d 389, 288 P.2d 623 [1955]).

Questions

1. How do conditions precedent affect contracts? Give some examples.
2. Give some examples of conditions concurrent.
3. How does a condition subsequent differ from a condition precedent?
4. What is the difference between a condition and a covenant?
5. When will the courts imply conditions and covenants?

8.2 Statute of Frauds

Some people believe that all contracts must be in writing. Otherwise, they wonder, how can one prove the existence of the contract and its provisions? In fact, only a few types of contracts are required to be in writing, and even then there are exceptions.

An oral contract is proved in court by the parties to the agreement and by witnesses, if any. At a trial there is often conflicting testimony and confusion about the actual terms of the contract, in which case it is difficult for the judge or the jury to make a correct decision. If the contract is in writing, it is less likely to wind up in litigation. A saying attributed to movie mogul Sam Goldwyn states, "An oral contract is not worth the paper it's written on."

Most contracts are important enough—or there is such an opportunity for fraud in the making of the contract—that every state has a statute of frauds declaring which type of contracts must be in writing. These statutes differ only in their classifications of contracts required to be written. This subchapter considers the most common and important types of these contracts.

Statute of Frauds
Statutory requirement that certain types of contracts be in writing to be enforceable.

Purpose of Statute

Perhaps statute of frauds is a misnomer, since the statute has nothing to do with the law of frauds discussed in Chapter 6. The original statute was passed in England in 1677, and its title was "An Act for the Prevention of Frauds and Perjuries," which was shortened to "Statute of Frauds," which still persists. The real purpose of the law was to cut down the number of fraud and perjury incidents related to contracts by requiring certain types of common agreements to be put in writing. Perhaps a better name for the law would be the statute of writings, since it requires certain contracts to be in writing and signed by the party "to be charged" (not necessarily the paying party, but the one who is the defendant in a lawsuit) in order to be enforced by the court.

Writing

The writing required may be a note or memorandum, may be informal, and may consist of one or more writings (e.g., separate escrow instructions

Writing
Many acts are required to be set forth in a written instrument in order to have legal effect.

and signed by one of the parties, or two letters). The writing may be made at the time the agreement is entered into or at a later date. The writing should meet the test of reasonable certainty and should contain the names of the parties, the subject matter, the terms and conditions of all the promises, and by whom and to whom made. Under this rule, the absence of a description of the property or the names of the parties in the sale of real estate is fatal.

Under the UCC, which is applicable to the sale of goods, the test of reasonable certainty has been greatly relaxed. A check in the seller's hands may be held to be a sufficient memorandum of the sale if it refers to the goods in question. The seller's indorsement is evidence of receipt and acceptance.

Under the UCC, signature of the party includes any symbol executed or adopted by a party with the intention of authenticating a writing (§ 1–201[39]). Authentication may be printed, stamped, or written. It may be by initials or by thumbprint. In *Automotive Spares Corp.* v. *Archer Bearings Co.* (382 F.Supp. 513 [(N.D.Ill. 1974]), the court held that authentication may be on any part of the document and in appropriate cases may be found in a billhead or letterhead.

Sale of Goods Over $500

Section 2–201(1) of the UCC states that a contract for the sale of goods for the price of $500 or more is not enforceable unless there is some writing sufficient to indicate that a contract for sale has been made between the parties. (See UCC § 2–105 in Appendix A for definition of *goods*). The writing must be signed by the defendant (the party against whom enforcement is sought), who is the one denying the contract or some of its provisions. The writing may be informal, since the only purpose of the rule is for the parties to establish that there is in fact a contract for the sale and purchase of goods. Although details regarding price, place of delivery, etc., may be omitted, the quantity must be stated unless it is a "need" or "output" agreement. (Refer to Subchapter 5.3.)

Exceptions to Writing

There are exceptions to the above rule.

1. Section 2–201(2) states that as between merchants, an oral contract of sale is enforceable if one of the merchants sends a written confirmation of the contract to the other merchant and the merchant receiving the information does not object to the contents of the confirmation within ten days after receiving it. Both merchants are bound (i.e., the merchant who signed the confirmation and the merchant who received it and failed to object). (For a definition of *merchant,* see UCC § 2–104 in Appendix A. A farmer was held to be a merchant in *Campbell* v. *Yokel* [20 Ill.App.3d 702, 313 N.E.2d 628 (1974)].)

2. Section 2–201(3)(a) states that a writing is not necessary if the goods are to be specially manufactured for the buyer and if, before receiving repudiation by the buyer, the seller has made a substantial beginning of the goods' manufacture or has made commitments for their procurement

Goods
All types of property except real estate and some legal documents.

Party to be Charged
The party sought to be bound by the contract, usually the defendant.

Merchants
Persons who deal in goods or hold themselves out as experts in dealing with goods involved in a transaction.

and the goods are not suitable for sale to others in the ordinary course of the seller's business. The following case illustrates this section.

Facts

Plaintiff sued defendant for damages because defendant refused to accept certain shoes manufactured for him. Defendant ordered one hundred dozen "brog. oxford" shoes from plaintiff. The shoe is specially made, very fancy, and of an unusual size. The shoes were not suitable for sale in the ordinary course of business. The price was over $500.

Decision

Because the transaction comes within § 2–201(3)(a), the contract did not have to be in writing.

Adams v. *Cohen*, 242 Mass. 17, 136 N.E. 183 (1922).

3. Section (2)–201(3)(c) states that the contract does not have to be in writing if payment for the goods has been made and accepted or the goods have been received and accepted by the buyer. If the goods have been partly paid for or partially delivered, the oral contract is enforceable only to the extent of the partial payment or partial delivery. However, when the goods are not divisible, such as an automobile, part payment will be sufficient to make the contract totally enforceable.

Starr v. Freeport Dodge, Inc.
54 Misc.2d 271, 282 N.Y.S.2d 58 (1967).

Bernard Tomson, Judge Plaintiff's action is for breach of contract and arises out of the attempted purchase by him of a new automobile from the corporate defendant, a car dealer, through the individual defendant, the salesman involved in the transaction. The plaintiff alleges that he signed an order form for a new automobile which described the subject matter of the sale, the price, which was in excess of $500, and the identity of both buyer and seller. The form is not signed by the dealer. . . .

It further appears that the plaintiff made a $25 down payment to the dealer, which was accepted by the dealer and for which deposit a credit was noted on the form. . . .

The defendants urge that there was no contract between the parties and that the order form, unsigned as it is by the dealer, falls within the purview of Section 2–201 of the Uniform Commercial Code as unenforceable since it was not signed by the party to be charged.

Section 2–201 of the UCC provides in part as follows:

(1) Except as otherwise provided in this section a contract for the sale of goods for the price of $500 or more is not enforceable by way of action or defense unless there is some writing sufficient to indicate that a contract for sale has been made between the parties and signed by the party against whom enforcement is sought or by his authorized agent or broker. . . .

(3) A contract which does not satisfy the requirements of subsection (1) but which is valid in other respects is enforceable. . . .

> (c) with respect to goods for which payment has been made and accepted or which have been received and accepted (Section 2–606). . . .
>
> Under the code, part payment takes the case out of the statute only to the extent for which payment has been made. . . .
>
> Even if subparagraph (c) validates, as the writers seem unanimously to agree, a divisible contract only for as much of the goods as have been paid for, it does not necessarily follow that such a rule invalidates an indivisible oral contract where some payment has been made and accepted. Any other conclusion would work an unconscionable result and would encourage rather than discourage fraud if the facts as pleaded (known as "low balling" in the trade) were proven at a trial. The statute of frauds would be used to cut down the trusting buyer rather than to protect the one who, having made his bargain, parted with a portion of the purchase price as an earnest of his good faith. Certainly here the $25 deposit was not intended as a purchase of a portion of the automobile. It was intended as payment towards the purchase of the entire article if the facts alleged in the complaint are proven at the trial.
>
> [Part payment will take the case out of the statute of frauds for all of the goods when the goods are not divisible. Judgment for plaintiff.]

Minerals

Mineral
Any naturally occurring substance that is neither animal nor vegetable.

Section 2–107(1) states that a contract for the sale of minerals (including oil and gas) or for the sale of a structure or its materials to be removed from the land is a contract for the sale of goods if the goods are to be severed by the seller. Thus, § 2–201 applies. However, if the goods are to be severed by the buyer, the contract is one affecting land, and § 2–201 does not apply.

Timber

Timber
Wood suitable for building, whether cut or in the form of trees.

Section 2–107(2) states that a contract for the sale of growing timber or growing crops is a contract for the sale of goods whether severed by the seller or the buyer.

Securities

Securities
Stock certificates, bonds, or other evidence of a secured indebtedness creating a right in the holder to participate in profits or distribution of assets.

Section 8–319 provides that every contract for the sale of securities, regardless of the amount, must be in writing and signed by the party to be charged (normally the defendant in the lawsuit) or his authorized agent or broker. Delivery of the securities or a confirmatory writing will satisfy the statute.

$5,000 Property

Section 1–206 provides that other types of personal property sales, such as royalty rights, patent rights, and general intangibles in an amount over $5,000 are within the statute (i.e., must be in writing and signed by the party to be charged).

Sale of Land

Contracts for the sale of land, or any interest therein, must be in writing and signed by the party to be charged regardless of the amount involved. This also applies to mortgages, easements, and real estate brokers' commission contracts. However, construction contracts are service contracts and do not fall within this section. Most states have statutes that provide that a lease of real property for more than one year must be in writing.

A few courts hold that in the case of a sale of land, the seller must sign the contract or the contract is unenforceable against either party. If the seller does sign, both parties are bound.

An oral agreement subject to the Statute of Frauds may become enforceable if some writing is subsequently drawn confirming the existence of the agreement. An oral agreement concerning a real estate broker's commission becomes enforceable when the seller and buyer execute escrow instructions providing for payment of the commission.

On occasion, a buyer and seller enter into an oral contract for the sale of land; and the buyer, in reliance on the oral contract, goes into possession of the land and/or makes valuable improvements on the land. In other words, the buyer, relying on the oral contract, changes his or her position in equity. Can the seller use the statute of frauds as a basis for refusal to perform the contract? Most courts will hold for the buyer under the doctrine of part performance even though there is nothing in the statute that aids the buyer in this situation. Since it would be unfair to permit the seller to use the statute for a defense after such reliance by the buyer, the seller is barred from using the statute to avoid the oral contract. A minority rule followed by some courts, relying on literal language that makes no exceptions regarding part performance, disallows relief to the buyer and will not enforce any oral contract for the sale of land.

Land
The earth and the things of a permanent nature found there or affixed thereto.

Contracts of More Than One Year

A contract which by its terms is impossible to perform within a year from the time it is made is within (included in the listed situations) the statute and must be in writing and signed by the party to be charged (again, the defendant in the lawsuit).

The one-year period of time begins on the day that the agreement is actually made, not on the day when performance is to commence. Thus, a contract to perform services for exactly one year starting today can be oral. However, if the agreement is made today but the work is not to start until two days from now, it would be impossible to complete the contract in one year, according to its terms, and the oral agreement would not be enforceable. Most states permit a one-day grace period.

Terms
Conditions of a contract that limit or define its scope.

Facts

Albert Hodge, age 54, was unhappy with his bank job in Pittsburgh. He also wanted to move back to his old home in Washington, D.C. Tilley, president of Evans Financial Corp. in Washington, orally offered Hodge the job of vice president and general counsel. Hodge started working in September and was fired the following May. He sued Evans for breach of contract, saying that he had an oral contract for a "permanent" job to last until his retirement at age 65. A jury awarded Hodge $175,000, and Evans appealed.

Decision

Since Hodge was 54 and said that the contract, by its terms, was to last until he was 65, the contract was for a fixed period of eleven years. Hodge argued that since he could have died within one year, the contract could have been fully performed and was enforceable. The court found that this would be true only if the contract hired Hodge "for life." Since the contract was for a stated period of more than one year, it could not be performed within one year even if Hodge died before then. Without a written contract, Hodge was not entitled to judgment.

Hodge v. Evans Financial Corp., 778 F.2d 794 (D.C.Cir. 1985). (Many states enforce oral "lifetime" contracts, since they could be performed in one year by death. Other states require writing.)

Contracts Performed Within One Year

If it is possible to perform a contract within one year, the statute does not apply. For example, a promise by A to loan money to B when A receives her inheritance from her father who is still living could be performed within a year because the father could die within a year. To service and maintain equipment "as long as you need it" could be completed within a year by not needing it within a year. To support another person until he or she dies could be performed within a year by the death of the person to be supported.

Requirement and output contracts are not subject to the statute, because the party could go out of business within a year and thus have no more requirements and no output.

Employment Contracts

Employment contracts of indefinite duration (employee is hired but not for any period of time) are enforceable even though oral, since either party could terminate the contract within one year from the making thereof. This has been held even where the employer promised "permanent" employment but retained the right to discharge for cause or otherwise.

Exceptions for Oral Contracts

Two common exceptions to the contracts not to be performed in one year section of the statute of frauds are as follows:

1. Where one of the parties has fully performed in a bilateral contract, most courts hold the contract enforceable against the other party even though the contract was impossible to perform within a year. For example, Bob buys an automobile from Sam on an oral contract that provides that Bob will pay to Sam the price of the car in fifteen monthly payments. Sam delivers the auto to Bob, so the court will enforce Bob's oral promise to pay the installments.
2. There is a modern tendency to enforce an oral contract if the plaintiff, in reliance on the agreement, has so changed his position that financial or unconscionable injury would be suffered, or when the defendant, having accepted the benefits, would be unjustly enriched by the plaintiff's technical legal inability to enforce the oral contract. As an example, the plaintiff made an oral lease of property for a period of two years, took

possession of the property, and made permanent improvements to the property.

The following case is an example of the equitable enforcement of an oral contract.

Facts
The plaintiff, Lucas, sued to recover the balance due him on an alleged two-year oral employment contract. An oral agreement was made between the plaintiff and the defendant whereby the plaintiff was to act as general manager for the defendant company at an annual salary of $27,000 for a fixed period of two years. In reliance on the oral contract, plaintiff resigned his employment in Missouri and moved his family to Colorado, where he assumed his new duties. After thirteen months, he was discharged without cause. The defendant invokes the statute of frauds as a defense.

Decision
The court held that the defendant was estopped to invoke the statute of frauds as a defense, because the plaintiff suffered unconscionable injury as a result of his reliance on the oral agreement. The plaintiff had resigned from a secure job with a company for whom he had worked for nine years. The plaintiff had sold a custom-built house in which he and his family had lived for only eight months. He gave up business and social contacts.

Lucas v. Whittaker Corporation, 470 F.2d 326 (10th Cir. 1972).

Wills

It is generally held that a contract to make a will must be in writing if it involves the devise of land or personal property where the statutory amount has been exceeded. Since such transactions would have to be in writing under the statute of frauds, so would an agreement to transfer them by will. Some states require that any contract to make a will must be written.

Will
A person's declaration of how he desires his property to be disposed of after his death.

Promise to Pay Another's Debt

Generally, a promise to the creditor to pay the debt of another must be in writing and signed by the party to be charged. For example, Richard wants to buy a car, so he and his father go to the "Honest John Used-car Lot." Richard chooses a car, makes a down payment, and signs an installment contract for the balance. "Honest John" is concerned about Richard's ability to pay and asks the father if he will guarantee payment. The father says, "If Richard doesn't pay, I will." This promise made to the creditor must be in writing or it is not enforceable.

There are exceptions to this type of agreement:

1. Where the third party makes the promise to the *debtor*, the oral promise is enforceable. For example, if the father tells his son (for consideration) that he will pay the son's debt to "Honest John," the promise is enforceable, since the statute of frauds does not apply.
2. Where the *leading benefit* of the transaction is for the promisor, the statute does not apply, even though the promise is made to the creditor. For example, the father wants his son to buy a car so that the father

Debt
The obligation of one person to pay or compensate another.

Debtor
One who owes a debt.

Creditor
One to whom money is owed by the debtor.

Novation
The substitution of a party for one of the original parties to a contract with the consent of the other party.

does not have to drive his son and two other children to and from three different schools, as it interferes with his busy work schedule. An oral promise to "Honest John" by the father is enforceable because the father is getting the real benefit of the agreement.

3. Where there has been a *novation* or substitution of debtors, the statute does not apply. For example, if "Honest John," the father, and the son all agree orally that the father will take over the son's debt and the son is no longer responsible, the oral agreement is enforceable because the debt has now become the father's debt. To complete a novation, there is a substitution of a party for one of the original parties to a contract with the consent of the remaining party, which, in effect, creates a new agreement.

4. Where the promisor is the original debtor, the statute does not apply. For example, if a mother calls a jeweler and tells her to send a $400 watch to her daughter as a birthday gift, the promise is enforceable because the mother is promising to pay her own debt and not that of another.

Yarbro v. Neil B. McGinnis Equipment Co.
101 Ariz. 378, 420 P.2d 163 (1966).

Bernstein, Vice Chief Justice . . . McGinnis Equipment Co. brought suit to recover payments due it pursuant to a conditional sales contract for the sale of one used Allis-Chalmers Model HD-5G tractor. The contract was negotiated in August of 1957 and called for twenty-three monthly installments of $574.00 each. The buyer, Russell, failed to make the first monthly payment, and on his suggestion a McGinnis company representative met with the appellant, Yarbro, to ask if he would help with the payments. As a result of this meeting Yarbro agreed to, and did, pay the September installment.

In the months that followed there was a continued failure on the part of Russell to make any of the monthly installment payments. . . .

In May, 1958 when McGinnis Co. indicated that the tractor soon would have to be repossessed, Yarbro again assured the company that it would be paid as soon as two pending real estate escrows were closed. This promised payment was not made. A similar promise was made by Yarbro in July on the strength of proceeds that were to be forthcoming from an oat crop in New Mexico but again no payment was made. . . . The tractor was finally repossessed in January of 1959. Subsequently, the McGinnis Co. brought an action to recover the payments due under the conditional sales contract, naming Russell and Yarbro as defendants. A default judgment was entered against Russell and the only question before this court now concerns the liability of the defendant, Yarbro. The trial court found Yarbro liable for the entire balance under the conditional sales contract. . . .

Although the promises made by Yarbro clearly were of the type covered in [the statute of frauds] the plaintiff contends that the leading object or primary purpose exception is applicable. . . . Simply stated, this rule provides that where the leading object of a person promising to pay the debt of another is actually to protect his own interest, such promise if supported by sufficient consideration, is valid, even though it be oral.

. . . Although a third party is the primary debtor, situations may arise where the promisor has a personal, immediate and pecuniary interest in the transaction, and is therefore himself a party to be benefitted by the performance of the promisee. In such cases the reason which underlies and which prompted the above statutory provision fails, and the courts will give effect to the promise. Recognizing the leading object rule as a well reasoned exception, the question remains whether the facts presently before this court make the exception applicable. . . . Further evidence of Yarbro's interest in the tractor comes from the fact that after its purchase he had borrowed it on a series of occasions. When repairs were needed shortly after Yarbro had made the first installment payment, the McGinnis Co. repairman found the machine on Yarbro's land. . . . Yarbro had asked on several occasions that the McGinnis Co. not repossess the tractor because he needed it. These requests were usually in conjunction with a promise to pay what was owing on the tractor. . . . It is when the leading and main object of the promisor is *not* to become surety or guarantor of another, even though that may be the effect, but is to serve some purpose or interest of his own, that the oral promise becomes enforceable. . . .

[Judgment for plaintiff affirmed.]

Marriage as Consideration

If a person makes a promise to pay a sum of money or to give property to another in consideration of that person's promise to marry, the agreement must be in writing. For example, if "Honest John" promises the father's daughter that if she will marry him he will give her the choice of any car on his lot and she agrees, the oral contract is not enforceable. It is universally held that the marriage itself does not constitute such part performance as to make the oral antenuptial contract valid. This provision of the statute does not apply to mutual promises to marry.

Facts

Eusebio Tellez, now deceased, proposed marriage to Guadalupe Diaz, now his widow, orally promising that if she would marry and care for him as his wife until his death, he would give her all of his property, both real and personal. After they married and were still living together, without her knowledge or consent, he conveyed all of the land to his children and grandchildren by a former marriage. He then had a stroke and moved in with his daughter, where he lived until his death. His widow now sues to recover the property promised to her under the oral contract made before their marriage.

Decision

The deceased's agreement to leave his property to Guadalupe Diaz was in consideration of her marrying him and caring for him until his death. This contract was within the statute of frauds in that it was an oral contract made upon consideration of marriage and had to be in writing to be enforceable. *Tellez* v. *Tellez*, 51 N.M. 416, 186 P.2d 390 (1947).

Contract Modification

Generally, a contract that is required to be in writing under the statute of frauds cannot be modified except in writing.

Modification
A change in the form or terms of a contract.

Under UCC § 2–209(3), if the contract as modified is within the statute of frauds, § 2–201 must be satisfied. For example, buyer and seller orally agree to buy and sell certain goods for $400 and later wish to increase the quantity of goods in an amount that will increase the price to $600. The modified agreement must meet the requirements of writing under the statute of frauds.

If the contract is in writing but did not have to be under the statute of frauds, would the modification have to be in writing? In most courts it would not. However, the modification would need the essential elements of a contract to be valid.

Facts

Harold Dougherty wanted to sell some property. He entered into an exclusive listing agreement with the United Farm Agency, agreeing in writing that United Farm would be entitled to a commission even if Dougherty found a buyer for the property on his own. He did just that, and when United Farm found out, it demanded its commission. Dougherty refused, claiming that there had been an "oral rescission" of the written exclusive listing contract. The trial court found for Dougherty, and United Farm appealed to the Texas Supreme Court.

Decision

United Farm was entitled to its commission of $30,000. Where a written contract is required under the statute of frauds, an oral rescission is not effective. The policy behind the statute is to remove uncertainty, prevent fraudulent claims, and reduce litigation. Permitting the use of oral agreements to rescind contracts that had to be written would promote all of the "evils" that the statute was intended to discourage, effectively nullifying the rule. Therefore, no rescission had occurred, and the commission must be paid.

Givens v. *Dougherty*, 671 S.W.2d 877 (1985).

Questions

1. What is the purpose of the statute of frauds?
2. Explain some exceptions to the requirement that contracts for the sale of goods over $500 have to be in writing.
3. When may part performance of an oral contract to sell land make the agreement enforceable?
4. How can you reconcile the encapsulated cases of *Hodge* v. *Evans Financial Corp.* and *Lucas* v. *Whittaker Corporation*?
5. Give some examples where the requirement of writing for a promise to pay the debt of another is excused, and explain why.

8.3 Parol Evidence Rule

Parol Evidence
A witness's testimony that is not written.

The previous subchapter discussed the rule that contracts required to be in writing under the statute of frauds can be modified or changed only by another writing. The next subchapter discusses the rules followed by the courts in trying to interpret what the parties intended in their contracts. One of the principles that apply to both situations is the *parol evidence rule*. This rule is one that relates to the presentation of evidence in court rather than to the making of contracts.

Parol Evidence Rule
A rule that disallows any evidence offered to show a prior or contemporaneous understanding of the parties that contradicts or modifies a written contract.

Oral Negotiations and the Written Contract

Before signing a written contract, the parties usually negotiate the various terms orally. When the oral discussion has been completed and the issues are settled, the contract agreement is then reduced to writing and signed by the parties. All of the negotiations and oral understandings are merged into the written contract. Since it is logical that the signed written document correctly contains all of the oral terms agreed upon by the parties, it is not reasonable for one party to claim that the parties really agreed to something other than that which is stated in their written contract.

The parol (oral) evidence rule states that oral testimony is not admissible in court if offered to vary the terms of a written contract when such oral testimony relates to spoken statements made before the signing of the contract or at the same time as the contract was signed.

The Rule as a Warning

This rule should serve as a warning to any party making a written contract, especially to buyers. *Never* sign a contract unless you are certain that it contains *all* of the terms agreed upon. Sometimes the salesperson's oral promise may be denied when it comes time to enforce it; and even if you are allowed to prove your point in court under one of the exceptions to the rule, the litigation may be more costly than the value of the promise. Another common-sense point to remember is that some innocent-looking documents, such as purchase orders or deposit receipts, can be written contracts.

Exceptions to the Rule

When ambiguity (something having more than one interpretation) exists in any of the words or provisions of a written contract, an exception to the rule is allowed, and oral testimony is admissible to explain the meaning of the ambiguity. For example, an implement dealer sold a farmer a reaper, and the dealer warranted in writing that the reaper was capable of cutting and raking 12 to 20 acres of grain a day by one good man and a team of horses. The dealer orally told the farmer before they signed the contract that he meant a team like the one the farmer currently owned. However, when the farmer's team was unable to do the work satisfactorily, the seller claimed that if *any* sort of team could pull the machine, the farmer should be bound by the contract. The farmer was allowed to give oral testimony to explain that the contract meant his team.

Ambiguity
An expression with more than one possible meaning.

Mistake of Fact

Most of the exceptions to the parol evidence rule allow evidence not to change the written agreement but rather to explain it or the conditions under which it was made. Thus, in the case of mutual mistake of fact, fraud, duress, illegality, undue influence, or lack of capacity, the court will admit oral testimony, not to vary the terms of the contract but to ascertain the true circumstances involved. For example, where a mistake is made in reducing the contract to writing because the typist used the wrong figures and the parties did not notice the error, oral evidence is allowed so that the court can determine the intent of the agreement and correct it to comply with the original terms.

Fraud

In another example, the plaintiff contractor signed a contract that contained the following clause: "[Contractor] is not relying upon any statement made by the company." The contractor was allowed to testify that the contract was procured by fraud. Again, he was not changing the terms of the agreement but was showing that the contract was fraudulently obtained and should be voided. It is obvious that since acts of fraud would not be set forth in the written contract, they could be proved only by outside oral testimony.

Lack of Capacity

Lack of capacity ordinarily would not be reflected in the body of the written contract, so minority or insanity could be established only by extraneous evidence.

Incomplete Contract

When a contract is incomplete on its face, such as the omission of important terms or blanks left unfilled, oral testimony is admissible to supply the missing items.

Condition Precedent

Where the parties have orally agreed to a condition precedent that the written contract is to have no effect unless a certain act or event occurs, such requirement for validity of the contract can be established by oral evidence. The party is not trying to vary or change the written contract but is attempting to prove that there is no contract in existence because the condition precedent did not happen. For example, a politician promises a person employment if the politician is elected to office. In such a case, the election to office is a condition precedent to handing out the job.

Conditional Clauses

Other common conditions occur when a buyer of a house puts a clause in the contract that the purchase of the property is contingent upon the buyer's being able to procure a loan in a certain amount at a set interest rate and upon certain terms, such as monthly payments and the length of time to pay off the loan. If the buyer were unable to obtain such a loan, the condition would not be met, and he would not have to purchase the house. Other conditional clauses frequently found in real estate contracts is that the sale is contingent upon the buyer's approval of a report regarding such things as termite inspection, plumbing, electrical system, soil, roof, foundation requirements, and the general construction of the property.

Long v. Jones
319 S.W.2d 292 (Ky. 1958).

Milliken, Judge The appellee, Mrs. Jones, recovered a judgment of $800, with interest, covering the down payment made by her on the proposed purchase of a house from the appellant, Dan Long, in Lexington. A written contract covering the terms of the proposed purchase was signed by her and by the vendor through his agent, and the $800 down payment was referred to therein "as evidence of good faith to bind this contract" and it was "to be applied on the purchase price upon passing of deed, or refunded, should title prove not merchantable, or acceptable, or if this offer is not accepted." . . .

As an explanation of her failure to go through with the purchase within the terms of the agreement, Mrs. Jones testified that at the time she signed the printed contract form and made the $800 down payment it was understood between her and the agent of the appellant-seller that she could not complete the proposed purchase within the time allotted unless she sold her home in Flemingsburg, and the trial court accordingly instructed the jury to find for Mrs. Jones if they believed what she said. It was proper for such testimony to be admitted for the consideration of the jury, not for the purpose of varying the terms of a written agreement, but on the issue of whether a contract in fact existed. . . .

> Evidence is generally held admissible to show that the parties made an agreement before or at the time they entered into a written contract of sale that such contract of sale should become binding only on the happening of a certain condition or contingency, the theory being that such evidence merely goes to show that the writing never became operative as a valid agreement and that there is therefore no variance or contradiction of a valid written instrument. . . .

The motion for an appeal is overruled, and the judgment is affirmed. [Caveat: Put the clause in the written contract and avoid litigation.]

Later Changes

The rule applies only to oral changes of provisions made prior to or contemporaneous with the written contract and not to later oral changes or additions. Although the parol evidence rule would not apply, certain other rules might prevent the later oral change or addition from being effective (e.g., statute of frauds). Although the later oral changes may be testified to in court, the other party may deny that oral changes were made, and the court may believe this denial. The point to remember here is that all potential oral changes should be put in writing.

Consideration

Frequently, certain types of instruments, such as deeds, leases, notes, and bonds, will contain a statement that the consideration has been received when in fact it has not; or the instrument will contain a nominal recital of consideration, whereas it is greater. Generally, in such cases, the courts will permit parol evidence to show that the consideration was not paid or that it is different than stated. This is because the document was not intended to be an integration of the agreement supplanting prior negotiations. Under this rule, it would be proper to permit testimony to show that in addition to the consideration stated in the deed, there was an oral promise to convey certain land by a will. However, if the terms are fully and correctly embodied in the contract, parol evidence is not generally admissible. Under this rule, if the contract sets out the purchase price, payable pursuant to certain terms, oral testimony is inadmissible to vary the contract.

UCC Provisions

In addition to the exceptions already mentioned, the UCC contains several provisions relating to the interpretation of contracts for the sale of goods. Sections 1–205, 2–202, and 2–208 provide that in the sale of goods, a written contract may be explained or supplemented in the following four ways:

Course of Dealing
Previous conduct between the parties to a transaction which fairly establishes a common basis of understanding between them.

Usage of Trade
A practice widely accepted and relied upon in many transactions in a particular trade or industry.

Course of Performance
Performance according to the common practices and customs of such commercial transactions.

1. By showing that there has been a *prior course of dealing* between the same buyer and seller which could be regarded as establishing a common basis for interpreting their expressions and other conduct.
2. By establishing a *usage of trade* that has such regularity in the place or business as to justify an expectation that it would be followed in the transaction in question.
3. By presenting evidence of *consistent additional terms* unless the court finds the writing to have been intended as a complete and exclusive statement of the terms of the agreement.
4. By making a contract of sale that involves repeated acts of performance by either party with knowledge of the nature of the performance and opportunity for objection to it by the other, in which case, any *course of performance* accepted without objection may be offered to determine the true meaning of the agreement.

In considering these exceptions, the court will first look to the express terms of the agreement, then apply the course of dealing and usage of the trade and, if reasonable, construe them all as being consistent with each other. When such a result would be unreasonable, the express terms shall control the course of performance and the course of performance shall control both the course of dealing and usage of trade.

QUESTIONS

1. How does the parol evidence rule apply to contracts?
2. What is meant by an ambiguity in a contract or its clauses? How does the court solve such a problem?
3. Suppose that you want to sell your car and run an ad in the paper. A young prospect shows up and shows you a phony ID that says he's 20 years old, and you draw up a contract that states his age as 20 and that he will pay you $100 a month until the car is paid for. You both sign the agreement, and he calls you up a few days later saying that the car is totaled, he is only 17, he disaffirms the contract, and he does not intend to make the payments. How can the parol evidence rule be applied in this situation?
4. A friend tells you that he is expecting a tax refund check next week, and if it comes he'll buy your car. You draw up a valid written contract setting forth the item, the parties' names, and the price to be paid for the car. Both of you sign it. Instead of getting a refund check, he gets a deficiency notice from the IRS. Can you hold him to the contract? How would the parol evidence rule apply in this case?
5. What are the UCC exceptions to the parol evidence rule that pertain to the sale of goods?

PROBLEMS

1. Walker, an employee, had a group life insurance policy with his company. The policy had a clause that it could be converted to an individual policy provided that it was done within thirty-one days after the termination of an employee's employment. Walker was suspended from his job in April, termination for cause was later announced by the boss, and negotiations ended in a settlement in November. Walker then tried to exercise his conversion privilege, and the insurance company said that the thirty-one-day period had expired. Walker died, and his widow sued to enforce the policy, saying that Walker should have been given notification of the date of termination of his employment. Decide.

2. Van Norden, an engineer, had a contract that provided an additional fee to him for preparing a case for arbitration, payable "after the arbitration is completed." Through no fault of the other party, the contemplated arbitration never took place, and the claim was successfully prosecuted by a lawsuit. When the fee was not paid, Van Norden sued to recover it. Decide.

3. On June 1, buyer and seller entered into an oral contract for the sale of 100 office chairs at $50 each, delivery by freight. On June 3, seller sent a signed letter to buyer that reaffirmed the terms of the oral contract. Buyer received the letter on June 4. On June 4, seller shipped the chairs to buyer. On June 15, before the chairs arrived, buyer changed her mind and tried to get out of the oral contract. Discuss.

4. Defendant made an oral contract with plaintiff for a tombstone to be made according to a pattern and design in a catalog at a price of $600. After the plaintiff selected the proper design and cut the inscription upon the tombstone, the defendant refused to accept it although it was complete and ready for delivery. Defendant pleads the statute of frauds. Discuss.

5. Buyer and seller entered into an oral contract for the sale of a boat at a price of $1,000. Buyer made a down payment in the amount of $50. Now buyer wants to cancel the contract, arguing that the contract should have been in writing. Discuss.

6. Buyer orally contracts with seller to purchase a garage on the seller's property for the sum of $450. Seller is to dismantle the garage and have it ready for pickup within three months from the date of the contract. Seller dismantles the garage and has it ready for pickup within the period; however, buyer refuses to pick up or pay for the garage. Seller brings suit, and buyer defends on the ground that the contract was for real estate and is unenforceable under the statute of frauds. Decision?

7. Seller and buyer enter into an oral contract for the sale of a parcel of land for the price of $499, to be paid in monthly installments. In reliance on the oral contract, buyer takes possession and builds a cabin on the land. After buyer has paid $200 in monthly installments, he discovers gold on the land. Seller brings an action to evict the buyer on the grounds that the contract was for real estate and there was nothing in writing. Decision?

8. In the middle of March, A orally employs B to manage a farm for one year upon specified terms

beginning April 1. In December, A discharges B without cause. B brings suit for breach of contract. Decision?

9. Seller and buyer entered into a written contract for the sale of a truck. The contract provided that the writing contained the whole agreement and that anything not incorporated therein was not to be regarded as part of the agreement between the parties. The seller fraudulently substituted a different motor for the one that he had led the buyer to believe he was buying. The buyer now sues for the fraud, but the seller contends that in view of the provisions in the written contract, oral testimony as to the alleged fraud may not be heard by the court. What should the court decide?

10. A and B entered into a written contract in which A was to manufacture and install a canopy in front of B's restaurant. It was orally agreed at the time the contract was entered into that A was to obtain the permission of the owner of the building prior to manufacture and installation of the canopy. A manufactured and installed the canopy without obtaining the owner's permission. B refuses to pay, since the owner objects to the canopy. At the trial, B wants to testify as to the oral agreement. May he do so?

CHAPTER NINE

Interpretation and Third Parties

9.1 Judicial Interpretation
Court Interpretation
Intent of the Parties
   Reasonable Interpretation
   Contract as a Whole
   Conflicts Within a Contract
   Usage and Custom
   Subsequent Conduct
Party Causing Uncertainty
Insurance Contracts
Conflict of Laws

9.2 Third-Party Beneficiaries
Donee Beneficiary
Creditor Beneficiary
Incidental Beneficiary
Intended Beneficiary
Change of Insurance Beneficiary

9.3 Assignments
Assignable Contracts
Delegation of Duty
Express Provisions
Employment Contracts
Judgment
Prohibited Contracts
Effect of Assignment
   Liability of Assignor
   Liability of Assignee
Acceptance by Assignee
Right to Assurances
Rights of Assignee
Defense Waivers
Priorities Among Successive Assignees

9.1 Judicial Interpretation

Court Interpretation

Judicial Interpretation
The explanation by a court of the meaning of a contract.

Legalese
A term referring to technical, formal legal language.

Verbosity
Using or containing more words than necessary.

Each contract should contain all the important terms of the agreement. The terms should be clearly stated, since ambiguous terms can result in different interpretations by the parties and can then lead to unnecessary litigation. The modern trend in drafting contracts is away from the use of "legalese" in favor of plain, concise language. In old England, at a time when most persons were unable to write, scribes were hired to draw up written agreements and were paid by the word. Some contend that this ancient practice led to the verbosity still found in many contracts. One cynical attorney said that he likes to make all of his contracts ambiguous because he could then argue them either way and, when he wrote agreements his clients could understand, they thought he lacked expertise and had overcharged them.

Where disagreements of the parties cannot be resolved and the case goes to trial, the court applies certain principles of construction and interpretation to the contract.

Intent of the Parties

Intention of the Parties
A mutual determination to do a specified thing or to act in a particular manner.

The primary purpose of the interpretation of a contract is to determine and give effect to the mutual intention of the parties. The modern approach is to search for the *expressed* intent in the words actually used. The secret or undisclosed intention of a party has no effect on the outcome. In other words, the court is interested only in what the parties said and not in the parties' undisclosed thoughts.

Reasonable Interpretation

An interpretation that gives a reasonable, lawful, and effective meaning to manifestations of the intent of the parties is preferred to one that makes the parties' words and acts unreasonable, unlawful, or of no effect.

Contract as Whole

A contract must be read and interpreted as a whole or in its entirety so as to give effect to every part. The intention of the parties is to be gathered from the entire instrument and not from detached or isolated words or parts.

If several writings exist between the parties regarding one transaction, they are all to be construed as one writing. However, terms on a printed letterhead or billhead or those placed on the reverse side of a printed contract form are not a part of the contract unless a reasonable person would regard them as such. Likewise, important provisions placed in fine print are generally unenforceable. Items that are called to the attention of a party *after* the contract has been entered into, such as terms in an employer's manual that are pointed out to the employee after the hiring contract has been made, may not be binding on such party.

Conflicts Within a Contract

When a contract is partly handwritten or typewritten and partly printed and the written part conflicts with the printed part, the written part prevails.

When there is a conflict between an amount expressed both in words and figures, the amount expressed in words prevails (e.g., One Hundred Twenty Dollars [$1.20]), the One Hundred Twenty Dollars would prevail.

Punctuation and rules of grammatical construction may be used to aid in the ascertaining of intent but are not used when they are in conflict with the real intent of the parties.

Facts

Penthouse magazine printed nude photographs of Barnes under a fictitious name and got from Barnes a signed release on a printed form that gave *Penthouse* the right to republication of the photos "in connection with my own or a fictitious name." When the photographer took the pictures and obtained the signed release, he wrote the letters "AKA" on the printed form which, he assured Barnes, meant that the photos would be used only under a fictitious name. Now that Barnes is well known, *Penthouse* wants to republish the nude pictures using her real name. She objects, and *Penthouse* claims it has that right under the contract.

Decision

The handwritten "AKA" controls over typewritten and printed terms for the purpose of interpreting the contract. If the terms of a promise are in any respect ambiguous or uncertain, they must be interpreted in the sense in which the promisor believed, at the time of making the promise, that the promisee understood them. Any language in the printed release form that is inconsistent with the added terms "AKA" must be disregarded. In cases of uncertainty, contract language is interpreted most strongly against any party causing the uncertainty. Parol evidence may be introduced to resolve the ambiguity. *Penthouse* cannot publish under Barnes's real name.

Penthouse Intern., Ltd. v. *Barnes*, 792 F.2d 943 (9th Cir. 1986).

Usage and Custom

Usage and custom may be used to explain the meaning of language in a contract and to imply terms when no contrary intention appears from the terms of the contract (e.g., in agency agreement to sell automobiles, the custom of taking used cars as trade-ins established such authority of agent; in a sale of real estate, custom may properly determine details regarding opening of escrow, furnishing of deeds and title insurance, and prorating of taxes; a layaway or will-call plan customarily means that the buyer has an option to purchase the goods within a specified time during which the seller will not sell the goods).

To enable custom to be used to interpret a contract, the parties must agree to it, or one party must know or have reason to know that the other party intends custom to govern the contract, or it must be so well known that a reasonable person would be aware of it.

Usage and Custom
Frequent or established use or practice.

Subsequent Conduct

Subsequent Conduct
The way one acts after an agreement was made.

Acts of the parties that take place after the execution of the contract but before any controversy arises may be looked to in determining the meaning of the contract. The parties themselves are most likely to be correct as to their real intent.

Facts

Crestview owned some property that it wanted to develop as a cemetery which was at the time against the county zoning law. It hired Dieden, an attorney, on a contingent fee of $7,500 and gave him three months to complete the action. Dieden filed an application for rezoning, argued it at several hearings against vigorous opposition, and finally got it passed by a 4–3 vote. Crestview congratulated Dieden and sent him a check for $5,000 "on account of your legal fee." The opposition then put together a referendum election, which overthrew the decision. Crestview did not get its cemetery permit and thus sued for a return of the $5,000. Dieden countered for the $2,500 he claimed still due him.

Decision

For Dieden. When he got the rezoning ordinance passed, Crestview congratulated him for it and paid him $5,000 on account. Even though no cemetery could be had, this conduct of the parties indicated that Dieden had done what he contracted to do.

Crestview Cemetery Assn. v. Dieden, 54 Cal.2d 744, 8 Cal.Rptr. 427, 356 P.2d 171 (1960).

Party Causing Uncertainty

The language of a contract should be interpreted most strongly against the party who caused the uncertainty to exist (i.e., the person who prepared the contract). The rule is particularly applicable to a contract prepared by an expert or experienced party, and especially where the party using the ambiguous language seeks to defeat the contract because of such language. The rule is also particularly applicable where the contract is on a printed form prepared by one of the parties. However, this rule of interpretation is to be used only after all other rules of interpretation have been used and no satisfactory result has been obtained.

Insurance Contracts

Insurance contracts are interpreted against the insurance company because the company prepared the contract and because the policy of the law favors coverage for losses to which the policy of insurance relates. It has been said that courts construe against insurance companies because people do not read their policies and would not understand them if they did. Whether the coverage relates to the peril insured against, the amount of liability, or the person or persons protected, the language will be interpreted in its most inclusive sense for the benefit of the insured.

Exception clauses are construed strictly. In other words, if the insurance company does not want to cover a particular loss related to the policy, the company must clearly exclude this loss or the insured will be covered.

Gray v. Zurich Insurance Co.
65 Cal.2d 263, 54 Cal.Rptr. 104, 419 P.2d 168 (1966).

Tobriner, Justice Plaintiff, Dr. Vernon D. Gray, is the named insured under an insurance policy issued by defendant. . . .

The policy contains a provision that "[T]his endorsement does not apply . . . to bodily injury or property damages caused intentionally by or at the direction of the insured."

The suit which Dr. Gray contends Zurich should have defended arose out of an altercation between him and a Mr. John R. Jones. . . . Dr. Gray notified defendant of the suit, stating that he had acted in self-defense, and requested that the company defend. Defendant refused on the ground that the complaint alleged an intentional tort which fell outside the coverage of the policy. Dr. Gray thereafter unsuccessfully defended on the theory of self-defense; he suffered a judgment of $6,000 actual damages although the jury refused to award punitive damages.

Dr. Gray then filed the instant action charging defendant with breach of its duty to defend.

The . . . court rendered judgment in favor of defendant. . . . In interpreting an insurance policy we apply the general principle that doubts as to meaning must be resolved against the insurer and that any exception to the performance of the basic underlying obligation must be so stated as clearly to apprise the insured of its effect. . . .

. . . No one can determine whether the third party suit does or does not fall within the indemnification coverage of the policy until that suit is resolved; in the instant case, the determination of whether the insured engaged in intentional, negligent or even wrongful conduct depended upon the judgment in the Jones suit, and, indeed, even after that judgment, no one could be positive whether it rested upon a finding of plaintiff's negligent or his intentional conduct. The carrier's obligation to indemnify inevitably will not be defined until the adjudication of the very action which it should have defended. . . . The insured is unhappily surrounded by concentric circles of uncertainty; the first, the unascertainable nature of the insurer's duty to defend; the second, the unknown effect of the provision that the insurer must defend even a groundless, false or fraudulent claim; the third, the uncertain extent of the indemnification coverage. Since we must resolve uncertainties in favor of the insured and interpret the policy provisions according to the layman's reasonable expectations, and since the effect of the exclusionary clause is neither conspicuous, plain nor clear, we hold that in the present case the policy provides for an obligation to defend and that such obligation is independent of the indemnification coverage.

. . . The judgment is reversed and the trial court instructed to take evidence solely on the issue of damages alleged in plaintiff's complaint including the amount of the judgment in the Jones suit, and the costs, expenses and attorney's fees incurred in defending such suit.

Conflict of Laws

A conflict of laws exists when there is a difference in the laws between municipalities, between states, or between countries. The law of New York is different from the law of California regarding revocation of an offer. For example if the buyer (offeror) is in Los Angeles and the seller (offeree-

Conflict of Laws
Where the laws are different in two jurisdictions and the court must decide which to follow.

acceptor) is in New York and no intent is indicated as to which law should apply, which law do we use? The validity of the contract is ordinarily determined by the law of the place where the contract was made, and this would be where the last act is necessary for its validity. This has been called the "more favored rule." In our example, we would use the law of New York, since the last act necessary to make the contract, namely the acceptance, would take place in New York. If the contract is entered into by telephone, the place of making is the place where the acceptor speaks.

Some courts follow the rule that the place where the contract is to be performed governs. Some courts follow the rule that the intent of the parties governs (i.e., the law of the place where the parties intended or presumed to have intended).

Center of Gravity Theory
In conflicts of laws the law of the jurisdiction with the most significant contacts regarding the subject matter of the conflict is followed.

A growing tendency by the courts is to follow the "center of gravity" or "grouping of contacts" theory, under which the courts emphasize the law of the place that has the most significant contacts with the matter in dispute. Even under this theory, the courts place heavy emphasis on the parties' intention, the place of making the contract, and the place of performance. Under this theory, the courts examine all of the points of contact that the transaction has with the two or more states involved, with a view to determining that aspect of the contract immediately before the court. When the court has identified the state with which the matter at hand is predominantly or most intimately concerned, it concludes that this is the proper law of the contract that the parties intended at the time of the contracting.

Under UCC § 1–105(1), the parties have the right to choose their own law. This right is subject to the firm rules stated in subsection (2) and is limited to jurisdictions to which the transaction bears a "reasonable relation." Ordinarily, the law chosen must be that where a significant enough portion of the making or performance of the contract is to occur.

Questions

1. What is meant by judicial interpretation of contracts?
2. Where the printed terms of a contract differ from handwritten entries on the agreement, which will prevail? What is the reason for this rule?
3. How can custom and usage affect contract terms?
4. What principles do the courts follow when interpreting insurance contracts?
5. When the contracting parties are in different states and the laws of their respective states are not the same, how do you determine which law to apply in contract disputes?

9.2 Third-Party Beneficiaries

Often contracts are made between two parties for the express purpose of benefiting a third party. A common example is a contract between an insurance company and a husband under which the husband's life is insured so that on his death the amount of the policy will be paid to his wife. In such a case, his wife is the beneficiary of the contract. Even though she is not a party to the insurance contract, she has a direct, personal cause of action for any breach of the promised performance.

The third party cannot enforce the contract unless it was made expressly for his benefit. Also, the beneficiary can recover only if there was an enforceable contract between the original parties to the contract. Thus, any defense between the original parties will also be effective against the third party.

There are three types of third-party beneficiary contracts: (1) donee, (2) creditor, and (3) incidental. In practically all states, *donee* or *creditor* beneficiaries may bring actions to enforce contracts made for their benefit. However, the courts will not enforce contracts for *incidental* beneficiaries.

Third Party
Someone other than the parties directly involved in the contract.

Donee Beneficiary

A contract whose purpose is to make a gift to the third party is called a third-party donee beneficiary contract. Thus, the insurance illustration is an example of a donee beneficiary contract. The wife is the donee beneficiary of the contract.

Donee Beneficiary
A person not a party to a contract but for whom the agreement confers a benefit as a gift.

Facts

Saylor opened a bank account of over $6,500 from the sale of his separately owned bonds and later added another $2,100 of his own money to it. He put the account in the name of "Mr. and Mrs. Adrian M. Saylor." His wife never signed a signature card, and no withdrawals were ever made from the account. Saylor died, and his administrator claims the account as part of the estate. The widow contends that it belongs to her.

Decision

For the widow. A person depositing an account in his own name and that of another creates a third-party beneficiary contract. Such agreements do not require consideration from the beneficiary. The donee beneficiary has the right to enforce a promise made for her benefit. It is not essential that the third person knew of the contract for her benefit at the time the contract was made. By causing the account to be established and maintained in the names of himself and his wife, in the absence of evidence to the contrary, there is a presumption that Saylor intended to and did make his wife a third-party beneficiary to the contract.

Saylor v. Saylor, 389 S.W.2d 904 (Ky. 1965).

Creditor Beneficiary

A contract between the original parties whose purpose is to satisfy an obligation to a third party is a creditor beneficiary contract. A creditor beneficiary is a creditor of the debtor promisee whose obligation will be discharged to the extent that the promisor agrees to perform. For example, if a tenant assigns a lease to a subtenant and the latter agrees to perform all of the terms of the lease, the agreement between the tenant and the subtenant is for the benefit of the landlord lessor. The landlord, as a creditor beneficiary, may now sue the subtenant but still retains any legal rights he has against the original tenant.

Creditor Beneficiary
A creditor beneficiary is a third party who has an obligation settled by agreement between the contracting parties.

Similarly, if a business is sold and the buyer assumes the liabilities of the seller's business, the creditors of the business are creditor beneficiaries of the agreement between the buyer and the seller. The creditors then have the right to sue the buyer of the business but still maintain their right to recover from the seller if the buyer does not pay. If the owner of an automobile that was financed by a bank, and upon which some money is still due, sells the automobile to a buyer who agrees to pay off the balance of the loan, the bank is a third-party creditor beneficiary of the contract of sale between the seller and buyer and can hold the buyer to the promise to pay the balance due.

Incidental Beneficiary

Incidental Beneficiary
A third party who is only remotely or incidentally benefited by a contract.

A person who is only remotely benefited by a contract cannot enforce it. In such case, it is not the intention of either the promisee or the promisor that the third person benefit from the contract. Thus, where a city makes a contract with a contractor to pave Balboa Avenue, property owners living along Balboa Avenue cannot sue the contractor if he fails to perform, because they are only incidental beneficiaries. The city made the contract to benefit all the members of the public and not primarily for the individual property owners on Balboa Avenue. Similarly, if Smith hires Jones to paint and relandscape his house, such work may well increase the value of a neighboring house owned by Dickson, but Dickson is merely an incidental beneficiary and cannot enforce the contract between Smith and Jones.

Intended Beneficiary

Intended Beneficiary
A person who is intended to receive a benefit or advantage from a contract.

Under the modern view, which is the majority rule, both donee and creditor beneficiaries of a contract are classified as *intended beneficiaries*. The parties to the contract that creates the donee or creditor beneficiary lose their power to modify or revoke the agreement made for an intended beneficiary whenever that beneficiary learns about the contract *and* (1) brings suit against the promisee *or* (2) materially changes his position in reasonable reliance on the contract *or* (3) manifests his assent to the benefits at the request of either the promisor or the promisee.

Change of Insurance Beneficiary

Beneficiaries of life insurance policies may be named revocably or irrevocably. In an irrevocable designation, the owner has no power to change the beneficiary. Some states control this problem by statute. For example, in California, life insurance policy beneficiaries may be changed unless expressly made irrevocable. In other states, they cannot be changed unless made revocable.

Questions

1. How does one become a donee beneficiary?
2. Give some examples of incidental beneficiaries.
3. What is the difference between a creditor beneficiary and a donee beneficiary?
4. What rights do intended beneficiaries have under the contracts that created them?
5. How can a wife who is the donee beneficiary on a life insurance policy make sure that her husband doesn't change the beneficiary and name an old girlfriend in her place?

9.3 Assignments

Assignable Contracts

An *assignment* is a transfer by one party to a contract of some or all of the rights under the contract to another party who was not a party to the original agreement. For example, a patient owes $500 to his doctor and does not pay. The doctor may then assign her right to collect the money to a collection agency. The doctor who makes the assignment is called the *assignor,* and the collection agency would be the *assignee.*

Assignment
The transfer of an interest in a right or property to another.

No particular language or form is necessary to make an assignment. Therefore, an oral assignment is valid unless the subject matter is one required by statute to be in writing. For example, wage assignments must be in writing in most states.

An assignment can be total or partial. For example, a creditor could assign part of his claim and retain the remainder.

Since consideration is not required for an assignment, assignments may be made as gifts.

Whether a contract is assignable depends upon its terms and the nature of the contract. Ordinarily, a contract is assignable. Although an offer is not assignable, an option contract, which is a contract whereby the seller keeps the offer open, is assignable.

Delegation of Duty

While contract *rights* are *assignable,* contract *duties* are only *delegable.* Where the duty is mechanical or ministerial in nature and requires no special feature or action by a person having special abilities, it is normally freely delegable. Some examples of persons with special abilities are actors, artists, musicians, doctors, lawyers, architects, and certified public accountants. The party delegating a contractual duty to another becomes the *obligor* and remains responsible to see that the duty is done. The one who holds the right of performance of the duty is called the *obligee* and can hold respon-

Delegable Duty
A duty that an obligor is able to transfer to another.

sible the obligor or the consenting delegate of the obligor to see that the duty is done.

La Rue v. Groezinger
84 Cal. 281, 24 P. 42 (1890).

Hayne, C. This was an action for damages for the breach of a contract to buy grapes. The substance of the material portions of the contract was as follows:

One Hopper agreed to sell all the grapes which he might raise during a period of ten years. . . . In consideration whereof the defendant agreed to accept the grapes and pay for them (after delivery).

The parties performed this contract for five years. At the end of that time, . . . Hopper conveyed the vineyard and assigned the contract to the plaintiff. . . . The crop of the following year was grown, gathered, and tendered by the plaintiff. The defendant refused to accept it, saying that he had no contract with the plaintiff, and . . . that the contract was not assignable. . . . The Civil Code of this state provides that written contracts "for the payment of money or personal property" may be transferred. . . . It is clear, however, that the provision cannot be construed to render assignable all contracts whatever, regardless of their nature or effect, but must be taken with some qualification.

In the first place, it was not intended to render null any agreement that the parties may have made on the subject. Hence, if the contract itself provides in terms that it is not transferable, it certainly cannot be transferred, although it otherwise might be so. . . .

In the next place, although the language may not show an intention that the contract should not be assigned, yet the nature of the case may be such that performance by another would be *an essentially different thing* from that contracted for. Thus a picture by one artist is an essentially different thing from a picture on the same subject by another artist; and so of a book composed by an author, or any other act or thing where the skill, credit, or other personal quality of circumstance of the party is a distinctive characteristic of the thing contracted for, or a material inducement to the contract. . . .

If, therefore, the case before us comes within either of the qualifications above stated, then it must be conceded that the contract was not assignable. . . . There is nothing in the language which excludes the idea of performance by another . . . and . . . there is nothing in the nature or circumstances of the case which shows that the skill or other personal quality of the party was a distinctive characteristic of the thing stipulated for, or a material inducement to the contract. There is no evidence that grapes for wine-making, containing a specified amount of saccharine matter, raised upon a particular vineyard by one man, would necessarily or probably be different from grapes raised from the same vines by another man. . . .

It is not impossible that one man might have some peculiar skill or secret by which he could raise better grapes from the same vines than other men could. But there is no evidence that there was any such peculiarity about the original owner of this vineyard, and we do not think that the court will *assume* that there was. . . . We cannot see any reason that would make this contract nonassignable. . . . [Judgment for plaintiff.]

Unless there is an express provision against it, an assignment of the rights of a contract normally include a delegation of the duties. However, a contract that calls for the skill, credit, or other personal quality of the promisor is not assignable or delegable by the promisor, since the performance received would be different from that required by the contract. For example, a famous singer who has a contract to perform a concert could not assign or delegate that contract to another singer. An exception may occur, however, when such an assignment has been ratified by subsequent acts of the parties.

Seale v. Bates
145 Colo. 430, 359 P.2d 356 (1961).

Doyle, Justice Plaintiffs in error will be referred to by name or as they were designated in the trial court where they were plaintiffs in an action against John Bates, individually, the Bates Dance Studio, Inc. and the Dance Studio of Denver, Inc. The Seales sought to recover $2,040 which had been paid to the Bates Dance Studio to defray the cost of 300 hours of dance instruction. . . . From their complaints it would appear that the contracts which the plaintiffs entered into with the Bates Dance Studio had been assigned to the Dance Studio of Denver, doing business as Dale Dance Studio. . . . The Seales were told that the "students and the instructors, the entire organization was transferred to the Dale Studios; that we would have the same instructors, the same instruction, a continuation of what we had had at Bates." They proceeded to take lessons at Dale, but after some 30 one-half hours of instruction they became dissatisfied with the conditions. . . . This dissatisfaction arose from the fact that the room was much smaller and more crowded and the music from another room interfered with the lessons. Each of the Seales did not have his or her own instructor, Mr. Seale being required to take his lessons from a male instructor; there were difficulties in getting appointments and on some occasions when appointments were made an instructor would not be available. . . . As a result of this dissatisfaction, Mr. and Mrs. Seale stopped taking lessons in May of 1957. The following August they complained to Mr. John Bates of the Bates Studio and demanded that he refund their money or make proper arrangements for completing their contract. Bates informed them that his school was then closed and that there was no money to reimburse them.

In seeking reversal, plaintiffs assert that the trial court erred. . . .

In failing to hold that the duties under these contracts were personal, therefore non-assignable.

. . . The argument of plaintiffs that this was a personal service contract and therefore non-assignable without their consent is valid. . . . This, however, does not furnish a reason for holding that plaintiffs are now entitled to recover. On the contrary, there is evidence to support the trial court's finding and conclusion that the plaintiffs accepted the assignment as such; they did not elect to rescind when it was brought to their attention that the contracts had been assigned to Dale Dance Studio. The undisputed evidence shows that they accepted the assignment and proceeded to take lessons from the Dale Dance Studio. This conduct is inconsistent with plaintiff's present theory that they at all times objected to the assignment. Had they refused to receive instruction from Dale and had they taken the position that their contract was with Bates and no other, there would be substance to their present contention that this violation justified the rescission. . . . Accordingly the trial court's finding and conclusion that the plaintiffs waived any rights which may have arisen from the assignment must be upheld. . . .

[Judgment for defendant.]

Express Provisions

If the contract contains an express provision against assignment ("This contract is not assignable by either party, and any attempted assignment will make this contract void"), generally the provision will be upheld and the contract will not be assignable (e.g., lease containing express provision against assignment without written permission of landlord is generally upheld). However, this clause can be waived (e.g., implied waiver when nonassigning party [landlord] accepted rent from assignee [new tenant]). Also, there is a modern rule followed in many states that holds that the landlord cannot be arbitrary and unreasonable in the refusal to accept an assignment of a lease.

A provision against assigning a contract would not, however, prohibit an assignment of the money due or to become due under the agreement, nor of an action for money damages arising from breach of the contract.

Employment Contracts

Where there is a valid, existing contract of employment, money to become due and other rights thereunder may be assigned. However, since the general rule is that possible future earnings may not be assigned, where the contract of employment is not yet in existence, an assignment under it would not be enforceable.

Judgment

Judgment
The determination by a court of matters submitted to it.

A right of action based on a wrong of purely personal nature, such as slander, assault and battery, or negligence, cannot be assigned. However, if successful in the trial, a *judgment* based on the action would be assignable.

Prohibited Contracts

Under UCC § 2–210(2), a court can prohibit an assignment of contracts for the sale of goods in any one of the following cases:

1. Where is would materially affect the duty of the nonassigning party. For example, A contracts to sell to B all of B's requirements of a certain product during a certain period. If B's requirements are materially different from C's, a potential assignee, B cannot assign the contract to C.

2. Where the assignment would increase the burden or risk on the nonassigning party. For example, A contracts to sell B goods according to B's specifications as to quality. B assigns to C, whose specifications as to quality vary materially from B's. B cannot assign to C, as this would materially increase the burden or risk on A.

3. Where the assignment would impair materially the nonassigning party's chance of obtaining a return performance. For example, assume that a seller has a continuing obligation in regard to goods already delivered

(such as servicing such goods) under contract to the buyer, who is to pay part of the price at a future date. Seller may not assign his right to payment, since such assignment may diminish his interest in continuing his obligation to service the goods.

Effect of Assignment

Liability of Assignor

Since the assignor cannot escape the burdens of the contract by an assignment, he still remains liable as a surety to the original party. To hold otherwise would allow persons to avoid their obligations by assigning them to irresponsible parties. This is true even though the assignee assumes all of the obligations of the agreement. In other words, the assignor can assign all of the benefits of a contract but remains liable for the burdens. For example, a buyer of goods assigns his right to purchase to a new buyer assignee. If the new buyer defaults, the original party is still liable.

Surety
One who undertakes to pay money or perform other acts in the event that his principal fails to do so.

Liability of Assignee

Under the minority and traditional view, the assignee does not become bound to perform the obligations of the assignor by merely accepting the assignment. However, if the assignee expressly assumes the assignor's promise to perform, he is liable to the creditor, since the creditor would be a third-party beneficiary to such an assignment if it appeared that it was made for the creditor's benefit. For example, S sells his business to B and as part of the contract, B promises to pay off all of the existing creditors of the business. B has assumed the seller's promise to perform. If B fails to pay off the debts, he is also liable to S for breach of the assumption agreement.

Acceptance by Assignee

Under the modern view, the Restatement of Contracts, and § 2–210(4) of the UCC, an acceptance by the assignee of an assignment of a contract constitutes a promise by the assignee to perform the duties of the assignor (in the absence of language or circumstances to the contrary). The promise is enforceable by either the assignor or the other party to the original contract. This type of assignment is the normal commercial assignment (substitution of the assignee for the assignor both as to rights and duties). For example, S sells, transfers, and assigns to B all of his rights and obligations in connection with a specified business. Although B promised nothing, it will be implied that he promised to pay off the obligation from the acceptance of the assignment.

Right to Assurances

Under § 2–210(5) of the UCC, the nonassigning party has a stake in the reliability of the person with whom the original contract was made and is therefore entitled to due assurance that any delegated performance will be carried out. Thus, the assignment may be treated as creating reasonable grounds for insecurity, and the nonassigning original party may demand assurances from the assignee. For example, a buyer of goods to be specially made feels insecure when the contracting manufacturer assigns the contract to a second unknown manufacturer. The purchaser can then demand a provision for withholding stated amounts of the purchase price until satisfactory completion of the agreement.

Assurances
Guarantees or promises that make one confident that the assured thing will occur.

Rights of Assignee

When the assignment is completed, the assignee has all of the legal rights of the assignor. However, to assert these rights, the assignee must give notice to the nonassigning original party (obligor). After notice of the assignment has been given, the obligor must perform his obligation to the assignee. If the obligor gives performance to the assignor after receiving notice of the assignment, the obligation is still owed to the assignee. For example, after a seller (obligor) learns that the buyer (assignor) has assigned his right to purchase goods to a new buyer (assignee), the seller must deliver the goods to the assignee to fulfill his obligation. Also, after a doctor assigns his fee to a collection agency, the patient debtor must pay the collection agency rather than the doctor to end the debt obligation.

After an assignment, the assignee is said to "stand in the shoes" of the assignor. In other words, the assignee takes all the rights of the assignor but subject to any defenses that the obligor has against the assignor before the notice of assignment. For example, a painter may assign to a collection agency a debt payment due him for painting a home. However, if the painter did not properly perform the contract, any claim for damages that the homeowner had against the painter could be asserted against the collection agency as well. The assignee collection agency might therefore be liable to the homeowner for the expenses incurred by paying a second painter to correct the defective work.

Defense Waivers

Waiver
A voluntary and intentional giving up or surrender of some known right.

Clauses are often inserted in installment contracts that state that the buyer will not assert any defenses he may have (such as a defective product) against an assignee of the contract (usually a finance company). These clauses have caused much litigation, and their present validity under case law is unsettled. However, the majority rule, and the modern trend, is that the clause is ineffective. In some jurisdictions, the clauses have been held to be void on the grounds of public policy. In many states, such defense waivers have been invalidated by consumer protection laws (e.g., California Civil Code Section 1804.2) or deemed to be unconscionable. In other states, courts have found such waivers invalid because of the close connection between the assignee of the contract and the original transaction.

In 1977, the Federal Trade Commission invalidated waiver of defense provisions in consumer credit transactions. Under UCC § 9–206(1), such waivers are enforceable only if the assignee (finance company or lender) purchased the contract *for value,* in *good faith,* and *without notice* of any defenses that the obligor might have against the assignor.

Priorities Among Successive Assignees

Occasionally, an assignor, because of mistake or fraud, may assign the same claim to more than one assignee. For example, a creditor may on the first of the month assign an account to Acme Collection Agency for collection and, through mistake, assign the same claim to Zenith Collection Agency at the end of the month. Or a land speculator with an option contract to buy some valuable property assigns the contract to Adam for $1,000, then fraudulently assigns the same option to Zeke for $1,000. In such instances, which assignee prevails? The majority rule adopted in most states, including New York, gives priority to the assignee first in time on the theory that the legal title or rights passed from the first assignor to the assignee at the first assignment. Thus, the assignor has nothing left to assign to the second assignee. Of course, the second assignee has a right to sue the assignor for any damages suffered.

There is a minority rule followed in some states, including California and Florida, that gives priority to the assignee who first gives notice to the obligor on the theory that an assignment should be governed by equitable rules. If the first assignee does not perfect his right by giving notice to the debtor or other obligor, he makes it possible for the assignor to deceive a second assignee, an innocent party, by making another assignment.

Priority
The right to a precedence or preference in claims.

Notice
Information concerning a fact actually communicated to a person or derived by him from a proper source.

QUESTIONS

1. What is the general rule regarding assignment of contracts? What is the reason for the rule?
2. In general, what kinds of contracts cannot be assigned?
3. What are the advantages and disadvantages of defense waiver clauses in contract assignments?
4. Under what conditions may the courts prohibit assignment of contracts for the sale of goods?
5. Who prevails when the same contract has been assigned to more than one assignee? In your opinion, what is the best way to handle this problem?

PROBLEMS

1. Plaintiff was insured by X Automobile Insurance Company. The policy had a provision whereby the company would pay all "reasonable medical expenses" incurred by the plaintiff as a result of an automobile accident. The plaintiff was injured in an automobile accident, and his doctor prescribed medicines and an orthopedic (very hard) mattress and spring for the plaintiff's low-back injury. The plaintiff submitted all medical bills as requested by the company; however, the company will not pay for the special mattress and spring. What decision?

2. A, an architect, made a written contract with B to design a building for which A was to be paid 10 percent of the cost of the building. There was nothing in the written contract as to the maximum cost of the building. After A finished his work, he demanded payment based on the actual cost of the building. B claims, however, that they had agreed on a maximum cost for the building and that A's fee could not exceed 10 percent of that maximum cost, which was considerably lower than the actual cost. Will the court permit B to testify as to the oral agreement?

3. Tenant signs a printed form lease stating that a garage is not included in the apartment rent. In a blank space at the end of the lease above the sig-

natures of the parties, the landlord writes "garage included in rent." A dispute arises as to whether the printed words in the lease or the written words prevail. Decision?

4. Mr. Hernandez takes out a policy of insurance on his life with his mother as the beneficiary. Several years later, Mr. Hernandez marries and wants to change the beneficiary of the policy to his wife. Discuss his right to do so without permission of his mother.

5. A has been injured in an automobile accident and retains B as his attorney to represent him. Later B assigns the retainer contract to T without A's permission. A seeks your advice as to whether he must accept T as his new attorney.

6. Tenant assigns the balance of his five-year store lease to assignee, who assumes all of the burdens of the lease. Shortly after the assignment, the assignee becomes bankrupt. The landlord seeks unpaid and future rentals for the balance of the term from the tenant. Tenant defends on the grounds that he had assigned the lease and the assignee expressly assumed the burdens of the lease. Decision?

7. A contracted with B to do some plumbing work in B's home. A did not have a license, although a statute required a license as a condition to recovering for plumbing work. After A completed the work, he assigned the right to the money for the work to T. B refuses to pay T, so T sues B on the contract between A and B. Decision?

8. Debtor owes creditor $1,000. Creditor assigns the claim to T, who promptly mails notice to the debtor. The debtor, however, fails to read the notice of the assignment from T and pays the creditor in full without knowing of the assignment. T seeks payment from debtor, and debtor contends that his payment to creditor without notice is a defense. Decision?

9. Debtor owes creditor $1,000. Creditor assigns the claims to A on June 1 and then by mistake assigns the same claim to B on June 4. On June 4, B gives notice of the assignment to debtor. On June 5, A gives notice of the assignment to the debtor. Both A and B claim the $1,000 from debtor. Who prevails?

10. Buyer purchased a new car from the seller on the installment plan. The installment contract contained a clause waiving any defenses the buyer had in the sale against any assignee of the contract. The bank purchased the installment contract for value, in good faith, and without notice of the buyer's defense. Buyer does not want to pay on the installment contract because the car has proven defective. Discuss.

CHAPTER TEN

Discharging the Contract

10.1 Termination
Performance
    Payment
    Time of Performance
    Substantial Performance
    Personal Satisfaction
Actions of the Parties
    Conditions
    Mutual Release
    Novation
    Accord and Satisfaction
    Account Stated
    Material Alteration
    Prevention of Performance
Impossibility
    Act of God
    Strikes and Other Hazards
    Act of an Enemy
    Destruction of Subject Matter
    Unforeseen Difficulty
    Commercial Frustration
    Disability or Death
Operation of Law
    Bankruptcy
    Insolvency
    Statute of Limitations

10.2 Damages
Compensatory Damages
    Construction Contracts
    Attorney's Fees
    Emotional Reactions
    Computer Error
    Loss of Profits
Punitive Damages
Liquidated Damages
Late Payments
Mitigation of Damages
    Goods and Services
Interest

10.3 Equitable Relief
Specific Performance
    Real Estate and Personal Property
    Personal Services
Rescission
    Restitution
Reformation

10.1 Termination

Performance

Performance
The fulfillment of an obligation.

Most contracts are terminated by performance of the terms of the agreement by the parties. Termination can also occur because of actions of the parties, because of impossibility of performance, or by operation of law.

Payment

Payment
Delivery of money in fulfillment of an obligation.

When payment is required by the contract, performance is completed by the payment of the money. Payment by check is a conditional payment and is not a discharge of the debt until the check is paid (i.e., credited to the bank account of the creditor). The creditor can refuse payment by check on the grounds that a check is not legal tender.

Tender
An unconditional offer to perform coupled with the ability to do so.

Valid Tender   A valid tender of payment consists of an unconditional offer by the debtor to the creditor of the exact amount due on the date the debt or claim is due. If the tender is refused, the debt is not discharged. The refusal stops the running of interest, discharges liens, and prevents the awarding of court costs if the debtor is sued, although the debtor must keep the tender open (i.e., keep the money available for the creditor). Statutes in some states provide that when tender is refused, the debtor can deposit the money in a bank in the name of the creditor and thereafter notify the creditor, at which time the obligation is extinguished (California Civil Code 1500).

Statute of Limitations
The statutory time beyond which an action may not be brought.

Partial Payment   Occasionally a debtor will owe one creditor more than one debt, and the debtor may send the creditor a partial payment. To which debt should this payment be applied? The decision may be important, because one or more of the debts may by barred by the statute of limitations (law that fixes time within which parties must take judicial action to enforce rights), but in most states, if the creditor applies the payment to such a debt, it will revive the right to sue. The debtor can specify how the payment should be applied, and the creditor is bound by that choice. However, if no choice is specified, the payment may be applied to any one or more of the debts in any manner that the creditor chooses.

Time of Performance

If the contract terms specify a date of performance, such performance should be done on that date. However, a short delay normally does not justify rescission of the agreement or a lawsuit for damages. However, the nature of the contract itself might be such that even a brief delay is actionable. For example, in contracts of a mercantile nature (for manufacture and sale of goods), or where there is a sale of property of a speculative or fluctuating value (oil, gas, or mining rights), time is considered to be important, and slight delays may be grounds for a lawsuit.

Time of Essence The contract itself may contain a clause that states "time is of the essence," in which case delayed performance is treated as a breach of contract unless refusal to grant a reasonable delay would be unconscionable.

Time of the Essence
A term used in contracts that fixes time of performance as an essential requirement.

Reasonable Delay In contracts for the manufacture of special products or in building contracts, time is not of the essence, and a reasonable delay is permitted because of the great hardship that might otherwise occur. In the usual real estate contract, time is not regarded to be of the essence.

The following case is an example of a delay in performance excused because it involved a contract for skill.

Facts
The plaintiff contracted with the defendant to furnish certain fine stationery and advertising matter "in the course of the year." The work was not finished in time, and delivery was not made until one week after the expiration of the year. The defendant refused to pay for the goods on the grounds that the goods were not furnished within the time specified in the contract. Plaintiff sued for the price of the goods.

Decision
In contracts for work or skill and for the materials upon which the work or skill is to be bestowed, a statement fixing the time of performance of the contract is not ordinarily of its essence, and a failure to perform within the time stipulated—followed by substantial performance after a short delay—will not justify the aggrieved party in repudiating the entire contract but will simply give the party his action for damages for the breach of the stipulation.

Judgment for plaintiff.

Beck & Pauli Lithographing Co. v. Colorado Mining Co., 3 C.C.A. 248, 52 Fed. 700 (1893).

Substantial Performance

When one of the parties to a contract fails to perform, the other may terminate the agreement and sue for breach of contract. In such a case, there has been a failure of consideration. To apply this rule strictly in all cases could result in great hardship. For example, if a building contractor built a home for a person and complied with the contract except for some minor detail, it would be unfair to permit rescission. Therefore, where there has been substantial compliance, or *substantial performance*, the court will not rescind the contract but will allow money damages for any part not completed.

Surety Development Corp. v. Grevas
42 Ill.App.2d 268, 192 N.E.2d 145 (1963).

Smith, Justice When is a house a home? In our context a house is a home when it can be lived in. But when is that: When substantially completed or completely completed? We posit the question, because the answer is decisive.

Plaintiff sells prefabricated houses. Defendants selected one of their models, styled "Royal Countess, elevation 940". A contract was signed. The cost was

$16,385.00; completion date September 27, 1961. Around 4:00 P.M. on that date defendants refused to accept the house asserting non-completion. Plaintiff then sued for the balance due and defendants counter-claimed for their downpayment. Both alleged performance by them and non-performance by the other. The legal issue is therefore relatively simple: Who performed and who didn't. The facts are more elusive—plaintiff at times says one thing, defendants another. We narrate them briefly.

On the morning of the twenty-seventh, "Royal Countess, elevation 940" was far from being a house, let alone a home. Racing the clock, plaintiff initiated a crash program. When defendants arrived on the scene at 4:00, at plaintiff's behest for final inspection, the crash program was still crashing—workmen were all over the place, slapping on siding, laying the floors, bulldozing the yard, hooking up the utilities, and so on. Defendants' tour was not a success, to put it mildly. Instead of a home, they found, to their dismay, a hive buzzing with activity. They did not tarry, in spite of the foreman's assurances that all would be right by 5:30. Nor did they come back. They should have. Believe it or not, the foreman was right. The job was substantially completed by 5:30, with only a service walk, some grading and blacktopping left undone.

The trial court found that the house had been substantially completed and concluded that there had been, therefore, substantial compliance with the contract and with this we agree. But because the house was not completely completed, it found that there had not been *complete* compliance. With this, too, we agree, but such finding is beside the point. Substantial—not complete—compliance in a construction contract is all that is required. By 5:30, there had been just that, in other words, substantial performance of the contract. Plaintiff's contretemps in having inspection set for 4:00 o'clock was hardly the way to make friends and influence people, but such happenstance is of no moment in determining whether or not there had been substantial compliance, unless such can be said to indicate bad faith. We do not think that it does. What it indicates is bad timing, not bad faith. . . .

No substantial sum was required to complete the items left undone. Nor were they of so essential a character that defendants could not have been ensconced in their new home that night if they had so desired. We have thus answered our question: A house is ready to be lived in, to become a home, when it has been substantially completed.

[Judgment for plaintiff.]

Personal Satisfaction

Satisfaction
Something that gratifies fully the wants, wishes, likes, or desires of a person.

When a contracting party inserts a conditional clause requiring personal satisfaction with the results and the promisee asserts dissatisfaction, the courts first look to the subject matter of the agreement before making a decision. If the contract involves matters of fancy, taste, or judgment and the promisee in good faith asserts that he is not satisfied, the courts will not consider the reasonableness of his attitude but will hold that his subjective personal decision controls. Typical examples are agreements to paint a portrait, write a literary article, or produce a play as well as many employment contracts. But where cases seem to involve objective factors, such as operative fitness or mechanical utility, courts will apply the term *reasonable satisfaction*, and if a reasonable person would be satisfied with the results, the agreement will be enforced. In the following encapsulated case, the court considered these rules:

Facts

Johnson was a school bus operator for two years, and his contract had an option to renew for three more years "if a bus is run and his service has been satisfactory." He tried to exercise his option, and the school district refused to accept it but instead operated its own bus. The school district officials said that "satisfaction" meant personal (subjective) judgment and that lack of such satisfaction could not be reviewed by the courts.

Decision

Personal satisfaction cases fall into two categories: one involves taste, fancy, or personal judgment; the other involves utility, fitness, or value (which can be measured objectively and in which performance need be only reasonably satisfactory). Where, as in this case, in a given contract the category is doubtful, the objective interpretation is to be adopted. In any event, the personal dissatisfaction must be actual and honest and not feigned to escape liability. If the plaintiff could prove that his performance would satisfy a reasonable person under the circumstances, his contract should be renewed.

Johnson v. School District No. 12, 210 Or. 585, 312 P.2d 591 (1957).

Express Provision Most authorities agree that even in mechanical utility types of contracts where a provision clearly calls for performance to personal satisfaction, the subjective test will be applied. Thus, as in most contract problem areas, the distinction can be avoided by the use of sufficiently emphatic and clear language in the agreement.

Mechanical Utility
Something useful done as if by a machine.

Third-Person Satisfaction If the parties agree that the sufficiency of performance shall be determined by some third person, such as an architect or attorney, that person's determination is conclusive in the absence of fraud or mistake. Suppose a doctor makes a contract with a contractor for the building of an expensive home and, realizing that she is not a construction expert, has her attorney put a clause in the agreement that the contractor will not be paid in full until the architect is satisfied with the job and issues his certificate of approval. The architect's certificate would be a condition precedent to the payment unless the architect withheld it arbitrarily, through mistake or fraud, or in bad faith. If any of these factors could be proved, the contractor could recover without the certificate.

Certificate
A written or printed statement testifying to a fact, qualification, or promise.

Actions of the Parties

Conditions

The parties themselves may act to end the contract. They may place conditions in the agreement (refer to Subchapter 8.1) that provide that the contract shall terminate upon the happening of a certain event. For example, a provision may be in an insurance policy that provides that unless the insured gives the company notice of loss by fire within a stated period of time, the right to recovery is lost. Or a seller may sell property with a condition that the property may be returned if it does not comply with certain specifications, thereby giving the buyer a title with right to rescind. Some contracts have provisions that either party may terminate the agreement upon giving a written notice to the other within a definite time period.

Specifications
A particular and detailed account or description of a thing.

Mutual Release

Release
The act or writing whereby some claim, right, or interest is given up to the person against whom it could have been enforced.

The parties to a contract may agree to rescind the contract and place each other in status quo by returning any property or money that had been delivered or paid. An oral mutual rescission is valid except in the case of a sale of an interest in land, in which case the mutual rescission must be in writing pursuant to the same formalities as required by the statute of frauds. The parties may agree to replace the original contract with a new one. If they do so, the original contract is terminated by substitution.

Novation

Novation
The substitution of a new agreement for an old one.

A novation is a substitution of a new contract or obligation for an old one, which is thereby extinguished. It can involve the substitution of a new debt or obligation where the debtor and creditor remain the same (debtor to paint creditor's house instead of paying creditor a certain sum of money), where the debt remains the same but a new creditor is substituted for the previous creditor, or where the debt remains the same but a new debtor is substituted for the previous debtor.

Novation of debtors is the most frequent form of novation. For example, John purchases a new car on an installment contract. While still owing $1,000 on the contract, John loses his job and is unable to keep up the payments on the car. Theresa, John, and the finance company agree that Theresa will take over the payments and the ownership of the car and John will be released from the installment contract.

Although a novation may be made orally, it is a much better practice to put the substitute agreement in writing.

Accord and Satisfaction

Accord and Satisfaction
The payment of money or other thing of value, usually less than the amount owed, in exchange for cancellation of a debt.

An *accord* is an agreement for a substituted performance in satisfaction of the original obligation. When the accord is carried out, there is an *accord and satisfaction,* and the original obligation is discharged. The usual purpose is to settle a claim with a different performance. Thus, debtor owes creditor $1,000. The parties agree that debtor shall paint the creditor's house in satisfaction of the debt. The agreement is an accord. When the house is painted, there has been an accord and satisfaction, and the debt is discharged.

Account Stated

Account Stated
An agreement between parties who have had previous transactions, fixing the amount due from one to the other and stating the liability of the debtor.

An account is a right to payment under a contract. An *account stated* is an agreement between parties who have transacted business with each other as to the amount of the final balance due from one to the other. This is a new and independent executory contract. The items in the orignal accounts are merged into the account stated. No right of action remains as to the items. For example, A and B have been doing business with each other over a period of time, which has created a relationship of debtor and creditor between them. A and B agree that a certain amount is due, and B promises to pay that amount. This is called an account stated. The agreement discharges the obligations arising under the prior transactions.

The account stated may be implied, as where a creditor renders a statement to the debtor and the debtor fails to object within a reasonable time.

Material Alteration

Generally a material, fraudulent alteration of a written contract by one who asserts a right under the contract extinguishes the person's right to recover on the contract. The test of materiality is whether the alteration makes any change in the meaning or legal effect of the contract. The following are exceptions to the general rule: (1) where the alteration is not material, (2) where it is made by a stranger to the instrument, (3) where it is made accidentally or innocently, (4) where it is made to show the actual agreement of the parties, or (5) where the alteration is ratified by the other party.

Where the alteration is intentional but not fraudulent, the effectiveness of the instrument is destroyed. The party who made the innocent alteration can generally recover on the original consideration. For example, A borrowed $10,000 from B and signed a note and mortgage, which created a lien on his farm. B innocently made a material alteration of the mortgage document without A's knowledge. Under the general rule, B will be able to get a judgment on the note but will not be able to enforce the mortgage lien against the farm.

Where one party signs an incomplete instrument containing blanks and the other party without authority fills them in, a fraudulent alteration has occurred that prevents the formation of any contract.

> **Material Alteration**
> Any alteration of a document that changes its legal effect.

Prevention of Performance

Where one party prevents the other party from performing, the latter is excused from performance. Also, where one party waives performance by the other, performance is excused. For example, landlord habitually accepts rental payments many days after payments are due. In such a case, before the landlord can insist that the payments be made on due date, the landlord must give a timely notice to the tenant of the reinstatement of the requirement. The following case is an example of prevention of performance constituting a breach of contract.

Facts

Velma Jacobs, owner of a farm, entered into a contract with Earl Walker in which Walker agreed to paint the barns and improvements on the farm. Walker purchased the paint from Charles Jones, doing business as Chas. Jones Lumber Company. Before the work was completed, Jacobs ordered Walker to stop because she was dissatisfied with the results. Offers were made by Jones and Walker to complete the job, but Jacobs declined to permit Walker to fulfill his contract.

Decision

Jacobs, by her order to Walker to cease work and by refusing to permit either Walker or Jones to complete the work (which the trial court found they were willing to do), breached the contract and excused further performance on the part of Walker. Under the circumstances, the law implies a promise on the one party not to prevent, hinder, or delay the performance of the other party.

Under the facts, as found by the trial court, Jones was entitled to be paid for the value of the paint furnished for use and used upon Jacobs' barns and improvements and Walker was entitled to recover for the reasonable value of the work he completed in accordance with the contract.

Jacobs v. Jones, 161 Colo. 505, 423 P.2d 321 (1967).

Anticipatory Breach
A breach of contract committed before the time of required performance, usually by repudiation.

Anticipatory Breach An actual breach does not take place until the time for performance has arrived. There may, however, be a total breach by anticipatory repudiation. A repudiation of a contract prior to the date fixed by the contract for performance is called an anticipatory breach. For example, in February, Jones and Elwell enter into a contract in which Elwell will act as a lifeguard for Jones from May through September. In March, Jones informs Elwell that he has hired someone else to be the lifeguard. This action by Jones is an anticipatory breach of the contract between Jones and Elwell.

If a party to a contract informs the other party prior to performance date that he is not going to perform, the aggrieved party has an election of remedies: (1) he may wait until the time for performance and exercise his remedies for the actual breach, or (2) he may treat the repudiation as an anticipatory breach and exercise his remedies immediately.

The doctrine does not apply to unilateral contracts. For example, debtor owes creditor $100 on a note that is not yet due and informs the creditor that he is not going to pay the note when it becomes due. Creditor cannot bring suit until after the note is due.

The doctrine does not ordinarily apply to a lease between a landlord and tenant. In the absence of a special provision in the lease, the lessor cannot sue at once to recover damages based on the entire balance due when the tenant defaults.

An anticipatory breach can be retracted if the injured party has not in the meantime changed his position. The injured party does not waive his remedies by urging performance.

Section 2–610 of the UCC provides that the aggrieved party following an anticipatory breach may suspend performance on his part and bring an action for breach of contract even though he has urged retraction of the repudiation.

Repudiation
An act or declaration by a contracting party indicating definitely that he or she will not perform, or further perform, the contract.

Section 2–611 of the UCC provides that if the aggrieved party has not changed his position or cancelled the contract, the repudiation may be retracted. However, although the repudiation may be retracted, the aggrieved party can demand assurance of due performance and until he receives such assurance may suspend any further performance on his part (UCC § 2–609).

Impossibility

Impossibility
A defense to breach of contract when performance is impossible.

If performance of a contract was physically impossible at the time the contract was made and this fact was not known to the parties, performance is excused. For example, T leases a dance hall from L. Unknown to the parties, the building has been destroyed by fire. This is usually referred to as objective impossibility (i.e., impossible in the nature of things rather than because of the inability of the party to perform).

Impossibility because a party is or becomes financially unable or because he personally lacks the capability or competence to perform is usually referred to as subjective impossibility and generally does not excuse performance. The following case is an example of subjective impossibility.

Kennedy v. Reece
225 Cal.App.2d 717, 37 Cal.Rptr. 708 (1964).

Conley, Presiding Justice This is an appeal by the plaintiff from a judgment adverse to him on his complaint and favorable to the defendants on their counterclaim. The plaintiff, Fred Kennedy, made a contract with Reece and Thomas, mining partners, to drill a water well for them. . . .

The cause was tried by the court sitting without a jury, and resulted in a judgment for the defendants on their counterclaim in the sum of $1,307.15, besides interest and costs. . . .

The evidence shows that Mr. Kennedy was an experienced water well driller carrying on his trade in the area; that he assured Mr. Reece that he was certain of getting an acceptable well and that there would be no trouble in reaching the 400-foot level contemplated by the written contract. However, the first hole drilled by the plaintiff, after being carried to a depth of 130 feet, was abandoned at the instance of the appellant because he claimed that he had struck hard rock.

The defendants did not complete the well, although the evidence indicates that two contractors stated to Mr. Reece that they would be willing to drill to the 400-foot level at a cost estimated at $5.00 per foot, besides the necessary expense of setting up and taking down their equipment. . . .

It is obvious that the finding that the plaintiff failed to comply with the terms of his contract is supported by substantial evidence; the well driller did not dig the well to a depth of 400 feet; he did not case it; he did not gravel pack, or wash, or bail it. Appellant contends, however, that he was relieved from the duty of completing his contract because of "impossibility" resulting when he hit hard rock at the 270 foot level.

The enlargement of the meaning of "impossibility" as a defense, (which at common law originally meant literal or physical impossibility of performance) to include "impracticability" is now generally recognized. . . . However, this does not mean that any facts, which make performance more difficult or expensive than the parties anticipated, discharge a duty that has been created by the contract. . . . Facts which make performance harder or more costly than the parties contemplated when the agreement was made do not constitute a ground for the successful interposition of the defense of "impracticability" unless such facts are of the gravest importance. If it be noted that this is merely a difference of degree rather than a difference in kind, such notation is accurate. . . .

[I]ncreased difficulties and heightened costs of a reasonable nature, even though originally unforeseen, do not render the performance of a contract "impracticable". . . . For example, if a contractor agrees to build a structure and it is destroyed by fire or other casualty when only partly completed, the contractor is not relieved from his duty to rebuild merely because of the additional expense he must incur or the added difficulties he must overcome. . . .

In the present case, neither the pleadings nor the facts as found by the court warrant the application of the doctrine of impossibility, or impracticability. . . .

[Judgment for defendant.]

Act of God

Act of God
An act resulting exclusively from natural causes and not brought on by any human interference.

Many courts hold that an act of God or nature (flood, tornado) does not excuse performance of a contract unless performance is excused in the contract. By statute or case law in many jurisdictions, an act of God or nature that renders a contract impossible of performance is a defense to performance.

Strikes and Other Hazards

Strike
A combined effort by a group to exert pressure on a person or entity to yield to certain demands.

Unless provided for in the contract, such hazards as strikes, picketing, riots, fire, business threats, inevitable or unavoidable accidents, and breaking of machinery or equipment generally do not constitute a defense for failure to perform. Hazards such as these are generally foreseeable or are only of a temporary nature. For a strike to be used as a defense, two things are necessary: (1) the strike must be unexpected and unforeseeable, and (2) the strike must have rendered performance commercially impracticable.

Act of an Enemy

The act of an enemy is generally no defense unless it renders performance impossible or illegal or destroys the basis or subject matter of the contract, in which case most courts excuse performance.

Destruction of Subject Matter

When a contract requires the transfer of a *specific* thing, the destruction of the thing makes the performance impossible and excuses performance (e.g., a contract to manufacture goods in a particular factory is discharged by the destruction of the factory; a contract to paint a specific building is discharged by the destruction of the building; a contract to carry goods by a particular ship is discharged by the loss of the ship; a sale of the wheat crop growing on a specific parcel of land is discharged if the crop is destroyed). (See UCC § 2–613[a].)

If there is a contract to sell only a given quantity of wheat and not a particular crop of wheat, the seller is not discharged by the destruction of the wheat. In such a case, the seller makes an absolute undertaking to deliver the wheat, which is not limited or restricted in any way to any particular wheat. Thus, if the seller is unable to deliver the quantity of wheat, he is liable for breach of contract. Moral: Sellers, put in an escape clause (e.g., destruction of the wheat excuses performance); buyers, keep it out.

Unforeseen Difficulty

Mere unforeseen difficulty or expense does not constitute impossibility and ordinarily is not a defense. The modern trend, however, is to allow the defense of impossibility when performance is impracticable because of excessive and unreasonable expense or extraordinary difficulty that was not reasonably foreseeable. The following case illustrates the rule.

Facts

The plaintiff entered into a contract with the defendant in which the plaintiff agreed to repair and upgrade the upstream face of Cooper Lake Dam. The contract provided that the plaintiff would quarry at a designated site across the lake. The parties assumed that the rock could be transported to the dam during the winter across the frozen ice. However, in attempting the crossing, the plaintiff lost three trucks and the lives of two drivers when the trucks broke through the ice.

Decision

The court held that the contract was impossible to perform and that the plaintiff was discharged. The court said: "[A] party is discharged from his contract obligations, even if it is technically possible to perform them, if the costs of performance would be so disproportionate to that reasonably contemplated by the parties as to make the contract totally impractical in a commercial sense."

Northern Corp. v. Chugach Electric Ass'n, 518 P.2d 76 (Alaska 1974).

Commercial Frustration

The doctrine of commercial frustration is similar to the doctrine of impossibility or impracticability in that both require extreme hardship to excuse performance. Commercial frustration is different in that it assumes the possibility of literal performance but excuses performance because a supervening event that was not contemplated by the parties and not reasonably foreseeable essentially destroyed the purpose for which the contract was made (e.g., lease of neon advertising sign followed by governmental blackout order frustrating primary purpose justified termination). Commercial frustration cannot be used to withdraw from a poor bargain (e.g., tenant leases a gas station that does not produce the profit anticipated because of governmental regulations).

Commercial Frustration
When an implied condition in a contract does not occur or ceases to exist without fault of either party and "frustrates" a party's intentions.

Disability or Death

When one party to a contract must perform an act that requires personal skill (author, painter, lawyer), death or disability of the person who was to perform the act discharges the contract. However, if all the work or services are of such a character that they may be performed by others as well, the obligation will not be discharged (e.g., building contract). The following case is an example of disability as an excuse for performance.

Disability
The state of not being fully able to function, whether physical or mental.

Facts

Plaintiff entered into a contract with the Arthur Murray Dance Studio. The contract stated in bold-type words "NON-CANCELLABLE NEGOTIABLE CONTRACT" and "I UNDERSTAND THAT NO REFUNDS WILL BE MADE UNDER THE TERMS OF THIS CONTRACT." Plaintiff was severely injured in an automobile collision rendering him incapable of continuing his dancing lessons. At that time, he had contracted for a total of 2,734 hours of lessons for which he had paid $24,812.80. Despite written demands, defendant refused to return any of the money.

Decision

Defendants do not deny that the doctrine of impossibility of performance is generally applicable to this type of case. Rather, the defendants contend that the bold-type words were a waiver of the doctrine of impossibility and that the words indicated a contrary intention. The court held that this type of construction was unacceptable. Judgment for plaintiff.

Parker v. Arthur Murray, Inc., 10 Ill.App.3d 1000, 295 N.E.2d 487 (1973).

Operation of Law

Generally, a contract is discharged and performance is excused if, after the contract has been entered into, the performance is made unlawful by a governmental order or decree. Under such circumstances, performance would constitute a violation of public policy (e.g., change in zoning law prior to beginning of construction that prohibited construction of apartment building in that locality).

Bankruptcy

A discharge in bankruptcy is the result of a proceeding in a federal court by which the bankrupt is released from the obligation of certain provable debts. The bankrupt is not released from such debts as back taxes accruing within three years prior to bankruptcy, claims based on willful or malicious injury to the person or property of another, alimony and child support, certain claims involving fraud, certain fines and penalties payable to governmental units, and certain student loans. (Refer to Chapter 31 for a discussion of bankruptcy.)

Insolvency

Section 1–201(23) of the UCC states that a person is insolvent when unable to pay debts as they become due or has ceased to pay debts in the ordinary course of business. Whenever a person's liabilities exceed his assets, he is insolvent under the Federal Bankruptcy Act definition.

States differ as to whether insolvency constitutes a breach of contract. Some courts hold that there is an implied condition in every contract that the promisor will not permit himself to be disabled from performance due to insolvency; therefore, insolvency amounts to a breach of contract.

Other courts hold that insolvency does not result in a breach of contract unless the contract contains an express provision to that effect. They say that if the seller is selling on credit and the buyer becomes insolvent, if the buyer can make payment, the seller must deliver the goods. In other words, the seller is not excused from performance by the insolvency of the buyer.

However, under UCC § 2–702, the seller may demand cash from an insolvent buyer prior to making delivery and may reclaim goods sold to an insolvent buyer. Under UCC § 2–502, the buyer can recover identified goods from an insolvent seller when the buyer has paid all or part of the purchase price. (See Subchapter 18.3, Remedies in Sales.)

Statute of Limitations

All jurisdictions have statutes that require lawsuits to be filed within a specified time after the right to sue accrues. If the time limit is not met, the plaintiff is forever barred from bringing the action. The period of time varies for different types of civil actions and for the state's prosecution of different types of crimes. It also varies from state to state, and local statutes thus must be consulted. Section 2–725 of the UCC specifies a four-year period for actions on contracts for the sale of goods.

Waiver Statute The majority rule is that a debtor may waive the statute of limitations after the time for filing has run by promising to pay the debt

---

Operation of Law
The determination of rights and duties through the automatic effects of the law and not by agreement or acts of the parties.

Bankruptcy
Federal law designed to give a debtor a fresh start either by reorganization or by collecting assets to discharge most debts.

Insolvency
A financial condition in which one is unable to meet obligations as they mature or where one's liabilities exceed assets.

DISCHARGING THE CONTRACT

(in most states, the new promise must be in writing) or by making a part payment, which then revives the obligation. In addition, there are certain other exceptions to the application of the statute. The statute does not apply to the government, nor does it apply where a party has been misled by the other party into delaying the filing of an action, such as when an insurance company adjuster promises an injured claimant that the suit will be settled and then withdraws the promise after the time limit for filing has expired.

Partial Payment A customer may owe a seller on an open account for goods purchased at different times over a period of many years. When the customer sends a partial payment to the seller, the general rule is that the seller can apply the payment to the oldest items in the account, thereby preventing the statute of limitations from running on the oldest items. However, the debtor can change that rule by instructions accompanying the payment (e.g., a notation on the check "By endorsement this check when paid is accepted in full payment of the following account [here state the specific items or invoice numbers and amounts so that the payment is made on current accounts and not on those barred or about to be barred by the statute of limitations]"). A letter containing similar instructions should accompany the check.

Limitation Clauses Some contracts (e.g., insurance contracts) contain a time limitation, such as ninety days, within which suit must be brought. Because suits against the government or its agencies are allowed by consent only, all statutory requirements, including time for filing, must be strictly followed.

Questions

1. When are contracts required to be performed exactly at the time stated in the agreement? When is delayed performance excused?
2. What does it mean to make a contract stating that performance will be to the contracting party's personal satisfaction? When will the court enforce the contract, and what rules will be applied?
3. What are the differences between mutual release, novation, and accord and satisfaction?
4. What does anticipatory breach mean? When it occurs, what are the rights of the other party?
5. What kind of impossibility excuses performance of a contract? What are some examples of impossibility that do not excuse performance?

10.2 Damages

Compensatory Damages

If one party breaks a contract, the other party may be entitled to money damages. When this happens, the law attempts to compensate the plaintiff

Compensatory Damages
Proven losses directly resulting from the breach of contract.

and place him in as good a position as if the defendant had performed the contract. This is based on the theory of awarding just compensation for losses that are the immediate, direct, and natural result of the act complained of; that were normal or usual; and that might have been expected. For example, an electric power company was held liable to food retailers for the spoiling of perishable food items when the company interrupted service without warning for six hours during a summer heat wave.

The injured party is entitled only to damages that were within the contemplation of the parties at the time the contract was made. Unusual or unexpected damages resulting from facts unknown to the defendant or that reasonably could not be foreseen at the time the contract was made are not recoverable. For example, plaintiff flour mill had a broken crankshaft that it sent to a nearby town for repairs. Defendant common carrier agreed to take the shaft and return it as soon as the repair was completed but neglected to make prompt delivery as promised. The plaintiff had not advised the defendant that the mill could not be operated without the shaft. As a result of the defendant's delay, the plaintiff lost several days' profits and sued for the lost profits. The court held for the defendant on the grounds that the plaintiff had not communicated to the carrier that the mill could not be operated without the shaft and the defendant could not reasonably foresee that the mill would be shut down due to the delivery delay.

The amount of damages recoverable is a fact for the jury to decide or for the court alone if there is no jury trial. Court costs (filing fees, witness fees, jury fees, deposition costs, but not attorney's fees) are usually charged to the losing party. If the plaintiff wins but did not suffer a loss or cannot prove a loss, the court may award nominal damages, such as one dollar plus court costs.

Nominal Damages
A nominal sum awarded in recognition that a legal injury was sustained, though slight.

Construction Contracts

In construction contracts where the contractor breaches the contract, damages are generally measured by the reasonable cost of completion in accordance with the contract (the amount extra it costs above the contract price to get the building done), plus reasonable compensation for any delay in performance. Generally this is true whether the contractor refused to finish the work or not and whether the breach was total or partial. However, if there would be an unreasonable economic waste (tearing down the building and starting over), generally the damage rule is based on the difference between the value of full performance as promised and the value of the defective performance actually rendered. Some courts refuse to follow the economic waste rule if the contractor is guilty of willful or intentional breach. In such courts, the contractor would be liable for the actual cost of completion.

Attorney's Fees

Generally, attorney's fees are not recoverable for breach of contract. Reasonable fees can be granted, however, when provided for in the contract, by statute, or when punitive damages are awarded. Some states (California by statute) provide for attorney's fees to the prevailing party when there is a clause in the contract providing for attorney's fees, whether or not the

Emotional Reactions

Emotional reactions peculiar to a particular individual that might result from a breach of contract are too subjective and variable to be reasonably contemplated prior to the breach or ascertainable afterward and are therefore generally not awarded. Where the subject matter of the contract directly concerns the comfort, happiness, or personal welfare of one of the parties, damages may be allowed for mental suffering. Some breaches of contract may justify a tort action for emotional distress.

Mental Suffering
Compensible injury resulting from mental pain, as opposed to mere physical pain, including deep grief distress, anxiety, and fright.

Pettaway v. Commercial Automotive Service
49 Wn.2d 650, 306 P.2d 219 (1957).

Finley, Justice This is an action for damages for the breach of an alleged contract for the purchase and sale of an automobile.

The defendant company displayed a special model, a 1953 Buick "Skylark," automobile in its show window. The plaintiff saw the car and discussed its purchase with a Mr. Shaw, one of defendant corporation's salesmen. Thereafter, the plaintiff signed one of the defendant corporation's order forms on which the price of the new car was stated as $5,667, and $1,500 was designated as a credit allowance for plaintiff's 1948 Chrysler.

. . . Plaintiff's testimony further indicated . . . that he was informed the defendant corporation had sold the 1953 Buick "Skylark" model to someone else. Apparently, the manufacturer had allotted only three automobiles of the particular model to the defendant company, and defendant company failed to produce one for the plaintiff. Thereupon, plaintiff commenced this action for damages for breach of contract. . . .

The jury awarded $1,325 to plaintiff. By answer to special interrogatories, it set (a) $825 as the market value of plaintiff's Chrysler; (b) $300 for plaintiff's disappointment, mental anguish, loss of sleep, humiliation, and damages to his reputation, allegedly resulting from the breach of the contract and the deprivation of the allegedly unique chattel; and (c) $200 by reason of deprivation of use of an automobile. The defendant corporation appealed.

. . . Now, as to the question of damages: Appellant contends that the court erred in submitting to the jury the issue of damages for deprivation of the use of respondent's Chrysler. The evidence was inadequate for the jury to make an award in any amount for that item. There is testimony in the record that respondent hired a taxicab a couple of times for six dollars; but these events were not connected with the breach of the contract in question. The award is the result of pure speculation. . . .

The jury awarded respondent three hundred dollars for the mental anguish occasioned by the failure to deliver the "Skylark" for "conspicuous consumption." The appellant contends that the court erred in submitting that issue to the jury and instructing upon it. We agree. Consequential damages are sustainable

> if they flow naturally and inevitably from a breach of contract and are so related to it as to have been within the contemplation of the parties when they entered into it.... The emotional reactions peculiar to a particular individual which might flow from a breach of a contract of sale of an automobile are too subjective and variable to be contemplated prior to a breach of contract, or ascertainable afterward. Such suffering, if any, is not compensable in an action for damages for breach of contract....
>
> For the reasons stated hereinbefore, it was error to allow the respondent damages in the amounts of $300 for mental anguish and $200 for loss of use of an automobile, and the judgment must be modified and reduced in this respect. [Note: Loss of use is recoverable in many jurisdictions.]

Computer Error

In the modern world there seems to be a tendency to blame the computer for common errors. Is such a computer error a good defense against a claim for damages? For example, Swarens sued the Ford Motor Credit Company for damages for the wrongful repossession of his automobile. Ford defended on the grounds that the repossession was the result of a computer error. The court said, "Men feed data to a computer and men interpret the answer the computer spews forth. In this computerized age, the law must require that men in the use of computerized data regard those with whom they are dealing as more important than a perforation on a card. Trust in the infallibility of a computer is hardly a defense, when the opportunity to avoid the error is as apparent and repeated as was here presented" (*Ford Motor Credit Company* v. *Swarens,* 447 S.W.2d 53 [1969]).

Loss of Profits

The injured party may recover for loss of profits if the loss can be established with reasonable certainty. Reasonable certainty—not mathematical certainty—is all that is required. As long as there is no uncertainty as to the *fact* of damages, there is no objection that the *amount* cannot be determined exactly.

Speculative Damages
Theoretical, not actual damages.

Speculative Damages Speculative (theoretical) damages, including speculative profits, are not recoverable. For example, the loss of future profits from a new business would be speculative, since there would be no evidence to show even a profitable operation, let alone what the amounts of return might be. However, loss of future profits from an *established* business could be awarded if there were a reasonably certain basis for the calculation of the plaintiff's probable loss resulting from the breach. Such loss might be shown by projecting the statistics of past profits into reasonable future performance.

Where the plaintiff is unable to prove the loss of profits, courts may award the amount of expenditures made plus the value of services performed in reliance upon the contract.

Punitive Damages

Exemplary or punitive damages are awarded to one party to punish the other party and to discourage others from similar wrongful conduct. Generally, punitive damages are limited to situations involving willful and wanton torts, such as fraud or libel. Courts have awarded punitive damages for deliberate breach of a fiduciary duty (to act primarily for the benefit of another, such as attorney for client), persistent and repeated wrongful conduct in the operation of a business, and fraud arising from a contract. The more reprehensible the act, the greater the amount of punitive damages that may be ordered. Another measure used by the courts is the amount of compensatory damages found. If the actual harm suffered is small, even a serious wrongful act might not support a large punitive damage award.

Punitive Damages
Compensation in excess of actual damages as a form of punishment to the wrongdoer.

Liquidated Damages

The parties may agree in the contract that a certain amount shall be paid to the injured party in case of default. This is known as a liquidated damage clause. However, any such stated amount must be the result of a reasonable effort by the parties to reach a sum that bears a reasonable relationship to actual damages. If the amount specified is in the nature of a penalty or forfeiture rather than damages, the clause will not be enforced. Further, the contract must be such that it would be extremely difficult or impractical for the court to determine the actual amount of damages.

A common example of a liquidated damage clause is found in building contracts where the contractor is required to pay a stated sum for each day of delay. In *Oregon State Highway Commission* v. *DeLong Corp.* (9 Or.App. 550, 495 P.2d 1215 [1972]), the court held that $2,000 a day for each day of delay by the contractor was reasonable in view of the losses by the state.

Liquidated Damages
An amount agreed in the contract by the parties as a reasonable estimate of damages owing to one in event of breach by the other.

Facts

Plaintiffs were realtors and leased offices from the defendant in Portland, Oregon. Shopping center developers told the defendant that they wanted to acquire the building. As a result, plaintiffs and defendant made a contract wherein defendant agreed to build another building on the opposite corner of the same intersection and lease a portion of it to plaintiffs for five years. They included a clause for $5,000 liquidated damages if the defendant did not perform. The defendant did not erect the building, and the plaintiffs sued. The plaintiffs were awarded $5,000 under the clause, and the defendant appealed.

Decision

Affirmed for the plaintiffs. There are two main criteria to use in deciding whether such a clause is an unenforceable penalty or actual liquidated damages. One requires the sum to bear a reasonable relationship to anticipated damages, and the other requires that the actual damages would be difficult to determine. If the answer to both requirements is yes, the clause is valid. Here, the amount was reasonable, and since the plaintiffs were given no local space, they could suffer loss of business and other imponderables for which it would be difficult to fix damages.
Medak v. *Hekimian*, 241 Or. 38, 404 P.2d 203 (1965).

Late Payments

In *Garrett* v. *Coast* (9 Cal.3d 731, 108 Cal.Rptr. 845, 511 P.2d 1197 [1973]), the court held that a late payment charge based on the percentage of unpaid balance of the loan obligation was punitive in character and unenforceable. However, the court said the plaintiff could recover damages for a late payment based on the period of time the money was wrongfully withheld, plus the administrative costs reasonably related to collecting and accounting for the late payment.

Mitigation of Damages

Mitigation of Damages
The requirement that the injured party act reasonably to avoid or limit losses.

An injured party is under a duty to mitigate, or minimize, the amount of damages. This means that one who was wronged must act reasonably to avoid or limit his losses. The courts will not allow recovery of damages that could reasonably have been avoided. For example, a person who is wrongfully discharged from an employment contract must use reasonable means to find a similar job. Even though improperly fired, one cannot sit idly by and expect to continue to draw the salary. If the same kind of work was readily available and refused by the person discharged, the employer would be allowed to deduct what the earnings could have been from the damages claimed. However, if the person discharged cannot find similar suitable work, he would be entitled to recover his full salary for the contract term.

Goods and Services

A buyer who receives inferior goods under a contract cannot increase the damages by continuing to use the goods after learning of their unfitness. And a buyer who does not receive goods or services according to the contract cannot recover damages for doing without such goods or services when it is possible to substitute the same from another source. Sections 2–602(2)(b) and 2–603(1) of the UCC cover the buyer's duties to minimize damages under certain conditions. (See Subchapter 18.3, Sales.)

Interest

Interest at the legal rate (that set by statute) may be awarded from the time of breach where the amount of money due is determined, from the time it becomes so, or from the date of judgment. Even though the demand is not for a specific sum, interest may be recovered where the damages are capable of being fixed by calculation, such as market value. If damages cannot be made certain, interest is not allowed prior to judgment.

Questions

1. What is meant by compensatory damages?

DISCHARGING THE CONTRACT

2. Are attorney's fees part of court costs? When are you able to collect your lawyer's fees from the other party?
3. Under what circumstances will the court award loss of profits as damages under breach of contract? When will such loss be disallowed?
4. Why will a court award punitive damages in a contract action? What facts are required before the court will make such an award?
5. What are liquidated damages? Why is the winning party in a lawsuit required to minimize damages in certain cases?

10.3 Equitable Relief

Specific Performance

There may be times when a plaintiff is not interested in money damages because he feels that money alone is not the solution to the defendant's breach of contract. For example, plaintiff finds a rare Picasso painting that she wants to add to her art collection. Plaintiff then makes a contract with defendant for the purchase of the painting. Later, when the plaintiff offers the money, the defendant refuses to deliver the work of art. In such a case, the plaintiff is not interested in money damages but wants the painting. Courts have the power to order the defendant to deliver the painting or, if he refuses, to sentence him to confinement for contempt of court. This order is called a decree of specific performance. It is not granted lightly. Several requirements must be met before a court will order specific performance:

Specific Performance
A court order to a party guilty of breach of contract to perform or complete performance of the obligations.

1. The contract must be definite and certain.
2. Money damages must be inadequate.
3. The agreement must be legal and without fraud or immorality.
4. The decree must not work a hardship or injustice on the defendant (e.g., consideration grossly inadequate at the time the contract was entered into or contract unconscionable).
5. The court must be able to supervise the performance of the ordered act.

Real Estate and Personal Property

Since no parcel of land is like any other on earth, each parcel is unique, and courts will generally order specific performance of real estate contracts. The same rule applies to items of personal property that are rare or unique. In addition to including works of art, courts have held that heirlooms, family portraits, and articles held under patent monopolies are of the type that would justify an action for specific performance of contract.

Contracts for ordinary personal property are not specifically enforceable, because the plaintiff could purchase identical goods on the open market. If the plaintiff has a loss, money damages would be adequate to cover such loss.

Because of the difficult or prolonged supervision required by the details involved, the court will usually not order specific performance of building construction or repair contracts.

When a court orders specific performance of a contract, it may at the same time award to the plaintiff any money damages that have resulted from the attempted breach.

Facts

Buelow, as the seller, and Bravo, as the buyer, entered into a written contract for the sale of an unimproved Bel Air residential lot for the purchase price of $93,000. A down payment of $27,000 was put in escrow, and the balance was to be a two-year note secured by a deed of trust. At close of escrow, Buelow refused to sign the escrow instructions or to complete her part of the transaction. The court awarded Bravo specific performance and $70,000 as an offset allowance for increased building costs from 1978 to 1983. Buelow appealed.

Decision

"Compensation as an incident to specific performance need not be limited by contract concepts of foreseeability, so long as said compensation is reasonable." There was sufficient evidence to support the increased construction costs as well as sufficient evidence that Buelow had notice of the fact that Bravo was planning to build, since a condition to the sale was securing a soil report.

Bravo v. Buelow, 168 Cal.App.3d 208, 214 Cal.Rptr. 65 (1985).

Personal Services

Personal services contracts are ordinarily not specifically enforceable because of the difficulty of court control. In such cases, a long and detailed supervision would usually be required. It is obvious that a court would have difficulty in gauging what would be a proper performance to the best of the defendant's ability. Further, it might be undesirable to compel continuation of personal associations after disputes have arisen and confidence and loyalty are gone. Also, there may be a constitutional problem, as the Thirteenth Amendment prohibits involuntary servitude. Conversely, and for the same reasons, courts will not order specific performance of a contract to employ someone.

Injunction In some restricted instances, contracts involving services of special, unique, unusual, extraordinary, or intellectual character—a type of "quasi-specific performance"—may be available in reverse by the granting of an *injunction* (a court order requiring a party to refrain from doing or continuing to do a particular act or activity) against the performance of such services for someone else. For example, an opera singer who had agreed to sing at plaintiff's theatre and nowhere else for a definite time contracted to sing elsewhere. The court held that the singer could not be forced to sing at the theatre but could be prevented from singing anywhere else during that period. Generally, an injunction of this type will be granted only if the services are unique or extraordinary, such as those of an opera singer, actor, jockey, or athlete. Further, an injunction will not be granted when it would cause unjust or harmful results, such as depriving the defendant of a reasonable means of livelihood.

Limitations A number of states by statute limit the court's power to enjoin breach of negative covenants in certain kinds of contracts. For example, under California Civil Code Section 3423, the breach of a contract for personal services will be restrained only if the services are unique and the salary is $6,000 or more per year. In *Foxx* v. *Williams* (244 Cal.App.2d 223, 52 Cal.Rptr. 896 [1966]), Redd Foxx was not enjoined, because his royalty contract for making phonograph records did not guarantee a minimum of $6,000 a year.

Facts
In 1982, Beverly Glen Music signed unknown singer Anita Baker to a recording contract. In 1984, Baker notified Beverly Glen that she had accepted an offer from Warner Communications, Inc., and would no longer perform under her contract. Beverly Glen sued to enjoin Baker from performing for any other recording studio, and the injunction was denied because of California Civil Code Section 3423. Beverly Glen then sought to enjoin Warner from employing Baker.

Decision
"What one was forbidden by statute to do directly, one cannot accomplish through the back door." No injunction will be granted to prohibit all those who might employ Baker, since Beverly Glen was prohibited from enjoining her from performing.

Beverly Glen Music, Inc. v. *Warner Communications, Inc.*, 178 Cal.App.3d 1142, 224 Cal.Rptr. 260 (1986).

The modern rule does not require an express negative covenant in a contract for injunctive relief. This is because the affirmative promise in a contract *implies* a promise not to do anything that defeats the required performance.

Rescission

Rescission is the unmaking of a contract. One of the parties may not unilaterally rescind the agreement unless legal grounds exist for such rescission. Statutes in some states enumerate the grounds that are the basis for rescission. The most common grounds for which rescission may be allowed are illegality, commercial frustration, fraud, undue influence, duress, mistake, insanity, intoxication, complete or substantial failure of consideration, substantial nonperformance or breach by the other party (failure of a building contractor to duly and properly carry out the contract), and inability of a party to perform.

A right to rescind must be exercised promptly or within a reasonable time after discovery of the facts that justify the rescission. Failure to act promptly can be considered a waiver of the right of rescission.

The party seeking rescission must offer to restore everything of value he has received under the contract on the condition that the other party do likewise, unless the latter is unable to do so.

Rescission
The cancellation of a contract and the return of the parties to their original position.

Restitution

When a rescission takes place, the successful party is entitled to *restitution* (the recovery of any consideration he gave plus any other compensation

Restitution
Contract remedy usually limited to the value of the performance by the injured party.

necessary to make him whole). Thus, a buyer who placed improvements on land was entitled to the value of the improvements when he rescinded the contract because of the seller's failure to perform.

Reformation

Reformation
An equitable remedy consisting of rewriting the contract in cases where the writing does not express what was actually agreed upon.

Under some circumstances, a party may want to correct a contract to reflect the true intent of the parties rather than rescind it. This is called a *reformation*. Typical cases in which the court will reform a contract are where there has been mutual mistake or fraud in the making of the agreement.

City of Baltimore v. DeLuca-Davis Construction Co.
210 Md. 518, 124 A.2d 557 (1956).

Hammond, Judge The Bureau of Highways of the Mayor and City Council of Baltimore issued a notice of letting of a contract for the construction of the Jones Falls Expressway storm water conduits and, in response, DeLuca-Davis Construction Co., Inc., the appellee, submitted a bid that by reason of clerical error was at least $589,880 less than it intended it to be, and some $700,000 less than the engineer's estimate and the next lowest bid. . . . As soon as the bids were announced, the appellee realized that it had made a mistake. After several hours of checking the precise form of the mistake was turned up and the Director of Public Works was notified immediately. Five days after the bids were opened, DeLuca-Davis wrote the Board of Estimates, explaining in detail how the mistake had occurred and that the actual bid should be $2,385,944.25 instead of $1,769,064.25, the bid submitted. The letter requested the Board either to correct the bid accordingly or to return the bid and the certified check for $50,000, which had accompanied it pursuant to the applicable charter provisions and the notice of letting. . . .

In transferring the estimated unit cost for unclassified excavation of $13.34 per cubic yard from the detail work sheet to the summary sheet the estimator by mistake entered the figure of $3.34 for Item 2 and Item 11. There seems little doubt that the mistake came about because the first figure in $13.34—the figure "1" was on a vertical ruled line in the work sheet apparently accentuated by the paper having been folded. . . .

It is manifest to us that the City is correct in saying that there cannot be reformation, for at least two reasons. In the first place, to warrant the equitable remedy of reformation the mistake must have been mutual. . . . Here the mistake was entirely that of the contractor and not induced by any act or omission of the City, so that it is entirely unilateral even under the perhaps fictional theory that if the act of one party is induced by the other, the mistake is mutual. More important than the first reason why there cannot be reformation is the second, namely, that a court will never in the name of reformation rewrite a contract or make a contract for the parties or act unless there is clear, convincing and satisfying proof of a mutual understanding and bargain that has not been accurately expressed. . . .

Although reformation requires that the mistake be mutual, rescission may be granted whether the mistake be that of one or both of the parties. . . . The general rule as to the conditions precedent to rescission for unilateral mistakes may be

> summarized thus: 1, the mistake must be of such grave consequences that to enforce the contract as made or offered would be unconscionable; 2, the mistake must relate to a material feature of the contract; 3, the mistake must not have come about because of the violation of a positive legal duty or from culpable negligence; 4, the other party must be put in status quo to the extent that he suffers no serious prejudice except the loss of his bargain. . . .
>
> There are numerous cases in many states that have granted contractors cancellation of bids based on clerical, material, palpable, bona fide mistakes. Where, as in the case at bar, the mistake has been brought to the attention of the contracting authority before the acceptance of the bid, the courts have been almost unanimous in granting relief. . . .
>
> We find that DeLuca-Davis is entitled to cancellation of its bid and the return of its deposit.

QUESTIONS

1. What are the prerequisites for obtaining a court order of specific performance of a contract?
2. Why are the courts reluctant to order specific performance for personal service contracts?
3. How does an injunction differ from an order for specific performance?
4. When may a party have a contract rescinded?
5. Under what circumstances may a contract be reformed?

PROBLEMS

1. Russell promises to paint Smith's portrait on or before July 15, and Smith promises to pay Russell the sum of $500, "provided I am satisfied with your work." Russell completes his work on July 14, whereupon Smith examines the painting, declares that he is not satisfied, and refuses to pay. Russell's work is excellent. Smith is in good faith. Discuss.

2. Moore had a fire policy on his home with the Phoenix Insurance Company that had a clause as follows: "If the above-mentioned premises shall become vacant and unoccupied for a period of more than ten days, this policy shall be void." Moore and his family left the premises for a two-week vacation. One month after their return, the home burned to the ground. The insurance company refuses to pay on the grounds that the policy was terminated by a violation of the policy. Decision?

3. "Whirlwind" White had a contract to fight "Madman" Morris at the Forum on June 14. On June 10, while hitting the punching bag, Morris sprained his wrist, causing a postponement of the fight. The prefight ticket purchasers now sue Morris for spraining his wrist, White for refusing to fight a man with a sprained wrist, and the Forum for postponing the fight. Result?

4. T leased a neon advertising sign from L for a period of one year. A few days after T and L entered into the lease, a governmental order forbade the use of neon signs in T's area. T seeks to rescind the lease. Decision?

5. Plaintiff ordered from defendant two dresses for his prospective bride to be made after model 46A and to be used on the honeymoon. Plaintiff told defendant at the time that the wedding was to take place on January 10 and that he was incurring great expense for the wedding. Defendant promised to have the gowns ready on or before January 9 but did not do so. Plaintiff alleges that as a result of the defendant's failure, his prospective bride changed the wedding date and he suffered a loss in the amount of $1,000 for foods, wines, entertainment, and other expenses. Decision?

6. Defendant signed a contract with plaintiff for the installation of a fire detection system on their premises for $498. The contract had a cancellation clause that read, "In the event of cancellation of this agree-

ment, the owner agrees to pay 1/3 of the contract price as liquidated damages." About 9:00 the next morning, following the signing of the contract and before the plaintiff had done anything with respect to the contract, defendant cancelled. Plaintiff sues to enforce the liquidated damage clause. Decision?

7. Plaintiff wrote a telegram in a secret code and tendered it to the telegraph company for transmission to T. Because of the carelessness of the telegraph company employee, the message never reached T. As a result, plaintiff lost a very valuable business deal with a profit of $10,000. Plaintiff now sues the telegraph company for the loss of profit. Decision?

8. Plaintiff purchased a demonstrator automobile from defendant. The odometer on the car was set back by defendant approximately 7,000 miles showing mileage of only 165 miles. Defendant represented to plaintiff that the mileage on the odometer was the correct mileage. Immediately upon learning of the true mileage, plaintiff sued for rescission, compensatory damages, and punitive damages. Defendant claims punitive damages should not be awarded. Discuss.

9. "Tricky" Blowhard was a candidate in the primary election for the U.S. Senate. He had a contract with the XYZ Television Corporation to televise two important political speeches one week before the election. Through a mixup in programming, the speeches were never televised. "Tricky" lost the election and now sues for breach of contract, claiming damages consisting of campaign expenses and the salary he would have received as a senator. Decision?

10. Primo Carnera, a heavyweight boxer, had a contract with the Madison Square Garden Corporation to fight the winner of the Schmeling-Scribling contest. The contract provided that Carnera could not render services as a boxer in any major boxing contest pending the fight between Schmeling and Scribling. Thereafter, Carnera made a contract to fight Jack Sharkey on a date prior to the S-S fight. Madison Square Garden Corporation seeks an injunction to prevent the Carnera-Sharkey fight. Carnera claims the prohibition violates the Thirteenth Amendment. Decision?

PART THREE

Agency

CHAPTER ELEVEN
Introduction to Agency Law

CHAPTER TWELVE
Principal and Agent Relationship

CHAPTER THIRTEEN
Agency and Third Parties

Agency

In the conduct of business and personal affairs most of us soon realize that a person can only be in one place at any given time. If it were not for the law of agency we would be limited to face to face dealings restricted to available time. Agency law involves the legal rights and duties when one person acts for another. For example, when you run an errand, work for or hire someone, employ an attorney, or sell something for others you are in an agency relationship. Through the use of agents it is possible to do many things in many places at the same time.

Agency is based on a voluntary contract wherein one party, the agent, agrees to represent another, the principal, in dealing with third parties.

Chapter 11 discusses the fiduciary nature of the agency relationship, how it is created and ended, and some agency problems raised by the rapidly expanding franchise industry.

Chapter 12 considers some of the general legal rules of agency and the duties of the agent and of the principal.

Chapter 13 analyzes the authority given an agent, and the liabilities of the principal, the agent, and third parties.

CHAPTER ELEVEN

Introduction to Agency Law

11.1 Nature of Agency
Agency Defined
   Servants and Employees
   Independent Contractor
   Liability

11.2 Creation and Termination
Capacity to Act as Agent
Creation
   Agreement
   Estoppel
   Implied Agency
   Ratification
   Operation of Law
Termination
   Agreement
   Contract Expiration
   Revocation
   Renunciation by Agent
   Option

Operation of Law
   Death
   Insanity
   Bankruptcy
   Impossibility
   War
   Change in Business Conditions
Irrevocable Agency

11.3 Franchises
Definition
Legal Implications
Disclosure Acts
Control
   Lanham Act
   Determining Amount of Control
   Independent Contractor Versus Agent
   Absence of Control
Franchise Contracts

11.1 Nature of Agency

Agency Defined

Agency
Relation in which one party is authorized to act for another.

Fiduciary
Legal duty requiring one to act for the benefit of another.

Agency is a voluntary legal fiduciary relationship created by contract, either express or implied, between two parties in which one of the parties (*agent*) acts for or represents the other party (*principal*) in dealings with a *third party,* such as a real estate broker representing a homeowner. A fiduciary relationship in law is one that requires the highest standard of faithful performance of duty.

Servants and Employees

Servant
One who works for and is under the control of a master.

Employee
One who accepts a job for wages and works under the control of the employer.

Ministerial
Requiring little or no judgment or discretion.

Agent
One who by mutual consent acts for another.

Although most of the laws relating to servants and employees are the same as those relative to agents, the relationship is not identical. Normally, a servant or employee is one who gives personal service as a member of a business or domestic household and is subject to control by the employer as to the physical duties performed or activities undertaken. A servant or employee usually does work that is more ministerial in nature, has no discretion as to the means to accomplish the ends for which he is employed, and seldom has the authority to represent the master or employer in business dealings. A servant or employee usually sells or gives time, while a non-servant agent is paid primarily for the results accomplished rather than for the time the work takes.

Sometimes an employee might act in a dual relationship as an agent. For example, a chain store manager might be an employee regarding internal affairs but becomes an agent when purchasing inventory. Often, the lines are not clearly drawn as to whether a person is acting as an employee or as an agent.

Independent Contractor

Independent Contractor
One who contracts to do work using his own methods without employer control.

The agency relationship is created when the servant or employee represents the employer in transactions with third persons. The employee or servant then becomes the agent, and the employer or master is the principal. An independent contractor is a person who contracts to do a piece of work according to his own methods and without being subject to the control of his employer except as to the result of the work (e.g., building contractor), whereas in an agency, the right of the principal to direct what the agent shall do or not do is basic. Also, an independent contractor does not represent the employer in business dealings.

Liability

Respondeat Superior
Let the superior reply, meaning that an employer is liable for the torts of an agent committed in the scope of the employment.

It is important to distinguish between an agent, servant, or employee on the one hand and an independent contractor on the other hand. Under the doctrine of *respondeat superior,* the principal, master, or employer is liable for the tort of his agent, servant, or employee committed while acting within the scope of his employment, whereas the employer generally is not liable for the tort of an independent contractor.

The following case illustrates the general rule concerning liability of independent contractors:

Facts
Plaintiff was injured by tripping over a piece of wire left on a sidewalk by a newsboy. The issue was whether the newsboy was an agent of the newspaper under the doctrine of *respondeat superior* or was operating as an independent contractor.

Decision
The court observed that ruling on control exercised over newspaper carriers was a difficult problem. It found in this case that the managers sold papers directly to the newspaper carriers, who then resold the papers at a profit. Any losses on unpaid accounts were borne by the newspaper carriers, who had no assigned territories and could sell competitors' papers. Finding practically no control to exist, the judge found the newsboy to be an independent contractor and granted the newspaper's motion for summary judgment.

Mirto v. *News-Journal Co.*, 50 Del. (11 Terry) 103, 123 A.2d 863 (1956).

Exceptions The courts have applied several exceptions to the liability rule and have found employers to be liable for the acts of their independent contractors in certain situations. The following are some of these exceptions:

1. Where the thing contracted to be done is unlawful.
2. Where the acts performed create a public nuisance.
3. Where a duty is imposed by law.
4. Where the hirer is under a nondelegable personal duty to perform the services promised.
5. Where the work to be performed is inherently dangerous, such as blasting.
6. Where the employer was negligent in the selection, instruction, or supervision of the contractor.
7. Where the hirer assumes a specific duty by contract.
8. Where the employer has knowledge of a dangerous situation created by the contractor and fails to halt or correct it.

Inherently Dangerous
Dangerous from the nature of the work itself.

The following case illustrates this last exception and reaches a different result from the *Mirto* decision.

Peairs v. Florida Publishing Company
132 So.2d 561 (1961).

Carroll, Chief Judge . . . The plaintiffs alleged in their complaint that prior to November 23, 1957, the defendant, a newspaper publisher, in the course of distributing its papers carelessly and negligently permitted a wire loop used for binding bundles of its papers, to remain and be on the parking lot of a certain restaurant in the City of Jacksonville, and that on that date the plaintiff Louise

> Peairs, a patron of the said restaurant, while walking from the restaurant to her car in the parking lot, tripped upon the said wire loop and fell, fracturing the bones in both of her wrists....
>
> ... The defendant, the publisher of a Jacksonville newspaper, distributed its newspapers to route carriers under a carrier lease contract in which the defendant leased to the carrier a certain route, together with its subscription list, and the carrier undertook to deliver the papers to the subscribers on the route. Under this contract the defendant sold the papers to the carrier at a stipulated price and agreed not to interfere with or attempt to control the carrier with respect to the ways, means, or methods of performance, distribution, solicitation, or collection....
>
> ... There was evidence also that, unless a distribution point was cleaned up, wires and trash would be left about a drop area. It was against the defendant's policy to leave wires and other trash around the distribution points, and the defendant's circulation manager had given instructions to the district managers to see that the wires and trash were picked up at the distribution points. Some of the carrier lease contracts had been terminated by the defendant because of the carriers' failure to pick up trash at the distribution points after being told to do so. If the carriers did not pick up the trash, usually the defendant's district managers would do so....
>
> ... When, at the close of the plaintiffs' case, the trial court granted the defendant's motion for a directed verdict, the court said, "... but this is the basis of the Court's feeling, that the carriers themselves were independent contractors and independent of the defendant's negligence for which they alone are responsible."...
>
> ... In their brief the appellants have called our attention to another recognized exception, which they claim is applicable to the facts of the present appeal—"Where a company gains knowledge of a dangerous situation created by its independent contractor, it may incur liability through its failure to halt the operation or correct it...."
>
> ... Applying these principles to the case before us, we are of the opinion that the jury could have fairly and reasonably concluded from the evidence produced at the trial that the defendant-appellee was liable to the plaintiffs for the negligent acts of the newsboy carriers, even though those carriers bore the relation of independent contractors to the defendant, under one or more of the exceptions to the general rule of nonliability for acts of independent contractors, as discussed above....
>
> Our conclusion is that the trial court erred in taking the case away from the jury and directing a verdict for the defendant....
>
> Reversed and remanded.

Some situations exist where it is important to determine whether or not the person is an employee or an independent contractor. If one is injured on the job, only employees, not independent contractors, are covered by workers' compensation laws. However, independent contractors may sue the employer directly under tort law for such injuries, but they must submit proof of negligence. Only employees can collect unemployment insurance payments. Independent contractors are excluded from the provisions of the National Labor Relations Act.

Right to Control It is not always easy to determine which status applies to the relationship. Courts hold that the chief factor to consider is whether the employer has any right to control the method of doing the work contracted for.

ABC Test The unemployment insurance acts in most of the states apply what is known as an ABC Test to determine whether or not a person is an employee. Under this test, to be an independent contractor requires that the person

(A) Has been and will continue to be free from direction and control over the performance of service under the contract.
(B) Performs a service that either is outside the usual course of business for which the service is performed or is performed outside of all places for which the service is performed.
(C) Is customarily engaged in an independently established trade, occupation, profession, or business.

The jury instruction given by California courts to help jurors decide the issue is: "The most important factor in determining whether one is . . . an independent contractor is whether the principal has the right to control the manner and means of accomplishing the result desired." If the principal has the authority to exercise complete control, whether or not that right is exercised with respect to all details is immaterial.

Sykee v. Ruolo
122 Ill.App.3d 331, 77 Ill. Dec. 857, 461 N.E.2d 480 (1984).

McGloon, Justice: Plaintiff, Catherine Sykee, brought this action for an order of replevin to recover possession of photographic negatives allegedly taken at plaintiff's request at her home on November 11, 1981.

Catherine Sykee testified that she had planned a cocktail party in honor of the 89th birthday of an artist named Erte. Defendant, Ms. Georgia Lee Ruolo, telephoned plaintiff at the suggestion of a mutual friend and said she was available to take pictures at the party. Plaintiff explained the nature of the party and said she would like three or four rolls of color film used with 36 pictures per roll. She agreed to defendant's fee of $150, and it was arranged that defendant would arrive one-half hour before the guests. There was no discussion with respect to photographic proofs, negatives or any additional charges above $150. Defendant took pictures at the party, which was attended by between 100 and 150 people, under the direction of plaintiff and her husband. She did not accompany defendant during the entire evening or direct her as to each photograph, but did direct that certain photographs be taken at the beginning and the end of the party and at various times in between. A few days later, plaintiff paid defendant the $150 fee, plus an additional $50 fee for proof sheets which defendant brought to plaintiff's home to show to her. Defendant offered to make enlargements for $35 or $40 each, but plaintiff thought this was too high and asked defendant for the negatives. Defendant refused, although she did offer to have enlargements made for as little as $7.50 each.

[U]nless the photographs were produced as a work for hire, copyright ownership is in defendant.

. . . "A 'work made for hire' is—(1) a work prepared by an employee within the scope of his or her employment; . . . Plaintiff maintains that defendant's work

> was "work prepared by an employee within the scope of his or her employment," that is, it falls within subsection (1). Defendant maintains plaintiff did not have the right to direct and supervise the manner in which defendant performed her work, and she was an independent professional who bought her own film and paid her own expenses.
>
> In our opinion, whether the defendant was either an employer or an independent contractor presented a question of fact. The crucial question is if plaintiff had the right to control the work even if she did not exercise it.
>
> But, plaintiff testified she did exercise control over the manner in which defendant performed the work. Thus, the plaintiff, for whom the work was prepared, is the author under section 201(b), since the photography was "a work made for hire," that is, done by an employee within the scope of her employment as stated in subsection (1) of the definition of a "work made for hire" in section 101. The evidence presented warranted the inference that the negatives were produced by defendant who was employed by plaintiff in her home for this very purpose and who was paid to make them.
>
> [Defendant ordered to give negatives to plaintiff.]

A dissenting judge in the preceding case argued that Sykee should not be the owner of the negatives, since she made the claim only after the price asked for the prints was more than she wanted to spend. The easiest way to avoid this type of misunderstanding is to write a simple agreement and get a signature. However, a statement in a contract that a party is an independent contractor does not determine such status. The right to control the work done remains the key element in reaching that decision.

Questions

1. What are the differences in the three cases used in this subchapter?
2. What is a fiduciary relationship?
3. Why is it important to determine whether a worker is an employee or an independent contractor?
4. When may an employer be liable for the acts of an independent contractor he has hired for a job?
5. How can you determine whether a person should be classified as an employee or an independent contractor?

11.2 Creation and Termination

An agency can be created by agreement, by estoppel, by ratification, or by operation of law.

Capacity to Act as Agent

Since the law treats one who acts through an agent as doing the act himself, the capacity to act by an agent depends on the capacity of the principal to do the act himself if he were present. Thus, a person who has the capacity to contract may appoint an agent, but an appointment by a person without capacity (e.g., a minor) would be voidable.

Any person can act as an agent except a person who does not understand the legal importance of making contracts for another. For example, a minor can act as an agent but not if he is an infant of tender years. Thus, agents are not required to possess the same qualifications as are principals. That is, a person can act as an agent for someone else although he is not capable of acting for himself. The principal cannot complain of the lack of mental capacity of one whom he has chosen to represent him. Generally, anyone except a lunatic, imbecile, or infant of tender years is capable of acting as an agent.

Capacity
Mental ability to make a rational decision.

Creation

Agreement

The usual method of creating an agency is by agreement (i.e., one person expressly authorizes another to act for him). In most instances, the authorization may be oral. If the agent is authorized to enter into a contract for the sale of real property for the principal, most states require that such authorization be in writing. In some states, the authorization must be in writing in any case in which the agent will enter into any of the types of contracts required by the statute of frauds to be in writing (e.g., sale of real property, sales of goods of a value of $500 or more). This is called the equal dignities rule (i.e., the authorization of an agent who is to make contracts required to be in writing must be created by a method of equal dignity, namely, a written instrument).

Authority
The permission or power delegated to another.

Equal Dignities
Express authority given to an agent must be written if a contract the agent is making for the principal is required to be in writing.

Estoppel

Agency by estoppel (apparent authority) arises when the principal intentionally or by want of ordinary care causes a third person to believe another to be his agent who is not really employed by him. For example, if the owner of a store places another person in charge of the store, third persons might assume that the person in charge is the agent of the owner of the store. The agent has apparent authority because he appears to be the agent, and the principal is estopped from denying the agency even if none exists.

The situation of agency by estoppel also occurs where there is an actual agency but the principal leads third persons to believe that the agent has greater powers than actually exist.

Agency by Estoppel
Occurs when principal causes a third person to believe reasonably that another is his agent.

Lindstrom v. Minnesota Liquid Fertilizer Co.
264 Minn. 485, 119 N.W.2d 855 (1963).

Murphy, Justice Action for labor and materials furnished by plaintiff, Anund T. Lindstrom, to defendant Minnesota Liquid Fertilizer Company, a Minnesota corporation. The jury returned a verdict in plaintiff's favor for $2,338.90, and defendant appeals from an order denying its motion for judgment notwithstanding the verdict or for a new trial.

The labor and material furnished by plaintiff were ordered by one Hurley Weaver, who represented to plaintiff that he was acting for defendant in the transactions. Defendant denies that he was its agent or employee and contends that the evidence compelled a finding that his status was merely that of a lessee of defendant's plant and equipment, without authority to bind defendant in any way. . . .

Weaver undertook to use defendant's equipment solely for the sale of defendant's products under defendant's trade name, and to maintain a sales volume in the area, which, in defendant's opinion, would represent a reasonable amount of business. He was directed to promote the sale of defendant's products in cooperation with defendant and to use defendant's equipment in applying the products sold. . . . Any provisions in the agreement constituting a limitation on Weaver's authority were certainly unknown to the public or to plaintiff.

. . . Further, at all times its corporate name was painted in large letters on the buildings, tanks, and equipment of this branch, with nothing thereon to indicate that Weaver was lessee of such business or operated it as an independent contractor. It is well settled that, in so far as third parties are concerned, the relationship of principal and agent may be evidenced by acts on the part of the alleged principal or appearances of authority he permits another to have which lead to the belief that an agency has been created. . . . It has been held that, where a party permits his name to be used on property or equipment which is placed under the control or direction of another and thus makes such other an ostensible agent, an agency by estoppel will result. . . .

The jury's finding that a principal and agent relationship existed between defendant and Weaver would render defendant liable for acts performed by Weaver within the scope of his apparent authority as plant manager. Any secret limitations placed thereon by defendant would not absolve it from liability to third persons such as plaintiff who dealt with Weaver as defendant's manager and who were unaware of any limitations upon his authority as such. . . .

Affirmed.

Implied Agency

Implied Agency
An agency agreement implied from the actions of the parties.

An agency agreement may also be implied from the actions of the parties, and the courts may find an actual agency relationship to exist notwithstanding a denial by the principal. Such an agency may be indicated by the prior habits or course of dealing between the two persons, subsequent acts, or the acquiescence or ratification of previous similar acts.

Although implied agencies are similar to those created by estoppel, the latter can be invoked by a third person only when he knew or relied upon the conduct of the principal. Since an implied agency is an *actual* agency, this limitation does not apply. The following case illustrates an implied agency.

Facts

Plaintiff's Cadillac was parked by Buster Douglas and was stolen while plaintiff dined in defendant's restaurant.

The issue of the case was whether defendant restaurant, by permitting an individual to park patrons' cars, held such individual out as its employee for such purposes.

Buster Douglas was not an employee in the usual sense, but with the knowledge of defendant, he did station himself in front of the restaurant, wore a doorman's uniform (which he himself had purchased), and parked defendant customers' autos.

Decision

The court held that the restaurant owner knew of and did not object to Buster Douglas's parking cars. Therefore, although Buster was not an actual employee, he had been held out to customers as being an authorized agent to park their vehicles. Because no suitable disclaimer was posted, plaintiff was justified in assuming that Buster Douglas represented the restaurant. Motion to dismiss was denied and the case set for trial.

Weingart v. Directoire Restaurant, Inc., 70 Misc. 2d 419, 333 N.Y.S.2d 806 (1972).

Ratification

An agency may be created by ratification (i.e., acceptance by the principal of the benefits of the acts of the purported agent). Nearly all courts hold that the agent must be purporting to act for the principal at the time of the contract with the third person, as prerequisite for ratification.

Ratification may be express or implied. It is implied when the principal, with knowledge of the material facts surrounding the agent's unauthorized act, receives and retains the benefits thereof.

The principal must ratify before the third person withdraws from the transaction. Until the principal ratifies, the third person can withdraw for any reason. This is because until affirmance, the third person and the purported principal are similar to an offeror and an offeree before acceptance. No mutuality of obligation exists until the principal ratifies the transaction; if the principal cannot be bound, neither can the third person. Since the agent has acted without authority, the principal who chooses to do so may repudiate the act.

The following case is an example of the failure to meet the prerequisite for ratification.

Ratification
The approval or validation of a previous action.

Affirmation
A person's indication that what one said or did was true.

Repudiation
The denial of the validity of an act or agreement.

Prerequisite
Something required beforehand.

Facts

Plaintiff brings this action to compel defendant, Armiger Body Shop, to transfer and deliver to him the title certificate evidencing ownership of a certain 1960 Ford Falcon. On September 30, 1960, plaintiff purchased the car from Roy Hitchens, a dealer in used automobiles, for $1,995. The Falcon was delivered to plaintiff on the day of the sale and has been in plaintiff's possession ever since. The vehicle is titled in the name of defendant, and the title certificate is in defendant's possession.

Decision

The court held that there had been no proof of an actual principal-agent relationship between the defendant body shop and Hitchens granting the latter the authority to sell the Falcon. Plaintiff could recover only if he could establish an agency authority by ratification. However, at the time of sale, Hitchens purported to act as the owner, not as an agent. The general agency rule is that acts done by one person in his individual capacity cannot be ratified by another person. Judgment for defendant.

Taylor v. Armiger Body Shop, 40 Del. Ch. 22, 172 A.2d 572 (1961).

Operation of Law

Agency implied by law can arise by statute. For example, most states have adopted a nonresident motorist statute that provides that the operation of a motor vehicle upon the highway of a state is an appointment of the secretary of that state as the agent of the nonresident for service of process in any action arising out of the operation of the motor vehicle in the state.

Agency can also be implied by law when the acts of a self-constituted agent are, by reason of the neglect of the principal or an act of God, necessary for the self-preservation of the principal or the well-being of society. Examples are a principal's being so incapacitated by injuries that he cannot act for himself or a merchant's furnishing necessities to a wife and charging them to her husband's account (no agency relationship exists, but the husband is liable for the necessities by virtue of a social policy that is in furtherance of the welfare of a neglected wife and the well-being of society as a whole).

Termination

An agency may be terminated by act of the parties or by operation of law.

Agreement

Since the agency was created by an agreement between the parties, it can be terminated in the same manner.

Contract Expiration

The contract of agency may provide that the agency shall terminate at a definite time (e.g., one year). In such case, the agency terminates in one year by virtue of the terms of the contract. Or the agency may be created for a particular purpose, in which case the agency terminates when the agent accomplishes the particular purpose (e.g., real estate broker sells the house).

Revocation

The principal may at any time revoke the authority given his agent by reasonable notice with or without good cause. When the agency is created for an indefinite time, it can be revoked by either party after reasonable notice without incurring liability. However, when the agency is contracted for a definite period of time, revocation without cause by either party may result in damages for the breach.

Renunciation by Agent

The agent may also at any time, with or without good cause, renounce the power conferred upon him by giving reasonable notice to the principal. If the agency is created for a definite period, renunciation by the agent before the expiration of the period subjects the agent to liability for damages for breach of contract.

Option Clause

An agency agreement may provide that either party may terminate the agency by giving a specified notice or paying a specified sum of money.

Operation of Law

When an agency contract is terminated by operation of law, it ends because of a statute rather than by consent of the parties. Some examples are death, insanity, bankruptcy, impossibility, war, and changes in the law or other circumstances.

> **Operation of Law**
> By the automatic effects of the law and not by private agreement or act of the party involved.

Death

Because an agency is a personal service contract with a fiduciary responsibility, the authority given to an agent terminates upon the principal's death. Also, the agent's death ends the agency relationship. To avoid the hardship that might result from personal liability of the agent for an unwitting breach of his implied warranty of authority, some states have modified the rule and will not terminate the agency until the agent is notified of the principal's death.

Under UCC § 4–405, death of a customer does not revoke the authority of a bank to accept, pay, collect, or account until the bank is notified of the death and has a reasonable opportunity to act on it.

In many states, a third person can rely on the agent's authority until the third person receives notice of the principal's death. An exception may exist where there is an irrevocable agency (discussed in the following subsection).

Ordinary contracts already made do not terminate upon death but become an obligation of the principal's estate.

Insanity

Insanity of the principal or the agent generally terminates an ordinary agency. In some states, a third person who has no knowledge of the principal's insanity and who deals in good faith with the agent will be protected if it would work an injustice on him. However, if the principal has been judicially declared insane, the third person is not protected, since all persons are deemed to know the status of a judicially declared incompetent. Under UCC § 4–405, incompetency of a customer does not revoke the authority of a bank to accept, pay, collect, or account until the bank is notified of the incompetency.

Bankruptcy

Bankruptcy of the principal terminates the agency as to matters affected by the bankruptcy. Bankruptcy of the agent terminates the agency if the agent should realize that the state of his credit would so affect the interests of his principal that the principal, if he had knowledge of the facts, would no longer consent to the agency.

Impossibility

The agency terminates when it becomes impossible to perform the agency (e.g., change in the law that makes the performance of the authorized act illegal or criminal, destruction of the subject matter, death of the third person with whom the agent has been dealing, insanity of the third person).

War

If the outbreak of war places the principal and agent in the position of alien enemies, the agency is terminated, or at least the agent's authority is suspended until peace is restored. War can also make it impossible or impractical for the agency to continue, in which case the agency will terminate.

Change in Business Conditions

The agency is terminated by the occurrence of an unusual event or a change in value or business conditions of such a nature that the agent should reasonably infer that the principal would not desire him to continue to act under the changed circumstances (e.g, broker to sell land at a certain price should regard authority to sell the land at that price as terminated if the land suddenly doubles in value).

Irrevocable Agency

Irrevocable Agency
An agency which can only be terminated under the terms of the original contract or with the consent of the agent.

Agency Coupled with an Interest
An irrevocable contract made when an agent paid consideration to exercise the authority granted in an agreement made for the agent's or a third party's benefit.

Power Given as a Security
Another term that means the same as irrevocable agency or agency coupled with an interest.

Ordinarily, an agency is created for the benefit of the principal, and since the relationship is fiduciary and confidential, the principal is free to terminate the agency at any time. This is true even though there is a valid contract for a fixed period. If, however, the agency is created for the benefit of the agent or a third person, the agent and not the principal is most concerned with the continuance of the agency, and it would not be fair to permit the principal to terminate the agency at will. Consequently, such agencies are held to be irrevocable by the principal and are not terminated by the death or incapacity of the principal. Such an irrevocable agency is usually called an *agency coupled with an interest,* or a *power given as a security.*

Suppose that the principal owns valuable real estate or diamonds and wishes to borrow money from his agent. As security for the loan, the principal gives the agent a mortgage on the land or a pledge on the diamonds together with the power to sell the property in the event he does not repay the money. If the agent then sells the property or the diamonds, he gives the purchaser a deed to the land or a bill of sale for the diamonds in the principal's name by the agent, as such. This type of agency contract is irrevocable.

The mere declaration of the parties in a written contract that the agency is irrevocable or coupled with an interest is ineffective.

Where the agent's interest is only in compensation, it is not one coupled to the subject matter of the agency but only an interest in the proceeds and is therefore revocable. For example, an attorney hired to pursue the claims of an heir took for his fee an assignment of part of what would come from the estate. This interest was held to be wholly dependent upon performance of duties of the agency and therefore was merely an interest in the proceeds. This ruling applies to most attorney contingency fee agencies, and although the lawyer may have a lien upon the money, he can be discharged and other counsel substituted in his place.

Even when the agency is irrevocable, unless the principal has actually transferred some sort of ownership interest in the subject matter to the agent, such as the mortgage or pledge, together with the power of sale, most courts will terminate the agency upon the death or insanity of either of the parties.

Questions

1. What are the limitations on your hiring someone to act as your agent?
2. What is meant by an agency by estoppel?
3. How can an agency be created by ratification?
4. What is meant by termination of an agency by operation of law? Give some examples.
5. What is an irrevocable agency? How is one created?

11.3 Franchises

The terms *agent* and *agency* are often used in everyday conversation to refer to franchise relationships that usually are not intended to be agencies. Franchising is a major modern business phenomenon. The Department of Commerce estimated in 1985 that more than one-third of all retail transactions were conducted through franchised outlets, and the volume continues to grow. With nearly a million franchises operating varied enterprises around the world, many new legal problems have been created.

Aided by advertising campaigns that emphasize the profits and satisfaction available to a person who is his own "boss," there has been tremendous growth in this type of operation. The system depends upon an effective monopoly in which a franchisee will pay to participate. The attractiveness of a franchise is that it enables a person to operate a small, local business with expert managerial help and mass media advertising from a central source.

Franchise
The right given to market another's product within a certain location or area.

Definition

A *franchise* is a contract by which a franchisee is given the right to engage in the business of offering, selling, or distributing goods or services under a marketing plan or system offered by the franchisor and associated with the franchisor's trademark, service mark, trade name, or other commercial symbol.

Franchisor
One granting to another (franchisee) the right to market products, use trade marks and methods in the sale of goods or services.

Legal Implications

Franchisee
One who receives from another (franchisor) the right to market products within a certain location or area.

Although the degree and quality of control exercised by the franchisor may be decisive in assuring success, they may also lead to many agency legal problems. Because of the varying degrees of control imposed by the contracts, courts tend to classify the franchisees as either agents or independent contractors. If the franchisee is an agent, the franchisor could become liable for both contract and tort obligations of the franchisee.

Most franchises are designed to permit extensive control of the system by the franchisor. If the contract is too one-sided or unfair, it may be stricken as unconscionable under the UCC (refer to Subchapter 6.3).

Disclosure Acts

Franchise Disclosure Acts
State laws requiring franchisors to register with the state and to furnish disclosure facts to prospective franchisees.

Beginning in 1970, states have been passing franchise disclosure acts requiring sellers of franchises to register with the state and to furnish disclosure statements to prospective buyers. Most states have now passed such acts. In 1979, the Federal Trade Commission issued a rule on franchise disclosure. Such laws are designed to help prospective franchisees make informed decisions. They require the franchisor to provide detailed background information to all potential buyers, including who is behind the franchise, what the franchise costs, and how it ends. State laws have different requirements, but most mandate a disclosure of any litigation against the franchisor, earnings projections for the franchise, audited balance sheets, and detailed contract terms. Failure to comply with these state disclosure laws can result in civil and criminal liability for the violator.

Facts

My Pie International had franchised thirteen pizza parlors through the country, including one to Dowmont, Inc., to operate in Illinois and another to Debould, Inc., for a location in Colorado. Within a few years, both stopped using the My Pie name and substituted "Arnold's." Later, My Pie sued these franchisees, claiming they had failed to pay royalties due, had broken their contract, and had infringed on My Pie's trademark. The franchisees defended on the basis that My Pie had failed to provide the franchise disclosures required by Illinois law. My Pie had accepted money for certain supplies, including menus and employees' T-shirts, before providing the disclosure statements.

Decision

The U.S. Seventh Circuit Court of Appeals held that failure to comply with the Illinois Franchise Disclosure Act made the franchise agreements voidable, which the franchisees did, so there were no rights under the agreements and no recovery for royalties or damages. The objective of the Act was to protect uninformed franchisees, which would be seriously undermined, if the franchisor could collect income without having first made the required disclosures. It didn't matter that the franchise *fee* had not been paid.

My Pie International v. *Debould, Inc.*, 687 F.2d 919 (7th Cir. 1982).

Control

Lanham Act

Franchisors face another problem because of the federal Lanham Act (15 USC, § 1051 *et seq.*), which requires the owner to exercise control over the nature and quality of goods and services sold by franchisees under the licensed trademark or face possible trademark abandonment. Accordingly, controls that the franchisor has inserted in the franchise agreement or its procedure manual in order to safeguard trademark integrity may have the unintended result of subjecting that franchisor to claims of liability for the torts and contracts of its franchisees.

Lanham Act
A federal law that requires trademark owners to exercise control over franchisees or face loss of their trademarks.

Determining Amount of Control

Since practically all franchise agreements contain clauses that control or restrict the activities of the parties, the real issue is determining how much control is sufficient to tilt the relationship to that of agency rather than independent contractor. Typical contracts may specify, for example, standards of quality, service, physical appearance, business hours, recordkeeping system, and forms of reports to be made to the franchisor. Other provisions may fix selling prices, provide training, guarantee exclusive sales territories, and require the purchase of certain services and supplies. The franchisor usually agrees to provide advertising and the use of a trademark. The purpose of such agreements is to protect the trademark and the trade name through standardized operations, appearance, and product quality.

Independent Contractor Versus Agent

Disclaimer In a franchise contract, an actual agency can arise by an express agreement between the franchisor and the franchisee, appointing the franchisee as an agent. However, since most franchisors want to avoid an agency relationship, the typical franchise contains a clause that expressly disavows the existence of an agency relationship and purports that the franchisee is an independent contractor. Such a disclaimer is not binding, however, where an agency may be implied or ostensible. If a franchisee is allowed to believe that he has authority to act on behalf of the franchisor, an actual agency exists by implication. Where acts of the franchisor are such that a third-party customer believes that the franchisee has the authority to act for the franchisor, an ostensible agency is created.

Facts

A Texaco dealer refurbished a used auto at his service station and sold it there to the plaintiff. Because the dealer had not fixed the brakes properly, the brakes failed, causing an accident. Texaco claimed that the dealer was an independent contractor and that such activities were beyond the scope of the franchised business.

Decision

The dealer had ostensible authority to make auto repairs, and plaintiff reasonably believed that Texaco would be responsible. Much media advertising and signs on the premises stated "Trust your car to the man who wears the star." This slogan was intended to convince the public that Texaco's franchised dealers were skilled mechanics, causing plaintiff to rely on such skill. Texaco was held liable.

Gizzi v. Texaco, Inc., 437 F.2d 308 (3d Cir. 1971).

Cases Many recent cases have dealt with the problem of whether or not the franchisee is the agent of the franchisor. In a case against Century 21

Real Estate Corporation, the judge held that there were sufficient facts to submit to a jury for the determination of the existence of an agency. The employees had stated that they represented Century 21; they had advertised that the franchisee was a "neighborhood professional" who belonged to a "nationwide organization that more people had put their trust in"; they wore gold blazers bearing the Century 21 service mark; the franchisor sponsored commercials that stated that Century 21 was the largest real estate organization in the United States and emphasized nationwide resources; it provided training and sales materials for the franchisee's employees; it prepared pictures of the franchisee's employees for local advertising; and the franchisee displayed the Century 21 service mark and logo (*Whitfield* v. *Century 21 Real Estate Corp.*, 484 F.Supp. 984 [S.D.Tex. 1979]).

In another case, when Southland Corporation, franchisor of 7-11 stores, was sued for death and injuries caused by the sale of alcoholic beverages to a minor by one of their franchisees, the court decided as a matter of law that no agency existed. Although the franchisor provided most things, the franchisee had personally applied for the "off-sale" beer license; only she and her employees sold the beer; she hired and fired all employees; she set the wages; she conducted all of the day-to-day operations; and a sign specifically said that she was an independent contractor. This was sufficient for the court to conclude that in this case the franchisee was an independent contractor (*Wickham* v. *Southland Corp.*, 168 Cal.App.3d 49, 213 Cal.Rptr. 825 [1985]).

Apparently, the test applied by the courts is the same for franchises as it is for employment contracts, and the amount of control exercised determines the relationship.

Nichols v. Arthur Murray, Inc.
248 Cal.App.2d 610, 56 Cal.Rptr. 728 (1967).

Coughlin, Associate Justice Defendant appeals from a judgment awarding plaintiff the amount prepaid by the latter under contracts for dancing lessons which were not furnished.

Defendant Arthur Murray, Inc., was engaged in the business of licensing persons to operate dancing studios using its registered trade name "ARTHUR MURRAY" and the Arthur Murray method of dancing. . . .

In determining whether an agency relationship exists between parties to a business enterprise, which is the subject of an agreement between them, the right to control is an important factor. If, in practical effect, one of the parties has the right to exercise complete control over the operation by the other an agency relationship exists; the former is the principal and the latter the agent. [Citations.]

The subject agreement, in substance, conferred upon defendant the right to control the employment of all employees of the franchise holder whether or not their duties related to teaching or supervising dancing instruction; to fix the minimum tuition rates to be charged; to select the financial institution handling, financing or discounting all pupil installment contracts; to designate the location of the studio, its layout and decoration; to make refunds to pupils and charge the amounts paid to the franchise holder; to settle and pay all claims against defendant arising out of the operation of the contemplated enterprise; to reimburse itself for the payment of any such refunds or claims, and the expense of any litigation in connection therewith, from a fund consisting of weekly payments by the franchise holder to defendant in an amount equal to 5% of the gross receipts; to invest the proceeds of this fund and pay the franchise holder only such portion of the income therefrom as defendant "shall determine should be properly allocated"; to control all advertising by the franchise holder, which was required to be submitted to defendant for approval prior to use; and to exercise a broad control over the operation of the enterprise under a provision requiring the franchise holder "to conduct the studio, to be maintained and managed by Licensee, in accordance with the general policies of the Licensor as established from time to time", and directing that failure to maintain such policies shall be sufficient cause for immediate cancellation of the agreement.

Many of the controls conferred were not related anywise to the protection of defendant's trade name, including its dancing and teaching methods, good will and business image. Other controls, although related to the protection of the trade name, because the exercise thereof was not limited to effecting such purpose, enabled defendant to impose its will upon the franchise holder in areas wholly unrelated to that purpose.

Defendant directs attention to provisions in the agreement which it claims expressly declare the intention of the parties that no agency relationship is intended; refers to the established principle that agency is a consensual relationship; and contends these circumstances dictate the conclusion no agency was created by the subject agreement. This contention disregards the fact that the agreement, as such, was consensual; both parties consented to the provisions imposing controls; and the agency relationship was created by the legal effect of those provisions.

The judgment is affirmed.

Agency Factors Some of the more important factors the courts have considered in deciding whether or not the franchisee is the agent of the franchisor include the following:

1. Controls over the day-to-day activities, whether specifically given or broadly stated, such as product packaging and merchandising; appearance of the franchised outlet; advertising and promotional activities; store signs; employee uniforms; method of preparing or furnishing goods and services; insurance; financial reporting obligations; selection of banks; maintenance requirements; inventory control systems; and selection of vendors.
2. Duty to promote franchised products.
3. Franchisor's right to determine prices to be charged.
4. Supervisory control over franchisee's employees.
5. Right to inspect franchised location.
6. Franchisor's right to terminate upon breach by the franchisee.

Product Promotion
Stirring up interest in an enterprise.

Supervisory Control
Actual management and direction.

Absence of Control

Factors that have been accepted as evidence to show an absence of control by the franchisor include the following:

1. Franchisee's right to set own prices.
2. Franchisee's establishment of its own course of operations.

3. No compensation, commission, or other remuneration from the franchisor.
4. No report requirements to franchisor.
5. No requirement to share profits with franchisor.
6. Payment by franchisee of all its own expenses and taxes.
7. Right to control employment relationships, including the right to hire and fire and to set wages and conditions of work.

Report Requirements
Obligation to give accounts and information at regular intervals.

Franchise Contracts

Because of the potential for *respondeat superior* liability, franchisors should carefully screen prospective franchisees. All franchise agreements should have indemnity and insurance clauses requiring the maintenance of liability insurance in reasonable relationship to the nature of the business and naming the franchisor as an additional insured. Finally, when making the contract, only such controls as are reasonably necessary for the efficient operation of the franchised system should be included.

QUESTIONS

1. What are franchise contracts? Why are they used?
2. What are some advantages and disadvantages of franchise agreements?
3. How effective is a disclaimer clause in a franchise contract that states that the franchisee is an independent contractor and not the agent of the franchisor?
4. How do you determine when the franchisee is the agent of the franchisor?
5. If you were advising a prospective franchisor, what provisions would you suggest to be included in the franchise contract?

PROBLEMS

1. Defendant, a milk route distributor, struck and injured plaintiff while defendant was on his milk route. The defendant distributed milk for the Mt. Meadow Creameries, but the Mt. Meadow company had no control over the activities of the defendant. Plaintiff joins the company in the lawsuit. Company defends on the grounds that the defendant was an independent contractor and the doctrine of *respondeat superior* therefore does not apply. Decision?

2. Plaintiff, owner of an antique shop, asked his friend Richard to mind the store while he went to the post office to mail a package. While the plaintiff was gone, a woman came into the store and purchased a rare painting for a very low price. When the plaintiff returned, Richard told him about the sale. Plaintiff brings action against the woman for the return of the painting on the grounds that Richard did not have authority to make the sale. Decision?

3. Jones, the secretary of the defendant's corporation, purchases some personal property for the corporation that he knows the corporation needs. Jones does not have authority to make the purchase. Defendant, after learning of the purchase, accepts the benefits of the purchase and is pleased to get the goods. Plaintiff, seller of the goods, brings action against the corporation for the purchase price. Defendant takes the position that Jones acted without authority. Decision?

4. Plaintiff, a real estate broker, asks defendant, a homeowner, if he wants to sell his house. Defendant replies that he does. Plaintiff asks defendant if he can represent him and make a sale of the house for him. Defendant tells him that it is all right with him

if the price is at least $25,000 and if the commission is not over five percent. Plaintiff agrees. A few days later, plaintiff enters into a contract for the sale of the house with a third party; however, defendant refuses to confirm the sale. Plaintiff brings action to force defendant to specifically perform the oral contract and the sale and to pay the commission. Decision?

5. P, a manufacturer, employs A as a traveling saleswoman to contract for the sale of goods manufactured by P. P is killed, but A does not know of this and continues to make contracts. A makes a contract with T, who now brings action against P's estate. Decision?

6. Atwood employed Bade, aged 17, as an agent. Acting within the scope of his authority and on behalf of Atwood, Bade made a contract with Sibley, who demanded that Atwood perform the contract. Atwood sues to rescind on the grounds that Sibley's contract was made with a minor. Decision?

7. The National Life Insurance Company employed Brown as its district agent. Brown died and in his will stated that his son was to carry on his work as district agent. When the son attempted to write an insurance policy for Sullivan, Sullivan claimed that the son could not legally do so. Decision?

8. Bill, the driver of a school bus carrying fifty small children to school, discovered that the brakes did not work. To avoid dissaster, Bill drove to a garage and had the brakes repaired, then drove on to the school. The garage sues Mac, the bus owner, for the cost of the repairs. Decision?

9. Joe, a skilled photographer, was hired by the ABC Company to photograph the new models of equipment the company was preparing for market. Before Joe could take the pictures, he was arrested for a felony, failed to make bail, and was put in prison. ABC claims its agency contract with Joe is terminated. Decision?

10. Jim, wanting to go into business for himself, makes a franchise contract with Firehouse Dogs to use its trademark, controls, and advertising for operation of a hot dog stand. The agreement requires Jim to pay a set fee for the franchise and to follow its instructions in the preparation of sandwiches. It allows Jim to keep all profits he makes, set his own business hours, hire and fire his employees, and pay all his own expenses and taxes. A customer, injured when he fell off a stool at the stand, sued Firehouse Dogs on the basis that Jim was their agent in the operation of this business. Decide.

CHAPTER TWELVE

Principal and Agent Relationship

12.1 General Rules
General Agent
Special Agent
Power of Attorney
Durable Power

12.2 Duties of Agent
Duty of Care
Good Conduct
Duty to Inform
Accounting
Duty to Be Practicable
Obedience
Loyalty
Dual Agency

Termination
Remedies of Principal
Defenses of Agent

12.3 Duties of Principal
Performance
No Interference
Duty to Inform
Accounting
Good Conduct
Duty to Indemnify
Compensation
Duty Not to Terminate
Agent Actions
Defenses of Principal

12.1 General Rules

Principal
One who has permitted or directed another to act for his benefit and subject to his direction or control.

Third Party
In agency, the party an agent deals with when representing the interests of the principal.

Scrupulous Good Faith and Candor
Conscientious honesty, sincerity, frankness, fairness and uprightness.

Since an agent represents a principal in dealing with third parties, the relationship is one in which the agent owes a duty of scrupulous good faith and candor to the principal. This agent-principal affiliation is one of great trust and is personal in nature. It is a classic example of fiduciary responsibility. Each party owes several duties and legal obligations to the other. While an agent normally represents only one party, his principal, in a transaction, sometimes he may represent both sides. For example, a real estate broker may act as agent for both the seller and the buyer. When this occurs, it must be with full knowledge and consent of the parties, and the agent must be careful, since he is required to play fair with both sides.

Facts

Jake Fretty, a salesman for Assam Real Estate, approached Van Zee about buying some land as an investment. Assam had a listing contract with the property's owner, Shawd, who wanted $90,000 for the land. Zee offered $80,000 with $15,000 down if Shawd would pay half the title insurance premium. Shawd approved the price but wanted $18,000 down and no part of the title cost. Assam people said it was a good deal and advised Zee not to let the "title insurance thing blow the deal," because title insurance would be a waste of money. Zee signed the contract but, on a banker's advice, asked for abstract of title and learned that there was a bank encumbrance as well as money still owed on a former contract. Zee told Assam and was informed for the first time that Shawd had called the bank from Assam's office to get permission to sell the land. Zee had to pay $13,560 more than the $80,000 to clear up the title. Zee sued Assam for the additional costs.

Decision

This was a breach of an agent's fiduciary duty as well as negligence. The broker had approached Zee on this deal, and Zee had asked Assam to handle the negotiations with Shawd. Zee had also relied on Assam. The broker's failure to investigate when it learned that the bank had a hold on the land was negligent, and the failure to tell the buyer everything it knew was a breach of the agent's duty. Assam was liable for the extra costs and expenses.

Zee v. Assam, 336 N.W.2d 162 (1983).

General Agent

General Agent
An agent authorized by the principal to do all necessary acts concerning the trade or business involved.

Agents may be general or special. A general agent is one who acts for the principal for many transactions over a prescribed period of time as authorized by the agreement between the agent and the principal. For example, a store owner may give the store manager (the owner's agent) the authority to operate the store in its day-to-day business. Or a large manufacturer may give its purchasing agent the authority to buy all of the parts needed to assemble its products.

Special Agent

Special Agent
An agent authorized to do a specific act or to take care of limited business transactions.

A special agent is one authorized by the principal to do a specific act or to take care of one transaction or a few specified business transactions.

Power of Attorney

An attorney-in-fact is an agent who is given either general or specified powers in a written power of attorney. For example, if you were going to be out of the country for a period of time and wanted to sell your car while you were away, you could give a special power of attorney to a friend to do that for you during your absence. Many military service people have given general powers of attorney to their spouses to manage all of their affairs during an overseas absence. This can be a risky business, because the general agent with such power is able to do anything that the principal would be able to do, such as selling off all of his property.

Attorney-in-Fact
An agent given authority by another to act in that person's place or name.

Power of Attorney
The document giving the attorney-in-fact the power and authority to act.

Durable Power

A recent development, enacted in over half the states, permits a durable power of attorney. Such an agency is supposed to survive the insanity or physical incapacity of the principal. One of the requirements is that the power of attorney contain language such as "shall not be affected by subsequent incapacity" or "becomes effective upon the incapacity" of the grantor principal. Another condition is that a written warning be given to the person signing the power, advising as to what rights are being given the agent. The main purpose for such a document is to avoid the necessity of having a court declare a person legally incapacitated before another could manage his affairs. Such a power has been referred to as senility insurance.

Durable Power of Attorney
A power of attorney designed to survive the insanity or physical incapacity of the principal.

Questions

1. What type of fiduciary duty does an agent owe to the principal?
2. Can an agent represent both parties to a transaction? If so, under what circumstances may it be done?
3. What is the difference between a general agent and a special agent?
4. When would one use a power of attorney? Give some examples.
5. What is a durable power of attorney?

12.2 Duties of Agent

In the fiduciary capacity, an agent owes certain duties to the principal.

Duty of Care

The agent owes a legal duty to use reasonable care, diligence, and skill in his work for the principal. However, the agent is not required to render perfect service and is not liable for errors in judgment unless based on negligence, fraud, or unfair dealing. For example, an insurance agency must

Legal Duty
That which the law requires to be done by a person.

not neglect to keep insurance in force for the specified amount agreed; an attorney must file a lawsuit or an appeal within the required time; and an insurance broker must obtain insurance covering the designated risk.

Good Conduct

Good Conduct
Behavior which does not discredit one or cause disrepute.

The agent owes a duty to conduct himself in such a manner so as not to bring discredit or disrepute upon the principal or his business or to make it impossible to continue friendly relations (e.g., a waitress should not become a call girl).

Duty to Inform

It is the duty of an agent to keep the principal informed of all facts relevant to the agency so that the principal can protect his interests (e.g., a broker must reveal all offers to purchase property). Since notice to the agent is generally held to be the same as notice to the principal, it is obvious that the agent must keep the principal informed. The following case is an example.

Facts

Mr. & Mrs. Miles were buying a house, and Mr. Russell was their agent for procuring a loan. A termite inspection had been made for Russell and the lender savings and loan company for $15. Later that day, the savings and loan company and Russell were advised that the house was termite infested and treatment would cost $450. Mr. and Mrs. Miles were not told about the termites and did not discover them until after the sale was completed and they had taken possession of the property.

Decision

The court held that an agent owes the principal a duty to disclose all material information that the agent learns concerning the subject matter of the agency relation and about which the principal is uninformed. Russell and the savings and loan company were agents to secure the termite inspection, and they had a duty to inform the plaintiffs of the result. Since they were duty bound to disclose the facts relating to the termite infestation prior to recording the deed and distributing the funds, they were liable to the plaintiffs for the cost of repairing the termite damage.

Miles v. Perpetual Savings and Loan Company, 58 Ohio St. 2d 93, 388 N.E.2d 1364 (1979).

Accounting

Accounting
Detailed statement of debt and credit between the parties arising out of the fiduciary relationship.

It is the duty of an agent to account to the principal for all property or money belonging to the principal that comes into the agent's possession.

Duty to Be Practicable

Practicable
Capable of being done, effected, or performed.

The agent owes a duty not to continue to render service that subjects the principal to risk of expense if it reasonably appears to the agent to be impossible or impracticable to accomplish the objects of the principal and if the agent cannot communicate with the principal.

Obedience

The agent is subject to a duty to obey all reasonable and lawful directions in regard to the manner of performing a service that he has contracted to perform. If the agent disobeys a reasonable order, the principal can terminate the employment. The agent owes a duty not to act in the principal's affairs except in accordance with all lawful instructions given to the agent by his principal.

Obedience
Compliance with a known law, prescribed rule, direction, order, command, or prohibition.

Loyalty

An agent must be loyal and faithful to the principal. The agent must not obtain any secret profit or advantage from the agency relationship. An agent must not enter into any transaction within the scope of the agency in which he has a personal interest unless he obtains the consent of the principal. An agent must not compete with the principal concerning the subject matter of the agency or represent a person whose interests conflict with the principal. Unless otherwise agreed, an agent has a duty to act in the principal's name and not to appear as the owner of the principal's property (e.g., attorney must not put money he has collected for a client in his own personal bank account). The agent's loyalty must be undivided.

Loyalty
In agency, faithfulness to one's principal.

General Automotive Manufacturing Co. v. Singer
19 Wis.2d 528, 120 N.W.2d 659 (1963).

Brown, Chief Justice Study of the record discloses that Singer was engaged as general manager of Automotive's operations. Among his duties was solicitation and procurement of machine shop work for Automotive. Because of Singer's high reputation in the trade he was highly successful in attracting orders. . . . As time went on a large volume of business attracted by Singer was offered to Automotive but which Singer decided could not be done by Automotive at all, for lack of suitable equipment, or which Automotive could not do at a competitive price. When Singer determined that such orders were unsuitable for Automotive he neither informed Automotive of these facts nor sent the orders back to the customer. Instead, he made the customer a price, then dealt with another machine shop to do the work at a lesser price, and retained the difference between the price quoted to the customer and the price for which the work was done. Singer was actually behaving as a broker for his own profit in a field where by contract he had engaged to work only for Automotive. We concur in the decision of the trial court that this was inconsistent with the obligations of a faithful agent or employee.

Singer finally set up a business of his own, calling himself a manufacturer's agent and consultant, in which he brokered orders for products of the sort man-

> ufactured by Automotive—this while he was still Automotive's employee and without informing Automotive of it. Singer had broad powers of management and conducted the business activities of Automotive. In this capacity he was Automotive's agent and owed a fiduciary duty to it. . . . Under his fiduciary duty to Automotive Singer was bound to the exercise of the utmost good faith and loyalty so that he did not act adversely to the interests of Automotive by serving or acquiring any private interest of his own. . . . He was also bound to act for the furtherance and advancement of the interest of Automotive.
>
> . . . If Singer violated his duty to Automotive by engaging in certain business activities in which he received a secret profit he must account to Automotive for the amounts he illegally received. . . .
>
> The trial court found that Singer's side line business, the profits of which were $64,088.08, was in direct competition with Automotive. However, Singer argues that in this business he was a manufacturer's agent or consultant, whereas Automotive was a small manufacturer of automotive parts. The title of an activity does not determine the question whether it was competitive but an examination of the nature of the business must be made. In the present case the conflict of interest between Singer's business and his position with Automotive arises from the fact that Singer received orders, principally from a third-party called Husco, for the manufacture of parts. As a manufacturer's consultant he had to see that these orders were filled as inexpensively as possible, but as Automotive's general manager he could not act adversely to the corporation and serve his own interests. . . .
>
> Rather than to resolve the conflict of interest between his side line business and Automotive's business in favor of serving and advancing his own personal interests, Singer had the duty to exercise good faith by disclosing to Automotive all the facts regarding this matter. . . . By failing to disclose all the facts relating to the orders from Husco and by receiving secret profits from these orders, Singer violated his fiduciary duty to act solely for the benefit of Automotive. Therefore he is liable for the amount of the profits he earned in his side line business.

Dual Agency

Dual Agency
A dual agency exists when an agent represents both parties to a transaction.

Real estate brokers are agents licensed by the state to represent sellers and buyers of real property. Their authority is usually limited to identifying the property and quoting a price in accordance with the seller's listing agreement. However, in many instances, as when a buyer comes into a realty office to purchase property, the broker may have a loyalty problem when trying to get the best price for the seller and the lowest price for the buyer.

Some states have passed laws that require realtors to specify in advance which party they represent as agent or, if representing both the buyer and the seller, to explain the relationship up front and obtain the consent of both parties.

A solution to this dual agency dilemma is to classify such a broker as either a "seller's" or a "buyer's" agent.

Termination

An agent is subject to a duty not to act as such after the termination of his authority.

Facts

Husband and wife listed property with a broker to sell for $15,000. Several weeks later, the broker offered to buy the property himself, first for $11,000 and then for $14,000, which the parties accepted. After twenty-seven days, broker resold the property to another purchaser for $25,000. Husband and wife sued for breach of fiduciary duty.

Decision

Agency ended when the plaintiffs agreed to sell to the broker, and there was no duty to disclose after that happened. The broker didn't conceal the fact that he was the purchaser, and the couple consented to the price. To recover, the plaintiffs would have had to prove that as of the time he bought the property, the defendant failed to disclose fully all the facts within his knowledge. Defendant wins.

Sylvester v. Beck, 406 PA. 607, 178 A.2d 755 (1962).

Remedies of Principal

When an agent violates or threatens to violate his duties, the principal has several remedies available to him. He may, of course, sue the agent for breach of the service contract and for any losses resulting from any breach of duty. An equity action may be brought for an accounting or for an injunction to prevent the agent from further acts. The principal may discharge the agent, refuse to pay compensation, or rescind the contract of service.

Accounting Action
An equity action asking for judicial determination of the rights of parties in a shared asset.

Defenses of Agent

If the principal brings an action against the agent, some defenses are available to the latter. They may include incapacity of the agent to act; illegality as an excuse for nonperformance; criminality as an excuse for failure to account; impossibility of performance; statute of frauds; principal's breach of contract, contributory fault, or failure to minimize damages; ratification or affirmance of an unauthorized act; superior rights of a third person; protection of the principal's own superior interests; discharge by release or accord and satisfaction; agent's insolvency or bankruptcy; and a setoff against principal's debt to agent.

Questions

1. What is meant by a duty of good conduct owed by the agent to the principal?
2. Since the agent has a duty to keep the principal informed, what facts must be related to the principal, and when must they be presented?
3. When is an agent required to make an accounting to his principal?
4. When is an agent allowed to retain any secret profits he makes in furtherance of the agency business?

12.3 Duties of Principal

Performance

The primary duty of the principal is to carry out the contract made with the agent. To accomplish this, there are several specific duties owed by the principal to enable the agent to properly perform the assigned tasks.

No Interference

Interference
To come in between, intervene or intermeddle for some purpose.

A principal has a duty to refrain from unreasonably interfering with the agent's work (e.g., terminating the agent's authority to act; supplying the agent with inferior goods; competing with the agent when the agent's services are exclusive, such as appointing an agent to collect a debt and then collecting it himself).

Duty to Inform

The principal owes a duty to use care to inform the agent of risks of physical harm or pecuniary loss [monetary] that exist in the performance of authorized acts and that he has reason to know are unknown to the agent. The principal's duty to give other information to the agent depends on the agreement between the principal and the agent or on the custom of the business (e.g., furnishing a list of prospective customers to the selling agent).

Accounting

A master has a duty to keep and render accounts of the money due from the master to the servant. An agent can sue a principal for an accounting as an equitable remedy. However, the extent of the principal's duty in this area depends upon such factors as the contract between the principal and the agent, the custom of the business, the method of compensation, and whether the agent operates an independent business.

Good Conduct

The principal owes a duty to conduct himself in such a manner so as not to harm the agent's reputation or to make it impossible for the agent, consistent with his reasonable self-respect or personal safety, to continue in the employment (i.e., agent does not have to continue to act for one whom he discovers to be an unsavory person or for one who physically or verbally abuses him or insults him).

Duty to Indemnify

It is the duty of the principal to indemnify the agent for any losses or damages suffered without his fault (e.g., payments of damages to third persons that the agent is required to make on account of the authorized performance of an act that constitutes a tort or a breach of contract; expenses of defending actions by third persons brought because of the agent's authorized conduct, such actions being unfounded but not brought in bad faith; obligations arising from the possession of things that the agent is authorized to hold on account of the principal; authorized payments made by the agent on behalf of the principal; payments resulting in benefits to the principal made by the agent under such circumstances that it would be inequitable for indemnity not to be made; and losses caused by the failure of the principal to give the agent required information, such as failure to give the agent proper instructions for grading a street).

Indemnify
To provide compensation for or to repair loss or damage suffered.

McKinnon and Mooney v. Fireman's Fund Indemnity Co.
288 F.2d 189 (6th Cir. 1961).

Per Curiam Plaintiff-appellee, as agent for The Fireman's Fund Indemnity Company, defendant-appellant, issued a liability policy for the appellant on an automobile owned by Fitzgerald. On October 17, 1954, it cancelled the policy for nonpayment of premium. On October 23, 1954, Fitzgerald was involved in an automobile accident in which one Davis was injured.

Davis recovered a $10,000.00 judgment in the state court against Fitzgerald, and thereafter filed a supplemental petition against the Indemnity Company asserting that Fitzgerald was covered by the insurance policy of the Indemnity Company in that the alleged cancellation of the policy was fraudulent. At the request of the Indemnity Company, appellee's employees testified in this action with respect to the cancellation of the policy. The Indemnity Company was successful in its defense of the action.

Thereafter, Davis sued appellee in the United States District Court alleging that appellee fraudulently conspired to manufacture evidence depriving him of a recovery under the supplemental petition in the state court. Appellee notified the Indemnity Company of this suit and requested it to defend the action, which the Indemnity Company refused to do. Appellee employed its own attorney and successfully defended this action on the ground of res judicata.

. . . The attorney submitted his bill for attorney's fee for his services in the matter and expenses in the amount of $5,236.09, which the appellee paid. Appellee then brought the present action against the Indemnity Company for reimbursement of this expense.

The District Judge rendered judgment for the appellee in the amounts of $4,000.00 for a reasonable attorney's fee plus $500.00 for expenses. This appeal followed.

We agree with the reasoning of the District Judge that an agent may recover from his principal any expenditures necessarily incurred in the transaction of his principal's affairs and that under this well settled rule of principal and agent, an agent, compelled to defend a baseless suit, grounded upon acts performed in his principal's business, may recover from the principal the reasonable and necessary expenses of his defense. . . . The judgment is affirmed.

Compensation

Compensation
Pay for work done.

The principal is under a duty to pay the agent the compensation agreed upon. If no sum was agreed upon, the agent may recover the customary compensation for such services; and if there is no customary compensation, the agent may recover the reasonable value of his services. The following case illustrates how the court determines when the compensation is due.

Facts
Floyd sued Morristown European Motors, Inc., for commissions he claimed were due. Between January 8 and February 13, at a time when the new models were not in stock and prices had not been set, Floyd took signed orders for three cars, and the buyers paid 10 percent of the expected price. Floyd took a leave of absence in March and was gone when the cars arrived and the buyers took delivery. Morristown refused to pay Floyd the $721.25 in commissions, claiming that when the cars were paid for and turned over to the customers, Floyd was not an employee.

Decision
The court held that so long as a salesperson is the "procuring cause of the sale," he is entitled to the commission even though the actual consummation was by the principal or through another agent. Judgment for Floyd.

Floyd v. Morristown European Motors, Inc., 138 N.J.Super. 588, 351 A.2d 791 (1976)

Duty Not to Terminate

The principal also has a duty not to repudiate or terminate the agency relationship in violation of the terms of the contract of employment.

Agent Actions

If the principal breaks the agreement, the agent has the right to sue for damages or bring an equity action for an accounting. The agent may also refuse to render any further service.

Defenses of Principal

Insubordination
The act of not submitting to authority or of being disobedient.

If sued by the agent, the principal may use as defenses any illegality, the statute of frauds, and any disloyalty or insubordination on the part of the agent.

QUESTIONS

1. What type of interference with the agent's work is denied to the principal?

2. What kind of information is the principal required to furnish to his agent?

3. Since the principal and the agent are both required to make an accounting to the other, what types of accounts must each prepare?
4. How does the good conduct duty owed by the agent to the principal differ from that owed by the principal to the agent?
5. Considering the highly personal nature of an agency and the liabilities that could result from it, why is there a duty on the part of the principal not to terminate the relationship?

PROBLEMS

1. Roumel, the owner of an apartment building, employed Robbins as manager to live in the building and, among other things, to collect rent from the tenants. Robbins kept the rental money in an unlocked desk in her apartment, although banking facilities were available nearby. Tenants and workers had frequent access to the desk. Rent money in the amount of $200 was left in the desk and apparently stolen. Roumel brought action against Robbins for the rent money. Decision?
2. Homeowner employed broker to sell his home. Broker sold the home to his own wife for $10,500. Some months later, broker sold the home to a third person for $11,500. Homeowner sues broker for the $1,000 profit. Decision?
3. Principal gave agent an exclusive territory to sell the principal's products. During the exclusive contract, the principal invaded the territory and made sales of his own. Agent brings action against principal for the profits he would have made on the sales. Decision?
4. Isaacs bought chances on an automobile, which was to be presented to the winner at a picnic on a certain date. Isaacs offered Leake $25 to take his tickets to the picnic and receive the car for him if he was the winner. Leake agreed. One of Isaacs' tickets was the lucky one, and the car was turned over to Leake, who refused to give the car to Isaacs, maintaining that the lottery was illegal and that by the rules the winner had to be present. Isaacs sues for the car. Decision?
5. As an agent for Alberts, Doyle received $1,000 from the sale of certain merchandise. He deposited this amount in his personal bank account. The bank failed, and Alberts sued Doyle for the $1,000. Decision?
6. Evans, the credit manager for ABC Corporation, attended a regional credit meeting held in San Francisco. He submitted an expense account, including reasonable amounts for airfare, hotel, meals, taxi, and registration fee. The firm's accountant questions these expenses, and Evans claims he is entitled to reimbursement. Decision?
7. Moe, hired by Super TV as a repairman, went on a house call and, while repairing the television set, received a high-voltage shock that resulted in medical care and a long period of curative treatments. Moe claims that Super TV is liable for these expenses. Decision?
8. Custom Video Games hired Benjamin as sales manager at a salary of $5,000 a month. After working with the company for several years and building up a large sales volume, Benjamin quit and immediately went to work for nearby competition. Custom Video Games claims that Benjamin has violated his fiduciary duty as an agent. Decision?
9. Wilbur opens a store and hires Oscar as his general manager. Before leaving on a lengthy cruise, Wilbur tells Oscar not to spend over $2,000 on any non-inventory item during his absence. Shortly after Wilbur sails, Oscar receives a call from the city building inspector indicating that certain wiring in the store has to be replaced within 24 hours or the company's business permit will be cancelled. If the lowest bid on the rewiring is $3,000, is Oscar authorized to have it done?
10. Williams instructed his agent, Shoreham, to ship goods from Los Angeles to San Francisco on the Southern Pacific Railroad. Shoreham checked rail schedules and decided that the goods would get to San Francisco faster if he shipped them on the Santa Fe Railway. The goods were lost en route and never arrived. Williams sues Shoreham for the value of the goods. Decision?

CHAPTER THIRTEEN

Agency and Third Parties

13.1 Principal's Liability for Agent's Contracts
Types of Authority
   Express Authority
   Implied Authority
   Customary Authority
   Apparent Authority
   Ostensible Authority
Equal Dignities Rule
Delegation of Authority
Undisclosed Principal
   Election Rule

13.2 Principal's Liability for Agent's Torts
Scope of Employment
   Personal Business
   Substantial Deviation
   Business Disputes and Property Protection
   Fraud
Auto Statutes

13.3 Other Liabilities
Agent Liability
   Tort Liability
   Contract Liability
   Incompetency Nondisclosure
   Wrongful Receipt of Money
Third-Party Liability to Principal
   Contract Liability
   Tort Liability
Third-Party Liability to Agent
   Undisclosed Principal
   Intention to Bind Agent
   Agent as Assignee
   Wrongful Acts
   Agent as Bailee

13.1 Principal's Liability for Agent's Contract

The principal alone is liable for contracts made by the agent within the agent's authority.

Types of Authority

Authority
The permission or power delegated to another.

Once an agency relationship has been created, it becomes important to determine the existence and extent of the agent's authority to act on behalf of the principal. The authority is determined by the words and conduct of the principal.

Express Authority

Express Authority
Authority expressly given by words or in writing.

Express authority is the actual authority given to the agent in words or in writing. The principal must express to the agent those acts that the agent is to perform. Express authority may also be inferred from silence if the agent informs the principal of acts he intends to do and the principal has no objections.

Implied Authority

Implied Authority
Authority implied from the words or acts of the principal.

Incidental Authority
Right to do acts necessary to carry out an assignment.

Unless the principal expressly limits the authority of the agent by orders or by clear implication, the authority to carry out a task or an instruction includes the authority to do those things that are usually or customarily done by an agent to reasonably accomplish the objective. Implied authority may be inferred from the words or conduct of the principal (e.g., the principal employs an agent to manage an apartment building at a certain salary per month and the agent has implied authority to employ necessary labor to keep the building clean and make minor repairs when needed.

Implied authority is often referred to as incidental authority, meaning the right to do those acts incidental to carrying out an assignment. For example, if an agent is asked to buy goods but given no money to pay for them, authority to buy on credit would be implied as incidental to such purchase.

Coblentz v. Riskin
74 Nev. 53, 322 P.2d 905 (1958).

Merrill, Justice Appellants are owners of the Thunderbird Jewel Shop in Clark County, Nevada. Respondent Riskin is a diamond broker and wholesale jeweler of Los Angeles, California. In August, 1955 appellants employed Hyman Davidson for services in connection with their store. In January, 1956 Davidson entered into a consignment agreement with Riskin pursuant to which he received, for purposes of retail sale, two expensive items of jewelry. In his dealings with Riskin, Davidson represented himself as manager of the jewel shop with full authority to receive merchandise on consignment. Riskin did not check these representations with appellants but did check with others in the jewelry trade and satisfied himself as to Davidson's authority. The jewelry pieces were reconsigned by Davidson without Riskin's approval or consent. The person to whom they were reconsigned has disappeared. Riskin demanded of appellants the return of the jewelry or its agreed value pursuant to the terms of the agreement. Upon failure of appellants to comply with his demand this action was brought. Judgment in favor of Riskin was given in the sum of $16,300. . . .

Riskin testified that it was the custom in the jewelry trade to take expensive pieces of jewelry on consignment rather than by purchase at wholesale. . . . By consignment retail merchants are not financially committed to the purchase of expensive items until they have themselves resold the items. Until resale their only financial commitment is that of safekeeping. Thus there is substantial benefit to be realized at the minimum of financial commitment. It can hardly be questioned that the engaging in consignment transactions would be regarded by those in the jewelry trade as a customary, proper and necessary function of store management. . . .

Davidson testified positively that he had been employed as manager of the store with instructions to run the store as he saw fit; that he had discussed with appellants the matter of taking merchandise on consignment and that appellants had approved; . . . that appellants had indicated approval of Davidson's success in securing such quality pieces and had never said anything about restrictions upon his authority to deal on consignment.

. . . Actual authority includes both implied authority and incidental authority. . . . Implied authority is that which the agent reasonably believes himself to possess as a result of representations by the principal or of acts of the agent permitted by the principal over a course of time in which the principal has acquiesced. . . . Incidental authority is that which is reasonably necessary, proper and usual to carry into effect the main authority granted. . . .

The trial court has found that Davidson was employed to serve as manager and that he did so serve. The evidence we have recited presents a clear case of both implied authority and incidental authority. We conclude that the trial court's determination of actual authority is supported by the record and that appellants are bound by Davidson's actions in their behalf in committing them to the consignment agreement with Riskin.

Affirmed.

Customary Authority

Implied authority is sometimes referred to as customary authority—that which is customary in a particular community for the type of activity involved. The following case is an example of customary authority.

Customary Authority
Authority customary in a particular community for the type of activity involved.

Facts

A hotel manager offered a reward for information leading to the arrest of the suspected murderer of one of his night clerks. Jackson located the suspect and claimed the reward but was turned down on the basis that the manager had no authority to make the offer. Jackson sued and won a jury verdict, which was set aside by the judge as a matter of law. Jackson appealed.

Decision
The court stated that the authority to contract for rewards may be inferred from the authority to manage a business. Such authority is limited to those contracts that are incidental to the business, are usually made in it, or are reasonably necessary in its conduct. The judge added that a factor to be considered is the custom of similar businesses at the same time and place. Since a jury reflects the community sense of a locale and the jury in this case had decided that the plaintiff had reasonably believed the authority to exist, the court found for the plaintiff and reinstated the verdict.

Jackson v. Goodman, 69 Mich.App. 225, 244 N.W.2d 423 (1976).

Apparent Authority

Apparent Authority
When it is reasonably apparent to a third person that the agent has authority to act.

Apparent authority results when the principal, by words or conduct, manifests that another is his agent and such manifestation is made to a third person rather than to the agent. It is that authority that is apparent to the third persons with whom the agent deals (i.e., the authority that a third party might reasonably attribute to the agent). For example, a landowner writes a letter to a broker hiring the broker as agent to sell a piece of property and sends a copy of the letter to a prospective buyer. The broker now has actual authority to sell the property to anyone, but as to the prospect, the broker has apparent authority.

Ostensible Authority

Ostensible Authority
When a principal causes a third person to believe the agent can act, the authority is ostensible.

Ostensible authority (or authority by estoppel) is similar to apparent authority, and the terms are often confused or used interchangeably. The difference is that ostensible authority is not really authority at all but a rule applied to prevent a principal who has misled another from profiting thereby. It is invoked whenever a principal has intentionally or negligently caused or allowed a third person to believe that an agent has authority to do that which, in fact, he is not authorized to do and the third person reasonably relies thereon. Under such circumstances, it would be unjust to allow the principal to deny the agent's authority. For example, a local manager of a business had express authority to receive checks but no authority to endorse and cash them. He did so for some time, however, without complaint from his principal. The court found ostensible authority by estoppel and held the principal to be liable.

The acts or declarations of the *agent alone* cannot establish ostensible authority; there must be some conduct on the part of the alleged principal. However, if the principal knows that the agent is holding himself out as having certain authority but keeps quiet about it, that conduct on the part of the principal might be enough to create ostensible authority.

Equal Dignities Rule

Equal Dignities Rule
The rule applies to authority as well as to the agency agreement, so written authority is needed if a contract made by the agent is required to be in writing.

Like agency itself, authority may be given by precedent authorization or subsequent ratification. Likewise, the equal dignities rule applies; written authority is thus necessary to enter into a contract required by law to be in writing.

Delegation of Authority

Because of the personal nature of the relationship and the potential for liability, an agent is generally not allowed to delegate his authority to a subagent unless expressly granted by the principal. Some states have enacted laws governing delegation of an agent's authority. For example, California Civil Code, Section 2349, states, "An agent, unless specifically forbidden by his principal to do so, can delegate his powers to another person in any of the following cases, and in *no others*": (a) when the act is purely mechanical, (b) when it is such as the agent cannot himself and the subagent can legally perform, (c) when it is the usage of the place to delegate such powers, and (d) when the principal has authorized the delegation.

Authority Delegation
Unless a principal has authorized an agent to delegate authority, the right to do so is limited.

Undisclosed Principal

Where the principal is named in the contract and not excluded by the contract's terms and the fact of agency appears, the principal will be liable for the acts of the agent, actually or apparently authorized, as a *disclosed* principal. However, on occasion, an agent may enter into a transaction on behalf of a principal without disclosing to the third party that he is acting only as an agent. For example, a movie star wants to purchase a certain house but realizes that if the owner of the house knows who the prospective buyer is, he may raise the price. The movie star appoints an agent to make the purchase for her without disclosing that he is an agent. This would be a transaction by an agent for an *undisclosed* principal. In the case of an undisclosed principal, the contract can be enforced by the principal against the third party, and the third party can enforce the contract against *either* the agent *or* the undisclosed principal, but not against both.

Suppose that an agent enters into a contract with a third party disclosing that he is an agent but not disclosing the name of the principal (e.g., agent signs contract "John Doe, agent"). The general rule is that oral evidence may be introduced at the trial to show that the parties intended to bind only the principal and not the agent. However, absent such showing, the principal is still undisclosed or partially disclosed.

Disclosed Principal
A disclosed principal is one named in the agency contract or of whom the third party has notice.

Undisclosed Principal
A principal is undisclosed when the third party has no notice of identity of the principal.

Partially Disclosed Principal
A principal is partially disclosed if the third party has knowledge of the existence but not the identity of the principal.

Election Rule

Since the third party cannot hold both the undisclosed principal and the agent liable under a contract, he must make an election as to which one to pursue. There are two situations, however, where this election rule does not apply. Suppose that the third party sues both the undisclosed principal and the agent jointly for breach of the contract and neither of them requests that an election be made. Instead, they allow the trial to proceed to judgment against both of them without asserting their right to compel an election. In such a case, the right has been waived. The other situation occurs when a third party sues the agent alone and obtains a judgment against him before learning of the identity of the principal. Under such circumstances he may then recover from the principal.

Election Rule
A rule that requires a third party to decide whether to sue the agent or the undisclosed principal.

Exceptions Although the principal, whether disclosed or undisclosed, may claim the benefits of a contract made by his agent, there are some exceptions to this rule. For example, where exclusive credit is given to the agent or the skill or other personal quality of the agent is an important part of the agreement, the undisclosed principal cannot sue. Also, if the third person has agreed to do personal services for the agent, he cannot be forced to perform them for an undisclosed principal. In addition, if the agent says that he has no principal and the third party would not have dealt with the principal, the third party cannot be held to the contract but will be permitted to rescind it. Finally, until the principal actually discloses his identity, the third party may deal directly with the agent on the contract, such as paying the agent or taking advantage of any defaults caused by the agent.

Questions

1. Why is it important to determine the limits of an agent's authority before contracting with the agent?
2. What is the difference between actual and apparent authority?
3. What is meant by ostensible authority?
4. When is the authority of an agent required to be in writing? Give an example.
5. If you make a contract with a person and later discover that the person was acting as the agent for an undisclosed principal, what are your rights and obligations under the agreement?

13.2 Principal's Liability for Agent's Torts

Whereas the principal alone is liable for contracts made by the agent on his behalf, both principal *and* agent are liable for torts committed by the agent against a third party within the scope of his employment. An agent may cause injury to a third person by his malicious or negligent acts, such as assault and battery, fraud, larceny, or embezzlement. The agent himself is of course not exculpated simply because he was acting in the interest of his principal (*Ralls* v. *Mittlesteadt,* 268 Ark. 471, 596 S.W.2d 349 [1980]). However, if the tort is committed within the scope of the agency, then the principal too is liable. Hence, it is important to know what is within or without the scope of the agent's employment.

Scope of Employment

Scope of the Employment
An act done in the course of the agency and by virtue of the authority as agent.

The co-liability of a principal, employer, or master, only exists if the torts and wrongful acts of an agent, employee, or servant are done within the scope of the agency or employment. This generally means doing the task that the agent, employee, or servant was hired to perform and doing it during working hours. This is a form of liability without fault and is based on the doctrine of *respondeat superior* (let the superior respond). It is immaterial that the agent may have acted in excess of his authority or

AGENCY AND THIRD PARTIES

contrary to instructions. Courts justify this doctrine on the theory that the employer can spread the risk of loss through insurance and carry the cost as part of his overhead.

To impose *respondeat superior* liability, it is essential that the agent, employee, or servant be acting for the principal or employer within the scope of employment when the tort is committed. An agent's scope of employment means that the act was done in the course of the agency and under the authority given the agent for the conduct of the principal's business. In other words, when doing the act, the agent is trying to promote the principal's business within the scope of the authority conferred on him for that purpose. Although the act may not be in the best interests of the principal or even in the prosecution of the principal's business, it may still be within the agent's authority and within his scope of employment. If the agent's departure from authorized conduct is not serious as to manner or space and is done in part by a motive to serve the principal, it may still be within the scope of employment. Any act that is required or incidental to the agent's duties or could be reasonably foreseen by the employer falls within the scope.

Facts

Garcia was hired by Van Groningen to disk some orchards. There was a company rule prohibiting passengers on the tractor. One day Garcia asked his nephew, Perez, to ride along with him on the tractor while he disked the fields. Since there was only one seat, Perez sat on the toolbox. A low-hanging tree branch knocked Perez off the tractor and into the blades, causing loss of use of an arm and the lower part of a leg. Perez sued on the basis that the uncle was acting in the scope of his employment when the accident occurred.

Decision

Perez was injured while his uncle was performing a task assigned to him by his employer, and the fact that Perez was an unauthorized passenger did not negate the fact that the uncle was engaged in his employer's business in disking the orchard. (One dissenting judge argued that the violation of safety rules and willful disobedience of company rules took it outside the scope of employment.)

Perez v. Van Groningen and Sons, 41 Cal.3d 962, 227 Cal.Rptr. 106, 719 P.2d 676 (1986).

In another case, the driver of a bread truck while on his route saw a woman with her car stranded in a ditch. He stopped to assist her and was injured. The court held that this was not a personal deviation but a Good Samaritan act. The driver had been told by his employer that every member of the public was a potential customer and should be treated with courtesy and consideration. Thus, rendering assistance to a disabled motorist was still in the scope of the driver's employment (*Bunny Bread* v. *Shipman,* 591 S.W.2d 692 [Ark., 1980]).

Personal Deviation
The turning aside from a course or a duty for personal reasons.

Good Samaritan
One who unselfishly helps others.

Personal Business

Acts necessary for the comfort, convenience, health, and welfare of an employee while at work, though strictly personal, do not take the employee outside the scope of employment. Cessation of work for such acts as eating, drinking, and warming oneself is necessary to employment and contributes to the furtherance of an employee's work. This has been extended to such

Lunch Hour Rule
Taking lunch is reasonably incidental to employment.

things as taking a shower in a locker room provided by the employer and even to such recreational activity as playing with a frisbee. Under the lunch hour rule, taking lunch is reasonably incidental to employment.

Substantial Deviation

When an agent or employee makes a *substantial* deviation or departure from his job to take care of personal business or to engage in activities for his own pleasure, he is engaging on a "frolic and detour" of his own and is outside the scope of his employment. However, if the main purpose of the activity is still within the scope of the principal's business, the activity is within the scope even though there may be incidental personal acts, slight delays, or a deviation from the most direct route. For example, a truck driver starts out on a direct route from the employer's factory to the railroad depot to deliver some goods. On the way, he stops at his home, which is only a block off the direct route. As he leaves his home, he has an accident. Since the deviation was slight, his principal or employer would be liable.

Frolic and Detour
Acts for personal pleasure outside the scope of one's employment.

It is obvious that courts may have difficulty at times in deciding the extent of deviation necessary to take the act out of the scope of employment.

Facts

Martha White, while driving after midnight, was pulled over by a deputy sheriff and without explanation was placed in the deputy's patrol car. The deputy drove White to an isolated place and threatened to rape and murder her. After she promised to go out with him that weekend, he returned her to her car. She then complained to authorities, and the deputy was arrested for kidnapping and false imprisonment and was convicted. White sued the deputy as well as the County of Orange on the theory of *respondeat superior*.

Decision

White had a good cause of action for vicarious liability against Orange County, since the government must be held responsible for acts done during the exercise of police authority. In this case, the wrongful acts flowed from the very exercise of such authority by the deputy sheriff.

White v. County of Orange, 166 Cal.App.3d 566, 212 Cal.Rptr. 493 (1985).

In a similar case, a Los Angeles police sergeant, in uniform and driving a black-and-white and flashing red lights, pulled over a vehicle being driven erratically by a young woman. The woman had been drinking and did not do well on a field sobriety test. The sergeant took the woman's keys, put the woman in the patrol car, and drove her home. Instead of leaving her there, he entered the house and forcibly raped her. However, a different appellate court held that the rape surely was not required by nor incidental to the sergeant's police duties. Instead, it was not work-related conduct contemplated by the employer but was a substantial deviation for personal purposes. It was also so unusual, startling, and uncharacteristic of the duties of a law enforcement officer that it was not "foreseeable" in the *respondeat superior* context. A strong dissent in the case argued that a police officer carries the authority of law with him into the community. He is supplied with a conspicuous automobile, a badge, and a gun to ensure immediate compliance with his directions. "The officer's method of dealing with this

AGENCY AND THIRD PARTIES

authority is certainly incidental to his duties: indeed it is an integral part of them" (*Mary Anna M.* v. *City of Los Angeles,* 200 C.A.3d 758, 246 Cal.Rptr. 487 [1988] [Rehearing granted]).

Exceptions to Substantial Deviation   The *going and coming rule* refers to situations, such as going to or coming from work or meals, that are considered to be substantial deviations or departures by the agent or employee and therefore outside the scope of employment. However, the rule has exceptions, some of which are as follows:

1. *Bunkhouse rule.* Where the employee or agent lives at his place of work, such as a bunkhouse on a ranch, going to the work area and coming back from the work area to the living quarters are usually regarded as within the scope of employment.
2. *Traveling salespeople.* Traveling salespeople are generally regarded to be within the scope of their employment the entire time that they are away on the job, even when not actually working.
3. *Travel paid by employer.* Where the employer provides transportation to the work, compensates the worker for travel time, or defrays travel expenses, the courts have held that such employee is exempt from the going and coming rule insofar as workers' compensation cases are concerned. However, if tort liability in *respondeat superior* is involved, the activity must be of some benefit to the employer's business, and the employer should have some right to control it.
4. *Special errand or dual purpose.* Where the agent's or employee's going and coming has some additional business purpose, the employee may be considered to be within the scope of employment for the entire trip. For example, an employee who works nights goes home to get certain tools and then goes to dinner. On his return to work, he has an accident. Because his dual purpose was to obtain the tools and to eat, he was within the scope of his employment.

Going and Coming Rule
Going to and from work and meals is generally considered outside the scope of one's employment.

Bunkhouse Rule
Where agent or employee lives at place of work, going and coming to work is in the scope of employment.

Gipson v. Davis Realty Co.
215 Cal.App.2d 190, 30 Cal.Rptr. 253 (1963).

Molinari, Justice   This is an appeal from a judgment in favor of the defendant, Davis Realty Company, a corporation, in an action for damages for personal injuries....

On April 4, 1957, Mrs. Jane Gipson, who was pregnant with child, was being transported by ambulance to the Stanford Hospital where her child was to be delivered. A collision between the ambulance and an automobile owned and driven by Roland Shugg occurred at the intersection of 26th Avenue and Clement Street in San Francisco. The accident occurred at about 12:20 p.m. The child was born about 40 minutes after the accident. The child showed signs of brain damage immediately after the accident, it being subsequently determined that such damage was permanent and that the child was suffering from a disability diagnosed as cerebral palsy.... A personal injury action was thereafter instituted by the child's father, Edward T. Gipson, as guardian ad litem on behalf of the child, ... and against Shugg and Davis Realty Company, a corporation, as the alleged employer of Shugg....

> The important question is whether, at the time of the accident in question, Shugg, as such agent, was acting within the course and scope of his employment. . . .
>
> The facts leading up to the accident appear to be undisputed. Shugg testified: that on the morning of the accident he was at the office of Davis Realty; that he left the office for the purpose of going to 38th Avenue and Clement Street to try to obtain a listing on a house at that corner on behalf of Davis Realty; that his sole intention upon leaving the office was to look at that property; . . . that as he started out on Clement Street he noticed it was around noon, so he decided to stop by at his home for lunch and then continue out to look at the property after lunch; . . . that the respondent did not instruct its salesmen as to when or where they should eat lunch; that it was the usual practice to stop at a convenient location for lunch and then continue on with the business of Davis Realty; that he ate lunch at home if he happened to be in the area; . . .
>
> . . . Therefore, whether or not the principal or employer is responsible for the act of the agent or employee at the time of the injury depends upon whether the agent or employee was engaged at that time in the transaction of the business of his principal or employer, or whether he was engaged in an act which was done for his own personal convenience or accommodation and related to an end or purpose exclusively and individually on his own. . . . Accordingly, it is the general rule that an employee on his way to lunch, even though he is driving an automobile which is the property of the master, is not engaged in furthering any end of the employer, and that therefore under such circumstances, the servant is not acting within the scope of his employment. . . .
>
> The so-called "lunch hour rule," . . . is, however, subject to an exception termed the "dual or combined purpose rule." . . .
>
>> "[W]here the servant is combining his own business with that of his master, or attending to both at substantially the same time, no nice inquiry will be made as to which business the servant was actually engaged in when a third person was injured; but the master will be held responsible, unless it clearly appears that the servant could not have been directly or indirectly serving his master."
>
> . . . In the instant case it cannot be said that at the time of the accident Shugg was engaged in an act which was done for his own personal convenience or accommodation and related to an end or purpose exclusively and individually his own. The testimony shows that, initially, his sole intent was to attend to the business of his principal at 38th Avenue and Clement Street. Enroute, he decided to combine his business with that of Davis Realty. This is the extent of his deviation. . . . The extent and substantiality of Shugg's deviation, if any, was a question of fact for the jury.
>
> The judgment is reversed.

Business Disputes and Property Protection

The employer or principal may be liable for the malicious acts of the employee or agent if committed in the scope of the employment. An assault and battery inflicted by an agent that results from a business dispute connected with the agent's employment can result in liability for the agent's principal. However, where the tort is over a personal grudge unrelated to the job, the principal is not liable, even though the act occurs on the employer's premises and during business hours.

Facts

Rubin was driving on a city street when he inadvertently obstructed the path of a taxicab, causing the latter to swerve and contact his vehicle. Angered by plaintiff's sudden blocking of his traffic lane, the cabbie got out of his taxi, approached Rubin, and hit him about the head and shoulders with a metal pipe. Rubin sued the cab company under *respondeat superior*.

Decision

An employer may be liable for the negligent, willful, malicious, or criminal acts of its employees where committed in the course of employment and in furtherance of the business but not when done for the sole benefit of the employee. While bartenders or bouncers might use force to protect property and maintain order for their employers, cab drivers would be unlikely to attack anyone who is neither a passenger nor connected with the cab company. This assault was a deviation from conduct usually associated with cab driving. The driver's assault was not undertaken in furtherance of cab business but was due to his own anger and frustration.

Rubin v. Yellow Cab Co., 154 Ill.App.3d 336, 107 Ill. Dec. 450, 507 N.E.2d 114 (1987).

Where the employment itself involves the risk of force and the tort is connected with the employment, such as an injury caused by a security guard throwing stones at a trespasser on posted property, the employer would be liable. Another example would be the assault on a noisy customer by a nightclub bouncer.

Fraud

Generally, the principal is liable for fraudulent representations of a type that are normally incidental to sales (i.e., those that the principal might reasonably expect would be the subject of representations by the agent). The principal is not liable, however, for representations that are unusual or exceptional unless the principal with knowledge of the fraud retains the benefits of the transactions. For example, the owner of a business employs a broker to sell the business for him. The broker misrepresents to a buyer that the net income is much greater than it really is and that the Exxon Corporation is purchasing the surrounding area to erect a tract of homes that will greatly increase the business. The first misrepresentation is one that a principal might reasonably expect a salesperson to make, and the principal is thus liable for the fraud of the agent. However, the second misrepresentation is so unusual to the sale of a business that there would be no liability on the part of the principal.

In some states, the principal is held liable for the fraud of an agent even when the fraudulent statement is unusual or extreme under the doctrine of *respondeat superior*. In some states (e.g., California), the courts hold that an innocent principal is not liable for the fraud of the agent if the written contract provides that the agent has no authority to make any representations not contained in the written contract, and is signed by the third party. Such a provision gives notice to the third person that the agent's representations are not authorized. In such a case, although the third party cannot hold the principal liable for fraud, he can hold the agent for fraud and can rescind the contract.

Auto Statutes

Automobile Statutes
State laws that hold owners of vehicles liable for harm caused by anyone driving with the owner's consent.

By operation of law in many states, automobile owners may be vicariously liable. Statutes hold the owner responsible up to a stated amount for any injury or damage caused by the negligent operation of the vehicle by anyone driving with the owner's consent.

Minor's Driver's License
Most states have laws making parents liable for damages caused by minor drivers if the parents signed the driver's license application.

Most states require that parents sign the application for a minor's driver's license. This usually imposes financial responsibility up to a limited amount for the negligent acts of the minor while driving the vehicle.

Questions

1. What is the legal meaning of the phrase *respondeat superior*?
2. What rules should be applied in determining whether or not a peace officer is acting in the scope of his employment or is only acting on his own?
3. What does the *going and coming rule* mean? What are some of the exceptions to the rule?
4. When is a principal liable for an assault and battery committed by his agent upon a third person?
5. How may a principal avoid liability for the fraudulent misrepresentations of his agent to third parties?

13.3 Other Liabilities

Agent Liability

A number of situations exist in which an agent may become liable to third persons and some where third persons may be liable to the principal or to the agent.

Tort Liability

If an agent commits a tort or wrongful act, he is personally liable for any injuries or damages caused regardless of the liability of the principal. For example, if a truck driver while negligently driving on the job hits a pedestrian in a crosswalk, the driver is liable to the injured person even though the principal may also be liable.

Reimbursement
If an innocent agent is required to pay damages, he is entitled to be repaid by the principal.

The agent is liable even though he acted pursuant to the principal's directions. However, an innocent agent who is required to pay damages for such a tort is entitled to reimbursement from the principal.

Contract Liability

If the agent's name appears alone on the contract without either the name of the principal or a statement of the fact of agency, the agent is personally liable.

Under the Restatement of Agency and the law of nearly all of the states, an agent who signs as an agent but does not set forth the name of the

AGENCY AND THIRD PARTIES

principal is liable on the contract unless otherwise agreed. However, extrinsic evidence is permitted to show the intent of the parties (i.e., that the agent was not to be bound).

Other courts (e.g., California) go further and hold the agent liable regardless of the disclosure of the agency unless the name of the principal is disclosed so that it appears on the face of the instrument that only the principal is to be bound (e.g., plaintiff proposed a contract to "Hotel Berry Systems," and defendant Berry wrote on the contract as follows: "Signed and accepted, B. S. Berry"). Plaintiff knew that the defendant was acting only as an agent. Defendant was held personally liable, since he had signed his name without disclosure of the principal or of the fact of agency. The fact that the proposed contract was submitted to the hotel company was not enough, since the contract may have intended to hold the agent as well.

Undisclosed Principal After the third person has discovered the identify of the undisclosed or partially disclosed principal, he may hold either the principal or the agent on the contract but not both of them. The third party has a choice, and once the choice is made, he is bound by it.

The following example illustrates the necessity of disclosing the principal if the agent seeks to avoid personal liability:

Facts
Defendants had placed orders for materials furnished on credit by plaintiff in the amount of $20,711.95, ordered before and after the date defendants incorporated. Defendants now state that they were acting as agents for the corporation and are not personally liable for the bill.

Decision
The court held that at the time the first purchases were made the defendants were individually liable because the corporation had not yet been formed and thus could not exist as a principal. After incorporation, no notice was given to the plaintiff of the corporate status. Where agents fail to disclose their principal when it is within their power to do so, the agents are personally liable. Judgment for plaintiff.

Tarolli Lumber Co., Inc. v. *Adreassi,* 59 A.D.2d 1011, 399 N.Y.S.2d 739 (1977).

If the facts show that the agent was acting on behalf of a principal rather than personally, he is a disclosed agent and is not liable on any agreement made in that capacity.

Guillory v. Courville
158 So.2d 475 (La.App., 1963).

Culpepper, Judge This is a suit on an open account. From an adverse judgment the plaintiff appeals.

The substantial issue is whether defendant has proved his defense that he was acting as a disclosed agent of a corporation.

. . . There is no dispute as to the law. An agent is responsible to those with whom he contracts when he does not disclose that he is acting as an agent. . . .

> The facts show that in January of 1958 the defendant, Claude Courville, and several other parties formed a corporation known as "Basile Flying Service, Inc.", domiciled in Evangeline Parish, Louisiana, for the purpose of engaging in the business of providing flying services to farmers. This concern purchased gasoline from the plaintiff at various times, from February, 1958 down through July of 1959, on an open account. Although occasionally delinquent, the account was paid except for the sum of $1,834.48 for purchases made during the period July 4, 1959 through July 30, 1959. Plaintiff's statements of account were addressed to "Basile Flying Service."
>
> Plaintiff testified that he did not know the business was incorporated and that he was relying on the credit of defendant, with whom he had done satisfactory business before. Defendant testified that he personally told plaintiff before the purchases in question were made, that the business was incorporated. At least one other witness corroborated defendant in this respect. Furthermore, several checks received by plaintiff's office, in payment of previous amounts on this open account, were clearly marked "Basile Flying Service, Inc.", although plaintiff denied seeing any of these checks. . . .
>
> The record amply supports the following finding of facts by the district judge:
>
> The court is of the opinion that plaintiff was informed by the defendant and other stockholders of the corporation of the fact that he was doing business with the corporation; that plaintiff cashed checks from the corporation; that an account was opened for the corporation and a credit check was made on the corporation. It is further the opinion of the court that the present action against defendant is a result of plaintiff's inability to effect collection against the corporation to whom the gasoline was originally billed or charged. The court is of the opinion that no action of defendant in this matter created a personal obligation toward plaintiff.
>
> For the reasons assigned the judgment appealed is affirmed.

Warranty of Authority
Every agent guarantees to third parties that he is authorized by the principal to do what is being done.

Warranty of Authority Every agent implicitly warrants or guarantees that he is authorized by the principal to do what he is doing. An agent who does not have authority to bind the principal is bound by the contract unless the principal ratifies it.

Incompetency Nondisclosure

Under the majority rule, the agent does not warrant the competency of the principal (e.g., that the principal is not a minor or is not mentally incompetent). However, the agent has a duty to inform third persons of the principal's lack of capacity and is liable for fraud in the form of nondisclosure if he does not do so.

Wrongful Receipt of Money

If an agent obtains a payment of money from a third person by the use of illegal methods, the agent is liable to the third person. When a third person makes an overpayment to the agent or a payment when none is due, the agent who knows that the payment was not proper is liable to the third person.

Third-Party Liability to Principal

The third person in an agency transaction may under some circumstances be liable to the principal in either contract or tort.

Contract Liability

A third person who has contracted with an agent representing a disclosed principal is as liable to the principal as though the contract had been made personally with the principal. Where the contract was unauthorized, it is not binding on the third party until the principal ratifies it.

A third person is liable to an undisclosed principal on a contract made on his behalf by the agent unless the terms of the contract expressly bar any principal or unless the third party would not contract with that particular principal and the agent or the principal knows this. In such a case, it is fraudulent for the agent not to reveal the principal's identity. However, in the normal case where the agent enters into a contract in his own name, concealing the fact that he is an agent and contracting as if he were the principal, the contract inures to the benefit of the principal, who may at any time come forward and claim all of the benefits from the third party.

Tort Liability

A third person is liable in tort to a principal for injuries he commits to the principal's property or interests in the hands of an agent, whether or not the principal had been disclosed at the time, in the same manner and to the same extent as though such agency did not exist and as if the third person had dealt with him directly.

A person who knowingly induces or assists an agent to violate a fiduciary duty to the principal is liable to the principal (e.g., bribing an agent for obtaining confidential information).

A third person who colludes with the agent to have the agent act for the third person rather than the principal is liable for fraud in the absence of a reasonable belief that the principal acquiesces.

A third person who causes an agent to fail in his performance (e.g., to leave his employment prematurely) will be liable to the principal for damages.

Third-Party Liability to Agent

Third persons normally are not liable to an agent who acts on behalf of a disclosed principal, just as such agent has no right of action against the third person for breach of contract. However, there are some exceptions.

Undisclosed Principal

If an agent executes a contract without informing the third person of the existence of the agency and the identity of the principal, the agent may maintain an action against the third person for breach of contract. Of course,

Intention to Bind Agent

If the parties intend that the agent be bound to the contract even though the third person knew the agent was acting as an agent, the agent may bring action against the third person for breach of contract.

Agent as Assignee

When the principal has assigned or otherwise transferred his claim or right to the agent (e.g., for purpose of collecting money for the principal), the agent has a cause of action against the third person for breach of his obligation to the principal.

Wrongful Acts

The third person is liable for fraudulent or other wrongful acts causing injury to the agent. If the third person wrongfully injures the agent's property or person, the agent has a cause of action against the third person. If the third person wrongfully causes the agent to be discharged, the agent has a cause of action against the third person.

Agent as Bailee

Agent as Bailee
An agent may sue the third party for any damage to principal's property in agent's possession since the agent would be liable to account to the principal.

An agent, such as a bailee, in possession of the principal's property has a general or special interest in the property and therefore may maintain an action against a third person who disturbs his possession or unlawfully injures the property. The third person's liability is not merely to the extent of the agent's special interest but is also for the full measure of damages caused by the injury, the agent being liable to account to the principal for the balance beyond his own interest.

QUESTIONS

1. In an agency transaction, who is responsible for damages caused by torts or wrongful acts committed on the job?
2. Suppose that you are an agent making a contract that does not disclose the principal, but you sign it, "John Doe, Secretary." What is your responsibility under the contract?
3. What is meant by an agent's warranty of authority?
4. Suppose that a third person with whom you do business as an agent has been billed twice for the same item and makes both payments to you. What are your responsibilities?
5. If a principal supplies an agent with a company car to use on the job, and the car is destroyed by the negligence of a third person, what are the agent's rights?

PROBLEMS

1. P is a bread manufacturer. He employs A to purchase wheat for him, but he instructs A not to purchase any wheat in a quantity greater than 100 bushels without first contacting P for approval of

the price. A represents to T, who knows he is P's agent, that he has authority to purchase 500 bushels of wheat for P. However, he does not inform T that he has no such authority without approval of P. Without obtaining P's approval, A purchases 500 bushels of wheat from T. P now refuses to take the wheat, and T sues P for breach of contract. Decision?

2. S, a deliveryman for M's liquor store, delivers a case of whiskey to a customer's home. After leaving the customer's home, S drives five miles farther to a hospital to visit his sick mother. As he is driving out of the hospital parking lot, he negligently runs into a child in the crosswalk. The child, through her guardian ad litem, brings suit against M. Decision?

3. Pacific Tuna Company hired Charlie as a purchasing agent to buy fish for it. After several transactions, Pacific Tuna Company advised Charlie that future purchases should be made only on consignment but did not notify the suppliers of the change. Despite these instructions, Charlie bought some fish outright and then bought ice to keep the fish fresh. Discuss Charlie's authority and Pacific Tuna Company's liability.

4. A bus driver for a local bus company asked a passenger who was slightly intoxicated to please get off the bus because he was making a general nuisance of himself. The passenger refused. The bus driver and the passenger exchanged words, and tempers flared. Finally, the bus driver pushed the passenger off the bus. With that, the passenger referred to the bus driver's ancestors with some unkindly remarks. The bus driver then got off the bus and hit the passenger in the mouth, breaking some front teeth. Passenger brings action against the bus company. Bus company defends on the grounds that the bus driver went beyond the scope of employment, since the company does not hire bus drivers to go around hitting people. Decision?

5. Burkovits sued Morton Gregson Co. and Kleeburger for return of overpayments for meat. Kleeburger was a salesman for Morton Gregson Co., delivering meat to Burkovits and collecting weekly. Over a period of time, Kleeburger wrongfully altered statements to Burkovits, and consequently, Burkovits made large overpayments. Burkovits sued Morton Gregson to recover the amounts overpaid, which had been retained by Kleeburger. Decision?

6. Reilly, president of Rock Wool Insulating Company, borrowed money from Huston on behalf of the corporation and executed a promissory note for the amount of the loan. The minutes book of the corporation showed that Reilly had general authority to make loans for the company but indicated nothing regarding execution of notes. When Houston sued on the note, Rock Wool Insulating Company claimed that Reilly had no authority to execute the note. Decision?

7. Pete operated a service station for the Southern Oil Company and was one of its most successful retailers. Pete told several customers that the products of his neighboring competitors were from foreign-owned companies, were inferior, and tended to cause irreparable damage to motors when used. Southern Oil had permitted Pete to make these statements, knowing that they were false and slanderous. The competitors sued Southern Oil Company for damages due to Pete's misrepresentations. Decision?

8. A contract was put on the letterhead of a corporation principal and signed, "The Feldheym Co., Inc. *Dave Schwebel.*" T brings action against Dave Schwebel personally. T contends that Schwebel did not indicate by his signature that he was acting only as an agent and that he should have used the word "by" before his signature. Schwebel contends that he was acting only as an agent and that this fact is easily inferred from the letterhead and from the name of the company before the signature. Decision?

9. Luke was fired by the ABC Company because of arguments he had with the sales manager. Shortly thereafter, Luke visited the XYZ Company, one of the accounts he had serviced for the ABC Company, and collected $250 that was due the ABC Company. Luke absconded with the money. No notice had been given to XYZ Company concerning Luke's discharge. ABC Company sues XYZ Company for the $250. Decision?

10. Ace Corporation, wishing to acquire an adjoining site for its factory expansion but without provoking a rise in price, hired Lott Realty to purchase the land without disclosing Ace's name. Lott Realty did so and signed a contract in its own name with Landers to purchase the site. If Ace changes its mind and refuses to complete the sale, what are Landers' legal rights?

PART FOUR

Property

CHAPTER FOURTEEN
Personal Property

CHAPTER FIFTEEN
Multiple Ownership and Real Property

CHAPTER SIXTEEN
Landlord and Tenant

CHAPTER FOURTEEN

Property

Property is the right to possess, use, and dispose of something. Concern for the protection of property rights has led to the development of much of our law. Most people think of property as the thing or things owned. In that sense, property may be personal, that which is usually moved around with a person, or real, which is land and those things imbedded therein or permanently attached thereto. Personal property can be tangible, that which can be touched (dog, stereo, auto, tennis racket) or intangible (patents, copyrights, stocks, bonds).

Chapter 14 discusses personal property, including bailments (transfer of possession to another for a particular purpose) and some special types of regulated bailments.

Chapter 15 considers multiple ownership of all kinds of property, interests in real property, and the acquisition of title to land.

Chapter 16 examines landlord and tenant relationships under leasehold tenancies, including covenants usually contained in leases and potential liabilities of the lessor and the lessee.

CHAPTER FOURTEEN

Personal Property

14.1 Acquisition of Title
Property Defined
- Tangible Property
- Intangible Property
Acquisition of Property Rights
- Gift
- Creation
- Accession
- Confusion of Goods
- Possession
- Operation of Law
Fixtures
- Trade Fixtures

14.2 Bailments
Bailment Defined
- Essential Elements
- Distinguished from Sale
- Distinguished from Pledge or Pawn
- Distinguished from Lease or License
Bailee's Duty of Care
- Sole Benefit of Bailor
- Mutual Benefit
- Sole Benefit of Bailee
Liability Limitations
Bailee's Lien
Duty to Return Property

Termination of Bailment
- Performance
- Agreement of Parties
- Breach
- Destruction of Property
- Operation of Law

14.3 Special Bailments
Liability of Hotel Keepers
- Negligence
- Theft
- Baggage Lien
Liability of Common Carriers
- Exceptions to Absolute Liability
- Termination of Strict Liability
- Limited Liability
- Passenger Safety
Liability of Warehousepersons
- Duty Under UCC
- Personal Property Lessor
- Bailee Liability
Liability of Parking Lot Operators
- Checkrooms
Liability of Safe Deposit Box Lessors
Container Contents
Constructive Bailments

14.1 Acquisition of Title

Property Defined

In our individualistic society, property refers to the rights one has in anything that can be owned. Property can be classified as real property, consisting of land and those things intended to be permanently attached thereto by people or by nature, such as buildings and vegetation, or personal property, referring to all other things, including tangible movable items and certain intangibles, such as contract rights. A single piece of property might be classified as either real or personal, depending upon its nature and intended use. Personal property includes all things that are not real property and that are generally movable. Such things can be either tangible or intangible.

Tangible Property

Tangible personal property consists of those objects that we recognize through our physical senses. Some examples are furniture, automobiles, books, food, perfume, and stereo equipment. The legal term *chattel* refers to such items.

Intangible Property

Intangible personal property is that which has no physical dimension but does represent a legal right to receive ownership or possession. Some examples are patent rights, shares of stock, negotiable instruments, currency, insurance policies, and executory contract rights. Such documents are not intrinsically valuable but represent specific rights. Accounts receivable (unpaid obligations owed by one party to another) are also intangible.

Acquisition of Property Rights

Title and right to possession of personal property may be acquired in many different ways. The UCC has standardized the law on the sale of goods (see Part V, The Law of Sales). The UCC also sets forth the legal rules for the acquisition and transfer of title to negotiable instruments (see Part VII, Commercial Paper). In addition to acquisition by these standard commercial transactions, personal property rights may be acquired by gift, through creation, because of accession or confusion of moveable goods, and by operation of law.

Gift

A gift is the voluntary transfer of property from the owner (the donor) to another (the donee) without payment of compensation. This lack of consideration is the basic difference between a gift and a contract. To be effective, a gift must be completed by delivery and acceptance. A gratuitous promise to make a gift in the future would not be enforceable. Gifts of personal property may be *inter vivos, causa mortis,* or testamentary. The latter occurs when the property is made as a gift through a validly executed will of a deceased person.

Property
Rights one has in anything that may be owned.

Real Property
Land and things imbedded in it or permanently attached to it.

Personal Property
Moveable things.

Tangible Property
Recognizable property that can be touched.

Intangible Property
A legal right to ownership of property.

Acquisition
To obtain possession of something.

Gift
A voluntary transfer of property made without consideration.

Inter Vivos An *inter vivos* gift is one made between two living persons. The legal requirements are as follows:

1. Donor's expressing an intent to transfer title.
2. Delivery of property by the donor.
3. Right of the donee to disclaim the gift and divest title within a reasonable time after notice of the gift.

Inter Vivos
Between living persons.

Facts

When Catherine Soupcoff died, her mother and sister went to visit her husband, Norman, and to attend the funeral. While sorting through the deceased's clothing, they came across a jewelry box. The will gave all jewelry to Norman, but a niece called him into the bedroom and suggested that the jewelry box be given to Catherine's mother. Norman agreed, saying he wouldn't have any use for it. When the sister returned home, she tried to give the jewelry box to her mother, but the mother was too upset at her daughter's death and said she "just couldn't accept it." Meanwhile, the sister retained possession of the box. A few weeks later, Norman and his attorney demanded the return of some items from the box. When they couldn't agree, the probate court said that Norman had made a gift of the box and its contents to the mother and the box should go to her. Norman appealed.

Decision

A gift requires donative intent, delivery, and acceptance. If a gift is beneficial to the donee, acceptance is ordinarily presumed. But in this case, the mother never took possession of the jewelry box, preventing completion of the gift. When she later changed her mind, it was too late. By that time, the gift had been revoked by Norman.

In re Estate of Soupcoff, 329 Pa.Super. 130, 477 A.2d 1388 (1984).

Symbolic Delivery The delivery may be actual or symbolic. A symbolic delivery would be the handing over of the keys to a new automobile, thereby making a gift of the vehicle.

Since there is no consideration, a prospective donee cannot sue to compel the gift, and if the donor dies before making delivery, the gift fails.

Symbolic Delivery
Delivery of a token with intent to pass title.

Conditional Delivery A gift may also be conditional, requiring that some condition occur before the transfer of title to the gift is completed. The typical example is the gift of an engagement ring, which usually is made in contemplation of the condition of subsequent marriage. Consequently, if the party who received such a conditional gift of the ring breaks the engagement, she would have to return the ring. However, there is a modern trend in many states that have adopted no-fault divorce laws to apply the same public policy to suits for recovery of gifts conditioned on marriage, therefore making it irrelevant how the engagement was ended.

Conditional Delivery
A condition must occur before title is transferred.

Causa Mortis Gift A *causa mortis* gift is one made when the donor, believing he is nearing death, delivers personal property to a donee intending that the donee shall retain it after the donor dies. This is a conditional gift, and the property must be returned under the following circumstances:

1. Donor does not die.
2. Donor revokes gift before his death.
3. Donee predeceases the donor.

Causa Mortis
In anticipation of approaching death.

Custodian
One who has immediate care or charge of something or someone.

Uniform Gifts to Minors Act All states have enacted laws providing for the making of gifts of money or securities to minors. Under the Uniform Gifts to Minors Act, adopted by a majority of jurisdictions, adults can make a gift to the minor by depositing the cash or registering the securities with another adult, broker, or financial institution with trust powers as custodian for the minor. This is considered an irrevocable gift but may be used by the custodian for the minor's benefit.

Creation

Creation
The act of bringing something into existence.

Artists and inventors may obtain exclusive rights to their creations under patent, copyright, and trademark laws.

Patent
A document giving an inventor exclusive right to the use of his invention.

Patents A creator who has given physical expression to an idea may be granted a patent by the U.S. Patent Office. A patent is the grant of a monopoly to the inventor for a period of seventeen years and is not renewable. The item must be something new and useful, not previously known and used.

Facts
Black & Decker has a popular Workmate workbench that it patented and sold over 10 million of in less than twenty years. Sears wanted to get it on the market, so it put out its Work Buddy workbench, and Black & Decker sued for patent infringement. Sears claimed that the patent should be invalidated, because the bench was "obvious" and could have been designed and built by anyone good with his hands. A jury disagreed and awarded Black & Decker $86,500 in damages. Sears appealed.

Decision
Unlike prior inventions, Workmate was a combination of workbench and vise ideal for use by amateur woodworkers. Its vise mechanism differed from others and was more versatile. By mimicking it, Sears had infringed on a valid patent. Since so many were sold, it was unlikely that it could have been "obvious" to a skillful person when first patented. Affirmed.
Black & Decker Mfg. Co. v. Sears, 679 F.2d 1101 (4th Cir. 1982).

The courts tend to protect patent rights because the Patent Office grants the monopoly only after making a thorough examination of the prior art in the field and then determining that the invention, process, product, design, or organism does not conflict with a prior pending or issued patent. The following case illustrates a modern trend in the expansion of patent areas.

Diamond v. Chakrabarty
447 U.S. 303, 100 S.Ct. 2204, 65 L.Ed.2d 144 (1980).

Burger, Chief Justice ... In 1972, respondent Chakrabarty, a microbiologist, filed a patent application . . . related to Chakrabarty's invention of "a bacterium from the genus Pseudomonas containing therein at least two stable energy-generating plasmids, each of said plasmids providing a separate hydrocarbon degradative pathway." This human-made, genetically engineered bacterium is capable of breaking down multiple components of crude oil. Because of this property, which is possessed by no naturally occurring bacteria, Chakrabarty's invention is believed to have significant value for the treatment of oil spills.

... The Constitution grants Congress broad power to legislate to "promote the Progress of Science and useful Arts, by securing for limited Times to Authors and Inventors the exclusive Right to their respective Writings and Discoveries." The patent laws promote this progress by offering inventors exclusive rights for a limited period as an incentive for their inventiveness and research efforts. . . . The authority of Congress is exercised in the hope that "[t]he productive effort thereby fostered will have a positive effect on society through the introduction of new products and processes of manufacture into the economy, and the emanations by way of increased employment and better lives for our citizens."

. . . This is not to suggest that [the patent law] has no limits or that it embraces every discovery. The laws of nature, physical phenomena, and abstract ideas have been held not patentable. . . . Thus, a new mineral discovered in the earth or a new plant found in the wild is not patentable subject matter. Likewise, Einstein could not patent his celebrated law that $E = mc$; nor could Newton have patented the law of gravity. Such discoveries are "manifestations of . . . nature, free to all men and reserved exclusively to none."

. . . Judged in this light, respondent's micro-organism plainly qualifies as patentable subject matter. His claim is not to a hitherto unknown natural phenomenon, but to a nonnaturally occurring manufacture or composition of matter—a product of human ingenuity "having a distinctive name, character [and] . . . use." . . . We are told the genetic research and related technological developments may spread pollution and disease, that it may result in a loss of genetic diversity, and that its practice may tend to depreciate the value of human life. These arguments are forcefully, even passionately presented; they remind us that, at times, human ingenuity seems unable to control fully the forces it creates—that, with Hamlet, it is sometimes better "to bear those ills we have than fly to others that we know not of." . . .

. . . The grant or denial of patents on micro-organisms is not likely to put an end to genetic research or to its attendant risks. The large amount of research that has already occurred when no researcher had sure knowledge that patent protection would be available suggests that legislative or judicial fiat as to patentability will not deter the scientific mind from probing into the unknown any more than Canute could command the tides. Whether respondent's claims are patentable may determine whether research efforts are accelerated by the hope of reward or slowed by want of incentives, but that is all.

Accordingly, the judgment of the Court of Customs and Patent Appeals [allowing the patent] is affirmed.

A patentee who believes that an infringement of his patent rights has occurred may be required to sue in federal court to determine the validity of the patent.

Infringement
A violation or encroachment upon the rights of another.

Copyrights A copyright is a grant by the government of the exclusive right to print, publish, and sell books, written material, musical compositions, lectures, works of art, photographs, motion pictures, data systems, videotapes, and other creations in a tangible medium of expression. The Copyright Revision Act of 1976 was the first major change in the law since 1909 and changed the former time period of twenty-eight years plus a twenty-eight year renewal to the life of the person plus fifty years. Existing copy-

Copyright
A protection giving artists and writers exclusive rights to their works.

rights in their first twenty-eight year period may be extended for an additional forty-seven years.

The exclusive right now attaches upon creation rather than publication. Fair use is permitted but not infringement upon creator's rights. Reproduction for classroom use is fair if certain tests are met. In making such a determination, the following factors are considered:

Fair Use
Permitted use of copyrighted material by others for limited purposes.

1. Purpose and character of the use (commercial or nonprofit).
2. Nature of the work.
3. Proportion of the work used.
4. Effect of use upon the potential market and value of the work.

Where an anthology has been compiled, the copyright belongs to each original author for his contribution unless it has been expressly granted to the compiler.

The following case is an example of the application of fair use in connection with historical biographies.

Facts

Gardner, author of *The Rosenberg Story*, sued Nizer, author of *The Implosion Conspiracy*, for copyright infringement, alleging that Nizer copied material from Gardner's book while writing about the Rosenbergs' case.

Decision

The court held that historical facts, as such, are not protected by copyright. Biographies are similar of necessity, and infringement occurs only where there is a substantial or material taking from a copyrighted work. Also, the fair use doctrine applied in this case. Fair use is the right to use copyrighted matter in a reasonable manner. Since the rule is liberally applied to biographies because of the public benefit from such works, infringement requires similarity that is virtually complete or verbatim. The case was dismissed.

Gardner v. Nizer, 391 F.Supp. 940 (S.D.N.Y. 1975).

Trademark
Any word, name, symbol, or device used by a manufacturer or merchant to identify certain goods.

Lanham Act
Federal law providing for federal registration and protection of trademarks.

Trademarks Chevron, Burger King, United Airlines, and Century 21 are common examples of names and designs that identify specific products or services. Such distinctive "word, name, symbol, or device or combination thereof adopted and used by a manufacturer or merchant to identify his goods to distinguish them from those manufactured or sold by others" is known as trademark and is sometimes referred to as a brand name. It is eligible for legal protection under the laws dealing with unfair competition.

The controlling federal law is the Trademark Act of 1946, popularly known as the Lanham Act (15 USC, Secs. 1051–1127). Under this law, a trademark may be registered by its owner or user. However, the right to use a mark exclusively comes into existence on the date it first is used in a public manner to identify particular products or services. The right lasts as long as the mark is used continuously and properly. The name must be used before it is eligible for registration, and it must occur in interstate commerce for federal registration. Once registered with the U.S. Patent and Trademark Office, the trademark becomes nationwide notice of the registrant's exclusive right to use it throughout the country. Violation of this right gives the registrant a cause of action for recovery of the defendant's profits, any damages caused by the infringement, plus court costs. In as-

PERSONAL PROPERTY

sessing damages, the court may award treble damages. A registration may also be used to stop at customs the importation of goods bearing an infringing mark.

Rights under the mark may be lost through abandonment either by nonuse or by permitting others to use it without retaining the right to control the nature and quality of the goods or services provided. (Refer to Subchapter 11.3 for how this affects franchise operations.)

When a trademark becomes so common that it is used in a generic sense and becomes a part of the language, the exclusive rights to its use are lost. Some examples of former trade names are linoleum, aspirin, trampoline, brassiere, and tollhouse cookies.

Generic
Related to a general group or class of related things not protected by a trademark.

Accession

Acquisition of title by accession or by confusion has special legal significance related to the moveable nature of personal property. Accession refers to an owner's right to any increase in the value of his property caused by artificial or natural means. Examples are the newborn young of animals, repairs made by a finder of a lost watch, or equipment added to a stolen automobile. When courts are asked to rule on whether title to the added value goes to the rightful owner of the property, an equitable result is sought by analyzing such factors as intent and willfullness. The following case illustrates rightful ownership of property with added value.

Accession
Something added to property either naturally or artificially.

Facts
Lane bought a dump truck on credit and had its bed and hoist replaced by Texas Hydraulic. When the finance company repossessed the truck, it claimed the improvements by accession. The court agreed. Texas Hydraulic appealed.

Decision
Although Texas Hydraulic claimed that it could remove the body and the hoist without damaging the truck, the court held that since the work had been completed and delivered to the owner without the requirement of a security document, the sale was complete and the items had become part of the truck by accession.

Texas Hydraulic and Equipment Co. v. Associates Discount Corp., 414 S.W.2d 199 (Tex., 1967).

Confusion

Confusion of goods occurs when property belonging to different owners is commingled. If the mixing is done willfully and wrongfully by one of the parties so that the total mass is indistinguishable, the innocent party acquires title to all. This rule does not apply if the following circumstances exist:

Confusion of Goods
Property of more than one owner becomes intermingled so that it cannot be identified except as part of the mass.

1. Commingling was done by consent of all owners.
2. Commingling was done by accident or mistake.
3. When the goods are of equal kind and grade of fungibles (oil, grain, etc.).
4. When the owners can still identify their goods.

Possession

Possession
Control of property.

Under certain circumstances, the taking of physical possession of property, if done lawfully, creates ownership rights. If lost property is found, the finder has title that is good against everyone except the owner. Title to property that has been abandoned or over which no prior title rights have been established rests with the person who takes and holds possession.

Lost Property
Property involuntarily parted with by the owner through neglect, carelessness, or inadvertence.

Mislaid Property
Property placed somewhere by its owner and then forgotten.

Lost or Mislaid Property Property is lost or mislaid when its rightful owner cannot locate it but does not intend to give up title or ownership. However, "finders keepers, losers weepers" is not the law, and title remains with the loser. To acquire legal title, the finder, who is considered an involuntary bailee, must comply with the requirements of local statutes, which usually require that the item be turned over to the police or other authority for a period of time. If the owner does not claim the property, the property is ordinarily returned to the finder. If the owner reclaims the property, the finder is not entitled to a reward or compensation unless a contract has been made with the owner or statutory provision grants such award.

Private Property The general rule that the finder's rights to goods are superior to all but the rightful owner may not apply when the goods are discovered on privately owned property. Under the following certain circumstances, the owner of the place rather than the finder is entitled to the goods:

1. If the goods are found in a private rather than a public area of the place (e.g., a private room for examining safe deposit boxes in a bank rather than the bank's public lobby).
2. If the goods are determined to be mislaid or placed somewhere and then forgotten rather than lost, since the owner, if and when he remembers, would probably return to the place where he left them.
3. If the goods are found by an employee, such as a chambermaid, who has the duty to turn the goods over to the employer.
4. Where the finders are trespassers.

Dolitsky v. Dollar Savings Bank
203 Misc. 262, 118 N.Y.S.2d 65 (1952).

This was an action by Betty Dolitsky (plaintiff) against Dollar Savings Bank (defendant) to recover $100 allegedly found by Dolitsky.

Betty Dolitsky rented a safe-deposit box from Dollar Savings Bank. The safe-deposit vault of the bank was in the basement, and the vault area was walled off from all other parts of the bank. Only box renters and officers and employees of the bank were admitted to this area. To gain access to the area, a box renter had to obtain an admission slip, fill in the box number and sign the slip, have the box number and signature checked by an employee against the records of the bank, and then present the slip to a guard who admitted the renter to the vault area.

On November 7, 1951, Dolitsky requested access to her box. While Dolitsky was in the booth she was looking through an advertising folder which the bank had placed there and found a $100 bill, which she turned over to the attendant. Dolitsky waited one year, and during that time the rightful owner of the $100 bill made no claim for it. Dolitsky then demanded that the bank surrender the bill to her, claiming that she was entitled to the bill as finder. The bank claimed that the bill was mislaid property and that it owed a duty to keep the bill for the rightful owner.

Trimarco, Justice At common law property was lost when possession had been casually and involuntarily parted with, so that the mind had no impress of and could have no knowledge of the parting. Mislaid property was that which the owner had voluntarily and intentionally placed and then forgotten.

Property in someone's possession cannot be found in the sense of common-law lost property. If the article is in the custody of the owner of the place when it is discovered it is not lost in the legal sense; instead it is mislaid. Thus, if a chattel is discovered anywhere in a private place where only a limited class of people have a right to be and they are customers of the owner of the premises, who has the duty of preserving the property of his customers, it is in the possession of the owner of the premises.

In the case of mislaid property discovered on the premises of another, the common-law rule is that the proprietor of the premises is held to have the better right to hold the same for the owner, or the proprietor has custody for the benefit of the owner, or the proprietor is the gratuitous bailee of the owner. The effect of the cases, despite their different description of the relationship, is that the proprietor is the bailee of the owner. Thus, the discoverer of mislaid property has the duty to leave it with the proprietor of the premises, and the latter has the duty to hold it for the owner. New York statutory requirements do not change this rule.

The recent case of *Manufacturers Savings Deposit Co. v. Cohen,* which held that property found on the floor of a booth located in an outer room used by a safe-deposit company in conjunction with a bank, access thereto not being limited to box holders or officials of the safe-deposit company, was lost property and as such should have been turned over to the property clerk of the Police Department, can be distinguished from the present case. In the *Cohen* case the court found that the booth on the floor of which the money was found was not located within the safe-deposit vault but rather in an outer room adjoining said vault and in a part of the bank which was accessible to the ordinary customer of the bank for the purchase of bonds and the opening of new accounts; as such the court considers the room in which the booth was located a public place which was not restricted to safe-deposit officials and persons having safe-deposit boxes in the vault. The case is further distinguished from the present case since its facts disclose that the money was found on the floor of the booth, which indicated to the court that the money was not mislaid.

Judgment for Dollar Savings Bank.

Buried Property Where lost property is found buried in the ground, the owner of the land generally has a claim superior to the finder. An exception is the common law treasure trove rule, followed in many jurisdictions, which gives the finder of bullion or coin in the soil the right to possession.

Abandoned Property Personal property is abandoned when the owner gives up possession with an intent to disclaim title. The items you put in your trash can are usually abandoned. The first person to take possession and control of abandoned property becomes the property's owner.

Treasure Trove
Hidden property whose owner is unknown and to which the finder usually has the best legal claim.

Abandonment
Knowingly giving up one's right to property.

Wild Animals Wild animals and fish, living freely in nature, are not owned by any person. However, under the state's police power, most wildlife is protected by game regulations and conservation laws. Absent such restrictions, anyone who legally obtains possession and control of such wild creatures becomes their owner. If the animal should be captured or killed while the hunter is trespassing on private property, title would belong to the landowner.

Operation of Law

Title to personal property may be transferred by operation of law. For example, it may be sold by a trustee in bankruptcy for the benefit of creditors.

Judgements Personal property not exempted by statute may be seized by proper authority and sold to satisfy court-awarded damages of the judgment creditor. Ordinarily, judgments against personal property have no effect upon the title unless the determination of title was the purpose of the lawsuit. A person claiming ownership of personal property in the possession of another may elect to either sue to recover the property, thereby determining title, or treat the matter as an involuntary transfer and sue for the value of the property together with any money damages in an action for conversion (the wrongful conversion of another's property to one's own use).

Escheat
The passing of property to the state because there is nobody to inherit it.

Escheat If a person dies without having disposed of his property by will, the personal property will go to the heirs by operation of law in accordance with the laws of succession in the state where the person resided at the time of his death. If there were no heirs, the property will go to the state by *escheat*. Various state escheat laws also provide that the title to unclaimed property such as stock dividends, bank deposits, and insurance proceeds shall revert to the state after a prescribed period of time. It is estimated that over a billion dollars a year of such intangibles are never claimed by those entitled to ownership.

Fixtures

Fixtures
Personal property attached to land in such a way as to be considered part of the real estate.

Fixtures are usually defined as personal property that has been affixed to the land or made a part of buildings in such a way that they are considered part of the real property. The key test for making such a determination is the intent of the parties concerned. The method of attachment, the purpose for which placed, and the ordinary custom and usage may all be considered in ascertaining the intent.

Paul v. First National Bank of Cincinnati
52 Ohio Misc. 77, 369 N.E.2d 488 (1976).

Black, Judge As the purchaser for $575,000 of an elegant residence known as Long Acres, located in Indian Hill, Hamilton County, a plaintiff Lawrence M.

Paul sues the defendants for removing and converting from the buildings and grounds certain items of property. . . .

. . . On July 13, 1971, plaintiff entered into a purchase contract with the defendant Executor, which contained the following provisions, among others:

. . .: "II. Together with . . . *all fixtures relating to said real estate*. . . . [Emphasis added.]

When possession was delivered to plaintiff on January 15, 1972, he noticed that a number of items were missing that had been on the property both before and after the date of the purchase contract. The defendants admit that these items had been removed by the individual defendants before surrendering possession.

Decedent Augustine J. Long, his wife and one of his children died on September 9, 1969, in an airplane accident. . . . The First National Bank of Cincinnati was duly appointed Executor of the Long Estate.

The will left to the decedent's surviving children "*all household furnishings, appliances, decoration and equipment* owned by me and used in or about any principal or seasonal residence." [Emphasis added.]

. . . [T]he Ohio Supreme Court designated . . . six "facts" to be considered in determining whether an item is a fixture:

1. The nature of the property;
2. The manner in which the property is annexed to the realty;
3. The purpose for which the annexation is made;
4. The intention of the annexing party to make the property a part of the realty;
5. The degree of difficulty and extent of any loss involved in removing the property from the realty; and
6. The damage to the severed party which such removal would cause.

. . . Using the Supreme Court's considerations, the light "fixtures" (there is no other available word) from the swimming pool, the stable apartment and the chapel are clearly fixtures in contemplation of law. . . . [T]hey were designed and produced solely and only for the swimming pool, from the same design as was used for the light fixture in the porte cochere (which was not removed). Further, the poles from which they were taken are barren and incomplete without them.

To allow the heirs to walk off with an organ bench, leaving the built-in organ behind would be plainly ridiculous. You cannot play an organ while standing up, and no ordinary bench will do.

The Mercury statue is pictured in two photographs included in the appraisal of Long Acres which was considered by plaintiff before purchase. . . .

As fixtures . . . these articles are classified legally as items which pass to the purchaser on sale of the real estate. . . .

. . . The plaintiff is entitled to recover the sum of $9,675 (with interest at the legal rate from January 15, 1972) from The First National Bank of Cincinnati, as Executor, for breach of contract. . . .

Trade Fixtures

Trade fixtures are those fixtures placed in a rented building by a tenant for use in business or trade. They may ordinarily be removed by the tenant if done before the expiration of the lease and if they can be removed without damaging the property. These factors were considered by the court in the following case.

Trade Fixtures
Articles put by a tenant on leased premises for the conduct of business.

Facts

The city of Rockford had condemned an office building, and an appraisal of the building included a payment for immovable fixtures. The tenant, an architectural firm, had installed decorative wall coverings, carpets, and cabinets which it claimed were trade fixtures that entitled it to the sum paid by the city. The corporate landlord also claimed the money, contending that the items were part of the building. No material damage resulted to the building by removal of the items.

Decision

Deciding that the items were trade fixtures, the court held that when tenants add fixtures to premises, there is a presumption that they so do for their own benefit and not for that of the landlord. This rule is construed liberally, and the tenant is allowed to remove such fixtures if the tenant does so before the lease expires and without causing any material damage to the property. Judgment for tenant.

Empire Building Corp. v. Orput and Associates, Inc., 32 Ill. App.3d 839, 336 N.E.2d 82 (1975).

Questions

1. What is the difference between real property and personal property?
2. What are the requirements for a binding *inter vivos* gift?
3. How are personal property rights created by patent?
4. What is the purpose of a trademark? How can a person obtain one and then protect it from being used by others?
5. What are the legal rights of someone who finds some money that was lost or mislaid by someone else?

14.2 Bailments

Bailment Defined

Bailment
Transfer of possession of property to another for a particular purpose.

A bailment is the transfer of possession of personal property for a particular purpose. For example, the owner of a watch gives the watch to a jeweler for repair. No transfer of title is made. The owner and the transferor of the property is the bailor; the person receiving the property is the bailee. Real property cannot be the subject matter of a bailment.

Essential Elements

The essential elements of a bailment are as follows:

Bailor
Person who delivers personal property to another for purpose of a bailment.

1. Retention of title by bailor.
2. Delivery of possession to the bailee.
3. Acceptance of possession by the bailee.
4. Possession and temporary control of property by the bailee for a specific purpose.

Bailee
One to whom bailment property is delivered.

5. Ultimate possession of the property to revert to bailor unless bailor orders it transferred to another person.

The necessity of acceptance of possession by the bailee is illustrated by the following case.

Facts
Trushin loaned his car to Acker, who drove the car to the Harbor Lounge. When Acker stopped at the front of the lounge, he left the lights of the car on and the motor running. Acker waved to one of the attendants who waved back. Acker then entered the lounge. None of the attendants parked the car, which was not seen thereafter; the car had been stolen.

While the thief was allegedly operating the vehicle in a negligent manner, the plaintiffs were injured; they sued several defendants, including the Harbor Lounge.

The trial court entered summary judgment in favor of the lounge, and the plaintiffs appealed.

Decision
The court held that the keys had been left in the car by Acker. There was no evidence that the car had been accepted by any employee of the lounge, nor was there any proof that any of the employees of the lounge were negligent. Affirmed.

Almeida v. *Trushin*, 368 So.2d 346 (Fla. 1979).

Distinguished From Sale

A bailment should be distinguished from a sale, a pledge or a pawn, and a lease or a license.

A bailment differs from a sale in three ways:

1. A sale is a transfer of title. A bailment is a transfer only of possession; it is still a bailment even though the goods are to be returned in a different form (e.g., wheat taken to a mill to be ground into flour and returned). However, if the person to whom the goods are given is to return only similar goods, the transaction may be a sale (e.g., a five-year lease of a farm and a herd of cows, with the provision that the lessee return cows of equal age and quality at the expiration of the lease).
2. A sale requires consideration. A bailment may be either for consideration or gratuitous.
3. A sale contemplates a permanent change of possession. A bailment is only a temporary change.

Sale
Contract by which title to property is transferred from the seller to the buyer.

Distinguished from Pledge or Pawn

A pledge or a pawn is a security device by which an owner of personal property gives possession of the property to secure a debt or to assure the performance of some obligation (e.g., debtor gives possession of a ring to a pawnshop owner to secure a loan). The debtor is the pledgor, and the pawnshop owner is the pledgee. A pledge arises when stocks, bonds, or negotiable paper is put up as security for a debtor, whereas a pawn exists when any other type of personal property is used as security for a loan. A pledge is similar to a bailment in that neither the pledgee nor the bailee has title to the property but has merely a special interest. However, there are two differences:

Pledge
A deposit of personal property as security for a debt.

1. In a pledge, the pledgee can assign the interest in the property to another person even without permission of the pledgor. In a bailment, the bailee cannot assign the property to anyone else.

2. In a pledge, the pledgee always has the right to sell the property if the debtor does not pay the debt. In a bailment, the bailee cannot sell the property to satisfy money due unless expressly permitted by statute. See Division 9 of the UCC, Appendix A, for the pledgee's rights in the event of default by the pledgor.

Distinguished from Lease or License

In a lease or license, the acceptor of the owner's goods has neither the right to possession nor the exclusive control of the goods. The lessor or licensor is merely making space or goods available for the lessee or licensee. (e.g. use of a locker or parking space.)

Bailee's Duty of Care

The amount of care owed towards the property by the bailee depends on the type of bailment, local statutes, and the contract of bailment. While the type of bailment may be important in determining the liability of the bailee for loss or damage to the bailed property, the modern trend is for courts to consider the overall question of negligence rather than to rely on these distinctions.

Sole Benefit of Bailor

In this type of bailment, the sole benefit of the bailment is for the bailor (e.g., bailor leaves her dog with a neighbor while bailor goes away on vacation). In this case, the bailee owes a duty of *slight* care towards the property.

Mutual Benefit

In this type of bailment, both the bailor and the bailee benefit from the bailment (e.g., bailor leaves her dog with bailee with the understanding that the bailee can use the dog to go hunting while the bailor is on vacation). In this case, the bailee owes a duty of *ordinary* care. Ordinary care means reasonable care under the circumstances.

Sole Benefit of Bailee

In this type of bailment, the sole benefit of the bailment is for the bailee (e.g., bailee borrows the bailor's dog to go hunting, but bailor is not going on a vacation and is receiving nothing for the use of her dog). In this type of bailment, the bailee owes a duty of *great* care.

Liability Limitations

Many local statutes contain exemptions from or limitations on liability in the case of certain bailees and in certain situations (e.g., California Civil Code Section 1840, which provides that where the bailee is informed of the value of the property by the bailor or has reason to assume the property's actual value, the liability cannot exceed such amount).

The act of bailment may be accompanied by an agreement that enlarges the liability of the bailee (e.g., "You are responsible for any damages to any of our cylinders while in your possession or care"). A lease of a furnished house provided that lessee would redeliver furniture in good condition and that lessee assumes all liability; the court held that lessee was an insurer and liable for a stolen rug.

Except where permitted by statute, contracts that attempt to exclude or limit liability are illegal if the bailee is quasi-public in character (e.g., common carrier, public parking lot, public warehouse, hotel). Even where local statutes permit limitation of liability, the amount must be reasonable or the limitation is ineffective. Private bailees can limit their liability if the clause does not defeat the real purpose of the contract. However, any such limitation must be brought to the attention of the bailor before the property is bailed. A limitation by a private bailee printed on a stub or ticket given to the bailor or posted on a sign or on the walls of the bailee's place of business ordinarily will not bind the bailor unless the bailee calls the bailor's attention to the writing and informs the bailor that it contains a limitation of liability (refer to Subchapter 6.3).

Bailee's Lien

By statute in most states, the bailee is given the right to a lien on the goods for payment for work or services rendered in connection with the bailed goods. The lien carries with it the right to sell the goods at public sale if the bailor does not pay for the work or services. In the absence of a statute to the contrary, the lien is lost if the bailee voluntarily returns the goods to the bailor. No lien arises on the goods when the work is done on credit.

Bailee's Lien
The right of a bailee to hold goods until paid for work or services.

Duty to Return Property

The bailee has a duty to return the bailed property to the bailor upon termination of the bailment, with a few exceptions:

1. Where the goods are taken by legal process while in the bailee's possession (e.g., attached by the sheriff for a debt due by bailor).
2. Where the person to whom the bailee delivers the property is better entitled to its possession than the bailor. In such a situation, if the bailee is in doubt as to which of two claimants is entitled to the goods, he is protected in most states by being permitted to interplead the parties

(surrendering the goods to a court and requiring the claimants to establish their rights in court) or by requiring the claimant who was not the bailor to indemnify the bailee against any liability to his bailor.
3. Where the goods are lost, stolen, or destroyed through no fault of the bailee.
4. Where the bailee has a lien on the goods. In such a situation, the bailee is entitled to keep possession of the goods until paid the amount of the lien.

Termination of Bailment

A bailment may be terminated by performance, acts of the parties, destruction of the bailed property, or operation of law.

Performance

Complete performance by both parties of the bailment contract terminates the bailment. This may occur by completion of the particular purpose of the bailment or, where the bailment was created for a particular time, by the expiration of the period of time.

Agreement of Parties

The bailment may be terminated by a subsequent agreement of the parties or, where it was created for an indefinite time, by the will of either party or, where it was created for the sole benefit of one party, by the will of either party.

Breach

If either party causes a material breach of the bailment, the other party may terminate (e.g., bailee sells the bailed property to a third person). If the bailor elects not to terminate the bailment, the bailee remains liable for any damages caused by his breach.

Destruction of Property

If the bailed property is destroyed by a third person or by an act of God or if it becomes unfit for use for the purpose of the bailment, the bailment is terminated.

Operation of Law

Death terminates a bailment at will. Insanity and bankruptcy terminate a bailment at will if it becomes impossible for the bailee to perform his duties. However, if the bailment is for a definite period, death or incapacity will not terminate the bailment, but rather the rights of the deceased party pass to the decedent's estate.

Questions

1. What is meant by a bailment?
2. How does a bailment differ from a sale, a pledge, and a license?
3. What are the three types of bailments? How does a court decide when a bailee is liable for damage to the bailed property?
4. What is meant by a bailee's lien?
5. Under what circumstances is a bailee excused from returning the bailor's property?

14.3 Special Bailments

Some classes of bailees regularly serve the public and are largely regulated by statutes. They include hotel keepers, common carriers, warehousepersons, parking lot operators, and safe deposit box lessors.

Liability of Hotel Keepers

Liability of hotel keepers is largely controlled by statute. The typical statute provides that if the proprietor provides a fireproof safe or some similar place for the keeping of valuable property and if the proprietor notifies the guests of such depositary, he is not liable for the loss of any property that the guest may fail to turn over to the proprietor for safekeeping. A guest who delivers valuables to the proprietor must inform the proprietor that the articles are of unusual value or there will not be any extraordinary liability.

Facts

Eliza and Sarah were guests at the Mayfair Regent, a Manhattan luxury hotel. Each was travelling with a jewelry collection allegedly worth $1,000,000. The hotel had posted notices that a safe was available in the manager's office for valuables. Both guests delivered their jewelry over to the management for deposit, signed receipts, and were given keys. The safe deposit boxes were broken into and the jewelry stolen. The hotel claimed it had done all that the law required and was liable only for the $500 statutory limit. The trial court agreed with the hotel; the women appealed.

Decision

The hotel safe deposit boxes were in a room made of sheetrock, and access to them was limited only by two hollow-core doors, one with an ordinary tumbler lock and the other with no lock at all. The guests claimed that the room was left unlocked and open to the public and the card file showing which guest used which box was exposed to public view. The court held that to avail itself of the liability limitation, the hotel must provide an adequate facility sufficient to protect against fire, theft, and other reasonably foreseeable risks.

Goncalves v. Regent International Hotels, Ltd., 58 N.Y.2d 206, 460 N.Y.S.2d 750, 447 N.E.2d 693 (1983).

In another New York case, the Court of Appeals said that an innkeeper who chooses not to make a safe available loses the statutory protection. When a resort hotel closed its vault from 11:00 p.m. to 8:00 a.m., it was responsible without limit for losses of guests returning too late to put their valuables in the safe (*Modell* v. *Kiamesha Concord, Inc.*, 48 N.Y.2d 107, 421 N.Y.S.2d 858, 397 N.E.2d 370 [1979]).

Negligence

When wearing apparel is left in the guest's room and is stolen, some statutes provide that the proprietor is liable only if he was negligent. Even when there is liability, most statutes limit that liability to a certain amount, which is usually small (for example, $100 for each trunk; $50 for each traveling bag and contents; $10 for each box, bundle, or package and contents; and $250 for all other personal property of any kind).

However, where actual negligence of the hotel owner or his employees is the cause of the loss of property of the guests, most states will not limit the recovery allowed.

Theft

The hotel keeper is liable for an employee's theft of a guest's property if the theft was within the scope of the employee's employment (e.g., clerk in charge of safe steals valuables deposited by guest). However, even where the theft is within the scope of the employment, the hotel keeper's liability may be limited to the sums specified in the statute.

Baggage Lien

The hotel keeper has a lien on the baggage of guests for the agreed charges and, if no express agreement was made, for the reasonable value of the accommodations that were furnished.

Liability of Common Carriers

Common Carrier
One in the business of transporting goods or persons for hire.

Common carriers are those who offer to the general public that they will carry goods and passengers from place to place for compensation. Common carriers involved in interstate commerce are regulated by the Interstate Commerce Commission, and those operating intrastate are regulated by state governmental authority such as, in many states, the Public Utilities Commission.

Exceptions to Absolute Liability

A common carrier is absolutely liable for any loss or damage to goods in its possession unless it can prove that the loss or damage was due solely to one of the following five exceptions:

1. Act of God. Unforeseen, unusual, violent, and superhuman events or catastrophes, such as an unprecedented wind or storm, earthquake, ex-

PERSONAL PROPERTY

treme temperature, severe flood, or stroke of lightning (a fire of human origin has been held not to be an act of God).

2. Act of public enemy. Nations, persons, or groups engaged in violent activities directed at an attempt to overthrow the government are the public enemy. Thieves, rioters, arsonists, and other criminals are not included in this definition unless they are attempting to overthrow the government.
3. Acts of state or public authority. Seizure of narcotics by the government and attachment of goods by the sheriff.
4. Acts of shippers. Improper packing; however, if this is apparent upon visual inspection and the carrier still accepts the goods, it has full liability for the goods.
5. Inherent nature of the goods. Carrier is not liable for perishable fruits and vegetables when shipper fails to obtain refrigerated or heated cars, nor is carrier liable for normal percentage of evaporation of oil or other liquids in transit.

If the carrier unnecessarily exposed the goods to damage by incorrect routing, it will be liable even though the damage was caused by one of the five exceptions stated.

Termination of Strict Liability

Three different rules are followed as to when the strict liability terminates. Some states hold that it ends when the goods are unloaded from the car into the freight house, at which time the duties of the warehouseperson begin. Some states hold that it ends after the consignee (person to whom the shipment has been made) has had a reasonable time to inspect and remove the goods. Some states hold that the consignee has the right to notice of the arrival of the shipment and that the strict liability of the carrier does not end until after notice and after the consignee has a reasonable time in which to remove the goods.

When the goods remain in possession of the carrier after strict liability terminates, the carrier's liability is reduced to that of a warehouseperson (ordinary care) until the goods are claimed.

Limited Liability

Under some laws, a carrier may be able to limit the amount of its liability as follows:

1. Under federal law. Carriers in interstate commerce are subject to federal law. Under the Carmack Amendment to the Interstate Commerce Act, the carrier may limit its liability to a stated amount by a provision in the bill of lading provided that the shipper is allowed to obtain a higher amount at an increased rate.
2. Under state laws. Most states provide by statute that a common carrier may, in intrastate commerce, limit its liability for injury to or loss of baggage or packages from ordinary negligence but not for such loss or injury caused by gross negligence. UCC § 7–309(2) provides that dam-

Limited Liability
Limitation placed on the amount of money that one can lose in a lawsuit.

ages may be limited "if the carrier's rates are dependent upon value and the consignor by the carrier's tariff is afforded an opportunity to declare a higher value."

Van Steinburg v. Pacific Southwest Airlines
102 Cal.App.3d 842, 160 Cal.Rptr. 612 (1980).

Kingsley, Associate Justice Plaintiffs appeal from a summary judgment in an action for loss of baggage checked on defendant airlines. We affirm the judgment.

Plaintiff Fink, an employee of plaintiff Van Steinburg, purchased a ticket on a flight of defendant airline from Oakland to Hollywood-Burbank airport. He checked, as regular baggage, sample cases belonging to his employer that contained expensive jewelry. On arrival, the sample cases were not delivered and Fink was told that, through some error, they had been flown to Los Angeles airport. On checking at the latter airport, one of the sample cases was missing and has never been found. Plaintiffs sued for the value of the jewelry, and for damages resulting from plaintiff's inability to use the contents of that case at a show in Dallas to which Fink had intended to go. The defense, raised on a motion for summary judgment, was that defendants' liability was limited, by an applicable tariff provision, to $500 for the missing case. The trial court accepted that defense and entered a judgment limiting recovery to $500.

It is admitted that plaintiff Fink was aware of the tariff provision and of the availability to him of additional protection if he disclosed the high value and paid an additional fee for that additional protection and that he deliberately did not disclose the high value or seek the additional protection. Plaintiffs here rely on *Muelder v. Western Greyhound Lines* (1970) 8 Cal.App.3d 319, 87 Cal.Rptr. 297. However, as the court in that case elaborately spelled out, not only was there gross negligence on the part of the carrier, but the shipper was a member of the general public, admittedly unaware of, and not told of, either the tariff limitation or the availability of additional protection. The opinion expressly distinguishes cases, such as this, where the owner was an experienced businessman, well aware of both the tariff and the availability of additional protection.

The judgment is affirmed.

Passenger Safety

Common carriers of passengers are not insurers of the safety of the passengers. However, because of the public nature of the business, they are held to the highest degree of care, skill, and diligence. Common carriers of passengers are subject to extensive state and federal regulation.

Facts

Several juveniles riding on an RTD bus started an argument with several other passengers, and the ensuing fight resulted in serious injuries. Before the argument had become physical, the bus driver had been warned of the problem but kept on driving and made no attempt to call police or stop the fight. The injured passengers sued RTD, contending that the bus company had a duty to protect its passengers from assaults by other passengers. RTD argued that such a duty would require placing armed guards on its buses which would create a disastrous financial burden. Case dismissed; passengers appealed.

Decision

A common carrier has a duty of "utmost care and diligence" for the carriage of its passengers. The duty of protection does not mean carriers are held to ensure the safety of their passengers under all circumstances. However, the driver in this instance took no measures at all to stop the fight. He could have ordered disorderly passengers to leave the bus or radioed police or headquarters for help. The passengers have a right to sue RTD for the injuries suffered.

Lopez v. Southern California RTD, 40 Cal.3d 780, 221 Cal.Rptr. 840, 710 P.2d 907 (1985).

Liability of Warehousepersons

A warehouseperson is a person engaged in the business of storing goods of others for compensation. In the absence of special statute, the warehouseperson owes a duty of *ordinary* care towards goods in his or her possession. Because of the public nature of their activities, warehousepersons are subject to extensive state and federal regulation.

Warehouseperson
One engaged in the storing of goods of others for compensation.

Duty Under UCC

UCC § 7–203 places a duty on the warehouseperson to deliver goods that conform to the description in the warehouse receipt or to answer in damages. The warehouseperson may avoid this liability, however, by an honest disclaimer on the receipt to the effect that he or she does not know whether the goods conform to the description. This can be done by writing *conspicuously* such words as "said to contain" or "contents unknown."

Personal Property Lessor

In a bailment of personal property for lease (e.g., automobile rental), the lessee is the bailee and the lessor is the bailor. The bailor must deliver the personal property in a condition fit for the purpose of letting, repair all deteriorations not caused by the bailee or the natural result of use, and secure quiet title in the bailee from any lawful claimant.

If the bailee is injured or his property damaged because of defective condition of the bailed property, the bailor may be liable as follows:

1. The bailor of dangerous personal property is liable to the bailee for injuries resulting from negligence (bailee may be barred by contributory negligence or assumption of the risk).

2. The bailor of personal property warrants that the property is fit for its particular use, and if it is not, the warranty is breached for failure to exercise reasonable care to ascertain that it was safe. For example, in hiring a horse for riding purposes, there is an implied warranty that the stable keeper used reasonable care to ascertain the habits of the horse. A stable keeper who should have discovered a horse's dangerous propensities and did not is liable (*Kersten* v. *Young*, 52 Cal.App.2d 1, 125 P.2d 501 [1942]). Modern cases have extended the bailor's liability of fitness for a particular use at the time of the bailment to a fitness during the entire period of the bailment and to third persons.

Bailee Liability

Where property is leased for a particular use and the bailee uses it for another purpose, the bailor may recover damages or terminate the hiring. Most courts hold the bailee absolutely liable for injury or loss occurring during such unauthorized use even though the bailee was not negligent.

Liability of Parking Lot Operators

Many bailment cases have dealt with damage or loss to vehicles while left in parking lots. The courts generally hold that when an owner locks his automobile and takes the keys, there is no bailment but merely the rental of a space in which to park. The theory is that the parking lot attendant, if there is one, is not given sufficient physical control over the car to make him a bailee. However, when the owner leaves the key in the automobile at the request of the parking lot attendant, a bailment is created, and the bailee owes a duty of ordinary care for the protection of the car. Many fact situations are not that simple, and the court then looks at all the circumstances in determining whether or not a bailment has been created.

Parking Management, Inc. v. Gilder
343 A.2d 51 (D.C.App. 1975).

Gallagher, Associate Judge . . . Appellee parked his car at the Parking Management, Inc. parking area which is enclosed within the Washington Hilton Hotel in this city. He was directed to a space by an attendant. He locked his car and kept the keys. He then opened the trunk in plain view of a group of employees and placed his lady friend's cosmetic bag in it and then locked the trunk. The rear of the car was exposed to the aisle. Upon his return, he found the trunk lid damaged from being pried open and reported it to the management.

The principal question for the court, initially at least, is the nature of the legal relationship of the parties. More particularly, it must be determined at the outset whether the parking lot operator owed the car owner any duties and, if so, what they were. In order to resolve this, it is necessary to examine the nature of the parking operation. It is not enough simply to ascertain whether the car owner locked his car and kept the keys ("park and lock"). These are material factors to be considered, but they do not end the inquiry.

. . . Appellant is correct in its assertion that this court has stated in those cases that a bailment did not exist where the car owner (a) parked his car and (b) kept the car keys. However, those cases simply involved those two factors and nothing more. Here there was additional evidence on the parking arrangement involved, e.g., the presence of 5 employees to service the customers in an enclosed area of the hotel and the acknowledgment that security of the cars is a major concern of PMI, which, according to the PMI supervisor, includes watching for thefts and tampering with the vehicles, as well as the acknowledged exertion of "control . . . in respect to housekeeping and any general operations that might pertain to the parking industry." Although, strictly speaking, the finding that a bailment existed may be open to debate, we believe the trial court reached the correct result in any event by way of its alternative finding that the protection the car owner was entitled to believe existed was not provided.

> The car owner was entitled under the circumstances to expect that reasonable care would be utilized to prevent tampering with his auto; and that this was not an unreasonable expectation on his part was demonstrated by testimony of the management of PMI to the effect that this was in fact among the duties of the employees. . . .
>
> While there has been a tendency to consider a showing of a "park and lock" arrangement as creating a lease agreement, we doubt the sophistication of this doctrine. Unlike the usual tenant of realty, the car owner has utterly no control of the so-called lease space as he is by definition always absent and helpless to protect his property, for all practical purposes. There is in most instances no fixed term, the duration of the parking being usually at the option of the car owner. Lastly, the car owner may not remove the car until the parking fee is paid. . . .
>
> On the facts here presented, we believe an operator may be required to exercise reasonable care to avoid malicious mischief to, or theft of, vehicles parked on a commercial parking lot (a going concern), even though the arrangement was "park and lock." The car owner was necessarily absent when the car damage occurred and should not be disadvantaged as a matter of law because of this reality. We do not feel that a car owner may fairly be regarded as a virtual stranger to the lot operator except for the payment of a parking fee.
>
> . . . Consequently, the judgment [for Gilder] is affirmed.

Checkrooms

A similar problem exists with checkrooms. The courts generally hold that when a patron hangs his coat on a hook in a restaurant, barbershop, or other place serving the public, no bailment is created. The reasoning is that there was no actual delivery of the item to the proprietor for safekeeping. However, if the establishment provides an attendant to receive the article, a bailment is created. Another question sometimes arises as to whether the proprietor is liable for something left in the pocket of a coat or for the contents of any checked item that is lost or stolen during the bailment. Courts generally hold that there is no liability, because the proprietor did not intend to assume possession of such things unless he was advised of such contents or reasonably should have known of their existence when he accepted custody of the item. The following case illustrates a typical checkroom bailment situation:

Checkroom
A room in which hat, coats and baggage may be left until called for.

Facts

Plaintiff and a companion went to the defendant's restaurant for dinner. Sometime after they were seated, they decided to check their coats and took the coats to the checkroom. The room was full, and Patty, the checkroom attendant, said that she was out of checks but that she knew the plaintiff and would accept the coats. When the plaintiff started to leave the restaurant, the checkroom was unattended. Patty later appeared but could not find the plaintiff's black Persian lamb coat. The trial court awarded $500 damages to the plaintiff, and the defendant appealed.

Decision

The court held that checkroom service was incident to the restaurant business and that Patty had the implied authority to accept the coat without giving a claim check. Since Patty had left the checkroom unattended, she failed to exercise the ordinary care required of a bailee under a mutual benefit bailment. Judgment was affirmed.

Johnson v. B. and N., Inc., 190 Pa. Super. 586, 155 A.2d 232 (1959).

Liability of Safe Deposit Box Lessors

Safe-Deposit Box
A strong metal container for storing valuables, usually in a bank vault.

A person who rents a safe deposit box will have one key for access to the box while the bank retains the other. Both keys are necessary to gain admittance to the box. The bank has control of the premises. Nearly all courts hold that the customer is the bailor and the bank is the bailee. Since this is a mutual benefit type of bailment, the bank must use ordinary care regarding the contents of the box.

Container Contents

Questions as to whether the bailment of a safe deposit box, coat, automobile, or other item is also a bailment of the item's contents are resolved by a determination of whether the contained articles are of a nature that are reasonably or normally found within the container. If they are, a bailment exists. However, a bailee of a container is not liable for the contents that are not visible when the container is bailed to him unless, from the nature of the container itself or from the surrounding circumstances, the bailee reasonably should have expected the presence of such contents. Of course, if the bailee is given express notice of the contents by the bailor and accepts them, there is a bailment. These rules are illustrated in the following case.

Facts
The plaintiff left his car in the defendant's parking lot. The keys, including the trunk key, were left in the car. The car was taken from the lot by persons unknown. The car was later recovered, but the plaintiff's golf clubs, valued at $373.53, which had been locked in the trunk, were missing and were not recovered. The plaintiff was not asked and did not voluntarily advise the defendant about the presence of the golf clubs when he left his car in the defendant's lot.

The plaintiff brings this civil action for the value of the golf clubs.

Decision
The court held that a parking lot bailee's duty depends upon notice, actual or constructive, of the presence of golf clubs or other items in a vehicle. Since no actual notice was given, constructive notice might be established by the property's being in plain view. But where, as in this case, the property was locked out of sight in the trunk, it would not be reasonable to assume that a driver would be carrying golf clubs in the trunk of the car. Judgment for defendant.

Allen v. Houserman, 250 A.2d 389 (Del. Super., 1969).

Constructive Bailments

Constructive Bailment
A bailment imposed by law requiring a person in possession of property to deliver it to another.

The law recognizes certain types of bailments wherein the bailee's obligation is imposed by law rather than by agreement of the parties, and the courts usually hold that such person is a gratuitous bailee (e.g., finder of lost or misplaced property; police officer taking possession of stolen goods; animal from one farm strays upon land of adjoining farm owner; property placed on property of another by mistake). A seller of goods who has not yet delivered the goods to the buyer is a bailee of the goods if the title has passed to the buyer. Similarly, the buyer who is in possession of goods but does not have title is a bailee of the goods.

In the finder, or voluntary, type of bailment, the finder must take possession of and care for the lost property. However, the finder will be entitled to recover for the value of his time and expense in caring for the property.

In the unwilling type of bailment, where property is thrust upon a stranger through some act beyond the control of either party, such as a tornado or other act of God, most courts hold that the bailee has only a moral duty to care for the property. A person who undertakes to do so becomes a bailee and is liable for negligence in caring for the personal property. Some states, by statute, impose a duty of care on the unwilling bailee regardless of the bailee's undertaking to care for the property.

The preceding are all constructive bailments made by law.

Shamrock Hilton Hotel v. Caranas
488 S.W.2d 151 (Tex.Civ.App. 1972).

Barron, Justice This is an appeal in an alleged bailment case from a judgment in favor of plaintiffs below.

Plaintiff's, husband and wife, were lodging as paying guests at the Shamrock Hilton Hotel in Houston on the evening of September 4, 1966, when they took their dinner in the hotel restaurant. After completing the meal, Mr. and Mrs. Caranas, plaintiffs, departed the dining area leaving her purse behind. The purse was found by the hotel bus boy who, pursuant to the instructions of the hotel, dutifully delivered the forgotten item to the restaurant cashier, a Mrs. Luster. The testimony indicates that some short time thereafter the cashier gave the purse to a man other than Mr. Caranas who came to claim it. There is no testimony on the question of whether identification was sought by the cashier. The purse allegedly contained $5.00 in cash, some credit cards, and ten pieces of jewelry said to be worth $13,062. The misplacement of the purse was realized the following morning, at which time plaintiffs notified the hotel authorities of the loss.

Plaintiffs filed suit alleging negligent delivery of the purse to an unknown person and seeking a recovery for the value of the purse and its contents.

. . . We find after a full review of the record that there is sufficient evidence . . . to support the jury findings on the special issues to the effect that the misdelivery was negligence and a proximate cause of the loss to appellees. Article 4592, Vernon's Tex.Rev.Civ.Stat.Ann. (1960), does not apply to limit the hotel's liability to $50.00 since its proviso declares that the loss must not occur through the negligence of the hotel, and such limiting statute is not applicable under the circumstances of this case.

Contrary to appellant's contention, we find that there was indeed a constructive bailment of the purse. The delivery and acceptance were evidenced in the acts of Mrs. Caranas' unintentionally leaving her purse behind in the hotel restaurant and the bus boy, a hotel employee, picking it up and taking it to the cashier who accepted the purse as a lost or misplaced item. . . .

Appellants urge that if a bailment is found it existed only as to "the purse and the usual petty cash or credit cards found therein" and not to the jewelry of which the hotel had no actual notice. . . .

> We believe appellants' contention raises the question of whether or not it was foreseeable that such jewelry might be found in a woman's purse in a restaurant of a hotel such as the Shamrock Hilton under these circumstances.
>
> ... It is known that people who are guests in hotels such as the Shamrock Hilton, a well-known Houston hotel, not infrequently bring such expensive jewelry with them, and it does not impress us as unreasonable under the circumstances that one person might have her jewelry in her purse either awaiting a present occasion to wear it or following reclaiming it from the hotel safe in anticipation of leaving the hotel.
>
> ... It follows that the findings of negligence and proximate cause of the loss of the purse apply to the jewelry as well, which is deemed to be a part of the bailment. ...
>
> ... The bus boy and cashier assumed possession and control of the purse per instructions of the hotel with respect to articles misplaced or lost by customers. The active cause which produced the loss was wholly independent of the negligence of Mrs. Caranas, and the hotel's primary duty of ordinary care to its paying guest was clear.
>
> The judgment of the trial court is affirmed.

QUESTIONS

1. What are the responsibilities and liabilities hotel keepers owe to their registered guests?
2. When are common carriers excused from absolute liability for goods in their custody?
3. What responsibility do buses and airlines as common carriers have to their passengers?
4. How do you know whether or not a bailment exists when you leave your car in a parking lot?
5. Under what circumstances does a bailment include the contents of the bailed container?

PROBLEMS

1. Homer Havens, owner of an apartment hotel, leased an apartment to Hal Turner. One night, Sheila Hart, Hal's mother-in-law, was invited to spend the night and to sleep in the folding bed in the living room. While Sheila was making up the bed, she found a diamond ring caught in the springs under the mattress. When the true owner could not be found following diligent search, Homer, Hal, and Sheila each claimed the ring. Who is entitled to its possession? Would it make any difference if Sheila had been a maid employed by Homer rather than Hal's mother-in-law?

2. Ruth purchased a female pedigreed miniature poodle dog from Pierre's Kennels. Unknown to either party, the dog was pregnant. When the litter was born, both Ruth and Pierre claimed the right of ownership. Who is correct?

3. Handler, shopping in a department store, takes his purchase to a cashier's checkstand and while waiting for a clerk to assist him notices a billfold on the counter. He examines it and finds that it contains $100 but no identification. The clerk arrives and demands that the billfold containing the money be turned over to the store. Does Handler have a better right to it than the store? Would it make any difference if Handler had found the billfold on the floor in an aisle?

4. Arnold and Jack were playing golf, and Jack complained that his putter was no good. Arnold then promised Jack that when they played next week Arnold would give him an old putter that Jack had always admired. Before they finished their game, the two men got into an argument over their scores, and Arnold told Jack that he could forget all about the putter. Jack claims that Arnold must either deliver the putter or pay damages. Decision?

5. Sears provided Seven Palms Motor Inn with drapes, which were installed on steel traverse rods attached

to the walls of the rooms above the windows, and with matching bedspreads made from the same material as the drapes. In asserting a mechanic's lien, Sears claims that these items were fixtures that had become a part of the real property and were therefore subject to the lien. What decision?

6. Plaintiff left her diamond ring with the defendant jeweler for cleaning. Before closing his store, the defendant placed the ring in the safe and locked the safe. During the night, a burglar opened the safe and stole the contents, including the plaintiff's ring. Plaintiff brings action for the value of the ring. Decision?

7. Ace Rudder, while flying his private plane, had an engine failure and made an emergency landing in Rudy Hayes's oat field. Ace returned to the wrecked plane to disassemble it for salvage, but Rudy refused to allow Ace to remove the plane until he paid for the damages to his field. Several days later, an insurance agent representing Ace came by and paid for the damages, whereupon Rudy allowed Ace and the agent to remove the plane. During the interval, no one had been watching the site, and many people had visited the oat field to view the spot. About $2,000 worth of equipment had been stolen from the plane. Ace sued Rudy for the damage caused by the thefts, claiming a bailment and negligence. Decision?

8. Plaintiff was a guest in the defendant's hotel. She left a valuable fur piece in her locked room when she went downstairs to dinner. On her return, she found the fur piece missing. The bedroom had a notice posted on the inside of the entrance door which she had not read that stated that the hotel provided a safe, free of charge, for the deposit of all valuable articles and that the hotel would not be liable for any valuable articles stolen from a room. Plaintiff brings action against the hotel for the value of her fur. Decision?

9. Plaintiff ships goods from New York to Chicago by defendant's railroad. During transit, the goods are destroyed by rioters. Plaintiff sues railroad as an insurer for the value of the goods. Defendant contends that it is not liable, since the damage was beyond its control. Decision?

10. Mrs. Chown saw a brood of turkeys along the highway that she believed to be hers and took them to the protection of her chicken yard. She then learned that the turkeys belonged to Ryan, her neighbor, and she put them back on the highway where they were all killed. Ryan sues Chown for the value of the turkeys. Decision?

CHAPTER FIFTEEN

Multiple Ownership and Real Property

15.1 Multiple Ownership of Property
Types of Ownership
   Tenants in Common
   Joint Tenancy
   Community Property
   Tenants by the Entirety
   Condominium Ownership
   Cooperative

15.2 Real Property
Real Property Defined
Estates
   Freehold Estates
   Dower and Curtesy
Easement
   Appurtenant
   Easement in Gross
   Prescriptive Easement
   Implied Easement
License
Operation of Law
   Rights to Space
   Riparian Rights
   Lateral Support
   Percolating Water
   Zoning
   Nuisances

15.3 Title Acquisition
Government Ownership
   Eminent Domain
   Police Power
   Zoning
   Escheat
   Homestead Laws
Transfer of Title
The Deed
   Deed Elements
   Quitclaim Deed
   Warranty or Grant Deed
   Delivery of Deed
   Recordation
   Title Insurance
Transfer through Operation of Law
Forced Sale
Adverse Possession
   License
Transfer of Property by Death
   Wills
   Intestate Succession
   Administration of Estate
Transfer by Action of Nature

15.1 Multiple Ownership of Property

Types of Ownership

The ownership of any property, personal or real, may be held by one individual, known as in severalty, or it may be held concurrently by two or more persons or entities. Joint owners are referred to as co-tenants, with each entitled to an undivided interest in the entire item and no one owner having a sole claim to any specific portion thereof. The two major types of concurrent ownership are tenancy in common and joint tenancy. Other forms of multiple ownership are community property, tenancy by the entirety, condominium, and cooperative.

Severalty
Ownership of property by one individual.

Tenants in Common

When title to property is transferred or deeded to two or more persons, in the absence of an express statement to the contrary, the majority rule is that such property is held in tenancy in common. The distinctive feature of such tenancy is that it is an estate of inheritance. Upon the death of any joint owner, such owner's interest in the property passes to the heirs or devisees. The ownership shares do not have to be co-equal but may be in any proportion, and profits and costs are shared in the same proportion as the ownership interest. The only common right that is shared equally is the right of possession. In the case of real property, a tenant in common may petition the court to divide the land in kind between the tenants. Such an action is called partition.

Tenants in Common
Ownership by two or more persons, each with a possessory interest that can be partitioned, sold, willed, or encumbered.

Joint Tenancy

Joint tenancy is created when exactly equal interests are transferred at the same time by one instrument that expressly states that the parties are to take possession as joint tenants.

The important characteristic of this tenancy is the right of survivorship. Upon the death of one of the joint tenants, such tenant's interest passes equally to the surviving joint tenants or tenant.

A transfer by one joint tenant of that tenant's interest to another party severs the joint tenancy as to the interest conveyed. If there are two joint tenants, such a conveyance ends the joint tenancy. If there are three or more, the joint tenancy continues between the remaining joint tenants as to their remaining interests. In either case, the transferee takes his share as a tenant in common with the other or others.

Joint tenancy property does not go through probate, since title is assumed to pass automatically to the survivors upon the death of a joint tenant. The property is, however, subject to the payment of appropriate estate and inheritance taxes.

Co-owners of real property may use the legal action of partition to terminate their joint ownership at any time, as illustrated by the following case.

Joint Tenants
Ownership by two or more persons where on the death of one, his or her interest passes to the survivor or survivors.

Partition
A judicial separation of the respective land interests of joint owners.

Facts

Plaintiff sued her brother seeking to partition 500 acres of farmland in Nebraska. The trial court held that the parties were owners as joint tenants with right of survivorship rather than as tenants in common and that the property should be partitioned equally between them. Defendant brother appeals.

Decision

Brother argued that a distinction should be made between a joint tenancy grant and their deed, which was joint tenancy with right of survivorship. The court held that the survivorship phrase made no difference. Once a joint title to real property has been established, partition is a legal right. When a joint tenant acts to end any of the required coexisting unities, as by partition or deed, the joint tenancy and the right of survivorship are ended. Affirmed.

Yunghans v. O'Toole, 199 Neb. 317, 258 N.W.2d 810 (1977).

Community Property

In some states, including all of those in the southwestern United States area acquired from Mexico, the system of community property is followed. This form of ownership refers to all property, real and personal, acquired by the earnings or efforts of the husband or the wife during the marriage, which each then owns co-equally with the other. In addition, each spouse may have separate property. This refers to that property already owned by either at the time of marriage or acquired by gift or inheritance during the marriage or to community property that has been converted by agreement. Commingling separate property with community property to the extent that it can no longer be traced may also change the separate property to community property. Originally, the husband was designated the manager of the community and its property. Recent sex discrimination court decisions have declared equal management rights to both spouses.

Community Property
All property, real and personal, acquired by the efforts and earnings of a husband and wife during marriage.

Tenants by the Entirety

Several states permit married persons to take title to real property as tenants by the entirety. Upon the death of either spouse, the entire property goes to the other. Neither spouse can transfer title or force a partition without the written consent of the other. In the event of a divorce, title is then held as tenants in common.

Tenants by the Entirety
Ownership of property by husband and wife together and neither can transfer an interest without consent of the other.

Facts

Elizabeth and Ed, husband and wife, owned property in Pennsylvania as tenants by the entireties. They made a separation agreement that provided that Elizabeth wouldn't receive support payments but would have the right to continue living in the family home with the children. She would make all payments of the mortgage, utilities, and taxes. If she should stop using the premises as her residence, the house was to be sold at a price agreeable to both and the net proceeds divided equally. Under state law, upon divorce, tenancy changed to tenants in common, and either party could force a sale of the property. However, Ed waived this right in the separation agreement. Following the divorce, Elizabeth lived in the house and paid off the mortgage. Ed sued to force a partition sale of the property. The trial court held that the waiver of the right to sell was contrary to the state's policy of encouraging free transferability of real estate and ordered the sale. Elizabeth appealed.

Decision

The appellate court acknowledged that the separation agreement imposed a limit on transferability but held that Ed's agreement to waive was limited to a "discernible and reasonable" period of time. Ed could sell the property and get half the proceeds when Elizabeth stopped living in the house or when she died. Decision overruled.

Kopp v. Kopp, 339 Pa.Super. 230, 488 A.2d 636 (1985).

Condominium Ownership

Condominium
A system of separate ownership of real property in individual units of multiunit projects.

Condominium ownership, particularly in urban and resort areas, has experienced rapid growth in recent years. In a condominium complex, each resident buys a unit in the building or group of buildings, and all residents own as tenants in common the common areas, such as hallways, parking lots, garages, storage areas, roads, and recreational facilities. Residents establish an association of which each one is a member, and the association is responsible for the operation of the building or buildings and common grounds. However, individual owners, not the association, are responsible for any loans they make for the purchase of their specific units. Residents usually pay a monthly fee to the association to cover the costs of operation. Most states now have statutes regulating the ownership of condominium units. Condo ownership can also lead to unexpected liabilities, as illustrated in the following case.

Facts

Dutcher owned a condominium apartment, which he leased to the Owenses. Dutcher's ownership included a 1.572 percent pro rata undivided ownership in the common elements of the condo complex. One day a fire began in a corridor light fixture and spread to Dutcher's apartment, causing a substantial loss to the Owenses. The Owenses sued Dutcher, among others, and were awarded $69,000 by the jury. Dutcher was ordered to pay $1,000+ as his pro rata share. The Owenses appealed, claiming that Dutcher should have been found jointly and severally liable for the entire $69,000 so that they could collect the entire amount from him and he could try to recover indemnity from all the other owners, including the association. The state court of appeals agreed, ruling that each condo owner was jointly and severally liable for any damage that arose from the common areas of the complex. Dutcher appealed to the supreme court of Texas.

Decision

Because of the uniqueness of the type of ownership involved in condominiums, the responsibility for the management of a condo's common areas should be connected to the actual control exercised by the person being sued. This limits the liability of the individual unit owner to that owner's pro rata share interest in the common areas.

Dutcher v. Owens, 647 S.W.2d 948 (1983).

California and a few other states have also concluded that a condominium complex and the condominium association are to be considered as separate legal entities from the individual unit owner. However, because of the potential liability for accidents and damages in the common area and the lack of legal precedent in many jurisdictions, condominium unit owners should have a lawyer check their legal documents and make sure that they have adequate insurance coverage. Condominium units are freely transferable and subject to any legal restriction that might be contained in the original agreement. Ownership generally has some advantages over ordinary rental in that an investment is obtained and the allowable expense deductions provide an income tax benefit.

Cooperative

Cooperative ownership is a form of joint ownership similar to condominium ownership, but the residents own shares in a corporation or association that owns the building. Share ownership entitles each resident to lease a unit in the building and to use the common areas. Normally, each resident makes a monthly payment as a prorated share of the loan or price of the building and the resident's share of the maintenance costs. Since most states hold that each tenant is jointly and severally liable for the loan, if one tenant misses a payment, the others must make it to prevent a foreclosure. The many problems caused by this rule of joint and several liability was an important factor in the evolvement of the condominium system.

Cooperative
A business entity that holds title to premises and grants rights to occupancy of specific units.

Questions

1. How many owners are involved when property is held in severalty?
2. What are the important differences between property held in tenancy in common and that held in joint tenancy?
3. What is meant by a partition action?
4. What is the difference between community property and tenancy by the entirety?
5. What is the difference between owning a unit in a condominium and owning one in a cooperative?

15.2 Real Property

Real Property Defined

Real property is land; those things intended to be affixed permanently thereto or embedded therein; and the various interests in its ownership, use, or possession.

Estates

Estates in real property are generally classified as either freehold or leasehold. Leasehold estates pertain to the law of landlord and tenant, discussed in the next chapter. Other interests in land may be easements or licenses.

Estate
Interest, right, or ownership in land.

In the previous subchapter, we discussed the modern trend of condominium ownership.

Freehold Estates

Freehold estates are usually classified as either fee simple estates or life estates.

Fee Simple Estate A fee simple estate is the greatest interest one can possess in land and gives the owner the absolute right of disposal or of transmitting by inheritance. It is possible, however, to grant a fee simple subject to a condition, such as "until a person remarries" or for "so long as used for church purposes" and then provide that upon the occurrence of the condition, the property reverts to the grantor or his heirs.

Life Estate The typical life estate is the grant or devise of real property to a grantee for life, creating an estate that will terminate upon the death of the grantee, called the life tenant. In such cases, upon the death of the life tenant, the property would revert to the grantor or his heirs, called a reversionary interest. However, the grantor may designate some other party to take the estate upon the death of the life tenant, in which event the one so named would be a remainderman and the estate received would be a remainder. Although a life tenant may transfer his interest, he may grant only what he has—an estate for the duration of his lifetime.

Fee Simple
A freehold estate in land with the right of absolute inheritance.

Life Estate
An estate whose duration is measured by the life of the person holding it or that of some other person.

Remainder
That part of an estate left upon the termination of a preceding estate.

Martin v. Heard
239 Ga. 816, 238 S.E.2d 899 (1977).

Per Curiam The plaintiffs appeal from a judgment rendered in favor of the defendants refusing to reform a warranty deed and refusing to issue an injunction.

On October 19, 1970, Mr. Coy Martin executed an option to Waymon Heard Farms, Inc., to convey 612 acres of land "reserving a life estate for himself and his wife on 12 acres which is to include the home site." . . . Heard Farms exercised the option. The warranty deed, however, does not describe the reservations in the same terms as the option. Following a description of the 612 acres, the deed provides: "Grantor reserves unto himself and his wife the right to reside in the residence located on the following described property for and during their natural life." A description of the 12 acres follows and then a forfeiture clause: "In the event that the grantor or his wife should discontinue the use of the house on the above described property for their personal residence, then and in that event all rights herein reserved will be forfeited to the grantee."

. . . In 1975 the Martins learned of the variances between the reservations in the option and the reservations in the deed. They filed suit to reform the deed to conform with the option and to enjoin Mr. Heard and the Heard corporation from interfering with the Martins' exercise of their rights. After a trial without a jury, the court held the deed valid as written, and interpreted the forfeiture clause to mean that if either Mr. or Mrs. Martin discontinued use of the property by death or otherwise, the remaining party would have to vacate the property within a reasonable time. . . . Finally the court ruled that the reservation of fishing privileges to the Martins terminated when their right to use the 12 acres ended. The Martins appeal.

. . . We conclude that the Martins each have a life estate subject to divestiture in the house and acreage. . . .

The appellant owned a large tract of land, conveying out of himself title to all except the interests reserved. He reserved unto himself and his wife "[T]he right to reside in the residence located on the following described property for and during their natural life." Then the deed described a definite 12.5 acres of land carved out of the larger 612 acre tract. The term of the reservation was for life, subject to forfeiture only if the grantor or his wife should discontinue the use of the house on the property for their personal residence. It is not reasonable to conclude that these parties who owned the land in fee, intended to reduce their rights thereon to rights comparable to those that may be granted to a tenant. Although the reservation is not as clear as the words contained in the original option to sell, they are clear enough to indicate that the granting parties were reserving to themselves, full use and enjoyment of the house for their lifetime.

. . . We also conclude that the condition upon which the life estates terminate occurs when the Martins *both* cease living on the property, whether by both vacating it or by the death or removal of the survivor of them. This conclusion follows in part from a reading of the testimony of the attorney who drew the deed, who stated that it was the parties' intent to incorporate into the deed in substance the same provisions as were contained in the option contract. The mere fact that the estate may terminate on some condition earlier than death does not destroy its character as a life estate. . . .

. . . The trial court erred. . . .

Dower and Curtesy

In some states, the common law rules of dower and curtesy create by operation of law what amounts to a life estate to a spouse of a one-third interest in all the real property owned by the couple during marriage. This rule does not apply in community property states, where each spouse has a half interest in all the property acquired by the work and efforts of either or both during marriage.

Dower and Curtesy
The right of a husband or wife to a life estate of a one-third interest in their real property upon the death of a spouse.

Easement

An easement is a limited right to make use of the land of another in a specific manner and is created either by deed, by acts of the parties, or by operation of law. Easements may be granted in writing by an express grant, reservation, or exception in the deed transferring title to the property, or they may be granted in a separate document. For example, the grantor may transfer title to a portion of his land and also expressly grant an easement for right of way over the rest of the land, or the grantor might reserve a right-of-way easement for himself over the land granted.

Easements can be created for many purposes, such as the laying of utility lines or the use of a common driveway.

Easement
A right of one to make beneficial use of the land of another.

Reservation
A clause in a conveyance which creates a lesser estate to be retained by the grantor.

Facts

Salvaty acquired property on which there was an easement of record in favor of Pacific Telephone for the construction and operation of a pole line for the stringing of telephone and power wires. In 1979, Falcon Cable TV made a license agreement with Pacific to place its equipment on Pacific's conduit system and poles. Falcon was required to obtain any permits and grants needed for the lawful exercise of the license. In 1980, the City of Alhambra awarded Falcon a franchise to provide cable television within the city limits and adopted an ordinance making it unlawful for a private property owner to interfere with Falcon's access to private property. When Falcon began using telephone lines on Salvaty's property, Salvaty sued for wrongful taking, trespass, and other torts. The court dismissed the case, and Salvaty appealed.

Decision

Under state law, public utilities have dedicated some of the surplus space on poles and other equipment to cable TV use. Although such television did not exist at the time the easement was created, it is part of the natural evolution of communications technology and therefore within the scope of the easement.

Salvaty v. Falcon Cable Television, 165 Cal.App.3d 798, 212 Cal.Rptr. 31 (1985).

Appurtenant

Appurtenant Easement
An easement that relates to adjoining land.

Easements that relate to adjoining land are usually called easements appurtenant. The land benefited is known as the dominant tenement, while the one giving up the right is designated as the servient tenement. Such easements usually are said to run with the land and are transferred with it in subsequent change of ownership.

Easement in Gross

Easement in Gross
Easement not tied to adjoining land, but one granted to an individual.

Easements not tied to adjoining land but granted to an individual, such as rights of way for utility companies, are called easements in gross, and their transferability varies according to the laws of the state in which they occur.

Prescriptive Easement

Prescriptive Easement
An easement acquired through the uninterrupted use of another's land for the prescribed statutory period of time.

An easement by prescription is similar to the acquisition of title by adverse possession and may be obtained by the actual use of the land for easement purposes openly and notoriously, in a manner adverse to the rightful owner's use, continuously and uninterruptedly for the period of time set forth in the state's statute of limitations. The continuous and uninterrupted use requirement can usually be stopped by the owner's placing an obstruction blocking the user's path.

Facts

Austin bought a parcel of land on which he built an apartment building. A driveway on one side of the property was finished in December 1968 and thereafter used continuously by tenants and tradespeople. In January 1978, Pierce bought an adjoining lot. His new survey showed that the Austin driveway encroached on his property. On May 6, 1978, Pierce drove stakes into the blacktop at his line. He connected the stakes with string and posted a sign denying use. Police advised Pierce to remove the stakes. He complied but notified Austin that he was claiming title to part of the driveway. When the case got to court, Austin said that he had a prescriptive easement by reason of adverse use for more than ten years (the time period in Missouri). A jury found for Pierce, and Austin appealed.

Decision

The ten-year period did not begin to run until the driveway was completed in December 1968, and it was interrupted by Pierce's staking it in May 1978. A true owner may reenter land to assert dominion over it as against an adverse user as long as entry is peaceable. Affirmed.

Pierce v. Austin, 651 S.W.2d 161 (Mo.App. 1983).

Implied Easement

An easement by implied grant or reservation may arise when an owner of adjacent properties establishes an apparent and permanent use, such as a common driveway, in the nature of an easement and then transfers one of the properties without mention of any easement.

Another implied easement may be created through reason of necessity. Where an owner grants part of his land to another and the portion granted is so situated that there is no access to it except across the grantor's remaining land, the law implies a grant of the right-of-way easement. However, it must be based on necessity rather than mere inconvenience. The following case illustrates an easement by implication.

Easement of Necessity
An easement necessary for the continued use of the land.

Facts

The trial court awarded the Millers and the Howells an easement for ingress and egress over the land of the Burrows, and the latter have appealed.

The opposing parties are coterminous landowners. Their common source of title is J. C. Clark. The Howells' land is located south of the Burrows'.

The Howells' right of ingress and egress was a road separating the lands of the Burrows and of Flurrie Shotts. Testimony was given to the effect that this road was the only one to the Howells' land and that it had been continuously used since 1948.

Decision

The court held that the two requirements for an easement of necessity had been established. First, the property came from a common source, J. C. Clark. Second, reasonable necessity existed, since this was the only practical avenue of ingress and egress. Although necessity does not of itself create a right of way, it is evidence of the grantor's intention to do so. The underlying principle is that anyone who conveys property also conveys whatever is necessary for the property's beneficial use, realizing that it is for the public good that land be occupied. Affirmed.

Burrow v. Miller, 340 So.2d 779 (Ala. 1976).

License

A license is the right to use the land of another based upon the permission granted by the owner. It creates no interest in property and in most cases is exercised only at the will of and subject to revocation by the owner at any time. However, when use or occupation of property is under license, no adverse or prescriptive rights will accumulate.

License
A license of real property is the right to use the land of another with the permission of the owner.

Operation of Law

Under operation of law, without regard to the intent of the parties, certain rights are attached to the ownership of land. Some of the more common refer to space, riparian, lateral support, disposition, and freedom from nuisance.

Rights to Space

Before the advent of modern air traffic, a landowner was deemed to own his land and the rights thereto from the center of the earth to the outermost limits of space. However, aviation law has changed the outer range to a height within which the owner has reasonable control. Air rights are now being sold for the construction of buildings in the space over other structures. Subterranean rights still belong with the land and include such oil and minerals as might lie thereunder. The boring or drilling under the property of another without his consent, regardless of the depth, constitutes an illegal trespass.

Facts

Daniel was seriously injured when an overhanging limb broke off a tree during a strong windstorm and struck him as he was working in the driveway of his parents' home. The branch came from a large maple tree that stood on adjacent property owned by Mary Olmstead. Many of the tree's branches overhung the neighbor's property. Daniel sued Mary for negligence and for trespass, claiming that Mary had allowed the tree limb to invade the airspace of his parents' property. A jury awarded Daniel $3,500 damages. Both parties appealed, Daniel because of the small amount awarded and Mary because of the verdict.

Decision

There was no proof that Mary had any reason to be aware of any alleged defective condition of the tree, so she was not guilty of negligence. The court also concluded that Mary (who didn't even plant the tree) had merely allowed an apparently healthy tree to grow naturally and cross over into Daniel's parents' airspace. This did not amount to an intentional act, which must be present to impose liability for trespass. Judgment for Mary.

Ivancic v. Olmstead, 66 N.Y.2d 349, 497 N.Y.2d 326, 488 N.E.2d 72 (1985).

Riparian Rights
Rights that result from ownership of land on the banks of waterways.

Lateral Support
An owner of property has the right to have his land, in its natural condition, supported and held in place by the adjoining land.

Riparian Rights

The rights of landowners to a natural watercourse within their property are referred to as riparian rights. An owner may not pollute, divert, or diminish the flow of such stream to the detriment of other downstream landowners. If the stream is not navigable, adjoining owners have title to the soil to the middle of the stream. If the waterway is navigable, the landowners have title to the low water mark, but the stream belongs to the federal government.

Lateral Support

Enjoyment and use of land depends upon the lateral support the land receives from adjacent land. No owner is allowed to excavate so near to the boundary as to cause his neighbor's land to cave in or the buildings to be damaged.

The California Supreme Court has imposed a duty on a landowner to use reasonable care to protect a neighboring lot from any condition on his own land, whether natural or artificial, that might damage the neighbor (*Sprecher* v. *Adamson Cos.*, 30 Cal.3d 358, 178 Cal.Rptr. 783, 636 P.2d 1121 [1981]).

Percolating Water

Percolating waters are those under the earth's surface. At common law, the owner of property had an absolute right over such water; however, this use is now regulated by statute. In most states, the reasonable use rule is followed (i.e., the landowner can take as much as is reasonably needed for the ordinary purposes of living on the land but not for commercial use).

Percolating Water
The water under the earth's surface.

Zoning

In theory, the owner of land has the right to freely use and dispose of the land as he wishes. However, this right is subject to government controls and restrictions, such as planning, zoning, and building construction standards laws. Furthermore, many private restrictive covenants may be placed in deeds or subdivision plans that further limit this right. They may include setting setback limits; prohibiting construction within a certain distance from the property lines; controlling the size, cost, and architectural design of any houses to be built; and prohibiting the sale of liquor thereon. Although restrictions are not popular in law, if it appears that they will operate to the general benefit of all concerned landowners, the courts will usually enforce them. However, racial, religious, and ethnic restrictive covenants have been declared unconstitutional.

Zoning
Legislative action to control or limit the use of private land.

Restrictive Covenants
Promises in an agreement that restrict the use of real property.

Facts

The McDonalds lived in a residential neighborhood in Emporia, Kansas, and the Janaceks lived next door. The Janaceks decided to build a garage on their lot and learned that under the city's building code, buildings had to be set back 30 feet from the road. Their deed contained a similar restriction. When Janacek and the builder examined the survey, they confused the property line with the curb line. As a result, the builder put the foundation 30 feet from the property line instead of the curb. Because of this mistake, the garage foundation was too close to the street. The Janaceks applied to the county zoning board and got a variance, but the board noted that it had no authority over the restrictive covenant in the deed. When the Janaceks resumed construction, the McDonalds sued. The court agreed that the covenant was violated and ordered removal of the "encroaching portion."

Decision

Zoning laws are intended to protect the public's safety and welfare. In contrast, the limitations on building imposed by a restrictive covenant stem from a private agreement and are incorporated in the owner's deed. Such restrictions will be enforced unless they are illegal, for example, racially discriminatory. Therefore, a variance from zoning laws does not take precedence over the limitations imposed by a valid restrictive covenant. The Janaceks must remove that portion of the garage that extends beyond the 30-foot boundary line.

McDonald v. *Emporia-Lyon County Joint Board,* 10 Kan.App.2d 235, 697 P.2d 69 (1985).

Since restrictive covenants are contrary to the general public policy in favor of full use and ready transferability of land, they are strictly construed by the courts, as illustrated in the following case.

North Cherokee Village Membership v. Murphy
71 Mich.App. 592, 248 N.W.2d 629 (1977).

Riley, Judge   We are asked to decide whether a restrictive covenant banning "house trailers and tents" can be interpreted to include within its prohibition the placement of a "double-wide" mobile home on appellants' lot.

Appellants' deed, like those of all other property owners in the North Cherokee Village subdivision, contains the following restrictive covenant:

> No house trailers or tents allowed on subdivision.

Aware of the restriction, appellants consulted their real estate agent and township officials to ask whether a "double-wide" mobile home would fall within the language of the covenant. In addition, they made somewhat half-hearted but unsuccessful attempts to seek the advice of the president of the homeowners association in their subdivision. The real estate agent advised them that as long as the structure complied with other deed restrictions, they could place the mobile home on their lot. They did so.

The mobile home, manufactured in two halves and carted separately to the premises, bore a certificate of title denominating it as a "trailer coach, double-wide." Pursuant to a Denton Township building permit the two sections were placed on a concrete block foundation and bolted together after removal of the two separate chassis. As conjoined the edifice has dimensions of 44 feet by 24 feet with three bedrooms, two baths, living room, dining room and kitchen, totaling 1,056 square feet of living space. Its purchase price was $12,000. It is equipped with connections to gas, electric, water and sewage lines. The roof is gabled with asphalt shingles. In all other respects, the structure complies with applicable deed restrictions, namely, clauses prohibiting structures with less than 900 square feet of usable floor space or those with flat roofs.

Two months after the mobile home had been placed on the lot, appellee brought suit seeking removal of the structure. The court below, holding that the wording of the restriction could reasonably be construed to embrace appellants' dwelling, issued an injunction commanding appellants to remove or raze the structure.

We begin with recognition of the general rule that covenants are construed strictly against those claiming the right of enforcement and all doubts are resolved in favor of the free use of property. In addition, it is well settled that a court of equity will not enlarge the scope of a covenant beyond the clear meaning of the language employed.

. . . Even assuming *arguendo* we were to infer an intent to ban transient structures by reading the phrase "house trailer and tent" in a light most favorable to plaintiff, we do not believe appellants' modular unit can accurately be described as any less permanent than other kinds of sectional, prebuilt dwellings currently on the market. Surely, factory-built housing would not violate the covenant; we discern, therefore, no significant reason why the appellants' summer home is any greater encroachment on the sparse language of the restriction.

. . . This cause is reversed and remanded to the trial court for rescission of the injunction.

Nuisances

Nuisances are such things as loud noises, polluted air, obnoxious odors, continual vibrations, and similar results from activities that unreasonably interfere with the enjoyment of property by adjacent landowners. If the condition affects the entire neighborhood or community, it is a public nuisance; if it affects only one or a few property owners, it is a private nuisance. Victims of such impositions have the right to seek a court order abating the nuisance and to recover damages suffered as a result of the condition. An example of the nuisance problem is set forth in the following case.

Facts

Del Webb built Sun City in Arizona on a site near a large stockfeeding operation. People hesitated to buy property near the feedlot because of the odor and the flies. Webb brought suit to abate the nuisance.

Decision

The court held that the difference between a private nuisance and a public nuisance was generally one of degree, the former affecting a few but the latter affecting the rights of many citizens as a part of the public. Since the entire community of the southern portion of Del Webb's Sun City was concerned, a public nuisance was created and the court ordered it to be abated. However, since Spur Industries feeding operation had been located there first, Del Webb was required to pay to Spur a reasonable amount for the cost of moving or shutting down.

Spur Industries, Inc. v. Del E. Webb Development Co., 108 Ariz. 178, 494 P.2d 700 (1972).

Questions

1. What is the difference between a fee simple estate and a life estate in land?
2. What is meant by an easement? Give some examples.
3. How does a license to use land differ from an easement?
4. How do zoning laws differ from restrictive covenants?
5. What are legal nuisances? If one bothers you, what can you do about it?

15.3 Title Acquisition

Ownership and title to real property may be acquired by original occupancy, voluntary transfer by the owner, involuntary transfer through operation of law, adverse possession, will, intestacy succession, or action of nature.

Government Ownership

A nation, through its power, is the ultimate owner of all the land within its boundaries. In many totalitarian countries, the state retains title to most of the real property. Most governments, however, permit private ownership of land with the right to transfer title freely in such manner as the owner chooses. In the United States, the government still owns much land, has the right under eminent domain to retake whatever it deems desirable for public use provided payment is made to the owner, and has the ability to take without payment what is considered necessary under its police power.

Eminent Domain

Eminent Domain
The right of the government to take private property for public use.

Under the power of eminent domain, the government may take private property for public use but is required to pay the owner the reasonable value thereof.

Police Power

Police Power
Limits imposed on private rights and property by the government under its inherent power to maintain health, safety, and public welfare.

However, if property is taken by public authority under its police power for the protection of the public health, safety, and welfare, no compensation is required.

Facts

Phillip Teresi, a produce grower in Santa Clara County, had his 1980 pepper crop damaged as a result of the state's Medfly Eradication Program. Ten acres were quarantined and fumigated with methyl bromide, which allegedly caused the peppers to rot. Teresi claims he is entitled to just compensation for private property taken or damaged by the state. The suit was dismissed, and Teresi appealed.

Decision

An exception to the right for just compensation exists when the damage is caused as a result of a valid exercise of police power to abate a nuisance in the face of an emergency. The urgency of governmental conduct is important enough to override the policy of compensation. Since the decision to quarantine and fumigate Teresi's crops was clearly one involving discretion, there would be no tort liability. The medfly eradication program was a valid exercise of police power.

Teresi v. State of California, 180 Cal.App.3d 239, 225 Cal.Rptr. 517 (1986).

Zoning

The government may also, through zoning and city-planning laws, restrict the use that an owner may make of his property if the interest of the state is more compelling than that of the owner and if the restrictions are reasonable.

Escheat

If an owner dies, leaving neither will nor heirs, the property returns to the state by escheat.

Homestead Laws

Homestead
Original federal homestead law grants of land from the government to private individuals.

All original title to land in the continental United States was acquired either by grant or patent from the federal government under homestead laws or from a nation that had previously held the land.

Transfer of Title

How can a person claim ownership of a real property? The fact that a person occupies a house does not necessarily mean that he is the owner. How can he say that the title of a certain property has been transferred to him?

Under early English common law, real property was transferred symbolically by the transferor, standing on the described land, delivering a twig or piece of soil therefrom to the transferee, and announcing the transfer. Later, a written instrument called *deed* was delivered to the transferee to signify the transfer of property.

Dedication
A private owner's gift or grant of land to a public agency.

The Deed

The most common way of transfer of title to real property today is by a deed of conveyance. The party who transfers his interest is called the grantor, and the recipient is called the grantee. In a sale of real property, the buyer usually is given a grant deed or a warranty deed. There are other types of deeds, such as the quitclaim deed, gift deed, i.e., when no monetary or other consideration is involved, commissioner's deed, sheriff's deed, trustee's deed, executor's deed, or tax deed.

Most prevalent are the grant deed or warranty deed and the quitclaim deed. A gift deed is used when both grantor and grantee are alive, whereas an executor's or administrator's deed is used for a testamentary gift. A commissioner's deed is executed by a court-appointed commissioner, for instance, in a proceeding involving a judicial foreclosure of a mortgaged property. A sheriff's deed is one delivered to the purchaser at some execution sale.

The deed is a document of title by which the grantor can claim ownership of a certain real property.

Grant Deed
A written instrument transferring an interest in land from the owner, the grantor, to another, the grantee.

Deed Elements

Most deeds contain the following elements:

1. Names of the grantor and grantee.
2. The consideration paid, if any.
3. Words of conveyance, such as "grant and convey," or a similar statement of intent.
4. Property description, which should be formal, describing the actual land, not the street address, and expressed either by lot and block number, metes (measures) and bounds (direction), or government survey.
    a. Most subdividers of real estate file plat maps with the clerk of the county in which the land is located, identifying the parcel by lot and block number.
    b. Metes and bounds describe land by beginning at a certain point and then, by direction and measured distance, circumscribing the parcel until the point of beginning is reached.
    c. Most of the United States has been surveyed by the government into a

grid system, wherein the north and south lines are called meridians and the east and west lines are called parallels or base lines. The grids are then broken down into townships of six square miles each which, in turn, are divided into 36 numbered sections of one square mile each, containing approximately 640 acres. Once the section is identified by number, regular parcels to be described by acreage may be expressed in halves or quarters, referring to the north, east, south, or west halves and the northeast, northwest, southeast, or southwest quarters.

5. Listing of any exceptions or reservations that might be excluded from the grant, such as mineral rights.
6. Quantity of the estate conveyed, usually with the words, "To have and to hold."
7. Covenants or promises of warranty. In many states, however, these are implied from the words of conveyance.
8. Executed and signed by the grantor or grantors. For a deed to be recorded, it must be acknowledged before a competent officer, usually a notary public, who guarantees that the signature is genuine.

Quitclaim Deed

Quitclaim Deed
A deed wherein the grantor grants to the grantee all of the rights, if any, that the grantor has in the deeded land.

Quitclaim is the simplest form of deed. It states that the grantor transfers to the grantee all of his rights, if any, in the property described. This instrument could then transfer the entire estate, any part thereof, or nothing. It might be used to relinquish property ownership in a marital dissolution.

Warranty or Grant Deed

Warranty Deed
A deed that guarantees that the grantor has good title to the land being deeded.

A warranty deed, or grant deed, is one by which the owner warrants or guarantees that he has a good and merchantable title to the described property being conveyed. A warranty deed may imply more specific covenants, such as the right to quiet enjoyment of the property and no existing encumbrances other than those stated in the deed. If any of these covenants are broken, the grantee has the right to recover damages from the grantor.

Delivery of Deed

Delivery
A voluntary transfer of title from one person to another.

Actual conveyance is not completed until the deed has been delivered. This may be done directly to the grantee, or it may be done in escrow to a third person for delivery to the grantee upon the completion of the escrow instructions by all of the parties.

Recordation

Recordation
Constructive notice of land transfers through the recording of deeds with proper local authorities.

Recordation, although not required to effect transfer, serves to give notice to the world of the conveyance, and if the same property has been deeded to more than one grantee, the first one to record has the good title. Recording is accomplished by depositing the deed with the proper authority for that purpose, usually the recorder or clerk of the county where the land is situated.

Title Insurance

In addition to obtaining recordation, a buyer may seek further protection by procuring a policy of title insurance in many states or, in others, by obtaining an abstract of title, usually prepared by a lawyer, which is a summarized report of the recorded transactions concerning the property.

Transfer Through Operation of Law

Title to land may be obtained by a buyer at a sale conducted by a sheriff or other proper official. This may be brought about by a judgment sale under a writ of execution obtained by a judgment creditor to secure money for payment of the amount owed. It may also result from a foreclosure action on an unpaid mortgage or trust deed.

Forced Sale

A worker or materials supplier who has contributed to making improvements on the property may force a sale under statutory mechanic's lien rights to recover payment for his goods or services. Nonpayment of property taxes or of special assessments against the realty may also lead to a forced sale of property. When buying realty at a forced sale, the purchaser should make careful inquiry as to all liens or other obligations against the property. This can be done by making a title search in those states using title insurance policies or obtaining an abstract in the other jurisdictions. The following case shows what might happen if such care is not taken.

Tax Sale
A sale of land for the nonpayment of taxes.

Facts

The Simons purchased real property at a Los Angeles County tax auction. The property had been deeded to the State of California because of the previous owner's failure to pay delinquent property taxes. The county tax collector did not provide written notice of the sale to the Secretary of the Treasury as required by law. The property thus was sold without disturbing a $200,000 income tax lien on it. The Simons bought the property for $32,000, part of which was applied to state and county property taxes, with the rest levied upon by the IRS, leaving a large balance still remaining as a lien against the property. The Simons filed a claim against the federal government to discharge the tax lien. The court dismissed the claim, and the Simons appealed.

Decision

It is true that had proper notice been given to the Secretary of the Treasury by the county tax collector, the federal tax lien would have been discharged, although the government would have retained the right to redeem the property. Without such notice, the Simons bought the property subject to the lien. The Simons were not innocent third parties. As potential purchasers, they were under a duty to ascertain the facts and legal requirements surrounding the sale. Because they were buying as volunteers and not trying to protect an existing interest, they had no rights against the government.

Simon v. United States, 756 F.2d 696 (9th Cir. 1985).

Adverse Possession

Title may also be acquired by adverse possession, which occurs when a person enters into actual possession of the land of another and remains there openly and notoriously for the period of time prescribed by the state's statute of limitations. This time period varies from state to state, ranging from five to thirty years. Such possession must be hostile to that of the true owner and must be continuous for the time period. Some states also require that the holding be under claim of title, while others require payment of taxes on the property during the occupation. Although it is not essential that the owner be actually aware that the land is being occupied, the possession must be of such a nature that a reasonably diligent owner would know of the adverse claim. Government-owned land is exempt from adverse possession.

Adverse Possession
A method of acquiring title to land by doing certain acts over an uninterrupted period of time as defined by state statute.

License

An individual who is on another's land with permission of the owner occupies by license, and the holding is not hostile or adverse.

License
Owner's revocable permission for use of his land by another.

Facts

Mesnick had his property surveyed before putting in a swimming pool. The survey showed that a grapestake fence built by his next-door neighbor was inside his property line and deprived him of the use of 319 square feet. Mesnick demanded that the neighbor, Caton, remove the fence, but Caton refused. Mesnick sued to force removal. Caton argued that he had acquired title by adverse possession, since the fence had been there since 1955. The court ruled for Mesnick and quieted title to the 319 square feet.

Decision

Adverse possession requires an adverse or hostile use of the land and payment of property taxes on it. Caton did not meet either of these requirements. Nor was there an easement by prescription, since the fence was dilapidated and had not been tended for many years. There was no evidence of any continuous adverse use of the property. Affirmed.

Mesnick v. Caton, 183 Cal.App.3d 1248, 228 Cal.Rptr. 779 (1986).

Transfer of Property by Death

Will

Any property, real or personal, may be transferred by the owner through a will, a written expression of a person's desires for the distribution of his property after death. In addition to disposing of property, the will may cover such items as the conduct of the funeral, a gift of the body or parts thereof for scientific or medical use, the choice of a guardian for any minor children, the establishment of testamentary trusts, and the appointment of an executor (male) or executrix (female) as the representative of the estate. (See Subchapter 32.1 for a detailed discussion of wills.)

Will
A written expression of a person providing for the disposal of property after his or her death.

MULTIPLE OWNERSHIP AND REAL PROPERTY

Terminology A person who dies leaving a will is said to have died testate. A male is called a testator; a female is referred to as testatrix. Real property granted by will is called a devise, and the recipient is a devisee. A gift of money is a legacy made to a legatee, and a gift of any other form of personal property is a bequest.

Form Any person of legal age and sound mind may make a will. It can be either a formal, witnessed will, drafted by a lawyer in accordance with the laws of the state of the testator's residence and witnessed by two witnesses in some states and three in others. In most states, holographic wills (written and signed in the handwriting of the testator or testatrix) are valid. Requirements vary from state to state, including the requirement that the will be dated, that there be no printed matter on the will, and that there be no signing witnesses.

Intestate Succession

Under the U.S. system of property ownership, when the owner dies, the property must pass to someone else. If the person dies intestate (without a will), the property passes to the heirs by descent under the laws of succession of the state of residence at the time of death. Priority of distribution is usually to the decedent's spouse and surviving descendants, followed, if necessary, by the most nearly blood related next of kin. (See Subchapter 32.2 for details of intestate succession.)

Administration of Estate

State probate laws provide for descent and for the administration of the estate. The person charged with this function is the personal representative, who may be the executor or executrix named in a will or, in the absence thereof, the administrator or administratrix, usually the nearest heir, appointed by the court for that purpose. The personal representative is charged with gathering the assets, paying the creditors' claims, filing and paying the tax returns, and assuring that the distribution of the remaining property is made in accordance with the will or by the laws of succession.

Transfer by Action of Nature

An action of nature through water flow or floods may add to property or take away property from an adjacent owner, either gradually or suddenly. Gradual deposits of land by water along the water's banks is known as accretion. Soil being washed up and deposited on the land is known as alluvium. Under such circumstances, the addition or deletion of property falls upon the owner abutting the water course. However, a severe storm or flood causing a river to change its course suddenly is called avulsion, and there is no change in the title to the land so shifted.

Testate
When the decedent leaves a will.

Devise
Real property granted by will.

Legacy
Gift of money made by will.

Holographic Will
A will that is written and signed in the personal handwriting of the maker, the testator.

Intestate
When a person dies without leaving a will.

Succession
The process by which property rights of a deceased person are transferred by will or through the state law of descent.

Administration
The process of settling the property affairs of a deceased person.

Alluvium
Deposits accumulated gradually along a stream bank.

Accretion
The adding on or adhering of something to real property.

Avulsion
An abrupt change in the course of a stream boundary resulting in loss of land by one owner and increase by the other.

QUESTIONS

1. What are the rights of the government under eminent domain and police power? What is the difference between the two?
2. What is the difference between a grant deed and a quitclaim deed?
3. How can a person acquire title to land by operation of law?
4. How can someone get title to a parcel of land by adverse possession?
5. What is the difference between accretion, alluvium, and avulsion?

PROBLEMS

1. Jonathan B. Good's will left all of his apartment building to his wife Bea for life and the remainder to his two daughters, Annie and Ima, as tenants in common. All beneficiaries are alive and adults. Annie wants to sell her interest now, but Bea and Ima contend that she cannot do so without their permission. Decide.
2. Roy, Gene, and Hoot owned a horse as tenants in common. Hoot kept the horse on his ranch, fed him, and used him for farm work. Gene visited the ranch one day and saw that the horse was hauling heavy loads of produce. Gene claimed that Hoot was working the horse too hard and ordered him to take it easier. Hoot told Gene that care of the horse was his responsibility and none of Gene's business. Is Hoot correct?
3. Houseman deeded his land to Koehler "for the term of Koehler's life." Two years later, Koehler deeded the land to Quentin "for the term of Quentin's life." A year later, Koehler died and Houseman claimed the land from Quentin under Houseman's reversion. Does Houseman have the title? Why?
4. In 1950, Grizzly Ben built a cabin on some remote forestland in California belonging to the U.S. government. Government agents discovered Ben at the site in 1979 and learned that he had been living there openly and continuously during the entire period. When the government attempted to evict him, Grizzly Ben claimed that he had title to the property by adverse possession. Is Grizzly Ben right?
5. Archer gave Gonzales permission to take a shortcut over Archer's land to reach Gonzales' orchard, thereby saving Gonzales a long trip around Archer's farm. Gonzales had been taking this shortcut regularly for ten years. Archer then sold his farm to Sharp, who fenced the farm in and told Gonzales that he could no longer use the shortcut. Gonzales claims that Sharp is required to permit him to use the shortcut, since Gonzales had been using it for ten years and the statute of limitations in the state for easement by prescription was only seven years. Is Gonzales legally entitled to continue to use the shortcut? Suppose he had been using it for ten years without Archer's consent, express or implied. Would it make a difference?
6. Pop Wise wanted to make a gift of his mountain lot to his daughter Vera. Vera had a grant deed to the lot drawn up and gave it to Pop, who later signed it before a notary public and put it in his desk drawer. Pop died before doing anything else. His will didn't mention the lot, but the residuary clause of the will left everything not otherwise disposed of to Pop's son Les. Both Vera and Les claim title to the lot. Who gets it?
7. Rod Reddy wasn't sure whether or not he owned Rancho Dunrovin, but Owen Fields wanted to buy it from him. Rod sold it to Owen and conveyed it by means of a quitclaim deed, which Owen had recorded. Later, Rod discovered that he actually had owned the full title to Rancho Dunrovin in fee simple. He sold the property to Hy Walls and gave Hy a general warranty grant deed to the property. Hy took the warranty grant deed and sued to evict Owen from the property on the theory that his general warranty grant deed gave him better title to Rancho Dunrovin than Owen's quitclaim deed. Is Hy entitled to the land?
8. Heavenly Acres, Inc., subdividers, put restrictive covenants in the grant deeds delivered to all purchasers of lots or houses in their development. Included among the restrictions placed in all of the deeds were the following: (1) No laundry may be hung outside for drying. (2) No animal pets may be kept inside or outside the premises. (3) No more than four people can be in any house at any one time. (4) Houses or lots cannot be sold to anyone except members of the Caucasian race. Are any of these restrictions enforceable? Are any unenforceable? Why?

9. Ray Kane came home from work one day and found that the city had installed parking meters in front of both his home and the other homes in the block. Ray disregarded the meter and did not put in the required money. When he got a traffic ticket, Ray argued to the court that by the deed to his house he owned the land to the middle of the street and that the city had no right to make him pay for parking on his own property. Is Ray correct?

10. The Fountain of Youth Drinking Water Company, serving thousands of customers throughout the county, drilled three artesian wells near Pine Mountain on some land the company owned. When Fountain of Youth started pumping, many property owners at Pine Mountain complained that the water level in their wells had dropped too low to provide for their domestic needs. The other property owners seek an injunction to stop Fountain of Youth from pumping. What result?

CHAPTER SIXTEEN

Landlord and Tenant

16.1 Leasehold Tenancies
Terminology
Types of Leasehold Tenancies
   Estate for Years
   Periodic Tenancy
   Tenancy at Will
   Tenancy at Sufferance
Termination of Lease
   Lease Terms
   Destruction or Loss of Premises
   Breach of Covenants

16.2 Covenants
Common Covenants
   Rent
   Security or Cleaning Deposit
   Use of Premises
   Assignment or Sublease
   Quiet Enjoyment
   Full Enjoyment

Exculpatory Clause
Retaliatory Eviction
Landlord's Remedy to Tenant's Breach
Tenant's Remedy to Landlord's Breach
   Constructive Eviction
Rent Control

16.3 Liabilities
Common Law Rule
Modern Liability Laws
   Landlord's Responsibility
Tort Liability
   Due Care Test
   Tenant Liability
   Lessor Liability
   Duty to Repair
   Building Code Violations
   Latent Defects
   Maintenance

16.1 Leasehold Tenancies

Terminology

Lease
A contract whereby the owner of real property (lessor) gives up possession of the property to another (lessee).

Rent
The consideration paid for a lease.

When an owner of real property (the lessor) gives up the right to possession of the property to another (the lessee), the agreement made for this purpose is called a lease and the consideration normally paid is called rent. When the lessee actually takes possession, he becomes the tenant and the lessor is the landlord. The lease contract may be express or implied and is required to be in writing only if a period of time is set that falls within the statute of frauds, usually that exceeding one year from the time it is made. (Refer to Subchapter 8.2, Statute of Frauds.)

Types of Leasehold Tenancies

Leasehold
The estate in real property of a lessee, created by a lease.

Tenancy
The right of the lessee (tenant) to occupy the premises of the lessor (landlord).

Leasehold tenancies, referred to as estates, are of four types:

1. Estate for years.
2. Periodic tenancy.
3. Tenancy at will.
4. Tenancy at sufferance.

Estate for Years

Estate for Years
A lease for a definite period of time.

An estate for years is one fixed for a definite period of time, with a stated date for beginning and ending. Since a lease is a contract, it may be ended at any time during its term by mutual agreement of the parties, by a condition stated in the lease, by operation of law such as bankruptcy, or by a merger if the lessee acquires fee simple title to the leased property.

Periodic Tenancy

Periodic Tenancy
A tenancy for a particular period, such as week, month, or year.

A periodic tenancy is often referred to as a tenancy from year to year or from month to month, depending on the period of time for which rental payment is made. Usually the period is from month to month, from one month to the next. It may be either written or oral and may be terminated at the end of any period by giving notice, usually of equal length of time as the period stated. In the absence of any notice to the contrary, it automatically renews for the next period.

Waldrop v. Siebert
286 Ala. 106, 237 So.2d 493 (1970).

McCall, Justice The appellees brought this action to recover possession of leased premises from the appellant. . . . The trial court rendered judgment for the plaintiff and the defendant has appealed therefrom. The basic question in the case being one of law, is "Does the lease between the parties give the appellant lessee the right to perpetually renew it."

On July 20, 1963, the appellees executed a written lease of the premises to the appellant for an original term of two years to run from July 20, 1963, to July 19, 1965. The rent was $720, payable in equal monthly installments of $30 on July 20, 1963, and on the 20th day of each month thereafter. The lease provides for an optional tenancy in the following language:

> Lessor grants to Lessee the option to renew at end of term for an additional term of Three (3) years, and year to year thereafter.

. . . The original term of this lease created a leasehold estate in the lessee for two years. The estate granted, being one limited to endure for a definite and ascertained period, fixed in advance, is what is known as a term for years. . . . By the provisions of the lease, the appellant is granted an option, at the end of the first term of two years, to renew or continue his tenancy "for an additional term of Three (3) years, and year to year thereafter." A tenancy from year to year is a periodic tenancy, measured by the year. This optional tenancy is part of the original demise.

While the language of the renewal clause may be susceptible of different meanings, we construe it to grant the appellant a single option, to renew ". . . for an additional term of Three (3) years, and year to year thereafter." The renewal creates a term of three years, which thence proceeds with a year to year tenancy, constituting one leasehold estate. The words of controversial import are "and year to year thereafter." We conclude that the conjunction joins this periodic tenancy from year to year to the tenancy for three years, not to the option to renew. After the appellant exercised the option, there was no second option or consecutive options conferred for subsequent renewals from year to year. The singular, "option," is employed. These words "and year to year thereafter" indicate to us the parties' intention, at the expiration of the three years, to continue the leasehold estate as transformed from a term of years to a year to year tenancy. The year to year tenancy continues in being for successive periods of a year until terminated by either party at his will at the end of any year by giving the previous legal notice.

. . . Therefore the additional term is at least for the three definite years plus one year, because such specifies for three years, and year to year thereafter. . . .

Having decided upon this the appellant had four additional years under the renewal option rather than three. Therefore, appellees' notice to quit the premises on July 19, 1968, was premature and inefficacious to terminate the lease, because the notice was given when appellant's leasehold estate was yet to run for another year, to wit, to July 19, 1969.

For this reason the case must be reversed and remanded.

Tenancy at Will

A tenancy at will is one that may be terminated by either party at any time. Since no period of time is stated, it is "at the will" of either party and may be either express or implied. Most states require that notice be given to terminate the tenancy relationship.

Tenancy at Will
A tenancy that may be terminated by either party at any time.

Tenancy at Sufferance

Tenancy at Sufferance
A tenancy that exists when a tenant continues to occupy premises after termination of the lease.

A tenancy at sufferance exists when a tenant continues to occupy the premises after the expiration of the lease. If the tenant continues to remain on the premises, it is at the sufferance of the landlord. However, most states require that notice to quit be given such tenants, and if they are permitted to stay, the leasehold implicitly becomes a periodic tenancy. An example of this type of tenancy is set forth in the following case.

Facts

The plaintiff brought an action for damages against the defendants alleging that she was the widow of W. R. Teston, who died May 30, 1973; that the defendants are her stepsons; that her deceased husband had deeded their home to the defendants reserving therein a life estate; that on the day after W. R. Teston's death the defendants threw her out of the house, took certain property, padlocked the house containing the plaintiff's clothing and other personal property, and told the plaintiff not to come back. The complaint set forth special damages sustained by the plaintiff and sought such damages plus $10,000 punitive damages for mistreatment of the plaintiff.

Decision

The court held that the plaintiff did not become an intruder after the death of her husband. Where a husband was a tenant at sufferance, after his death his wife and children succeeded to that same relation. If another has the right of possession, he may recover damages even from the owner. A tenant holding over wrongfully may not be ". . . forcibly dispossessed by the landlord without subjecting the latter to an action of trespass; he having an appropriate remedy for her summary dispossession." Judgment for plaintiff.

Teston v. Teston, 135 Ga.App. 321, 217 S.E.2d 498 (1975).

Termination of Lease

A lease may be terminated in accordance with the terms stated in the body of the agreement, by the destruction or loss of the premises, and by the breach of certain covenants (promises).

Lease Terms

An estate for years is terminated in accordance with the terms set forth in the lease. Periodic tenancies renew automatically unless notice is given by one party to the other, generally at least one period in advance. However, most states have statutes governing the maximum length of notice required, usually either thirty days or sixty days, regardless of the period involved. In a tenancy at will, no notice was required at common law for termination. Today, however, most states require legal notice, which makes the tenancy practically identical to a period-to-period type of tenancy. In a tenancy at sufferance, since the tenant has already held over beyond the terms of the lease, notice should not be required. Nevertheless, if the landlord has not commenced formal eviction, the tenancy converts to a periodic one and must be ended with proper notice and legal action.

Destruction or Loss of Premises

At common law, destruction of the premises did not terminate the lease, because the land was still available. Today, however, destruction of all or a material part of the premises terminates the lease under the doctrine of commercial frustration. Where changes in zoning laws have required the business to cease or to remove to another location, the same rule applies. Most leases have covenants providing for this contingency.

Condemnation When land is taken by the government for public use under the right of eminent domain in a condemnation proceeding, the tenant usually has no claim against the landlord. To avoid legal entanglements and the difficulty of apportioning damages, each lease should have a clause either stating that the lessee receives nothing or setting a distribution ratio agreeable to all parties.

> **Condemnation**
> A proceeding by which the government takes real property for public use under the eminent domain power.

Mortgage If the premises were mortgaged at the time the lease was made, the mortgage has priority, and a foreclosure would end the tenancy. However, if the lease was already in effect when the mortgage was executed, the mortgage is subject to the tenancy, and a foreclosure would not affect the lease. (See subchapter 29-1 for detailed discussion.)

> **Mortgage**
> A transfer of interest in real property as security for a loan, usually for the purchase price.

Breach of Covenants

Covenants are the clauses or promises in a lease agreement that set forth the rights and obligations of the parties. If a party breaks an important covenant, termination of the lease may result. Covenants can be drafted in such a way as to provide for termination of the lease in the event of violation. Some of the more common provisions are discussed in the next subchapter.

Unlawful Detainer When a tenant holds over after proper legal notice to quit the premises or breaches an important covenant, the landlord has the right to dispossess the tenant by eviction. The legal action is known as unlawful detainer. The eviction is accomplished lawfully by giving proper statutory notice and serving the necessary papers on the tenants; proceeding to a court hearing, usually summary in nature; obtaining a judgment; and, if necessary, accomplishing actual ejectment through the appropriate law enforcement agency.

> **Unlawful Detainer**
> When a tenant remains after a lease has ended or been terminated.

Questions

1. Are oral leases binding upon the parties?
2. What is the difference between an estate for years and a periodic tenancy?
3. When a lease expires but the tenant remains on the premises, what are the legal consequences?
4. How may a lease be terminated?
5. How can you lawfully evict a tenant?

16.2 Covenants

Common Covenants

Covenant clauses (promises) in leases may be drafted to cover almost any contingency that is not unlawful or against public policy. Some of the more common covenants found in the typical lease are for rent, security or cleaning deposits, use of the premises, duty to make repairs, assignment and subleasing, fixtures, option to renew or purchase, and quiet enjoyment.

Rent

Rent is the compensation paid or furnished the landlord in return for the use and possession of the leased premises. Most agreements now provide that rent be paid in advance, many requiring that the last month or two be advanced as a hedge against the possibility of the tenant's unlawfully detaining the property. If no figure is stated as rent, a reasonable amount is due, payable at the end of the lease period.

The usual lease is a gross lease, which calls for rental at a fixed rate per month. Some businesses operate with a net lease, under which the tenant pays the taxes, assessments, and all operating expenses in connection with the premises, turning the balance net figure over to the landlord. Many modern store leases are percentage leases, a type in which the rental is based on either a flat fee plus a percentage of gross or a percentage of the net income received from the tenant's business conducted on the premises. The latter type may contain a recapture clause permitting the landlord to take back the premises if the tenant's business does not reach a certain gross or net.

Security or Cleaning Deposit

Security Deposit
A money deposit paid in advance to a landlord to cover possible damage or breakage during the tenancy.

A security deposit or cleaning deposit is a sum required to be paid in advance to cover possible damage, breakage, or cost of cleaning when the tenant moves. When the term expires and the tenant leaves, if no rent is due, nothing has been damaged or broken beyond fair wear and tear, and the premises have been properly cleaned, the landlord must return the deposit. In many states, an improper refusal by the landlord to refund the deposit may result in punitive damages. A few courts have held that the landlord must also pay the state's legal rate of interest on the deposit for the time it was held.

Use of Premises

Waste
Tenant's damage that diminishes property value.

For most practical purposes, the tenant becomes the owner of the premises during the period of the lease and may use the property in any legal manner unless there is a covenant in the lease to the contrary. An exception is that the tenant is not permitted to damage or injure the landlord's interest, and any diminishment of the property's value because of damage caused by the tenant is known as waste, for which the tenant is liable. The owner may include a covenant stating that the use of the premises will be limited to "no other use" or "only for," such as "clothing store and no other use" or "use only for a clothing store," and provide for forfeiture in the event of breach.

The following case involving use of the property where the lease had a covenant restricting occupancy to "tenant and members of immediate family" presents an interesting solution by the court.

Facts
Landlord claims that tenant has violated a substantial obligation of his tenancy by sharing his apartment with a young lady "without the benefit of clergy" (or even the blessings of a civil court judge). However, she was the tenant's fiancee.

Decision
The tenant breached a substantial obligation of the tenancy by permitting undertenant (a person other than a member of his immediate family) to occupy the apartment. The breach is material and sufficient to warrant termination of the tenancy. If, however, undertenant becomes a member of tenant's immediate family (as appears imminent) or removes from the apartment within sixty days, issuance of the warrant will be stayed.

Fraydun Enterprises v. *Ettinger*, 91 Misc.2d 119, 397 N.Y.S.2d 301 (1977).

Discrimination In another New York case with similar facts, the tenant claimed that the clause was discriminatory because it was based on marital status; however, the court said that the tenant wasn't able to prove discrimination (*Hudson View Properties* v. *Weiss*, 109 Misc.2d 589, 442 N.Y.S.2d 367 [1981]). Some state laws, such as the California Housing Act, prohibit discrimination based on marital status, including that against unmarried couples.

Assignment or Sublease

In the absence of a provision to the contrary, a tenant may assign the lease or sublet the premises to another. A sublease is something less than all of the tenant's leasehold rights. To prevent the obtaining of undesirable tenants, the landlord usually insists on a covenant by which the tenant agrees not to sublet or assign without the written consent of the landlord.

To avoid arbitrary action, the tenant may request an addition that the landlord will not unreasonably withhold such consent. The modern rule followed in many courts is that the landlord's covenant is unenforceable where the withholding of consent is deemed unreasonable. However, this is still the minority rule, followed in Alabama, Alaska, Arkansas, California, Florida, Idaho, New Mexico, and Ohio. Hawaii and New York apply the rule to residential property only. Because of this changing trend, tenants should have a covenant put in the lease that the landlord's consent shall not be unreasonably withheld.

Sublease
The transfer by a tenant to another of some, but not all, of the tenancy rights.

Homa-Goff Interiors, Inc. v. Cowden
350 So.2d 1035 (Ala. 1977).

Jones, Justice This summary judgment case involves a counterclaim filed by the appellants, Homa-Goff Interiors, Inc., against Geraldine Cowden, the appellee, claiming interference with a contractual relationship and unlawful refusal, by Mrs. Cowden, to grant consent to a sublease agreement between Homa-Goff and certain named prospective subtenants.

In February of 1974, a lease was entered into by Mrs. Cowden and Homa-Goff, John Goff, Pal Shoemaker, Henry Goff, and Thomas Gallion for a ten-year period. . . . The lease contained a clause which restricted the lessees' power to sublet subject to the landlord's written consent.

In October, Homa-Goff opened a furniture store on the leased premises. After several months in business, however, it became apparent to the appellants that, because of financial problems, they could not continue their operation. Therefore, they began seeking a subtenant. After some negotiation with the State of Alabama, the appellants, according to their counterclaim, reached a tentative agreement with the State to sublease the premises at a rental rate in excess of the rate paid by the lessees. Mrs. Cowden, exercising her option provided in the lease, refused to approve the State as a sublessee.

. . . [T]he trial Judge ruled: "[t]he landlord's withholding of consent can be arbitrary and unreasonable." From the order based on these rulings, Homa-Goff appeals. We reverse.

The threshold question is whether Mrs. Cowden, pursuant to ¶ 15(a) of the lease, may arbitrarily and capriciously reject a subtenant proposed by the lessee. . . .

. . . The general rule throughout the country has been that, when a lease contains an approval clause, the landlord may arbitrarily and capriciously reject proposed subtenants. This rule, however, has been under steady attack in several states in the past twenty years; and this for the reason that, in recent times, the necessity of reasonable alienation of commercial building space has become paramount in our ever-increasing urban society.

. . . Guided by this rationale, we hold that, even where the lease provides an approval clause, a landlord may not unreasonably and capriciously withhold his consent to a sublease agreement. The landlord's rejection should be judged under a test applying a reasonable commercial standard. This question, of course, becomes a question of fact to be determined by the jury. Therefore, we hold that the trial Judge erred in granting a summary judgment in favor of Mrs. Cowden regarding appellant's claim alleging Mrs. Cowden was arbitrary and capricious in rejecting the prospective subtenants. It is a jury question whether Mrs. Cowden acted reasonably, and there is sufficient conflict of material fact to mandate a reversal.

. . . **Almon, Justice** (dissenting): I would adhere to the view adopted by a majority of jurisdictions in this country. Citizens should have the right to contract.

Waiver If the landlord accepts rent from an assignee or sublessee, such acceptance is considered to be a waiver of the restriction against assigning or subletting and amounts to a ratification by the landlord.

Quiet Enjoyment

Quiet Enjoyment
The right of unimpaired use and enjoyment of the leased property.

Most leases, either expressly or by implication, carry a covenant for quiet enjoyment. This means that the tenant will not lose possession by any act of the landlord through failure of the landlord's title or by the enforcement of any lien superior to the landlord's title. It also implies that the landlord will not personally disturb the possession of the tenant. Any breach of this covenant constitutes an eviction of the tenant, and the tenant has a right to recover damages and the option of terminating the lease. The following case is an example of failure to provide quiet enjoyment of the premises.

Facts

Tenant's dog had disturbed neighbors who complained to the apartment house manager. Management asked tenant to move out. When she refused to move, management cut off her electricity. The weather was cold, so she took her children to her parent's home for the night, leaving the dog on the patio at the apartment. The manager let the dog inside the apartment, where the dog caused extensive damage to the tenant's property. Tenant sued landlord for damages; the trial court awarded tenant $1,745 actual damages and $1,200 punitive damages. Landlord appeals.

Decision

The court found this to be a violation of tenant's quiet enjoyment right. Since a wrong had been committed as well as breach of contract, the award of both actual and punitive damages was affirmed.

Clark v. Sumner, 559 S.W.2d 914 (Tex.Civ.App., 1977).

Full Enjoyment

In addition to quiet enjoyment, a tenant is entitled to full enjoyment of the premises—the right to use the premises lawfully as he sees fit.

Exculpatory Clause

It has been customary for many landlords to include a clause in their leases that provide a waiver of their responsibility for condition of the property, including common areas. However, such waiver is now held void as against public policy in practically all states, either by statute or court decision. (Refer to Subchapter 6.3 on public policy.)

Retaliatory Eviction

A modern rule followed in many states prohibits retaliatory eviction. For example, when a tenant reports illegal or substandard conditions to the proper authorities and the landlord is required to make the necessary corrections, an eviction of the tenant for revenge is held to be against public policy and will not be enforced.

Eviction
The expulsion of the tenant from all or some of the leased premises.

Retaliatory Eviction
Eviction as retaliation against the tenant for reporting illegal or substandard conditions.

Landlord's Remedy to Tenant's Breach

When a tenant defaults in the performance of any major covenant of the lease, particularly the one requiring payment of rent, the landlord has the option of terminating the tenancy. If the landlord elects to evict, a notice of default must be served on the tenant demanding either that the breach be corrected or that the tenant quit. If the tenant fails to do either, the landlord may then proceed with legal action to terminate the tenancy and recover possession. The following case is an example of a tenant's breach.

Facts

Landlord seeks to evict tenant, claiming a violation of a lease covenant prohibiting tenant from defacing the premises or making any alteration, addition, or improvement without the prior written consent of the landlord. Tenant had installed a permanent air-conditioning unit.

Decision

The court noted that the landlord and the tenant were unfriendly but observed that lack of a "mutual admiration" society was no reason for terminating a lease. However, the judge found that the lease had been violated by the installation of a permanent air conditioner that had defaced the premises. He noted that cases permitting the placement of a window air conditioner were different, since no alterations were required. The tenant was ordered to remove the air conditioner and to restore the property to its original condition within sixty days or the court would order the lease terminated.

Kaminoff v. *Spiegel*, 93 Misc.2d 458, 402 N.Y.S.2d 777 (1978).

In a similar case, the American Can Company, as tenant of a one-story commercial building, added a dividing wall and additional truck docks without the landlord's consent. In this case, however, an Illinois court found that the purpose of the additions was to make the premises more useful to the occupants and that the building could be restored to substantially the same condition as when leased. Since the changes did not affect a substantial part of the premises or the appearance or fundamental purpose of the building, they were not considered structural alterations (*Justine Realty Co.* v. *American Can Co.*, 119 Ill.App.3d 582, 75 Ill.Dec. 50, 456 N.E.2d 871 [1983]).

Tenant's Remedy to Landlord's Breach

The failure of the landlord to perform covenants in the lease does not alone entitle the tenant to terminate, and the tenant's remedy is generally only for damages for breach of covenant. There are exceptions to this rule when the landlord breaches the covenant for quiet enjoyment or causes a constructive eviction.

Constructive Eviction

Constructive Eviction
Some act or omission by the landlord that makes the premises uninhabitable.

The landlord's failure to perform a covenant that materially impairs the tenant's ability to enjoy the premises will be treated by analogy as a breach of quiet enjoyment and as a constructive eviction of the tenant. A constructive eviction may also exist if the premises have been made uninhabitable because of some act or omission of the landlord.

Rent Control

Because of an acute housing shortage in some areas of the country, many local communities have passed ordinances that, among other things, control the amount of rents that landlords can charge and limit any annual increases;

LANDLORD AND TENANT

allow evictions only for limited reasons; and specify what improvement costs, if any, may be passed on to the tenants.

Questions

1. If you were a homeowner and wanted to rent your house for two years while you took an overseas job, what covenants would you insist on including in the lease?
2. Suppose that you were required to give a $200 cleaning deposit on a one-year lease of an apartment. You leave the property clean and in good condition. You can hire your regular cleaning crew to make it spotless for $50, but the landlord insists that he always uses his own crew after a tenant moves out and that it charges $200. He says he'll use the deposit for that purpose. What are your rights?
3. When a lease has a provision prohibiting any assignment or sublease without express written consent of the lessor, how arbitrary can the lessor be in refusing to approve an assignment?
4. What is meant by covenants of quiet and full enjoyment?
5. What is a retaliatory eviction?

16.3 Liabilities

Common Law Rule

At common law, the old rule of *caveat emptor* (let the buyer beware) applied. The landlord was held to have no responsibility concerning the condition of the premises, since the lease transferred his interest to the tenant for the period of the leasehold. The tenant's only obligation was not to damage the property or commit waste (to destroy, damage, or injure property beyond normal wear and tear).

Caveat Emptor
Let the buyer beware, a common law rule that buyers and renters contracted at their own risk.

Modern Liability Laws

Today's building, housing, and zoning laws require that someone be responsible for the condition of the premises, and statutes may place the liability on either the landlord or the tenant. Covenants, unless prohibited by state or local law, may also fix this obligation. The tenant's liability exists only to that part of the premises leased to the tenant.

Landlord's Responsibility

Common Areas The landlord is responsible for the common areas, as such areas are deemed to have remained with the landowner. Common areas are those parts where no individual tenant is entitled to exclude any other from use or enjoyment, including entryways, common stairs, halls, parking

Common Area
Portions of the premises used in common by all tenants.

lots, and other facilities shared by all of the tenants. Exterior walls, heating, air conditioning, and plumbing systems have also been placed in this category.

Shackett v. Schwartz
77 Mich.App. 518, 258 N.W.2d 543 (1977).

O'Brien, Judge Jack H. Kaufman was a tenant in an office building owned by Charles E. Schwartz. Kaufman is a doctor. One of Kaufman's patients slipped, fell and injured herself in the parking lot behind the office in question. She brought action against both, alleging joint and several liability.

The lease requires the lessee to maintain his own premises, and the lessor the roof and outer walls. At trial, Kaufman stated that he did not maintain the parking lot. Schwartz testified he made no arrangements for parking lot maintenance.

The jury returned a verdict for the plaintiff against both defendants for $25,000.
. . . A general statement of the landlord's duties is stated as follows:

. . . The lessor, absent agreement to the contrary, surrenders possession and holds only a reversionary interest. Under such circumstances, he is under no obligation to look after or keep in repair premises over which he has no control.

An exception to the general lack of obligation is that a landlord has a duty to keep in safe condition any portion of a building under his control. The duty extends to a tenant's invitees, such as plaintiff.

. . . However, the landlord has retained his responsibility for the common areas of the building which are not leased to his tenants. The common areas such as the halls, lobby, stairs, elevators, etc., are leased to no individual tenant and remain the responsibility of the landlord. It is his responsibility to insure that these areas are kept in good repair and reasonably safe for the use of his tenants and invitees.

The lease here demised only a portion of the premises to Kaufman. The other portion of the building was vacant at the time of the accident. The lease states that the vacant area at the rear of the building is to be used in common with other tenants. This portion would appear to be the parking lot.

While it is true that Kaufman was the only tenant, the provisions of the lease stated the amount of control of the premises surrendered under the lease. The fact that Kaufman was the only tenant should not change the result.

It would seem clear that under the general rule the landlord is responsible for common areas. The fact that there were no other tenants using the common area should be of no consequence.

. . . The lease taken as a whole shows that Kaufman had exclusive control of *only* the rooms enumerated in the lease.

Here, the lease is silent as to any allocation of risk. Since the lease did not transfer any right of control over the parking lot to the tenant, Kaufman, risk should remain with Schwartz, the landlord.

Reversed [as to Kaufman].

Habitability
The condition of residential or other premises being reasonably fit for occupation.

Habitability Most states now have habitability statutes requiring the landlord of residential premises to keep the premises in a habitable condition. Such laws usually permit the tenant, after giving notice, to make required repairs and deduct up to one month's rent to cover the cost. If the landlord covenants to make repairs and refuses to do so, the tenant would be entitled to make them and recover the entire cost from the landlord as damages for breach of contract.

Green v. Superior Court of City and County of San Francisco
10 Cal.3d 616, 111 Cal.Rptr. 704, 517 P.2d 1168 (1974).

Tobriner, Justice Under traditional common law doctrine, long followed in California, a landlord was under no duty to maintain leased dwellings in habitable condition during the term of the lease. In the past several years, however, the highest courts of a rapidly growing number of states and the District of Columbia have reexamined the bases of the old common law rule and have uniformly determined that it no longer corresponds to the realities of the modern urban landlord-tenant relationship. Accordingly, each of these jurisdictions has discarded the old common law rule and has adopted an implied warranty of habitability for residential leases. . . .

On September 27, 1972, the landlord Jack Sumski commenced an unlawful detainer action in the San Francisco Small Claims Court seeking possession of the leased premises and $300 in back rent. The tenant admitted non-payment of rent but defended the action on the ground that the landlord had failed to maintain the leased premises in a habitable condition.

. . . Some of the more serious defects described by the tenants included (1) the collapse and non-repair of the bathroom ceiling, (2) the continued presence of rats, mice, and cockroaches on the premises, (3) the lack of any heat in four of the apartment's rooms, (4) plumbing blockages, (5) exposed and faulty wiring, and (6) an illegally installed and dangerous stove.

. . . At common law, the real estate lease developed in the field of real property law, not contract law. . . . The typical city dweller who frequently leases an apartment several stories above the actual plot of land on which an apartment building rests, cannot realistically be viewed as acquiring an interest in land; rather, he has contracted for a place to live. . . .

First, the increasing complexity of modern apartment buildings not only renders them much more difficult and expensive to repair than the living quarters of earlier days, but also makes adequate inspection of the premises by a prospective tenant a virtual impossibility; complex heating, electrical and plumbing systems are hidden from view, and the landlord, who has had experience with the building, is certainly in a much better position to discover and to cure dilapidations in the premises.

Second, unlike the multi-skilled lessee of old, today's city dweller generally has a single, specialized skill unrelated to maintenance work. Furthermore, whereas an agrarian lessee frequently remained on a single plot of land for his entire life, today's urban tenant is more mobile than ever; a tenant's limited tenure in a specific apartment will frequently not justify efforts at extensive repairs. Finally, the expense of needed repairs will often be outside the reach of many tenants for "[l]ow and middle income tenants, even if they were interested in making repairs, would be unable to obtain any financing for major repairs since they have no long-term interest in the property."

. . . We have concluded that a warranty of habitability is implied by law in residential leases in this state and that the breach of such a warranty may be

> raised as a defense in an unlawful detainer action. Under the implied warranty which we recognize, a residential landlord covenants that premises he leases for living quarters will be maintained in a habitable state for the duration of the lease.
>
> . . . In most cases substantial compliance with those applicable building and housing code standards which materially affect health and safety will suffice to meet the landlord's obligations under the common law implied warranty of habitability we now recognize.
>
> [Judgment vacated and remanded for trial.]

Tort Liability

Tort liability of landowners and occupiers of premises refers to the responsibility for damages or injury suffered by an individual because of substandard conditions on the property resulting from a negligent act or omission by the party having the duty of care for the premises.

Due Care Test

The older rules of law set different standards of reasonable care, depending upon whether the injured person was a licensee, invitee, or trespasser. The modern view followed in most states establishes the test of due care as the reasonable application of all facts and circumstances, with the status of the injured party as only one of the considerations. Therefore, an injured party is now usually referred to as a "visitor," irrespective of the various status categories.

Tenant Liability

The tenant, as the possessor and occupier of leased premises, has the primary liability to other persons who are injured because of unreasonable conditions of the premises.

Lessor Liability

Although there was no common law of responsibility for the landlord over leased premises, the modern rule treats the lessor as a seller to the tenant, and new rules have been applied that are similar to those found in product liability (see Chapter 19). As a result, landlords have been found liable in many situations.

Duty to Repair

When the lease has a covenant charging the landlord with the duty to repair, the landlord has been held liable for failure to maintain the premises in a proper condition. Under such circumstances, both the landlord and the tenant may be liable to the injured visitor.

Building Code Violations

Violations of building codes that lead to injury of a visitor have been held to be the landlord's responsibility. Since such codes involve safety statutes, it is reasoned that visitors are a class intended to be protected and may sue as beneficiaries. At the same time, the tenant may also be liable for negligence in failing to care for the premises.

Latent Defects

Latent, or hidden, defects are also the landlord's problem if they were known to the landlord and not disclosed to the tenant. This rule is based on the fraud theory of the duty to disclose such information. Some recent court decisions have expanded this logic to require warning against dangerous social conditions, such as the high incidence of burglary and rape in a building or its vicinity.

Latent Defect
A defect not discoverable even by the use of ordinary and reasonable care.

Holley v. Mt. Zion Terrace Apartments, Inc.
382 So.2d 98 (Fla. App. 1980).

Schwartz, Judge On May 31, 1976, the plaintiff-appellant's decedent, Shirley Bryant, was raped and murdered while a tenant in the defendant-appellee's apartment complex. The crime was committed by an intruder, thought to have been a co-tenant, who apparently gained access into Ms. Bryant's second story apartment through a window which fronted onto a common outside walkway. The basis of the plaintiff's wrongful death action against the landlord was its allegedly negligent failure to provide reasonable security measures in the building's common areas. The trial judge entered summary judgment for the defendant and the plaintiff has taken this appeal. We reverse.

The Mt. Zion Terrace Apartments consists of twelve separate two-story buildings with over 130 apartments in all. It is located in the heavily populated Opa-Locka-Carol City area of Dade County. For a long period prior to the tragedy involved in this case, the complex had been plagued by the high incidence of serious crime which is unfortunately all too characteristic of our urban society. In the calendar year immediately before the murder, it had been the scene of no less than twenty "class one" crimes, those involving violence, which were reported to the police. Of these, there were six cases of violent assaults and seven in which apartments in the project were burglarized. The record shows that the landlord had itself recognized the dangerous nature of its premises in at least two ways. First, it would accept no cash at its office in the complex and took only checks or money orders in rental payments. Second, and far more importantly, Mt. Zion had in the past taken significant steps, which had been abandoned by the time that Ms. Bryant was killed, to safeguard the security of its apartments. Between 1972 and 1974 (Ms. Bryant moved in during 1973), it hired uniformed armed guards to patrol and protect the complex. During these years, the landlord had charged each tenant an additional five dollars a month for this service. Although the Federal Housing Administration put a stop to the practice, there is an unresolved indication in the record that the charge was thereafter added to and included in the rent. Notwithstanding the guard service was terminated. In

> 1974, Mt. Zion spent $4,924 for security; in 1975, $1,113; in 1976, the year of the murder, nothing.
>
> On these facts, we hold that the defendant failed to carry its required burden to demonstrate conclusively that it was not liable for Ms. Bryant's death.... Without repeating the extensive legal analyses they contain, we approve and follow those cases in other jurisdictions which have recognized such potential liability in similar circumstances. [California, District of Columbia, Georgia, Hawaii, Illinois, Michigan, New Jersey, New York, and Wisconsin.] Furthermore, two particular features of this case make the plaintiff's position even more convincing than in most, if not all, of the prior precedents:
>
> 1. Mt. Zion's prior practice of providing armed guards constitutes an admissible indication of the defendant's own "knowledge of the risk and the precautions necessary to meet it." W. Prosser, Law of Torts, § 33 at 168 (4th ed. 1971); and
>
> 2. The showing that part of Ms. Bryant's rent may have been expressly for security creates a genuine issue concerning the landlord's contractual responsibility to provide that protection.
>
> For these reasons, the judgment under review is reversed and the cause remanded for further consistent proceedings.

Maintenance

Maintenance
The upkeep and preservation of property.

Most states now hold that the landlord must use due care in maintaining the premises, and the fact that the landlord is not in actual possession is merely one of the factors to be considered in determining the question of fault in a negligence action.

QUESTIONS

1. What was the landlord's responsibility concerning leased property under common law rules?
2. Who is liable for damages resulting from accidents that occur on common areas in leased shopping malls?
3. What is meant by a habitable condition of the premises?
4. When might both landlord and tenant be liable for injuries caused by defective premises?
5. When may a landlord be liable to victims of crimes committed on his premises?

PROBLEMS

1. Larry Lease made an oral agreement with Tommy Tate under which Tommy would take possession of Larry's beach house for five years at a monthly rental of $300. After Tommy had moved in and lived there for six months, Tony Trapp offered Larry $400 a month rent for the house; Larry gave Tommy a thirty-day notice to quit. Tommy says Larry cannot break their valid lease. Who wins?

2. Lucy Lesser rented a furnished apartment to Tim Teller for the period of one year under a written lease. There was no covenant in the lease concerning liability for the furniture during the period of the tenancy. Tim liked to give wild parties, and the furniture suffered during his occupancy. When Tim moved out at the end of the lease, Lucy sued him for the loss in value of the furniture during Tim's tenancy. Is Tim liable?

3. Theus Temple leased one of the twenty apartments in the Hamilton House for two years. After he had lived there for six months, the building caught fire and burned to the ground. Theus stopped making rent payments, and the landlord sued him for the rents due under the balance of the lease. Is Theus liable for these payments?

4. Ted Tinsley rented a suite of rooms in a luxury apartment building, redecorated the rooms, stocked the place with antiques, and advertised that he was opening an interior decorating business. City inspectors contacted Ted and advised him that the building was in an area zoned for residential purposes only and the business could not be conducted on the premises. Ted advises the landlord that he considers the lease broken, since he had rented the suite for business purposes. Is Ted correct? Would it make any difference if the suite had been zoned for commercial purposes at the time Ted made the lease and had been rezoned as residential only after he had taken possession?

5. Thelma Thorne leased an apartment for one year beginning on April 1 at a rental of $300 per month. When the lease expired the following April, Thelma did not move but paid the landlord another $300 for the next month, which amount was accepted. In June, the landlord gave Thelma a thirty-day notice to vacate. Thelma refuses to move, saying that she has a binding lease until the next April 1. Does Thelma have to give up the apartment before the following March 31?

6. Les Lockett leased an apartment to Tessie Todd. There was no provision in the lease giving Les the right to enter and make inspections. Tessie suspected that Les was entering the premises and making inspections during her absence, so Tessie had the locks changed. When Les discovered this fact, he sought to evict Tessie on the grounds that he is entitled to make reasonable inspections but that she has prevented it by locking him out. Does Les have the right he claims?

7. Leroy Little, a carpenter and handyman, built his own home. Later, he leased the house to Tyrone Tripp, who moved in with his family. One afternoon, Tyrone's small daughter got up on a chair to remove a toy from a marble mantel above the brick fireplace in the living room. The mantel was not attached in any way to the wall or fireplace and fell away to the floor, falling on the child and causing her serious injuries. Tyrone claims that Leroy is liable, but Leroy says that he is not responsible for the condition of the leased premises. Who is correct?

8. Travis Thatcher had a lease for two years of a house from Liza Lott. When the lease still had four months to run, Liza entered the house with a passkey and noticed that some of Travis' furnishings had been removed. Liza then changed the locks on the house. A week later, Travis returned, broke one of the locks and removed the remainder of his belongings. He then wrote to Liza and said that he no longer would be responsible for the lease. Liza then sued Travis for the unpaid rent for the balance of the term of the lease. What result?

9. Lilly Lodge covenanted to keep her tenant's premises in good repair. Terry Taylor, the tenant, noticed that the hot water faucet handle in the bathroom shower was loose and asked Lilly to have it fixed. Lilly did nothing about the condition. A few weeks later, while a guest of Terry's was taking a shower, the handle and faucet broke and the guest was scalded. The guest sued both Lily and Terry for damages for his injuries. Who is liable?

10. Tillie Tyson leased a house from Louise Lowe on a month-to-month tenancy. Louise orally agreed to make reasonable repairs within a reasonable time. Tillie notified Louise by mail, demanding repair of leaky pipes, kitchen ceiling, and back porch, stating that rent would be withheld if the repairs were not made within thirty days. Two weeks later, Tillie obtained an inspection by the city building and safety officer, who cited Louise for eight violations of the city housing and maintenance code. Louise, at the end of the month, served Tillie with a proper thirty-day notice to quit. Tillie withheld the rent for the ensuing month and deposited it with the court. At the end of the thirty days, Louise brought an unlawful detainer action to evict Tillie. What result?

PART FIVE

Law of Sales

CHAPTER SEVENTEEN
Sales (I)

CHAPTER EIGHTEEN
Sales (II)

CHAPTER NINETEEN
Product Liability

CHAPTER TWENTY
Consumer Protection

Law of Sales

Marketing is perhaps the most important aspect of business. After all, the object of business is making profit and this is achieved through sale. Hence, however well the product is manufactured, it doesn't mean too much for the company, if it doesn't sell.

From the business point of view, the success of selling is a matter of having a good product for a competitive price. As simple as this may sound, there are legally many sales related issues and problems which the business person should know if he or she is to succeed in the enterprise. In fact, ignorance of the legal aspects of sales may be catastrophic, since it may lead to the loss of assets and profits, or may even result in the company's bankruptcy. Caution is of paramount importance particularly in the area of product liability and consumer law, where the rules demand a higher standard of conduct on the part of the business person or "merchant" who under UCC §2-104(1) "hold himself out as having knowledge and skill."

The subject matter of sales is regulated in Article 2 of the Uniform Commercial Code. The Article applies to transactions of "goods" meaning things "which are movable at the time of identification to the contract for sale other than the money in which the price is to be paid, investment securities and things in action" (§2-105[1]). Thus, the sale of real property, stocks, bonds, trademarks, patents, copyrights, and other intangibles, is outside the scope of this Article.

CHAPTER SEVENTEEN

Sales (I)

17.1 Concept of Sales
Sale
   Definition
   Present Sale, Contract to Sell
   Bailment, Gift
   Option
   Bulk Sale
   Auction
   Conditional Sale
Fungible Goods
Merchant
Contracts for Labor or Services

17.2 Title and Risk of Loss (1)
Title Transfer
Risk Transfer
Parties' Own Rules
Role of UCC
Identification
   When Identification Occurs
   Identification and Buyer's Rights
   Identification and Seller's Rights
Sale by Nonowner
Resale by Fraudulent Buyer

17.3 Title and Risk of Loss (2)
With Movement of Goods
   Shipment Contracts
   Destination Contracts
   C.O.D.
   Sale on Approval
   Sale or Return
   Consignment
   Auction
   Automobiles
Without Movement of Goods
   With Document of Title
   Without Document of Title

17.1 Concept of Sales

Sale

Definition

Sale
Passing of title from seller to buyer for a price.

A *sale* consists of the passing of title from the seller to the buyer for a price (UCC § 2–106[1]). The basic principles of the law of contracts apply. Thus, if a seller promises to sell and the buyer promises to buy, a binding agreement exists, provided that all the legal requirements for a valid contract are met.

Present Sale, Contract to Sell

Contract to Sell
Concerns the sale of future goods, i.e., goods presently not existing.

Sales contracts include both *present sales*—i.e., if the sold goods are "existing and identified" (UCC § 2–106[2])—and *contracts to sell*—i.e., the goods are "future goods," such as future crops, fish to be caught, or goods to be manufactured. A contract to sell is a contract, but title to the goods naturally cannot pass from the seller to the buyer before the goods are existing and identifiable.

Facts

A fishing schooner owner sold halibut that was to be caught on the next trip. The buyer, Low, paid the full price of the fish at the time the contract was made. The voyage was successful, but the boat owner became bankrupt before the vessel returned. Low claimed to be the owner of the fish and tried to obtain possession. Pew, the bankrupt's representative, contended that no title could pass to property not owned by the seller at the time the contract was made.

Decision

Judgment for Pew. "In the case at bar, the sellers, at the time of the sale, had no interest in the thing sold. There was a possibility that they might catch halibut; but it was a mere possibility and expectancy, coupled with no interest. We are of opinion that they had no actual or potential possession of, or interest in, the fish; and that the sale to the plaintiff was void."

Low v. Pew, 108 Mass. 347 (1871).

Bailment, Gift

Bailment
Transfer of possession of personal property.

Gift
A voluntary transfer of property to another made without consideration.

A sale differs from a bailment in that a *bailment* is the transfer of possession of personal property, not the transfer of title. Moreover, in a bailment, consideration is not always required.

A sale differs from a gift since a *gift* is a gratuitous transfer of the title to property with no consideration. A promise to make a gift is not a valid contract. Execution of a gift takes place by the delivery of the property, whereas delivery of the goods is not always necessary in a sale.

Option

Option
Gives optionee the right to accept or reject the offer.

An option *to buy* is not a sale of goods and there is no transfer of title to physical merchandise. It is a right or a privilege for which the owner of the option has paid and that gives the owner the right to buy a certain property from a seller at any time within an agreed period and at a fixed price. An option *to sell*, on the other hand, gives the owner the right to sell.

Bulk Sale

A *bulk sale* is a transfer in bulk, not in the ordinary course of business, of a substantial part of materials, supplies, merchandise, inventory, or equipment of the business (UCC § 6–102).

Bulk Sale
A transfer in bulk, not in the ordinary course of seller's business.

To protect the creditors of the merchant from the possibility that the merchant may sell all of the inventory and disappear with the money, the UCC, Article 6, sets up two requirements. First, a bulk transfer is ineffective against a creditor unless the buyer requires the seller to furnish a list of existing creditors, signed and sworn to by the seller (§ 6–104). Second, the buyer must send a notice containing the pertinent information to all the creditors listed at least ten days before either taking possession of the goods or paying for them, whichever is done first (§ 6–105).

More than a third of the states have adopted an additional requirement in their bulk sales statutes that requires the buyer to hold off payment to the seller for thirty days after the sale. During this period, omitted creditors may find out about the sale and can put in their claims against the money still held by the buyer. For those states that have not adopted this additional requirement, it is advisable to place such provision in the contract of sale.

A sales contract that does not comply with Article 6 may still be valid between the buyer and the seller. Article 6 is only for the protection of the creditors of the seller.

The following case illustrates a typical bulk sale dispute:

Facts

Johnson entered into a two-year employment contract with Mid States Screw and Bolt Company in 1974. In 1975, Johnson was terminated for reasons other than cause and brought suit under the employment contract to recover his compensation. After the suit was filed, Vincent Brass and Aluminum Company contracted to buy the assets of Mid States. As part of the sale, Mid States agreed to remain liable to Johnson. In addition, it did not include Johnson in the list of creditors it furnished to Vincent Brass (UCC § 6–104). Therefore, Johnson did not receive formal notice of the transfer of Mid States's assets. The trial court awarded Johnson his compensation against Mid States. Johnson subsequently filed a garnishment action against Vincent Brass.

Decision

The court concluded that Johnson can collect from Vincent Brass. The UCC requires that the transferor, Vincent, provide formal notice to all creditors and "To all other persons who are known to the transferee to hold or assert claims against the transferor" (UCC § 6–107[3]). Although Johnson was not included in the list of creditors, Vincent Brass had actual knowledge (UCC § 1–201[25]) that Johnson had asserted a claim against Mid States. Therefore, Vincent Brass was required to provide Johnson formal notice. That was not done.

Johnson v. Vincent Brass & Aluminum Co, 244 Ga. 412, 260 S.E. 2d 325 (1979).

Auction

Auction sales are covered by § 2–328 of the UCC. In a sale by auction, if goods are put up in separate lots, each lot is the subject of a separate sale. An auction sale is complete when the auctioneer so announces by the fall of the hammer or by other customary manner signifying the acceptance of a bid.

The normal procedure is an auction with reserve, in which the auctioneer may withdraw the goods at any time before the acceptance of any bid. If the sale is without reserve, the auctioneer cannot withdraw the article or lot after calling for bids unless no bid is made within a reasonable time. An auction is with reserve unless the goods are in explicit terms put up without reserve.

Hawaii Jewelers Association v. Fine Arts Gallery, Inc.
51 Hawaii 502, 463 P.2d 914 (1970).

Abe, Justice The defendant, Fine Arts Gallery, Inc., commenced business on July 5, 1968, at 2270 Kalakaua Avenue, in Waikiki, Honolulu, Hawaii, advertising its business as "auction." It also gave notice of "auction" to the public by bulkmail. At the premises there were several signs reading "auction."

The plaintiff, Hawaii Jewelers Association, an unincorporated trade association, brought this action against the defendant corporation and Stanton M. Bier, as principal stockholder and "auctioneer," pursuant to HRS § 445–32 to enjoin the operation by the defendants of a public auction without having first obtained a license as required by HRS § 445–7; without designating a public auction room as required by HRS § 445–29; and without obtaining a bond as required by HRS § 445–31.

The defendants contended in the trial court that the following statement or notice "OUR GOLDEN RULE 30 day money back guarantee on every sale" appearing in newspaper advertisements and on the inside back cover of the catalogue gave a buyer a right to return any article for any or no reason within 30 days and to a refund of the purchase price. Therefore, they argue that though the sale was conducted by competitive bidding, they were not conducting an auction.

The trial court on July 15, 1968, . . . issued a preliminary injunction.

Subsequently, after a hearing on October 25, 1968, the preliminary injunction was made permanent and the final order was entered on November 6, 1968. Defendants appealed. . . .

The defendants' contention is that the "thirty day money back guarantee" postpones the transfer to purchasers of title to articles and therefore the operation was not an auction within the provisions of the Uniform Commercial Code, HRS § 490:2–328. The pertinent portion of the provision reads as follows:

> *Sale by auction.* (1) In a sale by auction if goods are put up in lots each lot is the subject of a separate sale.
> (2) A sale by auction is complete when the auctioneer so announces by the fall of the hammer or in other customary manner. . . .

We believe that defendants and successful bidders intended that title would pass upon the fall of the hammer and that purchasers could do as they pleased with the goods purchased—give or sell them to third parties. The "thirty day money back guarantee" was either an option given a successful bidder to return the goods and get a refund of money paid within 30 days or a continuing offer of defendants to repurchase the goods for a period of 30 days from the date of sale. It was similar to a satisfaction or money back guarantee given purchasers under a "sale or return" contract which gives the buyer an option or right to return the goods. . . .

> As we have stated the "thirty day money back guarantee" did not prevent or postpone the transfer of the title to chattels upon the fall of the hammer and we hold that defendants were conducting a public auction within the meaning of HRS §§ 445–21 to 38, but without meeting the requirements of HRS §§ 445–7, 445–29, and 445–31. Therefore, the trial court properly issued a permanent injunction under the provisions of HRS § 445–32 to enjoin from conducting an auction. . . .

Conditional Sale

A *conditional sale* is a transfer of title on a condition—usually the payment of money (e.g., the seller sells a car or television set to the buyer transferring the possession at the time of the contract but *withholding* the transfer of the *title* until the buyer makes complete payment). The contract provides the seller with the right to peaceably retake possession of the property if the buyer defaults. If the property is destroyed before full payment, the seller loses his security and the buyer loses the property but must still pay the balance due on the contract. To cover this loss, the typical contract provides that the buyer take out an insurance policy with a loss payable clause to the seller.

Under the UCC, a conditional sales contract is known as a "security agreement" rather than as a conditional sale.

Conditional Sale
Seller reserves title until buyer pays the total price at which title passes to buyer.

Fungible Goods

"Fungible" with respect to goods or securities means goods or securities of which any unit is, by nature or usage of trade, the equivalent of any other like unit (UCC § 1–201[17]). For example, oil, corn, flour, and wheat are considered fungible goods by nature. Goods such as bales of cotton, sacks of sugar, and cases of canned goods, can be considered as fungible by usage of trade.

In the case of fungible goods where the seller purports to sell a portion of the mass to the buyer, the buyer becomes an owner in common with the seller in the proportion the amount sold bears to the amount in the mass at the time of the sale. For example, the seller has 1,000 bushels of wheat in a bin. The buyer and the seller enter into a contract whereby the buyer purchases 500 of the bushels in the bin. When the contract is entered into, the seller and the buyer own the wheat in common even though the wheat has not been divided (UCC § 2–105[4]). The buyer cannot own title to a specific 500 bushels of wheat until that amount of wheat has been separated from the mass. Precisely how and when title passes to the buyer is discussed in the following sub-chapters.

Fungible Goods
Any unit of such goods is identical with every other like unit.

Merchant

A *merchant* is a person who deals in goods that are the subject of the contract or who purports to have special knowledge or skill regarding such goods or employs an agent appearing to have such special knowledge or skill (UCC § 2–104[1]). Manufacturers, jobbers, wholesalers and retailers are merchants. The law demands a higher standard of conduct from merchants than it does to casual sellers.

Contracts for Labor or Services

The UCC does not govern contracts to provide services; it covers "transactions in goods." Nonetheless, some courts have applied UCC principles to service transactions where the transaction is mixed (i.e., it contains elements of both a sale of goods and performance of services). The test applied is whether the major or predominant element of the transaction was a sale of goods or the performance of a service. If "sale" predominates and the plaintiff is injured by the product sold, UCC rules relative to a breach of warranty govern. On the other hand, if the plaintiff is injured by a product used in the service, tort rules pertaining to negligence apply.

Facts

Mrs. Epstein was treated in a beauty parlor owned and operated by Marie Giannattasio. The treatment involved the use of "Zoto's 30-day color" manufactured by defendant Sales Affiliates, Inc., and a prebleach manufactured by defendant Clairol, Inc. Plaintiff alleged having suffered acute dermatitis, disfigurement resulting from loss of hair, and other injuries and damages. Plaintiff sued on the basis of negligence and a breach of warranty. The defendants demurred to the claim for a breach of warranty—Giannattasio and Sales Affiliates on the ground that the transaction was not for the sale of goods under the UCC, and Clairol on the same ground as well as on the ground that any warranties would not have been extended to the plaintiff. The lower court sustained the demurrers. Plaintiff appealed.

Decision

The lower court's decision was upheld, and the case was remanded for trial on the cause of action in negligence. "The issue reduced itself to the simple one of whether or not the use of the product involved in the course of the beauty treatment amounts to a sale or a contract for sale of goods under the pertinent sections of the code. . . . As the complaint alleges, the plaintiff asked Giannattasio for a beauty treatment, and not for the purchase of goods. From such language, it could not be inferred that it was the intention of either party that the transaction be a transaction in goods within the meaning of the code. . . . There is another line of cases which involves blood transfusions received by patients in the course of medical care and treatment in hospitals. These concern the claim that injuries caused by such transfusions ground a recovery under the Sales Act. This claim has been universally rejected. Such a contract is clearly one for services, and just as clearly, it is not divisible. . . . It has long been recognized that, when service predominates, and transfer of personal property is but an incidental feature of the transaction, the transaction is not deemed a sale within the Sales Act."

The court also referred to cases involving the service of food in a restaurant and quoted from a Connecticut precedent: "The only thing 'sold' is the personal service rendered in the preparation and presentation of the food, the various essentials to its comfortable consumption or other facilities provided, and the privilege of consuming so much of the meal ordered as the guest may desire. Service is the predominant feature of the transaction. If there is a transfer of title to the food actually consumed, it is merely incidental and does not constitute a sale of goods within the contemplation of the Sales Act . . ., and there is therefore no implied warranty of its quality under the law of sales."

Epstein v. Giannattasio, 25 Conn.Sup. 109, 197 A.2d 342 (Com. Pl. 1963).

SALES (I)

Questions

1. What is a sale, and what is the difference between a present sale and a contract to sell?
2. How does a sale differ from a bailment and a gift?
3. What is an option?
4. What is a bulk sale and what are the governing rules?
5. What is the difference between a contract for labor or service and a sales contract? How does the law resolve situations where a transaction is neither purely a service nor purely a sale but a combination of the two?

17.2 Title and Risk of Loss (1)

Title Transfer

A valid sales contract is executed by the seller's delivery of the goods and the buyer's payment of the purchase price. With respect to delivery of the goods, when do title to those goods and risk of loss transfer from the seller to the buyer? In a simple over-the-counter sale, they transfer at the time the seller releases the possession of the goods to the buyer. But trade transactions are not always this simple, and the larger they are, the more complicated the legal aspects of the delivery of the goods become. The point at which title passes is important for several reasons.

1. *Creditors' Claim.* If title is still with the seller, the goods may be subject to claims of the seller's creditors. If title has transferred to the buyer, the buyer's creditors may seize the goods.

Facts

Shabny shipped goods to Hargo, but Hargo did not want to purchase the goods at that time. Hargo agreed to store the goods on its premises until it needed the goods. Hargo subsequently went bankrupt. At issue was who owned the goods. The lower court applied UCC § 2–401(1) and held that title had passed from the seller to the buyer upon delivery.

Decision

The Supreme Court reversed. The common law viewed title as the main factor in solving sales problems. The UCC deliberately deemphasizes that view (UCC § 2–101). The parties' agreement concerning the delivered goods created no contract for sale. The parties showed no intent to pass title, and therefore title remained with Shabny.

Meinhard-Commercial Corp. v. Hargo Wollen Mills, 112 N.H. 500, 300 A.2d 321 (1972)

---

2. *Repossessory Right.* If the buyer defaults in the payment, can the seller recover the goods or the purchase price from the buyer? In a conditional

Repossession
Seller's recovery of goods delivered to buyer.

sale, the seller retains title even though the buyer has possession of the goods. The seller's primary remedy upon the buyer's default is repossession.

3. *Impact on Taxes.* The place where title to the goods transfers is also relevant to determine which local tax rules will apply.

Facts
Custom Built Homes bought unassembled prefabricated houses from Page-Hill in Minnesota to be delivered by the seller "F.O.B. building site . . . Kansas." The seller brought the houses to the building site by tractor-trailer, where he would unhitch the trailer and unload the shipment. The State of Kansas taxed Custom Built on the sale. Custom Built argued that the sale took place in Minnesota.

Decision
Judgment for Tax Commission. Under the terms of the contract, the seller was required to deliver the goods to the buyer at the building site in Kansas without additional charge for transportation to that point. As there was no contrary intention in the contract, the title to the goods passed at the building site. The sale therefore took place in Kansas and was subject to tax there.

Custom Built Homes Co. v. Kansas State Commission of Revenue, 184 Kan. 31, 334 P.2d 808 (1959).

Insurable Interest
Interest in property which may be insured against loss or damage.

4. *Insurable Interest.* The question of title is significant to determine whether the seller or the buyer or both have an insurable interest in the goods. Without this interest, no claim can be made on any insurance policy. As explained later in this section, the buyer may have insurable interest even before obtaining title, i.e. upon "identification" of the goods.

Risk Transfer

Apart from insurance protection, the point at which risk of loss passes from the seller to the buyer is equally important to determine who must suffer the loss if the goods are lost, stolen, destroyed, or damaged.

Facts
Caudle bought a house trailer from Sherrard, the plaintiff. A down payment by a check in the amount of $2,685 was made, and a promissory note for $4,005 for the balance was signed by the buyer. Delivery of the trailer was apparently to take place when the sale was made, but for some reason Caudle was unable to take delivery of the vehicle that very day. The trailer was stolen before Caudle had a chance to pick it up. Caudle placed a stop payment on his down payment check and cancelled the entire sale, upon which Sherrard brought suit for the full contract price. The trial judge entered a judgment n.o.v. for Sherrard in the amount of $6,285.70. Caudle appealed.

Decision
Judgment reversed. The court first rejected Sherrard's two arguments as to when the risk of loss passed. Sherrard argued that since it was "acting as" a bailee and

since the goods were to be delivered without being physically moved further, risk of loss had passed under UCC § 2–509(2)(b). The court stated that this section referred to goods in the possession of a commercial bailee who had issued a document of title (a bill of lading or a warehouse receipt) on them. The section was not intended to cover the situation where the seller was a "bailee" because title had already passed to the buyer.

Sherrard also argued that the contract itself provided for the passing of risk to the buyer under § 2–509(4). The contract said: "No transfer, renewal, extension or assignment of this agreement or any interest hereunder, and no loss, damage or destruction of said motor vehicle shall release buyer from his obligation hereunder." The court found that this language was not sufficiently clear to pass the risk to the buyer before delivery of possession but rather that it was intended to cover what happened after the buyer had taken delivery and was primarily for the benefit of the bank or finance company to which Sherrard assigned the contract. "To hold otherwise would be to set a trap for the unwary. If parties intend to shift the burden of the risk of loss from the seller to the buyer before delivery of the goods, then such must be done in clear and unequivocal language."

The court applied UCC § 2–509(3), which stated that where the seller was a merchant, risk of loss did not pass to the buyer until he or she received the goods. Since Caudle never received possession of the goods, Sherrard still had the risk of loss when the theft occurred, and since Caudle did not get his trailer, he was not liable for the contract price.

Caudle v. *Sherrard Motor Company,* 525 S.W.2d 238 (Tex.Civ.App. 1975).

Parties' Own Rules

Through provisions in their sales agreement, parties under the freedom of contract doctrine are at liberty to decide for themselves when and where title and risk of loss shall transfer from the seller to the buyer. As UCC § 2–401(1) says, . . . "title to goods passes from the seller to the buyer in any manner and on any conditions explicitly agreed on by the parties." Hence, many companies stipulate on their printed sales agreement that "title and risk of loss shall pass to Buyer upon Seller's delivery to the carrier at shipping point." Under such an arrangement, the buyer becomes owner and carries the risk of loss immediately after the seller makes the delivery to the carrier. Especially in foreign trade, where the foreign party often does not understand and is not always subject to American law, it is highly recommended to include such specific provisions in the sales contract to prevent misunderstandings and disputes.

Role of UCC

In the absence of expressed sales conditions, the UCC governs the transfer of title and risk of loss as discussed in this chapter.

The Code regulates title and risk of loss separately. Although title and risk of loss normally transfer from the seller to the buyer at the same time, as in a simple over-the-counter sale, in some situations they transfer independently of one another. For instance, in a documentary transfer, title may transfer when the seller delivers the document of title to the buyer, but the risk of loss remains with the seller until the buyer takes possession of the goods or a third party as bailee takes possession on the buyer's behalf.

Facts

Ramos, (plaintiff/buyer) bought a motorcycle from Wheel Sports Center (defendant/seller). Ramos paid the price in full and was given the documents to register the ownership. In addition he took liability insurance policy to protect himself. However, since he was leaving on vacation, he did not take possession of the motorcycle but was to pick up the merchandise when he returned. Meanwhile, during a city power blackout, the motorcycle was stolen from the seller's premises. Ramos sued to recover the purchase price.

Decision

Judgment for the plaintiff/buyer. The court cited UCC § 2–509(3), which provides that ". . . the risk of loss passes to the buyer on his receipt of the goods if the seller is a merchant. . . ." Section 2–103(1)(c) states that receipt of goods means taking physical possession of them. If physical delivery of the goods is to take place at the merchant's place, the merchant continues to control the goods until actual delivery of the merchandise. The court also refuted the existence of bailment, contructive or otherwise, between the buyer and the seller.

Ramos v. Wheel Sports Center, 96 Misc.2d 646, 409 N.Y.S.2d 505 (1978).

Identification

Identification
Exact designation of the particular goods involved in the sale.

Before title can transfer from the seller to the buyer, the goods sold must be identified. *Identification* means the exact designation of the particular goods as those to which the contract refers. Goods can be identified in many ways, such as by being described in the contract, by sending the goods to the buyer, by being marked, or by being set aside. In other words, identification means that the parties can say that these are the exact goods involved in the sale (UCC § 2–501).

The Official Comment to § 2–501 states: "In view of the limited function of identification there is no requirement in this section that the goods be in a deliverable state or that all of the seller's duties with respect to the processing of the goods be completed in order that identification occur. For example, despite identification the risk of loss remains on the seller under the risk of loss provisions until completion of his duties as to the goods and all of his remedies remain dependent upon his not defaulting under the contract."

Identification alone does not necessarily pass title, but title cannot pass to the buyer until the goods have been identified. Identification and passage of title can occur at the same time, but often identification precedes the passage of title and gives the seller and the buyer certain rights that are independent of title. Thus, in a binding sales contract for one GE refrigerator Model X-100, the seller already has the obligation to deliver one such refrigerator and the buyer already has the obligation to pay the seller the agreed purchase price, but nothing else has happened. Identification then takes place when a specific GE refrigerator Model X-100 serial number 12345-R is designated as the actual merchandise sold.

When Identification Occurs

It is important to know when identification of existing goods as the goods to which the contract refers occurs, since title cannot pass to the buyer until the goods are identified to the contract and because the buyer and the seller do not obtain certain rights as stated below until the goods are identified to the contract.

In the absence of specific agreement, identification of the goods to the contract occurs in the following ways:

1. When the contract is made, if it is for the sale of goods already existing and identified (e.g., undivided shares in an identified fungible bulk—grain in an elevator or oil in a storage tank—can be sold, and the mere making of the contract would be sufficient to effect an identification, even though the seller has not yet performed his duties to segregate and deliver the amount stated in the contract (buyer and seller become owners in common)(§ 2–105[3][4]).
2. If the contract is for the sale of future goods (existing goods not yet identified or not yet in existence), other than unborn young or future crops, identification occurs when the goods are shipped, marked, or otherwise designated by the seller as the goods to which the contract refers (§ 2–501[1][b]).
3. Unborn young or future crops are identified to a contract when the crops are planted or otherwise become growing crops or when the young are conceived (§ 2–501[1][c]). If the contract is made after the young are conceived or the crops are planted, such goods are identified by the making of the contract (§ 2–501[1][a]).

Identification and Buyer's Rights

Identification invests the buyer with a special property and an insurable interest in the goods (§§ 2–401[1], 2–501[1]).

1. The *special property interest* includes (a) the right of the buyer to reclaim goods from an insolvent seller (§ 2–502), (b) the right of the buyer to inspect the goods (§ 2–513[1]), (c) the right of possession if the seller fails to deliver (§ 2–716), and (d) the right to sue third parties for injuries to the goods (§ 2–722).
2. The *insurable interest* that is created in the buyer on identification of the goods is the interest a person must have in property to be able to insure it. Without an insurable interest, the insurance policy would be invalid as a wagering contract. The buyer can insure goods to the extent of his interest even though the goods are still in the seller's possession (§ 2–501[1]). For example, the buyer may carry insurance to protect himself from damage to his business by interruption due to nondelivery of necessary materials—this could be a loss not collectible from the seller because the seller is excused by casualty or unforeseen circumstances under § 2–613. The practical solution regarding insurance is to have a clause in the contract stating which party is to obtain the policy and who is to pay the premiums. Such a policy should name the buyer and the seller as insureds with benefits payable according to their respective interests.

If the seller subsequently breaches the contract before the buyer accepts or rejects the goods (e.g., the seller fails to deliver or ships nonconforming goods), risk of loss will still remain with the seller (§ 2–510[1]), while title may pass to the buyer pursuant to § 2–401.

Identification and Seller's Rights

If the buyer repudiates or breaches the contract after identification is made, the seller can (1) shift to the buyer the risk of loss that occurs within a reasonable time and for which the seller is not insured (§ 2–510[3]).

Identification of goods that are subsequently destroyed through no fault of the seller before passage of risk of loss to the buyer (2) relieves the seller of liability for breach of contract (§ 2–613). Identification entitles the seller to fix damages by (3) reselling the goods at a public sale (§§ 2–706[4], 2–704[2]).

In the event of the buyer's anticipatory breach or wrongful refusal to accept the goods, title remains with or revests in the seller (§§ 2–610, 2–401[4]), enabling the goods to be resold to a third party.

If the buyer breaches the agreement after acceptance or a wrongful attempt to revoke acceptance of the merchandise, title will remain with the buyer.

Sale by Nonowner

Nonowner
A bailee, a thief, or a finder is a nonowner without title to the goods.

It is a fundamental rule of law that a thief, finder, or bailee of goods cannot transfer title even to a bona fide purchaser for value. This principle is illustrated by the following case:

Facts

Connelly acquired a refrigeration trailer at a judicial foreclosure sale to satisfy his mechanic's lien for repair and storage costs. He then sold the trailer to a good faith purchaser, Marvin, for value. Unknown to both the seller and the buyer, the trailer had been stolen from its rightful owner. The original owner claimed title to the trailer, and the buyer sued the seller to recover the purchase price.

Decision

The seller purchased only title rights belonging to his predecessor, the thief. Thus, he obtained no title. UCC § 2–312, there is an implied warranty that the title conveyed is good unless otherwise stated. The court held that the seller breached that warranty of good title and found for the buyer.

Marvin v. Connelly, 272 S.C. 425, 252 S.E.2d 562 (1979).

An exception as to a bailee is found in UCC § 2–403(2)(3), which provides that an owner of goods who entrusts the possession of the goods to a merchant who deals in goods of that kind gives the merchant the power to transfer all rights of the owner to a buyer in the ordinary course of business. For example, B purchases a watch from a jeweler and leaves it with the jeweler to have his initials engraved on it, but the jeweler sells it to a buyer in the ordinary course of business. Some states (California UCC § 2403[3]) have enacted legislation giving greater protection to the owner by providing that the entrustment must be for the purposes of sale, obtaining offers to purchase, locating of buyer, etc., for the owner's rights to be defeated by a sale to a bona fide purchaser for value. Thus, in the preceding example, the owner could reclaim the watch.

Resale by Fraudulent Buyer

The general rule is that when the buyer of goods perpetrates a fraud on the seller and thereby gains possession of the goods, a sale of the goods by the fraudulent buyer to a bona fide purchaser for value passes title to the goods to the purchaser. The theory for passing a good title to the bona fide purchaser for value is that as between two innocent persons, namely the seller and the bona fide purchaser, the person who permitted the transaction to take place should suffer the loss (i.e., the innocent seller). The exception to the rule is in the case of fraud in the inception or execution (e.g., the buyer obtains the seller's signature by trick so that the seller either does not know he is signing a contract or believes he is signing a document different from the one he is actually signing).

The general rule has been expanded by UCC § 2–403(1), which provides that the bona fide second purchaser prevails over the original seller who has been deceived as to the identity of the original buyer when delivery of the goods was paid by a check which is later dishonored or when it was agreed that the transaction was a cash sale and the buyer did not pay.

Questions

1. Name several reasons why the point in time when title transfers from the seller to the buyer is important.
2. Give an example where the seller has the title, while risk of loss is with the buyer, and vice versa.
3. When does identification occur?
4. What does identification do for the buyer and the seller?
5. What is the answer to the question of title when a nonowner sells? How about a resale by a fraudulent buyer?

17.3 Title and Risk of Loss (2)

With Movement of Goods

The general rule is that title passes to the buyer at the time and place at which the seller completes the agreed performance, whereas risk of loss usually falls upon the party who has control over the goods (UCC § 2–401[2]). In the absence of an agreement to the contrary, transfer of title and risk of loss depend on whether the contract requires the goods to be delivered through a so-called shipment contract or a destination contract.

Shipment Contracts

A *shipment contract* requires or authorizes the seller to send the goods to the buyer but does not require the seller to deliver the goods to a particular

Shipment Contract
Title and risk of loss pass to buyer upon seller's delivery of the goods to the carrier.

place. The shipment contract is the normal shipping arrangement. If nothing is stated in the sales agreement, the arrangement is presumed to be a shipment contract.

Facts

Pestana is the representative of the estate of the deceased buyer, Amar, who purchased sixty-four electronic watches from Karinol for $6,006. The invoice/contract read: "Please send the merchandise in cardboard boxes duly strapped with metal bands via air parcel post to Chetumal. Documents to Banco de Commercio de Quintano Roo S.A." The document did not include F.O.B., F.A.S., C.I.F., or C. & F. (defined in Chapter 18) provisions and did not refer to any risk of loss. As there were no direct flights from Miami to Chetumal, Mexico, the parties agreed to have the merchandise flown to Belize City, Belize, where it would be picked up by Amar's agent, Smith, and land transported to Chetumal. The goods arrived in Belize City, Smith was notified, and Amar paid the balance due. When the boxes subsequently went through customs inspection, they were found empty. Karinol and its insurance company refused to refund the contract price, arguing that the risk of loss was with the buyer from the moment the goods were delivered to the common carrier. Amar sued for the refund of the paid contract price. The trial court decided in favor of Karinol, and Amar appealed.

Decision

Judgment affirmed. After reviewing the facts, the court noted that a shipment contract is a normal contract, and a destination contract is the variant contract. The normal presumption is that the seller is only obligated to get the goods to the carrier and that the goods travel at the buyer's risk. There was nothing in the sales agreement to contradict this presumption.

"All agree that there is sufficient evidence that the defendant Karinol performed its obligations as a seller under the Uniform Commercial Code if this contract is considered a shipment contract. Karinol put the goods sold in the possession of a carrier and made a contract for the goods' safe transportation to the plaintiff's decedent; Karinol also promptly notified the plaintiff's decedent of the shipment and tendered to said party the necessary documents to obtain possession of the goods sold.

"The plaintiff Pestana contends, however, that the contract herein is a destination contract in which the risk of loss on the goods sold did not pass until delivery on such goods had been tendered to him at Chetumal, Mexico—an event which never occurred. He relies for this position on the notation at the bottom of the contract between the parties which provides that the goods were to be sent to Chetumal, Mexico. We cannot agree. A 'send to' or 'ship to' term is a part of every contract involving the sale of goods where carriage is contemplated and has no significance in determining whether the contract is a shipment or destination contract for risk of loss purposes. . . . (T)he 'send to' term contained in this contract cannot, without more, convert this into a destination contract.

"It therefore follows that the risk of loss in this case shifted to the plaintiff's decedent as buyer when the defendant Karinol as seller duly delivered the goods to the defendant freight forwarder American under a reasonable contract of carriage for shipment to the plaintiff's decedent in Chetumal, Mexico."

Pestana v. Karinol Corp., 367 So.2d 1096, Florida (1979).

The seller's duties in a shipment contract are stated in § 2–504 (discussed in Chapter 18). They may vary because of the use of a certain shipping term, such as F.O.B. or F.A.S.; by an agreement between the parties; or by the open term provisions of the UCC, for example, delivery in single or multiple lots (§ 2–307), the seller's choice of shipment arrangements (§ 2–311[2]), and time for delivery (§ 2–309[1]).

Title and risk of loss pass on completion of the seller's duty of physically putting the goods into the *carrier's possession* (§§ 2–401[2][a], 2–509[1][a]). Depending upon the shipping term used, this duty sometimes includes actually loading the goods on board. The seller usually loads rail carloads, but any load smaller than a carload is usually loaded by the railroad.

Destination Contracts

A *destination contract* is one that requires the seller to deliver the goods at a named destination. For example, a contract calling for "ex warehouse" requires the seller to deliver the goods to the buyer's warehouse at a certain address. *Title and risk* of loss pass to the buyer when the goods are *tendered at the destination* (§§ 2–401[2][b], 2–509[1][b]). It is the tender of delivery and not the delivery itself that causes title to pass. The seller must perform certain duties before title can pass at the destination; such duties are stated in § 2–503 (e.g., put and hold goods at the buyer's disposition at a reasonable hour and for a reasonable time, give the buyer notice so he can take delivery, tender appropriate documents).

Destination Contract
Title and risk of loss pass to buyer upon tender of delivery at destination.

Facts

Rheinberg, a West German wine producer, sent a shipload of 1,245 cases of wine to its buyer, Vineyard. The shipping term used was "F.A.S. Charlotte, NC," which was the point of destination. The ship, MS München, disappeared at sea with all hands and cargo in her voyage to Charlotte. Rheinberg sought payment for the lost wine, and Vineyard refused to pay.

Decision

The court decided for the defendant. As the arrangement made was "F.A.S. Charlotte, NC" it was a destination contract. Title and risk of loss did not pass from Rheinberg to Vineyard before tender of delivery of the merchandise at Charlotte which of course never took place.

Rheinberg-Kellerei GMBH v. Vineyard Wine Co., 53 N.C.App. 560, 281 S.E.2d 425 (1981).

C.O.D.

In a C.O.D. (collect on delivery) contract, the seller retains control over possession of the goods by preventing the buyer from obtaining delivery until he pays for them.

The UCC fails to define C.O.D. or state whether it creates a shipment contract or a destination contract. However, courts often see C.O.D. contracts as *shipment contracts*, which means that title and risk of loss pass to the buyer upon delivery to the carrier. To avoid possible problems in C.O.D. contracts, parties should use a shipping term such as F.O.B. shipment point or F.O.B. destination or insert explicit terms in the contract regarding title and risk of loss.

C.O.D.
Collect on Delivery.

Facts

Auburn Motor Company sold five automobiles to Levasseur of Rhode Island to be shipped C.O.D. via the Adams Express from Indiana to Rhode Island. While the goods were in transit, Levasseur borrowed money from New England Auto Insurance Company to pay for the cars by executing a mortgage on the cars to secure payment of the loan. When the cars arrived, Levasseur transferred one of them to Whitten Motor Company, which sold the car to Andrews. Levasseur defaulted on the mortgage, and New England sought to recover the car from Andrews in accordance with the terms of the mortgage. Andrews argued that the mortgage was invalid, since Levasseur did not have title to the car when the mortgage was executed. He claimed that the C.O.D. shipment to Levasseur prevented the title from passing from Seller to Buyer.

Decision
Judgment for New England. Title to the car passed from Auburn Motor to Levasseur upon delivery of the goods to the carrier. Accordingly, Levasseur was the owner when the cars were in transit and at the time the mortgage was executed. The mortgage was therefore valid. A C.O.D. shipping term does not prevent title from passing from Seller to Buyer. It merely gives the carrier the right to retain possession of the goods on behalf of the seller until paid by the buyer.

New England Auto Investment Co. v. Andrews, 47 R.I. 299, 132 A 883 (1926).

Sale on Approval

Sale on Approval
Sale becomes final upon buyer's approval of the goods.

In a *sale on approval*, neither title nor risk of loss passes to the buyer until he indicates approval of the goods (§ 2–327[1][a]). Obviously, this is the best method of making a purchase as far as the buyer is concerned. If the buyer decides not to accept the goods, he must seasonably notify the seller of his election to return them. The risk and expense of returning the goods is on the seller, but a merchant buyer must follow any reasonable instructions (§ 2–327[1][b][c]). "Seasonably" means an action taken at or within the time agreed or, if no time is agreed, at or within a reasonable time (§ 1–204[3]). It is not a sale on approval if the buyer's right to return the merchandise is not clearly expressed in the arrangement.

Facts
Buyer purchased furniture on credit and made a number of payments thereafter. When he stopped making payments, Seller claimed the right to repossess the furniture on the theory that it had been sold on approval and that the buyer never gave his approval.

Decision
Judgment for the buyer. A sale cannot be a sale on approval when there is no express provision for the return of the goods at the option of the buyer. The fact that the sale was on credit did not make it a sale on approval. As the sale was an absolute sale, seller had no right of repossession.

Gantman v. Paul, 203 Pa.Super. 158, 199 A.2d 519 (1964) (Usually, Seller in such a case has a lien on the furniture to secure Buyer's continued payments, in which event he may exercise his rights on the furniture through court procedure.)

Sale or Return

Sale or Return
An executed sale, but buyer has the option to cancel it by returning the goods.

In a *sale or return* contract, the goods are delivered to the buyer with an option to return them. Title and risk pass to the buyer pursuant to rules related to delivery requiring movement of goods and delivery without moving goods. Return of the goods is at the buyer's risk and expense (§ 2–327). *Title revests in the seller* when the goods are returned and delivered to the seller at the place from which they were sent (§ 2–401[2][b]).

Sale or return contracts may be the arrangement between a manufacturer and a dealer who will use the goods for resale, though the normal mode of business in such a situation is consignment.

Consignment

In a *consignment,* a consignor, who is often the manufacturer or distributor, supplies goods to a consignee—the dealer or retailer—for the purpose of selling the goods to the ultimate buyer, who is usually the consumer. The consignee either returns to the consignor the unsold merchandise or pays the consignor the proceeds of sold goods minus the agreed commission. There is therefore an agency and a bailment; the consignor is principal and bailor, and the consignee is the agent and bailee. *Title* to the goods does not pass to the consignee but transfers *directly from consignor to* the ultimate *purchaser.* As to risk of loss, since the bailment is for mutual benefit, consignee is to exercise ordinary care and is liable for ordinary negligence. As a cautionary note, UCC § 2–326(3) provides that "(W)here goods are delivered to a person for sale and such person maintains a place of business at which he deals in goods of the kind involved, under a name other than the name of the person making delivery, then with respect to claims of creditors of the person conducting the business the goods are deemed to be on sale or return"; such goods are not on consignment.

Consignment
Entrusting of goods to consignee to sell for consignor.

Auction

UCC § 2–328 is silent as to when title and risk of loss pass to the successful auction bidder. However, since "(A) sale by auction is complete . . . by the fall of the hammer," title and risk are in practice regarded to transfer at this very moment. Until that time, a consignment exists whereby the auctioneer acts as consignee, sales agent, and bailee for the original owner of the goods. Subsequent to the fall of the hammer, the auctioneer becomes bailee for the new owner until delivery of the goods, with or without documents, takes place.

Auction
A sale of property to the highest bidder.

Automobiles

The UCC does not specifically refer to automobiles, nor does it attempt to set out a specific line of interpretation where a public regulation is concerned. Thus, it does not expressly affect preexisting motor vehicle registration statutes.

The modern trend followed by most courts is that ownership does not pass until requirements of the motor vehicle statutes have been complied with. Thus, tort liability remains with the seller until the statute is complied with.

Some courts hold that title passes pursuant to the provisions of the UCC, particularly § 2–401(2), upon physical delivery of the vehicle without completion of the statutory registration formalities. Most of these cases are from states that do not have statutes providing a mandatory and exclusive method of transferring title to motor vehicles.

Without Movement of Goods

With Document of Title

Document of Title
Documentary evidence of ownership of certain goods.

Ownership of goods in the possession of a bailee is usually evidenced by a so-called document of title issued by the bailee. For example, a bill of lading is issued by the common carrier that is transporting the goods; a warehouse receipt is issued by the warehouseman who is keeping the merchandise. The document of title may be negotiable, permitting the owner to sell the goods based upon the document alone, or it is not negotiable. The seller's performance in a sale of goods on a negotiable title document is completed by the seller's voluntarily delivering the document to the buyer. The seller's endorsement is required if the document is an order instrument rather than a bearer instrument (see chapter on Commercial Papers). The law says that title to the goods and risk of loss pass from the seller to the buyer when the buyer takes possession of the title document (UCC §§ 1–201[14][15], 2–401[3][a], and 2–509[2][a][c]).

Without Document of Title

(1) If goods already *identified* are to be delivered without a document of title and without being moved (e.g., buyer is to load and haul away without seller's help), *title passes* as soon as the *contract is made* (§ 2–401[3][b]). (2) If the contract is for the sale of *future goods* without a document of title and without being moved, title passes when the goods are *identified*. The goods do not have to be in a deliverable state. Thus, title to a machine to be specially manufactured may pass as soon as it is in an identifiable form, even though it is not finished. Title to crops may pass as soon as the crops are planted (§ 2–501[1][c]).

(3) If the *seller is to help* load the goods, title does not pass until the seller *completes* the physical duties (§ 2–401[2]).

Risk of loss passes to the buyer on receipt of the goods if the seller is a merchant (usual case). If the seller is a nonmerchant, risk of loss passes on tender of delivery to the buyer (§ 2–509[3]).

If the goods are in possession of a bailee, risk of loss passes when the bailee acknowledges the buyer's right to possession of the goods (§ 2–509[2][b]).

Facts

Russell, a boat dealer, sold a 19-foot boat to Clouser. Clouser made a down payment and agreed to pay the balance due when he took delivery of the boat. Meanwhile, Russell was to install a new engine and a drive train. While the boat was in Russell's possession, it was destroyed when it struck a seawall. Transamerica, which insured Russell for watercraft under 26 feet that were not owned by Russell, refused to honor Russell's claim, arguing that Russell was still the owner at the time of the accident.

Decision

Judgment for policyholder. If delivery is to be made without moving the goods and no documents of title are involved, title passes at the time of contracting if the goods are already identified at the time of contracting (§ 2–401[3][b]). The goods do not need to be in a deliverable state to be identified to the contract. Since the boat was identified at the time the parties contracted, there was no requirement for documents of title for boats in this state, and the delivery was to be made without the seller's moving the boat, title passed to Clouser at the time of the contracting. Russell still had the risk of loss because he retained possession of the boat.

Russell v. Transamerica Insurance Co., 116 Mich.App. 93, 322 N.W.2d 178 (1982).

Transfer of Title and Risk of Loss Chart

Type of Delivery or Sale	When Title Passes	When Risk Passes
Delivery by Movement of Goods		
1. Shipment contract (usual type of sale between merchants)	Delivery to carrier	Delivery to carrier
2. Destination contract	Tender at destination	Tender at destination though in possession of carrier
3. Other contracts requiring physical delivery by seller		
a. Merchant seller (usual type of sale between merchant and nonmerchant)	Completion of seller's duties of delivery	Buyer's taking physical possession of goods
b. Nonmerchant seller	Same as (a)	Tender of delivery
Delivery Without Movement of Goods		
1. Goods in seller's possession		
a. Merchant seller (usual type of sale between merchant and nonmerchant)	Identification of goods or making sales contract (whichever is later)	Buyer's taking physical possession of goods
b. Nonmerchant seller	Same as (a)	Tender of delivery
2. Goods in bailee's possession		
a. Delivery by negotiable document of title	When buyer takes possession of document	When buyer takes possession of document
b. Delivery by nonnegotiable document of title	Same as (a)	Honoring of document by bailee or buyer's inaction for reasonable time after receiving it
c. Delivery by procuring bailee's acknowledgement without a document of title	Identification of goods or making of contract (whichever is later)	Bailee's acknowledgement
d. Delivery by giving buyer written direction to bailee	Same as (c)	Honoring of document by bailee or buyer's inaction for reasonable time after receiving it
Sale on Approval	Signifies approval	Signifies approval
Sale or Return	Title passes pursuant to rules above except sale on approval	Risk of loss passes pursuant to rules above except sale on approval

QUESTIONS

1. Explain shipment and destination contracts.
2. What are the rules concerning C.O.D. transactions?
3. What is the difference between a sale or return arrangement and a consignment?
4. How and when do title and risk of loss pass in a transaction involving a document of title without moving the goods?
5. What are the rules regarding title and risk transfer if no document of title is involved and the buyer is to pick up the goods?

PROBLEMS

1. P was a patient in XYZ Hospital. During the course of his treatment, P was given a blood transfusion. The transfusion was listed as a separate item on P's hospital bill. P contracted serum hepatitis from the blood used in the transfusion, resulting in his death. P's heirs bring suit against the hospital on the theory that the transfusion was a sale of blood that carried with it an implied warranty that the blood was fit for use. XYZ does not argue the law of implied warranty but claims that the transfusion was merely a service and not a sale. Decision?

2. P, a book publisher, sold its entire book inventory to B. At that time, P owed D and others sums greatly in excess of the sale price. No notice of the sale was sent to P's other creditors. The entire proceeds of the sale were credited to D. These creditors seek your advice as to their respective rights against B and D.

3. Buyer purchases a refrigerator-freezer combination from the seller on an installment plan, whereby the seller is to retain legal-security title until the buyer completes all payments. Shortly after the purchase, the appliance is destroyed by fire in the buyer's home. Buyer refuses to pay the balance, arguing that since Seller retained legal title, Seller must bear the loss. Decision?

4. B in New York ordered 1,000 pitons for use in mountain climbing from S in Chicago. B sent a check for partial payment of the purchase price with the order. S put the pitons aside in his factory and put B's name on the box containing them. Eight days later, S became insolvent. B tendered the balance of the purchase price and demanded the pitons. C, a creditor of S, wants to seize all of the goods, including the pitons, as they have gone up in value since B's order. Who should get the pitons, and why?

5. Buyer purchases and pays for a large, expensive painting from Seller who deals in goods of that kind. Since the buyer does not have the means to take the painting with him, he leaves it with the seller with the understanding that he will pick it up the next day. Later that day, Seller wrongfully sells the painting to a bona fide purchaser for value in the ordinary course of business. Seller absconds with the money from the two sales. Buyer sues the bona fide purchaser to recover the painting. Decision?

6. Buyer, representing himself to be Henry Ford II, offers to purchase a stereo from Seller on credit. Seller, quite willing to sell Ford on credit, sells the stereo to Buyer. Buyer then sells the stereo to T, a bona fide purchaser for value, who has no knowledge of the buyer's fraud. When Seller discovers the fraud, he attempts to repossess the stereo. Decision?

7. Buyer in Illinois and Seller in New York enter into a contract for the sale of 1,000 cases of dog food F.O.B. New York, C.O.D. Seller delivers the dog food to the carrier in New York, but the goods are destroyed in transit by an unusual flood in Ohio. Seller demands payment, but Buyer contends that since he did not have an opportunity to inspect the goods he does not have to pay for them. Decision?

8. Buyer in Los Angeles and Seller in New York enter into a contract whereby the seller will ship to the buyer F.O.B. Los Angeles 1,000 sweaters #R 15. Seller ships the sweaters, which arrive at the freight depot in Los Angeles. The freight depot agent telephones the buyer and tenders delivery of the goods. Two days later, and before the buyer picks up the goods, an earthquake and fire destroy the freight depot and the sweaters. Seller demands payment, but Buyer contends that neither title nor risk passes until the goods are delivered. Decision?

9. Buyer, a business law student, and Seller enter into a contract whereby Buyer purchases a typewriter on a thirty-day approval. Twenty days after the purchase, the typewriter is stolen from the buyer's locked room due to no fault of the buyer. Buyer

immediately notifies Seller of the theft and states that he does not approve of the typewriter and disclaims all liability for the purchase price. Seller brings suit. Decision?

10. Buyer, a housewife, enters into a contract with the Reynolds television retail store at 11:00 a.m. for the purchase of a radio tape recorder combination at a price of $1,000. Reynolds tells the buyer that the set will have to be checked out by one of his employees and that she can pick it up the next day. Buyer says she will bring a station wagon and asks Reynolds if she should bring someone along to help load the set. He tells her this is not necessary, because his employees will load the set. She then pays Reynolds $500 on account and leaves the store. At 4:00 p.m. the same day, Seller calls Buyer and informs her they were able to get the set ready ahead of time and he is now tendering delivery to her. Buyer states that she cannot get the set until the next day as previously arranged. During the night, the set is stolen. Seller demands the balance of the purchase price, contending that title to the set passed at the time the contract was made because the goods were identified to the contract, and if not at that time, then certainly when tender was made. Decision?

CHAPTER EIGHTEEN

Sales (II)

18.1 Shipping Terms and Buyer's Performance
Shipping Terms
 F.O.B.
 F.A.S.
 C. & F.
 C.I.F.
 No Arrival, No Sale
 Ex Ship
Buyer's Payment
 Tender of Payment
 Installment Contract Payments
 Payment and Inspection

18.2 Seller's Performance
Seller's Delivery
 Duty to Ship
 Tender of Delivery
 Inspection, Acceptance, or Rejection
 Perfect Tender Versus Substantial Performance
 Seller's Right to Cure
 Duties Upon Rejection
 Substitution
 Uncertainty of Performance
 Goods in Possession of Seller
 Goods with Bailee
 Installment Contracts
Shipment With Reservation

18.3 UCC Remedies in Sales
Seller's Remedies
 Withholding of Goods
 Stop Carrier's Delivery
 Identify Goods to Contract
 Cancel the Contract
 Reclaim the Goods
 Resell the Goods
 Recover Damages
 Recover Contract Price
Buyer's Remedies
 Recover Identified Goods
 Replevin the Goods
 Specific Performance
 Cancel the Contract
 Revoke Acceptance
 Coverage
 Price Reduction
 Damages
 Retain Security Interest

CHAPTER EIGHTEEN

18.1 Shipping Terms and Buyer's Performance

Shipping Terms

The UCC defines mercantile shipping terms in Sections 2–319 through 2–324. Sometimes the definitions conflict with those in the American Foreign Trade Definitions (AFTD). In case of conflict, the parties should incorporate one or the other in the contract. The AFTD definitions can be obtained from the National Foreign Trade Commission, Inc., 10 Rockefeller Plaza, New York, NY 10020. Depending upon the shipping term used, the law designates the answer as to when title and risk of loss transfer from the seller to the buyer. In actual practice, mercantile shipping terms are commonly considered to refer basically to quotation or pricing of the merchandise offered or sold.

F.O.B.

F.O.B.
Free on board

F.O.B. (free on board) Place of Shipment requires the seller to bear the expense and the risk of putting the goods into possession of the carrier. It is basically a shipment contract. Title and risk therefore pass when physical delivery to the carrier is completed (§ 2–319[1][a]).

Facts

A California clothing manufacturer sued to recover the purchase price of merchandise sold to a Connecticut retail clothing store owner. All orders filled by the manufacturer were shipped "F.O.B. Los Angeles" and "Via Denver-Chicago," a common carrier. All orders contained the printed phrase, "Goods shipped at purchaser's risk." Old Colony, the second connecting carrier, attempted to deliver the merchandise to the retailer's store. The carrier refused to place the merchandise inside the store premises, and the shipment was not delivered. The merchandise thereupon disappeared. Defendant argued that the plaintiff's refusal to deliver inside the store excused payment for the merchandise, since risk of loss remained with the seller absent a proper delivery.

Decision

Judgment for the plaintiff. The use of the phrase "F.O.B. Los Angeles" was the controlling factor as to risk of loss of the merchandise upon delivery to Denver-Chicago. Title to the goods and risk of loss passed to the defendant at Los Angeles. The court stated: "The law erects a presumption in favor of construing the agreement as a 'shipment' contract, as opposed to a 'destination' contract. Under . . . a 'shipment' contract, plaintiff's liability for loss or damage terminated upon delivery to the carrier at the FOB point, to wit, Los Angeles. . . . Accordingly, at the FOB point, when the risk of loss shifted, Denver and Old Colony, as carriers, became the agents or bailees of defendant (buyer)."

Ninth Street East, Ltd. v. Harrison, 5 Conn. Cir. 597, 259 A.2d 772 (1968).

As a general and most used shipping term in trade, the term F.O.B. is usually followed by a certain geographical point, whereby the aforesaid basic meaning of the term may be modified.

SALES (II)

F.O.B. Shipment Point means that the seller must arrange the shipping; the buyer pays the cost of freight, cost of loading unless carrier requires the seller to load, insurance, export and import charges, custom duties, fees, and document expenses needed to bring the goods into the country (§§ 2–311[2], 2–319[1][a], 2–504).

F.O.B. Carrier, Vessel, Truck, etc., means that the seller must arrange the shipping and pay for and bear the risk of loading the goods on board the carrier. Title and risk pass after loading. Buyer must pay for the remaining expenses (§§ 2–311[2], 2–319[1][a][c], 2–504).

F.O.B. Destination, Buyer's Warehouse, etc., means that the seller must arrange shipping and pay costs, insurance, and freight (§ 2–319[1][b]). Title to the goods and risk of loss pass to the buyer only upon tender of delivery at the destination point, as illustrated in *Custom Built Homes Co. v. Kansas State Commission of Revenue* in Chapter 17.

F.A.S.

F.A.S. (free alongside) Vessel requires the seller to deliver the goods alongside the vessel, and title and risk pass when that is completed. The buyer must arrange shipping and pay for all the expenses after this point (§§ 2–319[2][3][4], 2–401[2][a]).

F.A.S.
Free alongside ship

C. & F.

C. & F. (cost and freight) requires the seller to arrange shipping and pay for loading, freight, and cost of export licenses, fees, and similar exportation charges, while the buyer must pay for insurance and cost of import charges, custom duties, fees, and document expenses to bring the goods into the country (§§ 2–311[2], 2–320[2][b], 2–320[3]).

C. & F.
Cost and freight

C.I.F.

C.I.F. (cost, insurance, freight) means that the price includes the cost of the goods, the insurance, and the freight to the named destination. Thus, the seller must arrange shipping and pay for everything except import duties. Title and risk pass on shipment, i.e., when the seller completes the duty of physical delivery to the carrier (§§ 2–320[1][2], 2–504).

C.I.F.
Cost, insurance, freight

Facts

Mexican Produce Company sold merchandise to Sonny Mohamed "C.I.F. Trinidad." Mexican Produce delivered the goods to Sea-Land Service, Inc., a carrier in Puerto Rico. The goods were damaged in transit. Mexican Produce sued Sea-Land Service, Inc., for the damage.

Decision

The court decided for Sea-Land Service, Inc. Under a C.I.F. contract, risk of loss transfers from the seller to the buyer when the goods are delivered to the carrier. The buyer therefore carried the risk of damage while in transit, and the seller, who did not sustain any damage, could not sue. (After accepting the delivery, Sea-Land became the carrier/bailee for buyer Sonny Mohamed.)

Mexican Produce Co. v. Sea-Land Service Inc., DC Puerto Rico, 429 F.Supp. 552 (D.P.R. 1974).

No Arrival, No Sale

No Arrival, No Sale
Title and risk pass to buyer upon arrival of goods.

No Arrival, No Sale means that the seller must arrange shipping and pay for all the cost of transportation up to the point of the arrival of the goods in the buyer's possession. Title and risk pass to the buyer upon arrival. However, the UCC provides that "where without fault of the seller the goods are in part lost or have so deteriorated as no longer to conform to the contract or arrive after the contract time, the buyer may proceed as if there had been casualty to identified goods (§ 2–613). Accordingly, although the buyer does not have title to the goods that fail to arrive, there is already an insurable interest establishing the possibility of a valid insurance claim (§ 2–324).

Ex Ship

Ex Ship
Title to goods passes to buyer upon their leaving the ship.

Ex Ship also requires the seller to arrange shipping and pay for everything. "(R)isk of loss does not pass to the buyer until the goods leave the ship's tackle or are otherwise properly unloaded" (§ 2–322).

Buyer's Payment

Tender of Payment

Tender of Payment
The offer of money in satisfaction of a claim for payment.

Generally, the buyer must offer or tender payment before he has the right to obtain the goods (§§ 2–507[1], 2–511[1]). Unless the seller committed an anticipatory breach by refusing to deliver the merchandise, *tender of payment* is a prerequisite to placing the seller in default.

Facts

On April 14, 1937, Defendant/Seller agreed to sell and Plaintiff/Buyer agreed to buy four used airplanes that the seller owned. The price was stipulated, and payment was to be made by certified check upon delivery of the airplanes to the buyer at the Municipal Airport, Kansas City, Missouri. The date for delivery was stated to be June 1, 1937.

On June 1, the seller was ready, able, and willing to deliver one of the planes described in the contract. Between June 1 and July 10, the seller was ready, able, and willing to deliver all of the four airplanes at the place specified. Meanwhile, the buyer did not on June 1 or any other date either tender payment on any or all of the machines or request delivery but brought an action against the seller for nondelivery of the merchandise. The trial court dismissed the buyer's complaint.

Decision

Judgment affirmed. "[T]here was a simple contract promising delivery by the seller to the buyer of specified goods at a definite time and place and neither party demanded performance from the other or tendered his own. Has either a right against the other? Payment and delivery are concurrent conditions since both parties are bound to render performance at the same time. Restatement, Contracts, § 251. In such a case . . . neither party can maintain an action against the other without first making an offer of performance himself. Otherwise, if each stayed at home ready and willing to perform each would have a right of action against the other. . . . to maintain an action at law the plaintiff must not only be ready and willing but he must have manifested this before bringing his action, by some offer of performance to the defendant, . . . It is one of the consequences of concurrent conditions that a situation may arise where no right of action ever arises against either party . . . so long as both parties remain inactive, neither is liable. . . . This statement . . . not only has the force of (the author's) authority and that of many decisions from many states, but is also sound common sense. It is not an unfair requirement that a party complaining of another's conduct should be required to show that the other has fallen short in the performance of a legal obligation. . . .

The conclusion is, therefore, that the defendant is not in default. Neither side having demanded performance by the other, neither side is in a position to complain or to assert any claim in an action of law against the other. This view of the case makes it unnecessary to examine the testimony which asserts that the buyers either abandoned or repudiated the contract prior to the time of the performance."

Vidal v. Transcontinental & Western Air, Inc., 120 F.2d 67 (3d Cir. 1941).

All sales are for cash unless the seller agrees to extend credit. If credit has been extended, the goods have been delivered, and the buyer subsequently does not make the payment as promised, the buyer's nonpayment is under the law not to be regarded as a repudiation of the sales agreement or a wrongful rejection of the goods, but the seller should simply bring action against the buyer to obtain payment.

Facts
Seller sold goods to the buyer on thirty-day credit. The thirty days passed, and payment was not made. The seller wrote the buyer a letter requesting payment. Thirty more days elapsed, and payment was still not made. The seller claimed that the buyer had repudiated the contract.

Decision
Seller was incorrect. The sales contract was not repudiated by the buyer. Failure to perform—in this case, failure to pay—is not a repudiation. To constitute a repudiation, there must be a clear expression of intent to be not bound by a contract. This is distinct from merely failing to perform the obligation under a contract.

National Ropes, Inc. v. National Diving Service, Inc., 513 F.2d 53 (5th Cir. 1975).

A tender of payment is sufficient when made by any means or in any manner current in the ordinary course of business, including check, unless the seller demands payment in legal tender and gives the buyer a reasonable amount of time to procure it (§ 2–511[2]).

UCC § 2–511(3) states that a "payment by check is conditional and is defeated as between the parties by dishonor of the check on due presentment." If the check is dishonored, the buyer has no right to retain the goods or dispose of them (§ 2–507[2]). A seller who has been paid by a dishonored check may sue for breach of the sales contract or sue on the instrument that has been dishonored (§§ 1–106[2], 3–802[1][b]).

As discussed in Chapter 17, a good faith second purchaser from a fraudulent buyer who has paid for the goods with a bad check will prevail over the original seller (§ 2–403[1]). However, the fraudulent buyer's creditors do not prevail over the original seller.

Installment Contract Payments

If the buyer defaults on an installment payment and if the breach substantially impairs the value of the whole contract to the seller, there is a breach

Installment Contract Payments Partial payments made on account of a debt due.

of contract (§§ 2–612[3], 2–703). What is substantial impairment is a difficult question of fact. However, it has been held that nonpayment of an installment can be a substantial impairment of the value of the contract either by creating financial difficulties for the seller, making it virtually impossible for the seller to assign the contract for financing, or giving the seller reasonable apprehension that the buyer would not make future payments.

If the buyer fails to pay for one or more installments, the seller can stop delivery of the goods not paid for and, if uncertain about future performance, can demand adequate assurances of performance from the buyer (e.g., demand that the buyer post a surety bond or submit a good credit report from his bank [§ 2–609]).

Republic-Odin Appliance Corp. v. Consumers Plumbing & Heating Supply Co.
24 Ohio Opinions 2d 226, 192 N.E.2d 132 (1963).

Hoddinott, Judge Plaintiff is a manufacturer of home water heaters. For about seven years, it did a large-scale business with defendant, which sold at wholesale to building contractors and at retail to home owners. This dual mode of business apparently offended the notions of orderly marketing procedure held by plaintiff and plaintiff's other customers who competed with defendant, and gave rise to friction.

Defendant's dominating figure is Richard Friedman, its president. He is a skillful bargainer in a business which is highly competitive, and adept at obtaining substantial price discounts in his purchases. He is proud of taking cash discounts for prompt payment of all his bills; over the years, however, there were frequent disputes about items on the bills rendered by plaintiff. Defendant was a good, but hardly a favorite, customer of plaintiff. . . .

On December 10, a balance was due on the account and on December 12 defendant purported to pay it, except that defendant held back $7,000 which was to be paid "when instructed by R. C. Friedman."

Then, on December 19th, plaintiff's vice president and general manager, William Lennon, wrote in a letter to Friedman, the following: . . .

> "In light of your past record of arbitrary deductions, 'misunderstanding of terms,' arbitrary withholding of $7,000.00 and your violation of our selling agreement, and in keeping with our desire to improve our channels of distribution, we are hereby notifying you that we are unwilling to ship to your account for any and all of your four locations.
>
> "Unless payment for your account in full is received in this office by December 23, 1958, we will be forced to take necessary legal action to insure collection." . . .

Plaintiff brought this action on its account with defendant for heaters sold, freight and parcel post, and prayed for a judgment of $7,465.58 and interest. . . .

The failure to pay the substantial amount due on this order, following on the heels of the troubled relations of the parties and the unprecedented demands of the defendant put forth as conditions for doing business in the future, is a material breach of contract within the purview of the statute. Plaintiff was justified in repudiating this order. . . .

Plaintiff was also justified in repudiating the other unfilled orders of defendant. . . .

> To state it in its simplest terms: If there is one installment contract between seller and buyer and one party breaches it under circumstances indicating he will not perform his duties in the future, then the other party is excused from further performance.
>
> The Uniform Commercial Code, which went into effect in 1962, recognizes that a party to an installment contract has a right to "a continuing sense of reliance and security that the promised performance will be forthcoming when due," the Code makes provision for an adequate assurance of performance. . . .
>
> Judgment shall be awarded to plaintiff against defendant on the petition for $7,465.58 with interest.

If the buyer persists, over the seller's objections, in wrongfully rejecting installments or failing to pay for them, the buyer will then be held to have repudiated the contract permitting the seller to exercise his remedies (see subchapter 18.3). However, if the seller accepts the payments without notification of cancellation of the contract or brings an action with respect to past installments or demands performance as to future installments, he reinstates the contract (§ 2–612[3]). The seller's acceptance of late payments may also be regarded as a waiver or modification of the contract (§§ 1–205[3], 2–208[3]).

Payment and Inspection

If a sale involves a documentary transaction (bill of lading) and the contract terms call for payment upon presentation of the bill of lading or for C.O.D., the buyer must pay for the goods before inspecting them (§ 2–513[3][b]).

If the sale is F.O.B. vessel, F.A.S. vessel, C.I.F., or C.F. terms, the buyer must pay before inspection of the goods (§§ 2–310[c], 2–319[4], and 2–320[4]). In a sale using C.I.F. or C.F. terms, but the documents are not to be presented for payment until after arrival of the goods, § 2–321(3) provides for preliminary inspection before payment when feasible.

In all other cases, the buyer may inspect the goods before making payment (§ 2–513[1]). The buyer is allowed a reasonable time to inspect the goods and may test or analyze them in the process of inspecting them. Although the buyer must pay for the inspection, if the goods do not conform to the contract, the buyer may recover from the seller necessary expenses of inspection (§§ 2–513[2], 2–515[a]).

If the goods are nonconforming and the buyer knows this, the buyer does not have to pay for the goods before inspection (§ 2–512[1]).

Section 2–512[1] does not provide any remedy for a seller against an alert buyer who refuses to pay for nonconforming goods. Furthermore, the seller's suit for damages would be ineffective, because the seller could not prove damages. The buyer can be aware that the goods are nonconforming by simple observation (this is not considered inspection), for example, damaged boxes that rattle, wrong quantity, or routine weighing before unloading that reveals an incorrect weight.

In cases where the buyer does not have the right of inspection before payment of the goods and the goods are nonconforming, the buyer must pay first and complain later of the defects.

Payment and Inspection
Shipping terms govern relative time of payment for and inspection of goods.

Questions

1. What does "F.O.B." stand for? What is its basic meaning, and what are the variations?
2. What does "C.I.F." mean?
3. What is the buyer's legal position if the goods do not arrive in a "No Arrival, No Sale" arrangement?
4. If the sales agreement is silent, must the buyer pay first, or must the seller deliver the merchandise first?
5. Under what terms must the buyer pay first before inspecting the goods? Under what terms may the buyer inspect the goods first before making payment?

18.2 Seller's Performance

Seller's Delivery

Seller's Delivery
Transfer of goods by seller to buyer.

In every sale, the obligation of the seller is to transfer and deliver the goods and the obligation of the buyer is to accept and pay in accordance with the contract (§ 2–301). This is true whether the sale involves a bottle of milk at the neighborhood grocery store or millions of bushels of wheat. Section 2–301 is adequate to govern performance in almost all sales transactions. Only mercantile sales (e.g., between manufacturer and wholesaler, distributor and retailer) are likely to involve different problems regarding delivery, acceptance, or payment.

Duty to Ship

Duty to Ship
Obligation of seller to deliver goods to carrier.

In a shipment contract, the seller's obligation is performed when the seller starts the goods on their way by delivery to the carrier. The seller does not guarantee arrival of the shipment (§ 2–504). In a destination contract, however, the seller has the duty to get the goods to their destination (§ 2–503). In the absence of a special provision, the contract will be considered a shipment contract rather than a destination contract.

The seller's duties in a shipment contract are as follows:

1. The seller must make a reasonable contract with a reasonable carrier (§ 2–504[a]) (e.g., the seller cannot ship perishable goods from New York to Los Angeles by a slow freighter going around the Horn); the seller must also provide for the care of the goods in transit if needed (e.g., refrigeration of perishables and feeding and watering of livestock).
2. The seller must have the goods classified and described as to their true worth.
3. The seller must arrange for the goods to be properly loaded.
4. The seller must promptly procure and offer to the buyer any document the buyer needs to obtain possession of the goods when they arrive, such as a bill of lading (§ 2–504[b]).
5. The seller must promptly notify the buyer that the shipment has been made (§ 2–504[c]). A standard manner of notification is sending an

invoice or bill of lading to the buyer. Frequently the agreement expressly requires prompt notification (e.g., by wire or cable). Failure of the seller to promptly notify the buyer that shipment has been made or to make a reasonable contract for the transportation of the goods is grounds for rejection of the goods, but only if the failure results in material delay or if loss ensues.

Tender of Delivery

In the absence of an agreement to the contrary, the seller must tender his performance under the contract if he wants to be paid. A valid tender of delivery (as used in this section, "tender" contemplates an offer coupled with a present ability to fulfill all the conditions resting on the tendering party and must be followed by actual performance if the other party shows himself ready to proceed) has two requirements:

1. The seller must put and hold conforming goods at the buyer's disposition.
2. The seller must give the buyer any notification reasonably necessary to enable the buyer to take delivery (§§ 2–503[1], 2–503[3]).

Tender of Delivery
The offer of delivery of goods, with present ability of seller to deliver them.

The tender must be at a reasonable hour and must be kept available for a reasonable time so the buyer can take delivery (§ 2–503[1][a]). The tender must be at the place stated in the contract and, if no place is stated, at the seller's place of business (§§ 2–308, 2–503[1]). If there are documents (e.g., bill of lading), the seller must tender all documents in correct form (§ 2–503[5]).

The effect of tender of delivery is to entitle the seller to the buyer's acceptance of the goods at the place and time of tender (§ 2–507[1]) provided, of course, the goods tendered conform to the sales agreement.

Unless expressly stated in the contract to the contrary, tender of delivery and payment (as explained in subchapter 18.1) are concurrent conditions; that is, neither party is required to perform until the other performs or tenders performance (§§ 2–507[1], 2–511[1]). Neither party can claim the other party is in default until he first tenders performance. However, if one party refuses to perform, the other party does not have to tender performance, as this would be a useless act (§ 2–610).

Many contracts provide for credit (i.e., goods are to be delivered to the buyer on sixty-day credit). In credit cases, the seller must perform his part of the contract before he can demand performance from the buyer.

Inspection, Acceptance, or Rejection

If the goods fail to conform to the contract in any respect (e.g., greater quantity than ordered or goods of a different description mixed with the goods ordered), the buyer may (1) reject the whole, (2) accept the whole, or (3) accept any commercial unit or units and reject the rest (§ 2–601). Exact performance by the seller may be tempered, however, by usage of trade, prior course of dealing, or course of performance, any one of which may permit commercial leeway in performance.

If the buyer decides to reject nonconforming goods, such a *rejection* must take place within a *reasonable time*. What is "reasonable" is illustrated in the following case:

Facts

Smith bought a new 1966 Chevrolet from Zabriskie Chevrolet, making a cash deposit of $124 and thereafter tendering his check in full payment on February 9. The car was delivered to Mrs. Smith on February 10. The transmission seriously malfunctioned a short distance from the dealer's lot. On February 11, Smith called Zabriskie to tell him that he had sold him a lemon and that he was stopping payment on the check and cancelling the sale. Later Zabriskie replaced the transmission. Smith refused to accept the repaired car.

Plaintiff charges that since the defendant accepted vehicle he is therefore bound under the Code (§ 2–607[1]) to complete payment for it. Defendant asserts that he never accepted the vehicle and therefore under the Code properly rejected it. He further asserts that even if there had been acceptance he was justified under the Code in revoking the same. Defendant supports this claim by stating that what was delivered to him was not what he bargained for (i.e., a new car with factory new parts, which would operate perfectly as represented) and that therefore the Code remedies of rejection and revocation of acceptance were available to him.

Decision

Judgment for Defendant/Buyer. "Section 2–606 states in pertinent part:

(1) Acceptance of goods occurs when the buyer

(a) after a reasonable opportunity to inspect the goods signifies to the seller that the goods are conforming or that he will take or retain them in spite of their non-conformity; or

(b) fails to make an effective rejection (subsection [1] of 2–602), but such acceptance does not occur until the buyer has had a reasonable opportunity to inspect them; or

(c) does any act inconsistent with the seller's ownership; but if such act is wrongful as against the seller it is an acceptance only if ratified by him.

It is clear that a buyer does not accept goods until he has had a "reasonable opportunity to inspect." Defendant sought to purchase a new car. He assumed what every new car buyer has a right to assume—and, indeed, has been led to assume by the high-powered advertising techniques of the auto industry—that his new car, with the exception of very minor adjustments, would be mechanically new and factory-furnished, operate perfectly, and be free of substantial defects. The vehicle delivered to the defendant did not measure up to these representations. Plaintiff contends that the defendant had "reasonable opportunity to inspect" by the privilege to take the car for a typical "spin around the block" before signing the purchase order. If by this contention the plaintiff equates a spin around the block with "reasonable opportunity to inspect," the contention is illusory and unrealistic. To the layperson, the complicated mechanisms of today's automobiles are a complete mystery. To have the automobile inspected by someone with sufficient expertise to disassemble the vehicle in order to discover latent defects before the contract is signed is assuredly impossible and highly impractical.

Consequently, the first few miles of driving become even more significant to the excited new car buyer. This is the buyer's first reasonable opportunity to enjoy the new vehicle to see if it conforms to what it was represented to be and whether the buyer is getting what he bargained for. How long the buyer may drive the new car under the guise of inspection of new goods is not an issue in the present case. It is clear that the defendant discovered the nonconformity within seven tenths of a mile and minutes after leaving the plaintiff's showroom. Certainly this was well within the ambit of "reasonable opportunity to inspect." That the vehicle was grievously defective when it left the plaintiff's possession is a compelling conclusion, as is the conclusion that in a legal sense the defendant never accepted the vehicle.

Even if the defendant had accepted the automobile tendered, he has a right to revoke under UCC § 2–608:

(1) The buyer may revoke his acceptance of a lot or commercial unit whose non-conformity substantially impairs its value to him if he has accepted it. . . .

Accordingly, and pursuant to UCC § 2–711, judgment is rendered on the main case in favor of the defendant. On the counterclaim, judgment is rendered in favor of the defendant and against the plaintiff in the sum of $124 (the amount of the deposit), there being no further proof of damages."

Zabriskie Chevrolet, Inc. v. Smith, 99 N.J.Super. 441, 240 A.2d 195 (1968).

On the other hand, in the following case, the buyer's rejection was considered too late and therefore unacceptable:

Facts

Defendant/Buyer purchased a number of kitchen units for installation in a university dormitory. Plaintiff/seller delivered the units to the construction site, where they remained untouched and uninspected for three months. When they were subsequently installed, they were rejected by the architect for not meeting the contract specifications. The buyer returned the units to the seller, but the seller refused to take them back and sued the buyer for the purchase price.

Decision

Judgment for the plaintiff/seller. Defendant/Buyer had accepted the goods by (1) waiting three months before inspecting them and (2) incorporating them in the building, as this was inconsistent with the plaintiff's ownership. Defendant could not revoke the acceptance because of the delay, particularly since the defects could have been readily discovered.

Cervitor Kitchens, Inc. v. Chapman, 7 Wn. App. 520, 500 P.2d 783 (1972).

Perfect Tender Versus Substantial Performance

Some courts apply a *perfect tender rule* and reject the doctrine of *substantial performance* in contracts for the sale of goods. In the following case, the Supreme Judicial Court of Maine stated that perfect tender required that the vendor's tender conform to all the specifications of the contract.

Perfect Tender versus Substantial Performance
Tender of delivery meeting 100 percent of the contract requirements, as opposed to tender meeting most, but not all, of the contract terms.

Facts

Plaintiff agreed to sell molds meeting certain specifications to defendant Lyn-Flex. Plaintiff delivered the goods and sued to recover the contract price. At issue was whether the molds were delivered on time and whether they met the buyer's specifications. The trial judge instructed the jury that the plaintiff's performance did not need to be 100 percent complete to entitle the plaintiff to enforce the contract. He said that Maine law required "substantial performance." The jury awarded the plaintiff the contract price.

Decision

The appellate court reversed and ordered a new trial. The judge's instruction was incorrect, as Maine law applies a perfect tender rule. UCC § 2–601 gives the buyer the right to reject "if the goods or the tender of delivery fail in any respect to conform to the contract." The court held that the jury must decide whether the plaintiff is liable under the standard.

Moulton Cavity & Mold, Inc. v. Lyn-Flex Industries, Inc., 396 A.2d 1024 (Me., 1979).

The preceding rule has two important exceptions:

1. Installment contracts (the buyer can reject only if nonconformity substantially impairs the value of that installment and cannot be cured) (§ 2–612).
2. Limitations of remedy (the parties can contract to limit the buyer's rights) (§§ 2–718 and 2–719).

Seller's Right to Cure

If the tendered goods do not conform to the contract and the buyer refuses to accept them, the seller can "cure" the defective performance if time for performance has not yet expired by (1) giving reasonable *notice* to the buyer of his intention to cure and (2) making a conforming delivery *within the*

Seller's Right to Cure
The right of a seller to make a proper delivery of goods after having first tendered a defective delivery.

contract time (§ 2–508). Curing should not be confused with "warranty." It is the buyer's right to warranty, and it is the seller's right to cure, as illustrated in the following case:

Facts

Plaintiff/Buyer purchased a new color TV set that did not function properly (the picture had a reddish tinge). Defendant/Seller advised the buyer that the chassis of the set needed to be removed from the cabinet and taken back to the shop to determine the cause of the problem. Buyer rejected this suggestion and insisted upon a brand new set. While retaining the malfunctioning TV set, the buyer demanded the return of the purchase price. Seller refused.

Decision

Judgment for Defendant/Seller. The court cited the UCC provision: "Where any tender or delivery by the seller is rejected because nonconforming and the time for performance has not yet expired, the seller may seasonably notify the buyer of his intention to cure and may then within the contract time make a conforming delivery." Buyer's adamant refusal to allow examination essential to determine the cause of the excessive red tinge to the picture defeated any effort by the seller to provide timely repair or even replacement of the set if the difficulty could not be corrected. As the seller was denied access to the merchandise and a reasonable opportunity to cure, "seller has not shown a breach of warranty" entitling the buyer to a brand new set or to rescission of the sales contract.

Wilson v. Scampoli, 228 A.2d 848 (D.C.App., 1967).

On the other hand, as shown in the previously cited *Zabriskie Chevrolet, Inc.* v. *Smith,* where a new Chevrolet is not supposed to need a new transmission, the court under those circumstances denied the seller's right to cure.

The law furthermore requires the seller to exercise the right to cure within a reasonable time, subsequent to which the buyer is allowed to reject the merchandise and recover damages.

Facts

Plaintiff/Seller agreed to custom-make two molds to be used in manufacturing plastic containers. Plaintiff had difficulty meeting the buyer's specifications. Time and again the seller remade the molds, but the molds were never suitable. The trial court held that the seller had breached the contract and awarded the buyer damages.

Decision

Time was of the essence in the performance of the contract. The court held that the time for performance had expired and therefore the plaintiff no longer had the unfettered right to cure pursuant to UCC § 2–508(1). Although UCC § 2–508(2) gives a seller some opportunity to extend the time for performance and cure—within a reasonable time—the seller here in no way complied with that section.

Hayes v. *Hettinga,* 228 N.W. 2d 181 (Iowa 1975).

Duties Upon Rejection

A merchant buyer who rightfully rejects delivered goods must follow the reasonable instructions of the seller regarding the disposition of the goods unless the seller has an agent or place of business at the market of rejection.

If the goods are perishable or threaten to decline speedily in value, the buyer must make reasonable efforts to sell the goods for the seller even in the absence of instructions. The buyer is entitled to reimbursement for reasonable expenses (§§ 2–603, 2–604).

A nonmerchant buyer who rightfully rejects delivered goods is only under a duty to hold the goods with reasonable care at the seller's disposition for a time sufficient to permit the seller to remove them (§ 2–602[2][b][c]).

In case of the buyer's rejection, and in any case before the buyer's acceptance, *risk of loss* of delivered *nonconforming goods* remains with the *seller*.

Facts
Defendant/Buyer purchased three reels of underground cable from the plaintiff/seller. Seller delivered only one reel of underground cable and two reels of aerial cable that the buyer could not use. Buyer notified the seller that the aerial cable was rejected and that it was placed in a well-lighted storage space for the seller to pick up. Seller did not pick up the merchandise within a three-month time period and within that time the reels were stolen. Seller sued the buyer for the price of the stolen cable.

Decision
Judgment for the defendant/buyer. The court cited UCC § 2–510(1): "Where a tender or delivery of goods so fails to conform to the contract as to give a right of rejection the risk of their loss remains on the seller until cure or acceptance."

Graybar Electric Company v. *Shook*, 283 N.C. 213, 195 S.E.2d 514 (1973).

A similar case is *Moses* v. *Newman*, 658 S.W.2d 119 (Tenn. App. 1983), in which a newly purchased mobile home was destroyed by a windstorm during the course of installing.

Substitution

"Where without fault of either party the agreed berthing, loading or unloading facilities fail or an agreed type of carrier becomes unavailable or the agreed manner of delivery otherwise becomes commercially impracticable but a commercially reasonable substitute is available, such substitute performance must be tendered and accepted" (§ 2–614[1]). Neither party is excused from performance, because the express manner of delivery is impractical when there is a substitute available.

Substitution
Commercially reasonable alternate performance.

Uncertainty of Performance

When reasonable grounds for insecurity arise with respect to the performance of either party (e.g., financial problems or strike against manufacturer/seller), the other may in writing demand adequate *assurance* of performance and until receiving such assurance may *suspend* his *own performance* (§ 2–609). Adequate assurance of due performance depends on the factual situation. Where the buyer can make use of a defective delivery, a mere promise by a seller of good repute that he will give the matter his immediate attention and that the defect will not be repeated is sufficient assurance.

Uncertainty of Performance
Grounds for demand by either party for assurance that performance will be forthcoming.

However, this would probably be insufficient if the statement were made by a known corner cutter, unless accompanied by a surety bond or, if so demanded by the buyer, by a speedy replacement of the defective product. If the defective product cannot be used by the buyer, a mere verbal assurance would not be adequate unless accompanied by replacement or other commercially reasonable cure.

Goods in Possession of Seller

The UCC does not specifically provide rules for tender of delivery when the goods are in the possession of the seller and are not to be moved by him. For passage of title, see § 2–401(3).

If the seller tenders delivery by putting and holding conforming goods for the buyer and gives required notice, and if the buyer accepts the goods, probably the seller has completed delivery (§§ 2–503[1], 2–606).

Goods with Bailee

When the goods are to be picked up by the buyer from a bailee, a valid tender of delivery can be made either by tendering to the buyer a negotiable document of title (bill of lading or warehouse receipt covering the goods) or by an acknowledgment from the bailee that the buyer is entitled to possession of the goods (§ 2–503[4][a]).

Installment Contracts

Installment Contracts
Contracts permitting delivery of goods in more than one shipment.

An *installment contract* is one that requires or authorizes the delivery of goods in separate lots to be separately accepted (§ 2–612[1]). The buyer may reject any installment that is nonconforming *if* the nonconformity substantially impairs the value of that installment *and* cannot be cured (§ 2–612[2]). If the nonconformity of an installment does not impair the value of the whole contract, the buyer must accept that installment if the seller gives adequate assurance of its cure. Impairment of the value of an installment can turn not only on the quality of the goods but also on such factors as quantity, time, and assortment.

In *Holiday Manufacturing Company* v. *B.A.S.F. Systems, Inc.*, the seller did not conform strictly to the terms of an installment contract. The court analyzed the buyer's behavior and concluded that the nonconforming deliveries did not substantially impair the value of the whole contract.

Facts

Defendant agreed to purchase six million plastic cassettes in installments. From the start, the plaintiff had trouble meeting the defendant's specifications, and delays occurred. During the following year, the plaintiff delivered only a fraction of the ordered cassettes. The seller corrected many quality problems. The buyer continued to work with the seller and even increased its order. Finally, the buyer cancelled all orders, citing "continuous quality problems and delivery delays."

Decision

Judgment for the seller. The court held that the buyer's cancellation was improper under UCC § 2–612(3). Throughout the year, the buyer did not protest or communicate any dissatisfaction. Rather, it encouraged the seller to continue production and even ordered more. The buyer saw in these cassettes a potentially profitable business venture and tolerated the delays. The seller was able to cure all the problems over time. The court concluded that the nonconformities with respect to the installments did not "substantially impair the value of the whole contract" (UCC § 2–612[3]). Therefore, the buyer did not have any right to cancel.

Holiday Manufacturing Co. v. B.A.S.F. Systems, Inc., 380 F.Supp. 1096 (D.Neb. 1974).

Shipment with Reservation

Shipment with reservation is a shipment in which the seller reserves security interest in the goods that have not been paid for by the buyer (§ 2–505).

In a situation where the buyer has already paid for the merchandise, the seller will ship the goods, have the carrier issue a bill of lading, usually in the name of the buyer as consignee for the goods, and have this document of title forwarded to the buyer to enable the buyer to receive the goods when they arrive at the point of destination. However, if the seller has not been paid, the seller will ship the goods to the buyer but may need to retain a security interest to assure the buyer's payment. In such a shipment with reservation, the seller will instruct the carrier to issue a bill of lading normally in the seller's own name or the name of the seller's agent. The seller may then send the title document to that agent or to the seller's bank at the buyer's locality with the instructions to collect the buyer's payment and release to the buyer the bill of lading. This is called "documentary collection," whereby the seller retains control over the goods in order to be paid.

The time at which title and risk of loss are transferred, and the method used in pricing the goods have basically little to do with the seller's security interest retention. They are determined mainly by the terms of the sales contract itself and the common rules of sales.

It is understandable that shipment with reservation places the seller in a position of uncertainty as to the successful completion of the transaction. A possibility always exists that the buyer will renege on the contract and fail to make the payment. Hence, major exporting countries such as Japan and West Germany do not favor this method of dealing but use letters of credit for their international trade (discussed in Chapter 28 "Commercial Papers" hereafter).

Shipment with Reservation
Shipment of goods in which seller has reserved a security interest to guarantee payment by buyer.

Questions

1. What does the buyer have to do after the seller's tender of delivery?
2. Discuss the seller's right to cure.
3. Who has the risk of loss after the buyer's rejection of nonconforming goods?
4. Discuss the "perfect tender" requisite and the "substantial performance" and installment concepts.
5. What is shipment with reservation?

18.3 UCC Remedies in Sales

If the sales agreement does not specifically provide for remedies on breach of contract, the UCC attempts to meet the problem in Part 7, Sections 2–701 through 2–724. Remedies provided by the UCC are to be liberally administered to the end that the aggrieved party may be put in as good a position as if the other party had fully performed (§ 1–106[1]).

Seller's Remedies

Withholding of Goods

Section 2–703(a) permits the seller to withhold delivery of the goods when:

1. The buyer wrongfully rejects or revokes acceptance of the goods.
2. The buyer fails to make a payment due on or before delivery.
3. The buyer repudiates the contract in whole or in part.
4. The buyer fails to cooperate with the seller so as to enable the seller to perform (§ 2–311[3][a]).

If the seller discovers the buyer is insolvent, the seller can withhold delivery until he is paid cash for the goods. A seller who has already delivered can demand cash (§ 2–702[1]). Since the Code does not state what constitutes discovery, the seller must have good evidence before using this remedy or the seller will be in breach of contract if the buyer is solvent. Therefore, if the seller is not quite certain that the buyer is insolvent, it would be better for him to use the remedy of demanding assurances of performance under § 2–609(1).

Stop Carrier's Delivery

The seller can stop delivery of goods when:

1. The buyer is insolvent (§ 2–702[1]).
2. The buyer repudiates or fails to make a payment due before delivery (§ 2–705[1]).
3. The seller has any other right to withhold or reclaim the goods (e.g., when the buyer fails to cooperate or when the seller is waiting for justifiably demanded assurances (§ 2–705[1]).

The right of the seller to stop delivery ends when:

1. The buyer or someone holding under the buyer, such as a subpurchaser, actually receives the goods (§ 2–705[2][a]).
2. A bailee of the goods, except the original carrier, acknowledges to the buyer that it holds the goods for the buyer, thereby obligating the bailee to deliver the goods to the buyer (§ 2–705[2][b]) (an example of such a bailee would be a warehouseperson).
3. A reshipping carrier or a carrier acting as a warehouseperson acknowledges to the buyer that it holds the goods for the buyer (§ 2–705[2][c]).

A diversion of a shipment is not a reshipment when it is merely an incident to the original contract of transportation and an acknowledgment by the carrier as a warehouseperson requires a contract of a truly different character from the original shipment (i.e., a contract not in extension of transit but as a warehouseperson).

4. A negotiable document of title covering the goods is negotiated to the buyer (§ 2–705[2][d]).

To stop delivery, the seller must notify the carrier or other bailee so that the bailee by reasonable diligence can prevent delivery (§ 2–705[3]). To stop delivery, the seller usually notifies the freight agent who handled the shipment. The agent will need information from the bill of lading, such as names of the shipper and consignee, the routing, the car number, the shipping point, and the destination point. If a negotiable bill of lading is outstanding, the carrier will probably demand a bond. The seller can probably avoid this, however, by simply diverting the goods to some other destination (§ 7–303). Although the seller is not required to notify the buyer that he is stopping delivery, it is usually good practice to give such a notice.

Identify Goods to Contract

The seller may identify goods to the contract (refer to Chapter 17) on the buyer's breach if conforming goods are in the seller's possession or control when learning of the breach.

The effect of identification to the contract is that the seller can resell the goods and hold the buyer for damages (§ 2–704). A seller who cannot resell the goods, can hold the buyer for the contract price (§ 2–709[1][b]).

Cancel the Contract

When the buyer wrongfully rejects the goods or revokes acceptance, fails to make a payment due, or repudiates the contract, the seller may cancel the contract (§ 2–703[f]). Cancellation permits the seller to end his obligations while retaining the right to damages for breach of contract.

Reclaim the Goods

The seller can reclaim goods sold on credit to the buyer if he discovers that the buyer was insolvent when receiving the goods. To reclaim the goods, the seller must demand return of the goods within *ten days* after the buyer has received them (§ 2–702[2]).

The seller loses the right to reclaim if the buyer has resold the goods to third persons in the ordinary course of business or to other good faith purchasers (§ 2–702[3]).

Resell the Goods

The seller may resell the goods when the buyer wrongfully rejects them or revokes acceptance, fails to make a payment due on or before delivery, or repudiates the contract in whole or in part (§ 2–706).

The seller may recover from the buyer the difference between the resale price and the contract price together with any incidental damages (§ 2–706[1]).

The resale may be at public or private sale (§ 2–706[2]). If at private sale, the seller must give the buyer reasonable notice of intention to resell (§ 2–706[3]). If at public sale, the seller must give the buyer reasonable notice of the time and place of the resale unless the goods are perishable or threaten to decline speedily in value (§ 2–706[4][b]).

The seller may purchase the goods at a public sale (§ 2–706[4][d]). The seller is not accountable to the buyer for any profit made on a resale (§ 2–706[6]).

Recover Damages

The seller is entitled to recover damages after the buyer's wrongful rejection of the goods, revocation of acceptance, failure to make a payment due, or repudiation of the contract (§§ 2–703[d][e], 2–706[1], 2–708).

The normal measure of damages is the difference between the contract price and the market price at the time and place for tender, plus any incidental damages sustained, less any expenses saved as a result of the buyer's breach (§ 2–708[1]).

If the seller resells the goods, the damages will be the difference between the contract and the resale price, plus any incidental damages, less any expense saved as a result of the buyer's breach (§ 2–706[1]).

Facts

Plaintiff/Buyer purchased a new boat from Defendant/Seller for $12,587.40 with a down payment of $4,250. Six days after the agreement, the buyer's lawyer wrote to the seller rescinding the sales contract because the buyer was about to be hospitalized. The seller refused to refund the deposit, the buyer sued, and the seller countersued. Meanwhile, the ordered boat was sold four months later to another purchaser for the same contract price. The buyer argued that the seller's loss on the sale was thereby recouped, but the seller maintained that the first sale was nevertheless lost, since two boats could have been sold. The seller claimed that the would-be profit on the lost sale was $2,579 and that incidental expenses were incurred totalling $674 for storage, upkeep, finance charges, and insurance. The seller also asked for recovery of attorney's fees of $1,250.

Decision

Plaintiff/buyer was awarded restitution of the deposit of $4,250, and defendant/seller was awarded the total sum of $3,253, representing the loss of profit and incidental damages prayed for. ". . . . Closely parallel to the factual situation now before us is that hypothesized by Dean Hawkland as illustrative of the operation of the rules: 'Thus, if a private party agrees to sell his automobile to a buyer for $2,000, a breach by the buyer would cause the seller no loss (except incidental damages, i.e., expense of a new sale) if the seller was able to sell the automobile to another buyer for $2000. But the situation is different with dealers having an unlimited supply of standard-priced goods. Thus, if an automobile dealer agrees to sell a car to a buyer at the standard price of $2000, a breach by the buyer injures the dealer, even though he is able to sell the automobile to another for $2000. If the dealer has an inexhaustible supply of cars, the resale to replace the breaching buyer costs the dealer a sale because, had the breaching buyer performed, the dealer would have made two sales instead of one. The buyer's breach, in such a case, depletes the dealer's sales to the extent of one, and the measure of damages should be the dealer's profit on one sale. Section 2–708 recognizes this, and it rejects the rule developed under the Uniform Sales Act by many courts that the profit cannot be recovered in this case.'

"The record which in this case establishes defendant's entitlement to damages in the amount of its prospective profit, at the same time confirms defendant's cognate right to 'any incidental damages provided in this Article (§ 2–710)' (§ 2–708[2])."

Neri v. *Retail Marine Corp.*, 30 N.Y.2d 393, 334 N.Y.S.2d 165, 285 N.E.2d 311 (1972).

If the measure of damages (difference between contract price and market price or between contract price and resale price) is inadequate to put the seller in as good a position as performance would have done, the UCC attempts to remedy the situation by providing the seller with an alternative measure of damages. Section 2–708(2) provides that the seller may recover his profit, including reasonable overhead, which he would have realized from full performance by the buyer, plus any incidental damages, less expenses saved as a result of the buyer's breach.

Although the aggrieved contracting party has the duty to mitigate damages, recovery of the full contract price is obtainable if the goods are specially manufactured, custom-built, and not resaleable.

Facts
Defendant/Buyer purchased truck and wheel assemblies to be used in manufacturing skateboards. When the skateboard fad terminated, the buyer returned without the seller's consent the remainder of the purchased merchandise. Seller was unable to resell the goods, as they were not suitable for any other uses; after seven months, the units were disassembled and rebuilt to make them suitable for roller skates. Seller then brought this action to recover the net loss after resale.

Decision
Judgment for Plaintiff/Seller. ". . . . In accordance with § 2–709, UCC, plaintiff was entitled to hold the merchandise for defendant and recover the full contract price of $12,860. Plaintiff did not elect to enforce this right, but recognizing that there was no market for the goods or resale value and that they were consequently worthless for the purpose for which they were designed, it attempted to mitigate defendant's damages by converting the goods to other uses and credited defendant with the reasonable value of the goods as converted or rebuilt for use in roller skates. In so doing, plaintiff was evidencing good faith and conforming to the general rule requiring one damaged by another's breach of contract to reduce or mitigate damages. . . ."

Chicago Roller Skate Manufacturing Company v. Sokol Manufacturing Company, 185 Neb. 515, 177 N.W.2d 25 (1970).

Recover Contract Price

The seller can recover from the buyer the price of the goods and incidental damages in three situations:

1. When the buyer has accepted the goods (§ 2–709[1][a]).
2. When conforming goods are lost or damaged after risk of loss has passed to the buyer (§ 2–709[1][a]).
3. When the goods have been identified to the contract and the seller is unable to resell them for a reasonable price (§ 2–709[1][b]).

Buyer's Remedies

Recover Identified Goods

The seller's insolvency gives the buyer the right to obtain identified goods that are still in the seller's possession (§§ 2–502, 2–711[2][a]). The following four conditions must be met:

1. Buyer has paid all or part of the price, and if the buyer has not paid all of the price, he has tendered the unpaid portion of the price (§ 2–502[1]).

2. Seller has failed to deliver the goods or has repudiated the contract (§§ 2–502[1], 2–711[2]).
3. The goods have been identified to the contract by the seller (§ 2–502[1]).
4. Seller became insolvent within *ten days* after receiving the first installment on the price (§ 2–502[1]).

A buyer who is concerned that the seller is having financial trouble should demand assurances of performance (§ 2–609).

Replevin the Goods

Replevin
Legal action to physically recover property wrongfully held by another.

Replevin is an action to recover specific goods in which the buyer has an interest and that are unlawfully withheld from the buyer. The buyer's right to such action is stated in § 2–716[3] of the UCC. This remedy is given the buyer in cases in which *cover is reasonably unavailable* and goods have been *identified* to the contract. This right is in addition to the buyer's right to recover identified goods on the seller's insolvency. The purpose of this section of the Code is to give a buyer rights to goods that are comparable to a seller's rights to the price.

Specific Performance

Specific Performance
Legal action to compel a party to perform as required by a contract.

The buyer can get specific performance of a contract when the goods are *unique* or in other proper circumstances (§ 2–716[1]). Thus, the UCC broadens the right to obtain specific performance. For example, various situations that could justify specific performance are output and requirement contracts involving a particular or peculiarly available source or market, unavailability of cover, and insolvency of the seller.

The decree for specific performance may include such terms and conditions as to payment, damages, or other relief as the court may deem just (§ 2–716[2]).

Cancel the Contract

The buyer, after notice to the seller, may cancel the contract if the seller fails to deliver the goods or repudiates the contract or the buyer rightfully revokes acceptance (§ 2–711[1]).

Facts

McDonald (defendant/buyer) contracted with AMF (plaintiff/seller) to install a computerized cash register system. Problems developed after initial installation, including lengthy breakdowns. Buyer met the seller to discuss the problems as well as the fact that the seller was late in delivering some additional ordered units. Buyer's representatives also found out at the seller's plant that none of those remaining units were being assembled. When progress was not made six weeks later, the buyer notified the seller that the contract was cancelled. Seller argued that demand for adequate assurance of performance must be in writing.

Decision

Judgment for Defendant/Buyer. The court found that the buyer did have reasonable grounds to cancel. The prototype that was installed was not working properly, and the seller did not have the engineering talent to solve the problems in the system. Moreover, the seller's internal memos showed the seller's knowledge of the buyer's concern about the seller's ability to perform. A written notice is not required for a buyer to cancel the contract when the seller was already aware of all these facts.

AMF, Incorporated v. *McDonald's Corporation*, Seventh Circuit Court of Appeals, 536 F.2d 1167 (7th Cir. 1976).

The buyer's right to cancel the contract is subject to the seller's right to cure a defective performance under the previously explained rules.

Cancellation excuses further performance by the buyer but does not deprive the buyer of any remedy for past breaches. For example, the buyer may cover, claim damages for breach, obtain conforming goods through replevin, or obtain specific performance, as explained earlier in the chapter.

In addition to allowing the right to cancel, the UCC enables the buyer to escape responsibility for the *costs of removal* of the goods, as in the following case:

Facts

Defendant/Seller delivered defective flooring to the plaintiff, who rejected the goods within a reasonable time and notified the seller. The flooring was not removed. The seller argued that the plaintiff's continued use of the goods bars a rescission of the contract.

Decision

Judgment for the plaintiff. The rejection was justified, and the plaintiff was therefore entitled to recover the purchase price of the merchandise. The plaintiff's only obligation was to hold the goods with reasonable care to permit the seller to remove them. The UCC puts the burden on the merchant to remove the rejected goods (§ 2–602).

Garfinkel v. *Lehman Floor Covering Co.*, 60 Misc. 2d 72, 302 N.Y.S.2d 167 (1969).

Revoke Acceptance

A buyer who has accepted goods that later prove to be defective can revoke his acceptance (i.e., withdraw his previous assent) (§ 2–608). (See § 2–607[2] regarding acceptance of nonconforming goods.) The buyer can revoke his acceptance only when the nonconformity is such as will cause a substantial impairment of value to the buyer. Generally, this remedy is resorted to only after attempts at adjustment have failed.

The buyer must notify the seller specifically of the revocation of the acceptance. In *Poole* v. *Marion Buick Co.* (14 N.C.App. 721, 189 S.E.2d 650 [1972]), Plaintiff/Buyer purchased a new car that had problems almost from the beginning. The buyer returned the automobile to the dealer on numerous occasions, and repairs were made by the dealer free of charge. The trouble nonetheless continued until the engine finally blew up eighteen months after the date of purchase and after the car had been driven 27,000 miles. The buyer then sued for recovery of the purchase price but lost, as he never notified the seller of a revocation.

In addition to notifying the seller, the buyer must revoke the acceptance within a reasonable time. In *Conte* v. *Dwan Lincoln-Mercury, Inc.* (172 Conn. 112, 374 A.2d 144 [1976]), a new Lincoln-Continental automobile

Revoke Acceptance
Buyer may withdraw acceptance where goods are subsequently discovered to be defective.

purchased by the plaintiff had spent six to eight weeks during the first year of ownership in the defendant/dealer's garage, receiving substantial repairs caused by inherent defects in the car. Each time, the plaintiff was told that the car was in good working order. The car had five times become undriveable on the highway and had to be towed to the dealer's garage. The plaintiff was entitled to revoke his acceptance because the nonconformity of the car substantially impaired the car's value to him.

The effect of a revocation of acceptance is that the buyer is in the same position as if he had rejected the goods and therefore has the same remedies and duties as a rejecting buyer (§ 2–608[b]—holding goods for seller; § 2–603[1]—disposing of goods; [3]). (See § 2–711[3]—security interest; §§ 2–602[2], 2–604—salvaging goods; § 2–602[a]—ownership; § 2–401[4]—revesting title in seller; §§ 2–327[1][c], 2–327[2]—sales on approval and sale or return; § 2–721—remedies for fraud.)

After a proper revocation of acceptance, the buyer is not liable for the price of the goods.

Coverage

Coverage
Purchase by buyer of substitute goods where goods shipped are defective.

When the seller fails to make delivery or repudiates the contract or when the buyer rightfully rejects goods or justifiably revokes acceptance (and the seller does not cure his defective performance), the buyer has the right to cover, i.e., to purchase goods in *substitution* for those due under the contract (§§ 2–711[a], 2–712).

The buyer is not required to cover, and failure to do so does not affect any of the other remedies under the UCC (§ 2–712[3]).

The buyer's damages are the *difference* between the *contract price* and the *cost of cover,* plus *incidental or consequential damages,* less expenses saved (§ 2–712[2]).

The supreme court of South Dakota has ruled that the cover rule is available to a nonmerchant as well as a merchant buyer. Also, the buyer must cover in a reasonable manner, as in the following case:

Facts
Before delivery was due, the seller notified the buyer that he would not deliver the equipment. The parties disagreed as to whether this was a breach or the seller's refusal to deliver was justified. The buyer covered, paying $1,000 more than the original contract price. The trial court directed a verdict for the seller.

Decision
The court reversed and remanded, holding that the case presented issues of fact for the jury to decide. A buyer may recover as damages the difference between the cost of cover and the contract price (§2–712[2]). The buyer must act in good faith and in a reasonable manner. Also, the cover remedy is available to both merchant and consumer buyer (§ 2–712[1] and comments 2 and 4).

Thorstenson v. *Mobridge Iron Works Co.,* 87 S.D. 358, 208 N.W.2d 715 (1973).

Price Reduction

A buyer who is damaged by the seller's breach may, after notice to the seller, offset all or part of the damages from the price still due on the contract (§ 2–717).

Damages

On the seller's repudiation of the contract, failure to deliver the goods, nonconforming delivery, or breach of warranty, the buyer is entitled to recover damages (§§ 2-711 through 2-715).

The normal measure of damages is the difference between the contract price and the market price of the cost of cover, plus incidental and consequential damages, less expenses saved (§§ 2-713, 2-714, 2-715).

In case of breach of warranty, the buyer's measure of damages is the difference between the value of the goods accepted and the value the goods would have had if they had been as warranted (§ 2-714[2]).

The burden of proof rests upon the buyer to establish the damages caused by the alleged breach of warranty. Courts will not allow recovery unless the buyer presents sufficient evidence of damages to the jury. See *State* v. *Travelers Indemnity Company* (250 Or. 356, 442 P.2d 612 [1968]).

Punitive or exemplary (penalty) damages are not covered in the Code. Such damages are normally not recoverable in contract cases, except when the breach is accompanied by a serious tort such as fraud or duress.

Damages
Money awarded to a party injured by the wrongful act or failure to act of another party.

Retain Security Interest

A buyer who has rightfully rejected goods or justifiably revoked acceptance of nonconforming goods that remain in his possession has a security interest in the goods to cover payments made on the price and the costs of inspection, receipt, transportation, care, and custody. The buyer may resell the goods in the same manner as an aggrieved seller (§ 2-711[3]).

Security Interest
Right of party in possession of goods to retain or sell them to recover his loss.

QUESTIONS

1. Name the remedies for the seller and for the buyer.
2. When can the seller reclaim goods that have been delivered to the buyer?
3. What damages can the seller recover upon the buyer's wrongful rejection, revocation of acceptance, failure to pay, or repudiation of the contract?
4. Who has the duty to remove the delivered goods upon cancellation by the buyer?
5. What is coverage?

PROBLEMS

1. A seller in New York enters into a contract for the sale of 1,000 bushels of wheat with a buyer in Florida. The seller takes out a negotiable bill of lading in his own name and ships the goods by reasonable contract to the buyer in Florida by independent carrier. The seller immediately notifies the buyer of the shipment. The goods are destroyed while in transit. The buyer refuses to pay for the wheat on the grounds that the seller reserved title in his own name by the use of the bill of lading and therefore the seller also retained the risk of loss. Decision?

2. Buyer and Seller enter into a contract for the sale of 100 cases of Beefeater Gin. On the contracted delivery date at 4:30 p.m., the seller delivers by truck to the buyer's place of business 80 cases of Beefeater Gin and 20 cases of Gordon's Gin. The buyer tells the truck driver that he will not accept delivery because he ordered 100 cases of Beefeater Gin, and there are only 80 cases on the truck. The truck driver returns the shipment to the seller the next morning, explaining to his employer why the shipment was refused. Five days later, the seller attempts

to cure his improper tender by delivering 100 cases of Beefeater Gin; however, the buyer refuses the shipment stating that he has purchased the goods from someone else. Decision?

3. B ordered 40,000 feet of half-inch, new steel pipe from S. The order specified that "the pipe not to be plugged." The order was shipped C.O.D. upon arrival. B permitted the carrier to unload a small portion of pipe and discovered that the pipe was plugged. B refused to accept the pipe. S sued, contending that the designation of shipment C.O.D. required B to accept and pay for the pipe. Decision?

4. Buyer and Seller enter into a contract for the sale of goods. The purchase price is $4,000. On Friday evening, the proper time for delivery, the buyer brings his truck to the seller's place of business to receive delivery of the goods and offers the seller his check in the amount of $4,000. Seller refuses the check demanding cash. Buyer states that the banks are closed, but he will bring the cash Monday morning. Seller refuses to give the buyer the extra time to raise the cash and declares the buyer is in breach of contract. Decision?

5. Buyer and Seller enter into a contract for the purchase of a television set. Payments are to be made in installments of $50 a month, payable on the first day of each month. Buyer makes his first payment on the first of the month; however, he makes his next five payments on the tenth of the month because of a change in salary payment dates. The seller does not complain about these late payments. On the seventh month, the seller repossesses the television set on the eighth day of the month. Seller claims this right because the buyer is late in his payment. Decision?

6. Seller, pursuant to a credit contract for the sale of 100 television sets, ships the sets from New York to the buyer in Chicago. Upon arrival of the goods, the freight agent for the carrier calls the buyer and acknowledges to him that he is holding the 100 television sets for him and asks him to pick them up. Before the buyer has an opportunity to pick up the sets, the seller learns that the buyer has become insolvent. The seller calls the representative of the carrier and asks him to stop delivery. The agent of the carrier states that he has already acknowledged to the buyer that he is holding the goods for him. Does the seller have the right to stop delivery?

7. A seller in Kentucky sold to a buyer in Florida a large quantity of tobacco, but the buyer refused delivery. After due notice, the seller sold the tobacco elsewhere for a price less than the contract price between the seller and the buyer. The seller brings suit for the difference between the resale price and the contract price, plus expenses in the transportation, care, and custody of the goods after the buyer refused delivery, together with the costs of the resale. The buyer contends that the seller's election to resell the property to another buyer released him from all liability on the contract. Decision?

8. S, a seller of soft water equipment, sold a unit to B. Approximately two weeks after the sale the equipment proved defective. B complained to S, who attempted to fix the unit. However, the unit continued to be defective. B continued to complain, and S continued to try to fix it. This procedure went on for approximately one year, when B finally sent a letter to S requesting him to pick up the equipment and refund the purchase price. S refuses to do either, claiming that B waited too long to revoke his acceptance. Decision?

9. B purchased a large quantity of toys from S to use as stock in his store for Christmas trade. Several shipments of toys were sent to B during October and November; however, the number was less than half of the toys ordered. B called S many times during October and November complaining that he was not receiving all the toys and each time was assured by S that the rest of the toys would be forthcoming. Finally, on December 1, B called S and angrily demanded the toys. When S gave B the same reply, an exasperated B said that he wanted no more toys. Apparently this call was too late, as B received a large shipment of the toys on December 2. This shipment completed the entire purchase order except for one small lot that was never sent. B did not open this shipment. The other toys were priced, put on display, and sold by B. In February, B sent all of the toys not sold to S and demanded S pay their value. S returned the shipment to B. Decision?

10. Saxon Livestock Co., pursuant to a written order, shipped a carload of livestock to Brink, a cattle dealer, F.O.B. at point of delivery to carrier. The purchase price was due and payable two days after Brink received the shipment. The carrier, P-C, issued a straight bill of lading for the shipment. While en route, Saxon learned that Brink was insolvent and had filed for bankruptcy. At that moment, Saxon ordered P-C to return the carload. The bankruptcy trustee then sued to recover the cattle on behalf of Brink's creditors. Decision?

CHAPTER NINETEEN

Product Liability

19.1 Warranty (1)
Bases of a Claim
Injury
Negligence
Statutory Duty
Warranty Defined
Privity
Express Warranties
   Affirmation or Promise
   Description
   Sample or Model

19.2 Warranty (2)
Implied Warranties
   Title
   Merchantability
   Fitness for Particular Purpose
Exclusion, Modification, and Disclaimer
   By Inspection: Express Warranties
   By Inspection: Implied Warranties
   Description Warranty
   Trade Usage Warranty
   Automobile Warranty
   Family Use of Goods
   Title Warranty
   Merchantability Warranty
   Particular Purpose Warranty
   Other Ways of Excluding Implied Warranties
Notice of Defect
Contributory Negligence
Assumption of Risk
Statute of Limitations
Federal Consumer Protection

19.3 Strict Liability in Tort
Definition
Buyer's Advantages
Concept Elements
   Unreasonably Dangerous
   Defective Product
Liable Parties
   Wholesaler
   Suppliers of Parts
   Secondhand Dealers
   Lessor or Bailor
   Seller of Real Estate
Services
Contributory Negligence
Assumption of Risk
Damages
Intentional Torts

19.1 Warranty (1)

Where profit is the paramount motive in a capitalistic society, business may tend to be careless or even callous toward the well-being of the ultimate user of its products. Indeed, consumers need to be adequately protected against the greed of some businesspeople. Yet, a too liberal imposition of product liability rules upon business could be detrimental to a nation's economic interest. In fact, our increasingly litigious society and the huge sums of money for damages that business is often forced to defray have undoubtedly prevented much American innovative and state-of-the-art merchandise from entering the market. This, in turn, reduces American competitiveness abroad which is ultimately reflected in our international balance of trade. Accordingly, a policy of moderation in law is necessary to establish and maintain an equilibrium between the often conflicting business and consumer interests.

Bases of a Claim

There are basically four legal theories upon which a person can base a claim for damages when injured by a defective product:

1. Negligence.
2. Violation of a statutory duty.
3. Breach of warranty.
4. Strict liability in tort.

A suit related to product liability may involve one or more of the above theories.

Injury

The plaintiff must have been actually injured to recover damages in a product liability suit. Thus, discovery of defective merchandise alone does not impose liability upon the seller if the defect has not caused any harm. The harm or damage may be caused to a *person*, to *property*, or to an *economic interest*.

Injury to property differs from injury to an economic interest in that the former involves a real physical loss or damage to property, whereas the latter refers to a loss in economic value without necessarily involving physical damage. For example, the defect itself may already be an economic loss, since it causes the merchandise to lessen in value. Furthermore, since the merchandise is defective, the buyer may have to cover, buy, or rent from someone else, thereby incurring consequential expenses that may well fall under the category of an economic or commercial interest.

In a strict liability case, there must be a personal and/or a property injury, as purely economic losses are not recoverable.

Facts

Ohio (defendant/seller) sold to National (plaintiff/buyer) welded steel tubing to be used in the manufacture of cranes. After five years of continuing business, cylinder failures began to occur in the manufactured cranes. The buyer and the seller agreed that those failures might be caused by imperfect welding. When the buyer was told by engineering consultants that the seller's tubing in the cranes was defective and dangerous, the buyer, after testing, replaced all defective cylinders at a cost of $1,078,960. Buyer brought the suit based on Seller's strict liability. Seller admitted liability for damages caused by the actual failures of the cranes but not for the expenses of refitting all the other cranes. The trial court sustained Seller's demurrer to the complaint.

Decision

Judgment for Seller/Defendant. In most cases, courts denied recovery of this type of damages under "strict liability." "In the case at bar, the facts pleaded establish that the damages sought to be recovered are the costs and expenses of removing the defective tubing manufactured by the defendant and replacing it. Such damages are not damages resulting from physical harm caused by the defective product. Instead, they are damages resulting from the purchase of defective or unsatisfactory products. . . .

"The proper relationship between tort law and the Uniform Commercial Code dictates that a cause of action for 'economic loss' under the facts of the present case be pursued under a warranty or contract theory. The fact that the incurring of replacement costs here also removed a potential future tort liability to ultimate users or consumers does not convert economic loss into physical harm, nor transform a contract warranty cause of action into a product liability tort action. It should again be noted that the 15 cases in which actual failures in defendant's product occurred are not involved in this litigation."

National Crane Corp. v. *Ohio Steel Tube Co.*, 213 Neb. 782, 332 N.W.2d 39 (1983).

Negligence

Independently of the UCC, a manufacturer will be liable to persons injured by a product when the manufacturer is negligent in the preparation or manufacture of the product and when as a reasonable person he could foresee that such negligence would injure such person or persons. Such liability extends to all persons that a reasonable person could foresee would be injured regardless of their relationship to the buyer. Recoveries have been allowed against manufacturers of automobiles on behalf of buyers, users, passengers, and bystanders based on negligence resulting in defective steering wheels, axles, brakes, tires, and other operating components.

In a negligence suit, the plaintiff has the burden of proof of the defendant's failure to exercise due care, thereby causing an injury to the plaintiff. A classic example of the application of negligence as a theory of product liability is *Macpherson* v. *Buick Motor Co.* (217 N.Y. 382, 111 N.E. 1050 [1916]), in which a purchaser of a Buick automobile was injured while driving the car when the spokes of one of the wheels collapsed. The evidence showed that a simple inspection of the vehicle by Buick (the manufacturer) would have disclosed the defective wheel and that Buick failed to conduct such an inspection and consequently failed to exercise due care.

Negligence, which more appropriately belongs under the heading "Tort," is discussed in Chapter 3.

Statutory Duty

State and federal statutes impose duties upon manufacturers of food, drugs, cosmetics, flammable materials, and toxic substances with respect to branding, labeling, description of contents, advertising, and the selling or offering for sale of adulterated, contaminated, or unwholesome products. (See Chapter 20, Consumer Protection.)

These statutes provide for enforcement by *criminal sanctions, seizure* of goods, and *injunctions*. They do not expressly impose civil liability based upon injuries to the user or consumer of a product that has been sold in violation of the statute. However, in a civil action for damages, a violation of statutory duty may be alleged, and if established by evidence, many courts hold that such violation constitutes negligence by itself. Examples are recovery for destruction of property resulting from faulty electrical wiring that did not comply with the building code and recovery for crop damage resulting from mislabeling of packages of seed in violation of a state statute.

Warranty Defined

Warranty
A promise by a seller regarding the goods sold.

Express Warranty
A warranty made by words or conduct of the seller.

Implied Warranty
A warranty created by operation of law.

A warranty is a promise by the seller concerning some aspect of the sale, such as the quality of the goods, the quantity, and the title. The subject of warranty is regulated by the UCC as part of the law of sales. There are two types of warranties, *express* and *implied*. An express warranty is made part of the contract by the words or conduct of the seller. An implied warranty is made part of the contract by operation of the law.

Under the UCC, a warranty may arise by the course of dealing or by custom and usage of the trade. A warranty carries with it strict liability. Thus, the seller of goods is liable even though he did not know or have reason to know the goods were defective.

Privity

Privity
A contractual or other legal relationship between two or more parties.

In most states, the warranties extend to any person who may reasonably be expected to use, consume, or be affected by the goods. This includes not only the purchaser of the goods but also a subpurchaser, as illustrated in the following case.

Facts
This was an action of contract and tort whereby the plaintiff sought to recover for himself and his minor son for an injury received when opening a beer bottle. The plaintiff bought from the defendant/seller a quart bottle of beer to take home. Upon his request, his nine-year-old son opened the bottle, and in the process, the neck of the bottle broke off, inflicting a cut on the boy's finger.

Decision
The appeals court cited, among others, UCC § 2–318, which states: "A seller's warranty whether express or

implied extends to any natural person who is in the family or household of his buyer or who is a guest in his home if it is reasonable to expect that such person may use, consume or be affected by the goods and who is injured in person by breach of the warranty. A seller may not exclude or limit the operation of this section." Children of this age are to be observed daily in modern stores handling bottled merchandise of all kinds at the invitation of sellers. It is reasonable to expect that they are thereby subject to being affected and injured.

Harris v. The Great Atlantic & Pacific Tea Co., Inc., 23 Mass. App. Dec. 169 (1962).

A customer of a store can bring a suit against the distributor or manufacturer from whom the store purchased the goods. In *Nobility Homes of Texas* v. *Shivers* (Tex. Civ.App., 539 S.W.2d 190 [Tex.Civ.App. 1976]), the court allowed a secondary purchaser of a mobile home to bring action against the original manufacturer directly, even though the loss was only economic in nature.

The majority rule also allows an employee to bring a suit against the manufacturer of the product or equipment purchased by the employer for use by the employee.

Facts

Federal Cartridge Company (FCC) purchased special flame-resistant clothing from Leef Brothers (defendant/seller) to be worn by employees working on FCC's premises. While the plaintiff was handling highly volatile powder, an explosion occurred, igniting his clothing, causing it to catch fire. Plaintiff suffered first-, second-, and third-degree burns all over the body.

Decision

The court refuted Defendant/Seller's argument that an employee may not recover for a breach of an express warranty made by a supplier to an employer. The evidence indicated that defendant Leef improperly applied the duPont product to the clothing used by FCC employees, causing an insufficient level of the product to remain in the fabric following processing and thus failing to make the fabric flame-resistant. "It is clear that even though plaintiff here was without knowledge of the warranties, he was the ultimate consumer of the treated garments and the intended beneficiary of the safety provisions provided by the express warranties in the agreement between his employer and defendant."

Froysland v. Leef Bros., Inc., 293 Minn. 201, 197 N.W.2d 656 (1972).

Express Warranties

Affirmation or Promise

UCC § 2–313(1)(a) provides that "*any affirmation of fact or promise* made by the seller to the buyer which relates to the goods and becomes part of the basis of the bargain creates an express warranty that the goods shall conform to the affirmation or promise." [Emphasis added.]

No particular words are necessary to create a warranty. The word "guarantee" is treated as the equivalent of "warranty."

UCC § 2–313(2) provides that a seller's statement as to the value of the goods or a statement that purports to be merely the seller's opinion or commendation of the goods does not create a warranty, since common experience discloses that such statements cannot fairly be viewed as entering

Guarantee
Has the same meaning as "warrantee."

Puffing
Statements of opinions made by a seller; not made as representations of fact.

into the bargain. Such statements are commonly referred to as "puffing" or "sales talk." However, a statement in which the seller gives market figures relating to sales of similar goods would be a statement of fact, not of value, and hence actionable.

Although not every chance remark of the seller is a warranty, a statement that has in the circumstances and in objective judgment become part of the basis of the bargain can be considered a warranty. Also, the more expert and experienced the seller, the more likely his words will be construed to be a warranty.

Examples of words construed to be warranties are as follows: glass is "shatterproof"; the machine is "durable" (a warranty that its parts will not wear out or break when put to use); goods are "number one" (an express warranty of good quality); seller will "stand behind the goods 100 percent"; oil-well suspension plug is "as good as" the plug of the competition; "this fabric is 100 percent wool."

Facts

Plaintiff Kates bought a used pressing machine from defendant Benay. Seller stated that the machine was only one year old. Actually it had been used for more than five years. Buyer brought an action against Seller for damages on account of a breach of express warranty.

Decision

The court decided for Plaintiff/Buyer. Seller's statement that the machine was one year old was a statement of fact that was an essential part of the bargain. Seller had therefore expressly warranted that the machine was one year old, and the fact that it was older amounted to a breach of warranty.

Kates Millinery, Ltd. v. *Benay-Albee Corp.*, 114 Misc.2d 230, 450 N.Y.S.2d 975 (1982).

Examples of statements considered as only opinion are as follows: goods are "first class"; peach kernel oil "as good as the best grade of olive oil"; caramel coloring matter "just as good as or perhaps better than any"; jukebox a "good machine" in "workable condition" and "would probably not require repair."

Facts

Chase Resorts (plaintiff) bought an automatic sprinkler system from Johns-Manville Corporation (defendant) to be used to water its golf course. For the purpose of inducing the buyer, the seller claimed that the system would provide "years of trouble-free service." The system turned out to require substantial repairs. Buyer claimed that Seller committed a breach of warranty.

Decision

Judgment for Defendant/Seller. "Years of trouble-free service" was merely a matter of opinion or "puffing" and did not constitute an express warranty. At the time of the sale it was impossible to determine when the system was going to need repairs.

Chase Resorts, Inc. v. *Johns-Manville Corp.*, 476 F.Supp. 633 (E.D. Mo. 1979).

A warranty may be made after the transaction is completed, and it need not be supported by consideration (§ 2–209[1]). However, if the sales contract as modified is within the statute of frauds, it must be in writing (§ 2–209[3]).

Section 2–313(1)(a) states that a warranty is made by a seller to a buyer. Can a buyer rely on a warranty made in a manufacturer's advertising so as to hold the manufacturer liable even though the buyer did not deal directly with the manufacturer? Most courts hold the manufacturer liable on the basis of an express warranty, even though the buyer did not contract with the manufacturer (i.e., the buyer recovers although there is no privity of contract between the buyer and the manufacturer).

Description

"Any description of the goods which is made part of the basis of the bargain creates an express warranty that the goods shall conform to the description" (§ 2–313[1][b]). Thus, a descriptive name constitutes a warranty (e.g., "black grapes," "Blue Goose" tomatoes, "No. 1 Saigon Long-Grain Rice," "export-cured boneless codfish").

Facts

Plaintiff/Buyer bought a can of boned chicken manufactured by C. A. Swanson Food Company. The words "boned chicken" were printed in bold on the can's label. Moreover, Swanson's advertisement in the *Los Angeles Times* described the product as having no bones and "all white and dark meat." Plaintiff broke his tooth on a bone while eating the chicken and sued on Seller's express warranty.

Decision

Judgment for Plaintiff. The court did not accept Defendant's claim that the term boned chicken was not intended as a warranty and that it was impossible to remove all of the bones from chicken. It was held that Swanson would have to either change the labeling and the ad or improve the processing method so as to exclude all the bones. A purchaser should be able to rely on the description on the label as well as on the ad promoting the product, since they constitute express warranties.

Lane v. C. A. Swanson and Sons, 130 Cal.App.2d 210, 278 P.2d 723 (1955).

The descriptive word or phrase can be an express warranty even though it is only in the invoice or in an advertisement and not in the sales contract. It has been held that a picture in an advertisement can constitute an express warranty.

Sample or Model

"Any sample or model which is made part of the basis of the bargain creates an express warranty that the whole of the goods shall conform to the sample or model" (§ 2–313[c]).

If the seller used the sample merely to suggest the character of the subject matter of the contract, it is not a warranty by sample. However, if the seller used the sample to indicate intent that it was to *be* the character of the subject-matter of the contract, it is a warranty. In other words, if the contract is based on the understanding that the seller will supply goods according to a particular description or that the goods will be the same as the sample or a model, the seller is bound by an express warranty that the goods shall conform to the description, sample, or model. A seller who does not want to make this warranty should label the samples and models in such manner as to indicate that they are only suggestive of the material he wishes to sell and that they did not come from the goods to be sold. A sample that has been drawn from an existing bulk is considered as describing values of the goods contracted for unless it is accompanied by a denial of warranty.

In *Alafoss, H. F. v. Premium Corporation of America* (448 F.Supp. 95 [D.Minn. 1978]), it was a breach of an express warranty where a manufacturer delivered to a distributor Icelandic coats, the collars of which had significant yellow discoloration, whereas the initial samples upon which the 8,255 coats were ordered showed full, solid white collars of a silky texture.

Questions

1. What are the four legal theories upon which a liability suit may be based? Are they all regulated by the UCC?
2. What are the types of injuries resulting from a defective product? Are they all recoverable under the four liability theories?
3. Discuss privity of contract in conjunction with product liability.
4. Do all sellers' claims related to merchandise quality or quantity amount to express warranties?
5. Name a few product descriptions that would be considered express warranties.

19.2 Warranty (2)

Implied Warranties

With or without express warranties, every sale is accompanied by certain warranties implied by operation of the law. The implied warranties include the warranties of title, merchantability, and fitness for a particular purpose.

Title

Every sale of goods contains a warranty of title, i.e., the title conveyed shall be good, and the goods shall be free from any security interest, encumbrance, or other lien of which the buyer has no knowledge (§ 2–312[1]).

A finder who sells a found item breaches the warranty of title, since he is not the owner of the property. It is equally a breach of title warranty if a seller sells merchandise as "free and clear" whenever there is in fact still an unpaid loan on the goods. The warranty of title assures the buyer an undisturbed use of the sold goods.

Facts

Thomas Jefferson (plaintiff) bought a Honda motorcycle from Lawrence Jones (defendant). The buyer paid on installments, and when the last installment payment was made, the seller signed over the title document and the buyer obtained a new title registration on his own name. Two years thereafter, the police seized the motorcycle when it was discovered in a routine check that the number on the new title certificate did not correspond with the one embossed on the motorcycle frame. The cycle was subsequently returned to the buyer. The buyer now brought an action against the seller to recover the legal fees incurred to regain the motorcycle. The two Maryland lower courts held for the seller, since the buyer had not shown that anyone else had a title superior to his.

Decision

The judgments were reversed on a broader interpretation of the warranty. "(I)n light of the legal standard . . ., we conclude that, as a matter of law, there exists a warranty of title that has been breached here. An undisputed aspect of possessing good title is that a purchaser be 'enable[d] . . . to hold the [property] in peace and, if he wishes to sell it, to be reasonably certain that no flaw will appear to disturb its market value.' . . . (A)ny substantial defect in that document necessarily creates a reasonable doubt as to that ownership. . . . To be valid, such a certificate must include, among other things, the vehicle's identification number, . . . and while the owner of the vehicle may prove his title by means other than the certificate, . . . any seller of a motor vehicle who executes an assignment of the vehicle's certificate of title that contains identifying information that is different from that on the vehicle itself, knows or should know that problems concerning the buyer's ownership would arise."

Jefferson v. Jones, 286 Md. 544, 408 A.2d 1036 (Maryland, 1979).

Merchantability

A warranty that the goods shall be merchantable is implied in a contract for their sale if the seller is a merchant with respect to goods of the kind at issue (§ 2–314[1]). Essentially, the goods sold by the merchant must (1) be of medium or *average quality* and (2) be fit for the *ordinary purpose* for which such goods are used (§ 2–314[2]) for specific situations.

Merchantability
Reasonable fitness of goods for use for the purpose for which such goods are sold.

Facts

Plaintiff Daniell locked herself up inside the trunk of her 1973 Ford Ltd., admittedly, to commit suicide. She stayed in the trunk for nine days, suffering physically and mentally, and was unable to free herself until a friend found her. She brought suit against Ford Motor Company for a breach of merchantability warranty, and on a breach of express warranty, based on demonstrations that the trunk was easy to open and close. There was no way to open the trunk from the inside.

Decision

Judgment for Ford Motor. No salesperson or literature ever mentioned opening the trunk from the inside. Since the demonstrations were limited to using the trunk from the outside, there was no express warranty made. The warranty of merchantability was not breached, because trunks need only be suitable for holding luggage, carrying items, and opening and closing from the outside. It was clear that Daniell did not rely on an express warranty, since she went into the trunk with the intention of dying.

Daniell v. Ford Motor Co., Inc., 581 F.Supp. 728 (D.N.M. 1984).

Restaurants In restaurant cases, the seller can be liable if the goods are not fit for human consumption. Whether food is unfit for human consumption is a question of fact. Food for human consumption need not be actually unfit; it is sufficient if the consumer has adequate grounds for believing that it is. The fact that some person on the witness stand would be willing to eat the food would not be a defense. In many states (California, Louisiana, Massachusetts, North Carolina), the warranty of fitness for human consumption does not apply if there is an object in the food that is not foreign to the food (e.g., cherry pit in cherry pie, bone in fish chowder, oyster shell in oyster soup, chicken bone in chicken pie)(*Mix v. Ingersoll Candy Co.*, 6 Cal.2d 674, 59 P.2d 144 [1936]). Other states (Maryland, Pennsylvania, Wisconsin) have rejected the so-called *foreign-natural* test in favor of what is known as the *reasonable expectation* test. Under this test, the jury must make a determination whether the buyer could reasonably have expected the object in the food. If he could not, the buyer will recover. Examples of recovery under this test are chicken bone in a chicken sandwich, oyster shell in canned oysters used in making oyster stew, and chicken bone in chow mein (*Zabner v. Howard Johnson's, Inc.*, 201 So.2d 824 [Fla.App. 1967]).

Self-Service Stores In the case of self-service stores, recent cases have found an implied warranty of merchantability when the customer has removed bottles from the display counter after which one of the bottles exploded causing injury (*Sheeskin v. Giant Foods, Inc.*, 20 Md.App. 611, 318 A.2d 874 [1974]; *Gillispie v. Great Atlantic & Pacific Tea Co.*, 14 N.C.App. 1, 187 S.E.2d 441 [1972]). In the Sheeskin decision, the court stated that the offer consisted in placing the goods on the shelf with a price stamped upon them. The acceptance consisted in the act of taking physical possession of the goods with the intent to purchase them, which manifested an intent to accept the offer and a promise to take them to the checkout counter and pay for them there. (This legal analysis and interpretation of the situation are perhaps arguable, for under those circumstances no sale has yet been made, but a bailment for mutual benefit may exist whereby bailor, who is the seller, may be liable for injuries caused to bailee by the bailed property.)

Secondhand Goods In the case of used or secondhand goods sold by a dealer, no court has excluded the possibility of an implied warranty of merchantability. However, some courts (because of the particular facts in the cases) have not found such an implied warranty. On the other hand, one court found the implied warranty in the sale of a secondhand airplane where damages were incurred in repairing the plane when a defect in the fuel supply system caused a fire three days after the sale (*Georgia Timberlands, Inc. v. Southern Airways Co.*, 125 Ga.App. 404, 188 S.E.2d 108 [1972]). In accord: *Overland Bond & Investment Corp. v. Howard* (9 Ill.App.3d 348, 292 N.E.2d 168 [1972]), used automobile from a dealer; *Hob's Refrigeration and Air Conditioning, Inc. v. Poche* (304 So.2d 326 [La. 1974], rebuilt compressor not fit for use.

In most courts, *leases* and *bailments* of chattels are covered by the implied warranty of fitness for ordinary purpose and, if sufficient facts are presented, by the implied warranty of fitness for a particular purpose.

Cintrone v. Hertz Truck Leasing and Rental Service
45 N.J. 434, 212 A.2d 769 (1965).

Francis, J. Plaintiff Francisco Cintrone was injured while a passenger in a truck leased by his employer from the defendant. In his complaint in this action he charged that the accident in which he was injured resulted from defendant's negligent inspection or maintenance of the leased vehicle or from a breach of defendant's warranty that the vehicle was fit and safe for use. (Whether the alleged warranty was express or implied was not specified.) The trial court dismissed the warranty claim, . . .

Defendant Hertz Truck Leasing & Rental Service is in the business of leasing and renting various types of motor vehicles to the public. Plaintiff's employer, Contract Packers, Inc., had leased nine trucks from defendant for use in its business. One of them was a 1959 Ford, 22 feet long and 11 feet high. . . .

On April 3, 1961 the Ford truck was scheduled for a delivery trip. Cintrone was to be the helper that day and one Robert Sottilare, another Contract Packers employee, the driver. . . .

After leaving Dover the men headed for Suffern, New York. About noontime, as Sottilare was going along Route 202, apparently within the limits of Suffern, he came around a bend in the road and saw an overhead bridge or trestle a hundred feet or so ahead of him. It was a low bridge, the clearance only 9 feet, 6 inches. Sottilare applied his brakes; they failed. The truck "just kept going" forward until the peak of its body hit the overhead structure. As Cintrone put it, he saw "the driver pumping the brakes. And he never stopped the truck because the brakes didn't work. . . . Plaintiff seeks a reversal of the adverse judgment, however, on the ground that the contractual relationship between Hertz and his employer gave rise to an implied continuing promissory warranty by Hertz that the truck in question was fit for the purposes for which plaintiff's employer rented it, i.e., operation and transportation of goods on the public highways. He urges further that under the proof adduced the failure of the brakes and the consequent accident created a factual issue for jury determination as to whether there was a breach of the implied warranty. Therefore he claims the court erred in refusing to submit that issue for jury consideration.

. . . The nature of the U-drive-it enterprise is such that a heavy burden of responsibility for the safety of lessees and for members of the public must be imposed upon it. The courts have long accepted the fact that defective trucks and cars are dangerous instrumentalities on highways. They present great potentiality for harm to other highway users as well as to their own drivers and passengers. Therefore the offering to the public of trucks and pleasure vehicles for hire necessarily carries with it a representation that they are fit for operation. This representation is of major significance because both new and used cars and trucks are rented. . . . The nature of the business is such that the customer is expected to, and in fact must, rely ordinarily on the express or implied representation of fitness for immediate use. . . .

. . . Accordingly, we are of the opinion (1) that the leasing agreement gave rise to a continuing implied promissory warranty that the leased trucks would be fit for plaintiff's employer's use for the duration of the lease, . . ., and (3) that the evidence created a factual issue for determination by the jury as to whether defendant Hertz had been guilty of a breach of that warranty which produced the collision and plaintiff's injury. . . .

For the reasons stated, the judgment for the defendant is reversed, and the cause is remanded for a new trial to be had in accordance with the views outlined.

Fitness for Particular Purpose

Where the seller has reason to know the particular purpose for which the goods are required and that the buyer is relying on the seller's skill or judgment to select or furnish the goods, there is an implied warranty that the goods shall be fit for such purpose (§ 2–315). For example, B told S, a retail paint merchant, that the paint on his stucco house was powdery and that he wanted advice as to what paint he should use to cover the walls. S recommended a certain paint, which B purchased and used according to the instructions S gave him. A few months later, the paint began to peel and blister. B has a cause of action for damages, because the seller knew the particular purpose of the buyer and had reason to know that the buyer was relying on the seller's skill and judgment in selecting the appropriate paint.

There is no breach of warranty of fitness for particular purpose if the buyer relied on his own skill and judgment, as shown in the following case.

Facts

Layne-Atlantic, a contractor constructing an underground well for United Geological Survey, needed to use a fiber-glass pipe manufactured by Koppers (defendant/seller). Seller recommended a pipe of 1.5 inches thick, but for budgetary reasons, UGS specified a pipe of .3 inch thick. When the pipe collapsed, Layne (plaintiff/buyer) brought an action on a breach of warranty of fitness for a particular purpose.

Decision

Judgment for Defendant/Seller. There was no breach of warranty of fitness for a particular purpose, since there was no evidence that Layne had relied on the skill and judgment of Koppers in making the purchase. The mere fact that the pipe had collapsed did not mean that it was not fit, and thus no breach of the warranty of merchantability occurred.

Layne-Atlantic Co. v. Koppers Co., Inc., 214 Va. 467, 201 S.E.2d 609 (1974).

Exclusion, Modification, and Disclaimer

Disclaimer
Renunciation or repudiation of a claim, power, or right of a person.

Disclaimers or exclusions of both express and implied warranties are construed against the seller. In some states, disclaimers are prohibited by consumer protection laws or by public policy.

UCC § 2–719(3) provides that a limitation of consequential damages for injury to the person in the case of consumer goods is prima facie unconscionable, but limitation of damages where the loss is commercial is not. An exception is where it is a recognized practice of the trade to exclude consequential damages or where they have been consistently excluded in prior dealings.

In *Majors* v. *Kalo Laboratories, Inc.* (407 F.Supp. 20 [M.D. Ala. 1975]), the court allowed a farmer consequential damages to his crop. It found the exclusionary clause unconscionable, because the damages it allowed (merely a refund of the purchase price) were grossly disproportionate to the damages it knew buyers would suffer if the product (soybean inoculant) did not work. Furthermore, the court noted the product's defects were latent. In *Collins v. Uniroyal, Inc.* (64 N.J. 260, 315 A.2d 16 [1974]), action was brought for death of a tire buyer in an accident occurring when the automobile went out of control due to failure of the manufacturer's tire. In holding for the plaintiff, the court held that the clause that limited the buyer's damages to replacement of the tire was unconscionable. To the same effect, see *McCarty v. E. J. Korvette, Inc.* (28 Md.App. 421, 347 A.2d 253 [1975]), citing and following *Collins*.

By Inspection: Express Warranties

A buyer does not have to inspect or examine the goods but may rely solely on the seller's express warranties. When the seller makes an express warranty and the buyer does not inspect, although an inspection would have revealed that the seller's representations were false, the seller is liable, since the buyer is justified in believing the seller's representations.

By Inspection: Implied Warranties

In the case of implied warranties, the seller can demand that the buyer inspect the goods or a sample or a model. If the buyer refuses, all implied warranties are disclaimed. If the buyer does examine the goods, there is no implied warranty as to defects that such examination should have revealed (§ 2–316[3][b]).

It has been held that where defects cannot be uncovered by inspection but only after use, the buyer can ignore a clause that requires inspection and still recover for the breach of warranty.

In *Twin Lakes Manufacturing Co. v. Coffey* (222 Va. 467, 281 S.E.2d 864 [1981]), a buyer inspected and bought an unassembled mobile home. After the home was assembled, major defects became evident. The court awarded the buyer the full price paid. Buyer's inspection of the unassembled home did not waive the implied warranty, as the defects were latent and could not have been discovered before the home was assembled.

Description Warranty

A clause excluding all warranties, express or implied, will not disclaim the warranty of description unless it is within the contemplation of both parties that such warranty is to be disclaimed. To make the disclaimer effective, the seller should state in conspicuous language that there is no warranty of description and place the disclaimer after the language of description.

Trade Usage Warranty

An effective disclaimer in the course of dealing or trade usage should be conspicuous and should state that the buyer acknowledges that (1) no warranties implied by custom or usage have become part of the contract, (2) in their trade, it is customary not to give warranties, and (3) prior dealings do not imply any warranties. But note the effect of the Magnuson-Moss Warranty Act, discussed at the end of this subchapter.

Automobile Warranty

Automobile disclaimers of warranties are usually so strict as to be misleading. Liability is usually limited to repair or replacement of defective parts. Although UCC § 2–316(4) permits contractual limitation of warranties, the courts treat disclaimers that are too strict as ineffective. One of the leading cases in the United States held an automobile disclaimer void on public policy grounds (because the buyer has no bargaining power with automobile manufacturers as to disclaimers) and permitted the wife of the buyer of the automobile to recover for personal injury damages from the manufacturer for breach of implied warranty of merchantability (*Henningsen v. Bloomfield Motors, Inc.*, 32 N.J. 358, 161 A.2d 69 [1960]). Other courts have followed the same reasoning. The California Supreme Court held not only that the disclaimer was invalid but also that the manufacturer and retailer were strictly liable in tort for the buyer's personal injuries (*Vandermark v. Ford Motor Co.*, 61 Cal.2d 256, 37 Cal.Rptr. 896, 391 P.2d 168 [1964]). (See subchapter 19.3 for a discussion of strict liability in tort.)

Family Use of Goods

UCC § 2–318 provides that a seller's warranty extends to any natural person who is in the family or household of the buyer or who is a guest in the buyer's home if it is reasonable to expect that such person may use, consume, or be affected by the goods and thus could be injured by breach of the warranty. The purpose of this section is to give a limited class of beneficiaries the benefit of the same express or implied warranty that the buyer received regardless of lack of privity of contract. Virginia adopted a provision in lieu of § 2–318 that eliminates the requirement of privity in all actions against the manufacturer and seller of goods for negligence and breach of warranty. California and Utah did not adopt § 2–318, since prior case law went further and did not require privity of contract in the sale of food and drugs or in the case of an express warranty made by a manufacturer. Some states ignore the requirement that a guest must be in the buyer's home at the time of the damage.

Modern decisions permit recovery for property damages as well as for personal injuries.

The last sentence of § 2–318 forbids the seller from excluding liability to persons to whom the warranties that benefit the buyer would extend under this section. It does not mean that a seller is precluded from excluding or disclaiming a warranty that might otherwise arise in connection with a sale if the exclusion is permitted under § 2–316; nor does it preclude the seller from limiting the remedies of his own buyer and therefore of any beneficiaries under §§ 2–718 and 2–719. Provisions that exclude or modify warranties or limit remedies for breach of contract apply equally to the beneficiaries and the buyer under this section.

Title Warranty

A warranty of title can be excluded only by specific language or by circumstances that give the buyer reason to know that the person selling does not claim title in himself or that the seller is purporting to sell only such right or title as he or a third person may have (§ 2–312[2]). The language should include the word "title" and be conspicuous. No warranty of title arises when the seller makes the sale in a representative capacity, such as a sheriff, an auctioneer, or an administrator of a decedent's estate.

Merchantability Warranty

A disclaimer of the implied warranty of merchantability must specifically mention merchantability and, in in writing, must be conspicuous (§ 2–316[2]). "Conspicuous" means clear and distinct language and prominently set forth in large, bold print in such position as to compel notice. An effective disclaimer would state that the seller does not warrant the goods to be merchantable.

Particular Purpose Warranty

A disclaimer of an implied warranty for a particular purpose must be in writing and must be conspicuous. In *Smith v. Sharpenstein* (13 UUC Reporting Service 609 [C.A.Okl., 1973]), the plaintiff entered into a written equipment lease with an option to purchase a used truck-tractor from the defendants. The court held that the inconspicuous disclaimer of the implied warranty of fitness for a particular purpose was ineffective, even though the plaintiff had read the disclaimer. (See § 2–316[2] for an example of an effective disclaimer.)

Other Ways of Excluding Implied Warranties

If the contract states that the buyer is taking the goods "as is" or "with all faults" or "as they stand," all implied warranties are excluded (§ 2–316[3][a]). A case in point is *Hutchinson Homes, Inc. v. Guerdon Industries, Inc.* (143 Ga.App. 664, 239 S.E.2d 553 [1977]), where a statement in boldface "NOTE: SOLD AS IS" on the invoice in a purchase of a mobile home was considered sufficient.

However, a catch phrase disclaimer, such as "all warranties, express or implied, are excluded," is probably ineffective to exclude express or implied warranties, especially if the words are not conspicuous (§ 2–316). Although a disclaimer may be effective to disclaim warranties, the same disclaimer would be ineffective in a suit based on negligence or strict liability in tort where the product was unreasonably dangerous to the user or consumer. This is the trend even where the product is secondhand.

Usage of trade may disclaim warranties (e.g., buyer who purchased from a junk dealer or at a sheriff's sale cannot rely on implied warranties). Also, course of dealing can exclude implied warranties (§ 2–316[3][c]).

Notice of Defect

UCC § 2–607(3)(a) states that the buyer must notify the seller within a reasonable time after he discovers or should have discovered any breach or be barred from any remedy. This notice requirement is not necessary where the buyer does not bring suit against the immediate seller.

Contributory Negligence

Contributory Negligence
Conduct on the part of the plaintiff which contributes to or causes plaintiff's injury, and may be used as a defense by the defendant.

In most courts, the fact that the plaintiff's actions or inactions contributed to the injury is not available as a defense for the seller of the product. For example, the plaintiff was reading a book and began eating a candy bar. She noticed that the candy did not taste just right. After eating about one third of the candy bar, she looked at it and saw that it was covered with worms and webbing. The court held for the plaintiff and said that in an implied warranty case there is no duty to inspect a candy bar before eating it (*Kassouf* v. *Lee Brothers, Inc.*, 209 Cal.App.2d 568, 26 Cal.Rptr. 276 [1962]).

Comparative Negligence
Negligence of an injured plaintiff which reduces the amount of damages recoverable from a negligent defendant.

In those states where the doctrine of Comparative Negligence is adopted, the injured party's own negligence reduces the amount of recovery proportionately.

Assumption of Risk

Assumption of Risk
Voluntarily exposing oneself to a known danger.

In an action for breach of warranty, it is necessary for the plaintiff to prove the existence of the warranty, that the warranty was broken, and that the breach was the proximate cause of the loss sustained.

In most courts, assumption of the risk is a defense in an action for breach of warranty, because the plaintiff's conduct rather than the seller's breach is the proximate cause of the loss. For example, a buyer who was drinking a soft drink from a bottle gagged on a foreign substance. She spit out the substance and proceeded to finish the drink. As she finished the drink, she gagged again and discovered she had suffered injuries from the foreign substance (ground glass) still in the bottle. Her action in finishing the drink (following an examination of the contents that should have indicated the defect complained of) could be shown as a matter bearing on whether the breach itself (the particles of glass) was the cause of the injury. It could be found that her behavior broke the causal chain between the breach of warranty and her injury. In other words, she assumed the risk of injury.

Statute of Limitations

An action for breach of any contract for sale must be begun within four years after the cause of action has accrued (§ 2–725[1]). A cause of action accrues when the breach occurs, regardless of the aggrieved party's lack of knowledge of the breach. A breach of warranty occurs when tender of delivery is made (§ 2–725[2]).

Federal Consumer Protection

In 1974, Congress enacted the Magnuson-Moss Warranty Act, effective in January of 1975, to provide purchasers of consumer products adequate information concerning written warranties made for such products and to prevent false and deceptive warranties. The Act is administered and enforced by the Federal Trade Commission (FTC).

The Act was a response to various warranty problems:

1. Many warranties were not understandable.
2. Many implied warranties were disclaimed (no responsibility claimed for breach).
3. Many warranties were unfair.
4. Many warranties were not honored.

To remedy these practices, the Act requires the following:

1. Disclosure clearly stated and in understandable language of the warranty.
2. A statement that the warranty is either full or limited.
3. A prohibition against disclaiming any implied warranty where a written warranty is provided.
4. A means of informally settling warranty disputes which is optional with the warrantor.

The Act is applicable only where a consumer product containing a written warranty is put on the market. A consumer product is defined as any item of tangible personal property normally for family, household, or personal use that is transmitted in interstate commerce.

The Act differentiates between a full and a limited warranty, one of which, for any product costing $10 or more, must be designated on the written warranty itself. A full warranty requires the warrantor to repair without charge the product to conform to the warranty, to place no time limit on the duration of any implied warranty, to give the consumer the option of a full refund or replacement if repair is unsuccessful, and to exclude consequential damages (damages caused by the product's failure to function as warranted) only if such an exclusion is clearly noted. A limited warranty cannot disclaim or modify any implied warranty but can limit the duration to that of the written warranty, provided that any such limitation is reasonable, conscionable (not totally one-sided and oppressive), and conspicuously stated. No other new or expanded remedies are provided.

The Magnuson-Moss Act preempts only provisions of the UCC that conflict with it. However, the Act provides that any state law that is more protective of consumers may prevail and be enforced. In practice, the Act would nullify UCC provisions that permit disclaimers of implied warranties of merchantability and fitness for intended purpose.

A consumer product buyer who does not give the warrantor a reasonable opportunity to repair the product cannot avail himself of the right to a refund of the purchase price under the Act. In *Pratt* v. *Winnebago Industries, Inc.* (463 F.Supp. 709 [W.D.Pa. 1979]), the requirement that the buyer return the product for repair was found reasonable and voluntarily accepted and thus not an impermissible duty under the Act.

Questions

1. What are the implied warranties in a sale?
2. Discuss restaurant cases.
3. What are the basic rules concerning warranty exclusions and disclaimers?
4. Does the buyer's inspection of the goods prior to purchase exclude the warranties?
5. What are Contributory Negligence and Assumption of Risk? Are they applicable as a seller's defense in a product liability suit?

19.3 Strict Liability in Tort

Definition

Strict Liability
Liability without proof of negligence.

The most important remedy in product liability cases today is strict liability in tort, which basically means liability without proof of negligence or liability without fault. The remedy is meant to compensate for the unequal economic and bargaining power between business on the one hand and the product user or consumer on the other hand. As the court concluded in *Price* v. *Shell Oil Co.* (2 Cal.3d 245, 85 Cal.Rptr. 178, 466 P.2d 722 [1970]): "Essentially, the paramount policy to be promoted by the rule is the protection of otherwise defenseless victims of manufacturing defects and the spreading throughout society of the cost of compensating them."

Although this legal policy is laudable, it is obvious that a too liberal application of the strict liability concept may suffocate business as noted earlier.

Buyer's Advantages

From the plaintiff's point of view, strict liability in tort has several advantages over breach of warranty:

1. It is a simpler remedy, requiring only that the product be defective, that the defect existed at the time the product left the seller's hands, and that the defect caused the plaintiff's damages.
2. The requirement of privity of contract is completely eliminated.
3. The injured party does not have to give notice, as in the case of a breach of warranty.
4. The producer of a product cannot use his superior bargaining power or knowledge to disclaim liability, as disclaimers are ineffective.
5. The plaintiff may be any person foreseeably affected by the goods (e.g., buyer, user, consumer, employee, or bystander).
6. Contributory negligence generally is not a bar to the action.

Concept Elements

The following description of the rules of strict liability in tort has been adopted in most courts. The Restatement, Second, Torts, § 402A, provides:

1. One who sells any product in a defective condition unreasonably dangerous to the user or consumer or to his property is subject to liability for physical harm thereby caused to the ultimate user or consumer or to his property if
   a. The seller is engaged in the business of selling such a product.
   b. The product is expected to and does reach the user or consumer without substantial change in the condition in which it is sold.
2. The rule stated in (1) applies although
   a. The seller has exercised all possible care in the preparation and sale of his product.
   b. The user or consumer has not bought the product from or entered into any contractual relation with the seller.

   Regarding (1), the courts in some states (e.g., California) hold that it is not necessary to prove the product is unreasonably dangerous.

Unreasonably Dangerous

A seller, whether a manufacturer or retailer, who knows or has reason to know that the product is dangerous or is likely to be dangerous is liable for injury caused by that product unless the seller warns of the danger.

The modern trend is that the seller is liable, even though he did not know or did not have reason to know of the dangerous character, such as in the sale of a product in a sealed container.

In *Matthews* v. *Campbell Soup Co.* (380 F.Supp. 1061 [S.D.Tex. 1974]), the federal district court applying *McKisson* v. *Sales Affiliates Inc.* (416 S.W.2d 787 [Tex. 1967]) construed unwholesome or unfit food products to be unreasonably dangerous under Restatement, Second, Torts, Section 402A.

The product by itself does not have to be dangerous. Strict liability may exist for an injury resulting from the wrong use of merchandise that is intrinsically harmless if the manufacturer does not explain how the device operates or give sufficient information concerning the danger involved or warn of the harmful effect of an overdose, such as of a drug, etc. If the damage in fact occurs, the product that is initially harmless can be considered or equated with a defective product. Section 402A requires the seller to provide sufficient *warnings* and *instructions* "in order to prevent the product from being unreasonably dangerous."

Facts

Kresge (defendant/seller) sold a refracting telescope to Midgley, a 13-year-old child. The warning on the package stated that the sun should be viewed only through a filter to be attached, but it did not explain how to attach the filter. Midgley improperly attached the filter, and Midgley's eyesight was damaged permanently.

Decision

Judgment for the plaintiff/buyer. The court considered the instructions on the package inadequate. The warning pertained only to the use of a filter, but there were no adequate instructions on how to install the filter.

Midgley v. S.S. Kresge Co., 55 Cal.App.3d 67, 127 Cal.Rptr. 217 (1976).

Whether or not a product is "unreasonably" dangerous and whether or not there is "sufficient" warning are questions of facts, which are usually for the jury to decide.

Defective Product

The original formula for "strict liability in tort" refers to any product in a "defective condition unreasonably dangerous."

1. A product may be defective owing to the careless production of the product involving the *failure to follow* an adequate *design*. For example, the steering mechanism may turn loose, causing the driver to lose control of the car; oil may leak from the brake system, rendering the brakes inoperative; the wires of an electrical appliance may not be properly insulated, causing a severe shock to the user.

2. A product may also be defective because of *improper design,* e.g., placing the fuel tank in an automobile in such a location as to cause a fire on impact, as in the case of *Arbet* v. *Gussarson,* involving a 1967 Rambler station wagon (66 Wis.2d 551, 225 N.W.2d 431 [1975]).

The absence of an adequate safety system may also amount to a defective design of the equipment, as shown in the following case.

Facts

An accident occurred on September 24, 1972, at the Clark factory in Reading, Pennsylvania, as Heckman (plaintiff) was operating the press. When Heckman placed a piece of metal in the machine to be cut, the ram came down on his hand, resulting in the amputation of several fingers along with other damage. Federal Press (defendant/manufacturer) did not provide any safety device for the machine when it sold the machine to Clark factory. Clark did purchase a protection guard from another source, but the guard was not being used at the time the injury occurred. Heckman brought a suit to recover damages caused by the injuries.

Decision

Judgment for the plaintiff. "If a manufacturer fails to provide reasonable safety devices for a product and thus creates an unreasonable risk of harm to the user, the fact that the manufacturer may expect the user to provide a protective appliance is not sufficient to preclude liability in most circumstances. [Citations.] The issue is one which should be decided by a jury in light of such matters as the feasibility of incorporating safety features during manufacture of the machine, the likelihood that users will not secure adequate devices, whether the machinery is of a standard make or built to the customer's specifications, the relative expertise of manufacturer and customer, the extent of risk to the user, and the seriousness of injury which may be anticipated."

Heckman v. *Federal Press Co.*, 587 F.2d 612 (3d Cir. 1978).

A similar case is *Kennedy* v. *Custom Ice Equipment Co., Inc.*, (Supreme Ct. of South Carolina, 271 S.C. 171, 246 S.E.2d 176 [1978]), in which a manufacturer of industrial ice equipment was held strictly liable for injuries sustained by a 15-year-old employee, who lost an arm when operating an unprotected ice conveyor. The absence of protective shields rendered the product defective as designed by the manufacturer.

If there is no defect in the product itself, however, and the use of the product *per se* will not bring about any dangerous effect, the fact that an injury nevertheless occurs because of some extraneous circumstances will not impose upon the seller the burden of strict liability.

Facts

On July 23, 1970, Thriftway Market in Pasco, Washington, received a box of Chiquita brand bananas from Associated Grocers. Later in the morning, when Tom Anderson, the produce manager, removed the box from the top of the stack, a banana spider of six inches in diameter—a Heteropoda Venatoria—leaped from some wet burlap onto his left hand and bit him. Tom Anderson died of heart failure nine months later. His wife brought this action to recover damages for the alleged wrongful death of her husband. In addition to negligence, the action was based upon (1) strict liability for a defect in product and (2) breach of implied warranty of merchantability and fitness, both of which were rejected by the trial court in a summary judgment.

Decision

Judgment confirmed. The bananas were not in any way defective or unfit for the purpose intended. The court noted that the spider was neither in the bananas nor in the container and ruled that although the container may have transported the spider, the product was not defective or unfit. In these circumstances, neither the doctrine of strict liability nor breach of implied warranty of fitness applies.

Anderson v. Associated Grocers, Inc., 11 Wash.App. 774, 525 P.2d 284 (1974).

Liable Parties

The basic policy of the strict liability rule is to protect "the defenseless victims of manufacturing defects." The remedy is not available in cases where the parties are of equal economic and bargaining power. It was denied, for instance, when Scandinavian Airline System sued United Aircraft for some defective jet engines it purchased. The federal court referred to *Kaiser Steel Corp. v. Westinghouse Elec. Corp.*, a California case, in which it stated: ". . . (T)he doctrine of products liability does not apply as between parties who: (1) deal in a commercial setting; (2) from positions of relatively equal economic strength; (3) bargain the specifications of the product; and (4) negotiate concerning the risk of loss from defects in it."

When the strict liability rule is applicable, all parties involved in the marketing process, whether manufacturer, distributor, retailer, manufacturer of the component part, assembler, lessor, licensor, or bailor, may be held liable.

Wholesaler

The Restatement, Second, Torts, § 402A, provides that strict liability is imposed on any person engaged in the business of selling products for use or consumption who sells a defective product. This includes not only a manufacturer or retail seller but also a wholesaler or distributor.

Suppliers of Parts

Frequently the manufacturer of a finished product purchased some of the components that went into the finished product from manufacturers of those components. Let us assume that an automobile manufacturer uses a component part for the brake system that has been made by another manufacturer and that the component part was defective. Most courts hold that the manufacturer of the defective component part is liable for injuries sustained by the user of the finished product as a result of that defective part if no essential change has been made in it by the manufacturer of the finished product. The liability is based on strict liability in tort. It is no defense that the manufacturer of the finished product failed to discover the defect by inspection or testing.

The manufacturer of the finished product is not excused from liability because of a defective condition resulting exclusively from a defective component part. Liability is based on breach of warranty, strict liability in tort, or negligence. If the manufacturer of the component part had a good reputation and if there had been no prior complaints or defects with respect to that part, such evidence would tend to show absence of negligence on the part of the manufacturer of the finished product. However, this should not preclude recovery on the grounds of breach of warranty or strict liability in tort.

Secondhand Dealers

The trend is to hold secondhand dealers in strict tort liability for defective products.

Lessor or Bailor

A lessor or bailor of personal property is liable for injuries caused by the defective condition of goods that makes the goods unreasonably dangerous (Restatement, Second, Torts, § 408). California has extended its strict liability rule to include such lessors and bailers (*Price* v. *Shell Oil Co.*, 2 Cal.3d 245, 85 Cal.Rptr. 178, 466 P.2d 722 [1970]).

Facts

A truck was leased by the defendant, Ryder Truck Rental, Inc., to Gagliardi Brothers, Inc., in the regular course of Ryder's truck rental business. The truck, operated by a Gagliardi employee, was involved in a collision in an intersection. Because of a failure of its braking system, the truck did not stop for a traffic light and struck the rear of an automobile that had stopped for the signal, causing that automobile to collide with the vehicle driven by the plaintiff, Dorothy Martin. As a result, Martin was injured, her car was damaged, and she and her husband brought suit against Ryder. The lower court decided in favor of Ryder.

Decision

Judgment reversed. "... In *Cintrone* v. *Hertz Truck Leasing, etc.* (45 N.J. 434, 212 A.2d 769 [1965]), the New Jersey Supreme Court applied strict liability in tort to a motor vehicle bailment situation because '(a) bailor for hire, such as a person in the U-drive-it business, puts motor vehicle in the stream of commerce in a fashion not unlike a manufacturer or retailer'; subjects such a leased vehicle 'to more sustained use on the highways than most ordinary car purchasers'; and by the very nature of his business, exposes 'the bailee, his employees, passengers and the traveling public ... to a greater *quantum* of potential danger of harm from defective vehicles than usually arises out of sales by the manufacturer.' . . . The extension of the doctrine of strict tort liability to bailors-lessors has been limited, however, to leases made in the regular course of a rental business, the doctrine being applicable only in a commercial setting by its very nature."

The court stated, furthermore, "Bystander recovery is the prevailing rule in the application of the doctrine of strict tort liability by the overwhelming weight of authority. Fairness and logic, as well as the philosophy underlying the doctrine, require that an injured bystander be covered in its application. . . . It is noteworthy that under the UCC § 2–318 an injured bystander may be protected as one 'affected by' a defective product in a direct sale situation covered by an implied warranty."

Martin v. Ryder Truck Rental, Inc., 353 A.2d 581 (Del. 1976).

Seller of Real Estate

Court decisions have extended the strict liability tort theory to the sale of real estate. In *Schipper* v. *Levitt & Sons, Inc.* (44 N.J. 70, 207 A.2d 314 [1965]), the court held a home developer liable on the theories of negligence, implied warranty, and strict liability where a hot water system had been installed in an apparently defective manner, resulting in the scalding of the infant plaintiff (Schipper negligence principles held applicable to all builders in *Totten* v. *Gruzen,* 52 N.J. 202, 245 A.2d 1 [1968]). In *Kreigler* v. *Eichler Homes, Inc.* (269 Cal.App.2d 244, 74 Cal.Rptr. 749 [1969]), the home developer was held liable for the failure of a radiant heating system in a concrete slab foundation that failed after eight years of use. In *Avner* v. *Longridge Estates* (272 Cal.App.2d 607, 77 Cal.Rptr. 633 [1969]), the defendant was held liable for slope failure and pad subsidence due to inadequate soil compaction.

A builder-seller may be insolvent or uninsured, in which case the only remedy may be against the financier of the project. The lender may be liable (1) on the theory of negligence based on the fact that the lender exercised extensive control over the project and therefore assumed a duty of reasonable care to the ultimate purchasers (*Connor* v. *Great Western Savings and Loan,* 69 Cal.2d 850, 73 Cal.Rptr. 369, 447 P.2d 609 [1968]), (2) as a joint venturer with the builder-developer, or (3) as an independent lot manufacturer who wholesales the subdivided lots to the developer. *Cf. Callaizakis* v. *Astor Development Co.* (4 Ill.App.3d 163, 280 N.E.2d 512 [1972]).

Services

The general trend is to impose strict liability in tort in the case of services (e.g., patron's hair and scalp injured through the application of a permanent wave lotion). However, the doctrine is not used in the case of professional services, although a recent case held a hospital strictly liable for defective services rendered to a patient (*Johnson* v. *Sears, Roebuck and Co.,* 355 F.Supp. 1065 [E.D.Wis. 1973]).

Contributory Negligence

Generally, when a plaintiff fails to discover a defect or to guard against the possibility a defect exists, such negligence is not a bar to recovery. This is true even when the consumer or user is careless in the use of the product, since in most courts, contributory negligence on the part of the plaintiff is no defense to the seller.

However, there can be no recovery when the plaintiff's conduct is the sole proximate cause of the injury (e.g., plaintiff was in a semiconscious state from a sleeping pill and her combustible nightgown caught fire while she was smoking a cigarette in bed).

Assumption of Risk

Assumption of Risk
Voluntarily exposing oneself to a known danger.

Generally, the user of a product who voluntarily and unreasonably proceeds to use the product in the face of danger that he knows or should know exists is barred from recovery on the grounds that he assumed the risk of danger. Thus, if a conspicuous warning was on the label of a product, the use of the product could amount to an assumption of the risk and preclude recovery.

Generally, misuse or mishandling of the product will bar recovery (e.g., where a bottled beverage is knocked against a radiator to remove the cap). However, where the misuse is foreseeable, the maker has a duty to protect against the misuse by proper manufacture or design or by warning the user.

The Supreme Court of California in *Daly* v. *General Motors Corp.* (20 Cal.3d 725, 144 Cal.Rptr. 380, 575 P.2d 1162 [1978]) held that assumption of the risk or product misuse will no longer be a complete bar to recovery and, instead, applied the comparative negligence doctrine (i.e., the plaintiff's recovery is reduced to the extent that his own lack of reasonable care contributed to the injury).

Damages

Strict Liability
Liability without proof of negligence.

It has been held that while an injured or damaged plaintiff can recover for both his personal injuries and property damage in an appropriate strict liability case, the plaintiff cannot recover for purely economic or commercial losses. However, the plaintiff may be able to recover under the theory of breach of express warranty, if that is applicable to the facts of the case.

Recent cases have awarded punitive damages and attorney fees in strict liability cases where the defendant has been guilty of concealing material facts concerning the safety of the product, where there has been an intentional misrepresentation of the product, or where the manufacturer has deliberately neglected for business reasons to caution customers and the public of a known defect (e.g., failure to redesign television set or warn of fire hazard that resulted in severe burns to plaintiff (*Gillham* v. *Admiral Corp.*, 523 F.2d 102 [6th Cir. 1975], certiorari denied, 424 U.S. 913, 96 S.Ct. 1113, 47 L.Ed.2d 318 (1976)).

In *Grimshaw* v. *Ford Motor Co.* (119 Cal.App.3d 757, 174 Cal.Rptr. 348 [1981]), the Court of Appeals of California permitted a passenger who was badly burned in an explosion of a defective Pinto to collect both compensatory and punitive damages but disallowed recovery to the heirs of the deceased driver of the vehicle. The personal representative of the driver could have recovered punitive damages. The court reaffirmed the expectation of safety rule in such cases enunciated in *Barker* v. *Lull Engineering Co.* (20 Cal.3d 413, 143 Cal.Rptr. 225, 573 P.2d 443 [1978]).

Intentional Torts

In *Sprague* v. *Frank J. Sanders Lincoln Mercury, Inc.* (120 Cal.App.3d 412, 174 Cal.Rptr. 608 [1981]), the plaintiff, injured because of the dealer's failure to repair known defects in a new car, introduced evidence of pain and suffering. The California reviewing court held that the suit was not in contract but properly alleged a tort (deceit, Civil Code Sec. 1709), thus supported recovery of punitive damages.

QUESTIONS

1. What is "strict liability in tort?" What is the basic policy underlying the rule?
2. Does a product have to be defective for the remedy to apply?
3. What are the two ways in which a product is defective?
4. In light of the character of the parties in the case, when is the strict liability rule not applicable?
5. How do "contributory negligence" and "assumption of risk" affect strict liability?

PROBLEMS

1. Cutter Laboratories manufactured and sold Salk polio vaccine. One shipment mistakenly contained live virus instead of only inactivated virus. The vaccine was injected into children and caused poliomyelitis. In the action against them, Cutter Laboratories defends on the grounds that there was no privity of contract between the manufacturer and the buyer, since the buyer purchased the vaccine from the pharmacy and not from them, and since the plaintiff's children were not the actual buyers, but their doctors. Decision?

2. P, the manager of a hotel, purchased on behalf of his employer four bottles of champagne produced and bottled by D. The champagne was to be consumed by guests of the hotel. While P was preparing the champagne for use, a cap from one of the bottles suddenly ejected and hit P in the eye, causing serious injury. P sues D for breach of warranty. D defends on the grounds that the warranty does not extend to an employee. Decision?

3. P's wife, after reading a manufacturer's brochure, purchased a combination power tool. Because of defective design and construction, the tool could hurl a piece of wood through the air and hit the user. P was so injured and brings action for his injuries. The retailer and the manufacturer defend on the grounds that there was no breach of warranty and that only the wife, who purchased the tool, can recover. Decision?

4. B purchased a two-year old International Harvester tractor truck "as is" from S. About two years after the purchase, B was doing some work on the engine. To get at the motor required raising the cab and securing it with a latch. The cab suddenly collapsed because of a defective latch, fell on B, and killed him. B's widow sued both S and International Harvester for breach of warranty and strict liability in tort. Discuss.

5. Buyer informed seller that he wanted a weedkiller to use on some weeds between his orange trees.

Seller sold buyer a particular brand that would kill the weeds but could also damage his orange trees, even if used in the normal manner. Seller did not warn the buyer that the product would damage the trees if the buyer used it as he planned. Buyer used the product as he planned and damaged his trees. Decision?

6. B purchased a wooden sailing sloop from S. During the course of negotiations before the sale, S orally stated that the sloop would "make up" and become watertight within a short time after being put into the water. The sloop leaked after allowance for "make up" in the water. B thereafter sued to cancel the contract and recover the purchase price. S argued that there was no express warranty of seaworthiness at the time of the sea trial of the sloop, but if there was any warranty, it existed only at the time of sale. S also argued that there was no proof of what caused the sloop to leak. Decision?

7. The Hafens purchased a mobile home from Tyson, the owner of the home, who had previously purchased the home from Progress Homes, the manufacturer. Tyson was not an employee or selling agent of Progress Homes. Many defects uncovered by the Hafens after the purchase revealed the home to be substantially lower in value than the contract price. The Hafens sued Progress Homes for the difference in value. Progress Homes defended on the grounds that it did not sell the home to the Hafens and was not liable to the Tysons for economic loss in the absence of a direct contractual relationship. Decision?

8. C, a consumer, purchased from S, a butcher, a raw pork roast sliced into pork chops. C did not ask S for how long and at what temperature pork chops should be cooked to render them free of trichinosis parasites. (Such parasites are present in raw pork and can cause serious illness to those who eat improperly cooked pork products.) C prepared the chops by frying them for fifteen minutes and then boiling them for one hour over a medium gas flame. The temperature required to make pork safe for consumption, 137°F, was not achieved by this cooking method. After eating the pork, C became very ill and was hospitalized. C sued S for strict liability in tort. Decision?

9. While cleaning her home, M put a closed can of crystal drain opener on a table next to her infant's crib. The family cat jumped upon the table and tipped the can of drain opener over into the crib. The impact of the fall caused the can to open. The infant, attracted to the can by its pretty packaging, began to play with the crystals and suffered serious injuries. M, suing on behalf of the infant, sought to recover damages for faulty packaging of the compound. Decision?

10. Ruth, driving a van manufactured by Elway Motors, suffered a rear-end collision caused by another vehicle. Upon collision, Ruth's head was forced backward against the rear window of the van's cab, causing serious injuries. No head-rest was installed in the van, and no such safety equipment was mandated by law at that time. Ruth sued to recover under strict liability in tort. Decision?

CHAPTER TWENTY

Consumer Protection

20.1 Advertising and Sales Practice
Advertising
  Deceptive Product Advertising
  Bait and Switch
Sales Practice
  Door-to-Door
  Referral Sales and Leases

20.2 Consumer Credit (1)
Credit Advertising
Equal Credit Opportunity
Credit Reporting
Disclosure of Credit Terms

20.3 Consumer Credit (2) and Other Consumer Legislations
Credit Cards
Balloon Payments
Credit Billing
Collection Practices
Consumer Defenses
Other Federal Legislation
State Legislation

20.1 Advertising and Sales Practice

Consumer law is a relatively new and dynamic area of law. Rules for the protection of consumers have increased substantially in recent years. Many consumer-oriented organizations, such as Common Cause and Center for Law in the Public Interest, as well as consumer advocates have worked and lobbied successfully for new and progressive consumer regulations. Cases concerning buyers' rights have been argued in court quite frequently. All of these activities have led to a general trend to enhance the protection of the average citizen from socially irresponsible and unscrupulous business operators. Further expansion in this direction should be expected to continue in the foreseeable future.

Many long-established civil and criminal law provisions, such as those concerning fraud, duress, illegality, warranties, and product liability as discussed earlier in this textbook, are already aimed at the protection of the less advantaged consumer. This chapter covers some additional and more typical consumer topics.

Advertising

Advertising regulations, like most consumer protection provisions, generally fall within the realm of administrative law (refer to Subchapter 2.3). The authority in charge of the enforcement of such law is primarily the Federal Trade Commission (FTC), an administrative agency of the federal government.

The policy underlying rules of advertising is the protection of the public interest rather than retribution or punishment of the deceptive advertiser. Whether the advertiser had any ill intent or innocently made the wrong statement, the primary goal of advertising regulation is to stop the dissemination of false presentation of facts to prevent the consumer from being misled.

Deceptive Product Advertising

Deceptive Advertising
Contains statements of facts that are false, less than the truth, or merely unproven.

The FTC is authorized to (1) require (a) that advertisements be limited to such statements as can be proven by the advertiser and (b) that the name of a product be changed if it misleads or tends to mislead the public and (2) seek voluntary agreement from an advertiser to (a) halt false or misleading advertising and, in some cases, (b) retract or correct such deceptive advertisements. The FTC bases its authority concerning regulation of advertising on Section 5 of the Federal Trade Commission Act (15 U.S.C.A. § 41 *et seq.*), which reads, "Unfair methods of competition in commerce and unfair or deceptive acts in commerce are declared unlawful." The FTC's power to order corrective advertising was confirmed *inter alia* in the "Listerine" case of *Warner Lambert Co. v. Federal Trade Comm.* (562 F.2d 749 [D.C. Cir. 1977]).

In light of the rules requiring truth in advertising, the advertiser is obliged to make an accurate and complete description of the product as well as the conditions on which the product is being offered. It is mandatory for an advertiser to maintain proper files, records, and videotapes containing facts claimed relative to performance, quality, safety, and price of the product advertised as well as the competitor's product attributes.

Commercials showing tests of products must be actual and not merely a deceptive mockup. The FTC has the power to demand an advertiser to produce substantiating evidence of a product's attributes. With the exception of trade secrets and privileged matters, the advertiser can be required to make the information public.

Facts

The Colgate-Palmolive Co. had a TV commercial demonstrating how its "Rapid Shave" shaving cream could soften even the toughness of sandpaper. The shown sandpaper test was in fact not actual. Instead of real sandpaper, a sheet of plexiglas sprinkled with sand was used in the shooting of the commercial. The FTC ruled that the advertisement was deceptive and issued a cease and desist order against Colgate-Palmolive. The U.S. Court of Appeals set aside the Commission's ruling. The FTC appealed.

Decision

The U.S. Supreme Court agreed with the Commission's ruling that the TV commercial was deceptive. The advertisement made the TV viewer believe that he was witnessing an actual test. This would tend to be more persuasive to him than it would if he knew that what he was seeing was only an imitation. "(W)hen the commercial not only makes a claim, but also invites the viewer to rely on his own perception of the demonstrative proof of the claim, the (advertiser) will be aware that the use of undisclosed props in strategic places might be a material deception."

Federal Trade Commission v. *Colgate-Palmolive Co.*, 380 U.S. 374, 85 S.Ct. 1035, 13 L.Ed.2d 904 (1965).

Nowadays, comparative commercials have become increasingly common. Such commercials, however disparaging and damaging to the competitor, are no longer regarded as unfair trade practice. From the consumer's point of view, such comparisons may be even commendable, since the consumer is usually not in the position to be involved with precise quality, price, and technical analyses. However, since factual truthfulness is absolutely required, a distortion in presentation may amount to deceptive advertising, as illustrated in the following case.

Facts

Bristol-Myers Co. ran a TV commercial depicting the high-fashion model, Cristina Ferrare, holding its shampoo product "Body on Tap" and claiming: "(I)n shampoo tests with over nine hundred women like me, Body on Tap got higher ratings than Prell for body. Higher than Flex for conditioning. Higher than Sassoon for strong, healthy-looking hair."

It was undisputed that there were no nine hundred women making product-to-product comparisons between the four competing shampoo products. Actually, groups of about two hundred women were asked to test only one shampoo and rate it on a qualitative scale, from "excellent" to "poor," with respect to twenty-seven attributes such as body and conditioning. Bristol-Myers' advertising claim was based on a conclusion of the test that was arguable, since it was obtained by arbitrarily combining some of the high ratings and discarding some of the lower ones. Furthermore, one third of the "women" were age thirteen to eighteen.

Sassoon brought this action, claiming that the Ferrare-900 women advertisement violated the prohibition of § 43(a) of the Lanham Trademark Act against false and misleading advertising. Bristol-Myers was charged with false and misleading representation, since (1) only about two hundred women, not "over nine hundred women," tested each shampoo; (2) the women tested only one shampoo without making product-to-product comparisons; (3) only two thirds of the test participants were adult women; (4) the advertisements failed to portray the test results accurately, since Bristol-Myers used only the top two qualitative rating categories.

Decision

Judgment for the plaintiff. "The inaccuracies alleged concern the number and age of the women in the tests, how the comparisons were made, and how the results were tabulated. . . . (W)e are persuaded that § 43(a) does prohibit the misrepresentations alleged here. . . .

"We do not hold that every misrepresentation concerning consumer test results or methodology can result in liability pursuant to § 43(a). But where depictions of consumer test results or methodology are so significantly misleading that the reasonably intelligent consumer would be deceived about the product's inherent quality or characteristics, an action under § 43(a) may lie. . . .

"The district court preliminarily enjoined the dissemination of the shampoo advertisements at issue. Because we believe that the Lanham Trademark Act addresses the misrepresentations alleged here, relating to a consumer preference test, we affirm the court's order."

Vidal Sassoon, Inc. v. Bristol-Myers Company, 661 F.2d 272 (2d Cir.1981).

Comparative Advertisement
Promotes one's product by comparing it with that of the competitor.

A comparison commercial or, for that matter, any advertisement cannot be considered deceptive if it concerns merely an opinion about a product, without involving any factual statements. A commercial stating that "our product is the best buy in town" or "is better tasting" than some other product cannot result in false representation. A comparative advertisement is not misleading, even though the persons taking the test for the comparison in fact did not tell the truth, as long as it can be substantiated that they indeed voiced the particular opinion.

The term *advertising* extends to written messages contained in newspaper and magazine advertisements, window displays, price tags, and audiovisual messages such as those seen on television and heard on radio. Under the FTC Improvement Act of 1980 (15 U.S.C. § 45 *et seq.*), Congress curtailed the FTC's investigative authority with respect to unfair or deceptive practices. Currently, rule making in specified areas may be vetoed by action of both houses of Congress within ninety days after promulgation.

Bait and Switch

Bait and Switch
Advertising of one price or product with the intention of inducing responding customers to buy a different product or at a different price.

The FTC *Guides on Bait Advertising,* 16 CFR § 238 (1968), established certain practices as evidence of bait advertising (i.e., an item is advertised at a very low price, and the consumer finds upon going to buy the item that the salesperson tries to induce him to buy another, more expensive item or that the store does not have the advertised item available and never did, in fact, have a significant number of the item advertised). Such tactics, referred to as bait-and-switch advertising, are as follows:

1. Refusing to show the advertised item.
2. Disparaging the advertised item.
3. Failing to have the advertised item available in reasonable quantities.
4. Refusing to promise delivery of the advertised item within a reasonable time.
5. Discouraging sales personnel from selling advertised products.

In applying sanctions to this practice, the FTC has not looked solely for evidence of salespersons switching customers to the more expensive item but rather has relied on the number of sales of the less expensive item advertised. If that number is minimal in comparison to the expensive item, the violation is established.

People v. Block & Kleaver, Inc.
103 Misc. 2d 758, 427 N.Y.S.2d 133 (1980).

Block and Kleaver, Inc., the defendant, was in the business of selling bulk beef at retail. It advertised the meat at prices less than the defendant itself had paid for it and less than those charged by two other retail bulk meat businesses. Each customer who responded to the advertisement was shown the sale beef. It was fatty, discolored, and unappetizing. The customer was told that there would be a weight loss averaging about 54 percent to trim the meat for use. The customer was also shown more appetizing and more expensive beef that had been pretrimmed. Employees represented that its weight loss in preparation for use would be only about 10 percent and that a side of beef would last for about 11 months. As a result customers purchased the more expensive beef. However, the average percentage of its waste in 17 purchases was 31 percent and the beef did not last as long as had been represented.

The defendant was charged with violating sections 190.20 and 190.65 of the Penal Law, proscribing misleading advertising and consumer fraud. After a nonjury trial, the defendant was convicted of both offenses. Pertinent parts of the trial court's opinion follows.

Mark, Judge . . . Section 190.20 of the Penal Law may be construed in conjunction with Section 396 of the General Business Law. . . . Both statutes proscribe the sale promotional practice known as "bait and switch advertising," "bait advertising," or "fictitious bargain claims." . . . This practice consists of advertising a product at a very low price; a pattern of conduct discouraging the purchase of the advertised article by disparaging the same and exhibiting a poor-appearing specimen of the advertised article; and the resulting switch to the purchase of a product costing more than the one advertised. . . .

This is the exact factual predicate in the instant case, as it was in *People* v. *Glubo* [158 N.E.2d 699 (N.Y. 1959)].

In that case, the defendant advertised via television a sewing machine which cost $45, for the price of $29.50. A customer who responded was visited by a salesman who would undertake to prove the advertised machine inoperable and point out that it was basically defective and inferior. The salesman would then attempt to persuade the customer to order a better machine at a much higher price. . . . The sole claim of falsity was that the defendant had no intention whatever of selling the advertised machine. . . . The People's case rested on the fact that the defendant advertised for sale a sewing machine it did not intend to sell in order to obtain leads so that it might sell the higher-priced machine. The defendant made no false representation concerning the machines they did sell and the sewing machines sold by the defendants were worth the money paid therefor.

The Court of Appeals held that the conduct of the defendant constituted false advertising and that it was properly convicted. . . .

Accordingly, the defendant corporation [Block & Kleaver, Inc.] is found guilty of the crime of False Advertising in violation of Section 190.20.

The defendant corporation cannot defend upon the ground that the misrepresentations of its employees were mere seller's talk. . . . The federal courts have constructed two tests for distinguishing fraudulent representations from puffing.

> Under the first test, a seller engages in a fraudulent misrepresentation when he actually invents non-existent attributes. . . . False declarations of value constitute fraud because values are facts. . . . Under the second test, the purchaser is entitled to receive a product conforming to his expectation, and he is defrauded if his expectation is not met. . . . When a buyer receives a product not meeting the specifications represented . . . or the value of the product is less than represented . . . he has been defrauded. . . .
> Accordingly, the defendant corporation is found guilty of the crime of Scheme to Defraud . . . in violation of Section 190.65(1) of the Penal Law.

A similar case is *All-State Indus. of North Carolina, Inc.* v. *Federal Trade Commission* (U.S. Court of Appeals, Fourth Cir., 423 F.2d 423 [4th Cir. 1970]). Here, the company's ads featured the "ADV" lower-cost grade of aluminum for residential aluminum siding, storm windows, and other products. However, when the company's salespeople contacted the customers, they attempted to sell instead the "PRO" grade pursuant to the sales training manual.

Sales Practice

Door-to-Door

Door-to-Door Sale
A sale concluded in the consumer's home.

Because of widespread high-pressure methods by door-to-door salespeople resulting in consumers' buying products they do not want or cannot pay for, many statutes and other regulations have been passed concerning this type of sale.

A door-to-door sale is a sale concluded in the consumer-buyer's home. Section 1689.5 of the California Civil Code provides a broader definition: "(a) 'Home solicitation contract or offer' means any contract, whether single or multiple, or any offer which is subject to approval, for the sale, lease or rental of goods or services or both made at other than appropriate trade premises in an amount of twenty-five dollars ($25) or more including any interest or service charges. . . . [¶](b) 'Appropriate trade premises,' means premises at which either the owner or seller normally carries on a business, or where goods are normally offered or exposed for sale in the course of a business carried on at those premises." Thus, a sales contract executed at the seller's office is not "door-to-door" as explained in *Nu Dimensions Figure Salons* v. *Becerra* (73 Misc.2d 140, 340 N.Y.S.2d 268 [1973]).

The FTC provides for a *three-day cooling-off period* on a door-to-door sale of $25 or more. The salesperson is required to provide the buyer a written contract, inform him of the right to cancel, and furnish him with two copies of a notice of cancellation form. A customer having second thoughts after the salesperson has left must sign a copy of the cancellation form and send or deliver the form to the seller within three business days. Exceptions include sales made entirely by mail or telephone; some emergency repair sales or repairs to personal property in the buyer's home; and sales of real estate, insurance, or securities. This regulation supersedes state laws if such laws do not give the buyer as much time to cancel, permit a fee or penalty for cancellation, or do not require substantially the same notice to the buyer.

Facts

Consumers/Defendants telephoned the plaintiff, who sent a representative to their home on February 5, 1974. The representative showed the defendants a sample of an insulated wall system. After some conversation, an agreement was reached between the defendants and the plaintiff's representative for the installation of such a system in the defendants' residence. The defendants signed a contract at their residence and gave the plaintiff's representative a $100 deposit, leaving a balance due of $1,650. The written contract did not contain a notice of the buyer's right to cancel such as is required in a home solicitation contract.

Plaintiff installed the wall system on February 20, 1974. The defendants were dissatisfied with the work. No accommodation was reached, and the defendants failed to pay the balance due. Plaintiff brought the present action on March 26, 1975. On May 12, 1975, after consulting counsel, the defendants mailed a written notice of cancellation to the plaintiff. On May 14, 1975, the defendants answered the plaintiff's complaint and filed a cross-complaint. Thereafter, the defendants moved for summary judgment on the basis of their having cancelled the contract. The trial court granted the summary judgment.

Decision

Judgment affirmed. ". . . If the contract was a home solicitation contract within the meaning of Civil Code section 1689.5, then, the notification required by section 1689.7, subdivisions (a) and (c) not having been given, defendants retained a right to cancel. (Civil Code, § 1689.7, subd. (e).) The trial court ruled, as a matter of law, that the contract, having been signed at defendants' home, was a home solicitation contract within the meaning of the statute, and granted defendants' motion for summary judgment. . . .

"If this result appears to deal harshly with merchants who have fully performed under their contracts, it seems clear to this court that the message which the Legislature has attempted to convey by enactment of sections 1689.5 et seq. of the Civil Code is "Caveat Vendor." Merchants, put on notice by the statute, can easily and inexpensively protect themselves, however, by including a right to cancel provision and an accompanying notice of cancellation as a matter of course in all contracts signed outside their trade premises. . . .''

Weatherall Aluminum Products Co. v. *Scott,* 71 Cal.App.3d 245, 139 Cal.Rptr. 329 (1977).

Part 5 of the *Uniform Consumer Credit Code* (UCCC) provides that within ten days after a notice of cancellation has been received by the seller or an offer to purchase has been otherwise revoked, the seller shall tender to the buyer any payments made, any note or other evidence of indebtedness, and any goods traded in. In the case of goods traded in, they must be in substantially the same condition as when traded. If the seller fails to tender the goods in said condition, the buyer may elect to recover an amount equal to the trade-in allowance stated in the agreement. The Code further provides that until the seller has complied with all of the regulations imposed by this section, the buyer may retain possession of goods delivered to him by the seller and has a lien on the goods in his possession or control for any recovery to which he is entitled.

Under the UCCC, the buyer must take reasonable care of the goods in his possession for a reasonable time. The buyer does not have to tender the goods to the seller at any place but his residence. If the seller fails to demand possession of goods within a reasonable time (here presumed to be forty days) after a home solicitation sale has been cancelled or an offer to purchase has been revoked, the goods become the property of the buyer without obligation to pay for them.

If a home solicitation is cancelled, under the UCCC the seller is not entitled to compensation for any services he performed pursuant to such sale.

The *Uniform Consumer Credit Code* has been adopted in only nine states: Colorado, Idaho, Indiana, Iowa, Kansas, Maine, Oklahoma, Utah, and Wyoming; and even in these states, the UCCC has been revised considerably.

Referral Sales and Leases

Referral Sales
For a purportedly reduced purchase price, commission, or bonus, the buyer is required to find other buyers for the product.

Referral sales and leases schemes are widespread. Typically, a company will induce a buyer to purchase or a tenant to lease at one price with a promised reduction or "bonus" to the purchaser or lessee for every prospective buyer or lessee furnished by the buyer for the same product. The mere giving of a list of names of persons the buyer feels might be interested in the product at the time of the sale is permitted if the price is not contingent on whether or not the persons named do purchase or on whether or not other events occur in the future. In actual practice, referral sales are often accompanied by fraud and by exorbitant pricing. As a result, the referral selling system has been condemned as unconscionable under the UCC and specifically prohibited by the UCCC.

Facts

Plaintiff brings action for $1,364.10, alleging that the amount is owed by the defendants to the plaintiff for a refrigerator-freezer for which the defendants agreed to pay $1,145.88. The balance of the amount consists of a claim for attorney fees in the amount of $227.35 and a late charge of $22.87. The only payment made on the account of the original indebtedness was for $32.00.

The contract for the refrigerator-freezer was negotiated orally in Spanish between the defendants and a Spanish-speaking salesman representing the plaintiff. In that conversation, the defendant/husband told the salesman that he had but one week left on his job and he could not afford to buy the appliance. The salesman distracted and deluded the defendants by advising them that that the appliance would cost them nothing, because they would be paid bonuses or commissions of $25.00 each on the numerous sales that would be made to their neighbors and friends. Thereafter there was submitted to and signed by the defendants a retail installment contract entirely in English. The retail contract was neither translated nor explained to the defendants. In that contract, there was a cash sales price set forth of $900. To this was added a service charge of $245.88, making a total of $1145.88 to be paid for the appliance.

The plaintiff admitted that the cost to the plaintiff corporation for the appliance was $348.00.

Decision

Judgment in favor of the defendants. ". . . In the instant case the court finds that it was 'too hard a bargain' and the conscience of the court will not permit the enforcement of the contract as written. Therefore the plaintiff will not be permitted to recover on the basis of the price set forth in the retail installment contract, namely $900.00 plus $245.85 as a service charge.

"However, since the defendants have not returned the refrigerator-freezer, they will be required to reimburse the plaintiff for the cost to the plaintiff, namely $348.00. No allowance is made on account of any commissions the plaintiff may have paid to salesmen or for legal fees, service charges or any other matters of overhead.

"Accordingly the plaintiff may have judgment against both defendants in the amount of $348.00 with interest, less the $32.00 paid on account, leaving a net balance of $316.00 with interest from December 26, 1964."

Frostifresh Corporation v. *Reynoso*, 52 Misc.2d 26, 274 N.Y.S.2d 757 (1966).

Questions

1. What is the policy underlying the regulation of advertising?
2. Discuss briefly the two cited cases involving deceptive advertisement.
3. When does a sales transaction fall under "bait and switch"?
4. What are the basic rules regarding door-to-door sales?
5. Why does the law condemn referral sales?

20.2 Consumer Credit (1)

Credit Advertising

Under the Consumer Credit Protection Act (15 U.S.C. 1601 *et seq.*), also known as the Truth-in-Lending Act, certain rules must be followed when advertising credit terms.

Credit Advertising
Offers money loans to the consumer for the purchase of certain goods.

No advertisement to aid, promote, or assist directly or indirectly the extension of consumer credit under an open end credit plan (e.g., typical department store credit plan) may set forth any of the specific terms of that plan or the appropriate rate determined under section 127(2) 5 unless it also clearly and conspicuously sets forth all of the following items:

(1) The time period, if any, within which any credit extended may be repaid without incurring a finance charge.
(2) The method of determining the balance upon which a finance charge will be imposed.
(3) The method of determining the amount of the finance charge, including any minimum or fixed amount imposed as a finance charge.
(4) Where periodic rates may be used to compute the finance charge, the period rates expressed as annual percentage rates.
(5) Such other or additional information for the advertising of open end credit plans as the Board may by regulation require to provide for adequate comparison of credit costs as between different types of open end credit plans (§ 143).

Finance Charge
Consists of interest and other costs of borrowing money.

Section 144 establishes certain provisions for advertising of credit other than open-end plans. Most important of these is the provision that the finance charge must be expressed as an annual percentage rate.

The burden of following all of the provisions of credit advertising falls on the advertising body, since there is no liability under this chapter on the part of any owner or personnel, as such, of any medium in which an advertisement appears or through which it is disseminated (§ 145).

A special rule provides that any advertisement to aid, promote, or assist directly or indirectly the extension of consumer credit repayable in more than four installments shall, unless a finance charge is imposed, clearly and conspicuously state, in accordance with the regulations of the Board:

"THE COST OF CREDIT IS INCLUDED IN THE PRICE QUOTED FOR GOODS AND SERVICES" (§ 146).

Equal Credit Opportunity

Regulations have been issued by the Board of Governors of the Federal Reserve System pursuant to the Equal Credit Opportunity Act (15 U.S.C.A. § 1691 *et seq.*) stating that a creditor shall not discriminate against any applicant on the basis of sex or marital status with respect to any aspect of a credit transaction. The regulations are known as Equal Credit Opportunity Regulations (Regulation B) Title 12—Banks and Banking, Part 202—Equal Credit Opportunity, and are a part of the Consumer Credit Protection Act. These regulations have been in effect since October 28, 1975.

On March 23, 1977, the regulations were amended to provide that discrimination in this matter cannot be used on the basis of race, color, religion, national origin, age, receipt of income from a public assistance program, or good faith exercise of rights under the Consumer Protection Act.

A case in point is *United States* v. *American Future Systems, Inc.* 743 F.2d 169 [3d Cir. 1984]), in which white female applicants for a certain credit program were treated as preferred sales targets. They received immediate credit, and orders by this group were always executed on an immediate shipment basis. Other applicants, on the other hand, were in the nonpreferred credit program. Goods ordered were not shipped out until the applicant made three successive monthly payments, and failure to make any of such payments would result in the company's retaining the payments made as well as the goods ordered.

Although an application for a multi-signature loan may ask whether the applicants are single, married, or separated, an application for a single-signature unsecured loan must state that no information as to the applicant's marital status or spouse is required. The applicant may be requested to furnish this information, however, if the spouse will be liable on the account or will also use the account or if the applicant is relying on the spouse's income, community property, alimony, or child support to pay the loan.

Specifically, the creditor cannot do any of the following:

1. Assign a value to sex or marital status in evaluating applications.
2. Assign a value to the existence of a telephone listing in evaluating applications.
3. Request, require, or use information about birth control practices or childbearing capability.
4. Terminate, require reapplication, or change terms based solely on change of name or marital status.
5. Discount all or part of the income (including part-time income) of the applicant or the applicant's spouse.
6. Use prohibited information in evaluating applications.
7. Prohibit an applicant from using any particular name.
8. Fail to act or unreasonably delay action upon an application.
9. Discourage a "reasonable person" from applying for credit.

To prevent liability, a denial of a consumer credit application should be accompanied by specific reasons, showing no violation of any of these equal credit opportunity rules.

Facts

Kathleen Carroll (plaintiff), a single working woman, applied for an Exxon credit card. She had no previous credit, nor did she have a savings account. She had been employed for only one year and had no dependents. Her application was denied with no reason given. Carroll then asked Exxon for an explanation. She was advised that there was not sufficient information on her credit report showing established credit. Exxon's letter did not name the reporting credit bureau. Plaintiff filed a lawsuit, claiming violation of the Fair Credit Reporting Act and the Equal Credit Opportunity Act.

Decision

Judgment for the plaintiff. Under the Fair Credit Reporting Act, Exxon was required to disclose the name and address of the credit reporting agency on the basis of whose information the credit was denied. This information should have been given to Carroll when she was notified of the denial of credit. Exxon also failed to give Carroll proper notice of the reasons for the denial of credit as required by the Equal Credit Opportunity Act. The real reasons were the absence of another major credit card, no savings account, a short job history, and no dependents. No definitive information on these reasons was provided to her.

Carroll v. *Exxon*, 434 F.Supp. 557 (E.D. La. 1977).

Section 202.8 rules on separate accounts in relation to state law. Any provision of state law that prohibits the separate extension of consumer credit to each spouse shall not apply in any case where each spouse voluntarily applies for separate credit from the same creditor. In any case, where such a state law is preempted, each spouse shall be solely responsible for the debt so contracted.

Further, when each spouse separately and voluntarily applies for and obtains a separate account with the same creditor, the accounts shall not be aggregated or otherwise combined for purposes of determining permissible finance charges or permissible loan ceilings under the laws of any state or of the United States. Such loan ceilings shall be construed to permit each spouse to be separately and individually liable up to the amount of the loan ceiling less the amount for which both spouses are jointly liable. For example, in a state in which there is a permissible loan ceiling of $1,000, if a married couple were jointly liable for $250, each spouse could subsequently become individually liable for $750 under this section.

Except for the provisions of § 202.8 set forth above, the Equal Credit Opportunity Act does not preempt state laws prohibiting credit discrimination based on sex or marital status. To date, over half the states have adopted such laws. For example, California Civil Code §§ 1812.30–1812.35 have been amended to prohibit discrimination on the basis of marital status as well as sex and to include an award of attorney's fees for violation thereof.

Facts

Plaintiffs, a couple to be married, were buying a house and applied to Illinois Federal for a joint mortgage. The application was denied, and the reasons given were "separate income not sufficient for loan, and job tenure." A suit was filed alleging violation of the Equal Credit Opportunity Act.

Decision

Judgment for the plaintiffs. The Act prohibits discrimination against a credit applicant on the basis of "sex or marital status." The obligations of joint debtors are the same whether or not they are married to each other. Illinois Federal would have aggregated the incomes had the applicants been married, and in this case, it did not aggregate them because the applicants were not married. Thus, it treated the applicants differently on the basis of their marital status—which is precisely the kind of discrimination that is barred by the Equal Credit Opportunity Act.

Markham v. Colonial Mortgage Service Co., 605 F.2d 566 (D.C. Cir. 1979).

Credit Reporting

In 1970, Congress enacted the Fair Credit Reporting Act, Title VI of the Consumer Credit Protection Act. The Act focuses on requirements for consumer reporting agencies, requirements for users of consumer reports, the rights of consumers, and remedies.

Section 603(f) of the Act defines "consumer reporting agency" as any person that regularly engages in whole or in part in the practice of assembling or evaluating consumer credit information or other information on consumers for the purpose of furnishing consumer reports to a third party or parties and for which monetary fees or dues are paid or, when acting on a cooperative nonprofit basis, for the purpose of preparing or furnishing consumer reports.

If the information is being assembled or evaluated for the business or person's own use, there would be no third party involved, and such a person or business would not be considered a consumer reporting agency.

Section 606 provides that no one may procure or cause to be prepared an investigative consumer report on any consumer unless

> (1) it is clearly and accurately disclosed to the consumer that an investigative consumer report including information as to his character, general reputation, personal characteristics, and mode of living, whichever are applicable, may be made, and such disclosure (A) is made in a writing mailed, or otherwise delivered, to the consumer, not later than three days after the date on which the report was first requested, and (B) includes a statement informing the consumer of his right to request the additional disclosures provided for under subsection (b) of this section; or
> (2) the report is to be used for employment purposes.

The consumer can then request in writing, within a reasonable time after receiving notice of the requested report, a complete and accurate disclosure of the nature and scope of the investigation. This disclosure must be in writing, mailed or otherwise delivered to the consumer not later than five days after the date on which the request for such disclosure was received from the consumer or the date such report was first requested, whichever is the later.

In addition, under § 609, any consumer upon proper identification can request that the consumer reporting agency clearly and accurately disclose the nature and substance of all information (except medical information) in its files on the consumer at the time of the request. The agency must reveal the sources of the information (with certain exceptions).

The Act provides for procedure in case of disputed accuracy, compliance procedures, restrictions on investigative consumer reports, and requirements on users of consumer reports, among other provisions.

Facts

Plaintiff Millstone bought a new automobile insurance policy, which was subsequently cancelled because of a report obtained by the insurance company from O'Hanlon Reports. After repeated requests, O'Hanlon provided Millstone with some selective information from his credit file, which revealed, among other things, that Millstone's neighbors disliked him and regarded him as a "drug-using hippie" with long hair and beard and that Millstone had participated in many public demonstrations. Millstone brought a lawsuit against O'Hanlon Reports for violation of the Fair Credit Reporting Act, seeking actual and punitive damages.

Decision

Judgment for the plaintiff. Millstone was awarded a judgment of $2,500 in actual damages, $25,000 in punitive damages, and $12,500 for attorney's fees. O'Hanlon had not used reasonable care to assure the maximum possible accuracy of its information about Millstone. It had also failed to disclose to Millstone, as required by the Act, the nature and substance of all the information contained in its files on him. O'Hanlon Reports had willfully violated the Act and had evaded its legal responsibilities to Millstone, who was deprived of his equal credit opportunity rights.

Millstone v. O'Hanlon Reports, 383 F.Supp. 269 (E.D. Mo. 1974).

Section 611 gives the consumer an opportunity to make limited corrections to the information on file.

The Federal Trade Commission has principal responsibility for administrative enforcement of the Fair Credit Reporting Act. Other boards and administrators are each given authority to enforce the requirements of the Act when applicable to concerns subject to their respective federal regulatory provisions.

Section 619 of the Act provides for a fine of not more than $5,000 or imprisonment for not more than one year or both for anyone who knowingly and willfully obtains information on a consumer from a consumer reporting agency under false pretenses.

Section 920 provides for a fine of not more than $5,000 or imprisonment for not more than one year or both for any officer or employee of a consumer reporting agency who knowingly and willfully provides information concerning an individual from the agency's files to a person not authorized to receive that information. The issue of giving consumer credit information to an unauthorized party arose in *Heath v. Credit Bureau of Sheridan, Inc.* (618 F.2d 693 [10th Cir. 1980]), in which the Progressive Mine Workers Union of America obtained from a credit bureau a consumer report on plaintiff Heath, a reform-seeking union member, in order to "embarrass, humiliate, and discredit" that member in the eyes of the public, his co-workers, and his fellow union members.

Sections 616 and 617 provide for certain civil liabilities for willful and negligent noncompliance with the provisions of the Act. However, there are many problems connected with establishing a cause of action under these sections. Any consumer reporting agency using "reasonable" procedures will be discharging its statutory obligations.

Disclosure of Credit Terms

The Consumer Credit Protection Act (15 U.S.C. 1601 *et seq.*), known as the "Truth-in-Lending Act," is implemented by Regulation Z, prescribed by the Board of Governors of the Federal Reserve System. (For a free copy of Regulation Z, write to the Federal Trade Commission, Division of Consumer Credit, Washington, DC 20580, or contact your local office of the FTC.)

The purpose of Regulation Z is to let borrowers and customers know the cost of credit so that they can compare costs with other credit sources. It does not fix maximum, minimum, or any charges for credit. The most important feature of Regulation Z is the requirement that the borrower be given a disclosure statement that shows the total finance charges translated into an annual percentage rage (A.P.R.) expressed in a dollar amount the borrower pays per year for the loan. The regulation applies to any individual or organization that in the ordinary course of business regularly extends or arranges credit for which a finance charge is or may be payable or which by agreement is repayable in more than four installments. It is enforced by both civil and criminal penalties.

Disclosure Statement
Shows the total finance charge translated into A.P.R. (annual percentage rate).

Facts

The Myricks (plaintiffs) had Ole South Building Supply install siding. Credit was based on a signed property improvement contract, a home improvement sales contract, and a mortgage agreement on their house. The documents did not show the total purchase price or the annual percentage rate and the credit insurance charge. The total transaction called for 84 monthly installments. Ole South assigned the contract to Finance America (defendant), and when the plaintiffs defaulted, Finance America attempted to foreclose on the house. Plaintiffs sued to rescind the agreement based on the Truth-in-Lending Act.

Decision

Judgment for the plaintiffs. Ole South violated the Truth-in-Lending Act by failing to disclose to the Myricks the finance charge, the annual percentage rate, and the cost of credit insurance. When the required disclosures are material and are never made, the debtor has the right to rescind the contract. Upon proper rescission of the contract, the mortgage became void. The finance company, however, was entitled to recover either the siding or its reasonable value.

Myrick v. Finance America Credit Corp., 404 So.2d 700 (Ala.Civ.App. 1981).

Similar cases are *Mourning* v. *Family Publication Service, Inc.* (411 U.S. 356, 93 S.Ct. 1652, 36 L.Ed.2d 318 [1973]), involving a thirty-monthly payment transaction on a magazine subscription, and *Chapman* v. *Miller* (575 S.W.2d 581 [Tex. Civ. App. 1978]), involving the sale of a used car on one down payment, six weekly payments, and eighteen monthly payments.

The finance charge in connection with any transaction shall be determined as the sum of all charges, payable directly or indirectly by the consumer and imposed directly or indirectly by the creditor as an incident to or as a condition of the extension of credit, whether paid or payable by the customer, the seller, or any other person on behalf of the customer to the creditor or to a third party. It includes any of the following types of charges:

1. Interest, time price differential, and any amount payable under a discount or other system of additional charges.

CONSUMER PROTECTION

Figure 20.1 Example of Disclosure Statement

First Interstate Bank

SIMPLE INTEREST PERSONAL LOAN AGREEMENT AND DISCLOSURE

Primary Borrower's Name _____ Loan No. _____

Co-Borrower's Name _____

Thank you for choosing First Interstate Bank of California ("Bank") to service your financial needs. This is the Agreement that covers your responsibilities and obligations to repay your loan. PLEASE READ THE ENTIRE AGREEMENT BEFORE SIGNING. If you have any questions, please ask any First Interstate Bank of California Loan Officer for help.
Thank you.

Loan Officer's Name _____ Telephone No. _____

ANNUAL PERCENTAGE RATE The cost of your credit as a yearly rate.	FINANCE CHARGE The dollar amount the credit will cost you.	Amount Financed The amount of credit provided to you or on your behalf.	Total of Payments The amount you will have paid after you have made all payments as scheduled.
_____ %	$ _____	$ _____	$ _____

Your payment schedule will be:

Number of Payments	Amount of Payments	When Payments Are Due

Security: You are giving a security interest in: ☐ the goods or property being purchased. ☐ this loan is unsecured.
☐ _____
Collateral securing other loans with us may also secure this loan.

Filing fees: $ _____

Variable rate: The annual percentage rate may increase during the term of this transaction if:
• the automatic payment authorization with the Bank is terminated for any reason.
• you terminate your United Account relationship.
In the event your interest rate is increased, your monthly payments will increase. Example: Your loan is in the amount of $ _____ at _____ % with a term of _____ months. There are _____ regular monthly payments of $ _____ and a final payment of $ _____ . If your interest rate were increased to _____ % at the beginning, your regular monthly payment would increase to $ _____ , and the final payment would be $ _____ . The interest rate will not increase above _____ %.

Late Charge: If a payment is late you will be charged 5% of the payment, with a minimum of $1.00 and a maximum of $10.00.

Prepayment: If you pay this loan off early: you will not have to pay a penalty.
you will not be entitled to a refund of part of the finance charge.

See this contract document and other appropriate contract documents for any additional information about nonpayment, default, any required repayment in full before the scheduled date, prepayment refunds and penalties, and security interests.

TERMS OF LOAN

By signing this Agreement you promise to pay First Interstate Bank of California the amount shown above in the Total of Payments and according to the payment schedule. The interest rate on the loan is _____ %, which rate may change as outlined above.

Unless otherwise agreed to, the Bank does not intend to refinance any "Balloon Payment" shown above. A "Balloon Payment" is any payment more than twice the amount of the regular monthly payment. You can mail your payment, personally pay it at any one of our statewide offices, or authorize us to automatically transfer each payment from your First Interstate Bank of California checking account.

All of the above terms are based on the presumption that you will make your payments on the date due. If any payments are early, your FINANCE CHARGE could be less. If any payments are late, your FINANCE CHARGE could be greater and you agree to pay the greater amount.

Itemization of the Amount Financed of $ _____
A. **Proceeds of Loan**
    Amount credited to your account . . . . $ _____
    Amount given to you directly . . . . $ _____
    Amount paid on your loan. . . . . $ _____
    Loan fee . . . . $ _____
    Amount paid to others on your behalf
    To public officials . . . . $ _____
    Filing and recording fees . . . . $ _____
    License and registration fees . . . . $ _____
    To _____ $ _____
    To _____ $ _____
    TOTAL AMOUNT BORROWED . . . .(A) $ _____
B. **Prepaid finance charges**
    Loan fee . . . . $ _____
    Document Preparation Fee . . . . $ _____
    TOTAL PREPAID FINANCE CHARGES . . . (B) $ _____
C. Amount financed (A) − (B) . . . . $ _____

CREDIT LIFE INSURANCE APPLICATION AND DISCLOSURE

Neither Single nor Joint Credit Life Insurance is required by the Creditor. Neither coverage will be provided unless you check off the coverage you want and sign below. The insurance covers the amount due on your loan at death (excluding unearned finance charges) up to $50,000. The insurance is only available to persons under age 65. Joint life insurance is only available to individuals or business partners who are both under age 65.

INSURANCE COVERAGE SELECTED

Please check one box:
☐ Yes ☐ No
Single Life Insurance   Daily Charge Rate Per $100 $ _____
On Primary Borrower   Estimated Total Charge $ _____
☐ Yes ☐ No
Joint Life Insurance   Daily Charge Rate Per $100 $ _____
On Joint Borrowers   Estimated Total Charge $ _____

The Estimated Total Insurance charge for the duration of your loan is shown above. The charge for your insurance accrues daily at the rate shown above based on your daily insured outstanding principal balance. The estimated charge represents the sum of the daily charges that will accrue on your loan if you make all monthly payments precisely on time. If you make any payments late, additional insurance charges could accrue (over the estimate) on your loan. If you make any payments early your total insurance charge could turn out to be less than the estimate. You will get periodic statements from the Bank that show your actual accrued insurance charges.

If you apply for the credit insurance marked above, your signature below means that you agree that you are not eligible for insurance if you have reached your 65th birthday.

Date _____ Primary Borrower's Signature _____ Age _____

Date _____ Co-Borrower's Signature _____ Age _____
(See Notice of Proposed Insurance on Reverse Side)
ORD 83914-1   I.D. 26 Non-Standard

I, (We) have read this Agreement and accept all of its terms and conditions. If this loan has two or more signers, each of us understands that each of us is jointly and severally liable under this Agreement. I, (We) have received a copy of this statement.

_____ _____ _____
Signature of Primary Borrower   Signature of Co-Borrower   Date

IC-2120 (9/86)   NOTE: See reverse side of this document for additional loan terms and conditions.
ORIGINAL

2. Service, transaction, activity, or carrying charge.
3. Loan fee, points, finder's fee, or similar charge.
4. Fee for an appraisal, investigation, or credit report.
5. Charges of premiums for credit life, accident, health, or loss-of-income insurance written in connection with any credit transaction (with certain exemptions).

Certain items are excludable as finance charges. In particular, if itemized and disclosed to the customer, any charges of the following types need not be included in the finance charge:

1. Fees and charges prescribed by law that actually are or will be paid to public officials for determining the existence of or for performing or releasing or satisfying any security related to the credit transaction.
2. Certain premiums payable for any insurance in lieu of perfecting any security interest otherwise required by the creditor in connection with the transaction (with certain limitations).
3. Taxes not included in the cash price.
4. License, certificate of title, and registration fees imposed by law.

In addition, late payment, delinquency, default, and reinstatement charges if imposed for actual unanticipated late payment, delinquency, default, or other such occurrence are not finance charges. Nor are overdraft charges imposed by a bank for paying checks that overdraw or increase an overdraft in a checking account, unless the payment of such checks and the imposition of such finance charges were previously agreed upon in writing.

Certain real property transactions charges, such as appraisal fees, credit reports, title examination, abstract of title, title insurance, required property surveys, fees for preparations of deeds, settlement statements, and notary fees, are not included in the finance charge.

Certain transactions are exempted under § 226.3 of this regulation:

1. Business or governmental credit, other than for agricultural purposes.
2. Certain transactions in security or commodities accounts.
3. Credit transactions, other than real property transactions, in which the amount financed is over the sum of $25,000.
4. Certain public utility bills.
5. Agricultural credit transactions, including real property transactions, in which the amount financed exceeds $25,000 or in which the transaction is pursuant to an express written commitment by the creditor to extend credit in excess of $25,000.

Because the many disclosure requirements of the Truth-in-Lending Act are very detailed and complex, the student is referred to Regulation Z for further particulars.

Overdraft
Takes place when a bank pays its customer's check without funds available in the account.

Questions

1. What does the Truth-in-Lending Act require of credit advertising?
2. What is prohibited by the Equal Credit Opportunity Act?

3. Under the Fair Credit Reporting Act, what should a lender do when denying a consumer credit application?
4. What can a consumer do when he disagrees with the content of his credit report?
5. Discuss the Truth-in-Lending Act in conjunction with credit term disclosure.

20.3 Consumer Credit (2) and Other Consumer Legislations

Credit Cards

Section 226.13 of Regulation Z provides that a credit cardholder is liable for the unauthorized use of the credit card up to $50, and then only if:

1. The credit card is an accepted credit card (an accepted credit card is one that the credit cardholder has requested and received, has signed or has used, or has authorized another to use).
2. The card issuer has given adequate notice to the cardholder of his potential liability.
3. The card issuer has provided the cardholder with an addressed notification requiring no postage to be paid to him that may be mailed by him in the event of the loss, theft, or possible unauthorized use of the credit card.
4. The card issuer has provided a method whereby the user of such card can be identified as the person authorized to use it, such as by signature, photograph, or fingerprint on the credit card or by electronic or mechanical confirmation.
5. The unauthorized use occurred before the cardholder notified the issuer that an unauthorized use occurred or may occur as a result of loss or theft.

Facts

Defendant Gloria Harlan asked for and obtained from Walker Bank two Visa cards, one for her husband and one herself, on the same account. When the couple separated, Mrs. Harlan requested the bank to close the account and to deny further extension of credit to her husband. To comply with her request, the bank required the return of the cards, but the cards were submitted three months later. Meanwhile, Mr. Harlan made use of his credit card, and the bank sued to recover the charges. Mrs. Harlan contended that her liability was limited to $50 because the charges made by her husband were unauthorized after her notification.

Decision

Judgment for Walker Bank. At the defendant's own request, the bank had issued a card to Mr. Harlan in his name. The card was a representation to merchants that Mr. Harlan was authorized to make a charge on the account. Accordingly, because the contract between the cardholder and the bank provided that all cards issued on the account had to be returned to close the account, Mrs. Harlan remained liable for the charges made on the card she had authorized until she surrendered the card.

Walker Bank & Trust Co. v. Harlan, 672 P.2d 73 (Utah 1983).

A similar case is *Martin v. American Express, Inc.* (361 So.2d 597 [Ala.Civ.App. 1978]), where a cardholder allowed his business associate to use his American Express card, supposedly up to the amount of $500. Instead, the associate charged the account for the total sum of $5,300. The cardholder was held liable for the total balance.

Notice may be given to the card issuer or his designee in person or by telephone or by letter, telegram, radiogram, cablegram, or other written communication that sets forth the pertinent information.

Some states have legislation similar to the above (e.g., New York [Section 512 of the General Business Law]).

In addition to statutory limitation of liability in credit card cases, courts have refused to permit the card issuer to recover any sums when the person dealing with the cardholder was negligent in assuming that the holder of the card was the lawful owner of it and in failing to take steps to identify the holder.

Regardless of whether a credit card is to be used for personal, family, household, agricultural, business, or commercial purposes, no credit card shall be issued to any person except in the following instances:

1. In response to a request or application therefor.
2. As a renewal of, or in substitution for, an accepted credit card, whether such card is issued by the same or a successor card issuer (§ 226.13[a]).

Balloon Payments

Balloon Payment
An installment payment substantially greater than the other installments (usually a final payment).

A balloon payment is an installment greater than the other installments as a provision of an installment sales contract or in an installment loan. Section 226.8(b)(3) of Regulation Z provides "If any payment is more than twice the amount of an otherwise regularly scheduled equal payment, the creditor shall identify the amount of such payment by the term 'balloon payment' and shall state the conditions, if any, under which that payment may be refinanced if not paid when due."

The consumer, in certain cases, as set forth under §§ 3.308(1) and 3.308(2) of the UCCC, has the right to refinance, without penalty, the amount of that payment at the time it is due, and the terms of the refinancing shall be no less favorable to the consumer than the terms of the original transaction. This does not apply to the following:

1. A consumer lease.
2. A transaction pursuant to open-end credit.
3. A transaction to the extent that the payment schedule is adjusted to the seasonal or irregular income or scheduled payments or obligations of the consumer.
4. A transaction of a class defined by rule of the administrator as not requiring for the protection of the consumer his right to refinance.

However, as previously mentioned, the UCCC has been adopted in only nine states and is changed and revised by many of those states.

Balloon payments can be helpful to consumers with seasonal or otherwise irregular sources of payment. They can also be deceptive to the consumer, since the regularly scheduled payments will be so low that the consumer will be enticed into the agreement because the "day of reckoning" is delayed.

Credit Billing

The Fair Credit Billing Act (15 U.S.C.A. 1666 *et seq.*) became effective in 1975. Because of the heavy volume of consumer complaints over billing errors in accounts, the Fair Credit Billing Act sets forth various remedies to the consumer. Section 127(b) of the Act requires the disclosure of the address to which billing inquiries shall be sent. Section 127(a) provides that the creditor must provide the consumer with a statement in the form prescribed in Regulation Z 226.7(a)(9), explaining the consumer's rights and obligations under the Fair Credit Billing Act at the time of the opening of the account and at semiannual intervals thereafter.

Section 161(b) describes billing errors as follows:

1. An extension of credit not made to the complaining customer or not made in the amount reflected on the billing statement.
2. Credit extensions for which documentation or clarification is requested.
3. Undelivered or unaccepted goods or services.
4. Incorrect payments or credits.
5. Clerical or computational errors.

Section 161 provides for requirements to be followed by the consumer regarding clerical and computational errors. Communication must

1. Be by a written notice.
2. Be received at the creditor's disclosed address.
3. List information enabling the creditor to identify the name and account number (if any) of the consumer.
4. Indicate that the consumer believes that there is a billing error.
5. Set forth the amount of such billing error.
6. Set forth the reasons for the consumer's belief.

Each creditor who receives such a proper claim of error must make either a written acknowledgement of receipt or a written response within *thirty days*.

Until the creditor responds to the claim of error, it may not take any action to collect the disputed amount. A creditor cannot restrict the use of an open-end account, pending the response to such claim, solely because the amount disputed has not been paid. Once the information has reached the creditor, the creditor may not report or threaten to report the disputed amount delinquent until ten days after its response has been sent to the consumer.

If a creditor fails to make the necessary requirements set forth in the Act, the creditor forfeits its right to collect the amount in dispute, whether or not such account was in error, and any corresponding finance charges, provided that the amount so forfeited shall not exceed $50 for each item or transaction on a periodic statement indicated by a customer as being in error.

Collection Practices

The Fair Debt Collection Practices Act (FDCPA) (Pub.L.No. 95–109, 91 Stat.874) brings debt collection procedures under federal regulation for the first time. The Act is intended to eliminate abusive debt collection practices in the consumer credit industry. Debt collectors who violate any of the Act's provisions will be subject to civil suits in the federal courts by injured parties or classes or to administrative enforcement by the FTC or certain other agencies.

First and foremost, the collector must ascertain the legitimacy of the collection as illustrated in the following case.

Facts

When Mr. Pullins was late in paying his bill to Baylor Medical Center, Baylor assigned the account to Credit Exchange of Dallas for collection. Meanwhile, Mr. Pullins paid directly to Baylor, but Credit Exchange was not informed thereof. It continued to attempt to collect from the debtor's wife, who told the collector that the bill had been fully satisfied. Because of the persistent collection efforts, Mrs. Pullins became upset and ill, and she sued Credit Exchange for damages.

Decision

Judgment for the plaintiff. Credit Exchange was blamed for its continuous efforts to collect without even verifying Mrs. Pullins' information about the bill's having been paid off. Accordingly, Credit Exchange was held liable for the harm caused by its collection efforts.

Pullins v. Credit Exchange of Dallas, Inc., 538 S.W.2d 681 (Tex.Civ.App. 1976).

Not all debt collectors are subject to the provisions of the Act, which is primarily intended to reach third-party collectors of overdue accounts. The most important exception to the Act's reach is the collection of debts by the original creditor itself or by an employee of the original creditor. Other excluded groups include attorneys-at-law who are collecting on behalf of and in the name of a client and purchasers of a debt that is not in default at the time of purchase.

Only debts arising from transactions that are primarily for personal, family, or household purposes are covered by the Act.

Most of the regulations in the Act concern direct contacts between the collector and the debtor. The collector may not communicate with the debtor at an unusual place or time.

Harassment and abuse of the debtor are prohibited, as are false and misleading representations and unfair practices. The following are among the listed unfair practices:

1. The use or threat of use of violence or other criminal activity to the person, reputation, or property of the debtor.
2. The use of obscene language.
3. The publication of "deadbeat lists."

4. Excessive or anonymous telephone calls.
5. The threat of legal action that cannot be taken or is not intended to be taken, including arrest.
6. Use of collect phone calls, telegrams, etc., concealing the true purpose of the communication.
7. Taking or threatening to take nonjudicial action upon property.
8. The use of a postcard or any other sign or symbol or company name on an envelope that would indicate that the communication involves debt collection.

Facts

Plaintiff Rutyna was a 60-year-old widow suffering from high blood pressure and epilepsy. She incurred a debt for medical purposes, but she believed that all her bills had been paid by Medicare and private health insurance. Nonetheless, an agent of Collection Accounts called her, informing her that she still owed $56. When she denied the debt, the collector said: "You owe it, you don't want to pay, so we're going to have to do something about it." A month thereafter, Collection Accounts sent a letter stating: "You have shown that you are unwilling to work out a friendly settlement with us to clear the above debt. Our field investigator has now been instructed to make an investigation in your neighborhood and to personally call on your employer. The immediate payment of the full amount, or a personal visit to this office, will spare you this embarrassment." Plaintiff claimed that she felt threatened and became very nervous, upset, and worried. She was particularly concerned about the embarrassment if her neighbors came to know about her debt and medical problems. She sued for damages under the Fair Debt Collection Practices Act.

Decision

Judgment for the plaintiff. The defendant's letter had the natural consequence of harassing, oppressing, and abusing the recipient. The tone of the letter was one of intimidation and was intended as such to effect a collection. The threat of an investigation and resulting embarrassment to the alleged debtor was clear, and the actual effect on the recipient is irrelevant. The FDCPA prohibits a debt collector form using any "false, deceptive, or misleading representation or means in connection with the collection of any debt." Among the threats precluded are any "to take any action that cannot legally be taken or that is not intended to be taken." Defendant's letter threatened embarrassing contacts with Mrs. Rutyna's employer and neighbors. This constitutes a false representation of the actions that the defendant could legally take. With certain limited exceptions, the Act prohibits communication by the collector with third parties.

Rutyna v. Collection Accounts Terminal, Inc., 478 F.Supp. 980 (N.D. Ill. 1979).

A comparable case is *Callarama v. Associates Discount Corp. of Delaware, Inc.*, 69 Misc.2d 287, (329 N.Y.S.2d 711 [1972]).

Other federal regulations govern the use of the mails and the telephone. For example, collection abuses under use of the mails have been prosecuted under 18 U.S.C.A. § 1341 and 18 U.S.C.A. § 1718 (Mail Fraud Statute).

Section 5.108(2) of the UCCC provides, "With respect to a consumer credit transaction, if the court as a matter of law finds that a person has engaged in, is engaging in, or is likely to engage in unconscionable conduct in collecting a debt arising from that transaction, the court may grant an injunction and award the consumer any actual damages he has sustained."

Section 5.108(5) further provides factors applicable to Subsection (2). A creditor is forbidden to do any of the following:

1. Use or threaten to use force, violence, or criminal prosecution against the consumer or members of his family.

2. Communicate with the consumer or a member of his family at frequent intervals or at unusual hours or under other circumstances so that it is a reasonable inference that the primary purpose of the communication was to harass the consumer.
3. Use fraudulent, deceptive, or misleading representations that simulate legal process or that appear to have been authorized, issued, or approved by a government, governmental agency, or attorney at law, when in fact they were not, or threaten or attempt to enforce a right with knowledge or reason to know that such right does not in fact exist.
4. Cause or threaten to cause injury to the consumer's reputation or economic status by disclosing information affecting the consumer's status and reputation for creditworthiness with knowledge or reason to know that the information is false.

Even though a debtor is able to establish all of the elements just discussed, he still faces the problem of proving damages.

General state laws are utilized in extreme cases involving assault, blackmail, slander, libel, disorderly conduct, or fraud.

Consumer Defenses

Ordinarily, the consumer is not required to pay the seller (or lessor) for goods or services that are defective in violation of express or implied warranties. Since sellers often sold their credit sales contracts to third parties such as banks and finance companies, they usually attempted nevertheless to preclude the consumer from asserting his legitimate defenses against a third party by a waiver in the credit agreement.

Consumer Defenses
Defenses that a consumer may use against the seller who demands payment.

The FTC has adopted a regulation prescribing that in every sale or lease to a consumer, the contract contain a provision affirming the consumer's defenses, not only against the seller or lessor but also against third parties. The following notice in boldface type of at least ten-point size is required:

NOTICE
ANY HOLDER OF THIS CONSUMER CREDIT CONTRACT IS SUBJECT TO ALL CLAIMS AND DEFENSES WHICH THE DEBTOR COULD ASSERT AGAINST THE SELLER OF GOODS OR SERVICES OBTAINED PURSUANT HERETO OR WITH THE PROCEEDS HEREOF. RECOVERY HEREUNDER BY THE DEBTOR SHALL NOT EXCEED AMOUNTS PAID BY THE DEBTOR HEREUNDER.

Apart from the above regulation, under the basic rules of contract assignment, an assignee cannot have better rights than the assignor. Thus, defenses good against the assignor are equally good against the assignee.

Facts

Donnelly (defendant) bought a TV set on credit from D.W.N. Advertising, Inc. In addition, he bought a service agreement with the company for the set. The seller sold the sales contract to Fairfield Credit Corporation and went out of business without ever performing on the service contract. Donnelly refused to make further payments on the TV set, since the accompanying service contract was defaulted upon. Fairfield claimed that the defense could not be used against it, as the sales contract contained a waiver.

Decision

Judgment for the defendant. All defenses that the consumer could have asserted against the seller-assignor are applicable to the contract assignee. A waiver of defenses by the consumer would be contrary to public policy. The assignee should not be able to recover from the consumer when the assignor himself would not be able to do so. Accordingly, the defendant could assert his defenses against the plaintiff.

Fairfield Credit Corp. v. *Donnelly,* 158 Conn. 543, 264 A.2d 547 (1969).

Other Federal Legislation

1. The Magnuson-Moss Warranty—Federal Trade Commission Improvement Act (15 U.S.C.A. § 2301 *et seq.*, 1975)—was passed to improve the adequacy of information available to consumers, prevent deception, and improve competition in the marketing of consumer products and to establish rules required in the written warranty of products. The Act designates federal minimum standards for warranties, designates warranties, establishes rules for terms and conditions of service contract disclosure, designates representatives, limits disclaimer of implied warranties, and covers full and limited warranting of a consumer product.

2. The Interstate Land Sales Full Disclosure Act (15 U.S.C.A. § 1701) requires that anyone selling or leasing fifty or more lots of unimproved land as part of a common promotional plan in interstate commerce or by utilization of the mails must first file a statement of record with the Office of the Interstate Land Sales Registration, a division of the Department of Housing and Urban Development. The statement of record contains very detailed information about the land and the developer. After the statement of record is approved by HUD as being on its face accurate and containing the required information, a developer may proceed to offer land for sale or lease, but he will also be required to furnish each purchaser a property report.

3. The Real Estate Settlements Procedure Act (12 U.S.C.A. § 2601, effective June 20, 1975) applies to all federally related mortgage loans. Virtually all mortgage lenders are covered. The property must be a one- to four-family residential dwelling. The Act requires disclosure of charges, prohibits kickbacks and splitting of fees except for services actually rendered, and limits the amount that a borrower must pay into a special or escrow fund for taxes and insurance.

4. The Motor Vehicle Information and Cost Savings Act (15 U.S.C.A. § 1901 *et seq.*, 1972) requires disclosure to the buyer of various elements in the cost of an automobile and prohibits selling an automobile without informing the buyer that the odometer has been reset below the true mileage.

5. The Fur Products Labeling Act (15 U.S.C.A. §§ 69–69j), Textile Fiber Products Act (15 U.S.C.A. §§ 70–70k), and the Wool Products Labeling Act (15 U.S.C.A. §§ 68–68j) provide standards for the labeling of the various products stated in the respective titles. The FTC has

regulatory jurisdiction and has issued regulations directing the manner and form of disclosing required labeling information. The regulations are enforced by cease-and-desist orders, restitution, affirmative disclosure, rescission of contracts, seizure of mislabeled goods, and willful violations by criminal penalties (these methods of enforcement are generally true in all of the acts.)

6. The Flammable Fabrics Act (15 U.S.C.A. §§ 1191–1204) covers wearing apparel, fabric for wearing apparel, and household furnishings. Recent FTC activities have been in the area of carpet and rug standards, bedding and mattress standards, and children's no-burn sleepwear standards.

7. The Federal Hazardous Substances Labeling Act (15 U.S.C.A. §§ 1261–73), through regulations issued by the Secretary of HEW, declares certain products to be hazardous and subject to labeling requirements to warn consumers of dangers. Some of the children's products relate to thermal, mechanical, electrical, toxic, and eye hazard protection.

8. The Mail Fraud Statute (18 U.S.C.A. §1341; 26 Stat. 466; 39 U.S.C. § 259) provides civil and criminal penalties when a party is found to be conducting a scheme or device of obtaining money or property through the mails by means of fraudulent practices.

9. The Fair Packaging and Labeling Act (15 U.S.C.A. §§ 1451–61) assists the consumer in determining values of products. Foods, drugs, cosmetics, and other consumer commodities must be labeled to show net quantity and other product information.

10. The National Traffic and Motor Vehicle Safety Act of 1966 (15 U.S.C.A. §§ 1381–1425) covers motor vehicle safety standards, labeling standards relating to tires, and notification to purchasers of automobile parts, including tires, of defects discovered by the manufacturer.

11. The Radiation Control for Health and Safety Act (42 U.S.C.A. §§ 263(b)–263(h)) provides that the Secretary of HEW shall set standards for radiation emissions for products covered by the statute. Standards for television receivers manufactured after January 15, 1970, have been set in addition to standards for other electronic products.

12. The Federal Postal Reorganization Act (39 U.S.C.A. § 101 at 3009, 1970) provides that a person who receives unsolicited goods in the mail has the right to retain, use, discard, or dispose of them in any manner he sees fit without any obligation to the sender. Some states have similar laws.

13. Under the Consumer Protection Safety Act (15 U.S.C.A. § 2051 *et seq.*, 1972), consumer products became subject to federal regulation. The government has authority to set safety standards for products and to ban those products that present real hazards to consumers. A consumer product is any article or part of an article produced or distributed for sale for personal use, consumption, or enjoyment in a household or school, in recreation or otherwise, except foods, drugs, cosmetics, motor vehicles, insecticides, firearms, cigarettes, radiological hazards, and certain flammable fabrics. The exceptions are covered by the Food, Drug and Cosmetic Act (21 U.S.C.A. § 301), the Poison Prevention Packaging Act of 1970 (70 U.S.C.A. § 1471), and other acts mentioned

in this chapter. The Act provides for civil and criminal penalties. In addition to providing for the usual state court action based upon product liability, the Act provides that suit will lie in any U.S. district court for a person injured through a failure to knowingly observe a consumer product safety rule. The Act grants broad power to the Consumer Product Safety Commission to preempt state or local consumer product safety standards but allows the agency to grant an exemption if the proposed local rule imposes a higher standard than the federal standard.

14. The Wholesome Meat Act (21 U.S.C.A. §§ 601–695, 1967), the Wholesome Poultry Products Act (21 U.S.C.A. §§ 451–570, 1968), the Public Health Service Act (42 U.S.C.A. §§ 201–300 u-5, 1974), and numerous related enactments provide consumers protection in those areas exempt from the Consumer Products Safety Act, unless otherwise noted. Standards are provided, as are civil and criminal remedies.

State Legislation

Many states have adopted legislation modeled on the federal enactments, some of which provide stronger remedies than are available under federal law. In general, Congress has authorized an exemption from its own legislation where comparable state laws offer greater consumer protection.

In the following two instances, uniform state enactments have been adopted:

1. The Uniform Consumer Credit Code (UCCC) sets forth the regulation of retail installment sales, consumer credit loans, and insurance. As previously discussed, when adopted, the UCCC supersedes all other related enactments and controls consumer transactions in each adopting state.
2. The Uniform Commercial Code (UCC) also provides consumer protection. Referral sales contracts, where the buyer is given a price reduction for referring customers to the seller, have been outlawed as unconscionable under UCC § 2–302.

QUESTIONS

1. When is a cardholder liable up to the limited amount of $50 for unauthorized use of a credit card?
2. What is a balloon payment, and what are the rules regarding it?
3. What does the law provide in the event of a consumer billing error?
4. Name several collection practices prohibited by law.
5. Discuss the consumer's waiver of defenses.

PROBLEMS

1. On Monday, a salesman called on an elderly widow at her home and identified himself, the company he worked for, and the product he sold. He made a contract to sell her an expensive vacuum cleaner

with a lifetime guarantee. The contract provided that she pay 10 percent down and the balance within one year. Delivery of the vacuum cleaner was subject to the widow's credit being approved by the home office of the seller. On Tuesday, the widow calls you for advice, as she wants to cancel the contract. Discuss.

2. In September, B purchased a stereo on credit from Montgomery Ward through its catalogue. The catalogue contained a statement, "NO MONTHLY PAYMENTS TILL FEBRUARY when you order stereo on Credit at Wards." It was not disclosed that the credit charge was computed by the seller from the date of purchase in September and not from the February date when payment was due. B claims the seller failed to disclose the financing terms in its advertising, making it liable for failure to disclose. Discuss.

3. The XYZ Company ran a commercial on television that purported to give viewers proof that its shaving cream could soften sandpaper. Unknown to viewers, the substance that appeared to be sandpaper in the commercials was in fact a prop made of plexiglas covered with sand. Could the FTC prohibit the use of this type of undisclosed simulation?

4. B applied for life insurance to the N Company and the S Company. These companies requested credit information on B from the R Credit Company, a mercantile reporting agency. R erroneously reported that B was an excessive drinker. This credit report caused both insurance companies to refuse to insure B. In addition, the report caused B's automobile insurance carrier to cancel his policy. B sues R for damages for defamation. Decision?

5. Ramis, a real estate developer, advertised nationally a massive development of one-acre unimproved lots in a southwestern state. Griswold, an out-of-state resident, learns of it and requests information about the project. Ramis provides Griswold with a small advertising brochure lacking in information about the company or the land. The brochure makes vague descriptions of the joys of home ownership and nothing else. Griswold purchases a lot. Two weeks later, Griswold wishes to cancel the land sales contract. Ramis sues to enforce the contract. Decision?

6. Plunkett obtains gas credit cards from Mobil for himself and his wife. Each card states: "This card is valid unless expired or revoked. Named holder's approval of all purchases is presumed unless written notice of loss or theft is received." Later, Plunkett returns his card to Mobil, stating that he is cancelling it, but having separated from his wife, he cannot return the card in her possession. Mobil thereafter sues Plunkett for charges made by his wife with the card in her possession. Plunkett defends on the grounds that he had lawfully cancelled the credit card agreement and is not responsible for his wife's credit card purchases. Decision?

7. The management of the Andrews Hotel wished to increase its revenues. It added a 2 percent "sundries charge" to the bill of every hotel guest. Over time, the total charges yielded the hotel $100,000. Gardner, a guest, protested the charge and complained to the state attorney general's Consumer Frauds Bureau when the hotel refused to remove the charge from his bill. The attorney general sued to compel the hotel to stop this practice and to refund charges already collected to all affected guests. The hotel managers argued that a messenger service used by 77 percent of the guests justified the charge. Decision?

8. Knopf applied for a loan at a bank, which sought a credit check to assure itself of Knopf's financial responsibility. Howe and Associates, a consumer credit reporting agency, confused Knopf's credit file with that of another individual of the same name and reported Knopf as bankrupt. This mistake delayed the granting of a bank loan. Knopf sued Howe for damages, claiming that their report, which took forty-nine days to make, was unreasonably delayed. Howe argued that such a complaint does not state a good cause of action. Decision?

9. Buyer purchased an automobile from seller on credit. Seller listed a $16 charge for "tag, title, and fees" and for a "documentary service fee" under the heading "Official Fees" on the sales contract but failed to itemize the amounts charged. Buyer complains that because components of the "official fees" were not itemized, the amount charged under that heading should not have been included in the computation of the finance charge. Decision?

10. Webb Foods, a retail grocery outlet, purchased debt collection forms from a collection agency. Although it wrote the collection agency's name and address on the mailing envelope, Webb did not include that address on the form letter or telegram when it mailed the forms to Stack, a debtor. Webb was demanding payment from Stack on checks returned for insufficient funds. Webb did not disclose that it had no legal right to collect certain charges or the fact that it, and not the collection agency, was sending the dunning notices. Is Stack liable to Webb on the checks?

PART SIX

Business Organizations

CHAPTER TWENTY-ONE
Forms of Business Organizations and Partnership (I)

CHAPTER TWENTY-TWO
Partnership (II)

CHAPTER TWENTY-THREE
Corporation (I)

CHAPTER TWENTY-FOUR
Corporation (II)

CHAPTER TWENTY-ONE

Business Organizations

Business is the foundation of our capitalistic society. There are big and small businesses everywhere in the United States. They may be sole proprietorships, partnerships, or corporations. Some are successful, others are not. How do they come about?

If a person has some money, talents, and the willingness to work, how should he or she start a business? Should he or she remain a sole proprietor, is a partner necessary, or is a corporation the proper form for the undertaking? Any chosen form of organization will have a profound effect on such important matters as capitalization of the enterprise, establishment procedure, length of the company's existence, transferability of its ownership, taxes, managerial control, and liability. Indeed, the success of the business depends to a considerable degree on how it is organized.

This Part VI deals mainly with partnerships and corporations. In addition to answering the above matters, it explains the rights and duties of the organization and its participants, and their liabilities to outsiders. The last chapter discusses corporate stock acquisition and securities regulations which should be of great interest to those who have dollars to invest or wish to work in a stock brokerage firm.

CHAPTER TWENTY-ONE

Forms of Business Organizations and Partnership (I)

21.1 Business Structures
Basic Considerations
   Capital
   Creation and Duration
   Taxes
   Control
   Liability
   Transferability

Forms of Business
   Sole Proprietorship
   Partnership
   Corporation
   Joint Venture
   Cooperative
   Syndicate
   Joint Stock Company
   Business Trust
   Franchise
   Unincorporated Association

21.2 Partnership Formation
Partnership Versus Corporation
Partnership Defined
Creation
   By Agreement
   By Estoppel
   Determining the Existence
Fictitious Name

21.3 Limited Partnership and Partnership Property
Limited Partnership
Partnership Property
   Capital
   Title
   Possessory Rights
   Assignability
   Execution, Charging Order
   Death of a Partner

21.1 Business Structures

Businesses range from the little girl with a five-dollar capital selling lemonade for twenty-five cents a glass to giant enterprises, like IBM, with multibillions of dollars in capital base and annual sales. Regardless of size, businesses are conducted under three basic forms of organization: (1) individual or sole proprietorship, (2) partnership, and (3) corporation. Other types of enterprising organizations, such as joint ventures, cooperatives, syndicates, joint stock companies, business trusts, franchises, and unincorporated associations, are in essence deviations and variations of the partnership and corporation.

Basic Considerations

A person who starts a new business may have a number of reasons, depending upon the circumstances and objectives, for preferring one business organization over another.

Capital

A successful businessperson is a realistic businessperson. Of course, dreaming of success is free, but to establish a viable business, one must realistically consider, first and foremost, whether he has sufficient capital for the kind of enterprise he is contemplating to establish. Capital includes diligence, personal skills, experience, and, ultimately, money.

Creation and Duration

Some businesses cost little or nothing to set up. Others are more complicated, as statutory regulations need to be met that may require efforts and money for professional advice, filing fees, etc. A pertinent question at this point is whether the organization is supposed to last for only one business endeavor or is expected to last "forever." Is the company expected to survive the founder?

Taxes

How do the tax consequences of the business affect the entrepreneur's total financial picture? For income tax purposes, certain business organizations may have profits and losses that can be combined with the owner's personal income and expense rather than taxed separately.

Control

Everyone should like to have complete managerial power over the business. Financial, physical, and other limitations may render such absolute one-person control not always possible. When others are involved in financing the business, decision-making powers must naturally be shared with those people having a stake in the company.

Liability

The entrepreneur may not be willing to assume personal liability for his conduct of business. He may want to protect a part of his personal wealth from the risk of doing business. In such a case, he may choose a form of business organization by which his liability is limited to the assets he has in the company. This mainly depends on whether the business organization is considered a separate entity under the law. If it is, the company may sue or be sued; if it is not, the person or persons owning the business are the ones to sue or be sued. Some business activities may result in the members of the organization being jointly liable, while other activities may impose joint *and* several liabilities.

Transferability

In some cases, ownership of business organizations can be transferred freely; in other cases, such transfers are restricted or even proscribed.

Forms of Business

Sole Proprietorship

Most beginners start business as a sole or individual proprietor, especially when the need for capital is limited and the proposed business is not too complicated. A sole proprietorship is comparatively simple to create. Except for some licensing requirements that may have to be met, anyone may commence a business as a sole proprietor without intricate formalities. A *regulatory* license may be needed for one who wishes to do business as a contractor, plumber, electrician, barber, lawyer, medical doctor, etc. Certain fees may also have to be paid to the local taxing authority for the necessary *revenue* license.

So far as income taxes are concerned, there is no distinction made between the business and the person. The proprietorship does not pay taxes. All company profits and losses are to be reported on the individual tax return.

A sole proprietor has complete managerial control over the business. Subject to certain rules concerning discrimination in employment, the proprietor may employ and terminate his employees at will. Since a sole proprietorship is not a separate legal entity, it cannot be a party in a litigation. An action must be brought personally against the owner. If the business uses a fictitious name such as "ABC Company," both the proprietor's name and the fictitious name must appear in the suit, for example, "John Smith, doing business as ABC Company."

With regard to exposure to creditors' claims, there is no difference between company assets and personal assets. The sole proprietor is personally liable for all business debts arising from company transactions as well as for torts committed by himself or his employees in the course of their employment.

Sole Proprietorship
A business owned by one person.

Regulatory License
Allows the licensee to do business based on her/his qualifications.

Revenue License
Allows the licensee to do business upon payment of the required fees or taxes.

The sole proprietor is free to transfer the entire business or part of his interest to another person or company. When he dies, the company is part of his estate.

Partnership

Partnership
An undertaking in which two or more persons do business for profit.

For various reasons, a person starting a new business may need another person or persons to work with. The reason may be financial, for instance, if one person alone would not have sufficient capital to establish the company. Another reason may be that the nature of management or operation requires more than one person who can trust and rely upon one another. In the restaurant business, it is not uncommon for the floor manager and the chef to be partners.

The Uniform Partnership Act Section 6 (1) defines partnership as "an association of two or more persons to carry on as co-owners a business for profit." The partnership is established by an agreement between the parties. No governmental approval or statutory filing is required. The agreement can be made orally, unless the Statute of Frauds requires a writing.

When all partners are active in the business, the company is called a *general* partnership; a *limited* partnership is one in which one or more of the partners do not participate in the conduct of business. As in the case of a sole proprietorship, if the partnership uses a fictitious name, proper notice must be filed.

Since a contract between the partners is all that is necessary to create a partnership, the cost of establishing the company normally is minimal. People such as physicians, lawyers, and accountants often become partners to share the burdens of doing business.

Unlike a corporation, a partnership is not intended to have a perpetual existence. A partnership may be terminated by agreement of the partners. It can also be terminated less amicably if there is serious dissension among the partners. In any event, the company cannot last longer than the life of any of its members.

The partnership itself is not subject to income tax. Each partner must report on his individual tax return his distributive share, whether or not actually distributed, of the partnership income or loss. Internal Revenue Code § 6031 requires the partnership to file Form 1065 ("U.S. Partnership Return of Income") to report its annual profits and losses as well as its distributions to the individual partners.

Regardless of the size and nature of the contribution, each general partner has an equal voice in managing and controlling the partnership. Liability for business debt is unlimited. Thus, each partner is personally liable for contractual obligations and tort liabilities attributable to the partnership. Under the law, each partner acts as an agent for all the other partners. Since managerial powers are shared equally among the general partners and each partner is liable with all his assets—business and personal—one must think carefully before entering into a partnership.

Although a partnership may have assets in its own name, it is under the Uniform Partnership Act not a separate legal entity. Unless otherwise provided by procedural rules, a partnership may not be a party in a civil action. A lawsuit must then be directed to the individual members doing business as partners in the partnership. The interest of a partner in the company is basically not transferable.

Corporation

Although a corporation may be created and owned entirely by one person, this form of business organization is usually chosen when a large capital for the enterprise is needed and funds from other sources are to be channeled in. An inventor of a product who wishes to do the manufacturing by himself but does not have the required capital may establish a corporation and attract funds from other people who expect to participate in the profits of the enterprise.

To establish a corporation, articles of incorporation must be filed by the incorporator(s) with the state government. The corporate articles must be approved by the secretary of state, and a fee must be paid. In some states, filing of the articles must be accompanied by the incorporators' pledge to provide a certain amount of paid-in capital upon approval. Compared with a sole proprietorship or a partnership, more cost is usually involved in creating a corporation.

Unlike a sole proprietorship and a partnership, the corporate existence is meant to be perpetual. Shares in the company are transferable and inheritable. Furthermore, unlike a sole proprietorship and a partnership, a corporation is a legal entity. Consequently, a corporation can sue and be sued.

A corporation is taxed on its income. The shareholders also pay income tax on the dividends they receive from the corporation. Therefore, there is double taxation on corporate profits. An exception to this rule is Subchapter S of the Internal Revenue Code, which allows a business corporation with no more than thirty-five shareholders under certain conditions to be treated as a partnership. In this event, the corporation does not pay corporate taxes, but each shareholder reports on his individual tax return his pro rata share, whether or not actually distributed, of the corporation profits or losses.

Although shareholders are legally the owners of a corporation, they may elect only a certain number of directors who represent them in overseeing the corporate business. In turn, these directors appoint executive officers who are in charge of the day-to-day management and operation of the company.

With regard to corporate debts, shareholders are not personally liable. Their liability for corporate debts is limited to the shareholders' equity in the company.

Corporation
A business organization created pursuant to statute, owned by one or more shareholders.

Joint Venture

A joint venture is similar to a partnership in that its members associate together as co-owners in a business enterprise for the purpose of making a profit. However, a partnership is usually intended to continue for a definite or indefinite period, whereas a joint venture is formed for a *single* transaction or a single series of transactions. Thus, the joint venture is more limited in scope and duration. An example of a joint venture is an agreement between

Joint Venture
A partnership for a special or limited purpose.

an owner of a parcel of land and a building contractor to build houses for sale and divide the profits. Business ventures range in size from very small enterprises to multimillion-dollar projects. The members of a joint venture can be individuals, partnerships, or corporations.

The relationship between the parties in a joint venture is governed by the rules of partnership. The Uniform Partnership Act applies to such matters as dissolution, fiduciary duty, accounting for profits and losses, and representation within the scope of business. Like a partnership, a joint venture is not a legal entity. Only the members individually can sue and be sued. The venture does not pay income taxes; the members do, upon distribution of the profits and losses.

An example case is *Wheatley* v. *Halvorson* (213 Or. 228, 323 P.2d 49 [1958]), in which the court ruled that there was a joint venture when three corporations and two individuals pooled their equipment, services, and other assets for the performance of a contract to construct a tunnel.

Cooperative

Cooperative
A group of individuals organized to gain some commercial advantage for their members.

Cooperatives are usually groups of individuals who gather their resources for the purpose of gaining a certain advantage in the marketplace. To obtain the lowest purchase price, consumers may pool their purchases and buy goods in bulk; to obtain the highest price, farmers may pool their farm products and sell them at an agreed price. Since such cooperatives aim at fixing prices, their agreements are in fact in restraint of trade and in violation of antitrust laws. Cooperatives, however, are generally considered exempt from those laws prohibiting monopoly practices. Farmers' and dairy farmers' cooperatives, for example, are explicitly exempted by the Capper-Volstead Act of 1922 from the operation of the federal Sherman Antitrust Act, provided they do not conspire with outsiders to fix prices.

Since cooperatives are created basically to marshal the members' resources, in general, they are for tax purposes nonprofit business organizations. If they are incorporated, dividends or profits are distributed to the members on the basis of their transactions with the cooperative rather than on the basis of the amount of capital contributed. Cooperatives are treated like partnerships if they are unincorporated.

Syndicate

Syndicate
Two or more investors joined in a partnership or corporation to finance a business project.

A syndicate consists of two or more investors who are financing a business project, such as the building or purchasing of an apartment complex or shopping center. The actual form of business organization may vary depending upon the financial objectives of the investors. Syndicates may be partnerships, limited partnerships, or corporations. The liability of a participating member depends upon the form of organization chosen.

Real estate syndicates in the form of limited partnerships are particularly favored, since the limited partners may offset fictitious partnership losses against their individual real income, that is, in a situation where the tax rules relative to active and passive income and expense permit such an offset.

Joint Stock Company

In a joint stock company, business management powers are given to directors and officers. As a business organization, the joint stock company is typically a hybrid of a partnership and a corporation. It has shareholders who may freely transfer their shares of stock. Its existence is meant to be perpetual, and the shareholders are not agents of one another, as would be the case in a partnership.

Unlike a corporation, which is created by statute, the joint stock company is established by an agreement between the shareholders. The company is not a legal entity and therefore cannot sue and be sued. For income tax purposes, the joint stock company is treated like a partnership and does not pay income tax. The principal disadvantage is that members are unlimitedly and personally liable for company debts.

Joint Stock Company
An unincorporated business organization whose owners are issued shares of stock to evidence their ownership.

Business Trust

The business trust, or *Massachusetts trust,* is established by a written trust agreement whereby trustors' ownerships to certain properties are deeded over to a trustee or a board of trustees who manage the properties for the benefit of the contributors. The trust agreement sets forth the powers and obligations of the trustees toward the trustors, who may at the same time be beneficiaries. The business trust is like a corporation in that death or bankruptcy of a beneficiary does not terminate the trust. Also, the beneficiaries are not personally liable for business debts. In some states, business trusts pay corporate taxes. The number of business trusts is declining, as such organizations may be subject to antitrust laws.

Business Trust
A trust created and operated to hold and manage properties for the benefit of investors who contribute money or other assets to the trust.

Franchise

The Federal Trade Commission (FTC) defines franchise as "an arrangement in which the owner of a trademark, tradename, or copyright licenses others, under specified conditions or limitations, to use the trademark, tradename, or copyright in purveying goods or services." A franchise is a contract between two independent individuals or companies. The grantor of the franchise is called the "franchisor," and the grantee is called the "franchisee." The agreement usually stipulates the duration of the relationship as well as the reasons for its termination, such as franchisee's debt, bankruptcy, or failure to meet the franchise obligations. The law of sales in Article 2 of the UCC applies when the franchise is established for the marketing of products manufactured by the franchisor.

As some franchises tend to be a mode of exploitation of the franchisee by the franchisor, to protect the franchisee, who is often in a lesser bargaining position, the FTC requires that the franchisor provide a disclosure statement concerning the franchisor's finances, operations, involvements in litigation, etc. This disclosure statement must be issued ten days before the franchisee signs the contract or pays for the franchise. Violation of this rule is subject to a fine of $10,000.

Since a franchise is not an agency, the franchisor is not liable for the franchisee's business dealings or for tort committed by the franchisee to a third party.

Franchise
An arrangement for licensing use of trademarks, copyrights or proprietary processes to persons who wish to use them in a business.

Facts

B.P. Oil Corporation granted a franchise on an automobile service station to Laison. The contract called for Laison to lease the station and buy the gas from B.P. Oil. Laison had complete control over the entire operation of the service station. One day when Mabe drove his car into the station for service, an attendant poured water into the radiator, causing an explosion. The water apparently contained some gasoline. Mabe sued B.P. Oil for his injuries, claiming that B.P. Oil was liable for Laison's negligence.

Decision

Judgment for B.P. Oil. The court ruled that Laison, the franchisee, was an independent contractor. B.P. Oil, the franchisor, did not make any operational decisions for the service station. There is no apparent agency, despite the fact that B.P.'s products were sold on the premises and the building was painted with B.P. Oil's colors, since it is common knowledge that such stations are independently owned and operated.

B.P. Oil Corp. v. Mabe, 279 Md. 632, 370 A.2d 554 (1977).

Unincorporated Association

Unincorporated Association
A nonprofit organization such as a social, fraternal or political club.

An unincorporated association is created by two or more individuals for the furtherance of a common *nonprofit* purpose. Social clubs, political parties, and fraternal organizations are common examples of unincorporated associations. No particular form of organization is required. Conduct or agreement indicating the existence of such an association is sufficient.

The unincorporated association usually does not have any legal existence. It can therefore not be a party to a litigation. Membership of the association does not automatically lead to personal liability for the association's conduct of business. A member becomes personally and unlimitedly liable if it is evident that he authorized or ratified a certain act or transaction by the association, as demonstrated in the following case.

Facts

Maine National Guard units held an annual New Year's Eve dance in the Augusta State Armory. Libby was a paying guest at the dance and, on leaving, fell on the ice in the parking lot and was injured. Perry was a member of the Armory Committee, which planned and operated the dance, as was Turner. Turner, however, took no part in the activities and was absent from all committee meetings. Judgment was against the entire committee, and it appealed.

Decision

The court held that although the Armory Committee was a voluntary unincorporated association formed to accomplish a common purpose and was duty bound to use the same care to avoid injury to others as natural persons are individually, mere membership in the body does not create liability. It was error to find Turner responsible with the other defendants on the mere evidence that he was a member of the Armory Committee. All the other defendants actively participated, aided, and abetted in the affair and were responsible to the plaintiff for the wrongful acts of omission of their associates or their agents in carrying out the social event duly authorized by the association. Judgment reversed as to Turner but sustained as to the other defendants.

Libby v. Perry, 311 A.2d 527 (Me. 1973).

Questions

1. Name several reasons why one would prefer a certain form of business organization over another.

2. How does one start a sole proprietorship?
3. Discuss the legal existence and liability aspects of a partnership as opposed to a corporation.
4. What is a joint venture?
5. Discuss the features of a franchise.

21.2 Partnership Formation

Partnership Versus Corporation

Most businesses owned by two or more persons or companies are either partnerships or corporations. The following table emphasizes once more the difference between these two business organizations.

Table 21.1 Partnership versus Corporation

Partnership	Corporation
Created by agreement.	Created by statutory authorization.
Not a legal separate entity in most states.	Legal entity separate and distinct from its owners (i.e., a legal person for the ownership of property and appearance as a party to litigation).
Each partner subject to unlimited liability for debts, contracts, and torts of the other partners arising out of the partnership business.	Shareholders not liable for the debts of the corporation.
A partner's interest not transferable without the consent of all of the other partners.	Shares of stock freely transferable.
Each partner has a direct and equal voice in the management of the business.	Management indirect through elected directors.
The partnership terminated by the agreement or by the death, bankruptcy, or withdrawal of a partner.	May have perpetual existence.
Each partner pays an income tax on his share of the net profits whether distributed or not.	Corporation pays an income tax on net profits, and the shareholders pay an income tax on the dividends they receive. There can be a tax advantage depending on the amount of net profits distributed and the shareholder's tax bracket.

Partnership Defined

According to the Uniform Partnership Act quoted earlier, a partnership is an association of two or more persons to carry on a business as co-owners for the purpose of making profits. It is *created by agreement* between the parties. A *trading* partnership is a business involved in buying and selling goods or real property. A *nontrading* partnership is a business that provides services, such as a medical office, a law firm, or an accounting firm.

The members of a partnership can be individual persons, partnerships, corporations, and other associations. To become a partner, an individual person must have the legal capacity to make a contract. A partner under the age of eighteen may avoid his partnership obligations or withdraw from the partnership entirely at any time before reaching majority. All basic contract rules relative to insanity, intoxication, etc., apply.

The question whether a corporation should be able to become a partner in a partnership, as acknowledged by the Uniform Partnership Act, is often disputed. The reason for disagreement is the rule that a natural person who is a general partner is absolutely and personally liable with all his assets, whereas a corporation in the same situation would be liable only with its corporate equity while the shareholders are not personally affected. In practice, the answer to this question is provided by the articles of incorporation and the relevant corporate laws applicable in the particular state. In any event, in dealing with the partnership, it is essential for one to know who the partners are to prevent future surprises.

Creation

By Agreement

A partnership may be established by an oral agreement, except when a writing is required by the Statute of Frauds.

Facts

Athene Cooper and Jacquelyn Hunt (then Saunders) orally agreed to undertake a business venture of the purchase, renovation, and operation of several rooming houses, a restaurant, and a grocery store. When Saunders became Hunt, her husband urged her to terminate the venture with Cooper, which she did. Cooper argued that the evidence did not establish a partnership between the parties but at most, a joint tenancy of the realty, and claimed that no agreements to operate any businesses were ever made. The court decided that there was a partnership and that Hunt was entitled to the amount she had contributed—$12,250. Cooper appealed.

Decision

The court held that a writing was not a partnership requirement. All that is needed is an association of two or more persons to carry on as co-owners of a business for profit. Receipt by a person of a share of the profits of a business is prima facie evidence that the person is a partner. Affirmed.

Cooper v. Saunders-Hunt, 365 A.2d 626 (D.C.App. 1976).

A similar case is *Stuart* v. *Overland Medical Center* (510 S.W.2d 494 [Mo.App. 1974]), which involved a physician practicing in a medical office without a written agreement of partnership. The court held that a valid partnership nevertheless existed, based on verbal arrangements and other conduct of the parties.

Although an oral agreement may be valid, it is desirable that the agreement be in writing to avoid subsequent disputes as to mutual rights and duties. Under the Statute of Frauds, a partnership contract must be in writing if the partnership is to continue for more than one year or if it will be engaging in the business of buying and selling real property.

A partnership agreement should include the following points:

1. Name of the firm.
2. Names and addresses of the partners.
3. Nature and purpose of the business.
4. Location of the partnership office and where the business is to be conducted.
5. Date of commencement of the partnership and how long it will exist.
6. Contributions by the partners which may consist of money, real and personal property, expertise, service, etc.
7. Rights of the partners to manage the company.
8. Obligations of the partners relative to the operation of the business.
9. Partners' salaries and drawing accounts.
10. Sharing of profits and losses.
11. Bookkeeping and accounting methods.
12. Qualifications for subsequent new partners.
13. Provisions regarding retiring and deceased partners.
14. Handling of grievance and arbitration.
15. Procedures for dissolution and distribution of assets.

Generally, the Uniform Partnership Act and other partnership regulations are ancillary in nature. They apply only where the contract between the parties is silent. It is the partnership agreement that primarily governs the relationships, rights, and duties of the partners, as shown in the following case.

Facts

Marshall (defendant) and Olsen were partners in a company dealing in billboard advertising. Marshall had an 80 percent interest and Olsen a 20 percent interest in the partnership. Olsen died, and Seattle-First National Bank (plaintiff) was executor of her estate. The partnership agreement required the surviving partner to purchase the interest of the deceased partner. It also stipulated the procedure for establishing the market value of that interest. In accordance with the stipulation, Seattle-First brought an action against Marshall to compel him to purchase Olsen's interest at a price of $164,649. Marshall argued that the price should be discounted by sales cost and capital gain taxes to be paid upon the sale of partnership interest.

Decision

Judgment for Olsen's estate. Since the partnership specifically set forth the method of valuing a partner's interest without providing allowances for any discount, the court rejected Marshall's contention, even though such discount may in other situations be appropriate. The agreement is the heart of the partnership, and its mandate must be enforced as written.

Seattle-First National Bank v. *Marshall,* 31 Wash. App. 339, 641 P.2d 1194 (1982).

Figure 21.1 Sample Partnership Agreement

This agreement, made and entered into as of the [*Date*], by and among [*Names*] (hereinafter collectively sometimes referred to as "Partners").

WITNESSETH:

Whereas, the Parties hereto desire to form a General Partnership (hereinafter referred to as the "Partnership"), for the term and upon the conditions hereinafter set forth;

Now, therefore, in consideration of the mutual covenants hereinafter contained, it is agreed by and among the Parties hereto as follows:

Article I
BASIC STRUCTURE

§ 1.1 Form

The Parties hereby form a General Partnership pursuant to the Laws of [*Name of State*].

§ 1.2 Name

The business office and place of business of the Partnership shall be conducted under the name of [*Name*].

§ 1.3 Place of Business

The principal office and place of business of the Partnership shall be located at [*Describe*], or such other place as the Partners may from time to time designate.

§ 1.4 Term

The Partnership shall commence on [*Date*], and shall continue for [*Number*] years, unless earlier terminated in the following manner:

(a) By the completion of the purpose intended, or
(b) Pursuant to this Agreement, or
(c) By applicable [*State*] law, or
(d) By death, insanity, bankruptcy, retirement, withdrawal, resignation, expulsion, or disability of all of the then Partners.

§ 1.5 Purpose —General

The purpose for which the Partnership is organized is _____.

Article II
FINANCIAL ARRANGEMENTS

§ 2.1 Initial Contributions of Partners

Each Partner has contributed to the initial capital of the Partnership property in the amount and form indicated on Schedule A attached hereto and made a part hereof. Capital contributions to the Partnership shall not earn interest. An individual capital account shall be maintained for each Partner.

§ 2.2 Additional Capital Contribution

If at any time during the existence of the Partnership it shall become necessary to increase the capital with which the said Partnership is doing business, then (upon the vote of the Managing Partner(s)):

Each party to this Agreement shall contribute to the capital of this Partnership within _____ days notice of such need in an amount according to his then Percentage Share of Capital as called for by the Managing Partner(s).

§ 2.3 Percentage Share of Profits and Capital

(a) The Percentage Share of Profits and Capital of each Partner shall be (unless otherwise modified by the terms of this Agreement) as follows:

Names	Initial Percentage Share of Profits and Capital

§ 2.4 Interest

No interest shall be paid on any contribution to the capital of the Partnership.

Figure 21.1 Continued

§ 2.5 Return of Capital Contributions
No Partner shall have the right to demand the return of his capital contributions except as herein provided.

§ 2.6 Rights of Priority
Except as herein provided, the individual Partners shall have no right to any priority over each other as to the return of capital contributions except as herein provided.

§ 2.7 Distributions
Distributions to the Partners of net operating profits of the Partnership, as hereinafter defined, shall be made at (*least monthly/such times as the Managing Partner(s) shall reasonable agree.*) Such distributions shall be made to the Partners simultaneously.

For the purpose of this Agreement, net operating profit for any accounting period shall mean the gross receipts of the Partnership for such period, less the sum of all cash expenses of operation of the Partnership, and such sums as may be necessary to establish a reserve for operating expenses.

§ 2.8 Compensation
No Partner shall be entitled to receive any compensation from the Partnership, nor shall any Partner receive any drawing account from the Partnership.

Article III
MANAGEMENT

§ 3.1 Managing Partners
The Managing Partner(s) shall be [*Names*] [*or* "all partners"].

§ 3.2 Voting
The Managing Partner(s) shall have the right to vote as to the management and conduct of the business of the Partnership as follows:

Names   **Vote**

Article IV
DISSOLUTION

§ 4.1 Dissolution
In the event that the Partnership shall hereinafter be dissolved for any reason whatsoever, a full and general account of its assets, liabilities and transactions shall at once be taken. Such assets may be sold and turned into cash as soon as possible and all debts and other amounts due the Partnership collected. The proceeds thereof shall thereupon be applied as follows:

(a) To discharge the debts and liabilities of the Partnership and the expenses of liquidation.

(b) To pay each Partner or his legal representative any unpaid salary, drawing account, interest or profits to which he shall then be entitled and in addition, to repay to any Partner his capital contributions in excess of his original capital contribution.

(c) To divide the surplus, if any, among the Partners or their representatives as follows:

    (1) First (to the extent of each partner's then capital account) in proportion to their then capital accounts.

    (2) Then according to each Partner's then Percentage Share of *Capital/Income*.

§ 4.2 Right To Demand Property
No Partner shall have the right to demand and receive property in kind for his distribution.

Witnesses   **Partners**

_____   _____

_____   _____

Dated: _____

Adopted from "West's Legal Forms," 2d ed. by Paul Lieberman. Copyright © 1981 by West Publishing Co. Reprinted with permission.

By Estoppel

Estoppel
A bar preventing a person from making a claim contrary to her/his previous claim or conduct the other party relied on.

A person who holds himself out as a partner or knowingly allows himself to be held out as a partner becomes liable as such to those who deal with the firm in the belief that he is a partner. A partnership by estoppel is similar to an agency created by estoppel covered in Chapter 11.

The following case illustrates the creation of a partnership by estoppel.

Calada Materials Co. v. Collins
184 Cal.App.2d 250, 7 Cal.Rptr. 374 (1960).

Vallée, Justice Appeal by defendant R. W. Walker from an adverse judgment in an action for the value of oil well drilling materials alleged to have been sold by plaintiff to defendants M. H. Collins and R. W. Walker. . . .

Plaintiff delivered mud and mud materials in connection with the drilling of two oil wells, Higdon No. 3 and C & W No. 1. Defendant concedes he is liable for an unpaid balance of $5,338.21 plus interest for materials furnished by plaintiff for Higdon No. 3. He denies he is responsible for any part of $5,795.28 for materials furnished by plaintiff for C & W No. 1. . . .

The court found that at all times mentioned in the complaint defendants Collins and Walker were doing business as a partnership under the firm name of Collins and Walker. . . . Collins and Walker testified the relationship between them was the same as to both wells. Plaintiff furnished the materials for both wells.

. . . On one occasion Walker, speaking of the lease on which C & W No. 1 was drilled, said "he was a partner with Collins and backing him and anything Collins did he was with him as long as it was all right with Mr. Collins." When Walker signed the drilling contract for C & W No. 1 he was asked, "You are partners in the deal, aren't you?" Walker replied, "Yes." During the drilling of C & W No. 1 there were signs on the rig and on trailers around the site reading, "Collins-Walker, C & W No. 1." On several occasions Collins introduced Walker as his partner with respect to C & W No. 1. Walker told plaintiff's manager that he and Collins were partners in C & W No. 1 and that plaintiff would get part of the money, if not all of it, in a few days and that Collins would pay him. . . .

A partnership need not be evidenced by a writing. It may be oral. . . .

And where there is no writing evidencing the agreement, the existence of a partnership may be evidenced by the conduct of the parties. . . .

Whether the acts and conduct of Walker were sufficient to lead plaintiff to believe he was a copartner and assumed responsibility as such was a question of fact for the trial court to determine from the evidence and the inferences to be drawn therefrom. . . .

Judgment affirmed.

Determining the Existence

Among all the circumstances that indicate the existence of a partnership, joint rights to manage and sharing profits and losses of the business are the most important tests as to whether a partnership exists. This is shown in the following case.

Facts

Defendant Bowen owned the Havana Club and all its physical assets located in a rented building. He made an agreement with plaintiff Cutler that she would operate the club, purchase supplies, pay bills, keep the books, and hire and fire employees. Bowen and Cutler were each to receive $100 per week and divide the net profits. A partnership form was filed by the business to the Internal Revenue Service. The redevelopment agency subsequently took the building to use for its own purposes and paid Bowen $10,000 damages for disruption of the business. Cutler brought this lawsuit against Bowen to recover one half of that sum on the claim that they were partners.

Decision

Judgment for Cutler. Even though all the physical assets of the Havana Club belonged to Bowen, there was a partnership in which Cutler contributed services. The partnership agreement called for equal sharing of the business profits. Moreoever, tax returns filed were for a partnership. Thus, the enterprise was not solely owned by Bowen.

Cutler v. Bowen, 543 P.2d 1349 (Utah 1975).

It should be noted that filing a partnership form to the IRS is significant only in determining whether there is a partnership as to the person(s) submitting the return. It is not controlling or binding either as to a person named as a partner on the return if the person is not aware of the filing or as to other third parties. Filing a partnership form of income tax, for example, does not change an employment relationship to a partnership.

Facts

The Delaware Employment Security Commission charged plaintiff Chaiken for failing to pay the unemployment compensation tax assessed against two barbers working in Chaiken's barbershop. Plaintiff defended on the ground that the two were not employees; they were all partners, as substantiated by the federal tax return filed for a partnership. Evidence showed that Chaiken owned the barbershop, that he used the same trade name long before the two other barbers joined him, and that he had a separate contract with each of the two barbers specifying the workdays and days off.

Decision

Judgment for Delaware Equipment. All the elements of co-ownership of a business conducted on the basis of profit sharing were missing. The facts that Chaiken had a separate contract with each of the two barbers rather than one partnership agreement and that each contract specified the workdays and days off confirmed that the other two barbers were only employees. Filing a return as a partnership did not render the enterprise a partnership.

Chaiken v. Employment Security Commission, 274 A.2d 707 (Del. Super. 1971).

Fictitious Name

Many partnerships as well as individuals operate under fictitious business names. Most states have statutes requiring the registration of such names if a business is conducted under a name that does not include the surname of each of the partners or under a name that suggests the existence of additional owners.

Fictitious Name
A business name different from the owner's real name.

Facts

Duris Enterprises was a company that leased property to Gahanna for one year. Gahanna broke the lease within the year, and Duris sued for a breach of contract. Gahanna argued that "Duris Enterprises" was an unregistered fictitious name, thereby preventing Duris from suing under that name.

Decision

Judgment for Duris Enterprises. It is true that a partnership could not sue under an unregistered fictitious name. "Duris Enterprises" is not, however, fictitious. A fictitious name is one that is "assumed, counterfeit, or pretended." "Duris" is the true surname of the partners, and adding the word *"Enterprises"* did not make the name fictitious. The statute requiring fictitious name filing is intended only to provide the public a way to find out who the members of the partnership are.

Duris Enterprises v. *Moore*, 9 Ohio App. 3d 99, 458 N.E.2d 451 (1983).

The purpose of the requirement is to make a public record of the individuals in the partnership for the benefit of those who deal with the partnership.

Such registration is usually necessary, because most banking procedures require such filing before they will open an account under a fictitious name and most courts will not permit lawsuits to be filed in the fictitious name until the required notice is executed, filed, and published.

The normal procedure is to file a fictitious business name statement—usually on a preprinted form provided by the clerk upon which is listed the names and addresses of all of the partners—with the county clerk of the county of the main place of business of the entity. After the record is filed with the clerk and the filing fee is paid, the statement must be published in a newspaper of general circulation in that county for a specified period of time (in California, once a week for four consecutive weeks).

Questions

1. Who may become members of a partnership?
2. Name the main points that should be included in a partnership agreement.
3. What is a partnership by estoppel?
4. What are the most important features that determine the existence of a partnership?
5. What is the purpose of fictitious name filing?

21.3 Limited Partnership and Partnership Property

Limited Partnership

A limited partnership is a statutory form of association, basically the same as a general partnership with the added provision for investors who wish to share in the profits but not in the management and thereby avoid the personal liability of general partners.

The main differences between limited and general partnerships are that the limited partnership

1. Must have at least one general partner.
2. Must file a Certificate of Limited Partnership.
3. May not include in its name the surnames of any limited partners without making them liable to creditors.
4. May not permit limited partners to take part in the control of the business.
5. Limits the liability of limited partners.

Limited Partnership
A partnership organized pursuant to statute, with provision for limiting the liability of some of the partners.

Delaney v. Fidelity Lease Limited
526 S.W.2d 543 (Tex. 1975).

Daniel, Justice The question here is whether limited partners in a limited partnership become liable as general partners if they "take part in the control of the business" while acting as officers of a corporation which is the sole general partner of the limited partnership. The trial court, by summary judgment, held that under such circumstances the limited partners did not become liable as general partners. The court of civil appeals affirmed with a dissent and a concurring opinion. We reverse and remand the case for trial on the merits.

Fidelity Lease Limited is a limited partnership organized under the Texas Uniform Limited Partnership Act, to lease restaurant locations. It is composed of 22 individual partners, and a corporate general partner, Interlease Corporation. Interlease's officers, directors and shareholders were W. S. Crombie, Jr., Alan Kahn, and William D. Sanders, who were also limited partners of Fidelity. In February of 1969, plaintiffs Delaney, et al. entered into an agreement with the limited partnership, Fidelity, acting by and through its corporate general partner, Interlease to lease a fast-food restaurant to the partnership. In accordance therewith, plaintiffs built the restaurant, but Fidelity failed to take possession or pay rent.

Plaintiffs brought suit for damages for breach of the lease agreement, naming as defendants the limited partnership of Fidelity Lease Limited, its corporate general partner Interlease Corporation, and all of its limited partners. . . . Plaintiffs appealed only as to limited partners Crombie, Kahn, and Sanders. Plaintiffs sought to hold these three individuals personally liable alleging that they had become general partners by participating in the management and control of the limited partnership.

Pertinent portions of the Texas Uniform Limited Partnership Act, Article 6132a, provide:

> Sec. 8. A limited partner shall not become liable as a general partner unless in addition to the exercise of his rights and powers as a limited partner, he *takes part in the control of the business.*

It was alleged by plaintiffs, and there is summary judgment evidence, that the three limited partners controlled the business of the limited partnership, albeit through the corporate entity. The defendant limited partners argue that they acted only through the corporation and that the corporation actually controlled the business of the limited partnership. In response to this contention, we adopt the

> following statements in the dissenting opinion of Chief Justice Preslar in the court of civil appeals:
>
>> I find it difficult to separate their acts for they were at all times in the dual capacity of limited partners and officers of the corporation. Apparently the corporation had no function except to operate the limited partnership and Appellees were obligated to their other partners to so operate the corporation as to benefit the partnership. Each act was done then, not for the corporation, but for the partnership. Indirectly, if not directly, they were exercising control over the partnership. Truly 'the corporation fiction' was in this instance a fiction.
>
> Thus, we hold that the personal liability, which attaches to a limited partner when "he takes part in the control and management of the business," cannot be evaded merely by acting through a corporation.
>   . . . Crombie, Kahn, and Sanders argue that, since their only control of Fidelity's business was as officers of the alleged corporate general partner, they are insulated from personal liability arising from their activities or those of the corporation. This is a general rule of corporate law, but one of several exceptions in which the courts will disregard the corporate fiction is where it is used to circumvent a statute. . . . That is precisely the result here, for it is undisputed that the corporation was organized to manage and control the limited partnership. Strict compliance with the statute is required if a limited partner is to avoid liability as a general partner. . . .
>   . . . Accordingly, the cause of action against the defendants Crombie, Kahn, and Sanders is severed, and as to that portion of the case the judgments of the lower courts are reversed and such cause as to them is remanded for trial in accordance with this opinion. . . .

The limited partners share in the profits but do not share losses beyond their capital investment. Limited partnership acts have been enacted in all states, most of them adopting the Uniform Limited Partnership Act (ULPA). In 1976, the ULPA was revised to resolve uncertainties existing in the original law and to permit certain actions by the limited partners that are not considered to be participation in the management or control of the business, such as being a contractor, employee, or agent of the partnership or general partner; consulting with or advising the general partner; and voting on specified extraordinary matters. Most states have either adopted the revised Act or further expanded their own. For example, California's statute, effective in 1983, treats limited partnerships more like corporations, requires that the firm name include the words "limited partnership," lists various activities that limited partners may engage in without exposing themselves to liability, and specifies new detailed procedures to be followed.

A limited partnership is not created by a mere informal agreement as is possible with a general partnership. It is created by a formal proceeding that must follow the statute. For example, the associates must sign, file, and record a certificate, which must set forth the partnership name, charter, location of business, the term to carry on the business, amount and character of contributions by special or limited partners, the share of profits or com-

FORMS OF BUSINESS ORGANIZATIONS AND PARTNERSHIP (I)

Figure 21.2 Sample Limited Partnership Certificate

CERTIFICATE OF LIMITED PARTNERSHIP

The undersigned, desiring to form a Limited Partnership under the Limited Partnership Act of the State of _____, make this certificate for that purpose.

§ 1. Name. The name of the Limited Partnership shall be "_____."

§ 2. Purpose. The business of the Limited Partnership shall be to [*describe*].

§ 3. Location. The location of the Limited Partnership's principal place of business is _____ County, _____.

§ 4. Agent for Service of Process. The agent for service of process on the Limited Partnership in the State of _____ shall be _____, whose business address is _____ .

§ 5. Members and Designation. The names and business addresses of the members, and their designation as General or Limited Partners, are

_____	[*Address*]	General Partner
_____	[*Address*]	General Partner
_____	[*Address*]	Limited Partner
_____	[*Address*]	Limited Partner

§ 6. Term. The term for which the Limited Partnership is to exist is _____ .

§ 7. Initial Contributions of Partners. The amount of cash and a description and statement of the agreed value of the other property or services contributed by each Partner are

[*Name*]	[*Describe*]
[*Name*]	[*Describe*]
[*Name*]	[*Describe*]
[*Name*]	[*Describe*]

§ 8. Subsequent Contributions of Partners. Each Partner may (but shall not be obliged to) make additional contributions to the capital of the Limited Partnership as follows:

§ 9. Profit Shares of Partners. The share of the profits that each Partner shall receive by reason of his contribution is

[*Name*]	_____%
[*Name*]	_____%
[*Name*]	_____%
[*Name*]	_____%

Signed _____, 19_____

Source: Reprinted with permission from Edmund O. Belsheim's "Modern Legal Forms." Copyright © 1971 by West Publishing Co.

pensation of each limited partner, and methods for changing personnel and continuing business after retirement of a general partner.

Limited partnerships are used primarily for investment purposes. The limited partners are not really partners but are investors with no personal liability beyond their investment.

There is an ever-increasing use of this method of acquiring investment capital, particularly in real estate development, oil and gas leases, film production, and the building of medical facilities. The limited partner is usually attracted to this mode of investing when he is subject to a progressive income tax rate schedule and his real personal income is for tax purposes allowed to be fictitiously reduced by *quasi* partnership losses, such as plant or equipment depreciations and research and development. Actually, utilizing a Subchapter S corporate organization, as explained earlier, would have more or less the same tax consequences. Lately, however, the U.S. Congress attempted to eliminate this tax advantage by denying the offset of "passive" losses against "active" income. Moreover, the U.S. Tax Reform Act of 1986 replaced the progressive tax bracket system with more uniform "flat" rate schedules.

Partnership Property

To ascertain the rights of the partners and the creditors to specific property, it is frequently important, especially when creditors of a partner are involved or upon dissolution, to ascertain exactly what property constitutes partnership property and what constitutes property of the individual partner.

What constitutes partnership property is ascertained from the agreement of the partners, from the partners' conduct, and from the purpose for and the way in which the property is used in the partnership business. The Uniform Partnership Act (UPA) states that all property originally brought into the partnership or subsequently acquired by purchase or otherwise on account of the partnership is partnership property. Unless a contrary intention appears, property acquired with partnership funds is partnership property (UPA § 8[1][2]).

Facts

Plaintiff Gauldin and defendant Corn entered into a partnership agreement to raise cattle and hogs. All cost of labor, profits, and losses were to be shared equally. Corn and his wife owned the land, which was used rent free for the business. The partnership paid for bulldozing and clearing the land, repairing and building fences, seeding, and fertilizing. A machine shed was built on the land for $2,487.50. A Cargill unit was built on the land for $8,000. When the partnership was dissolved after about ten years, Gauldin paid Corn $7,500 for the "removable" assets, which he apparently took. However, there was no agreement regarding the distribution of the barn and the Cargill unit. Gauldin sued to recover one half of the value of the two buildings.

Decision

Judgment for plaintiff Gauldin. It is a well-established rule that improvements made upon land owned by one partner, if made with partnership funds for purposes of the partnership business, are the property of the partnership. The partner who does not own the land is entitled to his proportionate share of the value of the improvements. This general rule applies where there is no agreement between the parties concerning this matter, as it is the case here. The barn and Cargill unit were acquired with partnership funds for the purpose of raising cattle and hogs. Hence, Gauldin is entitled to one half of the value of the two buildings at the time of the partnership's dissolution.

Gauldin v. Corn, 595 S.W.2d 329 (Mo. App. 1980).

Anything that is a proper subject of ownership may be partnership property. Examples of partnership property are cash, land, goods, the rendition of personal services, corporate stock, a seat on the stock exchange, an insurance policy on the life of a partner, and a patent.

In the absence of an express or implied agreement to the contrary, goodwill is a partnership asset. Goodwill means the public favor and patronage built up by the owner of a business. It has been defined as "nothing more than the probability that the old customers will resort to the old place." It includes the right to use the established firm name. In service partnerships, it may be so closely tied to the individual partners that none remains in the business. When a court is required to determine the value of the goodwill of a partnership business, the value is usually placed at what a reasonable person would be willing to pay.

Crops growing on partnership land are considered partnership property if that is the express or implied agreement of the partners.

Capital

Capital of a partnership is a monetary figure that represents the total of the sum contributed by the partners as a permanent investment. It is a fixed amount that the partnership under profitable circumstances is obligated to return to the partners at the time of dissolution. Distributed profits reinvested by the individual partners after paying taxes as well as other partners' extension of loans to the partnership are separate from the original capital. In the partnership balance sheet, these items do not belong to partnership equity but become partnership liabilities. From the individual partner's perspective, they are personal assets subject to claims by the partner's personal creditors.

Title

A partnership may hold and transfer title to personal property in the name of the partnership, whether the name is fictitious or consists of the names of the partners.

Under the Uniform Partnership Act (which has been adopted by all states except Georgia and Louisiana), real property may be acquired in the partnership name, whether it is fictitious or not. Title acquired in the partnership name must be conveyed in the partnership name.

Whenever real property is acquired by the partnership for partnership purposes, the rule of out-and-out conversion applies which converts the real property to personalty for all purposes, including descent and distribution.

Possessory Rights

A partner is a co-owner with the partners of specific partnership property (e.g., the factory, equipment, trucks). In the absence of an agreement to the contrary between the partners, each partner has an equal right with the partners to possess specific partnership property for partnership purposes. Each partner has no right, however, to possess such property for any other purpose without consent of the partners.

Assignability

Assignment
Transfer of one's contractural rights to a third party.

A partner may sell his *interest* in the assets of the partnership to a third person. Such a transfer does not pass the title of the partnership in the assets but passes only the interest of the individual partner. The *assignee* does *not* become a *member* of the firm because of the highly personal nature of a partnership and thus is not entitled to interfere in the management of the partnership business, to inspect the partnership books, or to require any information regarding partnership transactions. The assignee is entitled only to receive the profits to which the assignor would otherwise be entitled.

Execution, Charging Order

Charging order
A court order to satisfy a partner's personal debt by dissolving the partnership to reach the partner's interest.

A partner's right in specific partnership property is not subject to execution unless it is a claim against the entire partnership. In other words, a personal creditor of a particular partner cannot have that partner's interest in the partnership attached and sold to pay what is owed. The remedy of a personal creditor of a partner is to attempt to reach other assets of the partner; or if the creditor wishes to proceed against partnership property, he should get a charging order under which a receiver will be appointed to collect from the partnership the share of profits of the debtor-partner. UPA § 28 provides that the creditor can get a *charging order* whereby a receiver is appointed and the partner's interest in the profits and in corpus upon dissolution is applied to satisfy the judgment. If the partnership is a partnership at will (no definite time limit), a dissolution can be brought about immediately.

Facts

Goldblatt, one of the partners of a partnership, owed Buckman money. Upon a judgment against the debtor, Buckman attempted to foreclose on the land owned by the partnership. The partnership opposed this execution.

Decision

Judgment for partnership. A charging order is needed for a creditor of an individual partner to sell out that partner's interest in the firm. A creditor cannot sell a personal interest of any specific item of a partnership property. UPA § 25 allows execution against property of the partnership only on a claim against the partnership. Furthermore, UPA § 28 provides for the entry of a charging order against the interest of the debtor partner, by virtue of which the share of that interest that would be paid to the debtor partner, is to be paid instead to the receiver on behalf of the creditor.

Buckman v. Goldblatt, 39 Ohio App. 2d 1, 314 N.E.2d 188 (1974).

Death of a Partner

On the death of a partner, the partner's right (not ownership) in specific partnership property *vests in the surviving partner* or partners, except where the deceased was the last surviving partner, in which case the right in such property vests in the deceased's legal representative. This is to prevent the executor of the deceased's estate from coming into the partnership and taking custody of the deceased partner's interest which would probably cause confusion and difficulty. The surviving partners do not become the owners of the deceased partner's interest. They merely have the right of exclusive possession during the period that the partnership is liquidated and the net assets distributed to the partners, including the representative of the deceased partner. The liquidation of the partnership and distribution of the net assets must be done immediately after death of one of the partners in the absence of an agreement to the contrary.

QUESTIONS

1. What are the main features of a limited partnership?
2. How may a limited partner for income tax purposes benefit from a limited partnership?
3. What is partnership property?
4. Are all proceeds and contributions received from individual partners considered "capital" of the partnership?
5. What is a charging order?

PROBLEMS

1. A, B, and C agree that they will form a partnership but that C will not become a partner until he is discharged from the Army in one year. In the meantime, C lends the partnership $5,000 and agrees to take 5 percent of the profits as interest on the loan. A tells T, without C's knowledge, that C is a partner of the firm. T, relying on this information, sells the firm goods on credit. Six months later, the firm becomes insolvent. T brings action against C for the debt still due. Decision?

2. Defendant, a friend of the members of a partnership, was present when the partners requested goods on credit from the plaintiff and when, at the same time, they told Plaintiff that Defendant was a partner. Although Defendant heard the statement, he remained silent. Plaintiff brings action for the goods against Defendant. Decision?

3. A and B are partners in the garage business. They invest part of the profits from their business in land, taking title in their names as tenants in common. The land becomes very valuable, but their business becomes insolvent. B dies, leaving a wife. Creditors of the partners seek the land. B's wife and A also claim the land. Decision?

4. A, B, and C are partners. Nothing is said in the partnership agreement regarding the assignability of a partner's interest. C & A get into a dispute, after which A sells his entire interest to T, a responsible and wealthy businessman who is an expert in the business of the partnership. B and C refuse to permit T to participate in the management of the partnership business. Decision?

5. A and B are partners at will. C, a judgment creditor of B, wants to attach B's interest in the partnership property to collect his judgment. What advice would you give C?

6. A, B, C, and D, residents of Illinois, were partners doing business under the trade name of Morning Glory Nursery. A owned one-third interest, and B, C, and D owned two-ninths each. The partners acquired three tracts of land in Illinois for the partnership. Two of the tracts were acquired in the names of the partners, "trading and doing business as Morning Glory Nursery." The third was acquired in their individual names without the trade name appearing on the deed. B died intestate, leaving his wife and one son as his only heirs. The widow and

son sue to have B's interest in the real property transferred to them by descent. Decision?

7. Bolden, a minor, and Allen, an adult, formed a partnership to purchase and operate a machine shop. They purchased the shop from Plaintiff, and each contributed $5,000 toward the purchase price and gave the plaintiff a note for $5,000 for the balance. The project was unsuccessful, and the partnership became insolvent. Plaintiff brought an action against the partnership and Bolden and Allen individually to recover the $5,000 due on the unpaid note. Bolden claims that as a minor he has no liability. Decision?

8. Mather, a toy manufacturer, employed Stark as a saleswoman, agreeing to pay her a salary of 20 percent of the profits of the business. The business showed a loss of $1,500 at the end of the year. Mather claimed that since Stark was to get 20 percent of the profits, she was also liable for 20 percent of the losses. Is Mather correct?

9. Penner, Cory, and Sheldon decided to ask for contributions of food, clothing, and money from businesses in their town to be used for the poor. They considered themselves to be partners in the work and so identified themselves to others. All contributions made to the group were distributed by them as soon as received. Sheldon presented to Penner and Cory a bill of $25 for transportation and postage expense and insisted that as partners they must pay their proportionate shares. Are Penner and Cory partners with Sheldon in this enterprise?

10. Price and Mulford formed a partnership for the manufacture and sale of low-priced clocks. Price contributed $5,000, and Mulford contributed $10,000. The articles of co-partnership made no provision for the division of profits. At the end of one year, the profits amounted to $8,000. How should the profits be distributed?

CHAPTER TWENTY-TWO

Partnership (II)

22.1 Powers, Rights, and Duties
Powers
   Management
   Agency Authority
Rights
   Capital Contributions
   Profits and Losses
   Reimbursement and Indemnification
   Bookkeeping and Accounting
   Information
   Possession
Duties
   Fiduciary Duty
   Full Time, Reasonable Care, and Obedience
   Good Faith and Loyalty

22.2 Liabilities
In Contract
   In the Name of Partnership
   Within Authority
In Tort
In Crime

Extent of Partner's Liability
   Incoming and Outgoing Partners
   Upon Dissolution

22.3 Dissolution and Winding Up
Causes of Dissolution
   Acts of the Parties
   Operation of Law
   Court Decree
Effect of Dissolution
   On Powers
   On Rights and Duties
   Continuing the Business
Dissolution Notice
   To Co-partners
   To Third Parties
Winding Up
   Rules of Distribution
   Partnership Assets
   Capital Contribution
   Distribution in Kind
   Insolvency and Bankruptcy

22.1 Powers, Rights, and Duties

Powers

Management

Management Powers
Each partner has an equal vote in management of the partnership.

UPA § 18 (e) provides that "(A)ll partners have equal rights in the management and conduct of the partnership business." Accordingly, regardless of the amount of capital contributed by a partner or the fact that a partner contributes only his services, management decisions in the ordinary course of partnership business are made by *majority vote*. Where the number of the partners is even and there is an even division preventing a majority approval, the partnership is deadlocked, and no decision can be taken. If a basic issue is at stake and the deadlock cannot be broken to enable the business to continue properly, any partner may petition the court for an order to dissolve the partnership.

Where there is a general manager of the firm's business, partners usually delegate the day-to-day decision-making authority to the managing partner. It is simply impractical for all partners in a large organization, such as a law or accounting firm, to congregate every time a business decision is to be made. Normally, the partners meet only periodically to make basic policy and general management decisions, for which a simple majority vote is needed. This majority rule does not apply, however, if the decision contemplated contradicts the partnership agreement, such as changing the nature or purpose of the business. To alter the partnership agreement, a *unanimous vote* is required.

Summers v. Dooley
94 Idaho 87, 481 P.2d 318 (1971).

Donaldson, Justice This lawsuit, tried in the district court, involves a claim by one partner against the other for $6,000. The complaining partner asserts that he has been required to pay out more than $11,000 in expenses without any reimbursement from either the partnership funds or his partner. The expenditure in question was incurred by the complaining partner (John Summers, plaintiff-appellant) for the purpose of hiring an additional employee. The trial court denied him any relief except for ordering that he be entitled to one half of $966.72, which it found to be a legitimate partnership expense.

The pertinent facts leading to this lawsuit are as follows. Summers entered a partnership agreement with Dooley (defendant-respondent) in 1958 for the purpose of operating a trash collection business. The business was operated by the two men and when either was unable to work, the non-working partner provided a replacement at his own expense. In 1962, Dooley became unable to work and, at his own expense, hired an employee to take his place. In July, 1966, Summers approached his partner Dooley regarding the hiring of an additional employee but Dooley refused. Nevertheless, on his own initiative, Summers hired the man and paid him out of his own pocket. Dooley, upon discovering that Summers had hired an additional man, objected, stating that he did not feel additional labor was necessary and refused to pay for the new employee out of the partnership funds. Summers continued to operate the business using the third man and in October of 1967 instituted suit in the district court for $6,000 against his partner, the gravamen of the complaint being that Summers has been required to pay out more than $11,000 in expenses, incurred in the hiring of the additional man, without any reimbursement from either the partnership funds or his partner.

. . . In the instant case the record indicates that although Summers requested his partner Dooley to agree to the hiring of a third man, such requests were not honored. In fact Dooley made it clear that he was "voting no" with regard to the hiring of an additional employee.

An application of the relevant statutory provisions and pertinent case law to the factual situation presented by the instant case indicates that the trial court was correct in its disposal of the issue since a majority of the partners did not consent to the hiring of the third man. I.C. § 53–318(8) provides:

> Any difference arising as to ordinary matters connected with the partnership business may be decided by a *majority of the partners* . . . . [emphasis supplied]

. . . A careful reading of the statutory provision indicates that subsection 5 bestows *equal rights in the management and conduct of the partnership business* upon all of the partners. The concept of equality between partners with respect to management of business affairs is a central theme and recurs throughout the Uniform Partnership Law, which has been enacted in this jurisdiction. Thus the only reasonable interpretation of I.C. § 53–318(8) is that business differences must be decided by a majority of the partners provided no other agreement between the partners speaks to the issues.

A noted scholar has dealt precisely with the issue to be decided:

> . . . if the partners are equally divided, those who forbid a change must have their way (Walter B. Lindley, A Treatise on the Law of Partnership, Ch. II, § III, ¶ 24–8, p. 403 [1924]).

. . . In the case at bar one of the partners continually voiced objection to the hiring of the third man. He did not sit idly by and acquiesce in the actions of his partner. Under these circumstances it is manifestly unjust to permit recovery of an expense which was incurred individually and not for the benefit of the partnership but rather for the benefit of one partner.

Judgment affirmed. Costs to respondent.

Agency Authority

Every partner is an agent of the partnership for the purpose of carrying on the partnership business. An individual partner may have *express authority* to act for the partnership through the partnership agreement or because of a majority vote of the partners. In addition, a partner has *implied authority* to do those acts that are customarily done in his partnership or that are usual for similar partnerships. The agreement of the partnership determines the partnership's nature and scope of business. The agreement of the partnership can be changed only by the unanimous consent of the partners. If all of the partners agree to enlarge the scope of their business, the agreement is effective, and new powers are then conferred on the partners.

Agency
Every partner is an agent of the partnership.

Customary Powers The customary powers of a partner to bind the partnership depend on the nature of the business. The following are examples of customary powers held to bind the partnership due to the nature of the particular partnership:

1. Contracts made by a partner necessary to the transaction of business.
2. Sales of goods of the partnership in the regular course of business with warranties usual to such sales.
3. Purchases of property within the scope of the business, including purchases on credit.
4. Hiring and firing of employees.
5. Obtaining or canceling insurance.
6. Borrowing money and executing negotiable instruments in a trading partnership (a business of buying or selling for profit), but not in a nontrading partnership (e.g., lawyers, physicians, real estate business).
7. Compromising, adjusting, or paying claims against the partnership and compromising, adjusting, and receiving payment for claims by the partnership.

A transaction conducted by an individual partner in his own name will not bind the partnership even though the partnership business is the beneficiary of the transaction. When a partner executes a promissory note for and by himself, the partnership and the other partner do not become liable, although the proceeds borrowed are for the partnership business. This was illustrated in the case of *Edwards Feed Mill* v. *Johnson* (302 S.W.2d 151 [Tex.Civ.App. 1957]), in which one of the partners purchased feed in his own name to be used for their dairy partnership. The court ruled that the note to purchase the feed was not a partnership note but a personal obligation of the individual partner who executed the instrument. It was immaterial whether or not the other partner had in fact benefited in the transaction.

Apparent Authority
There must be at least a partnership necessity for a partner's act to bind the partnership.

Acts Not Within Apparent Authority An act of a partner that is not apparently necessary for the carrying on of the business of the partnership in the usual way does not bind the partnership unless authorized by the other partners. Examples of acts that are not within the authority of a partner in the usual type of partnership are contracts in which the partner assumes the debt of another, payment of a separate debt of the partner with partnership property, pledging partnership property to secure a partner's separate debt, giving away partnership property, and selling part of the partnership capital.

Unauthorized Acts Under the UPA UPA § 9(3) provides that a partner has no authority to perform the following acts unless authorized by the other partners or unless the other partners have abandoned the business:

1. Make an assignment of the partnership property for the benefit of creditors. Such an assignment may be avoided by the other creditors or by the other partners.
2. Dispose of the goodwill of the business (e.g., a partner has no implied power to bind the partnership by a promise not to compete with a competitor).
3. Do any other act that would make it impossible to carry on the ordinary business of the partnership (e.g., disposing of the stock of goods in one

of the departments in a department store or agreeing not to compete with a competitor).
4. Confess a judgment (e.g., one partner cannot abandon defenses in a lawsuit; one partner cannot permit a plaintiff to take a judgment without a contest, since all partners should have the right to defend in court).
5. Submit a partnership claim or liability to arbitration. It has been held that the partnership is not bound to perform an award unless all partners have agreed to the submission, nor can it enforce an award against the third person.

Rights

Capital Contributions

Depending upon the financial conditions upon dissolution of the partnership, each partner is to be repaid all the money and properties contributed as capital to the partnership. As noted in the previous chapter, these capital contributions are separate from a partner's loan advance to the partnership which is to be repaid prior to repayment of capital contributions.

Capital Contributions
Money or other property of value contributed as capital to the partnership.

Profits and Losses

Irrespective of the capital contributed by a partner, profits and losses—in the absence of a specific provision in the partnership agreement—are to be shared *equally* among all partners. The partners, however, may contractually agree to have profits and losses distributed in unequal proportions—for example, based proportionately on the different amounts of capital contributions, an individual partner's property used by the partnership, or personal services rendered to the partnership. In the absence of a specific provision in the partnership agreement with regard to partnership losses, such losses are to be shared in the same proportion as the profits.

The individual partner's right to profits is his personal property, and upon his death, the right passes directly to the partner's executor or administrator.

Reimbursement and Indemnification

The partnership must reimburse or indemnify all partners for all expenditures made and personal liabilities reasonably incurred by each partner in the ordinary and proper conduct of the partnership business or for the preservation of the partnership business or property. The right to reimbursement or indemnification does not exist if the partner has acted in bad faith, negligently caused the liability, or previously agreed to bear the expense by himself.

Indemnification
Reimbursement for expense or loss by one partner for the benefit of the partnership.

Bookkeeping and Accounting

UPA § 19 provides: "The partnership books shall be kept, subject to any agreement between the partners, at the principal place of business of the partnership, and every partner shall at all times have access to and may inspect and copy any of them."

Thus, each partner must keep or turn over to the proper person accurate records of a transaction he made on behalf of the partnership business. The task of keeping books and accounts of the firm may be given to one of the partners or to an employee who is liable for the accuracy of the books and accounts. The court may order an audit on the bookkeeping records by a neutral third party when an action is brought to compel a partner to account for charges made to the business.

A partner cannot sue a fellow partner on a partnership's obligation due him, such as reimbursement for an expense incurred or repayment of a loan to a partnership. Such matters are not isolated from the partnership's account as a whole. The proper remedy is a *suit in equity for an accounting*, subsequent to which the partnership may in such a case be dissolved. UPA § 22 provides for this remedy, stating that every partner has the right to a formal accounting as to partnership affairs:

1. If the partner is wrongfully excluded from the partnership business or from the possession of the partnership property by his copartners.
2. If the right exists under any partnership agreement.
3. If a partner has breached a fiduciary duty (UPA § 21).
4. Whenever other circumstances render it just and reasonable.

If a partnership conducts illegal business, such as providing services violative of a regulatory licensing requirement, a partner who participates in the illegal business activities cannot sue for an accounting by the partnership, as he is not in the position to require the other partners to account.

Information

Partners shall render on demand true and full information of all things affecting the partnership to any partner or his legal representative. Not only do the partners have the right to demand information, but it is the duty of a partner to voluntarily give information when it affects the partnership (e.g., partner must voluntarily disclose interest he has in property that is being purchased by the partnership).

Possession

The rights of a partner regarding partnership property, specifically relative to possession and use, were explained in Subchapter 21.3. Since all partnership property is *owned jointly* by the partners, one partner cannot be convicted of stealing the property from another, as illustrated in the following case.

Facts

Defendants Bogan and Kerr owned an automobile junkyard. They sold the business to the plaintiff, Patterson, who took possession of the junkyard. Defendants claimed that they had sold Patterson only a one-half interest and that they were his partners. Patterson claimed that he had purchased the entire operation and owed them nothing. To compel the return of the property, the defendants secured a warrant for the plaintiff's arrest for the crime of larceny. Patterson was arrested, but the charges were dismissed. Patterson then sued the defendants for the tort of malicious prosecution. Bogan and Kerr claimed that they had not acted maliciously but solely to secure the return of the property. Patterson was awarded $5,000 actual damages and $15,000 punitive damages. Defendants Bogan and Kerr appealed.

Decision

The court held that as a general rule, a partner cannot be convicted of larceny of partnership property, since each partner is the ultimate owner of an undivided interest in all of the partnership property. Thus, no partnership property with reference to any partner can be said to be the property of another. Patterson testified that he had bought the entire business, while the defendants said they sold him only one-half interest and were his partners. In either case, as sole owner or partner, the plaintiff could not have been guilty of larceny, and swearing out a warrant for his arrest was an act of malicious prosecution. Affirmed.

Patterson v. Bogan and Kerr, 261 S.C. 87, 198 S.E.2d 586 (1973).

Duties

Fiduciary Duty

Each partner is a trustee who must account to the partnership for any benefits and profits received from a transaction connected with partnership. The partners have a fiduciary relationship—one of trust and confidence—that prohibits a partner from taking advantage of his copartners. The following case is an example of a partner's duty to carry out his fiduciary responsibility.

Fiduciary Duty
Duty owed by a person in a position of trust.

Facts

Plaintiffs Lavin and Dillworth and defendant Ehrlich were partners in a storefront tax-preparing business. Ehrlich managed the business; Lavin and Dillworth were essentially investors. By letter dated October 9, 1978, Ehrlich announced his immediate withdrawal from and dissolution of the partnership. Later that month, he contacted to buy the storefront property from the landlord, and in January 1974, he took title. The lease on the storefront ran until April 30, 1971, and Ehrlich would not negotiate a new lease with the partnership, which he considered dissolved. His partners claim that Ehrlich breached his fiduciary duties in buying this property, and they ask the court to rule that he holds it in constructive trust for the partnership.

Decision

The court held that the opportunity to purchase the property and insure continued possession of the goodwill asset of the location should have been offered to the partnership. Ehrlich breached his fiduciary duty in not making that offer and in appropriating this important partnership asset to himself. He went out and grabbed the building and hoped—with this maneuver and his possession of the list of names of clients and prospects and past tax return files—to capitalize on the location and goodwill to the exclusion of his partners. The court found that Ehrlich held the property in constructive trust for the partnership and was ordered to surrender his right, title, and interest to the partnership if offered two thirds of the purchase price by the remaining partners, Lavin and Dillworth.

Lavin v. Ehrlich, 80 Misc.2d 247, 363 N.Y.S.2d 50 (1974).

The following case is another interesting situation involving a breach of fiduciary duty.

Facts

Paul G. Veale and Company was an accounting firm consisting of Larry Rose and four other partners. They were all CPAs. It was mentioned in the partnership agreement that Veale, Sr., and Rose had outside investments and other business commitments. The agreement also permitted all partners to pursue outside business activities and allowed a partner to be compensated privately, so long as such activities did not materially interfere with the partner's partnership duties or conflict with partnership business.

In light of these provisions, Rose provided accounting services to several of his personal clients, usually after office hours, and received compensation for his private services. He did not share these private earnings with his partners, although he used the partnership's secretarial help and computer time.

Rose's partners charged Rose with a breach of his fiduciary duty to the partnership and claimed damages, which are to be included in the partnership's winding up and accounting. Rose defended on the ground that the other partners were aware of his private practice and that they tacitly approved his use of partnership secretarial and computer facilities.

Decision

Judgment for the plaintiffs. By providing his personal clients the same services offered by the partnership, Rose violated the "will not compete" provision of the partnership agreement. Competing with one's own partnership, even after office hours, violates the common law fiduciary duty that partners owe their copartners. This duty requires the utmost good faith and honesty of partners in dealing with one another. A breach of the duty not to compete is to be corrected by giving the damaged partners their proportionate share of the wrongfully acquired profits. Misappropriation or misuse of partnership property constitutes constructive fraud. It was not clear whether Rose's partners were aware and approved of Rose's using partnership's facilities and having private clients on the side. Accordingly, the matter was returned to the trial court to obtain the facts.

Veale v. Rose, 657 S.W.2d 834 (Tex.App. 1983).

Constructive Fraud
An act or situation creating an inference of fraud.

Full Time, Reasonable Care, and Obedience

In the absence of an agreement to the contrary, it is the duty of each partner to give his entire time, skill, and energy to the partnership business. A partner is not entitled to compensation for his services unless there is an express or implied agreement for such payment.

A partner is under a duty to use reasonable care in the transaction of the partnership business and is liable for any loss resulting from the failure to use reasonable care.

A partner is under a contractual obligation to do all that is required of him by the partnership agreement. If a loss results from the failure to comply with the agreement, the partner must indemnify the partnership.

Good Faith and Loyalty

Good faith and loyalty toward the partnership and the other partners not only are legally required from each partner but also are the foundation of a healthy partnership. A partner is expected to fully devote himself to the company's business. He must not misrepresent or conceal business matters. He cannot use company property for personal use without permission from the other partners. A partner is not allowed to do other business, either individually or in concert with others, to compete with the partnership.

Facts

Whittier Hospital leased equipment from the Whittier Leasing Company, a partnership. Nine of the partners meanwhile established another partnership, the Friendly Hills Leasing Company, which took all of Whittier Hospital's business away from Whittier Leasing. Whittier Leasing's partners who did not join Friendly brought an action against Friendly's partners to obtain Whittier Leasing's dissolution and recover profits made from Whittier Hospital.

Decision

Judgment for the plaintiffs. The nine betraying partners clearly violated the duty of good faith and loyalty toward Whittier Leasing and the partners remaining in it. An order to dissolve Whittier Leasing was issued, since it is impossible to expect the partners thereafter to continue the partnership's business in harmony and with faith in one another. Furthermore, Friendly's partners were ordered to give up all the profits they made from leasing equipment to Whittier Hospital.

Olivet v. *Frischling,* 104 Cal.App.3d 831, 164 Cal.Rptr. 87 (1980).

Depending upon the nature of the partnership business, the partnership agreement may provide a valid anticompetitive restriction prohibiting a partner from competing with the partnership after its termination. The validity of such a restriction is usually governed by rules relative to trade restraint.

A partner must not make secret profits at the expense of the business or exploit a partnership business opportunity for personal gain, as shown in the following case.

Starr v. International Realty, Ltd.
271 Or. 396, 533 P.2d 165 (1975).

Tongue, Justice The case involves a group of prominent Portland doctors and others in high income tax "brackets" and in need of "tax shelters." They were persuaded by one Stanley G. Harris, a Portland "expert" in real property investments, that by investing $285,000 and joining with him in a partnership for the purchase of an apartment house then under construction, the entire down payment of $265,000 could be treated for federal income tax purposes as "prepaid interest," thereby saving large amounts otherwise payable in income taxes. . . .

Harris did not reveal to his partners that the property could have been purchased for $907,500 "net" to the seller . . ., and that a commission of $100,000, together with an escrow fee of $2,500, was to be paid to International Realty Ltd., of which Harris was president.

. . . The question to be decided in this case . . . is whether the $100,000 commission paid to International, of which Harris was the president, was a "secret" commission. . . .

It appears from the testimony that most of the plaintiffs knew or should have known that Harris and International were in the real estate business and that a realtor's commission in some amount would normally be paid to some realtor on the transaction. Apparently, because their interest in the income tax advantage of the transaction was so dominant and overriding, the doctors did not inquire whether such a commission would be paid to Harris or to International, or in

> what amount, and Harris did not tell them. It is contended by the doctors, however, that in this case they are entitled to the benefit of the equivalent of a rule more familiar to them in the practice of medicine—that of "informed consent."
>
> When, as in this case, a real estate broker undertakes to join as a member of a partnership or joint venture in the purchase of real property on which he holds a listing, he is also subject to the fiduciary duties of undivided loyalty and complete disclosure owed by one partner to another. Indeed, one of the fundamental duties of any partner who deals on his own account in matters within the scope of his fiduciary relationship is the affirmative duty to make a full disclosure to his partners not only of the fact he is dealing on his own account, but all the facts which are material to the transaction. . . .
>
> In this case, Harris did not inform plaintiffs or disclose to them the fact that this property could have been purchased for $907,500 "net" to the seller or that upon its purchase for $1,010,000 Harris or International (of which Harris was the president) would be paid a commission in the amount of $100,000. In the absence of such a disclosure there could be no effective "consent" by plaintiffs to the payment or retention by Harris of any such "benefit" from that transaction. . . .
>
> For these reasons, we must reject defendants' contention that the broker's commission paid to International was "neither secret nor concealed." For the same reasons, the trial court did not err in requiring defendants to account to the partnership for that commission.

Questions

1. How are management decisions made in a partnership?
2. Name a few customary powers of a general partner.
3. When can a partner sue in equity for an accounting?
4. Give some case examples regarding a partner's breach of fiduciary duty.
5. Discuss a partner's duty not to compete during the partnership's existence and after its termination.

22.2 Liabilities

The relationship between partners is that of an agency. Each partner is both a principal and an agent of his fellow partners. Hence, agency rules of liability as discussed in Chapter 13 of this textbook are applicable to partners in a partnership.

In Contract

In an agency, the principal alone is liable to a third party for a breach of contract and *vice versa* if the agency and the principal are disclosed by the agent to the third party. Accordingly, if (1) a partner enters into a contractual relationship in the name or on behalf of the partnership and the third party is aware or is led to believe that the agreement is made for the partnership and (2) the contract is made by the partner within his express or implied authority, the partnership is said to be *jointly* liable. As the partnership is not a legal entity, joint liability means that *all* the members of the firm are liable to the third party.

In the Name of Partnership

Whether or not a partner executes an agreement on behalf of the partnership or purely on his own personal account depends on the intention of the contracting parties expressed or inferred from the given circumstances.

In *Edwards Feed Mill* v. *Johnson* (302 S.W.2d 151 [Tex.Civ.App. 1957]) (cited in the previous subchapter), a partner was not held liable for a personal promissory note executed for the purchase of feed by the other partner, even though the feed was used to benefit the partnership. This case can be compared with the following case.

Costanzo v. Lawrence
64 Wash.2d 901, 395 P.2d 93 (1964).

Weaver, Justice Defendant Sam Lawrence appeals from a money judgment entered against him in the sum of $4,165.

March 15, 1959, defendants Lawrence and Harris formed a partnership to operate a livestock business to purchase, breed, feed and sell cattle. Defendant Lawrence purchased a substantial number of cattle and certain farm machinery from plaintiff. May 23, 1959, defendants entered into a written partnership agreement. Basically, it provided that Lawrence was to advance the money to purchase the cattle and Harris was to provide the expense of their care and maintenance and to do the work. . . .

A large quantity of chopped hay, which is the subject matter of this appeal, was stored on the ranch. The oral understanding concerning the hay is in dispute, but the written lease provided that the hay be "transferred, set-over and sold" to defendant Harris for $20 per ton if he exercised the option to purchase the ranch; otherwise he would have the option to pay for the hay consumed or to replace it.

Defendants' livestock venture was not successful. April 4, 1961, they terminated their partnership. About a month later defendant Harris exercised the option to purchase the ranch. He did not pay for the hay stored thereon.

Plaintiff brought this action against both defendants . . . for the value of the hay stored on the ranch in the spring of 1959.

The trial court found that the partnership was unjustly enriched to the extent of 199.5 tons of hay, having a market value of $3,990, which had been eaten by cattle *owned by the partnership* in the spring of 1959 and during the period between October 1, 1959, and May 1, 1960. . . .

The fact that plaintiff "transferred, set-over and sold" the hay to defendant Harris has no bearing on the question of whether the partnership was unjustly enriched. The fact remains that, to the extent found by the trial court, the hay was consumed by partnership cattle and the partnership was benefited. . . .

The judgment is affirmed.

Limited Partner
A partner who does not participate in management of the partnership and is not personally responsible for partnership losses beyond his agreed investment in the business.

Silent Partner
Does not take part in management of the partnership, but is jointly liable with the other general partners for all partnership debts.

In *Edwards Feed Mill* v. *Johnson* as well as in *Costanzo* v. *Lawrence*, the partnerships benefited from the transactions. However, in the former case, the seller sold the feed to the one partner individually, and allowing the partnership to benefit from the purchase was considered to be beside the point. In the latter case, the seller's hay was stored on the buyer's ranch. The seller knew that the buyer's business was a partnership and that the entire deal was basically between him and the partnership. The internal agreement between the partners Lawrence and Harris, whereby Harris was to pay for operational expenses, was not of the seller's concern. Furthermore, the fact that the hay was to be "transferred, set-over and sold" to Harris, if he exercised the option to buy the ranch upon the partnership's contemplated dissolution, was equally impertinent to the portion of the hay that was already consumed during the partnership's existence.

While a limited partner is not personally liable for partnership contracts, a silent or dormant partner is. All remedies available in a breach of contract in general are equally applicable to partnership contracts.

Within Authority

The partnership agreement and the way business is conducted by the partners are predominant factors in determining whether or not a business transaction by one of the partners is within his express or implied authority. For an important or extraordinarily unusual type of arrangement, a partner must, under the majority rule, have the consent of all of his fellow partners. Express authority would be required, for example, when major assets of the firm, such as equipment, are to be sold, by which sale the company's regular business would be impaired or rendered impossible.

Facts
Davis Nursing Home is a partnership owned and conducted by William and Charlotte Davis. William unilaterally sold the home, all its assets, and goodwill to plaintiff Feingold. Charlotte bitterly opposed the transaction. Feingold then sued William and Charlotte for a decree of specific performance of the sales agreement.

Decision
Judgment for the defendant. William Davis did not have the express authority to enter into such a contract. Since the performance or enforcement of the contract would make it impossible for the partnership business to continue, one partner alone cannot without the other partner's consent enter into such an arrangement. The partnership was not bound by that sale.

Feingold v. *Davis*, 444 Pa. 339, 282 A.2d 291 (1971).

If the contract is intended to be between the one partner personally and the third party, the other partners are not bound by it. This, however, is to be distinguished from a situation where the partnership is not disclosed but the transaction by the partner is in fact for the partnership and with the approval of the other partners. As in the case of an undisclosed agency (or partially disclosed agency), the other partners can be held liable.

In Tort

UPA § 13 states: "Where, by any wrongful act or omission of any partner acting in the ordinary course of the business of the partnership or with the authority of his co-partners, loss or injury is caused to any person, not being a partner in the partnership, or any penalty is incurred, the partnership is liable therefor to the same extent as the partner so acting or omitting to act." Section 15 of the Act provides: "All partners are liable (a) (J)ointly and severally for everything chargeable to the partnership under section(s) 13 . . . ."

Exactly as in an agency, where both the principal and agent are liable for a tort committed by the agent to a third party within the scope of the agency, in a partnership where the partners are principals and agents of one another, *all* and *each* of the partners are liable for a tort by one partner to a third party within the scope of partnership business. The partners' liability in tort is *joint* and *several*.

For example, on his way to show a customer a house for sale, a partner of a real estate brokerage firm ran a red light and collided with another car, causing injury to his passenger. Of course, this partner is individually liable for his wrongdoing, but all and each of the other partners are equally liable as principals.

Partnership Torts
All partners are jointly and severally liable for torts committed in the scope of the partnership business.

Facts

Art Seating Company was a partnership of which Zemelman was a partner. The company had a fire insurance policy issued by Boston Insurance Company. When there was a fire loss, Zemelman prepared and submitted a claim, which was asserted by the insurance company to contain false statements. The policy had an express provision stating that the insurance would be void upon such a false claim. The partnership defended on the ground that it was not bound by Zemelman's fraudulent statement, since Zemelman's conduct was not within his authority.

Decision

Judgment for Boston Insurance. Even though the commission of such fraud was not within the scope of the partner's authority, the partnership is liable for the consequences of the fraud.

Zemelman v. *Boston Insurance Co.*, 4 Cal.App.3d 15, 84 Cal.Rptr. 206 (1970).

Indeed, seldom is a tort perpetrated by a partner under the official authority of the partnership unless the company in its entirety is an organization involved in illegality. The civil liability criterion determining whether or not the wrongdoing by the partner is within the scope of business is usually the fact that the partnership did or would have profited from the wrongful act.

Since an injured third party may sue all or any of the partners, he may even sue an innocent partner without involving the tortfeasor. To prevent financial disaster resulting from such an awesome burden of responsibility, the partnership may carry liability insurance against such tort losses. Also, in addition to the general partnership rules pertaining to mutual indemnification, partners may have specific agreements to mutually indemnify one another. In the absence of such an agreement, the wrongdoing partner surely cannot collect from the innocent partners to cover tort damages he incurs.

Flynn v. Reaves
135 Ga.App. 651, 218 S.E.2d 661 (1975).

Clark, Judge The circumstances giving rise to this appeal may be summarized as follows: Seeking damages for medical malpractice, plaintiffs, husband and wife, brought suit only against defendant, Dr. Charles R. Moore, alleging him to have been negligent in his diagnosis and treatment of the eyes of plaintiff wife. Defendant answered, denying the allegations of negligence. Thereafter, defendant initiated a third-party action against his former co-partners, Dr. James T. Flynn, Jr., Dr. Robert E. Fokes, Jr. and Dr. James R. Paulk. (The events had occurred during the existence of the partnership which had been dissolved by mutual agreement prior to commencement of the present litigation.) . . . This pleading alleges that he had been an equal partner with the three third-party defendants, hereafter referred to as "co-partners," in a medical practice partnership operated under the name of "The Eye, Ear, Nose and Throat Clinic" at the time when he had diagnosed and treated plaintiff wife; that his diagnosis and treatment of plaintiff wife was performed within the course of the partnership business; that he and his co-partners shared equally in the profits and losses of the partnership; and that the three co-partners were liable to him for three-fourths of any sum which plaintiffs might recover against him in the principal suit. . . .

The law of partnership is the law of agency: "'Each partner being the agent of the firm, the firm is liable for his torts committed within the scope of his agency, on the principle of *respondeat superior,* in the same way that a master is responsible for his servant's torts, and for the same reason [that] the firm is liable for the torts of its agents or servants.' . . . Thus, "where several physicians are in partnership, they may be held liable in damages for the professional negligence of one of the firm."

. . . In the case at bar, therefore, the co-partners and defendant would be jointly and severally liable to plaintiffs if it were established that defendant in fact negligently diagnosed and treated plaintiff wife in the course of the partnership business. Therefore, plaintiffs had the choice of suing the defendant individually, or all of the partners including defendant jointly. But defendant cannot seek contribution from his co-partners simply because they are jointly liable to plaintiffs.

Here, the co-partners and defendant are not joint tortfeasors as among themselves. For the co-partners are subjected to liability only by the doctrine of respondeat superior. Thus, defendant whose negligence, if any, was actual, cannot seek contribution from his co-partners, who are merely constructively negligent. Of course, had defendant alleged that his co-partners were actual tortfeasors, a third-party action for contribution would lie. But such is not the case. . . .

Therefore, we hold, as other courts have held, that where a partner is sued individually by a plaintiff injured by the partner's sole negligence, the partner cannot seek contribution from his co-partners even though the negligent act occurred in the course of the partnership business. . . .

The rule of joint and several liability does not apply to a tort committed by one partner to another. Partners who are not involved are not liable for injuries sustained by the tort victim. In this situation, the aggrieved partner may sue only the wrongdoer.

In Crime

Other members of the partnership may be held liable for crimes perpetrated by one partner in the course of business. Examples of such business crimes include trading in stolen goods, performing transactions without the required regulatory license, dealing in contraband, and violating federal interstate transportation safety rules.

The general rule is that the innocent partner is not criminally liable for an act committed by another party so long as the partnership business itself has nothing to do with, or does not in any way profit from, the criminal conduct of the individual. Since a partnership is not a natural person, usually only fines may be imposed upon the firm, while the perpetrator may receive corporal punishment, such as incarceration.

The U.S. Supreme Court and many state courts have held in recent decisions that some partnerships are entities that can in certain situations be held criminally liable, as illustrated by the following case.

Partnership Crime
A partnership may be liable for crimes committed in its business by one or more of the partners.

Facts
Smithtown General Hospital, a partnership (defendant), was indicted for permitting an unauthorized person to participate in a surgical procedure and falsifying records to conceal the crime. The partnership moved to dismiss on the grounds that as a partnership it could not be indicted.

Decision
The court held that although a partnership has been defined as a relationship with no legal being as distinct from the members it comprises, there are exceptions. The partnership can be either an entity or an aggregate of its members, depending upon the nature of its activities and, in the case of criminal law, upon the nature of the infraction. The operation of a hospital is so intertwined with the public interest as to legally justify the imposition of extensive controls by all levels of government. The health care is provided by the facility and not necessarily by any of its proprietors. Accreditation, when given, is provided to the institution and not to the component members of the named proprietor. The hospital is in every sense an entity and not just an aggregate of the forty-two individual partners. The judge ruled that the defendant may be charged in an indictment as an entity with the commission of these crimes even though there is no showing of wrong on the part of the individual partners. Motion denied.

People v. *Smithtown General Hospital*, 92 Misc.2d 144, 399 N.Y.S.2d 993 (1977).

Extent of Partner's Liability

Each partner has *personal* and *unlimited* liability to the full extent of his personal assets for all business obligations incurred by the partnership. However, before a partner's personal assets can be reached to satisfy partnership debts, partnership assets must first be exhausted, as shown in the following case.

Partners' Liability
Each partner has personal and unlimited liability for all business obligations of the partnership that cannot be satisfied by the partnership's assets.

> **Horn's Crane Service v. Prior**
> *182 Neb. 94, 152 N.W.2d 421 (1967).*
>
> **Westermark, J.** Court sustained a general demurrer . . ., dismissed the action, and plaintiff appeals. We affirm the judgment.
>
> Plaintiff, a seller of equipment and supplies, in two causes of action in his amended petition seeks a personal judgment against the defendants, and each of them, for liability arising out of specific sums due under a written contract with (first cause of action) and for supplies and services furnished (second cause of action) a partnership . . . comprised of the two defendants, Wendell H. Prior and Orie Cook, and one C. E. Piper, the manager. . . . The partnership . . . was formed for the purpose of operating a quarry and rock-crushing business for profit, and the written contract was entered into and the supplies and services furnished pursuant thereto. Defendants' ultimate liability for personal judgment flowed out of the partnership's . . . original liability as a separate entity in the transactions.
>
> . . . In neither the original nor amended petition is it alleged, either directly or by inference, that the partnership . . . property was insufficient to satisfy its debts, or that there was no partnership property, and there is no allegation of dissolution or insolvency of said . . . partnership. This was fatal.
>
> In an action seeking a personal judgment against the individual members of a partnership . . . the petition does not state a cause of action if it fails to state that there is no partnership property or that it is insufficient to satisfy the debts of the partnership. . . . However, the partnership relation is such that the separate property of a partner cannot be subjected to the payment of partnership debts until the property of the firm is exhausted. . . . Firm property must also be subjected to the payment of the firm debts before it can be applied to the debts of the individual members of the firm. . . . The partners are personally, jointly, and severally responsible for partnership liabilities. But the benefits and liabilities of a partner arise from and are the result of the partnership relation. . . .
>
> There are several reasons for the rule. One of the most obvious is that credit having been extended to the partnership or firm, the members ought to have a right to insist that the partnership property be exhausted first. And to permit a firm creditor to by-pass the partnership property and exhaust the assets of an individual member leaving the partnership property extant, would be an obvious injustice, permit the other partners to profit at his expense, and place him in an adverse position with relation to his copartners. . . .
>
> The judgment of the district court in dismissing the action is correct and is affirmed.

Thus, to satisfy a business claim, partnership assets must be exhausted before a partner's personal assets can be reached, in which event the partnership creditor under the federal law of bankruptcy may be favored over the partner's personal creditor.

Facts

MHS Enterprises was a Michigan partnership owned by McElmurry (defendant) and three other partners. Commonwealth Capital Investment Corporation (plaintiff) won a suit against the partnership and obtained a judgment of $1,137,285 against the company. As the partnership was not able to satisfy the judgment, Commonwealth brought an action against McElmurry personally for satisfaction of the entire debt.

Decision

Judgment for Commonwealth. Under UPA § 15, all partners are jointly liable for partnership debts and obligations. Where there are no partnership assets left to satisfy the judgment, as in this case, the judgment creditor properly sought general partner McElmurry's individual assets to satisfy the debt. Under UPA § 18(a), McElmurry has the right to contribution from the other partners if they still have personal wealth.

Commonwealth Capital Investment Corporation v. McElmurry, 102 Mich.App. 536, 302 N.W.2d 222 (1980).

Incoming and Outgoing Partners

Theoretically, a new partnership is formed when a partner leaves the firm or a new partner is admitted to the business. Such a change is often not noticeable to the general public, particularly when a long-established company thrives upon its well-known name and good reputation. However, since general partners are personally and unlimitedly liable for partnership obligations, such a change in the partnership constellation is obviously important to partnership creditors. The law of partnership provides the following rules:

1. An "incoming" general partner is not personally liable for the firm's obligations existing prior to his entrance into the partnership. However, his capital contribution to the partnership as well as the other partnership assets is made available for the satisfaction of such prior business claims. This partner is, of course, personally liable for future partnership debts. He may also explicitly assume the obligation of paying previous debts.

2. An "outgoing" general partner continues to be personally liable for all partnership debts incurred prior to his departure from the partnership. He is not liable for business debts incurred after his leaving. The only way an outgoing partner is released of such prior partnership debts is by a novation, by which the respective creditor expressly agrees to have the outgoing partner substituted in his obligation by another person.

Upon Dissolution

Dissolution of the partnership does not discharge a partner's liability for existing debts. Unless expressly released by the creditor, a general partner remains liable after dissolution for all claims against the partnership that have not been satisfied. When a partnership is dissolved because of death of a partner, the estate of the deceased party continues to be liable for partnership obligations that originated from the time the deceased general partner was alive. It should be noted, however, that the deceased partner's creditors have priority over partnership creditors with regard to the estate property.

Dissolution
The termination and "winding up" of the partnership.

Questions

1. Explain the general partners' liability in contract and in tort.
2. What are the two requirements creating joint liability in contract?

3. When is express authority of all the partners required?
4. Can a wrongdoing partner compel his innocent partners to contribute for paying the damages. Do you remember a case illuminating this point?
5. What are the rules governing the liability of incoming and outgoing partners?

22.3 Dissolution and Winding Up

Termination of a partnership takes place upon (1) *dissolution* of the partnership and (2) *winding up* of the partnership business.

Dissolution designates the point in time when the partners cease to carry on the business together. Upon dissolution, the partnership is not immediately terminated but continues until the winding up is completed.

Facts
On June 11, 1919, the Bayer Bros. partnership, which owned two thirds of the stock of Montville Finishing Company, was dissolved. On August 13, 1919, before the winding-up process was completed, defendant bought seventy-six shares of Montville. The trial court found that the purchase of the stock was a breach of the defendant's fiduciary duty, as it was contrary to the interest of the partners.

Decision
The court held that upon the dissolution of the partnership, any fiduciary duty that the defendant owed toward the plaintiffs while the partnership existed ceased and that the defendant was free to purchase the stock. It is not unusual that the courts have failed to distinguish between the terms *dissolution, winding up,* and *termination* of a partnership. A partnership at will is dissolved when either of the partners expresses an intent not to continue any longer or when the partners decide to cease doing business for their mutual benefit. The partnership affairs are not terminated, however, until the winding up is completed. The partners' energies thereafter are devoted to the winding up of the business affairs of the partnership and to reaching an agreement as to the distribution of its assets. Reversed.

Bayer et al. v. Bayer, 215 App.Div. 454, 214 N.Y.S. 322 (1926).

Winding up is the process of settling partnership affairs after dissolution. During the period of winding up a dissolved partnership, the partnership is still in existence. The property is still held by the partners as tenants. The partners can sue and be sued regarding partnership rights and obligations. However, the partners should not undertake new business after the dissolution but should only liquidate and distribute the partnership property. Any new business transacted by a partner is solely for his own account.

Causes of Dissolution

A partnership can be dissolved (1) by the partners themselves, (2) by operation of law, and (3) by decree of the court.

Acts of the Parties

1. The partnership agreement itself may stipulate how long the business is supposed to last, subsequent to which the partnership is dissolved. It may also provide that the partnership is to be dissolved upon a condition subsequent. For example, the partners may agree to dissolve the partnership upon a loss of a certain amount of the capital.
2. In a situation where the agreement calls for the partnership to do business for a certain period of time, the firm can still be dissolved upon mutual unanimous agreement of the partners.
3. Since the partnership relationship is one of agency, and as this relationship is fiduciary and personal in nature, any partner may dissolve the partnership at any time even though it is in violation of the partnership agreement. The partner who wrongfully causes a dissolution is subject to liability for damages. To prevent undue hardship on the other partners, UPA § 38(2)(b) provides that they may buy out his interest.
4. If no definite time is mentioned in the partnership agreement, the partnership can be dissolved at will by any partner at any time.

Facts

Jebeles and his brother-in-law Costellos were partners in a business named "Dino's Hot Dog." Marital difficulties developed between Jebeles and his wife, who was Costellos' sister. As divorce proceedings began, Costellos, who devoted full time to the business, ceased remitting proceeds to Jebeles and changed the locks on the doors of the eating place. Jebeles sued Costellos for dissolution of the partnership and for an accounting of all profits. To preserve the valuable lease to the business premises and future profits, the trial court refused to dissolve the partnership and instead allowed Costellos to be the sole active partner and Jebeles a silent partner of the business. An accounting was also ordered by the court.

Decision

The appellate court found the refusal to dissolve the partnership erroneous. Jebeles and Costellos had not agreed on a definite duration of their partnership. When no definite term is specified in the partnership agreement, dissolution under UPA § 31(1)(b) can be caused by the express will of any partner. In this case, cause for dissolution existed simply because Jebeles desired a dissolution. Ordering an accounting without dissolving the partnership was also erroneous. According to UPA § 43, Jebeles' right to an accounting accrues at the date of dissolution.

Jebeles v. Costellos, 391 So.2d 1024 (Ala. 1980).

Operation of Law

1. UPA § 31(3) provides that a partnership is dissolved "(B)y any event which makes it unlawful for the business of the partnership to be carried on or for the members to carry it on in partnership. . . ." For example, a new local ordinance related to zoning may render illegal a previously legal business.
2. Where partners are the respective citizens of the belligerent countries in a state of war or armed conflict, the partnership is dissolved. However, this does not affect contracts made prior to the hostilities.

3. A partnership is dissolved by the adjudication of bankruptcy or insolvency of the partnership or an adjudication of bankruptcy or insolvency by one of the partners. Most courts hold that insolvency of the partnership or of one of the partners without an adjudication will not dissolve the partnership.
4. Death of one of the partners dissolves the partnership. In this respect, it might be desirable to provide in the partnership agreement for continuation of the business on the death of a partner and compensation to the deceased partner's estate.

Court Decree

A court may decree the dissolution of a partnership. The grounds are as follows:

1. Where the circumstances render it just and equitable (e.g., insolvency of a partner) or where it becomes unprofitable to carry on the business.
2. Misconduct of a partner to the extent that it is injurious to the partnership or to the other partners (e.g., misappropriation of funds) or excluding other partners from possession of partnership property.
3. Incapacity of a partner to discharge his duties (e.g., insanity).
4. Dissension among the partners where it is so serious and persistent as to make the successful continuance of the partnership impractical.

Effect of Dissolution

Dissolution terminates the existence of the partnership except for the purpose of winding up, e.g., performance of existing contracts, collection of money due, payment of debts, administering of firm assets, and the distribution of the assets in accordance with the partnership agreement (UPA §§ 33–43).

On Powers

Accounting
Each partner has a right to an accounting of profits and losses at the time of dissolution of a partnership.

Normally, dissolution terminates the power of a partner to bind the partnership except for the purpose of winding up. However, the partner may bind the partnership to third persons as follows:

1. To those who had extended credit to the firm prior to dissolution and had no knowledge or notice of the dissolution.
2. To those who had not extended credit but knew of the partnership prior to dissolution and had no knowledge or notice of the dissolution and the notice of the dissolution had not been advertised in a newspaper of general circulation (UPA § 35).

On Rights and Duties

Unless otherwise agreed, the partners who have not caused the dissolution have the right to wind up the partnership affairs (UPA § 37). The partner or partners in charge of the winding up are entitled to reasonable compensation for such services. In general, however, all partners have the right to be involved in the winding-up process.

A receiver may be appointed by the court to wind up the partnership business when the dissolution took place on account of a court decree. The winding-up procedures for the appointed receiver would be the same as those for a partner.

If the partnership is dissolved by death of a partner, the partnership property by operation of law vests in the surviving partners for the purpose of winding up the business. The surviving partners' fiduciary duty requires them to carry out the winding-up process and accounting to the deceased partner's estate representative with reasonable promptness and the highest degree of integrity.

Whether or not a partner upon dissolution of the partnership still owes fiduciary duty to his copartners often depends upon the nature of his disputed conduct and the interest of the other partners at stake. Where this interest is not, or is insufficiently, affected, the partner's act may be considered permissible, such as in *Bayer et al. v. Bayer* (cited earlier). In *Bovy v. Graham, Cohen & Wampold* (17 Wash. App. 567, 564 P.2d 1175 [1977]), a law partner who failed to disclose his contingent fee files to his copartners upon dissolution of the partnership was adjudged to have violated his fiduciary duty.

Partners' Right on Distribution
Upon dissolution, partners are empowered to do the things necessary to wind up the affairs of the partnership.

Receiver
A person appointed to take charge of assets under a court decree.

Continuing the Business

When the membership of the partnership changes by reason of death or retirement of a partner or by the entrance of another member and the business is continued, the creditors of the dissolved partnership are also creditors of the partnership continuing the business. The liability of the new member for prior obligations shall be satisfied out of partnership property only (UPA § 41). Thus, the incoming partner's liability is limited to his contribution, as explained in the previous subchapter.

Dissolution Notice

A dissolution notice is important to prevent unwanted liability.

Dissolution Notice
Necessary to prevent continuing liability by one partner for the acts of another partner.

To Copartners

When a partner wishes to dissolve or withdraw from the firm, a notice of his decision must be given to the copartners or his action, such as demonstratively destroying the partnership agreement, must clearly show his intent to depart from the partnership. Without such a notice, a disgruntled partner would continue to be liable for the actions of the other partners.

Jones v. Jones
15 Misc.2d 960, 179 N.Y.S.2d 480 (1958).

Brown, Jr., Justice   In this action for a dissolution of a partnership, accounting, etc., defendant moves for an order . . . dismissing the complaint on the ground that it does not set forth facts sufficient to constitute a cause of action. The action is brought by a wife against her husband. . . .

However, it appears from the complaint that the grounds upon which the action rests are that (1) one of the partners, defendant herein, is guilty of adultery and that an action for divorce has been instituted against him by the other party, and (2) defendant has refused to make a distribution of the assets or to account therefor.

Dissolutions of partnerships can only be brought about as provided by Sections 62 and 63 of the Partnership Law. An examination of Sec. 62 reveals that subdivision 1(b) is the only subdivision of this section that possibly could be applied to the situation presented herein provided the proper facts are pleaded. Subdivision 1(b) reads as follows:

> By the express will of any partner when no definite term or particular undertaking is specified.

The courts, however, have held in order to effect a dissolution of a partnership at will:

> there must have been a mutual agreement to dissolve, *or there must have been notice by a party desiring a dissolution to his copartners 'of his election to terminate the partnership, or his election must be manifested by unequivocal acts or circumstances brought to the knowledge of the other party which signify [the exercise of] the will of the former that the partnership be dissolved'.* . . .

Nowhere in the complaint has the plaintiff set forth such facts even though it may well be that such notice of election was given. The court, however, cannot assume from the facts as pleaded that such notice was given. In addition, while allegations of adultery and the institution of a divorce action could be the basis for terminating an alleged partnership at will, it cannot be said that these are unequivocal acts or circumstances signifying an election to dissolve for it is common knowledge that wives have divorced husbands without terminating businesses in which both parties were interested. . . . In an action for a dissolution of a partnership the accounting, impressing of a trust, appointment of a receiver, etc. are merely incidental relief sought in the dissolution of the partnership. . . .

Accordingly, the motion to dismiss is granted with leave to the plaintiff to serve an amended complaint if so advised within 20 days after service of a copy of the order to be entered herein, with notice of entry.

To Third Parties

A dissolution notice must be given to third parties in the event the partnership is dissolved by the decision of a partner or of the partners. Circumstances indicating the partnership's dissolution are usually not considered sufficient notice. For example, adding "Inc." to the partnership name on a letterhead and company's check is not sufficient information of the fact that the partnership has been incorporated.

Facts

House of Paul is a partnership that had its advertising material printed by Philipp Lithographing Co. Meanwhile, during the course of their dealing, House of Paul was incorporated, and Philipp was not informed of the change. When bills were not paid, Philipp sued the partners personally. The partners claimed limited liability as shareholders of the corporation.

Decision
Judgment for Philipp. The fact of the matter was that no notice has been given of the change from a partnership to a corporation. Since the plaintiff had done business with the same persons as partners, he could hold these partners individually liable until official notice to the contrary was given to him.

Philipp Lithographing Co. v. Babich, 27 Wis.2d 645, 135 N.W.2d 343 (1965).

An actual dissolution notice must be sent to persons who had dealt or are dealing with the partnership. As to people who have had no dealings with the company, public notice, such as newspaper ads, would be sufficient.

Winding Up

Upon dissolution, partnership business needs to be wound up. At this stage, the partners do not have the authority to create new obligations so as to delay or prevent the termination of the partnership. They do have the authority, however, to conduct ancillary transactions necessary to finish existing obligations. For example, when a contractor's partnership is dissolved in the middle of a project, a new purchase of material to complete that project is well within the authority of the partners.

Winding Up
Liquidating the operation when a partnership is dissolved.

Facts
Walnut Kernel is a newspaper published by a partnership owned by the Stoddard family, a father, mother, and son. After the parents passed away, the son kept running the paper. When King (plaintiff), the accountant for the paper, was not paid for his services, he sued the son and the executors of the two estates. The executors defended on the ground that continuing to employ King was beyond the authority of the surviving partner, since the partnership was legally dissolved and supposedly to be wound up. The answer to this defense was that the newspaper needed to be continued as a going concern so that it could be sold. Therefore, running of the paper was part of the winding-up process that would give the surviving partner the authority to employ the accountant on behalf of the partnership.

Decision
Judgment for the defendant. The court ruled that the son had no authority to continue publishing the newspaper indefinitely. The son was not winding up the estate but was continuing the business as usual after dissolution of the partnership. The accountant was not entitled to recover the value of his services.

King v. Stoddard, 28 Cal.App.3d 708 104 Cal.Rptr. 903 (1972).

Rules of Distribution

UPA § 40(b) provides the following:

"The liabilities of the partnership shall rank in order of payment, as follows:
  (I) Those owing to creditors other than partners, (II) Those owing to partners other than for capital and profits, (III) Those owing to partners in respect of capital, (IV) Those owing to partners in respect of profits."

Distribution
Paying out of partnership assets upon dissolution.

If there is insufficient partnership property to satisfy the liabilities, the partners must make contributions to the extent necessary to satisfy the liabilities (UPA § 40[d]). Where the partnership agreement is silent, business profits upon dissolution are to be shared equally among the partners regardless of the amounts of their capital contributions. In the absence of agreement, partners share losses in the same way as they share profits (UPA § 18[a]).

For example, assume that Partner A contributed $5,000, B $3,000, C $-0-; in addition, Partner B loaned the partnership $1,000. Upon dissolution, the balance sheet shows a *profit*.

Assets	$21,000	Liability to outsiders	$ 6,000
		Liability to B	$ 1,000
		Net worth	$14,000
	$21,000		$21,000

Distribution based on equal sharing is as follows:

Proceeds from asset liquidation	+$21,000	
To pay outside creditors	−$ 6,000	
To pay B loan	−$ 1,000	
To return capital	−$ 8,000	(A $5,000 B $3,000 C $ -0-)
To distribute profits	−$ 6,000	(A $2,000 B $2,000 C $2,000)
	$ -0-	A $7,000 B $5,000 C $2,000
		(amounts that partners receive)

On the other hand, suppose that upon dissolution the balance sheet shows a *loss*.

Assets	$21,000	Liability to outsiders	$27,000
		Liability to B	$ 1,000
		Net worth	$ (7,000)
	$21,000		$21,000

Distribution based on equal sharing is as follows:

Proceeds from asset liquidation	+$21,000	
To pay outside creditors	−$27,000	
To pay B loan	−$ 1,000	
Operation loss	−$ 7,000	
Capital loss	−$ 8,000	
Total loss	−$15,000 ÷ 3 =	−$5,000 share of loss for each partner

Partner A originally contributed $5,000, now pays	$ -0-
Partner B originally contributed $3,000, now pays	$2,000
Partner C originally contributed $ -0-, now pays	$5,000
	$7,000 to pay off all creditors

Partnership Assets

For the purpose of winding up partnership business, the first matter to ascertain is the partnership assets and their value. Partnership assets consist of all properties, real and personal, acquired at the beginning of and during the partnership. What is, or what is not, partnership property is often the subject of disputes, particularly with an expanding partnership business, where re-contributed shares of profits are converted into so-called after-acquired assets. In *Fortugno* v. *Hudson Manure Co.* (51 N.J.Super. 482, 144 A.2d 207 [1958]), where a growing family partnership owned the stocks of five corporations, the court considered those stocks to be subsequently acquired partnership assets that were to be liquidated upon dissolution of the partnership and the proceeds distributed to the partners in cash.

Capital Contribution

Without specific provisions to the contrary in the partnership agreement, only moneys and properties are to be considered capital contributions. This is illustrated in the following case.

Facts

Larsen and Claridge were partners in a farming operation from 1962 until the end of 1967. Claridge provided a net capital contribution of $141,940, plus the use of the land and living quarters for Larsen. Larsen agreed to provide services for the farming operation, and the partners agreed to share equally in profits and losses. Upon dissolution, the court awarded Claridge the full return of his capital contribution but would make no allowance for Larsen's contribution of labor. Larsen appealed.

Decision

The court held that there was no proof of any agreement between Larsen and Claridge that would equate the labor as provided by Larsen in monetary value with the actual capital contributed by Claridge. Without such an agreement, the court could not hold that labor was meant to provide an equal one-half contribution to the partnership venture. After the return of the $141,940 capital contribution to Claridge, $10,145 was left for distribution and was divided equally between them.

Larsen v. *Claridge*, 23 Ariz.App. 508, 534 P.2d 439 (1975).

Distribution in Kind

If, in accordance with the rules of distribution, creditors have been properly satisfied, a distribution in kind (i.e., distribution not in moneys but in properties) is not contrary to law so long as it is equitable and practical.

Distribution in Kind
Distribution in property other than money.

Facts

Five Logoluso brothers owned a farming partnership that had twelve parcels of real property valued at $2,000,000, subject to encumbrances of about $166,700. Upon dissolution, the trial court ordered the sale of all partnership property for the purpose of distributing the proceeds.

The brothers objected to the sale, since they had an agreement for a division of the real properties.

Decision

The appeals court ruled that the partners' agreement must be honored. Since the partnership had sufficient liquid assets to satisfy all partnership debts, there should be no reason to deny a distribution in kind.

Logoluso v. Logoluso, 233 Cal.App.2d 523, 43 Cal.Rptr. 678 (1965).

Insolvency and Bankruptcy

Where the partnership or a partner is insolvent or in bankruptcy, the rule of marshaling of assets is applied (UPA § 40(h)(i)). This rule is that partnership assets must be applied to the satisfaction of the claims of the partnership creditors and individual or personal assets of a partner to the satisfaction of his individual or personal creditors. Any balance of the personal estate of a partner is then applied to the satisfaction of partnership creditors. For example, if A is a partner in an insolvent business, the business creditors must first exhaust whatever interest A has in the business before going after his personal assets, even though he may be a very wealthy man. Conversely, if A should personally become insolvent, his nonpartnership-related creditors must first proceed against all of his personal assets before levying against his partnership interest. For this reason, many partnership creditors will require the individual partners to assume personal obligations on partnership debts.

Marshalling of Assets
Application of partnership assets to satisfy partnership obligations, and personal assets to satisfy personal obligations, before using personal assets for partnership obligations.

QUESTIONS

1. Name several grounds for dissolution of a partnership.
2. Can a partner dissolve a partnership "for a definite time" prematurely? Please explain.
3. Does a partner owe fiduciary duty to the copartners after the partnership is dissolved?
4. What does "winding up" mean?
5. Partner A contributed $9,000, Partner B $3,000, and Partner C $3,000. Upon dissolution, total assets are $-0- and total liabilities are $45,000. How much will each partner receive or pay?

PROBLEMS

1. A and B formed a partnership for five years. In the fourth year, A fraudulently converted property of the partnership to his own use. B, on discovering this fact, ousted A from the partnership. A brings an action for dissolution of the partnership, an accounting, and damages for the expulsion and loss of profits. Decision?

2. A and B were partners. They were performing a highway construction contract when A died. B continued performance of the contract. It was necessary for B to borrow a substantial sum of money from the bank to continue the project. When the partnership became insolvent, the bank sued the partnership. A's widow raised the defense that B could not enter a new transaction, such as borrowing money, and the partnership should therefore not be liable for the new loan. Decision?

3. A, B, and C are partners. C retired from the firm. A and B assumed the debts of the firm and paid C the value of his interest. D then became a partner of the firm with A and B, and the partnership of A, B, and D continued the business. T, a creditor of the firm of A, B, and C, brings action against A, B, C, and D for the debt. Decision?

4. A, B, and C formed a partnership. The capital was $5,000, to which A contributed $3,000; B, $2,000; and C, nothing. It was agreed that profits would be shared equally. Later, the partnership became

insolvent and was short $4,000 to pay the creditors. How shall the loss be adjusted?

5. A, B, and C were partners. The firm borrowed money from a bank and gave the bank the firm's note for the loan. In addition, each partner guaranteed the note personally. The partnership became insolvent. The bank claims that it has a right to file its claim as a partnership debt and has a right to a lien on the assets of the individual partners before the other general creditors of the partnership can look to the assets of the individual partners. Decision?

6. Phillips, Atkins, and Webb formed a partnership for the term of ten years. In the sixth year, Phillips withdrew without cause and Webb became bankrupt. A dispute then arose among the partners over the right to liquidate and wind up the firm's business. The exclusive right to do so was claimed by each of the partners and by Webb's trustee in bankruptcy. Who is entitled to wind up the business?

7. Golden was admitted into the partnership firm of Jackson and Smith. At the time of Golden's admission as a partner, the firm was indebted to several creditors, including Armen. The firm thereafter became insolvent, and the assets of the partnership and of the partners were insufficient to pay the partnership debts. Armen seeks to hold Golden personally liable for the deficit in his claim. Decision?

8. Riddle and Mohn form a ten-year partnership to practice surgery. During the second year, Mohn is involved in a serious motor accident, which necessitates the amputation of both arms. Riddle seeks to obtain a decree of dissolution of the partnership in a court of equity. Decision?

9. ABC partnership and its three partners, Ace, Best, and Conn, individually, were adjudged bankrupts. No assets remained in the estates of Ace and Best after the necessary expenses of administration had been paid. As to the estate of Conn and the ABC partnership, however, there remained the sums of $1,000 and $2,000, respectively. Can the ABC partnership creditors share in the assets remaining in the estate of Conn along with Conn's personal creditors?

10. Andy, who owned and operated a variety store, formed a partnership with Bill, who agreed to manage and operate the store as a partnership for half the profits. Bill made no capital investment in the enterprise. Later the partnership was dissolved. What proportion of the business assets should have been distributed to Bill?

CHAPTER TWENTY-THREE

Corporation (I)

23.1 Nature and Types of Corporations
Nature
- Personality
- Legal Entity

Types
- De Jure
- De Facto
- By Estoppel
- Private Versus Public
- Nonprofit
- Domestic Versus Foreign
- Close Corporation
- Professional Corporation

23.2 Promoters, Formation, and Termination
Promoters
- Disclosure
- Promoter's Contracts
- Preincorporation Stock Subscription

Formation
- Articles and Certificate of Incorporation
- Bylaws

Termination
- Dissolution: Voluntary, Involuntary, Merger and Consolidation
- Winding Up

23.3 Corporate Powers and Shareholders
Powers of the Corporation
- Express
- Implied
- Ultra Vires

Shareholders
- Meetings
- Election and Removal of Directors
- Bylaws and Resolutions
- Unusual Matters
- Inspection of Books
- Shareholders' Actions
- Other Rights
- Shareholder Liability

23.1 Nature and Types of Corporations

Compared to sole proprietorships, corporations are subject to greater governmental formalities and control. They involve the U.S. Constitution, federal laws, and state laws. This and the next chapter are not intended to be a comprehensive discourse of corporate law but are merely an introduction to the subject, with the emphasis on material important to the business student.

Nature

Personality

Corporate Personality
A corporation is a "person" created pursuant to statute, and has many, but not all, of the legal rights of a natural person.

A corporation is a legal "person" or entity. It has an existence separate from that of its shareholders. A corporation is a person within the meaning of the Fifth (due process) and Fourteenth (equal protection) Amendments to the Constitution of the United States. It is not a "citizen" within that part of the Fourteenth Amendment that has to do with the protection of privileges and immunities. It is, however, a citizen for the purpose of determining diversity of citizenship as a basis for jurisdiction of the federal courts in an action to which the corporation is a party.

Obviously, a corporation cannot be a person under a statute contemplating a natural person, such as one requiring mandatory imprisonment, giving preferences to a person over 65 years of age, or allowing a party to appear in person (*in propria persona*) in court. As a fictitious person, a corporation is represented by a licensed attorney at law.

Union Savings Ass'n v. Home Owners Aid, Inc.
23 Ohio St.2d 60, 262 N.E.2d 558 (1970).

Duncan, Justice The record, briefs and arguments of counsel raise the question: May a corporate litigant maintain a legal action *in propria persona* through an officer of the corporation who is not a licensed attorney? If a corporation cannot appear *in propria persona* through its officer, the order of the Court of Common Pleas, striking the corporate defendant's petition to vacate judgment, was proper.

Appellant, Home Owners, contends that corporate statutes in R.C. Chapter 1701, in essence, either provide or imply that a corporation is the same as a natural person in all respects and has all the capacities of a natural person, including the right to represent itself *in propria persona* through an appointed agent who need not be an attorney at law. Home Owners asserts constitutional protection for the right to litigate in this manner pursuant to its entitlement to due process and equal protection of the law, as guaranteed by the Ohio and United States Constitutions. In addition, Home Owners urges that a denial of the maintenance of this litigation through its officer unconstitutionally impairs the obligation of contract.

We cannot agree with appellant's contentions, which appear to be based upon the premise that a corporation and a natural living person are in all respects equal. A corporation is an artificial person, created by the General Assembly and deriving its power, authority and capacity from the statutes.

It is true that certain statutes make it appear that a corporation is to be treated as a natural person. Many other statutes, however, clearly reveal that the General Assembly did not intend a corporation to have all the attributes and powers of a natural person.

... In other jurisdictions, courts have held that a corporation cannot appear *in propria persona*. ...

The fallacy of defendant corporation's constitutional arguments is that they rest upon the faulty premise that a corporation is in all respects equal to a natural person.

... Beyond what has been concluded hereinabove in importance as a basis for our decision is the statutory prohibition regarding the practice of law. R.C. 4705.01 prohibits anyone from practicing law or commencing or defending an action "in which he is not a party concerned, ... unless he has been admitted to the bar by order of the Supreme Court. ..."

It is the responsibility of this court to provide effective standards for admission to the practice of law and for the discipline of those admitted to practice. Litigation must be projected through the courts according to established practice by lawyers who are of high character, skilled in the profession, dedicated to the interest of their clients, and in the spirit of public service. In the orderly process of the administration of justice, any retreat from those principles would be a disservice to the public. To allow a corporation to maintain litigation and appear in court represented by corporate officers or agents only would lay open the gates to the practice of law for entry to those corporate officers or agents who have not been qualified to practice law and who are not amenable to the general discipline of the court.

Judgment affirmed.

In Propria Persona
Appearing in court in person without being represented by an attorney.

It should be noted, however, that in a civil court with a limited jurisdiction, such as a Small Claims Court, parties are often not allowed to be represented by a professional attorney. In such a case, a corporation appears in court through one of its corporate officers, who may or may not be a practicing lawyer.

Legal Entity

A corporation is a legal entity with separate rights and liabilities. It may sue and be sued. It exists in the eyes of the law as though it were a person separate and distinct from the shareholders, as shown in the following case.

Facts
Kesner (plaintiff) is the treasurer of Hereford Realty, Inc., which had a checking account in Liberty Bank & Trust Co. (defendant). The bank improperly dishonored a check drawn by Hereford on the corporate account. Kesner personally sued the bank for wrongfully refusing to pay the check.

Decision
Judgment for Liberty Bank. Only the bank customer whose check has been dishonored has the right to sue for wrongful dishonor of that check. In this case, the customer is Hereford Realty, and only Hereford had the right to sue. Hereford Realty, Inc., is an entity separate and distinct from its officers and shareholders. Kesner, as an individual, could not sue the bank.

Kesner v. Liberty Bank & Trust Co., 7 Mass.App.Ct. 934, 390 N.E.2d 259 (1979).

The corporate entity starts exactly at the time the certificate of incorporation is issued by the appropriate state authority.

Facts

Robertson and Levy entered into an agreement whereby Levy agreed to form a corporation, Penn Ave. Record Shack, Inc., which was to purchase Robertson's business. Levy submitted articles of incorporation to the Superintendent of Corporations. Before the certificate of incorporation was issued, Levy, acting as president of the corporation, assumed Robertson's lease and signed a note payable to Robertson. Shortly thereafter, the corporation went bankrupt. Robertson sued Levy personally to recover the balance due on the note. Judgment for Levy was appealed.

Decision

Reversed. The court stated that § 56 of the Model Act provides that corporate existence begins only upon the issuance of the certificate of incorporation. Hence, before the certificate is issued, there is no corporation de jure, de facto, or by estoppel. That Robertson may have intended to deal with a corporation is immaterial. Levy is thus subject to personal liability for the obligations incurred prior to January 17, the date the certificate was issued, since he assumed to act as a corporation without any authority to do so (Model Act § 146).

Robertson v. Levy, 197 A.2d 443 (D.C. App. 1964).

Corporate Veil
Corporate shield which may be pierced to make the corporate owners personally liable.

Close Corporation
A corporation owned by a small number of people.

Because the debts of the corporation are not the debts of the shareholders, the directors, or the officers, the corporate entity absolves the shareholders and the managers from the liability of the corporation. This is one of the main advantages of a corporation.

However, this corporate entity or veil can under certain circumstances be broken or disregarded, in which event, the individuals who are attempting to use the corporate status to protect themselves from liabilities for their wrongs are held personally liable. The corporate entity veil will be disregarded when it is used to defeat public convenience, protect fraud, justify a wrong, evade the law, or defend crime. The courts will not recognize the entity protection to the managers or the shareholders if to do so would produce unjust or undesirable consequences inconsistent with the purpose of the entity concept. The question of disregarding the corporate entity, or as is often said, "piercing the corporate veil," usually arises with a one-person or family type of corporation. The one-person or close corporation is found where one or two persons own all of the corporation stock. This type of corporation may usually afford grounds for disregarding the entity unless the following two conditions are complied with:

1. The business must be conducted on a corporate rather than a personal basis.
2. The business must be established on an adequate financial basis.

Casanova Guns, Inc. v. Connally
454 F.2d 1320 (7th Cir. 1972).

Per Curiam This is an appeal by Casanova Guns, Inc. (Casanova Guns), a Wisconsin corporation, from the denial of its application for renewal of its federal firearms license by the Wisconsin Regional Commissioner of the Treasury Department's Alcohol, Tobacco and Firearms Division. The appellant brought an action in the district court under section 102 of the Gun Control Act of 1968, 18 U.S.C. § 923(f)(3), to review the commissioner's decision not to renew the license. The district court upheld the commissioner's decision.

The license was denied because of Casanova Guns' relationship with Casanova's, Inc. (Casanova's), a convicted felon. The Gun Control Act prohibits the issuance of federal firearms licenses to convicted felons and to companies directed or controlled by convicted felons. 18 U.S.C. § 923(d)(1)(B). Based upon their findings that Casanova's controlled or had the power to control Casanova Guns, the commissioner and the district court found the appellant ineligible for a renewal license. We are asked to review the finding that Casanova's controlled Casanova Guns.

It is apparent from the record that a substantial purpose for the incorporation of Casanova Guns was the circumvention of the statute restricting issuance of firearms licenses to convicted felons. Casanova Guns was formed after Casanova's was under federal indictment. Indeed, the testimony of John Casanova at the administrative hearing is a reluctant admission that the second corporation was formed to insure the continuation of the gun business.

Further, there is a significant unity of interest between the officers and stockholders of the two corporations and the business operations were closely integrated. The four officers of each corporation were the same, the only difference being that Clarence Casanova was the president of Casanova's and John Casanova was the president of Casanova Guns. Casanova Guns operated from the same building as Casanova's and was dependent on Casanova's for light, heat, telephone, bookkeeping and additional personnel when necessary. Casanova's provided these services on an informal "fee" arrangement, but the nature of that arrangement does not destroy the interlocking relationship between the management personnel and practices of the two companies.

In addition, the total assets of Casanova Guns derived from the inventory purchased from Casanova's. That inventory was purchased on a $424,000 unsecured note which is payable on demand. We believe a debt of this nature and magnitude warrants the inference that Casanova's possessed a substantial degree of control over Casanova Guns. That belief is bolstered by the admission of Clarence Casanova that he exercised some control over Casanova Guns in order to protect his investment. That control was made possible by the fact that the two corporations operated out of the same building; also Clarence Casanova's daughter was the bookkeeper for both corporations.

Under these circumstances, although we realize the hardship the denial works upon the Casanova enterprises, we find that the commissioner's denial of the application and the district court's affirmance of that decision were not clearly erroneous. The decision below is therefore affirmed.

Types

De Jure

A *de jure* corporation is formed when there is essential compliance with all of the mandatory provisions of the incorporation statute. The *de jure* corporation is legal for all purposes even though the corporation is not in

De jure Corporation
Established in compliance with applicable laws.

compliance with some minor provisions of the statute. Only the secretary of state might challenge such a corporation's corporate existence and authority.

De Facto

De facto Corporation
Not in substantial compliance with the law, but where a good faith effort has been made to organize under the law, and business has been transacted as a corporation.

A *de facto* corporation exists where there has not been substantial compliance with the mandatory provisions of the incorporation statute. In practice, it is a corporation in its dealings with all parties except the secretary of state of the state of incorporation, who may attack its corporate status and dissolve the corporation in a *quo warranto* court proceeding for that purpose.

To be a *de facto* organization, there must be the following:

1. A valid statute under which the corporation is formed.
2. A good faith attempt to organize under such statute.
3. Application of corporate powers, i.e., business has been transacted as a corporation.

A *de facto* corporation is entitled to act as a corporation until dissolved by direct state action. The shareholders of a *de facto* corporation are limitedly liable to the extent of their capital contributions to the company.

By Estoppel

Estoppel
A legal doctrine prohibiting a person from denying his own previous acts or deeds to the detriment of another person.

When an association represents itself to be a corporation, it cannot escape liability by denying its own corporate existence. Furthermore, if the association is not a *de jure* or *de facto* corporation, the members have unlimited liability as in a partnership. When a person contracts with an association as if it were a corporation, the general rule is that he cannot avoid liability on a contract by denying the corporate existence, since that person thereby admits the legal existence of the corporation for the purpose of any action that may be brought to enforce the contract.

Facts

James Bukacek was having serious financial problems. Bukacek and others agreed to form "Pell City Farms, Inc." Once formed, the corporation was to pay Bukacek's debts. In exchange, Bukacek was to deed his 300-acre farm to the corporation. Bukacek deeded the land to Pell City Farms, Inc., but Pell City Farms' articles of incorporation had not as yet been filed with the designated officer of the state. After the corporation was formed, Bukacek participated in corporate business involving the farm and took an active role as an officer, director, and shareholder. However, he later asserted that at the time he signed the deed, the corporation did not legally exist. He therefore argued that the corporation had been incapable of taking title to real property and that he still owned the farm. Bukacek (plaintiff) sued in equity to quiet title to the land. Judgment for Pell City Farms, Inc. Bukacek appealed.

Decision

Judgment for Pell City Farms, Inc. Bukacek was one of the incorporators; he dealt with the corporation as a corporation both before and after the articles of incorporation were filed. Under such facts, Bukacek is estopped to deny the existence of the corporation at the time he voluntarily executed a deed transferring property to the corporation even though the articles of incorporation had not been filed at that time.

"Our ruling here is limited. It is based on equitable grounds which preclude the [plaintiff] here from denying corporate existence. As against the state, of course, a corporation cannot be created by agreement of the parties . . . but they may, by their agreements or their conduct estop themselves from denying the fact of the existence of the corporation. We hold, therefore, that Bukacek is estopped to deny the existence of Pell City Farms, Inc., even though it may have been neither de facto nor de jure at the time he executed the deed making the corporation, *by its corporate name,* the grantee. . . ."

Bukacek v. Pell City Farms, Inc., 286 Ala. 141, 237 So.2d 851 (1970).

Private Versus Public

Private corporations are those organized for private purposes. Public corporations are created by the people or government for public purposes, political, or otherwise, e.g., United States, states, cities, towns, counties, school districts.

Nonprofit

A nonprofit corporation can be formed for religious, charitable, social, educational, or cemetery purposes. The business can be carried on at a profit as an incident to the main purpose of the corporation, and it is generally tax-exempt. The corporation cannot distribute any gains, profits, or dividends to any of its members, and under the Internal Revenue rules, its assets upon dissolution must be distributed to (an)other "qualified" organization(s), i.e., entities that also have tax-exempt status. A nonprofit corporation is a nonstock corporation. It can have memberships but no shares. The corporate officers receive salaries on which they pay individual income taxes.

Nonprofit Corporation
May make a profit, but cannot distribute it to its members; a charitable corporation.

Domestic Versus Foreign

A domestic corporation is one that is created by the laws of a particular state or country in which it does business. A foreign corporation is one created by the laws of another state or country but does business within the borders of a particular state. "Doing business" means that the corporation is doing a substantial amount of business with substantial regularity in the state. When a foreign corporation is doing business in the state, it must qualify as a foreign corporation. To qualify, it must, among other things, permit itself to be sued in the state. This is done by filing with the secretary of state in which it is going to do business a copy of its articles of incorporation, together with a statement setting forth its home office and office within the state and the name and address of a person or corporation within the state upon whom legal process may be served in any legal action against it. Failure to qualify as a foreign corporation can result in fines and the denial of the use of the courts of the state to enforce contracts.

In *Lincoln v. Fairfield-Nobel Co.* (76 Mich.App. 514, 257 N.W.2d 148 [1977]), where a salesman of a New York corporation was involved in a car accident in the state of Michigan that killed two other individuals, the court considered the corporation a foreign corporation doing business in the state of Michigan, where it could stand trial. The court stated: "(The) record discloses that defendant does a continuous and systematic business in Michigan. This is sufficient. The representative percentage of defendant's business conducted in Michigan is not of great importance as long as the business actually done in Michigan is continuous and systematic."

Close Corporation

Corporations are not all conglomerate giants. Today, because of the advantages of tax benefits and limited liability, many small firms that normally would be operated as sole proprietorships or partnerships are now incorporated. They may have only a few outstanding shares of stock, or all of the stock may be held by one person, a family, or a few friends. Since the stock is closely held by a few and not sold publicly, the entity is called a "close corporation." Many states now have separate statutes covering this type of corporation that permit simpler operation with less technical tax and accounting problems.

The following case illustrates the duty of a close corporation to its shareholders.

Facts

Donahue (plaintiff) was a minority shareholder in Rodd Electrotype. Harry Rodd and his children owned the remaining shares and served as officers and directors. Without informing the plaintiff, the board voted to reacquire Harry Rodd's shares. Upon learning of the transaction, the plaintiff objected and brought suit, claiming that the purchase was an unlawful distribution of corporate assets and that the Rodds breached the fiduciary duties owed by them as controlling shareholders to the minority shareholder. The trial court dismissed the suit.

Decision

On appeal, the court held that the Rodds had breached their fiduciary duty owed to the plaintiff. Close corporations are typified by (1) a small number of shareholders, (2) no ready market for corporate stock, and (3) substantial majority shareholder participation in the management, direction, and operations of the corporation. They resemble partnerships, requiring of the controlling owners utmost good faith, trust, fidelity, and absolute loyalty. Because Rodd was a member of the controlling group of shareholders, the corporation should have offered each shareholder an equal opportunity to sell a pro rata number of shares to the corporation at an identical price.

Donahue v. Rodd Electrotype Co., 367 Mass. 578, 328 N.E.2d 505 (1975).

Professional Corporation

Professional Corporation
A corporation for the practice of a profession such as law or medicine.

All states now permit a corporation to be organized for the purpose of conducting a profession, although most will not allow skilled individuals, such as doctors and lawyers, by incorporation to avoid personal liability for their own malpractice.

Questions

1. Discuss the personality status of a corporation.
2. What are the reasons for which the corporate veil can be broken?
3. What is a corporation by estoppel?
4. What is the tax status of a nonprofit corporation?
5. What is a domestic corporation and what is a foreign corporation?

23.2 Promoters, Formation, and Termination

Promoters

Large corporations are usually planned and formed by promoters. Their activities include researching the economic feasibility of the new business and assembling the necessary resources, property, and personnel. Promoters often continue in control of the corporation after the corporation's formation.

Promoters
Persons who plan and arrange for the formation of a new corporation.

Disclosure

Promoters are fiduciaries who owe a duty of good faith, fair dealing, and full disclosure to the corporation. They are liable to the corporation for any secret profits.

Frick v. Howard
23 Wis.2d 86, 126 N.W.2d 619 (1964).

Action to foreclose a mortgage on real estate. Plaintiff-respondent is the assignee of the promoter of a corporation. The purchase money mortgage being foreclosed was executed by the corporation in favor of the promoter and his wife when they sold certain real estate located in the city of Milwaukee to the corporation. Defendant-appellant is the receiver of the corporation. . . .

From a judgment of foreclosure in favor of the plaintiff for the amount of $77,159.57 defendant appeals. . . .

Beilfuss, Justice Did Preston, as a promoter, breach a fiduciary duty to the corporation? It appears without dispute that Preston was the organizer and promoter of the Pan American Motel, Inc.

He entered into the contract to purchase land for $240,000 on January 24, 1958. . . . He organized the corporation April 1, 1958 and was its sole stockholder until September 3, 1958. After successfully bringing an action on the contract to purchase, he obtained title to the land on August 29, 1958.

. . . Three days later, September 1, 1958, the corporation offered him $350,000 for the land. The offer was accepted and the corporation paid Preston $70,000 by cancellation of his debt of $35,000 to the corporation, issuing 35 shares of its stock to him, assuming the $170,000 mortgage, and giving him a note and mortgage for $110,000. The offer was signed by Preston as seller and Frank J. Mack for the corporation. At the time the offer to purchase was made by the corporation Preston was, as far as the record reveals, the sole stockholder and completely dominated the affairs of the corporation. There was a board of directors consisting of Preston and two others but the record does not show they owned any stock or that they were in any way independent of Preston. On April 1, 1959 the note of $110,000 and mortgage were signed by Preston as president of the corporation and by Frank J. Mack as secretary payable to Preston and his wife.

The trial court found that Preston committed a fraud upon the corporation but that the transaction was not secret.

> ... The fact that the transaction was not secret does not in all instances relieve a promoter of his fiduciary obligation to the corporation.
>
> "The promoters may deal with the corporation, but they must deal fairly, the burden of proof of fairness being on them. When they deal with the corporation, it must have independent directors; and the promoters cannot also be directors or dominate them as representatives of the other adversely interested parties.
>
> "Perfect candor, full disclosure, good faith, in fact, the utmost good faith, and the strictest honesty are required of promoters, and their dealings must be open and fair, or without undue advantage taken.
>
> "As a result of the fiduciary relation or relation of trust and confidence sustained by a promoter, an unfair advantage taken or secret profit gained thereby is a fraud. . . ."
>
> It is clear that at the time of the sale of the land to the corporation, and the execution of the note and mortgage, that the corporation had no independent board of directors. The actions of the corporation were completely dominated by Preston. The transaction to sell the land held for a very short period of time was controlled by Preston both as buyer and seller. This was not an agreement between an independent buyer and seller dealing at arm's length. Preston as an individual selling the property had a personal financial interest to obtain the highest price available; Preston as the alter ego of Pan American Motel, Inc. had a financial interest to purchase the property at the lowest price available. There could be no meeting of the minds.
>
> The fact that the land may or may not have been worth more than $240,000 cannot override Preston's fiduciary obligation as a promoter of the corporation.
>
> . . . Judgment reversed with directions to dismiss the complaint.

Promoter's Contracts

The acts of the promoters do not bind the corporation prior to the corporation's legal existence, since until the corporation legally exists, there cannot be a principal-agency relationship. The corporation is not liable on promoter contracts until it adopts or ratifies such contracts after incorporation.

The promoters themselves are liable on the contracts if they entered into them as individuals but not if they made the contracts in the name of the *contemplated* corporation and solely on its credit. If the other party to the contract is unaware that the corporation has not come into existence at the time he contracts with the promoter and if the promoter expressly or implicitly holds the corporation out to him as existing and that he has the right to bind the corporation by contract, the promoter will be personally liable on the contract on the theory that he has been guilty of a breach of warranty of his agency.

Preincorporation Stock Subscription

Preincorporation Stock Subscription
Agreement to purchase shares after the corporation is formed.

Before forming the corporation, the promoters may attempt to get people to pledge themselves to purchase stock after the corporation is formed. To take this action, the promoters must first secure a permit from the state to take preincorporation subscriptions. After they obtain the permit, they can solicit prospective investors for their promises to purchase stock.

These pledges (or offers) by the investors to purchase stock are usually revocable by the investor, in the absence of statute, until accepted by the corporation after it comes into legal existence. Modern statutes usually make preincorporation subscriptions irrevocable for a stated period of time, for example, six months under Model Business Corporations Act (MBCA) § 16.

Preincorporation agreements are not in common use. Today, it is more usual to first form the corporation and then attempt to sell the stock.

Formation

Although incorporation procedures may vary from state to state, a corporation is generally formed by filing the articles of incorporation followed by the issuance of a certificate of incorporation or charter by the designated state official.

Articles and Certificate of Incorporation

The incorporators may be natural persons or established corporations. Articles of incorporation are prepared, executed, and filed (usually in duplicate) by the incorporators with the secretary of state or designated state official.

The contents of the articles of incorporation are prescribed in the general incorporation statutes of the various states. Typical requirements are found in MBCA § 8:

Articles of Incorporation The written instrument governing and declaring the purposes and scope of a corporation.

1. The name of the corporation which under MBCA § 8(a) shall include such words as *Corporation, Incorporated, Limited, Corp., Inc.,* or *Ltd.*
2. The period of duration, which may be perpetual.
3. The purpose for which the corporation is organized.
4. The number of shares that the corporation shall have authority to issue and the par (equal) value of each share or a statement that the shares are without par value.
5. If the shares are to be divided into classes, the designation of each class and a statement of preferences, limitations, and relative rights of each class.
6. A statement that the corporation will not commence business until at least $1,000 has been received for issued shares.
7. Any provision limiting or denying to shareholders the right to acquire additional or treasury shares of the corporation on a preemptive basis.
8. Any provision the incorporators may choose to set forth for the regulation of the internal affairs of the corporation.
9. The address of the corporation's initial office and agent.
10. The number of directors constituting the original board of directors and the names and addresses of the persons who are to serve as the first board of directors until the first annual meeting of shareholders or until successors are elected.
11. The name and address of each incorporator (usually three or more and of legal capacity).

Figure 23.1 Sample of Articles of Incorporation

ARTICLES OF INCORPORATION OF [CORPORATE NAME]

The undersigned, acting as incorporator(s) of a corporation under the _____ Business Corporation Act, adopt(s) the following Articles of Incorporation for such corporation:

First: The name of the corporation is _____

Second: The period of its duration is _____

Third: The purpose or purposes for which the corporation is organized are: _____
_____

Fourth: The aggregate number of shares which the corporation shall have authority to issue is _____

Fifth: Provisions granting preemptive rights are:

Sixth: Provisions for the regulation of the internal affairs of the corporation are: _____

Seventh: The address of the initial registered office of the corporation is _____ and the name of its initial registered agent at such address is _____

Eighth: The number of directors constituting the initial board of directors of the corporation is _____, and the names and addresses of the persons who are to serve as directors until the first annual meeting of share holders or until their successors are elected and shall qualify are:

Name	Address
_____	_____
_____	_____

Ninth: The name and address of each incorporator is:

Name	Address
_____	_____
_____	_____

Dated _____, 19 ___.

_____
_____
_____
Incorporator(s)

Source: Reprinted with permission from Henn & Alexander, Corporations, 3rd ed. Copyright © 1983 by West Publishing Company.

If the articles of incorporation are found to be in order, the secretary of state will return an approved copy of the articles and issue a certificate of incorporation. Generally, the copy of the articles and the certificate are filed with the local county recorder. When the articles of incorporation and certificate are returned by the recorder, they are placed in the corporation minute book. Procedures may vary to some degree in some states.

According to MBCA § 56, the corporation starts to exist upon issuance of the certificate or charter. In some states, corporate existence commences with the filing of the articles of incorporation. In other states, it does not begin until the first meeting of the board of directors rendering the corporation in operation.

Bylaws

The MBCA prescribes that after issuance of the charter, a meeting of the board of directors is to be held primarily to adopt bylaws, elect officers, issue stock, and decide on matters necessary to start business. Bylaws are rules a corporation enacts to regulate its day-to-day business and the powers, rights, and duties of its directors, officers, and shareholders. However, they are not a necessary element of the formation and existence of a corporation.

Bylaws must conform to the articles of incorporation and local laws. Requirements relative to the contents of the bylaws and the procedures as to how the bylaws are to be adopted and amended may differ from state to state. Bylaws vary in length from a brief statement of rules for one corporation to a comprehensive booklet for another. In most states, the bylaws are not filed in any public office.

Bylaws
Rules governing the day to day operation of a corporation.

Termination

The corporate existence terminates upon the dissolution of the corporation and winding up of its business.

Dissolution: Voluntary, Involuntary, Merger and Consolidation

A corporation is dissolved voluntarily or involuntarily or by a merger or consolidation, which can be "friendly" or "hostile."

1. *Voluntary* dissolution takes place upon an agreement.
   a. Where the incorporators agreed at the beginning on the duration of the corporate life, as evidenced by the articles of incorporation, the corporation automatically desists upon expiration of this period.
   b. Without any pre-agreement, the shareholders, through the directors, may terminate the corporate existence voluntarily by surrendering the certificate of incorporation to the state government. Depending upon local statutes, one-half to two-thirds of the shareholders are needed for such a decision. Acceptance of the surrender of the articles by the state takes place after the corporate business is properly wound up. The corporation then ceases to exist, and all its liabilities are extinguished.
2. An *involuntary* dissolution takes place usually because of financial difficulties.
   a. Forced dissolution can be caused by creditors of a corporation or by petition of a percentage of the shareholders, which varies from 10 to 50

Dissolution
A corporation terminates upon its dissolution and winding up.

percent. Some of the reasons for a forced dissolution are fraud on the part of the directors, deadlocked factions of directors and shareholders, wasting of corporate property, misapplication of corporate property, mismanagement, abuse of authority, and unfairness to minority shareholders.

Insolvency and reorganization under the federal bankruptcy law do not by themselves terminate a corporate existence. However, such circumstances may be considered justifiable cause for creditors to commence proceedings to dissolve the corporate entity. Similarly, bankruptcy by itself does not dissolve the corporation, although continuing corporate business after sale of all of the corporation's assets would obviously be difficult, if not impossible.

b. Involuntary dissolution can also be caused by the act of the state legislature or by a decree of court initiated by the attorney general when it appears that the corporation has violated a corporation law, such as failure to pay franchise tax, abuse of powers, or fraud. In any event, the government can forfeit or revoke the certificate of incorporation with a good cause.

It should be noted that a mere suspension of the authority to do corporate business does not amount to termination of the corporate existence.

Facts

When Morse Bros. Painting and Weatherproofing, a corporation, failed to pay taxes to the State of California, the state suspended the company's authority to do business. In this state of suspension, the Bank of America loaned money to the company on a note signed: "Morse Bros. Painting and Weatherproofing, a Corporation By/s/J. L. Morse, President. By/s/Doris N. Morse, Secretary." Neither the bank nor the Morses knew at the time of the loan that the corporate authority had been suspended. Under the California statute, contracts made by a corporation while the corporation's powers were suspended were voidable at the election of the other contracting party. After J. L. Morse's death, the bank sued Doris Morse personally.

Decision

Judgment for Doris Morse. The suspension statute merely suspended the rights of the corporation to exercise its powers. It did not forfeit or terminate its existence, nor did it impose liabilities on officers for acting on behalf of the corporation during its suspension. Doris Morse had executed the note strictly in accordance with the Uniform Commercial Code. To avoid personal liability, she signed the paper in a representative capacity and identified her principal, i.e., the corporation. She was under the law of agency not held personally liable.

Bank of America National Trust and Savings Ass'n. v. *Morse,* 265 Or. 72, 508 P.2d 194 (1973).

Merger
Joining of two or more corporations to become one of the original corporations.

Surviving Corporation
The corporation that remains after a merger.

3. A *merger* of two or more corporations combines all of the corporations' total assets, with title held in one of them, called the surviving corporation. The other corporation or corporations, known as merged corporation(s), cease to exist as separate corporate entities. The debts and obligations of the merged corporation(s) are carried over and assumed by the surviving corporation as a matter of law, irrespective of any agreement to do so. The shareholders of the merged corporation receive stock issued by the surviving corporation, as outlined in the merger plan. The board of directors as well as a majority of the shareholders of each corporation must approve any merger.

As in the case of a purchase of all or substantially all assets, dissenting shareholders of either or all corporations (surviving and merged) are entitled to appraisal rights where authorized by statute.

The difference between a merger requiring shareholder approval and a reorganization agreement (not requiring such approval and thus not entitling shareholders to any appraisal rights) was noted in *Farris v. Glen Alden Corp.* The Supreme Court of Pennsylvania, in finding the transaction to be a merger, looked to the consequences of the transaction in making the determination.

Facts

The complaint stated that the notice of the annual shareholders' meeting did not conform to the requirements of the Business Corporation Law, 15 P.S. § 2852–1 et seq., in three respects: (1) It did not give notice to the shareholders that the true intent and purpose of the meetings was to effect a merger or consolidation of Glen Alden and List; (2) it failed to give notice to the shareholders of their right to dissent to the plan of merger or consolidation and claim fair value for their shares; and (3) it did not contain copies of the text of certain sections of the Business Corporation Law as required.

By reason of these omissions, plaintiff contended that the approval of the reorganization agreement by the shareholders at the annual meeting was invalid and unless the carrying out of the plan were enjoined, he would suffer irreparable loss by being deprived of substantial property rights.

Decision

"When use of the corporate form of business organization first became widespread, it was relatively easy for courts to define a 'merger' or a 'sale of assets' and to label a particular transaction as one or the other. But prompted by the desire to avoid the impact of adverse, and to obtain the benefits of favorable government regulations, particularly federal tax laws, new accounting and legal techniques were developed by lawyers and accountants which interwove the elements characteristic of each, thereby creating hybrid forms of corporate amalgamation. Thus, it is no longer helpful to consider an individual transaction in the abstract and solely by reference to the various elements therein to determine whether it is a 'merger' or a 'sale.' Instead, to determine properly the nature of a corporate transaction, we must refer not only to all the provisions of the agreement, but also to the consequences of the transaction and to the purposes of the provisions of the corporation law said to be applicable.

We hold that the combination contemplated by the reorganization agreement, although consummated by contract rather than in accordance with the statutory procedure, is a merger within the protective purview of the corporation law. The shareholders of Glen Alden should have been notified accordingly and advised of their statutory rights of dissent and appraisal. The failure of the corporate officers to take these steps renders the stockholder approval of the agreement at the shareholders' meeting invalid. The officers and directors of Glen Alden are enjoined from carrying out this agreement."

Farris v. Glen Alden Corporation, 393 Pa. 427, 143 A.2d 25 (1958).

A merger is called friendly if it is carried out with the approval of the management of the merged corporation. It is called hostile if what is known as "the corporate raider" purchases and accumulates the stock available in the open market without management's approval. Acquisition of a corporation through merger has become an important phenomenon in today's business arena. There are pros and cons, depending on one's point of view. Many merged corporations that have known products and good reputations retain their original names to preserve their goodwill.

4. A *consolidation* combines two or more corporations, including all assets, into a newly created consolidated corporation. The original corporations

Consolidation
Joining of two or more corporations to become a newly formed corporation.

cease to exist, and the debts and liabilities of each of them are assumed by the new corporation. The shareholders of each of the constituent corporations receive stock or other securities issued by the consolidated corporation. Like a merger, consolidation requires the approval of the board of directors and a majority of the shareholders of each constituent corporation.

Mergers and consolidations are often confused, as illustrated in the following case.

Akwell Corp. v. Eiger
141 F.Supp. 19 (S.D.N.Y., 1956).

Levet, District Judge Defendant has moved to dismiss the complaint in this action to recover damages for an alleged fraud on the ground that the Court lacks jurisdiction because (a) the plaintiff is not the real party in interest; and (b) the controversy is not between citizens of different states, in that the defendant is a citizen of the State of New York and that Killashun Export Corporation, the alleged real party in interest, is also a citizen of the State of New York.

It appears from the affidavits and annexed exhibits submitted on this motion that the defendant had been a customer of Killashun Export Corporation. It also appears that pursuant to an agreement of "Merger and Consolidation" between National Hygienic Products Corporation, The J. & E. Stevens Sales Co., and Killashun Exort Corporation a combination was effected which resulted in the continued existence of the National Hygienic Products Corporation. . . .

A photostatic copy of a certificate of the Secretary of State of Delaware, which is annexed to the answering affidavit, indicates that the agreement was filed in the Secretary's office on December 14, 1954.

There is also annexed a photostatic copy of a certificate of the Secretary of State of Delaware which states that on January 7, 1955 a certificate of amendment of the certificate of incorporation of National Hygienic Products Corporation was filed in the Secretary's office. Pursuant to said certificate of amendment, the name of the corporation was changed to The Akwell Corporation, the plaintiff in this action.

. . . Although the term "consolidation" is used in the agreement between the combining corporations in conjunction with the term "merger," it is manifest that the combination of corporate entities resulted in a merger. A merger consists in the uniting of two or more corporations by the transfer of all of the property to an existing corporation which survives the absorption. In this respect a merger differs from a consolidation wherein the existence of all the corporate entities terminates and a new corporation is created. . . .

It is well settled that subsequent to a merger the continuing corporation succeeds to the rights of the absorbed corporation and may itself sue on the claims of the absorbed corporation which have passed to the survivor or continuing corporation by reason of the merger.

. . . Accordingly, the plaintiff, The Akwell Corporation, is a proper party to this action and, therefore, this Court has jurisdiction to entertain the suit because there is a diversity of citizenship between the plaintiff, a Delaware corporation, and the defendant, who is a citizen of the State of New York.

Defendant's motion to dismiss is denied.

To protect the interest of minority shareholders, many states, including those adopting the Model Business Corporations Act, give a shareholder not wishing to approve a proposed sale or lease of corporate assets—merger or consolidation—the right to dissent. By dissenting and complying exactly with the statutory provisions, the shareholder is entitled to receive the fair value of his shares. Three requirements must be met:

1. Filing of a written objection to the proposed transaction prior to the vote of the shareholders.
2. Refraining from voting for the proposed transaction either in person or by proxy.
3. Making a written demand for appraisal upon the corporation within the time period specified by the corporation on the form provided, such time period to be not less than thirty days after the corporation mails the form.

The Model Act defines fair value of shares to mean the shares' value immediately before the completion of the proposed transaction, not to include any appreciation or depreciation that anticipated such action, unless disregarding such price fluctuations would be inequitable.

Winding Up

Usually, a certificate of election to dissolve the corporation must be filed with the secretary of state as the first step in winding up. The corporation must cease doing any business except that necessary to wind up its affairs. The directors must liquidate as much of the assets as they believe necessary to effect the winding up. After all the debts have been paid, the directors must distribute the balance of the assets to the shareholders. After distribution, the directors must file a certificate with the secretary of state showing that the corporation has been wound up, debts paid, and the balance of the assets distributed to the shareholders. Upon the filing of this certificate, the corporation terminates.

In an involuntary dissolution, the court decrees dissolution and orders the winding up by the directors under the supervision of the court. The procedure for winding up is similar to a voluntary dissolution.

Winding Up
Liquidating the operation when a corporation is dissolved.

Questions

1. Discuss the promoter's liabilities under preincorporation contracts.
2. What are the requirements for a corporation to come into existence?
3. What are corporation bylaws?
4. What is the difference between mergers and consolidations?
5. Discuss the corporation termination process.

23.3 Corporate Powers and Shareholders

Three groups participate in the management of a corporation: the shareholders, the directors, and the officers. The powers, qualifications, functions, and procedures relating to these three groups are prescribed in part by constitutions, statutes, administrative rules and regulations, articles of incorporation, bylaws, various shareholder and director resolutions and agreements, and proxies.

Powers of the Corporation

A corporation's powers are the things it is authorized to do and are derived from the articles of incorporation and the laws of the state under which the corporation was organized. A corporation has only such powers as are expressly or implicitly conferred by its charter. The difference between the powers of a natural person and those of a corporation is that a natural person can do anything not forbidden by law, whereas a corporation can do only what is expressly or implicitly authorized by the state. State laws can also specifically limit the powers of a corporation, as shown in the following case.

Facts

International Paper Co. (defendant) was sued by the State of Oklahoma for statutory penalty due to unlawful acquisition of rural land in violation of the state constitution prohibiting a corporation from owning such land "except such as shall be necessary and proper for carrying on the business for which it was chartered." The company defended on the grounds that the rural land was for reforesting and that the crop of timber needed for its production would not develop for forty to seventy years.

Decision

Judgment for International Paper. "Necessary and proper" does not mean absolutely necessary. The requirement is satisfied if the conduct in question is proper and useful and conducive to the accomplishment of the corporation's objectives. Owning rural land for the purpose of reforesting was a reasonable step to assure a continuous supply of wood pulp needed in the paper production. The court concluded that the acquisition of timberland by the corporation was not within the prohibition of the Oklahoma constitution.

State ex rel. Reidy v. *International Paper Co.*, 342 P.2d 565 (Okl. 1959).

Because corporate enterprise now engages in most types of activities, the modern trend is to grant almost unlimited powers. In California, for example, purpose statements are specified by statute. The one most commonly used is, "The purpose of this corporation is to engage in any lawful act or activity for which a corporation may be organized under the General Corporation Law of California other than the banking business, the trust company business or the practice of a profession permitted to be incorporated by the California Corporations Code."

Express

Express powers can be found in the corporation statutes, which are usually quite explicit and lengthy, or in the articles of incorporation. Common express powers granted by statutes to a corporation are as follows:

1. To have a corporate name.
2. To have perpetual existence.

3. To have a common seal.
4. To purchase and hold land and personal property for authorized corporate purposes.
5. To make bylaws for the governing of the corporation.
6. To borrow money when necessary to carry out the corporate purpose.
7. To sell, convey, mortgage, pledge, or lease part or all of its property.
8. To make contracts and incur liabilities.
9. To conduct its business within or outside of the state of incorporation.
10. To acquire its own shares.
11. To declare and pay dividends.
12. To amend its articles of incorporation.
13. To effect a merger or consolidation.
14. To have and exercise all powers necessary or convenient to effect any or all of the purposes for which it was formed.
15. To cease its corporate activities and surrender its corporate franchise.

Implied

In addition to the express powers granted by the state, corporations, in the absence of limitation by statute or by the articles, have the implied powers to do all acts that may be necessary to enable them to exercise the express powers. To be implied, the act must tend directly and immediately to accomplish the purpose of the corporation's creation. Examples of implied powers of a corporation are the following:

1. To take and hold property.
2. To borrow money and issue notes, bonds, or other obligations.
3. To loan corporate funds.
4. To reacquire its own shares of stock.
5. To acquire and hold shares and other securities of other corporations.
6. To contribute to charity.

Implied powers are often made express by statute or by the articles of incorporation.

Ultra Vires

An *ultra vires* act is one that is beyond the scope of the powers of the corporation, e.g., a business corporation engaging in a charitable enterprise such as operating a church or school or a corporation in the grocery business lending money to produce a stage or screen theatrical production.

MBCA § 7 and many statutes abolish *ultra vires* as a defense. This is to say that neither the respective corporation nor the other contracting party can avoid liability in contract because of the fact that the subject matter is outside the scope of the corporate power.

In *Total Automation* v. *Illinois National Bank & Trust Co.* (40 Ill.App.3d 266, 351 N.E.2d 879 [1976]), the court ruled, in effect, that the beneficiary of corporate conduct cannot subsequently avoid his obligation by claiming

Ultra Vires
Behavior on the part of a corporation that is not authorized by its articles or bylaws.

that the corporation had no authority to enter into the transaction. The case involved a corporation that had a checking account in the Illinois National Bank. When the corporation owed the bank's travel department money, the bank exercised its right of offset by deducting the amount of the bill from the checking account. The corporation claimed that the bank had no right of offset, since it was *ultra vires* for a national bank to operate a travel department.

MBCA § 7 furthermore provides that such lack of corporate capacity or power may be asserted in an affirmative action

1. By a shareholder against the corporation to enjoin it from further *ultra vires* acts.
2. By the corporation or a shareholder acting on behalf of the corporation to sue corporate officers or directors who committed the *ultra vires* act to recover damages for the corporation.
3. By the state attorney general to enjoin further *ultra vires* acts or to dissolve the corporation.

But even the state is not always successful in forfeiting a corporate charter based on an *ultra vires* concept, as shown in the following case.

Facts
Philadelphia Electric Co. was incorporated "for the purpose of supplying heating, lighting, and power by electricity to the public." In addition to supplying electricity, the company also sold household electrical appliances. The attorney general brought a lawsuit to forfeit the corporate charter on the ground that Philadelphia Electric, by the sale of appliances, was acting beyond the scope of its charter.

Decision
Judgment for Philadelphia Electric. The fact that the corporation was authorized to supply electricity did not mean that it could do nothing more. On the contrary, it is reasonable for a company to enhance the sale of its products—in this case electricity—by expanding the demand—in this case by selling electrical appliances. In doing so, Philadelphia did not act beyond the scope of its corporate charter.

Commonwealth ex rel. Baldridge v. *Philadelphia Electric Co.,* 300 Pa. 577, 151 A. 344 (1930).

In those states that still recognize the *ultra vires* defense, the defense is generally limited to executory or wholly unperformed contracts. Contracts fully performed by one side will prevent the other side from raising the defense on the grounds that the party benefited is estopped to do so. Contracts fully performed by both sides are immune to the defense; neither the corporations nor the other side may raise and rely on the *ultra vires* defense in such cases.

Obviously, committing torts or crimes are always beyond the corporate scope of authority. Nonetheless, under the agency rule of *respondeat superior*—i.e., let the master answer—a corporation today is liable for its agents' torts and crimes perpetrated in the course of employment. It is well settled that a corporation can be criminally punished by a fine or dissolution of its entity.

Shareholders

A shareholder is one who derives certain rights arising out of the ownership of one or more shares of corporate stock. Voting shareholders have a primary interest in the management and earnings of the corporation. They elect and remove directors, vote on extraordinary corporate transactions, such as a merger or a sale of assets, and vote to amend the articles of incorporation. They are entitled to receive dividends, subject to such dividends' being declared by the board of directors. Nonvoting shareholders are also entitled to vote on extraordinary corporate transactions and to receive dividends when declared but may not elect or remove directors.

In the absence of statute, shareholders cannot act for the corporation either individually or collectively. The management of the corporation is vested in the board of directors, although the shareholders have the indirect managerial powers noted above.

Shareholders
The owners of a corporation; also called "stockholders."

Meetings

Shareholders must act at a regular or special meeting or their actions have no legal effect. In has been held, however, that where all of the shareholders act together on behalf of the corporation without a regular meeting or formal vote, the action is valid.

Place of Meeting The articles, bylaws, or directors may prescribe the place of meeting. Most states permit a shareholders' meeting to be held outside the state of incorporation, and this is the position of MBCA § 28. Shareholders who participate in a meeting improperly held as to place or time waive their right to object to it.

Time of Meeting Regular meetings must be held at the time prescribed in the statute, articles, or bylaws. Statutes normally do not require notice of regular meetings, although it is the usual practice to give notice to all shareholders.

Special Meetings Special meetings are usually called by the board of directors pursuant to the bylaws, articles, or statutes for a special purpose. Notice of the day, hour, and place of the meeting must be given to all shareholders. The notice must state the nature of the business to be transacted at the meeting, and no other business may be conducted unless all of the shareholders waive this limitation. Shareholders who participate in a special meeting improperly called waive their right to object.

Quorum A quorum is the minimum number of shareholders who must be present in a shareholders' meeting to validate the decisions made in that meeting. Articles, bylaws, or statutes may provide that to constitute a quorum, a specified number of shareholders (usually a simple majority) must attend.

Quorum Shareholders' Meeting
Minimum number of shareholders, usually a simple majority, who must be present to make decisions of a shareholders' meeting valid.

Voting Rights In the absence of restrictions, each person who is registered as a shareholder on the corporation books has the right to vote. The general rule is that each shareholder has the right to one vote for each share of stock. The common law rule that each shareholder had one vote, regardless of the number of shares held, has been changed by statute or court decision in practically all jurisdictions.

Generally, those shareholders of voting stock in whose names the stock appears on the books of the corporation are entitled to vote. The directors may fix a controlling date to determine such eligibility.

The most common types of voting rights are (1) straight, (2) cumulative, and (3) class.

Straight voting means that each share has one vote for each business matter, including one vote for each director to be elected. Straight voting is the common method of voting on corporation business, except where cumulative voting is used in the election of directors.

Cumulative voting, which is required in some states, is a system of voting that applies only to the election of the board of directors. Each share has as many votes as there are vacancies to be filled, and the votes can be distributed among the candidates in any way the shareholder wishes, i.e., the shareholder can cumulate votes. For example, if ten directors are to be elected, a shareholder who owns one share has ten votes and may give all ten votes to one candidate or five votes to each of two candidates, etc. The purpose of cumulative voting is to permit minority shareholders to combine and secure some representation on the board of directors. The candidates for the positions to be filled are all elected at the same time. Cumulative voting is also permitted in the removal of directors.

Class or series voting is where there are two or more classes or series of stock outstanding and where each class or series of stock votes as a separate unit for one or more purposes, e.g., a classified board of directors with one class of stock voting for its class of directors and a board with another class of stock voting for its class of directors.

Proxy Voting   A proxy is an authority to vote stock. In the absence of an express requirement, a person does not have to be a shareholder to act as a proxy. The person acting as proxy to vote the stock is an agent for voting purposes. Most states permit voting by proxy but require that the proxy be in writing and signed by the shareholder. In the absence of an express requirement, no particular formality is required. Management normally asks shareholders before an election to allow management to vote on their behalf by proxy.

Voting Agreements   In most states, an agreement among shareholders to vote in a certain manner so as to concentrate their voting strength for the purpose of controlling the management is valid unless there is fraud or other illegal object. In most states, such agreements are valid even though they bind the directors in the exercise of their discretion, so long as they do not substantially limit the discretion of the directors.

Voting Trusts   A voting trust exists when, pursuant to an agreement, some or all of the shareholders transfer their shares to a voting trustee or trustees to hold and vote for them until the purpose of the trust is fulfilled or for a specified period. It is a device to concentrate shareholder control in one or more persons for the purpose of controlling management. Voting trusts are

---

Straight Voting
One share one vote for each business matter.

Cumulative Voting
Gives each share as many votes as there are vacancies at the board of directors.

Class Voting
Where there are different classes of stock, each class votes as a separate unit.

Proxy
Authorization or a person authorized to act for another person.

Voting Agreement
Agreement to vote in a certain way.

Voting Trust
Holds shares of a group of shareholders to accumulate voting power.

valid in most states, many of which have enacted statutes that provide for the procedures in setting up the trust, powers and duties of trustees, and the trust's duration. In California, an irrevocable voting trust can last up to twenty-one years.

Like the class or series voting, voting trusts are often used to enhance and perpetuate the position of the present corporate management by permitting management to act as a voting trustee for holders of a large number of shares. An investor, especially of over-the-counter stocks, should be aware of whether the shares purchased still carry voting rights. Such rights could have been relinquished in a voting trust, in which event, a so-called "voting trust certificate" instead of a regular stock certificate will be issued.

Election and Removal of Directors

At the annual or regular shareholder meeting, shareholders participate in the management of the corporation by electing the directors. In the absence of statute or bylaws to the contrary, shareholders elect directors to fill vacant and newly created directorates.

Shareholders have the power to remove a director for cause. A director can be removed without cause only if such right was reserved at the time the director was elected. The following case is an illustration.

Facts

A shareholder and member of the board of directors of the Willoughby Walk Cooperative Corporation sought to set aside the election of directors held six months previously. The petitioners here claimed that one newly elected director was not a member of the cooperative and was therefore not eligible to be on the board.

Decision

The court denied the petition. First, the court held that the petitioners, by participating at numerous subsequent meetings, effectively acknowledged the director's membership on the board and waived their rights to contest the election. The petitioners should have voiced their disapproval at an earlier time. Second, if the court were to have overturned the election, it would nullify six months of board work. Such a result would have been highly prejudicial to the members of the cooperative. Finally, the question of the director's eligibility was not a clear one, and there was no indication of bad faith.

Petition of Directors of Willoughby Walk Cooperative Apartments, Inc., 104 Misc.2d 477, 428 N.Y.S.2d 574 (1980).

Bylaws and Resolutions

Shareholders participate in management in some states by the power to adopt the initial bylaws and in most states by the inherent power to amend or repeal the bylaws.

Shareholders may pass resolutions that will affect the management of the corporations, e.g., endorsing the administration of a former president and demanding reinstatement. Shareholder resolutions can cover a wide variety of subject matters.

Shareholders' resolutions, unless approved by management, are seldom successful.

Unusual Matters

Shareholders exercise managerial powers in various unusual corporate business matters—e.g., approval of shareholders required for amendment of articles of incorporation, sale or lease of assets outside the regular course of corporation business, merger, consolidation, or dissolution—where such action is required by the articles, bylaws, or statute.

Inspection of Books

A shareholder personally or through an attorney or accountant has the right to inspect the books of the corporation at reasonable times for any legitimate purposes, e.g., to ascertain the financial condition of the corporation, to compile a list of shareholders to contact for the purchase of their stock so as to increase ownership and voting power, to obtain information in aid of bona fide litigation with the corporation. Improper or hostile purposes will justify a denial of inspection, e.g., to seek information to aid a competitor in business to secure advertising lists, to secure a list of shareholders to use for contacting business prospects.

In *Goldman* v. *Trans-United Industries, Inc.* (404 Pa. 288, 171 A.2d 788 [1961]), the court agreed that a relief to inspect corporate books for improper or unreasonable purposes will not be granted, but the burden of so proving is on the corporation. In this particular case, a shareholder's attempt to acquire the list of shareholders from the corporation was considered harmless.

May a corporation utilize the self-incrimination provision of the Fifth Amendment of the U.S. Constitution to deny a shareholder's right to inspect corporate books? The answer to this question is found in the following case.

Stone v. Martin
56 N.C.App. 473, 289 S.E.2d 898 (1982).

Whichard, Judge Plaintiffs, shareholders in defendant corporation, filed a complaint against the corporation and the individual defendants, who were officers, directors, and shareholders thereof, alleging numerous improper and unlawful acts and omissions in the operation of the corporation. They sought compensatory damages, punitive damages, and, as to the individual defendants, arrest and bail and execution against the person.

Plaintiffs served on defendant fifty-eight interrogatories and fifteen requests for admission. Defendant claimed with respect to each that because the complaint sought punitive damages, which are in the nature of a penalty, to answer would violate his privilege against compulsory self-incrimination under United States Constitution amendments V and XIV and North Carolina Constitution article 1, section 23. Plaintiffs moved under G.S. 1A–1, Rule 37(a), to compel defendant to comply with discovery. Judge Preston found that three of the interrogatories and three of the requests for admission called for potentially incriminatory answers and denied plaintiffs' motion with respect thereto. He ordered defendant to answer the remaining interrogatories and requests within thirty days.

Upon dependant's failure to comply, plaintiffs moved for imposition of Rule 37(b) sanctions. Judge Lee struck defendant's answer and ordered that he not oppose any claim or allegation set forth in plaintiffs' complaint. He further ordered judgment by default against defendant, the issue of damages being for jury determination.

Defendant contends the orders compelling him to respond, and imposing sanctions for his failure to do so, infringe upon his constitutional privilege against compulsory self-incrimination. He does not contend that answering may subject him to criminal punishment; rather, he contends that because plaintiffs seek punitive damages and body execution, he cannot be compelled to submit to discovery. On this record we find no infringement of defendant's constitutional privilege.

. . . Further, the requested discovery related almost entirely to the operation of defendant corporation, of which plaintiffs had been shareholders for more than six months preceding filing of their complaint. Plaintiffs thus had a statutory right, enforceable by an action in the nature of mandamus, to inspect the records of the corporation. They had the further right, similarly enforceable, to inspect the annual financial statement of the corporation and the record of shareholders. Plaintiffs alleged that defendants had denied their oral and written demands for opportunity to inspect the corporate records. The requested discovery to which the court ordered response sought information which the corporate records should have contained and which plaintiffs thus would have received had defendants complied with the statutory requirements for maintenance of corporate records and observed plaintiffs' right to inspect. "[T]he privilege against self-incrimination is a purely personal one," and "the official records and documents of [a corporation] that are held by [an individual] in a representative rather than in a personal capacity cannot be the subject of the personal privilege against self-incrimination, even though production of the papers might tend to incriminate [the individual] personally." It is thus evident that Judge Preston's order simply granted through discovery procedure access to information which plaintiffs could obtain in any event by mandamus.

It should be evident that tensions adhere within the law applicable to the area in which the problem presented falls, and that the standards prescribed for resolving those tensions are not necessarily easily applied in individual cases. We remain persuaded, however, from a careful examination of the standards and of the record in this case, that the standards were properly applied here.

For the foregoing reasons we affirm the order requiring defendant to comply with discovery. Because defendant failed to comply with that order, we find no abuse of discretion in the order imposing sanctions and judgment by default. . . .

Shareholders' Actions

A shareholder can sue the corporation in a direct action to enforce his shareholder's contract. A shareholder can also sue in a derivative action on behalf of the corporation against persons who have damaged the corporation when the corporation refuses to bring an action, e.g., suit against third persons for breach of contract with corporation. Shareholders may also join in an action on behalf of the corporation when the corporation refuses to defend itself. The case of *Saigh ex rel. Anheuser-Busch, Inc.* v. *Busch* (396 S.W.2d 9 [Mo., 1965], certiorari denied 384 U.S. 942, 86 S.Ct. 1465, 16 L.Ed.2d 541), cited in the next chapter, is an example of a share-

Derivative Action
Action taken on behalf of the corporation.

holders' derivative action involving some shareholders' objection to the allegedly excessive salary of the corporate president.

Other Rights

Other rights include the rights to have the shares recorded in the stock book of the corporation; to have issued to the shareholder a properly executed certificate as evidence of ownership of shares; to transfer shares as the shareholder chooses, subject to any valid restrictions; to receive a proportion of dividends as they are declared, subject to various preferences; and to receive any balance of the net corporate assets upon dissolution.

Shareholder Liability

Ordinarily, shareholders are limitedly and not personally liable for the debts of the corporation. The risk of the shareholder is limited to his capital investment. In some cases, the shareholder may have unlimited or further liability, e.g., when the corporate entity is broken, when a statute provides that a shareholder is liable for wages of corporation employees, or when a shareholder has not fully paid his stock subscription. When dividends are improperly paid out of capital, the shareholders are generally liable to creditors to the extent of the depletion of the capital.

QUESTIONS

1. Discuss the powers of a corporation. What are the sources of those powers?
2. Discuss the use of the *ultra vires* concept as a defense and in an affirmative action.
3. What are straight, cumulative, and class voting?
4. What are proxy voting, voting agreements, and voting trusts?
5. Discuss the shareholders' right to inspect corporate books.

PROBLEMS

1. A, B, and C decide to organize a corporation for the purpose of conducting a television repair service. The articles of incorporation are prepared and signed by A and B and acknowledged by a notary public. The articles are then given to C who signs them but forgets to have his signature acknowledged by a notary as required by statute. C files the articles and the required fee with the secretary of state. Thereafter, A, B, and C meet as the first directors of the ABC Corporation, elect officers, adopt bylaws, purchase a truck to be used in the business, employ D to drive the truck, and conduct other necessary corporate business. While D is driving the truck during the course of his employment, he negligently runs over a pedestrian. The pedestrian brings action against A, B, C, and D individually. A, B, and C defend on the ground that the corporate liability of the ABC Corporation does not extend to them individually. Decision?

2. A formed a corporation for the purpose of conducting a newspaper business so that he could publish untrue stories about B, a liberal politician who held a high office. A obtained a stock permit that gave the corporation permission to issue 100 shares of stock at $5 a share. The corporation issued 90 shares to A, 5 shares to A's wife, and 5 shares to A's son. Thereafter, A printed a libelous story about B, claiming that B was a communist sympathizer, which A knew was untrue. B brings action against A individually. A defends on the ground that only the corporation is liable. Decision?

3. The State of Oregon indicted the Pacific Powder Company, a corporation, for manslaughter when a

truckload of explosives belonging to the company was negligently parked and blew up during a fire, causing the death of a bystander. Oregon Criminal Statutes say: "'Person' includes corporations as well as natural persons." The statute on manslaughter states, "Every person convicted of manslaughter shall be punished by imprisonment in the penitentiary for not more than 15 years and by a fine not exceeding $5,000." Can the Pacific Powder Company be convicted of manslaughter?

4. A and two other persons were promoters for a new corporation: AT company. A retained K to perform legal services in connection with the incorporation of the new business and promised to pay K $1,500. K incorporated AT, and A and the other two promotors became AT's only directors. K was told at a director's board meeting that he should obtain a permit for AT to sell stock, because the directors wished to pay him for his prior professional services. When A and the other two failed to pay K, K sued AT. AT defended on the ground that it never obligated itself to pay K, either before or after incorporation. Decision?

5. L, acting as a promoter, made a preincorporation employment contract with M whereby M was hired as corporate comptroller for a one-year term. The corporation, T Company, was thereafter duly incorporated. M began his duties at that time. No formal action verifying M's contract was made by the board of directors, but all directors, officers, and shareholders had knowledge of M's contract. Two months later, M was terminated without cause. M sued T Company to recover for breach of contract. Decision?

6. R sought legal advice from MHV, a professional association duly incorporated under the laws of Maryland. R was a resident of Pennsylvania, and the legal advice was actually rendered in that state. The matter concerned the compromise of a medical disciplinary proceeding instituted against R by R's hospital. R ordered MHV to abandon the representation and then refused to pay a final bill rendered. When MHV sued to recover for its services, R defended on the ground that MHV's failure to register as a foreign corporation prevented MVR from suing R in Pennsylvania. Decision?

7. D Corporation and E Corporation duly consolidated to form DE Enterprises, Inc. Unpaid creditors of both D and E sued to recover payment against DE Enterprises. DE defended on the ground that the consolidation terminated any liability of D and E to creditors, absent express contractual assumption of such obligations by DE Inc. as part of the plan of consolidation. No such contractual assumption of preexisting obligations had been made. Decision?

8. A, B, and C, each own ten shares of stock in the X Corporation.

(a) A demands an inspection of the corporate books so that he can compile a list of shareholders for the purpose of contacting them to sell them some speculative oil stock. Does he have the right?

(b) B demands to see the corporate books so that he can obtain information to help his brother, a competitor of the X Corporation. Does he have the right?

(c) C demands to see the corporate books so that he can compile a list of shareholders for the purpose of trying to buy shares of stock from them. Does he have the right?

9. Plaintiff, a shareholder in defendant corporation, brings a shareholder derivative action against the directors of his corporation for losses alleged to be caused by mismanagement. The directors had formulated an anti-labor policy that resulted in the closing, dismantling, and removal of plants and equipment of the corporation, curtailing production. This was done not for any legitimate business purpose but only to punish and intimidate employees. The acts were illegal and intended to evade the obligations of the directors under the National Labor Relations Act; the acts constituted unfair labor practices and caused corporate losses of more than one million dollars. The corporation resists the action. Decision?

10. Smith was treasurer of Dram Inc. Smith wanted to buy an expensive automobile for his own use and tendered Jones, the automobile dealer, a corporate check in payment when the car was delivered. Jones asked Smith if he had corporate authority to pay by corporate check. Smith assured him that he controlled Dram's purse strings and could therefore spend Dram's corporate funds as he saw fit. Later Dram Inc. sued Jones to recover the price of Smith's car, claiming no express or implied authority was granted Smith to use a corporate check in payment of personal obligations. Decision?

CHAPTER TWENTY-FOUR

Corporation (II)

24.1 Corporate Management
Directors
    Qualifications
    Term and Removal
    Compensation
    Functions and Powers
    Meetings
    Fiduciary Duty
    Liability
Officers
    Qualifications
    Term and Removal
    Compensation
    Functions and Powers
    Fiduciary Duty
    Liability

24.2 Corporate Finance
Stock
    Par and No Par Value
    Shareholders' Equity
    Kinds of Stock
    Market Value
    Book Value
    Liability for Shares
Bonds
Retained Earnings
Dividends
    Sources
    Declaration by Board
    Persons Entitled to Dividend
    Stock Dividend
    Stock Split

24.3 Stock Acquisition and Securities Regulation
Subscription and Transfer
    Negotiability
    Restrictions
Government Regulatory Policies
    Securities Defined
    Securities and Exchange Commission
The Securities Act of 1933
    Registration Statement
    Liabilities and Defenses
    Exemptions
The Securities Exchange Act of 1934
    Registration and Periodic Reporting
    Antifraud Provisions
    Proxy Restrictions
    Insider Information and Short-Swing Profit
    Criminal Penalties
Other Enactments
    Public Utility Holding Company Act of 1935
    Trust Indenture Act of 1939
    Investment Company Act of 1940
    Investment Advisers Act of 1940
    Securities Investor Protection Act of 1970
    Insider Trading Sanctions Act of 1984
State Legislation
    Blue Sky Laws
    Uniform Securities Act
Industry Regulation

24.1 Corporate Management

Although shareholders are technically the owners of a corporation, they basically do not possess corporate managerial powers. They elect members of the board of directors, who manage the company on their behalf. The board of directors prescribes the corporation's objectives and policies, exercises the overall supervisory control, and approves or disapproves the company's operational conduct. The actual day-to-day business is conducted by officers, i.e., the president, secretary, treasurer, and other executives, who are appointed by the board of directors.

Often, a member of the board is at the same time an officer of the company. It is not unusual for the chairman of the board to be the president of the company. In so being, such a person's involvement and familiarity with the company's everyday affairs are expected to facilitate the flow of corporate information to the other directors as well as expedite the execution of board decisions.

Once the shareholders in the corporate structure elect the board of directors as their representatives, they have virtually little to say about the corporate business, as illustrated in the following case.

Directors
Persons elected by the owners (shareholders) of a corporation to manage the corporation on behalf of the shareholders.

Officers
Persons appointed by the directors to conduct the actual day to day business of the corporation.

Saigh ex rel. Anheuser-Busch, Inc. v. Busch
396 S.W.2d 9 (Mo.App. 1965), certiorari denied 384 U.S. 942, 86 S.Ct. 1465, 16 L.Ed.2d 541 (1966).

Ruddy, Judge This is a stockholders' derivative action.

The instant appeal before us is by plaintiffs from a judgment . . . wherein the trial court sustained the motion of a defendant August A. Busch, Jr., to dismiss . . . "with prejudice."

This suit was instituted by Fred Saigh and Elizabeth Saigh as stockholders of Anheuser-Busch, Inc., as a class action against August A. Busch, Jr., an individual defendant, and Anheuser-Busch, Inc. . . .

The general nature of the allegations . . . is that August A. Busch, Jr., as president of the nominal defendant is receiving salary and perquisites which are excessive and not based on the reasonable value of his services as president of the corporation. . . .

We now review what we consider to be the fundamental principles of law involved. The management and control of the property and business of a corporation is vested . . . in the Board of Directors, and this has been a fundamental principle of our statutory corporate law for many years. . . . Essentially, a corporation should be run for the benefit of its stockholders and not for that of its directors and officers, but no individual stockholder has the authority to take over the duties of corporate management. The management and control of the corporation being vested by statute in the board of directors . . . and the stockholders cannot control the directors in the exercise of the judgment vested in them by the statute. . . . If any or all of the directors perform improperly, the corporation itself is the proper party plaintiff to bring an action to recover any losses occasioned by the wrong. . . . In the event of the failure or refusal of the directors to litigate, then the stockholders may sue, however, it must be in right of the corporation, in which their petition and proof must make a case of wrongful refusal on the part of the directors to sue. . . .

If it is necessary for a stockholder to bring a derivative action because the corporate management wrongfully refuses to do so, it is conducted by the stockholder as the representative of the corporation and in such action the corporation is the real party in interest and it is brought for the benefit of the corporation. . . .

The management of a corporation is in the directors and the establishment and fixing of remuneration and perquisites for officers and managerial duties normally and initially are in the board of directors and, as we have pointed out in this regard, such duties being in the business and management area, any decision by the board of directors in connection therewith is usually controlling and exclusive and the shareholders cannot control the exercise of the judgment vested in them, unless this judgment is exercised in an arbitrary and capricious manner or contrary to by-laws or majority stockholders' action. . . .

The authorities . . . give support to our position that where the directors are charged to be under the influence of defendant Busch, the stockholders have the right to consider the matter and ratify, if they wish, any act of the directors, provided the act is not ultra vires, illegal or fraudulent. We rule that plaintiffs were under a duty to submit their grievance to the body of stockholders before bringing this action. . . .

The judgment of the trial court should be affirmed. It is so ordered.

Derivative Action
Action taken on behalf of the corporation.

Although officers' salaries are normally determined by the board of directors, in a situation where honesty and integrity of the directors themselves are challenged, courts may allow shareholders to intervene directly in corporate compensatory matters. This is demonstrated in the following case.

Facts

Harry Smith was a minority shareholder in Alabama Dry Docks and Shipbuilding Company, Inc. He brought a shareholder's derivative action to recover for the corporation's alleged excessive salaries and bonuses paid to four of the directors who acted at the same time as officers. As Smith was refused support by the other directors and shareholders for taking that action, he brought this derivative suit on behalf of the corporation. The trial court dismissed the suit on demurrer. Smith appealed.

Decision

Judgment for plaintiff Smith. "(W)here the amount of a bonus payment to officers of a corporation has no reasonable relation to the value of service for which it is given, it is in reality a gift and the majority stockholders have no power to give away corporate property against the protest of a minority stockholder. . . .

"The amount of compensation to be paid to an officer of a corporation is, in the first instance, within the business discretion of the corporation's board of directors, and with this discretion the courts are loath to interfere; generally the decision of the directors as to the amount of such compensation is final; where it appears, however, that the directors have not acted in good faith or that the compensation fixed by them is so excessive that it bears no reasonable relation to the services for which it is given, courts of equity have the power to inquire whether and to what extent payment to the officers constitutes misuse and waste of corporate assets. . . ."

Smith v. *Dunlap*, 269 Ala. 97, 111 So.2d 1 (Alabama, 1959).

Directors

Qualifications

Most statutes today make no requirement regarding qualifications. Some statutes require that the directors be of legal age to contract, be citizens of the United States, be residents of the state of incorporation, or be shareholders. Qualifications may be prescribed in the articles of incorporation or the bylaws.

Term and Removal

The first directors are usually named in the articles of incorporation or are elected by the incorporators. The term of office is usually until the next annual meeting and until the successor is elected. In larger companies, the tenures of the directors may be staggered to maintain the board's continuity. For instance, for a board with nine members, three positions are successively vacated and filled by shareholders' election each year.

Directors may be removed by the shareholders with cause, such as insanity, conviction of a felony, fraud, or gross abuse of authority. Many states have enacted statutes that spell out the removal of directors as well as cumulative and class voting rights for the shareholders.

Compensation

As representatives for the shareholders, directors are basically not entitled to compensation for ordinary representative services. Only if extraordinary services are performed as an officer or agent of the corporation, quasi-contractual recovery may be had. Directors have no inherent authority to vote a salary to any director, although it is becoming more common for a director's compensation to be provided for by statutes, articles of incorporation, bylaws, or shareholder resolutions. Directors are usually entitled to reimbursement of expenses incurred in furtherance of corporate business. In actual practice, board directors commonly receive an allowance for attending each board meeting.

Functions and Powers

The function of the board of directors is to set major policies and to direct the business of the corporation. The details of the operating management are usually left in varying degrees to the officers. Some of the usual functions and powers of the board of directors are as follows:

1. To select, supervise, remove, and fix the compensation, including retirement plans, for officers.
2. To determine dividend payments, financing, and capital changes.
3. To make policy decisions regarding products, prices, services, wages, and labor relations.

CORPORATION (II)

The following actions by the board of directors generally require a two-thirds approval of the shareholders.

1. Amendment of the articles of incorporation.
2. Increase or decrease of stock.
3. Consolidation, merger, sale of entire assets, or dissolution.

A director has an absolute right to inspect the corporation books, and his right cannot be denied even though his motive is ulterior and his purpose is improper.

Meetings

Notice Notice of a directors meeting is usually necessary, although it may be waived if a quorum is present and if each of the directors present signs a written approval of the meeting. It may also be waived by a director who is not notified of a special meeting but nevertheless attends without complaint as to the illegality of the meeting. A resolution passed at an improperly called board of directors meeting can be enforced by a third party who was unaware that the meeting was improperly called as the corporation is estopped from setting up such a defense. Innocent third persons have the right to assume that the meeting was duly held. Bylaws may dispense with notice of regular meetings but not of special meetings.

Place Regular meetings must be held at the place designated in the bylaws except when changed by approval of all the members of the board or by board resolution. Special meetings may be held at a place designated or at the principal office of the corporation. Meetings usually may be held within or without the state of incorporation unless restricted by statute, the articles, or bylaws.

Quorum Unless otherwise stated by statute, the articles, or bylaws, a quorum is a majority of the whole number of directors. An action of the board of directors usually requires a majority vote of the directors present at a meeting at which a quorum of the directors is present.

In a situation where a director is involved in a conflict of interest with regard to a decision to be made by the board, such a director may not be considered part of the quorum. In *Davis v. Heath Development Company* (558 P.2d 594 [Utah, 1976]), the board of directors consisted of five members. A board meeting attended by four directors approved a motion to sell all the corporate assets. However, two of the attending directors were the buyers in that sale. The court ruled that the corporation was not bound on the sales contract. "(A)ny director who has an interest in a proposed transaction with the corporation cannot participate in such business to bind the corporation, either to make up the quorum, or to vote on the proposal."

Quorum Directors' Meeting
The majority of the number of directors.

Proxy Directors vote personally as individuals and are not allowed to vote by proxy except where permitted by statute in a few states. This is because directors must attend personally to the business of the corporation and because of the value of their consultation and collective judgment.

Proxy Directors' Meeting
Is usually not allowed.

Fiduciary Duty

Directors are fiduciaries and must exercise their powers in good faith and in the interest of the corporation. A director cannot enter into any competing business with the corporation, take advantage of a business opportunity that could have been utilized by the corporation, have an interest that conflicts with the interest of the corporation, make secret profits, oppress minority shareholders, and, in a growing minority of states, sell stock to shareholders without revealing important inside information that he may have as to the value of the stock or as to the business of the corporation.

In the following case, the Arkansas Supreme Court ruled on the fiduciary duty of a corporate director.

Facts

Smith was a director and officer of Citation, an industrial cleaning equipment manufacturer. At the same time, Smith owned a company that distributed equipment. Citation made a series of sales to Smith's firm. Smith's company went bankrupt, and Citation could not collect on all its sales. Citation argued that Smith breached his fiduciary duty as director and officer by not disclosing his company's financial troubles and by accepting deliveries he was unable to pay for. Smith defended that Citation knew or should have known of his financial difficulties.

Decision

Citation knew of some of Smith's problems, but Smith did not disclose a great deal of information. Smith knew his company was unable to pay for certain shipments. Furthermore, Smith withdrew funds and equipment from his company to meet his personal debts. Citation knew of none of this. The court concluded that Smith had breached his fiduciary duty and was liable for Citation's losses incurred on these sales.

Smith v. Citation Manufacturing Co., Inc., 266 Ark. 591, 587 S.W.2d 39 (1979).

Liability

Directors owe a duty of ordinary and reasonable care to the corporation. When the required duty of care is violated, the directors are liable to the corporation for such corporate damage as was caused by their negligence. Directors are liable for losses caused by their bad faith, willfull and intentional departures from their duty, and fraudulent breaches of trust. Directors are also under a duty to act within their authority and are liable for any loss to the corporation from engaging in activities that are *ultra vires*. Examples of actions that have caused directors to be jointly and severally liable to the corporation are as follows:

1. Negligence in selecting or supervising an officer, agent, or employee.
2. Participation in the wrongful act of another director or officer.
3. Making false reports or entries in the corporate books.
4. Improperly expending corporate funds for management compensation.
5. Wrongful distribution of corporate assets among themselves or the shareholders.
6. Making unauthorized loans to directors, officers, or shareholders of corporate funds or other property.

7. Unauthorized purchase of corporation's own stock.
8. Unauthorized issuance of a dividend.
9. Closing down factory with loss of over one million dollars in furtherance of anti-labor policy.

Officers

Statutes usually provide that a corporation must have specified officers. Typical are the requirement of a president, vice president, secretary, and treasurer.

Qualifications

Some statutes provide that officers must have certain qualifications. In the absence of statute, there are no particular qualifications, except that an officer should have legal capacity, since he is an agent of the corporation.

Term and Removal

The officers are usually appointed by the directors. In many states, however, by statute, officers are elected by the shareholders. Officers usually serve at the pleasure of the board of directors. In most states, officers are removable with or without cause by the board of directors. When an officer has a valid contract of employment with the corporation, the board of directors has the power to remove the officer without cause but must pay damages for breach of contract.

Compensation

Officers who are not directors have the right to reasonable compensation for their services. Their compensation is normally fixed prior to the rendering of services.

Officers who are also directors are presumed to serve without compensation on usual board matters but are entitled to reasonable compensation for unusual services. It is becoming common for a director-officer to receive a fixed compensation on a prearranged basis. Sometimes the compensation is ratified by the shareholders.

In addition to fixed salaries and liberal expense accounts, there are other forms of compensation, e.g., profit sharing plans, stock bonuses, stock purchase plans, pensions, annuities, tax reimbursement plans, and deferred compensation plans.

Functions and Powers

Officers have such management functions and powers as are given them by the board of directors. The board is limited in such delegation by statutes, articles of incorporation, and bylaws.

President The corporate president is often considered second in command to the chairman of the board. As mentioned earlier, the chairman of the board of directors may simultaneously be the president of the corporation. The title of "chief executive officer" (CEO) may refer to a corporate president who is the board chairman at the same time. The president's real power depends on the internal structure of the corporation; the president may be only a figurehead or may be the controlling power.

Within the scope of his authority, the president may act as an agent on behalf of the corporation. He also has the implied power to do such acts as are necessary to carry out the business of the corporation.

Vice President A vice president assists the president and acts as his substitute when the president is unable to act. In large corporations, there are usually several vice presidents whose functions are to act as department heads. Their authority to act is derived from the executive powers of the president.

Secretary The secretary usually attends meetings of the corporation and keeps minutes and records of corporate transactions. The secretary also gives notices, certifies corporate records, and keeps the corporate seal.

Treasurer The treasurer takes charge of the financial records and disbursement of corporate funds. In most states, he may not bind the corporation. In large corporations, there is usually a controller in addition to the treasurer. In such a case, the controller keeps the records while the treasurer handles the money.

Fiduciary Duty

Officers, like directors, have a fiduciary relationship with the corporation. The law on the fiduciary relationship between the directors and the corporation is applicable here, i.e., cannot make secret profits, etc.

Liability

Officers owe a duty of ordinary and reasonable care to the corporation and are liable for willful or negligent acts that result in corporate loss.

An officer may incur personal liability when contracting on behalf of the corporation without authority. Even when an officer has authority, he can be liable on a contract if he does not indicate that he is contracting as an agent for the corporation. Otherwise, the corporation alone is liable on a contract entered into by its officers within their express, implied, or apparent authority when the corporation as a principal is disclosed to the other contracting party.

Joyner v. Alban Group, Inc.
541 S.W.2d 292 (Tex.Civ.App. 1976).

Evans, Justice Alban Group, Inc. brought this action on sworn account against Dean Joyner and Haversack Wine Company for certain design and art work

> performed on behalf of Haversack Wine Company. After a non-jury trial, the trial court rendered judgment against both defendants for the amount of the account in the sum of $12,720.37 plus interest, attorney's fees and costs. Both defendants have appealed.
>
> The question then is whether the evidence supports the trial court's judgment against Joyner. This court holds that it does not.
>
> Haversack Wine Company was incorporated in Texas on February 19, 1974. The plaintiff's president, Mr. Johnny Alban, testified that he was first contacted by Mr. Joyner in March or April 1974 to design the label or "corporate image" for Haversack Wine Company. Alban testified that when he first started doing the work he assumed he was dealing only with Joyner, but that he never made any inquiry to determine whether or not the Haversack Wine Company was incorporated.
>
> The use of the word "company" in a business name is sufficient to charge a person dealing with the business with notice that it may be incorporated. There is no question that Alban knew he was performing the work for Haversack Wine Company and he thus was placed upon inquiry of its corporate status. This court finds no evidence to support the trial court's finding that Joyner held himself out to Alban as doing business as a proprietorship.
>
> The judgment against Haversack Wine Company is affirmed. The judgment against Dean Joyner is reversed and rendered. . . .

An officer who commits a tort is personally liable to the victim of the tort; and if the tort is committed within his scope of employment, the corporation will also be liable under the doctrine of *respondeat superior*. However, unlike the innocent general partner in a partnership who is personally and unlimitedly liable for his fellow partner's wrongdoing, corporate shareholders do not have such personal and unlimited liability for a tort committed by an officer in the course of corporate business.

Respondeat Superior
Let the master answer; makes the corporation liable for tort committed by an officer within the scope of employment.

Facts

Plaintiff Birt claimed that his doctor was guilty of malpractice. The doctor was a shareholder of a professional corporation. Plaintiff also sued the corporation and all the officers, directors, and shareholders, who defended on the ground that they were protected by the corporate shield. Plaintiff claimed that relative to rendering medical services, they all should be held liable as partners in a partnership.

Decision

Judgment against the plaintiff as to the other defendants. The fact that the defendants were part of a corporation did not impose vicarious liability upon them for the conduct of anyone else. Since the legislature expressly authorized the formation of the professional corporation, there could not be partnership liability imposed upon the other defendants. The corporate entity therefore protected all persons connected with the corporation from malpractice liability rendered by an employee of the corporation.

Birt v. St. Mary Mercy Hospital, 175 Ind.App. 32, 370 N.E.2d 379 (1977).

Statutes in many states provide that officers are liable for corporate taxes, debts, wages, and crimes under specific circumstances, e.g., for failure to withhold taxes, for debts contracted before filing of certificate of paid-in capital, for antitrust violation. The corporate officer who commits a crime in the course of business cannot hide behind the corporate entity. In *Landex, Inc.* v. *State ex rel. List* (94 Nev. 469, 582 P.2d 786 [1978]), the court held that a president of a corporation could be criminally prosecuted for fraudulent land sales conducted by his salespeople.

Questions

1. How is a corporation managed?
2. What can shareholders do in the event that the directors breach their fiduciary duty, thereby endangering the corporation's well-being?
3. May directors be removed from office?
4. Can directors be held personally liable for corporate matters?
5. Discuss the officers' liability in contract and in tort.

24.2 Corporate Finance

The initial operating capital of a corporation is obtained through investments by investors. These investors in return receive shares of stock, also known as *equity securities,* which are reflected as shareholders' equity in the lower right-hand side of the balance sheet. When the corporation is operational and proves to be viable and creditworthy, further funding may be attained through direct borrowing or the issuance of corporate bonds, also called *debt securities.* Unlike stock, bonds are essentially corporate debts to outsiders and are reflected as liabilities in the corporate bookkeeping. Meanwhile, excess corporate profits that are not distributed as dividends to shareholders are accumulated and become retained earnings, also a part of shareholders' equity and a source of additional funding.

Stock

Stock
The shares of ownership of a corporation.

The ownership of a corporation is sold to the shareholders through issuance of shares of stock. Stock evidences a shareholder's proportionate ownership in the corporation. Proceeds received from the sale of stock are used to purchase corporate assets needed for the business to function. These assets are owned by the corporation, not by the shareholders who own the corporate stock. Yet, by owning stock, shareholders have an interest in the corporation in that they have a right to receive dividends, a right to participate in the distribution of capital upon dissolution, and a right to indirectly control corporate management through the elected directors of the board.

Authorized Stock
Number of shares that the corporation is authorized to issue.

Authorized shares of stock are the number of shares that the state of incorporation and the articles of incorporation approved and authorized the corporation to issue. Usually, the corporation does not issue those shares all at once, since only a portion of authorized capital is normally needed for the corporation to embark. *Issued shares* of stock are a part of authorized shares that have actually been issued to the shareholders. The more shares of stock that are issued, the more dividends the corporation usually has to

Issued Stock
Number of shares that the corporation actually has issued.

pay out. Therefore, it is advisable for a corporation not to issue more stock than needed. There may even be a situation in which the corporation needs to reduce its activities, such as during a depression or a recession, in which event, the corporation may wish to purchase back part of the issued stock. When this occurs, the stock that is still in the hands of shareholders is called *outstanding* shares of stock, whereas the portion repurchased by the corporation is called *treasury* stock. Treasury shares cannot be voted upon, and they do not participate in dividends or distribution of net assets on dissolution of the corporation.

Treasury Stock
Shares repurchased by the corporation.

Par and No Par Value

Par value is, in many states, the minimum price at which a share of stock is supposedly sold by the corporation. It is the price of one share that the board of directors deems proper and adequate. It can be any amount, but the higher the par value, the fewer the shareholders that are expected to purchase the stock, which may be the basic policy of a closely held corporation. Most states permit shares of stock with or without par value. The par value or no par value is printed on the face of the stock certificate.

Par Value
The minimum price at which a share of stock is supposedly sold by the corporation.

No-par Stock
Stock without a designated par value.

No par value issues are often favored on such grounds as

1. The stock could be sold at any time as "fully paid" without contingent liability of the subscriber to creditors. In the case of a par stock sold at a discount, the subscriber may still be liable to creditors for the unpaid portion of the so-called "watered stock."
2. Investors may be misled by the par value printed on the stock certificate, which in effect has nothing to do with the actual value of the stock at the market place.

On the other hand, some states collect capital tax on authorized shares, issued shares, and stock transfers. The rates of these taxes on stock without par value is often arbitrarily set at a figure of up to $100 a share, which can be exorbitant if the actual worth of a share is less than that amount.

Shareholders' Equity

Issued stock is usually to be sold at least at the stated par. If, for example, a share has a par value of $10, and is sold for $12, the $12 total is called *paid-in capital*. For purposes of bookkeeping, the $10 becomes *capital stock*, which in the confusing world of accounting terminologies may be called legal or stated capital. The $2 premium over par value is reported as *capital surplus*, also known as paid-in surplus or additional paid-in capital. When shares do not have a par value, laws of certain states may require the corporation to recognize the total consideration received for the shares as capital stock even when they are sold at different prices. Both capital stock and capital surplus are accommodated under shareholders' equity in the balance sheet.

Shareholders' Equity
Shareholders' net worth in the corporation.

Kinds of Stock

The rights and privileges of different classes of stock are controlled by the articles of incorporation in the absence of contrary statute. The most common division of classes of stock is into common stock and preferred stock.

Common Stock
The ordinary stock of the corporation, usually with voting rights and pro-rata dividend rights.

Common Stock Common stock is the ordinary stock of a corporation. Without priority over other types of stock, common shareholders among themselves are entitled to pro rata dividend and distribution of net assets upon dissolution of the corporation.

Common stock is usually the voting stock. Common shareholders, rather than preferred shareholders, elect the board of directors. In general, preferred shareholders, although owners of the corporation with other shareholders, are primarily interested in a fixed return in the form of a dividend and are not so concerned about management so long as their dividend is paid.

The common shareholder on the other hand, has a greater stake as owner of the corporation. He is taking a greater gamble on the success of the corporation and therefore should have the choice of management. If the corporation is a success, the common shareholder may receive the largest dividends; if the venture fails, he must absorb the initial and the heaviest losses.

Preferred Stock
Stock having a preference over the common stock, usually as to dividends. It may be cumulative or noncumulative, participating or nonparticipating, convertible or nonconvertible, callable or noncallable.

Preferred Stock Preferred stock is stock that has a preference over common stock. The preference is usually as to dividends, although it can take the form of various rights, powers, and privileges, including a priority on distribution of capital on dissolution of the corporation.

1. Preferred stock can be made either *cumulative* or *noncumulative*. Cumulative stock means that if there is no distribution of profits in the form of dividends in a particular year because there are no profits or because the profits are to be used for expansion, etc., the unpaid dividends accrue, and both back and current dividends must be paid in full before any dividend may be paid on common stock.

    In the case of noncumulative stock, the dividends that are unpaid during the current year are lost forever. Even if there is a large surplus available, a strong showing of fraud or abuse of discretion by the board of directors will be necessary before a court will compel a declaration of a dividend. Thus, unless the preferred stock is cumulative or unless the noncumulative shareholders have a contract with the corporation that makes a dividend mandatory, the noncumulative stock will lose its dividend unless declared each year.

2. Preferred stock also can be made *participating* or *nonparticipating*. Participating stock entitles the preferred shares to participate with the common shares in the annual distribution of surplus earnings after the common shares have received a dividend equal to that payable to the preferred. In essence, if there is a lavish amount of corporate net profits to be distributed as dividends, both participating preferred shareholders and common shareholders will ultimately receive the same amount per share.

    Upon dissolution and liquidation of the corporation, the owners of preferred stock with a par value usually receive the par value, and occasionally with a certain premium added. If no par value is stated, the corporation usually will pay a stated pre-agreed sum. Whether or not preferred shareholders participate with the common shareholders as to the distribution of net assets is a matter governed in the agreement. A preferred stock agreement may be found in the articles of incorporation and sometimes printed on the back of the preferred stock certificate.

Squires v. Balbach Co.
177 Neb. 465, 129 N.W.2d 462 (1964).

Brower, Justice . . . At the conclusion of the trial, the district court held that (upon dissolution of the corporation) the preferred stockholders were entitled to the par value of their stock with dividends at $8 per annum from January, 1962, to the date of payment less $2 per share which had already been paid, and that the common shareholders were entitled to the remainder. . . .

From this judgment plaintiffs have appealed assigning as error that the judgment is contrary to the law and the evidence. . . .

On the certificates of preferred stock the following appears: . . . . The dividends on the Preferred stock shall be cumulative, and shall be paid before any dividends are paid on the Common stock, and after dividends of eight per centum (8%) per annum have been paid on the Common stock, the Preferred and Common stock shall participate equally in all further dividends.

"In the event of the winding up or dissolution of the Corporation, whether voluntary or involuntary, the holders of the Preferred stock shall receive the par value of their shares with any unpaid dividends thereon, before any payments are made to holders of the Common stock."

. . . The question of participation rights upon dissolution had been somewhat obscured by a conflict of authority on the related problem of the right of preferred shareholders to participate in additional dividend distribution beyond their stated priority before dissolution. . . .

From the cases cited and those to be cited it appears that there are certain rules which have been generally announced in certain jurisdictions relating to the distribution of assets on liquidation of a corporation.

One is that in the absence of specified rights or limitations all stockholders are entitled to share equally in liquidated surplus assets.

Another is that courts universally adhere to the rule that the rights of respective classes of stockholders are determined by the terms of the articles and memorandum of the corporation except as may be limited by statute.

. . . We conclude that provisions in corporate articles and memoranda that holders of preferred stock shall be paid the par value of their stock before any liquidation dividends are paid to the holders of common stock is exhaustive and means that the preferred stock shall have its par preference on liquidation and nothing more.

3. Preferred stock can be *convertible* or *nonconvertible*. If it is convertible, the owner of the stock has the option of converting each preferred share into a certain number of common shares. The conversion ratio is specified when the convertible shares are issued. Because of this ratio, the value of convertible preferred stock fluctuates in accordance with the changing market price of the common stock.

4. Finally, preferred stock can be *callable* or *noncallable*. If it is callable, or redeemable, the corporation issues the preferred stock specifically conditioned upon its right to purchase the shares back at some future time. This mode of issuing preferred stock is devised primarily to protect the corporation against detrimental interest rate fluctuations. A fixed amount of dividend paid to a preferred shareholder may be reasonable at a given time, but when interest rates fall, paying the same amount

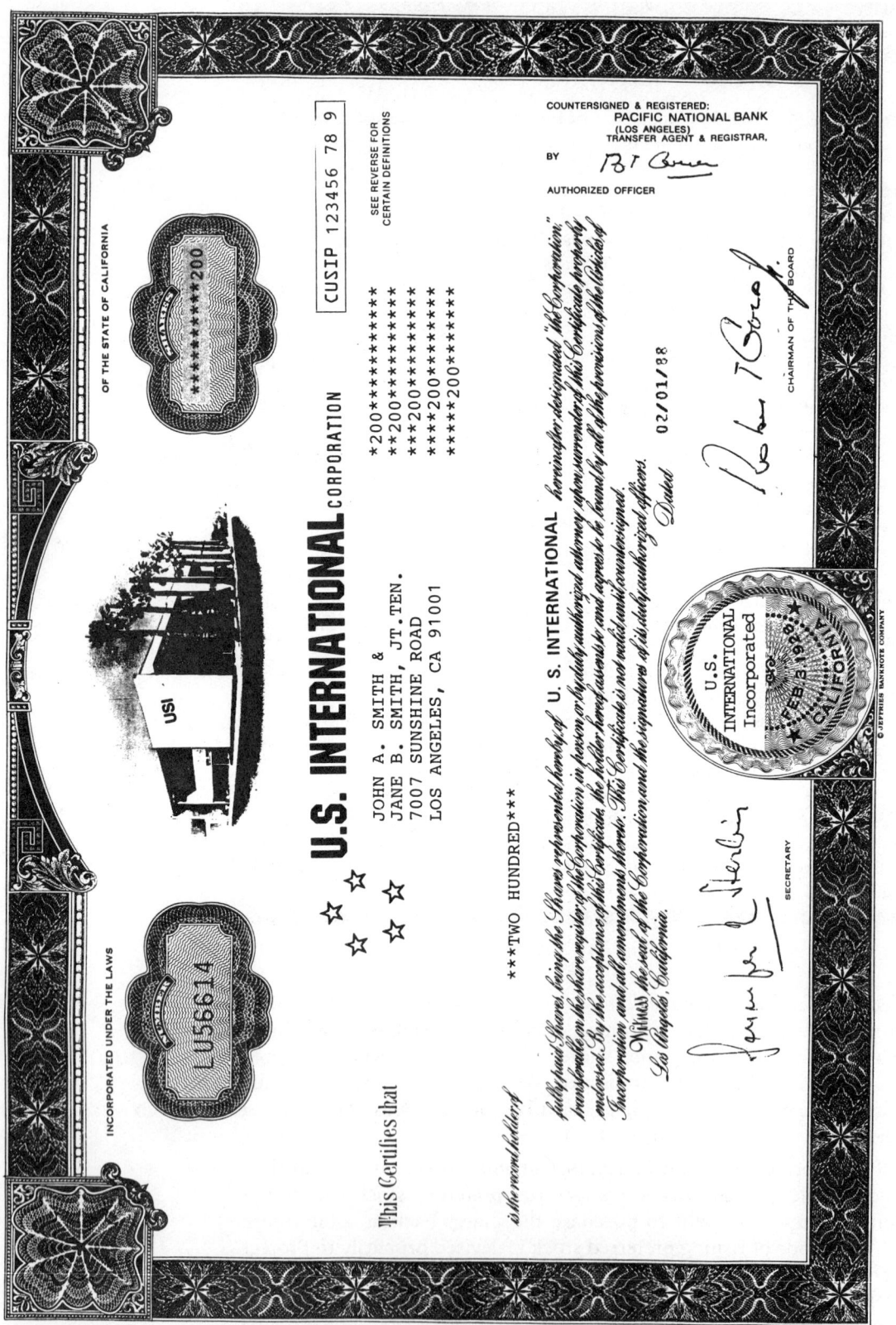

Figure 24.1 Sample of a Common Stock Certificate

can become economically unjustifiable. In such a situation, the company may wish to replace the high-cost preferred shares with shares at a lower cost.

Market Value

The stock market itself is, of course, not a subject matter for this book. Nevertheless, to have a basic idea of the market value of a stock, it is important for the business law student to understand the legal aspects and ramifications of corporate finance.

Basically, shares of stock can be bought and sold directly between buyers and sellers. In general, however, stock transactions are conducted through stock exchanges. The two major stock exchanges in the United States are the New York Exchange and the American Stock Exchange. Overseas, the important stock exchanges are the ones in Tokyo and London. All the stock listed with those exchanges are clustered, and each cluster is controlled by a stock specialist. A buyer or seller gives the instruction to a stock brokerage firm, which executes the order through the specialist. There is a five-business-day period for the executed transaction to be settled. The buyer may request a stock certificate to be issued in his name. If he does not need the certificate, he may leave the shares of stock in his brokerage account, in which event, the stock is held in "street name" (in the name of the stock brokerage company handling the account).

The market value of a stock is totally independent from the par value, if any; it fluctuates every minute of the day. If the general economy and the company are perceived to be promising, the stock goes up in price; otherwise, it goes down. In theory, the important factors influencing the stock market are the trend in interest rates, currency value, state budget and trade balances, inflation and deflation tendencies, option and future indices, etc. In practice, the stock market is simply unpredictable, yet it is considered an important barometer of the economy.

The price/earnings ratio, or P/E ratio, is the ratio between the market price per share and the earnings per share. Earnings per share is the amount derived from annual net profit divided by the number of outstanding common shares. The importance of the P/E ratio is again limited. Buyers of an "exploding" stock might not be deterred by a high P/E ratio.

Among all the indicators, Dow Jones Averages are the most popular and influential. They consist of continually updated averages of thirty industrial, twenty transportation, and fifteen utility companies.

Market Value
Share price determined by the stock market.

Book Value

When dealing with a small and closely held corporation and there is no certainty as to its continuation and perpetuity, the investor should be interested in the book value of his shares of stock. This book value, or net asset value, is the actual value per share that the owner is to receive upon dissolution of the corporation and liquidation of its assets. Upon accurate corporate financial statements, the book value is determined by dividing the total of all the entries in the shareholders' equity area, which is in essence the difference between total assets and total liabilities, by the total number of outstanding shares of stock.

Book Value
Actual value per share based upon the corporate assets.

Liability for Shares

Shares issued for improper consideration or for no consideration are often declared void by state law. Where permitted by statute, partly paid shares of stock may be issued, subject to assessment until the full amount has been paid. Most states and MBCA § 23(d) take the position that a stock certificate cannot be issued for stock that is only partly paid.

When a corporation issues shares of stock as fully paid and nonassessable for less than proper consideration, the stock is often described as "watered stock." The record owner of such stock is usually held liable for the unpaid consideration. A good faith transferee of watered stock is not liable for any unpaid balance. The original purchaser does not escape liability by such a transfer. Usually a person who holds shares in a fiduciary capacity is not liable for the unpaid balance, nor is a pledgee.

Bonds

Bonds
Certificates of indebtedness for money borrowed.

Debentures
Unsecured bonds.

MBCA § 4(h) provides that a corporation shall have the power "(T)o make contracts and guarantees and incur liabilities, borrow money at such rates of interest as the corporation may determine, issue its notes, bonds, and other obligations, and secure any of its obligations by mortgage or pledge of all or any of its property, franchises and income."

Bonds are usually issued in $1,000 denominations of face value. The corporation or its agent pays the interest on the bonds on a semiannual basis. *Term* bonds mature on one single date, whereas *serial* bonds mature on installments.

Bonds can be secured by the corporation's real or personal properties; or they can be unsecured, in which event, they are called *debenture* bonds. After a corporate reorganization, the company can issue income bonds, which pay interest only to the extent of the company's current earnings. Income bonds can be cumulative or noncumulative. Bonds can also be callable. Finally, convertible bonds can be converted into common stock.

Unlike shareholders, who are owners of the corporation, bondholders are creditors. Upon liquidation of the corporation, they are to be repaid before preferred and common shareholders receive any distribution. Bondholders do not participate in the sharing of the profits and losses of the business.

As with stocks, prices of bonds are determined by the market. The foremost determining factor influencing the bond market is the general trend in interest rates. When interest rates are increasing, bond prices should decrease to compensate for the spread between the market interest rate and the bond paying rate. Like stocks, bonds are rated in accordance with the relative strength and capacity of the company to repay its debts.

Retained Earnings

Retained Earnings
Portions of corporate profits reinvested in the business instead of distributed to shareholders.

Retained earnings, often called earned surplus, are the amounts that the corporation has reinvested in the business over the years. This is a cumulative figure. A newly organized corporation would have no retained earnings. As part of corporate equity, accumulated retained earnings are the primary source of funding and a good reason for a corporation's business expansion.

Dividends

The objective of a corporate shareholder is to gain profit, i.e., (a) when the price of the stock goes up and (b) when dividends on the stock are paid. Not all companies pay dividends. If there are no dividends, the shareholder's only expectation is rapid capital gain as the stock fluctuates in price. Utility stocks pay comparatively high dividends, but the stocks themselves are generally not volatile. All these strategic investment differences become important when income tax laws make a distinction between income and capital gain.

Dividends
Distributions of profit paid to shareholders by a corporation.

Dividends are distributed in cash, in property such as company products, or in shares of stock proportionate to a shareholder's relative interest in the corporation as reflected by the number of shares owned. Cash is the most customary type of dividend. Corporations usually pay dividends quarterly.

Sources

Although it varies with state law, corporations are basically not allowed to pay dividends from the corporation's stated capital. In so doing, the shareholder essentially receives funds taken from his own investment while the corporate creditors are thereby jeopardized. Ideally, dividends should be distributed from the annual net profits, and if this is not possible, the corporate retained earnings may be encroached. Some states allow dividends to be paid from the capital surplus account, which in effect also amounts to depletion of the shareholder's initial investment and weakening of the creditor's position.

Declaration by Board

The declaration of dividends is discretionary with the board of directors. Even where there is a large surplus, the shareholders cannot compel distribution of a dividend unless there has been an obvious abuse of discretion or there has been bad faith.

Doherty v. Mutual Warehouse Co.
255 F.2d 489 (5th Cir. 1958).

Rives, Circuit Judge This action is by a minority shareholder against a corporation to compel declaration and payment of dividends.
 . . . In Alabama, the law is well settled that a court of equity will not interfere with the internal business management of corporate affairs by the board of directors so long as they keep within the scope of the charter powers, and are not guilty of fraud, maladministration, or abuse of discretion. . . .

> The original capital of the corporation was $15,000.00, and as of the end of the year 1955 the surplus of the corporation was $188,738.38.
>
> Prior to the year 1955, the management of the corporation had determined that for sound business reasons the corporation should accumulate a surplus of $200,000.00. At the end of the year 1956 the surplus of the corporation, for the first time exceeded $200,000.00; the surplus being $206,314.30. Early in 1957 the directors of the corporation declared a dividend of $6,000.00 to stockholders of record—being a $40.00 dividend for each share of outstanding stock.
>
> The decision not to declare a dividend for the year 1955 and to use the profits of the corporation in the business was not an abuse of discretion, and such refusal to declare a dividend was not arbitrary, nor was there any bad faith or fraud, or maladministration destructive or injurious to the corporation. The decision not to declare a dividend for 1955 and to accumulate surplus was consistent with the character and needs of the business. At all times here material the directors, officers and management of the corporation have acted fairly and in the utmost good faith in the handling of the business, management and corporate affairs of the corporation in the interest of the corporation. . . .
>
> The judgment was right, and it is
> Affirmed.

The following older case, on the other hand, shows different circumstances leading to a different outcome.

Facts

Ford Motor Company had been profitable from 1903 to 1916. Its capital stock had increased from $150,000 to $2 million. Since 1911, the company had regularly paid quarterly dividends. In addition, special dividends had been declared amounting to $41 million from 1911 to 1915. In 1916, the board of directors decided to discontinue paying special dividends. At that point, Ford Motor had earned a surplus of $112 million. The earnings were $60 million per year, while the total liabilities were less than $20 million. There was cash in the amount of $54 million. Plaintiff Dodge, a shareholder, was unhappy with the withholding of the special dividend and brought a suit against the corporation. The company defended on the ground that it was planning a massive capital expansion, including the lowering of the Model T price from $440 to $360. "My ambition," said Mr. Ford, "is to employ still more men, to spread the benefits of this industrial system to the greatest possible number, to help them build up their lives and their homes."

Decision

Judgment for the plaintiff. Even if it were true that the shareholders, as Mr. Ford alleged, already made too much money, the duty of the corporation and its board of directors is to the shareholders. As the company was in such excellent financial condition, the court felt that by not appropriately distributing the company's earnings the board was not acting in the best interests of the shareholders.

Dodge v. Ford Motor Co., 204 Mich. 459, 170 N.W. 668 (1919).

Persons Entitled to Dividend

Generally, the board of directors declares dividends on a quarterly basis. From a corporate accounting point of view, there are essentially three important dates:

1. The *declaration* date is the day that the board makes the declaration and sets aside the funds needed for the dividend payment.

CORPORATION (II)

2. The *record* date is a future day specified by the board at the time of dividend declaration to determine that shareholders of corporate records on this particular date will be entitled to the dividend.
3. The *payment* date is some day after the record date when dividend payment is to be made.

When transfers of stock take place through brokerage firms and exchanges, it is obvious that a new purchaser of a stock cannot be on corporate record the same day, particularly where enormous volumes of stocks are floating and being transferred from person to person every minute of the day. In addition, a buyer of a stock through a brokerage firm has five business days to pay for the purchase. Therefore, under the security settlement regulation that governs stock transactions, it is not the record date but the *ex-dividend* date—which is four business days prior to the designated record date—that determines which shareholder has the right to the dividend declared. Accordingly, stock bought prior to the ex-dividend date entitled the new owner to the declared dividend. The new owner does not have that right if the purchase takes place on or after that date. For example, for American Telephone and Telegraph, the declaration date was March 16, 1988; the ex-dividend date, March 25, 1988; the record date March 31, 1988; and the payment date May 2, 1988. Persons owning this stock prior to March 25 would have the right to receive this dividend. Persons acquiring this stock on March 25 or later would not be paid this dividend.

Ex-Dividend Date
Determines which shareholder is entitled to the dividend declared.

Stock Dividend

A corporation may wish to preserve its cash if, for example, the business operation needs to be expanded. Yet the management may feel obligated to provide dividends to the loyal shareholders. Instead of paying cash, the corporation may issue stock dividends proportionate to the shareholders' respective interests in the company.

Stock dividends increase the number of outstanding shares as well as the amount of the corporation's stated capital amount. This increase is offset by a reduction of the retained earnings. It should be noted that since income tax liability is based on realized income, stock dividends are not taxable until the stock is actually sold at some future time.

Stock Dividend
Shares of stock issued to shareholders in place of cash dividends.

Stock Split

A stock split is simply a division of the outstanding shares into more units, each with proportionately less value. The shareholder's share of ownership, his rights on dissolution, and the total value of his investment remain essentially the same. The only changes are the issuance of a new certificate and a reduction in the market value of each share, which increases the marketability of the stock. For example, 100 shares following a 2-for-1 split would become 200 shares, with each share being worth one-half the previous price per share.

With a stock split, the dollar amount of the stated capital account remains the same. Only the number of outstanding shares increases. Where there is more than one class of shares outstanding, either a stock split or a stock dividend in one class may alter the relative voting strength of the

Stock Split
Division of stock shares into more units. The total value of the new shares remains basically the same as the old.

different classes. Both stock splits and stock dividends affect the book value per share.

Questions

1. How is a corporation financed?
2. How does preferred stock differ from common stock? What are the different kinds of preferred stock?
3. How is the book value per share determined?
4. How do bonds differ from stocks?
5. What is the difference between a stock dividend and a stock split?

24.3 Stock Acquisition and Securities Regulation

Subscription and Transfer

A person becomes a stockholder either by a preincorporation or a subsequent subscription of the stock directly from the corporation, its agent, or underwriter or by a transfer of the stock from another shareholder. The stock certificate issued by the corporation or its transfer agent is the evidence of ownership of the stated number of shares. MBCA § 23 requires that the certificate include the following: (1) the state of incorporation; (2) the name of the person to whom issued; (3) the number and class of shares represented by the certificate and the designation of the series, if any; and (4) the par value of each share represented by such certificate or a statement that the shares are without par value.

Negotiability

Under Article 8 of the Uniform Commercial Code, stocks and bonds are negotiable. A stock transfer takes place by the endorsement and delivery of the stock certificate by the transferor to the transferee. A stock certificate delivered but not endorsed amounts to an assignment instead of a negotiation.

Subscriptions and transfers of stock may be handled by the corporation itself when the company is small and has not gone public and the shareholders are limited in number. However, when stock of a larger corporation is sold to the public, the company necessarily depends on others to process subscriptions and transfers, which increases the corporation's exposure to endorsement forgeries. The law places a heavy burden of responsibility on brokerage firms, transfer agents, and the companies themselves for ensuring the authenticity of signatures.

Weller v. American Telephone and Telegraph
290 A.2d 842 (Del.Ch. 1972).

Marvel, Vice Chancellor . . . At the time of the acts complained of plaintiff was the registered holder of 500 shares of common stock of American Telephone and Telegraph Company and 100 shares of common stock of General Electric. Later, the shares of the latter company were split two for one.

In 1968, Gertrude L. Weller, a 94 year old widow, was invited to live in the home of Mr. and Mrs. Kenneth Jumper [her friends for many years]. . . .

In February, 1970, after having moved to her nephew's to live, following disclosure to some extent of Mr. Jumper's actual nature, Mrs. Weller ascertained that for over a period of almost two years she had been systematically defrauded by Mr. Jumper. In other words she became aware for the first time of the fact that Kenneth Jumper had used a form containing her signature for the purpose of opening a joint trading account with a stockbroker, namely the third party defendant Merrill Lynch, Pierce, Fenner & Smith, Inc., and that Mr. Jumper thereafter had apparently forged her name to the stock certificates here involved for the purpose of selling them on the market. . . .

Plaintiff thereupon notified the defendants American Telephone and Telegraph Company and General Electric Company on March 4, 1970 that the stock certificates representing her investments in such companies had been sold by means of forged signatures and requested the issuance to her of replacement certificates. The defendants having declined to issue such certificates as requested, this action ensued, the complaint naming as defendants the issuers of the certificates in question. Merrill Lynch was later joined as a third party defendant in its capacity as the broker which had guaranteed Mrs. Weller's signature.

. . . Section 8–404(2) of the Uniform Commercial Code provides that where an issuer has registered a transfer of a security in the name of a person not entitled to it, such issuer on demand must deliver a like security to the true owner, provided, inter alia, the owner has acted pursuant to subsection (1) of the section which follows. Section 8–404(2)(b). Subsection (1) of the following section provides that the owner of such a security must notify the issuer of the wrongful taking complained of within a reasonable time after he has notice of a lost or wrongfully taken certificate, Section 8–405(1). . . .

Accordingly, plaintiff is entitled to the entry of an order providing for the issuance to her of 500 shares of American Telephone and Telegraph Company common stock together with accrued and unpaid dividends as well as 200 shares of General Electric Company common stock together with accrued and unpaid dividends, summary judgment having been earlier granted to the defendants American Telephone and Telegraph Company and General Electric Company on their claim against the third party defendant Merrill Lynch, Pierce, Fenner and Smith, Incorporated on the basis of the latter's guarantee of Mrs. Weller's signature.

Restrictions

The corporation may impose certain restrictions on the transfer of stock. A closely held corporation may wish to provide existing shareholders preemptive privileges, whereby new issues may not be sold and outstanding shares may not be transferred without having been offered to the current shareholders. Unless clearly specified, such a restriction does not apply when the change of stock ownership is caused by a distribution of an estate of the original deceased owner. This is the case *(I)n the matter of the Estate of Spaziani* (125 Misc.2d 901, 480 N.Y.S.2d 854 [1984]). Furthermore, UCC § 8–204 requires such restrictions to be conspicuously noted on the stock certificate. In *Irwin* v. *West End Development Co.* (481 F.2d 34 [10th Cir. 1973]), a shareholder was considered not bound by a restriction that appeared in the articles of incorporation only.

Government Regulatory Policies

As trading in securities became attractive, more and more people became involved and were financially hurt because of the highly speculative character of the game and unethical schemes of unscrupulous operators. Securities are, by their very nature, different from most merchandise. A purchaser of a car or a piece of furniture can personally inspect and ascertain the quality of the product as well as scrutinize the reasonableness of the price. A buyer of a stock or bond does not have that opportunity. In the securities business, decisions are made for a great part on reliance upon available information.

Excessive speculation and outright fraud that surrounded the stock market crash of 1929 prompted the federal government to enact legislation to police the securities industry. The first objective was to provide investors adequate information necessary to make intelligent trading decisions. The second objective was to prevent unfair, deceptive, and manipulative conduct that had resulted in huge losses to the unsophisticated and powerless investors. The 1987 market crash and the recent Wall Street scandals will undoubtedly propel Capitol Hill to legislate even more protective measures.

Securities Defined

Securities
Includes stock, bonds, notes, and other modes of investment.

Courts apply the term securities liberally. Under the Securities Act of 1933, the term *security* means "any note, stock, . . . bond, debenture, evidence of indebtedness, certificate of interest of participation in any profit-sharing agreement, . . . preorganization certificate or subscription, . . . investment contract, voting trust certificate, . . . fractional undivided interest in oil, gas, or mineral rights, . . . or, in general, any interest or instrument commonly known as a 'security.'"

In *SEC* v. *Howey* (328 U.S. 293, 66 S.Ct. 1100, 90 L.Ed. 1244 [1946]), the U.S. Supreme Court said that an investment contract is a security if "the person invests his money in a common enterprise and is led to expect profits solely from the efforts of the promoter or a third party." This notion is sometimes called the *Howey test*.

How broadly courts define securities under federal securities law is illustrated in the following case.

Facts

Defendant company offered and sold certain courses. Under different plans, purchasers were privileged to attend seminars and receive course materials. They also had the opportunity to sell the courses to others for a commission. The court found that the courses and seminars had no value. The whole scheme was, in fact, an elaborate confidence game. The trial court held that the plans were securities under the federal securities laws and found certain securities laws violations.

Decision

Affirmed. The definitions of *securities* under federal securities laws include a wide variety of instruments and contracts. Federal securities law covers uncommon and irregular devices if they are widely offered or dealt with under terms or courses of dealing that establish their character in commerce as investment contracts. Here, the purchasers were really buying the possibility of deriving money from sales commissions. The court concluded that these deals were investment contracts and hence securities within federal securities law.

Securities and Exchange Commission v. *Glenn Turner Enterprises, Inc.*, 474 F.2d 476 (9th Cir. 1973), cert. denied 414 U.S. 821, 94 S.Ct. 117, 38 L.Ed.2d 53.

Securities and Exchange Commission

The primary enforcer of federal securities law is the Securities and Exchange Commission (SEC), a federal administrative agency. The SEC was established under the Securities Exchange Act of 1934. The Securities Act of 1933, the first major federal legislation regulating securities, was administered by the Federal Trade Commission before the SEC existed. Under the powers conferred by the 1934 Act, the SEC makes rules pertaining to the business conduct of all the securities exchanges and market participants, enforces them, and adjudicates cases involving violation of the rules. The SEC's decisions are subject to judicial review, as illustrated in *Medical Committee for Human Rights* v. *S.E.C.* (432 F.2d 659 [D.C. Cir. 1970]).

Securities and Exchange Commission
The Federal agency charged with the regulation of security transactions. Also called SEC.

The Securities Act of 1933

The main goal of the Securities Act of 1933, sometimes called the Truth-in-Securities Act, is to provide full and fair disclosure of information about securities offered to the general public. Regardless of whether the purchaser is ultimately going to win or lose, he should have complete and accurate information to make his decision.

Registration Statement

The company files the required information with the SEC in a registration statement, which is made available to investors in a *prospectus*. The prospectus contains specific and detailed information about the issuing company, its business, directors, officers, financial statements, assets and liabilities, etc.

When a registration statement is filed with the SEC, a preliminary offering, called "red herring," may be disseminated to inform potential buyers about the forthcoming issue. The cover must show the following statement printed in red:

Red Herring
Notice of a forthcoming stock issue which has not yet been approved by the SEC.

> A registration statement relating to these securities has been filed with the Securities and Exchange Commission, but has not yet become effective. Information contained herein is subject to completion or amendment. These securities may not be sold nor may offers to buy be accepted prior to the time the registration statement becomes effective. . . .

Usually, the waiting period for the Commission to approve the statement is twenty days. The SEC's approval of a registration statement means only that the commission is satisfied with the disclosure as fair and full information. The SEC does not attest to the accuracy or the merits or value of the securities offered. Hence, the cover page of the official prospectus shows the following disclaimer:

> THE SECURITIES HAVE NOT BEEN APPROVED OR DISAPPROVED BY THE SECURITIES AND EXCHANGE COMMISSION NOR HAS THE COMMISSION PASSED UPON THE ACCURACY OR ADEQUACY OF THIS PROSPECTUS. ANY REPRESENTATION TO THE CONTRARY IS A CRIMINAL OFFENSE.

Liabilities and Defenses

Anyone responsible for the presentation of a registration statement can be held liable for damages caused by the statement's errors and omissions. Such damages can be sought by any investor who lost money on securities because of such misstatements. A civil action can be brought against (1) the signers of the registration statement, including the issuer, the chief executive, the financial and accounting officers, and a majority of the board of directors; (2) all directors; (3) all persons who agree to be directors; (4) experts named in the registration statement, such as doctors, lawyers, engineers, and geologists; and (5) all underwriters. The civil liability of all such persons is joint and several.

Section 11 of the 1933 Act provides that the above defendants may assert the defenses of (1) due diligence, (2) immateriality, (3) purchaser's knowledge, (4) other causes of damages, (5) no reliance, and (6) statute of limitations. Courts are usually not too generous in applying these defenses.

Facts

A suit to recover a loss of their investment in debentures issued by BarChris Construction Corporation was brought by Escott and some other investors. The corporation became bankrupt, and the action was filed against those who signed the registration statement filed with the SEC. In its prospectus, sales, earnings, and current assets were overstated. Liabilities were understated. The company failed to disclose that a significant part of the proceeds from the debenture sale would be used to pay off old debts. Auslander was a director who had just joined the board before the debentures were registered. He had not read the registration statement. Trilling was the controller, who also claimed ignorance of the false and misleading statements. The registration statement was prepared and audited for the corporation by Peat, Marwick, Mitchell & Co., a public accounting firm. The defendants claimed the due diligence defense.

Decision

Judgment for the plaintiffs. The defendants are not shielded by the due diligence defense of § 11. The defense requires an investigation by the defendants to ascertain whether the presentation is true and complete. Auslander is liable, since he simply accepted the word of the management without conducting any examination. Trilling, being the controller, should have known of the inaccuracies. Peat, Marwick is liable, because as corporate auditor it should have been alerted by the misrepresentations.

Escott v. BarChris Construction Corp., 283 F.Supp. 643 (S.D.N.Y. 1968).

Under the Securities Act of 1933, it is a crime to commit fraud in the sale of securities or to willfully violate the Act. Criminal conviction may lead to a penalty of up to five years imprisonment and/or a fine of $10,000.

Exemptions

Some securities issues are exempted from the registration requirement of the 1933 Act:

1. Government-issued or government-guaranteed securities.
2. Short-term notes and drafts, maturing in no more than nine months.
3. Securities of nonprofit issuers.
4. Financial institution securities, such as those issued by banks and savings and loan institutions.
5. Securities issued by Interstate Commerce Commission-regulated entities, such as those in the railroads and trucking business.
6. Insurance policies and annuity contracts.

These securities are exempt from the registration requirement of the 1933 Act, but they are not exempt from the antifraud provisions of the Act.

The Securities Exchange Act of 1934

Whereas the 1933 Act basically requires registration of new issues, the 1934 Act not only imposes new and broader registration requirements but also focuses the attention on undesired business conduct in secondary securities markets. In addition to establishing the Securities and Exchange Commission, as mentioned earlier, the 1934 Act regulates securities exchanges, broker-dealer firms, and virtually all publicly held companies.

Registration and Periodic Reporting

While registration under the 1933 Act is limited to new offerings, the 1934 Act requires all securities traded on any national securities exchange to be registered unless exempt. The 1934 Act also requires all securities exchanges and broker-dealer firms as well as companies that have equity securities traded over the counter in interstate commerce and have assets exceeding $3 million with 500 or more shareholders to register with the SEC. Subsequent to the first-time registration, the registrant must file periodic reports to update the original information.

Antifraud Provisions

Section 10(b) of the 1934 Act makes it unlawful for anyone, while using the mails or any other facilities of interstate commerce, to purchase or sell securities and to

1. Employ any device, scheme, or artifice to defraud.
2. Make any untrue statement of a material fact.
3. Omit to state a material fact without which the information is misleading.
4. Engage in any act, practice, or course of business that operates or would operate as a fraud or deceit on any person.

Fraudulent conduct includes such practices as knowingly spreading false rumors to affect securities prices, "wash sales" (simultaneously buying and

Wash Sale on Securities
Simultaneously buying and selling the same security to influence the market.

Churning
Excessive trading by a broker on a customer's account to improperly gain commission.

selling the same security to influence its market activity), and "churning," which occurs when a stockbroker controls a customer's account and trades excessively to improperly gain commission. Whether or not churning took place is often a matter of judgment. In *Zaretsky* v. *E.F. Hutton & Co.* (509 F.Supp. 68 [S.D.N.Y. 1981]), the court decided in favor of the investors, whereas in *Van Alen* v. *Dominick & Dominick, Inc.* (441 F.Supp. 389 [S.D.N.Y. 1976]), the court decided in favor of the brokerage firm.

Proxy Restrictions

The 1934 Act proscribes solicitation of proxy involving any registered security "in contravention of such rules and regulations as the Commission may prescribe." The SEC rules require the solicitor to furnish the security holders with (1) a proxy statement covering all material facts concerning the matters being voted upon as well as (2) a proxy form for the solicited shareholder to state his approval or disapproval of the proposal presented. Providing such material information is required when shareholders are notified of a shareholders' meeting even if the corporation does not solicit proxies.

Insider Information and Short-Swing Profit

Insider Information
Information not available to the public at large.

Insider information is information not available to the public at large. Anyone who possesses privileged information material to the value of a corporation's securities, such as a company's invention, discovery, or windfall profit, must either disclose such information to the investing public or abstain from trading in the corporate securities until the information becomes public. Investors who sustain a loss because of insider information may recover damages from anyone who unlawfully used the undisclosed information.

Facts
While test drilling in Ontario, Canada, the Texas Gulf Sulphur Co. (TGS) found a drill core that was extremely rich in copper content. The drilling was stopped temporarily so that the company could purchase all the mineral rights on nearby land. Meanwhile, the company gave a misleading impression to the general public to the effect that most of the areas drilled were barren. During this period, several corporate directors, officers, and employees who knew about the discovery purchased shares of TGS stock through brokers on the New York Stock Exchange. The SEC brought an action for violation of Rule 10b–5.

Decision
Judgment for the SEC. Even though the extent of the ore body was uncertain, the information about the discovery was material when the purchases were made. The information, if public, might well have affected the price of TGS stock and would have been important to an investor who bought, sold, or held the stock. Individual defendants were ordered to pay profits into escrow for injured parties, and Texas Gulf settled most shareholders suits by a payment of $2.7 million.

SEC v. *Texas Gulf Sulphur Co.*, 401 F.2d 833 (2d Cir., 1968).

Subsequent to the above case is *Cannon* v. *Texas Gulf Sulphur Co.* (55 F.R.D. 308 [S.D.N.Y., 1972]). A more recent case related to the issue of "insider information" is *Basic, Incorporated* v. *Levinson* (108 S.Ct. 978 [1988]).

Dissemination of privileged information without personally benefiting from the information does not amount to insider trading condemned by the 1934 Act. This is illustrated in *Dirks* v. *Securities and Exchange Commission* (463 U.S. 646, 103 S.Ct. 3255, 77 L.Ed.2d 911 [U.S. Supreme Court, 1983]), where an officer of a New York broker-dealer firm came to know about fraudulent conduct by Equity Funding of America and revealed the story to his clients, who took advantage of the information. It was held that an insider is liable under Rule 10b–5 for insider trading only when he does not disclose material nonpublic information before trading on it and thus makes "secret profits."

To monitor insider trading, corporate directors, officers, and any person owning 10 percent or more of the company's registered company's stock must file monthly reports with the SEC showing any changes in stock ownership. Any profits made within six months by any of these persons from trading in the respective security is called "short-swing profit," which is recoverable by the corporation even if no insider information was involved.

Short-Swing Profit
Profit made within six months by an insider.

Criminal Penalties

Aside from civil damages, the 1934 Act provides penalties of up to five years imprisonment and/or up to $100,000 in fines for violating the prescribed rules and regulations.

Other Enactments

As time progresses, more and more legislation has been found necessary to regulate the securities business.

Public Utility Holding Company Act of 1935

This act regulates the financing and operations of gas and electric public utility holding companies.

Trust Indenture Act of 1939

This act regulates the sale of debt securities, such as bonds. The law requires these securities to be registered under the Securities Act. Certain debt arrangements require a trustee to represent the creditors' interest. As a fiduciary, the trustee must be independent and fully representing the investors.

Investment Company Act of 1940

This act empowers the SEC to regulate publicly owned companies involved in investing and trading in securities. The Act also prescribes the standards for selecting managers, managers' salaries, size of sales charges, investment strategies, etc.

Investment Advisers Act of 1940

The SEC is authorized by this act to regulate investment advisers—persons in the business of advising others on financial investments. In practice, there is comparatively little regulatory control over this business sector. Hence, unwarranted practices in this area are widespread. As fee schedules are not fixed, these advisers often charge their clients arbitrarily. The value of their services is usually open to question. It is not unusual for an adviser to recommend investments in which he himself has an additional personal interest.

Securities Investor Protection Act of 1970

This act established the Securities Investor Protection Corporation (SIPC) to oversee the operation and liquidation of member brokerage firms with financial problems. The SIPC accumulates and manages an insurance fund to indemnify brokerage customers' losses due to a firm's financial failure. In 1988, customers' protection consisted of SIPC coverage of up to $500,000 and excess SIPC insurance of up to $10 million obtained from London Insurers.

Insider Trading Sanctions Act of 1984

With the recent surge of corporate scandals involving insider trading, Congress promulgated this act to increase the risk of trading on insider information as well as the punishment for such activities. In addition to the remedies under the Securities Exchange Act of 1934, the Insider Trading Sanctions Act authorizes the SEC to bring an action in a U.S. district court to have civil penalties imposed upon a person who trades in securities through national security exchanges or broker-dealer firms, based upon information not available to the investing public. Criminal liability is extended to any person who aids and abets. The penalty, which may not exceed three times the profit gained or the loss avoided by such trade, is payable to the Treasury of the United States. Action must be filed within five years after the trading date.

State Legislation

Blue Sky Laws

Blue Sky Laws
State laws to prevent securities fraud, regulating both public and private securities offerings.

All the states except Delaware and Nevada require a corporation to obtain a state permit prior to solicitation or issuance of a stock. These state laws to protect the public from stock frauds are known as "blue sky" laws. The governmental agency, usually a division of corporations, will grant the permit only if it finds that the proposed corporate venture and the securities are fair, just, and equitable. Many state laws also have broker-dealer registration provisions. Generally, a sale of shares made by a corporation in violation of the blue sky laws or other noncompliance is voidable and may be rescinded by the purchaser.

Uniform Securities Act

In 1985, the National Conference of Commissioners on Uniform State Laws adopted a new Uniform Securities Act to replace previous law. The law contains provisions requiring securities registration, broker dealer registration, and antifraud rules.

Industry Regulation

In addition to government regulation, the securities industry itself undertakes in its own interest the task of self-policing. Securities exchanges carefully investigate the business operation of a brokerage firm before extending membership. They also provide rules governing activities both on and off the trading floors. Violating these rules may lead to fines and suspensions. They provide valuable assistance to government agencies investigating fraudulent conduct in the industry. Many brokerage firms maintain a vigilant watch over their floor personnel and account executives.

The National Association of Securities Dealers, Inc. (NASD) is a self-regulatory institution composed of brokerage firms. The purpose of NASD is, among others, to promote high standards of commercial honor, promote among members observance of federal and state securities laws, adopt and enforce rules of fair practice in the securities business, and promote self-discipline among members.

QUESTIONS

1. How does a person become a corporate shareholder?
2. What are the major federal securities regulations? Who enforces them?
3. What is the procedure for a corporation to go public?
4. Give some examples of fraudulent conduct in the securities business.
5. Discuss state involvement in securities regulations.

PROBLEMS

1. Plaintiff was the secretary and a director of the defendant corporation. The president and secretary of the corporation were directed by the board of directors to sign certain mortgage papers, but the plaintiff refused to sign them. Thereafter, the full board of directors at a duly called meeting removed the plaintiff by majority vote from the office of secretary, but not as a director. Plaintiff brings an action to enjoin the corporation from removing her as secretary. Decision?

2. Potent Products Company had a board of fifteen directors. The board, at a meeting attended by thirteen of the directors, voted to declare an illegal dividend. The roll call vote was 9 to 2. The dividend was paid and the company soon became insolvent. The creditors sued the fifteen directors personally for the amount paid out in the dividend. Which of the following directors, if any, are liable?
(a) Director Hart Manning was present and voted in favor of the dividend even though he knew it was illegal.
(b) Director Bill Podesta was present but knew nothing about the interpretation of financial statements. He voted in favor of the dividend because Les Cash, the company treasurer and a C.P.A., assured him that the dividend was legal.
(c) Director Les Cash, treasurer and a C.P.A., was present and voted in favor, stating that he thought the dividend was legal.
(d) Director Harry Grant was present but didn't vote.
(e) Director Valerie Lewis was present and voted no.
(f) Director Frank N. Ernst didn't attend the meeting because his daughter was getting married. It was the only meeting of the board that he had ever missed.

3. Y was the president of ACE Corporation. As part of his corporate duties, Y arranged financing for ACE. FSF Finance Company drew twelve checks payable to the order of ACE. These checks were then endorsed by Y in his corporate capacity as a president and were cashed at two different banks.

The BNB Bank, on which the checks were drawn, charged FSF, its depositor, with the amount of the checks. FSF then sued BNB to restore the amount of the checks to its account, arguing that BNB had improperly made payment to Y because Y had no corporate authority to endorse and cash the checks. Decision?

4. David subscribed for 200 shares of 8 percent cumulative, participating, redeemable, convertible, preferred shares of the Atlas Hotel Company with a par value of $100 per share. The subscription agreement provided that he was to receive a bonus of one share of common stock of $100 par value for each share of preferred stock. David fully paid his subscription agreement of $20,000 and received the aforementioned 200 shares of preferred and the bonus stock of 200 shares of the par value common. Subsequently the company became insolvent. Rogers, the receiver of the corporation, brings suit for $20,000, the par value of the common stock, against David. Decision?

5. Ray, a shareholder in Swanson Company, a corporation, delivered his stock certificate endorsed in blank to Turpin, a purchaser for value. Ray died the following day. His executor, believing that the certificate was lost, applied to the corporation for a new certificate which was issued and the share transferred to the executor's name on the books. The executor sold the new certificate to Upson, an innocent purchaser, delivering the certificate endorsed to his name, to him, three weeks after Ray's death. Two days later, Turpin presented the original certificate to the corporation, asking that appropriate action be taken to reflect his ownership of the shares. Turpin brings an action against Swanson Company, demanding that he be adjudged the owner of the stock, that Swanson Company be required to issue a new certificate in his name, and that he be paid a dividend that had accrued since the certificate was transferred to him. Decision?

6. Defendant corporation sold 100 shares of stock for $25,000 to the plaintiff without having obtained a permit from the state division of corporations as required by the Corporate Securities Act. Plaintiff knew the defendant had not obtained a permit to sell the stock. Plaintiff attended and participated in shareholder meetings for two years and accepted dividends. The defendant corporation is now insolvent, and the plaintiff sues to rescind the sale. Decision?

7. S learned that A, B, and C were about to form a corporation to produce and market a line of automobile accessories. S had patented a tamper-proof steering column lock but lacked funds to market it successfully. A, B, and C agreed to purchase S's patent rights for cash and 200 shares of preferred stock in the corporation. XYZ Inc., when formed, issued the stock to S but refused to make the promised cash payment. XYZ was very profitable due to S's patented lock and had a large earned surplus with a large cash balance on hand. XYZ was about to sell the remainder of the authorized preferred shares, ignoring S's demand to purchase a proportionate share of the stock sold. S sued both to recover the cash payment and to enforce his preemptive rights. Decision?

8. Chase, a certified public accountant, audited the books of Brine's Inc. She negligently certified incorrect information in financial statements on the form required and filed with the SEC. Brine's subsequently went bankrupt. After investigation, shareholders of Brine's discover that Donaldson, president of Brine's, had embezzled large sums from the company and has absconded to parts unknown. The shareholders sue Chase under Rule 10b–5. Chase admits negligence in failing to discover Donaldson's misconduct but defends on the grounds that she had no actual knowledge of the embezzlement. Decision?

9. Z Inc., in seeking to sell a new issue of common stock, registered the issue but made false statements in both the prospectus and registration statement. O was the underwriter of the stock, and RAF acted as the securities broker-dealer. T purchased shares based on the prospectus. The value of the shares fell drastically when the falsity of the information was made public. T sues Z Inc., O, and RAF under the Securities Act of 1933. Z Inc., O, and RAF assert the defense of due diligence and lack of knowledge of untrue statements. Decision?

10. Mr. and Mrs. S are shareholders in AB Inc. They brought a derivative action against AB Inc. and its president, AB Jr., to require AB Jr. to return to the company the value of salary and perquisites provided him in excess of the reasonable value of the services he rendered as president. AB Jr. and AB Inc. defended and requested dismissal of the action on the grounds that Mr. and Mrs. S had failed to try to persuade the directors to take the desired action. Mr. and Mrs. S responded that AB Jr. controlled the directors and that AB Jr. and the board controlled communication with shareholders. Decision?

PART SEVEN

Commercial Papers

CHAPTER TWENTY-FIVE
Negotiable Money Instruments

CHAPTER TWENTY-SIX
Transfer of Money Instruments

CHAPTER TWENTY-SEVEN
Presentment, Discharge, and Banking Procedures

CHAPTER TWENTY-EIGHT
Payment Assurances and Documents of Title

CHAPTER TWENTY-FIVE

Commercial Papers

Jane bought from Pete, a classmate, for $3,000 a used car which was supposed to have a new engine. Pete cheated her. The engine was only newly painted. It was in fact old and leaking oil. Jane immediately placed a stop payment on the $3,000 check she wrote to Pete. Meanwhile, Pete somehow managed to obtain from his bank cash for the check which he endorsed. Because of the stop payment instruction, Jane's bank refused to pay. Pete's bank now brought a suit against Jane. Does Jane have to pay?

This is only an example of the many problems related to negotiable instruments discussed in the following chapters.

Indeed, the subject matter of commercial papers has traditionally been considered intricate and difficult to understand. However, this should not be the case in this Part VII, since serious efforts have been made to explain the concepts in this rather wide area in a systematic and simple fashion. In addition to thorough discussions on negotiable instruments, prospective bankers may learn about banking procedures in Chapter 27. For future importers and exporters, Chapter 28 covers payments assurances, which include letters of credit, bankers' acceptances, and documents of title.

CHAPTER TWENTY-FIVE

Negotiable Money Instruments

25.1 Types of Commercial Papers
Commercial Papers Defined
   Title Documents
   Money Instruments
Promissory Note
   Types of Lending
   Nonnegotiable Loan Agreement
Draft
   Check
   Bank Draft
   Cashier's Check
   Certified Check
   Bill of Exchange

25.2 Requirements of Negotiability
Negotiability
   Writing and Signature
   Promise or Order
   Unconditional Promise or Order
   Sum Certain
   In Money
   Time of Payment
   Order or Bearer
   Additional Recitals
Execution by an Agent
   Disclosed Agency
   Undisclosed Agency

25.3 Other Parties to the Instrument, Endorsements, and Imposters
Parties to Money Instruments
   Bearer
   Holder
   Accommodation Party
   Co-Maker
   Guarantor
   Endorser-Endorsee
Endorsements
   Special
   Blank
   Restrictive
   Without Recourse
   Bank Endorsement
Imposter Provisions

25.1 Types of Commercial Papers

Commercial Papers Defined

Commercial Paper
Paper representing value that can be transferred.

Commercial papers in the broadest sense is a generic and collective term covering any paper representing value that can be bought, sold, or otherwise transferred. Webster defines commercial paper as "paper used in business having a monetary or exchangeable value." On such a broad notion, commercial papers include (1) documents evidencing title of ownership to property as well as (2) documents entitling the owner to certain sums of money. Some of these documents are commercial items that can be traded and transferred. Others are not, though they still represent title.

Title Documents

Title Document
Document evidencing ownership of a property.

Grant Deed and Quitclaim Deed
Documents evidencing title to real property.

Mortgage Agreement and Trust Deed
Documents evidencing lender's interest in borrower's real property.

As to real property, documents such as grant deeds or quitclaim deeds represent an owner's title to property, although as such they are not considered commercial papers and are not transferable. Each time an owner sells his real property, a new deed will have to be executed to transfer the ownership to the buyer. On the other hand, a mortgage agreement or a trust deed, which creates a money lender's interest in the borrower's real property as a security for the loan, constitutes an integral part of the lending arrangement which is usually transferable as an adjunct to the promissory note.

As to personal property, most executory contracts, such as contracts in futures, are commercial papers to the fullest extent. Stock certificates representing a holder's ownership in a corporation are title documents, which are freely bought and sold. In fact, a certificate of ownership of a motor vehicle, though hardly a commercial paper, usually needs to be signed and delivered by the seller to the buyer of the vehicle to signify transfer of ownership. However, the most prominent commercial papers substantiating ownership of goods in trade and commerce are the bill of lading and the warehouse receipt (discussed in Chapter 28).

Money Instruments

Commercial papers include all types of money instruments, such as currency itself, whether domestic or foreign, as well as government and corporate bonds, which are securities representing rights to certain sums of money. However, Article 3 of the Uniform Commercial Code, which is our main focus in this chapter and the following chapter, specifically governs only those money instruments listed in § 3–104(2), i.e.:

(a) a "draft" ("bill of exchange") if it is an order;
(b) a "check" if it is a draft drawn on a bank and payable on demand;
(c) a "certificate of deposit" if it is an acknowledgment by a bank receipt of money with an engagement to repay it;
(d) a "note" if it is a promise other than a certificate of deposit.

Two of the above listed instruments are for our study purposes particularly important, namely the *promissory note* and the *draft*. A check, as defined in the UCC, is essentially a draft.

Certificate of Deposit
A receipt for money, issued by a bank.

A certificate of deposit (CD), on the other hand, is neither a promissory note nor a draft. It is defined as an acknowledgement by a bank of a receipt of money with an engagement to repay the depositor with interest on a certain future date. The future date may be one week up to many years from the date of deposit. As such, it may perhaps be classified as a quasi-promissory note.

When interest rates for such term deposits of under $100,000 were federally regulated a few years ago, only accounts of $100,000 and over were called CDs. With the deregulation of the banking and savings and loan industries, any term deposits can now be called CDs. Withdrawal of the funds prior to the agreed maturity can result in significant penalties.

Banking and savings institutions often issue nontransferable CDs, specifically to minimize exposure to endorsement forgeries. After all, aside from a penalty for an early withdrawal, the depositor can always redeem the certificate virtually on demand. Where the depositor is allowed to negotiate the CD, both transferor and transferee are usually required to register with the depositary bank. A certificate of deposit is negotiable if it meets all the conditions of negotiability as required of a promissory note and a draft.

Figure 25.1 Example of a Non-Negotiable Time Certificate of Deposit

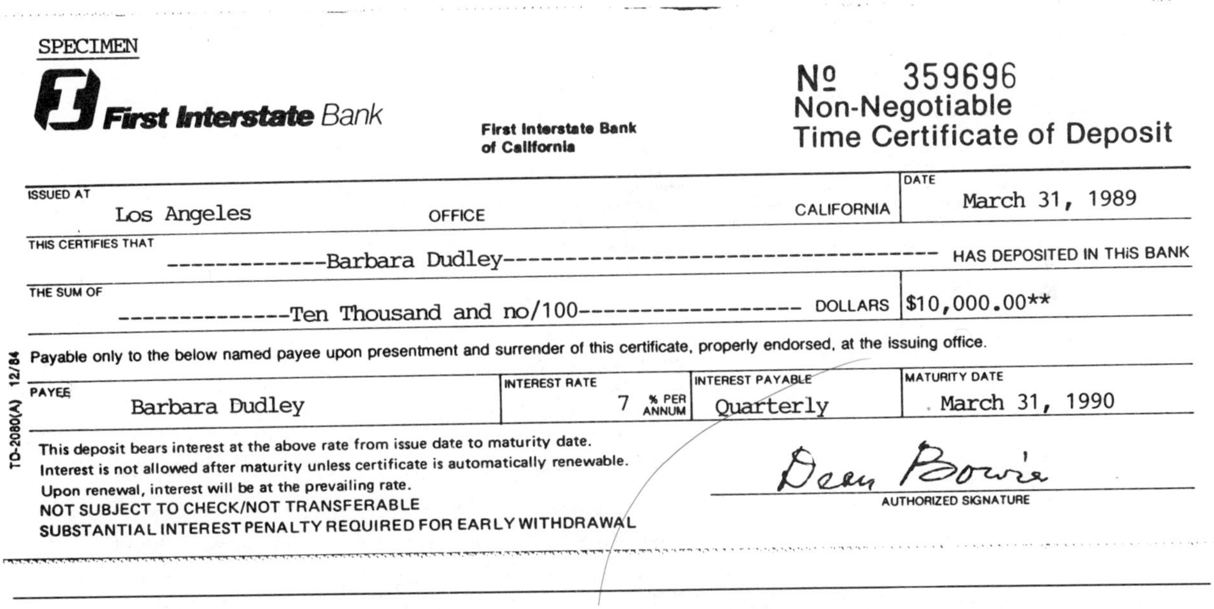
SPECIMEN

First Interstate Bank

First Interstate Bank of California

Nº 359696
Non-Negotiable
Time Certificate of Deposit

ISSUED AT Los Angeles OFFICE CALIFORNIA DATE March 31, 1989

THIS CERTIFIES THAT -------------Barbara Dudley----------------------------------- HAS DEPOSITED IN THIS BANK

THE SUM OF --------------Ten Thousand and no/100----------------- DOLLARS $10,000.00**

Payable only to the below named payee upon presentment and surrender of this certificate, properly endorsed, at the issuing office.

PAYEE	INTEREST RATE	INTEREST PAYABLE	MATURITY DATE
Barbara Dudley	7 % PER ANNUM	Quarterly	March 31, 1990

This deposit bears interest at the above rate from issue date to maturity date.
Interest is not allowed after maturity unless certificate is automatically renewable.
Upon renewal, interest will be at the prevailing rate.
NOT SUBJECT TO CHECK/NOT TRANSFERABLE
SUBSTANTIAL INTEREST PENALTY REQUIRED FOR EARLY WITHDRAWAL

Dean Bowie
AUTHORIZED SIGNATURE

TD-2080(A) 12/84

Promissory Note

Promissory Note
A promise by one party, the maker, to pay another party, the payee.

A promissory note is a lending instrument. The lender provides the borrower the money (or merchandise of equivalent value), and the borrower executes and delivers the promissory note to the lender.

A negotiable promissory note is an unconditional written promise by one party (the maker) to pay a certain sum of money to another party (the payee). It can be payable on demand (if this does not defeat the purpose

Figure 25.2 Example of a Promissory Note (Instalment Note)

First Interstate Bank

INSTALMENT NOTE
(Interest Extra)

$ _____

_____, California

_____, 19 ___

For value received, the undersigned ("Borrower") promises to pay to the order of FIRST INTERSTATE BANK OF CALIFORNIA ("Bank") at its _____ Office, at _____ the principal sum of _____ Dollars ($_____), with interest on the unpaid principal balance payable on demand from the date of this Note until maturity, breach, acceleration or demand, at a rate per annum of _____ percent (_____%), and thereafter, payable on demand, at the rate, calculated daily, which is the higher of (a) 2% per annum above the contractual rate set forth above or (b) 3% per annum above Bank's Prime Rate, until paid in full. Prime Rate is an index rate which Bank establishes from time to time in connection with pricing certain of its loans. Bank may make loans at, above or below its stated index rate. Information on the current index rate can be obtained by contacting Bank. Any change in the floating rate in (b) above shall be effective the day Prime Rate changes. Principal shall be payable in _____ instalments of _____ Dollars each on the _____ day of _____, beginning on the _____ day of _____, 19 ___, and continuing _____ until _____, 19___, on which last mentioned date all remaining principal and interest shall be due and payable.

Interest shall be calculated on the basis of a 365/366-day year for actual days elapsed. If interest is not paid when due, it shall thereafter bear like interest as principal.

Borrower may prepay this Note, without premium or penalty, in whole or in part, with accrued interest to the date of such prepayment on the amount prepaid. Borrower shall pay any loss resulting from such prepayment incurred by Bank in liquidating or redeploying deposits from which such loan funds were obtained. Any prepayment shall be applied to the instalment payments of principal in inverse order of maturity.

Any of the following shall constitute an event of default under this Note whether committed by or against Borrower, any endorser or any guarantor:
(a) The nonpayment when due of principal of or interest on this Note or any other obligation of any nature or description to Bank;
(b) The death, dissolution or termination of business of any of them;
(c) Any petition in bankruptcy being filed by or against any of them or any proceedings in bankruptcy, insolvency or under any other laws relating to the relief of debtors, being commenced for the relief or readjustment of any indebtedness of any of them, either through reorganization, composition, extension or otherwise;
(d) The making by any of them of an assignment for the benefit of creditors;
(e) The appointment of a receiver of any property of any of them;
(f) Any seizure, vesting of rights of or intervention by or under any authority of any government;
(g) The entry of a judgment against any of them which, in Bank's opinion, materially impairs the ability of any of them to meet their obligations to Bank;
(h) The failure to furnish any financial information upon the reasonable request of Bank; or
(i) Any misrepresentation to Bank in obtaining credit by any of them.

At any time after the occurrence of any such event of default, this Note and any other obligations to Bank of Borrower may, at Bank's discretion, become immediately due and payable.

Both principal and interest on this Note are payable in lawful currency of the United States of America without deduction for or on account of any present or future taxes, duties or other charges levied or imposed on this Note.

If this Note is placed in the hands of an attorney for collection, Borrower, each endorser and each guarantor agree to pay all costs and expenses of Bank, including reasonable attorneys' fees, whether or not a suit is brought. "Reasonable attorneys' fees" shall include reasonable attorneys' fees and allocated costs of in-house counsel incurred in any and all judicial, bankruptcy and other proceedings (including appellate level proceedings) whether such proceedings arise before or after entry of a final judgment.

All extensions of time for payment, whether by operation of law, judicial proceedings, or otherwise, shall be included in the computation of interest.

All obligations under this Note shall be the individual obligation of Borrower unless requisite corporate action has been taken to make this Note an enforceable corporate obligation, and all such obligations shall be the joint and several obligations of each Borrower where there is more than one.

Borrower, each endorser and each guarantor waive diligence, demand, presentment, protest and any type of notice.

This Note shall be governed and construed in accordance with the laws of the State of California.

Name of Borrower

Signature   Signature   Title

Address   Signature   Title

                                                       Signature   Title

NAME		LOAN NUMBER	DUE	
RATE	AMOUNT	CCI NUMBER	PRODUCT LINE	PURPOSE CODE

For value received, I endorse and guarantee the payment of the Note on the reverse, at the times and according to the terms expressed in the Note, with all costs of collection, including reasonable attorneys' fees in any action on said Note or on this guarantee, whether or not a suit is brought, and authorize the granting of extensions of time or other indulgences to maker and alterations and amendments of any instruments securing said Note and sales of and the taking and releasing of any security, the discharging or releasing of any party or parties, and the making of compositions or other arrangements with the maker or principal, all without notice to me and same shall not affect my liability. I waive the right to require the holder of this Note to proceed against the maker or any other party or to proceed against or apply any security the holder may hold, and waive the right to require the holder to pursue any other remedy for my benefit, and agree that the holder may proceed against me for the amount guaranteed without taking any action against the maker or any other party and without proceeding against or applying any security the holder may hold. Each married person who executes this guarantee agrees and assents to the liability of any separate property of that person now owned or hereafter acquired for any and all debts and obligations owed to the holder of this Note secured by any mortgage, deed of trust or other hypothecation of any of the community property. This guarantee shall be the joint and several obligations of each of the undersigned where there is more than one. Diligence, demand, presentment, protest and any type of notice are waived.

		PAYMENTS			
				CREDITED ON	
	DATE PAID	INTEREST PAID TO	INTEREST	PRINCIPAL	BALANCE OF PRIN UNPAID

of borrowing) or at a stated future time. It can be made payable to *order,* in which case the payee may order that it be paid to another person, or to *bearer,* i.e., the person in possession of the instrument (UCC § 3–104[1]). It is a two-party instrument.

Types of Lending

A loan can be unsecured or secured by collateral. If it is unsecured, the promissory note may be the only loan document. If the loan is secured by a real property, the note is accompanied by a mortgage agreement or a trust deed. If it is secured by a personal property, a security agreement and a financing statement may be attached to the note. The lending criteria, credit judgment, and interest rates for a secured loan are different from those of an unsecured loan. Moreover, institutional lenders usually make a clear distinction between a commercial and a consumer loan.

Nonnegotiable Loan Agreement

A loan agreement that does not meet the requirements of a negotiable promissory note is nevertheless valid between the lender and the borrower. For example, in a credit card arrangement, where the actual amount borrowed by the customer fluctuates within the line of credit extended, the credit agreement lacks negotiability. Such a loan agreement, though not negotiable, may under the general rule of contracts still be assigned. The difference between negotiation and assignment is explained in the next chapter.

Draft

A draft is an unconditional written order by one party (the drawer) to another party (the drawee) to pay a certain sum of money on demand or at a stated future time to a third party (the payee) (UCC § 3–104[2][a]). A draft is a three-party instrument.

    The reason for the drawee to make the payment on the drawer's draft is an account relationship between them in which the drawee owes money to, holds money for, or is prepared to lend money to the drawer. Anyone, whether a bank, a company, or an individual, can be a drawer or a drawee.

    A draft is an instrument of payment. If it is payable on demand, it is called a *sight draft,* as opposed to a *future draft,* which is payable at some future time.

Draft
An order by one party, the drawer, to another party, the drawee, to pay a third party, the payee.

Check

A check is a draft drawn by a bank customer on his bank and is payable on demand (UCC § 3–104[2][b]). Legally, the payee may immediately proceed to the drawee bank, and, upon proper identification, endorse and cash the check. Such personal identification is technically not required if the payee happens to be the customer of the same bank. If the payee deposits the check at his own bank, the depositary bank will usually not release the funds until the check is actually paid by the drawee bank.

Check
A draft drawn on a bank for payment on demand.

Figure 25.3 Example of a Draft

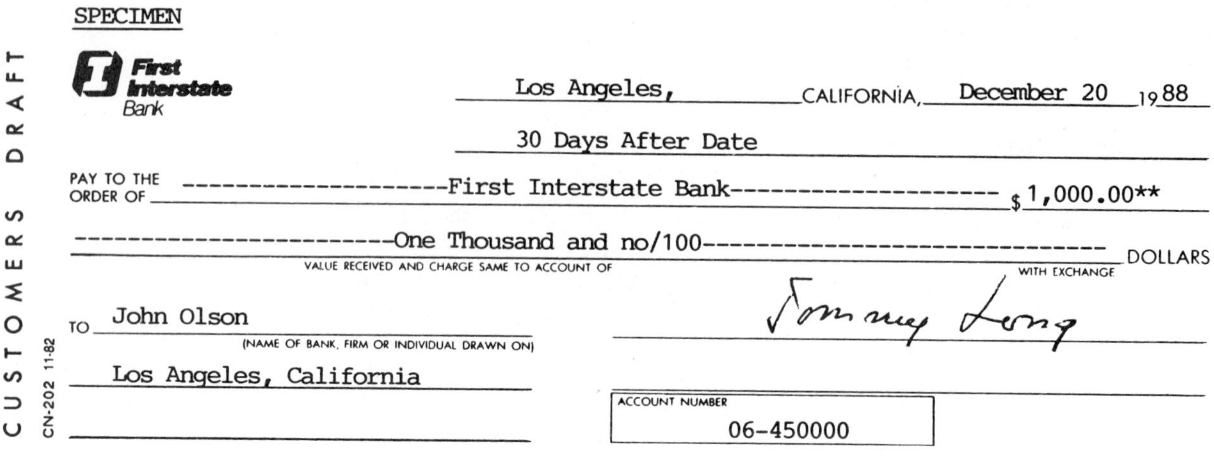
SPECIMEN

CUSTOMERS DRAFT

First Interstate Bank

Los Angeles, CALIFORNIA, December 20 1988

30 Days After Date

PAY TO THE ORDER OF --------------------First Interstate Bank-------------------- $1,000.00**

-----------------------One Thousand and no/100------------------------------ DOLLARS

VALUE RECEIVED AND CHARGE SAME TO ACCOUNT OF — WITH EXCHANGE

TO John Olson

(NAME OF BANK, FIRM OR INDIVIDUAL DRAWN ON)

Los Angeles, California

Tommy Long

ACCOUNT NUMBER 06-450000

CN-202 11-82

Figure 25.4 Example of a Check

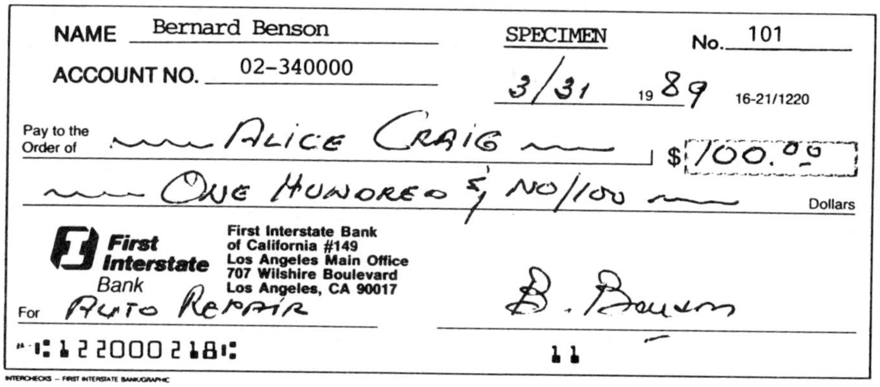
NAME Bernard Benson SPECIMEN No. 101

ACCOUNT NO. 02-340000 3/31 1989 16-21/1220

Pay to the Order of Alice Craig $100.00

One Hundred & no/100 Dollars

First Interstate Bank

First Interstate Bank of California #149 Los Angeles Main Office 707 Wilshire Boulevard Los Angeles, CA 90017

For Auto Repair B. Benson

⑆122000218⑆ 11

INTERCHECKS — FIRST INTERSTATE BANKGRAPHIC

Bank Draft

Bank Draft
A draft drawn by one bank upon another bank.

A bank draft is a draft drawn by one bank upon another bank. Here again, there must be an account relationship between the two banks so that the drawee bank is prepared to make the payment to the designated payee.

A bank draft is a convenient device for moving funds from place to place. A purchaser who plans to travel to another country to do some purchasing but does not wish to carry money may obtain a bank draft from his hometown bank drawn on a bank at the place of destination. This is especially true if a large amount of money is involved, in which case traveler's checks in small denominations become impractical.

Cashier's Check

A cashier's check is a draft drawn by a bank on itself ordering the payment of a certain sum of money to the named payee. From the payee's point of

Figure 25.5 Example of a Cashiers Check

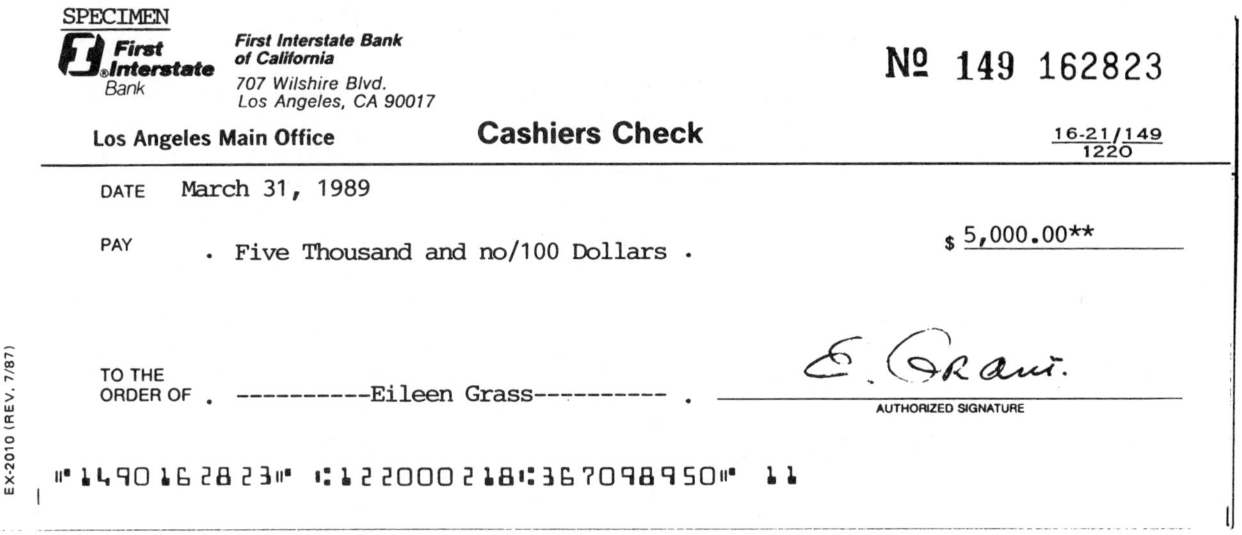
SPECIMEN
First Interstate Bank
First Interstate Bank of California
707 Wilshire Blvd.
Los Angeles, CA 90017
Nº 149 162823
Los Angeles Main Office
Cashiers Check
16-21/149
1220
DATE March 31, 1989
PAY . Five Thousand and no/100 Dollars .
$ 5,000.00**
TO THE ORDER OF . ----------Eileen Grass---------- .
AUTHORIZED SIGNATURE
EX-2010 (REV. 7/87)

view, a cashier's check is usually preferred over a personal check, particularly if the payor is unknown to the payee. Unlike a personal check, which is subject to sufficiency of the drawer's funds at the paying bank, a cashier's check renders the bank itself liable for payment of the instrument. It should be noted, however, that a cashier's check is not the same as cash. It is still a check subject to problems, such as a stop payment and the issuing bank's insolvency, which seldom occur.

Cashier's Check
A draft drawn by a bank on itself.

Certified Check

A certified check is a check drawn by a bank depositor across the face of which an officer of the bank or some other authorized person has stamped the word *certified* and signed his name on behalf of the bank. Such a certification signifies the bank's guarantee that sufficient funds have been set aside from the depositor's account to pay the check when payment is demanded. Essentially, certification of a check is similar to acceptance of a draft (discussed in Chapter 28). Again, a certified check is still a check, and apart from the question of liability, it may still be stop paid.

Certified Check
A check drawn by a bank depositor, and guaranteed by the bank to be backed with sufficient funds.

Since the stated check amount is only earmarked and not actually withdrawn from the customer's account, the bank is exposed to some administrative error or oversight, which can result in the account's being depleted before the certified check is presented for payment. Therefore, certifying a check has slowly become a practice of the past. Today banks more and more prefer to issue a cashier's check instead of certifying a customer's check. In so doing, the payment amount is deducted immediately from the customer's account.

As people are not expected to carry large sums of money, a cashier's check is usually considered as good as cash. There are occasions, however, in which the legal distinction between all these money instruments becomes important, as illustrated in the following case.

Perry v. West
110 N.H. 351, 266 A.2d 849 (1970).

Kenison, Chief Justice The issue in this case is whether a municipality can be compelled to accept a bid for property sold for taxes accompanied by a bank draft or a cashier's check when the municipal ordinance and the announced terms of the auction sale require the bid to be accompanied by "cash or certified check." The facts are not in dispute and the issues have been completely argued and briefed by the parties.

Plaintiffs submitted the highest bid at an auction sale of certain property within the City of Concord conducted by George M. West, Tax Collector, as real estate agent for the City. The City had previously acquired the property by tax sale. . . . The advertisements appearing in the *Concord Daily Monitor* . . . required that all bids be accompanied "by cash or certified check in an amount to at least 10% of the bid price." Plaintiffs' high bid was accompanied by a bank draft of the New Hampshire Savings drawn on the Mechanicks National Bank and payable to George West, Tax Collector. The second highest bid, submitted by Henry J. Love, was accompanied by a cashier's check of Concord National Bank payable to the City of Concord. The third highest bid was submitted by Pasquale Alosa and accompanied by United States currency. Lockwood Realty Company submitted the fourth highest bid accompanied by its check certified by the Mechanicks National Bank. . . .

On the day of the auction, November 17, 1969, defendant West, on the advice of the City Solicitor, sent a letter to Alosa and the Perrys advising them that Alosa was the successful bidder. On November 19, 1969, the City executed a quitclaim deed to the property in favor of Alosa, which was never recorded. After a hearing on November 20, 1969, in Merrimack County Superior Court on the petition of the Perrys, the City was ordered to execute and deliver a deed to the Perrys. None of the other bidders was made a party at this hearing. On November 21, the City executed a quitclaim deed in favor of the Perrys which was delivered and recorded.

Alosa filed a petition to enter the action as party defendant which was granted. After a hearing on November 25, 1969, the Court enjoined the Perrys from encumbering, transferring or dealing with any rights of ownership in the property. The other bidders were subsequently added as parties. Defendants' exceptions to the granting of the petition of the Perrys have been reserved and transferred by *Loughlin*, J.

Plaintiffs contend that the bank draft submitted with their bid was "cash" within the modern usage of the term and therefore their bid complied with the terms of the auction. . . .

. . . Although the meaning of "cash" may vary with the context of its use, the common meaning is United States currency. . . . Nothing in the present case indicates that the City Council intended to expand this meaning. Indeed the term "certified check" would be unnecessary if "cash" were to include various forms of commercial paper in addition to currency.

The various commercial instruments involved in this case have definite and distinct meanings. A bank draft is merely the instrument of one bank drawing upon its deposits with another bank. A cashier's check is the instrument of a bank drawing upon its own funds. . . . Certification of a check is acceptance by the drawee.

For this case the important distinction among these instruments is the number of parties liable on the instrument. Bank drafts and cashier's checks are "one-name paper." Only the drawer bank is liable on a bank draft until accepted by the drawee. Although a cashier's check is accepted upon issuance, there is only one bank involved and therefore only one party bound on the instrument.... However both the drawer and drawee are bound on a certified check.... There are therefore accepted and reasonable distinctions among "cash," "certified check," "bank draft" and "cashier's check" upon which the City Council could base its preference for cash or certified check. Within the context of the auction of property sold for taxation the phrase "cash or certified check" had a definite, unambiguous and accepted commercial meaning....

The general rule that a municipality must accept the highest bid, ... only requires acceptance of the highest bid which conforms to the terms of the auction sale consistent with the governing municipal ordinance.... The City did not waive the bidding requirements. It rejected the two highest bids which did not comply with the terms of the auction and accepted the bid accompanied by currency. Subsequent compliance with a court order was not a waiver of the terms by the City. Acceptance of the Perrys' bid by defendant West could have subjected him to personal liability....

Both the City and the public were entitled to rely upon the terms of the auction sale and the controlling ordinance and this court will not compel the City to waive the conditions in the advertisements and Ordinances.... All bidders must have equal opportunity and the city officials must not be required to make subjective evaluations of the apparent financial integrity of the bidders.... Certainty in bidding procedures by which all bidders are on an equal basis should not be discouraged in the disposition and sale of municipal property.

Pasquale Alosa, the highest bidder who conformed to the terms of the auction, is therefore entitled to the property upon full payment of his bid price....

Remanded.

Bill of Exchange

Although foreign trade may be conducted on a cash or an "open account" basis, the most common method of international payment is the bill of exchange, which, as recognized by UCC § 3–104(2)(a), is a draft. Both terms are used interchangeably, though draft is technically a general term that also includes checks and other three-party instruments. In a bill of exchange, the seller/exporter is the drawer. He draws a draft on the buyer/importer, designating himself or a third party, usually his bank, as the payee.

Bill of Exchange
A draft used primarily in foreign trade to facilitate payment for export/import goods.

Tenor or Usance The point in time when the drawee is required to pay or accept a bill of exchange is called tenor or usance. In this respect, the following are types of bills of exchange:

Tenor or Usance
Point in time when drawee is required to pay a bill of exchange.

1. A *sight draft* (S/D) calls upon the drawee to pay upon presentation. Since the bill of exchange is usually dispatched by mail, whereas the merchandise is transported by freight lines, its presentation might take place before the goods arrive, which may not be desirable for the importer/drawee.

Sight Draft
Draft payable upon presentation.

2. An *arrival draft* ("on arrival") requires payment by the drawee upon arrival of the shipment. As the arrival time is uncertain—or the entire shipment in fact may never arrive—such a bill of exchange is not negotiable because of its lack of a definite or ascertainable due date. To

Arrival Draft
Draft payable upon arrival of the shipment.

circumvent this problem, a sight draft, instead of an arrival draft, may be employed, followed by an instruction to the collecting bank to defer presentation of the draft until the goods have actually arrived.

3. A *future draft* is a draft payable some time in the future. The future date has little to do with the arrival of the merchandise. It is a date pre-agreed upon by the seller/exporter and the buyer/importer, and it is often nothing but an extension of credit to allow the importer to sell the goods before paying for the bill of exchange. Examples of a future draft are a draft payable "Thirty Days After Sight" (30 Days S/D) and "date" drafts, such as a draft payable "Ninety Days After Date" (90 Days D/D). Upon presentation of the draft by the payee or collecting bank, the drawee accepts the draft in recognition of his liability to pay on the specified future date. The bill of exchange then becomes an acceptance.

Future Draft
Draft payable at a certain future time.

Documents Since a bill of exchange is usually drawn in conjunction with a sale and shipment of merchandise, more often than not it is accompanied by documents pertaining to the goods, i.e., (1) an ocean bill of lading, (2) a marine insurance certificate, or (3) a commercial invoice. Such a bill of exchange is called a *documentary draft,* as opposed to a *clean draft,* which does not have such attachments.

Collection Because of geographic distances, the drawer/exporter uses a third party, usually a bank, to collect the funds from the drawee/importer. The bank can be the drawer's home bank, which in turn utilizes its branch office or a correspondent bank operating at the drawee's location. The drawer may also bypass the home bank and employ a bank at the drawee's location to facilitate the collection process. A future draft is presented to the drawee first for acceptance and then, at the maturity date, for payment. An international bill of exchange is commonly drawn in duplicate, with each copy dispatched separately. The second copy becomes valueless if the first copy arrives safely.

The collection of a documentary bill of exchange is called documentary collection or "Documents Against Payment" (D/P). The law of agency applies between the drawer as principal and the collecting bank/payee as agent. The authority of the collecting bank is derived from the drawer's explicit collecting instructions, which include the following:

Documentary Bill of Exchange
Bill of Exchange accompanied by documents relating to the shipment.

D/P
Documents Against Payment.

1. A clear identification of the drawee, his address, and other ways to reach him.
2. Whether the shipping documents are to be surrendered to the drawee against acceptance of the draft or against payment.
3. Whether or not acceptance or payment may be deferred until arrival of the goods.
4. Whether or not the drawee may inspect the merchandise before accepting or paying the draft.
5. What the collecting bank must do in the event of nonacceptance or nonpayment, including an instruction as to the disposition of the merchandise.
6. Whether interest and collection charges are to be borne by the drawee and whether these charges are to be waived if the drawee refuses to pay them.

NEGOTIABLE MONEY INSTRUMENTS

7. The name and address of the drawee's representative or attorney who should be informed if collection problems occur.

Questions

1. What is the meaning of the term "commercial papers" in the broadest sense?
2. What do money instruments include?
3. Describe a promissory note.
4. Describe the various types of drafts.
5. What is the bill of exchange? Who are the parties to the instrument?

25.2 Requirements of Negotiability

Negotiable instruments are contracts. As explained in Subchapter 9.3, most contracts are assignable. If a contract is assigned, the transferee under the general rules of contract will have the same rights and be exposed to the same defenses, such as fraud, duress, and incapacity, as the assignor.

A negotiable instrument is not only assignable but also negotiable. Negotiation differs from assignment in that the transferee, under given circumstances, may actually be in a better position than an assignee because of his immunity to some defenses, as explained in Subchapter 26.3. For example, a thief cannot pass title to stolen goods. But a thief of a negotiable instrument can pass a good title to the instrument to a purchaser for value without notice of the theft. For this reason, it is important to know the requirements of negotiability of such an instrument.

The requirements of negotiability must be met by the instrument itself without extraneous assistance from separate understandings or arrangements, as illustrated in the following case.

Negotiable Instrument
A contract that can be assigned as well as negotiated.

First State Bank at Gallup v. Clark
91 N.M. 117, 570 P.2d 1144 (1977).

Easley, J. First State Bank of Gallup (First State), Plaintiff-Appellee sued M. S. Horne (Horne), Defendant-Appellant on a promissory note. The trial court granted summary judgment against defendant and we affirm.

Horne had executed a $100,000 note in favor of R. C. Clark which contained a restriction that the note could not be transferred, pledged or assigned without the written consent of Horne. As part of the transaction between Horne and Clark, Horne gave Clark a separate letter authorizing Clark to pledge the note as collateral for a loan of $50,000 which Clark anticipated making with First State. Clark did make the loan and pledged the note, which was accompanied by Horne's letter authorizing the note to be used as collateral. First State also called Horne to verify that he was in agreement that his note could be accepted as collateral. First State attempted to collect from Horne on Horne's note to Clark which had been pledged as collateral. Horne refused to pay and this suit resulted.

The issues raised on appeal include (1) whether the note was a negotiable instrument for purposes of Article 3 of the Uniform Commercial Code (U.C.C.). . . . Article 3 of the U.C.C. defines a certain type of readily transferable instrument and lays down certain rules for the treatment of that instrument and rules concerning the rights, remedies and defenses of persons dealing with it.

In order to be a "negotiable instrument" for Article 3 purposes the paper must precisely meet the definition set out in § 3–104, since § 3–104 itself states that, to be a negotiable instrument, a writing "must" meet the definition therein set out. Moreover, it is clear that in order to determine whether an instrument meets that definition *only the instrument itself* may be looked to, *not* other documents, even when other documents are referred to in the instrument. [Citations.] As Hart & Willier, 2 Bender's U.C.C. Service, *Commercial Paper,* § 2.03[1] points out in its text and in footnote 3:

> The applicability of Article 3 must be determined from the instrument itself, without reference to other documents or oral agreements. The "four-corners test" is still applicable: the determination of negotiability under Article 3 must be made by inspecting only the instrument itself. . . . This is clear from the mandatory language of U.C.C. § 3–104, and from the following language from the Official Comment to U.C.C. § 3–105 found under the heading "Purposes of Changes": "The section is intended to make it clear that, so far as negotiability is affected, the conditional or unconditional character of the promise or order is to be determined by what is expressed in the instrument itself. . . .

We recognize the Official Comments to the U.C.C. as persuasive, though they are not controlling authority. [Citation.]

Section 3–104 thus requires that, in order to be a negotiable instrument for Article 3 purposes, one must be able to ascertain without reference to other documents that the instrument:

> (a) [is] signed by the maker or drawer; and (b) contain[s] an unconditional promise or order to pay a sum certain in money and no other promise, order, obligation or power given by the maker or drawer except as authorized by [Article 3]; and (c) [is] payable on demand or at a definite time; and (d) [is] payable to order or to bearer.

The note in question here failed to meet the requirements of § 3–104, since the promise to pay contained in the note was not unconditional. Moreover, the note was expressly drafted to be non-negotiable since it stated:

> This note may not be transferred, pledged, or otherwise signed without the written consent of M. S. Horne.

These words, even though they appeared on the back of the note, effectively cancelled any implication of negotiability provided by the words "Pay to the order of" on the face of the note. Notations and terms on the back of a note, made contemporaneously with the execution of the note and intended to be part of the note's contract of payment, constitute as much a part of the note as if they were incorporated on its face. [Citation.]

. . . Since the note in question is not negotiable for Article 3 purposes, First State cannot be a holder in due course under Article 3, and we need not discuss that issue.

. . . The summary judgment of the district court is hereby affirmed for the [other] stated reasons, although we reject the trial court's conclusion that the note in question was a negotiable instrument as contemplated by Article 3.

Negotiability

Under UCC § 3–104(1):

> "Any writing to be a negotiable instrument within this Article must
> (a) be signed by the maker or drawer; and
> (b) contain an unconditional promise or order to pay a sum certain in money and no other promise, order, obligation, or power given by the maker or drawer except as authorized by this Article; and
> (c) be payable on demand or at a definite time; and
> (d) be payable to order or to bearer."

An instrument that does not meet the requirements of negotiability may still be a valid agreement between the original parties, whose rights and obligations are governed by the general law of contracts.

Writing and Signature

A negotiable instrument must be in writing, which includes handwriting, typing, printing, and engraving. Ink or pencil may be used. Pencil is not advisable, however, because it is not so durable as ink and can be easily altered. Since a negotiable instrument is a written instrument, the parole evidence rule applies in that testimony to modify the instrument by proving the existence of a conflicting oral agreement alleged to have been made before or at the time of the execution of the commercial paper is not admissible.

The maker or drawer must sign the instrument. The signature may be in one's own handwriting or be printed, engraved, or stamped. The signature may consist of initials, figures, or a mark (UCC § 1–201[39]). It need not be at the end, but it must appear somewhere on the instrument. However, if a signature is placed on the instrument in such a manner so as to result in an uncertainty whether the signer was the maker, drawer, or acceptor, the signer may be considered only as an endorser.

Promise or Order

If the instrument is a promissory note, it must contain a promise to pay money; if it is a draft or check, it must contain an order to pay money. An acknowledgment of a debt is not a promise, e.g., "I.O.U., John Smith, the sum of $10,000 (signed) Robert Williams." An authorization to pay money is not an order, e.g., "We hereby authorize you to pay on our account, to the order of William Smith, the sum of $10,000." Such instruments are not negotiable, since there is no promise to pay and no order to pay.

Unconditional Promise or Order

The promise and the order must not be conditional. UCC § 3–105(2) states: "A promise or order is not unconditional if the instrument . . . states that it is subject to or governed by any other agreement. . . ." Thus, when the obligation to pay is dependent upon the delivery of merchandise, the completion of the construction of a building, or the rendering of certain services, the promise or order is conditional and nonnegotiable. An instrument is also conditional if "it is to be paid only out of a particular fund or source...."

However, an instrument that merely "indicates a particular account to be debited or any other fund or source from which reimbursement is expected" is not conditional, e.g., "charge my expense account" (UCC § 3–105[1][f]).

Facts

Liberty Advertiser executed a note in favor of the Bank of Viola that read:

> "For value received, the undersigned promises to pay to the Order of Bank of Viola, Viola, Illinois, the principal sum of *$15,884.54*, payable in installments or as follows: Or *payable $80.00 per week from Jack & Jill contract*, with interest at the rate of 8.00 percent per annum from date until paid." [Italicized segments handwritten in original]

At the trial, the "Jack & Jill" reference was identified as one of the defendant's advertisement contract. The trial court declared the note to be conditional, as it was to be paid from a particular fund.

Decision

Judgment reversed. "Negotiability is favored in the law.... It follows that construing an instrument as unconditional is favored in the law. An instrument may be unconditional which indicates a particular account or fund or source from which reimbursement is expected."

Bank of Viola v. Nestrick, 72 Ill.App.3d 276, 28 Ill.Dec. 469, 390 N.E.2d 636 (Illinois, 1979).

An instrument that is limited to payment out of a particular fund is not conditional if issued by the government (UCC § 3–105[1][g]).

Sum Certain

If the instrument is to be negotiable, it must call for the payment of a sum certain, i.e., definite on its face as to how much is to be paid. The sum payable is a sum certain even though it is to be paid with stated different rates of interest before and after default or a specified date (UCC § 3–106[1][b]) or with costs of collection or an attorney's fee, or both, upon default (UCC § 3–106[1][e]).

However, if the actual interest rate to be charged is not clearly specified and consequently the sum of money to be paid on the instrument is uncertain, the paper is not negotiable.

Facts

Hotel Evans executed a promissory note containing a promise to pay $1,600 with "interest at bank rate." Alport, a subsequent holder of the note, brought a lawsuit when Hotel Evans defaulted. Maker's defense was that the note was not negotiable as it contained an indefinite interest rate.

Decision

Judgment for the defendant. The promissory note was not negotiable, since it did not contain the unconditional promise to pay sum certain. As the instrument provided for "interest at bank rate," the amount due on the note could not be readily determined and thus did not qualify as a sum certain.

A. Alport & Sons, Inc. v. Hotel Evans, Inc., 65 Misc.2d 374, 317 N.Y.S.2d 937 (1970).

In Money

The instrument must call for payment in money. UCC § 3-107(1) provides: "An instrument is payable in money if the medium of exchange in which it is payable is money at the time the instrument is made. An instrument payable in 'currency' or 'current funds' is payable in money." An instrument payable in goods or services is not negotiable, even if such items are stipulated as a substitute for money.

Money includes foreign currency. Unless specifically stated that the instrument may only be paid in the specified foreign money, a foreign currency instrument may be paid in U.S. dollars, into which the foreign currency is to be converted "at the buying sight rate for that currency on the day on which the instrument is payable or, if payable on demand, on the day of demand" (UCC § 3-107[2]).

Time of Payment

An instrument is negotiable if it is payable on *demand* or at a *definite future* time. A stated future time is not definite if it refers to the happening of a certain event that may never take place, for example, "when John is 21 years old" or "when Jane marries." This is shown in the following case.

Facts

Barton executed in favor of SHRAM a promissory note for $3,000 due and payable "upon evidence of an acceptable permanent loan of $290,000 for Barton-Lugwig Cains Hill Place Office Building, Atlanta, Georgia, from one of SHRAM's investors and upon acceptance of the commitment by the undersigned." SHRAM managed to obtain a loan commitment for Barton, and Barton did execute the commitment. However, Barton refused to pay on the note on the grounds that the note did not contain a specific due date and that the loan had in fact not been made. The trial court entered a judgment in favor of SHRAM.

Decision

Judgment affirmed, although the promissory note was not negotiable. "This 'promissory note' by its terms was made payable 'upon evidence of an acceptable permanent loan . . . and upon acceptance of the (loan) commitment'; however under Code Ann. Ch. 109A-3-104(1)(c) a negotiable instrument must 'be payable on demand or at a definite time.' The 'note' here was not payable on demand under the language of S. 109A-3-108, and under S. 109A-3-109(2) '(a)n instrument which by its terms is otherwise payable only upon an act or event uncertain as to time of occurrence is not payable at a definite time even though the act or event has occurred.'" The trial court found that SHRAM earned the $3,000 when Barton accepted the loan commitment. Consequently, its summary judgment for SHRAM was correct, as there was a valid agreement between these original parties, although the instrument per se was not negotiable.

Barton v. Scott Hudgens Realty & Mortgage, Inc. (SHRAM), 136 Ga.App. 565, 222 S.E.2d 126 (1975).

Instruments payable on demand include those payable at sight or on presentation and those in which no time for payment is stated (§ 3-108). An instrument is payable at a certain future time if this future time can be determined from the face of the instrument itself. In *McLean* v. *Paddock* (78 N.M. 234, 430 P.2d 392 [1967]), a certain promissory note dated August 9, 1958, was declared negotiable, as it read:

> "For value received, I, we, or either of us promise to pay to Harper Realty, or order, the sum of Twelve Thousand Three Hundred Eighty-eight and 20/100

Dollars, said amount to be paid in equal installments of Seventy-Five and no/100 Dollars, each, payable monthly after date beginning _____ 1, 1958, and on the first day of each month thereafter until the whole amount first herein named and any interest or costs shall have been paid in full. . . ."

For the court, it was clear that the first payment was intended to be on September 1, 1958.

Under UCC § 3–109(1), an instrument has a definite time of maturity if it is payable (a) on or before a stated date, (b) at a fixed period after a stated date, (c) at a fixed period after sight, (d) at a definite time subject to any acceleration, (e) at a definite time subject to extension at the option of the holder, (f) at a definite time subject to extention to a further definite date at the option of the maker or acceptor, or (g) at a definite time subject to an extension to a further definite date upon or after the occurrence of a specified act or event.

The following case shows that an instrument does not lose its negotiability if it is antedated or postdated (§ 3–114).

Facts

In 1964, S. Gentilotti wrote a check for $20,000, payable to the order of his son, Edward J. Gentilotti. The check was postdated November 4, 1984, which would be his son's twentieth birthday. The father also wrote on the check that it should be paid from his estate if he died before November 4, 1984. The check was given to Edward's mother for safekeeping. The father died on May 31, 1972. When the check was presented to the bank, the bank refused payment. Mother and son sued the estate's executor, who claimed that the check was not negotiable, as it was postdated.

Decision

Judgment for the plaintiffs. The fact that a check is postdated does not affect its negotiability; it is simply payable on the stated date. However, the drawer's instructions to the bank to pay the check if the drawer died before November 4, 1984, accelerated the due date and rendered the check immediately payable from the drawer's estate.

Smith v. Gentilotti, 371 Mass. 839, 359 N.E.2d 953 (1977).

Unless some kind of fraud is involved, the date on the instrument is presumed to be the true date whether or not it was originally inserted. It should be noted, however, that regardless of the date on the instrument, the payee and any other holders acquire title to the instrument on the date of delivery.

An undated instrument is considered to be dated on the day it is executed and delivered to the payee. Without malicious intent, such as an attempt of forgery or unauthorized completion, the payee or any holder who knows the actual date may insert that date, specifically when the instrument is payable on a certain number of days, weeks, or months "after date."

Order or Bearer

The instrument to be negotiable must be made payable to order or to bearer. When it is stated on the instrument that it is payable to the order of a specified person (e.g., "Pay to the order of John Smith" or "Pay to John

Order Instrument
Is payable to a certain party and is negotiated by an endorsement and delivery.

Bearer Instrument
Is payable to the bearer and is negotiated by delivery alone.

Smith or order") it is an order paper. John Smith would have to *endorse and deliver* the instrument to negotiate it (UCC §§ 3–110, 3–202[1]).

An instrument is payable to bearer when it is payable to bearer or the order of bearer, a specified person or bearer, or cash or the order of cash (e.g., "Pay to bearer" or "Pay to John Smith or bearer") (UCC § 3–111). Bearer paper can be negotiated by *delivery alone* (UCC § 3–202[1]).

In *Hall* v. *Westmoreland, Hall & Bryan* (123 Ga.App. 809, 182 S.E.2d 539 [1971]), an attorney's client wrote the following letter: "I agree to pay to your firm as attorney's fees for representing me in obtaining property settlement agreement and tax advice, the sum of $2,760, payable at the rate of $230 per month for twelve (12) months beginning January 1, 1970. . . . Very truly yours, Barbara Hall Hodge." This instrument was not negotiable, as it was not made payable to order or to bearer.

A promissory note payable to order is also not negotiable if it does not specify a named payee (*Broadway Management Corp.* v. *Briggs* [30 Ill.App.3d 403, 332 N.E.2d 131 (1975)]). A traveler's check is a negotiable instrument provided it is written to the order of a named person or to bearer (*Gray* v. *American Express Company* [34 N.C.App. 714, 239 S.E.2d 621 (1977)]).

Additional Recitals

Many promissory notes and bonds of corporations contain additional recitals that may or may not affect negotiability. Negotiability is not affected by the following (UCC § 3–112):

1. Such recitals as an authorization of a confession of judgment (the debtor permits judgment to be entered against him for a stipulated sum without institution of legal proceedings; such proceedings are not permitted in many states).
2. Statement that collateral has been given for the instrument.
3. Statement that the debtor waives the benefit of any law intended for his benefit (not permitted in many states).
4. Statement that the endorsement by the payee is an acknowledgment of full satisfaction of the debt.
5. Notations on the check as to the purpose for which the check was given or the items discharged by the check.

A provision authorizing the holder of the instrument to require an act other than the payment of money (e.g., delivery of goods) makes the instrument nonnegotiable (UCC § 3–104[1][b]).

Execution by an Agent

The fact that an instrument is executed by an agent of the maker or drawer does not impair the instrument's negotiability. The Uniform Commercial Code does not prescribe any specific form of an agent's authorization. Except in a case of forgery, the maker or drawer can still be liable for the instrument executed by his agent or employee without authorization.

```
            ┌─────────────────────────────────┐
            │    U. S. International, Corp.   │
            │                                 │
            │         by  Nel Peterson        │
            │           Nel Peterson, President│
            └─────────────────────────────────┘
```

Disclosed Agency

An agent of a maker or drawer discloses the agency if on the instrument itself he identifies his principal *and* indicates that he executes the instrument in a representative capacity. Thus, if an officer of a corporation executes an instrument, the name of the corporation must appear on the face of the document and the officer's signature must be preceded or followed by his corporate designation. If these requirements are met as shown in the accompanying example, only the principal and not the agent is liable for payment on the instrument.

Undisclosed Agency

On the other hand, an agent is personally liable for executing an instrument if the agency is not disclosed, whether or not the nondisclosure was intended. Nondisclosure takes place when the principal is not identified on the instrument. An agent who discloses the principal but fails to state his representative capacity is jointly and severally liable with the disclosed principal for payment of the instrument (UCC § 3–403[2]).

Facts

Griffin, president of Greenway Building Company, was an authorized corporate signer who executed a number of drafts drawn on the Northeast Bank in favor of Ellinger. Griffin signed only his name on these drafts that had the corporation name printed at the top. The drafts were not paid, and Ellinger sued Griffin personally. Griffin defended on the ground that he was only acting in a representative capacity.

Decision

Judgment for Ellinger. The corporate name printed on the draft did not change the fact that Griffin signed his individual name without disclosing his representative capacity or his corporate designation. Accordingly, he was personally liable.

Griffin v. Ellinger, 538 S.W.2d 97 (Tex., 1976).

A similar case is *Tesoro Petroleum Corp. v. Schmidt* (210 Neb. 537, 316 N.W.2d 290 [1982]).

Questions

1. Explain the basic difference between assignment and negotiation.
2. What are the requirements of negotiability?

3. When is a promise or an order unconditional? When is it conditional?
4. Give a case example in which an instrument was not negotiable because of the absence of a specific date of maturity.
5. Who is liable for payment if an instrument is executed by an agent in a disclosed agency?

25.3 Other Parties to the Instrument, Endorsements, and Imposters

Parties to Money Instruments

There may be other parties to the paper in addition to the maker and payee of a promissory note and the drawer (or maker), drawee, and payee of a draft.

Bearer

Anyone who possesses an instrument made payable to "Bearer" or to "Cash" is called a bearer. Similarly, if an instrument is written to "the order of" a named payee, after the payee endorses the paper in blank, the instrument becomes a bearer paper, and anyone who has possession of it is also called a bearer. Unlike an order paper, which is negotiated by an endorsement of the named transferor and delivery of the instrument to the transferee, a bearer paper may be negotiated by the delivery of the instrument alone.

Bearer
Anyone possessing an instrument payable to "bearer" or to "cash."

Holder

A holder is a person who has the possession of the instrument made payable or endorsed to him or his order or made payable to bearer or endorsed in blank. Thus, all bearers are holders, but not all holders are bearers. For example, a note or a check written and delivered to Mary Smith makes Mary a payee and a holder but not a bearer. If Mary subsequently endorses the paper in blank and delivers it to Tom Fontain, Tom becomes not only a holder but also a bearer. If the instrument is endorsed by Mary to the order of Tom Fontain, the paper must be re-endorsed by Tom for further transference.

Holder
A person possessing an instrument made payable or endorsed to him or his order or in blank, or made to bearer.

A holder is simply a possessor of the instrument without necessarily having title to the paper. A thief or a finder of a bearer paper is certainly not an owner but is nonetheless a holder. Since a bearer paper as such does not need another endorsement for further transference, the thief or finder may, apart from questions related to defenses and adverse claims, legally negotiate the instrument to the next holder, who may become a holder in due course.

A holder "for value" is a holder who gives consideration for the instrument he receives. A holder "in due course" is a person who is a holder for value, in good faith, and without notice of any defense to the instrument. All of these are explained in the next chapter.

Accommodation Party

Accommodation Party
One who signs an instrument as a co-maker or guarantor, without receiving value therefor.

The term *accommodation party* is not well defined in the Uniform Commercial Code. Section 3–415(1) simply states: "(A)n accommodation party is one who signs the instrument in any capacity for the purpose of lending his name to another party to it." Black defines accommodation party as "(O)ne who has signed an instrument as maker, drawer, acceptor, or indorser without receiving value therefor, and for purpose of lending his name to some other person as means of securing credit."

In actual practice, specifically in banking, the term is seldom used. If a party, whether a natural person or a corporation, is to hold himself liable in the event that the real maker does not meet his obligation on a money instrument, he usually becomes either a *co-maker* or a *guarantor*. Particularly, when a bank is to lend money to a partnership or a corporation that is wholly owned by a few individuals, the partnership or the corporation becomes the maker of the promissory note, whereas the owners become co-signers or guarantors. The purpose is to make these owners liable with their personal assets if their firm or company fails to meet its obligation to the bank. Similarly, if Mary is unable to borrow from a bank because of her unsteady income, her older sister Jane, who is an established wage earner, may become a co-signer or guarantor to assure the bank that she will repay the loan in the event that Mary defaults.

In the event that the maker or drawer defaults in the payment, can the co-maker or guarantor deny liability on the ground that he did not receive any value from the instrument? Generally, the answer is no, since the benefit received by the real maker or drawer as well as the obligee's reliance on his participation in the arrangement is usually considered sufficient consideration to hold him liable.

Facts

Pitrolo Pontiac Co., a corporation, borrowed money from Community Bank. Paul Pitrolo and his wife, who ran the automobile dealership, wrote on the note that they guaranteed its payment. The corporation defaulted, and Community Bank sued the Pitrolos. The defenses raised were based on the grounds that (1) the note was made by the corporation and (2) the Pitrolos did not personally receive value for the guaranties.

Decision

Judgment for Community Bank. (1) The fact that the maker of the note was a corporation was immaterial, since the Pitrolos acted in their separate capacities as guarantors. (2) The fact that the bank lent money to the corporation, as requested by the Pitrolos, was sufficient consideration for the Pitrolos to be held responsible as guarantors. Indeed, as accommodation parties, the Pitrolos personally are not to receive any value from the arrangement.

Pitrolo v. *Community Bank & Trust Co.,* ___ W.Va. ___ 298 S.E.2d 853 (1982).

UCC § 3–415(5) states that "(A)n accommodation party is not liable to the party accommodated, and if he pays the instrument has a right of recourse on the instrument against such party."

Co-Maker

As to liability, there is nevertheless an important difference between a co-maker and a guarantor. A co-maker places his signature on the instrument itself adjacent to that of the maker and often on the same dotted line. Thus, although he does not receive actual consideration for signing the paper, he in fact makes the same promise or order as the maker himself. There is technically no necessity for the holder or obligee to prove default of the maker before he can reach the co-maker, since the co-maker is legally as liable as the maker for paying the instrument. It is common practice, however, that the lender does not call for the co-maker unless the actual borrower defaults.

Co-Maker
One who assumes liability equal to the maker, signing the instrument in the same place as the maker.

Guarantor

A guarantor, on the other hand, signs either on the instrument itself with the words "payment guaranteed" or "collection guaranteed" or on a separate guarantee agreement in which he agrees to pay in the event the primary obligor defaults. The term *guarantee* means assumption of liability upon default of the original promisor. UCC § 3–416(1) provides: " 'Payment guaranteed' or equivalent words added to a signature mean that the signer engages that if the instrument is not paid when due he will pay it according to its tenor without resort by the holder to any other party." Thus, default by the primary party is, in this situation, necessary before the guarantor becomes liable for payment. Yet, a legal action against him is not required as illustrated in the following case.

Guarantor
One who guarantees payment in the event the primary obligator defaults.

Facts
Brown University extended a student loan to Ruth Laudati, who wrote a promissory note guaranteed by her mother, Josephine. Ruth defaulted on the note, and Brown University brought an action against Josephine. Josephine raised the defense that the university had not sued Ruth for the repayment of the loan.

Decision
Judgment for Brown University. A guarantor on a money instrument may be sued upon default on the paper by its maker. The holder is not required to proceed against the maker before suing the guarantor. In fact, he may choose not to sue the maker at all.

Brown University v. *Laudati,* 113 RI 926, 320 A.2d 609 (1974).

The term *collection guaranteed* goes even further, in that the guarantor becomes liable "only after the holder has reduced his claim against the maker or acceptor to judgment and execution has been returned unsatisfied, or after the maker or acceptor has become insolvent or it is otherwise apparent that it is useless to proceed against him" (UCC § 3–416[2]). Indeed, financial institutions generally considered a guarantor as a secondary source of repayment, similar to a collateral.

Figure 25.7 Example of a Guarantee

GUARANTEE

1. This guarantee is given in consideration of any financial accommodations given, or to be given, or continued, by First Interstate Bank of California ("Bank"), to _____

("Customer"). The undersigned unconditionally guarantees the prompt payment of all indebtedness and liabilities of the Customer to the Bank according to the terms thereof or as agreed in any financial statement, application, note or other document executed by the Customer, which the Customer may now or at any time hereafter owe to the Bank, whether arising from dealings between the Bank and the Customer or from other dealings by which the Bank may be or become in any manner whatever a creditor of the Customer, to the extent of and not exceeding at any one time the principal sum of _____ Dollars, with such interest as may be due thereon from the Customer.

2. The undersigned agrees that the Bank may in its absolute discretion and without prejudice to or in any way limiting or lessening the liability of the undersigned under this Guarantee: (a) extend credit to the Customer in such amount and at such times as the Bank may determine, whether for a greater or lesser amount than is hereby guaranteed, and whether the Bank has knowledge of facts with respect to the Customer which might be construed as materially prejudicial to the interests of the undersigned, the Bank being hereby relieved of any duty to disclose any such facts to the undersigned; (b) grant extensions of time or other indulgences; (c) change the interest rate; (d) take or give up or modify, vary, exchange, renew or abstain from perfecting or taking advantage of any security; (e) accept or make compositions or other arrangements or file or refrain from filing a claim in any bankruptcy proceeding of the Customer or other guarantor; (f) discharge or release any party or parties; (g) realize or not realize on any security regardless of effect on the undersigned's subrogation or reimbursement rights; (h) apply payments in such manner and order of priority as the Bank sees fit; and (i) otherwise deal with the Customer and any co-guarantor and other parties and security as the Bank may deem expedient.

3. This shall be a continuing guarantee and shall cover all indebtedness and liabilities of the Customer, and where more than one, the several obligations of each as well as their joint obligations, including those incurred up to such time as the Bank shall have actually received written notice of revocation of this Guarantee by the undersigned. Such revocation shall not affect the undersigned's obligations to the Bank with respect to indebtedness or liabilities of the Customer to the Bank arising prior to actual receipt by the Bank of such revocation. Notwithstanding any notice of revocation, if at any time all or any part of any payment theretofore applied by the Bank to any indebtedness or liability of the Customer is or must be rescinded or returned by the Bank for any reason whatsoever, such indebtedness or liability shall for the purpose of this Guarantee, to the extent that such payment is or must be rescinded or returned, be deemed to have continued in existence notwithstanding such application by the Bank, and this Guarantee shall continue to be effective or be reinstated, as the case may be, as to such indebtedness or liability as though such application by the Bank had not been made.

4. This Guarantee shall secure any balance due or owing from time to time and at any time from the Customer to the Bank, notwithstanding any payments from time to time made to the Bank or any settlement of account or any other thing whatsoever; and no payments made by or on behalf of the undersigned to the Bank shall be held to discharge or diminish the continuing liability of the undersigned hereunder unless written notice is given to the Bank at the time of making such payments that the same are being made for the purpose of liquidating such liability; and, until full payment of all indebtedness and liabilities (including interest), present and future and whether or not payment thereof is guaranteed hereby, of the Customer to the Bank, the undersigned waives all right of subrogation and all benefit of or right to participate in any security now or hereafter held by the Bank.

5. All demands, presentments, notices of protest and of dishonor and notices of every kind or nature, including those of any action or non-action on the part of the Customer, the Bank, any co-guarantor, or any creditor of the Customer, the Bank, or any co-guarantor, or any other person whomsoever, are expressly waived by the undersigned. The undersigned hereby waives the right to require the Bank to proceed against the Customer, any co-guarantor or any other party or to proceed against or apply any security it may hold, and waives the right to require the Bank to pursue any other remedy for the benefit of the undersigned, and agrees that the Bank may proceed against the undersigned for the amount hereby guaranteed without taking any action against the Customer, any co-guarantor or any other party and without proceeding against or applying any security it may hold. The undersigned waives the right to plead any and all statutes of limitations as a defense to this Guarantee and to any indebtedness or liability hereby guaranteed, and agrees that any partial payments by or on behalf of the Customer on any indebtedness or liability hereby guaranteed, including interest, shall, as of the time each such payment is made, stop the running of the time within which an action may be commenced upon this Guarantee and shall constitute a further waiver by the undersigned of the right to plead any and all statutes of limitations as a defense to this Guarantee and to any indebtedness or liability hereby guaranteed. As to the Bank, the undersigned further waives any right of contribution the undersigned may have against any co-guarantor or other party.

Figure 25.7 Continued

6. All debts and liabilities, present and future, of the Customer to the undersigned, or any of them, are hereby postponed to the liabilities of the Customer to the Bank, and all moneys received by any of the undersigned or their representatives, successors or assigns thereon, shall be received as trustees for the Bank and shall be paid over to the Bank; and the undersigned and each of them further agree, upon any liquidation or distribution of the assets of the Customer, to assign to the Bank upon its request all claims on account of all such debts and liabilities, to the end that the Bank shall receive all dividends and payments on such debts and liabilities until payment in full of all liabilities of the Customer to the Bank; and this agreement shall constitute such an assignment in the event the undersigned shall fail or refuse to execute and deliver such other or further assignment of such claims as the Bank may request.

7. Where the Customer is a corporation, partnership, or other association or receiver, trustee or other fiduciary, the Bank is not to be concerned to see or inquire into the powers of the Customer or its directors, officers, partners, associates or other agents acting or purporting to act on its behalf, the undersigned hereby representing that such powers exist, and moneys in fact borrowed from the Bank in the professed exercise of such powers shall be deemed to form part of the liabilities guaranteed, even though the borrowing or obtaining of such moneys be in excess of the powers of the Customer or of the directors, partners, officers, associates or other agents thereof, or shall be in any way irregular or defective or informal.

8. When the Customer is a partnership or other association, this Guarantee is to extend to the person or persons for the time being and from time to time carrying on the business now conducted by the Customer, notwithstanding any change or changes in the name or membership of the Customer's firm.

9. Married persons who execute this Guarantee hereby agree and expressly assent to the liability of their separate property for any and all obligations hereunder.

10. The undersigned agrees to pay a reasonable attorney's fee and all other costs and expenses which may be incurred by the Bank in connection with this Guarantee or in the collection of any of said indebtedness or liabilities from the Customer or the undersigned.

11. This Guarantee is assignable with any or all of the indebtedness or liabilities which it guarantees, and when so assigned the undersigned shall be bound as above to the assignees without in any manner affecting the undersigned's liability hereunder on any part of said obligations retained by the Bank.

12. This Guarantee shall inure to the benefit of and bind the heirs, administrators, executors, successors and assigns of the Bank and each of the undersigned, and shall be construed as the joint and several obligation of each of the undersigned where there is more than one. Where there is more than one Customer named herein, reference herein to "Customer" shall mean all and any one or more of them and the words used herein in the singular shall be deemed to have been used in the plural where the context and construction so require. This Guarantee shall be construed in accordance with the laws of the State of California. Notice of acceptance of this Guarantee is hereby waived.

13. This Guarantee is in addition to and exclusive of the guarantee(s) of any other guarantor(s) and of any and all prior guarantees of any of the undersigned of indebtedness or liabilities of the Customer to the Bank; and this Guarantee shall in no way limit or lessen any other liability, howsoever arising, of any of the undersigned for payment of indebtedness or liabilities which are hereby guaranteed.

14. No terms or provisions of this Guarantee may be changed or amended without the written consent of the Bank. Should any provision of this Guarantee be determined to be unenforceable by a court of competent jurisdiction, all other provisions shall remain effective.

Dated: _____.at: _____ , California.

_____   _____
_____   _____

Endorser-Endorsee

A payee of a promissory note or a draft, especially if the instrument is payable at some future date, may transfer the instrument by endorsing (also spelled "indorsing") and delivering it to another party. This is called negotiation. The payee then becomes an endorser, and the transferee is called the endorsee.

Endorser
A person who transfers his right to an instrument by signing his name, usually on the back of it.

Endorsee
The recipient of a transfer made by an endorsement.

The usual way of endorsing a money instrument is to sign one's name on the back of the paper. A rubber stamp may also be used, particularly where the paper is not to be further negotiated. An endorsement may be made on the front of the paper, but this may expose the endorser to the possibility of being seen as a co-maker or a co-drawer of the instrument, even though UCC § 3–402 provides: "Unless the instrument clearly indicates that a signature is made in some other capacity it is an indorsement."

When there is no space left on the instrument for one's signature, an endorsement may made on a piece of paper, called an *allonge*, "so firmly affixed thereto as to become a part thereof" (UCC § 3–202[2]).

Lopez v. Puzina
239 Cal.App.2d 708, 49 Cal.Rptr. 122 (1966).

Molinari, Justice   Plaintiffs, John and Emanuela Lopez, as holders of a promissory note, brought this action against defendants, Milo and Nora Puzina, as alleged endorsers of this note. From the judgment of nonsuit entered against them plaintiffs appeal. The sole issue presented is whether defendants are endorsers of the subject note so as to give plaintiffs a right to recover against them upon the refusal of the makers to pay.

The subject note dated July 15, 1958 in the principal sum of $4,298.26, payable to the order of Anthony Joseph Caruso and Marie Doris Caruso, his wife, was executed by Robert W. Lesco and Willa Mae Lesco, his wife, and delivered to said payees. The note recited that it was secured by a deed of trust. The Carusos subsequently assigned the note to the Puzinas without recourse by an assignment affixed to the note. Thereafter, on July 23, 1958, the Puzinas delivered the note to plaintiffs as part payment for a parcel of real property sold by plaintiffs to the Puzinas. No endorsement or assignment was endorsed upon or physically affixed to the note. . . .

When the note became due and payable on July 15, 1963 it was presented by plaintiffs to the Lescos for payment of the face amount, plus interest then due in the sum of $1,719.30. Payment having been refused, plaintiffs brought the instant action on the subject note against the Lescos, as makers, and the Puzinas upon a complaint alleging that the Puzinas were endorsers of the note. A demurrer to the complaint, interposed by the Puzinas, was overruled and the cause proceeded to trial against them. At the conclusion of plaintiffs' case the Puzinas made a motion for nonsuit which was granted and judgment was entered thereon.

In order to hold defendants liable on the subject promissory note as endorsers thereof it was incumbent upon plaintiffs to establish that the note was endorsed by defendants. At all times relevant to this action Civil Code, section 3112 provided for the manner by which an endorsement must be made as follows: "The indorsement must be written on the instrument itself or upon a paper attached thereto."

. . . In the instant case there is no endorsement on the note itself. It is contended by plaintiffs, however, that the endorsement of the note is to be found on the instrument entitled "Assignment of Deed of Trust," bearing defendants' signatures and providing in the language hereinabove set out verbatim that they had "endorsed," assigned and transferred to plaintiffs the subject deed of trust together with the promissory note therein mentioned. It should be noted here that it is not contended by plaintiffs that the subject "Assignment of Deed of Trust" was physically attached to the subject promissory note.

> The crucial question presented, accordingly, is whether a promissory note can be endorsed by an instrument which is separate from the note. . . .
>
> Plaintiffs make the further contention that, since section 3112 provides that "The signature of the indorser, without additional words, is a sufficient indorsement," the "*allonge*" provided for in that section merely refers to a paper which contains only a signature. Accordingly, they argue, an endorsement consisting of a signature with additional words may be made on a separate paper or instrument. This contention is without merit. Section 3112 specifically provides that "*The indorsement*," if not written on the instrument itself, "*must* be written . . . upon a paper attached thereto."
>
> . . . Having determined that under California law defendants did not effectively endorse the subject note we conclude that they are, by the terms of the "Assignment of Deed of Trust," merely assignors of the note. . . . As such they are not liable upon the note upon the obligor's failure to pay, since an assignor of a promissory note does not by the mere fact of assignment warrant that the obligor is solvent or that the assignor will perform the obligor's obligations. . . .
>
> The judgment is affirmed.

In *Lamson* v. *Commercial Credit Corporation* (187 Colo. 382, 531 P.2d 966 [1975]), where an endorsement of two pages long was involved, the court was even more specific as to how an allonge must be attached to the instrument. To quote verbatim:

> The subject indorsement was typed on two legal size sheets of paper. It would have been physically impossible to place all of the language on the two small checks. Therefore, the indorsement had to be "affixed" to them in some way. Such a paper is called an allonge. In this case the allonge was affixed by stapling it to the checks.
>
> We agree with the Court of Appeals' statement that a separate paper pinned or paperclipped to an instrument is not sufficient for negotiation. However, we hold, contra to its decision, that the section does permit stapling as an adequate method of firmly affixing the indorsement. Stapling is the modern equivalent of gluing or pasting. Certainly as a physical matter is it just as easy to cut by scissors a document pasted or glued to another as it is to detach the two by unstapling. Therefore we hold that under the circumstances described, stapling an indorsement to a negotiable instrument is a permanent attachment to the checks so that it becomes "a part thereof."

The endorsee may again transfer the paper by endorsing and delivering it to another endorsee. This process may continue usually until the maturity date of the instrument is reached. UCC § 3–414(2) provides: "(U)nless they otherwise agree indorsers are liable to one another in the order in which they indorse, which is presumed to be the order in which their signatures appear on the instrument."

An endorsement pertains to the entire amount on the instrument. An endorsement referring to only a part of the amount due has the effect of an assignment, which prevents the transferee from becoming a holder in due course. When an instrument is made payable to a person under a misspelled name or one other than his own name, the person may endorse in that name or his own name or both, provided there is no criminal or malicious intent. Signature in both names may be required by a person paying or giving value for the instrument (UCC § 3–203).

Facts

Louis Agaliotis took out an insurance policy on his son Robert. Louis paid all the premiums and, under the terms of the policy, was entitled to all premium refunds. By mistake the insurance company sent Louis a refund check for $1,852 made payable to Robert L. Agaliotis. Louis endorsed the check "Robert L. Agaliotis" and cashed it. His son Robert sued Louis to recover the money.

Decision

Judgment for the defendant. There was a simple mistake by the insurance company. Under the insurance policy, the check was supposed to be written to the father, Louis Agaliotis. Louis could endorse the check (1) in the incorrect name, (2) in his own name, or (3) in both names. In any event, he was entitled in this case to endorse in the incorrect name and retain the proceeds.

Agaliotis v. *Agaliotis,* 38 N.C.App. 42, 247 S.E.2d 28 (1978).

A single endorsement or a bank endorsement is sufficient if the instrument is a check to be deposited to a joint account of both named payees (*Callahan* v. *C & S State Bank* (150 Ga.App. 62, 256 S.E.2d 666[Georgia, 1979]).

When an instrument is made payable to two or more persons jointly, e.g., "Pay to the order of Peter Gray *and* John Green," all of them must endorse to negotiate the instrument. When an instrument is made payable to two or more persons severally (i.e., in the alternative), for example, "Pay to the order of Peter Gray *or* John Green," the single endorsement of either of them is sufficient for further negotiation.

Like a guarantor, the endorser assumes liability if the instrument is not paid in accordance with its terms. In addition, the endorser provides certain warranties to the next holders of the paper. Subchapter 26.1 details these important legal consequences resulting from an endorsement.

Endorsements

The Uniform Commercial Code recognizes four kinds of endorsements: special, blank, restrictive, and "without recourse" (§§ 3–204, 3–205, 3–206, 3–414[1], 3–417[3]).

Special

Special Endorsement
Specifies to whom or to whose order the instrument is payable.

A special endorsement specifies the person to whom or to whose order the instrument is to be payable, e.g., "Pay to John Smith (signed) Robert Jones" or "Pay to the order of John Smith (signed) Robert Jones." The special endorsee's endorsement (Robert Jones) is necessary for further negotiation of the instrument. The special endorser may also endorse specially or in any other proper form.

The word *order* is not required in a special endorsement. Thus, "Pay to Maria Lopez, Paul Martin," is a valid special endorsement allowing the paper to be further negotiated.

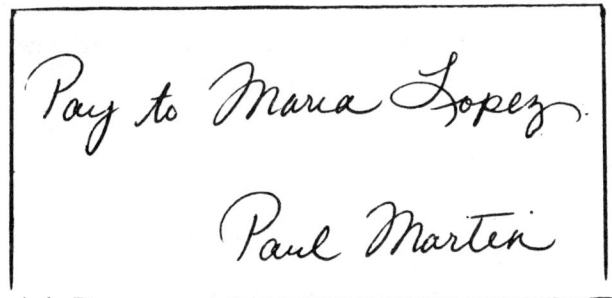

Facts

Fred Klomann was the payee on three promissory notes amounting to $13,000 issued by Robert J. Graff, one of the partners of Sol K. Graff & Sons. Subsequently, Klomann specially endorsed the notes to his daughter, Candice Klomann. Candice examined the notes and handed them back to her father, who was to collect the payment on her behalf. However, Klomann later scratched out Candice's name, inserted his wife Georgia's name, and delivered the notes to his wife. When the maker didn't pay, Georgia Klomann sued to collect.

Decision

The trial court's summary judgment for Georgia Klomann was reversed. Under UCC § 3–204(1), "(A)ny instrument specially indorsed becomes payable to the order of the special indorsee and may be further negotiated only by his indorsement." Merely scratching out the special endorsee's name and inserting Georgia Klomann's name was not the proper way to negotiate the note to her. Once Fred Klomann endorsed the notes to his daughter, he had no more interest in them and had no power to negotiate the notes further. Candice should have endorsed the notes herself and delivered them to Georgia.

Klomann v. *Sol K. Graff & Sons,* 22 Ill.App.3d. 572, 317 N.E.2d 608 (1974).

See also *Casarez* v. *Garcia* (99 N.M. 508, 660 P.2d 598 [1983]).

Blank

A blank endorsement specifies no endorsee and consists of a mere signature. For example, a check payable "to the order of Helen Parker" is endorsed

Blank Endorsement
An endorsement with signature only, not specifying any particular endorsee, thereby creating a bearer instrument.

in blank by Helen Parker simply by signing her name only. An instrument so endorsed is payable to the bearer and may be negotiated by delivery alone.

Facts
Reggie Bluiett received from her employer, the Silver Slipper Gambling Hall and Saloon, her weekly paycheck made out to her name. She endorsed the check in blank and left it on the dresser at home. Freddie Watkins broke into Reggie's house, stole her check and took it to a local auto parts store, where he bought two tires at a price of $71.21. He paid the store with Reggie's check and received the balance in cash.

Decision
The auto store was a holder in due course. After Reggie endorsed the check in blank, it became a bearer paper, which could be negotiated merely by delivery. The check was delivered to the auto store, who had given value for it, was in good faith, and was not aware of any defense.

Watkins v. *Sheriff of Clark County,* 85 Nev. 246, 453 P.2d 611 (1969).

A bearer paper can be converted to an order paper by writing a special endorsement over the blank endorsement, e.g., if John Smith endorses in blank and delivers to Richard Jones, Richard can write above John Smith's signature the words "Pay to Richard Jones." This will protect Richard Jones in case the instrument is stolen, since his signature is now necessary to transfer the instrument. Although blank endorsements are common, they are dangerous to use, since a finder or thief can negotiate by delivery alone.

The negotiation of a blank endorsement passes ownership of the instrument, imposes on the endorser a liability to pay the amount of the instrument under certain conditions, and creates certain warranties (UCC §§ 3–414, 3–417).

In *Palmer and Ray Dental Supply of Abilene, Inc.* v. *First Nat'l Bank,* the Court of Civil Appeals of Texas reviewed the question of whether a blank endorsement on a check was an authorized endorsement making the depositary bank free of liability for payment to a dishonest employee of the maker.

Facts
Palmer and Ray's bookkeeper, Wilson, was instructed to deposit certain checks in the company's account. Wilson brought the checks to the bank and dishonestly cashed them and did not account to the company for the money she received. Wilson endorsed the checks with a rubber stamp that printed only Palmer and Ray's company name and address. Palmer and Ray sued the bank for wrongful conversions of the checks.

Decision
The court dismissed the suit. It held that the endorsements, consisting of only the plaintiff's name and address, were authorized blank endorsements (UCC §§ 1–201[43], 3–204). When the bank delivered cash to Wilson, the bearer, it was not guilty of conversion.

Palmer & Ray Dental Supply of Abilene Inc. v. *First National Bank,* 477 S.W.2d 954 (Tex.Civ.App. 1972).

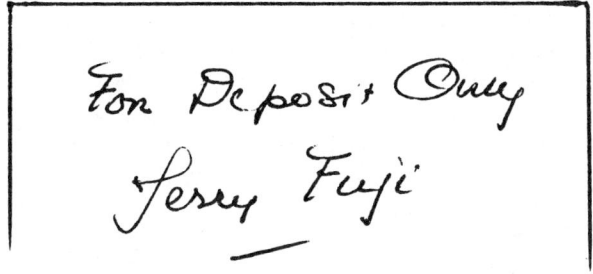

Restrictive

A restrictive endorsement specifies the use to be made of the paper. UCC § 3–205 makes the following endorsements restrictive:

1. A conditional endorsement states that it is to be effective only upon the satisfaction of a specific condition, e.g., "Pay to John Smith upon completion of building." Thus, while a condition imposed by a maker renders the money instrument nonnegotiable, a condition made in an endorsement does not affect the negotiability of the paper (UCC § 3–206[1]). In case of transfer of an instrument that has been endorsed conditionally, the transferee may become a holder in due course subject to satisfaction of the condition. For instance, a payee endorses a paper "Pay to the order of Mr. X, if Mr. X delivers the goods to payee before June 1." If Mr. X renegotiates the paper to Mr. Y, Mr. Y cannot collect from the maker of the note or drawee of the draft unless the merchandise is indeed delivered on or before June 1. In the event that the maker or drawee nevertheless pays Mr. Y, he may be liable again for another payment to payee, the conditional endorser, if the condition imposed by him is not met.

2. A "for collection" or "deposit" endorsement uses such words as "for deposit only, Jerry Fuji," "for collection," or "pay any bank" to show an intention as to the disposition of the instrument.

    Fultz v. *First National Bank in Graham* illustrates the effect of a bank's failure to comply with such an endorsement.

Restrictive Endorsement
An endorsement specifying use or conditions which are required to receive payment for the instruments.

Facts
Fultz (plaintiff) endorsed certain checks "for deposit only." Defendant bank paid part of the amount of the checks to an employee, McCoy, who was not authorized to sign checks on the account or to withhold cash amounts from the deposits made for Fultz and who misappropriated the funds.

Decision
The court held that the bank was liable to Fultz because it failed to follow his instructions carried on the restricted endorsement "for deposit only." The court also ruled that Fultz should have been able to rely on the bank to follow the deposit instructions and was under no further duty to ascertain whether the bank had followed his instructions.

Fultz v. *First Nat'l Bank in Graham*, 388 S.W.2d 405 (Tex. 1965).

A similar case is *O.K. Moving and Storage Co. v. Elgin National Bank* (363 So.2d 160 [Fla.App., 1978]). On the other hand, in *Palmer & Ray Dental Supply of Abilene, Inc. v. First National Bank* (477 S.W.2d 954 [Tex.Civ.App. 1972]) (quoted in the preceding subsection), where the rubber stamp endorsement showed the company's name and address but did not read "for deposit only," the checks became bearer instruments, and the depositary bank was not wrong for allowing the depositing employee to cash them.

Trust Endorsement
Makes endorsee agent or trustee of the endorser.

3. A trust endorsement that makes the endorsee the agent or trustee of the endorser is restrictive in that it states that the endorsement is for the benefit or use of the endorser or another person, e.g., "Pay John Smith as agent for Robert Jones (signed) Richard Paul," "Pay John Smith for account of Robert Jones (signed) Richard Paul," "Pay John Smith in trust for Robert Jones (signed) Richard Paul."

Under UCC § 3–206(1), an endorsement totally prohibiting further transfer of the instrument is ineffective. If a paper is endorsed "Pay to Carol Lake only" or "Pay to Carol Lake and no one else," the word *only* or the words *and no one else* can be ignored; Carol can endorse and negotiate the instrument without legal impediment. As Comment 2 to § 3–206 states, an "only" endorsement "does not of itself give notice to subsequent parties of any defense or claim, of the endorser." It is insufficient to indicate any defect in the instrument that would prevent a transferee from qualifying as a holder in due course. Thus, while a maker may effectively prohibit the further transfer of the instrument by the payee, as shown in *First State Bank at Gallup v. Clark* (91 N.M. 117, 570 P.2d 1144 [1977]) (cited in Subchapter 25.2), an endorser may not.

UCC § 3–206(2) stipulates that "(A)n intermediary bank, or a payor bank which is not the depositary bank, is neither given notice nor otherwise affected by a restrictive indorsement of any person except the bank's immediate transferor or the person presenting for payment." Accordingly, any valid restrictive endorsement on a check or a draft drawn on a bank in effect operates on the path of the instrument until it reaches the depositary bank. The bank clearinghouse or the paying bank does not have to abide by the restriction.

Without Recourse

Without Recourse Endorsement
An endorsement transferring the instrument but limiting the liability of the endorser.

"Without Recourse, Mary Sands," is an example of a nonrecourse endorsement. Such an endorsement limits the liability of the endorser in that the endorser is not liable to the subsequent transferee(s) if the maker becomes insolvent and is not able to pay. Also, an attorney may receive a check written to him for a payment to his client, in which event the attorney endorses the item "without recourse" to his client, as he is not expected to guarantee payment by the maker. A nonrecourse endorsement does not affect the passage of title or the negotiable character of the instrument.

Bank Endorsement

To facilitate the collection on commercial papers by one bank from another, UCC § 4–206 provides: "(A)ny agreed method which identifies the trans-

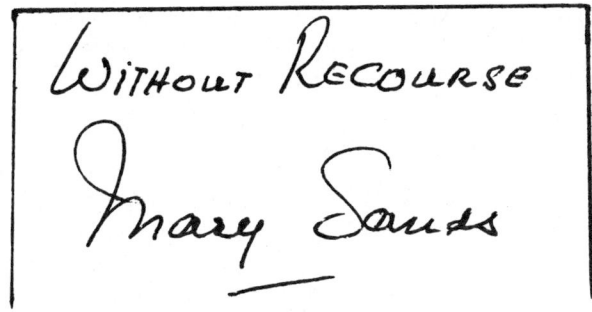

feror bank is sufficient for the item's further transfer to another bank." Hence, a bank may endorse an item with its name initials or its Federal Reserve number. The bank endorsement usually includes the letters "PEG" which stands for "prior endorsements guaranteed."

Unless the instrument specifically requires the payee's personal endorsement, the depositary bank may endorse on behalf of the payee. Simply stamping or marking any notation on the instrument showing that it was accredited to the customer's account is considered to be as effective as the depositor's own endorsement. An example of such a bank endorsement is: "Credited to the Account of the Within Named Payee, Absence of Endorsement Guaranteed."

Imposter Provisions

Only the named payee, the named endorsee, or his agent may endorse the money instrument. An endorsement by any other person is not effective to further negotiate the paper, although "it operates as the signature of the unauthorized signer in favor of any person who in good faith pays the instrument or takes it for value" (UCC § 3–404[1]). However, under UCC § 3–405, such an endorsement *remains effective* in the following situations.

1. An imposter by use of the mails or otherwise has induced the maker or drawer to issue the instrument to him or his confederate in the name of the payee. For example, Peter Crook assumes the name "Jon Bates" and induces the maker, who owes Jon Bates money, to write a note or a draft to the order of Jon Bates. Peter Crook then signs as Jon Bates and further negotiates the instrument.

Facts

A person who claimed to be Wallace Gloss sold a car that he did not own to A & D Motor Sales. A & D issued a check written to Wallace Gloss, and the person subsequently cashed the check at a currency exchange owned by Greenberg. When the check was dishonored, Greenberg sued to recover as a holder in due course.

Decision

Judgment for the plaintiff. ". . . (T)he authorities are fairly in accord in holding that, under the circumstances presented in the case at bar, the impostor's endorsement in the name by which the payee is described is to be regarded as a genuine endorsement between the drawer and the drawee who pays the paper on such endorsement—and is not a forgery. . . .

"The consequences of the mistake should fall upon the drawer rather than on the purchaser, since the mistake is primarily the former's, whether he has himself been deceived or has deliberately tried to shift the burden of identification by giving the imposter a negotiable instrument instead of cash."

Greenberg v. A & D Motor Sales, Inc., 341 Ill.App. 85, 93 N.E.2d 90 (1950).

2. A person signing as or on behalf of a maker or drawer intends the payee to have no interest in the instrument. For example, for tax purposes, Mr. Henry Twist, president of Twist Corporation and an authorized signer, writes an "expense" check to Jerry Ghost, which may be a fictitious or a real name. Twist endorses the check as Jerry Ghost, deposits the check with the drawee bank, and keeps the money.

3. An agent or employee of the maker or drawer has supplied him with the name of the payee intending the latter to have no such interest. For example, Jane Warp, a company's payroll clerk, pads the payroll by inserting some extra names of persons, whether fictitious or real, to it. She issues checks under these names, endorses under the names, and cashes the checks.

Apart from the criminal and civil liabilities of these imposters, their endorsements do not affect the further negotiability of the instrument, which means that the transferee may become a holder in due course. The law seems to consider the imposters in the preceding situations as nevertheless having title to the instrument, allowing them to validly endorse under the payee's name.

The imposter's rules do not apply to cases involving a thief, an embezzler, or a finder who forges the payee's name on a good check and further negotiates the paper. In the imposter cases, the maker is usually the victim of a fraud in the inducement, whereas a forgery by a thief, an embezzler, or a finder deprives the payee and renders the instrument nonnegotiable.

Facts

Magee, the superintendent of Snug Harbor Realty Co., was authorized to examine incoming bills and to instruct the bookkeeper to issue checks for the approved invoices. The checks were then signed by the authorized signer and picked up by Magee for delivery. Magee forged the signatures of certain payees and cashed the checks. Upon discovery of Magee's impropriety, Snug Harbor sued the bank to recover the total amount of the checks.

Decision

Judgment for the plaintiff. The imposter rules do not apply when there is a valid check written for the correct amount to the actual creditor and someone subsequently forges the payee's name, since there was no effective negotiation of the check and payment by the bank to the forger was improper. It is the duty of any bank to identify the presenter who demands payment of the check.

Snug Harbor Realty Co. v. First National Bank, 105 N.J.Super. 572, 253 A.2d 581, affirmed 54 N.J. 95, 253 A.2d 545 (1969).

A similar case is *Danje Fabrics* v. *Morgan Guaranty Trust Co.* (96 Misc.2d 746, 409 N.Y.S.2d 565 [1978]).

QUESTIONS

1. What is the difference between a co-maker and a guarantor?
2. What is an allonge?
3. What is a special endorsement? What is a blank endorsement?
4. Give some examples of a restrictive endorsement.
5. What are the imposter rules?

PROBLEMS

1. The following promissory note has just been executed:

    Atlanta, Georgia
    July 1, 1988
    One year after date, I promise to pay to the order of John Jones Three Hundred and no/100 dollars ($300), at the First National Bank. Value received.
    (signed) Richard Roe

    Who is the maker and who is the payee of this note?

2. The following bill of exchange has just been executed:

    Atlanta, Georgia
    July 1, 1988
    To Bill Brown
    Augusta, Georgia
    Ninety days after date, pay to the order of John Jones Three Hundred and no/100 Dollars ($300) and charge the same to my account. Value received.
    (signed) Richard Roe
    Acct. No. 43–751–02

    Identify the drawer, the drawee, and the payee of this bill.

3. Gordon received a certified check from Bain, a customer, in payment of a bill of goods. He kept the check for a week and then presented it for payment to the bank on which it was drawn. The bank refused to pay it, claiming that Bain had become insolvent since the check was issued and they are no longer liable on the check. Decision?

4. Ace Holder, heavy loser in a business transaction to Willie Win, gives Willie the following instrument: "I.O.U., Willie Win, $10,000. /s/ Act Holder." Is this a negotiable instrument that can be negotiated to a holder in due course? Why?

5. Buyer purchases an automobile from seller and executes a ninety-day note for $500 payable to seller's order. The note provides that buyer has the option of giving seller a color TV set in lieu of cash payment. Seller claims that this note is a negotiable instrument. Decision?

6. Jenson contracted to take a correspondence course and signed an agreement: "In consideration of receiving the lessons in this course, I promise to pay to the order of the Literary Writers Correspondence School $250 in equal installments of $25 each month for ten months, starting one month from the date of this contract."

    A few weeks after giving the note to the school, Jenson received a letter from the North American Bank, stating that the bank had purchased his note and instructing him to send all payments to the bank. Jenson refused, claiming that the agreement he had made was a contract with the school, not a negotiable instrument. Decision?

7. Robert Jones had signed the following instrument: "Los Angeles, California, 7/1/88. I promise to pay to the order of Paul Payee Ten Thousand Dollars ($10,000) one year from date with interest at the rate of 7% per annum from date. If this note is not paid at maturity, it shall bear interest at the rate of 9% per annum from maturity until paid and costs of collection and reasonable attorney fees. (Signed) Robert Jones." A dispute arises as to whether or not this is a negotiable instrument. Decision?

8. Randall was a salesman on a business trip to Tokyo. He called upon a client who purchased several thousand dollars worth of supplies from him and offered to Randall in payment a draft properly drawn on a San Francisco correspondent bank and made payable in yen. Randall refuses to accept, arguing that it is nonnegotiable, since it is made payable in Japanese yen. Decision?

9. Bill Smith was the payee of a check made out to his order. Before it was endorsed, he lost the check. John Finder found the check on the floor of the bank and transferred it without endorsement to Joe

Brown, a holder who paid value and took it without notice that it had been lost. Joe claims that it has been transferred to him by negotiation and that he is a holder in due course. Decision?

10. Wendy sued Harlan for divorce. As a result, Wendy received a property settlement. Under its terms, a demand note signed by Harlan and payable to the order of Wendy's father was later to be transferred to Wendy. Wendy's father delivered the note to Wendy but did not endorse the paper or write anything on the note. When Wendy's father died, Wendy sued Harlan on the note. Harlan refused to pay the note, arguing that Wendy could not sue because she was not the owner of the note. Decision?

CHAPTER TWENTY-SIX

Transfer of Money Instruments

26.1 Liability of the Parties
Promissory Note
Draft or Check
Transfer by Endorsement
    Payment Guarantee
    Warranties
Nonrecourse
Transfer by Delivery

26.2 Holder in Due Course
Basic Requirements
    Value
    Good Faith
    Ignorance of Impropriety
Other H.D.C.s
    The Payee
    Holder Through an H.D.C.
    Reacquirer

26.3 Defenses
Real Defenses
    Forgery
    Material Alteration
    Fraud in the Inception
    Absolute Duress
    Legal Incapacity
    Illegality as to Law
    Consumer Protection
Personal Defenses
    Failure of Consideration
    Lack of Delivery
    Prior Payment or Cancellation
    Unauthorized Completion
    Fraud in the Inducement
    Relative Duress
    Circumstantial Incapacity
    Illegality as to Public Policy
Adverse Claims

26.1 Liability of the Parties

Sooner or later, a money instrument needs to be paid. The holder of the paper, whether he is the original payee or a subsequent transferee, will demand the payment. For a promissory note or a draft payable at sight, the demand must be made within a reasonable time after the stated date or issuance of the instrument, whichever is later (UCC § 3–503[1][b]). For an instrument payable at a certain future date, the demand must be made on or before the date of maturity (UCC § 3–503[1][c]). Demand, also called "presentment," is to be made to the party liable for the payment. There may be more than one party obligated to pay on the instrument. However, one party is primarily liable, while the liability of the other parties is secondary in nature.

It should be understood from the outset that a money instrument is to be regarded separate from the underlying contractual obligation. There is no such underlying obligation if a check is simply a gift from the maker to the payee. However, if the check is written to pay for a sales transaction, the buyer/maker becomes liable for two obligations resulting in separate causes of action, namely his liability to pay for the merchandise bought and his liability to pay for the check. For the first obligation, the buyer is obligated only to the party with whom he has privity in contract based on the sales transaction, i.e., the seller (who is the payee on the check). For the second obligation, he is obligated to the ultimate holder of the check, whoever he may be. Payment on the instrument received by the payee/seller will obviously obliterate the obligation of the maker/buyer to pay for the merchandise. On the other hand, payment on the instrument to a holder other than a payee does not necessarily discharge the maker's obligation in the sales transaction. Suppose that A bought a car from B and paid B with a check. C stole the check from B, forged B's signature, and for some reason managed to cash the check at A's drawee bank. B, who has not been paid for the merchandise sold, may still demand payment from A. In turn, A may demand the bank to credit his account with the same amount of money paid to the forger. This is shown in the *Snug Harbor Realty* and *Danje Fabrics* decisions cited in Subchapter 25.3. In any event, understanding the distinction between these obligations and liabilities is necessary in the study of negotiable instruments.

Underlying Transaction
A transaction, such as a sale, for which a money instrument, such as a check, is written.

Promissory Note

In a promissory note, the liability of the *maker* is primary, which means that the maker will pay the instrument according to its terms at the time of his promise to pay (UCC § 3–413[1]). Despite a proper demand for payment, the maker may nevertheless not pay (1) if he is insolvent (i.e., he does not have the money to pay) or simply is not willing to pay and/or (2) because of certain defenses, i.e., justifications that he may have for non-payment, such as forgery or alteration of the instrument, mistake, fraud, duress, or undue influence. If payment is for some reason refused by the maker, the transferors, whether they are the payee or subsequent transferees, become secondarily liable to the unpaid holder of the instrument.

Maker/Drawer
Maker of a note or drawer of a draft is the party that executes the instrument.

TRANSFER OF MONEY INSTRUMENTS

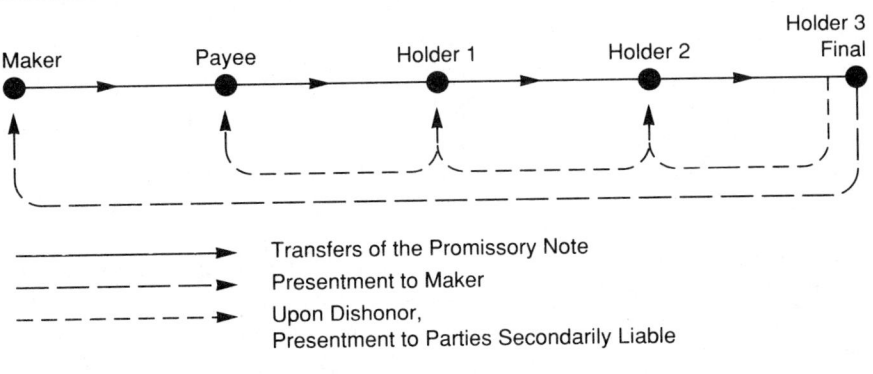

Draft or Check

In a draft, the *drawee or acceptor* is primarily liable for payment. Thus, even though the payee received the instrument from the drawer, he must demand payment from the drawee whether it is a bank or a nonbank party. The liability of the drawer and the other transferees are secondary in that they may have to pay only if the drawee dishonors the instrument (UCC § 3–413[2]). The reasons for a drawee not to pay may be similar to those of a maker of a note previously mentioned. In the case of a check, the maker may not have sufficient funds with the drawee bank, or the maker may have given the bank a stop-payment instruction.

Drawee
Party to whom payment order is directed.

Payee
Party to whom a money instrument is payable.

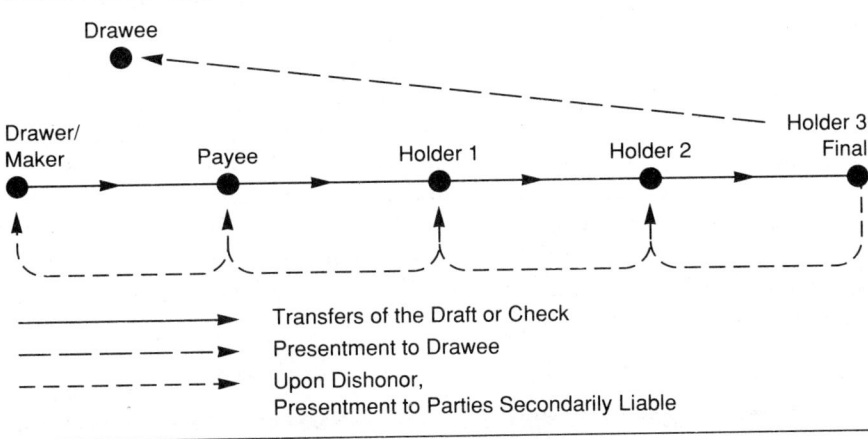

Transfer by Endorsement

As explained in the previous chapter, an order money instrument—as are all order commercial papers—is negotiated by an endorsement by the transferor and delivery of the document to the transferee. Thus, the paper must be delivered to the transferee, although the delivery does not need to be actual or physical, as shown in the following case.

Facts

In an injury settlement case, Catherine Wagner was the recipient of a check for $17,400. She endorsed the check in blank, making it a bearer paper, and placed it on the kitchen table in an apartment she had shared with Robert Scherer for fifteen years. Scherer was the official tenant of the apartment. She afterwards committed suicide by jumping to her death from the roof of the building. Two suicide notes were written, one of which stating that she wished to leave everything she owned to Scherer, including the check. When the police arrived, they took possession of the check. Hyland, the administrator of Wagner's estate, claimed that the check was part of the estate. Scherer claimed that the bearer instrument was effectively delivered to him.

Decision

Judgment for Scherer. Only Scherer had the other key to the apartment, and it was in his apartment where Wagner left the bearer check. Accordingly, the court felt that there was a constructive delivery. Wagner clearly intended to leave the check as a gift causa mortis to Scherer.

Scherer v. Hyland, 75 N.J. 127, 380 A.2d 698 (1977).

But what about the endorsement that the transferor makes? What legal consequence does it have? In essence, there are two types of liabilities that a regular endorser incurs:

1. He *guarantees payment* on the instrument if the primary party defaults.
2. He is liable for the *warranties* he extends to the subsequent transferees, as stipulated in UCC § 3–417.

Payment Guarantee

Here, the endorser's liability to pay on the instrument is related to the primary party's inability or unwillingness to meet his paying obligation. It does not involve defects of the instrument *per se*. Thus, in the event that the maker of a promissory note becomes bankrupt or insolvent, the payment-seeking holder has recourse to the prior endorsers, including the payee, as secondary parties. If the bank does not hold sufficient funds in the account of the maker of the check, the payment-seeking holder has recourse to the prior endorsers, including the payee and the maker, who are secondarily liable. Also, the endorser who signs on the instrument as an accommodation party takes up the same paying liability as a regular endorser. An interesting discourse on this subject of accommodation party endorser is found in the following case.

Jamaica Tobacco & Sales Corp. v. Ortner
70 Misc.2d 388, 333 N.Y.S.2d 669 (1972).

Hentel, J. Plaintiff corporation's secretary-treasurer Froehlich testified that G & R Stationery Corporation was indebted to plaintiff for goods supplied, and on or about July 28, 1971, Froehlich arrived at G & R's place of business along with a City Marshal to replevy against the goods of G & R. At that dramatic moment, Morris Stone, the president of G & R telephoned the defendant Jerry Ortner, which thereupon led to a telephone conversation between Froehlich and the defendant.

Froehlich testified that he had never met the defendant before; that he had previously done business with him over the telephone and thus recognized his voice; that defendant told him on this occasion Stone was a friend, and that he had loaned money to Stone before; that defendant asked Froehlich to call off the replevin proceeding and stated: *"I'll guarantee you will get your money."* [emphasis supplied]. Further, when defendant was asked by Froehlich "will you put it in writing?", the defendant reportedly answered "yes."

Later in this non-jury trial, defendant testified that he received a telephone call from Stone late in July 1971, to the effect that a City Marshal was at Stone's place of business and that he was going to close up his store because he owed money to the plaintiff. The defendant admittedly spoke to the Marshal who told him that Stone would be out of business if he did not pay plaintiff's outstanding bill. The defendant further stated he had done business with Stone for some six prior years, and he recalled his conversation with Froehlich on the telephone on that day and told Froehlich: "If you clean out the store, the store is finished, . . . the Stones are elderly people who are in tears, . . . *I'll sign for them* . . . they (the Stones) promised me they would make good." The defendant also stated that he felt sorry for the Stones and that he was trying to help keep them in business. All of this is corroborative of Froehlich's testimony.

In July 1971, the proof shows G & R owed the plaintiff $2439.80; and also owed the defendant approximately $400.

Following the reported telephone conversation, Froehlich released the City Marshal, the replevin proceeding was halted; and a series of six notes were executed dated July 29, 1971, each in the sum of $406.63 or $406.64, payable to the order of the plaintiff and which were signed by Stone as president of G & R, due on the first of every month commencing September 1, 1971, and concluding on February 1, 1972. After Stone signed the notes, Froehlich sent them over to the defendant by messenger for his signature pursuant to the telephone advice of the defendant. Froehlich instructed an employee to type on the reverse of each note this legend: *"In event of nonpayment then the total amount due of all notes shall become due and payable"* [emphasis supplied] over the blank, underscored line meant for defendant's signature. . . .

The six notes were introduced into evidence with defendant's signature on the back of each note immediately below the quoted italicized legend supra.

On September 1, 1971, the due date of the first of the notes, the same not being paid, an action was thereupon commenced by a complaint dated September 3, 1971, against the defendant indorser. No demand for payment was made first of G & R.

. . . With respect to the affirmative defense that the signature of the defendant on the reverse of the notes "does not legally constitute an endorsement or a promise to pay for the debt or default of the debtor herein," the court reserved decision.

The defendant's memorandum of law rightly asserts: "The controversial point involved in this action is the statement [legend] on the back [of each note]". [See italicized legend supra]. The questions to be answered by the court are: Does the legend bind the defendant to do anything? Is the legend applicable to him? Does his signature make him liable as an indorser regardless of the ambiguous legend? Is the defendant an accommodation indorser? Is he a guarantor? May the plaintiff sue the defendant directly on the notes as an individual of primary liability rather than secondary thereunder without first going through the procedures of presentment, notice of dishonor and protest?

The court answers all of these questions affirmatively—yes!

In the court's opinion, we have a very strong case here in favor of the plaintiff. . . . Here we have the plaintiff-creditor actually in the midst of protecting its rights to payment by levying on the goods of the debtor under process of law. This was

Replevin
Legal action to physically recover property.

Accomodation Endorser
A party who endorses an instrument for the purpose of providing a guarantee.

not an idle threat of foreclosure—the closing down of the plaintiff's business was actually in progress. At that moment of high drama, a friend of the debtor makes a plea to the creditor to exercise humane forbearance, halt the replevy proceeding and give the debtor six months to pay off the indebtedness. The creditor agrees to do so and then surrenders its immediate right to replevy relying upon the third party's extremely strong and unequivocal oral representation to guarantee payment of the indebtedness and his stated willingness to put such a guarantee in writing.

. . . It was upon defendant's promise and guarantee to pay that the plaintiff primarily relied and acted upon to its subsequent detriment. Plaintiff had already written the debtor G & R off its credit book as a bad risk, and was insuring a return on its money by levying on the goods of the debtor. That remedy came to a close when the replevin proceeding was aborted by virtue of the defendant's intervention and a new and primary debt came into being upon the defendant's promise to pay. The circumstances surrounding this negotiation identify the *defendant as being more in the guise of a comaker of these notes rather than an indorser*.

. . . Regardless of the ambiguity, artlessness and clouded meaning of the legend on the reverse side of the notes, the defendant's signature establishes him, at the very least, as an accommodation indorser with consequent liability to the plaintiff. Defendant's signature on the notes cannot be held to be an empty act without consequence or liability to the defendant. He put his signature on the notes as a guarantor of payment on condition that plaintiff would desist from exercising its swift and immediate right to replevy.

. . . The accommodation indorser, a stranger to the instrument, i.e., not a maker, drawer, acceptor or payee, *usually* indorses his name prior to the delivery of the note to the payee in order "to give credit to the principal obligor or maker, and often is one whom the payee himself requires as security before he will take the instrument or advance the funds represented thereby."

"The liability of an indorser is not a joint obligation with the maker, and he cannot compel the holder to sue the maker first.

. . . Thus, the holder may proceed against any or all indorsers." "*The contract of the indorser is a new and independent one, distinct from that of the maker.*" "The holder of a note may sue both the maker and the indorser or either. An indorser, sued upon his contract of indorsement, is absolutely liable therein." See U.C.C. § 3–414(1) and comment 1.

. . . The plaintiff, in the court's opinion, had the right—under the circumstances of this case—to sue the defendant directly and primarily on these notes not only as an accommodation indorser/guarantor but also as a de facto comaker.

. . . Keep in mind that an accommodation indorser is only secondarily liable unless he makes a special agreement (*such as proved in this case by parol evidence*) which makes him primarily liable.

. . . "An indorser who guarantees payment waives all demand on the maker or drawee, and his liability becomes indistinguishable from that of a co-maker (Comment U.C. C. § 3–416). When words of guaranty are used, presentment, notice of dishonor, and protest are not necessary to charge the user. (U.C.C. § 3–416(5))."

. . . The activist role of defendant in negotiating these notes imposed upon him, by operation of law, the responsibilities and obligations of a *co-maker* even though he appeared to be an indorser as a matter of form.

"An instrument should be considered as it would manifestly be understood by the *average businessman,* and the party signing it should be exonerated from liability when, according to such construction, it appears that he did not intend,

> and was not understood, to bind himself." Here, the court is convinced that defendant intended to bind himself on the same level as the maker of the notes.
>
> On the basis of this reasoning of the court, the plaintiff was not required to go against the maker, G & R, first in order to trigger liability on the part of the accommodation indorser. The creditor has the right to move directly against the accommodation party as it did here.
>
> ... Accordingly, ... judgment is rendered in favor of the plaintiff on the notes for $2439.80, plus interest, from September 1, 1971.

The way the case was written may seem to obscure the ruling. Can an endorser be held primarily liable? Can he be made to pay on the instrument without the maker's default? The answer is no. However, as in *Brown University* v. *Laudati* (113 R.I. 299, 320 A.2d 609 [1974]) (cited in Subchapter 25.3), a legal action against the primary obligor is not required to render the accommodation party liable.

Although endorsers as well as the drawer of a draft are secondarily liable, the ultimate holder whose payment is denied will normally reach his immediate transferor first, with whom he most likely has an underlying arrangement for which he was supposedly paid by the money instrument. It should be remembered that endorsers "are liable to one another in the order in which they indorse, which is presumed to be the order in which their signatures appear on the instrument" (UCC § 3–414[2]). This means that if there are five parties secondarily liable, #1 is liable to the remaining four, #2 is liable to the remaining three, etc. As far as #5 is concerned, he may demand payment from and take action against any four of the preceding transferors, who are severally liable. However, if Maker A writes a check to Payee B, then B endorses the check to C, and C endorses it to D, upon nonpayment by the drawee bank, D may sue C on the check *and* the underlying arrangement, such as a sales transaction in which he needs to be paid, whereas D may sue B or A on the instrument alone.

Warranties

For an instrument to be negotiated through several parties, the identification and integrity of whom may not always be ascertainable to a subsequent transferee, transferors who endorse the instrument are by law required to provide certain warranties or guaranties to the subsequent holders. Without such warranties or guaranties, no transferee would be willing to give value for an instrument, the soundness of which may be questionable.

Endorser's Warranties
An endorser gives certain guarantees to the transferee(s).

UCC § 3–417 provides that any person who transfers an instrument and receives consideration warrants to his transferee and, if the transfer is by endorsement, to any subsequent holder who takes the instrument in good faith, the following warranties:

1. The transferor has a good title to the instrument or is authorized to obtain payment or acceptance on behalf of one who has a good title and the transfer is otherwise rightful. In other words, he guarantees that he is not a thief or a finder. It should be noted that a donee of a bearer instrument is a proper owner of the paper and may effectively transfer the title to the instrument to another person. So is the transferee of an

instrument received from a minor, as long as the minor has not repudiated the transfer.

2. All signatures are genuine or authorized. This warranty covers not only the maker's signature but also the signatures of the prior endorsers.

3. The instrument has not been materially altered. A typical example of a material alteration is changing the maturity date of a promissory note or the figure and written amounts of a check. In *Williams* v. *Montana National Bank of Bozeman* (534 P.2d 1247 [Montana, 1975]) (cited in Subchapter 26.3), a con artist managed to change a check amount of $1.26 to $6,841.26 by making use of the available blank spaces on the instrument.

4. No defense of any party is good against the transferor. There may be all kinds of defenses that the maker and prior endorsers may assert, such as mistake, fraud, duress, undue influence, lack of consideration, incapacity, illegality, prior payoff of the instrument, unauthorized completion, or adverse claim. The transferor guarantees that none of such defenses can be successfully brought up against him.

5. The transferor has no knowledge of any insolvency proceeding instituted with respect to the maker or acceptor or the drawer of an unaccepted instrument. This is to say that he is not aware of the inability of the primary obligor to pay on the instrument.

Insolvency
State in which a person is unable to pay his debts.

The transferor by delivery extends these warranties to his transferee only. If the transferor also endorses the instrument, his warranties become valid for all the subsequent holders. A claim based on any of the warranties may not be made by the maker or any prior transferor against a subsequent endorser as illustrated in the following case.

Facts
Defendants executed a note to pay for certain materials. The note was endorsed twice, until it finally became payable to the plaintiff bank. Bank sued defendants to recover on the note. Defendants denied the genuineness of their signatures and of all endorsements.

Decision
Judgment for the bank. At trial, evidence showed that defendants' signatures on the note were genuine. Although there were some minor questions regarding one endorsement (the company name was abbreviated), the court ruled that (1) the evidence showed that the endorsement was genuine and (2) only the endorsee, and not the defendant, is in a position to question the genuineness of the endorsements under the Uniform Commercial Code (UCC § 3–203).

Watertown Federal Savings and Loan Assn. v. *Spanks*, 346 Mass. 398, 193 N.E.2d 333 (1963).

Nonrecourse

Nonrecourse Endorsement
An encorsement limiting the liability of the endorser.

Compared to the above-stated two types of liabilities of the full endorser, the liability of a person who endorses without recourse is limited in that (1) he *does not obligate himself* to pay on the instrument should the primary obligor default on account of insolvency or unwillingness to pay and (2) he provides the same five warranties to the subsequent holder, except that as to warranty (4), he has *no knowledge* of a good defense against him but does not guarantee that there is no good defense against him (UCC § 3–417[3]).

In addition to without recourse, the endorser may completely exclude all the warranties by also inserting the words "Without Warranties." One may ask why a holder for value would accept such a very limited endorsement. Indeed, such a transaction would, under normal circumstances, be undesirable. However, there are always situations in which accepting such a paper is the only hope for the transferee to prevent a potential loss. One should remember, furthermore, that if the nonrecourse and/or nonwarranty endorser negotiates the paper to pay for another underlying contractual obligation, he is not discharged of this obligation if the transferee fails to obtain payment on the money instrument so endorsed.

Transfer by Delivery

What happens if a negotiable instrument is transferred by delivery alone without an endorsement? A bearer instrument is negotiated by delivery alone. An order paper is assigned by delivery alone. Whether the paper is negotiated or assigned by delivery, the consequences are the same as to the two types of a full endorser's liabilities. (1) Since no endorsement is involved, the transferor by delivery does not guarantee payment if the primary obligor defaults. (2) However, like all transferors, he extends the same full warranties to his immediate transferee only and not to all the subsequent holders. For illustration, refer to *Lopez* v. *Puzina* (239 Cal.App.2d 708, 49 Cal.Rptr. 122 [1966]), cited in Subchapter 25.3

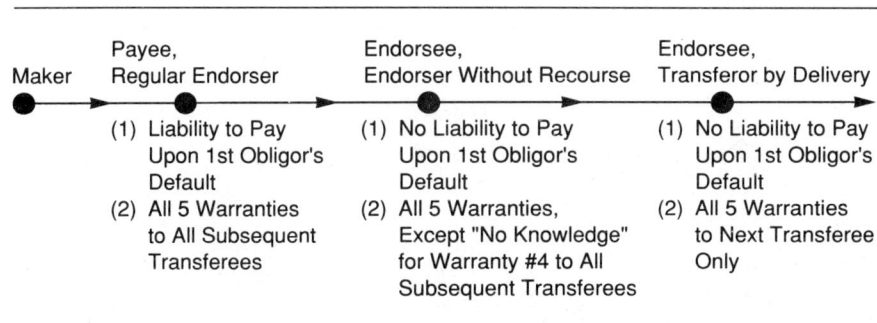

Figure 26.1 Liabilities of the Transferor: A Pictorial Summary

Questions

1. Who are the parties primarily and secondarily liable in a promissory note and in a draft?
2. Explain the money instrument as opposed to the underlying contractual obligation.

3. What are the liabilities of a full endorser?
4. How does a holder who is denied payment by the primary obligor recover the loss?
5. What are the liabilities of a nonrecourse endorser and of a transferor by delivery?

26.2 Holder in Due Course

The previous subchapter explained how a holder of a negotiable instrument may turn to his previous transferors if he is refused payment upon proper presentment due to insolvency or unwillingness to pay on the part of the obligor or due to defects in the instrument itself, such as forgery or material alterations. The obligor, whether he is primary or secondary in position, may also refuse payment on the instrument because of certain defenses he may assert, such as fraud or duress. However, if the payment-seeking holder of a negotiable paper is a holder in due course (H.D.C.), some of these defenses, however valid, cannot be used against him. (The defenses that are applicable or not applicable to an H.D.C. are discussed in the following subchapter.)

Basic Requirements

To be a holder in due course, a holder must take the instrument in the ordinary course of business:

1. For value.
2. In good faith.
3. Without notice that it is overdue or has been dishonored or of any defense against or claim to it on the part of any person.

A party who acquires the instrument not in the regular course of business does not become an H.D.C. The UCC lists three such instances:

1. Purchase of an instrument at a judicial sale or by taking it under legal process.
2. Acquiring an instrument through an estate.
3. Purchasing an instrument as part of a bulk transaction not in the regular course of business of the transferor.

Estate
The properties of a deceased person.

Value

A holder takes the instrument for value:

1. To the extent that the agreed consideration has been performed (UCC § 3–303[a]). For example, on June 1, payee endorses a $2,000 note to H for H's promise that he will pay payee the sum of $1,000 on July 1 and $1,000 on August 1. On July 1, H pays payee $1,000, at which time, H becomes an H.D.C. to the extent of $1,000. If after July 1 and before August 1, H should learn of a defense to the note, he will not be able to improve his position as an H.D.C.

2. When the holder takes the instrument in payment of or as security for an antecedent claim, whether or not it is due (UCC § 3–303[b]). For example, D owes C $1,000, which is due on June 1. On May 15, D receives a negotiable note for $1,000 from M which he transfers to C as payment for the debt. C is an H.D.C.

3. When the holder gives a negotiable instrument for the instrument or makes an irrevocable commitment to a third person (UCC § 3–303[c]). For example, payee gives holder a $1,000 negotiable note in exchange for holder's guarantee of a $1,000 loan by bank to P. Holder has made an irrevocable commitment to a third person (bank) and so is an H.D.C.

Antecedent
Prior in point of time.

As widely practiced, purchase of an instrument at a discount price generally does not affect the fact that the paper is acquired for value. Courts do not normally measure the value given unless it is so slight as to indicate the existence of fraud. Ordinarily, "value" in a negotiable instrument has the same legal meaning as "consideration" in contracts in general.

A depositary bank that paid wholly or partly on an instrument deposited by its customer may be an H.D.C.

Facts
Pazol issued a check payable to Eidson Construction Company. Eidson wrote "For Deposit" on the check and deposited it in its checking account with the Citizens National Bank. Eidson promptly withdrew the funds from its account. When Citizens presented the check for payment, the check was dishonored. Citizens sued Pazol to recover a judgment for the amount of the check. Pazol defended on the ground that Citizens was not a holder in due course of the check.

Decision
When Eidson withdrew the funds from its account, Citizens became a holder for value (UCC §§ 3–302[1][a], 4–208, 4–209). The court determined that Citizens met the other requirements of UCC § 3–302(1) and held it to be a holder in due course. The court concluded that it could therefore enforce payment against the drawer.

Pazol v. Citizens National Bank of Sandy Springs, 110 Ga.App. 319, 138 S.E.2d 442 (1964).

Good Faith

" 'Good faith' means honesty in fact in the conduct or transaction concerned" (UCC § 1–201[19]). Giving a small value for the instrument can cause the question of good faith to arise. Bad faith is established by proving that the transferee knew certain facts that rendered it improper for him to acquire the instrument, e.g., in a case where fraud was involved.

Good Faith
Honesty in the conduct of a transaction, and absence of all knowledge of facts which would render the transaction unconscionable.

Arcanum National Bank v. Hessler
69 Ohio St. 2d 549, 433 N.E.2d 204 (1982).

[Appellant Hessler executed some promissory notes payable to John Smith Grain Company. Without the knowledge or consent of appellant, John Smith Grain Company sold the notes to appellee, Arcanum National Bank. The bank sued Hessler to recover the amount of the notes.]

Krupansky, Justice The sole issue in this case is whether appellee is a holder in due course who takes the note free from appellant's defense of want of consideration.

In a suit by the holder of a note against the maker, the holder obtains a great advantage if granted the status of holder in due course. R.C. Chapter 1303 (Article 3, U.C.C.) provides that a holder in due course takes the instrument free from most defenses and claims. One such defense which is of no avail when raised against a holder in due course is want of consideration, the defense raised by appellant.

Whether one is a holder in due course is an issue which does not arise unless it is shown a defense exists. Once it is established a defense exists, the holder has the full burden of proving holder in due course status in all respects.

. . . Appellant contends appellee has not established holder in due course status because appellee took the instrument with notice of a defense against it. We agree.

. . . Appellant also contends, in essence, appellee bank failed in its burden of proving holder in due course status because appellee failed to establish it took the note in good faith as required under UCC 3–302(A)(2).

"Good faith" is defined as "honesty in fact in the conduct or transaction concerned" UCC 1–201(19). Under the "close connectedness" doctrine, . . . a transferee does not take an instrument in good faith when the transferee is so closely connected with the transferor that the transferee may be charged with knowledge of an infirmity in the underlying transaction. . . .

. . . According to White and Summers, noted authorities on the Uniform Commercial Code, the following five factors are indicative of a close connection between the transferee and transferor.

(1) Drafting by the transferee of forms for the transferor; (2) approval or establishment or both of the transferor's procedures by the transferee (e.g., setting the interest rate, approval of a referral sales plan); (3) an independent check by the transferee on the credit of the debtor or some other direct contact between the transferee and the debtor; (4) heavy reliance by the transferor upon the transferee (e.g., transfer by the transferor of all or substantial part of his paper to the transferee) and; (5) common or connected ownership or management of the transferor and transferee.

An analysis of the above factors in relation to the facts of this case, as set forth in the trial court's findings, reveals an unusually close relationship between appellee bank (the transferee), the John Smith Grain Company (the transferor-payee) and J & J Farms, Inc.

Appellee provided John Smith Grain Company with the forms used in the transaction and supplied the interest rate to be charged. At the time of the purchase of the first note, appellee bank ran an independent credit check on appellant. There is evidence of a heavy reliance by John Smith Grain Company upon appellee bank insofar as it was customary for the grain company to transfer substantially all of its commercial paper to appellee bank. There was not only a common director of appellee and John Smith Grain Company, but also common directors or management between John Smith Grain Company and J & J Farms, Inc. H. K. Smith was a director of appellee bank and the president and director of John Smith Grain Company. C. North, Jr., was an officer and director of both John Smith Grain Company and J & J Farms, Inc. John Milton Smith was officer and director of John Smith Grain Company and officer of J & J Farms, Inc. In addition, the trial court found that B. Henninger, the executive vice-president of appellee who had previously been employed by John Smith Grain Company, frequented John Smith Grain Company several times a week between November 1976 and January 1977 to advise the officers of John Smith Grain Company on

---

Close Connectedness
A close relationship in which the parties may be presumed to have special knowledge of each other.

Infirmity
Irregularity that impairs.

business practices. During that time, John Smith Grain Company was experiencing serious financial difficulties.

The facts of this case clearly indicate such close connectedness between appellee bank and John Smith Grain Company as to impute knowledge by appellee bank of infirmities in the underlying transaction. . . .

. . . Not only do the facts indicate appellee bank was aware of the impending bankruptcy of John Smith Grain Company, but they also show appellee had reason to know of a fatal infirmity in the underlying transaction, viz, there was no consideration given by John Smith Grain Company for the note. C. North, Jr., an officer and director of both John Smith Grain Company and J & J Farms, Inc., obtained appellant's signature and advised appellant to sign his wife's name on the note. As an officer and director of J & J Farms, Inc., C. North, Jr., undoubtedly was aware that at the time he obtained appellant's signature, the hogs had already been mortgaged by J & J Farms, Inc. It is well-established in Ohio a corporation can act only through its officers and agents, and the knowledge of the officers of a corporation is at once the knowledge of the corporation. If North, as officer and director of both John Smith Grain Company and J & J Farms, Inc., knew there was no consideration for the note, then such knowledge is imputed to both corporations. Thus, H. K. Smith, as president and director of John Smith Grain Company, had ample reason to know of the failure of consideration; and since H. K. Smith was also a director of appellee bank, his knowledge is imputed to appellee bank.

The executive vice-president of appellee bank, B. Henninger, who had previously been employed by John Smith Grain Company, was also in close contact with John Smith Grain Company at the time appellant signed the note. According to the trial court's conclusions, at the time appellant's signature was obtained on the note, B. Henninger was meeting several times a week with the officers of John Smith Grain Company to advise them on business practices. At that time, the officers of John Smith Grain Company included H. K. Smith, who was also a director of appellee bank, and C. North, Jr., who was also an officer and director of J & J Farms, Inc.

Given these facts, one cannot conclude with absolute certainty that appellee bank had actual knowledge of the failure of consideration. As appellant correctly states in his brief, however, the doctrine of close connectedness was developed in part because of the difficulty of proving the transferee's actual knowledge of problems in the underlying transaction. The doctrine allows the court to imply knowledge by the transferee when the relationship between the transferee and transferor is sufficiently close to warrant such an implication.

Under the circumstances of this case, we find the relationship between appellee bank and John Smith Grain Company was so entwined that it was error for the trial court not to apply the doctrine of close connectedness to find appellee bank failed to carry its burden of proving good faith.

If we accept the trial court's findings of fact and apply the close connectedness doctrine, we can reach only one conclusion, viz., appellee bank did not take the note in good faith.

Upon either one or both of the above reasoned theories, *i.e.*, (1) notice of a defense and (2) close connectedness doctrine, we find the Court of Appeals erred in affirming the trial court's finding that appellee bank was a holder in due course. The judgment of the Court of Appeals is, therefore reversed.

Similar cases are *General Investment Corp.* v. *Di Angelini* (58 N.J. 396, 278 A.2d 193 [1971]) and *Norman* v. *World Wide Distributors, Inc.* (202 Pa.Super. 53, 195 A.2d 115 [1963]).

Ignorance of Impropriety

Overdue Instrument
Instrument that has passed its maturity date.

Notice of Overdue or Dishonored Instrument To qualify as an H.D.C., the purchaser of an instrument must not know that the instrument was overdue or had been dishonored. When an instrument is not paid when due, it may be for the reason that the debtor has a good defense. Although the H.D.C. may not know this, the law assumes that he knows there is a defense when the paper is overdue; hence, the purchaser cannot be an H.D.C. A purchaser of an instrument with a fixed date must take the instrument before that date arrives. A demand instrument must be purchased within a reasonable time after its issue. A reasonable time for a check drawn and payable in the United States is presumed to be thirty days (UCC § 3-304[3][c]). A holder cannot be an H.D.C. if he has reason to know that an installment of principal is delinquent or that an acceleration of the instrument has been made (UCC § 3-304[3][a][b]). Knowledge of a delinquent interest installment does not disqualify such a holder. (UCC § 3-304[4][f]).

Ignorance of Defenses and Adverse Claims A purchaser cannot be an H.D.C. if he knows of defenses or adverse claims by prior parties to the instrument, e.g., that defective goods were given for the instrument, which may result in failure of consideration.

The purchaser has notice of a claim or defense in the following instances:

1. The instrument is so incomplete, bears such visible evidence of forgery or alteration, or is otherwise so irregular as to call into question its validity, terms, or ownership or to create an ambiguity (UCC § 3-304[1][a]).
2. The purchaser has notice that the obligation of any party to the instrument is voidable in whole or in part or that all the parties have been discharged (UCC § 3-304[1][b]).

Facts

Defendant Vanotti bought a parcel of land and executed a promissory note secured by a mortgage on the lot. Shortly thereafter, the plaintiffs purchased the note at a 40 percent discount. The sellers breached the sales contract, entitling Vanotti to rescind the contract. Vanotti stopped payment on the note. Plaintiffs claimed that they were holders in due course and therefore could collect on the note regardless of the buyer's defenses against the sellers.

Decision

The court held that the plaintiffs were not holders in due course. The issue was whether the plaintiffs, at the time they bought the note, had notice of any defense against the note on the part of any person (UCC § 3-302[1]). The Code provides that a holder meet this notice requirement if he has actual knowledge or has facts from which he has reason to know of the defenses when coming into possession of the note, such as the large discount of 40 percent. Here, the plaintiffs moreover knew from the contents of the documents delivered with the note that the buyer had possible defenses.

Salter v. Vanotti, 42 Colo.App. 448, 599 P.2d 962 (1979).

In a similar case, *United States Finance Company* v. *Jones* (285 Ala. 105, 229 So.2d 495 [1969]), the court made the following observation:

> "The mere fact that a note is purchased for an amount less than its face, or that an unusually large discount is accepted, is never of itself sufficient to charge the purchaser with notice of existing equities, unless the consideration is merely nominal. However, inadequacy is always a fact to be considered by the jury as evidence of bad faith, and may, with suspicious circumstances, authorize a finding of bad faith, especially if the consideration is grossly inadequate. . . ."

3. The acquirer purchased the instrument from an agent or fiduciary with the knowledge of the principal's claim of the agent's misappropriation of the instrument.

A holder is not prevented from becoming an H.D.C. if he acquires knowledge of the defense after the instrument was transferred to him. In *Kemp Motor Sales* v. *Statham* (120 Ga.App. 515, 171 S.E.2d 389 [1969], a payee of a check negotiated the instrument for value to a third party. Because of a dispute between the drawer and the payee, the drawer stopped payment on the check for lack of consideration. The third party sued the drawer, claiming that he was a holder in due course. This was refuted by the drawer, since the third party came to know about the defense before the check was deposited to his bank. The court decided for the third party, as knowledge of the defense after acquiring the instrument has no effect on the endorsee's status as an H.D.C.

Furthermore, discrepancies on the face of an instrument do not always preclude a holder from being an H.D.C. if his good faith can somehow be substantiated.

Facts

Compton wrote a check to Tabke drawn on Northwestern National Bank. The figure amount showed $3,430, as opposed to the handwritten amount of $13,430. When Tabke attempted to cash the check at McCook County National Bank, an officer of the bank contacted Northwestern Bank, who assured the officer that there were sufficient funds to cover the larger amount. The check was subsequently cashed for the larger amount. Northwestern dishonored the check based on Compton's stop-payment instruction. When McCook sued Compton, the latter claimed that the former could not be an H.D.C., *inter alia*, because of the irregularity on the face of the check.

Decision

Judgment for McCook. The $10,000 discrepancy would not prevent the holder bank from being a holder in due course, as it attempted to ascertain the correct amount from the drawee bank. It should be noted, furthermore, that handwritten amounts are generally considered to prevail over figure amounts.

McCook County National Bank v. *Compton*, 558 F.2d 871 (8th Cir. 1977).

Other H.D.C.s

The Payee

UCC § 3–302(2) provides that a payee can be a holder in due course if he satisfies all the requirements of an H.D.C. If a payee receives a money

H.D.C.
Holder in due course.

instrument as a seller in an underlying transaction, because of privity of contract, he is subject to all the defenses that the maker/buyer may have against him. Being an immediate party in the underlying contractual relation, the payee will not be able to claim ignorance of any possible defenses. Hence, such a payee cannot possibly qualify as an H.D.C.

It would be different if the maker of an instrument is not a buyer but another party. For example, buyer manages to trick maker to write a check directly to seller/payee. In this case, the seller/payee is an H.D.C. if he takes the instrument in good faith and without knowledge of the fraud by the buyer on the maker.

Facts

Drexler was an attorney for and a corporate secretary of Eldon's Super Fresh Stores, Inc. On August 12, 1969, Drexler purchased some stock through Merrill Lynch, where he maintained an active account. Drexler paid for the stock with a check written by Eldon's, made payable to Merrill Lynch, and signed by Eldon Prinzing, the corporate president and sole shareholder. Only after fifteen months, in November 1970, Prinzing inquired of Merrill Lynch as to the whereabouts of the stock certificate he claimed to have purchased. In his suit, he insisted that the check was given to Drexler for the purpose of purchasing the stock on his behalf.

Decision

Judgment for Merrill Lynch. The issue here is whether Merrill Lynch took the instrument with or without notice of Eldon's defense. It was found that Merrill Lynch did not have actual knowledge or inferable knowledge of Eldon's claim. The check was delivered to Merrill Lynch by Eldon's agent, Drexler, with the consent and knowledge of Eldon's president; it contained no restrictions or designations as to its use, and Eldon's had no trading account with Merrill Lynch. Merrill Lynch is an H.D.C. that took the check free from Eldon's claim of a wrongful delivery.

Eldon's Super Fresh Stores, Inc. v. Merrill Lynch, Pierce, Fenner & Smith, Inc., 296 Minn. 130, 207 N.W.2d 282 (1973).

Holder Through an H.D.C.

A holder who derives his title through an H.D.C. and who is not himself a party to any fraud or illegality has all the rights of an H.D.C. even though he cannot satisfy the requirements of an H.D.C. For example, a payee by fraud induces a drawer to issue a check to him. The payee negotiates the check to an H.D.C. The H.D.C. negotiates the check to John Smith, who knows of the fraud. Since John Smith takes the rights of the H.D.C., he can enforce the check against the drawer (UCC § 3–201[1]).

Reacquirer

A reacquirer is a holder of an instrument who negotiates the instrument and then reacquires it. A reacquirer who was an H.D.C. the first time he acquired the instrument will hold it as an H.D.C. even though the reacquiror was not an H.D.C. when he reacquired it. The reacquirer is remitted to his former position.

Questions

1. What are the basic requirements of an H.D.C.?
2. Must a holder pay the full value of the instrument to be an H.D.C.?
3. Explain the "close connectedness" doctrine.
4. Do irregularities on the face of a check prevent a holder from becoming an H.D.C.?
5. Explain how a payee can become an H.D.C.

26.3 Defenses

The maker or drawer of a negotiable instrument as well as a subsequent transferor may have so-called defenses justifying his refusal to pay the holder upon presentment. Obviously, it would seriously affect the economy in general and trade in particular if obligors to money instruments could use all kinds of excuses not to pay the rightful holder of the paper. True, it may be justifiable for a buyer and drawer of a check not to pay the seller/payee if he was cheated by the latter. But it is not always right for him to default against an innocent third party H.D.C., to whom the payee has negotiated the instrument and who may have had nothing to do with the deceit. After all, the H.D.C. took the instrument in the ordinary course of business for value, in faith, and without knowledge of such a defense. UCC § 3–305(2) prescribes that an H.D.C. purchases an instrument free from certain defenses of "any party to the instrument with whom the holder has not dealt."

Defenses that are applicable to an H.D.C. are called *real* or universal, whereas those against which an H.D.C. is protected are called *personal* or limited. There are certain apparent guidelines as to whether an obligor's defense is real or personal. Where the user of the defense is virtually blameless and the defense itself would under the rules of ordinary contracts lead to the transaction's becoming *void*, such a defense is real. On the other hand, where the obligor somehow carries some blame and the defense would lead to an agreement's becoming *voidable*, such a defense is personal. In light of these observations, the following hold true:

1. Forgery and material alteration are exclusively real defenses.
2. Failure of consideration, lack of delivery, prior payment or cancellation, and unauthorized completion are exclusively personal defenses.
3. Fraud, duress, incapacity, and illegality may either be real or personal, depending on their nature.

Real Defenses

The real defenses against which the H.D.C. is not protected are the following.

Forgery

Forgery
Making or altering of a writing with an intent to defraud.

Forgery is treated in negotiable instruments the same way we treat counterfeit money; both are valueless. If a signature is forged or signed without authority, the purported drawer or maker has a real defense against the holder in due course. Forgery can be ratified, in which case the drawer or maker would be liable. The defense of forgery can be lost under the doctrine of estoppel if one permits a forgery by negligence (UCC § 3–404).

UCC § 3–406 provides:

> "Any person who by his negligence substantially contributes to a material alteration of the instrument or to the making of an unauthorized signature is precluded from asserting the alteration or lack of authority against a holder in due course or against a drawee or other payor who pays the instrument in good faith and in accordance with the reasonable commercial standards of the drawee's or payor's business."

Whether or not negligence exists in a given case is a question of fact as shown in the following case.

Facts

As a correspondent bank, Central Jersey Bank kept blank checks drawn on the Chase Manhattan Bank. Despite the precautionary banking procedures followed, a number of checks were missing. One of the missing checks was used by a forger to purchase a car for $22,000. The check was made payable to the buyer, who endorsed it to Brogan Cadillac, the plaintiff/seller. The instrument was issued by actual authorized signers of the Central Jersey Bank, but the signatures were forged. At issue was whether the bank was negligent so as to contribute to the forgery.

Decision

Judgment for Central Jersey Bank. The bank's attempts to prevent such an occurrence were considered sufficient. All the checks were kept in the bank vault, and all the bank rules for safekeeping were properly observed. When the bank discovered that some of the checks were missing, it immediately notified all banks in the area to be on the lookout for persons attempting to forge those checks. "By way of analogy, if a woman secures a checkbook from her bank, places it into her handbag, enters the public street and is the victim of a purse-snatcher who subsequently forges her check, should a jury be permitted to determine if she was guilty of negligence?"

Brogan Cadillac-Oldsmobile Corp. v. Central Jersey Bank & Trust Co., 183 N.J.Super. 333, 443 A.2d 1108 (1981).

Material Alteration

Material Alteration
Fraudulent alteration of the essential terms of an instrument.

Where there has been a material fraudulent alteration of an instrument, such as a change of the maturity date of a promissory note of a bill of exchange, the defense against the H.D.C. is real. If only the amount in a money instrument has been fraudulently raised, the real defense is partial in that the H.D.C. can still enforce the instrument according to its original terms.

There is no real defense against an H.D.C. if the maker negligently permits such material alteration to take place. This is illustrated in *J. Gordon Neely Enterprises, Inc. v. American National Bank of Huntsville* (403 So.2d 887 [Alabama, 1981]), where a dishonest bookkeeper managed to embezzle

$17,005.18 by filling the blanks and increasing the original amounts of some company checks. Corresponding cases are *Nationwide Acceptance Corp. v. Henne* (194 So.2d 434 [La., 1967]) and *Williams v. Montana National Bank of Bozeman* (534 P.2d 1247 [Montana, 1975]). In *Ray v. Farmers State Bank* (576 S.W.2d 607 [Texas, 1979]), the maker of a check for $1.50—an 80-year-old woman who was taken by a con artist—was, under the circumstances, not considered negligent for allowing the check amount to be altered to $1,851.50.

Fraud in the Inception

As explained in Subchapter 7.1, fraud in the inception renders a contract void, whereas fraud in the inducement results in the contract's becoming voidable. As defenses against the H.D.C., the former is real, whereas the latter is personal. UCC § 3–305(2)(c) defines fraud in the inception as a "misrepresentation as has induced the party to sign the instrument with neither knowledge nor reasonable opportunity to obtain knowledge of its character or its essential terms." This is the case, for example, if an illiterate or blind person signs a negotiable note that is represented as a receipt or some other harmless document.

Fraud in the Inception
A misrepresentation causing a party to sign an instrument without knowledge or opportunity to learn of its essential terms.

Matthews v. Aluminum Acceptance Corp.
1 Mich.App. 570, 137 N.W.2d 280 (1965).

. . . In this action to enjoin defendant from enforcing any claims against plaintiffs and from foreclosing the mortgage upon plaintiffs' home, the questions on appeal are whether . . . constructive forgery or fraud was established. . . . and whether the entire transaction was shot through with usury.

In April of 1962, plaintiffs Robert and Katherine Matthews were approached by representatives of All-Style Builders, aluminum siding applicators. They allege that All-Style indicated that their modest home had been chosen as a demonstration site for aluminum siding for that area. New siding was to be applied over the tar paper on their home, and in addition they were to be given a loan of $650 in cash to fix their tractor and the total price for this was to be $3,250. Further, they were to receive $100 to apply against their contract for each potential customer which All-Style brought to view their newly-sided house.

When the smoke cleared, so to speak, the Matthews learned that the instrument they had signed included a promissory note and mortgage calling for 84 equal monthly installments at the rate of $61.04 per month for a grand total of $5,127.36, not the $3,250 they had anticipated, and the instruments had been assigned to defendant Aluminum Acceptance Corporation, a firm specializing in financing siding application.

All-Style Builders is not a party to this suit and defendant Aluminum Acceptance claims it is a bona fide holder of the paper, denies fraud and further claims that the instruments are not usurious because the agreement provides for a cash price, whereas the note and mortgage represent a "time price" and are a discount transaction.

As to the transaction itself, Mr. Matthews says that he was unable to read any but the largest print, and that only with difficulty, and Mrs. Matthews was able only to read the printed portion with her glasses and that the papers were stacked one on top of another at the time of the signing and with the upper portions

> covered, leaving visible only the area to be signed. The papers, they further allege, were blank at the time of signing.
>   Plaintiffs made only one payment and now seek to enjoin foreclosure of the mortgage and defendant counterclaims, seeking foreclosure, deficiency and such other relief "as shall be agreeable to equity and good conscience."
>   The latter phrase is a little difficult to digest when the record is studied closely.
>   . . . Judgment entered canceling the mortgage and giving defendant judgment on its counterclaim in the sum of $3,250. Aluminum Acceptance Corporation appeals this judgment. . . . The rule in Michigan is . . . that a signature deceptively procured is in law a forgery and those who subsequently acquire interest under the forged instrument are in no better position than if they had purchased with notice. . . .
>   The judgment of the court is affirmed.

Illiteracy as a real defense of fraud in the inception was recognized in *Schaeffer v. United Bank and Trust Company* (32 Md.App. 339, 360 A.2d 461 [1976]).

If a person has reasonable opportunity to obtain knowledge of the character of the instrument or its essential terms and does not do so, his defense of fraud will be only personal and not applicable to an H.D.C.

Absolute Duress

Duress
A threat of force or coercion.

Absolute duress—a threat of physical force directed to death or great bodily harm—makes a contract void and affords the maker or endorser of an instrument a real defense against the H.D.C. The reasoning is that no one under ordinary circumstances is expected to brave such dire consequences. If the duress is less than absolute, we call it "relative," and such a defense is personal and limited.

Legal Incapacity

Incapacity
Legal inability to contract, such as that of a minor or insane person.

In many states, a minor under the age of 18 or a judicially declared insane person can repudiate a contract of which he is a party; if he does so, the contract is void. If the contract is a negotiable instrument, such a legal incapacity, if evoked, will result in a real defense against an H.D.C. This rule applies only when such a contractually incapable person writes a negotiable instrument as a maker or drawer but not when he endorses the paper.

Illegality as to Law

Illegality
The status of being prohibited by law or of being against public policy, such as a promissory note for a gambling debt.

Contracts are void if they are illegal by statutory or case law. Such illegality is a real defense. Unlike some states, such as Nevada and California, where some types of gambling are permitted, New York and Virginia have statutes specifically declaring that an instrument given in payment of a gambling debt is void, thereby providing the obligor of an instrument a real defense against the H.D.C.

Glassman v. Federal Deposit Insurance Corp.
210 Va. 650, 173 S.E.2d 843 (1970).

Snead, C.J. The trial court held, first, that if the notes were given for gambling losses, they would be invalid under Code, § 11–14, even in the hands of a holder in due course. Code, § 11–14 declares, in part, that "All . . . contracts and securities whereof the whole or any part of the consideration be money or other valuable thing, won . . . at any game . . . shall be utterly void."

. . . We therefore agree with the trial court's holding that even though Crown Savings was a holder in due course . . . the note should be held invalid under Code, § 11–14, if Glassman proved that the notes were given for gambling losses.

Glassman testified that the gambling losses resulted from a gin rummy game that took place during August and September of 1963 at the Golden Triangle Motor Hotel in Norfolk, Virginia. He stated that his losses totaled about $100,000. The participants in the game, besides Glassman, were George Vantraub, and the two Halprin brothers, Jack and Burt.

After losing a substantial sum, and after the notes were given, Glassman discovered that the cards with which the game had been played were marked.

Richard B. Keeley testified for Glassman. Keeley at the time of the game was manager of the Golden Triangle Motor Hotel. He stated that of his own knowledge he knew of the gin game and had been present at some of the sessions. He corroborated Glassman's testimony as to the participants in the game, the general period during which it was played, and that the cards were marked. He stated that he saw scores kept and knew that Glassman was losing. He also testified that he did not actually see the notes or any money passed.

Glassman stated that after he had lost all his cash, "I had no money coming in, and I gave these notes, and it was a gambling debt." On advice of counsel Glassman notified the banks with which he did business not to honor the notes. Crown Savings was not among those banks.

Although the trial court sat as a jury and heard the witnesses (with the exception of Ridley) we cannot agree with the determination that Glassman failed to prove by a preponderance of the evidence the facts on which his defense rests. To establish his case by a preponderance it is not necessary that he eliminate every doubt or question in the mind of the trier of fact. In our view his testimony established the existence of the gin game, its participants, its location, the general period during which it was played and the fact that it was rigged against him. All this was corroborated by Keeley. . . .

[Reversed.]

In *Middle Georgia Livestock Sales* v. *Commercial Bank & Trust Co.* (123 Ga.App. 733, 182 S.E.2d 533 [1971]), a buyer who unknowingly bought stolen cattle instructed his bank to stop payment on his check. Meanwhile, the seller's bank had paid the seller cash for the check. Can the seller's bank recover from the buyer? The answer is no. The buyer had a real defense. "A sale of stolen goods although to a bona fide purchaser for value, cannot transfer any lawful interest in the property." If the underlying transaction is void, the H.D.C. is not protected.

In *Pacific National Bank* v. *Hernreich* (240 Ark. 114, 398 S.W.2d 221 [Ark., 1966]), some promissory notes written in favor of a foreign corporation that did not qualify to operate in Arkansas were declared void, thereby extending a real defense to the maker of the instrument.

Consumer Protection

The Federal Trade Commission (FTC) promulgated a regulation in 1975 to protect consumers against unscrupulous sellers who immediately after a questionable credit transaction negotiate the paper that the buyer executes to a third party for value. As noted in Subchapter 20.3, the FTC rule requires a notice on the promissory note or contract that reads:

> ANY HOLDER OF THIS CONSUMER CREDIT CONTRACT IS SUBJECT TO ALL CLAIMS AND DEFENSES WHICH THE DEBTOR COULD ASSERT AGAINST THE SELLER OF GOODS OR SERVICES OBTAINED PURSUANT HERETO OR WITH THE PROCEEDS HEREOF. RECOVERY HEREUNDER BY THE DEBTOR SHALL NOT EXCEED AMOUNTS PAID BY THE DEBTOR HEREUNDER.

In effect, the rule makes all valid defenses by a consumer real, without regard to their nature. Any defense that a maker/buyer may have against the seller can also be asserted against the H.D.C. The holder in due course is no longer privileged in such consumer credit transactions.

Facts

A representative of Aluminum Industries, Inc. sold Pedro and Paula de la Fuente aluminum siding for their home. The buyers executed a retail installment contract and a promissory note for $9,138.24, to be paid in ninety-six monthly installments at an A.P.R. of 12 percent. The contract granted the holder of the note a lien on their home. The promissory note contained a notice in bold type as required by the FTC to warn future H.D.C.s. The job was not done, and the makers defaulted against Home Savings, to whom the credit transaction was transferred. Did the makers have an applicable defense against Home Savings, who claimed to be an H.D.C.?

Decision

Judgment for the de la Fuentes. The FTC rule requiring the notice is to deny any subsequent holder in due course a protection against claims by a consumer buyer. The makers' defense, which was good against Aluminum Industries, was equally good against Home Savings.

de la Fuente v. Home Savings Association, 669 S.W.2d 137 (Tex.App. 1984).

The rule does not apply when a buyer makes out a check as a full cash payment for the purchase.

Personal Defenses

The following are the defenses against which the H.D.C. is protected.

Failure of Consideration

Consideration
Something of value given to support a contract, such as a promise of payment.

The most common defense is the failure of consideration. This occurs whenever a party to a contract receives nothing or less than he bargained for. For example, the merchandise purchased was never delivered or was defective. If the payee/seller defaults in his obligation, the maker/buyer's defense of "want or failure of consideration" against him is effective. However, the defense cannot be used against an innocent H.D.C.

Lack of Delivery

Failure to deliver a negotiable instrument is also a personal defense, which is not good against an H.D.C. For example, a drawer makes out a check to cash, or a payee endorses a check in blank and leaves the check someplace, allowing it to be stolen or found. Since the thief or finder can pass good title to his transferee, the transferee may become an H.D.C. against whom the maker's or the blank endorser's defense of lack of delivery does not apply. This is illustrated in *Watkins v. Sheriff of Clark County* (85 Nev. 246, 453 P.2d 611 [1969]) (cited in Subchapter 25.3).

Lack of Delivery
When an executed or endorsed instrument is not actually delivered to payee or endorsee.

Prior Payment or Cancellation

A maker of a negotiable promissory note who pays off the debt should always take possession of the instrument or be certain that it is destroyed. If he does not, a dishonest holder may negotiate the paper to a holder in due course, who takes it free of the defense of prior payment. It should be noted that even lender banks often violate this rule of returning the promissory note to the borrower after it has been paid off, particularly if it concerns a long-term installment loan. Where there is an early payoff and the actual maturity has not been reached, the promissory note may certainly be further negotiated to an H.D.C. against whom the borrower's defense of prior payoff does not apply.

Returning the instrument to the maker or drawer is also necessary if the holder for some reason agrees to cancel the obligation on the paper.

Prior Payment
Paying an instrument prior to its maturity date.

Unauthorized Completion

When a person signs a check or note and leaves blank the name of the payee, the amount, or any other term, and the instrument falls into the hands of a thief or a dishonest person who fills in the check or note and then negotiates it to an H.D.C., the drawer or maker has no defense (UCC § 3–407[3]). In fact, it is not uncommon for an obligor of a money instrument under certain circumstances to intentionally leave the payment amount blank for the trusted obligee to complete at a later time.

Unauthorized Completion
Completing the blanks on an instrument without permission of the party who executed it.

Trade Acceptance
An acceptance on a money instrument provided by a nonbank entity.

Facts

Woodard, a regular customer of Moody Manufacturing Company, made a purchase and paid for it by accepting a trade acceptance drawn by Moody on him. He signed the acceptance while the money amount was still blank because it had not yet been determined what goods he would be purchasing. Subsequently, Moody filled in the amount and negotiated the acceptance to Illinois Valley Acceptance Corp. Woodard defaulted on the acceptance, and when Illinois Valley sued him, he raised the defense of fraud, in that he had never received the merchandise, as well as the defense of unauthorized completion, as he accepted the trade acceptance in blank. Illinois Valley purchased the instrument from Moody on the basis of a continuing business relationship.

Decision

Judgment for Illinois Valley. Plaintiff was an H.D.C., and both defenses of fraud in the inducement and unauthorized completion were not applicable in this case. It should be noted that Woodard obviously could bring an action against Moody based upon those allegations of impropriety.

Illinois Valley Acceptance Corp. v. Woodard, 159 Ind.App. 50, 304 N.E.2d 859 (1973).

Fraud in the Inducement

Fraud in the Inducement
Fraud where the defrauded party knows what he is signing, but his consent has been induced by misrepresentation as to the benefit he will receive.

A person who knows that he is signing a negotiable instrument and knows its contents but is induced into signing it by false representations can raise the defense of fraud only against the party with whom he bargained but not against an H.D.C. For example, M signs a promissory note to P for the purchase of a used automobile, relying on false representations by P as to the condition of the automobile. P negotiates the note to an H.D.C. M has no defense against the H.D.C. M's remedy will be a suit for fraud against P.

Facts

A representative of Gracious Living Inc. installed water-softening equipment for the Hutchinsons for a supposedly four-month trial. After the job was done, the Hutchinsons claimed that they were asked to sign a form so that the sales rep could show the form to his boss to prove he had made the demonstration and use said form as a bond to cover the unit while it was on the Hutchinson's property. The Hutchinsons were surprised when they received a payment book from the Reading Trust Company, at which time they realized that they had been tricked into signing a contract with Gracious Living. Reading Trust acquired the promissory note from Gracious Living for value, in good faith, and without knowledge of any defense. Mr. Hutchinson was a high school graduate, and Mrs. Hutchinson had completed the junior year in high school. Both could read and write the English language. Reading Trust sued them when they refused to pay on their obligation.

Decision

Judgment for Reading Trust. In this situation, the Hutchinsons were not induced to sign the instrument "with neither knowledge nor reasonable opportunity to obtain knowledge of its character or its essential terms." It is not a fraud in the inception, but it is only a fraud in the inducement, which cannot be used as a defense against an H.D.C.

Reading Trust Co. v. Hutchinson, 35 Pa. D&C.2d 790 (1964) (Unpublished Case).

Prior to the FTC regulation of 1975, there have been numerous cases in which defrauded customers were compelled to honor their commitment on a negotiable instrument acquired by an H.D.C. *Burchett v. Allied Concord Financial Corporation* (74 N.M. 575, 396 P.2d 186 [New Mexico, 1964]), involving aluminum siding, is just such a case.

Relative Duress

A contract executed under a threat less than a threat against life or grave bodily harm is voidable, as the victim might or might not have felt threatened. Under the law of negotiable instruments, such a defense is only personal; it does not apply to an H.D.C. Under this category fall such threats as economic duress, e.g., "If you don't sign, I will start a bankruptcy proceeding against you," or blackmail, e.g., "I will reveal you are an ex-convict."

Circumstantial Incapacity

Claims of insanity without judicial declaration or claims of having been under the influence of drugs or intoxication or under undue influence are personal defenses against which the H.D.C. is protected. If such claims are used against the payee, courts usually look into the underlying transaction as well as the instrument itself to determine the validity of the claim.

Illegality as to Public Policy

Although the underlying arrangement of a negotiable instrument is not illegal by statute or by case law, it still may under given circumstances be considered to violate public policy or morality. Even in the state of Nevada, where gambling is permitted, courts still refuse to honor claims based on gamling debts. This is illustrated in *Sea Air Support, Inc.* v. *Hermann* (96 Nev. 574, 613 P.2d 413 [1980]).

Adverse Claims

An adverse claim is a claim by a third person that he and not the holder is the real owner of the instrument. For example, a check is made payable to payee. Subsequently, it is endorsed to A, B, and C. A then claims that B induced him into transferring the check to him by fraud, that he rescinds said transfer, and that he is therefore the true owner of the check. A will not prevail against C, the H.D.C. This is shown in *Bricks Unlimited, Inc.* v. *Agee* (672 F.2d 1255 [5th Cir., 1982]).

A minor who endorses a negotiable instrument does not have any valid claim against an H.D.C.

An H.D.C. takes free of all adverse claims except a forged endorsement. For example, a thief steals a note from payee, endorses the payee's name to it, and sells it to the H.D.C. The payee will be able to recover the note from the H.D.C. (UCC §§ 3–207, 3–305[1], 3–306, 3–404[1]).

Adverse Claim
Claim of ownership of an instrument by a third party.

QUESTIONS

1. Are there any apparent guidelines for a defense to be real or personal?
2. Explain material alteration as opposed to unauthorized completion as a defense.
3. What is the difference between fraud in the inception and fraud in the inducement as a defense against an H.D.C.?
4. When is legal incapacity a real defense? When is it a personal defense?
5. When is illegality a real defense? When is it a personal defense? Can you cite some illustrative cases?

PROBLEMS

1. Ace Holder gave Bill Betton his promissory note for money won by Bill in a game of cards. State law made notes given for gambling debts unenforceable. Bill endorsed the note in due course and for value to California Bank. After due presentment and notice of dishonor, California Bank sues Bill for the

amount of the note. Bill interposes the defense that the note was given for an amount won in an illegal gambling transaction. Decision?

2. Francis issued and delivered a check to Lee in payment of an automobile. On the face of the check was written "car to be free and clear of liens." The check was endorsed and delivered by Lee to the Lance Company. When Lance sued Francis, Francis defended on the ground that Lance was not a holder in due course because the words "car to be free and clear of liens" gave notice of defenses of fraud in the inducement and failure of consideration. Decision?

3. Payee represented that certain land is readily irrigable and that the soil is good for raising oranges. M, in reliance on the representations, gives the payee his negotiable note for the purchase price. Payee negotiates the note to an H.D.C. M learns that the property is in the desert and is not irrigable and that the soil is poor for oranges. M refuses to pay the note. Decision?

4. M executes a note payable to bearer and accidentally leaves it on a counter at the bank. X finds the note and negotiates it to an H.D.C. May the H.D.C. recover from M?

5. D gave an order check to P for $5.00. The check was so drawn that figures could be inserted between the dollar sign ($) and the number 5. On the line where the word "five" appeared, there was room to the left to insert several words. P inserted the numbers "90" next to the number 5, and the words "nine hundred and" next to the word five. P then negotiated the check for the sum of $905 to H. D refused to pay H. Decision?

6. M gave an order check to P for value. P negotiated the check to a minor. The minor negotiated the check to A, who negotiated it to an H.D.C. The minor rescinds the transfer to A and claims the check. Decision?

7. P represented to M that an instrument he was asking M to sign was a contract by which P was hiring M as an employee. M was unable to read, and there was no one nearby to read the instrument to him. M signed the note. P negotiated it to an H.D.C. Can the H.D.C. recover from M?

8. A, by fraudulent representations, induced B to buy 100 shares of Acme Company stock. The shares were worthless. On May 5, B delivered to A a promissory note for $5,000 in full payment for the shares, due six months after that date. On May 25, A endorsed and sold the note to C for $4,800. In October, B made aware that C held the note, told C of the fraud and stated that he refused to pay the note. On December 1, C negotiated the note to D, who, while not involved in the fraud, knew of the fraud perpetrated upon B. D sues B on the note, claiming holder in due course status. Decision?

9. M signed a note on January 1, 1979, payable on June 1, 1980, and delivered it to P. P changed the date from June 1, 1980, to June 1, 1989, and on July 1, 1980, negotiated it to H. Can H recover from M?

10. Penn installed equipment in Morgan's store. Morgan signed and delivered to Penn a promissory note payable to the order of Penn for $1,100, the purchase price, due in thirty days. Ten days later Penn, short of funds, returned to Morgan's store and told Morgan he would accept $1,000 in cash now as full payment for the note. Morgan paid the $1,000 but forgot to obtain the note from Penn. Two days after this cash payment, Penn endorsed the note in blank and negotiated it for value to Quinn. The next day, Quinn learned that Morgan had already paid Penn for the note, whereupon Quinn gave the note to his mother as a birthday present, without further endorsement. Quinn's mother was not aware of Morgan's prior payment. Quinn's mother sued Morgan on the note. Decision?

CHAPTER TWENTY-SEVEN

Presentment, Discharge, and Banking Procedures

27.1 Presentment and Notice of Dishonor
Presentment
Who Presents
To Whom Presentment Is Made
Manner of Presentment
Time of Presentment
Place of Presentment
When Presentment Is Excused
Nonpayment
Notice of Dishonor
Who Gives Notice
To Whom Notice Is Given
Form of Notice
Time of Notice
Protest

27.2 Discharge
Grounds for Discharge
Payment or Satisfaction
Tender of Payment
Cancellation or Renunciation
Impairment
Reacquisition
Material Alteration
Certification
Acceptance
Unexcused Delay
Effect of Discharge

27.3 Banking Procedures
The Depositary Bank
Endorsements
Depositor's Warranties
Presentment
Notice of Dishonor and Charge-Back
Bank as H.D.C. and Its Security Interest
The Payor Bank
Promptness and Due Care
Signature Card
Overdraft
Stop Payment
Termination of Bank's Authority
Customer's Duty
Bank's Recovery Rights
Subrogation
Other Recoveries
Electronic Banking
Types of Transfers
Procedural Provisions
Liability Limitations

27.1 Presentment and Notice of Dishonor

As explained in Subchapter 26.1, in a promissory note, the liability of the maker is primary, whereas the liability of the subsequent transferor, if any, is secondary. In a draft, the drawee or acceptor is primarily liable, whereas the drawer and the subsequent transferors are secondarily liable.

If it is a sight instrument, the primary obligor is to pay for it upon presentation. If it is a future instrument, payment is to be made on or before the maturity date. A notice or demand by the holder of the instrument is not required for the primary party to become liable for payment. The instrument itself is sufficient to create the liability. On the other hand, before the maturity of the instrument, the primary obligor does not have any legal obligation to pay, as shown in the following case.

Facts
Burke, who executed a promissory note, informed Bertolet, the holder of the paper, that he would not honor the note when it became due. Upon this notice, Bertolet immediately brought an action against Burke. The defendant moved for a summary judgment in his favor.

Decision
Judgment for Burke. A negotiable instrument is payable at sight or on a specific future date. It does not become due simply because the maker declares that he will default and not honor the instrument when due. The general contract rule on anticipatory repudiation does not apply to a commercial paper.

Bertolet v. *Burke,* 295 F.Supp. 1176 (D.V.I. 1969).

To hold the secondary obligor liable, the payment-seeking holder of an instrument must have (1) *presented* a demand for payment to the primary obligor who refused to pay and (2) given a *notice of dishonor* to the secondary obligor. Since parties to a negotiable instrument are severally liable, each of these secondary obligors may be held responsible for the entire payment of the paper.

Presentment

Presentment
Demand for payment due on commercial paper.

UCC § 3–504(1) defines presentment as "a demand for acceptance or payment made upon the maker, acceptor, drawee, or other payor by or on behalf of the holder."

Who Presents

Presentment for payment is to be made by the holder of an instrument or by his agent who is authorized to receive the payment on his behalf. In any event, the party from whom payment is demanded is entitled to require a definite proof of personal or corporate identification of the presenter and, if the presenter is an agent, some specific evidence of his authority to represent.

To Whom Presentment Is Made

Presentment for payment is to be made to the primary obligor, i.e., the maker of a promissory note or the drawee/acceptor of a draft. If the paper is a check drawn on a multibranch banking institution, presentment must be made at the particular branch at the address as indicated on the check. Unless the presenter is its own customer, another branch of that bank would not be willing to honor the check, since it does not keep the facsimile and cannot ascertain the genuineness of the drawer's signature.

Manner of Presentment

The demand for payment may be made in any manner, so long as it is clearly a demand and not a mere inquiry as to whether the obligor is able or willing to pay. Actual presentation of the instrument itself is not always required, except in a case, such as that of a check, where the paper needs to be immediately surrendered to the payor upon payment. In addition to the paid instrument, the payor may also require a signed receipt. In the event of a partial payment while the paper remains in the possession of the holder, it is advisable for a notation to be made on the instrument itself to inform any possible subsequent transferee, unless the terms on the instrument clearly refer to such a partial payment. Presentment for payment may be made in person, by mail, or through a bank's clearinghouse. Where private parties are involved, complicated payoffs on an instrument may be executed through a neutral escrow.

Time of Presentment

A sight negotiable instrument must be presented for payment within a reasonable time—thirty days after the date on the paper or the date of its issuance, whichever is later. UCC § 3–503(2) provides, "(A) reasonable time for presentment is determined by the nature of the instrument, any usage of banking or trade and the facts of the particular case." Unless it is a certified check, a bank has, under UCC § 4–404, no obligation to pay a check presented more than six months after its date. Since a bank is expected to exercise reasonable care in paying its depositors' checks, it may refuse to pay even before the six-month guideline if it suspects irregularity.

An instrument payable at a stated future date must be presented for payment on or before that date. If the maturity of a promissory note for some reason has been accelerated, presentment must be made within a reasonable time subsequent to such acceleration (UCC § 3–503[1][d]).

When calculating the number of days of interest, the day of the loan inception does not count, but the due date is to be included. For example, if a loan commences on June 1 and is to be paid off on June 9, there are eight days for which interest is to be paid. For the calculation of interest, the number of days in a particular month or year may differ among the various financial institutions. Sometimes it depends on whether it is an interest-earning or an interest-paying account.

If the due date of an instrument falls on a full or partial business holiday, the day for presentment is extended to the first working day for both the obligor and obligee.

UCC § 3–511 states that a delay in presentment is excused when it is caused by circumstances beyond the control of the holder. However, § 3–502(1) provides that an unexcused delay discharges any endorser's liability for payment of the instrument.

Place of Presentment

Presentment for payment is to be made at the place specified in the instrument. If no address is stated, presentment is to be made at the place of business or residence of the obligor from whom payment is demanded.

When Presentment Is Excused

According to UCC § 3–511(2) and (3), presentment for payment is excused under the following conditions:

1. If the primary obligor has already refused to pay.
2. If the party secondarily liable has waived such a presentment to the primary obligor.
3. If such a presentment cannot be made despite the exercise of due diligence on the part of the holder.
4. If the obligor has died or has gone into insolvency proceedings.
5. If the secondary party has no reason to expect or has no right to require that the instrument be paid.

Nonpayment

Nonpayment
Failure to pay before close of business on the day of presentment.

Dishonor
Failure or refusal to accept or pay commercial paper.

Upon presentment of an instrument that is due and payable, payment "may be deferred without dishonor pending reasonable examination to determine whether it is properly payable, but payment must be made in any event before the close of business on the day of presentment" (UCC § 3–506[2]) subsequent to which the instrument is considered dishonored by nonpayment. A delay in payment in violation of this rule may result in an additional liability for the obligated party to whom the paper is presented, such as payment of a late charge.

Notice of Dishonor

Notice of Dishonor
Notice to be given to any secondary parties who are to be made liable for payment of an instrument.

In addition to the presentment to and nonpayment by the primary obligor, a notice of dishonor must be given to a secondary party to create his liability for payment of the instrument.

Facts

Hane was an assignee of a note signed by Theta Electronic Labs and endorsed by Exten. Theta defaulted, and Hane sued Exten to recover the balance of the note. Hane waited over a year before presenting the note, and he waited almost two months before giving notice of dishonor. The trial court dismissed the suit.

Decision

Affirmed. Hane must show that Exten was given notice of presentment and dishonor before he can hold them on their endorsement. Unless presentment or notice of dishonor is waived or excused, unreasonable delay will discharge an endorser (UCC §§ 3–502[1][a] and 3–508[2]). The court affirmed the lower court's finding that Hane had delayed presentment and notice of dishonor and dismissed the suit.

Hane v. Exten, 255 Md. 668, 259 A.2d 290 (1969).

Who Gives Notice

The payment-seeking holder gives the notice of dishonor after he himself has received such a notice from the maker of a note or the drawer of a draft from whom payment was first sought. UCC § 3–508(1) says that such a notice may be given by "any party who has himself received notice, or any other party who can be compelled to pay the instrument." The dishonor of the paper by the primary obligor must in any event be conveyed to the secondary obligor for him to become liable, although it is not always necessary for the notice to be given by the aggrieved party himself. UCC § 508(8) provides, "Notice operates for the benefit of all parties who have rights on the instrument against the party notified." For example, a promissory note went from payee to A and then to B through negotiation. The maker defaulted against B, the payment-seeking holder. B, who could give a notice of dishonor to both the payee and A, gave a notice only to A, whereupon A gave a notice to payee. Although the payee did not receive a notice from B, he is nonetheless secondarily liable to B because of A's notice to him.

To Whom Notice Is Given

The notice of dishonor may be directed to any person who may be liable on the instrument. Thus, if a promissory note is dishonored by the maker, notices may be given to all the subsequent transferors. If a draft is dishonored by the drawee, the drawer as well as the subsequent transferors may be given such notices. Although the payment-seeking holder may then sue any of these secondary obligors on the instrument, against his immediate transferor he may, in addition, have a claim based on the transaction underlying the transfer.

If a corporation as the primary obligor defaults on an instrument, no notice of dishonor needs to be sent to the corporate executives for them to become secondarily liable if the executives endorsed the paper as accommodation parties.

Facts

Tiber Construction Company, Inc. borrowed $30,000 from Schenectady Trust on a demand note executed by the corporate officers, Sciocchetti and Downey, who also personally endorsed the paper in their individual capacity as accommodation parties. When the corporation defaulted, the payee immediately brought a suit against the endorsers, who denied liability, since no notice of dishonor had been sent to them personally.

Decision

Judgment for the payee. Under these given circumstances, the endorsers were actually involved in all the corporate affairs; they were fully cognizant of the corporate financial matters; and they were the persons to whom the presentment was made and who defaulted for the corporation on the paper. Giving a notice of dishonor would in this case be redundant.

Schenectady Trust Company v. *Sciocchetti*, 82 Misc.2d 1075, 371 N.Y.S.2d 36 (1975).

A notice to one partner of a partnership is a notice to all the partners. A notice to a party who becomes insolvent may be given to the party himself or to his estate representative. A notice to a party who has died or has become incompetent may be sent to his last known address or personal representative (UCC § 3–508[5–7]).

Form of Notice

There is in fact no particular form prescribed for a notice of dishonor. UCC § 3–508(3) states that a notice may be given in any reasonable manner.

> "It may be oral or written in any terms which identify the instrument and state that it has been dishonored. A misdescription which does not mislead the party notified does not vitiate the notice. Sending the instrument bearing a stamp, ticket or writing stating that acceptance or payment has been refused or sending a notice of debit with respect to the instrument is sufficient."

Time of Notice

UCC § 3–508(2) provides, "(A)ny necessary notice must be given by a bank before its midnight deadline and by any other person before midnight of the third business day after dishonor or receipt of notice of dishonor."

Bank violation of this midnight deadline rule is unfortunately not uncommon. It should be understood that an unexcused delay violative of this rule discharges the secondary obligor from his liability on the instrument, even when the delay was not attributable to negligence of the payment-seeking party (UCC § 3–502).

Nevada State Bank v. Fischer
93 Nev. 317, 565 P.2d 332 (1977).

Thompson, J. The Nevada State Bank charged Lucile Fischer's account $2,000 when it received notice that a check in that amount, endorsed by her, had been dishonored. Therefore, she commenced this action against the Bank for wrongfully so debiting her account.

The district court ruled that her liability as endorser was discharged since notice of dishonor was not timely given her. Judgment was entered in her favor together with interest, costs, and attorney fees. The Bank appeals from that judgment. We affirm.

The facts are not disputed. On May 1, 1970, Mrs. Fischer endorsed a $2,000 check payable to the drawer and drawn on the Clayton Bank of Clayton, Missouri. She did this as an accommodation to the payee-drawer. The Nevada State Bank cashed the check for the payee-drawer and initiated collection through Valley Bank of Nevada that same day.

On July 28, 1970, the Valley Bank of Nevada notified Nevada State Bank that the check had been dishonored stating "original lost in transit—account closed." On July 29, 1970, the Nevada State Bank debited Mrs. Fischer's account for $2,000 and notified her in writing of the payor bank's dishonor of the check.

The record does not disclose which of the several banks involved in the collection process either lost the check or delayed action with regard to it. It is clear, however, that Nevada State Bank acted promptly upon receiving notice of dishonor. Whether it was permissible in these circumstances for that bank to charge its innocent depositor rather than to look to one of the other banks involved is the issue of our decision.

Lucile Fischer endorsed the check as an accommodation party and is liable in the capacity in which she signed. NRS (Nevada Revised Statutes) 104.3415. By endorsing the check she engaged that upon dishonor and any necessary notice of dishonor and protest, she would pay the instrument according to the tenor at the time of her endorsement. NRS 104.3414(1).

An endorser is a secondary party, NRS 104.3102(1)(d), whose liability is subject to the preconditions of presentment, NRS 104.3501(1)(b), and proper notice of dishonor NRS 104.3501(2)(a). Where, without excuse, any necessary presentment or notice of dishonor is delayed beyond the time it is due, an endorser is discharged. Such is the command of NRS 104.3502(1).

It is the contention of Nevada State Bank that since it initiated collection within one day of the endorsement and notified the endorser of dishonor within one day of receipt of such notice by it, "delay" does not exist and Mrs. Fischer, as endorser, is not discharged from liability.

An uncertified check must be presented for payment, or collection initiated thereon, within a reasonable time, which in this case is presumed to be seven days. NRS 104.8503(2)(b). Although the record does not advise us when presentment was made to the proper party, NRS 104.3504, we do know that Nevada State Bank initiated collection within one day after cashing the check. Consequently, bank collection was timely initiated.

In our view, however, the second precondition to liability of the endorser, that is, timely notice of dishonor, was not met. Although the Nevada State Bank notified Mrs. Fischer within its midnight deadline, NRS 104.4104, after receipt of notice of dishonor from Valley Bank of Nevada, this fact, alone, does not resolve the timeliness issue.

The record does not disclose at what point in time the check first was dishonored. We know only that almost ninety days elapsed between Mrs. Fischer's endorsement of the check and her receipt of notice of its dishonor. It is apparent that one of the several banks involved in the collection process violated its midnight deadline in giving notice of dishonor. Had such bank given timely notice, Mrs. Fischer would have learned within a reasonable time that the check had been dishonored.

Prompt action by all parties to the transaction is contemplated before an endorser may be held liable. As stated in the official comment to sec. 3–503 of Uniform Commercial Code (our NRS 104.3503):

> The endorser who has merely received the check and passed it on and does not expect to have to pay it, is entitled to know more promptly whether it is to be dishonored, in order that he may have recourse against the person with whom he has dealt.

As already expressed, at sometime in the chain of collection a midnight deadline was violated. Notwithstanding such violation, we are asked to conclude that notice of dishonor given ninety days after initiation of bank collection was timely. We decline to so conclude. Mrs. Fischer's liability as an endorser was discharged when the violation of the midnight deadline by a bank, identity unknown, resulted in unreasonable delay in notice of dishonor. The Nevada State Bank may look to the violator for its recovery. Its customer-endorser should not be held responsible for a violation of law committed by another bank involved in the chain of collection.

Protest

Protest
Formal declaration or certification of dishonor.

A protest is a formal certificate of dishonor (UCC § 3–509). It declares that the instrument was on a certain day presented for payment or acceptance and that such payment or acceptance was refused, stating the reasons given, if any, for the refusal. The holder protests against all parties to such an instrument and declares that the parties will be held responsible for all losses or damages arising from the instrument's dishonor. It is required only on a draft that is drawn or payable outside the United States, although a holder may protest a dishonor on any instrument. It is "under the hand and seal of a United States consul or vice consul or a notary public or other person authorized to certify dishonor by the law of the place where dishonor occurs." The advantage of a protest is that it is evidentiary in character and may save expenses in obtaining or proving evidence through such devices as depositions.

Questions

1. What are the conditions for a secondary party to an instrument to become liable?
2. When should a sight draft be presented for payment? How about a future draft? When must a money instrument be paid subsequent to its presentment?
3. Name some of the reasons for which a presentment may be excused.
4. When and to whom is a notice of dishonor given?
5. What is a protest?

27.2 Discharge

A party to a negotiable instrument may be discharged individually, such as by a one-party release, or by some act that discharges all of the parties to the instrument at one time, such as a payment by the maker. Basically, all the reasons for which a party to an ordinary contract may be discharged from his contractual obligation are also applicable to an obligor on a negotiable instrument. What are those grounds and how does a discharge affect the rights of the other parties to the instrument?

Grounds for Discharge

Part 6 of the Uniform Commercial Code regulates the discharge of a party from liability on an instrument. UCC § 3–601 provides a list of these grounds for discharge.

Payment or Satisfaction

(1) The obligor is wholly (or partly) discharged *by paying* the entire amount (or part thereof) to the holder or his agent. (2) A discharge *by satisfaction* takes place when the payor, with the holder's consent, may substitute the payment of money with a transfer of property, rendering of services, or even payment of a lesser sum. If the holder agrees, payment or satisfaction may be made by any person, including a stranger to the instrument, in which event the surrender of the instrument to such a person gives him the rights of a transferee, who may be a holder in due course (UCC § 3–603).

Discharge from liability does not take place under the following circumstances:

1. The payor pays or satisfies in bad faith a holder who acquired the instrument by theft or who acquired the instrument through a thief. For example, the maker of a note pays the holder with the knowledge that the holder stole the paper from the payee. The maker is not discharged from his liability to the payee.
2. The payor who is not a clearing bank pays or satisfies the holder in violation of a restrictive endorsement of the instrument. As discussed in Subchapter 25.3, if the payee of a note endorses the instrument conditionally to the holder, the maker is not discharged from his liability to the payee if he pays the holder in violation of the condition.

A payment or satisfaction made by a party who is secondarily liable gives the party the rights of a holder who reacquired the paper through negotiation and to whom the primary obligor remains liable.

Facts

K & S International, which sold farm equipment to Howard, received as payment a promissory note executed by the purchaser. The note was negotiated to a Jonesboro bank. When Howard defaulted, K & S paid the bank the remaining balance on the note. K & S then sued Howard to recover the money. One of Howard's claims was that he was discharged, since the note was already marked "paid."

Decision

Judgment for K & S International. Although the holder of the instrument had been paid and had marked the paper as "paid," the primary obligor was not discharged from his liability to the secondary party who made the payment. Because of the payment, K & S International, the secondary party, became the holder of the instrument, which was entitled to payment from the primary obligor, even though there was no re-endorsement by the paid Jonesboro bank to the secondary party.

K & S International, Inc. v. Howard, 249 Ark. 901, 462 S.W.2d 458 (1971).

Tender of Payment

Tender of Payment
Offer to pay the full amount due.

If the obligor offers to pay the full amount when the instrument is due and the holder for some reason refuses to accept the offer, the obligor is discharged "to the extent of all subsequent liability for interest, costs and attorney's fees" (UCC § 3–604). The holder's refusal of such tender of payment "wholly discharges any party who has a right of recourse against the party making the tender." Thus, if the payee has negotiated the paper to the holder, he is also discharged from his liability to the holder if the holder refuses the maker's valid tender of payment. On the other hand, the obligor is not discharged in any way if, on an unliquidated claim, he offers to pay less than the actual full amount.

Cancellation or Renunciation

Cancellation
Intentionally marking or destroying the instrument or its face or endorsement so as to void it.

Cancellation takes place when the holder of an instrument, with or without consideration, makes the cancellation "in any manner apparent on the face of the instrument or the indorsement, as by intentionally cancelling the instrument or the party's signature by destruction or mutilation" (UCC § 3–605[1][a]). Accidental destruction or mutilation of the paper does not amount to cancellation. The fact that in such a situation the negotiability of the instrument may become impossible does not by itself extinguish the obligatory relationship between the parties to the paper. Thus, aside from the problem of proving, the debtor still owes the creditor.

Renunciation
Surrender of the instrument, or a written release cancelling it.

Renunciation takes place (1) by signing and delivering a writing representing a release or (2) by surrendering the instrument to the obligor to be discharged (UCC § 3–605[1][b]). Surrender of the executed writing representing the release is an absolute requirement in a renunciation.

Greene v. Cotton
457 S.W.2d 493 (Ky. 1970).

Action against executors of payee's estate and others by makers of note for declaration that balance of note was released on payee's death. The Grant Circuit Court, James R. Ford, J., rendered judgment for plaintiff and defendants appealed. . . . **Davis, Commissioner.** The critical question is whether a writing by decedent S. R. Jones legally accomplished the cancellation and release of a promissory note which B. C. Cotton and his wife, appellees, had executed to Jones. The circuit court held that it did. There are other questions presented by appellants, but our view of the case makes it unnecessary to consider or discuss them.

On August 17, 1955, the Cottons executed and delivered to S. R. Jones their promissory note in the sum of $72,000 bearing 5% interest and secured by mortgage on real estate in Grant County owned by the Cottons. Various payments on the note had reduced the principal due to $38,400 at the date of the death of Jones on May 2, 1967.

The appellants, executors of the will of Jones, found among Jones' effects a key to a lockbox at Citizens Bank of Dry Ridge. Upon inspecting the contents of that lockbox, they found an envelope bearing the typewritten address:

"To admrs. of my estate
S. R. Jones"

Within the envelope was found a typewritten paper signed by S. R. Jones, which recited:

"I, S. R. Jones hereby request that if B. C. Cotton be living at the time of my death and if there is an unpaid balance on his note and mortgage to me that same be released and the note and mortgage returned to him marked paid. Dated July 7, 1966.

/s/ S. R. Jones"

B. C. Cotton was president of Citizens Bank of Dry Ridge, and there was evidence that Cotton knew that Jones had executed a paper purporting to cancel the note. However, Cotton never received physical possession of the paper, nor did he (or anyone other than Jones) have a key to Jones' lockbox. It appears that the last credit on the note was made on July 7, 1966, the date of the purported release. It also appears that Jones kept the typed release in his own office until Tuesday, April 28, 1967, on which date he placed it in the lockbox at Dry Ridge. His death ensued on Saturday, May 2, 1967. . . .

Patently, Jones was mindful when the release was typed that Cotton might make further payments on the note—indeed that it might be fully paid. Clearly, he did not purport to remit the debt except on the contingency that Jones should die before the death of B. C. Cotton. Most importantly, Jones never delivered the release to Cotton and never parted with dominion over it. Nobody but Jones, or his qualified personal representatives at his death, had any right to enter the lockbox. If Jones had elected to sue on the note, Cotton could not have interposed the release as a defense. If Jones had changed his mind, he could have destroyed the release or modified it, and Cotton would have had no recourse. In short, we agree with the trial judge that Jones thought he had done all that was legally required but that fact, without more, did not accomplish the intended result.

KRS (Kentucky Revised Statutes) 355.3–605(1)(b), in treating the legal requirements for cancellation and renunciation of a note, provides that the result may be achieved:

". . . by renouncing his rights by a writing signed *and delivered* or by surrender of the instrument to the party to be discharged." [Emphasis supplied.]

[1] The rationale of Baldwin's Ex'r v. Barber's Ex'rs, 151 Ky. 168, 151 S.W. 686, is particularly apposite here. As noted in Baldwin's Ex'r, a test respecting sufficiency of a writing attempting to effect a gift is irrevocability, *vel non*. Since there is no claim of a contract to release supported by consideration, the release must stand or fall as a gift. It falls.

> The view we have expressed is generally accepted. Cf. 63 A.L.R.2d 278, where it is written in part:
>
>> "It may be stated as a general rule that a mere statement, declaration, or memorandum by the creditor to the effect that he gives, has given, or intends to give the debt to the debtor, that he does not desire or intend that the debt shall be paid or collected or that the amount remaining unpaid at his death is to be forgiven, is ineffectual for such purpose." . . .
>
> [2] As was recently observed in Compton v. Compton, Ky., 435 S.W.2d 76, despite the *intention* of a donor to effect a transfer of a bank account, the failure to comply with legal requirements cannot be supplied merely by noting the abortive attempt to carry out an intention.
>
> It follows that the court erred in entering judgment for appellees and dismissing appellants' counterclaim on the note.
>
> The judgment is reversed for proceedings consistent with the opinion.

Impairment

Impairment
Impairment of certain rights of an obligor resulting in discharge from his liability.

Impairment of the right of recourse or of the collateral discharges the obligor from his liability on a negotiable instrument. Under UCC § 3–606(1)(a), an *impairment of the right of recourse* takes place when "the holder discharges any party to the instrument to the extent that, without such party's consent, the holder without express reservation of rights (1) releases or agrees not to sue any person against whom the party has to the knowledge of the holder a right of recourse, (2) or agrees to suspend the right to enforce against such person, the instrument, or collateral, (3) or otherwise discharges such person." [Emphasis added.]

Thus, a holder may by a release discharge one party A while expressly reserving the right to proceed against another party B. B is still liable to the holder, and his right of recourse against A is, by virtue of the holder's release alone, not impaired.

Facts

Hallowell held a promissory note executed by Kohntopp and Turner. In consideration of some payment to Hallowell by Kohntopp, Hallowell executed without Turner's consent or knowledge an agreement not "to execute" against Kohntopp, but Hallowell expressly reserved the right to proceed against Turner. Hallowell subsequently sued Turner on the note. Turner's defense was that Hallowell's releasing Kohntopp resulted in Turner's discharge. The trial court decided in Turner's favor.

Decision

Judgment reversed. Hallowell released Kohntopp with the express reservation of his right against Turner. Neither Turner's ignorance of the release nor the absence of his consent had any effect upon his obligation to pay. However, Hallowell's release of Kohntopp did not impair Turner's right to proceed against Kohntopp.

Hallowell v. Turner, 95 Idaho 392, 509 P.2d 1313 (1973).

Unjustifiable *impairment of the collateral* takes place when a holder of a negotiable instrument for some reason destroys, harms, or diminishes the value of the collateral. Since a collateral securing an obligation not only benefits the payment-seeking holder but also strengthens the position of the secondary obligor(s), impairment of it by the holder discharges the secondary obligor(s) (UCC § 3–606[1][b]).

Facts

Garren agreed to cosign a promissory note written by Marshall and his wife in favor of Beneficial Finance Co., with the understanding that Beneficial took a security interest in Marshall's Harley Davidson motorcycle to also protect Garren's interest as a cosigner. When the Marshalls defaulted, Beneficial agreed for the Marshalls to sell the motorcycle and use the proceeds to reduce the amount of the loan. However, the Marshalls absconded with the money, and Beneficial sued on the note. The trial court decided for Garren.

Decision

Judgment upheld. When the motorcycle was sold with Beneficial's consent, not only Beneficial but also Garren lost the right of recovery against the collateral. The sale of the motorcycle without Garren's consent was an unjustifiable impairment of the collateral directly affecting Garren's interest as a cosigner.

Beneficial Finance Company of Norman v. Marshall, 551 P.2d 315 (Okl.App. 1976).

Reacquisition

UCC § 3–208 provides, "Where an instrument is returned to or reacquired by a prior party, he may cancel any indorsement which is not necessary to his title and reissue or further negotiate the instrument; but any intervening party is discharged as against the reacquiring party and subsequent holders not in due course and, if his indorsement has been cancelled, is discharged as against subsequent holders in due course as well."

Reacquisition
Return of an instrument to a prior party who may cancel unnecessary endorsements on the paper.

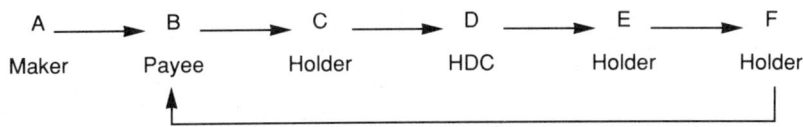

B, the payee, reacquired the above promissory note from F. C, D, and E, the intervening parties, are all discharged as against B; the liability of these parties vis-à-vis B's liability vitiates each other. Also, C and D are discharged as against E. If B cancels C's endorsement, C is discharged as against D as well.

Material Alteration

Fraudulent and material alteration by the holder discharges the party whose obligation is thereby changed unless the alteration takes place with such party's consent or the party is precluded from asserting the defense. As discussed in Subchapter 25.3, a maker of an instrument does not have a defense against an H.D.C. if he negligently allows such a material alteration to take place (UCC § 3–407[2][a]).

Material Alteration by Holder
Fraudulent alteration having material significance.

Certification

When a drawee bank certifies a check at the holder's request, all prior endorsers are discharged from their obligation (UCC § 3–411[1]). In prac-

Certification by Drawee Bank
Certification of the availability of funds to cover the check.

Acceptance

Acceptance
A draft accepted by drawee for future payment.

A holder of a draft may refuse an acceptance by the drawee that varies from the original terms of the instrument. However, "(W)here the holder assents to an acceptance varying the terms of the draft each drawer and indorser who does not affirmatively assent is discharged" (UCC § 3–412[3]).

Unexcused Delay

Unexcused delay in presentment, notice of dishonor, or protest discharges the obligor. This was discussed in the previous subchapter.

Effect of Discharge

When a maker of a promissory note is discharged by payment to the holder, the holder as well as the prior transferors are subject to the discharge. This means that they no longer have a claim against the maker. The maker at this point is discharged even if the instrument is not canceled and/or surrendered to him.

If the holder retains the negotiable paper and transfers it to another holder, the following holds true:

1. If the latter is an assignee or a holder not in due course, the maker's discharge by a prior payment applies to him, since an assignee cannot acquire better rights than those of the assignor.
2. If he is an H.D.C., which is possible, especially if the instrument was paid prior to its maturity, he is immune to the maker's discharge, which is only a personal defense as explained in Subchapter 26.3 (UCC § 3–305).

Questions

1. What happens if a secondary obligor pays the payment-seeking holder?
2. What are the consequences of a tender of payment?
3. What is the difference between a cancellation and a renunciation?
4. Explain impairment of the right of recourse and impairment of the collateral.
5. Against whom is the maker's discharge by payment effective?

27.3 Banking Procedures

Check
A check is a draft drawn on a bank.

Among the various types of commercial papers, the check is undoubtedly predominant in volume and importance. Many people carry a checkbook to pay for their expenses. Thus, a person may have, so to say, a million dollars in his pocket without carrying any cash. How does this work?

PRESENTMENT, DISCHARGE, AND BANKING PROCEDURES

As we already know, a check is a draft drawn on a bank. The maker has money in his checking account at the bank. He writes a check and gives it to the payee. The payee takes the check to the maker's bank to have it cashed or to his own bank to have it cashed if it agrees to do so or to have the check credited to his checking account. The payee's bank, which is called the *depositary* or collecting bank, then forwards the check for collection to the maker's bank, called the *payor* bank. This is done either directly or through a clearinghouse. The payor bank pays the check, debits the maker's checking account, and returns the canceled check together with his account statement to the maker.

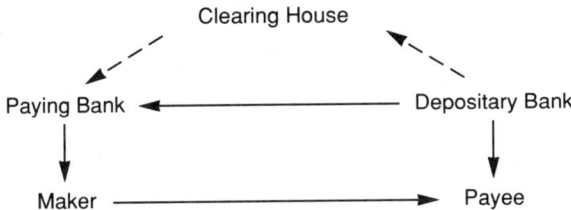

In general, the depositary bank does not allow the payee to make use of the amount of the check deposited until the check is cleared, i.e., the funds are collected from the payor bank. With our modern-day computer and communications systems, clearing checks is done quite rapidly, particularly where the banks may have a direct account relationship with each other. Banks may also be members of the Federal Reserve Bank (the bank of banks), through which checks may be processed. In fact, under the Expedited Funds Availability Act, effective September 1, 1988: (1) Funds deposited in the form of cashier's checks, certified checks, and government checks must be made available to depositors the next business day. (2) Funds from local checks written on an institution in the same metropolitan area or within the same Federal Reserve check-processing region must be made available within three business days. (3) Banks, thrifts, and credit unions are permitted to hold funds written on out-of-town institutions for as many as seven business days after deposit. In 1990, the maximum hold periods are reduced to two days for local checks and five days for out-of-town checks.

In actuality, each bank is a depositary and a payor bank at the same time. As an agent acting for its principal, the bank receives checks deposited by a customer for collection and pays checks drawn by the customer on his account. In addition to servicing checking accounts, called demand deposit accounts (DDA), and savings accounts, called term deposit accounts (TDA), banks provide other services, such as business financing, commercial and consumer loans, documentary collection, letter of credit issuance, and foreign currency exchange. Some banks trade in precious metals or may even conduct business in securities.

Clearance
Collection of funds on a check from payor bank.

The Depositary Bank

The basic tasks of a depositary bank are to *present* the deposited check for payment and to give its customer a *notice of dishonor* if the payor bank

Depositary Bank
Bank where payee deposits the check.

for any reason refuses to pay. There are certain rules to be followed when processing a check for collection.

Endorsements

As explained in Subchapter 25.3, the depositor is ordinarily required to endorse the instrument deposited. In so doing, the instrument is actually negotiated to the bank. In the absence of the depositor's endorsement, the depositary bank is by law authorized to endorse the check on behalf of the customer. As UCC § 4–205(1) reads: "A depositary bank which has taken an item for collection may supply any indorsement of the customer which is necessary to title unless the item contains the words 'payee's indorsement required' or the like." Government and insurance claim checks usually require personal endorsements or a power of attorney given to the bank authorizing the bank to make the endorsement. Many bank escrow services require an endorsement on an escrow check, since they use such endorsements as receipts for the money delivered. Some individual checks may also request or specify that a personal endorsement is required. "In the absence of such a requirement a statement placed on the item by the depositary bank to the effect that the item was deposited by a customer or credited to his account is effective as the customer's indorsement."

Since the payor bank has the signature facsimile of the maker only, the depositary bank is required to guarantee the payee's signature by marking "P.E.G." (Prior Endorsements Guaranteed). (This is apparently the reason that bankers prefer to spell *endorsement* with an *e* rather than an *i*.) Because of this endorsement guarantee, the depositary bank should understandably be reluctant to accept a third-party check (an item deposited by a holder other than the payee himself), as the authenticity of the payee's signature cannot be verified.

A depositary bank's stamp stating "Pay Any Bank" means that only a bank may acquire the rights of a holder except when (1) the check needs to be returned to the depositor or (2) a bank specially reendorses the item to a person other than a bank (UCC § 4–201[2]).

Figure 27.3 Depositary Bank's Stamp

```
JA '88 19
PAY ANY BANK, P.E.G.
BANK of AMERICA, NT & SA
LOS ANGELES, CA.
```

Meanwhile, the deposited check is immediately credited to the depositor's account. If the account is interest bearing, the interest on the deposited amount accrues from the date of deposit. Within the check-clearance days prescribed by the Expedited Funds Availability Act, the computer will show "uncollected funds" for the amount deposited, meaning that the funds are not available to the depositor for cash withdrawal or check writing.

Depositor's Warranties

The depositary bank, the depositor of the check, and any prior holder who obtains payment for the check give the payor bank as well as the maker

Facts

Central Bank, the collecting bank, presented to Birmingham Trust, the drawee bank, a check with a forged endorsement. The check was paid, and when the forgery was discovered, Birmingham sued Central on the grounds that it had breached its warranty of genuineness of prior endorsements. Central countered that Birmingham was contributorily negligent in accepting the check. The trial court entered judgment for Central.

Decision

Reversed. UCC § 4–207 provides that the collecting bank warrants to the payor bank that it has good title to the check. A drawee bank has no duty to verify the endorsement of a check that comes to it from a collecting bank under warranty. Thus, Central's plea of contributory negligence is no defense to the breach of warranty action, and Birmingham should prevail.

Birmingham Trust National Bank v. *Central Bank & Trust Co.,* 49 Ala. App. 630, 275 So.2d 148 (1973).

who pays in good faith such warranties as good title, no knowledge of unauthorized signatures, and no material alteration (UCC § 4–207).

Presentment

UCC § 4–202(1)(a) requires a depositary bank to exercise ordinary care in presenting checks or other collection items to a payor bank or to any nonbank payor for payment. As emphasized in UCC § 4–204(1): "A collecting bank must send items by reasonably prompt method taking into consideration any relevant instructions, the nature of the item, the number of such items on hand, and the cost of collection involved and the method generally used by it or others to present such items."

Notice of Dishonor and Charge-Back

There are a number of reasons that a payor bank refuses to pay a check: not sufficient funds (NSF) and a stop-payment order by the maker, among others. The bank must then return the check with a stamp stating the reason, whatever it may be, for nonpayment. Upon such a returned item, the depositary bank must (1) forward the unpaid check together with a notice of dishonor to the depositor customer "before its midnight deadline following receipt of the item" (UCC § 4–202[2]) and (2) if the check has been credited to the depositor's account, "charge back the amount of any credit given for the item" (UCC § 4–212[1]).

As demonstrated in *Nevada State Bank* v. *Fischer* (93 Nev. 317, 565 P.2d 332 [1977]) (cited in the previous subchapter), the depositor is discharged from liability if the depositary bank violates the midnight deadline rule, although "taking proper action within a reasonably longer time may be seasonable but the bank has the burden of so establishing" (UCC § 4–202[2]).

If the maker and the payee are customers of the same bank, the bank acts as both depositary and payor bank. In such a case, the bank's endorsement on a deposited check is not to be considered an acceptance for which it is liable if subsequent to endorsing the check the bank discovers the insufficiency of the maker's account and decides to dishonor the instrument.

Charge-back
Cancellation of credit given to a customer's account due to nonpayment of a deposited check.

Douglas v. The Citizens Bank of Jonesboro
244 Ark. 168, 424 S.W.2d 532 (1968).

Harris, J. This litigation involves two separate causes of action, which however, by agreement, were set forth in one set of pleadings, and disposed of at one hearing. Appellants, Weldon Douglas, and Janie Chandler, each maintained a checking account in the Citizens Bank of Jonesboro. Rees Plumbing Company, Inc. (which is not presently a party to this proceeding), was a customer of the bank, and maintained checking accounts. On August 19, 1966, the plumbing company delivered its check in the amount of $1,000.00 to Douglas. On that same day Douglas presented the check to the bank for deposit to his own checking account; an employee at the teller's window prepared a deposit slip, dated as of that day, reflecting that the check was being deposited to Douglas' account. He was given a duplicate of the deposit slip, and an employee of the bank thereafter affixed to the back of the check a stamp in red ink, denoting the August 19th date, and stating, "Pay to any bank—P.E.G., Citizens Bank of Jonesboro, Jonesboro, Arkansas." Under date of August 20, 1966, the bank dishonored the check because of insufficient funds, and charged the amount back to the account of Douglas. This same statement of facts applies to Mrs. Chandler, except that the check she presented was originally made payable to a Richard R. Washburn (in the amount of $1,600.00) by the same Rees Company, and this check had been properly endorsed by Washburn before coming into the hands of Mrs. Chandler.

. . . After first demurring, and moving to make the complaint more definite and certain, the bank filed an answer setting out that the accounts of Rees were insufficient on August 19 to honor the checks, and further, that both were charged back to the accounts of the respective appellants on August 20, and the appellants so notified. The bank further denied that the endorsement stamp, heretofore mentioned, constituted an acceptance stamp. The bank asserted that the stamp was no more than a method of identification. . . .

The principal question of issue is, "Did the bank, by stamping the endorsement upon the checks deposited by appellants, and by delivering to appellants the deposit slips, accept both of said checks for payment?" The answer is, "No." . . . This case is controlled by the following sections of the Code: Ark.Stat.Ann. § 85–4–212(3), 85–4–213 and § 85–4–301(1) (Add.1961).

Subsection (3) of Section 85–4–212 reads as follows:

> A depositary bank which is also the payor may charge back the amount of an item to its customer's account or obtain refund in accordance with the section governing return of an item received by a payor bank for credit on its books (Section 4–301 (§ 85–301)).

Subsection (1) of Section 85–4–301 provides:

> Where an authorized settlement for a demand item (other than a documentary draft) received by a payor bank otherwise than for immediate payment over the counter has been made before midnight of the banking day of receipt the payor bank may revoke the settlement and recover any payment if before it has made final payment (subsection (1) of Section 4–213 (§ 85–213)) and before its midnight deadline it
> (a) returns the item; or
> (b) sends written notice of dishonor or nonpayment if the item is held for protest or is otherwise unavailable for return.

Sometimes a maker, when notified by the payee of his bounced check, asks the payee to resubmit the item, as he has since remitted additional money to his account to cover the check. Banks are usually willing to present an item twice, but no more.

Bank as H.D.C. and Its Security Interest

If for any reason, such as a long-established customer relationship, the depositary bank allows the depositor to make use of uncollected funds and if the check covering these funds is returned by the payor bank, the depositary bank becomes a holder in due course to the extent of the actual amount taken by the customer. To facilitate recovery from the depositor, UCC § 4–208(1) provides:

> "A bank has a security interest in an item and any accompanying documents or the proceeds of either
> (a) in case of an item deposited in an account to the extent to which credit given for the item has been withdrawn or applied;
> (b) in case of an item for which it has given credit available for withdrawal as of right, to the extent of the credit given whether or not the credit is drawn upon and whether or not there is a right of charge-back; or
> (c) if it makes an advance on or against the item."

This is illustrated in *Citizens Nat. Bank of Englewood* v. *Fort Lee Savings & Loan Ass'n* (89 N.J.Super. 43, 213 A.2d 315 [1965]), in which the court commented:

> "It would hinder commercial transactions if depositary banks refused to permit withdrawal prior to clearance of checks. Apparently banking practice is to the contrary. It is clear that the Uniform Commercial Code was intended to permit the continuation of this practice and to protect banks who have given credit on deposited items prior to notice of a stop payment order or other notice of dishonor."

The Payor Bank

A bank is under a duty to honor checks drawn by a customer when there are sufficient funds in his account, the check is not over six months old, and the check is in proper form.

Payor Bank
Drawer's bank that pays drawer's check.

Promptness and Due Care

Under UCC § 4–302, a payor bank is accountable for the amount of the presented check if it does not pay or return the item or send a notice of dishonor before the midnight deadline following receipt of the item. Furthermore, "(A) payor bank is liable to its customer for damages proximately caused by the wrongful dishonor of an item. When the dishonor occurs through mistake, liability is limited to actual damages proved" (UCC § 4–402).

Signature Card

Signature Card
Contains the agency's agreement between the customer and the customer's bank.

The signature card, which the customer signed when opening the account, is essentially the agency agreement between the customer and the payor bank, whereby the latter is specifically authorized to pay checks drawn by the customer/principal. Bankers should pay particular attention to signature requirements stipulated on the signature card, especially with regard to co-ownership accounts, corporations, and partnerships. If, for instance, in the case of a partnership, two signatures are required on the partnership's business checks, the payor bank is liable for paying checks with only one signature (*Jewett* v. *Manufacturers Hanover Trust Co.*, 48 Misc.2d 1094, 266 N.Y.S.2d 607 [1965]).

Overdraft

Overdraft
Overdrawing one's checking account.

The payor bank may charge against a drawer's account any check that is properly payable even though it creates an overdraft (UCC § 4–401[1]). If there is an overdraft, the bank has an implied promise from the customer for reimbursement. In fact, most signature cards give the payor bank the right of offset, i.e., the right to debit one customer account to cover an amount owed on his other account. In *City Bank of Honolulu* v. *Tenn* (469 P.2d 816 [Hawaii, 1970]), Harry Tenn, a drawer, had a personal account and a business account at the City Bank. He drew a check for $6,000 on his personal account to pay for a tentative business deal, with the knowledge of the insufficient funds in this account. He even informed the payee that this check was only a token of good faith and that the payee should not immediately present the check for payment. However, the check was deposited at another bank, and when it reached the City Bank, the latter cashed the check after failing to reach Tenn. The payment was executed by transferring $4,700 from Tenn's business account to his personal account. Is the bank authorized to do so in the absence of the customer's express authority? The answer is yes. The court noted, "The authority was impliedly given by the drawing of the check and its delivery to the payee."

In reality, it is more an exception than the rule for a bank to allow an account to be overdrawn without some type of credit arrangement (called "instant cash," "ready reserve," "balance plus," etc.) on the basis of which the bank charges interest on the amount overdrawn.

Stop Payment

Stop Payment
Customer's instruction to his bank to refuse payment on a check written by him.

The drawer has the right to stop payment on checks drawn on his account (UCC § 4–403). The order to stop payment must be received at such time and in such manner as to afford the bank a reasonable opportunity to act on it. Under the UCC, an oral stop payment is binding upon the bank for fourteen days unless confirmed in writing. A written order is effective for six months unless renewed in writing. To avoid involvement in a dispute between the drawer and the payee, banks as a rule do not accept a stop-payment instruction through the telephone.

The bank is liable for paying a check after it has been stop paid. But is the bank's negligence a requisite of its liability?

Facts

Tusso wrote a check for $600, drawn on the Security National Bank, to Adamson Construction Company. When he realized that it was a double payment, he instructed the bank at 9:00 the next morning to stop pay the check. At 10:40 that morning, the check was presented and honored by the bank. When Tusso sued the bank to recover the amount, the bank defended that the customer had to prove negligence on the part of the bank.

Decision

Judgment for Tusso. The depositor was not required to prove the bank's negligence in paying over the stop-payment instruction. Violation of the instruction *per se* was sufficient to hold the bank liable.

Tusso v. Security National Bank, 76 Misc.2d 12, 349 N.Y.S.2d 914 (1973).

Under UCC § 4–403(3), however, it is necessary for the customer to prove the fact and the actual amount of loss to recover on such a wrongful payment. In *Cicci v. Lincoln Nat. Bank & Trust Co. of Central N.Y.* (46 Misc.2d 465, 260 N.Y.S.2d 100 [1965]), the court ruled for the bank when the customer could not establish his loss subsequent to the bank's payment of a stop-paid check.

A drawer cannot stop payment on a check that has been certified by the bank.

Although under UCC § 4–103(1) a bank may not disclaim its "responsibility for its own lack of good faith or failure to exercise ordinary care," it may require the customer to execute an agreement to indemnify the bank if, for some reason irrelevant to the bank's due care, the bank incurs damages because of a stop-payment instruction. This is especially the case when a bank is willing to accept a stop payment instruction on its cashier's check which a customer has purchased. Payment on a cashier's check may and should be refused if the check is stolen or lost and subsequently presented by the thief or the finder. In general, however, payment on a cashier's check cannot be stopped if it is demanded by the payee or a rightful holder. This is demonstrated in *State of Missouri ex rel. Chan Siew Lai v. Powell,* 536 S.W.2d 14 (Mo. 1976), where the court observed: ". . . A cashier's check, unlike an ordinary check, is a check drawn by a bank on itself and is accepted by the mere act of its issuance. . . . People accept a cashier's check as a substitute for cash because the bank stands behind it, rather than an individual."

A check payable to cash cannot have a stop payment executed on it, since it is a bearer item. In those instances where the drawer has used a check guarantee card to negotiate his check, payment cannot be stopped, since the bank has agreed to pay any check up to the guaranteed amount, usually $100, provided that the necessary information has been put on the front or back of the check indicating that a check guarantee card was used.

The following is a stop-payment case, the outcome of which is certainly arguable.

Facts

FJS wrote a check for $1,844.98. Ten days later, FJS called its bank and stopped payment on the check. FJS provided all the necessary information to the bank but misstated the amount of the check by 50 cents. The mistake was repeated in FJS's written confirmation of the stop-payment instruction. Because of Fidelity's particular computer system, the 50-cent error was fatal, and the stop payment was never recorded. Fidelity honored the check, and FJS sued to recover the amount of the check.

Decision

Judgment for FJS. UCC § 4–403(1) requires that a customer ordering a stop payment do so in a reasonable manner. The amount of the check was only one piece of information that FJS provided. FJS had no way of knowing that the perfect accuracy of the amount of the check was crucial. The court concluded that FJS described the check with sufficient particularity and should recover.

FJS Electronics, Inc. v. Fidelity Bank, 288 Pa. Super. 138, 431 A.2d 326 (1981).

Termination of Bank's Authority

Death or incompetence of the drawer does not by itself revoke the bank's authority to pay checks drawn by the drawer until the bank is informed of the death or the adjudication of incompetency and has a reasonable time to act on such information (UCC § 4–405[1]). Even though the bank knows of the death of a drawer, it may still pay or certify checks for a period of ten days thereafter unless ordered to stop payment by a person claiming an interest in the account (UCC § 4–405[2]). This point of law is illustrated in *Cirar* v. *Bank of Hartshorne* (567 P.2d 96 [Okl. 1977]). The reason for the rule is to permit holders of checks drawn by the deceased to cash the checks without the necessity of filing a claim against the deceased's estate.

Customer's Duty

A customer of a payor bank has a duty to examine his bank statement and canceled checks for forgeries or alterations within a reasonable time after the checks are returned or made available to him. The law does not specify the period of time within which the customer must report forgeries or alterations. UCC § 4–406(1) simply states that "the customer must exercise reasonable care and promptness to examine the statement and items to discover his unauthorized signature or any alteration on an item and must notify the bank promptly after discovery thereof."

Banks may attempt to limit their liability by provisions in the signature cards stating that errors must be reported within ten days after receipt of monthly statements and canceled checks. Most courts hold that these provisions are invalid. In any event, without regard to care or lack of care of either the customer or the bank, a customer under UCC § 4–406(4) is precluded from asserting a claim against his bank if he does not discover and report (1) within one year his unauthorized signature or any alteration on the face or back of the check or (2) within three years any unauthorized endorsement.

Facts

From 1965 to 1973, Winkie's employee forged hundreds of checks. Over that period, Winkie never examined any checks, nor did he reconcile any bank statements. Winkie sued the bank to recover for the amounts of the checks. Winkie argued that the bank was negligent in failing to ascertain whether the checks were properly endorsed.

Decision
Judgment for bank. Winkie was negligent by his failure to both examine the checks and set up a system of internal control. The forgeries of Winkie's signature caused the loss. Thus, the bank's lack of care with respect to the forged endorsements was of no consequence.

Winkie, Inc. v. Heritage Bank of Whitefish Bay, 92 Wis.2d 784, 285 N.W.2d 899 (1979).

A similar case is *Huber Glass Co. v. First National Bank of Kenosha* (29 Wis.2d 106, 138 N.W.2d 157 [1965]).

Where there are successive forgeries or alterations, the failure of the customer to examine and notify the bank within a period of fourteen days after the first statement and canceled checks were delivered to the customer would preclude him from asserting forgeries or alterations of later checks presented by the same wrongdoer and paid by the bank (UCC § 4–406[2][b]).

Bank's Recovery Rights

The law furnishes the bank certain means to protect itself against losses and to recover damages in the event errors are made due to its negligence or in spite of its exercise of due care.

Subrogation

Under UCC § 4–407, if a payor bank has paid an item over a stop-payment order of the drawer or otherwise under circumstances giving a basis for objection by the drawer to prevent unjust enrichment, and only to the extent necessary to prevent loss to the bank by reason of its payment, the payor bank shall be subrogated, i.e., substituted, to the rights of the following parties:

Subrogation
To recover loss incurred by its failing to honor a stop-payment order, a bank may assert the rights of certain other parties.

1. Any holder in due course against the drawer. Thus, when the payor bank is sued by the drawer for a wrongful payment, it may assert the defense that the drawer did not suffer a loss, since he would have been liable to the H.D.C. whether the bank had obeyed the stop payment or not.

2. The payee or any other holder of the item against the drawer, either on the item or under the transaction out of which the item arose. Thus, if the bank for some reason cannot claim any defense on the instrument itself, it still may use the contractual arrangement underlying the drawer's check as an argument that the drawer does not suffer any loss. This is the case, for example, if the drawer has not paid for the merchandise he received from the payee.

3. The drawer against the payee or any other holder of the item with respect to the transaction out of which the item arose. For instance, the drawer ordered a stop payment, as the payee did not deliver the merchandise. Since the bank may substitute for the drawer, it may sue the payee to recover the payment erroneously made to him.

Other Recoveries

Can a payor bank in the case of a forgery of the maker's signature, a forged endorsement, or a material alteration recover from an innocent holder not in due course? The answer should in general be in the affirmative. If the paid holder has endorsed the item, he is bound by the endorser's warranties that cover all these irregularities. If the transferor is a depositary bank, it should have the opportunity to charge back the depositor's account, as discussed earlier. The midnight deadline rule, which applies in NSF and stop-payment situations, does not apply in cases involving forgery and material alteration.

The imposter rules of UCC § 3–405, explained in Subchapter 25.3, also provide the payor bank, which is a holder in due course, adequate protection against such losses.

Electronic Banking

EFT Act
Electronic Funds Transfer Act.

With the increased use of computer technology in banking, in 1978 Congress passed the Electronic Funds Transfer (EFT) Act to provide certain answers to some of the emerging legal issues. The Act applies not only to banks but also to other financial institutions, such as savings and loans and credit unions.

Types of Transfers

Modern-day electronic technology can be used by the banking industry in numerous ways. Presently, the following four types of EFT systems are commonly available:

1. Automatic Teller Machine (ATM), which allows the bank's customer, who is given a personal identification card and number (PIN), to conduct various types of transactions, such as deposits and withdrawals, through the use of electronic terminals available twenty-four hours a day.
2. Direct Deposit, which allows paychecks, pension checks, and Social Security checks to be automatically deposited by the payor straight to the recipient's bank account, thus eliminating the problems of late and stolen checks.
3. Point of Sale Transfers (POS), conducted through terminals at a merchant's store. By using the identification card and code, the customer can pay for his purchases by instantly transferring funds from his bank account to the merchant's account.
4. Pay-By-Telephone, which allows a customer by prearrangement to call his bank to instruct the transfer of funds from his account to pay bills that are due periodically, such as utility bills.

Procedural Provisions

Under the EFT Act, the financial institution is to provide the customer with an easily understandable contract explaining the system, his rights, and his liabilities. All EFT transactions must be shown on the monthly bank statement. The customer is to examine the statement and report errors within sixty days. Upon receipt of such a report, the bank is given ten days to investigate the error and, if found, correct the error within one day. Instead of having to investigate the error within the ten-day limit, the bank may also immediately credit the customer's account with the disputed amount, in which event it has forty-five days to investigate.

Liability Limitations

A customer is liable for a maximum of $50 for unauthorized transfers made prior to his notification to the bank of the loss of his identification card or code. If such a notice is not given to the bank within two business days after discovery, the customer can be held liable for up to $500. Over sixty days, the customer's liability is unlimited.

Where does the customer stand relative to computer errors and modern-day electronic thefts?

Facts

Citibank issued to Judd an EFT card and a personal identification code for access to its automatic teller machines. On a monthly statement, Judd discovered two withdrawals totaling $800, which she allegedly had not made. The withdrawals took place on February 26, 1980, between 2:13 p.m. and 2:14 p.m. and on March 28, 1980, between 2:30 p.m. and 2:32 p.m. According to Judd's testimony, which was corroborated by her employer, Judd was at those times at work. Citibank refused to recredit her account.

Decision

Judgment for Judd. It was held that the EFT Act relieves account holders from such a liability except if the bank can prove negligence on the part of the customer or that the customer contributed to the unauthorized use of the EFT facility. As the judge observed: "It is too commonplace in our society that when faced with the choice of man or machine, we readily accept the 'word' of the machine every time. This, despite the tales of computer malfunctions that we hear daily."

Judd v. Citibank, 107 Misc.2d 526, 435 N.Y.S.2d 210 (1980).

QUESTIONS

1. What are the rules entitling the depositary bank to charge back?
2. Explain the position of a bank as an H.D.C.
3. What is an overdraft? What may the bank do when an overdraft is made?
4. In what situations can a stop payment not be made?
5. Explain the bank's subrogation rights.

PROBLEMS

1. D drew a check on June 1 payable to P. P negotiated to an H.D.C. The H.D.C. presented the check to the drawee bank on June 10. The drawee dishonored the check. The H.D.C. did not give D or P

notice of dishonor. D and P claim that failure to give due notice of dishonor is an absolute discharge of their liability. Decision?

2. The H.D.C. of a check that had been dishonored sent notice of the dishonor to the drawer by a properly stamped and addressed envelope deposited in a U.S. Postal Service box. The drawer states that he never received the notice. Was the notice valid?

3. The drawer of a check delivered the check to the payee, who negotiated it to H. H altered the check by increasing the amount from $50 to $500 and cashed it at the payor bank. The payor bank made a debit of the drawer's account in the amount of $500. The drawer promptly notified the bank of the alteration after he received his bank statement and checks. Does the bank have the right to debit the drawer's account for $500?

4. The drawer of a check in the amount of $5,000 delivered the check to P, who endorsed it to H. H took the check to the payor bank for collection. The drawer had only $4,000 in his account, but the bank paid H the sum of $5,000. The drawer refuses to pay the bank $1,000, since the bank had no authority to pay the additional sum. Decision?

5. A check was forged, negotiated, and paid by the drawee. The drawee debited the account of the purported drawer. A few days after the purported drawer received his bank statement and checks, he noticed the forgery and complained to the bank demanding that the bank remove the debt. Decision?

6. Jones borrowed $3,000 from Brown, giving Brown in return a promissory note for $3,000 payable to the order of Brown. The note, dated September 15, was due in thirty days. On October 12, Brown endorsed the note to the Acme Company. Three days later, Acme learned that Jones was seriously ill. Acme wrote Jones that they were discharging him from liability on the instrument. On the due date, Acme demanded payment from Brown as an endorser and sued when Brown refused payment. Brown defended on the grounds that his liability was terminated by Acme's discharge of Jones from liability. Decision?

7. The drawer of a check had the check certified and then delivered it to P, who negotiated it to an H.D.C. The drawer and P now claim they are discharged of liability by the certification. Decision?

8. The payee of a note endorsed the note to H. H, without consent of the payee, extended the time for payment of the note. The maker failed to pay, so H looked to the payee for payment. Decision?

9. D sent a $600 check drawn on City Bank to P. D then realized that he had already paid P. D went to City Bank at 9:00 on the following morning when the bank opened and notified it to stop payment on the $600 check he had written the day before. At 10:40 P arrived at the bank with the check. The bank certified the check and charged it to D's account. D sued City Bank to recover the amount so charged. The bank defended on the ground that D was required to prove that it was negligent. Decision?

10. Booker drew a check on National Bank payable to FMX Corporation. FMX requested National to certify Booker's check, on which basis the bank did so. National later refused to make payment on Booker's check. FMX sued National Bank, which defended on the ground that a dispute existed between Booker and FMX Corporation as to the amount due the latter. Decision?

CHAPTER TWENTY-EIGHT

Payment Assurances and Documents of Title

28.1 Letters of Credit (I)
Basic Concept
   Letter of Credit Defined
   Negotiability
   A Guaranty?
The Parties
   Account Party
   Issuer
   Advising Bank
   Confirming Bank
   Paying Bank and Negotiating Bank
   A Beneficiary
Contractual Bases
Governing Law
Form
   Self-Containing Document
   Duration
Types of Letters of Credit

28.2 Letters of Credit (II) and Bankers' Acceptances
Liabilities
   Transferability
   Documentary Draft
   Payment
   Reimbursement
Account Party's Remedies
Bankers' Acceptances
   Definition
   Form
   Liabilities
   Acceptance Financing
   Eligible Acceptances

28.3 Documents of Title
Definitions
   Bill of Lading
   Warehouse Receipt
Transferability
   Documentary Collection
   Duly Negotiated
   Unduly Negotiated
Liability
   On Warranties
   Bailee's Liability

28.1 Letters of Credit (I)

Letter of Credit
A promise by its issuer to honor a demand for payment upon the fulfillment of certain conditions.

Perhaps the most reliable device to ensure payment of money is the letter of credit (L/C), particularly if it is issued by a large and reputable bank. In essence, an L/C is a unilateral act by the issuer whereby he promises to pay the addressee, who is the beneficiary, a stated sum upon presentation of documents certifying the fulfillment of certain conditions.

Basic Concept

Letter of Credit Defined

UCC § 5–103(1)(a) states that a letter of credit, or credit, means an engagement by a bank or another person made at the request of a customer that the issuer will honor drafts and other demands for payment upon compliance with the conditions specified in the credit.

The L/C is used in all kinds of situations to ensure such performance as payment for a contractual obligation, payment for damages, and repayment of loans. Traditionally, it is used in commerce and especially in foreign trade. A *commercial letter of credit* is an instrument usually issued by a bank at the request of its customer, who is the buyer/importer, whereby the bank undertakes to pay sight drafts or accept time drafts drawn on it by the beneficiary, who is the seller/exporter, upon presentation of certain documents specified in the letter evidencing proper delivery of the merchandise. There are, of course, other modes of payment, such as cash, open account, and documentary collection, but because of geographical distances and the fact that importers and exporters often do not know each other personally, the letter of credit has been of paramount importance and the most widely used payment vehicle in international transactions. In fact, some exporting countries refuse to issue an export permit unless it is accommodated by a letter of credit.

Commercial Letter of Credit
An L/C used to assure payment for merchandise delivered.

Open Account
Seller allows buyer to purchase goods on unsecured credit.

Documentary Collection
A draft accompanied by a title document which is to be surrendered to drawee upon payment.

Negotiability

The fact that the L/C is used in commerce, has value, and may be transferable does not mean that it is a negotiable instrument. It is not an unconditional promise or order to pay, and it is not payable to order or bearer as prescribed by UCC § 3–104(1). It is merely a unilateral undertaking stipulating the conditions precedent upon which the issuer will pay the beneficiary.

A Guaranty?

Although the payment-assuring aspect is common to both the L/C and the guaranty, they are by their very nature not the same. In a guaranty, the guarantor is required to pay upon the primary obligor's default. As an accommodation party, the guarantor is only secondarily liable. In an L/C, the issuer is required to pay upon presentation of documents and is primarily liable under the terms of the letter *per se*.

PAYMENT ASSURANCES AND DOCUMENTS OF TITLE

Figure 28.1 Example of a Letter of Credit

First Interstate Bank

First Interstate Bank
of California
International Division
Box 54191
Los Angeles, California 90054

Cable Address:
FICALBANK Telex No. 674421

SPECIMEN [7]

OUR NUMBER: I100
IRREVOCABLE DOCUMENTARY CREDIT

PLACE AND DATE OF ISSUE: DATE AND PLACE OF EXPIRY:
LOS ANGELES, 27SEP88   10JAN89 AT NEGOTIATING BANK

APPLICANT: U.S. International Corp.   BENEFICIARY: Globe Motor Company
           100 Orchard Blvd.   77 Changan East Road
           Los Angeles, CA 90000   Taipei, Taiwan

ADVISING BANK:
FIRST INTERSTATE BANK OF CALIFORNIA
TAIPEI BRANCH
221 NANKING EAST ROAD SEC 2
TAIPEI, TAIWAN

AMOUNT: USD ***********7,680.00
SEVEN THOUSAND SIX HUNDRED EIGHTY AND 00/100 USD

THIS LETTER OF CREDIT IS AVAILABLE WITH:
ADVISING BANK
BY: NEGOTIATION, AGAINST PRESENTATION OF THE DOCUMENTS DETAILED HEREIN AND OF YOUR
DRAFT(S) AT SIGHT DRAWN ON FIRST INTERSTATE BANK OF CALIFORNIA, LOS ANGELFS, CALIFORNIA

   PARTIAL SHIPMENTS PROHIBITED

   TRANSHIPMENT PROHIBITED

   SHIPMENT/DISPATCH TAKEN IN CHARGE
   FROM/AT: ANY PORT IN TAIWAN
   NOT LATER THAN: 10DEC88
   FOR TRANSPORTATION TO: LOS ANGELES, CALIFORNIA PORT

   SIGNED COMMERCIAL INVOICE IN SIX-FOLD

   INSURANCE POLICY COVERING ALL RISKS

   GENERALIZED SYSTEM OF PREFERENCES CERTIFICATE OF ORIGIN FORM "A"

   FULL SET OF CLEAN ON BOARD MARINE BILLS OF LADING PLUS ONE NON-NEGOTIABLE COPY TO
   ORDER OF SHIPPER, BLANK ENDORSED, NOTIFY U.S. International Corp.
   MARKED "FREIGHT PREPAID"

   COVERING SHIPMENT OF:
   THIRTY (30) T.G. - 40 MIXERS WITHOUT MOTORS, TWENTY (20) T.G. - 55 MIXERS WITHOUT MOTORS,
   ALL 304 STAINLESS STEEL SHAFT PROPELLERS TO ACCEPT 56 C FRAME MOTORS

   CIF LOS ANGELES, CALIFORNIA PORT

   ALL BANKING CHARGES OUTSIDE OF THE USA ARE FOR THE ACCOUNT OF THE BENEFICIARY

   DRAFTS AND DOCUMENTS MUST BE PRESENTED THROUGH FIRST INTERSTATE BANK OF CALIFORNIA,
   TAIPEI. PAYMENT WILL ONLY BE EFFECTED UPON RECEIPT OF DOCUMENTS FROM THEM

   DOCUMENTS TO BE PRESENTED WITHIN 31 DAYS AFTER THE DATE OF ISSUANCE OF THE SHIPPING
   DOCUMENTS(S), BUT WITHIN THE VALIDITY OF THE CREDIT

WE HEREBY ISSUE THIS DOCUMENTARY CREDIT IN YOUR FAVOR. IT IS SUBJECT TO THE UNIFORM CUSTOMS
AND PRACTICE FOR DOCUMENTARY CREDITS (1983 REVISION, INTERNATIONAL CHAMBER OF COMMERCE,
PARIS, FRANCE PUBLICATION NO. 400) AND ENGAGES US IN ACCORDANCE WITH THE TERMS THEREOF. THE
NUMBER AND DATE OF THE CREDIT AND THE NAME OF OUR BANK MUST BE QUOTED ON ALL DRAFTS REQUIRED.
IF THE CREDIT IS AVAILABLE BY NEGOTIATION EACH PRESENTATION MUST BE QUOTED ON THE REVERSE OF
THIS ADVICE BY THE BANK WHERE THE CREDIT IS AVAILABLE.

****

Donala S. Yanaro
AUTHORIZED SIGNATURE

ORIGINAL

Prudential Ins. Co. of American v. Marquette Nat. Bank
419 F.Supp. 734 (1976).

Donald D. Alsop, District Judge This action was initiated by plaintiff against the defendant to recover the amount of $62,000, plus interest, based on defendant's refusal to honor Prudential's sight draft. The matter is presently before the court upon plaintiff's motion for summary judgment.

The relevant facts are established by the complaint and defendant's answer thereto. On December 6, 1972, a Minnesota corporation by the name of McGlynn-Garmaker Company entered into a loan commitment agreement with plaintiff with respect to a loan by plaintiff to McGlynn-Garmaker Company of $3,100,000. As a part of that agreement, McGlynn-Garmaker Company secured an Irrevocable Credit in favor of plaintiff as a commitment standby fee in the amount of $62,000. The letter of Irrevocable Credit, No. 892, was issued on January 2, 1973, by defendant, at the request of McGlynn-Garmaker Company, in favor of plaintiff. In December of 1974, defendant received plaintiff's draft in the amount of $62,000 together with a letter designed to meet the documentary requirements of the letter of Irrevocable Credit. Defendant thereafter dishonored the draft.

[1, 2] Plaintiff alleges that defendant's letter of January 2, 1973, constituted an irrevocable letter of credit under the provisions of Minn.Stat. §§ 336.5–102 and 336.5–103 and that plaintiff's draft should have been paid by defendant upon presentation of the draft and the appropriate documents. Defendant argues that its letter of January 2, 1973, is not a letter of credit, but rather is in the nature of a guaranty. The issuance of a guaranty, defendant argues, is beyond the scope of powers granted to a national bank pursuant to 12 U.S.C. § 24 and is therefore unenforceable. *Border Nat'l Bank v. American Nat'l Bank*, 282 F. 73 (5th Cir. 1922). The defendant further argues that even if the Irrevocable Credit is not ultra vires, it is, nevertheless, unenforceable because the contract between McGlynn-Garmaker Company and plaintiff requiring the payment of a $62,000 fee upon failure of the loan to close is an invalid penalty provision. As a final argument in defense of plaintiff's motion for summary judgment, defendant argues that there are material facts yet to be resolved making the entry of summary judgment inappropriate.

"A guaranty is a promise to answer for the payment of some debt . . . in case of the default of another person, who is in the first instance liable for such payment . . ." while a "letter of credit confers authority upon the person to whom it is addressed to advance money or furnish goods on the credit of the writer." *Border Nat'l Bank v. American Nat'l Bank, supra*, 282 F. at 77. A significant difference in these two concepts is that in the former the guarantor is secondarily liable and in the latter, the issuer of the letter of credit is primarily liable. *Barclays Bank D.C.O. v. Mercantile Nat'l Bank*, 481 F.2d 1224, 1236 (5th Cir. 1973), cert. denied, 414 U.S. 1139, 94 S.Ct. 888, 39 L.Ed.2d 96 (1974). The court is persuaded that defendant's letter of January 2, 1973, labeled Irrevocable Credit, No. 892, is a letter of credit within the provisions of Minn.Stat. §§ 336.5–102 and 336.5–103 and that its issuance is not beyond the powers of a national bank. As such, it is an appropriate device to be used as a loan commitment standby fee. *Fidelity Bank v. Lutheran Mutual Life Ins. Co.*, 465 F.2d 211 (10th Cir. 1972).

[3] Defendant does not allege that plaintiff failed to provide the appropriate documents as required by the letter of credit. Rather defendant argues that the commitment standby fee as required by the contract between plaintiff and McGlynn-Garmaker is an illegal penalty provision and therefore defendant did not have to honor the plaintiff's draft. Plaintiff argues that the loan commitment agreement

> and the agreement between McGlynn-Garmaker and defendant for the issuance of a letter of credit are separate contracts and that defendant cannot allege a defense in this action that may or may not be available to McGlynn-Garmaker under the loan commitment agreement.
> ... The court rules that the contract of McGlynn-Garmaker Company with plaintiff is independent of the obligations of defendant as issuer of the letter of credit and that the alleged illegality of the commitment standby fee is not a defense which may be asserted by defendant in this action. *Barker v. National Boulevard Bank of Chicago, supra.* ...
>
> [Judgment for Prudential Ins.]

(What is a commitment standby fee? In a loan commitment agreement, which usually involves large loan amounts to finance construction projects, the funds are disbursed portion by portion. However, the lender is required to keep the money available, and in consideration of this commitment, the borrower pays a commitment standby fee.)

The Parties

The letter of credit may involve several parties whose designations and functions should be understood.

Account Party

The account party, who is also called customer, opener, buyer, or importer, initiates the entire process by requesting the bank to issue the L/C to pay a beneficiary. He promises to reimburse the bank if the payment is made. "A 'customer' is a buyer or other person who causes an issuer to issue a credit. The term also includes a bank which procures issuance or confirmation on behalf of that bank's customer" (UCC § 5–103[1][g]).

Account Party
Is the bank's customer who requests the issuance of an L/C.

Issuer

"An 'issuer' is a bank or other person issuing a credit" (UCC § 5–103[1][c]). Technically, a nonbank enterprise, such as a large, well-established company, may issue a credit, although the practice is rather uncommon. The strength of an L/C depends on the stature of the issuer. The bank issues a letter for the customer when the customer has sufficient cash, is sufficiently creditworthy, or has a collateral to ensure reimbursement. Although the issuing bank has the ultimate liability to honor the draft drawn on it based on its L/C, it does not have to be the actual paying or accepting bank, as explained hereunder.

Issuer
Is the bank, or the nonbank enterprise, which issues the L/C.

Advising Bank

"An 'advising' bank is a bank which gives notification of the issuance of a credit by another bank" (UCC § 5–103[1][e]). An advising bank is necessary

Advising Bank
Is the bank which, at the request of the issuing bank, notifies the beneficiary.

if the beneficiary is not at the same location as the issuing bank, such as in international trade. The issuer is the importer's bank, whereas the advising bank is the bank located in the exporter's country. Where a large bank nowadays operates worldwide, the advising of an L/C may be conducted by its own branch or office at the exporter's place.

An advising bank does not assume any obligation to honor drafts drawn or demands for payment made under the credit, but it does assume obligation for the accuracy of its own statement (UCC § 5–107[1]). The advice usually includes the wording: "This letter is solely an advice of the opening of the aforesaid credit and conveys no engagement by us." If the advising bank incorrectly transmits the terms of a credit, the issuer may still be bound by the original terms (UCC § 5–107[3]).

Confirming Bank

Confirming Bank
Is the bank which promises to honor an L/C written by its issuing bank.

"A 'confirming bank' is a bank which engages either that it will itself honor a credit already issued by another bank or that such a credit will be honored by the issuer or a third bank" (UCC § 5–103[1][f]). The confirming bank is a bank at the beneficiary's location that confirms a letter of credit at the request of the issuing bank. The confirming bank and the advising bank are often the same bank.

Paying Bank and Negotiating Bank

Paying Bank
Is the bank which pays on an L/C on behalf of the issuing bank.

To facilitate payment to the beneficiary, the issuer may designate a paying bank accessible to the payee. Upon such a payment, the paying bank is to be reimbursed by the issuer. The beneficiary may also offer to sell his draft drawn on the letter of credit to a negotiating bank. The negotiating bank pays or accept the draft on its own volition for profit. It charges a straight fee and discounts the amount of the draft. Both paying bank and negotiating bank may become holders in due course on the drafts purchased. A draft drawn by a seller/beneficiary in international trade is called a bill of exchange, and if it is accepted by a bank, it becomes a banker's acceptance. The advising bank may be the confirming bank as well as the paying bank.

A Beneficiary

Beneficiary
Is the addressee whose demand for payment is to be honored under the L/C.

"A 'beneficiary' of a credit is a person who is entitled under its terms to draw or demand payment" (UCC § 5–103[1][d]). He is usually a seller/exporter in whose favor the credit is opened.

Contractual Bases

Essentially three independent contracts are involved with a letter of credit:

1. The contract between account party and beneficiary, under which the former owes money to the latter subject to certain agreed terms and conditions. If the contract concerns a sale of goods, payment to the seller/beneficiary is conditioned upon the delivery of the merchandise,

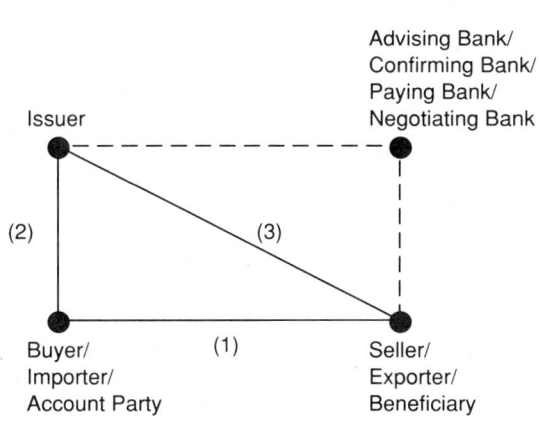

Figure 28.2
Parties to a Letter-of-Credit Transaction

which is to be substantiated by a bill of lading that the seller receives from the carrier.

2. The contract between account party and issuer (called the reimbursement agreement). This agreement serves as the account party's application for a letter of credit specifying the terms as well as his promise to repay the issuer for payments made to the beneficiary.

3. The letter of credit itself issued for the account of the customer. This is the unilateral promise of the issuer to honor the drafts drawn by the beneficiary when all the terms and conditions are met.

Reimbursement Agreement
Is the contract in which the account party promises to repay the issuer for payments made to the beneficiary.

Governing Law

Article V of the Uniform Commercial Code is generally applicable in all fifty states and the District of Columbia. The principles concerning conflict of law obviously play an important role. To facilitate a judicial settlement, parties are at liberty to choose the applicable law as well as the judicial forum for the transaction. In addition, the Uniform Customs and Practice for Documentary Credit (UCP) (revised in 1974), as published in the International Chamber of Commerce Publication No. 290, is an important authority that is often made part of and fully incorporated in both the letter of credit and the reimbursement agreement.

As the L/C is used in various situations, it is possible that in a credit transaction each of the three contracts discussed above may be governed by a different set of rules. In *Intraworld Indus., Inc.* v. *Girard Trust Bank* (461 Pa. 343, 336 A.2d 316, 17 UCC Rep.Serv. 191 [1975]), the lease agreement between the account party and the beneficiary that gave rise to the letter of credit was governed by the laws of Switzerland, the reimbursement agreement between the account party and the issuer was to be construed under the laws of Pennsylvania, whereas the letter of credit itself made a reference to the UCP.

Form

UCC § 5–104(1) states that an L/C does not have to be in any particular form. It must be in writing and signed by the issuer, as much as a confirmation must be written and signed by the confirmer. Furthermore, "(A) telegram may be a sufficient signed writing if it identifies its sender by an authorized authentication. The authentication may be in code and the authorized naming of the issuer in an advice of credit is a sufficient signing" (UCC § 5–104[2]).

Self-Containing Document

A letter of credit should be complete and precise. Yet, by no means should excess details of the underlying transaction, such as quality and condition of the merchandise, be included. It must state the amount of credit in domestic or foreign currency, the expiration date, the documents to be presented, the tenor of the draft, and, where applicable, a brief description of the merchandise. Ambiguities in a letter of credit are to be interpreted and resolved against the issuer (*East Girard Savings Ass'n.* v. *Citizens Nat'l. Bank & Trust Co.*, 593 F.2d 598, 26 UCC Rep.Serv. 475 [5th Cir., 1979]).

A letter of credit should be drafted to be absolutely self-contained. Even though other arrangements may underlie the credit, the letter itself is an independent engagement that is to be construed pursuant to its own terms and without reference to any other agreements. In *Prudential Ins. Co. of America* v. *Marquette Nat. Bank* (419 F.Supp. 734 [1976]) (cited above), the U.S. District Court ruled that the question of whether or not the disputed commitment standby fee constituted an illegal penalty provision is irrelevant to the issuer's duty to abide by the terms of its letter of credit. This is also pointed out in *Shaffer* v. *Brooklyn Park Garden Apts.* (311 Minn. 452, 250 N.W.2d 172, 20 UCC Rep.Serv. 1269 [1977]), where a limited partnership agreement between the account party and the beneficiary was the reason for the L/C to be written.

Duration

A letter of credit may be written for any duration, but the future drafts drawn on it may be limited in time by the law applicable to the issuer. In *National Surety Corp.* v. *Midland Bank* (551 F.2d 21 [1977]), the U.S. appellate court observed "that under New Jersey statute giving banks power to issue letters of credit authorizing holders thereof to draw drafts on it at sight or on time not exceeding one year, the one-year limitation applies not to letters of credit but only to drafts which are drawn on such letters and that instant letters were valid, notwithstanding that they exceeded one year in duration, specifically, were open-ended."

Types of Letters of Credit

The letter of credit is a flexible document that may be used for all kinds of purposes and in all kinds of circumstances. The following paragraphs describe the most common types of letters of credit.

PAYMENT ASSURANCES AND DOCUMENTS OF TITLE

A *straight credit* is an undertaking by the issuer to honor a draft drawn by the named beneficiary only. In a *negotiation credit,* the issuer's undertaking is upon certain conditions extended to a third party who purchases the beneficiary's draft under the credit.

Straight Credit
Allows the named beneficiary only to draw the draft(s) for payment.

A letter of credit may be *revocable* or *irrevocable*. A revocable credit may be canceled or changed anytime by the issuer without notice to or consent from the account party or the beneficiary (UCC § 5–106[3]). However, an issuer remains obligated to a third party who has acted in reliance on the letter prior to receiving notice of its cancellation.

Negotiation Credit
Allows a third party, who purchases the beneficiary's draft, to receive payment under the L/C.

A *standby* letter of credit is a letter to ensure a certain performance by the account party. This device may be used in a lending arrangement whereby the letter takes the place of a collateral. For payment, the sight draft drawn on such a credit needs to be accomplished by a simple statement from the beneficiary giving notice of the performance failure.

Standby L/C
Ensures payment to the beneficiary upon a default by the account party.

Back-to-back letters of credit involve a situation whereby one credit is used as a collateral for the issuance of another. For example, A sells to B, and B sells to C. C may ask his bank to issue an L/C in favor of B which in turn can be used by B as a security to obtain an L/C from his bank in favor of A.

Back-to-Back Letters of Credit
Where one credit is used as a collateral for the issuance of another.

A *revolving* letter of credit is typically used where a series of shipments are involved. The letter may be issued to cover the purchase price of one or two shipments only, with the provision that each time a shipment arrives and an amount is drawn, the credit will be amended to reinstate the original amount.

Revolving Letter of Credit
Is an L/C covering the payment of a series of shipments.

A *red clause* letter of credit permits the seller to draw drafts as an advance toward delivery of the merchandise. The account party/importer who allows such a credit assumes the risk of nondelivery by the exporter. The device is currently seldom utilized.

Red Clause Letter of Credit
Allows the beneficiary to receive an advance toward delivery of the goods.

Questions

1. What is a letter of credit? How does it compare with a guaranty?
2. May a party become an H.D.C. pursuant to a letter of credit?
3. What is an advising bank? Confirmer? Paying bank? Negotiating bank?
4. What are the three contracts involved with an L/C?
5. Name a few types of letters of credit.

28.2 Letters of Credit(II) and Bankers' Acceptances

Liabilities

On the part of the beneficiary/payee, problems related to an L/C lie mainly in the area of documentation required by the letter. On the other hand, a draft drawn on a letter of credit may for various reasons be dishonored, such as insolvency of the issuer, a plain default, or a misunderstanding of the law.

Transferability

The UCC is silent as to the transferability of the letter of credit. In general, an L/C may be used by the addressee only. Under Article 46e of the UCP, a transferable letter of credit may be transferred once. This is sometimes necessary, viz., when a letter of credit is written to a trader or an agent who needs to transfer the credit to the manufacturer or the actual seller. Transferability is also popular for traveler's L/Cs that a person on a business trip may use to pay for purchases. The letter must be addressed to "Mr. X and/or transferee(s)."

The issuer as well as the confirming bank must be informed of the name of the new beneficiary. Since a letter of credit is not a negotiable instrument, the transfer made may only be an assignment. Accordingly, the assignee acquires no more rights and duties than those of the assignor.

Documentary Draft

Some L/Cs require the draft to be presented to the issuing or confirming bank only, whereas others allow the instrument to be negotiated to other banks. It should be noted that while the letter itself is not negotiable, the draft or bill of exchange is, thereby making it possible for the payor or acceptor to become a holder in due course.

Documentary Draft
Draft to be presented with documentation evidencing fulfillment of the conditions.

Drafts drawn on an L/C are documentary drafts, i.e., drafts to be presented in the company of documentation verifying whether the conditions stipulated in the letter have been met. By its very nature, a letter of credit operates on documentation alone, and it has nothing to do with the underlying transaction between the account party and the beneficiary, such as a sale that the document purports to reflect.

What happens if the document is forged or its contents are untrue? In this respect, UCC § 5–109(2) provides that "(A)n issuer must examine documents with care so as to ascertain that on their face they appear to comply with the terms of the credit but, unless otherwise agreed, assumes no liability or responsibility for the genuineness, falsification or effect of any document which appears on such examination to be regular on its face."

Facts

Instituto Nacional (Indeca), a Guatemalan quasi-national corporation, sought to purchase 6,000 metric tons of black beans from RuMex International Inc. A letter of credit was issued by Banco de Guatemala, and since the beans were located in the United States, Banco engaged Continental Illinois National Bank's services to confirm the letter. When the documents were presented by RuMex to Continental, Continental at first found that they were nonconforming. However, after changes were made, the documents were accepted, and RuMex's draft was honored. Continental credited RuMex's and debited Banco's accounts. The beans never arrived. Indeca brought a suit against Continental alleging, among others, gross negligence in examining the documents. Indeca contended that some of the documents never truly conformed and were so blatantly nongenuine.

Decision

The court decided in favor of Indeca. Although the absence of contractual privity between the confirming bank and the account party was recognized, a suite on a tort

PAYMENT ASSURANCES AND DOCUMENTS OF TITLE 659

theory may generate a different conclusion. As the court observed: "A confirming bank owes no duty to the issuing bank's customer. That customer has a remedy against its own issuer. But as to any evidence of wrongdoing that becomes evident only in the revision process, the ultimate customer cannot look to its own issuer. There the confirming bank owes the duty to the ultimte customer as someone who might foreseeably be harmed."

Instituto Nacional v. Continental Ill. Nat. Bank, 530 F.Supp. 279 (1981).

Indeed, the paying bank's accuracy when examining the documents is of great importance. Strict compliance with the wording of the letter is an absolute requisite for the beneficiary's draft to be honored. Even when the underlying sales transaction is executed perfectly, the paying bank may still be held liable for documentary noncompliance.

Facts

North Carolina Bank opened a letter of credit in favor of Courtaulds in the amount of "up to" $135,000 for the purchase of acrylic yarn by Adastra Knitting Mills, Inc. The credit expired on August 15, 1973. On August 13, 1973, the bank refused t honor Courtaulds' draft for $67,346.77, since the documentation did not agree with the letter's condition, viz., that the draft be accompanied by a "Commercial invoice in triplicate stating [inter alia] that it covers . . . 100% acrylic yarn." The fact of the matter was that Adastra was unable to waive any discrepancies in documentation because it was meanwhile bankrupt, and such a waiver needed the trustee's consent. At the trial, Courtaulds prevailed on the contention that the invoices in actuality met the specifications of the letter of credit, in that the packing lists attached to the invoices disclosed on their faces that the packages contained "cartons marked:—100% acrylic." On this premise, it was urged that the lists were a part of the invoice, since they were appended to it, and the invoices should be read as one with the lists, allowing the lists to detail the invoices.

Decision

The U.S. appellate court decided in favor of the bank. "The obligation of the drawee bank was graven in the credit. Indeed, there could be no departure from its words. Bank was not expected to scrutinize the collateral papers, such as the packing lists. . . . Had Bank deviated from the stipulation of the letter and honored the draft, then at once it might have been confronted with the not improbable risk of the bankruptcy trustee's charge of liability for unwarrantably paying the draft moneys to the seller, Courtaulds, and refusal to reimburse Bank for the outlay."

Courtaulds North America, Inc. v. North Carolina National Bank, 528 F.2d 802 (1975).

The expiration date of the letter of credit must also be observed. In *Chase Manhattan Bank* v. *Equibank* (550 F.2d 882 [1977]), a documentary draft presented ten days after the expiration date of the letter was considered a good reason for a dishonor by the issuer.

Payment

UCC § 5–112(1) provides "(A) bank to which a documentary draft or demand for payment is presented under a credit may without dishonor of the draft, demand or credit, defer honor until the close of the third banking day following receipt of the documents." When the beneficiary presents a complete documentation to the bank, whether it is a negotiating bank, a paying bank, or the issuing bank itself, the bank must pay the full amount of the sight draft, and if it is a future draft, it must accept the paper, thereby rendering itself primarily liable for payment on the maturity date. There is an abundance of cases emphasizing the paying bank's obligation to honor the draft on the basis of the documents alone and not on the underlying transaction or other extraneous factors. Under UCC § 5–115(1), a wrongful dishonor may result in the bank's having to pay not only the amount of the draft but also incidental damages plus interest.

Since the paying bank's liability is solely dependent upon the completeness of the documents alone, it is not wrong in accepting a document, such as a bill of lading evidencing a shipment of merchandise, even though the crates are in fact empty. Since a confirmer under UCC § 5–107(2) acquires the rights of the issuer, he may expect reimbursement not only from the issuer but, in some cases, also from the issuer's account party, although this point was also disputed in the above-cited case of *Instituto Nacional v. Continental Ill. Nat. Bank* (530 F.Supp. 279 [1981]).

Reimbursement

UCC § 5–114(3) states, "Unless otherwise agreed an issuer which has duly honored a draft or demand for payment is entitled to immediate reimbursement of any payment made under the credit and to be put in effectively available funds not later than the day before maturity of any acceptance made under the credit." However, instead of an immediate cash payment, the reimbursement agreement between the issuer and the account party may provide for the former extending credit to the latter. The contract may further provide for the interest to be charged on the loan as well as the collateral to secure the delayed reimbursement. UCP Article 14a requires the reimbursement agreement to "state precisely the documents against which payment, acceptance, or negotiation is to be made."

Account Party's Remedies

An irrevocable letter of credit cannot be retracted or canceled by the issuing bank or by the account party. Once it is issued to the beneficiary, there is little the account party can do to prevent a draft from being honored if it is accompanied by documents completely complying with the terms of the letter.

Only when the issuing bank is called upon to pay and accept the beneficiary's draft can the account party obtain a temporary restraining order (TRO) to prevent his bank from honoring the presentment. A permanent injunction may be issued if the account party has a valid defense against the presenter. As discussed in Subchapter 26.3, defenses such as fraud in the inducement or failure of consideration are personal in nature and are applicable only to the drawer, who is the seller/beneficiary of the letter. They cannot be asserted against an H.D.C., which the paying bank may well be. In the latter case, it is for the H.D.C. to prove that the instrument was acquired for value, in good faith, and without notice of default.

Injunction
A prohibitive writ issued by a court.

Facts

Cambridge Sporting Goods was purchasing 27,936 pairs of boxing gloves at a price of $42,576.80 from Duke Sports in Pakistan. Two Pakistani banks, United Bank Limited and The Muslim Commercial Bank, were to finance Duke in the sale. A letter of credit was issued by Manufacturers Hanover Trust Company at the request of Cambridge in favor of Duke. When Duke could not meet the delivery deadline, Cambridge advised Duke on June 18, 1971, that the sales contract was canceled and that the letter of credit should be returned. Cambridge simultaneously notified United of the cancellation. Nonetheless, on July 17, 1971, Cambridge was informed by Manufacturers of the receipt of documents from United purporting to evidence a shipment of the merchandise. The merchandise shipped turned out to be old, unpadded, ripped, and mildewed gloves, showing an obvious fraud. Cambridge commenced an action against Duke and obtained a preliminary injunction prohibiting Manufacturers from paying the drafts. Subsequently, Cambridge levied on the funds subject to the letter of credit and drafts, which were delivered by Manufacturers to the sheriff. The Pakistani banks then sued Cambridge to vacate the levy and to obtain payment of both their drafts, claiming that they were holders in due course. The trial court decided in favor of the Pakistani banks.

Decision

On appeal, the judgment was reversed. "We conclude that the defense of fraud in the transaction was established and in that circumstance the burden shifted to petitioners to prove that they were holders in due course and took the drafts for value, in good faith and without notice of any fraud on the part of Duke." As Cambridge notified United of the cancellation of the sale prior to United's honoring Duke's draft, denying knowledge of a defect would be difficult for United to do.

United Bank Ltd. v. *Cambridge Sporting Goods* (392 N.Y.S.2d 265 [1976]).

Bankers' Acceptances

A check, which is a sight draft or a demand instrument, is certified for the single purpose of obtaining an assurance of payment by the drawee bank. Usually, the drawer asks his drawee bank for a certification to assure the payee that the check is good. If the payee possesses the check, the best assurance he can have is, of course, an immediate payment.

If a future or time draft is certified by the drawee, it is called an acceptance. Letters of credit often authorize the drawing of time drafts that call for acceptance by the paying bank upon its presentment. An acceptance by a drawee bank is called a *banker's acceptance*. An acceptance executed by a nonbank is a *trade acceptance*.

Banker's Acceptance
A draft accepted for payment by the drawee bank.

Trade Acceptance
A draft accepted for payment by the drawee other than a bank, such as a company.

In addition to an assurance of payment, an acceptance of a time draft is also a financing device that is widely used in commerce.

Definition

UCC § 3–410(1) provides "Acceptance is the drawee's signed engagement to honor the draft as presented. It must be written on the draft, and may consist of his signature alone. It becomes operative when completed by delivery or notification." In addition to being regulated by some UCC provisions, the subject matter of a banker's acceptance is regulated in detail by Section 13 of the Federal Reserve Act of 1914, which was followed by numerous legislative amendments and rulings by the Federal Reserve Board of Governors.

Figure 28.3 Example of a Banker's Acceptance

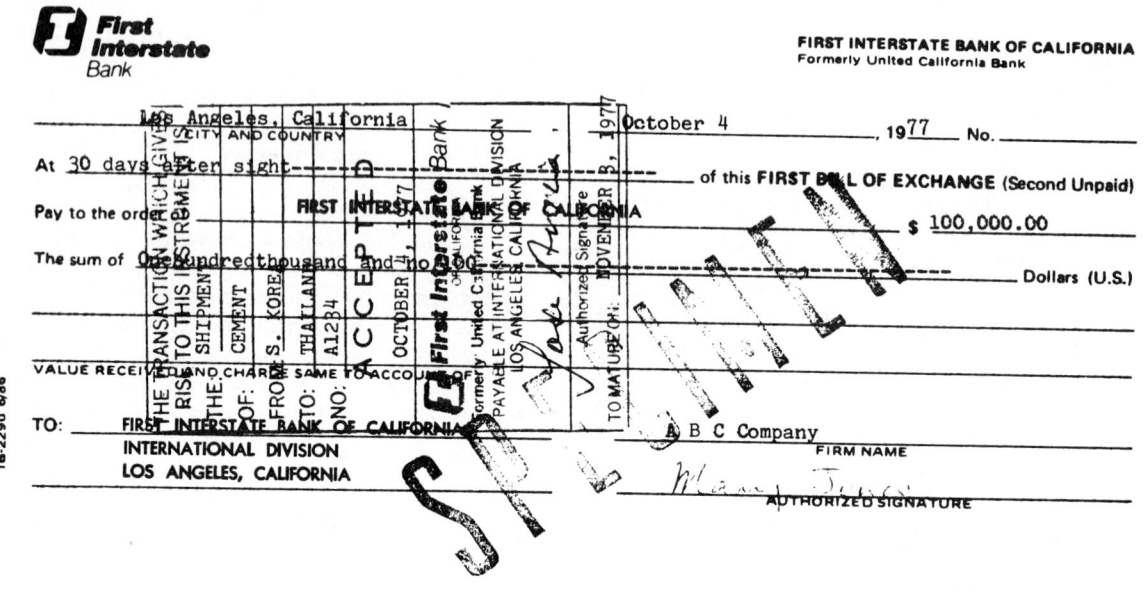

Form

A common form of a banker's acceptance is the use of the word "ACCEPTED" stamped across the face of the draft, dated and signed by the drawee. Other forms may be as effective, such as the use of the word "certified," "good," or "O.K." followed by the signature, or even the signature alone, so long as they do not express or represent a negative response to the drawee's liability to pay. As a high court stated in *Lawless* v. *Temple* (150 N.E. 176 [Massachusetts, 1926]), "(A) drawee may be charged as acceptor although he writes merely his name upon the bill, and that anyone taking the bill has the right to fill up a blank acceptance on the same principle that any holder may fill up a blank endorsement." However, a signature is always required.

Facts

Menke Plumbing-Heating & Sheet Metal Work submitted a bid to perform construction work for West Burlington High School. The rules called for all bidders to submit a certified check with their bid as a show of good faith. Menke's bid was the lowest, but the Board of Education refused to award the contract because Menke's check was actually not certified. The check had a bank's stamp as follows:

There was no signature in the designated space. Menke sued both State Central Savings Bank, on whom

CERTIFIED

June 30, 1970

The State Central Savings Bank

West Point Office, West Point, Iowa

_____

Manager

$6,300.00

the check was drawn, and the Board of Education. The trial court ruled that the check was not certified.

Decision

Judgment affirmed. "The principal issue presented by the Bank's appeal is whether a check stamped as was the check in the case here is properly certified as a matter of law. The Bank claims the stamp placed upon the check by it is adequate to constitute a certification. The lower court held, and plaintiff Menke and defendant Board assert in this appeal that the stamped words indicating certification without the signature of a bank official do not as a matter of law suffice to effect proper certification of the check. We are persuaded the trial court was correct in its ruling, and agree with plaintiff and defendant Board."

Menke v. Board of Education, Independent School District of West Burlington, 211 N.W.2d 601 (Iowa, 1973).

In *Home Savings Bank* v. *General Finance Corp.* (10 Wis.2d 417, 103 N.W.2d 117 [1968]), an oral acceptance was held invalid.

Liabilities

As discussed in Subchapter 26.1, when a check or any kind of draft is drawn, the drawee is primarily liable, whereas the drawer is secondarily liable. What does an acceptance do if the drawee is already primarily liable?

1. As to privity in contract, although with an unaccepted draft the drawee is primarily liable, if he dishonors the instrument, the payee's only recourse is the drawer, whom he may sue for nonpayment. The payee may not sue the drawee, since there is no privity in contract between him and the drawee. On the other hand, if the draft is accepted by the drawee, the payee may maintain an immediate action against the drawee/acceptor, since the acceptance creates a direct contractual relationship between them *(Exchange Bank & Trust Co. v. Arkansas Grain Co., 277 S.W. 871 [Arkansas, 1925])*.

2. As to assurance of payment, a bank drawee, though primarily liable, does not have to pay a check if the drawer's funds are insufficient, but when a draft is accepted, the drawee/acceptor's primary liabiity to pay at maturity is entirely disjoined from the question whether or not he will be reimbursed by the drawer.

In light of these differences, the acceptor's liability is similar to the issuer's in a letter of credit. As much as the strength of the letter of credit depends upon the issuer, the soundness of an acceptance depends on the acceptor. The secondary liability of the drawee becomes significant only if the acceptor does not honor the acceptance for reasons irrelevant to the drawer, such as his insolvency.

Privity in Contract
Refers to the relationship between the interested parties of a contract.

Acceptance Financing

The assuring aspect of an acceptance led to the acceptance being used as a major tool of financing commercial activities in certain areas.

Acceptance Financing
Acceptance created to finance commercial activities.

Foreign Trade For the importation of rubber, for example, an importer needs to borrow money for ninety days, as this time is required for him to resell the merchandise and pay the seller. He may be able to use acceptance financing by drawing a draft for ninety days on his bank, making the draft payable to himself or to bearer, have the bank accept the draft, sell the draft immediately to the bank at a discount, and receive the money. For this arrangement, he enters into an acceptance credit agreement with the bank by which he is to pay the bank the amount of the draft he draws on or before its maturity. The accepting bank may take a security interest in the merchandise to be imported or in some other type of collateral. After purchasing the acceptance at a discount from the importer, the bank may rediscount the negotiable instrument in the acceptance market, an open-counter market located mainly in New York. As the commercial paper travels from hand to hand, the discount rate diminishes, and upon the paper's maturity, the holder receives the full amount of the draft from the acceptor. By then, the importer has resold the rubber and repaid his bank.

Similarly, a wheat exporter who allows his foreign buyer sixty days to pay may utilize acceptance financing as follows. He instructs the importer to have his bank issue a letter of credit authorizing the exporter/beneficiary to draw a sixty-day draft. Upon delivery of the wheat to the carrier, he presents the draft with the documents to the paying bank and has the draft accepted by executing an acceptance credit agreement, using the sales proceeds to be paid after sixty days as authorized by the letter of credit as a security. Upon the acceptance, he resells the paper to the bank at a discount and obtains money without having to wait for the sixty days, while the bank can rediscount it to the public. The proceeds from the sale after sixty days are to be used to reimburse the acceptor.

Shipment of Goods Within the United States This acceptance financing requires the accepting bank to obtain possession of the title documents on the merchandise, such as a warehouse receipt.

Storage of Readily Marketable Staples This type of acceptance financing, too, requires possession of the title documents. Such an arrangement was originally intended to provide financing for basic agricultural commodities only, but the Board of Governors has since been liberalizing the list to also include certain manufactured goods.

Creation of Dollar Exchange With the Board of Governors' permission, a member bank may accept drafts drawn on it by certain approved foreign banks for the purpose of furnishing dollar exchange. This vehicle is often needed to facilitate payments in international trade.

A banker's acceptance to finance a commercial transaction is based on a "self-liquidation" premise; i.e., the transaction itself is the primary source of repayment of the money loaned. By providing the services and lending its credit and reputation, the accepting bank profits on the commission charged for creating the acceptance as well as in the discounting of the instrument.

Eligible Acceptances

On an acceptance, the bank in essence lends money to the drawer without having to use its own funds, since the bank may immediately rediscount the acceptance in the market. This may lead to the conclusion that the bank "creates money" for itself to lend out by simply using its preferred credit position, the abuse of which may eventually result in monetary catastrophe. Therefore, to prevent undesired contingencies, such as the bank's inability to collect reimbursement, the law imposes strict limitations on the issuance of acceptances, according to which only "eligible acceptances" may be discounted in the open market.

Eligible Acceptances
Acceptances which may be discounted in the open market.

Under Paragraph 7 of Section 13 of the Federal Reserve Act, no financial institution may accept in the aggregate an amount for all customers' drafts exceeding 150 percent of the bank's capital and surplus; with the Federal Reserve Board's authority, the percentage may be increased to 200 percent. Furthermore, an acceptance financing for importation and exportation, shipment of goods within the United States, and storage of readily marketable staples is limited to a maximum of six months from the date of inception, whereas the maturity of drafts drawn by foreign banks for the creation of dollar exchange is limited to three months. There are other such restrictions that the acceptance department of a bank's international division must observe.

Questions

1. What is the duty of a paying bank in a letter of credit?
2. Is the paying bank liable if the documents accepted turn out to be forged?
3. Explain the remedies for the account party.
4. What is the effect of an acceptance on the accepting bank in view of its liability?
5. What are the commercial areas for acceptance financing?

Subchapter 28.3 Documents of Title

A document of title is a proof of ownership of certain goods. It is a commercial paper that is bought and sold, and as it travels from hand to hand, the successive holders supplant each other in the ownership without having to transfer the possession of the goods. A title document, therefore, serves an important function in the sale of goods, since no physical delivery is necessitated, as well as in the reserving and transferring of security interest in the property it represents.

The UCC does not cover interstate shipments or foreign commerce and is expressly subject to applicable federal statutes, including the Federal Bills of Lading Act, the Interstate Commerce Act, the Harter Act of 1893 regulating offshore ocean commerce, the Carriage of Goods by Sea Act, and the United States Warehouse Act.

Documents of title include bills of lading, dock warrants, dock receipts, warehouse receipts, and any other documents that in the regular course of business or financing represent title to property. The person named in such a document has the right to receive, hold, and dispose of the document and the goods it covers. The document must state that it was issued by a bailee (e.g., a carrier or warehouse) and must purport to cover goods in the bailee's possession that are identified (UCC §1–201[15]).

Definitions

Among all the documents representing title, the bill of lading (B/L) and the warehouse receipt are certainly the most commonly known and used.

Bill of Lading

Bill of Lading
Document issued by a carrier evidencing receipt of goods for shipment.

A bill of lading (B/L) is a document evidencing the receipt of goods for shipment issued by a person engaged in the business of transporting or forwarding goods and includes an airbill (UCC 1–201[6]). The B/L is both a receipt for goods by a carrier from the shipper or consignor and a contract stating the terms of the transportation and delivery of the goods to the consignee.

While a domestic bill of lading must be issued on a single copy only, an international B/L may be written on more than one copy. This practice stems from the days when postal services were not reliable and consignors felt it necessary to dispatch to the consignee one copy after another for safety. A "full set" of a bill of lading consists of three copies.

Under UCC §§ 7–304(2) and (3), "(W)here a bill of lading is lawfully drawn in a set of parts, each of which is numbered and expressed to be valid only if the goods have not been delivered against any other part, the whole of the parts constitute one bill." Furthermore, "(W)here a bill of lading is lawfully issued in a set of parts and different parts are negotiated to different persons, the title of the holder to whom the first due negotiation is made prevails as to both the document and the goods even though any later holder may have received the goods from the carrier in good faith and discharged the carrier's obligation by surrender of his part."

Under no circumstances, however, may a bailee release the possession of the property without surrender and cancellation of the negotiable title document.

Koreska v. United Cargo Corp.
23 App.Div.2d 37, 258 N.Y.S.2d 432 (1965).

Per Curiam Plaintiff, an Austrian manufacturer and seller of thermographic copying paper, appeals from an order denying his motion for summary judgment for the value of paper allegedly converted by defendant United Cargo Corporation. United, a carrier, having issued a negotiable order bill of lading for the goods, consisting of four large packages, delivered them to the New York purchaser without requiring or taking up the bill of lading, and before plaintiff had received his purchase price.

The substantial question presented is whether United has raised a triable issue of fact in contending that it was excused from its duty of requiring surrender of the bill of lading before delivering the goods. United urges that it was so excused by an oral waiver made by plaintiff's agent and also by a binding trade custom or course of dealing. . . .

A further reason why United may not avail itself of the alleged waiver, is that the waiver was oral only, and would modify the express term of the bill that delivery was to be made at the order of the New York bank consignee. One of the conditions printed on the back of the bill provides:

> "None of the terms of this bill of lading shall be deemed to have been waived by any person unless by express waiver signed by such person, or his duly authorized agent."

Ordinary prudence, moreover, would dictate that the carrier require that such instructions be noted on the bill itself (cf. U.C.C. § 7–303[2]).

For similar reasons evidence of the course of dealing or trade custom is also without significance. The express term, requiring delivery in accordance with the consignee's order, is controlling, whenever the course of dealing or trade custom is inconsistent with it . . . (U.C.C. § 1–205[4]).

In the absence of a triable issue of fact, summary judgment must be granted. Summary relief is, moreover, particularly appropriate in commercial cases, such as this, where the injured party is far away and has relied on documentary rights and evidence. If a trade custom or the oral waiver by an unknown purported agent, contrary to the plain terms of trade documents, were given the effect contended for by United, the ability of such a distant person to engage in foreign trade in reliance on negotiable documents of title would be severely and unduly handicapped. Allowance of such a practice is certainly destructive of the integrity of documents used in international trade throughout the world.

Accordingly, the order denying plaintiff Koreska's motion for summary judgment should be reversed on the law, and summary judgment for $13,939.72, the invoice price, in favor of plaintiff, granted, with costs and disbursements to plaintiff-appellant against defendant-respondent.

Warehouse Receipt

A warehouse receipt is a receipt issued by a person engaged in the business of storing goods for hire (UCC § 1–201[45]). It is an acknowledgement by the warehouseman that certain goods have been received from the depositor for storage. It is also a contract between the two parties on the terms of the service rendered. Occasionally, the owner of the property has his own storage place, but without a warehouse receipt, he may have difficulty in selling the merchandise or borrowing on it, since he is unable to prove his rightful ownership. Such a problem may be solved by the warehouser's taking exclusive control over the goods at the location where they are stored and issuing a *field warehousing receipt,* which is as legal and valuable as a regular receipt.

Warehouse Receipt
Document issued by a warehouseman evidencing receipt of goods for storage.

Transferability

Documentary Collection

Documents of title are either negotiable or nonnegotiable. A bill of lading, warehouse receipt, or other document of title is negotiable if, by its terms, the goods are to be delivered to the bearer or to the order of a named person. If the document calls for delivery of the goods "to the bearer," negotiation may take place by delivery of the instrument. If the document provides for delivery "to the order of" a named person, it is negotiated by the transferor's endorsing and delivering the paper to the transferee. On the other hand, if the document specifically consigns the goods to a named person, it is nonnegotiable, which is the case with a *straight bill of lading*.

A negotiable document of title is also a convenient vehicle for a seller to collect the purchase price from the buyer. For example, a seller in New York who wants to sell goods to a buyer in California can have a bill of lading issued to the order of himself, in which case he is both the consignor and the consignee. The seller endorses the B/L to the buyer and draws a draft on the buyer, making the draft payable to his bank or himself. He presents it with the bill of lading to his bank in New York with the instruction to forward the document to and collect the purchase price from the buyer through a correspondent bank in California. The bank in California presents the draft to the buyer, and upon payment of the purchase price, the buyer is given the bill of lading. The buyer then surrenders the B/L to the carrier and is given the goods. This is a typical documentary collection, or a D/P, which stands for *documents against payment*.

Documentary Collection
A draft accompanied by a title document which is to be surrendered to drawee upon payment.

Duly Negotiated

UCC § 7–501(4) states, "A negotiable document of title is 'duly negotiated' when it is negotiated in the manner stated in this section to a holder who purchases it in good faith without notice of any defense against or claim to it on the part of any person and for value." The holder of a duly negotiated document obtains title to the document and title to the goods. His ownership is not defeated by delivery of the goods by the warehouseman to some other party, including the consignor. Personal defenses discussed in Subchapter 26.3, such as failure of consideration, lack of delivery of the documents, and fraud in the inducement, cannot be asserted by a previous holder against a holder on due negotiation.

However, since "(A) document of title confers no right in goods against a person who before issuance of the document had a legal interest or a perfected security interest in them" (UCC § 7–503[1]), the holder of a duly negotiated title document is not protected against the rights of the true owner or a secured party who has a valid claim against the goods. Thus, if a title document issued on stolen goods is duly negotiated, the true owner will prevail over the holder.

Duly Negotiated Document
Document negotiated to a holder who purchases it in good faith without notice of any defenses.

Unduly Negotiated

UCC § 7–504(1) provides, "A transferee of a document, whether negotiable or nonnegotiable, to whom the document has been delivered but not duly negotiated, acquires the title and rights which his transferor had or had actual authority to convey." Accordingly, (1) a nonnegotiable document, such as a straight bill of lading, may still be transferred through assignment, and (2) a negotiable document may still be transferred, though unduly negotiated, for example, if the transferee gave no value for it or knew of the defect of the instrument. In either instance, the transferee or assignee remains vulnerable to personal defenses that any of the previous holders may have.

Liability

The liabilities related to a document of title are generally on the part of the previous transferor(s) and the bailee who has the ultimate obligation to deliver the property to the rightful owner.

On Warranties

The party negotiating or transferring a document of title for value (other than an intermediary or a secured party) warrants to his immediate purchaser only that

1. The document is genuine. Thus, one who purchases a forged document of title may recover from the person who sold it to him.
2. The person has no knowledge of any fact that would impair the document's validity or worth.
3. The person's negotiation or transfer is rightful and fully effective with respect to the document and the goods it represents (UCC § 7–507).

The intermediary, such as a collecting bank entrusted with documents, warrants only good faith and authority to act (UCC § 7–508). The endorser is not liable for any default of the bailee or previous endorsers (UCC § 7–505).

Bailee's Liability

The duties and liabilities of the common carrier and the warehouser were discussed in Subchapter 14.3 on the topic of bailments. Without prejudice to the absolute liability of a common carrier, the law imposes upon the carrier in general and the warehouser the duty to exercise reasonable care over the goods entrusted to them. Each is liable for damages for the loss of, or injury to, the property caused by failure to perform the bailee's obligation "as a reasonably careful man" (UCC §§ 7–204[1] and 7–309[1]).

The following is a case involving the liability of an interstate common carrier.

Facts

Refrigerated Transport Co. (RTC) carried a load of beef shipped by Frosty Land Foods in Montgomery, Alabama, to Scott Meat Company in Los Angeles. The bill of lading provided for delivery of the load to the consignee in Los Angeles on Friday, December, 9, 1977, at 6 a.m., but the drivers actually arrived at approximately 3:30 p.m. that Friday. Because of the late arrival, Scott informed the drivers that it was not possible for the shipment of meat to be processed at that time, upon which the drivers checked into a motel for the weekend. The beef was delivered to Scott on Monday, December 12. Upon inspection, Scott found that the meat had become "off condition" and refused the shipment. After extensive trimming, Frosty Land sold the meat at a loss of $13,529 and brought a suit against RTC to recover the loss.

Decision

Judgment for Frosty Land. The load of beef was in good condition when entrusted to Refrigerated Transport. Apart from the late delivery, it was obvious that the merchandise was damaged while in the custody of RTC. Unless RTC could show that the loss was to be attributed solely to one or more of the excepted causes (act of God, act of public enemy, act of public authority, act of shipper, and the inherent nature of the goods), RTC as a common carrier was liable for the damage. It was not established that the loss was from any of these causes.

Frosty Land Foods v. *Refrigerated Transport Co.*, 613 F.2d 1344 (Ala., 1980).

The following case involved the liability of a warehouseman. Note that the court imposed the burden of proving the absence of negligence on the defendant/bailee.

Facts

Singer's air conditioners had been stored in Stoda warehouses for several years. When Singer's transport manager, Guy Bataglia, in May 1974, visited the Stoda's Hoffman Plant, where 133 cartons of Singer's air-conditioning units were kept, he inquired about the sprinkler system and was told by Larry Ellis, Stoda's president, that the system was operative, although he knew that it had been turned off. A fire broke out on July 7, 1974, destroying Singer's property. Singer sued Stoda to recover the value of the destroyed air conditioners.

Decision

Judgment for Singer. The facts were that the defendant had the custody of the plaintiff's property. This was sufficient to establish a prima facie case of defendant's liability. It was for Stoda to prove that it was not negligent on its part, and the warehouse had not offered any such evidence. On the strength of the prima facie case, Singer was entitled to recover the loss.

Singer Co. v. *Stoda*, 79 App.Div.2d 227, 436 N.Y.S.2d 508 (1981).

What is the liability of a shipping company for delivering the merchandise to a holder of a forged bill of lading?

David Crystal, Inc. v. Cunard Steam-Ship Co.
223 F.Supp. 273 (D.C.N.Y., 1963), affirmed 339 F.2d 295 (2d Cir.), certiorari denied 380 U.S. 976, 85 S.Ct. 1339, 14 L.Ed.2d 271 and 380 U.S. 976, 85 S.Ct. 1340, 14 L.Ed.2d 271.

Levet, District Judge This action in admiralty, brought by the libellant, David Crystal, Inc. (Crystal), seeks to recover the value of twenty-eight of its shipment of twenty-nine cases of shirts transported by the respondent, Cunard Steam-Ship Co. (Cunard), pursuant to an ocean bill of lading consigning the goods to Crystal's customs broker in New York, Penson & Company (Penson). . . .

A single sentence suffices to express the essential facts in this case: The cargo in question was discharged from Cunard's vessel to the pier by Clark, the stevedore, and from there misdelivered by Clark upon the presentation of a forged delivery order of the customs broker, Penson, obtained by the thieves through the complicity of one of Penson's employees. While pilferage on the New York

> docks is not new, the cool assurance with which the conspirators completed the necessary formalities and waited at the pier almost nine hours until the cargo was finally loaded aboard their truck, gives some indication that this was a masterly executed plot to obtain the cargo by persons more than casually familiar with the procedures of the piers and the customs brokers. . . .
>
> At the outset is the question of Cunard's liability. It was undisputed at the trial that the misdelivery occurred after the cargo had been discharged from the vessel in the same good order and condition, segregated on the pier by the stevedore, and notice given to the consignee of the time and place of the delivery.
>
> The bill of lading provides:
>
>> Packages merchandise to be delivered subject to the exceptions, restrictions and conditions of the undermentioned clauses, from the ship's deck where the Shipowner's responsibility shall cease. . . .
>
> . . . Were a literal reading of the bill of lading permitted, the case would clearly come to a swift end in favor of the carrier. But so easy a solution is not possible. . . .
>
> Cunard's liability as a carrier had ceased and both it and its agent Clark stood as warehouseman in relation to the cargo. The question becomes, what is the liability of a carrier, as warehouseman, for a delivery of the goods to the wrong persons. . . .
>
> The libellant argues that a warehouseman is absolutely liable for a misdelivery without any question as to his negligence. . . . As Professor Braucher of Harvard states, "Delivery to the wrong person, under the Code as under prior law, would seem to subject the bailee to an absolute liability to the person entitled under the document, even though, for example, the bailee relied on a skillfully forged delivery order."
>
> . . . Libellant Crystal is entitled to an interlocutory decree sustaining its claim for liability against the respondent-petitioner Cunard.

While under UCC §§ 7–204(2) and 7–309(2) the warehouseman and the carrier may limit the amount of liability, they may not stipulate exculpatory clauses in the title document so as to modify and reduce their obligation to exercise due care.

Facts

Kimberly-Clark had merchandise stored at Lake Erie Warehouse, which sustained water damage allegedly caused by the warehouseman's negligence. Lake Erie defended on the ground that the rate schedule agreement contained, among others, the following exculpatory clause:

> "Sec. 7(c) Warehouseman shall not be liable for damage to customer's goods which are damaged or destroyed by perils insured against by customer; as evidence of which customer waives any and all right of recovery from warehouseman for losses caused by any other perils against which customer has insured."

Decisions

Judgment for Kimberly-Clark. Although under UCC § 7–202(3) a warehouseman may insert in his receipt any terms, the terms may not be contrary to his obligation of delivery or his duty of care under UCC § 7–204.

Kimberly-Clark Corp. v. *Lake Erie Warehouse,* 49 A.D.2d. 492, 375 N.Y.S.2d 918 (1975).

QUESTIONS

1. What are the functions of a document of title?
2. What is field warehousing?
3. Explain a documentary collection.
4. What is the difference between due negotiation and undue negotiation?
5. What is the limitation for a bailee when setting forth the terms of his service?

PROBLEMS

1. Cashmere Inc., a small textile manufacturer in London, purchased wool from Auckland Export in New Zealand through the Phoenix Traders in Arizona, a large wholesale enterprise. To ensure payment for the commodity, Phoenix issued at Cashmere's request a letter of credit allowing Auckland to draw a sight draft accompanied by the necessary documents evidencing shipment of the merchandise. Upon presentation of the documentary draft, Phoenix defaulted and claimed that as a nonbank it was not allowed to issue a commercial letter of credit. Decision?

2. Both Mary Marion and Paul Paulson were established customers of the Boston Fishermen's Bank. Mary borrowed $10,000 from Paul on a promissory note accompanied by a letter executed by the bank stating: "We hereby guarantee Mary Marion's payment obligation on the promissory note of 1-1-1988 in the amount of $10,000 in favor of Paul Paulson, payable 60 days after date." Sixty days went by and Mary did not pay. Paul immediately sued the bank. Decision?

3. The Portland Bank wrote a letter of credit in favor of Farmer Olson in Iowa for delivery of corn. Portland requested the Progressive Farmers' Bank in Des Moines to advise Olson of the letter. Upon fulfillment of all the conditions in the letter, Olson drew a draft on Portland and presented it with the necessary documents to Progressive Farmers' for payment. The bank refused to pay and denied any liability resulting from Portland's letter of credit. Decision?

4. The Dallas Importers Bank issued a letter of credit in favor of Mercedes Exports in Hamburg, West Germany, authorizing the beneficiary to draw a sight draft upon presentation of a bill of lading evidencing the shipment to Cindy Olivares, Dallas, Texas, of one 1989 Mercedes Benz Model 450 SL "as specified in the sales agreement dated 6-1-1988." The draft was presented and paid by the bank on the presentation of a bill of lading covering "one 1989 Mercedes Benz Model 450 SL." Cindy refused to pay the bank, since the car was a right-hand-drive, whereas the sales agreement specifically required a steering wheel on the left side of the car. Decision?

5. Mary Moore lent $20,000 to Rodolfo Rivera, payable on or before 12-31-1990. At Rivera's request, the First Bank of Oklahoma issued a letter of credit in favor of Moore, ensuring Rivera's repayment of the loan. Rivera defaulted. Moore drew a draft on the bank in accordance with the tenor of the letter of credit. The bank dishonored the draft, claiming that the letter could not have been a letter of credit, since it was to guarantee a loan and not to ensure the payment of goods in a commercial transaction. Decision?

6. Charmant Handbag Manufacturers deposited $45,000 at the Orlando Security Bank and executed a reimbursement agreement, requesting the bank to issue a letter of credit in favor of Exotic Leather Enterprises in Lusaka, Zambia, for the importation of crocodile skin. When the merchandise arrived in the United States, it was confiscated by U.S. Customs for violation of the law protecting wildlife. Charmant immediately instructed Orlando Security not to pay the draft, and when the bank refused to obey the instruction, Charmant asked the court to enjoin the bank from making the payment. Decision?

7. Kiddie Fun Dealers in Philadelphia purchased toys from Toy World in Hong Kong. A letter of credit was issued by The Entertainment Bank, which instructed its correspondent in Hong Kong—the Bank of Kowloon—to pay the beneficiary in accordance with the terms and conditions of the letter. Toy World presented to Kowloon Bank the documentary draft exactly as stipulated in the letter. The bank examined the documents carefully, found them to be in order, and made the payment. The crates arrived. However, they contained only worthless papers and no merchandise. Kiddie Fun sued the Bank of Kowloon, as it did not ascertain the contents of the crates when they were shipped. Decision?

8. Tommy Saito drew a time draft on the Apple Valley Bank, payable to David Cooperman, on 12-31-1990. The bank accepted the draft, but it meanwhile went bankrupt and out of business. Upon maturity of the time draft, David presented the acceptance to Tommy, who refused to pay because the draft was already

accepted by the bank and the acceptor alone was to be held liable for the payment. Decision?

9. An exporter in Osaka, Japan, shipped ten Toyota Corollas, Model 1989 LE, and acquired a set of a bill of lading consisting of three copies. He sold one copy to A, then a copy to B, and then a copy to C, all through due negotiation. Sakura Maru, the common carrier, released the cargo to B upon presentation of his copy of the bill of lading. A sued Sakura to recover the value of the ten Toyotas. Decision?

10. Liza stored all of her goods in the Watchman Warehouse, obtaining for them a negotiable warehouse receipt making the goods deliverable to Liza's order. Liza then duly negotiated the warehouse receipt to Bill for value. Liza returned to Watchman Warehouse and demanded her goods, which were turned over to her by an employee of the warehouse. Liza then disappeared with the goods and the money Bill had paid her for the receipt. Bill went to pick up the goods and presented the receipt, but, of course, the goods were not available. Bill sued Watchman Warehouse for the wrongful release of the goods. Will Bill be able to collect?

PART EIGHT

Secured Transactions, Insurance, Bankruptcy, Estates and Trusts

CHAPTER TWENTY-NINE
Secured Transactions

CHAPTER THIRTY
Insurance

CHAPTER THIRTY-ONE
Bankruptcy

CHAPTER THIRTY-TWO
Estates and Trusts

Secured Transactions, Insurance, Bankruptcy, Estates and Trusts

This last part of the textbook covers miscellaneous subject matters related to business.

Chapter 29 explains secured transactions which concern credit as an integral part of business. When a businessman extends credit and takes a collateral for the lending arrangement, how does he know whether his interest in the collateral is enforceable through the court of law, especially if the property is in the borrower's possession?

Chapter 30 deals with insurance. For sure, no one would doubt the importance of insurance in business. After all, one's shop may be destroyed by fire. A shipment of merchandise from overseas may be lost. A company's car may be involved in a traffic accident. A business partner, on whom the company depends, may die.

Chapter 31 discusses bankruptcy. Although bankruptcy is generally considered undesirable, occasionally, it cannot be avoided. What is then the procedure? What are the rights and duties of the bankrupt individual or company? What are the rights and duties of the creditors? Is liquidation the only resort for a person or a business having financial troubles?

Chapter 32 covers estates and trusts. Since the business person usually accumulates a considerable amount of wealth throughout the years, proper planning is in order should death occur. Through wills, trusts, and other legal devices, not only can frustration and dissension among the surviving relatives be avoided, but also death taxes may be reduced significantly, and a long winding and expensive probate may be eliminated.

CHAPTER TWENTY-NINE

Secured Transactions

29.1 Security Interest in Real Estate
Unsecured Credit
Secured Credit
Real Estate Security Devices
Mortgage
    Form
    Transfer of the Property
    Collateral Impairment
    Foreclosure
Deed of Trust
    Form
    Property Transfer and Impairment
    Foreclosure
Land Contract
    Form
    Transfer by Vendor
    Transfer by Vendee
    Default

29.2 Security Interest in Personal Property (I)
Creation of Security Interest
Possession
Security Agreement

Attachment
    Value
    Debtor's Right in the Collateral
Perfection
    By Attachment
    By Possession
    By Filing a Financing Statement

29.3 Security Interest in Personal Property (II)
Priorities
    Between Perfected Interests
    Between Perfected and Unperfected Interests
    Between Nonperfected Interests
    After-acquired Property
    Purchase Money
    Future Advances
    Special Priorities
    State Regulation
Default of the Debtor
    Remedies
    Secured Party's Right to Possession
    Sale of Collateral
    Distribution of Proceeds

29.1 Security Interest in Real Estate

Credit has been and will perhaps always be an indispensable and important part of the American economy. Financial institutions (i.e., commercial banks, savings and loan associations, and finance companies), large and small businesses, individual merchants, and people at large lend and borrow money to and from one another for all kinds of reasons and purposes. All these borrowings take place either as unsecured or secured transactions.

Unsecured Credit

Unsecured Credit
Credit extended without the security of a collateral.

Unsecured transactions are quite common. For example, a friend borrows $10 "until pay day"; credit cards and department store charge accounts are largely based on unsecured credit; a bank customer borrows money from his bank "on his signature"; or a retailer needs thirty days or more to pay his wholesaler for the supplies. Such an unsecured lending means that the creditor gets nothing more than the debtor's promise to pay under the agreed terms. This promise can be formalized by a promissory note that may or may not be a negotiable instrument (discussed in the earlier chapters).

If the debtor does not keep his promise, the creditor's only recourse is to sue the debtor in court. When a judgment is obtained and a writ of execution is issued, property owned by the debtor may be used to satisfy the creditor. Salaries, wages, and other income to which the debtor is entitled may be garnished. The problem, however, is that the debtor is often "judgment proof" if he does not own property of any significance or any collectible income, in which event the creditor must simply take the loss. Under our civil law system, no judgment debtor can be incarcerated or otherwise punished for not being able to satisfy the judgment.

Unsecured credit, therefore, is mainly a matter of trust. What the creditor is looking at is the character and reputation of the prospective borrower, whether an individual or a company, as well as his or its expected capacity to service the debt. By proving to be trustworthy, the debtor enhances his credit standing in the world of finance. The unsecured creditor may, of course, improve his position by requiring a cosigner or guarantor who will repay the loan if the debtor defaults.

Secured Credit

Secured Credit
Credit extended with the security of a collateral.

Collateral
Something of value pledged to secure the payment of a debt.

To minimize the risk of nonpayment, the creditor may ask for a collateral to secure the loan. Real as well as personal property, such as cars, boats, airplanes, household appliances, farm equipment, factory machineries, or business inventories, can all be used as collateral. The loan is said to be wholly collateralized if the value of the collateral is higher than the amount of the debt. Otherwise, the loan is only partly collateralized. Should the debtor default, the creditor then has the collateral as a secondary source of repayment.

While the debt itself in a secured transaction is signified by a promissory note, there is, in addition, something else, such as a document that establishes the creditor's security interest in the given collateral. No doubt, the legality of this security interest is of utmost importance, for in the absence of this legality, the supposedly secured loan remains, in effect, unsecured.

Promissory Note
Written evidence of a debt and a promise to pay it.

Real Estate Security Devices

The purchase of residential, commercial, and other income properties always involves so much money that few people can afford to pay the total price with their own available funds. A buyer usually pays only a small down payment, such as 10 to 20 percent of the agreed price, and borrows the remaining funds from a commercial or savings bank or other source. In so doing, he defers the payment on the property over a period of time, sometimes twenty or thirty years, or even longer. As one can make considerable profits in the real estate business out of borrowed funds, the game of buying property is often to make as small as possible a down payment and borrow the remainder. This is called "leverage."

In addition to the promissory note evidencing the debt, there are several devices and many variations thereof through which the lender can acquire his security interest in the real property. Commonly known are the mortgage, the deed of trust, and the land contract.

Mortgage

A mortgage is usually defined as a contract between the borrower, who is the *mortgagor,* and the lender, who is the *mortgagee,* by which a specific property belonging to the debtor is hypothecated to ensure repayment of the loan. To "hypothecate" means to pledge, whereby the ownership and possession of the property remain with the pledgor. Under this lien theory, the debtor's legal title and right to possession can be divested only upon default through the prescribed foreclosure proceedings. Some states follow the common law title theory that upon the making of the mortgage, title passes to the mortgagee subject to a condition subsequent of payment of the debt. When the obligation is paid, title reverts to the mortgagor.

Mortgage
A pledge of property, where title of the property remains with the debtor.

Hypothecate
To use real property as collateral for a loan.

Form

The mortgage instrument can be written in the form of an ordinary conveyance by the mortgagor to the mortgagee. It is executed with the same formalities used in the completion of deeds conveying title. It differs only in that there is usually a statement to the effect that the mortgage is void when the mortgagor completes payment of the debt. Such a provision is referred to as a "defeasance," which can also be accomplished through a separate document of "reconveyance." The New York statutory mortgage Form M simply states that the mortgagor mortgages to the mortgagee the property concerned.

Defeasance
Provision voiding the mortgage upon complete repayment of the debt.

Constructive Notice
Notice implied by law.

To impart constructive notice to subsequent purchasers of the property and encumbrancers, the mortgage instrument may usually be recorded. It should be noted, however, that an unrecorded mortgage is still valid and binding between the mortgagor and mortgagee. Also, the mortgagor's heirs and donees cannot deny the mortgage on the ground that it has not been recorded.

Transfer of the Property

In the absence of provisions to the contrary, the mortgagor is ordinarily permitted to transfer the property without the mortgagee's permission. Such a transfer passes only the mortgagor's interest or "equity" in the property and does not in anyway defeat or impair a properly recorded mortgage. Without an express release by the mortgagee, the mortgagor remains liable for the debt, regardless of whether the mortgagor's transferee agrees to assume the loan. On the other hand, the mortgagee is usually free to transfer or assign the mortgage at any time.

Collateral Impairment

Collateral Impairment
Decreasing the value of a collateral.

During the mortgage period, the mortgagor is generally entitled to possession of the property. Mortgagors in possession are responsible for the property and are expected to refrain from any conduct that may impair the value of the collateral. For example, in *Berns Construction Co. v. Highley* (332 F.2d 240 [7th Cir. 1964]), a mortgagor was held liable for removing and selling dirt and gravel from the mortgaged land, since the act was considered to reduce the value of the collateral.

Foreclosure

Foreclosure
Sale of mortgage property on default by mortgagor in satisfaction of the mortgage debt.

If the mortgagor fails to make the payments, the remedy for the mortgagee is through foreclosure of the mortgage. Most states have a procedure of foreclosure by judicial sale conducted by an officer of the court. In many jurisdictions, the mortgagor has a statutory right of redemption to recover the property by paying the full amount of the loan obligation plus costs within a specified time after the sale.

Some states permit a power of sale clause in the mortgage agreement, which allows the mortgagee to foreclose the property by sale without the necessity of a court decree. Such a power of sale is, in essence, similar to a power of attorney. The mortgagee as an attorney-in-fact is to execute the deed in the name of the mortgagor to convey the title to the new purchaser.

If foreclosed property sells for more than the amount due on the secured note, the surplus should be returned to the mortgagor. However, if it sells for less, the difference is a deficiency that normally remains the liability of the original mortgagor or any subsequent purchaser who had expressly assumed the mortgage. A deficiency judgment may in most cases be obtained unless the mortgage was executed by the buyer for purchase money needed to buy the property.

Figure 29.1 Example of a Mortgage

Mortgage

This mortgage, made the _____ day of _____, nineteen hundred and _____, between _____, (insert residence) the mortgagor, and _____ (insert residence), the mortgagee.

Witnesseth, that to secure the payment of an indebtedness in the sum of ____ dollars, lawful money of the United States, to be paid on the _____ day of _____, nineteen hundred and _____, with interest thereon to be computed from _____, at the rate of _____ per centum per annum, and to be paid _____, according to a certain bond or obligation bearing even date herewith, the mortgagor hereby mortgages to the mortgagee (description).

And the mortgagor covenants with the mortgagee as follows:

1. That the mortgagor will pay the indebtedness as hereinbefore provided.
2. That the mortgagor will keep the buildings on the premises insured against loss by fire for the benefit of the mortgagee; that he will assign and deliver the policies to the mortgagee; and that he will reimburse the mortgagee for any premiums paid for insurance made by the mortgagee on the mortgagor's default in so insuring the buildings or in so assigning and delivering the policies.
3. That no building on the premises shall be removed or demolished without the consent of the mortgagee.
4. That the whole of said principal sum and interest shall become due at the option of the mortgagee: after default in the payment of any installment of principal or of interest for ____ days; or after default in the payment of any tax, water rate or assessment for ____ days after notice and demand; or after default after notice and demand either in assigning and delivering the policies insuring the buildings against loss by fire or in reimbursing the mortgagee for premiums paid on such insurance, as hereinbefore provided; or after default upon request in furnishing a statement of the amount due on the mortgage and whether any offsets or defenses exist against the mortgage debt, as hereinafter provided.
5. That the holder of this mortgage, in any action to foreclose it, shall be entitled to the appointment of a receiver.
6. That the mortgagor will pay all taxes, assessments or water rates, and in default thereof, the mortgagee may pay the same.
7. That the mortgagor within _____ days upon request in person or within days upon request by mail will furnish a written statement duly acknowledged of the amount due on this mortgage and whether any offsets or defenses exist against the mortgage debt.
8. That notice and demand or request may be in writing and may be served in person or by mail.
9. That the mortgagor warrants the title to the premises.

In witness whereof this mortgage has been duly executed by the mortgagor.
In presence of:

_____

Deed of Trust

A deed of trust is a conveyance made by the indebted property owner, the *trustor*, to a third party, the *trustee*, with the instruction to hold the property

Deed of Trust
A conveyance of title of property to a trustee, as security for the payment of a debt.

Figure 29.2 Example of a Deed of Trust

RECORDING REQUESTED BY

AND WHEN RECORDED MAIL TO

Name
Street Address
City & State

——— SPACE ABOVE THIS LINE FOR RECORDER'S USE ———

SHORT FORM DEED OF TRUST AND ASSIGNMENT OF RENTS (INDIVIDUAL)   A.P.N._____

This Deed of Trust, made this _____ day of _____, between _____ , herein called TRUSTOR,

whose address is _____ ,
(number and street)   (city)   (state)   (zip)

_____ , a California corporation, herein called TRUSTEE, and

_____ , herein called BENEFICIARY,

Witnesseth: That Trustor IRREVOCABLY GRANTS, TRANSFERS AND ASSIGNS to TRUSTEE IN TRUST, WITH POWER OF SALE, that property in _____ County, California, described as:

TOGETHER WITH the rents, issues and profits thereof, SUBJECT, HOWEVER, to the right, power and authority given to and conferred upon Beneficiary by paragraph (10) of the provisions incorporated herein by reference to collect and apply such rents, issues and profits.

For the Purpose of Securing: 1. Performance of each agreement of Trustor incorporated by reference or contained herein. 2. Payment of the indebtedness evidenced by one promissory note of even date herewith, and any extension or renewal thereof, in the principal sum of $_____ executed by Trustor in favor of Beneficiary or order. 3. Payment of such further sums as the then record owner of said property hereafter may borrow from Beneficiary, when evidenced by another note (or notes) reciting it is so secured.

To Protect the Security of This Deed of Trust, Trustor Agrees: By the execution and delivery of this Deed of Trust and the note secured hereby, that provisions (1) to (14), inclusive, of the fictitious deed of trust recorded in Santa Barbara County and Sonoma County October 18, 1961, and in all other counties October 23, 1961, in the book and at the page of Official Records in the office of the county recorder of the county where said property is located, noted below opposite the name of such county, viz.:

(which provisions, identical in all counties, are printed on the reverse hereof) hereby are adopted and incorporated herein and made a part hereof as fully as though set forth herein at length; that he will observe and perform said provisions; and that the references to property, obligations, and parties in said provisions shall be construed to refer to the property, obligations, and parties set forth in this Deed of Trust.

  The undersigned Trustor requests that a copy of any Notice of Default and of any Notice of Sale hereunder be mailed to him at his address hereinbefore set forth.

STATE OF CALIFORNIA,
COUNTY OF_____ } SS.
On_____ before me, the undersigned, a Notary Public in and for said State, personally appeared
_____
_____, known to me
to be the person___ whose name___ subscribed to the within
instrument and acknowledged that___ executed the same.
WITNESS my hand and official seal.

Signature_____

Signature of Trustor
_____
_____
_____

Title Order No._____
Escrow or Loan No._____

(This area for official notarial seal)

―――― **DO NOT RECORD** ――――

The following is a copy of provisions (1) to (14), inclusive, of the fictitious deed of trust, recorded in each county in California, as stated in the foregoing Deed of Trust and incorporated by reference in said Deed of Trust as being a part thereof as if set forth at length therein.

To Protect the Security of This Deed of Trust, Trustor Agrees:

(1) To keep said property in good condition and repair; not to remove or demolish any building thereon; to complete or restore promptly and in good and workmanlike manner any building which may be constructed, damaged or destroyed thereon and to pay when due all claims for labor performed and materials furnished therefor; to comply with all laws affecting said property or requiring any alterations or improvements to be made thereon; not to commit or permit waste thereof; not to commit, suffer or permit any act upon said property in violation of law; to cultivate, irrigate, fertilize, fumigate, prune and do all other acts which from the character or use of said property may be reasonably necessary, the specific enumerations herein not excluding the general.

(2) To provide, maintain and deliver to Beneficiary fire insurance satisfactory to and with loss payable to Beneficiary. The amount collected under any fire or other insurance policy may be applied by Beneficiary upon indebtedness secured hereby and in such order as Beneficiary may determine, or at option of Beneficiary the entire amount so collected or any part thereof may be released to Trustor. Such application or release shall not cure or waive any default or notice of default hereunder or invalidate any act done pursuant to such notice.

(3) To appear in and defend any action or proceeding purporting to affect the security hereof or the rights or powers of Beneficiary or Trustee; and to pay all costs and expenses, including cost of evidence of title and attorney's fees in a reasonable sum, in any such action or proceeding in which Beneficiary or Trustee may appear, and in any suit brought by Beneficiary to foreclose this Deed.

(4) To pay: at least ten days before delinquency all taxes and assessments affecting said property, including assessments on appurtenant water stock; when due, all incumbrances, charges and liens, with interest, on said property or any part thereof, which appear to be prior or superior hereto; all costs, fees and expenses of this Trust.

Should Trustor fail to make any payment or to do any act as herein provided, then Beneficiary or Trustee, but without obligation so to do and without notice to or demand upon Trustor and without releasing Trustor from any obligation hereof, may: make or do the same in such manner and to such extent as either may deem necessary to protect the security hereof, Beneficiary or Trustee being authorized to enter upon said property for such purposes; appear in and defend any action or proceeding purporting to affect the security hereof or the rights or powers of Beneficiary or Trustee; pay, purchase, contest or compromise any incumbrance, charge or lien which in the judgment of either appears to be prior or superior hereto; and, in exercising any such powers, pay necessary expenses, employ counsel and pay his reasonable fees.

(5) To pay immediately and without demand all sums so expended by Beneficiary or Trustee, with interest from date of expenditure at the amount allowed by law in effect at the date hereof, and to pay for any statement provided for by law in effect at the date hereof regarding the obligation secured hereby not to exceed the maximum allowed by law at the time when said statement is demanded.

(6) That any award of damages in connection with any condemnation for public use of or injury to said property or any part thereof is hereby assigned and shall be paid to Beneficiary who may apply or release such moneys received by him in the same manner and with the same effect as above provided for disposition of proceeds of fire or other insurance.

(7) That by accepting payment of any sum secured hereby after its due date, Beneficiary does not waive his right either to require prompt payment when due of all other sums so secured or to declare default for failure so to pay.

(8) That at any time or from time to time, without liability therefor and without notice, upon written request of Beneficiary and presentation of this Deed and said note for endorsement, and without affecting the personal liability of any person for payment of the indebtedness secured hereby, Trustee may: reconvey any part of said property; consent to the making of any map or plat thereof; join in granting any easement thereon; or join in any extension agreement or any agreement subordinating the lien or charge hereof.

(9) That upon written request of Beneficiary stating that all sums secured hereby have been paid, and upon surrender of this Deed and said note to Trustee for cancellation and retention and upon payment of its fees, Trustee shall reconvey, without warranty, the property then held hereunder. The recitals in such reconveyance of any matters or facts shall be conclusive proof of the truthfulness thereof. The grantee in such reconveyance may be described as "the person or persons legally entitled thereto." Five years after issuance of such full reconveyance, Trustee may destroy said note and this Deed (unless directed in such request to retain them).

(10) That as additional security, Trustor hereby gives to and confers upon Beneficiary the right, power and authority, during the continuance of these Trusts, to collect the rents, issues and profits of said property, reserving unto Trustor the right, prior to any default by Trustor in payment of any indebtedness secured hereby or in performance of any agreement hereunder, to collect and retain such rents, issues and profits as they become due and payable. Upon any such default, Beneficiary may at any time without notice, either in person, by agent, or by a receiver to be appointed by a court, and without regard to the adequacy of any security for the indebtedness hereby secured, enter upon and take possession of said property or any part thereof, in his own name sue for or otherwise collect such rents, issues and profits, including those past due and unpaid, and apply the same, less costs and expenses of operation and collection, including reasonable attorney's fees, upon any indebtedness secured hereby, and in such order as Beneficiary may determine. The entering upon and taking possession of said property, the collection of such rents, issues and profits and the application thereof as aforesaid, shall not cure or waive any default or notice of default hereunder or invalidate any act done pursuant to such notice.

(11) That upon default by Trustor in payment of any indebtedness secured hereby or in performance of any agreement hereunder, Beneficiary may declare all sums secured hereby immediately due and payable by delivery to Trustee of written declaration of default and demand for sale and of written notice of default and of election to cause to be sold said property, which notice Trustee shall cause to be filed for record. Beneficiary also shall deposit with Trustee this Deed, said note and all documents evidencing expenditures secured hereby.

After the lapse of such time as may then be required by law following the recordation of said notice of default, and notice of sale having been given as then required by law, Trustee, without demand on Trustor, shall sell said property at the time and place fixed by it in said notice of sale, either as a whole or in separate parcels, and in such order as it may determine, at public auction to the highest bidder for cash in lawful money of the United States, payable at time of sale. Trustee may postpone sale of all or any portion of said property by public announcement at such time and place of sale, and from time to time thereafter may postpone such sale by public announcement at the time fixed by the preceding postponement. Trustee shall deliver to such purchaser its deed conveying the property so sold, but without any covenant or warranty, express or implied. The recitals in such deed of any matters or facts shall be conclusive proof of the truthfulness thereof. Any person, including Trustor, Trustee, or Beneficiary as hereinafter defined, may purchase at such sale.

After deducting all costs, fees and expenses of Trustee and of this Trust, including cost of evidence of title in connection with sale, Trustee shall apply the proceeds of sale to payment of: all sums expended under the terms hereof, not then repaid, with accrued interest at the amount allowed by law in effect at the date hereof; all other sums then secured hereby; and the remainder, if any, to the person or persons legally entitled thereto.

(12) Beneficiary, or any successor in ownership of any indebtedness secured hereby, may from time to time, by instrument in writing, substitute a successor or successors to any Trustee named herein or acting hereunder, which instrument, executed by the Beneficiary and duly acknowledged and recorded in the office of the recorder of the county or counties where said property is situated, shall be conclusive proof of proper substitution of such successor Trustee or Trustees, who shall, without conveyance from the Trustee predecessor, succeed to all its title, estate, rights, powers and duties. Said instrument must contain the name of the original Trustor, Trustee and Beneficiary hereunder, the book and page where this Deed is recorded and the name and address of the new Trustee.

(13) That this Deed applies to, inures to the benefit of, and binds all parties hereto, their heirs, legatees, devisees, administrators, executors, successors and assigns. The term Beneficiary shall mean the owner and holder, including pledgees, of the note secured hereby, whether or not named as Beneficiary herein. In this Deed, whenever the context so requires, the masculine gender includes the feminine and/or neuter, and the singular number includes the plural.

(14) That Trustee accepts this Trust when this Deed, duly executed and acknowledged, is made a public record as provided by law. Trustee is not obligated to notify any party hereto of pending sale under any other Deed of Trust or of any action or proceeding in which Trustor, Beneficiary or Trustee shall be a party unless brought by Trustee.

―――― **DO NOT RECORD** ――――

REQUEST FOR FULL RECONVEYANCE
To be used only when note has been paid.

To _____, **Trustee:** Dated _____

The undersigned is the legal owner and holder of all indebtedness secured by the within Deed of Trust. All sums secured by said Deed of Trust have been fully paid and satisfied; and you are hereby requested and directed, on payment to you of any sums owing to you under the terms of said Deed of Trust, to cancel all evidences of indebtedness, secured by said Deed of Trust, delivered to you herewith together with said Deed of Trust, and to reconvey, without warranty, to the parties designated by the terms of said Deed of Trust, the estate now held by you under the same.

MAIL RECONVEYANCE TO:

By _____

By _____

Do not lose or destroy this Deed of Trust OR THE NOTE which it secures. Both must be delivered to the Trustee for cancellation before reconveyance will be made.

in trust as security for the payment of the debt to the lender, who is the *beneficiary*. Indeed, the trust deed is theoretically rather anomalous. In actual practice, the entire transaction is usually executed exclusively between the borrower/trustor and the lender/beneficiary, often without the appointed trustee's knowledge. Without an acceptance by the grantee, there is actually no title conveyance in the real sense. Hence, although under the title theory, ownership of the property is supposed to be retained by the trustee, in general, the deed of trust is simply regarded as similar to a mortgage with the power of sale. For all intents and purposes, the trustor or his successor is considered owner of the property with all the rights to transfer the estate, subject to the provisions of the trust deed.

Form

There is no statutorily standardized form of a trust deed. The written instrument, however, must contain words of conveyance, such as *grant, transfer,* or *convey,* for the specific purpose of securing the debt to the beneficiary. Rules pertaining to recording apply to trust deeds the same as they do to any other conveying deed. Upon due recordation, a trust deed's interest is superior to any interest or lien subsequently attaching to the property or previously created but not then recorded unless the lender has knowledge thereof. However, there is no superiority over federal, state, or local taxes or assessments if these liens are statutorily accorded preference over private interests. Also, subsequently recorded mechanic liens may sometimes be given priority.

Property Transfer and Impairment

Due-on-sale Clause
Provision rendering the entire debt due and payable upon sale of the property by debtor.

Rules relating to property transfer by the trustor and impairment are basically the same as those under a mortgage agreement. Trust deeds often contain acceleration provisions, such as *due-on-sale, alienation,* and *encumbrance* clauses. However, in a landmark case, *Wellencamp* v. *Bank of America* (21 Cal.3d 943, 148 Cal. Rptr. 379, 582 p. 20 970 [1978]), the validity of such a due-on-sale clause was overruled, mainly because it is considered to provide an unwarranted restraint on the borrower.

Foreclosure

An important difference between a deed of trust and a mortgage, which difference makes the former quite popular, is the possibility of a trustee foreclosure without judicial proceedings. When the debtor ceases to make payments on the trust deed loan, the creditor-beneficiary calls on the trustee to act, usually by providing him with the promissory note and the deed of trust and a notice of default that is to be recorded. A copy of the notice is sent to the trustor and any party, such as a junior lien holder, who has requested such a notice. Upon recordation of the notice of default, the debtor as well as any other junior lien holder is given the opportunity, usually within three months, to cure the default and *reinstate* the loan obligation by paying the beneficiary all sums then due. Upon expiration of this period, the lender/beneficiary is entitled to a full *redemption* of the loan. Actual notice of default is therefore most important, as shown in the following case.

Facts

The Lupertinos (plaintiffs) purchased a certain real property from the Carbahals (defendants) for a total purchase price of $150,000, paid by a down payment of $43,500 and a note secured by a deed of trust in the amount of $106,500. Transamerica Title Insurance Company was the designated trustee. The trust deed called for the notice of default and notice of sale to be forwarded to the then trustors' address at Sunnyvale, California. Meanwhile, the plaintiffs/trustors moved to Winters, California. When the plaintiffs/trustors first defaulted in February 1971, the trustee for some reason came to know of their new address, and a notice of default and election to sell was properly transmitted. In response, the plaintiffs/trustor cured the default by bringing the loan up to date. Trustors defaulted again in November 1971, but this time Transamerica negligently mailed the notice to the trustors' old address at Sunnyvale and not to their new address in Winters, California. The ninety-day reinstatement period had run. When the trustors learned that a sale of the property was pending, they immediately attempted to cure the default again, but the lenders/beneficiaries denied the request and insisted upon the accelerated balance of the loan in the sum of $94,440.22.

Decision

Judgment for the plaintiffs. "We hold that after a *trustee* communicates with the trustor at a given address, leading the trustor to believe that his address is recognized as the receiving point of communication, the trustee cannot later refuse or fail to recognize that address. At that point the trustee ceases to act as an impartial common agent. Instead the trustee becomes the instrumentality, however innocent or negligent, of a deception which wrongfully deprives the trustor of a statutory right to reinstate the delinquent obligation."

Lupertino v. *Carbahal*, 35 Cal.App.3d 742, 111 Cal.Rptr. 112 (1973).

After the trustee executes the notice of sale, the property will be sold in public. The purchaser of the property obtains title through a trustee's deed. There is usually no deficiency judgment or a redemption right after a trustee sale.

Foreclosure of a deed of trust may also be pursued through a court proceeding, in which event all mortgage rules apply. The trustor is usually given the opportunity to reinstate the loan prior to entry of the court decree. A deficiency judgment is possible under this proceeding. Subsequent to the judicial sale, the judgment debtor is given a period of redemption.

Land Contract

Another mode of real estate financing is the installment land contract, whereby the seller or *vendor* retains the title to the property and the buyer or *vendee*, although usually given possession, does not acquire the ownership until the last installment has been made. Such an agreement passes to the vendee a so-called *equitable ownership* to the extent of the payments made, leaving the legal title in the vendor to secure payments under the contract and other performances agreed on.

Land Contract
A real estate instalment sale contract in which title to the property remains in the vendor to secure payment by the vendee.

Form

The written contract contains simply the names and signatures of the parties, a sufficient description of the property, the agreed purchase price, and how the installments are to be made. Unless acknowledged by the vendor, the vendee is usually not entitled to record the contract, which may be quite disadvantageous to him.

Figure 29.3 Example of a Land Contract

THIS AGREEMENT, made this ____ day of _____, 19___, between _____, herein called "Vendor," and _____, herein called "Vendee," concerns the following: The Vendor hereby agrees to sell and the Vendee agrees to buy all that certain piece or parcel of land being in the County of ____ and State of _____, and more particularly described as follows:

subject to all easements, laws, ordinances, reservations applying to this property, for the principal sum of _____ Dollars ($ _____), payable as follows: _____ Dollars ($ ____), cash downpayment upon signing of this contract and the balance shall be payable in _____ installments of _____ Dollars ($ ____), each on the ____ day of each _____, beginning on the ____ day of _____, 19___, and continuing _____ until _____, 19 ___, on which last mentioned date all remaining principal and interest shall be due and payable. Interest at the rate of _____ percent (____ %) per annum, starting _____, shall be deducted from each and every monthly payment and the balance applied on the principal. Principal and interest are payable in lawful money of the United States. It is understood and agreed that the above monthly payment includes taxes and insurance that may become due and payable subsequent to the date of this contract, said amounts to be paid by Vendor and added to the principal balance.

Vendee also agrees to pay all taxes and assessments that may be levied on the property, including taxes for the year 19___, and also deferred payments on special assessments that shall become due and payable after the date thereof to be prorated to date.

Vendee shall keep all buildings and improvements now existing or hereafter erected on the premises insured against loss by fire by such company and in such amount as agreed by Vendor. Such policy shall be delivered to, and remain in possession of Vendor.

Vendee agrees to keep the buildings and other improvements on the premises in good condition and repair. In case the Vendee shall fail to pay taxes, effect insurance, or make necessary repairs, the Vendor may do any or all of these things and the amount paid therefore by the Vendor shall be deemed a part of the principal sum under this contract and become payable immediately with interest at the rate of _____ percent (____ %) per annum until paid.

The Vendor on receiving payment in full of the principal and interest, and of all other sums chargeable under the contract, agrees, at his own proper cost and expense, to execute and deliver to the Vendee, or to his assigns, upon surrender of this contract, a good and sufficient conveyance in fee simple of the above described premises, free and clear of all liens and encumbrances, except such as may have accrued thereon subsequent to the date of this contract by or through the acts or negligences of others than the Vendor, and at the option of the Vendor furnish the Vendee an abstract of title or a policy of title insurance in an amount equal to the purchase price under this contract. The Vendor hereby reserves the right to mortgage said premises at any time in an amount not in excess of the amount then due on this contract, and the Vendee agrees that the said mortgage shall be a first lien on the premises.

It is mutually agreed that the Vendee shall have possession of said premises from and after _____ .

If the Vendee shall fail to comply with the terms of this contract, the Vendor may take possession of the property and all the improvements on it and treat the

Figure 29.3 Example of a Land Contract

Vendee as a tenant holding over without permission and remove him therefrom and retain any money paid hereon as stipulated damages for nonperformance of this contract. It is hereby expressly understood and declared that time is of the essence of this contract. Notice of said forfeiture may be given by depositing the notice in post office, addressed to Vendee at his last known address.

It is agreed that the provisions contained in this contract are to apply to and bind the heirs, executors, administrators, and assigns of the respective parties to this contract.

This contract shall be governed and construed in accordance with the laws of the State of _____.

IN WITNESS WHEREOF, the said parties have hereunto set their hands the day and year first above written.

In presence of:

_____)   _____
                                Vendor
_____)   _____
                                Vendee

Transfer by Vendor

The vendor may transfer his rights to a third party. He may convey to his transferee the legal title to the property as well as the right to receive the installment payments from the vendee. The grantee has the duty to notify the contract vendee of the transfer. He is bound to convey the ownership to the vendee upon completion of the terms of the contract.

The vendor may also incumber his interest in the property by a mortgage or deed of trust, in which event his interest in the property as well as his interest under the land contract are used as a collateral for the loan. An arrangement may be made in which the vendee is requested to make the installment payments directly to the vendor's lender.

Transfer by Vendee

The vendee, too, is usually allowed to transfer his interest under the land contract. This can take place by an assignment or by a deed of conveyance. Even if there is a covenant in the contract prohibiting such a transfer by the vendee without the vendor's consent, such a provision does not affect the validity of the transaction between the vendee and the third party. The vendor may also waive such a restraining clause, either expressly or impliedly, by accepting payments directly from the new transferee.

Default

Under *Glock* v. *Howard & Wilson Colony Co.* (123 Cal. 1, 55 P. 713 [1898]), it was formerly the rule in California that upon a *declaration of forfeiture* by the vendor to terminate the contract, the vendor has the right

Default
Failure to keep a promise to pay or to do some other act required by a contract.

to retain all the installment payments made without having to refund anything to the vendee. Later decisions have modified this rule, as it is considered to unjustly enrich the vendor (*Freedman* v. *Rector,* 37 Cal.2d 16, 230 P. 2d 629 [1951]). Even upon a willful default, courts most likely permit the vendee to recover such portions of the payments made in excess of the vendor's actual damages.

As in the case of a purchase money mortgage or a deed of trust, no deficiency judgment against the vendee can be obtained in a foreclosure proceeding upon default. It should be noted, however, that a land contract is legally not the same as a mortgage or a trust deed, as demonstrated in the following case.

Kosloff v. Castle
115 Cal. App. 3d 369, 171 Cal.Rptr. 308 (1981).

This appeal arises out of a dispute over real property in Sonoma County. After a nonjury trial, the court granted recovery to respondent on her complaint to quiet title and recover possession and denied recovery to appellant on her cross-complaint for specific performance.

Appellant contends that a willfully defaulting vendee under an installment land contract is legally entitled to an equity of redemption, i.e., that she should have been allowed to reinstate the contract and tender full performance. She also maintains that an installment land contract is in fact a mortgage under Civil Code section 2924, giving a right of redemption to mortgagors.

For the most part the facts are not disputed. In 1966, respondent purchased a home in Sonoma County for $15,000 which she rented to appellant in 1970 for $150 per month. Appellant continued to rent the house at that rate for the next three years. On July 1, 1973, the parties entered into a written agreement for the sale of the property to the appellant for $15,000. The purchase price was payable in installments of $150 per month for two years, and the balance of $11,400 in a single balloon payment was due on or before July 1, 1975. There was no provision for interest. The respondent would retain title to the property until the final payment was made, and appellant would forfeit her interest in the property if she breached the contract. In the event of a breach appellant's monthly payments would be deemed rental payments for the use of the property. Time was of the essence.

From July 1, 1973, until April 1976, appellant paid $114 per month directly to the lending institution for the monthly loan installment and impound account and remitted the balance of $36 to respondent. Appellant failed to tender the balloon payment of $11,400 on July 1, 1975, when due. From May 1976 through January 1977, she paid a reduced monthly amount of $98.77 to the lending institution and continued to remit $36 to respondent. From February 1977 through September 1977 appellant paid only the $98.77 and failed to make any payments to respondent; after suit was filed, appellant paid to respondent $288, representing the $36 per month for this latter eight-month period. From December 1976 through February 1978, appellant paid directly to the county treasurer three installments totalling $808 on property taxes.

. . . Respondent took no steps to enforce payment of the $11,400 until December 15, 1976, at which time respondent's attorney informed appellant by letter that her rights under the contract had terminated. Respondent served appellant with a notice to quit on April 1977 and filed an action for unlawful detainer and to quiet title in August 1977.

In September of 1977, appellant tendered the amount of $9,372.72 which sum represented the $11,400 minus the payments made from July 1975 to September 1977, with an allowance for interest on the $11,400. The offer was refused.

Over appellant's objections, the court found that respondent believed, following the breach of contract, that appellant had once again assumed the role of tenant. The court also found that the value of the property at the time of the contract was $20,000 to $22,000 and that the reasonable rental in April 1977 was $200 per month.

. . . The trend has been toward judicial recognition that where the installment land contract is used as a security device, it is for all intents and purposes a mortgage; the total judicial equation of the two, however, has never been completed.

. . . Appellant urges us to complete the land sale reform initiated by *Barkis v. Scott, supra,* 34 Cal.2d 116, and ending prematurely with *MacFadden v. Walker, supra,* 5 Cal.3d 809, by today holding that the land sale contract is a mortgage under Civil Code section 2924. That section states in part that, "Every transfer of an interest in property, other than in trust, made only as a security for the performance of another act, is to be deemed a mortgage . . ." If we were to so hold, appellant would then be entitled to a right of redemption under Civil Code 2924c. One of the area's foremost commentators argues persuasively for appellant's position. (Hatland, Secured Real Estate Transactions (1974) § 2.12, pp 59–61.)

We decline to hold that the agreement in the case before us is a mortgage as defined in Civil Code section 2924. We believe that any reform in this area is more appropriately initiated by the Legislature which is in a better position to effect and coordinate comprehensive answers to the many-faceted questions that such a determination would evoke.

Questions

1. What is the remedy for an unsecured creditor if the debtor defaults?
2. Describe the basics of a mortgage.
3. Describe the basics of a deed of trust.
4. What is the difference between a mortgage and a deed of trust in view of foreclosure?
5. Describe the basics of a land contract.

29.2 Security Interest in Personal Property (I)

The creditor who wants to obtain a security interest in a personal property belonging to the debtor also needs to be sure of the validity of the transaction and where his rights stand *vis-à-vis* claims by other creditors on the same property. Secured transactions relating to personal property are regulated in Article 9 of the Uniform Commercial Code which applies "to any transaction (regardless of its form) which is intended to create a security interest in personal property or fixtures including goods, documents, instruments, general intangibles, chattel paper or accounts" (UCC § 9–102[1]). An example of such a secured transaction is an owner of a business who borrows money from his bank and uses his inventory or store equipment as collateral for the loan. If the borrower defaults on the loan, the bank may use the security as a secondary source of repayment.

Prior to the UCC, many devices were used for giving the creditor a security interest in personal property. There were pledges, assignments, chattel mortgages, trust receipts, trust deeds, inventory liens, equipment trusts, conditional sales, and leases and consignments intended as security. These devices are now considered "security agreements." The interest created is called "security interest;" the borrower or credit buyer, a "debtor;" and the lender, credit seller, or buyer of accounts, contract rights, or chattel paper, a "secured party" (UCC §§ 1–201[37]) and 9–105).

Article 9 of the UCC covers nearly all security interests in personal property and fixtures. The principal exceptions are state statutes that regulate consumer installment sales and consumer loans; security interests perfected under a federal statute; wage assignments; interests in real estate, except fixtures; mechanic liens; claims arising out of judicial proceedings; equipment trusts covering railway rolling stock; transfers of claims under insurance policies; transfer of deposit, savings, and other accounts maintained with a bank, savings and loan association, credit union, or similar organization.

Creation of Security Interest

Security Interest
The right of a secured creditor to the protection afforded by the security.

For a secured transaction to be effective, three requirements are necessary:

1. The collateral must be in the *possession* of the secured party, i.e., the lender or seller *or* the debtor must execute a *security agreement*.
2. There must be an *attachment* of the secured party's security interest to the collateral.
3. There must be a *perfection* of the security interest.

Possession

A pledge or a pawn, as discussed in subchapter 14.2, is typically a security interest established by possession. The property is delivered to the creditor/bailee with the express or implied authority that in the event the debtor defaults, the property may be sold and the sale proceeds used to pay off the debt. For example, a bank customer borrows $10,000 from his bank and gives the bank the possession of his stock certificate representing a value of $18,000. The bank usually requires the borrower to execute a *stock power* that authorizes the bank as an attorney-in-fact to endorse the certificate in the name of the debtor and sell the stock in case the debt is not paid. Similarly, a pawnbroker may take in a gold ring worth $500 to secure a debt of $200.

Security Agreement

Another way to establish a security interest in personal property is through a security agreement, especially when the borrower retains possession of the collateral. A security agreement must be in writing, be signed by the debtor, and contain a description of the collateral sufficient to reasonably identify it. The security agreement may contain any terms and provisions that the parties desire, but the agreement must be fair to the debtor.

The importance of a sufficient description of collateral in both the financing statement and the security agreement is discussed in the following case.

Facts

The security agreement between American Restaurant Supply Company (plaintiff) and Wilmark (debtor) described the collateral as "Foodservice equipment and supplies delivered to San Marco Inn at St. Marks, Florida." The trial court held that the description was inadequate (UCC § 9–203[1]) and that the security interest was not legally enforceable.

Decision

Affirmed. A security agreement should describe collateral with details sufficient for third parties to be able to reasonably identify the particular assets covered. The agreement here did not make possible the identification of the equipment and was therefore not legally sufficient to be enforced.

American Restaurant Supply Co. v. Wilson, 371 So.2d 489 (Fla.App. 1979).

On the other hand, if the description of the collateral is adequate, a simple reference to it in the promissory note is sufficient to create a valid security interest.

Facts

Plant Reclamation sold equipment to Amex-Protein in exchange for a promissory note. The note included the following line: "This note is secured by a security interest in subject personal property per invoices." The referee held that the note did not create a valid security interest.

Decision

The federal court reversed the referee, holding that the language of the note created or provided for a security interest (UCC § 9–105[h]). No magic words or precise form are necessary to create or provide for a security interest so long as the minimum formal requirements of the Code are met. Although the promissory note did not describe the collateral, it made reference to other available documents that provided an adequate description (UCC § 9–110).

Matter of Amex-Protein Development Corp., 504 F.2d 1056 (9th Cir. 1974).

692　　CHAPTER TWENTY-NINE

Figure 29.4　Example of a Security Agreement

SECURITY AGREEMENT AND POWER OF ATTORNEY　　　　　　　　　　　　Loan No. _____
(VEHICLES)

This Agreement, made _____, 19_____, by _____
of _____, County of _____
California, herein called Debtor (whether one or more), in favor of **FIRST INTERSTATE BANK OF CALIFORNIA**, a California corporation,
of _____, County of _____, California,
herein called Bank, _____

WITNESSETH:

　　That the Debtor hereby grants to Bank a security interest, pursuant to the California Commercial Code, in the certain motor vehicle(s) (herein called vehicle, whether one or more) owned by Debtor free of liens, security interests or encumbrances and described as follows to wit:

Year Model	Trade Name	No. Cyls.	Body Type	Serial No.	Motor No.	License No.

now and to be permanently garaged at _____ in _____ County, California, together with all equipment, parts, appliances and accessories appertaining thereto or used in connection therewith and whether heretofore or hereafter acquired, all of which shall be and become a component part thereof and is included under the terms of this agreement, as security for:

1. The payment to Bank of:
　　(a) Th   certain Simple Interest Personal Loan Agreement and Disclosure Statement (herein Note) executed by Debtor in favor of Bank, and further described as follows:
　　Note for $_____ dated _____
　　payable
　　and bearing interest at the rate and payable in the manner set forth in said note(s); and any and all extensions and/or renewals of said note(s) or any amounts owing thereon;
　　(b) Any and all sums hereafter advanced and expenditures hereafter made (in addition to any advancements or expenditures necessarily made pursuant to the provisions of paragraphs 2 and 3 hereof) by Bank to or for Debtor, and all indebtedness and obligations now or hereafter owing or due or becoming or due from Debtor to Bank;
2. Any and all costs incurred by Bank hereunder including reasonable attorney's fees and all expenditures made by Bank in connection with discovering, locating, taking possession of, towing, repairing, rehabilitating, storing or otherwise caring for and protecting vehicle or other property covered hereby and constituting any of Bank's security hereunder;
3. The repayment of any and all sums and amounts that are necessarily advanced or expended by Bank or assigns for the maintenance or preservation of the property, or any part thereof, described in this agreement;
4. The payment and performance of each and every of the obligations and promises of Debtor herein contained.
　　Debtor does hereby irrevocably, coupled with an interest, make, constitute and appoint First Interstate Bank of California or any officer thereof Debtor's true and lawful attorney-in-fact, with full power of substitution, to sign in the name, place and stead of Debtor any and all Certificate(s) of Ownership, Registration Card(s), applications therefor, affidavits and/or any other documents required or necessary to transfer or convey any and all right, title and interest, registered, legal and/or equitable, in and to the within described vehicle, to any person or persons and empower said attorney-in-fact to collect, receive and receipt for any and all licenses, Registration Cards or Certificates of Ownership and to do and perform any and all other acts necessary or incident to the execution of the powers herein expressly granted as fully to all intents and purposes as the Debtor might or could do if personally present.
　　Debtor agrees not to misuse said vehicle or make any material change therein without Bank's written consent and agrees not to use or permit to be used said vehicle for the purpose of illegally transporting or concealing intoxicating liquors, drugs, narcotics or contraband goods of any kind or in the violation of any Federal, State or Municipal law, statute or ordinance, or for hire or military purposes or in any race or speed contest, and agrees not to allow any person to operate or use said vehicle who is not permitted to do so under the terms of the insurance policies thereon. Should a substantial decrease in the value of said vehicle occur from any cause and further security satisfactory to Bank be not given to Bank to offset such decrease in value, or should Bank deem said vehicle in danger of misuse or removal from the State of California or should Bank for any reason feel insecure, Bank may at Bank's option declare all sums secured hereby immediately due and payable.
　　Should Debtor's title to said property be other than sole and unencumbered ownership (except as to this agreement), or should Debtor default hereunder, or should such property be attached or should bankruptcy proceedings be instituted by Debtor or against Debtor and not dismissed in ten days, then in any such event all sums secured by this agreement shall at the option of Bank become immediately due and payable, and Bank shall have the remedies of a secured party under the California Commercial Code, including, without limitations, the right to require Debtor to assemble the property and make it available to Bank at a place designated by Bank and to take possession of

IC-2020 4/83

Figure 29.4 Continued

the property covered hereby with or without process of law and sell and dispose of the same or any part thereof at public or private sale upon legal notice to Debtor, and with or without having said property present or in view at time or place of sale, and upon such terms and in such manner as Bank may determine, and Bank may be the purchaser at any such sale. Bank shall deduct and retain from the proceeds of such sale all of Bank's expenditures made and costs incurred pursuant to this agreement, including costs of sale and reasonable attorney's fees and the interest unpaid on said note, and shall apply any remainder of said proceeds of sale upon the balance unpaid on the aforesaid indebtedness and obligations secured hereby, in such manner and order as Bank may elect. Any overplus shall be paid to the person or persons legally entitled thereto upon proof of such right.

Debtor will obtain, pay for and keep Property, Bank and Debtor, insured through agents and in companies approved by Bank against loss by collision, fire, theft, and such other risks as may be mutually agreed upon by Debtor and Bank. All policies are to contain a loss payable clause in form acceptable to Bank naming Bank and loss payee, and will be delivered to Bank and held by Bank as security for the Note, and in the event of repossession, as Bank's sole property. Bank is hereby authorized to make any claim thereunder, to cancel same upon default, and to receive payment of, to endorse any instrument in payment of loss or return premium, and to apply any money so received on amount due hereunder. Debtor's failure to obtain insurance coverage as specified above shall constitute an event of default. However, Bank has the option of obtaining either Vendor's Single Interest (Covers Interest of Bank Only) or Dual Interest Coverage (Covers Interest of Debtor and Bank for physical damage only) and adding the cost of the insurance premium together with any Finance Charge and any other cost incurred to the **unpaid balance** of the Note and apportioning this added cost between the instalment payments remaining to be paid by **Debtor**. In the alternative at Bank's option, the cost of such insurance coverage together with any Finance Charge therefore or other costs then due may be either made due and payable on the due date of the next "monthly instalment" or on the date of the final payment due on the Note, or Bank may bill Debtor for the above amounts according to a schedule apportioning said amount over a period of months ending on or before the date of the final instalment due on the Note.

Each of the following shall constitute a default on the part of the Debtor hereunder:

(a) Failure to keep any promise or agreement herein contained or to pay or perform when due any obligation secured hereby;

(b) Failure to immediately repay all advancements and expenditures made by Bank for the protection or preservation of the property or in the enforcement of Bank's rights hereunder, including interest at legal rate from date of advancement or expenditure to date of repayment, Bank being hereby empowered to make such advancements or expenditures whenever in Bank's opinion the same shall be necessary for any of said purposes, including expenditures for repossession of the property or for the counsel or any person or collection agency to collect any past due amounts owing to Bank and secured hereby.

(c) Any statement, representation, or warranty of Debtor herein contained being or becoming untrue, it being understood and agreed that each statement herein contained as to the ownership or description of or title to the property is intended to be and shall constitute a representation and warranty on the part of Debtor;

(d) Failure at any time during the existence of this agreement to keep said vehicle properly registered and licensed in the State of California and to have the license and certificate of legal ownership show the Bank as the legal owner of said vehicle and to deliver such Certificate of Ownership to Bank;

(e) Without Bank's prior written consent, the removal of said vehicle from the State of California or a sale, transfer, rental, creating a security interest in, or other encumbering or disposal of said vehicle or any interest therein or the incurring of any bill for repairs to or storage of said vehicle in excess of $25.00 or permitting to exist any unpaid bill in any amount for or on account of any such repairs or storage;

(f) Failure on demand of Bank to exhibit said vehicle and any other property covered hereby to Bank and to allow inspection thereof at any time;

(g) Abandonment or concealment of said vehicle or failure to house the same in suitable shelter or failure to keep the same in good condition and repair or failure to promptly replace any lost, worn or broken parts;

(h) Failure to take out and keep in force and effect and deliver to Bank, a policy or policies of insurance with coverage satisfactory to Bank and with loss payable to Bank as its interest may appear; it being agreed that if Bank takes possession of said vehicle, any insurance policy or policies thereon and all unearned or return premiums thereon shall be and become the sale property of Bank, the same being hereby assigned to Bank.

Bank shall have the right to enforce any one or more of its remedies herein mentioned or provided by law, successively or concurrently, and no action taken hereunder shall stop or prevent the Bank from pursuing any other or future remedy which Bank may have.

Bank may accelerate payment of the unpaid amount and, as permitted by law, repossess and remove the vehicle, including any attachments, without notice, demand or legal process, and for such purposes may enter any unsecured premises where the vehicle is located.

The right to plead any and all statutes of limitations as defense to any demand secured by or mentioned in this agreement is hereby waived.

Each married person who joins in executing this agreement and any note or notes secured thereby, hereby agrees and expressly assents, pursuant to Section 5123 of the Civil Code of the State of California, to the liability of his/her separate property of all his/her debts and obligations herein mentioned.

DEBTOR

Attachment

Attachment
Enforceability of a security interest.

UCC §§ 9–203(1) and (2) provide that a security interest is not enforceable against the debtor or third parties with respect to the collateral and does not attach unless:

(1) (a) the collateral is in the possession of the secured party pursuant to agreement, *or* the debtor has signed a security agreement which contains a description of the collateral and in addition, when the security interest covers crops growing or to be grown or timber to be cut, a description of the land concerned;

(b) value has been given; and

(c) the debtor has rights in the collateral.

(2) A security interest attaches when it becomes enforceable against the debtor with respect to the collateral. [Emphasis added.]

Value

A security interest does not attach until "value has been given." In essence, this means that for the lender to obtain an enforceable security interest in the borrower's property, the debtor must receive from the secured creditor sufficient consideration. For example, a lender and a borrower agree on May 1 that the lender will loan $10,000 against the borrower's inventory. A security agreement is executed on May 1, but the funds are not disbursed to the borrower until June 1. The security interest in the debtors's inventory does not attach until June 1, when the debtor receives value. It should be noted that value could have been given earlier, such as is the case with a preexisting debt.

After-Acquired Property
Additional property acquired after the creditor's security interest has attached.

Similar to the right to security in after-acquired property is the floating lien (§§ 9–204 and 9–205). This is a security interest in constantly changing collateral. It has been called a floating lien, a lien on shifting stock, an inventory lien, a free-handed mortgage, and a floating charge. In this type of lien, the debtor (e.g., a retail seller) has the right to use, commingle, or dispose of all or part of the collateral; to collect or compromise accounts, contract rights, or chattel paper; or use, commingle, or dispose of proceeds. It is not necessary for the secured party to require the debtor to account for the proceeds or to replace the collateral.

The floating lien can be used only with respect to inventory or accounts receivable; but, of course, it can be used to tie up all of a debtor's assets. It is a highly useful lien in inventory and accounts receivable financing in that it permits a businessperson to pledge property to be obtained in the future and to use the collateral to make money rather than hold it as a stationary asset and gives the secured party an automatically perfected security interest in each item of after-acquired collateral immediately on its acquisition by the debtor.

Debtor's Right in the Collateral

It is understandable that the borrower must own or at least have rights in the collateral for the lender's security interest to attach to it. In short, no one may borrow on a property that in fact belongs to another. For example, the pawnshop's security interest does not attach to the guitar that John brought in if the guitar is actually owned by Peter.

Perfection

After the debtor and the secured party make the security agreement and after the secured party's security interest attaches to the collateral, it is necessary to perfect the security interest to make it *valid against third parties,* i.e., other secured parties, attaching creditors, or a trustee in bankruptcy. Perfecting is not necessary for the secured party to enforce his interest against the debtor. That is done by the security agreement and the attaching of the security interest. However, it is necessary to perfect the security interest to make it good against third parties. The purpose of perfection is to give notice to all persons who may be dealing with the debtor that the secured party has or may have a security interest in the collateral.

Perfection
Validation of a security interest as against third parties.

In re McFadden
18 B.R. 758 (Bkrtcy. Ark. 1982).

The Bankruptcy Court held herein that a Sony Betamax video cassette recorder, owned by the debtor, was used substantially for business and income purposes of the debtor; and that, since appellant did not file on the equipment with the Secretary of State and the County Clerk, as required for business equipment in Arkansas by *Ark.Stat.Ann.* § 85–9–401(c) (Add.1961), appellant was a general creditor and dismissed its Petition for Reclamation.

Appellant seeks a remand, contending that the Bankruptcy Court refused to allow appellant to present rebuttal testimony and to otherwise present evidence to support its position.

. . . The debtor received the subject video cassette recorder in September, 1977.

. . . Based on . . . testimony, the debtor conclusionarily estimates that 60% of his use of the recorder was for business and 40% was personal. But this opinion is not borne out. . . . Even at the outset of his use of the recorder, from September 8, 1977, to the termination of his employment . . . , the debtor, according to his own testimony, used the recorder for business purposes only on an average of once a week. . . . This testimony, rendered by the debtor who should have had the motive and been willing to specify the average time per week spent on business use if it in fact exceeded the average spent on personal use, warrants an inference that the average weekly hour [sic] spent on personal use exceeded the average per week spent on use for business purposes. This finding is sufficient to warrant a conclusion that the "primary" use . . . was personal rather than business. . . .

Even if the subsequent use of the recorder is relevant to the matter of filing, then the evidence . . . shows that, after the debtor terminated his employment . . . he made . . . no business use of the recorder. All his use of it thereafter was personal. Therefore, inasmuch as his use of the recorder was primarily personal, the recorder is properly classifiable as "consumer goods" within the meaning of § 9–109 of the Uniform Commercial Code and single filing is sufficient under § 9–401 of that Code to perfect the security interest.

> . . . But, even if it should be found that the claimant's security interest is not perfected . . . perfection of a security interest is not a necessary element in a creditor's *inter partes* suit to recover specific property from the debtor. Perfection is necessary only to defeat the claim or defense of a third party, such as the trustee in bankruptcy, who it appears, makes no claim to this property on behalf of the creditors or estate. Nor is it anywhere represented that the value of the recorder will be used for the creditors' or the estate's benefit. A security interest has efficacy between the parties without any of the incidents of perfection. Therefore, in the case at bar, it must be held that the plaintiff, Walloch TV, may reclaim the cassette recorder without demonstrating perfection. . . .

A security interest can be perfected by *attachment*, by *possession*, or by filing a *financing statement*.

By Attachment

UCC § 9–302(1) lists a few types of security interests that are automatically perfected when they are attached. This means that the security interest is perfected without the secured party's having to do anything more. A most common type of a security interest perfected when it it attaches is the purchase money security interest in consumer goods other than motor vehicles and fixtures.

Facts

As an engagement present for his fiancée, Nicolosi purchased a diamond ring on credit from Rike-Kumber. A purchase money security agreement was executed, giving the store a security interest in the ring until it was fully paid for. No financing statement covering the security interest was filed. When Nicolosi subsequently became bankrupt, the bankruptcy trustee claimed that the diamond ring belonged to the bankruptcy estate, since Rike-Kumber did not perfect its security interest in the collateral.

Decision

Judgment for Rike-Kumber. The store had a perfected security interest in the ring, since the ring was a consumer good purchased for personal use. Rike-Kumber established a perfected security interest in the diamond ring upon mere attachment. This took place when Nicolosi signed the security agreement, according to which Rike-Kumber extended the credit.

In re Nicolosi, 4 UCC Rep.Serv. 111 (S.D.Ohio 1966) (unpublished case).

Kimbrell's Furniture Company, Inc. v. *Sig Friedman, d/b/a Bonded Loan* (261 S.C. 172, 198 S.E.2d 803 [1973]), involved the sale by a store of a television set and a tape player to a consumer. The security interest of a pawnbroker, a subsequent transferee, established by possession, had to yield to the security interest of the original seller who took in a security agreement without filing a financing statement.

Whether or not collateral under given circumstances qualifies as a consumer good may be a subject of dispute, as demonstrated in the above-cited *In re McFadden.* Therefore, although filing to perfect a purchase money security interest in consumer goods is not required, it may on occasion still be advantageous to the secured party to do so. Moreover, under UCC

§ 9–307(2), a subsequent consumer buyer "... takes free of a security interest even though perfected if he buys without knowledge of the security interest, for value and for his own personal, family or household purposes unless prior to the purchase the secured party has filed a financing statement covering such goods."

By Possession

UCC § 9–302 provides that possession of the collateral by the secured party gives notice of his security interest, making it unnecessary to file a financing statement.

Facts

Burnett was a tenant at the Regency East Apartments in Providence, Rhode Island. When he became delinquent in the rent, the Regency took him to court and obtained a judgment against him. To secure payment of the judgment, Burnett gave the Regency's manager a five-dollar gold piece as collateral, and they both signed an agreement as follows:

> October 14, 1975
>
> As collateral on the $600.00 owed by Mr. Robert Burnett, I have received one (1) 1811 Five-Dollar Gold Piece to be kept until 12 Noon on Thursday, October 16, or until said rent is paid in full, whichever comes first.

Subsequently, Burnett filed for bankruptcy, and the question then arose whether the Regency had a perfected security interest in Burnett's gold piece.

Decision

The judgment creditor's security interest in the gold piece was established and perfected when the creditor took possession of the collateral. (Other than for the purpose of evidence, the written agreement between the Regency and Burnett was not even necessary for the former's security interest to be perfected. The gold piece was owned by Burnett, and value was given for the security interest when Burnett gave the manager the property and the manager accepted Burnett's promise to satisfy the judgment.)

In re Burnett, Little v. *Regency East,* 21 UCC Rep. 1471 (D.R.I. 1977) (unpublished case).

Possession is the required and exclusive method of perfecting a security interest in an instrument. The word "instrument" includes the following: (1) negotiable instruments (§ 3–104), (2) securities (§ 8–102), and (3) other rights to payment evidenced by writings that are in the ordinary course of business transferred by delivery with any necessary endorsement or assignment, e.g., government warrants (§§ 9–304 and 9–305).

By Filing a Financing Statement

The most common method of perfecting a secured party's security interest in the collateral is by filing a financing statement with the proper governmental agency. A financing statement is a document that is signed by both the debtor and the secured party and contains the names and addresses of the parties and a description of the types or items of collateral covered. Any description of personal property or real estate is sufficient whether or not it is specific if it reasonably identifies what is described. Minor errors that are not seriously misleading will not destroy the statement's effectiveness (see §§ 9–110 and 9–402).

Financing Statement
Statutory filing with a government agency to perfect security interest.

Figure 29.5 Example of a Financing Statement

This FINANCING STATEMENT is presented for filing pursuant to the California Uniform Commercial Code.

1. DEBTOR (LAST NAME FIRST—IF AN INDIVIDUAL)
1A. SOCIAL SECURITY OR FEDERAL TAX NO.
1B. MAILING ADDRESS
1C. CITY, STATE
1D. ZIP CODE
2. ADDITIONAL DEBTOR (IF ANY) (LAST NAME FIRST—IF AN INDIVIDUAL)
2A. SOCIAL SECURITY OR FEDERAL TAX NO.
2B. MAILING ADDRESS
2C. CITY, STATE
2D. ZIP CODE
3. DEBTOR'S TRADE NAMES OR STYLES (IF ANY)
3A. FEDERAL TAX NUMBER
4. SECURED PARTY
NAME
MAILING ADDRESS
CITY STATE ZIP CODE
4A. SOCIAL SECURITY NO., FEDERAL TAX NO. OR BANK TRANSIT AND A.B.A. NO.
5. ASSIGNEE OF SECURED PARTY (IF ANY)
NAME
MAILING ADDRESS
CITY STATE ZIP CODE
5A. SOCIAL SECURITY NO., FEDERAL TAX NO. OR BANK TRANSIT AND A.B.A. NO.

6. This FINANCING STATEMENT covers the following types or items of property **(include description of real property on which located and owner of record when required by instruction 4).**
As security for and in consideration of all present and any future advances or other obligations debtor hereby grants United California Bank a security interest in all of the following types or items of property ("Collateral" herein) in which the debtor now has or hereafter acquires any right, title, or interest, or rights present and future, wheresoever located and whether in the possession of the debtor, a warehouseman, bailee, trustee or any other person, and all increases, therein and replacements, products, and proceeds thereof. Proceeds include but are not limited to inventory, returned merchandise, accounts, chattel paper, general intangibles, insurance proceeds, documents, money, goods, equipment, instruments, and any other tangible or intangible property arising under the sale, lease or other disposition of collateral:

7. CHECK IF APPLICABLE ☒
7A. ☐ PRODUCTS OF COLLATERAL ARE ALSO COVERED
7B. DEBTOR(S) SIGNATURE NOT REQUIRED IN ACCORDANCE WITH INSTRUCTION 5(a) ITEM: ☐(1) ☐(2) ☐(3) ☐(4)

8. CHECK IF APPLICABLE ☒
☐ DEBTOR IS A "TRANSMITTING UTILITY" IN ACCORDANCE WITH UCC § 9105 (1) (n)

9. DATE:
►
SIGNATURE(S) OF DEBTOR(S)

TYPE OR PRINT NAME(S) OF DEBTOR(S)
►
SIGNATURE(S) OF SECURED PARTY(IES)

TYPE OR PRINT NAME(S) OF SECURED PARTY(IES)

CODE
1
2
3
4
5
6
7
8
9
0

10. THIS SPACE FOR USE OF FILING OFFICER (DATE, TIME, FILE NUMBER AND FILING OFFICER)

11. *Return copy to:*
NAME
ADDRESS
CITY
STATE
ZIP CODE

(1) FILING OFFICER COPY
FORM UCC-1—FILING FEE $3.00
Approved by the Secretary of State

MS-336 10-78

A financing statement is *not* a substitute for a security agreement. A security agreement may be filed as a financing statement if it contains the required formalities. But because a security agreement often contains details that the parties prefer not to reveal in a public notice, the parties prefer to file the simple financing statement. A person searching the records to ascertain if the debtor's property is subject to a security interest will learn very little from a financing statement except that the property may be subject to a security interest. The person must therefore go to the parties for further information, and a procedure exists for obtaining such information.

Section 9–401 provides for three alternatives regarding the place where the financing statement is to be filed: local filing (county), central filing (Secretary of State), or a combination of both local and central. Because states have used all three alternatives plus variations, local rules must be consulted in this area.

Filing a financing statement is required in the following secured transactions: (1) intangible collateral (i.e., contract rights, accounts, and general intangibles) (examples of general intangibles are any interest or claim in or under any policy of insurance, goodwill, literary rights, patents, and copyrights) and (2) goods (i.e., inventory and equipment in general) (for definitions, see §§ 9–106, 9–109[1], 9–109[1], 9–109[2][4], and 9–109[3]).

Filing is permissive in secured transactions involving chattel paper and negotiable instruments (§ 9–304).

A filing is effective for only five years. Unless a continuation statement is filed before the expiration of the five-year period, the perfection of the security interest terminates. A continuation statement is a declaration by the secured party that identifies the original filing statement by its file number and declares that it is still effective. Successive continuation statements will continue the perfection indefinitely. A termination statement must be filed promptly by the secured party when the debtor pays off the debt.

Questions

1. How is a security interest in personal property created?
2. Give two examples of a security interest through possession.
3. When does attachment take place? Please explain.
4. Give an example of a perfection by attachment.
5. Describe briefly the procedure for filing a financing statement.

29.3 Security Interest in Personal Property (II)

Priorities

What is the rule if the same collateral is used to secure more than one debt? The principle in such a situation is that the collateral is not to be divided equally or prorated among the creditors, but whoever is given the highest priority under the law is to be paid in full before the subsequent priority is to be met. The UCC provides certain rules to determine which of the conflicting security interests shall prevail. This question of priority is specifically important in the event the debtor becomes bankrupt and all kinds of creditors come out to retrieve their money.

Between Perfected Interests

Between perfected interests, priority goes to the secured party whose interest was perfected first. For example, lender A advances funds to debtor and files on June 1, knowing that another lender B has a prior security interest in the same collateral, but B's interest has then not been perfected. Subsequently, B files on June 5. Lender A's interest is entitled to priority, even though A knew of the prior unperfected interest. This is similar to the priority rule of first and second recorded mortgage in real estate.

Between Perfected and Unperfected Interests

Between a perfected and an unperfected security interest, the former will prevail. For example, if related to a nonpossessory and nonpurchase money collateral, one security interest is established by a security agreement and perfected by filing a financing statement whereas the other is based on a security agreement alone, the perfected interest will be given priority.

It should be emphasized, however, that the purpose of filing a financing statement is solely to give constructive notice to other persons, and by itself, such a filing, without an underlying security agreement, does not create a security interest. This is illustrated in the following case.

Mid-Eastern Electronics, Inc. v. First Nat. Bank of So. Md.
380 F.2d 355 (4th Cir. 1967).

Albert V. Bryan, Circuit Judge A security interest under the Maryland Uniform Commercial Code in personal property of its debtor, with lien primacy therefor, was denied the appellant, First National Bank of Southern Maryland, by the District Court. Instead, priority of lien was accorded Mid-Eastern Electronics, Inc., appellee, under an attachment upon its judgment against this debtor. We uphold the decision. . . .

This judgment was obtained in the District Court by Mid-Eastern (ME) against the debtor, Continental Electronics, Inc. for the sum of $30,763.32 on July 14, 1965. In seeking to collect it, ME levied upon the chattel assets, including inventory and equipment, of the judgment debtor and a garnishment was also served upon the Bank. . . . It later appeared that the Bank was asserting a security interest in the debtor's personalty for the payment of certain notes it held of the debtor. Reliance for its claim as a secured party was placed upon a financing statement filed pursuant to the UCC, § 9–302, with the appropriate State office. . . . Assuming arguendo that the financing agreement met the requisites of the UCC § 9–402, it alone did not create a security interest. It was but notice that one was claimed, a single step in the means by which the rights and priorities of a secured party are "perfected."

> We begin with § 9–204(1) of the code, which provides:
> "(1) A security interest cannot attach until there is agreement . . . that it attach and value is given and the debtor has rights in the collateral. It attaches as soon as all of the events in the preceding sentence have taken place unless explicit agreement postpones the time of attaching."
>
> A security interest, additionally, is unenforceable unless, under the Code's statute of frauds, the "debtor has signed a security agreement which contains a description of the collateral . . . ." § 9–203(1)(b). Under the UCC, " 'Collateral' means the property subject to a security interest, and includes accounts, contract rights and chattel paper which have been sold . . . ." § 9–105(1)(c). " 'Agreement' means the bargain of the parties in fact. . . ." § 1–201(3) (Accent added). As the appellant can proffer no writing signed by the debtor giving, even sketchily, the terms of the security agreement it is unenforceable. So found the District Judge and we affirm.

Between Nonperfected Interests

When neither of the conflicting security interests has been perfected, the rule is that the first interest that attaches is given priority. Thus, the time of attachment is pertinent. However, this priority lasts only as long as both interests remain unperfected. If a later interest perfects first, it takes priority.

Between a nonperfected interest and other interests, a nonperfected interest generally loses. For example, a secured party who has not perfected his interest loses to a lien creditor or trustee in bankruptcy even if the creditor or trustee had notice of the secured interest. Likewise, the secured party loses to a purchaser or assignee of the collateral to the extent that the purchaser gave value and took without notice of the security interest.

After-acquired Property

As a general rule, the secured party under an after-acquired property clause will prevail against other creditors or interest holders, including the debtor's trustee in bankruptcy (§ 9–108). A secured party's interest covering after-acquired property means that in addition to the presently designated collateral, anything added to it is subject to the same debt. This is usually the case when an entire store or factory or only its inventory or equipment is used to secure a loan. For example, a lender loaned money to D and took a security interest in D's inventory, both present and after-acquired. Later D, while insolvent, purchased raw material on credit from a seller. When the seller discovered D's insolvency, he attempted to reclaim the raw material under § 2–702. The lender claimed the goods under the after-acquired clause. The lender prevails unless the seller timely secures a perfected purchase money security interest (§§ 2–702[3] and 9–108).

Purchase Money

A purchase money security interest is a security interest taken or retained by the seller of collateral to secure repayment of all or a part of the purchase price. The seller of property finances the sale with his own property, retaining the right to recover the property so as to satisfy any outstanding loan balance in case the buyer fails or refuses to pay.

Purchase Money
Loan funds to purchase property used as collateral for the loan.

A purchase money interest generally takes priority over conflicting security interests in the same collateral if the interest is perfected when the debtor takes possession of the collateral *or* within ten days thereafter (§ 9–312[3], [4]). For example, a secured party, A, takes a security interest in equipment owned by D and equipment to be after-acquired by D. A promptly files. Later, seller B sells new equipment to D and takes back a security interest in the new equipment to secure payment of the unpaid purchase price. If seller B promptly files, his interest will prevail. Making use of the ten-day filing period, therefore, is most important to a subsequent purchase money creditor.

Facts

When Firestone made a loan to Edmund Carroll (dba Kozy Kitchen) on November 18, 1960, a security agreement was executed listing all equipment and fixtures on the business premises. The agreement included the following words: "together with all property and articles now, and which may hereafter be, used or mixed with, added or attached to, and/or substituted for any of the described property." A proper financing statement was filed with the town clerk on November 18, 1960, as well as with the secretary of state on November 22, 1960. Subsequently, on November 25, 1960, National Cash Register sold and delivered to Carroll a cash register on a conditional sales contract. NCR filed with the town clerk on December 20 and with the secretary of state on December 21, 1960, almost a month after the delivery of the merchandise. When Carroll defaulted to both Firestone and NCR, Firestone repossessed and sold all the property covered by its security agreement, including the cash register. NCR sued for conversion, claiming that it was the rightful owner of the cash register.

Decision

Judgment for Firestone. Firestone had a perfected security interest on all the properties on Carroll's premises, including after-acquired property. NCR failed to protect its interest, as it did not file within ten days after delivery of its merchandise.

National Cash Register Company v. *Firestone & Company, Inc.*, 346 Mass. 255, 191 N.E.2d 471 (1963).

In *Sherman County Bank* v. *Kallhoff* (205 Neb. 392, 288 N.W.2d 24 [1980]), a Nebraska appellate emphasized that in counting the ten-day grace period, the time of the debtor's actual physical possession of the subsequently purchased merchandise, rather than the date of the sales contract, is the deciding factor.

The *ten-day rule* applies only if the purchase is a *noninventory purchase,* such as acquisition of equipment. If it is an inventory purchase, the secured party's interest must be perfected at the time the debtor receives the collateral *and* the secured party must give written notice to any other security interest holder who has previously filed a financing statement covering inventory of the same type of goods (§ 9–312[3][a][b]).

In *Paramount Finance Co.* v. *United States* (379 F.2d 543 [6th Cir. 1967]), a federal lien imposed by 26 U.S.C. § 6321 was held invalid against a lender's previously perfected purchase money security interest.

Future Advances

Using the same collateral, a lender may extend future advances. This is the case, for instance, with a construction loan where the building-to-be is given as a security for the lender's loan commitment while the loan proceeds are actually disbursed in a staggered fashion as future advances until the construction is completed. The secured party is protected in making future advances to the debtor so long as he originally perfected the security interest by filing or taking possession (§ 9–312[7]). The financing statement need not mention anything about future advances. The statement gives constructive notice that some sort of security interest exists, and it is up to the searcher to find out the nature of the interest and what it secures.

Special Priorities

Certain classes of creditors and interest holders have a priority over perfected security interests: holders of mechanic liens (§ 9–310); good-faith purchasers in the ordinary course of business (§ 9–307[1]); the holder in due course of a negotiable instrument, e.g., a check (§ 9–309); and certain purchasers of chattel paper and nonnegotiable instruments (§ 9–308). The following is an example of the superiority of the right of a good-faith purchaser in the ordinary course of business.

Facts

Sterling Acceptance lent money to Hornish, a franchise Dodge dealer, and had a perfected security interest in the dealership's inventory. Subsequently, Grimes, a good-faith purchaser, bought one of the new cars taken from Hornish's inventory. When Hornish defaulted on the loan, Sterling attempted to recover the Dodge from Grimes.

Decision

Judgment for Grimes. He was a buyer in the ordinary course of business, and as such, he bought the car free from Sterling's security interest. When a car dealership borrows money from a lender by flooring (i.e., by using the car inventory as security), it is indeed the purpose of such a credit extension for the dealer to sell the inventory and use the proceeds to repay the lender. Accordingly, the creditor must look to the dealer for repayment and not to the car that has been sold to a good-faith purchaser.

Sterling Acceptance Co. v. Grimes, 194 Pa.Super. 503, 168 A.2d 600 (1961).

It should be noted that a purchaser in the ordinary course of business is protected only if the merchandise was bought *directly* from the inventory collateral covered by the perfected security interest. Such a purchaser will be denied the protection if he purchased the property through another source, as shown in the following case.

"Flooring"
Where inventory is used to secure a business loan.

Facts

An automobile dealer sold a car on credit for private use and sold the financing paper to the plaintiff bank. Later the original buyer sold the car to another car dealer, who sold to defendant Jones. Jones purchased the car in good faith and without notice that his purchase was in violation of the bank's security interest. The plaintiff brought suit in the amount outstanding under the original credit agreement. The defendant argued that he was a buyer in the ordinary course of business (UCC § 1–201[9]) and thus took free of the perfected security interest.

Decision

The defendant is liable to the plaintiff for the outstanding amount of the original sales agreement. UCC § 9–307(1) provides that the buyer of goods in the ordinary course of business takes free of a security interest created by the seller. Here, the bank's security interest was created not by the defendant's seller but by the first dealer. Thus, UCC § 9–307(1) does not apply, and the defendant does not take free of the plaintiff's security interest.

National Shawmut Bank of Boston v. *Jones,* 108 N.H. 386, 236 A.2d 484 (1967).

State Regulation

Section 9–302(3) expressly exempts from the filing requirements of Article 9 any personal property covered by a certificate of title, e.g., automobiles, mobile homes, trailers, boats. In those states that have a certificate title system, compliance with that law is the only way in which a security interest can be perfected in collateral subject to such laws. In the few states that do not have a certificate of title system, filing under the UCC is the proper method of perfecting a security interest.

Default of the Debtor

The security agreement determines when the debtor defaults. Some of the typical default clauses that define a debtor's default are noninsurance of collateral, removal of collateral, loss or destruction of collateral, bankruptcy or assignment for benefit of creditors, and nonpayment.

Remedies

The secured party's remedies and conduct in the event of default are limited by implied standards of good faith and constitutional due process.

The three basic remedies of the secured party are (1) sale or other disposition of the collateral (§ 9–504), (2) retention of the collateral (§ 9–505[2]), and (3) an action for the debt (§ 9–501[1]).

Secured Party's Right to Possession

Repossession
Taking possession of the collateral by creditor from debtor.

Section 9–503 gives the secured party the right to take possession of the collateral upon the debtor's default; however, the secured party must do so peaceably.

The question has arisen several times as to whether or not § 9–503 is constitutional. That is, is taking a debtor's property without court proceedings a violation of the constitutional guarantee that property shall not be taken without due process of law under the Fourteenth Amendment to the Constitution of the United States? Is some notice to the debtor and an opportunity for hearing necessary?

The majority of the courts have held that § 9–503 is constitutional. For example, in *Adams* v. *Southern Calif. First Nat. Bank* 492 F.2d 324 [9th Cir. 1973], certiorari denied 419 U.S. 1006, 95 S.Ct. 325, 42 L.Ed.2d

282 (1974), the court held that the State of California was not so significantly involved in the self-help repossession procedures undertaken by the creditors as to permit the court to find the state action (conduct under color of state law) required to establish a federal cause of action. In other words, due process is a limitation only where state action is involved, and repossessions by private persons pursuant to the provisions of the security agreement do not involve state action. The U.S. Supreme Court has refused to decide the constitutionality of § 9–503 up to this time.

If a creditor repossesses the collateral when the debtor is not in default, the creditor commits a conversion. This is also the case when the creditor repossesses the wrong collateral. In addition to compensatory damages for the conversion, the debtor can recover punitive damages when the creditor has acted recklessly and with willful indifference.

Sale of Collateral

Section 9–504(1) provides, that a secured creditor after debtor's default may dispose of any or all of the collateral, but in doing so must attempt to obtain the highest price for the benefit of both himself and the debtor.

Prior to the sale, the creditor must give the debtor proper notice of the time and place of the sale to provide the debtor the opportunity to object to the foreclosure sale and protect his interest.

Facts

Gibson borrowed from Hagberg, a pawnbroker, on two pieces of rare old Indian jewelry. He received $45 for a belt and $50 on a necklace. When he defaulted on both loans, Hagberg, without giving any notice, sold the belt for $240 and the necklace for $80. At that time, the interest owed was $22. It was alleged that the two pieces of jewelry were worth $500 each. Gibson sued Hagberg for improperly disposing of the collateral.

Decision

Judgment for Gibson. He was awarded the difference between the reasonable value of the jewelry and the amount owed on the loan. Hagberg violated the Code's provision requiring proper notice prior to a foreclosure sale. Moreover, Hagberg was found not to have made a commercially reasonable sale of the rare jewelry. Hence, he was liable for damages.

Gibson v. *Hagberg,* 11 UCC Rep. 655 (N.M. 1972) (unpublished case).

Under UCC § 9–505, if the creditor's purchase money security interest involves a consumer good and the debtor has paid 60 percent or more of the cash price or of the loan, the creditor must under given circumstances sell the repossessed collateral. If less than 60 percent has been paid, the creditor may propose that he retain the collateral without a sale in satisfaction of the debt. The debtor then has twenty-one days to object in writing, in which event the creditor must nevertheless sell the collateral. Before the collateral is actually disposed of, the consumer creditor has under § 9–506 the right of redeeming it by paying off the debt.

Distribution of Proceeds

Section 9–504(1) also points out the order in which the proceeds of the collateral sale are to be distributed. First are the expenses of repossessing, storing, and selling the collateral as well as legal fees. Second is satisfaction of the debt. Third is satisfaction of junior liens in accordance with their seniority. Any proceeds remaining are to be returned to the debtor. In the event that the sales proceeds are not sufficient to satisfy the debt, the creditor is usually entitled to a deficiency judgment.

QUESTIONS

1. If concerning the same collateral, creditor A has a security agreement only and creditor B files a financing statement only, who has the valid security interest and why?
2. When is the ten-day filing period required?
3. What are future advances? Give an example.
4. What is the rule related to the disposal of repossessed consumer merchandise?
5. What is the rule on distribution of proceeds from the sale of repossessed property?

PROBLEMS

1. Jerry Gold bought an office building from Rob Baker for $200,000. Jerry took the building subject to a preexisting $150,000 mortgage held by the Fidelity Trust Company. Jerry's business failed, and the office building was sold through foreclosure by the Fidelity Trust Company At public auction, the building brought $140,000. Fidelity Trust Company got a deficiency judgment in the amount of $10,000. Does Jerry have to pay this $10,000 out of his other personal assets? Would it make any difference if he had assumed the mortgage?
2. Bank lent the borrower $150,000 on 7 percent annual interest by taking a deed of trust on the borrower's real property appraised at $250,000. Two years after the loan was made, the borrower sold the property for $300,000 to the purchaser, with the condition that the purchaser might assume the loan. At this point in time, real estate interest had increased to about 10 percent annually. The bank rejected the purchaser's request for assuming the loan and intended to implement the due-on-sale clause stated in the trust deed. Decision?
3. A borrowed $10,000 from B and gave B as security a mortgage on his property. The mortgage was not recorded. A defaulted on the loan, and B attempted to foreclose. A argued that B did not have the right to do so, since the mortgage was never recorded. Decision?
4. Secured party A has a perfected security interest in the debtor's present and future inventory, pursuant to a properly filed financing statement. S sells new inventory to the debtor, taking back a security interest in the new inventory. S files the financing statement eight days later. Debtor becomes insolvent. S claims a priority over A as to the new inventory on the basis that S had a purchase money interest that he had perfected. Discuss.
5. Stoddard obtained a new automobile loan from National Bank and gave National a security interest in the automobile to protect his loan. National perfected the security interest in compliance with Article 9 of the UCC. Stoddard later took the automobile to Levy Auto Mechanics for repairs. Stoddard then stopped paying loan installments to the bank. National sought to repossess the automobile from Levy. Levy refused to surrender the automobile until the repair bill was paid. National sued Levy to recover the vehicle, claiming its perfected security interest was entitled to priority over Levy's common law possessory lien for unpaid repairs. Decision?
6. B and G each bought automobiles for personal use from S, a private owner. Neither B or G knew that each vehicle was subject to an unfiled security interest in favor of the original seller D, a dealer in such vehicles. When S failed to make payment in accordance with the security interests of D, D repossessed the vehicles. B and G sue D, arguing that they had clear title by reason of their purchase from S. Decision?
7. S sold B a new tractor-truck worth $30,000 with a down payment of $3,000 and the balance to be paid

in thirty monthly installments. The agreement provided that upon default in any payment, S could take "immediate possession of the property—without notice or demand. For this, vendor may enter upon any premises the property may be. . . ." B defaulted, and S notified him that the truck would be repossessed. B had the truck, attached to a loaded trailer, in a locked loading area of a company that had employed B to drive the loaded trailer to the West Coast. S found the truck. When no one was around, S removed the wire screen over a ventilator hole by unscrewing it from the outside with his penknife. S then reached through the ventilator hole with a stick and unlocked the door of the tractor-truck. He then disconnected the trailer and had the truck towed away. B sued S for unlawful repossession of the truck by committing a breach of the peace. Decision?

8. C held a security agreement that covered furniture, fixtures, and inventory at the bankrupt's old drugstore. The security agreement contained an after-acquired property clause. The drugstore and its contents were destroyed by fire. The owner purchased a new store eight months later in a community 270 miles away. Afterward, he filed bankruptcy. C claims the new inventory as against the trustee in bankruptcy. Decision?

9. Kottke is a maker of dyed fabrics from textile goods. She purchased and paid for goods from a third party who had bought the goods from Lang, a textile manufacturer. The goods were still in Lang's warehouse at the time of sale. Lang refused to deliver the goods to Kottke because the third party had not paid Lang on other accounts. Kottke sued Lang in tort for conversion of the goods. Lang argued that he had a perfected security interest in the goods. Decision?

10. Beniquez had a security agreement with Dixon covering the sale of certain trailers. Beniquez did not file a financing statement or repossess the property when Dixon defaulted in payment. The United States filed a tax lien on the trailers. Beniquez claimed his prior security agreement prevailed over the tax lien. Decision?

CHAPTER THIRTY

Insurance

30.1 Insurance Concept (I)
Regulatory Authority
Insurance Company
The Insurance Contract
    Binder
    Interpretation
    Modification
Agents and Brokers
Premium

30.2 Insurance Concept (II) and Life Insurance
Commencement
Termination
    Lapse
    Cancellation
Claim and Coverage
Life Insurance
    Types of Policies
    Beneficiary
    Insurable Interest in Life Insurance
    Incontestability
    Surrender and Cancellation

30.3 Property and Liability Insurance
Insurable Interest in Property Insurance
Fire Insurance
    What Is Covered
    Who Is Covered
    Extent of Coverage
Automobile Insurance
    Collision Coverage
    Liability Coverage

30.1 Insurance Concept (I)

Insurance is a matter of protection against risk. Unfortunately, risk exists almost everywhere. A person might die, leaving a helpless child alone. Fire might burn down a home or a business, destroying all the savings and equity the owner had. Automobile accidents causing injury and damage to persons and property are common. An importer might lose his shipment because of a shipwreck or war. The loss of a key employee might cause irreparable damage to the company's business.

To counter such losses, one may, of course, privately maintain adequate savings or reserves. This does not always work, however, particularly in the case of a catastrophic incident. In such an event, sharing risk with others is a more sensible and practical solution, and the most common way of such risk sharing is through insurance.

Regulatory Authority

The federal government regulates only certain aspects of the insurance business, such as in matters related to stock security issuance. As far as its operation is concerned, the industry is almost exclusively governed by state regulation. The state ordinarily has the power to charter and license an insurance company, provide the essential terms of insurance policies, approve or supervise rate schedules, and oversee insurance agents and brokers.

Insurance Company

Stock Insurance Company
An insurance company owned as a corporation by shareholders.

Mutual Insurance Company
An insurance company whose policyholders are simultaneously the insurers.

There are basically two types of insurance companies: *stock* and *mutual*. A stock insurance company is a corporation that obtains its initial capitalization through the issuance of stock to subscribers. Thus, the company is owned by the shareholders, and the corporate rules discussed in Part VI of this book apply. A mutual insurance company, on the other hand, is essentially a cooperative, consisting of members who are simultaneously insurers and policyholders. These members contribute to the company by paying premiums and other assessments to enable the business to cover claims, losses, and other expenditures. Proportionate to their interests, the members gain from the operation's accumulated profits.

The Insurance Contract

Insurance Policy
The written contract of insurance between the insurer and the insured policyholder.

The insurance policy is a written contract between the *insurer* or *underwriter* and the *insured*, whereby the latter pays or promises to pay the premium as a consideration for the former to promise to pay a certain sum if a certain event takes place. That event may be the death, injury, or illness of a person or the loss, destruction, or damage of property. Elementary contractual requirements, such as the existence of mutual consent, consideration, capacity, and legality, as well as other contractual principles, apply to insurance.

INSURANCE

Although insurance agents and brokers are the ones soliciting business, the first move is ordinarily made by the insurance-seeking applicant, whose application may be seen as an offer to contract. This offer may be accepted or rejected by the insurance company. If it is accepted, the insurer may send the applicant a notice of acceptance before issuing a policy.

Binder

Before the insurer formally accepts the application, the company or its agent may temporarily insure the applicant. Such temporary insurance—called a binder—is provided either in writing in the form of an interim receipt or orally, even by telephone. If the binder is in writing, it usually states the essentials of the policy-to-be. The temporary agreement terminates when the formal policy is issued or the application is rejected by the insurer.

Binder
A temporary insurance agreement.

Interpretation

Basic rules governing ordinary contracts apply to insurance policies. Since policies are drawn by the insurance company and the ordinary policyholder's difficulty in understanding the technical and legal terms of the contract is widely recognized, any ambiguity is generally interpreted against the insurer and in favor of the insured.

An abundance of cases exist related to the question of interpretation of an insurance policy. The following is a case resulting from a well-known hijacking incident in the 1970s.

Northwest Airlines, Inc. v. Globe Indemnity Company
303 Minn. 16, 225 N.W.2d 831 (1975).

Yetka, Justice . . . On September 29, 1965, defendant (insurer) and plaintiff (insured) executed an insurance agreement entitled "Blanket Crime Policy" and providing indemnity for covered losses not to exceed $250,000, with a $20,000 deductible clause. This policy was in effect at the time of the alleged loss.

. . . On November 24, 1971, . . . (A) male passenger, ticketed under the name of D. B. Cooper, boarded Flight 305 at Portland, Oregon. . . . At or near the time of takeoff, at approximately 3 p.m., he proceeded to "hijack" Flight 305 by threatening to detonate what appeared to be a bomb concealed in his briefcase unless the following demands were met:

1. $200,000 in cash, to be delivered to the plane at Seattle.
2. Four parachutes, to be delivered with the money.
3. No police interference.
4. Refueling of the plane at Seattle.

. . . Captain Scott decided to cooperate with the hijacker. . . . Stewardess Tina Larson (, who) carried the money into the airplane and surrendered direct physical custody of it to the hijacker. Upon receipt thereof, Cooper allowed the passengers to leave the airplane. Stewardess Larson also delivered the parachutes and other items to Cooper, who was still in the rear cabin of the aircraft. At that time, he allowed two other stewardesses to leave the airplane. Cooper, Stewardess Larson, and the cockpit crew of three men remained on board.

Pursuant to Cooper's instructions, the airplane took off for the stated destination of Mexico. However, intermediate fuel stops were negotiated with Cooper, the first of which was to be Reno, Nevada. The hijacker instructed the crew as to altitude, speed, and other details of the flight. After takeoff, Cooper ordered the remaining crew members to stay in the forward area of the aircraft and to keep the curtains to the tourist section closed. Shortly after takeoff, approximately 7:30 p.m., Cooper lowered the rear stairs of the airplane. Approximately halfway between Seattle and Portland, the instruments of the aircraft indicated that Cooper had jumped from these stairs. Upon landing in Reno, Nevada, the crew discovered that Cooper, the bomb, the money, and two parachutes were not on board. Neither Cooper nor the money has ever been located.

. . . Plaintiff seeks recovery under the following insuring agreements, which state in relevant part:

"LOSS INSIDE THE PREMISES COVERAGE

"II. Loss of Money and Securities by the actual destruction, disappearance or *wrongful abstraction* thereof *within the Premises* or within any Banking Premises or similar recognized places of safe deposit.

. . . "LOSS OUTSIDE THE PREMISES COVERAGE

"III. Loss of Money and Securities by the actual destruction, disappearance or *wrongful abstraction* thereof outside the Premises while being conveyed by a *Messenger* or any armored motor vehicle company, or while within the living quarters in the home of any Messenger.

"Loss of other property by Robbery or attempt thereat outside the Premises while being conveyed by a *Messenger* or any armored motor vehicle company, or by theft while within the living quarters in the home of any Messenger." (Italics supplied.)

. . . To recover, defendant correctly states that plaintiff must establish:

1. That it suffered a loss of money.
2. That the loss resulted from the actual wrongful abstraction thereof.
3. That the wrongful abstraction is a risk covered in the policy.

. . . Defendant attacks the first element on grounds that the trial court's finding that plaintiff "suffered a loss of $200,000 in money by means of wrongful abstraction thereof within the meaning of the contract of insurance" is too general.

. . . (W)e cannot agree that the taking of the $200,000 is not a "loss of money" as defined in the policy.

. . . The second requisite element, wrongful abstraction, is not defined in the policy and the parties agree that said term is unambiguous.

. . . Defendant characterizes the hijacking as extortion, which is "wrongful" according to the definition of extortion provided by defendant. Thus, the hijacking was wrongful. The term "abstract" is defined in Webster's New International Dictionary (2d ed. 1947) p. 10, as "to take secretly or dishonestly." . . . (I)t would appear clear that airline hijacking for ransom is indeed wrongful abstraction.

Defendant argues also that extortion is not a peril insured against by the policy. Defendant proposes that the rule of "expressio unius est exclusio alteris" (expression of one thing is an exclusion of another) is applicable because the inclusion of coverage for wrongful abstraction thereby excludes coverage for extortion and hijacking losses. We do not agree with these contentions.

. . . Defendant contends the third requisite element for coverage under Insuring Agreement II, wrongful abstraction within the premises, has not been fulfilled. It argues that the wrongful abstraction took place when Cooper assumed control of the airplane. Thus, it concludes that, since the $200,000 was not at the covered premises *at that moment,* there was no loss of money due to wrongful abstraction. This argument, too, must fail in the cold light of the fact that the hijacking consisted of a continuing course of related events beginning with the takeover of the airplane and culminating with the hijacker's successful escape with the money which was, *when taken,* owned by plaintiff.

. . . When that policy is read as a whole, we find it to be in the nature of a blanket or all-risk policy, as opposed to one which covers only specified risks. As defendant's counsel admitted in oral argument, mere unforeseeability of the manner in which the loss was sustained will not *per se* constitute grounds for the insurer to deny coverage. In the present case, where there is blanket coverage and the risk at issue was not excluded, the insurer must fulfill its contractual obligation to indemnify the insured.

. . . Affirmed.

Indeed, most insurance cases involve the question of interpretation of a policy, and it is a generally accepted trend for courts to read insurance terms to the advantage of the insured.

Facts

C & J Fertilizer (plaintiff) was insured by Allied Mutual (defendant) under two policies titled "Broad Form Storekeepers Policy" and "Mercantile Burglary and Robbery Policy." Both policies defined burglary as "the felonious abstraction of insured property (1) from within the premises by a person making felonious entry therein by actual force and violence, of which force and violence there are visible marks made by tools, explosives, electricity or chemicals upon, or physical damage to, the exterior of the premises at the place of such entry." The policies explicitly excluded an "inside job." One morning, when the employees came in for work, all the doors of the premises were locked except the front office door. There were no marks caused by the use of tools, explosions, electricity, or chemicals, nor was there any physical damage to the exterior of the building. However, physical damage by tools was visible on the door leading to the room wherefrom chemicals and equipment worth about $10,000 were stolen. The trial court denied recovery by the plaintiff, since there was no physical damage to the exterior of the building to indicate felonious entry by force and violence.

Decision

Judgment for C & J Fertilizer. The Iowa Supreme Court reversed the lower court's decision on the basis of the reasonable expectation, implied warranty, and unconscionability theories. Regarding the first theory, reference was made to the concept adopted in *Rodman* v. *State Farm Mutual Ins. Co.* (208 N.W.2d 903, 905–908 [Iowa 1973]), i.e., that "the objectively reasonable expectations of applicants and intended beneficiaries regarding the terms of insurance contracts will be honored even though painstaking study of the policy provisions would have negated those expectations" (208 N.W.2d at 906). Aside from the letter of the policies referring to exterior damage of the premises, the party under the policies clearly wished to exclude only an "outside job," which is not the case here. As to an implied warranty, the higher court felt that the plaintiff should prevail under the UCC concept of fitness for the particular purpose. The plaintiff is also entitled to a reversal, because the liability-avoiding provision in the definition of the burglary is, in the circumstances of this case, considered unconscionable.

C & J Fertilizer, Inc. v. *Allied Mutual Insurance Company,* 227 N.W.2d 169 (Iowa 1975).

On the other hand, there are cases showing a stricter construction of a policy. In *Miller* v. *Underwriters at Lloyd's, London* (398 So.2d 654 [La.App. 1981]), where a fire insurance policy covered an "owner-occupied" house and the insured was required to notify the insurer in the event that the house became vacant or was unoccupied for more than sixty days, the insured did not recover when the house burned down while it was unoccupied for more than sixty days, even though the owner had from time to time visited the place to make some repairs. In *Stack* v. *Hanover Ins. Co.* (57 Ala.App. 504, 329 So.2d 561 [1976]), where the policy covered vandalism, the insured was denied recovery for damage caused by a large deer crashing into a glass door of the house.

In interpreting a policy, the insured's initial application is often considered part of the agreement. This is particularly relevant if fraud is involved. The incorporation of the application may be formalized by an express provision in the policy. Furthermore, policies are tacitly considered to contain all the terms prescribed by statute, whether or not they actually do so.

Modification

Rider
A separate document to change terms of a policy.

The insurer and the insured may agree to certain changes in the policy. A unilateral modification by the insurer is permissible if this right is specifically reserved in the policy. A change in the term of a policy is accomplished by an endorsement on the policy or by a separate *rider*.

Agents and Brokers

Fiduciary Duties
Duties of trustworthiness.

Insurance is bought and sold through insurance agents and brokers. An insurance agent is a person representing a specific insurance company. Although there may be several types of agents under the state statute, all agents owe fiduciary duties and loyalty to the respective insurance companies. The law of agency applies to the relationship between an insurer and its agent. As a principal, the insurer is liable for agreements made by the agent in its behalf as well as for the agent's tort committed within the scope of authority.

On the other hand, an insurance broker is usually an independent contractor who acts as a middleman between the insured and the insurer, whoever the latter may be. Thus, a broker is not an employee or agent of any insurer. He solicits business from the public that needs all kinds of insurance and matches those needs with the programs available in the insurance market. He receives from the company commission for deals made in the company's favor. Since a broker is an independent contractor, it is more difficult for the insurer to be held liable for his actions. In fact, it is the insured party who, under given circumstances, may be considered the employer of the broker.

In *Lazzara* v. *Howard A. Esser, Inc.* (604 F.Supp. 1205 [N.D.Ill. 1985]), where liability of the insurer depended on whether the procurer of the policy was an agent or a broker, a U.S. District Court set forth a four-prong test, namely: (1) Who set him in motion first? (2) Who could control his actions? (3) Who pays him? (4) Whose interest was he to protect?

> "In the present case, the documents before this Court clearly show that Esser was acting as Lazzara's broker for the purpose of procuring the insurance. . . . Esser was set in motion by Lazzara. Also, Lazzara was the person who could control Esser's actions. . . . Esser was contacted and directed by Lazzara to protect the interests of Lazzara, not the insurers. Moreover, that Esser received its commission checks from Aetna and Reliance is not a factor that supports Esser's assertion that it did not act as Lazzara's broker. The contracts between Esser and Etna and Reliance provided that the commissions would be derived from the premiums paid by Lazzara, as required by Illinois law. . . . In fact, for at least the first premium payment, Lazzara paid Esser the premium, who in turn paid the insurance companies, *after* deducting its commission."

Both the insurance agent and the broker are expected to show good faith as well as exercise due care and proper diligence in transacting the business. They are supposed to proceed strictly in accordance with the instructions given them. They can be held liable for damages caused by departure from their scope of authority and dereliction of duty, such as failure to procure insurance requested by an applicant, renew an expired policy, or adequately service an existing policy. In *Joseph Forest Products, Inc. v. Pratt* (278 Or. 477, 564 P.2d 1027 [1977]), an agent who failed to obtain fire insurance requested by the owner was held liable for damages caused by fire on the applicant's plant. "As a general rule the liability of the agent with respect to a loss, by reason of his breach of duty, is that which would have fallen on the company had the insurance been properly effected, together with such other damages as proximately result from the breach, and less the amount of unpaid premiums or cost of the insurance."

Premium

The premium is the consideration that the insured pays for the insurer's promise to indemnify him in the event of a casualty resulting in injury to a person or damage to property. In addition to the net premium, which is the charge for the coverage itself, a "loading" fee may have to be paid by the insured for the insurer's handling cost, agent commission, physical examination, and other office expenses.

The amount of the premium primarily depends on the *risk* factor, or the likelihood that a loss may occur, and the *value* of the object insured that would determine how much the insurer would have to pay. Obviously, there may be other variables, such as the insured's medical records in a life insurance policy, the location of the property in a fire insurance policy, or one's driving record in automobile insurance coverage.

Usually, the applicant submits the application to the agent or broker, together with the first premium. At this point, he may be issued a binder. However, the application still needs to be accepted by the insurer, prior to which there is no permanent agreement. This means that the applicant also may still reject the deal if he subsequently does not agree with the terms or premium set forth in the insurer's acceptance.

Premium
The consideration paid by insured to the insurer for insurance.

Facts

Mrs. Green, Hall's sister, went to McKenzie & Mouk Insurance Agency to obtain auto insurance for Hall. An employee completed a binder-application form (which Mrs. Green did not sign) and accepted from Mrs. Green a check for $99 as the quoted premium for six months. The application was submitted to an insurance company, and after checking Hall's driving record, the agency was informed that the premium should be $343 for the six-month period. The agency wrote to Mrs. Green concerning the increased premium and claimed that it never received a response. Mrs. Green, on the other hand, claimed that she called the agency to reject the coverage. The agency sued Hall for the additional charge.

Decision

Judgment for Hall. Neither Mrs. Green nor Hall ever agreed to pay the additional charge. An application for coverage merely constitutes a contractual offer. The insurance contract is not completed until the application is accepted by the insurer. In this case, the insurance company's higher premium charge was nothing but a counteroffer, which the applicant can accept or reject. The question of whether or not Mrs. Green responded to the agency's letter became immaterial, since there was in any event no definite acceptance by the defendant.

McKenzie & Mouk, Inc. v. Hall, 467 So.2d 1220 (La.App. 1985).

The general rule is that the insurer is entitled only to earned premium. Consequently, if the policy is canceled before expiration of the term for which the premium has been paid, the insurer is required to reimburse the insured any unearned portion of the paid premium.

A statute or the policy itself may provide that the insurance shall not automatically lapse if the premium for the following term is not paid when due. There is ordinarily a grace period of thirty days for the premium to be paid. As to life insurance, the insurer may upon default in payment of the premium statutorily be compelled to undertake such arrangements as issuing a paid-up policy in a smaller amount or an extended term policy or returning the cash surrender value of the policy. This is further explained in the next subchapter.

Questions

1. What is an insurance policy? What is a binder?
2. How are policy terms generally interpreted?
3. What legal principles were applied in interpreting the policy terms in *C & J Fertilizer, Inc.* v. *Allied Mutual Insurance Company*?
4. What is the difference between an insurance agent and an insurance broker?
5. Define insurance premium.

30.2 Insurance Concept (II) and Life Insurance

Commencement

Commencement
The time at which the insurance coverage takes effect.

When the insurance becomes effective is basically a matter of agreement between the parties. Usually, the applicant informs the agent or broker when he wishes the policy to take effect. The issuance of the policy itself or payment of the premium is not necessarily a condition precedent for insurance to commence, although most policies state precisely when they actually become effective.

Ordinarily, fire as well as automobile insurance is effective upon issuance of a written or oral binder by the agent or broker. On the other hand, for life insurance to take effect, delivery of the policy to the insured while in a state of good health and payment of the initial premium are usually required, although in the following case a "conditional receipt" instead of a formal policy was considered sufficient for a life insurance contract to be enforceable.

Facts

On September 24, 1972, Mr. Collister went to Nationwide Life's agent to apply for life insurance. He paid the agent $60.66 for the first two-month premium and received from the agent a "conditional receipt." He was killed on November 4, 1972, in a car accident. At that time, neither a formal policy had been issued nor had the application been rejected. Moreover, Mr. Collister had not taken the medical exam required by the application and the conditional receipt. Nationwide Life denied any liability, and Mrs. Collister sued the company.

Decision

Judgment for the plaintiff. The court recognized that insurance contracts are in fact not freely negotiated agreements between parties with equal bargaining power. It is the insurer who, for the most part, dictates the contractual terms, while the insured has little to negotiate on. To accept Nationwide's argument would be to permit an insurer to hold itself immune from liability while it considers whether to accept or reject the risk and at the same time enjoy the benefits that flow from immediate collection of the premium. In the absence of an understanding to the contrary between the parties, coverage will be deemed to be that which would be expected by the ordinary person, namely, complete and immediate coverage upon payment of the premium.

Collister v. *Nationwide Life Insurance Co.*, 479 Pa. 579, 388 A.2d 1346 (1978).

Consistent with the above ruling is *Gillilan* v. *Federated Guaranty Life Insurance Co.* (447 So.2d 668 [Ala. 1984]), in which the circumstances are similar. The application for coverage of $40,000 was submitted on November 29, 1980. The application specifically made the coverage conditional upon the insurer's underwriting department's investigation of the applicant's insurability. Furthermore, it stated that if the application was not accepted and approved within sixty days, no contract would be issued. On December 31, 1980, the applicant died; and on January 9, 1981, about forty days after the application, the insurer refunded the insured's premium to his estate, rejecting the application for insurance. The court felt that there could, in this case, not be an insurance contract at the time of the insured's death.

Coverage
The protection provided by an insurance policy.

Certain policies may stipulate a waiting period with regard to coverage of certain types of risks. This means that a certain period of time after the policy becomes binding must elapse before the specific risk is actually covered. A waiting period, as such, is an exception rather than the rule. In most instances, a policy takes immediate effect when there is a binding agreement and sometimes even as soon as the insured submits the initial application.

Facts

Metts (plaintiff) mailed on May 15 a completed polio insurance application form distributed by Central Standard Life (defendant). The printed form clearly stated "immediate first-day coverage automatically covers the entire family." The company received the application on May 23. Meanwhile, on May 21, Metts's son was stricken with polio, of which the insurer was notified on May 28. Metts sued the company, as it refused to pay on the ground that the application had not been accepted.

Decision

Judgment for Metts. The application unequivocally provided for Central Standard Life to be bound immediately and automatically after the completed application was mailed. There was no waiting period contemplated. Since the language was clear, there was no room for interpretation, but even if there were ambiguity, it was to be construed in favor of the insured.

Metts v. Central Standard Life Insurance Co., 142 Cal.App.2d 445, 298 P.2d 621 (1956).

Termination

Insurance terminates upon lapse or cancellation of the policy.

Lapse

Lapse
Termination for failure to pay a premium when due or within a grace period.

Grace Period
A time period after a premium is due, within which the premium may still be paid to prevent lapse of the policy.

Failure to pay the required premium can result in the policy to lapse. Except for policies issued for a specified term without further extension being contemplated, failure to pay the premium within the grace period (previously discussed) will cause the insurance policy to actually expire. It should be noted that life insurance policies may ordinarily be reinstated within a reasonable time by paying all the premiums due, as long as the insured is still insurable.

Cancellation

Policies usually state whether they can or cannot be canceled. In general, the insured may cancel property or liability insurance at any time before its expiration, in which event he is entitled to reimbursement of the unused portion of the premium. On the other hand, the insurer is normally required to give the insured a certain number of days written notice of cancellation. However, a life insurance contract generally cannot be canceled, since this would virtually allow an insurer to terminate policies of older, feeble, or sick people to avoid paying anticipated benefits.

Claim and Coverage

Proof of Loss
The formal written statement of a claimant under an insurance policy.

To recover, the insured must promptly notify the insurer of any claim arising under the policy, or at least within a reasonable time after he has knowledge of the loss. A proof of loss, a formal written statement by the claimant—is to be submitted to the insurer within a certain number of days. The insurer then has the right to investigate and settle the case. This must be conducted in good faith. A liability insurance policy may stipulate that the insurer is obligated to defend the policyholder against lawsuits. The policy may also provide a deadline for the policyholder to be able to sue the insurance company.

The insurance policy states the risks or perils for which the insured is covered. In addition, it contains *exceptions,* or exclusions, for which the insurer will not pay a loss. Not only are these exceptions interpreted strictly against the insurer, but judicial policy calls for an exception to be ignored if there is no causative connection between the loss or injury and the situation contemplated under the exception. For instance, in *South Carolina Insurance Company* v. *Collins* (269 S.C. 282, 237 S.E.2d 358 [1977]), the court decided in favor of the estate of a pilot who was killed when the plane he was piloting crashed. The policy clearly excluded the situation in which the Piper Colt airplane was being flown by a person without a valid medical examination certificate. Nevertheless, even though in this case the insured's medical certificate had expired at the time of the crash, the court insisted that there was no immediate relationship between the accident and the expired certificate, and there was therefore no reason to deny the estate's claim.

If the insurer pays the entire amount of the claim, it may take over the position of the insured against the third party who caused the damage. This is called *subrogation,* which entitles the insurer to bring action against the third party. For example, an automobile insurer who pays a claim of a policyholder may sue the third party whose negligence was the cause of the car accident, in which event the insured is required to cooperate with the insurer in all matters related to the claim.

Life Insurance

In a life insurance contract, the insured pays a premium for the insurer's promise to pay a third party (the beneficiary) the face amount of the policy (or more) upon the death of the insured. The character of life insurance is somewhat different from property insurance in that it does not indemnify a measurable loss but is meant to assist the beneficiary in the absence of the deceased person's pecuniary support. Accordingly, life insurance is often seen as an investment for the benefit of the living rather than a remedy for an actual damage.

Life Insurance
Requires insurer to pay beneficiary upon death of the insured.

Types of Policies

Life insurance can be classified as follows:

1. Straight life insurance, under which premiums are to be paid throughout the entire life of the insured.
2. Limited payment insurance, under which premiums need to be paid only for a certain period of time, e.g., twenty years, or until the death of the insured if it takes place during this period.
3. Endowment insurance, which requires the insurer to pay a specific amount when the policyholder reaches a certain age or upon his death, whichever occurs earlier. This is similar to a retirement plan.

Straight Life Insurance
Premiums are paid throughout entire life of insured.

Limited Payment Life Insurance
Premiums are paid only for a specified length of time.

Endowment Insurance
Provides for payment to the policyholder when he reaches a certain age or upon his death if it occurs earlier.

Term Insurance
Provides for insurance only for a certain time period.

Group Insurance
Insurance provided at a reduced rate for people associated with the same organization.

4. Term insurance, which requires the insurer to pay a specific amount only if the policyholder dies within a certain period of time, e.g., ten years after the inception. Such a policy is appropriate, for instance, for a breadwinner to protect a minor dependent.

A group of employees or professionals may take insurance under a group policy. Each member of the group may designate his or her own beneficiary, though the group premium may be paid by the employer. *Double indemnity* means that the insurer will pay double the policy face value if the insurer dies as a result of an accident.

Beneficiary

Beneficiary
A person who is to receive the proceeds of a life insurance policy.

Contingent Beneficiary
Receives the policy proceeds if the primary beneficiary predeceases the insured.

A beneficiary is a person who is to receive the proceeds of a life insurance policy upon the death of the insured. One or more persons as well as the insured's estate may be named beneficiary. A contingent beneficiary is to receive the insurance's benefits only if the primary beneficiary predeceases the insured. If no contingent beneficiary is designated and the only beneficiary predeceases the insured or dies simultaneously with the insured, the proceeds of the policy become payable to the insured's estate.

Life insurance generally permits the policyholder to change the beneficiary without the latter's consent. This takes place by a written notification to the insurer, who formalizes the change by an endorsement of the policy. As shown in *Pena* v. *Salinas* (536 S.W.2d 671 [Tex.Civ.App. 1976]), a change of the beneficiary by the insured in his last will, without an endorsement in the policy, was ruled to be ineffective. (Refer to discussion on donee beneficiary in Subchapter 9.2).

A life insurance beneficiary who murders or feloniously causes the death of the insured is precluded from obtaining any benefits arising from the policy. Also, suicide committed by the insured within a certain period of time, such as two or three years after commencement of the policy, may result in denial of policy benefits to the beneficiary.

Insurable Interest in Life Insurance

Insurable Interest
Interest held by purchaser of an insurance policy.

Insurable interest in life insurance is the interest that one must have in the life of the insured person. The question may be seen in two ways: (1) Since any person ordinarily has an interest in preserving his own life, there is obviously an insurable interest, and if such a person purchases a policy on his own life and pays the premiums, he may designate his own estate or any other person as beneficiary. Thus, the beneficiary himself does not have to prove an insurable interest in the insured's life. (2) On the other hand, if a person purchases a policy on someone else's life, he must be able to show an insurable interest in order to receive benefits from the policy. He must have a real financial or equitable interest in the life of the insured. It would not be insurance, but rather gambling or speculation, if one could purchase a policy on any other person's life.

Insurable interest can be based on a blood, pecuniary, or affinity relationship in which the beneficiary prefers the insured to stay alive. Thus, an insurable interest exists between husband and wife, between parents and children, or between partners in a partnership. A company may have insurable interest in the life of its key executive. A creditor has an insurable interest in the life of his debtor. In *Mutual Savings Life Ins. Co. v. Noah* (291 Ala. 444, 282 So.2d 271 [1973]), the court recognized an insurable interest between brothers. "(A)n insurable interest may arise from blood relationship alone without regard to whether the beneficiary has any pecuniary interest in the life of the insured or is dependent upon him." However, the following relationships have been held not to create an insurable interest: i.e., cousin and cousin, the wife of a man's wife's brother, aunt and niece, aunt-in-law and niece, niece and uncle.

Questions related to insurable interest may be raised by the insurer alone. It may not be brought up by a beneficiary who seeks to disqualify another beneficiary (*Mullenax* v. *National Reserve Life Insurance Co.*, 29 Colo.App. 418, 485 P.2d 137 [1971]). It should also be noted that the insurable interest, if required, need exist only at the time the policy is issued and not at the later time or when the insured dies.

Secor v. Pioneer Foundry Company
20 Mich.App. 30, 173 N.W.2d 780 (1969).

Levin, Judge Plaintiff is the widow of Jack A. Secor and the administratrix of his estate. She commenced this action to recover the proceeds of an ordinary life insurance policy on his life which were paid to his former employer, defendant Pioneer Foundry Company, Inc. The trial court entered a judgment of no cause of action and the plaintiff appeals. We affirm.

Pioneer Foundry employed Secor for a period of 9 years, 1954 to July, 1963. In March, 1960, Pioneer Foundry obtained a $50,000 policy on his life; it was the applicant, the owner and the beneficiary, and it paid the premiums on the policy. After the employment relationship terminated in July, 1963, Pioneer Foundry paid the March, 1964 annual premium. Secor died the following month.

Plaintiff argues that after the termination of Secor's employment Pioneer Foundry lost whatever insurable interest it had in Secor's life and that a constructive trust should be impressed on the proceeds in favor of Secor's widow and estate.

A preliminary issue—whether the plaintiff has standing to complain—is dispositive of plaintiff's contention that Pioneer Foundry no longer had an insurable interest after Secor left its employ. In *Hicks* v. *Cary* (1952), 332 Mich. 606, 52 N.W.2d 351, on facts similar to those before us, the Michigan Supreme Court declared that the insurer alone may assert that the beneficiary of a life policy does not have an insurable interest. . . . The rule that only the insurer can raise the question of lack of insurable interest appears to be well supported in other jurisdictions.

. . . In the present case, the insurer . . . paid the proceeds of the policy to Pioneer Foundry in May, 1964, without asserting this possible defense.

. . . The purchaser of ordinary life insurance, as distinguished from casualty or property insurance, buys not only indemnification in a specific amount against a particular peril or potential loss but also makes an investment. To terminate the rights of the owner or beneficiary of ordinary life insurance because the relationship to the life insured has changed, perhaps after many years of making premium payments, at a time when death is bound to be more imminent than it was at the time the policy was issued, would not only adversely affect this investment quality of life insurance but would also confer an unanticipated and unwarranted windfall on the insurer.

In recognition of these considerations the almost universal rule of law in this country is that if the insurable interest requirement is satisfied at the time the policy is issued, the proceeds of the policy must be paid upon the death of the life insured without regard to whether the beneficiary has an insurable interest at the time of death. It has, accordingly, been held that an employer who is the beneficiary of a policy insuring the life of one of his employees may collect proceeds which become payable under the policy even though the employee's death occurs after the termination of his employment.

The ordinary life insurance policy issued to the defendant corporation is referred to in the insurance industry as "keyman" life insurance. The plaintiff emphasizes that the typical life insurance policy is purchased to provide for loss by family members who may be expected to suffer a personal as well as a financial loss upon the death of the life insured. From this she argues that keyman life insurance should not be governed by the same rules as apply to life insurance generally. The proffered distinction is not, in our opinion, meaningful. Life insurance is not meant to assuage grief; its primary function is monetary. It serves fundamentally the same purpose whether the beneficiary is a widow or a business; it seeks to replace with a sum of money the earning capacity of the life insured.

The plaintiff's analogy to the public policy against a murderer collecting insurance on the life of the victim is inapposit. Pioneer Foundry's act of paying the yearly premium after Secor left its employ is not (contrary to plaintiff's argument) at all analogous to murdering him. Given the general rule that the beneficiary of a life policy may collect its proceeds although the insurable interest which existed when the policy was issued subsequently terminates, it would make no sense to hold that the act of paying the premium (necessary to the full preservation of the owner's rights under the policy) somehow or other brings about a termination of the owner-beneficiary's rights.

We also decline to limit Pioneer Foundry's recovery to the amount of its investment in the policy and its financial loss (probably nil) upon Secor's death. Pioneer Foundry's investment in the policy was large both quantitatively and relatively. It chose to make the premium payment due 8 months after Secor's employment terminated to preserve recovery of its prior expenditures. It did this in its own interest; it has not been suggested that it was acting for, or because of any obligation it had assumed to, Secor or his family. . . .

Affirmed. . . .

Incontestability

Incontestability
Prohibits insurer to contest the policy for misstatements in the insured's application, after the insurance has been in force for a certain length of time.

An application for life insurance may contain intentional or unintentional misrepresentations without which the application could be rejected or for which different terms or higher premiums might be required. Relevant are such items as age, medical history, or health condition of the applicant. Subsequent discovery of misinformation prejudicial to the insurer's interest entitles the insurer to cancel or rescind the policy or use the misrepresentation as a defense of fraud in the procurement of the policy.

It would be most unfair to the policy owner, however, particularly where the misinformation is innocent, if the insurer may contest the policy at any time, since the insurer might simply withhold its discovery of the falsity until a claim is presented. Hence, all states' rules, except those of Missouri and Rhode Island, require that life insurance contracts contain an incontestability clause that prohibits the insurer to contest the policy after a certain date or passage of a certain period of time, e.g., one or two years after the policy is issued.

Surrender and Cancellation

Ordinarily, the insured may surrender or cancel a life insurance policy at any time. If he does so, he may ask for the cash surrender value of the policy, borrow against it, or ask for a paid-up or an extended-term policy.

The cash surrender value of a life insurance policy depends on the accumulated premiums thus far paid. Therefore, the longer the policy has been paid for, the larger its cash value. Usually, the insured may ask for the cash surrender value if the policy has been in existence for at least two or three years. The insured may also borrow against the cash value to meet a temporary financial need. He will have to pay interest on the loan, and the policy cash value is used as collateral. Term policies do not carry a cash surrender value.

Under a state regulation, a policyholder is allowed to ask for a *paid-up* policy if he no longer wishes to pay the premium. In essence, a paid-up policy is a policy covering an amount smaller than the amount of the old policy. The smaller amount is based on the cash value of the lapsed policy. Another alternative in such a situation is the issuance of an *extended-term* policy, under which the length of the extended period of coverage again depends on the value of the lapsed policy.

Cash Surrender Value
Value of a life insurance policy based on premiums thus far paid.

Questions

1. What are exceptions in an insurance policy, and how are they interpreted?
2. What are the basic types of a life insurance?
3. What is a primary and what is a contingent beneficiary on a life insurance policy?
4. In which situation must a beneficiary have an insurable interest in the life of the insured?
5. Explain cash surrender value of a policy.

30.3 Property and Liability Insurance

Almost any property can be insured against loss, destruction, or damage. Marine insurance protects import and export shipments to and from abroad. There is property insurance to protect cargoes on trucks, trains, and airplanes. A passenger's luggage or a postal package can also be insured.

Liability insurance, on the other hand, is designed to idemnify the policyholder if he for some reason becomes liable for an injury to the person or property of a third party. For example, a manufacturer may purchase product liability insurance to protect himself against damages resulting from the use or consumption of his product. A building owner may need protection against liability to people injured on the premises. A motorist may accidentally injure another person or damage another vehicle.

Property Insurance
Protects policyholder against loss, destruction, or damage to his property.

Liability Insurance
Protects policyholder against liability for injuring a third party's person or property.

Two most commonly known types of insurance involving both property and liability coverage are discussed in this subchapter, namely *fire* and *automobile* insurance.

Insurable Interest in Property Insurance

A claim for property damage is valid only if the insured has an insurable interest in the property. This means that the damage to the property translates to an immediate pecuniary or financial loss to the insured. In Subchapter 17.2, we learned that insurable interest for a buyer of goods exists at the moment the goods are identified. This can take place before the buyer takes possession of the merchandise. Indeed, insurable interest in property is given a rather broad connotation. It includes not only legal or equitable title but also possession of the property as well as the interest of a lien holder in a collateral.

Facts

In 1972, Joseph and Betty DeWitt purchased a house, taking title in Betty's name. In 1979, they were divorced, and as part of a divorce settlement, Betty moved out of the house. She was also required to execute a quitclaim deed conveying the title to the house to Joseph, which she never did. Joseph died in 1980, after which Betty reoccupied the property with her son from the marriage. American Family Mutual subsequently issued a new fire policy on the house to Betty without knowledge of the divorce settlement. The house was thereafter totally destroyed by fire in an explosion. When American learned about the divorce and the property settlement, it denied liability. A legal action by Betty DeWitt ensued.

Decision

Judgment for the plaintiff. The court found merit in the plaintiff's claim that the decree of divorce and the settlement agreement were not sufficient to effectuate a conveyance without an affirmative act by her to convey her interest. It further emphasized that a person has insurable interest in the property "if she will derive pecuniary benefit or advantage from its preservation, or will suffer pecuniary loss or damage from its destruction, termination, or injury by the happening of the event insured against." Insurable interest may be derived from possession, enjoyment, or profits of the property, security, or lien resting upon it, or it may be other certain benefits growing out of or dependent upon it. Here, Betty's insurable interest was based not only on her former status as sole owner but also on her personal liability as mortgagor, the expenses she defrayed to repair and improve the property, and her possession and occupancy of the house as a dwelling place.

DeWitt v. American Family Mutual Insurance Co., 667 S.W.2d 700 (Mo. 1984).

In fact, almost any kind of financial interest can qualify as an insurable interest. A general contractor who builds a house for the owner has an insurable interest in the building, since the building's destruction could cost him the profits he is to receive. Even an innocent purchaser of stolen merchandise may have an insurable interest in the property. In *Castle Cars* v. *United States Fire Ins. Co.* (221 Va. 773, 273 S.E.2d 793 [1981]), judgment was rendered in favor of a car dealer from whose lot a newly acquired car was stolen. The insurance carrier denied liability under a garagekeeper's liability insurance policy, since the dealer had actually bought a stolen car.

The dealer argued that he was only an innocent purchaser who unknowingly bought the vehicle on a falsified title certificate.

Whereas in life insurance, insurable interest of the beneficiary must exist at the inception of the policy, in property insurance, the policyholder is required to have insurable interest at the time of the loss.

Fire Insurance

Most residential and commercial properties in this country are covered by fire insurance. Fire insurance policies are basically indemnity contracts that obligate the insurance carrier to pay the policyholder for losses resulting from fire damage to the insured property. The policy may also include a liability coverage to protect the insured from damages arising from injuries sustained by third parties on the property.

Fire Insurance
Protects policyholder against losses resulting from fire.

What Is Covered

Fire insurance ordinarily covers losses resulting from a *hostile fire*. The fire must be the immediate or proximate cause of the loss. At least a reasonable connection is required. A hostile fire must be unintended, such as a fire caused by an electrical short circuit or by lightning. A fire may initially be "friendly," such as fire in a fireplace, but later escapes to other places and becomes incontrollable.

Hostile Fire
Unintended fire.

In *Schulze & Burch Biscuit* v. *American Protection Ins.* (96 Ill.App.3d 350, 51 Ill.Dec. 823, 421 N.E.2d 331 [1981]), the policyholder operated a baking business that used several large ovens to bake biscuits, crackers, and related products. The ovens employed natural gas. One day, at the end of a working shift, one of the ovens was inadvertently left to operate though no product was on the conveyer. This caused the oven temperature to rise excessively, which ultimately resulted in serious damage to the oven. The cost of repairing and replacing the oven was allegedly about $150,000. The court considered such a fire hostile and allowed the insured to recover the damages. On the other hand, in *Youse* v. *Employers Fire Insurance Co.* (172 Kan. 111, 238 P.2d 472 [1951]), the court rejected a claim of a policyholder who accidentally threw a valuable ring in a burning trash incinerator. This fire was not hostile.

The New York standard fire insurance form is commonly used as the *"standard policy." Extended coverage* protects the policyholder against losses caused by elements other than fire, such as smoke damage, explosion, windstorm, hail, and loss of rent.

Who Is Covered

The insured may make a claim on a policy unless he fraudulently or intentionally caused the fire. A fire negligently caused by the policyholder does not preclude him from recovery. A problem arises when there are two or more tenants on the policy and fraud is perpetrated by only one of them.

Morgan v. Cincinnati Ins. Co.
411 Mich. 267, 307 N.W.2d 53 (1981).

Kavanagh, Justice . . . Plaintiff and her husband, as tenants by the entireties, owned a home which was insured by defendant. On January 20, 1974, it was extensively damaged by a fire started by plaintiff's husband, who was living apart from plaintiff as divorce proceedings between them were then pending. Plaintiff filed a claim under the insurance policy, which the defendant denied. Defendant asserted that since plaintiff and her husband were the insured and owned inseparable interests in the property as tenants by the entireties the fraud of plaintiff's husband was imputed to plaintiff. Plaintiff's suit was dismissed on defendant's motion for summary judgment. The Court of Appeals affirmed "with extreme reluctance." *Morgan v. Cincinnati Ins. Co.*, 91 Mich.App. 48, 50, 282 N.W.2d 829 (1979). We reverse.

On appeal defendant contends that the question whether an innocent insured may recover on property insurance after another insured has committed some act of fraud depends on whether the interests of the insured are considered joint or several. Defendant asserts that the property interests of parties holding as tenants by the entireties are unified and cannot be separated and therefore plaintiff cannot show an interest in the insured property separate from that interest which has been tainted by fraud.

This argument misses the point, for no interest in the insured property was tainted by fraud, nor does that bear on the question before us. Claimant's right in this matter is determined not by interest in the insured property but by the rights under the contract of insurance.

In *Monaghan v. Agricultural Fire Ins. Co. of Watertown, N.Y.*, 53 Mich. 238, 18 N.W. 797 (1884), this Court addressed the issue of recovery by an innocent insured notwithstanding fraud by another insured. In *Monaghan* three minors owned a parcel of property and a house and barn on it by deed from their father. After the father's death their mother, who owned no interest in the real property, procured a fire insurance policy on the premises and contents, naming herself and the three minors as insured. After a fire damaged the house it was determined that the mother had committed fraud in reporting as destroyed certain items which she had removed from the house prior to the fire. The three minors instituted the action for recovery of fire insurance proceeds. The Court stated that recovery under the insurance contract was to be determined irrespective of the nature of ownership of the property insured. Recovery was to be determined according to the contracts interests held by the respective parties. The Court in *Monaghan* construed the contract interests created by the insurance policy to be joint. . . .

The rule stated in *Monaghan* is a general law of contracts. . . . Thus some courts have held that "[b]ecause the agreement not to commit fraud is joint, with each insured promising that he and the other would not commit fraud, the breach caused by intentional destruction is chargeable to both insureds and precludes recovery by the innocent joint insured." *Klemens v. Badger Mutual Ins. Co. of Milwaukee*, 8 Wis.2d 565, 567, 99 N.W.2d 865, 866 (1959).

. . . The standard fire insurance policy prescribed by statute provides:

> "This entire policy shall be void if, whether before or after a loss, the insured has wilfully concealed or misrepresented any material fact or circumstance concerning this insurance or the subject thereof, or the interest of the insured therein, or in case of any fraud or false swearing by the insured relating thereto." M.C.L. § 500.2832; M.S.A. 24.12832.

> The insurer in this case would have us read this provision as if it stated "[t]his entire policy shall be void if . . . any person insured" has committed fraud. We believe such a reading is unwarranted . . .
>
> We no longer consider the application of the theory of implied suretyship appropriate in insurance law. . . .
>
> . . . (S)ince the provision quoted above does not expressly create a joint obligation of suretyship, to read the fraud provision as creating one would be contrary to the reasonable expectations of an insured. An ordinary person seeing his or her name included in an insurance contract without limiting language would suppose his or her interest to be covered. . . .
>
> Henceforth whenever the statutory clause limiting the insurer's liability in case of fraud by the insured is used it will be read to bar only the claim of an insured who has committed the fraud and will not be read to bar the claim of any insured under the policy who is innocent of fraud.
>
> The summary judgment herein is set aside and the cause remanded for further proceedings. . . .

If property is used as a security in a mortgage agreement or a trust deed or is the object of a land contract, the lender and the borrower, or the vendor and the vendee, may purchase separate policies to protect each of their interests in the property. The common practice, however, is that one of the parties, usually the one who retains title to the property, is contractually required to obtain a policy covering the full value of the property. In case of a loss, the insurance proceeds are to be divided *pro rata* according to the parties' respective interests. The policy then contains a "loss payable" endorsement.

Extent of Coverage

Ordinarily, a policyholder may claim only up to the actual amount of the loss, and this amount may not exceed the maximum stipulated on the policy. The policy may also permit the insurer to replace or restore property rather than pay the cash value of the loss. Appraisers and arbitrators may be employed to determine the actual cash value of the loss, which is often disputed, such as in the case of *Allstate Insurance Company* v. *Kleveno* (81 A.D.2d 648, 438 N.Y.S.2d 384 [1981]), where a one-hundred-year-old residence in New York was involved. As opposed to the antique or historical value, personal attachment to property will usually not be considered.

A *valued policy* allows the insured to recover the face amount of the policy if the property is totally destroyed, regardless of the property's fair market value at the time of the loss and, thus, regardless of whether the property has meanwhile appreciated or depreciated. An *open policy* allows the insurer to pay only the fair market value of the property at the time of the property's destruction, but only up to the limit stated on the policy. Thus, if the policy face value is $100,000 and the fair market value at the time of the total loss is $80,000, only $80,000 may be recovered. On the other hand, if the fair market value has increased to $120,000, the recovery remains $100,000.

The insured party, who is allowed to obtain more than one policy on the same property, may not recover more than the actual loss incurred. The loss then is to be prorated among the insurance carriers.

A *coinsurance* provision requires that to fully recover the full value of a partial loss, the property must be insured for at least a specified percentage, usually 80 percent, of its fair market value. If the property is in fact insured for less than the amount required by the coinsurance clause, the insured would be entitled to only a proportionate part of a future claim. For example, if property with a fair market value of $100,000 is insured for only $60,000 and the policy has a coinsurance clause of 80 percent, on a partial loss of $30,000, the insurer will pay only $22,500. The reason is that under the 80 percent coinsurance clause, the property should have been insured for at least $80,000, and since the policy was for only $60,000, which is 75 percent of $80,000, the policyholder is entitled to only 75 percent of the actual loss, which is $22,500. The formula is as follows:

$$\frac{\text{Policy Face Value } (\$60,000)}{\text{Coinsurance } (80\%) \times \text{Fair Market Value } (\$100,000)} \times \text{Loss } (\$30,000) = \text{Recovery } (\$22,500)$$

> **Coinsurance**
> For full recovery of a loss, the property must be insured for a minimum percentage of its market value.

Automobile Insurance

Automobile insurance nowadays is a must for every motorist. Financial responsibility laws have been adopted by many states that in simple terms compel a motorist either to show some proof of ability to pay, such as a security deposit or a trust account sufficient to satisfy a judgment that may be rendered against him, or to have automobile insurance that contains, in addition to collision coverage, liability coverage to protect him against claims by others.

Collision Coverage

Collision coverage basically indemnifies the policyholder for damages to his own vehicle, regardless of the question of negligence. The coverage may also include personal injury to the owner, driver, or passenger of the vehicle if the vehicle is struck by another automobile. The word "collision" is broadly interpreted. It not only refers to an actual violent contact between the vehicle and another vehicle, wall, or tree but also includes the striking of a piece of gravel causing a hole in the windshield or the falling of a heavy branch of a tree on the car. A claim under the coverage is usually denied if the vehicle is used in violation of the law. Before honoring a claim, the insurer has a right to examine the vehicle to determine the extent of the damage as well as to detect any possible fraud. The insurer may subrogate for the policyholder in a suit against a third party whose fault caused the damage or injury.

> **Collision Coverage**
> Indemnifies policyholder for damage to his vehicle.

Uninsured motorist coverage insures the policyholder for loss due to the negligence of an uninsured motorist. As such, the coverage is unnecessary

> **Uninsured Motorist Coverage**
> Indemnifies policyholder for loss caused by an uninsured motorist.

in the presence of collision insurance, which provides protection to the insured regardless of whether or not the third party was at fault.

Facts

Plaintiff, as personal representative of the estates of his deceased children and as friend of another child, filed suit against his insurance carrier seeking recovery under the uninsured motorist provision of his insurance policy. Three of his minor children died and a fourth child was injured in an accident involving an uninsured automobile owned by a third party. The suit alleged that the vehicle was negligently operated by the plaintiff's wife, who also died. In a motion to dismiss the suit for failure to state the cause of action, the defendant insurance company claimed that no direct cause of action against the insurer could be maintained, and since the plaintiff was suing in the representative capacity, the suit was barred for public policy reasons prohibiting a child to sue a parent. The trial court granted the motion to dismiss.

Decision

Judgment for the plaintiff. The trial court decision was reversed. Suing the tortfeasor first to establish negligence is not a prerequisite for recovery under an uninsured motorist provision, as the insurer is not bound by such a suit. Besides, it was pointed out that judicially created intrafamily immunity is based upon public policies of preventing collusion and maintaining family relationships. These policies did not apply in this case. Thus, a suit may be maintained between a child and a parent, although it was not a condition for recovery under this coverage.

Guess v. Gulf Ins. Co., 96 N.Mex. 27, 627 P.2d 869 (1981).

Comprehensive coverage protects the policyholder against a variety of risks other than collision, such as theft, vandalism, or fire. Again, courts generally interpret the coverage liberally to favor the insured. In *Edwards v. State Farm Automobile Ins. Co.* (296 N.W.2d 804 [Iowa 1980]), "theft" was construed to include a situation of an apparent fraud whereby the policyholder, in selling his car, obtained a bad check from the buyer. "When the insurance company drafting and furnishing the policy of insurance had an opportunity to adequately define theft and failed to do so, it ran the risk that a court would adopt from those alternatives available the one which is most favorable to the insured."

Liability Coverage

Up to the maximum amount stated in the policy, the insurer is under liability coverage obliged to pay claims by third parties for damage to their person or property arising from ownership, maintenance, or use of the insured vehicle. Thus, in *McNeill v. Maryland Insurance Guaranty Association* (48 Md.App. 411, 427 A.2d 1056 [1981]), the policy was deemed to cover an injury sustained by a third party from an explosion of his car battery when he attempted to jump start his car from the battery of the policyholder's car.

The liability policy ordinarily does not cover only the insured himself. It may contain an *omnibus clause* to cover his family, employees, agents, or other persons who operate the vehicle with the policyholder's permission. The clause also applies to a situation where the person who is given permission by the insured allows another person to drive the car.

D.O.C. (*Drive-Other-Car*) coverage insures the policyholder or a family member against liability incurred while driving another person's vehicle.

The coverage is normally limited to "occasional use" of the other car. It excludes situations where the other car is used regularly. This is emphasized in *Mattox v. Cotton States Mutual Insurance Company* (156 Ga.App. 655, 275 S.E.2d 667 [1980]), where a policeman had been involved in a high-speed chase in which his police car collided with another vehicle, killing a person. When the mother of the deceased filed suit against the policeman, the policeman requested his own insurance carrier to join in his defense and provide coverage. The court denied the request, as the policeman was operating "a non-owned vehicle furnished or available for the regular use of his department and to him as part of that department."

Liability coverage may contain exclusions, e.g., when the harm is intentionally caused by the insurer or when liability is admitted by the insured to the injured third party or when the claim falls under workers' compensation laws.

Facts

Mrs. LeDoux was insured by Globe American Casualty when she drove her car directly into a pickup truck occupied by Denny Lyons and two other persons. All three occupants of the truck sustained personal injuries as a result of the collision. They filed a suit against Mrs. LeDoux for damages. Globe, the liability insurance carrier, then filed a complaint asking the court to declare that the policy provision excluding coverage for intentional acts was applicable to preclude insurance coverage. It argued that Mrs. LeDoux understood the physical consequences of her action and deliberately attempted to commit suicide. The trial court decided in favor of Globe.

Decision

Judgment reversed. "In light of the overwhelming testimony that Mrs. LeDoux was unable to act in accordance with reason at the time of the collision, we hold that appellee's policy exclusion for injury or property damage caused intentionally by its insured does not preclude Mrs. LeDoux from coverage pursuant to her policy."

Globe American Casualty Co. v. Lyons, 131 Ariz. 337, 641 P.2d 251 (1981).

The insurance carrier is obligated to defend the policyholder in a suit brought by a third party regarding a claim that falls within the policy. In the event that the insurer wrongfully refuses to defend, it may have to pay a judgment entered against the insured, even if the amount exceeds the maximum provided in the policy.

No-fault insurance, if it has not been adopted, has these days become a hot issue in many states. Essentially, it means that the insurer will pay the insured for injuries sustained while using the insured vehicle, regardless of whose fault caused the injury. Medical expenses and loss of wages are usually included in the coverage. However, pain and suffering may be recovered only under certain circumstances. The policy may also include other persons, such as the other driver or a pedestrian. Except for serious accidents resulting in disability, disfigurement, or death or where the medical bills and wage losses exceed a certain amount, the insured motorist is barred from suing the third party at fault. If under the policy the insured is allowed to sue the third party, he may first collect from the insurance carrier the maximum amount under the no-fault coverage and subsequently reimburse the insurer with the amount of the suit recovered from the third party.

No-fault Insurance
Covers injuries sustained by policyholder regardless of who was at fault.

QUESTIONS

1. How does insurable interest in life insurance differ from insurable interest in property insurance?
2. What does fire insurance cover? Please explain.
3. What is coinsurance in a fire insurance policy?
4. What is the difference between collision coverage and liability coverage?
5. What is an omnibus clause? What is D.O.C. coverage?

PROBLEMS

1. Plaintiff instructed the defendant, an independent broker, to obtain an insurance policy on her house. The defendant procured an insurance policy from Acme Insurance Co., issued a binder to the plaintiff, but never sent Acme the first premium that the plaintiff had paid to him. Fire broke out, and the house was damaged. Acme denied liability on the ground that it never received the premium from the plaintiff. Decision?

2. Rebecca obtained from United Insurance a life insurance policy on Lucille, her second cousin on her father's side. Rebecca did not live with Lucille, and she did not inform Lucille of the policy. Rebecca paid the premiums regularly. On Lucille's death, Rebecca sued United Insurance for the amount of the policy. Is she entitled to recovery?

3. Wisley bought a life insurance policy from National Reserve Life, naming his wife Sarah as a primary beneficiary and his father Rufus as a secondary beneficiary. Wisley and his wife were subsequently divorced, and Sarah remarried. When Wisley died, both Sarah and Rufus claimed the proceeds of the policy. Rufus argued that Sarah did not have an insurable interest in his son's life. Decision?

4. Policyholder obtained life insurance from an insurer by making false statements regarding his medical history. Within a few months after the policy was issued, the company learned about the misrepresentations and canceled the policy. Policyholder claimed that once the policy was issued, it could not be canceled, since the policy was a binding contract. Decision?

5. Catania had a life insurance policy for $10,000 from State Farm with a double-indemnity clause applicable in case of death that "resulted directly, and independently of all other causes, from bodily injury effected solely through external, violent, and accidental means." Suicide is explicitly excluded. Catania died from acute narcotism caused by a self-injected dose of heroin. Is his beneficiary entitled to double indemnity?

6. Plaintiff had a fire insurance policy on a grocery store he once owned. When he retired, he conveyed all his interest in the store to his daughter but came to the store from time to time to help in serving customers. He also lived on the proceeds of the store. One day, a fire destroyed the store and all its contents. The insurance carrier denied the plaintiff's claim on the ground that the plaintiff did not have an insurable interest. Decision?

7. Policyholder, who was intoxicated, dropped a lit cigarette in his bed, thereby causing a fire that destroyed the entire house. The insurance carrier denied liability, since the fire was caused by the policyholder's negligence. Decision?

8. Gruenberg purchased from Aetna Insurance Co. a fire policy on his restaurant and cocktail lounge in Los Angeles. Seven months later, the business was destroyed by fire. Gruenberg was suspected of committing arson to defraud the insurance company. When Aetna demanded that Gruenberg appear to answer questions in their office, Gruenberg refused to do so. The criminal charges against him were dismissed for lack of probable cause, but Aetna denied liability due to Gruenberg's refusal to cooperate in the investigation. Decision?

9. Scarola bought a stolen car in good faith and for value and obtained insurance on the vehicle. The car was subsequently severely damaged in an accident. The insurer denied liability, since Scarola did not have the title and therefore did not have an insurable interest in the car. Decision?

10. Mary had car insurance with an ambiguously written omnibus clause. One day she asked John to sell the car for her. When John allowed a prospective buyer to drive the vehicle, the car was damaged when the latter drove the car into a tree. It turned out that the prospective buyer was not licensed to drive. The insurance company denied liability, arguing that the omnibus clause covered only Mary's family and that the car was operated unlawfully. Decision?

CHAPTER 31

Bankruptcy

31.1 Chapter 7 (Part I)
Legislative Policies
Bankruptcy Regulation and Bankruptcy Courts
Chapter 7: Liquidation
   Voluntary Bankruptcy
   Involuntary Bankruptcy
   Automatic Stay

31.2 Chapter 7 (Part II)
Liquidation Continued
   Trustee Appointment
   Trustee's Duties
   Exemptions
   Voidable Transfers
   Provable Claims
   Distribution of Proceeds

   Discharge
   Reaffirmation

31.3 Chapters 11, 12, and 13
Chapter 11
   Petition
   Proceeding
   The Plan
   Confirmation
   Discharge
Chapter 13
   Petition and Proceeding
   The Plan
   Confirmation
   Discharge
Chapter 12
   Who May Petition
   Proceeding

CHAPTER THIRTY-ONE

31.1 Chapter 7 (Part I)

Bankruptcy
A federal court procedure to provide debtors relief from unsurmountable financial problems resulting from debts.

Bankruptcy involves a situation in which a business or a person becomes over-indebted and is unable to meet its or his financial obligations. There are plenty of reasons for one to be forced into bankruptcy. For a company, it may be a widespread economic depression, recession, or poor management; for an individual, it may be an unexpected layoff, a serious accident or illness, irresponsibility in borrowing and spending, or simply self-indulgence. Whatever the reason may be, a solution is needed if one's finances are plainly too depleted to satisfy the demands of creditors.

Legislative Policies

Servitude
Working for a creditor to repay debt.

The old idea was that debt could never be forgiven. In old England, a person unable to repay his debt was usually thrown into prison, where he remained until a relative or friend was able to redeem him by paying off the debt or by making some arrangements satisfactory to the creditor. Another solution was for the debtor to submit himself to servitude and work for the creditor for a period of time to repay his debt. The first bankruptcy legislation in England was adopted in 1542. It was designed to provide relief only to merchants who were stricken by some business misfortune.

In the United States, Article I, Section 8, of the federal Constitution provides that ". . . Congress shall have Power . . . (T)o establish . . . uniform Laws on the subject of Bankruptcies throughout the United States." Yet for decades, Congress seemed to be uncertain on what legislative policies to adopt. Indeed, to provide relief to a cornered debtor is humane and laudable, but this means that the person is allowed to escape an otherwise legitimate debt. Moreover, abuse is unquestionably a concern.

These days, bankruptcy is accepted as a practical and reasonable vehicle to rehabilitate the hopeless debtor who otherwise would be ruined. It is meant to provide the debtor with the opportunity to start anew. On the other hand, bankruptcy rules are also meant to protect creditors against an unscrupulous debtor who may take such detrimental actions as hiding available assets or giving undue preference to certain creditors.

Many authors feel that bankruptcy is increasingly condoned in our society. It is said that the stigma the bankrupt usually carried has now faded away. This, however, is not quite true in business. Generally, a lender is still considered imprudent to lend money to a person who has been bankrupt. Hence, a credit application ordinarily inquires about previous bankruptcies. The Fair Credit Reporting Act of 1970 allows bankruptcy to stay in a consumer credit report for fourteen years. Moreover, giving a lender untrue information in a loan application amounts to obtaining credit under false pretenses, and may be a criminal offense. In fact, if a lender extends new credit to an ex-bankrupt, he usually is a lender who looks primarily at the collateral as a source of repayment, and he usually charges higher than prevailing interest rates.

Another modern-day phenomenon is for huge and well-to-do companies to utilize the bankruptcy regulation as a tactical maneuver in encountering and solving undesirable financial liabilities. This is further explained in the discussion of Chapter 11 of the Bankruptcy Act.

Bankruptcy Regulation and Bankruptcy Courts

Bankruptcy was governed for a long time by the federal Bankruptcy Act of 1898. In 1978, major changes were made to the existing law when Congress passed the Bankruptcy Reform Act. The act became effective on October 1, 1979, with a transition period until April 1, 1984, when the new bankruptcy court would be phased in. Meanwhile, in 1982, the U.S. Supreme Court decided that Congress had conferred too much power to bankruptcy judges, who actually lacked the lifetime tenure and salary protection given to federal judges by Article III of the Constitution. A revision of the bankruptcy court system ensued after the following case was decided.

Tenure
The period of holding a job.

Facts
Under the Bankruptcy Reform Act of 1978, a U.S. bankruptcy court was established in each judicial district as an adjunct to the district court. Bankruptcy judges were appointed for fourteen years, subject to removal by the judicial council of the circuit in which they served. Grounds for removal were incompetence, misconduct, neglect of duty, and disability. The salaries were regulated by statute and were subject to adjustment. The question of propriety of the court system arose when Northern Pipeline, in conjunction with a petition for reorganization, brought in the bankruptcy court a suit against Marathon Pipe Line seeking damages for an alleged breach of contract and warranty and for misrepresentation, coercion, and duress. Marathon sought immediate dismissal of the suit on the ground that the Bankruptcy Reform Act unconstitutionally conferred Article III judicial powers upon judges who did not have life tenure or protection against salary diminution. Marathon's motion to dismiss was denied by the bankruptcy court; but on appeal, the district court granted the motion.

Decision
The U.S. Supreme Court decided for Marathon. In his opinion for the majority, Justice Brennan found that the broad grant of jurisdiction to bankruptcy judges in the 1978 bankruptcy law was in violation of Article III of the U.S. Constitution. " . . . The judicial power of the United States must be exercised by judges who have the attributes of life tenure and protection against salary diminution specified by Art. III. These attributes were incorporated into the Constitution to ensure the independence of the Judiciary from the control of the Executive and Legislative Branches. There is no doubt that bankruptcy judges created by the Act are not Art. III judges. . . . Congress does not have the same power to create adjuncts to adjudicate constitutionally recognized rights and state-created rights as it does to adjudicate rights that it creates. The grant of jurisdiction to bankruptcy courts cannot be sustained as an exercise of Congress' power to create adjuncts to Art. III courts."

Northern Pipeline Construction Co. v. *Marathon Pipe Line Company*, 458 U.S. 50, 102 S.Ct. 2858, 73 L.Ed.2d 598 (1982).

After this decision, the bankruptcy court system operated under some emergency rules until Congress enacted the Bankruptcy Amendments and Federal Judgeship Act of 1984. Bankruptcy judges are now appointed for a term of fourteen years by the U.S. Court of Appeals for the curcuit where the presiding district court is located. They are still not Article III judges; thus, jurisdiction of the bankruptcy courts is limited. All cases are first brought in the U.S. district court that may refer them to the bankruptcy court, which is then authorized to hear and determine such cases and "core proceedings," i.e., certain bankruptcy matters defined in the U.S. Code. The bankruptcy court's decision is subject to review by the district court. Unless the parties agree otherwise, noncore matters are only "heard" and proposed findings of fact and conclusions of law are sent to the district court for complete review. From the district court, the case may be appealed to the U.S. Court of Appeals.

The Bankruptcy Code has nine chapters contained in the U.S. Code as Title 11. They are all odd-numbered except Chapter 12, which was newly created in 1984 to aid family farmers. Chapters 1, 3 and 5 are general in nature and apply to all bankruptcies. Chapter 7 refers to liquidation in ordinary bankruptcy. Chapter 9 allows for the adjustment of debts by municipalities. Chapter 11 provides for business reorganization. Chapter 13 is for individuals with regular income and provides for adjustment of their debts. Chapter 15 provides for a national U.S. trustee system. It grants more powers to the trustees in bankruptcy matters. Chapter 31 of this text deals with Chapters 7, 11, 12, and 13 of the Bankruptcy Code.

Core Proceedings
Certain matters in the Code that may be adjudged by the Bankruptcy Court.

Chapter 7: Liquidation

Ordinary, or *straight*, *bankruptcy* is the most familiar type. The debtor is to list all of his debts and turn the nonexempt assets over to a trustee. The trustee converts the assets to cash and, after paying expenses, distributes the balance to his creditors. The debtor then obtains a *discharge* and, with some exceptions, is relieved of the obligation to pay the debts. Chapter 7 liquidation commences by filing a voluntary or involuntary petition in the federal district court and paying the filing fee.

Liquidation
Procedure for converting debtor's assets to cash, paying creditors, and discharging the debtor.

Discharge
Release of a debtor from his debts.

Voluntary Bankruptcy

Any indebted individual, partnership, corporation, or other legal entity—with the exception of railroads, government units, banks, savings and loan associations, and insurance companies—may file for bankruptcy. A joint voluntary petition may be filed by a husband and wife. In a 1984 legislative change, a consumer-debtor is required to state in the petition that although aware of the reliefs available under Chapters 11 and 13, he elects to proceed under Chapter 7. This requirement is meant to encourage him to use one of the other alternatives to liquidation.

Voluntary Bankruptcy
Bankruptcy proceeding initiated by the debtor.

Nearly all bankruptcy petitions are filed voluntarily. The petition forms provide for a listing of all the creditors, the amounts owed to each, and a statement of the debtor's financial affairs and of all his assets, including those that are exempt. In addition, the debtor must include a listing of current income and expenses. The debtor must accurately complete the petition forms and schedules, swear to them under oath, and sign them. It is a crime under the bankruptcy regulations to conceal assets or knowingly supply false information on the petition documents.

If the voluntary petition is found to be proper, the filing of the petition *per se* will constitute an *order for relief*. Otherwise a hearing may be held

Facts

When Reed filed for bankruptcy in December 1979, he owed a bank about $200,000 for a loan to a men's store he operated. He also owed money to some other business creditors. Shortly before declaring bankruptcy, Reed sold much of his property, including stock and collections of antiques, coins, and guns, and used the proceeds to pay off the mortgages on his home. In doing so, he created a homestead, which under Texas law is exempt from claims of general creditors in bankruptcy. The Bankruptcy Court's denial of Reed's voluntary petition was upheld by the District Court. Reed appealed.

Decision

Judgment affirmed. The Court of Appeals found ample evidence to support the finding that Reed had an actual intent to defraud his creditors. Reference was made to the rapid conversion of nonexempt assets to extinguish the mortgages on his home, which was done for the single purpose of creating exempted assets. While the Texas constitutional and statutory protection of homestead is absolute, the appeals court pointed out that the Bankruptcy Code set separate standards for determining whether the debtor shall be denied a discharge. The Code provides that such a denial is proper if the debtor has transferred property "with the intent to hinder, delay, or defraud a creditor" (11 U.S.C. § 727[a][2]).

In the Matter of Hugh D. Reed, 700 F.2d 986 (5th Cir. 1983).

Involuntary Bankruptcy

A petition for involuntary bankruptcy may be filed by the creditors under Chapter 7 or 11. (1) If there are twelve or more creditors, the petition may be filed by three or more of them who have unsecured claims totaling $5,000 or more. (2) If there are fewer than twelve creditors, one or more whose total claims equal at least $5,000 may file. In addition to the categories of debtors previously listed that may not file a voluntary petition, farmers and nonprofit organizations are also exempt from involuntary bankruptcy.

Involuntary Bankruptcy Bankruptcy initiated by the bankrupt's creditors.

In the Matter of Okamoto
491 F.2d 496 (9th Cir. 1974).

Ely, Circuit Judge On November 28, 1969, Hornblower & Weeks-Hemphill, Noyes (hereinafter "Hornblower") filed a petition that Okamoto be adjudged an involuntary bankrupt. Hornblower attempted to proceed as the sole petitioning creditor, pursuant to section 59(b) of the Bankruptcy Act, 11 U.S.C. § 95(b). Okamoto's answer alleged that he was indebted to more than eleven creditors, and the answer was accompanied by a schedule listing twenty-one creditors. The Referee in Bankruptcy conducted a hearing under section 59(d) and found that Okamoto had nineteen unsecured creditors which must be counted. Since a single creditor cannot proceed under section 59(b) unless the total number of claimants is less than twelve, the Referee dismissed Hornblower's petition. On review, the District Court affirmed the Referee's Order of dismissal.

[1] Here, Hornblower attacks the finding of the Bankruptcy Court that Okamoto had more than eleven creditors. Hornblower principally asserts that creditors

for relatively small current expenses should be excluded in computing the total number of creditors under section 59(b). Section 59(b) provides in part:

> "Three or more creditors who have provable claims not contingent as to liability against a person, amounting in the aggregate to $5,000 in excess of the value of any securities held by them, or, if all of the creditors of the person are less than twelve in number, then one or more of the creditors whose claim or claims equal that amount, may file a petition to have him adjudged a bankrupt . . . ."

If less than three creditors join in the petition, section 59(e) furnishes the guidelines for computing the total number of claimants. Although section 59(e) does not provide for the exclusion of creditors with small claims, Hornblower contends that the doctrine of *de minimis non curat lex* should be applied. Since eight of the debts here involved were for amounts less than sixty-five dollars, Hornblower argues that the total number of creditors meets the statutory limit.

> *De Minimus non Curat Lex*
> The law does not concern itself with trifling matters.

. . . In *Denham* the Court adopted a similar contention to that here advanced, holding that creditors claiming insignificant amounts are not to be included in determining the total number of creditors for the purposes of section 59(b). The Court explained:

> "It is our belief that whether or not a scheme was involved, it was not the intent of Congress to allow recurring bills such as utility bills and the like to create a situation which, by refusal of these small creditors to join in an involuntary petition, can defeat the use of the Bankruptcy Act by a large creditor, as in the subject case. This would be grossly inequitable, and for this reason this Court refuses to follow the *Colorado Lime* decision."

. . .We are not persuaded by *Denham*, for it appears to us that the *Denham* court ignored unambiguous Congressional direction. The Congress has explicitly prescribed the procedure that must be followed when less than three creditors join in the petition. In such circumstances the Act provides that the alleged bankrupt *must* have less than twelve creditors and expressly excludes certain types of creditors from the required computation. Since Congress made no distinction between large and small claims, we cannot arrogate unto ourselves the power to do so and thereby engraft an additional exception to the Act. Hornblower's argument properly should be addressed to the Congress. Our conclusion is reinforced by the fact that Congress has clearly and expressly excluded small claims when it has intended to do so. . . .

[2] Rejecting Hornblower's first contention, we reach its assertion that the small creditors should be discounted because Okamoto entered into a scheme to circumvent the provisions of the Act. The short answer to this contention is that the Referee concluded that no such scheme or device had existed. We cannot, in the light of the evidence, hold that this finding was clearly erroneous.

[3] Hornblower also attacks the inclusion of certain creditors as not being creditors of Okamoto. It asserts that two of the debts were incurred by others through the use of credit cards issued in Okamoto's name. The Referee found that the cards were used with Okamoto's consent and that the obligations were owed by him. This finding also has substantial evidentiary support and is not clearly erroneous.

Finally, Hornblower contends that Okamoto Enterprises, a partnership, is indebted to six of the creditors and that these claimants should not be included for section 59 purposes. Even if we assume, *arguendo*, that these creditors were improperly included, the number of creditors still exceeded eleven.

Arguendo
For the purpose of argument.

[4] Since Okamoto was indebted to more than eleven creditors and only one claimant filed the petition under section 59(b), the petition was properly dismissed.

Affirmed.

The debtor may challenge the involuntary petition within *twenty days* after he has been served with the petition and summons, in which case a hearing will be held. An order for relief will be entered only if the court finds any of the following:

1. The debtor is not paying debts as they become due, which is known as equitable or accounting insolvency, as opposed to a balance sheet insolvency, which shows the debtor's total liabilities exceeding total assets.

2. Within 120 days prior to the filing of the involuntary petition, an assignment has taken place as a collective creditor remedy outside bankruptcy, and a custodian, i.e., the assignee, has been appointed and has taken possession of the debtor's property to enforce a lien against it for the benefit of the creditors. (Such an assignment is the common law or state statutory version of Chapter 7 liquidation.) Creditors dissatisfied with the assignment may proceed with an involuntary bankruptcy petition within the above-prescribed timing.

Insolvency
The status of being unable to pay one's debts when due, or of having liabilities exceeding assets.

The Code provides penalties for filing a frivolous involuntary petition against a debtor. The petitioning creditors may be made to pay the debtor's costs and attorneys' fees if the involuntary petition is dismissed. Furthermore, a petition filed in bad faith is a tort, which can result in punitive damages for injury to the debtor's reputation.

If the court, on the other hand, grants an order for relief, the debtor will be required to supply information demanded in the bankruptcy schedules.

Automatic Stay

The filing of a voluntary or involuntary petition results in an automatic stay. This means that all forms of creditors' action against the debtor or his property are placed on hold. Such actions include (1) actions to commence or continue judicial proceedings against the debtor, (2) actions to acquire possession of the debtor's property, (3) actions to create, perfect, or enforce a lien against the debtor's property, and (4) actions to set off prior indebtedness owed to the debtor.

Stay
Placing court actions, orders, or remedies on "hold."

A relief from the stay may be given to a secured creditor who can show that the stay does not provide him adequate protection and endangers his interest in the collateral. Such a relief to a creditor may be given in the form of periodic cash payments or by providing a replacement lien or an additional lien on his property.

Adequate Protection
Sufficient protection of creditor's interest in the collateral in debtor's possession.

A creditor who knowingly violates an automatic stay may have to pay costs and attorneys' fees as well as punitive damages to any injured party.

Facts

Mr. Holland borrowed money from Dana Corporation Federal Credit Union and authorized his employer to transfer $80 from his weekly check to the credit union to repay the loan. The credit union deposited these weekly payroll deductions into Holland's share draft account and transferred every month the total amount of the deductions to the loan department. When Holland filed a bankruptcy petition on November 21, 1980, the bankruptcy court sent a notice of the bankruptcy and automatic stay to the credit union. Holland also went to the credit union to request termination of the payroll deductions. However, as he was never given the instruction on how to stop the arrangement, the payroll deductions continued. Holland filed a motion with the bankruptcy court, seeking an order to find the credit union in violation of the automatic stay.

Decision

Judgment for Holland. The credit union was found to have violated the automatic stay, as it had actual notice of the bankruptcy as well as the automatic stay and still continued to transfer funds from the debtor's share draft account to his loan account. "Congressional intent seems clear. 'The automatic stay is one of the fundamental debtor protections provided by the bankruptcy laws. It gives the debtor a breathing spell from his creditors. It stops *all collection efforts* (emphasis added), all harassment and all foreclosure actions.' H.R. Rep. No. 595, 95 Cong. 1st Sess. 340 (1977)."

In the Matter of Holland, 21 B.R. 681 (Bkrtcy. Ind. 1982).

Questions

1. What are the legislative policies pertaining to bankruptcy?
2. What are the types of bankruptcy?
3. What may be the basis for denying a voluntary petition?
4. What may be the grounds for approving an involuntary petition?
5. What does an automatic stay mean to the creditors?

31.2 Chapter 7 (Part II)

Liquidation Continued

The purpose of a liquidation proceeding is to satisfy the creditors in the best way possible and to subsequently discharge the debtor of further liability.

Trustee Appointment

Trustee in Bankruptcy
The court-appointed administrator of the bankrupt's property.

If, upon a voluntary or involuntary petition, an order for relief is entered, the court will designate an *interim trustee* who will take possession of the debtor's property until a permanent trustee is appointed. The court will also order a meeting of creditors, which is to be attended by the debtor, the creditors, and the interim trustee, without the judge. In this meeting, the debtor is expected to provide the creditors the necessary information concerning his assets and liabilities and anything of importance to the creditors. The debtor's full cooperation is required for a subsequent discharge of his obligations. If the creditors do not elect a permanent trustee, the court will make the interim trustee a permanent one.

Trustee's Duties

The trustee becomes the representative of the debtor's estate. He preserves the estate property to protect the interests of the creditors. The debtor's estate consists of all the property the debtor has at the commencement of the proceeding and any other property the debtor acquires within *180 days* subsequent to the date of petition filing. Except for nonexempt assets, the

BANKRUPTCY

debtor's estate is liquidated and the proceeds distributed to the creditors. A creditors' committee of three to eleven unsecured creditors may assist the trustee in the handling of all these affairs.

Meanwhile, disputes may arise as the bankruptcy trustee attempts to seize as many assets as possible available to the debtor. The following case is an example.

Facts

Creative Bath Products sold a molding machine to Measure Control Devices and obtained a purchase money security interest in the merchandise. To perfect the security interest, Creative Bath filed a financing statement with the Nassau County clerk but not with the secretary of state of New York, where the transaction took place. When Measure Control went bankrupt, the trustee sought to seize all the proceeds from the sale of the molding machine on the ground that its security interest was not properly perfected. Measure Control argued that since the trustee had actual notice of the Nassau filing prior to the sale, his argument must have failed because of the principle of good faith provided by UCC § 9–401(2) on secured transactions.

Decision

Judgment for the trustee. It was concluded that since a creditor's security interest was never perfected, it is in spite of UCC § 9–401(2) null and void as to the trustee in bankruptcy who is subject to bankruptcy rules. Under § 544(a) of the Bankruptcy Code, the trustee is allowed to void the lien. Accordingly, Creative Bath's security interest is to be stricken as a lien against the proceeds of the sale of the merchandise.

In re Measure Control Devices, Inc., 48 B.R. 613 (Bkrtcy. N.Y. 1985).

On the other hand, in *In the Matter of Turpin* (644 F.2d 472 [5th Cir. 1981]), where the bankruptcy trustee attempted to seize funds held for the debtor by the City National Bank of Austin as trustee of a profit sharing and pension plan created by the debtor's employer as retirement benefits, the court agreed with the debtor that his future interest in this account was not to be turned over to the bankruptcy trustee. The law prohibits garnishment of future earnings to pay past obligations. (See also *Low* v. *Pew*, 108 Mass. 347 [1871], discussed in Subchapter 17.1.)

Exemptions

The debtor may keep those assets that are statutorily exempt from the trustee's liquidation. Exemptions are regulated by the Bankruptcy Code as well as by state statutes; the debtor may choose only one set of exemptions. Some state laws compel the debtor to take only the state exemptions. Under the 1984 Amendments, a husband and wife in a joint petition filing are required to select the same set of exemptions.

The following property is exempt under the federal Bankruptcy Reform Act:

1. Equity in a residence up to $7,500.
2. Equity in a motor vehicle up to $1,200.
3. Household furnishings, clothing, and personal items up to $200 each to a maximum of $4,000.

Exemption
Property specified by the Bankruptcy Code and/or state statutes that is exempt from seizure by the bankruptcy trustee.

4. Jewelry up to $500.
5. Tools of a trade, including books, up to $750.
6. Prescription health aids.
7. Any other property up to $400, plus up to $3,750 not used in (1) above in any property.
8. Life insurance contracts other than credit life insurance policies.
9. Social Security, veteran's and disability benefits, alimony and child support payments, and like awards.

Facts

Lois Perry filed a voluntary petition under Chapter 7. Among the items of personal clothing that she listed as exempt under Virginia state law was a mink coat with a value of approximately $2,500. The state statute exempts all necessary wearing apparel of the debtor and his family. Unlike the federal Bankruptcy Code, which exempts items of clothing only up to $200 each, the State of Virginia places no such monetary limit. the trustee claimed the coat as a nonexempt asset.

Decision

Exemption allowed. The court decided that the state exemption was required to be used. Since the state did not place any monetary limit, the question of good faith should be considered in determining what is necessary. A coat is usually a necessary item of clothing, and the value, within reason, should not govern.

In re Perry, 6 B.R. 263 (Bkrtcy. Va., 1980).

Voidable Transfers

Voidable Transfers
The trustee may void and recover fraudulent transfers made by the bankrupt.

Fraudulent Conveyance
Fraudulent transfer of property made within one year prior to filing a bankruptcy petition.

Voidable Preference
Voidable payment by a bankrupt person to a creditor so as to prejudice the other creditors.

The trustee may void *fraudulent conveyances* and voidable preferences and recover on behalf of the creditors the properties so transferred or the moneys so paid. A fraudulent conveyance is a transfer of property made fraudulently within *one year* preceding the filing of the petition. Some state statutes extend this time period to two to five years, in which event, the trustee may use the rule most favorable to the creditors. The fraud may be actual or constructive. Fraud takes place if the debtor conveys a property to intentionally prevent the trustee and the creditors from recovering it. For example, in *In re Oesterle* (2 B.R. 122 [Bkrtcy. Fla. 1979]), a debtor had deeded his real property to his mother without receiving anything in return. The deed was not recorded until two days after the petition was filed. Under Georgia state law, a real property transfer is not effective until it has been recorded. The court recognized not only that the transfer was not completed but also that it was in fact fraudulent. It was without consideration and appeared to have taken place just prior to filing the petition. The transfer was void, and the trustee could rightfully claim the property as part of the bankruptcy estate.

A *voidable preference* is given if the debtor made a payment to one or more creditors so as to prejudice the position of the others. Under 11 U.S.C. § 547(b)(f), a preference is voidable *inter alia* if (1) it concerns a payment of a pre-existing debt and the payment was made when the debtor was already in a state of insolvency, within *ninety days* before the filing of the bankruptcy petition, and (2) the creditor has benefited more from the transfer than what he would have received from the bankruptcy proceeding.

Facts

On July 30, 1979, Duffy sent Avis Rent-a-Car a check for $400 postdated August 3 to pay for a car he had leased. The check was paid by the drawee bank on August 6. Duffy filed a voluntary petition eighty-eight days after the check was paid. The bankruptcy trustee chose to void the payment as a preference, since it was paid within ninety days of the petition.

Decision

Judgment for the trustee. The law of negotiable instruments states that a check is not paid until accepted and honored by the bank. Since in this case the check was honored within the ninety-day limit and the payment was for a preexisting debt, the rule of voidable preferences is applicable.

In the Matter of Duffy, 3 B.R. 263 (Bkrtcy. N.Y. 1980).

The trustee may set aside preferences made to insiders (relatives, partners, and corporate executives and directors) if they were made within *one year* before filing the petition and the recipient of the preference has reasonable cause to believe that the debtor was insolvent. This kind of preference was voided in *New York Credit Men's Adjustment Bureau, Inc. v. Adler* (2 B.R. 752 [S.D.N.Y. 1980]), where a bankrupt corporation transferred money to its president, its accountant, and the accountant's wife within one year prior to filing.

The trustee is not allowed to void a transfer if it is for (1) a new obligation, (2) a payment made in the ordinary course of business forty-five days prior to petition filing, (3) a payment on a purchase money security interest, (4) a payment on a fully secured claim, and (5) ordinary or routine payments if the payments total less than $600 per creditor.

Provable Claims

Within *six months* after the first creditors' meeting, a *proof of claim*, which is basically a creditor's written statement describing the claim against the debtor, may be filed. Generally, legitimate debts existing prior to the order for relief are provable. These claims are allowed to participate in the distribution of the bankruptcy estate.

Certain claims that are not provable or fully provable are listed in 11 U.S.C. § 101(4):

1. Claim based on contracts obtained by fraud or durress.
2. Interest on loans that accrued since the petition was filed.
3. Lease termination, in which event the lessor may prove only up to one year's rent or 15 percent of the remaining term of the lease not to exceed three years, whichever is greater, plus the unpaid rent already due and payable.
4. Breach of an employment contract in which the employee may claim up to one year's compensation and the unpaid wages that are due and payable.

Proof of Claim
A creditor's written statement describing his claim.

Distribution of Proceeds

Once the bankruptcy estate has been liquidated, the trustee has acknowledged the creditors' claims based on the creditors' list submitted by the debtor, and the proofs of claims have been filed by the creditors, the proceeds from the liquidation need to be disbursed.

A secured crditor, such as a mortgagee or a beneficiary of a trust deed, should not be affected too much by the bankruptcy, as he may fully enforce his security interest to obtain payment from the sale of the collateral. Under 11 U.S.C. § 507, the other creditors participate in the distribution of the proceeds according to the following priorities:

1. Fees and expenses of administering the estate, which includes trustee's, attorneys', and accountants' fees.
2. Claims rising in the ordinary course of business between the date of petition filing and the date the trustee is appointed.
3. Claims for employee wages and other employment benefits up to $2,000 per person, earned within 90 days before the date of petition filing.
4. Claims arising from contributions to an employee plan up to $2,000 per employee where the services have been rendered within 180 days prior to petition filing, with the understanding that the total of (3) and (4) may not exceed $2,000.
5. Farmers' claims for grain stored in the debtor's grain elevator and fishermen's claims for fish stored in the debtor's storage or processing facility up to $2,000 per creditor.
6. Claims up to $900 by a consumer creditor who gave money to the debtor as a deposit on merchandise or a service that was not delivered or rendered.
7. Federal, state, and local taxes due within three years prior to petition filing.

When all these priority claims have been paid, the remaining proceeds are to be disbursed to the general unsecured creditors on a *pro rata* basis. Usually, these creditors are left with far less money than the actual debts.

Discharge

Bankruptcy discharges the bankrupt individual, not a bankrupt corporation. Discharge means that the debtor is relieved of further liability for those debts that are dischargeable. He may for ethical or some other reasons file a written statement waiving his right to the discharge.

Under 11 U.S.C. § 727, a discharge will be denied if the debtor (1) within one year prior to filing, fraudulently transferred or concealed property with intent to hinder, delay, or defraud creditors, (2) failed to maintain proper financial records, (3) made a false statement under oath, (4) failed to provide satisfactory explanation of his finances, (5) disobeyed a court order, (6) had a prior voluntary discharge within the past six years, or (7) filed a written waiver of discharge.

Some of the debts that are not dischargeable under 11 U.S.C. § 523 are as follows:

1. Taxes due any governmental entity.
2. Debts obtained by fraud.
3. Claims that are not included in the proceeding, as they were not reported in the list of creditors submitted by the debtor.

4. Debts resulting from embezzlement, larceny, or defalcation while debtor was acting as a fiduciary.
5. Alimony and child support.
6. Claims resulting from willful and malicious torts.
7. Fines, penalties, and forefeitures payable to a governmental unit.
8. Student loans, unless they were due more than five years prior to the bankruptcy or they impose an undue hardship to the debtor.
9. Debts exceeding $500 per creditor for the purchase of "luxury goods" made within forty days preceding the order for relief.
10. Cash advances obtained within twenty days before the order for relief from an open-end credit arrangement, such as a credit card, totaling more than $1,000.
11. Debts based on a judgment or consent decree resulting from the debtor's operating a motor vehicle while intoxicated.

In re Conrad
6 B.R. 151 (Bkrtcy. Ky. 1980).

Paul George Conrad filed a voluntary petition in bankruptcy in October 1979, listing $37,354 in liabilities and $25 in assets.

Conrad's obligations consisted of a loan executed in connection with a business venture, Double Dip Ice Cream Company; signature loans; revolving credit card accounts and a student loan of $4,125.79 owed to the U.S. Department of Health, Education, and Welfare.

Conrad had used the GI Bill of Rights to study at five different colleges and had also obtained three federally guaranteed long-term, low-interest student loans. After receiving his bachelor's degree, he had been employed as a teacher. He was terminated as a full-time teacher in April 1979, and since that time he had been on call as a substitute teacher, for which he was paid $33 a day when he was called. He had not sought other full-time employment. He lived at home with his 75-year-old mother. He did not have a car of his own and used his mother's van.

. . . Accurately describing himself as "overweight," Conrad testified that his physical appearance "turns off a lot of people," including potential employers.

. . . One of the issues in the bankruptcy proceeding was whether the student loan was dischargeable in bankruptcy.

Dietz, Bankruptcy Judge   Section 523(a) of the Bankruptcy Code provides that a bankruptcy discharge will not extend:

>   (8) to a governmental unit, or a nonprofit institution of higher education, for an educational loan, unless . . .
>   (B) excepting such debt from discharge under this paragraph will impose an undue hardship on the debtor.

Before examining the facts of the case before us, we will briefly review current decisions on the point. Even a cursory reading of them reveals the obvious—that each undue hardship case ultimately rests upon its own facts.

Undue hardship was held to entitle the petitioner to a discharge of student debt in *In re Johnson*. The bankrupt was a young woman who was pregnant, being divorced, and recently been seriously injured in an automobile accident, and had been asked by her parents to move out of their home. She planned to rent a room, give birth to the child, and live on welfare.

The claim of undue hardship in this case rests upon two asserted facts: (1) Conrad must support and provide for his elderly mother, and (2) he is unable to obtain employment because of his physical appearance.

Upon the first point, we have some question as to who is supporting whom. The mother, who gave birth to this healthy young man while in her 44th year, and who fancies a mode of transportation generally associated with drivers two generations her junior, may be a vital woman indeed. Although the record does not indicate the extent of her income or financial substance, it is at least clear that Union Trust Bank would not extend credit to the son without the mother's hand being put to the note.

Upon the second point, we must observe, with neither cynicism nor cruelty, that corpulence is a condition which may swiftly diminish with continued impecuniosity.

This unemployed former president of the Double Dip Ice Cream Company, having double-dipped the available federal subsidies to obtain a superior education, should consider some alternatives. Enlightened self-interest would seem to suggest the virtue of a vigorous and energetic search for a proper workshop in which to use those intellectual tools which have been well honed at federal expense.

. . . Ordered that the indebtedness of Paul George Conrad to the Department of Health, Education and Welfare, United States of America, is not dischargeable in bankruptcy.

Judgment against Conrad.

Reaffirmation

Reaffirmation
A formal agreement by the bankrupt debtor to pay a debt that has been discharged.

In a reaffirmation agreement, the bankrupt debtor promises to pay the creditor on a debt that has been formerly discharged. To prevent undue pressure by the creditor, such a reaffirmation agreement may now be made only with the court's approval, while the debtor is given *sixty days* to rescind the reaffirmation. A court approval is not required if the reaffirmation concerns a loan secured by real property. The debtor may, of course, voluntarily pay any discharged obligation without entering into a reaffirmation arrangement.

Questions

1. What are the duties and responsibilities of a bankruptcy trustee?
2. What are exemptions? Name a few.
3. Name two categories of voidable transfers.
4. How are the proceeds in a liquidation distributed?
5. What is a discharge? What is a reaffirmation?

31.3 Chapters 11, 12, and 13

The Bankruptcy Code provides a debtor in trouble other alternatives short of going into Chapter 7 straight bankruptcy. Without necessitating liquidation of the debtor's assets, these supplementary proceedings can give creditors a better chance to recover more than what ordinary bankruptcy would avail while the debtor is given a breather to consolidate his resources.

Chapter 11

Chapter 11 covers *Reorganization*. It is designed to assist businesses (i.e., corporations, partnerships, and sole proprietorships) to cope with temporary and surmountable financial difficulties. The debtor is to submit a reorganization plan according to which the creditors will be best paid under the circumstances.

Reorganization
A procedure under the Bankruptcy Code for the relief of business organizations with financial difficulties.

Petition

Similar to a liquidation, a reorganization may be petitioned either *voluntarily* or *involuntarily*. Proceeding under Chapter 11 is available to all debtors who may become bankrupt under Chapter 7, including railroads, which are denied straight bankruptcy. Stockbrokers and commodity brokers are excepted.

Although under Chapter 7, an order for relief will not be issued if the voluntary petition is found to be a substantial abuse of the bankruptcy provision, the criteria for approving a reorganization petition are less stringent. Not only is it not necessary for the debtor to be insolvent and unable to pay debts, but the debtor's good faith is not a question at the time of the petition; it will be considered only when the court subsequently deliberates on the propriety of the reorganization plan. As noted earlier, Chapter 11 has lately been increasingly utilized by solvent and ongoing companies to ward off, protect themselves from, or at least cushion against the impact of potential losses.

In re Johns-Manville Corp.
36 B.R. 727 (Bkrtcy. N.Y. 1984).

Burton R. Lifland, Bankruptcy Judge . . . Whether an industrial enterprise in the United States is highly successful is often gauged by its "membership" in what has come to be known as the "Fortune 500." Having attained this measure of financial achievement, Johns-Manville Corp. and its affiliated companies (collectively referred to as "Manville") were deemed a paradigm of success in corporate America by the financial community. Thus, Manville's filing for protection under Chapter 11 of Title 11 of the United States Code ("the Code or the Bankruptcy Code") on August 26, 1982 ("the filing date") was greeted with great surprise and consternation on the part of some of its creditors and other corporations that were being sued along with Manville for injuries caused by asbestos exposure. As discussed at length herein, Manville submits that the sole factor necessitating its filing is the mammoth problem of uncontrolled proliferation of asbestos health suits brought against it because of its substantial use for many years of products containing asbestos which injured those who came into contact with the dust of this lethal substance. According to Manville, this current problem of approximately 16,000 lawsuits pending as of the filing date is compounded by the crushing economic burden to be suffered by Manville over the next 20–30 years by the filing of an even more staggering number of suits by those who had been exposed but who will not manifest the asbestos-related diseases until some time during this future period ("the future asbestos claimants"). Indeed, approximately 6,000 asbestos health claims are estimated to have arisen in only the first 16 months since the filing date. This burden is further compounded by the insurance industry's general disavowal of liability to Manville on policies written for this very purpose. Indeed, the issue of coverage has been pending for years before a state court in California. . . .

It is the propriety of the filing by Manville which is the subject of the instant decision. (However,) (t)he motions to dismiss Manville's petition filed by the Asbestos Committee, GAF, Whitman, and the Codefendants must be denied. Preliminarily, it must be stated that there is no question that Manville is eligible to be a debtor under the Code's statutory requirements. . . . (W)ith specific regard to Chapter 11, the Code eliminates the requirement . . . that the debtor be insolvent or unable to pay his debts as they mature.

. . . In the instant case, not only would liquidation be wasteful and inefficient in destroying the utility of valuable assets of the companies as well as jobs, but, more importantly, liquidation would preclude just compensation of some present asbestos victims and all future asbestos claimants. This unassailable reality represents all the more reason for this Court to adhere to this basic potential liquidation avoidance aim of Chapter 11 and deny the motions to dismiss. Manville must not be required to wait until its economic picture has deteriorated beyond salvation to file for reorganization.

. . . Manville's purported motivation in filing to obtain a breathing spell from asbestos litigation should not conclusively establish its lack of intent to rehabilitate and justify the dismissal of its petition. On the contrary, there has been submitted no evidence that Manville has not bargained to obtain a reorganization plan in good faith.

. . . In *Eden*, this Court stated:

Sine Qua Non
An indispensable condition.

> Good faith as the *sine qua non* for the filing and maintenance of a Chapter 11 case should be probed elastically and on a case-by-case basis. To do otherwise invites unnecessary rigidity in bankruptcy administration emasculating bright prospects of reorganization by slavish review of pre-petition dealings by debtors with their creditors.

Eden, 13 B.R. 578, 584.

. . . In *Manville*, it is undeniable that there has been no sham or hoax perpetrated on the Court in that Manville is a real business with real creditors in pressing need of economic reorganization.

. . . In short, there was justification for Manville to elect a course contemplating a viable court-supervised rehabilitation of the real debt owed by Manville to its real creditors.

. . . Manville is a financially besieged enterprise in desperate need of reorganization of its crushing real debt, both present and future. The reorganization

> provisions of the Code were drafted with the aim of liquidation avoidance by great access to Chapter 11. Accordingly, Manville's filing does not abuse the jurisdictional integrity of this Court.
>
> ... (T)he type of plan which emerges, *i.e.*, whether or not it treats with future claimants fairly, if at all, is irrelevant to the threshold determination made by this Court today as to the propriety or "good faith" of Manville's filing. These pejorative considerations are more appropriately left to the decision on confirmability of a concrete plan, as applied to a plan proponent, under Section 1129 of the Code....
>
> For the reasons set forth above ... all four of the motions to dismiss the Manville petition are denied in their entirety.
>
> It is SO ORDERED.

Proceeding

Upon filing a petition for reorganization, the court will issue an order for relief. The debtor is ordinarily allowed to continue with the management and operation of the business as well as retain possession of the business assets, in which event he is called a *debtor in possession*. Such as in ordinary bankruptcy, the petitioner for reorganization is also required to submit a creditors' list and complete financial statements. The court will appoint a committee representing the unsecured creditors and, if necessary, additional committees representing other classes of creditors and shareholders. The creditors' committees basically oversee the debtor in possession in managing the business affairs and participate in formulating the reorganization plan. Upon the committees' request, the court may appoint a trustee or an examiner (if the debtor is suspected of fraud, incompetence, mismanagement, or other irregularities).

Debtor in Possession
The debtor managing and operating a business under a plan for reorganization.

The Plan

The reorganization plan may be submitted within *120 days* subsequent to the order for relief. An organization plan is usually the result of intensive bargaining between all the parties concerned. The plan may be submitted by the debtor, but any other interested party may file a plan if a trustee is appointed, if the debtor does not file, or if the debtor's plan is not accepted by the creditors within *180 days* after the order for relief.

The plan must identify the classes of creditors who are impaired and those who are not. It may contain proposals to sell certain assets, to merge, consolidate or otherwise divest, to satisfy or change certain liens or claims, or to recapitalize the business, for example, by the issuance of new voting stock. A plan is accepted by a class of creditors if those holding at least two-thirds in dollar amount and more than one-half of the total number of the creditors approve it. An unimpaired class of creditors is not required to vote.

Reorganization Plan
The plan finally agreed upon for the restructuring of a debtor's liabilities under a reorganization.

Confirmation

The court will hold a confirmation hearing on the proposed plan. The plan is ordinarily confirmed if it is proposed in good faith and approved by all

Confirmation
The reorganization plan must be confirmed by the court before being placed in effect.

Cramdown
Court confirmation of a reorganization plan that has been rejected by a class of creditors.

the impaired classes of creditors. Even if the plan is rejected by a class of creditors, it still may be confirmed by the court if it feels that it is fair and equitable to all the creditors. Such a confirmation is known as a *cramdown*.

Facts

White, owner of a land-surveying business, filed a reorganization plan accepted by the creditors except Midland Bank, which had two claims against him. Under the plan, one claim for $12,000 was to be repaid $270 per month plus interest. The other claim for $88,200 was to be repaid over ten years with interest. The latter debt, secured by a real estate mortgage, would be prepaid if White succeeded in selling a portion of the property. White's projected income for the next year was $103,000. Midland argued that the plan was not proposed in good faith, that it was not feasible, and that it was not fair and equitable.

Decision

Reorganization plan confirmed. Essentially, a reorganization plan is proposed in good faith when there is a reasonable likelihood that the plan will achieve a result consistent with the objectives and purposes of the Bankruptcy Code. To determine whether a plan is feasible, the court must examine the adequacy of the capital structure, the business's earning power, and economic conditions, management's ability, the probability of the present management's continuation, and any other factors related to the successful performance of the plan. The court need not find that the plan is guaranteed of success but only find that a reasonable expectation of success exists. Based on testimonial evidence, the court determined that the plan was feasible. The plan allows Midland Bank to retain its lien on the property securing the claim. Furthermore, the plan meets both the fair and equitable requirement of § 1129(b)(2) and the requirement that the plan not discriminate unfairly pursuant to § 1129(b)(1).

In re White, 41 B.R. 227 (Bkrtcy. Tenn. 1984).

On the other hand, in *In the Matter of Landmark at Plaza Park, Ltd.* (7 B.R. 653 [Bkrtcy. N.Y. 1980]), the court denied confirmation of a Chapter 11 plan in which the interest of a first mortgagee would be significantly impaired. The plan involved a real estate lender who, on an originally agreed fully amortized loan, was to receive payments with interest at only 12½ percent, whereas the appropriate rate was 15 percent. The court felt, moreover, that it was highly unlikely that the debtor would meet his obligations anyway under the plan.

If the court finds that the plan is unfair or not feasible for successful implementation, it may recommend that a second plan be submitted or may order that the proceeding be converted to liquidation under Chapter 7. This may serve as a reason for all the parties to cooperate in finding a reasonable and practical solution to avoid straight bankruptcy.

Discharge

A confirmed reorganization plan is binding upon all the parties concerned. The company, its owners, and the creditors acquire new rights and obligations that completely substitute the old ones. Thus, the approved plan discharges the debtor from all debts and portions of debts that are not included in the plan. When the reorganization plan is subsequently implemented completely and all the creditors under the plan are paid accordingly, the debtor is discharged of all his previous liabilities similar to the bankrupt under Chapter 7.

Chapter 13

Chapter 13 provides for the *Adjustment of Debts of an Individual with Regular Income*. The proceeding is available to individuals, including sole proprietors, who have unsecured debts less than $100,000 and secured debts up to $350,000. The debtor is required to submit a repayment plan to be approved by the court.

Petition and Proceeding

A petition under Chapter 13 may be filed *only voluntarily* by the debtor. The petition must state that the debtor is unable to pay his debts as listed and wishes to propose a repayment plan that may include composition of debts, which is a reduction of the amount of debt, as well as extension of debts, which allows the debtor a longer period of time to repay. Upon filing the petition, a creditors' meeting will be called to determine the provable and allowable claims. A trustee will be appointed to oversee the debtor's financial affairs and to assist the debtor in formulating the repayment plan.

Composition of Debts
Reduction of the amount of debt.

Extension of Debts
Allowing the debtor a longer time to repay.

The Plan

The proposed repayment plan is to be submitted to the court within *ten days* of filing the petition. It must include (1) a submission to the trustee of the debtor's projected disposable income for a three-year period (which may be extended to five years) to repay the debts under the plan, (2) full payment of claims entitled to priority under Chapter 7, and (3) retention of the liens by secured creditors and provisions for equal treatment of the other creditors of the same class.

Confirmation

The repayment plan is to be approved by the court at a confirmation hearing. Creditors are not asked to vote on the plan. However, the court confirms the plan only if certain requirements are met:

1. The plan is in conformity with terms, requirements, and other provisions of the Bankruptcy Code in general and Chapter 13 in particular.
2. The filing fee has been paid.
3. The plan was proposed in good faith.
4. Secured creditors are protected under the plan as far as repayment of their loans and preservation of their liens are concerned.
5. Unsecured creditors are under the plan to receive not less than what they would receive under a Chapter 7 liquidation.
6. The debtor appears to be able to comply with the plan.

The court will confirm the plan over the objection of an unsecured creditor or the trustee only if (1) the plan provides for a full repayment of the protesting creditor's claim or (2) the plan calls for the debtor to submit in the ensuing three years all his disposable income (i.e., income not needed for family sustenance) to be used for payments under the plan. If the court rejects the plan, the debtor may file a new plan.

Abuse of Chapter 13 proceeding seems to be abundant. The repayment plan especially appears to be a convenient device in situations where the debt is not dischargeable under Chapter 7, such as willful and malicious tort liability, embezzled or stolen money, or a student loan that the debtor does not have the intention to ever pay.

In re Satterwhite
7 B.R. 39 (Bkrtcy. Tex. 1980).

William M. Schultz, Bankruptcy Judge The matter before the Court is the trustee's objection to confirmation of the debtor's Chapter 13 plan.

The debtor filed a Chapter 13 petition upon which he listed his monthly take-home pay as $1,458.00 and his monthly expenses as $2,072.24, leaving a negative balance of $614.24. He exempted all of his assets. He scheduled no secured debts and five unsecured debts totalling over $16,450.00, four of which could be barred by limitations. The largest of these debts, and likely the only debt, is evidenced by a judicial lien in the amount of $15,749.30 plus interest, which stems from an action for an assault committed by Satterwhite against A. R. Regan. Under the plan, Satterwhite proposes to make a one-time payment of $1.00 to each creditor. Approval of this "Dollar 13" plan would result in a payout to unsecured creditors of substantially less than one (1%) percent on their claims, which is still more than the sum the creditors would have received under a liquidation distribution.

The trustee's objection centers on Bankruptcy Code Section 1325(a)(3), which provides that confirmation will follow if ". . . the plan has been proposed in good faith. . . ." The trustee argues that because the debtor, who clearly is unable to fund a reasonable plan, proposes a one (1%) percent payout on unsecured debts composed of essentially one judgment debt which is potentially nondischargeable under Chapter 7, the debtor's plan is not proposed in good faith. The trustee contends that because the debtor is incapable of meeting all the requirements of the Bankruptcy Code, the only purpose behind the plan is to obtain the liberal Chapter 13 discharge as a way of disposing of a potentially nondischargeable debt.

The debtor counters that Section 1325 contains no express minimum payout as a threshold condition to confirmation.

The Court believes that Congress restructured Chapter 13 to function as a device through which debtors would be encouraged to repay their debts over an extended period of time. Bankruptcy Code Section 109(e) limits relief to debtors with regular income. The Code defines this debtor as an individual with income sufficiently regular ". . . to enable such individual to make *payments* under a plan . . . ". Bankruptcy Code Section 101(24) (emphasis added).

The Court agrees with the progeny of *In re Burrell*, 6 B.R. 360 (Bkrtcy., N.D.Cal. 1980), which held

> ". . . The correct approach, in this Court's view, is to treat the issues of substantiality and best effort as elements of good faith. . . ."

. . . In this case, considering the debtor's monthly expenses exceed the income, a plan is tantamount to a liquidation via Chapter 13. Therefore, the Court must carefully scrutinize the debtor's total circumstances. The Court believes the debtor's plan to be directed more toward the discharge of a nondischargeable debt to a major unsecured judgment creditor than to repayment of creditors.

> Chapter 13 may not be used as a substitute for Chapter 7 when the principal motive is to circumvent exceptions to discharge instead of meaningful payments of debts. To confirm a plan under such a scenario, in this Court's opinion, would make a mockery of Chapter 13.
>
> Other jurisdictions are in accord that marginal composition plans treating potentially nondischargeable debts will not be confirmed as the plans lack the requisite element of being proffered in good faith. . . .
>
> Because the plan fails to satisfy the good faith requirement of Section 1325(a)(3), confirmation is denied. . . .

In *In re Jonson* (17 B.R. 78 [Bkrtcy. Ind. 1981]), the plan was rejected as a debtor attempted to use Chapter 13 to repay only less than one-half of the student loan owed to Indiana University. In *In re Reynolds* (83 B.R. 684 [Bkrtcy. Mo. 1988]), the court denied a repayment plan according to which the debtor would make a monthly donation of $80 to the Assembly of God Church as his constitutional right and as a "reasonable necessary"personal expense, while his disposable income available for payment to his creditors was only $325. In *In re Yee* (7 B.R. 747 [Bkrtcy. E.D.N.Y. 1980]), a financial analyst with an annual income of $16,800, planned to pay only $30 a month for thirty-six months, a total of $1,080, to pay out debts totaling about $13,000 (including $380 in parking tickets). The court found that the plan demonstrated a lack of good faith. In many of these cases, the debtor's assets were exempt under Chapter 7 to pressure the creditor to accept the Chapter 13 repayment plan. It should be noted that the debtor under Chapter 13 has regular income that may be subject to garnishment as an alternative to bankruptcy.

Garnishment
Seizure by court order of money owed by a third party (such as an employer) to a debtor.

Discharge

Under the terms of the approved repayment plan, the debtor makes payments to the trustee, who in turn pays the creditors. The 1984 amendments require the payments to commence within thirty days after filing of the plan, subject to its confirmation. When the debtor has completed all the payments under the plan, he will be discharged of all debts covered by the plan. The debtor may even be discharged without having to carry out the entire plan due to hardship, i.e., if his failure to make further payments is attributed to circumstances beyond his control, the creditors have thus far already received at least what they would have received under Chapter 7 liquidation, and prescribing a new plan would be impractical.

Chapter 12

Chapter 12, *Family Farmer Bankruptcy Act,* became law only in 1986. The proceedings are basically similar to those under Chapter 13. The purpose of the legislation is to assist small family farmers who are having serious financial difficulties because of political or economic jolts as well as natural causes, such as droughts.

Who May Petition

To qualify as a family farmer, a person must derive at least 50 percent of his gross income from farming, while his debts are not to exceed the aggregate amount of $1.5 million, of which at least 80 percent is farm related. Chapter 12 is also available to partnerships and closely held corporations if at least one-half is owned by a farm family.

Subsequent to the petition and the order for relief, a repayment plan is to be filed within *ninety days*. Meanwhile, a secured creditor may object to the automatic stay if there is no adequate protection of his interest by the farm collateral, which is often the case. However, as opposed to Chapter 11, under which "lack of adequate protection" is to be understood as a situation where the collateral value has become less than the amount of the secured debt, Chapter 12 recognizes adequate protection if the distressed family farmer is simply willing to make reasonable rental payments on the farm. With this condition, the secured lender may not object to the plan if he is to take over a farm worth less than the loan. The deficiency is then treated as an unsecured credit.

Proceeding

The repayment plan under Chapter 12 is similar to a plan under Chapter 13. It is to be confirmed by the court within *45 days* subsequent to its submission. Chapter 12 requirements as to protection of secured creditors, protection of unsecured creditors, good faith, and willingness to make a three-year period disposable income available for repayment of debts, as well as provisions for discharge, are basically the same as those under Chapter 13.

QUESTIONS

1. What are the main differences between Chapters 11, 12, and 13?
2. As to the question of propriety, what is the difference between a liquidation voluntary petition and a reorganization voluntary petition?
3. What is a cramdown?
4. In which situations do debtors tend to manipulate Chapter 13 to deprive creditors?
5. How is the family farmer under Chapter 12 protected against foreclosure of the farm by a secured lender?

PROBLEMS

1. Peter Pan was unemployed and became unable to service any of his debts. He owed Big Joe Corporation $27,000 and fifteen other creditors small debts of less than $100 each. Could Big Joe on his own successfully file an involuntary bankruptcy petition against Peter Pan?
2. Mark Boles filed voluntary bankruptcy and submitted the necessary schedules of assets and liabilities with his petition. He was ordered to appear at the first meeting of his creditors. Here he was asked, under oath, many questions concerning his financial affairs. Boles felt that he shouldn't be required to answer some of these questions, because they invaded his privacy. Can he refuse to answer for this reason?
3. Tom Flute owed money to ten creditors. On January 15, he paid off in cash $1,500 to one of the creditors John Smiley. On July 15, he filed a voluntary petition. Would the bankruptcy trustee be able to retrieve the $1,500 payment from Smiley?

4. Willie Hyde, having engaged in embarrassing financial transactions, destroyed all of his records. Later, before he had paid off debts incurred during these transactions, Hyde filed voluntary bankruptcy. The story of the destruction of the records emerged during the conduct of the bankruptcy proceedings. Some of Hyde's creditors claimed he should not be granted a discharge from his debts due to this destruction of records. Were the creditors correct?

5. Williams got a judgment for $3,500 against Hart for injuries received in an auto accident. Hart filed a bankruptcy petition and sought to discharge this debt. Witnesses testified that they could smell alcohol on Hart's breath at the time of the accident. The state law determined DUI (driving under influence) based upon the weight of alcohol in a person's blood. No scientific evidence was presented to show this fact. Is this debt dischargeable?

6. The debtor owes $6,635 on an education loan, which she now wants to discharge in bankruptcy. She has a take-home pay of $650 a month and reasonable monthly expenses of $926 for her and her three children. Last winter a church had to pay her gas bill so that she could heat her home. She has many unpaid medical bills. She has been sued, and her wages have been garnished. She filed a voluntary bankruptcy petition. Are the unpaid student loans dischargeable?

7. Bingham received a discharge in bankruptcy. Several months later, a creditor of a debt that was discharged in the bankruptcy met Bingham in a bar. After a few drinks, the creditor got Bingham to agree to pay the old debt. However, the next day Bingham refused when the creditor reminded him of the agreement. The creditor sues on the debt. Decision?

8. Fresh Foods Inc. filed a voluntary petition for reorganization under Chapter 11, even though it was a highly successful business. The petitioner claimed that about 500 lawsuits had been filed against it and many more were anticipated in the future for injuries to persons caused by food poisoning after eating Fresh Foods' canned products. The creditors objected to the petition, since the petitioner was not insolvent. They argued that the petition was not filed in good faith and should be dismissed. How should the court rule?

9. Dr. Lewis filed a voluntary Chapter 7 bankruptcy. One of his listed debts was a $1,500 judgment entered against him for assault on Betty Durston. Lewis testified in the bankruptcy court that he "put both hands around (Durston's) neck and told her to leave his wife alone or he would break her neck." Will the court grant a discharge of this judgment claim? Would it make any difference if Lewis had filed a Chapter 13 plan?

10. Farmer Miller took a loan of $700,000 from Sunland Bank. His family farm, which was worth $1,000,000, was used as a collateral to secure the loan. Subsequently, the farm was badly hit by continuous droughts and its market value diminished rapidly to $500,000. The farm income had decreased so much that Miller became unable to pay his debts as agreed. Moreover, Sunland Bank threatened foreclosure. What can Miller do?

CHAPTER THIRTY-TWO

Estates and Trusts

32.1 The Will
Estate Planning
Will Defined
Validity Requirements
    Testamentary Capacity
    Testamentary Intent
    Proper Execution
Forms of Wills
    Holographic Wills
    Nuncupative Wills
    Modification
    Revocation
Testate Distribution
    Contesting a Will

32.2 Intestate Succession and Estate Administration
Heirs
Intestate Distribution
    Distribution per Stirpes
    Distribution per Capita

Probate
    Admitting a Will
    Representation
    Priority of Liabilities

32.3 Trust
Trust Defined
Express Trusts
    Validity Requirements
    Types of Trusts
    Form
    Trustee's Powers
    Trustee's Duties
    Beneficiary
    Remedies
    Termination
Implied Trusts
    Resulting Trusts
    Constructive Trusts

32.1 The Will

When a person dies, he leaves an estate. His estate consists of all the assets and liabilities, i.e., what he has and what he owes. There is not much to worry about if the estate is small and insignificant. But if the estate is considerable, a person may wish to arrange beforehand what needs to be done with his property.

Estate Planning

Estate
The assets and liabilities that a person owns and owes.

Will
An instrument or act expressing the wishes of a person regarding the disposition of his property at the time of his death.

The primary objective of estate planning is to ensure that the estate will be distributed according to the decedent's wishes. Two devices are ordinarily involved: the will and the trust.

Tax liability is usually an important consideration in estate planning. Taxes must be paid from the estate for the decedent's income prior to death. Then, federal estate taxes and state inheritance taxes need to be paid before the estate may be distributed. It is true that federal estate taxes have recently been considerably abated. Only a few years ago, tax was to be paid on the portion that the decedent's spouse received, and when this spouse died, the same portion would be taxed again before it could transfer to another beneficiary. Presently, the share for a surviving spouse is not taxed. Also, federal tax exemptions on gifts and estates have been significantly increased from $275,000 in 1983 to $600,000 in 1987.

Probate
Court procedure for carrying out the terms of a will, or for distributing the estate of an intestate person.

Avoidance of probate may be another consideration in estate planning. Probate is the court proceeding on the administration and disposition of a decedent's estate. It can be quite involved and costly, since attorneys, personal representatives, and other experts may need to be paid. Moreover, the proceeding can be time consuming. It is conducted in public, without regard to the parties' privacy. Probate may be prevented by the use of such devices as inter vivos gifts, joint tenancy, trusts, and life insurance policies.

Will Defined

Testate
The state of having a valid will.

Intestate
The state of having no valid will.

Testator
A man who makes a will.

Testatrix
A woman who makes a will.

Legitimate Portion
Portion of estate exclusively reserved for a decedent's immediate family.

A will or a testament is a legally executed document containing a person's instructions on the disposition of his estate after his death. There is then a *testate* distribution of his estate. If the person does not have a will, he dies *intestate,* and state intestacy laws determine who will inherit his property.

A man who leaves a will is called a testator; a woman, a testatrix. The will may dispose only of property that the testator personally owns at the time of his death. In the event a married decedent is subject to community property law, he may will out all his separate property but only one-half of the community property. In most civil law countries and also under Islamic law, members of the decedent's immediate family are given so-called legitimate portions of the estate which are exclusively reserved for them and which cannot be violated by a decedent's will. Such reservations do not exist in our laws. A testator may do whatever he wants, as long as the will pertains to property at his disposal.

Wills do not cover properties that are transferred to other persons through other legal avenues, such as to the survivor in a joint tenancy, the trustee of a living trust, or the beneficiary of a life insurance policy.

Validity Requirements

Basically three elements make a will valid: capacity, intent, and proper execution.

Testamentary Capacity

To be able to dispose of his property by a will, a testator must have reached the *legal age*, which is generally 18 years, and must be of *sound mind*. Since a person making a will may be already old, feeble, or sick, he is not expected to possess the same level of mental capacity as is required of someone to enter into a business contract. However, the testator must be able to understand the general meaning and nature of his will. He must be aware of the property involved and of his relationship to the beneficiary. Even a judicially declared insane person may have a valid will as long as the will was made at a time when the person was clear in his mind.

Testamentary Capacity
The capacity to make a legally valid will.

Facts

Gentry, a U.S. Army serviceman, was confined in the Walter Reed Hospital psychiatric ward when he was adjudicated incompetent in 1965. Pioneer Trust Company was appointed his guardian. Gentry had one daughter, but in his will that was drawn in 1969 while he was confined, he named his mother as sole beneficiary of his estate. When Gentry died, his daughter came to contest the validity of the will on the ground that her father lacked testamentary capacity. Gentry's ward physician, Dr. Esperson, testified that Gentry's mental illness was largely controllable by psychiatric medication and that Gentry was generally clear minded as long as he took the prescribed drugs. He would become psychotic only if he left the hospital for an extended period and stopped taking the medication.

Decision

The will was valid. It was drawn professionally and witnessed by the attorney and his secretary under circumstances indicating that Gentry was sane at that moment. His testamentary intent was clearly demonstrated by letters to Pioneer Trust as well as to his mother stating that "I want my mother to inherit my 4 or 5 thousand." The court observed that mental competency to make a will is determined at the precise moment the will is executed. A will made by an insane person may be valid if made during a lucid interval. ". . . (B)ecause the testator was under guardianship at the time of execution of the will is not conclusive of his mental incompetency at the time if the evidence shows that the testator possessed the requisite testamentary capacity at the time of the execution of the will." Gentry's mother was decreed the sole beneficiary of the estate.

Estate of Gentry, 32 Or.App. 45, 573 P.2d 322 (1978).

In *Koonce* v. *Mims* (402 So.2d 942 [Ala. 1981]), the court also endorsed the presumption that testamentary capacity exists unless there is evidence to the contrary.

On the other hand, testamentary capacity may under other circumstances be considered lacking, e.g., if the testator is so weakened by age, illness, and disease, that he is unable to understand the nature and consequences of his conduct. For example, in *In the Matter of Estate of Lockwood* (254 Cal.App.2d 309, 62 Cal.Rptr. 230 [1967]), an 89-year-old testatrix was considered mentally incompetent when she executed a codicil changing her previous will while she was extremely ill and semicomatose.

Testamentary Intent

Testamentary Intent
Actual and genuine intent to make a certain will.

Animus Testandi
Testamentary intent; testator's intent to make the will.

A will may be valid only if there is testamentary intent or *animus testandi* of the testator to transfer his ownership of a certain property to a certain person upon his death. The intent must be apparent and genuine. It may not be impaired by such factors as mistake, fraud, duress, or undue influence. For example, where babies at birth were innocently switched, the parents' mistaken presumption of kinship may be argued. Falsely claiming to be a testator's relative may result in fraud. However, most frequent is the allegation that the testamentary intent has been distorted because of undue influence.

Facts

During his life, Carlo Franco was quite close to his sister Caterina. With the idea of leaving everything he had to this sister, Carlo had more than 1,000 shares of American Telephone and Telegraph stock issued in his name together with Caterina's as joint tenants. Only two years before his death, his brother, John Franco, managed to instigate an incident whereby Carlo became angry with Caterina. Subsequent to the incident, John and his family pretended to care for Carlo. One day they brought Carlo, a bashful, uneducated, and trusting person, to John's attorney to execute a will that gave all of Carlo's estate to John's two sons, except for $300, which was to be given to Caterina. They also had Carlo ask Caterina to sign the stock certificates relinquishing all of her interest. Carlo seemed afterwards to regret the will. When Carlo died, Caterina contended that the will was obtained by undue influence.

Decision

The court decided in favor of Caterina. The court quoted *Estate of Lingenfelter* (38 Cal.2d 571, 585, 241 P.2d 990, 999 (1952)), in which the California Supreme Court observed:

> The indicia of undue influence have been stated as follows: '(1) The provisions of the will were unnatural. . . ; (2) the dispositions of the will were at variance with the intentions of the decedent, expressed both before and after its execution; (3) the relations existing between the chief beneficiaries and the decedent afforded to the former an opportunity to control the testamentary act; (4) the decedent's mental and physical condition was such as to permit a subversion of his freedom of will; and (5) the chief beneficiaries under the will were active in procuring the instrument to be executed.' (*Estate of Yale*, 214 Cal. 115, 122 [4 P.2d 153].) These, coupled with a confidential relationship between at least one of the chief beneficiaries and the testator, altogether were held 'sufficient to shift the burden to the proponents of the will to establish an absence of undue influence and coercion and to require the issues to be determined by the jury.' (*Estate of Yale, supra*, p. 123 [4 P.2d 153].)

In re Estate of Franco, 50 Cal.App.3d 374, 122 Cal.Rptr. 661 (1975).

Proper Execution

Execution
Signing the will.

State law generally requires a *formal will* to be written or typewritten, signed, and witnessed. It may be written on a piece of paper, on the wall, or anywhere, as long as the testamentary intent is apparent. Normally, the testator signs at the end of the will. If he is unable to sign his name, he may place an "X" or have another person sign his name on the document.

A will is usually not notarized or formally recorded. Two witnesses are ordinarily required for *attestation,* although some states may require three. A witness does not have to know the contents of the will. It is sufficient that he is made aware that he is witnessing the testator signing a will. This is called *publication.* The witness normally verifies that the testator has the required testamentary capacity, is of sound mind, and is not acting under duress, menace, or undue influence. Although states may not prescribe a certain age for a witness, it is preferable to have the witness be of legal age. For obvious reasons, it is advisable that a witness be younger than the testator himself. An additional witness may be required if one of the witnesses is to receive property or otherwise benefit from the will.

Attestation
Witnessing the will.

Publication
Making the witness aware that he is witnessing the testator signing a will.

Forms of Wills

In addition to the formal will, there are *holographic* and *nuncupative* wills.

Formal Will
Must be written or typewritten, signed and witnessed.

Holographic Wills

A holographic will is a will written by the testator entirely by hand. It is not attested or witnessed. If it is recognized, it has the same force as a formal will. Some states may specifically require a holographic will to be dated. Also, a holographic will may not be considered effective if some printing or typewriting appears in the document, in which case formal attestation is needed. Some jurisdictions may require that only the decedent's signature and material provisions be in the testator's handwriting.

Holographic Will
Written entirely by the hand of the testator. Need not be witnessed.

Facts

Cunningham, who died in September 1983, had a "Last Will and Testament" written on a preprinted stationery form dated December 27, 1977. The opening and closing clauses as well as the attestation clause were printed. The remaining, which included his name, Social Security number, and the main body of instructions, were all handwritten. Cunningham signed at the top of the document. Two witnesses who signed at the bottom of the instrument did not see Cunningham signing, nor could they recall being told by him that he had signed the document as required by New Jersey law.

Decision

The will was admitted to probate. It is true that the document did not meet the requirements for a formal will because it had not been witnessed by two persons who had either seen Cunningham sign it or been told by him that he had signed it. However, New Jersey law also provides for the admission to probate of holographic wills in which only the decedent's signature and the material provisions ought to be in handwriting. Cunningham's will met these requirements. The document was executed with the intent that it constituted his will.

In re Estate of Cunningham, 198 N.J. Super. 484, 487 A.2d 777 (1984).

Nuncupative Wills

Nuncupative Will
An oral will.

A nuncupative will is an oral will made in the presence of witnesses. A few states recognize this type of will, which can be made by the testator during his last illness or by a sailor or soldier in service. There are often statutory limitations on the amount of money and the type of property that may be disposed of by a nuncupative will. It may not be probated unless the witnesses reduce the will to writing and sign it within a specific period of time after it was orally declared. A nuncupative will made by a sailor or soldier may remain in force after termination of service. It may be modified or revoked in the same way as any other will.

Modification

Codicil
A document that modifies the terms of a will.

A will may not be changed by making additional notes, inserting words, or crossing out certain provisions on the already attested document. It is to be amended by a *codicil*, a separate document executed in the same manner required of the will itself. The original document remains in force except for the provisions changed by the codicil.

Revocation

Ambulatory
Is the status of a will before the testator dies.

A will does not become effective until the testator dies and the will is probated. Until then a will is called *ambulatory*, i.e., it can be revoked by an act of the testator or by operation of the law. A testator, while still having his testamentary capacity, can revoke his will by destroying or crossing out the provisions of the document with the intention to revoke. In *Franklin* v. *MacLean* (192 Va. 684, 66 S.E.2d 504 [1951]), a decedent's will written in ink was considered to have been revoked when the document was found with other papers in a locked closet in her bedroom, since pencil lines had been drawn through all the provisions as well as through her signature.

Revocation
Cancellation of the will, or of any document.

Usually, revocation by destruction of the will may be conducted by the testator only. However, Texas Probate Code § 63 provides: "No will in writing, and no clause thereof or devise therein, shall be revoked, except by a subsequent will, codicil, or declaration in writing, executed with like formalities, or by the testator destroying or canceling the same, or *causing it to be done in his presence*." [Emphasis Added.] In *Morris* v. *Morris* (631 S.W.2d 188 [Texas, 1982]), a will that at the testator's instruction was destroyed not in his presence by another person was admitted to probate.

Statutes may also provide that revocation of a will can be effected by operation of the law due to a change in the testator's circumstances. If a person marries subsequent to the execution of a will, the will is presumed to have been revoked unless it is specifically made in contemplation of the marriage. If the will in this case is considered revoked by operation of the law, the revocation may take effect only partly so as to allow the spouse to inherit what he or she would receive without the will. The same rule applies to a situation where a will was executed before the birth or adoption of a child. On the other hand, the testator's divorce does not by itself revoke his will unless there is a property settlement, in which case the will is considered revoked so far as it pertains to the divorced spouse (*Estate of Liles,* 435 A.2d 379 [D.C.App. 1981]).

Testate Distribution

A *devise* is a gift by will of real property. The recipient is called a devisee. A *bequest* or a *legacy* is a gift by will of personal property. A legatee is usually a recipient of a gift of money. These terms may in practice be used interchangeably, in which case it should not be construed to defeat the intent of the testator.

A devise, bequest, or legacy may be *general* or *specific,* depending upon whether or not the property concerned is specifically described in the will. It is called *residuary* if it refers to the property remaining after the general and/or specific bequests. For example, a will concerning an estate consisting of money in the amount of $200,000, a house, and a car, says: "$150,000 to Ralph, the house to Sandra, and the remaining to Tom." Ralph is a general legatee, Sandra is a specific devisee, and Tom is a residuary legatee. *Antilapse* statutes prescribe that in a situation where a named devisee or legatee predeceased the testator and the will does not provide for a contingent beneficiary, the devise or legacy will transfer to the heirs of the deceased recipient.

Abatement of legacies refers to a situation wherein after all probate costs, fees, and debts are paid, the remaining of the estate is not enough to fulfill the testator's wishes in the will. In such a case, the residuary legacy is to abate first, then the general, and lastly the specific legacy. Thus, if in the example above only $2,000 and the house are left in the estate, then Ralph takes $2,000, Sandra takes the house, and Tom takes nothing.

A specific devise or legacy is considered adeemed if it is not in the estate when the decedent dies. Whether it has been sold or given away, such an *ademption* of property operates as a cancellation of the legacy. The recipient may, of course, still be a beneficiary under other provisions of the will or an heir under the law of succession.

Devise
A testamentary gift of real property.

Bequest
A testamentary gift of personal property.

Residuary Bequest
Property remaining after the general and specific bequests.

Legacy
A bequest of money.

Abatement of Legacy
If the estate is not enough to meet the testator's wishes, residuary legacy is to be disregarded first, then the general, and then the specific legacy.

Ademption
If a specific devise is not in the estate when the decedent dies.

Facts
In Mary Eickholt's will of 1980, one half of her farm would be given to her brother and the other half to her sister. The residue of her estate was to be divided between them equally. Subsequently, in 1981, she executed a codicil providing that the residue should be given to four of her nephews. The codicil also directed the executor to sell the farm and to combine the proceeds with the residue.

Decision
There was an ademption of the farm, leaving Mary's brother and sister with nothing. The court must interpret a will and a codicil as one instrument, executed on the date of the codicil. Codicil provisions substitute for provisions in the will to the extent that they are incompatible. Accordingly, there may only be one residuary clause, i.e., the one provided in the codicil.

Matter of Estate of Eickholt, 365 N.W.2d 44 (Iowa App. 1985).

Disinheritance by the will takes place when a relative who would participate in the distribution under the law of succession takes nothing under the will, as all the estate properties are given to other persons. Usually, a

Contesting a Will

Will Contest
An attack in the probate court on the validity of a will.

A will may be contested when the testator dies and a probate proceeding ensues to determine its validity. Any person dissatisfied with the will may contest its propriety. He may be a person who feels that he should be, but is not, remembered in the will or a beneficiary who is unhappy with his share. It is not uncommon for a *pretermitted* or forgotten heir to contest the will.

A will may be contested on a number of grounds. Most common are (1) the lack of form or formality prescribed by law, (2) forgery, (3) the lack of testamentary capacity, and (4) mistake, fraud, duress, or undue influence. Undue influence is often the reason for the probate court to set a will aside.

In some circumstances, the court may even presume the presence of undue influence, unless the accused beneficiary can prove otherwise. This is the case, for example, in *In re Estate of Nelson* (274 N.W.2d 584 [S.D. 1978]), where the decedent's lawyer managed to make himself the sole beneficiary in his client's will, thereby completely disinheriting his heirs. "No evidence was presented indicating that Theodosen (the lawyer) took no unfair advantage of his dominant position. A prima facie case of undue influence was established and it required a finding of undue influence. . . ." Yet, the court does not always accept undue influence as a reason to void a will.

Facts

Mrs. Kleeb had two daughters and one son when she died in 1979. She was most of the time confined to a wheelchair. She had Parkinson's disease and had suffered a stroke. Shortly after her husband's death in 1972, one of her daughters, Velma, was appointed as Mrs. Kleeb's conservator. Disputes soon developed among the children concerning the handling of Mrs. Kleeb's affairs. As Mrs. Kleeb filed a court petition requesting Velma to be discharged as her conservator, both her daughters instituted proceedings seeking to place their mother under guardianship. Mrs. Kleeb felt very much offended in the belief that her daughters were trying to have her declared insane. At the advice of her son Stewart, Mrs. Kleeb was examined by two doctors, who declared her competent and capable of taking care of her own affairs. Subsequently, in June 1974, Stewart brought Mrs. Kleeb to an attorney who drew her last will, giving each of the daughters $10. The balance of the estate, which consisted principally of two farms, was given to Stewart. The daughters' guardianship proceedings were meanwhile dismissed because a court-ordered examination by the Richard Young Memorial Hospital in Omaha, Nebraska, revealed that there was "no evidence of gross mental incompetence." When Mrs. Kleeb died, her daughters brought a suit to set aside their mother's will on the grounds of testamentary incapacity and undue influence by her son Stewart.

Decision

The will was admitted to probate. The court found that although there was evidence to indicate that on certain of the psychological tests performed at the Memorial Hospital, Mrs. Kleeb displayed the judgment of one eight or nine years of age, it was amply established that at the time Mrs. Kleeb executed her will she met all of the necessary requirements to make her competent to execute a will. An important testimony was presented by Mrs. Kleeb's nephew and one nonrelative, who were asked to come to see her individually. Each of them was told the exact contents of her will as she desired them to be. The court also rejected the allegation of undue influence exercised by Stewart. "It is obvious that there was a tugging and pulling between the children. It is likewise clear, although perhaps without justification, that Mrs. Kleeb was incensed by her daughters' filing of the guardianship proceedings. Indeed that may have been what motivated her to take the action in 1974 she took, but the 5 years which expired between the time she executed the will and her death did not seem to change her view."

In re Estate of Kleeb, 211 Neb. 763, 320 N.W.2d 459 (1982).

Questions

1. What are the necessary elements of a valid will? Please explain.
2. How is a formal will executed? What is a holographic and what is a nuncupative will?
3. How is a will modified? How is it revoked?
4. How are legacies abated? When does ademption occur?
5. Who may contest a will, and on what grounds?

32.2 Intestate Succession and Estate Administration

When a person dies without leaving a will, his estate is distributed to his heirs in accordance with the intestacy law—also known as the law of succession or inheritance—of the state where the death occurs. Statutes of succession differ considerably from state to state, particularly where community property of married couples is involved. A Uniform Probate Code (UPC), which provides some uniformity, has been adopted by quite a number of the fifty states. If the decedent leaves no heir to inherit under the law of succession, the estate will *escheat* to the state.

Escheat
An estate belongs to the state if there is no will and no heir to inherit.

Heirs

Heirs must be relatives of the decedent. However, not all relatives are heirs. The inheritance status of an heir depends upon the proximity of the heir's relationship with the deceased person. Heirs are categorized into classes starting with the immediate family members, who are the spouse and children, and extending to the most distant relatives. The general rule as well as the rule under the UPC is that when there is a surviving member of one class, relatives of a subordinating class do not take any of the estate.

Heir
One who inherits or is entitled to inherit.

1. In the absence of any blood relatives of the decedent, a *surviving spouse* may take the entire estate. If, in addition to leaving the surviving spouse, the decedent left one child, the estate is to be divided equally between the two. If there are more than one issue or offspring, then one third of the estate is for the surviving spouse, and two thirds are for the children. Where community property of married people is recognized and the

Lineal Descendants
Children of the decedent.

Lineal Ascendants
Parents of the decedent.

Collateral Heirs
Decedent's relatives based on common ancestry, such as brothers, sisters, and their children.

deceased spouse did not dispose of his or her one-half share by a will, the property goes entirely to the surviving spouse.

2. *Lineal descendants* are the children or legal issue of the decedent who share the entire estate if the decedent did not leave a surviving spouse. If a child predeceased the decedent and left lawful issue, the share of the predeceased child goes to his or her offspring.

3. *Lineal ascendants* or parents of the decedent receive the entire estate if the decedent did not leave a surviving spouse or legal issue. If the decedent left a surviving spouse but no issue, the estate goes one-half to the surviving spouse and one-half to the parents.

4. *Collateral heirs* are the decedent's relatives based on common ancestry, such as brothers, sisters, and their children. Cousins may also be collateral heirs. They inherit only if the decedent did not have any other closer relatives. The law of succession provides for all kinds of contingencies as well as the disposition of the decedent's property to the next of kin in the absence of relatives of a preferred class.

Warpool v. Floyd
524 S.W.2d 247 (Tenn. 1975).

Harbison, Justice This case presents for decision the issue of whether children of half-brothers and sisters of an intestate take equal shares of his personal property with children of brothers and sisters of the whole blood. The chancellor held that they are entitled to equal shares, and the administrator has appealed here, seeking appropriate instructions as to the distribution of intestate personal property.

The decedent had one full brother and sister, both of whom predeceased him. The sister died without issue, but the brother left one child surviving. He is the administrator as well as the full nephew by blood of the decedent.

Decedent, who never married, was predeceased by both parents. His father, however, by a previous marriage had ten children, all of whom had predeceased the decedent. Eight of these, however, left surviving children, representatives of whom were named as defendants in the court below. There are some twenty-eight of these nephews and nieces of the half blood.

[1] Under the law of intestate distribution in this state, there is no representation among collateral kindred, after the children of brothers and sisters. T.C.A. § 31–202. Children of brothers and sisters, however, do take by representation, and it has been held that they take the intestate's personal property per stirpes, rather than per capita. *Housley v. Laster,* 176 Tenn. 174, 140 S.W.2d 146 (1940).

The statutes governing distribution of intestate personal property give priority to the surviving spouse and/or children of a decedent. Where there are no persons in these categories, however, the parents are preferred. The statutes then provide as follows:

> "If no father or mother, to brothers and sisters, or the children of such brothers and sisters representing them, equally." T.C.A. § 31–201(5).

The statutes provide that if there are neither brothers, sisters, nieces nor nephews, then the personal estate is distributed "to every of the next of kin of the intestate who are in equal degree, equally." T.C.A. § 31–201(6).

Kindred or Kin
Relatives; relationship by blood.

> In the case of *Kyle v. Moore,* 35 Tenn. 183 (1855), this Court expressly held that brothers and sisters of half blood shared equally in intestate personal property with brothers and sisters of the whole blood.
>
> The Court noted that under the statutes then in effect, which were derived from earlier North Carolina statutes, where there were no children, distribution was to be made "to the next of kindred, in equal degree, of or unto the intestate, and their legal representatives, and in no other manner whatsoever."
>
> The Court noted that in the computation of the degrees of kinship, there was no distinction between the half blood and the whole blood. The Court said:
>
>> "There is no law giving any preference to the half blood on the side of the transmitting ancestor, to the exclusion of the other line, in the distribution of personalty." 35 Tenn. at 185.
>
> ...Finding no legislative history which would lead us to believe that the General Assembly intended to prefer siblings of the whole blood over those of the half blood, we hold that half-brothers and half-sisters share equally with full brothers and sisters in the distribution of intestate personalty, and that their children, taking by representation, take equally with the children of full brothers and sisters.
>
> The decree of the chancellor is affirmed at the cost of appellants.

Intestate Distribution

State intestate succession laws may vary as to how all these heirs are to share in the decedent's estate.

Distribution per Stirpes

If relatives stand in different degrees of relationship with the decedent, the estate may be distributed on the basis of stirpes or family lines. This means that if a distributee predeceased the decedent, his children take a share in the estate by way of *representation,* i.e., by equally dividing among themselves the portion designated for the deceased parent. Thus, if decedent grandfather had three children—Anthony, Bill, and Cathy— and Bill died earlier, leaving one child Derrick, while Cathy also predeceased her father, leaving Edward, Frank, and Georgina, under the rule of stirpital distribution, Anthony receives ⅓ share, Derrick receives Bill's ⅓ share, while Edward, Frank and Georgina are to receive ⅓ of Cathy's ⅓ share, or ⅑ share each.

Per Stirpes
By right of representation; through deceased parents.

Distribution per Capita

When an estate is to be distributed per capita, all distributees standing in the same degree of relationship with the decedent share equally the portion of the estate designated for the particular class. Accordingly, Anthony in the above example is still to receive ⅓ share, but as both Bill and Cathy were to receive ⅔ share, their children who are relatives of the

Per Capita
Equal division by head-count among heirs of the same degree of relationship.

next generation are sharing this portion equally, i.e., each is to receive ¼ of ⅔ share, or ⅙ share.

Probate

Upon the decedent's death, all the properties belonging to the estate need to be identified, debts and taxes must be paid, and the remaining is to be distributed. Probate is the court procedure concerning the administration of a decedent's estate from the time of death until all the properties are disposed of. No probate is needed if there is nothing in the estate to be administered, if the decedent has given away all his belongings to another person or to a trust while he was alive, or if all the properties were held with another person(s) or with his spouse as joint tenants or as tenants by the entirety with the right of survivorship. It should be noted, however, that although probate may be avoided by these conditions, such property is still subject to federal estate and state inheritance taxes.

Admitting a Will

If the decedent left a will, the probate court must first determine whether the will is valid. Parties interested in the document or in the estate will be notified. A hearing will be held, and witnesses signing the will may be asked to testify. The court then decides whether or not the will was executed in compliance with all the statutory and other legal requirements. In the absence of any indication of a defect, the court will usually admit the will to probate. However, a will may be contested before or even after it has been admitted. The general rule is for the contestant to convince the court why the document should be set aside.

Representation

Personal Representative
The person responsible for administration and distribution of a decedent's estate.

Executor/Executrix
A personal representative appointed by a will.

Administrator/Administratrix
A personal representative appointed by the probate court.

Pendente Lite
Pending litigation.

During probate, the decedent's estate is managed by a *personal representative* who is the executor or executrix named in the will. He or she is appointed by the court by *letters of testamentary*. If there is no will or if the will does not mention anyone to represent the estate, *letters of administration* will be issued designating a court-appointed administrator or administratrix as the personal representative. He or she is usually an interested and close relative of the decedent. In *Tudor v. Southern Trust Co.* (193 Tenn. 331, 246 S.W.2d 33 [1952]), the court appointed a brother to administer a decedent's estate instead of a first cousin who petitioned for the position. The court observed that "next of kin" under Tennessee law must be a person who is to receive a share of the estate. The brother would in this case be the only beneficiary to inherit.

An *administrator pendente lite*, who is a temporary-personal representative, may be appointed if the will is contested.

The duties of a personal representative can be summarized as follows:

1. The personal representative must collect, inventory, and appraise the assets of the estate. State statutes may require that available cash be

deposited in a bank, in which event the name of the account is to read: "Sam Snow, Executor of the Estate of Ronald Winter, Deceased."

2. If, because of the composition or nature of the estate, or if, because of complicated litigations, the distribution of the estate may be subject to a long delay, the personal representative may be required to invest some of the liquid assets. He is ordinarily not expected to continue with the decedent's business without the decedent's explicit authorization in the will. Even then, the representative should be careful not to comingle accounts so as to jeopardize the interests of the beneficiaries of the estate.

Facts

Henry Muller, Jr., died testate on October 18, 1961, leaving two sons, Henry Muller III, the executor of the estate, and Edwin G. Muller, the objectant in this case. Muller's will was quite simple. It provided that his two sons were to share equally in his estate and that Henry be appointed executor. The will authorized the executor to continue the testator's businesses if, in the executor's discretion, it was for the best interests of the estate. The executor was also empowered to sell, mortgage, or lease the testator's real property under such terms and conditions as the executor deemed best. The main issue brought by Edwin against his brother, who as executor continued the father's enterprises, was that some general funds belonging to the estate were injected into the businesses.

Decision

The court held the executor liable for the amounts of the estate funds used. The intention of a testator to confer upon an executor power to use general assets of the estate to continue various businesses of the testator must be found in the direct, explicit, and unequivocal language of the will, or else it will not be deemed to have been conferred (*Willis* v. *Sharp,* 113 N.Y. 586, 21 N.E. 705 (1889); *Columbus Watch Co.* v. *Hodenpyl,* 135 N.Y. 430, 32 N.E. 239 (1892)). Although the decedent's will did authorize the executor to continue the various businesses, such authorization merely granted to the executor the power to continue the businesses with the funds already invested in them at the time of the testator's death.

In re Estate of Muller, 24 N.Y.2d 336, 300 N.Y.S.2d 341, 248 N.E.2d 164 (N.Y. 1969).

3. Creditors of the estate need to be notified of the decedent's death individually and/or by a local newspaper announcement. They may submit their proofs of claim within a certain period of time, which is usually not more than six months, subsequent to which a creditor's claim may be barred.
4. It is also the duty of the personal representative to pay out all legitimate claims and charges against the estate in the order of priority explained below.
5. Finally, the representative must identify the beneficiaries of the estate and distribute the properties when their respective rights have been determined.

The personal representative must exercise due care in administering the estate. He is fully accountable for managing the properties. Injury or damage to the estate resulting from his mismanagement or misconduct makes him personally liable for the loss. He has the duty to preserve the estate in the best way possible and to be prudent when probate expenses need to be incurred.

The personal representative is even liable for injury or damage to the estate resulting from misconduct by a person to whom he delegates his duties. In *Kaufman v. Kaufman's Administrator* (292 Ky. 351, 166 S.W.2d 860 [1942]), the decedent's son, a farmer with little knowledge of financial matters, reluctantly became the administrator of his father's estate. He agreed to serve as administrator only with the understanding that he could hire an attorney who would do most of the work. Despite his good name and reputation, the attorney embezzled the assets of the estate. The administrator was nevertheless held liable for the losses.

The representation of the estate terminates (1) when the court discharges the representative upon completion of the administration, (2) if the court grants the representative's request to resign, (3) if for some reason other than misconduct the court revokes the letters of representation, or (4) if the representative is removed by court order for reasons such as fraud, misappropriation, mismanagement, and conflict of interest.

Priority of Liabilities

The personal representative must pay all the decedent's debts before any distribution can take place. This is not too difficult if the estate's assets exceed the liabilities. But what is to happen if the estate has a negative equity and not all the creditors can be paid? Although state rules may differ, priority for the payment of debts is generally arranged as follows:

1. *Secured Debts.* Ordinarily a secured creditor will always be paid as long as the collateral is sufficient to cover the debt. If a mortgaged house is inherited or given away by a will, the beneficiary may usually assume the decedent's obligation under the mortgage arrangement, in which event the creditor's interest is not affected. If the house needs to be liquidated so that the decedent's equity in the property can be distributed, the sales proceeds will first be used to pay off the mortgage. Only the remainder belongs to the estate. If the sales proceeds are not sufficient to repay the entire mortgage obligation, the mortgagee becomes an unsecured creditor for the unpaid balance. Like other unsecured creditors, he ranks at the bottom of the list of priorities as far as the deficiency is concerned.

2. *Funeral and Burial Expenses.* Although funeral and burial of the decedent are usually arranged by the relatives before a personal representative is appointed, the decedent's estate must pay all the expenses duly incurred, including the cost or erecting a mausoleum, monument, or tombstone at the grave site.

3. *Administrative Expenses.* These are expenses related to the administration of the estate, such as court costs, costs of placing obituaries and notifying the creditors, costs of litigations brought by or against the estate, compensation for the personal representative, and attorney's fees.

4. *Family Allowance.* The decedent's spouse and children may need sustenance allowance while the estate is being administered. This financial assistance to the family is ordinarily recognized whether or not there is

a will and, if there is a will, whether or not the claimant is entitled to anything from the estate. The right to such an allowance, however, may be preempted by the claimant's adverse conduct, for instance, if a wife deserted the deceased husband before his death.

5. *Federal and Local Taxes.* These may consist of income, property, estate, and inheritance taxes. Payments due the United States may have priority over those due to state, county, and city governments.
6. *Expenses of the Last Illness.* These include medical expenses, such as physician's fees and hospital charges.
7. *Employee Salaries and Wages.* The decedent could have a business that employs people who have not been paid since the decedent died and his estate went into probate. While the personal representative without mandate by the will may not further conduct the business, he is, as a personal representative of the estate, obligated to pay the unpaid salaries and wages.
8. *Unsecured Debts.* After determining their validity, the personal representative pays all the unsecured claims.

If, under this system of priority, the proceeds of the estate are at a given stage insufficient to pay the claims of a certain class, these proceeds will then be divided pro rata among the claimants of this class. If the proceeds are enough to pay all the creditors in all the categories, the remaining proceeds will be distributed to the person or persons entitled to the estate under the will or under the law of inheritance. Upon proper publication of the decedent's death, there should normally be no creditors' claims after the estate has been distributed. Under the "Slayer's statutes," a person who murdered or feloniously caused the death of another person may not become a beneficiary of the victim's estate.

Questions

1. Who are heirs under the law of succession?
2. What is distribution per stirpes? What is distribution per capita?
3. Give a general description of the probate procedure.
4. What are the reasons for a representation of an estate to terminate?
5. Give a general picture of the priority of claims.

32.3 Trusts

Trust Defined

A trust is a legal device whereby a trustor—also known as the *settlor* or *grantor*—conveys his property in trust to a trustee for the benefit of a beneficiary. The device is used for various reasons, such as tax benefits and

Trust
A legal device for the management or distribution of property by a trustee for the benefit of one or more other persons.

Trustee
The manager and legal owner of property held for the benefit of another.

Trustor/Settlor
The originator of the trust, also called the settlor.

Beneficiary
The person for whose benefit a trust exists.

Cestui Que Trust
When the duration of a trust is measured by the life of the beneficiary.

Corpus
The assets in a trust.

avoidance of cumbersome probate proceedings. However, the basic idea is for a trustee to manage the trustor's property and take care of the beneficiary when the trustor himself is unable to do so because of prolonged illness, death, or other reasons.

The *trustee* may be anyone who is legally capable of holding title to property. Corporate trustees are sometimes preferred because of their expected perpetual existence. The trustee is a fiduciary of the trust beneficiary. His position calls for the highest standards of honesty, loyalty, and care.

The *beneficiary* of a trust may be any person, such as a minor child or a friend, or a group of persons, such as homeless people or university students. The beneficiary may also be an institution, such as a college, a church, a charitable organization, or a corporation. Dogs, cats, and other animals may be beneficiaries. The beneficiary is called *cestui que trust,* as the beneficiary's life or existence measures the duration of the trust.

The property entrusted to the trustee is called *trust corpus,* trust res, or trust estate. As the trustee usually manages the estate by investing the assets, the trust is ordinarily expected to generate income from interest earnings and other profits.

The settlor may appoint himself as trustee *or* as beneficiary. He cannot be both without defeating the basic purpose of a trust. The beneficiary may also be the trustee, although this is the exception rather than the rule.

Express Trusts

An express trust is created voluntarily by the settlor.

Validity Requirements

Several basic requirements need to be met for a trust to be valid.

1. The settlor must have interest in the property conveyed to the trust. The interest may be his ownership or some other rights, such as possessory or lien rights.

2. The settlor must have legal capacity to convey his interest in the property. The trustee, who is to transact business for the trust, must have contractual capacity to do so. However, the beneficiary who is to receive benefits from the trust is not required to have the capacity to hold property. Indeed, most trusts are established because of the beneficiary's lack of capacity or competence to handle business affairs.

3. The settlor must have the intention to create the trust. This intention may usually be determined from the provisions transferring the assets to the trust, specifying the duties of the trustee, and designating the beneficiary.

4. The beneficiary must be clearly identified. The settlor may name primary and contingent beneficiaries and may make himself a beneficiary.

5. The trust must be for a lawful purpose. A trust is void if it is created to violate a statutory or case law. It may also be voided and set aside if it contradicts public policy or if it is contrary to general morality.

Types of Trusts

A trust is a flexible device. There is a great variety of trusts to accommodate all kinds of purposes. A living trust, or an *inter vivos trust,* is created to operate during the lifetime of the settlor. A trust that is to take effect only upon the settlor's death is called a *testamentary trust.* This trust is created by a declaratory instrument that becomes an adjunct to the settlor's will that conveys the assets to the trust. It is possible that in addition to a living trust, the settlor wishes by testamentary disposition to add all or part of his remaining assets to it. This is called *pour-over trust.*

A *private trust* names one or more private individuals as beneficiaries who may be the settlor's spouse or children. The duration of such trust is usually limited by the rule against perpetuities which requires that the interest in the property conveyed must vest only for a maximum period measured by the life or lives of the beneficiary(ies) existing at the time of the inception of the trust plus twenty-one years.

A *charitable trust* is established to advance the public welfare or the public good. This includes such trusts as those that benefit religion; poor people; people suffering from a certain disease; cultural and educational institutions, including their teachers and students; public cemeteries; the construction and maintenance of certain public buildings, monuments, and facilities such as playgrounds; and organizations to prevent cruelty to animals. Assets transferred to charities may pass tax free. Unless specifically prohibited by the terms of the trust, a charitable trust does not automatically terminate in the event the initial purpose can no longer be attained or if the intended beneficiary no longer exists. Under the *cy pres doctrine,* the court will in such a situation designate another purpose or another beneficiary most similar or nearest to the original one specified in the trust.

Living Trust
More properly called an *inter-vivos* trust; a trust created during the lifetime of the trustor. It may continue beyond the trustor's lifetime.

Testamentary Trust
A trust created by a will or other testamentary document to take effect only after the death of the trustor.

Pour-Over Trust
When by testamentary disposition decedent's assets are to be added to an existing living trust.

Private Trust
Has private individual(s) as beneficiary(ies).

Charitable Trust
Is established to advance public welfare or public good.

Cy Pres Doctrine
Allows the court to designate another purpose most similar to the original one that can no longer be attained.

Wesley United Methodist Church v. Harvard College
366 Mass. 247, 316 N.E.2d 620 (1974).

Tauro, Chief Justice This is a bill in equity brought by the board of trustees of the Wesley United Methodist Church, as trustees under a charitable trust created by the will of one Harold E. Colson, seeking modification of the terms of the trust under the doctrine of cy pres. The defendant Harvard College did not file an answer, and the Attorney General waived his right to be heard. G.L. c. 12, § 8. The sole heirs at law of Harold E. Colson, Harold C. Guppy, Sr., and Mary F. Smith, contend that the doctrine of cy pres is inapplicable and that a resulting trust should be declared in their favor. The Probate Court granted the plaintiff the requested relief, and the heirs at law have appealed. We affirm.

The case is before us on a statement of agreed material facts which may be summarized as follows. Harold E. Colson died on December 28, 1968. His will, executed in September, 1957, contained the following provision: "Fourth: All the rest, residue and remainder of my estate, of whatsoever kind and wheresoever situate, I give, devise and bequeath unto Wesley Methodist Church of Salem, Massachusetts, to be used by the Board of Trustees of said church to establish a fund to be designated as the 'Frances L. Colson Memorial Scholarship Fund' and both the principal and income of such fund shall be used by said Board of Trustees to provide one five-hundred dollar scholarship each year to assist one worthy male member of the congregation or communicant of said church, to be selected each year at the discretion of said Board of Trustees, to attend Harvard College, Cambridge, Massachusetts for undergraduate education. In the event that the annual income from said fund shall exceed five hundred dollars, then the income in excess of that required for the scholarship above referred to shall be accumulated until such excess income exceeds the sum of five hundred dollars, at which time said Board of Trustees may, at its discretion, provide a second five-hundred-dollar scholarship, subject to the qualifications and limitations as above provided."

Frances L. Colson was the testator's mother. Both she and the testator had been members of the Wesley United Methodist Church, he having joined on December 29, 1907. When his will was executed in September, 1957, the decedent had a small estate, with modest investment in United States Savings Bonds. In time, his net worth increased significantly, and as of July 11, 1972, the funds given to the Wesley United Methodist Church for trust purposes exceeded $55,000, producing an annual income approximating $3,200.

To date, the church has given out no scholarships. In fact, it has not even received any applications from students or prospective students. It has only 236 members, most of whom are adults. The tuition charge at Harvard College has risen substantially since 1957, and as of 1973 was $2,600 a year. In 1957 the college did not admit women, but it does today.

The Probate Court found that "the express terms of the trust . . . are literally impracticable of operation in limiting the beneficiaries to male members or communicants of Wesley Methodist Church," and that "the testator's intention to provide scholarships for students attending Harvard College as a memorial for his mother may be fulfilled to promote and accomplish the general charitable intent of the testator under the application of cy pres." It was ordered that "the Board of trustees of the Petitioner apply income and accumulations of the trust fund in the awarding of annual scholarships, in their discretion, unlimited in amount, to worthy male or female applicants, not restricted to members or communicants of the petitioner if there are no such applicants, for undergraduate or graduate education in Harvard University."

. . . We hold that the Probate court's findings were warranted and the decree was not erroneous. . . . (W)e believe that the settlor displayed a general charitable intent, as distinguished from an intent "limited to . . . a specific charitable purpose." . . .

We are satisfied that the settlor would have wished that the funds be applied to a like charitable purpose rather than be removed from charitable use entirely. . . .

In view of the foregoing, we conclude that the case was a proper one for the application of the cy pres doctrine. . . .

Decree affirmed.

In *Trammell* v. *Elliott* (230 Ga. 841, 199 S.E.2d 194 [Georgia, 1973]), a decedent's will partially provided as follows:

All funds remaining after the aforementioned bequests are made or set aside, I wish made into an Endowment or Scholarship Fund in memory of my parents, the late William and Frances McCord Boyd, of Newton County, Georgia, said fund to be known as the Boyd-McCord Memorial Scholarship and placed with the Trustees of the Georgia Institute of Technology, Emory University, and Agnes Scott College, in equal proportions, to manage and keep reports on same. This scholarship is set side for benefit of deserving and qualified poor *white* boys and girls and interest only is to be used for said scholarships. [Emphasis supplied.]

The Georgia appeals court held that the mere existence of the racial classification was not sufficient to rebut the inference of general charitable intent. It affirmed the trial's court application of the *cy pres* doctrine by excluding the illegal racial reference from the charitable grant.

A trust may be *revocable* or *irrevocable*. If it is irrevocable, it may not be terminated during the specified period of time. Revocability or irrevocability may result in different tax consequences.

A trust may be *discretionary* or *nondiscretionary*. A discretionary trust gives the trustee a broad mandate to invest in a way he sees fit. A nondiscretionary trust instructs the trustee to make investments only as specifically directed, such as in IBM stock, municipal bonds, certificates of deposits, or gold. The trustee normally charges more on a discretionary trust, as it entails more efforts and responsibility.

Discretionary Trust
Allows the trustee to manage the trust in a way he sees fit.

With a *spendthrift trust,* the settlor usually intends to protect the beneficiary from irresponsible spending habits by prohibiting him to borrow or assign his interest in the trust, while his creditors are also barred from reaching it. The settlor may be even more strict by instructing the trustee to provide the beneficiary allowance only as necessary or to pay only those beneficiary expenses that he approves.

Spendthrift Trust
Prohibits the beneficiary to borrow or assign his interest in the trust.

A *tentative trust* or a *Totten trust,* which name is derived from a New York case, is a customer trust account at a bank or savings and loan. That account's name may read "Maggie Jones, in trust for Marie Jones." Maggie Jones is then trustor and trustee at the same time, and she alone may withdraw funds from the account or close it entirely. If Maggie Jones dies, the account belongs to Marie Jones, but not before Maggie's creditors have been paid. There is no trust created as far as creditors and taxes are concerned. Like any other trust, the assets of a tentative trust are excluded from probate.

Tentative Trust/Totten Trust
Customer trust account at a bank.

Facts

A decedent, Charles Wright, had a savings account at the Farmers State Bank which bore the name "Charles Wright, Pay on Death to Mary Lowe." Charles did not intend Mary to withdraw funds from the account while he was alive. When he died, he left a will giving the entire estate to his sons. The savings account was not mentioned. Mary as well as the sons claimed the assets in the account.

Decision

There was a tentative trust in favor of Mary. As Charles did not terminate the account when he was alive, the trust was never revoked. Also, there were no claims made by Charles's creditors. Thus, when Charles died, the title to the account transferred to Mary as the named beneficiary.

In re *Wright's Estate,* 17 Ill.App.3d 894, 308 N.E.2d 319 (1974).

To prevent conflict of interest, government ethics regulation may require a high-ranking government official to establish a *blind trust* to which he transfers his holdings, such as stocks and bonds, to a trustee. The trustee manages these assets for him during his tenure with the government. The settlor is not allowed to give the trustee any instructions or to advise on

Blind Trust
A trust providing for management solely by the trustee with no instructions or interference by the trustor.

investments, nor is he supposed to discuss financial matters with the trustee. The trustee is to provide the settlor periodic statements on the state of affairs and condition of the trust.

Form

A written trust is called a *trust declaration,* trust agreement, or deed of trust. No particular form or language is prescribed. A testamentary trust must always be in writing, since it is to accompany the settlor's last will. A formal trust declaration is usually witnessed. A trust does not always have to be in writing, however. An *inter vivos* trust conveying personal property may be created orally as long as the requirements of its validity are met.

Facts

A day before his death, decedent Cabaniss handed some endorsed checks over to his daughter Stephanie for her to set up a joint checking account with Carla, another daughter who was incompetent. He also wrote to his attorney requesting him to assist Stephanie in opening such an account. In this letter, he stated that Stephanie was "to act as trustee and withdrawals are to be used only for the benefit of Carla." The following day Cabaniss committed suicide. At issue was whether the checks in Stephanie's possession belonged to Cabaniss's estate or whether the checks were trust assets that had passed without probate.

Decision

An oral *inter vivos* trust was created for Carla's benefit. The court held that "decedent adequately manifested his intention to create a trust and subsequently complied with the formalities necessary to bring about that result. In his oral declarations to Stephanie and in his letters executed in Stephanie's presence, decedent imperatively and unambiguously designated his daughter Carla as beneficiary, appointed Stephanie trustee, and identified the endorsed checks as the trust property. Simultaneously, decedent unconditionally negotiated the checks to Stephanie by endorsing them in blank and by delivering them to, and leaving them in, Stephanie's exclusive possession."

Cabaniss v. *Cabaniss,* 464 A.2d 87 (D.C.App. 1983).

Depending upon the intention expressed in the trust instrument, a trust may even exist without a formal conveyance of the property to the trust estate. In *Barnette* v. *McNulty* (21 Ariz.App. 127, 516 P.2d 583 [1973]), a husband and owner of an incorporated business executed before he died a trust declaration acknowledging that he was holding 201 shares of his company as trustee for his wife. However, the stock certificates remained in his name. They were never transferred to the trust, and the corporation was never informed of any change of stock ownership. The court decided in favor of the surviving spouse/beneficiary. Since the husband was the original owner of the property and was also the trustee, no transfer was necessary for the trust estate to exist. Moreover, since it was an *inter vivos* trust established when the husband/settlor and trustee was still alive and since it did not involve any real property, the trust could be established orally.

Trustee's Powers

In addition to the express powers granted by the trust decree, the trustee may also exercise implied powers that are necessary to carry out the purpose of the trust. If the trustee is honest and capable, it would obviously be advantageous for the trust if the trustee had broad discretionary powers. It is equally obvious that such broad powers may easily be abused, particularly with a testamentary trust. A trustee is not liable for failing to use his discretionary powers.

The court may apply the *cy pres* doctrine if the circumstances during the life of a nondiscretionary trust have changed so as to render the execution of the express powers impossible, obsolete, or harmful to the trust estate. For example, a trustee may be instructed to invest in a certain company stock only, and the company has now gone bankrupt, or the investment directed by the nondiscretionary trust has deteriorated so much that to continue would jeopardize the well-being of the trust. His fiduciary duty may require the trustee in such a situation to obtain new instructions from the court. Most jurisdictions acknowledge this so-called *prudent man rule*.

Trustee's Duties

In administering the estate, the trustee is a fiduciary who owes the trust beneficiary honesty and loyalty. He is to protect and preserve the trust estate with reasonable care. In *Witmer* v. *Blair* (588 S.W.2d 222 [Missouri, 1979]), a trustee who innocently failed to deposit trust money in an interest-bearing bank account was held liable for the amount of interest that could have been earned had the funds been invested in an interest-yielding savings account. The emphasis is on negligence. As long as the trustee is not negligent, a loss to the trust *per se* does not amount to liability.

Facts

The Ettingers had a trust for the benefit of Bohart, their granddaughter. The principal asset of the trust consisted of Prentice-Hall stock. Settlors were the founders of this publishing firm. In 1965, United States Trust was appointed as the corporate trustee. Subsequently, the granddaughter died, and the entire trust estate became payable to her children. They claimed that the trustee breached its fiduciary duty in failing to diversify the trust assets. Prentice-Hall stock sold for $18.50 a share in 1965. By January 1970, the stock was worth $52.00, but after a few years of wide fluctuations, it went down to $24.00 in 1979, when the trust was to be distributed.

Decision

Judgment for United States Trust. It is true that United States Trust was accorded discretionary powers, but the trust instrument also provided: "The Trustee is specifically authorized to continue to hold the property as received from the Settlors. . . ." Accordingly, the court concluded that preserving family control over the company was an important part of the settlors' motivation. "While, in retrospect, the value of the trust could have been maximized had the plaintiff divined the downward course of the stock market in the 1970's, we cannot say that it abused the discretion specifically granted it in continuing to hold Prentice-Hall stock. 'A trustee is neither the insurer nor the guarantor of the value of a trust's assets. A trustee's performance is not judged by success or failure, and while negligence may result in liability, a mere error in judgment will not.' . . ."

United States Trust Co. v. *Bohart*, 197 Conn. 34, 495 A.2d 1034 (1985).

Without a specific court order, the trustee may not sell anything to or buy anything from the trust, nor is he allowed to engage in competition with the estate. He may not obtain any secret profits. He may not disclose to other parties information that may harm the trust. He does not escape liability by delegating his duties to another person. The trustee must account for all the assets of the trust. He may not comingle his personal or other accounts with the trust account. In *Northwestern Mutual Life Insurance Company v. Wiemer* (96 Ill.App.3d 549, 52 Ill.Dec. 139, 421 N.E.2d 1002 [1981]), a trustee was held guilty of self-dealing in violation of its fiduciary duty. The trust involved a farm on which Northwestern had a first mortgage of $70,000 and Havana Bank, the trustee, had a second mortgage. When the settlor died, Havana took $8,000 from the trust account to pay itself part of the second mortgage. This was not only violative of the trustee's duty to pay the first mortgage first, but it was also a classic case of a breach of trust.

The trustee has the duty to provide information to interested parties regarding the trust estate. He must also allow the settlor and the beneficiary to inspect the trust records. The trustee must defend the trust against unwarranted claims by third parties. On the other hand, he must take reasonable steps to enforce legitimate claims of the trust.

For all these duties and responsibilities, the trustee receives compensation that may be statutorily regulated. The larger the estate, the smaller the compensation percentage usually becomes. Nowadays, corporate trustees entertain estates in the millions of dollars.

A trustee designated in the trust instrument may accept or reject the appointment. A testamentary trust ordinarily names substitute or successor trustee(s). Also, the court may appoint a substitute trustee if the trust instrument fails to designate one.

Beneficiary

When a settlor conveys his interest in property to a trust, the trustee has the legal title to the property, while the beneficiary obtains the *equitable* or beneficial *interest* in the estate. Except when a spendthrift trust is involved, the beneficiary may usually transfer or assign, and third-party creditors may seize his beneficial interest for the payment of his debts.

In the event that the trust is created specifically to benefit a person during his lifetime, the trust terminates when the person dies. The trust corpus will then be distributed. If the trust designates a contingent or successor beneficiary, the primary beneficiary is the life tenant of the beneficial interest, and the successor the remainderman. If the trust has two or more primary beneficiaries, there is a cotenancy of the beneficial interest, by which they become either joint tenants, tenants in common, or otherwise. If the beneficiary is a thing, such as a tombstone or an animal, the trust is called an *honorary trust*. Although the beneficiary in this situation is incapable of enforcing the beneficial rights, a trust as such is generally recognized.

Honorary Trust
Designates a thing or an animal as beneficiary.

Remedies

The beneficiary and other interested parties may sue the trustee. The remedies available in the event of a trustee's breach of trust, misconduct, or mismanagement include money damages, injunction preventing the trustee from further damaging the trust estate, recovery of stolen or embezzled trust property, removal, and probably criminal prosecution. In *In the Estate of Gump* (180 Cal.Rptr. 219 [1982]), where the Wells Fargo Bank as a testamentary trustee negligently accepted an underpayment of rent on behalf of the trust, the court stated that the trustee could be charged for the shortage.

Termination

A trust may be set up for a certain period of time. It subsequently terminates. A trust also terminates if the objective becomes impossible or illegal to achieve. Termination of a trust may take place by revocation in the event that the trust is revocable as well as by a merger whereby the settlor becomes trustee and beneficiary at the same time. Finally, if continuation of the trust does not serve any purpose, the beneficiary may request its termination.

The trust instrument usually specifies how the trust corpus is to be distributed by the trustee upon termination. The property does not have to be distributed to the same beneficiary(ies) who benefited during the life of the trust. If the settlor did not give any such instructions, the property upon termination of the trust reverts back to the settlor's estate.

Implied Trusts

Trusts may be implied by operation of the law. There are two types of implied trusts: (1) resulting trusts and (2) constructive trusts.

Resulting Trusts

A resulting trust is based on the settlor's presumed or implied intent. This is manifested when the settlor disposes of certain property under circumstances indicating his intention that the property is ultimately to be returned to him or to be further transferred under his direction. This happens, for instance, if an owner of property conveys his title to another person for tax purposes or when a person asks another to keep his belongings while he is away for a while. Such a bailment is based on trust, and the bailee can be held liable as trustee.

Resulting Trust
Is created by circumstances indicating trustor's implied intention to have the property ultimately returned to him.

Constructive Trusts

A constructive trust, on the other hand, is a remedial device to redress a wrong or to prevent unjust enrichment. When property is unlawfully or unfairly acquired, the holder may be considered a constructive trustee for the person to whom the property actually belongs.

Constructive Trust
Is created to redress a wrong or to prevent unjust enrichment.

Facts

Counts and Leonard had agreed that the latter would bid for both of them on a tract of land being offered at an auction. They would jointly acquire title to the land and partition it, by which Counts would have the use of the rear portion, with a forty-foot easement over Leonard's front portion for a right-of-way to the public road. The bid was successful, but Leonard's wife complained about the sharing of the land with Counts. Without notifying Counts, Leonard obtained a deed conveying the entire tract to himself and his wife as tenants by the entirety with the right of survivorship. Subsequently, Leonard offered Counts a deed conveying the parcel with an easement of thirty feet rather than forty feet, including restrictions that would unreasonably limit Counts's use of his portion of the land.

Decision

Judgment for Counts. The court found that the Leonards had title to the real parcel of the land as constructive trustees for Counts. "The principle applicable to this class of contracts is stated in A.L.I. Restatement, Restitution § 194(2), p. 795, as follows: 'A person who agrees with another to purchase property on behalf of the other and purchases the property for himself individually holds it upon a constructive trust for the other, even though he is not under a duty to purchase the property for the other.' . . . A constructive trust arises not only when there has been actual fraud, but whenever one holding title to property 'is subject to an equitable duty to convey it to another on the ground that he would be unjustly enriched if he were permitted to retain it.' Scott, *supra*, § 462 at 3413."

Leonard v. Counts, 221 Va. 582, 272 S.E.2d 190 (1980).

QUESTIONS

1. What is a trust, and what are the requirements of its validity?
2. What is an *inter vivos*, testamentary, pour-over, private, discretionary, spendthrift, tentative, and honorary trust?
3. Please explain the *cy pres* doctrine. Give a case example.
4. Describe the trustee's duties.
5. What are implied trusts? Please explain.

PROBLEMS

1. Mary Houser was judicially declared incompetent ten years ago. Her sister Anna was appointed the guardian and served in this capacity until Mary died recently. Mary executed a will three years ago, leaving her entire estate to Anna. Mary left one son, who deserted her long ago. He reappeared and contested the will. Decision?

2. Mr. Dunhill, a widower in his nineties, had a will leaving his estate to two grandchildren. He had a few friends, but he was the closest with Mr. Bear, a somewhat younger man, who was with Mr. Dunhill every day to accompany and help him in many ways. Without formally revoking the existing will, Mr. Dunhill executed a subsequent will naming Mr. Bear as his sole beneficiary. He used to tell his friends that he would not even recognize his grandchildren, since they never came to visit him. Mr. Dunhill remained physically and mentally healthy until he died a year ago. The grandchildren contested the second will on the grounds that the former was never revoked, that Mr. Dunhill was already old and lacked testamentary capacity when he executed the second will, and that he was unduly influenced by Mr. Bear. Decision?

3. Mrs. Berry died intestate without leaving any relatives. She always told her neighbors that she would like her helper Sarah to have her house and all her personal belongings, but she never put her wishes in writing. What is going to happen with her estate?

4. Mrs. Faith bought from a stationery store a preprinted will form. She completed the essential parts in longhand, signed the paper, and kept it in one of her cabinet drawers. The document was never witnessed, and no one knew about it. Is it a valid will?

5. Mr. Brooks had a will leaving all his properties to Mrs. Brooks. The Brookses were subsequently divorced, and there was a property settlement. Since Mr. Brooks still cared for his ex-wife, he left the will as it was until he died. The couple's only daughter believed she and not her mother should inherit her father's property, and she therefore contested the father's will. Decision?

6. In his will, Mr. Booker left his hardware store to his son Hank, $70,000 to his daughter Marie, and the remainder to his daughter Anabela. When business deteriorated, he sold the store. When he died, the balance of his estate after all the expenses was

$20,000. How should this remaining money be distributed?

7. Bill Dooley died intestate as a bachelor. Both his parents predeceased him. He left one uncle Abe on his father's side who had two children Bruce and Connie, one sister Dianne who was not married, and one brother Ed who had one daughter Francis. There were two brothers who predeceased him. One had two daughters, Georgia and Ivonne, the other had four children, Jonathan, Kay, Lena, and Maude. How would a stirpital distribution be executed?

8. Van Overveen designated the Girls' Study Fund of Santa Maria Catholic High as beneficiary of his testamentary trust. Twenty years after his death, the school became co-ed, and the girls' study fund was replaced by the Catholic Scholarship Fund. Mr. Overveen's children requested the court to distribute the assets of the trust to them, since the beneficiary originally designated by the trust no longer existed. Decision?

9. Mary Calhoun purchased a certificate of deposit in the amount of $10,000 from Apple Valley Bank. The name on the certificate read: "Mary Calhoun, trustee for Vicky Calhoun." Vicky was Mary's daughter. One day, Mary was involved in a serious car accident and was in a coma for a number of weeks. As money was needed for her mother's medical expenses, Vicky went to the bank to redeem the certificate of deposit. The bank refused her because she was only 17. Decision?

10. Mr. Hara's testamentary trust consisted exclusively of IBM, GE, and AT&T stocks. The estate was worth about $300,000 in 1972 when he died. As trustee, Global Trust Incorporated, a well-established and reputable company, was given discretionary powers to buy and sell any stocks listed in the major stock exchanges. The only beneficiary of the trust, Mr. Hara's son Michael, was to receive $5,000 annually from the trust income derived from the stock dividends. The trustee genuinely attempted to preserve the estate the best way possible, but its repeated misjudgments and continuing misfortune as well as the stock market slump of the 70s caused the estate to shrink to about $50,000 in 1980. As the dividend income became insufficient to cover the $5,000 annual distribution, Michael sued the trustee on the ground of mismanagement. He contended that had the trustee done nothing but simply invest the estate in an interest-bearing bank account, the $300,000 would have grown to at least $500,000 in the 1980s. Decision?

Appendix A

The Constitution of the United States

Preamble

We the People of the United States, in Order to form a more perfect Union, establish Justice, insure domestic Tranquility, provide for the common defence, promote the general Welfare, and secure the Blessings of Liberty to ourselves and our Posterity, do ordain and establish this Constitution for the United States of America.

Article I

Section 1. All legislative Powers herein granted shall be vested in a Congress of the United States, which shall consist of a Senate and House of Representatives.

Section 2. The House of Representatives shall be composed of Members chosen every second Year by the People of the several States, and the Electors in each State shall have the Qualifications requisite for Electors of the most numerous Branch of the State Legislature.

No Person shall be a Representative who shall not have attained to the Age of twenty five Years, and been seven Years a Citizen of the United States, and who shall not, when elected, be an Inhabitant of that State in which he shall be chosen.

Representatives and direct Taxes shall be apportioned among the several States which may be included within this Union, according to their respective Numbers, which shall be determined by adding to the whole Number of free Persons, including those bound to Service for a Term of Years, and excluding Indians not taxed, three fifths of all other Persons. The actual Enumeration shall be made within three Years after the first Meeting of the Congress of the United States, and within every subsequent Term of ten Years, in such Manner as they shall by Law direct. The Number of Representatives shall not exceed one for every thirty Thousand, but each State shall have at Least one Representative; and until such enumeration shall be made, the State of New Hampshire shall be entitled to chuse three, Massachusetts eight, Rhode Island and Providence Plantations one, Connecticut five, New York six, New Jersey four, Pennsylvania eight, Delaware one, Maryland six, Virginia ten, North Carolina five, South Carolina five, and Georgia three.

When vacancies happen in the Representation from any State, the Executive Authority thereof shall issue Writs of Election to fill such Vacancies.

The House of Representatives shall chuse their Speaker and other Officers; and shall have the sole Power of Impeachment.

Section 3. The Senate of the United States shall be composed of two Senators from each State, chosen by the Legislature thereof, for six Years; and each Senator shall have one Vote.

Immediately after they shall be assembled in Consequence of the first Election, they shall be divided as equally as may be into three Classes. The Seats of the Senators of the first Class shall be vacated at the Expiration of the second Year, of the second Class at the Expiration of the fourth Year, and of the third Class at the Expiration of the sixth Year, so that one third may be chosen every second Year; and if Vacancies happen by Resignation, or otherwise, during the Recess of the Legislature of any State, the Executive thereof may make temporary Appointments until the next Meeting of the Legislature, which shall then fill such Vacancies.

No Person shall be a Senator who shall not have attained to the Age of thirty Years, and been nine Years a Citizen of the United States, and who shall not, when elected, be an Inhabitant of that State for which he shall be chosen.

The Vice President of the United States shall be President of the Senate, but shall have no Vote, unless they be equally divided.

The Senate shall chuse their other Officers, and also a President pro tempore, in the Absence of the Vice President, or when he shall exercise the Office of President of the United States.

The Senate shall have the sole Power to try all Impeachments. When sitting for that Purpose, they shall be on Oath or Affirmation. When the President of the United States is tried, the Chief Justice shall preside: And no Person shall be convicted without the Concurrence of two thirds of the Members present.

Judgment in Cases of Impeachment shall not extend further than to removal from Office, and disqualification to hold and enjoy any Office of honor, Trust, or Profit under the United States: but the Party convicted shall nevertheless be liable and subject to Indictment, Trial, Judgment, and Punishment, according to Law.

Section 4. The Times, Places and Manner of holding Elections for Senators and Representatives, shall be prescribed in each State by the Legislature thereof; but the Congress may at any time by Law make or alter such Regulations, except as to the Places of chusing Senators.

The Congress shall assemble at least once in every Year, and such Meeting shall be on the first Monday in December, unless they shall by Law appoint a different Day.

Section 5. Each House shall be the Judge of the Elections, Returns, and Qualifications of its own Members, and a Majority of each shall constitute a Quorum to do Business; but a smaller Number may adjourn from day to day, and may be authorized to compel the Attendance of absent Members, in such Manner, and under such Penalties as each House may provide.

Each House may determine the Rules of its Proceedings, punish its Members for disorderly Behavior, and, with the Concurrence of two thirds, expel a Member.

Each House shall keep a Journal of its Proceedings, and from time to time publish the same, excepting such Parts as may in their Judgment require Secrecy; and the Yeas and Nays of the Members of either House on any question shall, at the Desire of one fifth of those Present, be entered on the Journal.

Neither House, during the Session of Congress, shall, without the Consent of the other, adjourn for more than three days, nor to any other Place than that in which the two Houses shall be sitting.

Section 6. The Senators and Representatives shall receive a Compensation for their Services, to be ascertained by Law, and paid out of the Treasury of the United States. They shall in all Cases, except Treason, Felony and Breach of the Peace, be privileged from Arrest during their Attendance at the Session of their respective Houses, and in going to and returning from the same; and for any Speech or Debate in either House, they shall not be questioned in any other Place.

No Senator or Representative shall, during the Time for which he was elected, be appointed to any civil Office under the Authority of the United States, which shall have been created, or the Emoluments whereof shall have been increased during such time; and no Person holding any Office under the United States, shall be a Member of either House during his Continuance in Office.

Section 7. All Bills for raising Revenue shall originate in the House of Representatives; but the Senate may propose or concur with Amendments as on other Bills.

Every Bill which shall have passed the House of Representatives and the Senate, shall, before it become a Law, be presented to the President of the United States; If he approve he shall sign it, but if not he shall return it, with his Objections to the House in which it shall have originated, who shall enter the Objections at large on their Journal, and proceed to reconsider it. If after such Reconsideration two thirds of that House shall agree to pass the Bill, it shall be sent together with the Objections, to the other House, by which it shall likewise be reconsidered, and if approved by two thirds of that House, it shall become a Law. But in all such Cases the Votes of both Houses shall be determined by Yeas and Nays, and the Names of the Persons voting for and against the Bill shall be entered on the Journal of each House respectively. If any Bill shall not be returned by the President within ten Days (Sundays excepted) after it shall have been presented to him, the Same shall be a Law, in like Manner as if he had signed it, unless the Congress by their Adjournment prevent its Return in which Case it shall not be a Law.

Every Order, Resolution, or Vote, to Which the Concurrence of the Senate and House of Representatives may be necessary (except on a question of Adjournment) shall be presented to the President of the United States; and before the Same shall take Effect, shall be approved by him, or being disapproved by him, shall be repassed by two thirds of the Senate and House of Representatives, according to the Rules and Limitations prescribed in the Case of a Bill.

Section 8. The Congress shall have Power To lay and collect Taxes, Duties, Imposts and Excises, to pay the Debts and provide for the common Defence and

Commerce Clause

general Welfare of the United States; but all Duties, Imposts and Excises shall be uniform throughout the United States;

To borrow Money on the credit of the United States;

To regulate Commerce with foreign Nations, and among the several States, and with the Indian Tribes;

To establish an uniform Rule of Naturalization, and uniform Laws on the subject of Bankruptcies throughout the United States;

To coin Money, regulate the Value thereof, and of foreign Coin, and fix the Standard of Weights and Measures;

To provide for the Punishment of counterfeiting the Securities and current Coin of the United States;

To establish Post Offices and post Roads;

To promote the Progress of Science and useful Arts, by securing for limited Times to Authors and Inventors the exclusive Right to their respective Writings and Discoveries;

To constitute Tribunals inferior to the supreme Court;

To define and punish Piracies and Felonies committed on the high Seas, and Offenses against the Law of Nations;

To declare War, grant Letters of Marque and Reprisal, and make Rules concerning Captures on Land and Water;

To raise and support Armies, but no Appropriation of Money to that Use shall be for a longer Term than two Years;

To provide and maintain a Navy;

To make Rules for the Government and Regulation of the land and naval Forces;

To provide for calling forth the Militia to execute the Laws of the Union, suppress Insurrections and repel Invasions;

To provide for organizing, arming, and disciplining, the Militia, and for governing such Part of them as may be employed in the Service of the United States, reserving to the States respectively, the Appointment of the Officers, and the Authority of training the Militia according to the discipline prescribed by Congress;

To exercise exclusive Legislation in all Cases whatsoever, over such District (not exceeding ten Miles square) as may, by Cession of particular States, and the Acceptance of Congress, become the Seat of the Government of the United States, and to exercise like Authority over all Places purchased by the Consent of the Legislature of the State in which the Same shall be, for the Erection of Forts, Magazines, Arsenals, dock-Yards, and other needful Buildings;—And

To make all Laws which shall be necessary and proper for carrying into Execution the foregoing Powers, and all other Powers vested by this Constitution in the Government of the United States, or in any Department or Officer thereof.

Section 9. The Migration or Importation of such Persons as any of the States now existing shall think proper to admit, shall not be prohibited by the Congress prior to the Year one thousand eight hundred and eight, but a Tax or duty may be imposed on such Importation, not exceeding ten dollars for each Person.

The privilege of the Writ of Habeas Corpus shall not be suspended, unless when in Cases of Rebellion or Invasion the public Safety may require it.

No Bill of Attainder or ex post facto Law shall be passed.

No Capitation, or other direct, Tax shall be laid, unless in Proportion to the Census or Enumeration herein before directed to be taken.

No Tax or Duty shall be laid on Articles exported from any State.

No Preference shall be given by any Regulation of Commerce or Revenue to the Ports of one State over those of another: nor shall Vessels bound to, or from, one State be obliged to enter, clear, or pay Duties in another.

No Money shall be drawn from the Treasury, but in Consequence of Appropriations made by Law; and a regular Statement and Account of the Receipts and Expenditures of all public Money shall be published from time to time.

No Title of Nobility shall be granted by the United States: And no Person holding any Office of Profit or Trust under them, shall, without the Consent of the Congress, accept of any present, Emolument, Office, or Title, of any kind whatever, from any King, Prince, or foreign State.

Section 10. No State shall enter into any Treaty, Alliance, or Confederation; grant Letters of Marque and Reprisal; coin Money; emit Bills of Credit; make any Thing but gold and silver Coin a Tender in Payment of Debts; pass any Bill of Attainder, ex post facto Law, or Law impairing the Obligation of Contracts, or grant any Title of Nobility.

No State shall, without the Consent of the Congress, lay any Imposts or Duties on Imports or Exports, except what may be absolutely necessary for executing it's inspection Laws: and the net Produce of all Duties and Imposts, laid by any State on Imports or Exports, shall be for the Use of the Treasury of the United States; and all such Laws shall be subject to the Revision and Controul of the Congress.

No State shall, without the Consent of Congress, lay any Duty of Tonnage, keep Troops, or Ships of War in time of Peace, enter into any Agreement or Compact with another State, or with a foreign Power, or engage in War, unless actually invaded, or in such imminent Danger as will not admit of delay.

Article II

Section 1. The executive Power shall be vested in a President of the United States of America. He shall hold his Office during the Term of four Years, and, together with the Vice President, chosen for the same Term, be elected, as follows:

Each State shall appoint, in such Manner as the Legislature thereof may direct, a Number of Electors, equal to the whole Number of Senators and Representatives to which the State may be entitled in the Congress; but no Senator or Representative, or Person holding an Office of Trust or Profit under the United States, shall be appointed an Elector.

The Electors shall meet in their respective States, and vote by Ballot for two Persons, of whom one at least shall not be an Inhabitant of the same State with themselves. And they shall make a List of all the Persons voted for, and of the Number of Votes for each; which List they shall sign and certify, and transmit sealed to the Seat of the Government of the United States, directed to the President of the Senate. The President of the Senate shall, in the Presence of the Senate and House of Representatives, open all the Certificates, and the Votes shall then be counted. The Person having the greatest Number of Votes shall be the President, if such Number be a Majority of the whole Number of Electors appointed; and if there be more than one who have such Majority, and have an equal Number of Votes, then the House of Representatives shall immediately chuse by Ballot one of them for President; and if no Person have a Majority, then from the five highest on the List the said House shall in like Manner chuse the President. But in chusing the President, the Votes shall be taken by States, the Representation from each State having one Vote; A quorum for this Purpose shall consist of a Member or Members from two thirds of the States, and a Majority of all the States shall be necessary to a Choice. In every Case, after the Choice of the President, the Person having the greater Number of Votes of the Electors shall be the Vice President. But if there should remain two or more who have equal Votes, the Senate shall chuse from them by Ballot the Vice President.

The Congress may determine the Time of chusing the Electors, and the Day on which they shall give their Votes; which Day shall be the same throughout the United States.

No person except a natural born Citizen, or a Citizen of the United States, at the time of the Adoption of this Constitution, shall be eligible to the Office of President; neither shall any Person be eligible to that Office who shall not have attained to the Age of thirty five Years, and been fourteen Years a Resident within the United States.

In Case of the Removal of the President from Office, or of his Death, Resignation or Inability to discharge the Powers and Duties of the said Office, the Same shall devolve on the Vice President, and the Congress may by Law provide for the Case of Removal, Death, Resignation or Inability, both of the President and Vice President, declaring what Officer shall then act as President, and such Officer shall act accordingly, until the Disability be removed, or a President shall be elected.

The President shall, at stated Times, receive for his Services, a Compensation, which shall neither be increased nor diminished during the Period for which he shall have been elected, and he shall not receive within that Period any other Emolument from the United States, or any of them.

Before he enter on the Execution of his Office, he shall take the following Oath or Affirmation: "I do solemnly swear (or affirm) that I will faithfully execute the Office of President of the United States, and will to the best of my Ability, preserve, protect and defend the Constitution of the United States."

Section 2. The President shall be Commander in Chief of the Army and Navy of the United States, and of the militia of the several States, when called into the actual Service of the United States; he may require the Opinion, in writing, of the principal Officer in each of the executive Departments, upon any Subject relating to the Duties of their respective Offices, and he shall have Power to grant Reprieves and Pardons for Offenses against the United States, except in Cases of Impeachment.

He shall have Power, by and with the Advice and Consent of the Senate to make Treaties, provided two thirds of the Senators present concur; and he shall nominate, and by and with the Advice and Consent of the Senate, shall appoint Ambassadors, other public Ministers and Consuls, Judges of the supreme Court, and all other Officers of the United States, whose Appointments are not herein otherwise provided for, and which shall be established by Law; but the Congress may by Law vest the Appointment of such inferior Officers, as they think proper, in the President alone, in the Courts of Law, or in the Heads of Departments.

The President shall have Power to fill up all Vacancies that may happen during the Recess of the Senate, by granting Commissions which shall expire at the End of their next Session.

Section 3. He shall from time to time give to the Congress Information of the State of the Union, and recommend to their Consideration such Measures as he shall judge necessary and expedient; he may, on extraordinary Occasions, convene both Houses, or either of them, and in Case of Disagreement between them, with Respect to the Time of Adjournment, he may adjourn them to such Time as he shall think proper; he shall receive Ambassadors and other public Ministers; he shall take Care that the Laws be faithfully executed, and shall Commission all the Officers of the United States.

Section 4. The President, Vice President and all civil Officers of the United States, shall be removed from Office on Impeachment for, and Conviction of, Treason, Bribery, or other high Crimes and Misdemeanors.

Article III

Section 1. The judicial Power of the United States, shall be vested in one supreme Court, and in such inferior Courts as the Congress may from time to time ordain and establish. The Judges, both of the supreme and inferior Courts, shall hold their Offices during good Behaviour, and shall, at stated Times, receive for their Services a Compensation, which shall not be diminished during their Continuance in Office.

Section 2. The judicial Power shall extend to all Cases, in Law and Equity, arising under this Constitution, the Laws of the United States, and Treaties made, or which shall be made, under their Authority;—to all Cases affecting Ambassadors, other public Ministers and Consuls;—to all Cases of admiralty and maritime Jurisdiction;—to Controversies to which the United States shall be a Party;—to Controversies between two or more States;—between a State and Citizens of another State;—between Citizens of different States;—between Citizens of the same State claiming Lands under Grants of different States, and between a State, or the Citizens thereof, and foreign States, Citizens or Subjects.

In all Cases affecting Ambassadors, other public Ministers and Consuls, and those in which a State shall be a Party, the supreme Court shall have original Jurisdiction. In all the other Cases before mentioned, the supreme Court shall have appellate Jurisdiction, both as to Law and Fact, with such Exceptions, and under such Regulations as the Congress shall make.

The Trial of all Crimes, except in Cases of Impeachment, shall be by Jury; and such Trial shall be held in the State where the said Crimes shall have been committed; but when not committed within any State, the Trial shall be at such Place or Places as the Congress may by Law have directed.

Section 3. Treason against the United States, shall consist only in levying War against them, or, in adhering to their Enemies, giving them Aid and Comfort. No Person shall be convicted of Treason unless on the Testimony of two Witnesses to the same overt Act, or on Confession in open Court.

The Congress shall have Power to declare the Punishment of Treason, but no Attainder of Treason shall work Corruption of Blood, or Forfeiture except during the Life of the Person attainted.

Article IV

Section 1. Full Faith and Credit shall be given in each State to the public Acts, Records, and judicial Proceedings of every other State. And the Congress may by general Laws prescribe the Manner in which such Acts, Records and Proceedings shall be proved, and the Effect thereof.

Section 2. The Citizens of each State shall be entitled to all Privileges and Immunities of Citizens in the several States.

A Person charged in any State with Treason, Felony, or other Crime, who shall flee from Justice, and be found in another State, shall on Demand of the executive Authority of the State from which he fled, be delivered up, to be removed to the State having Jurisdiction of the Crime.

No Person held to Service or Labour in one State, under the Laws thereof, escaping into another, shall, in Consequence of any Law or Regulation therein, be discharged from such Service or Labour, but shall be delivered up on Claim of the Party to whom such Service or Labour may be due.

Section 3. New States may be admitted by the Congress into this Union; but no new State shall be formed or erected within the Jurisdiction of any other State; nor any State be formed by the Junction of two or more States, or Parts of States, without the Consent of the Legislatures of the States concerned as well as of the Congress.

The Congress shall have Power to dispose of and make all needful Rules and Regulations respecting the Territory or other Property belonging to the United States; and nothing in this Constitution shall be so construed as to Prejudice any Claims of the United States, or of any particular State.

Section 4. The United States shall guarantee to every State in this Union a Republican Form of Government, and shall protect each of them against Invasion; and on Application of the Legislature, or of the Executive (when the Legislature cannot be convened) against domestic Violence.

Article V

The Congress, whenever two thirds of both Houses shall deem it necessary, shall propose Amendments to this Constitution, or, on the Application of the Legislatures of two thirds of the several States, shall call a Convention for proposing Amendments, which, in either Case, shall be valid to all Intents and Purposes, as part of this Constitution, when ratified by the Legislatures of three fourths of the several States, or by Conventions in three fourths thereof, as the one or the other Mode of Ratification may be proposed by the Congress; Provided that no Amendment which may be made prior to the Year One thousand eight hundred and eight shall in any Manner affect the first and fourth Clauses in the Ninth Section of the first Article; and that no State, without its Consent, shall be deprived of its equal Suffrage in the Senate.

Article VI

All Debts contracted and Engagements entered into, before the Adoption of this Constitution shall be as valid against the United States under this Constitution, as under the Confederation.

This Constitution, and the Laws of the United States which shall be made in Pursuance thereof; and all Treaties made, or which shall be made, under the Authority of the United States, shall be the supreme Law of the Land; and the Judges in every State shall be bound thereby, any Thing in the Constitution or Laws of any State to the Contrary notwithstanding.

The Senators and Representatives before mentioned, and the Members of the several State Legislatures, and all executive and judicial Officers, both of the United States and of the several States, shall be bound by Oath or Affirmation, to support this Constitution; but no religious Test shall ever be required as a Qualification to any Office or public Trust under the United States.

Article VII

The Ratification of the Conventions of nine States shall be sufficient for the Establishment of this Constitution between the States so ratifying the Same.

Amendment I [1791]

Congress shall make no law respecting an establishment of religion, or prohibiting the free exercise thereof; or abridging the freedom of speech, or of the press; or the right of the people peaceably to assembly, and to petition the Government for a redress of grievances.

Amendment II [1791]

A well regulated Militia, being necessary to the security of a free State, the right of the people to keep and bear Arms, shall not be infringed.

Amendment III [1791]

No Soldier shall, in time of peace be quartered in any house, without the consent of the Owner, nor in time of war, but in a manner to be prescribed by law.

Amendment IV [1791]

The right of the people to be secure in their persons, houses, papers, and effects, against unreasonable searches and seizures, shall not be violated, and no Warrants shall issue, but upon probable cause, supported by Oath or affirmation, and particularly describing the place to be searched, and the persons or things to be seized.

Amendment V [1791]

No person shall be held to answer for a capital, or otherwise infamous crime, unless on a presentment or indictment of a Grand Jury, except in cases arising in the land or naval forces, or in the Militia, when in actual service in time of War or public danger; nor shall any person be subject for the same offence to be twice put in jeopardy of life or limb; nor shall be compelled in any criminal case to be a witness against himself, nor be deprived of life, liberty, or property, without due process of law; nor shall private property be taken for public use, without just compensation.

Amendment VI [1791]

In all criminal prosecutions, the accused shall enjoy the right to a speedy and public trial, by an impartial jury of the State and district wherein the crime shall have been committed, which district shall have been previously ascertained by law, and to be informed of the nature and cause of the accusation; to be confronted with the witnesses against him; to have compulsory process for obtaining witnesses in his favor, and to have the Assistance of Counsel for his defence.

Amendment VII [1791]

In Suits at common law, where the value in controversy shall exceed twenty dollars, the right of trial by jury shall be preserved, and no fact tried by jury, shall be otherwise re-examined in any Court of the United States, than according to the rules of the common law.

Amendment VIII [1791]

Excessive bail shall not be required, nor excessive fines imposed, nor cruel and unusual punishments inflicted.

Amendment IX [1791]

The enumeration in the Constitution, of certain rights, shall not be construed to deny or disparage others retained by the people.

Amendment X [1791]

The powers not delegated to the United States by the Constitution, nor prohibited by it to the States, are reserved to the States respectively, or to the people.

Amendment XI [1798]

The Judicial power of the United States shall not be construed to extend to any suit in law or equity, commenced or prosecuted against one of the United States by Citizens of another State, or by Citizens or Subjects of any Foreign State.

Amendment XII [1804]

The Electors shall meet in their respective states, and vote by ballot for President and Vice-President, one of whom, at least, shall not be an inhabitant of the same state with themselves; they shall name in their ballots the person voted for as President, and in distinct ballots the person voted for as Vice-President, and they shall make distinct lists of all persons voted for as President, and of all persons voted for as Vice-President, and of the number of votes for each, which lists they shall sign and certify, and transmit sealed to the seat of the government of the United States, directed to the President of the Senate;—The President of the Senate shall, in the presence of the Senate and House of Representatives, open all the certificates and the votes shall then be counted;—The person having the greatest number of votes for President, shall be the President, if such number be a majority of the whole number of Electors appointed; and if no person have such majority, then from the persons having the highest numbers not exceeding three on the list of those voted for as President, the House of Representatives shall choose immediately, by ballot, the President. But in choosing the President, the votes shall be taken by states, the representation from each state having one vote; a quorum for this purpose shall consist of a member or members from two-thirds of the states, and a majority of all states shall be necessary to a choice. And if the House of Representatives shall not choose a President whenever the right of choice shall devolve upon them, before the fourth day of March next following, then the Vice-President shall act as President, as in the case of the death or other constitutional disability of the President.—The person having the greatest number of votes as Vice-President, shall be the Vice-President, if such number be a majority of the whole number of Electors appointed, and if no person have a majority, then from the two highest numbers on the list, the Senate shall choose the Vice-President; a quorum for the purpose shall consist of two-thirds of the whole number of Senators, and a majority of the whole number shall be necessary to a choice. But no person constitutionally ineligible to the office of President shall be eligible to that of Vice-President of the United States.

Amendment XIII [1865]

Section 1. Neither slavery nor involuntary servitude, except as a punishment for crime whereof the party shall have been duly convicted, shall exist within the United States, or any place subject to their jurisdiction.

Section 2. Congress shall have power to enforce this article by appropriate legislation.

Amendment XIV [1868]

Section 1. All persons born or naturalized in the United States, and subject to the jurisdiction thereof, are citizens of the United States and of the State wherein they reside. No State shall make or enforce any law which shall abridge the privileges or immunities of citizens of the United States; nor shall any State deprive any person of life, liberty, or property, without due process of law; nor deny to any person within its jurisdiction the equal protection of the laws.

Section 2. Representatives shall be apportioned among the several States according to their respective numbers, counting the whole number of persons in each State, excluding Indians not taxed. But when the right to vote at any election for the choice of electors for President and Vice President of the United States, Representatives in Congress, the Executive and Judicial officers of a State, or the members of the Legislature thereof, is denied to any of the male inhabitants of such State, being twenty-one years of age, and citizens of the United States, or in any way abridged, except for participation in rebellion, or other crime, the basis of representation therein shall be reduced in the proportion which the number of such male citizens shall bear to the whole number of male citizens twenty-one years of age in such State.

Section 3. No person shall be a Senator or Representative in Congress, or elector of President and Vice President, or hold any office, civil or military, under the United States, or under any State, who having previously taken an oath, as a member of Congress, or as an officer of the United States, or as a member of any State legislature, or as an executive or judicial officer of any State, to support the Constitution of the United States, shall have engaged in insurrection or rebellion against the same, or given aid or comfort to the enemies thereof. But Congress may by a vote of two-thirds of each House, remove such disability.

Section 4. The validity of the public debt of the United States, authorized by law, including debts incurred for payment of pensions and bounties for services in suppressing insurrection or rebellion, shall not be questioned. But neither the United States nor any State shall assume or pay any debt or obligation incurred in aid of insurrection or rebellion against the United States, or any claim for the loss or emancipation of any slave; but all such debts, obligations and claims shall be held illegal and void.

Section 5. The Congress shall have power to enforce, by appropriate legislation, the provisions of this article.

Amendment XV [1870]

Section 1. The right of citizens of the United States to vote shall not be denied or abridged by the United States or by any State on account of race, color, or previous condition of servitude.

Section 2. The Congress shall have power to enforce this article by appropriate legislation.

Amendment XVI [1913]

The Congress shall have power to lay and collect taxes on incomes, from whatever source derived, without apportionment among the several States, and without regard to any census or enumeration.

Amendment XVII [1913]

[1] The Senate of the United States shall be composed of two Senators from each State, elected by the people thereof, for six years; and each Senator shall have one vote. The electors in each State shall have the qualifications requisite for electors of the most numerous branch of the State legislatures.

[2] When vacancies happen in the representation of any State in the Senate, the executive authority of such State shall issue writs of election to fill such vacancies: *Provided*, That the legislature of any State may empower the executive thereof to make temporary appointments until the people fill the vacancies by election as the legislature may direct.

[3] This amendment shall not be so construed as to affect the election or term of any Senator chosen before it becomes valid as part of the Constitution.

Amendment XVIII [1919]

Section 1. After one year from the ratification of this article the manufacture, sale, or transportation of intoxicating liquors within, the importation thereof into, or the exportation thereof from the United States and all territory subject to the jurisdiction thereof for beverage purposes is hereby prohibited.

Section 2. The Congress and the several States shall have concurrent power to enforce this article by appropriate legislation.

Section 3. This article shall be inoperative unless it shall have been ratified as an amendment to the Constitution by the legislatures of the several States, as provided in the Constitution, within seven years from the date of the submission hereof to the States by the Congress.

Amendment XIX [1920]

[1] The right of citizens of the United States to vote shall not be denied or abridged by the United States or by any State on account of sex.

[2] Congress shall have power to enforce this article by appropriate legislation.

Amendment XX [1933]

Section 1. The terms of the President and Vice President shall end at noon on the 20th day of January, and the terms of Senators and Representatives at noon on the 3d day of January, of the years in which such terms would have ended if this article had not been ratified; and the terms of their successors shall then begin.

Section 2. The Congress shall assemble at least once in every year, and such meeting shall begin at noon on the 3d day of January, unless they shall by law appoint a different day.

Section 3. If, at the time fixed for the beginning of the term of the President, the President elect shall have died, the Vice President elect shall become President. If the President shall not have been chosen before the time fixed for the beginning of his term, or if the President elect shall have failed to qualify, then the Vice President elect shall act as President until a President shall have qualified; and the Congress may by law provide for the case wherein neither a President elect nor a Vice President elect shall have qualified, declaring who shall then act as President, or the manner in which one who is to act shall be selected, and such person shall act accordingly until a President or Vice President shall have qualified.

Section 4. The Congress may by law provide for the case of the death of any of the persons from whom the House of Representatives may choose a President whenever the right of choice shall have devolved upon them, and for the case of the death of any of the persons from whom the Senate may choose a Vice President whenever the right of choice shall have devolved upon them.

Section 5. Sections 1 and 2 shall take effect on the 15th day of October following the ratification of this article.

Section 6. This article shall be inoperative unless it shall have been ratified as an amendment to the Constitution by the legislatures of three-fourths of the several States within seven years from the date of its submission.

Amendment XXI [1933]

Section 1. The eighteenth article of amendment to the Constitution of the United States is hereby repealed.

Section 2. The transportation or importation into any State, Territory, or possession of the United States for delivery or use therein of intoxicating liquors, in violation of the laws thereof, is hereby prohibited.

Section 3. This article shall be inoperative unless it shall have been ratified as an amendment to the Constitution by conventions in the several States, as provided in the Constitution, within seven years from the date of the submission hereof to the States by the Congress.

Amendment XXII [1951]

Section 1. No person shall be elected to the office of the President more than twice, and no person who has held the office of President, or acted as President, for more than two years of a term to which some other person was elected President shall be elected to the office of President more than once. But this Article shall not apply to any person holding the office of President when this Article was proposed by the Congress, and shall not prevent any person who may be holding the office of President, or acting as President, during the term within which this Article becomes operative from holding the office of President or acting as President during the remainder of such term.

Section 2. This article shall be inoperative unless it shall have been ratified as an amendment to the Constitution by the legislatures of three-fourths of the several States within seven years from the date of its submission to the States by the Congress.

Amendment XXIII [1961]

Section 1. The District constituting the seat of Government of the United States shall appoint in such manner as the Congress may direct:

A number of electors of President and Vice President equal to the whole number of Senators and Representatives in Congress to which the District would be entitled if it were a State, but in no event more than the least populous state; they shall be in addition to those appointed by the states, but they shall be considered, for the purposes of the election of President and Vice President, to be electors appointed by a state; and they shall meet in the District and perform such duties as provided by the twelfth article of amendment.

Section 2. The Congress shall have power to enforce this article by appropriate legislation.

Amendment XXIV [1964]

Section 1. The right of citizens of the United States to vote in any primary or other election for President or Vice President, for electors for President or Vice President, or for Senator or Representative in Congress, shall not be denied or abridged by the United States, or any State by reason of failure to pay any poll tax or other tax.

Section 2. The Congress shall have power to enforce this article by appropriate legislation.

Amendment XXV [1967]

Section 1. In case of the removal of the President from office or of his death or resignation, the Vice President shall become President.

Section 2. Whenever there is a vacancy in the office of the Vice President, the President shall nominate a Vice President who shall take office upon confirmation by a majority vote of both Houses of Congress.

Section 3. Whenever the President transmits to the President pro tempore of the Senate and the Speaker of the House of Representatives his written declaration that he is unable to discharge the powers and duties of his office, and until he transmits to them a written declaration to the contrary, such powers and duties shall be discharged by the Vice President as Acting President.

Section 4. Whenever the Vice President and a majority of either the principal officers of the executive departments or of such other body as Congress may by law provide, transmit to the President pro tempore of the Senate and the Speaker of the House of Representatives their written declaration that the President is unable to discharge the powers and duties of his office, the Vice President shall immediately assume the powers and duties of the office as Acting President.

Thereafter, when the President transmits to the President pro tempore of the Senate and the Speaker of the House of Representatives his written declaration that no inability exists, he shall resume the powers and duties of his office unless the Vice President and a majority of either the principal officers of the executive department or of such other body as Congress may by law provide, transmit within four days to the President pro tempore of the Senate and the Speaker of the House of Representatives their written declaration and the President is unable to discharge the powers and duties of his office. Thereupon Congress shall decide the issue, assembling within forty-eight hours for that purpose if not in session. If the Congress, within twenty-one days after receipt of the latter written declaration, or, if Congress is not in session, within twenty-one days after Congress is required to assemble, determines by two-thirds vote of both Houses that the President is unable to discharge the powers and duties of his office, the Vice President shall continue to discharge the same as Acting President; otherwise, the President shall resume the powers and duties of his office.

Amendment XXVI [1971]

Section 1. The right of citizens of the United States, who are eighteen years of age or older, to vote shall not be denied or abridged by the United States or by any State on account of age.

Section 2. The Congress shall have power to enforce this article by appropriate legislation.

Appendix B

The Uniform Commercial Code

(Adopted in 52 jurisdictions; all 50 States, although Louisiana has adopted only Articles 1, 3, 4, 5, 7, 8 and 9; the District of Columbia, and the Virgin Islands.)

The Code consists of 11 Articles as follows:

Art.
1. GENERAL PROVISIONS
2. Sales
2A. Leases
3. Commercial Paper
4. Bank Deposits and Collections
4A. Funds Transfers
5. Letters of Credit
6. Bulk Transfers (including Alternative B)
7. Warehouse Receipts, Bills of Lading and Other Documents of Title
8. Investment Securities
9. Secured Transactions: Sales of Accounts and Chattel Paper
10. Effective Date and Repealer
11. Effective Date and Transition Provisions

Article 1
GENERAL PROVISIONS

Part 1 Short Title, Construction, Application and Subject Matter of the Act

§ 1—101. **Short Title.**

This Act shall be known and may be cited as Uniform Commercial Code.

Copyright © 1987 by the American Law Institute and the National Conference of Commissioners on Uniform State Laws. Reproduced with permission.

§ 1—102. **Purposes; Rules of Construction; Variation by Agreement.**

(1) This Act shall be liberally construed and applied to promote its underlying purposes and policies.

(2) Underlying purposes and policies of this Act are

(a) to simplify, clarify and modernize the law governing commercial transactions;

(b) to permit the continued expansion of commercial practices through custom, usage and agreement of the parties;

(c) to make uniform the law among the various jurisdictions.

(3) The effect of provisions of this Act may be varied by agreement, except as otherwise provided in this Act and except that the obligations of good faith, diligence, reasonableness and care prescribed by this Act may not be disclaimed by agreement but the parties may by agreement determine the standards by which the performance of such obligations is to be measured if such standards are not manifestly unreasonable.

(4) The presence in certain provisions of this Act of the words "unless otherwise agreed" or words of similar import does not imply that the effect of other provisions may not be varied by agreement under subsection (3).

(5) In this Act unless the context otherwise requires

(a) words in the singular number include the plural, and in the plural include the singular;

(b) words of the masculine gender include the feminine and the neuter, and when the sense so indicates words of the neuter gender may refer to any gender.

§ 1—103. **Supplementary General Principles of Law Applicable.**

Unless displaced by the particular provisions of this Act, the principles of law and equity, including the law merchant and the law relative to capacity to contract, principal and agent, estoppel, fraud, misrepresentation, duress, coercion, mistake, bankruptcy, or other validating or invalidating cause shall supplement its provisions.

§ 1—104. **Construction Against Implicit Repeal.**

This Act being a general act intended as a unified coverage of its subject matter, no part of it shall be deemed to be impliedly repealed by subsequent legislation if such construction can reasonably be avoided.

§ 1—105. **Territorial Application of the Act; Parties' Power to Choose Applicable Law.**

(1) Except as provided hereafter in this section, when a transaction bears a reasonable relation to this state and also to another state or nation the parties may agree that the law either of this state or of such other state or nation shall govern their rights and duties. Failing such agreement this Act applies to transactions bearing an appropriate relation to this state.

(2) Where one of the following provisions of this Act specifies the applicable law, that provision governs and a contrary agreement is effective only to the extent permitted by the law (including the conflict of laws rules) so specified:

> Rights of creditors against sold goods. Section 2—402.
>
> Applicability of the Article on Leases. Sections 2A—105 and 2A—106.
>
> Applicability of the Article on Bank Deposits and Collections. Section 4—102.
>
> Bulk transfers subject to the Article on Bulk Transfers. Section 6—102.
>
> Applicability of the Article on Investment Securities. Section 8—106.
>
> Perfection provisions of the Article on Secured Transactions. Section 9—103.

§ 1—106. **Remedies to Be Liberally Administered.**

(1) The remedies provided by this Act shall be liberally administered to the end that the aggrieved party may be put in as good a position as if the other party had fully performed but neither consequential or special nor penal damages may be had except as specifically provided in this Act or by other rule of law.

(2) Any right or obligation declared by this Act is enforceable by action unless the provision declaring it specifies a different and limited effect.

§ 1—107. **Waiver or Renunciation of Claim or Right After Breach.**

Any claim or right arising out of an alleged breach can be discharged in whole or in part without consideration by a written waiver or renunciation signed and delivered by the aggrieved party.

§ 1—108. **Severability.**

If any provision or clause of this Act or application thereof to any person or circumstances is held invalid, such invalidity shall not affect other provisions or applications of the Act which can be given effect without the invalid provision or application, and to this end the provisions of this Act are declared to be severable.

§ 1—109. **Section Captions.**

Section captions are parts of this Act.

Part 2 General Definitions and Principles of Interpretation

§ 1—201. **General Definitions.**

Subject to additional definitions contained in the subsequent Articles of this Act which are applicable to specific Articles or Parts thereof, and unless the context otherwise requires, in this Act:

(1) "Action" in the sense of a judicial proceeding includes recoupment, counterclaim, set-off, suit in equity and any other proceedings in which rights are determined.

(2) "Aggrieved party" means a party entitled to resort to a remedy.

(3) "Agreement" means the bargain of the parties in fact as found in their language or by implication from other circumstances including course of dealing or usage of trade or course of performance as provided in this Act (Sections 1—205 and 2—208). Whether an agreement has legal consequences is determined by the provisions of this Act, if applicable; otherwise by the law of contracts (Section 1—103). (Compare "Contract".)

(4) "Bank" means any person engaged in the business of banking.

(5) "Bearer" means the person in possession of an instrument, document of title, or certificated security payable to bearer or indorsed in blank.

(6) "Bill of lading" means a document evidencing the receipt of goods for shipment issued by a person engaged in the business of transporting or forwarding goods, and includes an airbill. "Airbill" means a document serving for air transportation as a bill of lading does for marine or rail transportation, and includes an air consignment note or air waybill.

(7) "Branch" includes a separately incorporated foreign branch of a bank.

(8) "Burden of establishing" a fact means the burden of persuading the triers of fact that the existence of the fact is more probable than its non-existence.

(9) "Buyer in ordinary course of business" means a person who in good faith and without knowledge that the sale to him is in violation of the ownership rights or security interest of a third party in the goods buys in ordinary course from a person in the business of selling goods of that kind but does not include a pawnbroker. All persons who sell minerals or the like (including oil and gas) at wellhead or minehead shall be deemed to be persons in the business of selling goods of that kind. "Buying" may be for cash or by exchange of other property or on secured or unsecured credit and includes receiving goods or documents of title under a pre-existing contract for sale but does not include a transfer in bulk or as security for or in total or partial satisfaction of a money debt.

(10) "Conspicuous": A term or clause is conspicuous when it is so written that a reasonable person against whom it is to operate ought to have noticed it. A printed heading in capitals (as: NON-NEGOTIABLE BILL OF LADING) is conspicuous. Language in the body of a form is "conspicuous" if it is in larger or other contrasting type or color. But in a telegram any stated term is "conspicuous". Whether a term or clause is "conspicuous" or not is for decision by the court.

(11) "Contract" means the total legal obligation which results from the parties' agreement as affected by this Act and any other applicable rules of law. (Compare "Agreement".)

(12) "Creditor" includes a general creditor, a secured creditor, a lien creditor and any representative of creditors, including an assignee for the benefit of creditors, a trustee in bankruptcy, a receiver in equity and an executor or administrator of an insolvent debtor's or assignor's estate.

(13) "Defendant" includes a person in the position of defendant in a cross-action or counterclaim.

(14) "Delivery" with respect to instruments, documents of title, chattel paper, or certificated securities means voluntary transfer of possession.

(15) "Document of title" includes bill of lading, dock warrant, dock receipt, warehouse receipt or order for the delivery of goods, and also any other document which in the regular course of business or financing is treated as adequately evidencing that the person in possession of it is entitled to receive, hold and dispose of the document and the goods it covers. To be a document of title a document must purport to be issued by or addressed to a bailee and purport to cover goods in the bailee's possession which are either identified or are fungible portions of an identified mass.

(16) "Fault" means wrongful act, omission or breach.

(17) "Fungible" with respect to goods or securities means goods or securities of which any unit is, by nature or usage of trade, the equivalent of any other like unit. Goods which are not fungible shall be deemed fungible for the purposes of this Act to the extent that under a particular agreement or document unlike units are treated as equivalents.

(18) "Genuine" means free of forgery or counterfeiting.

(19) "Good faith" means honesty in fact in the conduct or transaction concerned.

(20) "Holder" means a person who is in possession of a document of title or an instrument or a certificated investment security drawn, issued, or indorsed to him or his order or to bearer or in blank.

(21) To "honor" is to pay or to accept and pay, or where a credit so engages to purchase or discount a draft complying with the terms of the credit.

(22) "Insolvency proceedings" includes any assignment for the benefit of creditors or other proceedings intended to liquidate or rehabilitate the estate of the person involved.

(23) A person is "insolvent" who either has ceased to pay his debts in the ordinary course of business or cannot pay his debts as they become due or is insolvent within the meaning of the federal bankruptcy law.

(24) "Money" means a medium of exchange authorized or adopted by a domestic or foreign government as a part of its currency.

(25) A person has "notice" of a fact when

(a) he has actual knowledge of it; or

(b) he has received a notice or notification of it; or

(c) from all the facts and circumstances known to him at the time in question he has reason to know that it exists.

A person "knows" or has "knowledge" of a fact when he has actual knowledge of it. "Discover" or "learn" or a word or phrase of similar import refers to knowledge rather than to reason to know. The time and circumstances under which a notice or notification may cease to be effective are not determined by this Act.

(26) A person "notifies" or "gives" a notice or notification to another by taking such steps as may be reasonably required to inform the other in ordinary course whether or not such other actually comes to know of it. A person "receives" a notice or notification when

(a) it comes to his attention; or

(b) it is duly delivered at the place of business through which the contract was made or at any other place held out by him as the place for receipt of such communications.

(27) Notice, knowledge or a notice or notification received by an organization is effective for a particular transaction from the time when it is brought to the attention of the individual conducting that transaction, and in any event from the time when it would have been brought to his attention if the organization had exercised due diligence. An organization exercises due diligence if it maintains reasonable routines for communicating significant information to the person conducting the transaction and there is reasonable compliance with the routines. Due diligence does not require an individual acting for the organization to communicate information unless such communication is part of his regular duties or unless he has reason to know of the transaction and that the transaction would be materially affected by the information.

(28) "Organization" includes a corporation, government or governmental subdivision or agency, business trust, estate, trust, partnership or association, two or more persons having a joint or common interest, or any other legal or commercial entity.

(29) "Party", as distinct from "third party", means a person who has engaged in a transaction or made an agreement within this Act.

(30) "Person" includes an individual or an organization (See Section 1—102).

(31) "Presumption" or "presumed" means that the trier of fact must find the existence of the fact presumed unless and until evidence is introduced which would support a finding of its non-existence.

(32) "Purchase" includes taking by sale, discount, negotiation, mortgage, pledge, lien, issue or re-issue, gift or any other voluntary transaction creating an interest in property.

(33) "Purchaser" means a person who takes by purchase.

(34) "Remedy" means any remedial right to which an aggrieved party is entitled with or without resort to a tribunal.

(35) "Representative" includes an agent, an officer of a corporation or association, and a trustee, executor or administrator of an estate, or any other person empowered to act for another.

(36) "Rights" includes remedies.

(37) "Security interest" means an interest in personal property or fixtures which secures payment or performance of an obligation. The retention or reservation of title by a seller of goods notwithstanding shipment or delivery to the buyer (Section 2—401) is limited in effect to a reservation of a "security interest". The term also includes any interest of a buyer of accounts or chattel paper which is subject to Article 9. The special property interest of a buyer of goods on identification of those goods to a contract for sale under Section 2—401 is not a "security interest", but a buyer may also acquire a "security interest" by complying with Article 9. Unless a consignment is intended as security, reservation of title thereunder is not a "security interest," but a consignment is in any event subject to the provisions on consignment sales (Section 2—326).

Whether a transaction creates a lease or security interest is determined by the facts of each case; however, a transaction creates a security interest if the consideration the lessee is to pay the lessor for the right to possession and use of the goods is an obligation for the term of the lease not subject to termination by the lessee, and

(a) the original term of the lease is equal to or greater than the remaining economic life of the goods,

(b) the lessee is bound to renew the lease for the remaining economic life of the goods or is bound to become the owner of the goods,

(c) the lessee has an option to renew the lease for the remaining economic life of the goods for no additional consideration or nominal additional consideration upon compliance with the lease agreement, or

(d) the lessee has an option to become the owner of the goods for no additional consideration or nominal additional consideration upon compliance with the lease agreement.

A transaction does not create a security interest merely because it provides that

(a) the present value of the consideration the lessee is obligated to pay the lessor for the right to possession and use of the goods is substantially equal to or is greater than the fair market value of the goods at the time the lease is entered into,

(b) the lessee assumes risk of loss of the goods, or agrees to pay taxes, insurance, filing, recording, or registration fees, or service or maintenance costs with respect to the goods,

(c) the lessee has an option to renew the lease or to become the owner of the goods,

(d) the lessee has an option to renew the lease for a fixed rent that is equal to or greater than the reasonably predictable fair market rent for the use of the goods for the term of the renewal at the time the option is to be performed, or

(e) the lessee has an option to become the owner of the goods for a fixed price that is equal to or greater than the reasonably predictable fair market value of the goods at the time the option is to be performed.

For purposes of this subsection (37):

(x) Additional consideration is not nominal if (i) when the option to renew the lease is granted to the lessee the rent is stated to be the fair market rent for the use of the goods for the term of the renewal determined at the time the option is to be performed, or (ii) when the option to become the owner of the goods is granted to the lessee the price is stated to be the fair market value of the goods determined at the time the option is to be performed. Additional consideration is nominal if it is less than the lessee's reasonably predictable cost of performing under the lease agreement if the option is not exercised;

(y) "Reasonably predictable" and "remaining economic life of the goods" are to be determined with reference to the facts and circumstances at the time the transaction is entered into; and

(z) "Present value" means the amount as of a date certain of one or more sums payable in the future, discounted to the date certain. The discount is determined by the interest rate specified by the parties if the rate is not manifestly unreasonable at the time the transaction is entered into; otherwise, the discount is determined by a commercially reasonable rate that takes into account the facts and circumstances of each case at the time the transaction was entered into.

(38) "Send" in connection with any writing or notice means to deposit in the mail or deliver for transmission by any other usual means of communication with postage or cost of transmission provided for and properly addressed and in the case of an instrument to an address specified thereon or otherwise agreed, or if there be none to any address reasonable under the circumstances. The receipt of any writing or notice within the time at which it would have arrived if properly sent has the effect of a proper sending.

(39) "Signed" includes any symbol executed or adopted by a party with present intention to authenticate a writing.

(40) "Surety" includes guarantor.

(41) "Telegram" includes a message transmitted by radio, teletype, cable, any mechanical method of transmission, or the like.

(42) "Term" means that portion of an agreement which relates to a particular matter.

(43) "Unauthorized" signature or indorsement means one made without actual, implied or apparent authority and includes a forgery.

(44) "Value". Except as otherwise provided with respect to negotiable instruments and bank collections (Sections 3—303, 4—208 and 4—209) a person gives "value" for rights if he acquires them

(a) in return for a binding commitment to extend credit or for the extension of immediately available credit whether or not drawn upon and whether or not a chargeback is provided for in the event of difficulties in collection; or

(b) as security for or in total or partial satisfaction of a pre-existing claim; or

(c) by accepting delivery pursuant to a preexisting contract for purchase; or

(d) generally, in return for any consideration sufficient to support a simple contract.

(45) "Warehouse receipt" means a receipt issued by a person engaged in the business of storing goods for hire.

(46) "Written" or "writing" includes printing, typewriting or any other intentional reduction to tangible form.

Amended in 1962, 1972, 1977, and 1987.

§ 1—202. **Prima Facie Evidence by Third Party Documents.**

A document in due form purporting to be a bill of lading, policy or certificate of insurance, official weigher's or inspector's certificate, consular invoice, or any other document authorized or required by the contract to be issued by a third party shall be prima facie evidence of its own authenticity and genuineness and of the facts stated in the document by the third party.

§ 1—203. **Obligation of Good Faith.**

Every contract or duty within this Act imposes an obligation of good faith in its performance or enforcement.

§ 1—204. **Time; Reasonable Time; "Seasonably".**

(1) Whenever this Act requires any action to be taken within a reasonable time, any time which is not manifestly unreasonable may be fixed by agreement.

(2) What is a reasonable time for taking any action depends on the nature, purpose and circumstances of such action.

(3) An action is taken "seasonably" when it is taken at or within the time agreed or if no time is agreed at or within a reasonable time.

§ 1—205. **Course of Dealing and Usage of Trade.**

(1) A course of dealing is a sequence of previous conduct between the parties to a particular transaction which is fairly to be regarded as establishing a common basis of understanding for interpreting their expressions and other conduct.

(2) A usage of trade is any practice or method of dealing having such regularity of observance in a place, vocation or trade as to justify an expectation that it will be ob-

served with respect to the transaction in question. The existence and scope of such a usage are to be proved as facts. If it is established that such a usage is embodied in a written trade code or similar writing the interpretation of the writing is for the court.

(3) A course of dealing between parties and any usage of trade in the vocation or trade in which they are engaged or of which they are or should be aware give particular meaning to and supplement or qualify terms of an agreement.

(4) The express terms of an agreement and an applicable course of dealing or usage of trade shall be construed wherever reasonable as consistent with each other; but when such construction is unreasonable express terms control both course of dealing and usage of trade and course of dealing controls usage trade.

(5) An applicable usage of trade in the place where any part of performance is to occur shall be used in interpreting the agreement as to that part of the performance.

(6) Evidence of a relevant usage of trade offered by one party is not admissible unless and until he has given the other party such notice as the court finds sufficient to prevent unfair surprise to the latter.

§ 1—206. **Statute of Frauds for Kinds of Personal Property Not Otherwise Covered.**

(1) Except in the cases described in subsection (2) of this section a contract for the sale of personal property is not enforceable by way of action or defense beyond five thousand dollars in amount or value of remedy unless there is some writing which indicates that a contract for sale has been made between the parties at a defined or stated price, reasonably identifies the subject matter, and is signed by the party against whom enforcement is sought or by his authorized agent.

(2) Subsection (1) of this section does not apply to contracts for the sale of goods (Section 2—201) nor of securities (Section 8—319) nor to security agreements (Section 9—203).

§ 1—207. **Performance or Acceptance Under Reservation of Rights.**

A party who with explicit reservation of rights performs or promises performance or assents to performance in a manner demanded or offered by the other party does not thereby prejudice the rights reserved. Such words as "without prejudice", "under protest" or the like are sufficient.

§ 1—208. **Option to Accelerate at Will.**

A term providing that one party or his successor in interest may accelerate payment or performance or require collateral or additional collateral "at will" or "when he deems himself insecure" or in words of similar import shall be construed to mean that he shall have power to do so only if he in good faith believes that the prospect of payment or performance is impaired. The burden of establishing lack of good faith is on the party against whom the power has been exercised.

§ 1—209. **Subordinated Obligations**

An obligation may be issued as subordinated to payment of another obligation of the person obligated, or a creditor may subordinate his right to payment of an obligation by agreement with either the person obligated or another creditor of the person obligated. Such a subordination does not create a security interest as against either the common debtor or a subordinated creditor. This section shall be construed as declaring the law as it existed prior to the enactment of this section and not as modifying it. Added 1966.

Note: *This new section is proposed as an optional provision to make it clear that a subordination agreement does not create a security interest unless so intended.*

Article 2
SALES

Part 1 Short Title, General Construction and Subject Matter

§ 2—101. **Short Title.**

This Article shall be known and may be cited as Uniform Commercial Code—Sales.

§ 2—102. **Scope; Certain Security and Other Transactions Excluded From This Article.**

Unless the context otherwise requires, this Article applies to transactions in goods; it does not apply to any transaction which although in the form of an unconditional contract to sell or present sale is intended to operate only as a security transaction nor does this Article impair or repeal any statute regulating sales to consumers, farmers or other specified classes of buyers.

§ 2—103. **Definitions and Index of Definitions.**

(1) In this Article unless the context otherwise requires

    (a) "Buyer" means a person who buys or contracts to buy goods.

    (b) "Good faith" in the case of a merchant means honesty in fact and the observance of reasonable commercial standards of fair dealing in the trade.

    (c) "Receipt" of goods means taking physical possession of them.

    (d) "Seller" means a person who sells or contracts to sell goods.

THE UNIFORM COMMERCIAL CODE

(2) Other definitions applying to this Article or to specified Parts thereof, and the sections in which they appear are:
"Acceptance". Section 2—606.
"Banker's credit". Section 2—325.
"Between merchants". Section 2—104.
"Cancellation". Section 2—106(4).
"Commercial unit". Section 2—105.
"Confirmed credit". Section 2—325.
"Conforming to contract". Section 2—106.
"Contract for sale". Section 2—106.
"Cover". Section 2—712.
"Entrusting". Section 2—403.
"Financing agency". Section 2—104.
"Future goods". Section 2—105.
"Goods". Section 2—105.
"Identification". Section 2—501.
"Installment contract". Section 2—612.
"Letter of Credit". Section 2—325.
"Lot". Section 2—105.
"Merchant". Section 2—104.
"Overseas". Section 2—323.
"Person in position of seller". Section 2—707.
"Present sale". Section 2—106.
"Sale". Section 2—106.
"Sale on approval". Section 2—326.
"Sale or return". Section 2—326.
"Termination". Section 2—106.

(3) The following definitions in other Articles apply to this Article:
"Check". Section 3—104.
"Consignee". Section 7—102.
"Consignor". Section 7—102.
"Consumer goods". Section 9—109.
"Dishonor". Section 3—507.
"Draft". Section 3—104.

(4) In addition Article 1 contains general definitions and principles of construction and interpretation applicable throughout this Article.

§ 2—104. Definitions: "Merchant"; "Between Merchants"; "Financing Agency".

(1) "Merchant" means a person who deals in goods of the kind or otherwise by his occupation holds himself out as having knowledge or skill peculiar to the practices or goods involved in the transaction or to whom such knowledge or skill may be attributed by his employment of an agent or broker or other intermediary who by his occupation holds himself out as having such knowledge or skill.

(2) "Financing agency" means a bank, finance company or other person who in the ordinary course of business makes advances against goods or documents of title or who by arrangement with either the seller or the buyer intervenes in ordinary course to make or collect payment due or claimed under the contract for sale, as by purchasing or paying the seller's draft or making advances against it or by merely taking it for collection whether or not documents of title accompany the draft. "Financing agency" includes also a bank or other person who similarly intervenes between persons who are in the position of seller and buyer in respect to the goods (Section 2—707).

(3) "Between merchants" means in any transaction with respect to which both parties are chargeable with the knowledge or skill of merchants.

§ 2—105. Definitions: Transferability; "Goods"; "Future" Goods; "Lot"; "Commercial Unit".

(1) "Goods" means all things (including specially manufactured goods) which are movable at the time of identification to the contract for sale other than the money in which the price is to be paid, investment securities (Article 8) and things in action. "Goods" also includes the unborn young of animals and growing crops and other identified things attached to realty as described in the section on goods to be severed from realty (Section 2—107).

(2) Goods must be both existing and identified before any interest in them can pass. Goods which are not both existing and identified are "future" goods. A purported present sale of future goods or of any interest therein operates as a contract to sell.

(3) There may be a sale of a part interest in existing identified goods.

(4) An undivided share in an identified bulk of fungible goods is sufficiently identified to be sold although the quantity of the bulk is not determined. Any agreed proportion of such a bulk or any quantity thereof agreed upon by number, weight or other measure may to the extent of the seller's interest in the bulk be sold to the buyer who then becomes an owner in common.

(5) "Lot" means a parcel or a single article which is the subject matter of a separate sale or delivery, whether or not it is sufficient to perform the contract.

(6) "Commercial unit" means such a unit of goods as by commercial usage is a single whole for purposes of sale and division of which materially impairs its character or value on the market or in use. A commercial unit may be a single article (as a machine) or a set of articles (as a suite of furniture or an assortment of sizes) or a quantity (as a bale, gross, or carload) or any other unit treated in use or in the relevant market as a single whole.

§ 2—106. Definitions: "Contract"; "Agreement"; "Contract for Sale"; "Sale"; "Present Sale"; "Conforming" to Contract; "Termination"; "Cancellation".

(1) In this Article unless the context otherwise requires "contract" and "agreement" are limited to those relating to the present or future sale of goods. "Contract for sale" includes both a present sale of goods and a contract to sell goods at a future time. A "sale" consists in the passing of title from the seller to the buyer for a price (Section 2—401). A "present sale" means a sale which is accomplished by the making of the contract.

(2) Goods or conduct including any part of a performance are "conforming" or conform to the contract when they are in accordance with the obligations under the contract.

(3) "Termination" occurs when either party pursuant to a power created by agreement or law puts an end to the contract otherwise than for its breach. On "termination" all obligations which are still executory on both sides are discharged but any right based on prior breach or performance survives.

(4) "Cancellation" occurs when either party puts an end to the contract for breach by the other and its effect is the same as that of "termination" except that the cancelling party also retains any remedy for breach of the whole contract or any unperformed balance.

§ 2—107. Goods to Be Severed From Realty: Recording.

(1) A contract for the sale of minerals or the like (including oil and gas) or a structure or its materials to be removed from realty is a contract for the sale of goods within this Article if they are to be severed by the seller but until severance a purported present sale thereof which is not effective as a transfer of an interest in land is effective only as a contract to sell.

(2) A contract for the sale apart from the land of growing crops or other things attached to realty and capable of severance without material harm thereto but not described in subsection (1) or of timber to be cut is a contract for the sale of goods within this Article whether the subject matter is to be severed by the buyer or by the seller even though it forms part of the realty at the time of contracting, and the parties can by identification effect a present sale before severance.

(3) The provisions of this section are subject to any third party rights provided by the law relating to realty records, and the contract for sale may be executed and recorded as a document transferring an interest in land and shall then constitute notice to third parties of the buyer's rights under the contract for sale.

Part 2 Form, Formation and Readjustment of Contract

§ 2—201. Formal Requirements; Statute of Frauds.

(1) Except as otherwise provided in this section a contract for the sale of goods for the price of $500 or more is not enforceable by way of action or defense unless there is some writing sufficient to indicate that a contract for sale has been made between the parties and signed by the party against whom enforcement is sought or by his authorized agent or broker. A writing is not insufficient because it omits or incorrectly states a term agreed upon but the contract is not enforceable under this paragraph beyond the quantity of goods shown in such writing.

(2) Between merchants if within a reasonable time a writing in confirmation of the contract and sufficient against the sender is received and the party receiving it has reason to know its contents, its satisfies the requirements of subsection (1) against such party unless written notice of objection to its contents is given within ten days after it is received.

(3) A contract which does not satisfy the requirements of subsection (1) but which is valid in other respects is enforceable

(a) if the goods are to be specially manufactured for the buyer and are not suitable for sale to others in the ordinary course of the seller's business and the seller, before notice of repudiation is received and under circumstances which reasonably indicate that the goods are for the buyer, has made either a substantial beginning of their manufacture or commitments for their procurement; or

(b) if the party against whom enforcement is sought admits in his pleading, testimony or otherwise in court that a contract for sale was made, but the contract is not enforceable under this provision beyond the quantity of goods admitted; or

(c) with respect to goods for which payment has been made and accepted or which have been received and accepted (Sec. 2—606).

§ 2—202. Final Written Expression: Parol or Extrinsic Evidence.

Terms with respect to which the confirmatory memoranda of the parties agree or which are otherwise set forth in a writing intended by the parties as a final expression of their agreement with respect to such terms as are included therein may not be contradicted by evidence of any prior agreement or of a contemporaneous oral agreement but may be explained or supplemented

(a) by course of dealing or usage of trade (Section 1—205) or by course of performance (Section 2—208); and

(b) by evidence of consistent additional terms unless the court finds the writing to have been intended also as a complete and exclusive statement of the terms of the agreement.

§ 2—203. Seals Inoperative.

The affixing of a seal to a writing evidencing a contract for sale or an offer to buy or sell goods does not constitute the writing a sealed instrument and the law with respect to sealed instruments does not apply to such a contract or offer.

§ 2—204. Formation in General.

(1) A contract for sale of goods may be made in any manner sufficent to show agreement, including conduct by both parties which recognizes the existence of such a contract.

(2) An agreement sufficient to constitute a contract for sale may be found even though the moment of its making is undetermined.

(3) Even though one or more terms are left open a contract for sale does not fail for indefiniteness if the parties have intended to make a contract and there is a reasonably certain basis for giving an appropriate remedy.

§ 2—205. Firm Offers.

An offer by a merchant to buy or sell goods in a signed writing which by its terms gives assurance that it will be held open is not revocable, for lack of consideration, during the time stated or if no time is stated for a reasonable time, but in no event may such period of irrevocability exceed three months; but any such term of assurance on a form supplied by the offeree must be separately signed by the offeror.

§ 2—206. Offer and Acceptance in Formation of Contract.

(1) Unless other unambiguously indicated by the language or circumstances

(a) an offer to make a contract shall be construed as inviting acceptance in any manner and by any medium reasonable in the circumstances;

(b) an order or other offer to buy goods for prompt or current shipment shall be construed as inviting acceptance either by a prompt promise to ship or by the prompt or current shipment of conforming or nonconforming goods, but such a shipment of nonconforming goods does not constitute an acceptance if the seller seasonably notifies the buyer that the shipment is offered only as an accommodation to the buyer.

(2) Where the beginning of a requested performance is a reasonable mode of acceptance an offeror who is not notified of acceptance within a reasonable time may treat the offer as having lapsed before acceptance.

§ 2—207. Additional Terms in Acceptance or Confirmation.

(1) A definite and seasonable expression of acceptance or a written confirmation which is sent within a reasonable time operates as an acceptance even though it states terms additional to or different from those offered or agreed upon, unless acceptance is expressly made conditional on assent to the additional or different terms.

(2) The additional terms are to be construed as proposals for addition to the contract. Between merchants such terms become part of the contract unless:

(a) the offer expressly limits acceptance to the terms of the offer;

(b) they materially alter it; or

(c) notification of objection to them has already been given or is given within a reasonable time after notice of them is received.

(3) Conduct by both parties which recognizes the existence of a contract is sufficient to establish a contract for sale although the writings of the parties do not otherwise establish a contract. In such case the terms of the particular contract consist of those terms on which the writings of the parties agree, together with any supplementary terms incorporated under any other provisions of this Act.

§ 2—208. Course of Performance or Practical Construction.

(1) Where the contract for sale involves repeated occasions for performance by either party with knowledge of the nature of the performance and opportunity for objection to it by the other, any course of performance accepted or acquiesced in without objection shall be relevant to determine the meaning of the agreement.

(2) The express terms of the agreement and any such course of performance, as well as any course of dealing and usage of trade, shall be construed whenever reasonable as consistent with each other; but when such construction is unreasonable, express terms shall control course of performance and course of performance shall control both course of dealing and usage of trade (Section 1—205).

(3) Subject to the provisions of the next section on modification and waiver, such course of performance shall be relevant to show a waiver or modification of any term inconsistent with such course of performance.

§ 2—209. Modification, Rescission and Waiver.

(1) An agreement modifying a contract within this Article needs no consideration to be binding.

(2) A signed agreement which excludes modification or rescission except by a signed writing cannot be otherwise modified or rescinded, but except as between merchants such a requirement on a form supplied by the merchant must be separately signed by the other party.

(3) The requirements of the statute of frauds section of this Article (Section 2—201) must be satisfied if the contract as modified is within its provisions.

(4) Although an attempt at modification or rescission does not satisfy the requirements of subsection (2) or (3) it can operate as a waiver.

(5) A party who has made a waiver affecting an executory portion of the contract may retract the waiver by reasonable notification received by the other party that strict performance will be required of any term waived, unless the retraction would be unjust in view of a material change of position in reliance on the waiver.

§ 2—210. **Delegation of Performance; Assignment of Rights.**

(1) A party may perform his duty through a delegate unless otherwise agreed or unless the other party has a substantial interest in having his original promisor perform or control the acts required by the contract. No delegation of performance relieves the party delegating of any duty to perform or any liability for breach.

(2) Unless otherwise agreed all rights of either seller or buyer can be assigned except where the assignment would materially change the duty of the other party, or increase materially the burden or risk imposed on him by his contract, or impair materially his chance of obtaining return performance. A right to damages for breach of the whole contract or a right arising out of the assignor's due performance of his entire obligation can be assigned despite agreement otherwise.

(3) Unless the circumstances indicate the contrary a prohibition of assignment of "the contract" is to be construed as barring only the delegation to the assignee of the assignor's performance.

(4) An assignment of "the contract" or of "all my rights under the contract" or an assignment in similar general terms is an assignment of rights and unless the language or the circumstances (as in an assignment for security) indicate the contrary, it is a delegation of performance of the duties of the assignor and its acceptance by the assignee constitutes a promise by him to perform those duties. This promise is enforceable by either the assignor or the other party to the original contract.

(5) The other party may treat any assignment which delegates performance as creating reasonable grounds for insecurity and may without prejudice to his rights against the assignor demand assurances from the assignee (Section 2—609).

Part 3 General Obligation and Construction of Contract

§ 2—301. **General Obligations of Parties.**

The obligation of the seller is to transfer and deliver and that of the buyer is to accept and pay in accordance with the contract.

§ 2—302. **Unconscionable Contract or Clause.**

(1) If the court as a matter of law finds the contract or any clause of the contract to have been unconscionable at the time it was made the court may refuse to enforce the contract, or it may enforce the remainder of the contract without the unconscionable clause, or it may so limit the application of any unconscionable clause as to avoid any unconscionable result.

(2) When it is claimed or appears to the court that the contract or any clause thereof may be unconscionable the parties shall be afforded a reasonable opportunity to present evidence as to its commercial setting, purpose and effect to aid the court in making the determination.

§ 2—303. **Allocations or Division of Risks.**

Where this Article allocates a risk or a burden as between the parties "unless otherwise agreed", the agreement may not only shift the allocation but may also divide the risk or burden.

§ 2—304. **Price Payable in Money, Goods, Realty, or Otherwise.**

(1) The price can be made payable in money or otherwise. If it is payable in whole or in part in goods each party is a seller of the goods which he is to transfer.

(2) Even though all or part of the price is payable in an interest in realty the transfer of the goods and the seller's obligations with reference to them are subject to this Article, but not the transfer of the interest in realty or the transferor's obligations in connection therewith.

§ 2—305. **Open Price Term.**

(1) The parties if they so intend can conclude a contract for sale even though the price is not settled. In such a case the price is a reasonable price at the time for delivery if

(a) nothing is said as to price; or

(b) the price is left to be agreed by the parties and they fail to agree; or

(c) the price is to be fixed in terms of some agreed market or other standard as set or recorded by a third person or agency and it is not so set or recorded.

(2) A price to be fixed by the seller or by the buyer means a price for him to fix in good faith.

(3) When a price left to be fixed otherwise than by agreement of the parties fails to be fixed through fault of one party the other may at his option treat the contract as cancelled or himself fix a reasonable price.

(4) Where, however, the parties intend not to be bound unless the price be fixed or agreed and it is not fixed or agreed there is no contract. In such a case the buyer must return any goods already received or if unable so to do must pay their reasonable value at the time of delivery and the seller must return any portion of the price paid on account.

§ 2—306. **Output, Requirements and Exclusive Dealings.**

(1) A term which measures the quantity by the output of the seller or the requirements of the buyer means such actual output or requirements as may occur in good faith, except that no quantity unreasonably disproportionate to any stated estimate or in the absence of a stated estimate to any normal or otherwise comparable prior output or requirements may be tendered or demanded.

(2) A lawful agreement by either the seller or the buyer for exclusive dealing in the kind of goods concerned imposes unless otherwise agreed an obligation by the seller to use best efforts to supply the goods and by the buyer to use best efforts to promote their sale.

§ 2—307. **Delivery in Single Lot or Several Lots.**

Unless otherwise agreed all goods called for by a contract for sale must be tendered in a single delivery and payment is due only on such tender but where the circumstances give either party the right to make or demand delivery in lots the price if it can be apportioned may be demanded for each lot.

§ 2—308. **Absence of Specified Place for Delivery.**

Unless otherwise agreed

(a) the place for delivery of goods is the seller's place of business or if he has none his residence; but

(b) in a contract for sale of identified goods which to the knowledge of the parties at the time of contracting are in some other place, that place is the place for their delivery; and

(c) documents of title may be delivered through customary banking channels.

§ 2—309. **Absence of Specific Time Provisions; Notice of Termination.**

(1) The time for shipment or delivery or any other action under a contract if not provided in this Article or agreed upon shall be a reasonable time.

(2) Where the contract provides for successive performances but is indefinite in duration it is valid for a reasonable time but unless otherwise agreed may be terminated at any time by either party.

(3) Termination of a contract by one party except on the happening of an agreed event requires that reasonable notification be received by the other party and an agreement dispensing with notification is invalid if its operation would be unconscionable.

§ 2—310. **Open Time for Payment or Running of Credit; Authority to Ship Under Reservation.**

Unless otherwise agreed

(a) payment is due at the time and place at which the buyer is to receive the goods even though the place of shipment is the place of delivery; and

(b) if the seller is authorized to send the goods he may ship them under reservation, and may tender the documents of title, but the buyer may inspect the goods after their arrival before payment is due unless such inspection is inconsistent with the terms of the contract (Section 2—513); and

(c) if delivery is authorized and made by way of documents of title otherwise than by subsection (b) then payment is due at the time and place at which the buyer is to receive the documents regardless of where the goods are to be received; and

(d) where the seller is required or authorized to ship the goods on credit the credit period runs from the time of shipment but post-dating the invoice or delaying its dispatch will correspondingly delay the starting of the credit period.

§ 2—311. **Options and Cooperation Respecting Performance.**

(1) An agreement for sale which is otherwise sufficiently definite (subsection (3) of Section 2—204) to be a contract is not made invalid by the fact that it leaves particulars of performance to be specified by one of the parties. Any such specification must be made in good faith and within limits set by commercial reasonableness.

(2) Unless otherwise agreed specifications relating to assortment of the goods are at the buyer's option and except as otherwise provided in subsections (1)(c) and (3) of Section 2—319 specifications or arrangements relating to shipment are at the seller's option.

(3) Where such specification would materially affect the other party's performance but is not seasonably made or where one party's cooperation is necessary to the agreed performance of the other but is not seasonably forthcoming, the other party in addition to all other remedies

(a) is excused for any resulting delay in his own performance; and

(b) may also either proceed to perform in any reasonable manner or after the time for a material part of his own performance treat the failure to specify or to cooperate as a breach by failure to deliver or accept the goods.

§ 2—312. Warranty of Title and Against Infringement; Buyer's Obligation Against Infringement.

(1) Subject to subsection (2) there is in a contract for sale a warranty by the seller that

(a) the title conveyed shall be good, and its transfer rightful; and

(b) the goods shall be delivered free from any security interest or other lien or encumbrance of which the buyer at the time of contracting has no knowledge.

(2) A warranty under subsection (1) will be excluded or modified only by specific language or by circumstances which give the buyer reason to know that the person selling does not claim title in himself or that he is purporting to sell only such right or title as he or a third person may have.

(3) Unless otherwise agreed a seller who is a merchant regularly dealing in goods of the kind warrants that the goods shall be delivered free of the rightful claim of any third person by way of infringement or the like but a buyer who furnishes specifications to the seller must hold the seller harmless against any such claim which arises out of compliance with the specifications.

§ 2—313. Express Warranties by Affirmation, Promise, Description, Sample.

(1) Express warranties by the seller are created as follows:

(a) Any affirmation of fact or promise made by the seller to the buyer which relates to the goods and becomes part of the basis of the bargain creates an express warranty that the goods shall conform to the affirmation or promise.

(b) Any description of the goods which is made part of the basis of the bargain creates an express warranty that the goods shall conform to the description.

(c) Any sample or model which is made part of the basis of the bargain creates an express warranty that the whole of the goods shall conform to the sample or model.

(2) It is not necessary to the creation of an express warranty that the seller use formal words such as "warrant" or "guarantee" or that he have a specific intention to make a warranty, but an affirmation merely of the value of the goods or a statement purporting to be merely the seller's opinion or commendation of the goods does not create a warranty.

§ 2—314. Implied Warranty: Merchantability; Usage of Trade.

(1) Unless excluded or modified (Section 2—316), a warranty that the goods shall be merchantable is implied in a contract for their sale if the seller is a merchant with respect to goods of that kind. Under this section the serving for value of food or drink to be consumed either on the premises or elsewhere is a sale.

(2) Goods to be merchantable must be at least such as

(a) pass without objection in the trade under the contract description; and

(b) in the case of fungible goods, are of fair average quality within the description; and

(c) are fit for the ordinary purposes for which such goods are used; and

(d) run, within the variations permitted by the agreement, of even kind, quality and quantity within each unit and among all units involved; and

(e) are adequately contained, packaged, and labeled as the agreement may require; and

(f) conform to the promises or affirmations of fact made on the container or label if any.

(3) Unless excluded or modified (Section 2—316) other implied warranties may arise from course of dealing or usage of trade.

§ 2—315. Implied Warranty: Fitness for Particular Purpose.

Where the seller at the time of contracting has reason to know any particular purpose for which the goods are required and that the buyer is relying on the seller's skill or judgment to select or furnish suitable goods, there is unless excluded or modified under the next section an implied warranty that the goods shall be fit for such purpose.

§ 2—316. Exclusion or Modification of Warranties.

(1) Words or conduct relevant to the creation of an express warranty and words or conduct tending to negate or limit warranty shall be construed wherever reasonable as consistent with each other; but subject to the provisions of this Article on parol or extrinsic evidence (Section 2—202) negation or limitation is inoperative to the extent that such construction is unreasonable.

(2) Subject to subsection (3), to exclude or modify the implied warranty of merchantability or any part of it the language must mention merchantability and in case of a writing must be conspicuous, and to exclude or modify any implied warranty of fitness the exclusion must be by a writing and conspicuous. Language to exclude all implied warranties of fitness is sufficient if

it states, for example, that "There are no warranties which extend beyond the description on the face hereof."

(3) Notwithstanding subsection (2)

(a) unless the circumstances indicate otherwise, all implied warranties are excluded by expressions like "as is", "with all faults" or other language which in common understanding calls the buyer's attention to the exclusion of warranties and makes plain that there is no implied warranty; and

(b) when the buyer before entering into the contract has examined the goods or the sample or model as fully as he desired or has refused to examine the goods there is no implied warranty with regard to defects which an examination ought in the circumstances to have revealed to him; and

(c) an implied warranty can also be excluded or modified by course of dealing or course of performance or usage of trade.

(4) Remedies for breach of warranty can be limited in accordance with the provisions of this Article on liquidation or limitation of damages and on contractual modification of remedy (Sections 2—718 and 2—719).

§ 2—317. **Cumulation and Conflict of Warranties Express or Implied.**

Warranties whether express or implied shall be construed as consistent with each other and as cumulative, but if such construction is unreasonable the intention of the parties shall determine which warranty is dominant. In ascertaining that intention the following rules apply:

(a) Exact or technical specifications displace an inconsistent sample or model or general language of description.

(b) A sample from an existing bulk displaces inconsistent general language of description.

(c) Express warranties displace inconsistent implied warranties other than an implied warranty of fitness for a particular purpose.

§ 2—318. **Third Party Beneficiaries of Warranties Express or Implied.**

Note: If this Act is introduced in the Congress of the United States this section should be omitted. (States to select one alternative.)

Alternative A
A seller's warranty whether express or implied extends to any natural person who is in the family or household of his buyer or who is a guest in his home if it is reasonable to expect that such person may use, consume or be affected by the goods and who is injured in person by breach of the warranty. A seller may not exclude or limit the operation of this section.

Alternative B
A seller's warranty whether express or implied extends to any natural person who may reasonably be expected to use, consume or be affected by the goods and who is injured in person by breach of the warranty. A seller may not exclude or limit the operation of this section.

Alternative C
A seller's warranty whether express or implied extends to any person who may reasonably be expected to use, consume or be affected by the goods and who is injured by breach of the warranty. A seller may not exclude or limit the operation of this section with respect to injury to the person of an individual to whom the warranty extends. As amended 1966.

§ 2—319. **F.O.B. and F.A.S. Terms.**

(1) Unless otherwise agreed the term F.O.B. (which means "free on board") at a named place, even though used only in connection with the stated price, is a delivery term under which

(a) when the term is F.O.B. the place of shipment, the seller must at that place ship the goods in the manner provided in this Article (Section 2—504) and bear the expense and risk of putting them into the possession of the carrier; or

(b) when the term is F.O.B. the place of destination, the seller must at his own expense and risk transport the goods to that place and there tender delivery of them in the manner provided in this Article (Section 2—503);

(c) when under either (a) or (b) the term is also F.O.B. vessel, car or other vehicle, the seller must in addition at his own expense and risk load the goods on board. If the term is F.O.B. vessel the buyer must name the vessel and in an appropriate case the seller must comply with the provisions of this Article on the form of bill of lading (Section 2—323).

(2) Unless otherwise agreed the term F.A.S. vessel (which means "free alongside") at a named port, even though used only in connection with the stated price, is a delivery term under which the seller must

(a) at his own expense and risk deliver the goods alongside the vessel in the manner usual in that port or on a dock designated and provided by the buyer; and

(b) obtain and tender a receipt for the goods in exchange for which the carrier is under a duty to issue a bill of lading.

(3) Unless otherwise agreed in any case falling within subsection (1)(a) or (c) or subsection (2) the buyer must seasonably give any needed instructions for making delivery, including when the term is F.A.S. or F.O.B. the

loading berth of the vessel and in an appropriate case its name and sailing date. The seller may treat the failure of needed instructions as a failure of cooperation under this Article (Section 2—311). He may also at his option move the goods in any reasonable manner preparatory to delivery or shipment.

(4) Under the term F.O.B. vessel or F.A.S. unless otherwise agreed the buyer must make payment against tender of the required documents and the seller may not tender nor the buyer demand delivery of the goods in substitution for the documents.

§ 2—320. **C.I.F. and C. & F. Terms.**

(1) The term C.I.F. means that the price includes in a lump sum the cost of the goods and the insurance and freight to the named destination. The term C. & F. or C.F. means that the price so includes cost and freight to the named destination.

(2) Unless otherwise agreed and even though used only in connection with the stated price and destination, the term C.I.F. destination or its equivalent requires the seller at his own expense and risk to

(a) put the goods into the possession of a carrier at the port for shipment and obtain a negotiable bill or bills of lading covering the entire transportation to the named destination; and

(b) load the goods and obtain a receipt from the carrier (which may be contained in the bill of lading) showing that the freight has been paid or provided for; and

(c) obtain a policy or certificate of insurance, including any war risk insurance, of a kind and on terms then current at the port of shipment in the usual amount, in the currency of the contract, shown to cover the same goods covered by the bill of lading and providing for payment of loss to the order of the buyer or for the account of whom it may concern; but the seller may add to the price the amount of the premium for any such war risk insurance; and

(d) prepare an invoice of the goods and procure any other documents required to effect shipment or to comply with the contract; and

(e) forward and tender with commercial promptness all the documents in due form and with any indorsement necessary to perfect the buyer's rights.

(3) Unless otherwise agreed the term C. & F. or its equivalent has the same effect and imposes upon the seller the same obligations and risks as a C.I.F. term except the obligation as to insurance.

(4) Under the term C.I.F. or C. & F. unless otherwise agreed the buyer must make payment against tender of the required documents and the seller may not tender nor the buyer demand delivery of the goods in substitution for the documents.

§ 2—321. **C.I.F. or C. & F.: "Net Landed Weights"; "Payment on Arrival"; Warranty of Condition on Arrival.**

Under a contract containing a term C.I.F. or C. & F.

(1) Where the price is based on or is to be adjusted according to "net landed weights", "delivered weights", "out turn" quantity or quality or the like, unless otherwise agreed the seller must reasonably estimate the price. The payment due on tender of the documents called for by the contract is the amount so estimated, but after final adjustment of the price a settlement must be made with commercial promptness.

(2) An agreement described in subsection (1) or any warranty of quality or condition of the goods on arrival places upon the seller the risk of ordinary deterioration, shrinkage and the like in transportation but has no effect on the place or time of identification to the contract for sale or delivery or on the passing of the risk of loss.

(3) Unless otherwise agreed where the contract provides for payment on or after arrival of the goods the seller must before payment allow such preliminary inspection as is feasible; but if the goods are lost delivery of the documents and payment are due when the goods should have arrived.

§ 2—322. **Delivery "Ex-Ship".**

(1) Unless otherwise agreed a term for delivery of goods "ex-ship" (which means from the carrying vessel) or in equivalent language is not restricted to a particular ship and requires delivery from a ship which has reached a place at the named port of destination where goods of the kind are usually discharged.

(2) Under such a term unless otherwise agreed

(a) the seller must discharge all liens arising out of the carriage and furnish the buyer with a direction which puts the carrier under a duty to deliver the goods; and

(b) the risk of loss does not pass to the buyer until the goods leave the ship's tackle or are otherwise properly unloaded.

§ 2—323. **Form of Bill of Lading Required in Overseas Shipment; "Overseas".**

(1) Where the contract contemplates overseas shipment and contains a term C.I.F. or C. & F. or F.O.B. vessel, the seller unless otherwise agreed must obtain a negotiable bill of lading stating that the goods have been loaded on board or, in the case of a term C.I.F. or C. & F., received for shipment.

(2) Where in a case within subsection (1) a bill of lading has been issued in a set of parts, unless otherwise agreed if the documents are not to be sent from abroad the buyer may demand tender of the full set; otherwise only one part of the bill of lading need be tendered. Even if the agreement expressly requires a full set

    (a) due tender of a single part is acceptable within the provisions of this Article on cure of improper delivery (subsection (1) of Section 2—508); and

    (b) even though the full set is demanded, if the documents are sent from abroad the person tendering an incomplete set may nevertheless require payment upon furnishing an indemnity which the buyer in good faith deems adequate.

(3) A shipment by water or by air or a contract contemplating such shipment is "overseas" insofar as by usage of trade or agreement it is subject to the commercial, financing or shipping practices characteristic of international deep water commerce.

§ 2—324. "No Arrival, No Sale" Term.

Under a term "no arrival, no sale" or terms of like meaning, unless otherwise agreed,

(a) the seller must properly ship conforming goods and if they arrive by any means he must tender them on arrival but he assumes no obligation that the goods will arrive unless he has caused the non-arrival; and

(b) where without fault of the seller the goods are in part lost or have so deteriorated as no longer to conform to the contract or arrive after the contract time, the buyer may proceed as if there had been casualty to identified goods (Section 2—613).

§ 2—325. "Letter of Credit" Term; "Confirmed Credit".

(1) Failure of the buyer seasonably to furnish an agreed letter of credit is a breach of the contract for sale.

(2) The delivery to seller of a proper letter of credit suspends the buyer's obligation to pay. If the letter of credit is dishonored, the seller may on seasonable notification to the buyer require payment directly from him.

(3) Unless otherwise agreed the term "letter of credit" or "banker's credit" in a contract for sale means an irrevocable credit issued by a financing agency of good repute and, where the shipment is overseas, of good international repute. The term "confirmed credit" means that the credit must also carry the direct obligation of such an agency which does business in the seller's financial market.

§ 2—326. Sale on Approval and Sale or Return; Consignment Sales and Rights of Creditors.

(1) Unless otherwise agreed, if delivered goods may be returned by the buyer even though they conform to the contract, the transaction is

    (a) a "sale on approval" if the goods are delivered primarily for use, and

    (b) a "sale or return" if the goods are delivered primarily for resale.

(2) Except as provided in subsection (3), goods held on approval are not subject to the claims of the buyer's creditors until acceptance; goods held on sale or return are subject to such claims while in the buyer's possession.

(3) Where goods are delivered to a person for sale and such person maintains a place of business at which he deals in goods of the kind involved, under a name other than the name of the person making delivery, then with respect to claims of creditors of the person conducting the business the goods are deemed to be on sale or return. The provisions of this subsection are applicable even though an agreement purports to reserve title to the person making delivery until payment or resale or uses such words as "on consignment" or "on memorandum". However, this subsection is not applicable if the person making delivery

    (a) complies with an applicable law providing for a consignor's interest or the like to be evidenced by a sign, or

    (b) establishes that the person conducting the business is generally known by his creditors to be substantially engaged in selling the goods of others, or

    (c) complies with the filing provisions of the Article on Secured Transactions (Article 9).

(4) Any "or return" term of a contract for sale is to be treated as a separate contract for sale within the statute of frauds section of this Article (Section 2—201) and as contradicting the sale aspect of the contract within the provisions of this Article on parol or extrinsic evidence (Section 2—202).

§ 2—327. Special Incidents of Sale on Approval and Sale or Return.

(1) Under a sale on approval unless otherwise agreed

    (a) although the goods are identified to the contract the risk of loss and the title do not pass to the buyer until acceptance; and

    (b) use of the goods consistent with the purpose of trial is not acceptance but failure seasonably to notify the seller of election to return the goods is acceptance, and if the goods conform to the contract acceptance of any part is acceptance of the whole; and

(c) after due notification of election to return, the return is at the seller's risk and expense but a merchant buyer must follow any reasonable instructions.

(2) Under a sale or return unless otherwise agreed

(a) the option to return extends to the whole or any commercial unit of the goods while in substantially their original condition, but must be exercised seasonably; and

(b) the return is at the buyer's risk and expense.

§ 2—328. **Sale by Auction.**

(1) In a sale by auction if goods are put up in lots each lot is the subject of a separate sale.

(2) A sale by auction is complete when the auctioneer so announces by the fall of the hammer or in other customary manner. Where a bid is made while the hammer is falling in acceptance of a prior bid the auctioneer may in his discretion reopen the bidding or declare the goods sold under the bid on which the hammer was falling.

(3) Such a sale is with reserve unless the goods are in explicit terms put up without reserve. In an auction with reserve the auctioneer may withdraw the goods at any time until he announces completion of the sale. In an auction without reserve, after the auctioneer calls for bids on an article or lot, that article or lot cannot be withdrawn unless no bid is made within a reasonable time. In either case a bidder may retract his bid until the auctioneer's announcement of completion of the sale, but a bidder's retraction does not revive any previous bid.

(4) If the auctioneer knowingly receives a bid on the seller's behalf or the seller makes or procures such as bid, and notice has not been given that liberty for such bidding is reserved, the buyer may at his option avoid the sale or take the goods at the price of the last good faith bid prior to the completion of the sale. This subsection shall not apply to any bid at a forced sale.

Part 4 Title, Creditors and Good Faith Purchasers

§ 2—401. **Passing of Title; Reservation for Security; Limited Application of This Section.**

Each provision of this Article with regard to the rights, obligations and remedies of the seller, the buyer, purchasers or other third parties applies irrespective of title to the goods except where the provision refers to such title. Insofar as situations are not covered by the other provisions of this Article and matters concerning title became material the following rules apply:

(1) Title to goods cannot pass under a contract for sale prior to their identification to the contract (Section 2—501), and unless otherwise explicitly agreed the buyer acquires by their identification a special property as limited by this Act. Any retention or reservation by the seller of the title (property) in goods shipped or delivered to the buyer is limited in effect to a reservation of a security interest. Subject to these provisions and to the provisions of the Article on Secured Transactions (Article 9), title to goods passes from the seller to the buyer in any manner and on any conditions explicitly agreed on by the parties.

(2) Unless otherwise explicitly agreed title passes to the buyer at the time and place at which the seller completes his performance with reference to the physical delivery of the goods, despite any reservation of a security interest and even though a document of title is to be delivered at a different time or place; and in particular and despite any reservation of a security interest by the bill of lading

(a) if the contract requires or authorizes the seller to send the goods to the buyer but does not require him to deliver them at destination, title passes to the buyer at the time and place of shipment; but

(b) if the contract requires delivery at destination, title passes on tender there.

(3) Unless otherwise explicitly agreed where delivery is to be made without moving the goods,

(a) if the seller is to deliver a document of title, title passes at the time when and the place where he delivers such documents; or

(b) if the goods are at the time of contracting already identified and no documents are to be delivered, title passes at the time and place of contracting.

(4) A rejection or other refusal by the buyer to receive or retain the goods, whether or not justified, or a justified revocation of acceptance revests title to the goods in the seller. Such revesting occurs by operation of law and is not a "sale".

§ 2—402. **Rights of Seller's Creditors Against Sold Goods.**

(1) Except as provided in subsections (2) and (3), rights of unsecured creditors of the seller with respect to goods which have been identified to a contract for sale are subject to the buyer's rights to recover the goods under this Article (Sections 2—502 and 2—716).

(2) A creditor of the seller may treat a sale or an identification of goods to a contract for sale as void if as against him a retention of possession by the seller is fraudulent under any rule of law of the state where the goods are situated, except that retention of possession in good faith and current course of trade by a merchant-seller for a commercially reasonable time after a sale or identification is not fraudulent.

(3) Nothing in this Article shall be deemed to impair the rights of creditors of the seller

    (a) under the provisions of the Article on Secured Transactions (Article 9); or

    (b) where identification to the contract or delivery is made not in current course of trade but in satisfaction of or as security for a pre-existing claim for money, security or the like and is made under circumstances which under any rule of law of the state where the goods are situated would apart from this Article constitute the transaction a fraudulent transfer or voidable preference.

§ 2—403. **Power to Transfer; Good Faith Purchase of Goods; "Entrusting".**

(1) A purchaser of goods acquires all title which his transferor had or had power to transfer except that a purchaser of a limited interest acquires rights only to the extent of the interest purchased. A person with voidable title has power to transfer a good title to a good faith purchaser for value. When goods have been delivered under a transaction of purchase the purchaser has such power even though

    (a) the transferor was deceived as to the identity of the purchaser, or

    (b) the delivery was in exchange for a check which is later dishonored, or

    (c) it was agreed that the transaction was to be a "cash sale", or

    (d) the delivery was procured through fraud punishable as larcenous under the criminal law.

(2) Any entrusting of possession of goods to a merchant who deals in goods of that kind gives him power to transfer all rights of the entruster to a buyer in ordinary course of business.

(3) "Entrusting" includes any delivery and any acquiescence in retention of possession regardless of any condition expressed between the parties to the delivery or acquiescence and regardless of whether the procurement of the entrusting or the possessor's disposition of the goods have been such as to be larcenous under the criminal law.

(4) The rights of other purchasers of goods and of lien creditors are governed by the Articles on Secured Transactions (Article 9), Bulk Transfers (Article 6) and Documents of Title (Article 7).

Part 5 Performance

§ 2—501. **Insurable Interest in Goods; Manner of Identification of Goods.**

(1) The buyer obtains a special property and an insurable interest in goods by identification of existing goods as goods to which the contract refers even though the goods so identified are non-conforming and he has an option to return or reject them. Such identification can be made at any time and in any manner explicitly agreed to by the parties. In the absence of explicit agreement identification occurs

    (a) when the contract is made if it is for the sale of goods already existing and identified;

    (b) if the contract is for the sale of future goods other than those described in paragraph (c), when goods are shipped, marked or otherwise designated by the seller as goods to which the contract refers;

    (c) when the crops are planted or otherwise become growing crops or the young are conceived if the contract is for the sale of unborn young to be born within twelve months after contracting or for the sale of crops to be harvested within twelve months or the next normal harvest season after contracting whichever is longer.

(2) The seller retains an insurable interest in goods so long as title to or any security interest in the goods remains in him and where the identification is by the seller alone he may until default or insolvency or notification to the buyer that the identification is final substitute other goods for those identified.

(3) Nothing in this section impairs any insurable interest recognized under any other statute or rule of law.

§ 2—502. **Buyer's Right to Goods on Seller's Insolvency.**

(1) Subject to subsection (2) and even though the goods have not been shipped a buyer who has paid a part or all of the price of goods in which he has a special property under the provisions of the immediately preceding section may on making and keeping good a tender of any unpaid portion of their price recover them from the seller if the seller becomes insolvent within ten days after receipt of the first installment on their price.

(2) If the identification creating his special property has been made by the buyer he acquires the right to recover the goods only if they conform to the contract for sale.

§ 2—503. **Manner of Seller's Tender of Delivery.**

(1) Tender of delivery requires that the seller put and hold conforming goods at the buyer's disposition and give the buyer any notification reasonably necessary to enable him to take delivery. The manner, time and place for tender are determined by the agreement and this Article, and in particular

    (a) tender must be at a reasonable hour, and if it is of goods they must be kept available for the period reasonably necessary to enable the buyer to take possession; but

(b) unless otherwise agreed the buyer must furnish facilities reasonably suited to the receipt of the goods.

(2) Where the case is within the next section respecting shipment tender requires that the seller comply with its provisions.

(3) Where the seller is required to deliver at a particular destination tender requires that he comply with subsection (1) and also in any appropriate case tender documents as described in subsections (4) and (5) of this section.

(4) Where goods are in the possession of a bailee and are to be delivered without being moved

(a) tender requires that the seller either tender a negotiable document of title covering such goods or procure acknowledgment by the bailee of the buyer's right to possession of the goods; but

(b) tender to the buyer of a non-negotiable document of title or of a written direction to the bailee to deliver is sufficient tender unless the buyer seasonably objects, and receipt by the bailee of notification of the buyer's rights fixes those rights as against the bailee and all third persons; but risk of loss of the goods and of any failure by the bailee to honor the non-negotiable document of title or to obey the direction remains on the seller until the buyer has had a reasonable time to present the document or direction, and a refusal by the bailee to honor the document or to obey the direction defeats the tender.

(5) Where the contract requires the seller to deliver documents

(a) he must tender all such documents in correct form, except as provided in this Article with respect to bills of lading in a set (subsection (2) of Section 2—323); and

(b) tender through customary banking channels is sufficient and dishonor of a draft accompanying the documents constitutes non-acceptance or rejection.

§ 2—504. **Shipment by Seller.**

Where the seller is required or authorized to send the goods to the buyer and the contract does not require him to deliver them at a particular destination, then unless otherwise agreed he must

(a) put the goods in the possession of such a carrier and make such a contract for their transportation as may be reasonable having regard to the nature of the goods and other circumstances of the case; and

(b) obtain and promptly deliver or tender in due form any document necessary to enable the buyer to obtain possession of the goods or otherwise required by the agreement or by usage of trade; and

(c) promptly notify the buyer of the shipment.

Failure to notify the buyer under paragraph (c) or to make a proper contract under paragraph (a) is a ground for rejection only if material delay or loss ensues.

§ 2—505. **Seller's Shipment under Reservation.**

(1) Where the seller has identified goods to the contract by or before shipment:

(a) his procurement of a negotiable bill of lading to his own order or otherwise reserves in him a security interest in the goods. His procurement of the bill to the order of a financing agency or of the buyer indicates in addition only the seller's expectation of transferring that interest to the person named.

(b) a non-negotiable bill of lading to himself or his nominee reserves possession of the goods as security but except in a case of conditional delivery (subsection (2) of Section 2—507) a non-negotiable bill of lading naming the buyer as consignee reserves no security interest even though the seller retains possession of the bill of lading.

(2) When shipment by the seller with reservation of a security interest is in violation of the contract for sale it constitutes an improper contract for transportation within the preceding section but impairs neither the rights given to the buyer by shipment and identification of the goods to the contract nor the seller's powers as a holder of a negotiable document.

§ 2—506. **Rights of Financing Agency.**

(1) A financing agency by paying or purchasing for value a draft which relates to a shipment of goods acquires to the extent of the payment or purchase and in addition to its own rights under the draft and any document of title securing it any rights of the shipper in the goods including the right to stop delivery and the shipper's right to have the draft honored by the buyer.

(2) The right to reimbursement of a financing agency which has in good faith honored or purchased the draft under commitment to or authority from the buyer is not impaired by subsequent discovery of defects with reference to any relevant document which was apparently regular on its face.

§ 2—507. **Effect of Seller's Tender; Delivery on Condition.**

(1) Tender of delivery is a condition to the buyer's duty to accept the goods and, unless otherwise agreed, to his duty to pay for them. Tender entitles the seller to acceptance of the goods and to payment according to the contract.

(2) Where payment is due and demanded on the delivery to the buyer of goods or documents of title, his right as against the seller to retain or dispose of them is con-

ditional upon his making the payment due.

§ 2—508. **Cure by Seller of Improper Tender or Delivery; Replacement.**

(1) Where any tender or delivery by the seller is rejected because non-conforming and the time for performance has not yet expired, the seller may seasonably notify the buyer of his intention to cure and may then within the contract time make a conforming delivery.

(2) Where the buyer rejects a non-conforming tender which the seller had reasonable grounds to believe would be acceptable with or without money allowance the seller may if he seasonably notifies the buyer have a further reasonable time to substitute a conforming tender.

§ 2—509. **Risk of Loss in the Absence of Breach.**

(1) Where the contract requires or authorizes the seller to ship the goods by carrier

    (a) if it does not require him to deliver them at a particular destination, the risk of loss passes to the buyer when the goods are duly delivered to the carrier even though the shipment is under reservation (Section 2—505); but

    (b) if it does require him to deliver them at a particular destination and the goods are there duly tendered while in the possession of the carrier, the risk of loss passes to the buyer when the goods are there duly so tendered as to enable the buyer to take delivery.

(2) Where the goods are held by a bailee to be delivered without being moved, the risk of loss passes to the buyer

    (a) on his receipt of a negotiable document of title covering the goods; or

    (b) on acknowledgment by the bailee of the buyer's right to possession of the goods; or

    (c) after his receipt of a non-negotiable document of title or other written direction to deliver, as provided in subsection (4)(b) of Section 2—503.

(3) In any case not within subsection (1) or (2), the risk of loss passes to the buyer on his receipt of the goods if the seller is a merchant; otherwise the risk passes to the buyer on tender of delivery.

(4) The provisions of this section are subject to contrary agreement of the parties and to the provisions of this Article on sale on approval (Section 2—327) and on effect of breach on risk of loss (Section 2—510).

§ 2—510. **Effect of Breach on Risk of Loss.**

(1) Where a tender or delivery of goods so fails to conform to the contract as to give a right of rejection the risk of their loss remains on the seller until cure or acceptance.

(2) Where the buyer rightfully revokes acceptance he may to the extent of any deficiency in his effective insurance coverage treat the risk of loss as having rested on the seller from the beginning.

(3) Where the buyer as to conforming goods already identified to the contract for sale repudiates or is otherwise in breach before risk of their loss has passed to him, the seller may to the extent of any deficiency in his effective insurance coverage treat the risk of loss as resting on the buyer for a commercially reasonable time.

§ 2—511. **Tender of Payment by Buyer; Payment by Check.**

(1) Unless otherwise agreed tender of payment is a condition to the seller's duty to tender and complete any delivery.

(2) Tender of payment is sufficient when made by any means or in any manner current in the ordinary course of business unless the seller demands payment in legal tender and gives any extension of time reasonably necessary to procure it.

(3) Subject to the provisions of this Act on the effect of an instrument on an obligation (Section 3—802), payment by check is conditional and is defeated as between the parties by dishonor of the check on due presentment.

§ 2—512. **Payment by Buyer Before Inspection.**

(1) Where the contract requires payment before inspection non-conformity of the goods does not excuse the buyer from so making payment unless

    (a) the non-conformity appears without inspection; or

    (b) despite tender of the required documents the circumstances would justify injunction against honor under the provisions of this Act (Section 5—114).

(2) Payment pursuant to subsection (1) does not constitute an acceptance of goods or impair the buyer's right to inspect or any of his remedies.

§ 2—513. **Buyer's Right to Inspection of Goods.**

(1) Unless otherwise agreed and subject to subsection (3), where goods are tendered or delivered or identified to the contract for sale, the buyer has a right before payment or acceptance to inspect them at any reasonable place and time and in any reasonable manner. When the seller is required or authorized to send the goods to the buyer, the inspection may be after their arrival.

(2) Expenses of inspection must be borne by the buyer but may be recovered from the seller if the goods do not conform and are rejected.

(3) Unless otherwise agreed and subject to the provisions of this Article on C.I.F. contracts (subsection (3)

of Section 2—321), the buyer is not entitled to inspect the goods before payment of the price when the contract provides

(a) for delivery "C.O.D." or on other like terms; or

(b) for payment against documents of title, except where such payment is due only after the goods are to become available for inspection.

(4) A place or method of inspection fixed by the parties is presumed to be exclusive but unless otherwise expressly agreed it does not postpone identification or shift the place for delivery or for passing the risk of loss. If compliance becomes impossible, inspection shall be as provided in this section unless the place or method fixed was clearly intended as an indispensable condition failure of which avoids the contract.

§ 2—514. When Documents Deliverable on Acceptance; When on Payment.

Unless otherwise agreed documents against which a draft is drawn are to be delivered to the drawee on acceptance of the draft if it is payable more than three days after presentment; otherwise, only on payment.

§ 2—515. Preserving Evidence of Goods in Dispute.

In furtherance of the adjustment of any claim or dispute

(a) either party on reasonable notification to the other and for the purpose of ascertaining the facts and preserving evidence has the right to inspect, test and sample the goods including such of them as may be in the possession or control of the other; and

(b) the parties may agree to a third party inspection or survey to determine the conformity or condition of the goods and may agree that the findings shall be binding upon them in any subsequent litigation or adjustment.

Part 6 Breach, Repudiation and Excuse

§ 2—601. Buyer's Rights on Improper Delivery.

Subject to the provisions of this Article on breach in installment contracts (Section 2—612) and unless otherwise agreed under the sections on contractual limitations of remedy (Sections 2—718 and 2—719), if the goods or the tender of delivery fail in any respect to conform to the contract, the buyer may

(a) reject the whole; or

(b) accept the whole; or

(c) accept any commercial unit or units and reject the rest.

§ 2—602. Manner and Effect of Rightful Rejection.

(1) Rejection of goods must be within a reasonable time after their delivery or tender. It is ineffective unless the buyer seasonably notifies the seller.

(2) Subject to the provisions of the two following sections on rejected goods (Sections 2—603 and 2—604),

(a) after rejection any exercise of ownership by the buyer with respect to any commercial unit is wrongful as against the seller; and

(b) if the buyer has before rejection taken physical possession of goods in which he does not have a security interest under the provisions of this Article (subsection (3) of Section 2—711), he is under a duty after rejection to hold them with reasonable care at the seller's disposition for a time sufficient to permit the seller to remove them; but

(c) the buyer has no further obligations with regard to goods rightfully rejected.

(3) The seller's rights with respect to goods wrongfully rejected are governed by the provisions of this Article on Seller's remedies in general (Section 2—703).

§ 2—603. Merchant Buyer's Duties as to Rightfully Rejected Goods.

(1) Subject to any security interest in the buyer (subsection (3) of Section 2—711), when the seller has no agent or place of business at the market of rejection a merchant buyer is under a duty after rejection of goods in his possession or control to follow any reasonable instructions received from the seller with respect to the goods and in the absence of such instructions to make reasonable efforts to sell them for the seller's account if they are perishable or threaten to decline in value speedily. Instructions are not reasonable if on demand indemnity for expenses is not forthcoming.

(2) When the buyer sells goods under subsection (1), he is entitled to reimbursement from the seller or out of the proceeds for reasonable expenses of caring for and selling them, and if the expenses include no selling commission then to such commission as is usual in the trade or if there is none to a reasonable sum not exceeding ten per cent on the gross proceeds.

(3) In complying with this section the buyer is held only to good faith and good faith conduct hereunder is neither acceptance nor conversion nor the basis of an action for damages.

§ 2—604. Buyer's Options as to Salvage of Rightfully Rejected Goods.

Subject to the provisions of the immediately preceding section on perishables if the seller gives no instructions within a reasonable time after notification of rejection the buyer may store the rejected goods for the seller's account or reship them to him or resell them for the seller's account with reimbursement as provided in the preceding section. Such action is not acceptance or conversion.

§ 2—605. **Waiver of Buyer's Objections by Failure to Particularize.**

(1) The buyer's failure to state in connection with rejection a particular defect which is ascertainable by reasonable inspection precludes him from relying on the unstated defect to justify rejection or to establish breach

(a) where the seller could have cured it if stated seasonably; or

(b) between merchants when the seller has after rejection made a request in writing for a full and final written statement of all defects on which the buyer proposes to rely.

(2) Payment against documents made without reservation of rights precludes recovery of the payment for defects apparent on the face of the documents.

§ 2—606. **What Constitutes Acceptance of Goods.**

(1) Acceptance of goods occurs when the buyer

(a) after a reasonable opportunity to inspect the goods signifies to the seller that the goods are conforming or that he will take or retain them in spite of their nonconformity; or

(b) fails to make an effective rejection (subsection (1) of Section 2—602), but such acceptance does not occur until the buyer has had a reasonable opportunity to inspect them; or

(c) does any act inconsistent with the seller's ownership; but if such act is wrongful as against the seller it is an acceptance only if ratified by him.

(2) Acceptance of a part of any commercial unit is acceptance of that entire unit.

§ 2—607. **Effect of Acceptance; Notice of Breach; Burden of Establishing Breach After Acceptance; Notice of Claim or Litigation to Person Answerable Over.**

(1) The buyer must pay at the contract rate for any goods accepted.

(2) Acceptance of goods by the buyer precludes rejection of the goods accepted and if made with knowledge of a non-conformity cannot be revoked because of it unless the acceptance was on the reasonable assumption that the non-conformity would be seasonably cured but acceptance does not of itself impair any other remedy provided by this Article for non-conformity.

(3) Where a tender has been accepted

(a) the buyer must within a reasonable time after he discovers or should have discovered any breach notify the seller of breach or be barred from any remedy; and

(b) if the claim is one for infringement or the like (subsection (3) of Section 2—312) and the buyer is sued as a result of such a breach he must so notify the seller within a reasonable time after he receives notice of the litigation or be barred from any remedy over for liability established by the litigation.

(4) The burden is on the buyer to establish any breach with respect to the goods accepted.

(5) Where the buyer is sued for breach of a warranty or other obligation for which his seller is answerable over

(a) he may give his seller written notice of the litigation. If the notice states that the seller may come in and defend and that if the seller does not do so he will be bound in any action against him by his buyer by any determination of fact common to the two litigations, then unless the seller after seasonable receipt of the notice does come in and defend he is so bound.

(b) if the claim is one for infringement or the like (subsection (3) of Section 2—312) the original seller may demand in writing that his buyer turn over to him control of the litigation including settlement or else be barred from any remedy over and if he also agrees to bear all expense and to satisfy any adverse judgment, then unless the buyer after seasonable receipt of the demand does turn over control the buyer is so barred.

(6) The provisions of subsections (3), (4) and (5) apply to any obligation of a buyer to hold the seller harmless against infringement or the like (subsection (3) of Section 2—312).

§ 2—608. **Revocation of Acceptance in Whole or in Part.**

(1) The buyer may revoke his acceptance of a lot or commercial unit whose non-conformity substantially impairs its value to him if he has accepted it

(a) on the reasonable assumption that its non-conformity would be cured and it has not been seasonably cured; or

(b) without discovery of such non-conformity if his acceptance was reasonably induced either by the difficulty of discovery before acceptance or by the seller's assurances.

(2) Revocation of acceptance must occur within a reasonable time after the buyer discovers or should have discovered the ground for it and before any substantial change in condition of the goods which is not caused by their own defects. It is not effective until the buyer notifies the seller of it.

(3) A buyer who so revokes has the same rights and duties with regard to the goods involved as if he had rejected them.

§ 2—609. Right to Adequate Assurance of Performance.

(1) A contract for sale imposes an obligation on each party that the other's expectation of receiving due performance will not be impaired. When reasonable grounds for insecurity arise with respect to the performance of either party the other may in writing demand adequate assurance of due performance and until he receives such assurance may if commercially reasonable suspend any performance for which he has not already received the agreed return.

(2) Between merchants the reasonableness of grounds for insecurity and the adequacy of any assurance offered shall be determined according to commercial standards.

(3) Acceptance of any improper delivery or payment does not prejudice the aggrieved party's right to demand adequate assurance of future performance.

(4) After receipt of a justified demand failure to provide within a reasonable time not exceeding thirty days such assurance of due performance as is adequate under the circumstances of the particular case is a repudiation of the contract.

§ 2—610. Anticipatory Repudiation.

When either party repudiates the contract with respect to a performance not yet due the loss of which will substantially impair the value of the contract to the other, the aggrieved party may

(a) for a commercially reasonable time await performance by the repudiating party; or

(b) resort to any remedy for breach (Section 2—703 or Section 2—711), even though he has notified the repudiating party that he would await the latter's performance and has urged retraction; and

(c) in either case suspend his own performance or proceed in accordance with the provisions of this Article on the seller's right to identify goods to the contract notwithstanding breach or to salvage unfinished goods (Section 2—704).

§ 2—611. Retraction of Anticipatory Repudiation.

(1) Until the repudiating party's next performance is due he can retract his repudiation unless the aggrieved party has since the repudiation cancelled or materially changed his position or otherwise indicated that he considers the repudiation final.

(2) Retraction may be by any method which clearly indicates to the aggrieved party that the repudiating party intends to perform, but must include any assurance justifiably demanded under the provisions of this Article (Section 2—609).

(3) Retraction reinstates the repudiating party's rights under the contract with due excuse and allowance to the aggrieved party for any delay occasioned by the repudiation.

§ 2—612. "Installment Contract"; Breach.

(1) An "installment contract" is one which requires or authorizes the delivery of goods in separate lots to be separately accepted, even though the contract contains a clause "each delivery is a separate contract" or its equivalent.

(2) The buyer may reject any installment which is non-conforming if the non-conformity substantially impairs the value of that installment and cannot be cured or if the non-conformity is a defect in the required documents; but if the non-conformity does not fall within subsection (3) and the seller gives adequate assurance of its cure the buyer must accept that installment.

(3) Whenever non-conformity or default with respect to one or more installments substantially impairs the value of the whole contract there is a breach of the whole. But the aggrieved party reinstates the contract if he accepts a non-conforming installment without seasonably notifying of cancellation or if he brings an action with respect only to past installments or demands performance as to future installments.

§ 2—613. Casualty to Identified Goods.

Where the contract requires for its performance goods identified when the contract is made, and the goods suffer casualty without fault of either party before the risk of loss passes to the buyer, or in a proper case under a "no arrival, no sale" term (Section 2—324) then

(a) if the loss is total the contract is avoided; and

(b) if the loss is partial or the goods have so deteriorated as no longer to conform to the contract the buyer may nevertheless demand inspection and at his option either treat the contract as voided or accept the goods with due allowance from the contract price for the deterioration or the deficiency in quantity but without further right against the seller.

§ 2—614. Substituted Performance.

(1) Where without fault of either party the agreed berthing, loading, or unloading facilities fail or an agreed type of carrier becomes unavailable or the agreed manner of delivery otherwise becomes commercially impracticable but a commercially reasonable substitute is available, such substitute performance must be tendered and accepted.

(2) If the agreed means or manner of payment fails because of domestic or foreign governmental regulation, the seller may withhold or stop delivery unless the buyer

provides a means or manner of payment which is commercially a substantial equivalent. If delivery has already been taken, payment by the means or in the manner provided by the regulation discharges the buyer's obligation unless the regulation is discriminatory, oppressive or predatory.

§ 2—615. Excuse by Failure of Presupposed Conditions.

Except so far as a seller may have assumed a greater obligation and subject to the preceding section on substituted performance:

(a) Delay in delivery or non-delivery in whole or in part by a seller who complies with paragraphs (b) and (c) is not a breach of his duty under a contract for sale if performance as agreed has been made impracticable by the occurrence of a contingency the nonoccurrence of which was a basic assumption on which the contract was made or by compliance in good faith with any applicable foreign or domestic governmental regulation or order whether or not it later proves to be invalid.

(b) Where the causes mentioned in paragraph (a) affect only a part of the seller's capacity to perform, he must allocate production and deliveries among his customers but may at his option include regular customers not then under contract as well as his own requirements for further manufacture. He may so allocate in any manner which is fair and reasonable.

(c) The seller must notify the buyer seasonably that there will be delay or non-delivery and, when allocation is required under paragraph (b), of the estimated quota thus made available for the buyer.

§ 2—616. Procedure on Notice Claiming Excuse.

(1) Where the buyer receives notification of a material or indefinite delay or an allocation justified under the preceding section he may by written notification to the seller as to any delivery concerned, and where the prospective deficiency substantially impairs the value of the whole contract under the provisions of this Article relating to breach of installment contracts (Section 2—612), then also as to the whole,

    (a) terminate and thereby discharge any unexecuted portion of the contract; or

    (b) modify the contract by agreeing to take his available quota in substitution.

(2) If after receipt of such notification from the seller the buyer fails so to modify the contract within a reasonable time not exceeding thirty days the contract lapses with respect to any deliveries affected.

(3) The provisions of this section may not be negated by agreement except in so far as the seller has assumed a greater obligation under the preceding section.

Part 7 Remedies

§ 2—701. Remedies for Breach of Collateral Contracts Not Impaired.

Remedies for breach of any obligation or promise collateral or ancillary to a contract for sale are not impaired by the provisions of this Article.

§ 2—702. Seller's Remedies on Discovery of Buyer's Insolvency.

(1) Where the seller discovers the buyer to be insolvent he may refuse delivery except for cash including payment for all goods theretofore delivered under the contract, and stop delivery under this Article (Section 2—705).

(2) Where the seller discovers that the buyer has received goods on credit while insolvent he may reclaim the goods upon demand made within ten days after the receipt, but if misrepresentation of solvency has been made to the particular seller in writing within three months before delivery the ten day limitation does not apply. Except as provided in this subsection the seller may not base a right to reclaim goods on the buyer's fraudulent or innocent misrepresentation of solvency or of intent to pay.

(3) The seller's right to reclaim under subsection (2) is subject to the rights of a buyer in ordinary course or other good faith purchaser under this Article (Section 2—403). Successful reclamation of goods excludes all other remedies with respect to them.

§ 2—703. Seller's Remedies in General.

Where the buyer wrongfully rejects or revokes acceptance of goods or fails to make a payment due on or before delivery or repudiates with respect to a part or the whole, then with respect to any goods directly affected and, if the breach is of the whole contract (Section 2—612), then also with respect to the whole undelivered balance, the aggrieved seller may

(a) withhold delivery of such goods;

(b) stop delivery by any bailee as hereafter provided (Section 2—705);

(c) proceed under the next section respecting goods still unidentified to the contract;

(d) resell and recover damages as hereafter provided (Section 2—706);

(e) recover damages for non-acceptance (Section 2—708) or in a proper case the price (Section 2—709);

(f) cancel.

§ 2—704. Seller's Right to Identify Goods to the Contract Notwithstanding Breach or to Salvage Unfinished Goods.

(1) An aggrieved seller under the preceding section may

(a) identify to the contract conforming goods not already identified if at the time he learned of the breach they are in his possession or control;

(b) treat as the subject of resale goods which have demonstrably been intended for the particular contract even though those goods are unfinished.

(2) Where the goods are unfinished an aggrieved seller may in the exercise of reasonable commercial judgment for the purposes of avoiding loss and of effective realization either complete the manufacture and wholly identify the goods to the contract or cease manufacture and resell for scrap or salvage value or proceed in any other reasonable manner.

§ 2—705. Seller's Stoppage of Delivery in Transit or Otherwise.

(1) The seller may stop delivery of goods in the possession of a carrier or other bailee when he discovers the buyer to be insolvent (Section 2—702) and may stop delivery of carload, truckload, planeload or larger shipments of express or freight when the buyer repudiates or fails to make a payment due before delivery or if for any other reason the seller has a right to withhold or reclaim the goods.

(2) As against such buyer the seller may stop delivery until

(a) receipt of the goods by the buyer; or

(b) acknowledgment to the buyer by any bailee of the goods except a carrier that the bailee holds the goods for the buyer; or

(c) such acknowledgment to the buyer by a carrier by reshipment or as warehouseman; or

(d) negotiation to the buyer of any negotiable document of title covering the goods.

(3) (a) To stop delivery the seller must so notify as to enable the bailee by reasonable diligence to prevent delivery of the goods.

(b) After such notification the bailee must hold and deliver the goods according to the directions of the seller but the seller is liable to the bailee for any ensuing charges or damages.

(c) If a negotiable document of title has been issued for goods the bailee is not obliged to obey a notification to stop until surrender of the document.

(d) A carrier who has issued a non-negotiable bill of lading is not obliged to obey a notification to stop received from a person other than the consignor.

§ 2—706. Seller's Resale Including Contract for Resale.

(1) Under the conditions stated in Section 2—703 on seller's remedies, the seller may resell the goods concerned or the undelivered balance thereof. Where the resale is made in good faith and in a commercially reasonable manner the seller may recover the difference between the resale price and the contract price together with any incidental damages allowed under the provisions of this Article (Section 2—710), but less expenses saved in consequence of the buyer's breach.

(2) Except as otherwise provided in subsection (3) or unless otherwise agreed resale may be at public or private sale including sale by way of one or more contracts to sell or of identification to an existing contract of the seller. Sale may be as a unit or in parcels and at any time and place and on any terms but every aspect of the sale including the method, manner, time, place and terms must be commercially reasonable. The resale must be reasonably identified as referring to the broken contract, but it is not necessary that the goods be in existence or that any or all of them have been identified to the contract before the breach.

(3) Where the resale is at private sale the seller must give the buyer reasonable notification of his intention to resell.

(4) Where the resale is at public sale

(a) only identified goods can be sold except where there is a recognized market for a public sale of futures in goods of the kind; and

(b) it must be made at a usual place or market for public sale if one is reasonably available and except in the case of goods which are perishable or threaten to decline in value speedily the seller must give the buyer reasonable notice of the time and place of the resale; and

(c) if the goods are not to be within the view of those attending the sale the notification of sale must state the place where the goods are located and provide for their reasonable inspection by prospective bidders; and

(d) the seller may buy.

(5) A purchaser who buys in good faith at a resale takes the goods free of any rights of the original buyer even though the seller fails to comply with one or more of the requirements of this section.

(6) The seller is not accountable to the buyer for any profit made on any resale. A person in the position of a seller (Section 2—707) or a buyer who has rightfully rejected or justifiably revoked acceptance must account

for any excess over the amount of his security interest, as hereinafter defined (subsection (3) of Section 2—711).

§ 2—707. "Person in the Position of a Seller".

(1) A "person in the position of a seller" includes as against a principal an agent who has paid or become responsible for the price of goods on behalf of his principal or anyone who otherwise holds a security interest or other right in goods similar to that of a seller.

(2) A person in the position of a seller may as provided in this Article withhold or stop delivery (Section 2—705) and resell (Section 2—706) and recover incidental damages (Section 2—710).

§ 2—708. Seller's Damages for Non-Acceptance or Repudiation.

(1) Subject to subsection (2) and to the provisions of this Article with respect to proof of market price (Section 2—723), the measure of damages for non-acceptance or repudiation by the buyer is the difference between the market price at the time and place for tender and the unpaid contract price together with any incidental damages provided in this Article (Section 2—710), but less expenses saved in consequence of the buyer's breach.

(2) If the measure of damages provided in subsection (1) is inadequate to put the seller in as good a position as performance would have done then the measure of damages is the profit (including reasonable overhead) which the seller would have made from full performance by the buyer, together with any incidental damages provided in this Article (Section 2—710), due allowance for costs reasonably incurred and due credit for payments or proceeds of resale.

§ 2—709. Action for the Price.

(1) When the buyer fails to pay the price as it becomes due the seller may recover, together with any incidental damages under the next section, the price

(a) of goods accepted or of conforming goods lost or damaged within a commercially reasonable time after risk of their loss has passed to the buyer; and

(b) of goods identified to the contract if the seller is unable after reasonable effort to resell them at a reasonable price or the circumstances reasonably indicate that such effort will be unavailing.

(2) Where the seller sues for the price he must hold for the buyer any goods which have been identified to the contract and are still in his control except that if resale becomes possible he may resell them at any time prior to the collection of the judgment. The net proceeds of any such resale must be credited to the buyer and payment of the judgment entitles him to any goods not resold.

(3) After the buyer has wrongfully rejected or revoked acceptance of the goods or has failed to make a payment due or has repudiated (Section 2—610), a seller who is held not entitled to the price under this section shall nevertheless be awarded damages for non-acceptance under the preceding section.

§ 2—710. Seller's Incidental Damages.

Incidental damages to an aggrieved seller include any commercially reasonable charges, expenses or commissions incurred in stopping delivery, in the transportation, care and custody of goods after the buyer's breach, in connection with return or resale of the goods or otherwise resulting from the breach.

§ 2—711. Buyer's Remedies in General; Buyer's Security Interest in Rejected Goods.

(1) Where the seller fails to make delivery or repudiates or the buyer rightfully rejects or justifiably revokes acceptance then with respect to any goods involved, and with respect to the whole if the breach goes to the whole contract (Section 2—612), the buyer may cancel and whether or not he has done so may in addition to recovering so much of the price as has been paid

(a) "cover" and have damages under the next section as to all the goods affected whether or not they have been identified to the contract; or

(b) recover damages for non-delivery as provided in this Article (Section 2—713).

(2) Where the seller fails to deliver or repudiates the buyer may also

(a) if the goods have been identified recover them as provided in this Article (Section 2—502); or

(b) in a proper case obtain specific performance or replevy the goods as provided in this Article (Section 2—716).

(3) On rightful rejection or justifiable revocation of acceptance a buyer has a security interest in goods in his possession or control for any payments made on their price and any expenses reasonably incurred in their inspection, receipt, transportation, care and custody and may hold such goods and resell them in like manner as an aggrieved seller (Section 2—706).

§ 2—712. "Cover"; Buyer's Procurement of Substitute Goods.

(1) After a breach within the preceding section the buyer may "cover" by making in good faith and without unreasonable delay any reasonable purchase of or contract to purchase goods in substitution for those due from the seller.

(2) The buyer may recover from the seller as damages the difference between the cost of cover and the contract

price together with any incidental or consequential damages as hereinafter defined (Section 2—715), but less expenses saved in consequence of the seller's breach.

(3) Failure of the buyer to effect cover within this section does not bar him from any other remedy.

§ 2—713. **Buyer's Damages for Non-Delivery or Repudiation.**

(1) Subject to the provisions of this Article with respect to proof of market price (Section 2—723), the measure of damages for non-delivery or repudiation by the seller is the difference between the market price at the time when the buyer learned of the breach and the contract price together with any incidental and consequential damages provided in this Article (Section 2—715), but less expenses saved in consequence of the seller's breach.

(2) Market price is to be determined as of the place for tender or, in cases of rejection after arrival or revocation of acceptance, as of the place of arrival.

§ 2—714. **Buyer's Damages for Breach in Regard to Accepted Goods.**

(1) Where the buyer has accepted goods and given notification (subsection (3) of Section 2—607) he may recover as damages for any non-conformity of tender the loss resulting in the ordinary course of events from the seller's breach as determined in any manner which is reasonable.

(2) The measure of damages for breach of warranty is the difference at the time and place of acceptance between the value of the goods accepted and the value they would have had if they had been as warranted, unless special circumstances show proximate damages of a different amount.

(3) In a proper case any incidental and consequential damages under the next section may also be recovered.

§ 2—715. **Buyer's Incidental and Consequential Damages.**

(1) Incidental damages resulting from the seller's breach include expenses reasonably incurred in inspection, receipt, transportation and care and custody of goods rightfully rejected, any commercially reasonable charges, expenses or commissions in connection with effecting cover and any other reasonable expense incident to the delay or other breach.

(2) Consequential damages resulting from the seller's breach include

    (a) any loss resulting from general or particular requirements and needs of which the seller at the time of contracting had reason to know and which could not reasonably be prevented by cover or otherwise; and

    (b) injury to person or property proximately resulting from any breach of warranty.

§ 2—716. **Buyer's Right to Specific Performance or Replevin.**

(1) Specific performance may be decreed where the goods are unique or in other proper circumstances.

(2) The decree for specific performance may include such terms and conditions as to payment of the price, damages, or other relief as the court may deem just.

(3) The buyer has a right of replevin for goods identified to the contract if after reasonable effort he is unable to effect cover for such goods or the circumstances reasonably indicate that such effort will be unavailing or if the goods have been shipped under reservation and satisfaction of the security interest in them has been made or tendered.

§ 2—717. **Deduction of Damages From the Price.**

The buyer on notifying the seller of his intention to do so may deduct all or any part of the damages resulting from any breach of the contract from any part of the price still due under the same contract.

§ 2—718. **Liquidation or Limitation of Damages; Deposits.**

(1) Damages for breach by either party may be liquidated in the agreement but only at an amount which is reasonable in the light of the anticipated or actual harm caused by the breach, the difficulties of proof of loss, and the inconvenience or nonfeasibility of otherwise obtaining an adequate remedy. A term fixing unreasonably large liquidated damages is void as a penalty.

(2) Where the seller justifiably withholds delivery of goods because of the buyer's breach, the buyer is entitled to restitution of any amount by which the sum of his payments exceeds

    (a) the amount to which the seller is entitled by virtue of terms liquidating the seller's damages in accordance with subsection (1), or

    (b) in the absence of such terms, twenty per cent of the value of the total performance for which the buyer is obligated under the contract or $500, whichever is smaller.

(3) The buyer's right to restitution under subsection (2) is subject to offset to the extent that the seller establishes

    (a) a right to recover damages under the provisions of this Article other than subsection (1), and

    (b) the amount or value of any benefits received by the buyer directly or indirectly by reason of the contract.

(4) Where a seller has received payment in goods their reasonable value or the proceeds of their resale shall be

treated as payments for the purposes of subsection (2); but if the seller has notice of the buyer's breach before reselling goods received in part performance, his resale is subject to the conditions laid down in this Article on resale by an aggrieved seller (Section 2—706).

§ 2—719. **Contractual Modification or Limitation of Remedy.**

(1) Subject to the provisions of subsections (2) and (3) of this section and of the preceding section on liquidation and limitation of damages,

(a) the agreement may provide for remedies in addition to or in substitution for those provided in this Article and may limit or alter the measure of damages recoverable under this Article, as by limiting the buyer's remedies to return of the goods and repayment of the price or to repair and replacement of non-conforming goods or parts; and

(b) resort to a remedy as provided is optional unless the remedy is expressly agreed to be exclusive, in which case it is the sole remedy.

(2) Where circumstances cause an exclusive or limited remedy to fail of its essential purpose, remedy may be had as provided in this Act.

(3) Consequential damages may be limited or excluded unless the limitation or exclusion is unconscionable. Limitation of consequential damages for injury to the person in the case of consumer goods is prima facie unconscionable but limitation of damages where the loss is commercial is not.

§ 2—720. **Effect of "Cancellation" or "Rescission" on Claims for Antecedent Breach.**

Unless the contrary intention clearly appears, expressions of "cancellation" or "rescission" of the contract or the like shall not be construed as a renunciation or discharge of any claim in damages for an antecedent breach.

§ 2—721. **Remedies for Fraud.**

Remedies for material misrepresentation or fraud include all remedies available under this Article for non-fraudulent breach. Neither rescission or a claim for rescission of the contract for sale nor rejection or return of the goods shall bar or be deemed inconsistent with a claim for damages or other remedy.

§ 2—722. **Who Can Sue Third Parties for Injury to Goods.**

Where a third party so deals with goods which have been identified to a contract for sale as to cause actionable injury to a party to that contract

(a) a right of action against the third party is in either party to the contract for sale who has title to or a security interest or a special property or an insurable interest in the goods; and if the goods have been destroyed or converted a right of action is also in the party who either bore the risk of loss under the contract for sale or has since the injury assumed that risk as against the other;

(b) if at the time of the injury the party plaintiff did not bear the risk of loss as against the other party to the contract for sale and there is no arrangement between them for disposition of the recovery, his suit or settlement is, subject to his own interest, as a fiduciary for the other party to the contract;

(c) either party may with the consent of the other sue for the benefit of whom it may concern.

§ 2—723. **Proof of Market Price: Time and Place.**

(1) If an action based on anticipatory repudiation comes to trial before the time for performance with respect to some or all of the goods, any damages based on market price (Section 2—708 or Section 2—713) shall be determined according to the price of such goods prevailing at the time when the aggrieved party learned of the repudiation.

(2) If evidence of a price prevailing at the times or places described in this Article is not readily available the price prevailing within any reasonable time before or after the time described or at any other place which in commercial judgment or under usage of trade would serve as a reasonable substitute for the one described may be used, making any proper allowance for the cost of transporting the goods to or from such other place.

(3) Evidence of a relevant price prevailing at a time or place other than the one described in this Article offered by one party is not admissible unless and until he has given the other party such notice as the court finds sufficient to prevent unfair surprise.

§ 2—724. **Admissibility of Market Quotations.**

Whenever the prevailing price or value of any goods regularly bought and sold in any established commodity market is in issue, reports in official publications or trade journals or in newspapers or periodicals of general circulation published as the reports of such market shall be admissible in evidence. The circumstances of the preparation of such a report may be shown to affect its weight but not its admissibility.

§ 2—725. **Statute of Limitations in Contracts for Sale.**

(1) An action for breach of any contract for sale must be commenced within four years after the cause of action has accrued. By the original agreement the parties may reduce the period of limitation to not less than one year but may not extend it.

(2) A cause of action accrues when the breach occurs, regardless of the aggrieved party's lack of knowledge of the breach. A breach of warranty occurs when tender of delivery is made, except that where a warranty explicitly extends to future performance of the goods and discovery of the breach must await the time of such performance the cause of action accrues when the breach is or should have been discovered.

(3) Where an action commenced within the time limited by subsection (1) is so terminated as to leave available a remedy by another action for the same breach such other action may be commenced after the expiration of the time limited and within six months after the termination of the first action unless the termination resulted from voluntary discontinuance or from dismissal for failure or neglect to prosecute.

(4) This section does not alter the law on tolling of the statute of limitations nor does it apply to causes of action which have accrued before this Act becomes effective.

Article 2A
LEASES

Part 1 General Provisions

§ 2A—101. Short Title.

This Article shall be known and may be cited as the Uniform Commercial Code—Leases.

§ 2A—102. Scope.

This Article applies to any transaction, regardless of form, that creates a lease.

§ 2A—103. Definitions and Index of Definitions.

(1) In this Article unless the context otherwise requires:

(a) "Buyer in ordinary course of business" means a person who in good faith and without knowledge that the sale to him [or her] is in violation of the ownership rights or security interest or leasehold interest of a third party in the goods buys in ordinary course from a person in the business of selling goods of that kind but does not include a pawnbroker. "Buying" may be for cash or by exchange of other property or on secured or unsecured credit and includes receiving goods or documents of title under a pre-existing contract for sale but does not include a transfer in bulk or as security for or in total or partial satisfaction of a money debt.

(b) "Cancellation" occurs when either party puts an end to the lease contract for default by the other party.

(c) "Commercial unit" means such a unit of goods as by commercial usage is a single whole for purposes of lease and division of which materially impairs its character or value on the market or in use. A commercial unit may be a single article, as a machine, or a set of articles, as a suite of furniture or a line of machinery, or a quantity, as a gross or carload, or any other unit treated in use or in the relevant market as a single whole.

(d) "Conforming" goods or performance under a lease contract means goods or performance that are in accordance with the obligations under the lease contract.

(e) "Consumer lease" means a lease that a lessor regularly engaged in the business of leasing or selling makes to a lessee, except an organization, who takes under the lease primarily for a personal, family, or household purpose, if the total payments to be made under the lease contract, excluding payments for options to renew or buy, do not exceed $25,000.

(f) "Fault" means wrongful act, omission, breach, or default.

(g) "Finance lease" means a lease in which (i) the lessor does not select, manufacture or supply the goods, (ii) the lessor acquires the goods or the right to possession and use of the goods in connection with the lease, and (iii) either the lessee receives a copy of the contract evidencing the lessor's purchase of the goods on or before signing the lease contract, or the lessee's approval of the contract evidencing the lessor's purchase of the goods is a condition to effectiveness of the lease contract.

(h) "Goods" means all things that are movable at the time of identification to the lease contract, or are fixtures (Section 2A—309), but the term does not include money, documents, instruments, accounts, chattel paper, general intangibles, or minerals or the like, including oil and gas, before extraction. The term also includes the unborn young of animals.

(i) "Installment lease contract" means a lease contract that authorizes or requires the delivery of goods in separate lots to be separately accepted, even though the lease contract contains a clause "each delivery is a separate lease" or its equivalent.

(j) "Lease" means a transfer of the right to possession and use of goods for a term in return for consideration, but a sale, including a sale on approval or a sale or return, or retention or creation of a security interest is not a lease. Unless the context clearly indicates otherwise, the term includes a sublease.

(k) "Lease agreement" means the bargain, with respect to the lease, of the lessor and the lessee in fact as found in their language or by implication from other circumstances including course of dealing or usage of trade or course of performance as provided in this Article. Unless the context clearly indicates otherwise, the term includes a sublease agreement.

(l) "Lease contract" means the total legal obligation that results from the lease agreement as affected by this Article and any other applicable rules of law. Unless the context clearly indicates otherwise, the term includes a sublease contract.

(m) "Leasehold interest" means the interest of the lessor or the lessee under a lease contract.

(n) "Lessee" means a person who acquires the right to possession and use of goods under a lease. Unless the context clearly indicates otherwise, the term includes a sublessee.

(o) "Lessee in ordinary course of business" means a person who in good faith and without knowledge that the lease to him [or her] is in violation of the ownership rights or security interest or leasehold interest of a third party in the goods, leases in ordinary course from a person in the business of selling or leasing goods of that kind but does not include a pawnbroker. "Leasing" may be for cash or by exchange of other property or on secured or unsecured credit and includes receiving goods or documents of title under a pre-existing lease contract but does not include a transfer in bulk or as security for or in total or partial satisfaction of a money debt.

(p) "Lessor" means a person who transfers the right to possession and use of goods under a lease. Unless the context clearly indicates otherwise, the term includes a sublessor.

(q) "Lessor's residual interest" means the lessor's interest in the goods after expiration, termination, or cancellation of the lease contract.

(r) "Lien" means a charge against or interest in goods to secure payment of a debt or performance of an obligation, but the term does not include a security interest.

(s) "Lot" means a parcel or a single article that is the subject matter of a separate lease or delivery, whether or not it is sufficient to perform the lease contract.

(t) "Merchant lessee" means a lessee that is a merchant with respect to goods of the kind subject to the lease.

(u) "Present value" means the amount as of a date certain of one or more sums payable in the future, discounted to the date certain. The discount is determined by the interest rate specified by the parties if the rate was not manifestly unreasonable at the time the transaction was entered into; otherwise, the discount is determined by a commercially reasonable rate that takes into account the facts and circumstances of each case at the time the transaction was entered into.

(v) "Purchase" includes taking by sale, lease, mortgage, security interest, pledge, gift, or any other voluntary transaction creating an interest in goods.

(w) "Sublease" means a lease of goods the right to possession and use of which was acquired by the lessor as a lessee under an existing lease.

(x) "Supplier" means a person from whom a lessor buys or leases goods to be leased under a finance lease.

(y) "Supply contract" means a contract under which a lessor buys or leases goods to be leased.

(z) "Termination" occurs when either party pursuant to a power created by agreement or law puts an end to the lease contract otherwise than for default.

(2) Other definitions applying to this Article and the sections in which they appear are:

"Accessions". Section 2A—310(1).
"Construction mortgage". Section 2A—309(1)(d).
"Encumbrance". Section 2A—309(1)(e).
"Fixtures". Section 2A—309(1)(a).
"Fixture filing". Section 2A—309(1)(b).
"Purchase money lease". Section 2A—309(1)(c).

(3) The following definitions in other Articles apply to this Article:

"Accounts". Section 9—106.
"Between merchants". Section 2—104(3).
"Buyer". Section 2—103(1)(a).
"Chattel paper". Section 9—105(1)(b).
"Consumer goods". Section 9—109(1).
"Documents". Section 9—105(1)(f).
"Entrusting". Section 2—403(3).
"General intangibles". Section 9—106.
"Good faith". Section 2—103(1)(b).
"Instruments". Section 9—105(1)(i).
"Merchant". Section 2—104(1).
"Mortgage". Section 9—105(1)(j).
"Pursuant to commitment". Section 9—105(1)(k).
"Receipt". Section 2—103(1)(c).
"Sale". Section 2—106(1).
"Sale on Approval". Section 2—326.
"Sale or Return". Section 2—326.
"Seller". Section 2—103(1)(d).

(4) In addition Article 1 contains general definitions and principles of construction and interpretation applicable throughout this Article.

§ 2A—104. **Leases Subject to Other Statutes.**

(1) A lease, although subject to this Article, is also subject to any applicable:

(a) statute of the United States;

(b) certificate of title statute of this State: (list any certificate of title statutes covering automobiles, trailers, mobile homes, boats, farm tractors, and the like);

(c) certificate of title statute of another jurisdiction (Section 2A—105); or

(d) consumer protection statute of this State.

(2) In case of conflict between the provisions of this Article, other than Sections 2A—105, 2A—304(3) and 2A—305(3), and any statute referred to in subsection (1), the provisions of that statute control.

(3) Failure to comply with any applicable statute has only the effect specified therein.

§ 2A—105. **Territorial Application of Article to Goods Covered by Certificate of Title.**

Subject to the provisions of Sections 2A—304(3) and 2A—305(3), with respect to goods covered by a certificate of title issued under a statute of this State or of another jurisdiction, compliance and the effect of compliance or noncompliance with a certificate of title statute are governed by the law (including the conflict of laws rules) of the jurisdiction issuing the certificate until the earlier of (a) surrender of the certificate, or (b) four months after the goods are removed from that jurisdiction and thereafter until a new certificate of title is issued by another jurisdiction.

§ 2A—106. **Limitation on Power of Parties to Consumer Lease to Choose Applicable Law and Judicial Forum.**

(1) If the law chosen by the parties to a consumer lease is that of a jurisdiction other than a jurisdiction in which the lessee resides at the time the lease agreement becomes enforceable or within 30 days thereafter or in which the goods are to be used, the choice is not enforceable.

(2) If the judicial forum chosen by the parties to a consumer lease is a forum that would not otherwise have jurisdiction over the lessee, the choice is not enforceable.

§ 2A—107. **Waiver or Renunciation of Claim or Right After Default.**

Any claim or right arising out of an alleged default or breach of warranty may be discharged in whole or in part without consideration by a written waiver or renunciation signed and delivered by the aggrieved party.

§ 2A—108. **Unconscionability.**

(1) If the court as a matter of law finds a lease contract or any clause of a lease contract to have been unconscionable at the time it was made the court may refuse to enforce the lease contract, or it may enforce the remainder of the lease contract without the unconscionable clause, or it may so limit the application of any unconscionable clause as to avoid any unconscionable result.

(2) With respect to a consumer lease, if the court as a matter of law finds that a lease contract or any clause of a lease contract has been induced by unconscionable conduct or that unconscionable conduct has occurred in the collection of a claim arising from a lease contract, the court may grant appropriate relief.

(3) Before making a finding of unconscionability under subsection (1) or (2), the court, on its own motion or that of a party, shall afford the parties a reasonable opportunity to present evidence as to the setting, purpose, and effect of the lease contract or clause thereof, or of the conduct.

(4) In an action in which the lessee claims unconscionability with respect to a consumer lease:

(a) If the court finds unconscionability under subsection (1) or (2), the court shall award reasonable attorney's fees to the lessee.

(b) If the court does not find unconscionability and the lessee claiming unconscionability has brought or maintained an action he [or she] knew to be groundless, the court shall award reasonable attorney's fees to the party against whom the claim is made.

(c) In determining attorney's fees, the amount of the recovery on behalf of the claimant under subsections (1) and (2) is not controlling.

§ 2A—109. **Option to Accelerate at Will.**

(1) A term providing that one party or his [or her] successor in interest may accelerate payment or performance or require collateral or additional collateral "at will" or "when he [or she] deems himself [or herself] insecure" or in words of similar import must be construed to mean that he [or she] has power to do so only if he [or she] in good faith believes that the prospect of payment or performance is impaired.

(2) With respect to a consumer lease, the burden of establishing good faith under subsection (1) is on the party who exercised the power; otherwise the burden of establishing lack of good faith is on the party against whom the power has been exercised.

Part 2 Formation and Construction of Lease Contract

§ 2A—201. **Statute of Frauds.**

(1) A lease contract is not enforceable by way of action or defense unless:

(a) the total payments to be made under the lease contract, excluding payments for options to renew or buy, are less than $1,000; or

(b) there is a writing, signed by the party against whom enforcement is sought or by that party's authorized agent, sufficient to indicate that a lease contract has been made between the parties and to describe the goods leased and the lease term.

(2) Any description of leased goods or of the lease term is sufficient and satisfies subsection (1)(b), whether or not it is specific, if it reasonably identifies what is described.

(3) A writing is not insufficient because it omits or incorrectly states a term agreed upon, but the lease contract is not enforceable under subsection (1)(b) beyond the lease term and the quantity of goods shown in this writing.

(4) A lease contract that does not satisfy the requirements of subsection (1), but which is valid in other respects, is enforceable:

(a) if the goods are to be specially manufactured or obtained for the lessee and are not suitable for lease or sale to others in the ordinary course of the lessor's business, and the lessor, before notice of repudiation is received and under circumstances that reasonably indicate that the goods are for the lessee, has made either a substantial beginning of their manufacture or commitments for their procurement;

(b) if the party against whom enforcement is sought admits in that party's pleading, testimony or otherwise in court that a lease contract was made, but the lease contract is not enforceable under this provision beyond the quantity of goods admitted; or

(c) with respect to goods that have been received and accepted by the lessee.

(5) The lease term under a lease contract referred to in subsection (4) is:

(a) if there is a writing signed by the party against whom enforcement is sought or by that party's authorized agent specifying the lease term, the term so specified;

(b) if the party against whom enforcement is sought admits in that party's pleading, testimony, or otherwise in court a lease term, the term so admitted; or

(c) a reasonable lease term.

§ 2A—202. **Final Written Expression: Parol or Extrinsic Evidence.**

Terms with respect to which the confirmatory memoranda of the parties agree or which are otherwise set forth in a writing intended by the parties as a final expression of their agreement with respect to such terms as are included therein may not be contradicted by evidence of any prior agreement or of a contemporaneous oral agreement but may be explained or supplemented:

(a) by course of dealing or usage of trade or by course of performance; and

(b) by evidence of consistent additional terms unless the court finds the writing to have been intended also as a complete and exclusive statement of the terms of the agreement.

§ 2A—203. **Seals Inoperative.**

The affixing of a seal to a writing evidencing a lease contract or an offer to enter into a lease contract does not render the writing a sealed instrument and the law with respect to sealed instruments does not apply to the lease contract or offer.

§ 2A—204. **Formation in General.**

(1) A lease contract may be made in any manner sufficient to show agreement, including conduct by both parties which recognizes the existence of a lease contract.

(2) An agreement sufficient to constitute a lease contract may be found although the moment of its making is undetermined.

(3) Although one or more terms are left open, a lease contract does not fail for indefiniteness if the parties have intended to make a lease contract and there is a reasonably certain basis for giving an appropriate remedy.

§ 2A—205. **Firm Offers.**

An offer by a merchant to lease goods to or from another person in a signed writing that by its terms gives assurance it will be held open is not revocable, for lack of consideration, during the time stated or, if no time is stated, for a reasonable time, but in no event may the period of irrevocability exceed 3 months. Any such term of assurance on a form supplied by the offeree must be separately signed by the offeror.

§ 2A—206. **Offer and Acceptance in Formation of Lease Contract.**

(1) Unless otherwise unambiguously indicated by the language or circumstances, an offer to make a lease contract must be construed as inviting acceptance in any manner and by any medium reasonable in the circumstances.

(2) If the beginning of a requested performance is a reasonable mode of acceptance, an offeror who is not notified of acceptance within a reasonable time may treat the offer as having lapsed before acceptance.

§ 2A—207. **Course of Performance or Practical Construction.**

(1) If a lease contract involves repeated occasions for performance by either party with knowledge of the na-

ture of the performance and opportunity for objection to it by the other, any course of performance accepted or acquiesced in without objection is relevant to determine the meaning of the lease agreement.

(2) The express terms of a lease agreement and any course of performance, as well as any course of dealing and usage of trade, must be construed whenever reasonable as consistent with each other; but if that construction is unreasonable, express terms control course of performance, course of performance controls both course of dealing and usage of trade, and course of dealing controls usage of trade.

(3) Subject to the provisions of Section 2A—208 on modification and waiver, course of performance is relevant to show a waiver or modification of any term inconsistent with the course of performance.

§ 2A—208. Modification, Rescission and Waiver.

(1) An agreement modifying a lease contract needs no consideration to be binding.

(2) A signed lease agreement that excludes modification or rescission except by a signed writing may not be otherwise modified or rescinded, but, except as between merchants, such a requirement on a form supplied by a merchant must be separately signed by the other party.

(3) Although an attempt at modification or rescission does not satisfy the requirements of subsection (2), it may operate as a waiver.

(4) A party who has made a waiver affecting an executory portion of a lease contract may retract the waiver by reasonable notification received by the other party that strict performance will be required of any term waived, unless the retraction would be unjust in view of a material change of position in reliance on the waiver.

§ 2A—209. Lessee under Finance Lease as Beneficiary of Supply Contract.

(1) The benefit of the supplier's promises to the lessor under the supply contract and of all warranties, whether express or implied, under the supply contract, extends to the lessee to the extent of the lessee's leasehold interest under a finance lease related to the supply contract, but subject to the terms of the supply contract and all of the supplier's defenses or claims arising therefrom.

(2) The extension of the benefit of the supplier's promises to the lessee does not: (a) modify the rights and obligations of the parties to the supply contract, whether arising therefrom or otherwise, or (b) impose any duty or liability under the supply contract on the lessee.

(3) Any modification or rescission of the supply contract by the supplier and the lessor is effective against the lessee unless, prior to the modification or rescission, the supplier has received notice that the lessee has entered into a finance lease related to the supply contract. If the supply contract is modified or rescinded after the lessee enters the finance lease, the lessee has a cause of action against the lessor, and against the supplier if the supplier has notice of the lessee's entering the finance lease when the supply contract is modified or rescinded. The lessee's recovery from such action shall put the lessee in as good a position as if the modification or rescission had not occurred.

§ 2A—210. Express Warranties.

(1) Express warranties by the lessor are created as follows:

(a) Any affirmation of fact or promise made by the lessor to the lessee which relates to the goods and becomes part of the basis of the bargain creates an express warranty that the goods will conform to the affirmation or promise.

(b) Any description of the goods which is made part of the basis of the bargain creates an express warranty that the goods will conform to the description.

(c) Any sample or model that is made part of the basis of the bargain creates an express warranty that the whole of the goods will conform to the sample or model.

(2) It is not necessary to the creation of an express warranty that the lessor use formal words, such as "warrant" or "guarantee," or that the lessor have a specific intention to make a warranty, but an affirmation merely of the value of the goods or a statement purporting to be merely the lessor's opinion or commendation of the goods does not create a warranty.

§ 2A—211. Warranties Against Interference and Against Infringement; Lessee's Obligation Against Infringement.

(1) There is in a lease contract a warranty that for the lease term no person holds a claim to or interest in the goods that arose from an act or omission of the lessor, other than a claim by way of infringement or the like, which will interfere with the lessee's enjoyment of its leasehold interest.

(2) Except in a finance lease there is in a lease contract by a lessor who is a merchant regularly dealing in goods of the kind a warranty that the goods are delivered free of the rightful claim of any person by way of infringement or the like.

(3) A lessee who furnishes specifications to a lessor or a supplier shall hold the lessor and the supplier harmless against any claim by way of infringement or the like that arises out of compliance with the specifications.

§ 2A—212. Implied Warranty of Merchantability.

(1) Except in a finance lease, a warranty that the goods will be merchantable is implied in a lease contract if the lessor is a merchant with respect to goods of that kind.

(2) Goods to be merchantable must be at least such as

(a) pass without objection in the trade under the description in the lease agreement;

(b) in the case of fungible goods, are of fair average quality within the description;

(c) are fit for the ordinary purposes for which goods of that type are used;

(d) run, within the variation permitted by the lease agreement, of even kind, quality, and quantity within each unit and among all units involved;

(e) are adequately contained, packaged, and labeled as the lease agreement may require; and

(f) conform to any promises or affirmations of fact made on the container or label.

(3) Other implied warranties may arise from course of dealing or usage of trade.

§ 2A—213. Implied Warranty of Fitness for Particular Purpose.

Except in a finance of lease, if the lessor at the time the lease contract is made has reason to know of any particular purpose for which the goods are required and that the lessee is relying on the lessor's skill or judgment to select or furnish suitable goods, there is in the lease contract an implied warranty that the goods will be fit for that purpose.

§ 2A—214. Exclusion or Modification of Warranties.

(1) Words or conduct relevant to the creation of an express warranty and words or conduct tending to negate or limit a warranty must be construed wherever reasonable as consistent with each other; but, subject to the provisions of Section 2A—202 on parol or extrinsic evidence, negation or limitation is inoperative to the extent that the construction is unreasonable.

(2) Subject to subsection (3), to exclude or modify the implied warranty of merchantability or any part of it the language must mention "merchantability", be by a writing, and be conspicuous. Subject to subsection (3), to exclude or modify any implied warranty of fitness the exclusion must be by a writing and be conspicuous. Language to exclude all implied warranties of fitness is sufficient if it is conspicuous and states, for example, "There is no warranty that the goods will be fit for a particular purpose".

(3) Notwithstanding subsection (2), but subject to subsection (4),

(a) unless the circumstances indicate otherwise, all implied warranties are excluded by expressions like "as is" or "with all faults" or by other language that in common understanding calls the lessee's attention to the exclusion of warranties and makes plain that there is no implied warranty, and is conspicuous;

(b) if the lessee before entering into the lease contract has examined the goods or the sample or model as fully as desired or has refused to examine the goods, there is no implied warranty with regard to defects that an examination ought in the circumstances to have revealed; and

(c) an implied warranty may also be excluded or modified by course of dealing, course of performance, or usage of trade.

(4) To exclude or modify a warranty against interference or against infringement (Section 2A—211) or any part of it, the language must be specific, be by a writing, and be conspicuous, unless the circumstances, including course of performance, course of dealing, or usage of trade, give the lessee reason to know that the goods are being leased subject to a claim or interest of any person.

§ 2A—215. Cumulation and Conflict of Warranties Express or Implied.

Warranties, whether express or implied, must be construed as consistent with each other and as cumulative, but if that construction is unreasonable, the intention of the parties determines which warranty is dominant. In ascertaining that intention the following rules apply:

(a) Exact or technical specifications displace an inconsistent sample or model or general language of description.

(b) A sample from an existing bulk displaces inconsistent general language of description.

(c) Express warranties displace inconsistent implied warranties other than an implied warranty of fitness for a particular purpose.

§ 2A—216. Third-Party Beneficiaries of Express and Implied Warranties.

Alternative A

A warranty to or for the benefit of a lessee under this Article, whether express or implied, extends to any natural person who is in the family or household of the lessee or who is a guest in the lessee's home if it is reasonable to expect that such person may use, consume, or be affected by the goods and who is injured in person by breach of the warranty. This section does not displace principles of law and equity that extend a warranty to or for the benefit of a lessee to other persons. The operation of this section may not be excluded, modified, or limited, but an exclusion, modification, or limitation of the warranty, including any with respect to rights and remedies, effective against the lessee is also effective against any beneficiary designated under this section.

Alternative B

A warranty to or for the benefit of a lessee under this Article, whether express or implied, extends to any natural person who may reasonably be expected to use, consume, or be affected by the goods and who is injured in person by breach of the warranty. This section does not displace principles of law and equity that extend a warranty to or for the benefit of a lessee to other persons. The operation of this section may not be excluded, modified, or limited, but an exclusion, modification, or limitation of the warranty, including any with respect to rights and remedies, effective against the lessee is also effective against the beneficiary designated under this section.

Alternative C

A warranty to or for the benefit of a lessee under this Article, whether express or implied, extends to any person who may reasonably be expected to use, consume, or be affected by the goods and who is injured by breach of the warranty. The operation of this section may not be excluded, modified, or limited with respect to injury to the person of an individual to whom the warranty extends, but an exclusion, modification, or limitation of the warranty, including any with respect to rights and remedies, effective against the lessee is also effective against the beneficiary designated under this section.

§ 2A—217. Identification.

Identification of goods as goods to which a lease contract refers may be made at any time and in any manner explicitly agreed to by the parties. In the absence of explicit agreement, identification occurs:

(a) when the lease contract is made if the lease contract is for a lease of goods that are existing and identified;

(b) when the goods are shipped, marked, or otherwise designated by the lessor as goods to which the lease contract refers, if the lease contract is for a lease of goods that are not existing and identified; or

(c) when the young are conceived, if the lease contract is for a lease of unborn young of animals.

§ 2A—218. Insurance and Proceeds.

(1) A lessee obtains an insurable interest when existing goods are identified to the lease contract even though the goods identified are nonconforming and the lessee has an option to reject them.

(2) If a lessee has an insurable interest only by reason of the lessor's identification of the goods, the lessor, until default or insolvency or notification to the lessee that identification is final, may substitute other goods for those identified.

(3) Notwithstanding a lessee's insurable interest under subsections (1) and (2), the lessor retains an insurable interest until an option to buy has been exercised by the lessee and risk of loss has passed to the lessee.

(4) Nothing in this section impairs any insurable interest recognized under any other statute or rule of law.

(5) The parties by agreement may determine that one or more parties have an obligation to obtain and pay for insurance covering the goods and by agreement may determine the beneficiary of the proceeds of the insurance.

§ 2A—219. Risk of Loss.

(1) Except in the case of a finance lease, risk of loss is retained by the lessor and does not pass to the lessee. In the case of a finance lease, risk of loss passes to the lessee.

(2) Subject to the provisions of this Article on the effect of default on risk of loss (Section 2A—220), if risk of loss is to pass to the lessee and the time of passage is not stated, the following rules apply:

(a) If the lease contract requires or authorizes the goods to be shipped by carrier.

(i) and it does not require delivery at a particular destination, the risk of loss passes to the lessee when the goods are duly delivered to the carrier; but

(ii) if it does require delivery at a particular destination and the goods are there duly tendered while in the possession of the carrier, the risk of loss passes to the lessee when the goods are there duly so tendered as to enable the lessee to take delivery.

(b) If the goods are held by a bailee to be delivered without being moved, the risk of loss passes to the lessee on acknowledgment by the bailee of the lessee's right to possession of the goods.

(c) In any case not within subsection (a) or (b), the risk of loss passes to the lessee on the lessee's receipt of the goods if the lessor, or, in the case of a finance lease, the supplier, is a merchant; otherwise the risk passes to the lessee on tender of delivery.

§ 2A—220. Effect of Default on Risk of Loss.

(1) Where risk of loss is to pass to the lessee and the time of passage is not stated:

(a) If a tender or delivery of goods so fails to conform to the lease contract as to give a right of rejection, the risk of their loss remains with the lessor, or, in the case of a finance lease, the supplier, until cure or acceptance.

(b) If the lessee rightfully revokes acceptance, he [or she], to the extent of any deficiency in his [or her] effective insurance coverage, may treat the risk of loss as having remained with the lessor from the beginning.

(2) Whether or not risk of loss is to pass to the lessee, if the lessee as to conforming goods already identified to a lease contract repudiates or is otherwise in default under the lease contract, the lessor, or, in the case of a finance lease, the supplier, to the extent of any deficiency in his [or her] effective insurance coverage may treat the risk of loss as resting on the lessee for a commercially reasonable time.

§ 2A—221. Casualty to Identified Goods.

If a lease contract requires goods identified when the lease contract is made, and the goods suffer casualty without fault of the lessee, the lessor or the supplier before delivery, or the goods suffer casualty before risk of loss passes to the lessee pursuant to the lease agreement or Section 2A—219, then:

(a) if the loss is total, the lease contract is avoided; and

(b) if the loss is partial or the goods have so deteriorated as to no longer conform to the lease contract, the lessee may nevertheless demand inspection and at his [or her] option either treat the lease contract as avoided or, except in a finance lease that is not a consumer lease, accept the goods with due allowance from the rent payable for the balance of the lease term for the deterioration or the deficiency in quantity but without further right against the lessor.

Part 3 Effect Of Lease Contract

§ 2A—301. Enforceability of Lease Contract.

Except as otherwise provided in this Article, a lease contract is effective and enforceable according to its terms between the parties, against purchasers of the goods and against creditors of the parties.

§ 2A—302. Title to and Possession of Goods.

Except as otherwise provided in this Article, each provision of this Article applies whether the lessor or a third party has title to the goods, and whether the lessor, the lessee, or a third party has possession of the goods, notwithstanding any statute or rule of law that possession or the absence of possession is fraudulent.

§ 2A—303. Alienability of Party's Interest Under Lease Contract or of Lessor's Residual Interest in Goods; Delegation of Performance; Assignment of Rights.

(1) Any interest of a party under a lease contract and the lessor's residual interest in the goods may be transferred unless

(a) the transfer is voluntary and the lease contract prohibits the transfer; or

(b) the transfer materially changes the duty of or materially increases the burden or risk imposed on the other party to the lease contract, and within a reasonable time after notice of the transfer the other party demands that the transferee comply with subsection (2) and the transferee fails to comply.

(2) Within a reasonable time after demand pursuant to subsection (1)(b), the transferee shall:

(a) cure or provide adequate assurance that he [or she] will promptly cure any default other than one arising from the transfer;

(b) compensate or provide adequate assurance that he [or she] will promptly compensate the other party to the lease contract and any other person holding an interest in the lease contract, except the party whose interest is being transferred, for any loss to that party resulting from the transfer;

(c) provide adequate assurance of future due performance under the lease contract; and

(d) assume the lease contract.

(3) Demand pursuant to subsection (1)(b) is without prejudice to the other party's rights against the transferee and the party whose interest is transferred.

(4) An assignment of "the lease" or of "all my rights under the lease" or an assignment in similar general terms is a transfer of rights, and unless the language or the circumstances, as in an assignment for security, indicate the contrary, the assignment is a delegation of duties by the assignor to the assignee and acceptance by the assignee constitutes a promise by him [or her] to perform those duties. This promise is enforceable by either the assignor or the other party to the lease contract.

(5) Unless otherwise agreed by the lessor and the lessee, no delegation of performance relieves the assignor as against the other party of any duty to perform or any liability for default.

(6) A right to damages for default with respect to the whole lease contract or a right arising out of the assignor's due performance of his [or her] entire obligation can be assigned despite agreement otherwise.

(7) To prohibit the transfer of an interest of a party under a lease contract, the language of prohibition must be specific, by a writing, and conspicuous.

§ 2A—304. Subsequent Lease of Goods by Lessor.

(1) Subject to the provisions of Section 2A—303, a subsequent lessee from a lessor of goods under an existing lease contract obtains, to the extent of the leasehold interest transferred, the leasehold interest in the goods

that the lessor had or had power to transfer, and except as provided in subsection (2) and Section 2A—527(4), takes subject to the existing lease contract. A lessor with voidable title has power to transfer a good leasehold interest to a good faith subsequent lessee for value, but only to the extent set forth in the preceding sentence. When goods have been delivered under a transaction of purchase the lessor has that power even though:

(a) the lessor's transferor was deceived as to the identity of the lessor;

(b) the delivery was in exchange for a check which is later dishonored;

(c) it was agreed that the transaction was to be a "cash sale"; or

(d) the delivery was procured through fraud punishable as larcenous under the criminal law.

(2) A subsequent lessee in the ordinary course of business from a lessor who is a merchant dealing in goods of that kind to whom the goods were entrusted by the existing lessee before the interest of the subsequent lessee became enforceable against the lessor obtains, to the extent of the leasehold interest transferred, all of the lessor's and the existing lessee's rights to the goods, and takes free of the existing lease contract.

(3) A subsequent lessee from the lessor of goods that are subject to an existing lease contract and are covered by a certificate of title issued under a statute of this State or of another jurisdiction takes no greater rights than those provided both by this section and by the certificate of title statute.

§ 2A—305. **Sale or Sublease of Goods by Lessee.**

(1) Subject to the provisions of Section 2A—303, a buyer or sublessee from the lessee of goods under an existing lease contract obtains, to the extent of the interest transferred, the leasehold interest in the goods that the lessee had or had power to transfer, and except as provided in subsection (2) and Section 2A—511(4), takes subject to the existing lease contract. A lessee with a voidable leasehold interest has power to transfer a good leasehold interest to a good faith buyer for value or a good faith sublessee for value, but only to the extent set forth in the preceding sentence. When goods have been delivered under a transaction of lease the lessee has that power even though:

(a) the lessor was deceived as to the identity of the lessee;

(b) the delivery was in exchange for a check which is later dishonored; or

(c) the delivery was procured through fraud punishable as larcenous under the criminal law.

(2) A buyer in the ordinary course of business or a sublessee in the ordinary course of business from a lessee who is a merchant dealing in goods of that kind to whom the goods were entrusted by the lessor obtains, to the extent of the interest transferred, all of the lessor's and lessee's rights to the goods, and takes free of the existing lease contract.

(3) A buyer or sublessee from the lessee of goods that are subject to an existing lease contract and are covered by a certificate of title issued under a statute of this State or of another jurisdiction takes no greater rights than those provided both by this section and by the certificate of title statute.

§ 2A—306. **Priority of Certain Liens Arising by Operation of Law.**

If a person in the ordinary course of his [or her] business furnishes services or materials with respect to goods subject to a lease contract, a lien upon those goods in the possession of that person given by statute or rule of law for those materials or services takes priority over any interest of the lessor or lessee under the lease contract or this Article unless the lien is created by statute and the statute provides otherwise or unless the lien is created by rule of law and the rule of law provides otherwise.

§ 2A—307. **Priority of Liens Arising by Attachment or Levy on, Security Interests in, and Other Claims to Goods.**

(1) Except as otherwise provided in Section 2A—306, a creditor of a lessee takes subject to the lease contract.

(2) Except as otherwise provided in subsections (3) and (4) of this section and in Sections 2A—306 and 2A—308, a creditor of a lessor takes subject to the lease contract:

(a) unless the creditor holds a lien that attached to the goods before the lease contract became enforceable, or

(b) unless the creditor holds a security interest in the goods that under the Article on Secured Transactions (Article 9) would have priority over any other security interest in the goods perfected by a filing covering the goods and made at the time the lease contract became enforceable, whether or not any other security interest existed.

(3) A lessee in the ordinary course of business takes the leasehold interest free of a security interest in the goods created by the lessor even though the security interest is perfected and the lessee knows of its existence.

(4) A lessee other than a lessee in the ordinary course of business takes the leasehold interest free of a security interest to the extent that it secures future advances

made after the secured party acquires knowledge of the lease or more than 45 days after the lease contract becomes enforceable, whichever first occurs, unless the future advances are made pursuant to a commitment entered into without knowledge of the lease and before the expiration of the 45-day period.

§ 2A—308. **Special Rights of Creditors.**

(1) A creditor of a lessor in possession of goods subject to a lease contract may treat the lease contract as void if as against the creditor retention of possession by the lessor is fraudulent under any statute or rule of law, but retention of possession in good faith and current course of trade by the lessor for a commercially reasonable time after the lease contract becomes enforceable is not fraudulent.

(2) Nothing in this Article impairs the rights of creditors of a lessor if the lease contract (a) becomes enforceable, not in current course of trade but in satisfaction of or as security for a pre-existing claim for money, security, or the like, and (b) is made under circumstances which under any statute or rule of law apart from this Article would constitute the transaction a fraudulent transfer or voidable preference.

(3) A creditor of a seller may treat a sale or an identification of goods to a contract for sale as void if as against the creditor retention of possession by the seller is fraudulent under any statute or rule of law, but retention of possession of the goods pursuant to a lease contract entered into by the seller as lessee and the buyer as lessor in connection with the sale or identification of the goods is not fraudulent if the buyer bought for value and in good faith.

§ 2A—309. **Lessor's and Lessee's Rights When Goods Become Fixtures.**

(1) In this section:

(a) goods are "fixtures" when they become so related to particular real estate that an interest in them arises under real estate law;

(b) a "fixture filing" is the filing, in the office where a mortgage on the real estate would be recorded or registered, of a financing statement concerning goods that are or are to become fixtures and conforming to the requirements of subsection (5) of Section 9—402;

(c) a lease is a "purchase money lease" unless the lessee has possession or use of the goods or the right to possession or use of the goods before the lease agreement is enforceable;

(d) a mortgage is a "construction mortgage" to the extent it secures an obligation incurred for the construction of an improvement on land including the acquisition cost of the land, if the recorded writing so indicates; and

(e) "encumbrance" includes real estate mortgages and other liens on real estate and all other rights in real estate that are not ownership interests.

(2) Under this Article a lease may be of goods that are fixtures or may continue in goods that become fixtures, but no lease exists under this Article of ordinary building materials incorporated into an improvement on land.

(3) This Article does not prevent creation of a lease of fixtures pursuant to real estate law.

(4) The perfected interest of a lessor of fixtures has priority over a conflicting interest of an encumbrancer or owner of the real estate if:

(a) the lease is a purchase money lease, the conflicting interest of the encumbrancer or owner arises before the goods become fixtures, the interest of the lessor is perfected by a fixture filing before the goods become fixtures or within ten days thereafter, and the lessee has an interest of record in the real estate or is in possession of the real estate; or

(b) the interest of the lessor is perfected by a fixture filing before the interest of the encumbrancer or owner is of record, the lessor's interest has priority over any conflicting interest of a predecessor in title of the encumbrancer or owner, and the lessee has an interest of record in the real estate or is in possession of the real estate.

(5) The interest of a lessor of fixtures, whether or not perfected, has priority over the conflicting interest of an encumbrancer or owner of the real estate if:

(a) the fixtures are readily removable factory or office machines, readily removable equipment that is not primarily used or leased for use in the operation of the real estate, or readily removable replacements of domestic appliances that are goods subject to a consumer lease, and before the goods become fixtures the lease contract is enforceable; or

(b) the conflicting interest is a lien on the real estate obtained by legal or equitable proceedings after the lease contract is enforceable; or

(c) the encumbrancer or owner has consented in writing to the lease or has disclaimed an interest in the goods as fixtures; or

(d) the lessee has a right to remove the goods as against the encumbrancer or owner. If the lessee's right to remove terminates, the priority of the interest of the lessor continues for a reasonable time.

(6) Notwithstanding paragraph (a) of subsection (4) but otherwise subject to subsections (4) and (5), the interest of a lessor of fixtures is subordinate to the conflicting

interest of an encumbrancer of the real estate under a construction mortgage recorded before the goods become fixtures if the goods become fixtures before the completion of the construction. To the extent given to refinance a construction mortgage, the conflicting interest of an encumbrancer of the real estate under a mortgage has this priority to the same extent as the encumbrancer of the real estate under the construction mortgage.

(7) In cases not within the preceding subsections, priority between the interest of a lessor of fixtures and the conflicting interest of an encumbrancer or owner of the real estate who is not the lessee is determined by the priority rules governing conflicting interests in real estate.

(8) If the interest of a lessor has priority over all conflicting interests of all owners and encumbrancers of the real estate, the lessor or the lessee may (a) on default, expiration, termination, or cancellation of the lease agreement by the other party but subject to the provisions of the lease agreement and this Article, or (b) if necessary to enforce his [or her] other rights and remedies under this Article, remove the goods from the real estate, free and clear of all conflicting interests of all owners and encumbrancers of the real estate, but he [or she] must reimburse any encumbrancer or owner of the real estate who is not the lessee and who has not otherwise agreed for the cost of repair of any physical injury, but not for any diminution in value of the real estate caused by the absence of the goods removed or by any necessity of replacing them. A person entitled to reimbursement may refuse permission to remove until the party seeking removal gives adequate security for the performance of this obligation.

(9) Even though the lease agreement does not create a security interest, the interest of a lessor of fixtures is perfected by filing a financing statement as a fixture filing for leased goods that are or are to become fixtures in accordance with the relevant provisions of the Article on Secured Transactions (Article 9).

§ 2A—310. Lessor's and Lessee's Rights When Goods Become Accessions.

(1) Goods are "accessions" when they are installed in or affixed to other goods.

(2) The interest of a lessor or a lessee under a lease contract entered into before the goods became accessions is superior to all interests in the whole except as stated in subsection (4).

(3) The interest of a lessor or a lessee under a lease contract entered into at the time or after the goods became accessions is superior to all subsequently acquired interests in the whole except as stated in subsection (4) but is subordinate to interests in the whole existing at the time the lease contract was made unless the holders of such interests in the whole have in writing consented to the lease or disclaimed an interest in the goods as part of the whole.

(4) The interest of a lessor or a lessee under a lease contract described in subsection (2) or (3) is subordinate to the interest of

(a) a buyer in the ordinary course of business or a lessee in the ordinary course of business of any interest in the whole acquired after the goods became accessions; or

(b) a creditor with a security interest in the whole perfected before the lease contract was made to the extent that the creditor makes subsequent advances without knowledge of the lease contract.

(5) When under subsections (2) or (3) and (4) a lessor or a lessee of accessions holds an interest that is superior to all interests in the whole, the lessor or the lessee may (a) on default, expiration, termination, or cancellation of the lease contract by the other party but subject to the provisions of the lease contract and this Article, or (b) if necessary to enforce his [or her] other rights and remedies under this Article, remove the goods from the whole, free and clear of all interests in the whole, but he [or she] must reimburse any holder of an interest in the whole who is not the lessee and who has not otherwise agreed for the cost of repair of any physical injury but not for any diminution in value of the whole caused by the absence of the goods removed or by any necessity for replacing them. A person entitled to reimbursement may refuse permission to remove until the party seeking removal gives adequate security for the performance of this obligation.

Part 4 Performance Of Lease Contract: Repudiated, Substituted And Excused

§ 2A—401. Insecurity: Adequate Assurance of Performance.

(1) A lease contract imposes an obligation on each party that the other's expectation of receiving due performance will not be impaired.

(2) If reasonable grounds for insecurity arise with respect to the performance of either party, the insecure party may demand in writing adequate assurance of due performance. Until the insecure party receives that assurance, if commercially reasonable the insecure party may suspend any performance for which he [or she] has not already received the agreed return.

(3) A repudiation of the lease contract occurs if assurance of due performance adequate under the circumstances of the particular case is not provided to the insecure party within a reasonable time, not to exceed 30 days after receipt of a demand by the other party.

(4) Between merchants, the reasonableness of grounds for insecurity and the adequacy of any assurance offered must be determined according to commercial standards.

(5) Acceptance of any nonconforming delivery or payment does not prejudice the aggrieved party's right to demand adequate assurance of future performance.

§ 2A—402. **Anticipatory Repudiation.**

If either party repudiates a lease contract with respect to a performance not yet due under the lease contract, the loss of which performance will substantially impair the value of the lease contract to the other, the aggrieved party may:

(a) for a commercially reasonable time, await retraction of repudiation and performance by the repudiating party;

(b) make demand pursuant to Section 2A—401 and await assurance of future performance adequate under the circumstances of the particular case; or

(c) resort to any right or remedy upon default under the lease contract or this Article, even though the aggrieved party has notified the repudiating party that the aggrieved party would await the repudiating party's performance and assurance and has urged retraction. In addition, whether or not the aggrieved party is pursuing one of the foregoing remedies, the aggrieved party may suspend performance or, if the aggrieved party is the lessor, proceed in accordance with the provisions of this Article on the lessor's right to identify goods to the lease contract notwithstanding default or to salvage unfinished goods (Section 2A—524).

§ 2A—403. **Retraction of Anticipatory Repudiation.**

(1) Until the repudiating party's next performance is due, the repudiating party can retract the repudiation unless, since the repudiation, the aggrieved party has cancelled the lease contract or materially changed the aggrieved party's position or otherwise indicated that the aggrieved party considers the repudiation final.

(2) Retraction may be by any method that clearly indicates to the aggrieved party that the repudiating party intends to perform under the lease contract and includes any assurance demanded under Section 2A—401.

(3) Retraction reinstates a repudiating party's rights under a lease contract with due excuse and allowance to the aggrieved party for any delay occasioned by the repudiation.

§ 2A—404. **Substituted Performance.**

(1) If without fault of the lessee, the lessor and the supplier, the agreed berthing, loading, or unloading facilities fail or the agreed type of carrier becomes unavailable or the agreed manner of delivery otherwise becomes commercially impracticable, but a commercially reasonable substitute is available, the substitute performance must be tendered and accepted.

(2) If the agreed means or manner of payment fails because of domestic or foreign governmental regulation:

(a) the lessor may withhold or stop delivery or cause the supplier to withhold or stop delivery unless the lessee provides a means or manner of payment that is commercially a substantial equivalent; and

(b) if delivery has already been taken, payment by the means or in the manner provided by the regulation discharges the lessee's obligation unless the regulation is discriminatory, oppressive, or predatory.

§ 2A—405. **Excused Performance.**

Subject to Section 2A—404 on substituted performance, the following rules apply:

(a) Delay in delivery or nondelivery in whole or in part by a lessor or a supplier who complies with paragraphs (b) and (c) is not a default under the lease contract if performance as agreed has been made impracticable by the occurrence of a contingency the nonoccurrence of which was a basic assumption on which the lease contract was made or by compliance in good faith with any applicable foreign or domestic governmental regulation or order, whether or not the regulation or order later proves to be invalid.

(b) If the causes mentioned in paragraph (a) affect only part of the lessor's or the supplier's capacity to perform, he [or she] shall allocate production and deliveries among his [or her] customers but at his [or her] option may include regular customers not then under contract for sale or lease as well as his [or her] own requirements for further manufacture. He [or she] may so allocate in any manner that is fair and reasonable.

(c) The lessor seasonably shall notify the lessee and in the case of a finance lease the supplier seasonably shall notify the lessor and the lessee, if known, that there will be delay or nondelivery and, if allocation is required under paragraph (b), of the estimated quota thus made available for the lessee.

§ 2A—406. **Procedure on Excused Performance.**

(1) If the lessee receives notification of a material or indefinite delay or an allocation justified under Section 2A—405, the lessee may by written notification to the lessor as to any goods involved, and with respect to all of the goods if under an installment lease contract the value of the whole lease contract is substantially impaired (Section 2A—510):

(a) terminate the lease contract (Section 2A—505(2)); or

(b) except in a finance lease that is not a consumer lease, modify the lease contract by accepting the available quota in substitution, with due allowance from the rent payable for the balance of the lease term for the deficiency but without further right against the lessor.

(2) If, after receipt of a notification from the lessor under Section 2A—405, the lessee fails so to modify the lease agreement within a reasonable time not exceeding 30 days, the lease contract lapses with respect to any deliveries affected.

§ 2A—407. Irrevocable Promises: Finance Leases.

(1) In the case of a finance lease that is not a consumer lease the lessee's promises under the lease contract become irrevocable and independent upon the lessee's acceptance of the goods.

(2) A promise that has become irrevocable and independent under subsection (1):

(a) is effective and enforceable between the parties or against third parties including assignees of the parties, and

(b) is not subject to cancellation, termination, modification, repudiation, excuse, or substitution without the consent of the party to whom the promise runs.

Part 5 Default
A. In General

§ 2A—501. Default: Procedure.

(1) Whether the lessor or the lessee is in default under a lease contract is determined by the lease agreement and this Article.

(2) If the lessor or the lessee is in default under the lease contract, the party seeking enforcement has rights and remedies as provided in this Article and, except as limited by this Article, as provided in the lease agreement.

(3) If the lessor or the lessee is in default under the lease contract, the party seeking enforcement may reduce the party's claim to judgment, or otherwise enforce the lease contract by self-help or any available judicial procedure or nonjudicial procedure, including administrative proceeding, arbitration, or the like, in accordance with this Article.

(4) Except as otherwise provided in this Article or the lease agreement, the rights and remedies referred to in subsections (2) and (3) are cumulative.

(5) If the lease agreement covers both real property and goods, the party seeking enforcement may proceed under this Part as to the goods, or under other applicable law as to both the real property and the goods in accordance with his [or her] rights and remedies in respect of the real property, in which case this Part does not apply.

§ 2A—502. Notice After Default.

Except as otherwise provided in this Article or the lease agreement, the lessor or lessee in default under the lease contract is not entitled to notice of default or notice of enforcement from the other party to the lease agreement.

§ 2A—503. Modification or Impairment of Rights and Remedies.

(1) Except as otherwise provided in this Article, the lease agreement may include rights and remedies for default in addition to or in substitution for those provided in this Article and may limit or alter the measure of damages recoverable under this Article.

(2) Resort to a remedy provided under this Article or in the lease agreement is optional unless the remedy is expressly agreed to be exclusive. If circumstances cause an exclusive or limited remedy to fail of its essential purpose, or provision for an exclusive remedy is unconscionable, remedy may be had as provided in this Article.

(3) Consequential damages may be liquidated under Section 2A—504, or may otherwise be limited, altered, or excluded unless the limitation, alteration, or exclusion is unconscionable. Limitation of consequential damages for injury to the person in the case of consumer goods is prima facie unconscionable but limitation of damages where the loss is commercial is not.

(4) Rights and remedies on default by the lessor or the lessee with respect to any obligation or promise collateral or ancillary to the lease contract are not impaired by this Article.

§ 2A—504. Liquidation of Damages.

(1) Damages payable by either party for default, or any other act or omission, including indemnity for loss or diminution of anticipated tax benefits or loss or damage to lessor's residual interest, may be liquidated in the lease agreement but only at an amount or by a formula that is reasonable in light of the then anticipated harm caused by the default or other act or omission.

(2) If the lease agreement provides for liquidation of damages, and such provision does not comply with subsection (1), or such provision is an exclusive or limited remedy that circumstances cause to fail of its essential purpose, remedy may be had as provided in this Article.

(3) If the lessor justifiably withholds or stops delivery of goods because of the lessee's default or insolvency (Section 2A—525 or 2A—526), the lessee is entitled to restitution of any amount by which the sum of his [or her] payments exceeds:

(a) the amount to which the lessor is entitled by virtue of terms liquidating the lessor's damages in accordance with subsection (1); or

(b) in the absence of those terms, 20 percent of the then present value of the total rent the lessee was obligated to pay for the balance of the lease term, or, in the case of a consumer lease, the lesser of such amount or $500.

(4) A lessee's right to restitution under subsection (3) is subject to offset to the extent the lessor establishes:

(a) a right to recover damages under the provisions of this Article other than subsection (1); and

(b) the amount or value of any benefits received by the lessee directly or indirectly by reason of the lease contract.

§ 2A—505. Cancellation and Termination and Effect of Cancellation, Termination, Rescission, or Fraud on Rights and Remedies.

(1) On cancellation of the lease contract, all obligations that are still executory on both sides are discharged, but any right based on prior default or performance survives, and the cancelling party also retains any remedy for default of the whole lease contract or any unperformed balance.

(2) On termination of the lease contract, all obligations that are still executory on both sides are discharged but any right based on prior default or performance survives.

(3) Unless the contrary intention clearly appears, expressions of "cancellation," "rescission," or the like of the lease contract may not be construed as a renunciation or discharge of any claim in damages for an antecedent default.

(4) Rights and remedies for material misrepresentation or fraud include all rights and remedies available under this Article for default.

(5) Neither rescission nor a claim for rescission of the lease contract nor rejection or return of the goods may bar or be deemed inconsistent with a claim for damages or other right or remedy.

§ 2A—506. Statute of Limitations.

(1) An action for default under a lease contract, including breach of warranty or indemnity, must be commenced within 4 years after the cause of action accrued. By the original lease contract the parties may reduce the period of limitation to not less than one year.

(2) A cause of action for default accrues when the act or omission on which the default or breach of warranty is based is or should have been discovered by the aggrieved party, or when the default occurs, whichever is later. A cause of action for indemnity accrues when the act or omission on which the claim for indemnity is based is or should have been discovered by the indemnified party, whichever is later.

(3) If an action commenced within the time limited by subsection (1) is so terminated as to leave available a remedy by another action for the same default or breach of warranty or indemnity, the other action may be commenced after the expiration of the time limited and within 6 months after the termination of the first action unless the termination resulted from voluntary discontinuance or from dismissal for failure or neglect to prosecute.

(4) This section does not alter the law on tolling of the statute of limitations nor does it apply to causes of action that have accrued before this Article becomes effective.

§ 2A—507. Proof of Market Rent: Time and Place.

(1) Damages based on market rent (Section 2A—519 or 2A—528) are determined according to the rent for the use of the goods concerned for a lease term identical to the remaining lease term of the original lease agreement and prevailing at the time of the default.

(2) If evidence of rent for the use of the goods concerned for a lease term identical to the remaining lease term of the original lease agreement and prevailing at the times or places described in this Article is not readily available, the rent prevailing within any reasonable time before or after the time described or at any other place or for a different lease term which in commercial judgment or under usage of trade would serve as a reasonable substitute for the one described may be used, making any proper allowance for the difference, including the cost of transporting the goods to or from the other place.

(3) Evidence of a relevant rent prevailing at a time or place or for a lease term other than the one described in this Article offered by one party is not admissible unless and until he [or she] has given the other party notice the court finds sufficient to prevent unfair surprise.

(4) If the prevailing rent or value of any goods regularly leased in any established market is in issue, reports in official publications or trade journals or in newspapers or periodicals of general circulation published as the reports of that market are admissible in evidence. The circumstances of the preparation of the report may be shown to affect its weight but not its admissibility.

B. Default by Lessor

§ 2A—508. Lessee's Remedies.

(1) If a lessor fails to deliver the goods in conformity to the lease contract (Section 2A—509) or repudiates the lease contract (Section 2A—402), or a lessee rightfully rejects the goods (Section 2A—509) or justifiably

revokes acceptance of the goods (Section 2A—517), then with respect to any goods involved, and with respect to all of the goods if under an installment lease contract the value of the whole lease contract is substantially impaired (Section 2A—510), the lessor is in default under the lease contract and the lessee may:

    (a) cancel the lease contract (Section 2A—505(1));

    (b) recover so much of the rent and security as has been paid, but in the case of an installment lease contract the recovery is that which is just under the circumstances;

    (c) cover and recover damages as to all goods affected whether or not they have been identified to the lease contract (Sections 2A—518 and 2A—520), or recover damages for nondelivery (Sections 2A—519 and 2A—520).

(2) If a lessor fails to deliver the goods in conformity to the lease contract or repudiates the lease contract, the lessee may also:

    (a) if the goods have been identified, recover them (Section 2A—522); or

    (b) in a proper case, obtain specific performance or replevy the goods (Section 2A—521).

(3) If a lessor is otherwise in default under a lease contract, the lessee may exercise the rights and remedies provided in the lease contract and this Article.

(4) If a lessor has breached a warranty, whether express or implied, the lessee may recover damages (Section 2A—519(4)).

(5) On rightful rejection or justifiable revocation of acceptance, a lessee has a security interest in goods in the lessee's possession or control for any rent and security that has been paid and any expenses reasonably incurred in their inspection, receipt, transportation, and care and custody and may hold those goods and dispose of them in good faith and in a commercially reasonable manner, subject to the provisions of Section 2A—527(5).

(6) Subject to the provisions of Section 2A—407, a lessee, on notifying the lessor of the lessee's intention to do so, may deduct all or any part of the damages resulting from any default under the lease contract from any part of the rent still due under the same lease contract.

§ 2A—509. Lessee's Rights on Improper Delivery; Rightful Rejection.

(1) Subject to the provisions of Section 2A—510 on default in installment lease contracts, if the goods or the tender or delivery fail in any respect to conform to the lease contract, the lessee may reject or accept the goods or accept any commercial unit or units and reject the rest of the goods.

(2) Rejection of goods is ineffective unless it is within a reasonable time after tender or delivery of the goods and the lessee seasonably notifies the lessor.

§ 2A—510. Installment Lease Contracts: Rejection and Default.

(1) Under an installment lease contract a lessee may reject any delivery that is nonconforming if the nonconformity substantially impairs the value of that delivery and cannot be cured or the nonconformity is a defect in the required documents; but if the nonconformity does not fall within subsection (2) and the lessor or the supplier gives adequate assurance of its cure, the lessee must accept that delivery.

(2) Whenever nonconformity or default with respect to one or more deliveries substantially impairs the value of the installment lease contract as a whole there is a default with respect to the whole. But, the aggrieved party reinstates the installment lease contract as a whole if the aggrieved party accepts a nonconforming delivery without seasonably notifying of cancellation or brings an action with respect only to past deliveries or demands performance as to future deliveries.

§ 2A—511. Merchant Lessee's Duties as to Rightfully Rejected Goods.

(1) Subject to any security interest of a lessee (Section 2A—508(5)), if a lessor or a supplier has no agent or place of business at the market of rejection, a merchant lessee, after rejection of goods in his [or her] possession or control, shall follow any reasonable instructions received from the lessor or the supplier with respect to the goods. In the absence of those instructions, a merchant lessee shall make reasonable efforts to sell, lease, or otherwise dispose of the goods for the lessor's account if they threaten to decline in value speedily. Instructions are not reasonable if on demand indemnity for expenses is not forthcoming.

(2) If a merchant lessee (subsection (1)) or any other lessee (Section 2A—512) disposes of goods, he [or she] is entitled to reimbursement either from the lessor or the supplier or out of the proceeds for reasonable expenses of caring for and disposing of the goods and, if the expenses include no disposition commission, to such commission as is usual in the trade, or if there is none, to a reasonable sum not exceeding 10 percent of the gross proceeds.

(3) In complying with this section or Section 2A—512, the lessee is held only to good faith. Good faith conduct hereunder is neither acceptance or conversion nor the basis of an action for damages.

(4) A purchaser who purchases in good faith from a lessee pursuant to this section or Section 2A—512 takes

the goods free of any rights of the lessor and the supplier even though the lessee fails to comply with one or more of the requirements of this Article.

§ 2A—512. **Lessee's Duties as to Rightfully Rejected Goods.**

(1) Except as otherwise provided with respect to goods that threaten to decline in value speedily (Section 2A—511) and subject to any security interest of a lessee (Section 2A—508(5)):

(a) the lessee, after rejection of goods in the lessee's possession, shall hold them with reasonable care at the lessor's or the supplier's disposition for a reasonable time after the lessee's seasonable notification of rejection;

(b) if the lessor or the supplier gives no instructions within a reasonable time after notification of rejection, the lessee may store the rejected goods for the lessor's or the supplier's account or ship them to the lessor or the supplier or dispose of them for the lessor's or the supplier's account with reimbursement in the manner provided in Section 2A—511; but

(c) the lessee has no further obligations with regard to goods rightfully rejected.

(2) Action by the lessee pursuant to subsection (1) is not acceptance or conversion.

§ 2A—513. **Cure by Lessor of Improper Tender or Delivery; Replacement.**

(1) If any tender or delivery by the lessor or the supplier is rejected because nonconforming and the time for performance has not yet expired, the lessor or the supplier may seasonably notify the lessee of the lessor's or the supplier's intention to cure and may then make a conforming delivery within the time provided in the lease contract.

(2) If the lessee rejects a nonconforming tender that the lessor or the supplier had reasonable grounds to believe would be acceptable with or without money allowance, the lessor or the supplier may have a further reasonable time to substitute a conforming tender if he [or she] seasonably notifies the lessee.

§ 2A—514. **Waiver of Lessee's Objections.**

(1) In rejecting goods, a lessee's failure to state a particular defect that is ascertainable by reasonable inspection precludes the lessee from relying on the defect to justify rejection or to establish default:

(a) if, stated seasonably, the lessor or the supplier could have cured it (Section 2A—513); or

(b) between merchants if the lessor or the supplier after rejection has made a request in writing for a full and final written statement of all defects on which the lessee proposes to rely.

(2) A lessee's failure to reserve rights when paying rent or other consideration against documents precludes recovery of the payment for defects apparent on the face of the documents.

§ 2A—515. **Acceptance of Goods.**

(1) Acceptance of goods occurs after the lessee has had a reasonable opportunity to inspect the goods and

(a) the lessee signifies or acts with respect to the goods in a manner that signifies to the lessor or the supplier that the goods are conforming or that the lessee will take or retain them in spite of their nonconformity; or

(b) the lessee fails to make an effective rejection of the goods (Section 2A—509(2)).

(2) Acceptance of a part of any commercial unit is acceptance of that entire unit.

§ 2A—516. **Effect of Acceptance of Goods; Notice of Default; Burden of Establishing Default after Acceptance; Notice of Claim or Litigation to Person Answerable Over.**

(1) A lessee must pay rent for any goods accepted in accordance with the lease contract, with due allowance for goods rightfully rejected or not delivered.

(2) A lessee's acceptance of goods precludes rejection of the goods accepted. In the case of a finance lease, if made with knowledge of a nonconformity, acceptance cannot be revoked because of it. In any other case, if made with knowledge of a nonconformity, acceptance cannot be revoked because of it unless the acceptance was on the reasonable assumption that the nonconformity would be seasonably cured. Acceptance does not of itself impair any other remedy provided by this Article or the lease agreement for nonconformity.

(3) If a tender has been accepted:

(a) within a reasonable time after the lessee discovers or should have discovered any default, the lessee shall notify the lessor and the supplier, or be barred from any remedy.

(b) except in the case of a consumer lease, within a reasonable time after the lessee receives notice of litigation for infringement or the like (Section 2A—211) the lessee shall notify the lessor or be barred from any remedy over for liability established by the litigation; and

(c) the burden is on the lessee to establish any default.

(4) If a lessee is sued for breach of a warranty or other obligation for which a lessor or a supplier is answerable over:

> (a) The lessee may give the lessor or the supplier written notice of the litigation. If the notice states that the lessor or the supplier may come in and defend and that if the lessor or the supplier does not do so he [or she] will be bound in any action against him [or her] by the lessee by any determination of fact common to the two litigations, then unless the lessor or the supplier after seasonable receipt of the notice does come in and defend he [or she] is so bound.
>
> (b) The lessor or the supplier may demand in writing that the lessee turn over control of the litigation including settlement if the claim is one for infringement or the like (Section 2A—211) or else be barred from any remedy over. If the demand states that the lessor or the supplier agrees to bear all expense and to satisfy any adverse judgment, then unless the lessee after seasonable receipt of the demand does turn over control the lessee is so barred.

(5) The provisions of subsections (3) and (4) apply to any obligation of a lessee to hold the lessor or the supplier harmless against infringement or the like (Section 2A—211).

§ 2A—517. Revocation of Acceptance of Goods.

(1) A lessee may revoke acceptance of a lot or commercial unit whose nonconformity substantially impairs its value to the lessee if he [or she] has accepted it:

> (a) except in the case of a finance lease, on the reasonable assumption that its nonconformity would be cured and it has not been seasonably cured; or
>
> (b) without discovery of the nonconformity if the lessee's acceptance was reasonably induced either by the lessor's assurances or, except in the case of a finance lease, by the difficulty or discovery before acceptance.

(2) Revocation of acceptance must occur within a reasonable time after the lessee discovers or should have discovered the ground for it and before any substantial change in condition of the goods which is not caused by the nonconformity. Revocation is not effective until the lessee notifies the lessor.

(3) A lessee who so revokes has the same rights and duties with regard to the goods involved as if the lessee had rejected them.

§ 2A—518. Cover; Substitute Goods.

(1) After default by a lessor under the lease contract (Section 2A—508(1)), the lessee may cover by making in good faith and without unreasonable delay any purchase or lease of or contract to purchase or lease goods in substitution for those due from the lessor.

(2) Except as otherwise provided with respect to damages liquidated in the lease agreement (Section 2A—504) or determined by agreement of the parties (Section 1—102(3)), if a lessee's cover is by lease agreement substantially similar to the original lease agreement and the lease agreement is made in good faith and in a commercially reasonable manner, the lessee may recover from the lessor as damages (a) the present value, as of the date of default, of the difference between the total rent for the lease term of the new lease agreement and the total rent for the remaining lease term of the original lease agreement and (b) any incidental or consequential damages less expenses saved in consequence of the lessor's default.

(3) If a lessee's cover does not qualify for treatment under subsection (2), the lessee may recover from the lessor as if the lessee had elected not to cover and Section 2A—519 governs.

§ 2A—519. Lessee's Damages for Non-Delivery, Repudiation, Default and Breach of Warranty in Regard to Accepted Goods.

(1) If a lessee elects not to cover or a lessee elects to cover and the cover does not qualify for treatment under Section 2A—518(2), the measure of damages for non-delivery or repudiation by the lessor or for rejection or revocation of acceptance by the lessee is the present value as of the date of the default of the difference between the then market rent and the original rent, computed for the remaining lease term of the original lease agreement together with incidental and consequential damages, less expenses saved in consequence of the lessor's default.

(2) Market rent is to be determined as of the place for tender or, in cases of rejection after arrival or revocation of acceptance, as of the place of arrival.

(3) If the lessee has accepted goods and given notification (Section 2A—516(3)), the measure of damages for non-conforming tender or delivery by a lessor is the loss resulting in the ordinary course of events from the lessor's default as determined in any manner that is reasonable together with incidental and consequential damages, less expenses saved in consequence of the lessor's default.

(4) The measure of damages for breach of warranty is the present value at the time and place of acceptance of the difference between the value of the use of the goods accepted and the value if they had been as warranted for the lease term, unless special circumstances show proximate damages of a different amount, together with incidental and consequential damages, less expenses saved

in consequence of the lessor's default or breach of warranty.

§ 2A—520. **Lessee's Incidental and Consequential Damages.**

(1) Incidental damages resulting from a lessor's default include expenses reasonably incurred in inspection, receipt, transportation, and care and custody of goods rightfully rejected or goods the acceptance of which is justifiably revoked, any commercially reasonable charges, expenses or commissions in connection with effecting cover, and any other reasonable expense incident to the default.

(2) Consequential damages resulting from a lessor's default include:

(a) any loss resulting from general or particular requirements and needs of which the lessor at the time of contracting had reason to know and which could not reasonably be prevented by cover or otherwise; and

(b) injury to person or property proximately resulting from any breach of warranty.

§ 2A—521. **Lessee's Right to Specific Performance or Replevin.**

(1) Specific performance may be decreed if the goods are unique or in other proper circumstances.

(2) A decree for specific performance may include any terms and conditions as to payment of the rent, damages, or other relief that the court deems just.

(3) A lessee has a right of replevin, detinue, sequestration, claim and delivery, or the like for goods identified to the lease contract if after reasonable effort the lessee is unable to effect cover for those goods or the circumstances reasonably indicate that the effort will be unavailing.

§ 2A—522. **Lessee's Right to Goods on Lessor's Insolvency.**

(1) Subject to subsection (2) and even though the goods have not been shipped, a lessee who has paid a part or all of the rent and security for goods identified to a lease contract (Section 2A—217) on making and keeping good a tender of any unpaid portion of the rent and security due under the lease contract may recover the goods identified from the lessor if the lessor becomes insolvent within 10 days after receipt of the first installment of rent and security.

(2) A lessee acquires the right to recover goods identified to a lease contract only if they conform to the lease contract.

C. Default by Lessee

§ 2A—523. **Lessor's Remedies.**

(1) If a lessee wrongfully rejects or revokes acceptance of goods or fails to make a payment when due or repudiates with respect to a part or the whole, then, with respect to any goods involved, and with respect to all of the goods if under an installment lease contract the value of the whole lease contract is substantially impaired (Section 2A—510), the lessee is in default under the lease contract and the lessor may:

(a) cancel the lease contract (Section 2A—505(1));

(b) proceed respecting goods not identified to the lease contract (Section 2A—524);

(c) withhold delivery of the goods and take possession of goods previously delivered (Section 2A—525);

(d) stop delivery of the goods by any bailee (Section 2A—526);

(e) dispose of the goods and recover damages (Section 2A—527), or retain the goods and recover damages (Section 2A—528), or in a proper case recover rent (Section 2A—529).

(2) If a lessee is otherwise in default under a lease contract, the lessor may exercise the rights and remedies provided in the lease contract and this Article.

§ 2A—524. **Lessor's Right to Identify Goods to Lease Contract.**

(1) A lessor aggrieved under Section 2A—523(1) may:

(a) identify to the lease contract conforming goods not already identified if at the time the lessor learned of the default they were in the lessor's or the supplier's possession or control; and

(b) dispose of goods (Section 2A—527(1)) that demonstrably have been intended for the particular lease contract even though those goods are unfinished.

(2) If the goods are unfinished, in the exercise of reasonable commercial judgment for the purposes of avoiding loss and of effective realization, an aggrieved lessor or the supplier may either complete manufacture and wholly identify the goods to the lease contract or cease manufacture and lease, sell, or otherwise dispose of the goods for scrap or salvage value or proceed in any other reasonable manner.

§ 2A—525. **Lessor's Right to Possession of Goods.**

(1) If a lessor discovers the lessee to be insolvent, the lessor may refuse to deliver the goods.

(2) The lessor has on default by the lessee under the lease contract the right to take possession of the goods. If the lease contract so provides, the lessor may require

the lessee to assemble the goods and make them available to the lessor at a place to be designated by the lessor which is reasonably convenient to both parties. Without removal, the lessor may render unusable any goods employed in trade or business, and may dispose of goods on the lessee's premises (Section 2A—527).

(3) The lessor may proceed under subsection (2) without judicial process if that can be done without breach of the peace or the lessor may proceed by action.

§ 2A—526. Lessor's Stoppage of Delivery in Transit or Otherwise.

(1) A lessor may stop delivery of goods in the possession of a carrier or other bailee if the lessor discovers the lessee to be insolvent and may stop delivery of carload, truckload, planeload, or larger shipments of express or freight if the lessee repudiates or fails to make a payment due before delivery, whether for rent, security or otherwise under the lease contract, or for any other reason the lessor has a right to withhold or take possession of the goods.

(2) In pursuing its remedies under subsection (1) the lessor may stop delivery until

(a) receipt of the goods by the lessee;

(b) acknowledgment to the lessee by any bailee of the goods, except a carrier, that the bailee holds the goods for the lessee; or

(c) such an acknowledgment to the lessee by a carrier via reshipment or as warehouseman.

(3) (a) To stop delivery, a lessor shall so notify as to enable the bailee by reasonable diligence to prevent delivery of the goods.

(b) After notification, the bailee shall hold and deliver the goods according to the directions of the lessor, but the lessor is liable to the bailee for any ensuing charges or damages.

(c) A carrier who has issued a nonnegotiable bill of lading is not obliged to obey a notification to stop received from a person other than the consignor.

§ 2A—527. Lessor's Rights to Dispose of Goods.

(1) After a default by a lessee under the lease contract (Section 2A—523(1)) or after the lessor refuses to deliver or take possession of goods (Section 2A—525 or 2A—526), the lessor may dispose of the goods concerned or the undelivered balance thereof in good faith and without unreasonable delay by lease, sale or otherwise.

(2) If the disposition is by lease contract substantially similar to the original lease contract and the lease contract is made in good faith and in a commercially reasonable manner, the lessor may recover from the lessee as damages (a) accrued and unpaid rent as of the date of default, (b) the present value as of the date of default of the difference between the total rent for the remaining lease term of the original lease contract and the total rent for the lease term of the new lease contract, and (c) any incidental damages allowed under Section 2A—530, less expenses saved in consequence of the lessee's default.

(3) If the lessor's disposition is by lease contract that for any reason does not qualify for treatment under subsection (2), or is by sale or otherwise, the lessor may recover from the lessee as if the lessor had elected not to dispose of the goods and Section 2A—528 governs.

(4) A subsequent buyer or lessee who buys or leases from the lessor in good faith for value as a result of a disposition under this section takes the goods free of the original lease contract and any rights of the original lessee even though the lessor fails to comply with one or more of the requirements of this Article.

(5) The lessor is not accountable to the lessee for any profit made on any disposition. A lessee who has rightfully rejected or justifiably revoked acceptance shall account to the lessor for any excess over the amount of the lessee's security interest (Section 2A—508(5)).

§ 2A—528. Lessor's Damages for Non-Acceptance or Repudiation.

(1) Except as otherwise provided with respect to damages liquidated in the lease agreement (Section 2A—504) or determined by agreement of the parties (Section 1—102(3)), if a lessor elects to retain the goods or a lessor elects to dispose of the goods and disposition is by lease agreement that for any reason does not qualify for treatment under Section 2A—527(2), or is by sale or otherwise, the lessor may recover from the lessee as damages for non-acceptance or repudiation by the lessee (a) accrued and unpaid rent as of the date of default, (b) the present value as of the date of default of the difference between the total rent for the remaining lease term of the original lease agreement and the market rent at the time and place for tender computed for the same lease term, and (c) any incidental damages allowed under Section 2A—530, less expenses saved in consequence of the lessee's default.

(2) If the measure of damages provided in subsection (1) is inadequate to put a lessor in as good a position as performance would have, the measure of damages is the profit, including reasonable overhead, the lessor would have made from full performance by the lessee, together with any incidental damages allowed under Section 2A—530, due allowance for costs reasonably incurred and due credit for payments or proceeds of disposition.

§ 2A—529. Lessor's Action for the Rent.

(1) After default by the lessee under the lease contract (Section 2A—523(1)), if the lessor complies with subsection (2), the lessor may recover from the lessee as damages:

> (a) for goods accepted by the lessee and for conforming goods lost or damaged within a commercially reasonable time after risk of loss passes to the lessee (Section 2A—219), (i) accrued and unpaid rent as of the date of default, (ii) the present value as of the date of default of the rent for the remaining lease term of the lease agreement, and (iii) any incidental damages allowed under Section 2A—530, less expenses saved in consequence of the lessee's default; and

> (b) for goods identified to the lease contract if the lessor is unable after reasonable effort to dispose of them at a reasonable price or the circumstances reasonably indicate that effort will be unavailing, (i) accrued and unpaid rent as of the date of default, (ii) the present value as of the date of default of the rent for the remaining lease term of the lease agreement, and (iii) any incidental damages allowed under Section 2A—530, less expenses saved in consequence of the lessee's default.

(2) Except as provided in subsection (3), the lessor shall hold for the lessee for the remaining lease term of the lease agreement any goods that have been identified to the lease contract and are in the lessor's control.

(3) The lessor may dispose of the goods at any time before collection of the judgment for damages obtained pursuant to subsection (1) and the lessor may proceed against the lessee for damages pursuant to Section 2A—527 or Section 2A—528.

(4) Payment of the judgment for damages obtained pursuant to subsection (1) entitles the lessee to use and possession of the goods not then disposed of for the remaining lease term of the lease agreement.

(5) After a lessee has wrongfully rejected or revoked acceptance of goods, has failed to pay rent then due, or has repudiated (Section 2A—402), a lessor who is held not entitled to rent under this section must nevertheless be awarded damages for non-acceptance under Sections 2A—527 and 2A—528.

§ 2A—530. Lessor's Incidental Damages.

Incidental damages to an aggrieved lessor include any commercially reasonable charges, expenses, or commissions incurred in stopping delivery, in the transportation, care and custody of goods after the lessee's default, in connection with return or disposition of the goods, or otherwise resulting from the default.

§ 2A—531. Standing to Sue Third Parties for Injury to Goods.

(1) If a third party so deals with goods that have been identified to a lease contract as to cause actionable injury to a party to the lease contract (a) the lessor has a right of action against the third party, and (b) the lessee also has a right of action against the third party if the lessee:

> (i) has a security interest in the goods;

> (ii) has an insurable interest in the goods; or

> (iii) bears the risk of loss under the lease contract or has since the injury assumed that risk as against the lessor and the goods have been converted or destroyed.

(2) If at the time of the injury the party plaintiff did not bear the risk of loss as against the other party to the lease contract and there is no arrangement between them for disposition of the recovery, his [or her] suit or settlement, subject to his [or her] own interest, is as a fiduciary for the other party to the lease contract.

(3) Either party with the consent of the other may sue for the benefit of whom it may concern.

Article 3
COMMERCIAL PAPER

Part 1 Short Title, Form and Interpretation

§ 3—101. Short Title.

This Article shall be known and may be cited as Uniform Commercial Code—Commercial Paper.

§ 3—102. Definitions and Index of Definitions.

(1) In this Article unless the context otherwise requires

> (a) "Issue" means the first delivery of an instrument to a holder or a remitter.

> (b) An "order" is a direction to pay and must be more than an authorization or request. It must identify the person to pay with reasonable certainty. It may be addressed to one or more such persons jointly or in the alternative but not in succession.

> (c) A "promise" is an undertaking to pay and must be more than an acknowledgment of an obligation.

> (d) "Secondary party" means a drawer or indorser.

> (e) "Instrument" means a negotiable instrument.

(2) Other definitions applying to this Article and the sections in which they appear are:
"Acceptance". Section 3—410.
"Accommodation party". Section 3—415.
"Alteration". Section 3—407.
"Certificate of deposit". Section 3—104.

"Certification". Section 3—411.
"Check". Section 3—104.
"Definite time". Section 3—109.
"Dishonor". Section 3—507.
"Draft". Section 3—104.
"Holder in due course". Section 3—302.
"Negotiation". Section 3—202.
"Note". Section 3—104.
"Notice of dishonor". Section 3—508.
"On demand". Section 3—108.
"Presentment". Section 3—504.
"Protest". Section 3—509.
"Restrictive Indorsement". Section 3—205.
"Signature". Section 3—401.

(3) The following definitions in other Articles apply to this Article:
"Account". Section 4—104.
"Banking Day". Section 4—104.
"Clearing House". Section 4—104.
"Collecting Bank". Section 4—105.
"Customer". Section 4—104.
"Depositary Bank". Section 4—105.
"Documentary Draft". Section 4—104.
"Intermediary Bank". Section 4—105.
"Item". Section 4—104.
"Midnight deadline". Section 4—104.
"Payor Bank". Section 4—105.

(4) In addition Article 1 contains general definitions and principles of construction and interpretation applicable throughout this Article.

§ 3—103. **Limitations on Scope of Article.**

(1) This Article does not apply to money, documents of title or investment securities.

(2) The provisions of this Article are subject to the provisions of the Article on Bank Deposits and Collections (Article 4) and Secured Transactions (Article 9).

§ 3—104. **Form of Negotiable Instruments; "Draft"; "Check"; "Certificate of Deposit"; "Note".**

(1) Any writing to be a negotiable instrument within this Article must

(a) be signed by the maker or drawer; and

(b) contain an unconditional promise or order to pay a sum certain in money and no other promise, order, obligation or power given by the maker or drawer except as authorized by this Article; and

(c) be payable on demand or at a definite time; and

(d) be payable to order or to bearer.

(2) A writing which complies with the requirements of this section is

(a) a "draft" ("bill of exchange") if it is an order;

(b) a "check" if it is a draft drawn on a bank and payable on demand;

(c) a "certificate of deposit" if it is an acknowledgment by a bank receipt of money with an engagement to repay it;

(d) a "note" if it is a promise other than a certificate of deposit.

(3) As used in other Articles of this Act, and as the context may require, the terms "draft", "check", "certificate of deposit" and "note" may refer to instruments which are not negotiable within this Article as well as to instruments which are so negotiable.

§ 3—105. **When Promise or Order Unconditional.**

(1) A promise or order otherwise unconditional is not made conditional by the fact that the instrument

(a) is subject to implied or constructive conditions; or

(b) states its consideration, whether performed or promised, or the transaction which gave rise to the instrument, or that the promise or order is made or the instrument matures in accordance with or "as per" such transaction; or

(c) refers to or states that it arises out of a separate agreement or refers to a separate agreement for rights as to prepayment or acceleration; or

(d) states that it is drawn under a letter of credit; or

(e) states that it is secured, whether by mortgage, reservation of title or otherwise; or

(f) indicates a particular account to be debited or any other fund or source from which reimbursement is expected; or

(g) is limited to payment out of a particular fund or the proceeds of a particular source, if the instrument is issued by a government or governmental agency or unit; or

(h) is limited to payment out of the entire assets of a partnership, unincorporated association, trust or estate by or on behalf of which the instrument is issued.

(2) A promise or order is not unconditional if the instrument

(a) states that it is subject to or governed by any other agreement; or

(b) states that it is to be paid only out of a particular fund or source except as provided in this section.

§ 3—106. **Sum Certain.**

(1) The sum payable is a sum certain even though it is to be paid

(a) with stated interest or by stated installments; or

(b) with stated different rates of interest before and after default or a specified date; or

(c) with a stated discount or addition if paid before or after the date fixed for payment; or

(d) with exchange or less exchange, whether at a fixed rate or at the current rate; or

(e) with costs of collection or an attorney's fee or both upon default.

(2) Nothing in this section shall validate any term which is otherwise illegal.

§ 3—107. **Money.**

(1) An instrument is payable in money if the medium of exchange in which it is payable is money at the time the instrument is made. An instrument payable in "currency" or "current funds" is payable in money.

(2) A promise or order to pay a sum stated in a foreign currency is for a sum certain in money and, unless a different medium of payment is specified in the instrument, may be satisfied by payment of that number of dollars which the stated foreign currency will purchase at the buying sight rate for that currency on the day on which the instrument is payable or, if payable on demand, on the day of demand. If such an instrument specifies a foreign currency as the medium of payment the instrument is payable in that currency.

§ 3—108. **Payable on Demand.**

Instruments payable on demand include those payable at sight or on presentation and those in which no time for payment is stated.

§ 3—109. **Definite Time.**

(1) An instrument is payable at a definite time if by its terms it is payable

(a) on or before a stated date or at a fixed period after a stated date; or

(b) at a fixed period after sight; or

(c) at a definite time subject to any acceleration; or

(d) at a definite time subject to extension at the option of the holder, or to extension to a further definite time at the option of the maker or acceptor or automatically upon or after a specified act or event.

(2) An instrument which by its terms is otherwise payable only upon an act or event uncertain as to time of occurrence is not payable at a definite time even though the act or event has occurred.

§ 3—110. **Payable to Order.**

(1) An instrument is payable to order when by its terms it is payable to the order or assigns of any person therein specified with reasonable certainty, or to him or his order, or when it is conspicuously designated on its face as "exchange" or the like and names a payee. It may be payable to the order of

(a) the maker or drawer; or

(b) the drawee; or

(c) a payee who is not maker, drawer or drawee; or

(d) two or more payees together or in the alternative; or

(e) an estate, trust or fund, in which case it is payable to the order of the representative of such estate, trust or fund or his successors; or

(f) an office, or an officer by his title as such in which case it is payable to the principal but the incumbent of the office or his successors may act as if he or they were the holder; or

(g) a partnership or unincorporated association, in which case it is payable to the partnership or association and may be indorsed or transferred by any person thereto authorized.

(2) An instrument not payable to order is not made so payable by such words as "payable upon return of this instrument properly indorsed."

(3) An instrument made payable both to order and to bearer is payable to order unless the bearer words are handwritten or typewritten.

§ 3—111. **Payable to Bearer.**

An instrument is payable to bearer when by its terms it is payable to

(a) bearer or the order of bearer; or

(b) a specified person or bearer; or

(c) "cash" or the order of "cash", or any other indication which does not purport to designate a specific payee.

§ 3—112. **Terms and Omissions Not Affecting Negotiability.**

(1) The negotiability of an instrument is not affected by

(a) the omission of a statement of any consideration or of the place where the instrument is drawn or payable; or

(b) a statement that collateral has been given to secure obligations either on the instrument or otherwise of an obligor on the instrument or that in case of default on those obligations the holder may realize on or dispose of the collateral; or

(c) a promise or power to maintain or protect collateral or to give additional collateral; or

(d) a term authorizing a confession of judgment on the instrument if it is not paid when due; or

(e) a term purporting to waive the benefit of any law intended for the advantage or protection of any obligor; or

(f) a term in a draft providing that the payee by indorsing or cashing it acknowledges full satisfaction of an obligation of the drawer; or

(g) a statement in a draft drawn in a set of parts (Section 3—801) to the effect that the order is effective only if no other part has been honored.

(2) Nothing in this section shall validate any term which is otherwise illegal.

§ 3—113. Seal.

An instrument otherwise negotiable is within this Article even though it is under a seal.

§ 3—114. Date, Antedating, Postdating.

(1) The negotiability of an instrument is not affected by the fact that it is undated, antedated or postdated.

(2) Where an instrument is antedated or postdated the time when it is payable is determined by the stated date if the instrument is payable on demand or at a fixed period after date.

(3) Where the instrument or any signature thereon is dated, the date is presumed to be correct.

§ 3—115. Incomplete Instruments.

(1) When a paper whose contents at the time of signing show that it is intended to become an instrument is signed while still incomplete in any necessary respect it cannot be enforced until completed, but when it is completed in accordance with authority given it is effective as completed.

(2) If the completion is unauthorized the rules as to material alteration apply (Section 3—407), even though the paper was not delivered by the maker or drawer; but the burden of establishing that any completion is unauthorized is on the party so asserting.

§ 3—116. Instruments Payable to Two or More Persons.

An instrument payable to the order of two or more persons

(a) if in the alternative is payable to any one of them and may be negotiated, discharged or enforced by any of them who has possession of it;

(b) if not in the alternative is payable to all of them and may be negotiated, discharged or enforced only by all of them.

§ 3—117. Instruments Payable With Words of Description.

An instrument made payable to a named person with the addition of words describing him

(a) as agent or officer of a specified person is payable to his principal but the agent or officer may act as if he were the holder;

(b) as any other fiduciary for a specified person or purpose is payable to the payee and may be negotiated, discharged or enforced by him;

(c) in any other manner is payable to the payee unconditionally and the additional words are without effect on subsequent parties.

§ 3—118. Ambiguous Terms and Rules of Construction.

The following rules apply to every instrument:

(a) Where there is doubt whether the instrument is a draft or a note the holder may treat it as either. A draft drawn on the drawer is effective as a note.

(b) Handwritten terms control typewritten and printed terms, and typewritten control printed.

(c) Words control figures except that if the words are ambiguous figures control.

(d) Unless otherwise specified a provision for interest means interest at the judgment rate at the place of payment from the date of the instrument, or if it is undated from the date of issue.

(e) Unless the instrument otherwise specifies two or more persons who sign as maker, acceptor or drawer or indorser and as a part of the same transaction are jointly and severally liable even though the instrument contains such words as "I promise to pay."

(f) Unless otherwise specified consent to extension authorizes a single extension for not longer than the original period. A consent to extension, expressed in the instrument, is binding on secondary parties and accommodation makers. A holder may not exercise his option to extend an instrument over the objection of a maker or acceptor or other party who in accordance with Section 3—604 tenders full payment when the instrument is due.

§ 3—119. Other Writings Affecting Instrument.

(1) As between the obligor and his immediate obligee or any transferee the terms of an instrument may be modified or affected by any other written agreement executed as a part of the same transaction, except that a holder in due course is not affected by any limitation of his rights arising out of the separate written agreement if he had no notice of the limitation when he took the instrument.

(2) A separate agreement does not affect the negotiability of an instrument.

§ 3—120. Instruments "Payable Through" Bank.

An instrument which states that it is "payable through" a bank or the like designates that bank as a collecting bank to make presentment but does not of itself authorize the bank to pay the instrument.

§ 3—121. Instruments Payable at Bank.

Note: If this Act is introduced in the Congress of the United States this section should be omitted.
(States to select either alternative)

Alternative A—

A note or acceptance which states that it is payable at a bank is the equivalent of a draft drawn on the bank payable when it falls due out of any funds of the maker or acceptor in current account or otherwise available for such payment.

Alternative B—

A note or acceptance which states that it is payable at a bank is not of itself an order or authorization to the bank to pay it.

§ 3—122. Accrual of Cause of Action.

(1) A cause of action against a maker or an acceptor accrues

    (a) in the case of a time instrument on the day after maturity;

    (b) in the case of a demand instrument upon its date or, if no date is stated, on the date of issue.

(2) A cause of action against the obligor of a demand or time certificate of deposit accrues upon demand, but demand on a time certificate may not be made until on or after the date of maturity.

(3) A cause of action against a drawer of a draft or an indorser of any instrument accrues upon demand following dishonor of the instrument. Notice of dishonor is a demand.

(4) Unless an instrument provides otherwise, interest runs at the rate provided by law for a judgment

    (a) in the case of a maker, acceptor or other primary obligor of a demand instrument, from the date of demand;

    (b) in all other cases from the date of accrual of the cause of action.

Part 2 Transfer and Negotiation

§ 3—201. Transfer: Right to Indorsement.

(1) Transfer of an instrument vests in the transferee such rights as the transferor has therein, except that a transferee who has himself been a party to any fraud or illegality affecting the instrument or who as a prior holder had notice of a defense or claim against it cannot improve his position by taking from a later holder in due course.

(2) A transfer of a security interest in an instrument vests the foregoing rights in the transferee to the extent of the interest transferred.

(3) Unless otherwise agreed any transfer for value of an instrument not then payable to bearer gives the transferee the specifically enforceable right to have the unqualified indorsement of the transferor. Negotiation takes effect only when the indorsement is made and until that time there is no presumption that the transferee is the owner.

§ 3—202. Negotiation.

(1) Negotiation is the transfer of an instrument in such form that the transferee becomes a holder. If the instrument is payable to order it is negotiated by delivery with any necessary indorsement; if payable to bearer it is negotiated by delivery.

(2) An indorsement must be written by or on behalf of the holder and on the instrument or on a paper so firmly affixed thereto as to become a part thereof.

(3) An indorsement is effective for negotiation only when it conveys the entire instrument or any unpaid residue. If it purports to be of less it operates only as a partial assignment.

(4) Words of assignment, condition, waiver, guaranty, limitation or disclaimer of liability and the like accompanying an indorsement do not affect its character as an indorsement.

§ 3—203. Wrong or Misspelled Name.

Where an instrument is made payable to a person under a misspelled name or one other than his own he may indorse in that name or his own or both; but signature in both names may be required by a person paying or giving value for the instrument.

§ 3—204. Special Indorsement; Blank Indorsement.

(1) A special indorsement specifies the person to whom or to whose order it makes the instrument payable. Any instrument specially indorsed becomes payable to the order of the special indorsee and may be further negotiated only by his indorsement.

(2) An indorsement in blank specifies no particular indorsee and may consist of a mere signature. An instrument payable to order and indorsed in blank becomes payable to bearer and may be negotiated by delivery alone until specially indorsed.

(3) The holder may convert a blank indorsement into a special indorsement by writing over the signature of the indorser in blank any contract consistent with the character of the indorsement.

§ 3—205. Restrictive Indorsements.

An indorsement is restrictive which either

(a) is conditional; or

(b) purports to prohibit further transfer of the instrument; or

(c) includes the words "for collection", "for deposit", "pay any bank", or like terms signifying a purpose of deposit or collection; or

(d) otherwise states that it is for the benefit or use of the indorser or of another person.

§ 3—206. Effect of Restrictive Indorsement.

(1) No restrictive indorsement prevents further transfer or negotiation of the instrument.

(2) An intermediary bank, or a payor bank which is not the depositary bank, is neither given notice nor otherwise affected by a restrictive indorsement of any person except the bank's immediate transferor or the person presenting for payment.

(3) Except for an intermediary bank, any transferee under an indorsement which is conditional or includes the words "for collection", "for deposit", "pay any bank", or like terms (subparagraphs (a) and (c) of Section 3—205) must pay or apply any value given by him for or on the security of the instrument consistently with the indorsement and to the extent that he does so he becomes a holder for value. In addition such transferee is a holder in due course if he otherwise complies with the requirements of Section 3—302 on what constitutes a holder in due course.

(4) The first taker under an indorsement for the benefit of the indorser or another person (subparagraph (d) of Section 3—205) must pay or apply any value given by him for or on the security of the instrument consistently with the indorsement and to the extent that he does so he becomes a holder for value. In addition such taker is a holder in due course if he otherwise complies with the requirements of Section 3—302 on what constitutes a holder in due course. A later holder for value is neither given notice nor otherwise affected by such restrictive indorsement unless he has knowledge that a fiduciary or other person has negotiated the instrument in any transaction for his own benefit or otherwise in breach of duty (subsection (2) of Section 3—304).

§ 3—207. Negotiation Effective Although It May Be Rescinded.

(1) Negotiation is effective to transfer the instrument although the negotiation is

(a) made by an infant, a corporation exceeding its powers, or any other person without capacity; or

(b) obtained by fraud, duress or mistake of any kind; or

(c) part of an illegal transaction; or

(d) made in breach of duty.

(2) Except as against a subsequent holder in due course such negotiation is in an appropriate case subject to rescission, the declaration of a constructive trust or any other remedy permitted by law.

§ 3—208. Reacquisition.

Where an instrument is returned to or reacquired by a prior party he may cancel any indorsement which is not necessary to his title and reissue or further negotiate the instrument, but any intervening party is discharged as against the reacquiring party and subsequent holders not in due course and if his indorsement has been cancelled is discharged as against subsequent holders in due course as well.

Part 3 Rights of a Holder

§ 3—301. Rights of a Holder.

The holder of an instrument whether or not he is the owner may transfer or negotiate it and, except as otherwise provided in Section 3—603 on payment or satisfaction, discharge it or enforce payment in his own name.

§ 3—302. Holder in Due Course

(1) A holder in due course is a holder who takes the instrument

(a) for value; and

(b) in good faith; and

(c) without notice that it is overdue or has been dishonored or of any defense against or claim to it on the part of any person.

(2) A payee may be a holder in due course.

(3) A holder does not become a holder in due course of an instrument:

(a) by purchase of it at judicial sale or by taking it under legal process; or

(b) by acquiring it in taking over an estate; or

(c) by purchasing it as part of a bulk transaction not in regular course of business of the transferor.

(4) A purchaser of a limited interest can be a holder in due course only to the extent of the interest purchased.

§ 3—303. Taking for Value.

A holder takes the instrument for value

(a) to the extent that the agreed consideration has been performed or that he acquires a security interest in or a lien on the instrument otherwise than by legal process; or

THE UNIFORM COMMERCIAL CODE

(b) when he takes the instrument in payment of or as security for an antecedent claim against any person whether or not the claim is due; or

(c) when he gives a negotiable instrument for it or makes an irrevocable commitment to a third person.

§ 3—304. **Notice to Purchaser.**

(1) The purchaser has notice of a claim or defense if

(a) the instrument is so incomplete, bears such visible evidence of forgery or alteration, or is otherwise so irregular as to call into question its validity, terms or ownership or to create an ambiguity as to the party to pay; or

(b) the purchaser has notice that the obligation of any party is voidable in whole or in part, or that all parties have been discharged.

(2) The purchaser has notice of a claim against the instrument when he has knowledge that a fiduciary has negotiated the instrument in payment of or as security for his own debt or in any transaction for his own benefit or otherwise in breach of duty.

(3) The purchaser has notice that an instrument is overdue if he has reason to know

(a) that any part of the principal amount is overdue or that there is an uncured default in payment of another instrument of the same series; or

(b) that acceleration of the instrument has been made; or

(c) that he is taking a demand instrument after demand has been made or more than a reasonable length of time after its issue. A reasonable time for a check drawn and payable within the states and territories of the United States and the District of Columbia is presumed to be thirty days.

(4) Knowledge of the following facts does not of itself give the purchaser notice of a defense or claim

(a) that the instrument is antedated or postdated;

(b) that it was issued or negotiated in return for an executory promise or accompanied by a separate agreement, unless the purchaser has notice that a defense or claim has arisen from the terms thereof;

(c) that any party has signed for accommodation;

(d) that an incomplete instrument has been completed, unless the purchaser has notice of any improper completion;

(e) that any person negotiating the instrument is or was a fiduciary;

(f) that there has been default in payment of interest on the instrument or in payment of any other instrument, except one of the same series.

(5) The filing or recording of a document does not of itself constitute notice within the provisions of this Article to a person who would otherwise be a holder in due course.

(6) To be effective notice must be received at such time and in such manner as to give a reasonable opportunity to act on it.

§ 3—305. **Rights of a Holder in Due Course.**

To the extent that a holder is a holder in due course he takes the instrument free from

(1) all claims to it on the part of any person; and

(2) all defenses of any party to the instrument with whom the holder has not dealt except

(a) infancy, to the extent that it is a defense to a simple contract; and

(b) such other incapacity, or duress, or illegality of the transaction, as renders the obligation of the party a nullity; and

(c) such misrepresentation as has induced the party to sign the instrument with neither knowledge nor reasonable opportunity to obtain knowledge of its character or its essential terms; and

(d) discharge in insolvency proceedings; and

(e) any other discharge of which the holder has notice when he takes the instrument.

§ 3—306. **Rights of One Not Holder in Due Course.**

Unless he has the rights of a holder in due course any person takes the instrument subject to

(a) all valid claims to it on the part of any person; and

(b) all defenses of any party which would be available in an action on a simple contract; and

(c) the defenses of want or failure of consideration, non-performance of any condition precedent, non-delivery, or delivery for a special purpose (Section 3—408); and

(d) the defense that he or a person through whom he holds the instrument acquired it by theft, or that payment or satisfaction to such holder would be inconsistent with the terms of a restrictive indorsement. The claim of any third person to the instrument is not otherwise available as a defense to any party liable thereon unless the third person himself defends the action for such party.

§ 3—307. **Burden of Establishing Signatures, Defenses and Due Course.**

(1) Unless specifically denied in the pleadings each signature on an instrument is admitted. When the effectiveness of a signature is put in issue

(a) the burden of establishing it is on the party claiming under the signature; but

(b) the signature is presumed to be genuine or authorized except where the action is to enforce the obligation of a purported signer who has died or become incompetent before proof is required.

(2) When signatures are admitted or established, production of the instrument entitles a holder to recover on it unless the defendant establishes a defense.

(3) After it is shown that a defense exists a person claiming the rights of a holder in due course has the burden of establishing that he or some person under whom he claims is in all respects a holder in due course.

Part 4 Liability of Parties

§ 3—401. Signature.

(1) No person is liable on an instrument unless his signature appears thereon.

(2) A signature is made by use of any name, including any trade or assumed name, upon an instrument, or by any word or mark used in lieu of a written signature.

§ 3—402. Signature in Ambiguous Capacity.

Unless the instrument clearly indicates that a signature is made in some other capacity it is an indorsement.

§ 3—403. Signature by Authorized Representative.

(1) A signature may be made by an agent or other representative, and his authority to make it may be established as in other cases of representation. No particular form of appointment is necessary to establish such authority.

(2) An authorized representative who signs his own name to an instrument

(a) is personally obligated if the instrument neither names the person represented nor shows that the representative signed in a representative capacity;

(b) except as otherwise established between the immediate parties, is personally obligated if the instrument names the person represented but does not show that the representative signed in a representative capacity, or if the instrument does not name the person represented but does show that the representative signed in a representative capacity.

(3) Except as otherwise established the name of an organization preceded or followed by the name and office of an authorized individual is a signature made in a representative capacity.

§ 3—404. Unauthorized Signatures.

(1) Any unauthorized signature is wholly inoperative as that of the person whose name is signed unless he ratifies it or is precluded from denying it; but it operates as the signature of the unauthorized signer in favor of any person who in good faith pays the instrument or takes it for value.

(2) Any unauthorized signature may be ratified for all purposes of this Article. Such ratification does not of itself affect any rights of the person ratifying against the actual signer.

§ 3—405. Impostors; Signature in Name of Payee.

(1) An indorsement by any person in the name of a named payee is effective if

(a) an impostor by use of the mails or otherwise has induced the maker or drawer to issue the instrument to him or his confederate in the name of the payee; or

(b) a person signing as or on behalf of a maker or drawer intends the payee to have no interest in the instrument; or

(c) an agent or employee of the maker or drawer has supplied him with the name of the payee intending the latter to have no such interest.

(2) Nothing in this section shall affect the criminal or civil liability of the person so indorsing.

§ 3—406. Negligence Contributing to Alteration or Unauthorized Signature.

Any person who by his negligence substantially contributes to a material alteration of the instrument or to the making of an unauthorized signature is precluded from asserting the alteration or lack of authority against a holder in due course or against a drawee or other payor who pays the instrument in good faith and in accordance with the reasonable commercial standards of the drawee's or payor's business.

§ 3—407. Alteration.

(1) Any alteration of an instrument is material which changes the contract of any party thereto in any respect, including any such change in

(a) the number or relations of the parties; or

(b) an incomplete instrument, by completing it otherwise than as authorized; or

(c) the writing as signed, by adding to it or by removing any part of it.

(2) As against any person other than a subsequent holder in due course

(a) alteration by the holder which is both fraudulent and material discharges any party whose contract is thereby changed unless that party assents or is precluded from asserting the defense;

(b) no other alteration discharges any party and the instrument may be enforced according to its original tenor, or as to incomplete instruments according to the authority given.

(3) A subsequent holder in due course may in all cases enforce the instrument according to its original tenor, and when an incomplete instrument has been completed, he may enforce it as completed.

§ 3—408. **Consideration.**

Want or failure of consideration is a defense as against any person not having the rights of a holder in due course (Section 3—305), except that no consideration is necessary for an instrument or obligation thereon given in payment of or as security for an antecedent obligation of any kind. Nothing in this section shall be taken to displace any statute outside this Act under which a promise is enforceable notwithstanding lack or failure of consideration. Partial failure of consideration is a defense pro tanto whether or not the failure is in an ascertained or liquidated amount.

§ 3—409. **Draft Not an Assignment.**

(1) A check or other draft does not of itself operate as an assignment of any funds in the hands of the drawee available for its payment, and the drawee is not liable on the instrument until he accepts it.

(2) Nothing in this section shall affect any liability in contract, tort or otherwise arising from any letter of credit or other obligation or representation which is not an acceptance.

§ 3—410. **Definition and Operation of Acceptance.**

(1) Acceptance is the drawee's signed engagement to honor the draft as presented. It must be written on the draft, and may consist of his signature alone. It becomes operative when completed by delivery or notification.

(2) A draft may be accepted although it has not been signed by the drawer or is otherwise incomplete or is overdue or has been dishonored.

(3) Where the draft is payable at a fixed period after sight and the acceptor fails to date his acceptance the holder may complete it by supplying a date in good faith.

§ 3—411. **Certification of a Check.**

(1) Certification of a check is acceptance. Where a holder procures certification the drawer and all prior indorsers are discharged.

(2) Unless otherwise agreed a bank has no obligation to certify a check.

(3) A bank may certify a check before returning it for lack of proper indorsement. If it does so the drawer is discharged.

§ 3—412. **Acceptance Varying Draft.**

(1) Where the drawee's proffered acceptance in any manner varies the draft as presented the holder may refuse the acceptance and treat the draft as dishonored in which case the drawee is entitled to have his acceptance cancelled.

(2) The terms of the draft are not varied by an acceptance to pay at any particular bank or place in the United States, unless the acceptance states that the draft is to be paid only at such bank or place.

(3) Where the holder assents to an acceptance varying the terms of the draft each drawer and indorser who does not affirmatively assent is discharged.

§ 3—413. **Contract of Maker, Drawer and Acceptor.**

(1) The maker or acceptor engages that he will pay the instrument according to its tenor at the time of his engagement or as completed pursuant to Section 3—115 on incomplete instruments.

(2) The drawer engages that upon dishonor of the draft and any necessary notice of dishonor or protest he will pay the amount of the draft to the holder or to any indorser who takes it up. The drawer may disclaim this liability by drawing without recourse.

(3) By making, drawing or accepting the party admits as against all subsequent parties including the drawee the existence of the payee and his then capacity to indorse.

§ 3—414. **Contract of Indorser; Order of Liability.**

(1) Unless the indorsement otherwise specifies (as by such words as "without recourse") every indorser engages that upon dishonor and any necessary notice of dishonor and protest he will pay the instrument according to its tenor at the time of his indorsement to the holder or to any subsequent indorser who takes it up, even though the indorser who takes it up was not obligated to do so.

(2) Unless they otherwise agree indorsers are liable to one another in the order in which they indorse, which is presumed to be the order in which their signatures appear on the instrument.

§ 3—415. **Contract of Accommodation Party.**

(1) An accommodation party is one who signs the instrument in any capacity for the purpose of lending his name to another party to it.

(2) When the instrument has been taken for value before it is due the accommodation party is liable in the capacity in which he has signed even though the taker knows of the accommodation.

(3) As against a holder in due course and without notice of the accommodation oral proof of the accommodation

is not admissible to give the accommodation party the benefit of discharges dependent on his character as such. In other cases the accommodation character may be shown by oral proof.

(4) An indorsement which shows that it is not in the chain of title is notice of its accommodation character.

(5) An accommodation party is not liable to the party accommodated, and if he pays the instrument has a right of recourse on the instrument against such party.

§ 3—416. **Contract of Guarantor.**

(1) "Payment guaranteed" or equivalent words added to a signature mean that the signer engages that if the instrument is not paid when due he will pay it according to its tenor without resort by the holder to any other party.

(2) "Collection guaranteed" or equivalent words added to a signature mean that the signer engages that if the instrument is not paid when due he will pay it according to its tenor, but only after the holder has reduced his claim against the maker or acceptor to judgment and execution has been returned unsatisfied, or after the maker or acceptor has become insolvent or it is otherwise apparent that it is useless to proceed against him.

(3) Words of guaranty which do not otherwise specify guarantee payment.

(4) No words of guaranty added to the signature of a sole maker or acceptor affect his liability on the instrument. Such words added to the signature of one of two or more makers or acceptors create a presumption that the signature is for the accommodation of the others.

(5) When words of guaranty are used presentment, notice of dishonor and protest are not necessary to charge the user.

(6) Any guaranty written on the instrument is enforcible notwithstanding any statute of frauds.

§ 3—417. **Warranties on Presentment and Transfer.**

(1) Any person who obtains payment or acceptance and any prior transferor warrants to a person who in good faith pays or accepts that

(a) he has a good title to the instrument or is authorized to obtain payment or acceptance on behalf of one who has a good title; and

(b) he has no knowledge that the signature of the maker or drawer is unauthorized, except that this warranty is not given by a holder in due course acting in good faith

(i) to a maker with respect to the maker's own signature; or

(ii) to a drawer with respect to the drawer's own signature, whether or not the drawer is also the drawee; or

(iii) to an acceptor of a draft if the holder in due course took the draft after the acceptance or obtained the acceptance without knowledge that the drawer's signature was unauthorized; and

(c) the instrument has not been materially altered, except that this warranty is not given by a holder in due course acting in good faith

(i) to the maker of a note; or

(ii) to the drawer of a draft whether or not the drawer is also the drawee; or

(iii) to the acceptor of a draft with respect to an alteration made prior to the acceptance if the holder in due course took the draft after the acceptance, even though the acceptance provided "payable as originally drawn" or equivalent terms; or

(iv) to the acceptor of a draft with respect to an alteration made after the acceptance.

(2) Any person who transfers an instrument and receives consideration warrants to his transferee and if the transfer is by indorsement to any subsequent holder who takes the instrument in good faith that

(a) he has a good title to the instrument or is authorized to obtain payment or acceptance on behalf of one who has a good title and the transfer is otherwise rightful; and

(b) all signatures are genuine or authorized; and

(c) the instrument has not been materially altered; and

(d) no defense of any party is good against him; and

(e) he has no knowledge of any insolvency proceeding instituted with respect to the maker or acceptor or the drawer of an unaccepted instrument.

(3) By transferring "without recourse" the transferor limits the obligation stated in subsection (2) (d) to a warranty that he has no knowledge of such a defense.

(4) A selling agent or broker who does not disclose the fact that he is acting only as such gives the warranties provided in this section, but if he makes such disclosure warrants only his good faith and authority.

§ 3—418. **Finality of Payment or Acceptance.**

Except for recovery of bank payments as provided in the Article on Bank Deposits and Collections (Article 4) and except for liability for breach of warranty on presentment under the preceding section, payment or acceptance of any instrument is final in favor of a holder in due course, or a person who has in good faith changed his position in reliance on the payment.

THE UNIFORM COMMERCIAL CODE

§ 3—419. Conversion of Instrument; Innocent Representative.

(1) An instrument is converted when

   (a) a drawee to whom it is delivered for acceptance refuses to return it on demand; or

   (b) any person to whom it is delivered for payment refuses on demand either to pay or to return it; or

   (c) it is paid on a forged indorsement.

(2) In an action against a drawee under subsection (1) the measure of the drawee's liability is the face amount of the instrument. In any other action under subsection (1) the measure of liability is presumed to be the face amount of the instrument.

(3) Subject to the provisions of this Act concerning restrictive indorsements a representative, including a depositary or collecting bank, who has in good faith and in accordance with the reasonable commercial standards applicable to the business of such representative dealt with an instrument or its proceeds on behalf of one who was not the true owner is not liable in conversion or otherwise to the true owner beyond the amount of any proceeds remaining in his hands.

(4) An intermediary bank or payor bank which is not a depositary bank is not liable in conversion solely by reason of the fact that proceeds of an item indorsed restrictively (Sections 3—205 and 3—206) are not paid or applied consistently with the restrictive indorsement of an indorser other than its immediate transferor.

Part 5 Presentment, Notice of Dishonor and Protest

§ 3—501. When Presentment, Notice of Dishonor, and Protest Necessary or Permissible.

(1) Unless excused (Section 3—511) presentment is necessary to charge secondary parties as follows:

   (a) presentment for acceptance is necessary to charge the drawer and indorsers of a draft where the draft so provides, or is payable elsewhere than at the residence or place of business of the drawee, or its date of payment depends upon such presentment. The holder may at his option present for acceptance any other draft payable at a stated date;

   (b) presentment for payment is necessary to charge any indorser;

   (c) in the case of any drawer, the acceptor of a draft payable at a bank or the maker of a note payable at a bank, presentment for payment is necessary, but failure to make presentment discharges such drawer, acceptor or maker only as stated in Section 3—502(1)(b).

(2) Unless excused (Section 3—511)

   (a) notice of any dishonor is necessary to charge any indorser;

   (b) in the case of any drawer, the acceptor of a draft payable at a bank or the maker of a note payable at a bank, notice of any dishonor is necessary, but failure to give such notice discharges such drawer, acceptor or maker only as stated in Section 3—502(1)(b).

(3) Unless excused (Section 3—511) protest of any dishonor is necessary to charge the drawer and indorsers of any draft which on its face appears to be drawn or payable outside of the states, territories, dependencies, and possessions of the United States, the District of Columbia and the Commonwealth of Puerto Rico. The holder may at his option make protest of any dishonor of any other instrument and in the case of a foreign draft may on insolvency of the acceptor before maturity make protest for better security.

(4) Notwithstanding any provision of this section, neither presentment nor notice of dishonor nor protest is necessary to charge an indorser who has indorsed an instrument after maturity.

§ 3—502. Unexcused Delay; Discharge.

(1) Where without excuse any necessary presentment or notice of dishonor is delayed beyond the time when it is due

   (a) any indorser is discharged; and

   (b) any drawer or the acceptor of a draft payable at a bank or the maker of a note payable at a bank who because the drawee or payor bank becomes insolvent during the delay is deprived of funds maintained with the drawee or payor bank to cover the instrument may discharge his liability by written assignment to the holder of his rights against the drawee or payor bank in respect of such funds, but such drawer, acceptor or maker is not otherwise discharged.

(2) Where without excuse a necessary protest is delayed beyond the time when it is due any drawer or indorser is discharged.

§ 3—503. Time of Presentment.

(1) Unless a different time is expressed in the instrument the time for any presentment is determined as follows:

   (a) where an instrument is payable at or a fixed period after a stated date any presentment for acceptance must be made on or before the date it is payable;

   (b) where an instrument is payable after sight it must either be presented for acceptance or negotiated within a reasonable time after date or issue whichever is later;

(c) where an instrument shows the date on which it is payable presentment for payment is due on that date;

(d) where an instrument is accelerated presentment for payment is due within a reasonable time after the acceleration;

(e) with respect to the liability of any secondary party presentment for acceptance or payment of any other instrument is due within a reasonable time after such party becomes liable thereon.

(2) A reasonable time for presentment is determined by the nature of the instrument, any usage of banking or trade and the facts of the particular case. In the case of an uncertified check which is drawn and payable within the United States and which is not a draft drawn by a bank the following are presumed to be reasonable periods within which to present for payment or to initiate bank collection:

(a) with respect to the liability of the drawer, thirty days after date or issue whichever is later; and

(b) with respect to the liability of an indorser, seven days after his indorsement.

(3) Where any presentment is due on a day which is not a full business day for either the person making presentment or the party to pay or accept, presentment is due on the next following day which is a full business day for both parties.

(4) Presentment to be sufficient must be made at a reasonable hour, and if at a bank during its banking day.

§ 3—504. How Presentment Made.

(1) Presentment is a demand for acceptance or payment made upon the maker, acceptor, drawee or other payor by or on behalf of the holder.

(2) Presentment may be made

(a) by mail, in which event the time of presentment is determined by the time of receipt of the mail; or

(b) through a clearing house; or

(c) at the place of acceptance or payment specified in the instrument or if there be none at the place of business or residence of the party to accept or pay. If neither the party to accept or pay nor anyone authorized to act for him is present or accessible at such place presentment is excused.

(3) It may be made

(a) to any one of two or more makers, acceptors, drawees or other payors; or

(b) to any person who has authority to make or refuse the acceptance or payment.

(4) A draft accepted or a note made payable at a bank in the United States must be presented at such bank.

(5) In the cases described in Section 4—210 presentment may be made in the manner and with the result stated in that section.

§ 3—505. Rights of Party to Whom Presentment Is Made.

(1) The party to whom presentment is made may without dishonor require

(a) exhibition of the instrument; and

(b) reasonable identification of the person making presentment and evidence of his authority to make it if made for another; and

(c) that the instrument be produced for acceptance or payment at a place specified in it, or if there be none at any place reasonable in the circumstances; and

(d) a signed receipt on the instrument for any partial or full payment and its surrender upon full payment.

(2) Failure to comply with any such requirement invalidates the presentment but the person presenting has a reasonable time in which to comply and the time for acceptance or payment runs from the time of compliance.

§ 3—506. Time Allowed for Acceptance or Payment.

(1) Acceptance may be deferred without dishonor until the close of the next business day following presentment. The holder may also in a good faith effort to obtain acceptance and without either dishonor of the instrument or discharge of secondary parties allow postponement of acceptance for an additional business day.

(2) Except as a longer time is allowed in the case of documentary drafts drawn under a letter of credit, and unless an earlier time is agreed to by the party to pay, payment of an instrument may be deferred without dishonor pending reasonable examination to determine whether it is properly payable, but payment must be made in any event before the close of business on the day of presentment.

§ 3—507. Dishonor; Holder's Right of Recourse; Term Allowing Re-Presentment.

(1) An instrument is dishonored when

(a) a necessary or optional presentment is duly made and due acceptance or payment is refused or cannot be obtained within the prescribed time or in case of bank collections the instrument is seasonably returned by the midnight deadline (Section 4—301); or

(b) presentment is excused and the instrument is not duly accepted or paid.

(2) Subject to any necessary notice of dishonor and protest, the holder has upon dishonor an immediate right of recourse against the drawers and indorsers.

(3) Return of an instrument for lack of proper indorsement is not dishonor.

(4) A term in a draft or an indorsement thereof allowing a stated time for re-presentment in the event of any dishonor of the draft by nonacceptance if a time draft or by nonpayment if a sight draft gives the holder as against any secondary party bound by the term an option to waive the dishonor without affecting the liability of the secondary party and he may present again up to the end of the stated time.

§ 3—508. **Notice of Dishonor.**

(1) Notice of dishonor may be given to any person who may be liable on the instrument by or on behalf of the holder or any party who has himself received notice, or any other party who can be compelled to pay the instrument. In addition an agent or bank in whose hands the instrument is dishonored may give notice to his principal or customer or to another agent or bank from which the instrument was received.

(2) Any necessary notice must be given by a bank before its midnight deadline and by any other person before midnight of the third business day after dishonor or receipt of notice of dishonor.

(3) Notice may be given in any reasonable manner. It may be oral or written and in any terms which identify the instrument and state that it has been dishonored. A misdescription which does not mislead the party notified does not vitiate the notice. Sending the instrument bearing a stamp, ticket or writing stating that acceptance or payment has been refused or sending a notice of debit with respect to the instrument is sufficient.

(4) Written notice is given when sent although it is not received.

(5) Notice to one partner is notice to each although the firm has been dissolved.

(6) When any party is in insolvency proceedings instituted after the issue of the instrument notice may be given either to the party or to the representative of his estate.

(7) When any party is dead or incompetent notice may be sent to his last known address or given to his personal representative.

(8) Notice operates for the benefit of all parties who have rights on the instrument against the party notified.

§ 3—509. **Protest; Noting for Protest.**

(1) A protest is a certificate of dishonor made under the hand and seal of a United States consul or vice consul or a notary public or other person authorized to certify dishonor by the law of the place where dishonor occurs. It may be made upon information satisfactory to such person.

(2) The protest must identify the instrument and certify either that due presentment has been made or the reason why it is excused and that the instrument has been dishonored by nonacceptance or nonpayment.

(3) The protest may also certify that notice of dishonor has been given to all parties or to specified parties.

(4) Subject to subsection (5) any necessary protest is due by the time that notice of dishonor is due.

(5) If, before protest is due, an instrument has been noted for protest by the officer to make protest, the protest may be made at any time thereafter as of the date of the noting.

§ 3—510. **Evidence of Dishonor and Notice of Dishonor.**

The following are admissible as evidence and create a presumption of dishonor and of any notice of dishonor therein shown:

(a) a document regular in form as provided in the preceding section which purports to be a protest;

(b) the purported stamp or writing of the drawee, payor bank or presenting bank on the instrument or accompanying it stating that acceptance or payment has been refused for reasons consistent with dishonor;

(c) any book or record of the drawee, payor bank, or any collecting bank kept in the usual course of business which shows dishonor, even though there is no evidence of who made the entry.

§ 3—511. **Waived or Excused Presentment, Protest or Notice of Dishonor or Delay Therein.**

(1) Delay in presentment, protest or notice of dishonor is excused when the party is without notice that it is due or when the delay is caused by circumstances beyond his control and he exercises reasonable diligence after the cause of the delay ceases to operate.

(2) Presentment or notice or protest as the case may be is entirely excused when

(a) the party to be charged has waived it expressly or by implication either before or after it is due; or

(b) such party has himself dishonored the instrument or has countermanded payment or otherwise has no reason to expect or right to require that the instrument be accepted or paid; or

(c) by reasonable diligence the presentment or protest cannot be made or the notice given.

(3) Presentment is also entirely excused when

(a) the maker, acceptor or drawee of any instrument except a documentary draft is dead or in insolvency proceedings instituted after the issue of the instrument; or

(b) acceptance or payment is refused but not for want of proper presentment.

(4) Where a draft has been dishonored by nonacceptance a later presentment for payment and any notice of dishonor and protest for nonpayment are excused unless in the meantime the instrument has been accepted.

(5) A waiver of protest is also a waiver of presentment and of notice of dishonor even though protest is not required.

(6) Where a waiver of presentment or notice or protest is embodied in the instrument itself it is binding upon all parties; but where it is written above the signature of an indorser it binds him only.

Part 6 Discharge

§ 3—601. Discharge of Parties.

(1) The extent of the discharge of any party from liability on an instrument is governed by the sections on

(a) payment or satisfaction (Section 3—603); or

(b) tender of payment (Section 3—604); or

(c) cancellation or renunciation (Section 3—605); or

(d) impairment of right of recourse or of collateral (Section 3—606); or

(e) reacquisition of the instrument by a prior party (Section 3—208); or

(f) fraudulent and material alteration (Section 3—407); or

(g) certification of a check (Section 3—411); or

(h) acceptance varying a draft (Section 3—412); or

(i) unexcused delay in presentment or notice of dishonor or protest (Section 3—502).

(2) Any party is also discharged from his liability on an instrument to another party by any other act or agreement with such party which would discharge his simple contract for the payment of money.

(3) The liability of all parties is discharged when any party who has himself no right of action or recourse on the instrument

(a) reacquires the instrument in his own right; or

(b) is discharged under any provision of this Article, except as otherwise provided with respect to discharge for impairment of recourse or of collateral (Section 3—606).

§ 3—602. Effect of Discharge Against Holder in Due Course.

No discharge of any party provided by this Article is effective against a subsequent holder in due course unless he has notice thereof when he takes the instrument.

§ 3—603. Payment or Satisfaction.

(1) The liability of any party is discharged to the extent of his payment or satisfaction to the holder even though it is made with knowledge of a claim of another person to the instrument unless prior to such payment or satisfaction the person making the claim either supplies indemnity deemed adequate by the party seeking the discharge or enjoins payment or satisfaction by order of a court of competent jurisdiction in an action in which the adverse claimant and the holder are parties. This subsection does not, however, result in the discharge of the liability

(a) of a party who in bad faith pays or satisfies a holder who acquired the instrument by theft or who (unless having the rights of a holder in due course) holds through one who so acquired it; or

(b) of a party (other than an intermediary bank or a payor bank which is not a depositary bank) who pays or satisfies the holder of an instrument which has been restrictively indorsed in a manner not consistent with the terms of such restrictive indorsement.

(2) Payment or satisfaction may be made with the consent of the holder by any person including a stranger to the instrument. Surrender of the instrument to such a person gives him the rights of a transferee (Section 3—201).

§ 3—604. Tender of Payment.

(1) Any party making tender of full payment to a holder when or after it is due is discharged to the extent of all subsequent liability for interest, costs and attorney's fees.

(2) The holder's refusal of such tender wholly discharges any party who has a right of recourse against the party making the tender.

(3) Where the maker or acceptor of an instrument payable otherwise than on demand is able and ready to pay at every place of payment specified in the instrument when it is due, it is equivalent to tender.

§ 3—605. Cancellation and Renunciation.

(1) The holder of an instrument may even without consideration discharge any party

(a) in any manner apparent on the face of the instrument or the indorsement, as by intentionally cancelling the instrument or the party's signature by destruction or mutilation, or by striking out the party's signature; or

(b) by renouncing his rights by a writing signed and delivered or by surrender of the instrument to the party to be discharged.

(2) Neither cancellation nor renunciation without surrender of the instrument affects the title thereto.

§ 3—606. Impairment of Recourse or of Collateral.

(1) The holder discharges any party to the instrument to the extent that without such party's consent the holder

(a) without express reservation of rights releases or agrees not to sue any person against whom the party has to the knowledge of the holder a right of recourse or agrees to suspend the right to enforce against such person the instrument or collateral or otherwise discharges such person, except that failure or delay in effecting any required presentment, protest or notice of dishonor with respect to any such person does not discharge any party as to whom presentment, protest or notice of dishonor is effective or unnecessary; or

(b) unjustifiably impairs any collateral for the instrument given by or on behalf of the party or any person against whom he has a right of recourse.

(2) By express reservation of rights against a party with a right of recourse the holder preserves

(a) all his rights against such party as of the time when the instrument was originally due; and

(b) the right of the party to pay the instrument as of that time; and

(c) all rights of such party to recourse against others.

Part 7 Advice of International Sight Draft

§ 3—701. Letter of Advice of International Sight Draft.

(1) A "letter of advice" is a drawer's communication to the drawee that a described draft has been drawn.

(2) Unless otherwise agreed when a bank receives from another bank a letter of advice of an international sight draft the drawee bank may immediately debit the drawer's account and stop the running of interest pro tanto. Such a debit and any resulting credit to any account covering outstanding drafts leaves in the drawer full power to stop payment or otherwise dispose of the amount and creates no trust or interest in favor of the holder.

(3) Unless otherwise agreed and except where a draft is drawn under a credit issued by the drawee, the drawee of an international sight draft owes the drawer no duty to pay an unadvised draft but if it does so and the draft is genuine, may appropriately debit the drawer's account.

Part 8 Miscellaneous

§ 3—801. Drafts in a Set.

(1) Where a draft is drawn in a set of parts, each of which is numbered and expressed to be an order only if no other part has been honored, the whole of the parts constitutes one draft but a taker of any part may become a holder in due course of the draft.

(2) Any person who negotiates, indorses or accepts a single part of a draft drawn in a set thereby becomes liable to any holder in due course of that part as if it were the whole set, but as between different holders in due course to whom different parts have been negotiated the holder whose title first accrues has all rights to the draft and its proceeds.

(3) As against the drawee the first presented part of a draft drawn in a set is the part entitled to payment, or if a time draft to acceptance and payment. Acceptance of any subsequently presented part renders the drawee liable thereon under subsection (2). With respect both to a holder and to the drawer payment of a subsequently presented part of a draft payable at sight has the same effect as payment of a check notwithstanding an effective stop order (Section 4—407).

(4) Except as otherwise provided in this section, where any part of a draft in a set is discharged by payment or otherwise the whole draft is discharged.

§ 3—802. Effect of Instrument on Obligation for Which It Is Given.

(1) Unless otherwise agreed where an instrument is taken for an underlying obligation

(a) the obligation is pro tanto discharged if a bank is drawer, maker or acceptor of the instrument and there is no recourse on the instrument against the underlying obligor; and

(b) in any other case the obligation is suspended pro tanto until the instrument is due or if it is payable on demand until its presentment. If the instrument is dishonored action may be maintained on either the instrument or the obligation; discharge of the underlying obligor on the instrument also discharges him on the obligation.

(2) The taking in good faith of a check which is not postdated does not of itself so extend the time on the original obligation as to discharge a surety.

§ 3—803. Notice to Third Party.

Where a defendant is sued for breach of an obligation for which a third person is answerable over under this Article he may give the third person written notice of the litigation, and the person notified may then give similar notice to any other person who is answerable over to him under this Article. If the notice states that the person notified may come in and defend and that if the person notified does not do so he will in any action against him by the person giving the notice be bound by any determination of fact common to the two litigations, then unless after seasonable receipt of the notice the person notified does come in and defend he is so bound.

§ 3—804. Lost, Destroyed or Stolen Instruments.

The owner of an instrument which is lost, whether by destruction, theft or otherwise, may maintain an action in his own name and recover from any party liable thereon upon due proof of his ownership, the facts which prevent his production of the instrument and its terms. The court may require security indemnifying the defendant against loss by reason of further claims on the instrument.

§ 3—805. Instruments Not Payable to Order or to Bearer.

This Article applies to any instrument whose terms do not preclude transfer and which is otherwise negotiable within this Article but which is not payable to order or to bearer, except that there can be no holder in due course of such an instrument.

Article 4
BANK DEPOSITS AND COLLECTIONS

Part 1 General Provisions and Definitions

§ 4—101. Short Title.

This Article shall be known and may be cited as Uniform Commercial Code—Bank Deposits and Collections.

§ 4—102. Applicability.

(1) To the extent that items within this Article are also within the scope of Articles 3 and 8, they are subject to the provisions of those Articles. In the event of conflict the provisions of this Article govern those of Article 3 but the provisions of Article 8 govern those of this Article.

(2) The liability of a bank for action or non-action with respect to any item handled by it for purposes of presentment, payment or collection is governed by the law of the place where the bank is located. In the case of action or non-action by or at a branch or separate office of a bank, its liability is governed by the law of the place where the branch or separate office is located.

§ 4—103. Variation by Agreement; Measure of Damages; Certain Action Constituting Ordinary Care.

(1) The effect of the provisions of this Article may be varied by agreement except that no agreement can disclaim a bank's responsibility for its own lack of good faith or failure to exercise ordinary care or can limit the measure of damages for such lack or failure; but the parties may by agreement determine the standards by which such responsibility is to be measured if such standards are not manifestly unreasonable.

(2) Federal Reserve regulations and operating letters, clearing house rules, and the like, have the effect of agreements under subsection (1), whether or not specifically assented to by all parties interested in items handled.

(3) Action or nonaction approved by this Article or pursuant to Federal Reserve regulations or operating letters constitutes the exercise of ordinary care and, in the absence of special instructions, action or nonaction consistent with clearing house rules and the like or with a general banking usage not disapproved by this Article, prima facie constitutes the exercise of ordinary care.

(4) The specification or approval of certain procedures by this Article does not constitute disapproval of other procedures which may be reasonable under the circumstances.

(5) The measure of damages for failure to exercise ordinary care in handling an item is the amount of the item reduced by an amount which could not have been realized by the use of ordinary care, and where there is bad faith it includes other damages, if any, suffered by the party as a proximate consequence.

§ 4—104. Definitions and Index of Definitions.

(1) In this Article unless the context otherwise requires

(a) "Account" means any account with a bank and includes a checking, time, interest or savings account;

(b) "Afternoon" means the period of a day between noon and midnight;

(c) "Banking day" means that part of any day on which a bank is open to the public for carrying on substantially all of its banking functions;

(d) "Clearing house" means any association of banks or other payors regularly clearing items;

(e) "Customer" means any person having an account with a bank or for whom a bank has agreed to collect items and includes a bank carrying an account with another bank;

(f) "Documentary draft" means any negotiable or nonnegotiable draft with accompanying documents, securities or other papers to be delivered against honor of the draft;

(g) "Item" means any instrument for the payment of money even though it is not negotiable but does not include money;

(h) "Midnight deadline" with respect to a bank is midnight on its next banking day following the banking day on which it receives the relevant item or notice or from which the time for taking action commences to run, whichever is later;

(i) "Properly payable" includes the availability of funds for payment at the time of decision to pay or dishonor;

(j) "Settle" means to pay in cash, by clearing house settlement, in a charge or credit or by remittance, or otherwise as instructed. A settlement may be either provisional or final;

(k) "Suspends payments" with respect to a bank means that it has been closed by order of the supervisory authorities, that a public officer has been appointed to take it over or that it ceases or refuses to make payments in the ordinary course of business.

(2) Other definitions applying to this Article and the sections in which they appear are:
"Collecting bank" Section 4—105.
"Depositary bank" Section 4—105.
"Intermediary bank" Section 4—105.
"Payor bank" Section 4—105.
"Presenting bank" Section 4—105.
"Remitting bank" Section 4—105.

(3) The following definitions in other Articles apply to this Article:
"Acceptance" Section 3—410.
"Certificate of deposit" Section 3—104.
"Certification" Section 3—411.
"Check" Section 3—104.
"Draft" Section 3—104.
"Holder in due course" Section 3—302.
"Notice of dishonor" Section 3—508.
"Presentment" Section 3—504.
"Protest" Section 3—509.
"Secondary party" Section 3—102.

(4) In addition Article 1 contains general definitions and principles of construction and interpretation applicable throughout this Article.

§ 4—105. "Depositary Bank"; "Intermediary Bank"; "Collecting Bank"; "Payor Bank"; "Presenting Bank"; "Remitting Bank".

In this Article unless the context otherwise requires:

(a) "Depositary bank" means the first bank to which an item is transferred for collection even though it is also the payor bank;

(b) "Payor bank" means a bank by which an item is payable as drawn or accepted;

(c) "Intermediary bank" means any bank to which an item is transferred in course of collection except the depositary or payor bank;

(d) "Collecting bank" means any bank handling the item for collection except the payor bank;

(e) "Presenting bank" means any bank presenting an item except a payor bank;

(f) "Remitting bank" means any payor or intermediary bank remitting for an item.

§ 4—106. Separate Office of a Bank.

A branch or separate office of a bank [maintaining its own deposit ledgers] is a separate bank for the purpose of computing the time within which and determining the place at or to which action may be taken or notices or orders shall be given under this Article and under Article 3.

Note: *The brackets are to make it optional with the several states whether to require a branch to maintain its own deposit ledgers in order to be considered to be a separate bank for certain purposes under Article 4. In some states "maintaining its own deposit ledgers" is a satisfactory test. In others branch banking practices are such that this test would not be suitable.*

§ 4—107. Time of Receipt of Items.

(1) For the purpose of allowing time to process items, prove balances and make the necessary entries on its books to determine its position for the day, a bank may fix an afternoon hour of 2 P.M. or later as a cut-off hour for the handling of money and items and the making of entries on its books.

(2) Any item or deposit of money received on any day after a cut-off hour so fixed or after the close of the banking day may be treated as being received at the opening of the next banking day.

§ 4—108. Delays.

(1) Unless otherwise instructed, a collecting bank in a good faith effort to secure payment may, in the case of specific items and with or without the approval of any person involved, waive, modify or extend time limits imposed or permitted by this Act for a period not in excess of an additional banking day without discharge of secondary parties and without liability to its transferor or any prior party.

(2) Delay by a collecting bank or payor bank beyond time limits prescribed or permitted by this Act or by instructions is excused if caused by interruption of communication facilities, suspension of payments by another bank, war, emergency conditions or other circumstances beyond the control of the bank provided it exercises such diligence as the circumstances require.

§ 4—109. Process of Posting.

The "process of posting" means the usual procedure followed by a payor bank in determining to pay an item and in recording the payment including one or more of the following or other steps as determined by the bank:

(a) verification of any signature;

(b) ascertaining that sufficient funds are available;

(c) affixing a "paid" or other stamp;

(d) entering a charge or entry to a customer's account;

(e) correcting or reversing an entry or erroneous action with respect to the item.

Part 2 Collection of Items: Depositary and Collecting Banks

§ 4—201. Presumption and Duration of Agency Status of Collecting Banks and Provisional Status of Credits; Applicability of Article; Item Indorsed "Pay Any Bank".

(1) Unless a contrary intent clearly appears and prior to the time that a settlement given by a collecting bank for an item is or becomes final (subsection (3) of Section 4—211 and Sections 4—212 and 4—213) the bank is an agent or sub-agent of the owner of the item and any settlement given for the item is provisional. This provision applies regardless of the form of indorsement or lack of indorsement and even though credit given for the item is subject to immediate withdrawal as of right or is in fact withdrawn; but the continuance of ownership of an item by its owner and any rights of the owner to proceeds of the item are subject to rights of a collecting bank such as those resulting from outstanding advances on the item and valid rights of setoff. When an item is handled by banks for purposes of presentment, payment and collection, the relevant provisions of this Article apply even though action of parties clearly establishes that a particular bank has purchased the item and is the owner of it.

(2) After an item has been indorsed with the words "pay any bank" or the like, only a bank may acquire the rights of a holder

(a) until the item has been returned to the customer initiating collection; or

(b) until the item has been specially indorsed by a bank to a person who is not a bank.

§ 4—202. Responsibility for Collection; When Action Seasonable.

(1) A collecting bank must use ordinary care in

(a) presenting an item or sending it for presentment; and

(b) sending notice of dishonor or non-payment or returning an item other than a documentary draft to the bank's transferor [or directly to the depositary bank under subsection (2) of Section 4—212] *(see note to Section 4—212)* after learning that the item has not been paid or accepted as the case may be; and

(c) settling for an item when the bank receives final settlement; and

(d) making or providing for any necessary protest; and

(e) notifying its transferor of any loss or delay in transit within a reasonable time after discovery thereof.

(2) A collecting bank taking proper action before its midnight deadline following receipt of an item, notice or payment acts seasonably; taking proper action within a reasonably longer time may be seasonable but the bank has the burden of so establishing.

(3) Subject to subsection (1)(a), a bank is not liable for the insolvency, neglect, misconduct, mistake or default of another bank or person or for loss or destruction of an item in transit or in the possession of others.

§ 4—203. Effect of Instructions.

Subject to the provisions of Article 3 concerning conversion of instruments (Section 3—419) and the provisions of both Article 3 and this Article concerning restrictive indorsements only a collecting bank's transferor can give instructions which affect the bank or constitute notice to it and a collecting bank is not liable to prior parties for any action taken pursuant to such instructions or in accordance with any agreement with its transferor.

§ 4—204. Methods of Sending and Presenting; Sending Direct to Payor Bank.

(1) A collecting bank must send items by reasonably prompt method taking into consideration any relevant instructions, the nature of the item, the number of such items on hand, and the cost of collection involved and the method generally used by it or others to present such items.

(2) A collecting bank may send

(a) any item direct to the payor bank;

(b) any item to any non-bank payor if authorized by its transferor; and

(c) any item other than documentary drafts to any non-bank payor, if authorized by Federal Reserve regulation or operating letter, clearing house rule or the like.

(3) Presentment may be made by a presenting bank at a place where the payor bank has requested that presentment be made.

§ 4—205. Supplying Missing Indorsement; No Notice from Prior Indorsement.

(1) A depository bank which has taken an item for collection may supply any indorsement of the customer which is necessary to title unless the item contains the words "payee's indorsement required" or the like. In the absence of such a requirement a statement placed on the item by the depositary bank to the effect that the item was deposited by a customer or credited to his account is effective as the customer's indorsement.

(2) An intermediary bank, or payor bank which is not a depositary bank, is neither given notice nor otherwise affected by a restrictive indorsement of any person except the bank's immediate transferor.

§ 4—206. Transfer Between Banks.

Any agreed method which identifies the transferor bank is sufficient for the item's further transfer to another bank.

§ 4—207. Warranties of Customer and Collecting Bank on Transfer or Presentment of Items; Time for Claims.

(1) Each customer or collecting bank who obtains payment or acceptance of an item and each prior customer and collecting bank warrants to the payor bank or other payor who in good faith pays or accepts the item that

(a) he has a good title to the item or is authorized to obtain payment or acceptance on behalf of one who has a good title; and

(b) he has no knowledge that the signature of the maker or drawer is unauthorized, except that this warranty is not given by any customer or collecting bank that is a holder in due course and acts in good faith

(i) to a maker with respect to the maker's own signature; or

(ii) to a drawer with respect to the drawer's own signature, whether or not the drawer is also the drawee; or

(iii) to an acceptor of an item if the holder in due course took the item after the acceptance or obtained the acceptance without knowledge that the drawer's signature was unauthorized; and

(c) the item has not been materially altered, except that this warranty is not given by any customer or collecting bank that is a holder in due course and acts in good faith

(i) to the maker of a note; or

(ii) to the drawer of a draft whether or not the drawer is also the drawee; or

(iii) to the acceptor of an item with respect to an alteration made prior to the acceptance if the holder in due course took the item after the acceptance, even though the acceptance provided "payable as originally drawn" or equivalent terms; or

(iv) to the acceptor of an item with respect to an alteration made after the acceptance.

(2) Each customer and collecting bank who transfers an item and receives a settlement or other consideration for it warrants to his transferee and to any subsequent collecting bank who takes the item in good faith that

(a) he has a good title to the item or is authorized to obtain payment or acceptance on behalf of one who has a good title and the transfer is otherwise rightful; and

(b) all signatures are genuine or authorized; and

(c) the item has not been materially altered; and

(d) no defense of any party is good against him; and

(e) he has no knowledge of any insolvency proceeding instituted with respect to the maker or acceptor or the drawer of an unaccepted item.

In addition each customer and collecting bank so transferring an item and receiving a settlement or other consideration engages that upon dishonor and any necessary notice of dishonor and protest he will take up the item.

(3) The warranties and the engagement to honor set forth in the two preceding subsections arise notwithstanding the absence of indorsement or words of guaranty or warranty in the transfer or presentment and a collecting bank remains liable for their breach despite remittance to its transferor. Damages for breach of such warranties or engagement to honor shall not exceed the consideration received by the customer or collecting bank responsible plus finance charges and expenses related to the item, if any.

(4) Unless a claim for breach of warranty under this section is made within a reasonable time after the person claiming learns of the breach, the person liable is discharged to the extent of any loss caused by the delay in making claim.

§ 4—208. Security Interest of Collecting Bank in Items, Accompanying Documents and Proceeds.

(1) A bank has a security interest in an item and any accompanying documents or the proceeds of either

(a) in case of an item deposited in an account to the extent to which credit given for the item has been withdrawn or applied;

(b) in case of an item for which it has given credit available for withdrawal as of right, to the extent of the credit given whether or not the credit is drawn upon and whether or not there is a right of chargeback; or

(c) if it makes an advance on or against the item.

(2) When credit which has been given for several items received at one time or pursuant to a single agreement is withdrawn or applied in part the security interest remains upon all the items, any accompanying documents or the proceeds of either. For the purpose of this section, credits first given are first withdrawn.

(3) Receipt by a collecting bank of a final settlement for an item is a realization on its security interest in the item, accompanying documents and proceeds. To the extent and so long as the bank does not receive final settlement for the item or give up possession of the item or accompanying documents for purposes other than collection, the security interest continues and is subject to the provisions of Article 9 except that

(a) no security agreement is necessary to make the security interest enforceable (subsection (1)(a) of Section 9—203); and

(b) no filing is required to perfect the security interest; and

(c) the security interest has priority over conflicting perfected security interests in the item, accompanying documents or proceeds.

§ 4—209. **When Bank Gives Value for Purposes of Holder in Due Course.**

For purposes of determining its status as a holder in due course, the bank has given value to the extent that it has a security interest in an item provided that the bank otherwise complies with the requirements of Section 3—302 on what constitutes a holder in due course.

§ 4—210. **Presentment by Notice of Item Not Payable by, Through or at a Bank; Liability of Secondary Parties.**

(1) Unless otherwise instructed, a collecting bank may present an item not payable by, through or at a bank by sending to the party to accept or pay a written notice that the bank holds the item for acceptance or payment. The notice must be sent in time to be received on or before the day when presentment is due and the bank must meet any requirement of the party to accept or pay under Section 3—505 by the close of the bank's next banking day after it knows of the requirement.

(2) Where presentment is made by notice and neither honor nor request for compliance with a requirement under Section 3—505 is received by the close of business on the day after maturity or in the case of demand items by the close of business on the third banking day after notice was sent, the presenting bank may treat the item as dishonored and charge any secondary party by sending him notice of the facts.

§ 4—211. **Media of Remittance; Provisional and Final Settlement in Remittance Cases.**

(1) A collecting bank may take in settlement of an item

(a) a check of the remitting bank or of another bank on any bank except the remitting bank; or

(b) a cashier's check or similar primary obligation of a remitting bank which is a member of or clears through a member of the same clearing house or group as the collecting bank; or

(c) appropriate authority to charge an account of the remitting bank or of another bank with the collecting bank; or

(d) if the item is drawn upon or payable by a person other than a bank, a cashier's check, certified check or other bank check or obligation.

(2) If before its midnight deadline the collecting bank properly dishonors a remittance check or authorization to charge on itself or presents or forwards for collection a remittance instrument of or on another bank which is of a kind approved by subsection (1) or has not been authorized by it, the collecting bank is not liable to prior parties in the event of the dishonor of such check, instrument or authorization.

(3) A settlement for an item by means of a remittance instrument or authorization to charge is or becomes a final settlement as to both the person making and the person receiving the settlement

(a) if the remittance instrument or authorization to charge is of a kind approved by subsection (1) or has not been authorized by the person receiving the settlement and in either case the person receiving the settlement acts seasonably before its midnight deadline in presenting, forwarding for collection or paying the instrument or authorization,—at the time the remittance instrument or authorization is finally paid by the payor by which it is payable;

(b) if the person receiving the settlement has authorized remittance by a non-bank check or obligation or by a cashier's check or similar primary obligation of or a check upon the payor or other remitting bank which is not of a kind approved by subsection (1)(b),—at the time of the receipt of such remittance check or obligation; or

(c) if in a case not covered by sub-paragraphs (a) or (b) the person receiving the settlement fails to seasonably present, forward for collection, pay or return a remittance instrument or authorization to it to charge before its midnight deadline,—at such midnight deadline.

§ 4—212. Right of Charge-Back or Refund.

(1) If a collecting bank has made provisional settlement with its customer for an item and itself fails by reason of dishonor, suspension of payments by a bank or otherwise to receive a settlement for the item which is or becomes final, the bank may revoke the settlement given by it, charge back the amount of any credit given for the item to its customer's account or obtain refund from its customer whether or not it is able to return the items if by its midnight deadline or within a longer reasonable time after it learns the facts it returns the item or sends notification of the facts. These rights to revoke, charge-back and obtain refund terminate if and when a settlement for the item received by the bank is or becomes final (subsection (3) of Section 4—211 and subsections (2) and (3) of Section 4—213).

[(2) Within the time and manner prescribed by this section and Section 4—301, an intermediary or payor bank, as the case may be, may return an unpaid item directly to the depositary bank and may send for collection a draft on the depositary bank and obtain reimbursement. In such case, if the depositary bank has received provisional settlement for the item, it must reimburse the bank drawing the draft and any provisional credits for the item between banks shall become and remain final.]

Note: *Direct returns is recognized as an innovation that is not yet established bank practice, and therefore, Paragraph 2 has been bracketed. Some lawyers have doubts whether it should be included in legislation or left to development by agreement.*

(3) A depositary bank which is also the payor may chargeback the amount of an item to its customer's account or obtain refund in accordance with the section governing return of an item received by a payor bank for credit on its books (Section 4—301).

(4) The right to charge-back is not affected by

(a) prior use of the credit given for the item; or

(b) failure by any bank to exercise ordinary care with respect to the item but any bank so failing remains liable.

(5) A failure to charge-back or claim refund does not affect other rights of the bank against the customer or any other party.

(6) If credit is given in dollars as the equivalent of the value of an item payable in a foreign currency the dollar amount of any charge-back or refund shall be calculated on the basis of the buying sight rate for the foreign currency prevailing on the day when the person entitled to the charge-back or refund learns that it will not receive payment in ordinary course.

§ 4—213. Final Payment of Item by Payor Bank; When Provisional Debits and Credits Become Final; When Certain Credits Become Available for Withdrawal.

(1) An item is finally paid by a payor bank when the bank has done any of the following, whichever happens first:

(a) paid the item in cash; or

(b) settled for the item without reserving a right to revoke the settlement and without having such right under statute, clearing house rule or agreement; or

(c) completed the process of posting the item to the indicated account of the drawer, maker or other person to be charged therewith; or

(d) made a provisional settlement for the item and failed to revoke the settlement in the time and manner permitted by statute, clearing house rule or agreement.

Upon a final payment under subparagraphs (b), (c) or (d) the payor bank shall be accountable for the amount of the item.

(2) If provisional settlement for an item between the presenting and payor banks is made through a clearing house or by debits or credits in an account between them, then to the extent that provisional debits or credits for the item are entered in accounts between the presenting and payor banks or between the presenting and successive prior collecting banks seriatim, they become final upon final payment of the item by the payor bank.

(3) If a collecting bank receives a settlement for an item which is or becomes final (subsection (3) of Section 4—211, subsection (2) of Section 4—213) the bank is accountable to its customer for the amount of the item and any provisional credit given for the item in an account with its customer becomes final.

(4) Subject to any right of the bank to apply the credit to an obligation of the customer, credit given by a bank for an item in an account with its customer becomes available for withdrawal as of right

(a) in any case where the bank has received a provisional settlement for the item,—when such settlement becomes final and the bank has had a reasonable time to learn that the settlement is final;

(b) in any case where the bank is both a depositary bank and a payor bank and the item is finally paid,— at the opening of the bank's second banking day following receipt of the item.

(5) A deposit of money in a bank is final when made but, subject to any right of the bank to apply the deposit to an obligation of the customer, the deposit becomes available for withdrawal as of right at the opening of

the bank's next banking day following receipt of the deposit.

§ 4—214. Insolvency and Preference.

(1) Any item in or coming into the possession of a payor or collecting bank which suspends payment and which item is not finally paid shall be returned by the receiver, trustee or agent in charge of the closed bank to the presenting bank or the closed bank's customer.

(2) If a payor bank finally pays an item and suspends payments without making a settlement for the item with its customer or the presenting bank which settlement is or becomes final, the owner of the item has a preferred claim against the payor bank.

(3) If a payor bank gives or a collecting bank gives or receives a provisional settlement for an item and thereafter suspends payments, the suspension does not prevent or interfere with the settlement becoming final if such finality occurs automatically upon the lapse of certain time or the happening of certain events (subsection (3) of Section 4—211, subsections (1)(d), (2) and (3) of Section 4—213).

(4) If a collecting bank receives from subsequent parties settlement for an item which settlement is or becomes final and suspends payments without making a settlement for the item with its customer which is or becomes final, the owner of the item has a preferred claim against such collecting bank.

Part 3 Collection of Items: Payor Banks

§ 4—301. Deferred Posting; Recovery of Payment by Return of Items; Time of Dishonor.

(1) Where an authorized settlement for a demand item (other than a documentary draft) received by a payor bank otherwise than for immediate payment over the counter has been made before midnight of the banking day of receipt the payor bank may revoke the settlement and recover any payment if before it has made final payment (subsection (1) of Section 4—213) and before its midnight deadline it

(a) returns the item; or

(b) sends written notice of dishonor or nonpayment if the item is held for protest or is otherwise unavailable for return.

(2) If a demand item is received by a payor bank for credit on its books it may return such item or send notice of dishonor and may revoke any credit given or recover the amount thereof withdrawn by its customer, if it acts within the time limit and in the manner specified in the preceding subsection.

(3) Unless previous notice of dishonor has been sent an item is dishonored at the time when for purposes of dishonor it is returned or notice sent in accordance with this section.

(4) An item is returned:

(a) as to an item received through a clearing house, when it is delivered to the presenting or last collecting bank or to the clearing house or is sent or delivered in accordance with its rules; or

(b) in all other cases, when it is sent or delivered to the bank's customer or transferor or pursuant to his instructions.

§ 4—302. Payor Bank's Responsibility for Late Return of Item.

In the absence of a valid defense such as breach of a presentment warranty (subsection (1) of Section 4—207), settlement effected or the like, if an item is presented on and received by a payor bank the bank is accountable for the amount of

(a) a demand item other than a documentary draft whether properly payable or not if the bank, in any case where it is not also the depositary bank, retains the item beyond midnight of the banking day of receipt without settling for it or, regardless of whether it is also the depositary bank, does not pay or return the item or send notice of dishonor until after its midnight deadline; or

(b) any other properly payable item unless within the time allowed for acceptance or payment of that item the bank either accepts or pays the item or returns it and accompanying documents.

§ 4—303. When Items Subject to Notice, Stop-Order, Legal Process or Setoff; Order in Which Items May Be Charged or Certified.

(1) Any knowledge, notice or stop-order received by, legal process served upon or setoff exercised by a payor bank, whether or not effective under other rules of law to terminate, suspend or modify the bank's right or duty to pay an item or to charge its customer's account for the item, comes too late to so terminate, suspend or modify such right or duty if the knowledge, notice, stop-order or legal process is received or served and a reasonable time for the bank to act thereon expires or the setoff is exercised after the bank has done any of the following:

(a) accepted or certified the item;

(b) paid the item in cash;

(c) settled for the item without reserving a right to revoke the settlement and without having such right under statute, clearing house rule or agreement;

(d) completed the process of posting the item to the indicated account of the drawer, maker or other person to be charged therewith or otherwise has evidenced by examination of such indicated account and by action its decision to pay the item; or

(e) become accountable for the amount of the item under subsection (1)(d) of Section 4—213 and Section 4—302 dealing with the payor bank's responsibility for late return of items.

(2) Subject to the provisions of subsection (1) items may be accepted, paid, certified or charged to the indicated account of its customer in any order convenient to the bank.

Part 4 Relationship Between Payor Bank and Its Customer

§ 4—401. When Bank May Charge Customer's Account.

(1) As against its customer, a bank may charge against his account any item which is otherwise properly payable from that account even though the charge creates an overdraft.

(2) A bank which in good faith makes payment to a holder may charge the indicated account of its customer according to

(a) the original tenor of his altered item; or

(b) the tenor of his completed item, even though the bank knows the item has been completed unless the bank has notice that the completion was improper.

§ 4—402. Bank's Liability to Customer for Wrongful Dishonor.

A payor bank is liable to its customer for damages proximately caused by the wrongful dishonor of an item. When the dishonor occurs through mistake liability is limited to actual damages proved. If so proximately caused and proved damages may include damages for an arrest or prosecution of the customer or other consequential damages. Whether any consequential damages are proximately caused by the wrongful dishonor is a question of fact to be determined in each case.

§ 4—403. Customer's Right to Stop Payment; Burden of Proof of Loss.

(1) A customer may by order to his bank stop payment of any item payable for his account but the order must be received at such time and in such manner as to afford the bank a reasonable opportunity to act on it prior to any action by the bank with respect to the item described in Section 4—303.

(2) An oral order is binding upon the bank only for fourteen calendar days unless confirmed in writing within that period. A written order is effective for only six months unless renewed in writing.

(3) The burden of establishing the fact and amount of loss resulting from the payment of an item contrary to a binding stop payment order is on the customer.

§ 4—404. Bank Not Obligated to Pay Check More Than Six Months Old.

A bank is under no obligation to a customer having a checking account to pay a check, other than a certified check, which is presented more than six months after its date, but it may charge its customer's account for a payment made thereafter in good faith.

§ 4—405. Death or Incompetence of Customer.

(1) A payor or collecting bank's authority to accept, pay or collect an item or to account for proceeds of its collection if otherwise effective is not rendered ineffective by incompetence of a customer of either bank existing at the time the item is issued or its collection is undertaken if the bank does not know of an adjudication of incompetence. Neither death nor incompetence of a customer revokes such authority to accept, pay, collect or account until the bank knows of the fact of death or of an adjudication of incompetence and has reasonable opportunity to act on it.

(2) Even with knowledge a bank may for 10 days after the date of death pay or certify checks drawn on or prior to that date unless ordered to stop payment by a person claiming an interest in the account.

§ 4—406. Customer's Duty to Discover and Report Unauthorized Signature or Alteration.

(1) When a bank sends to its customer a statement of account accompanied by items paid in good faith in support of the debit entries or holds the statement and items pursuant to a request or instructions of its customer or otherwise in a reasonable manner makes the statement and items available to the customer, the customer must exercise reasonable care and promptness to examine the statement and items to discover his unauthorized signature or any alteration on an item and must notify the bank promptly after discovery thereof.

(2) If the bank establishes that the customer failed with respect to an item to comply with the duties imposed on the customer by subsection (1) the customer is precluded from asserting against the bank

(a) his unauthorized signature or any alteration on the item if the bank also establishes that it suffered a loss by reason of such failure; and

(b) an unauthorized signature or alteration by the same wrongdoer on any other item paid in good faith by the bank after the first item and statement was available to the customer for a reasonable period not exceeding fourteen calendar days and before the bank receives notification from the customer of any such unauthorized signature or alteration.

(3) The preclusion under subsection (2) does not apply if the customer establishes lack of ordinary care on the part of the bank in paying the item(s).

(4) Without regard to care or lack of care of either the customer or the bank a customer who does not within one year from the time the statement and items are made available to the customer (subsection (1)) discover and report his unauthorized signature or any alteration on the face or back of the item or does not within three years from that time discover and report any unauthorized indorsement is precluded from asserting against the bank such unauthorized signature or indorsement or such alteration.

(5) If under this section a payor bank has a valid defense against a claim of a customer upon or resulting from payment of an item and waives or fails upon request to assert the defense the bank may not assert against any collecting bank or other prior party presenting or transferring the item a claim based upon the unauthorized signature or alteration giving rise to the customer's claim.

§ 4—407. **Payor Bank's Right to Subrogation on Improper Payment.**

If a payor bank has paid an item over the stop payment order of the drawer or maker or otherwise under circumstances giving a basis for objection by the drawer or maker, to prevent unjust enrichment and only to the extent necessary to prevent loss to the bank by reason of its payment of the item, the payor bank shall be subrogated to the rights

(a) of any holder in due course on the item against the drawer or maker; and

(b) of the payee or any other holder of the item against the drawer or maker either on the item or under the transaction out of which the item arose; and

(c) of the drawer or maker against the payee or any other holder of the item with respect to the transaction out of which the item arose.

Part 5 Collection of Documentary Drafts

§ 4—501. **Handling of Documentary Drafts; Duty to Send for Presentment and to Notify Customer of Dishonor.**

A bank which takes a documentary draft for collection must present or send the draft and accompanying documents for presentment and upon learning that the draft has not been paid or accepted in due course must seasonably notify its customer of such fact even though it may have discounted or bought the draft or extended credit available for withdrawal as of right.

§ 4—502. **Presentment of "On Arrival" Drafts.**

When a draft or the relevant instructions require presentment "on arrival", "when goods arrive" or the like, the collecting bank need not present until in its judgment a reasonable time for arrival of the goods has expired. Refusal to pay or accept because the goods have not arrived is not dishonor; the bank must notify its transferor of such refusal but need not present the draft again until it is instructed to do so or learns of the arrival of the goods.

§ 4—503. **Responsibility of Presenting Bank for Documents and Goods; Report of Reasons for Dishonor; Referee in Case of Need.**

Unless otherwise instructed and except as provided in Article 5 a bank presenting a documentary draft

(a) must deliver the documents to the drawee on acceptance of the draft if it is payable more than three days after presentment; otherwise, only on payment; and

(b) upon dishonor, either in the case of presentment for acceptance or presentment for payment, may seek and follow instructions from any referee in case of need designated in the draft or if the presenting bank does not choose to utilize his services it must use diligence and good faith to ascertain the reason for dishonor, must notify its transferor of the dishonor and of the results of its effort to ascertain the reasons therefor and must request instructions.

But the presenting bank is under no obligation with respect to goods represented by the documents except to follow any reasonable instructions seasonably received; it has a right to reimbursement for any expense incurred in following instructions and to prepayment of or indemnity for such expenses.

§ 4—504. **Privilege of Presenting Bank to Deal With Goods; Security Interest for Expenses.**

(1) A presenting bank which, following the dishonor of a documentary draft, has seasonably requested instructions but does not receive them within a reasonable time may store, sell, or otherwise deal with the goods in any reasonable manner.

(2) For its reasonable expenses incurred by action under subsection (1) the presenting bank has a lien upon the goods or their proceeds, which may be foreclosed in the same manner as an unpaid seller's lien.

Article 4A
FUNDS TRANSFERS*

Part 1 Subject Matter and Definitions

§ 4A—101. Short Title.

This Article may be cited as Uniform Commercial Code—Funds Transfers.

§ 4A—102. Subject Matter.

Except as otherwise provided in Section 4A—108, this Article applies to funds transfers defined in Section 4A—104.

§ 4A—103. Payment Order.

(1) "Payment order" means an instruction of a sender to a receiving bank, transmitted orally, electronically, or in writing, to pay, or to cause another bank to pay, a fixed or determinable amount of money to a beneficiary if:

    (a) the instruction does not state a condition to payment to the beneficiary other than time of payment,

    (b) the receiving bank is to be reimbursed by debiting an account of, or otherwise receiving payment from, the sender, and

    (c) the instruction is transmitted by the sender directly to the receiving bank or to an agent, funds transfer system, or communication system for transmittal to the receiving bank.

If an instruction is to make more than one payment to a beneficiary, the instruction is a separate payment order with respect to each of the payments.

(2) "Sender" means the person giving the instruction to the receiving bank.

(3) "Receiving bank" means the bank to which the sender's instruction is addressed.

(4) "Beneficiary" means the person to be paid by the beneficiary's bank.

(5) "Beneficiary's bank" means the bank in which the beneficiary has the account to which payment is to be made pursuant to a payment order or which is to otherwise make payment to the beneficiary if the payment order does not provide for payment to an account.

§ 4A—104. Funds Transfer.

(1) "Funds transfer" means the series of transactions, commencing with the originator's payment order, made for the purpose of making payment to the beneficiary of the order. It includes any payment order issued by the originator's bank or an intermediary bank intended to carry out the originator's payment order, and is completed by acceptance by the beneficiary's bank of a payment order for the benefit of the beneficiary of the originator's payment order.

(2) "Originator" means the sender of the first payment order in a funds transfer.

(3) "Originator's bank" means (i) the receiving bank to which the payment order of the originator is issued if the originator is not a bank, or (ii) the originator if the originator is a bank.

(4) "Intermediary bank" means a receiving bank other than the originator's bank or the beneficiary's bank.

§ 4A—105. Other Definitions.

(1) As used in this Article:

    (a) "Authorized account" means a deposit account of a customer in a bank designated by the customer as a source of payment of payment orders issued by the customer to the bank. If a customer does not so designate an account, any account of the customer is an authorized account if payment of a payment order from that account is not inconsistent with a restriction on the use of that account.

    (b) "Bank" means any person engaged in the business of banking, and includes a savings bank, savings and loan association, credit union or trust company. A branch or separate office of a bank is a separate bank for purposes of this Article.

    (c) "Customer" means a person, including a bank, having an account with a bank or from whom a bank has agreed to receive payment orders.

    (d) "Funds transfer business day" of a receiving bank means the part of a day during which the receiving bank is open for the receipt, processing, and transmittal of payment orders and cancellations and amendments of payment orders.

    (e) "Funds transfer system" means a wire transfer network, automated clearing house, or other communication system of a clearing house or other association of banks through which a payment order by a bank may be transmitted to the bank to which the order is addressed.

    (f) "Good faith" means honesty in fact and the observance of reasonable commercial standards of fair dealing.

    (g) "Issued" with respect to a payment order means the time it is sent to the receiving bank.

    (h) "Prove" with respect to a fact means the burden of establishing the fact (subsection (8) of Section 1—201) has been met.

---

*Approved in substance by the National Conference of Commissioners on Uniform State Laws and The American Law Institute. Subject to editorial revision.

(2) Other definitions applying to this Article and the sections in which they appear are:

"Acceptance"	Section 4A—207
"Beneficiary"	Section 4A—103
"Beneficiary's bank"	Section 4A—103
"Executed"	Section 4A—301
"Execution date"	Section 4A—301
"Funds transfer system rule"	Section 4A—501
"Funds transfer"	Section 4A—104
"Intermediary bank"	Section 4A—104
"Originator"	Section 4A—104
"Originator's bank"	Section 4A—104
"Payment by beneficiary's bank to beneficiary"	Section 4A—405
"Payment by originator to beneficiary"	Section 4A—406
"Payment by sender to receiving bank"	Section 4A—403
"Payment date"	Section 4A—401
"Payment order"	Section 4A—103
"Receiving bank"	Section 4A—103
"Security procedure"	Section 4A—201
"Sender"	Section 4A—103

(3) The following definitions in Article 4 apply to this Article:

"Clearing house"	Section 4—104
"Item"	Section 4—104
"Suspends payments"	Section 4—104

§ 4A—106. **Funds Transfer Business Day; Time Payment Order Is Received.**

(1) The time a payment order or cancellation or amendment of a payment order is received is determined by the rules applicable to receipt of a notice stated in subsection (27) of Section 1—201. A receiving bank may fix a time or times on any funds transfer business day as a cut-off time for the receipt and processing of payment orders and cancellations or amendments of payment orders. Different cut-off times may apply to receipt of payment orders, cancellations or amendments, or to different categories of payment orders, cancellations or amendments. A cut-off time may apply to senders generally or different cut-off times may apply to different senders or categories of senders. If a payment order or cancellation or amendment of a payment order is received after the close of a funds transfer business day or after the appropriate cut-off time on a funds transfer business day, the receiving bank may treat the payment order, cancellation or amendment as received at the opening of the next funds transfer business day.

(2) If this Article refers to an execution date or payment date or states a day on which a receiving bank is required to take any action, and the date or day does not fall on a funds transfer business day, the next day which is a funds transfer business day shall be treated as the date or day stated, unless the contrary is stated in this Article.

§ 4A—107. **Federal Reserve Regulations and Operating Circulars.**

Regulations of the Board of Governors of the Federal Reserve System and operating circulars of the Federal Reserve Banks supersede any inconsistent provision of this Article to the extent of the inconsistency.

§ 4A—108. **Exclusion of Consumer Transactions Governed by Federal Law.**

This Article does not apply to a funds transfer any part of which is governed by the Electronic Fund Transfer Act of 1978 (Title XX, Public Law 95—630, 92 Stat. 3728, 15 U.S.C. § 1693 et seq.) as amended from time to time.

Part 2 Issue and Acceptance of Payment Order

§ 4A—201. **Security Procedure.**

"Security procedure" means a procedure established by agreement of a customer and a receiving bank for the purpose of (i) verifying that a payment order or communication amending or cancelling a payment order is that of the customer, or (ii) detecting error in the transmission or the content of the payment order or communication. A security procedure may require the use of algorithms or other codes, identifying words or numbers, encryption, callback procedures or similar security devices. Comparison of a signature on a payment order or communication with an authorized specimen signature of the customer is not by itself a security procedure.

§ 4A—202. **Authorized and Verified Payment Orders.**

(1) A payment order received by the receiving bank is the authorized order of the person identified as sender if that person authorized the order or is otherwise bound by it pursuant to the law of agency or other applicable law.

(2) If a bank and its customer have agreed that the authenticity of payment orders issued to the bank in the name of the customer as sender will be verified pursuant to a security procedure, a payment order received by the receiving bank is effective as the order of the customer, whether or not authorized, if (i) the security procedure is a commercially reasonable method of providing security against unauthorized payment orders, and (ii) the

bank proves that it accepted the payment order in good faith and in compliance with the security procedure and any written agreement or instruction of the customer restricting acceptance of payment orders issued in the name of the customer. The bank is not required to follow an instruction that violates a written agreement with the customer or notice of which is not received at a time and in a manner affording the bank a reasonable opportunity to act on it before the payment order is accepted.

(3) Commercial reasonableness of a security procedure is a question of law to be determined by considering the wishes of the customer expressed to the bank, the circumstances of the customer known to the bank, including the size, type, and frequency of payment orders normally issued by the customer, alternative security procedures offered to the customer, and security procedures in general use by customers and receiving banks similarly situated. A security procedure shall be considered to be commercially reasonable if (i) the security procedure was chosen by the customer after the bank offered, and the customer refused, a security procedure that was commercially reasonable for that customer, and (ii) the customer expressly agreed in writing to be bound by any payment order, whether or not authorized, issued in its name, and accepted by the bank in compliance with the security procedure chosen by the customer.

(4) The term "sender" in this Article includes the customer in whose name a payment order is issued if the order is the authorized order of the customer pursuant to subsection (1), or if it is effective as the order of the customer pursuant to subsection (2).

(5) This section applies to amendments and cancellations of payment orders to the same extent it applies to payment orders.

(6) Except as provided in this section and in subsection (2)(a) of Section 4A—203, rights and obligations arising under this section may not be varied by agreement.

§ 4A—203. Unenforceability of Certain Verified Payment Orders.

(1) This section applies to an accepted payment order that is not, pursuant to subsection (1) of Section 4A—202, an authorized order of a customer identified as sender, but which is effective as the order of the customer pursuant to subsection (2) of Section 4A—202.

(2) The receiving bank is not entitled to enforce or retain payment of the payment order:

(a) to the extent provided in an express written contract of the bank, or

(b) if the customer proves that issuance of the order was not caused, directly or indirectly, by (i) a person entrusted at any time with duties to act for the customer with respect to payment orders or the security procedure, or (ii) a person with access to transmitting facilities of the customer or who obtained, without authority of the receiving bank, information facilitating breach of the security procedure from a source controlled by the customer, regardless of how the information was obtained or whether the customer was at fault. Information includes any access device, computer software or the like.

(3) This section applies to amendments of payment orders to the same extent it applies to payment orders.

§ 4A—204. Refund of Payment and Duty of Customer to Report With Respect to Unauthorized Payment Order.

If a receiving bank accepts a payment order issued in the name of its customer as sender which is (i) not authorized and not effective as the order of the customer under Section 4A—202, or (ii) not enforceable, in whole or in part, against the customer under Section 4A—203, the bank shall refund any payment of the payment order received from the customer to the extent the bank is not entitled to enforce payment, and shall pay interest on the refundable amount calculated from the date the bank received payment to the date of the refund. However, if the customer fails to exercise ordinary care to determine that the order was not authorized by the customer and to advise the bank of the relevant facts within a reasonable time not to exceed 90 days from the date the customer received notification from the bank that the order was accepted or that the customer's account was debited with respect to the order, the customer is not entitled to interest from the bank on the amount to be refunded. The bank is not entitled to any recovery from the customer on account of a failure by the customer to give notification as stated in this section.

§ 4A—205. Erroneous Payment Orders.

(1) This section applies to an accepted payment order transmitted pursuant to a security procedure for the detection of error, if the payment order (i) erroneously instructed payment to a beneficiary not intended by the sender, (ii) erroneously instructed payment in an amount greater than the amount intended by the sender, or (iii) is an erroneously transmitted duplicate of a payment order previously sent by the sender.

(2) If the sender proves that the sender or the sender's agent complied with the security procedure and that the error would have been detected if the receiving bank had also complied, the sender is not obliged to pay the order to the extent stated in subsection (3).

(3) If the funds transfer is completed on the basis of an erroneous payment order described in subsection (1)(i) or (iii), the sender is not obliged to pay the order and

the receiving bank is entitled to recover from the beneficiary any amount paid to the beneficiary to the extent the law governing mistake and restitution allows recovery. If the funds transfer is completed on the basis of a payment order described in subsection (1)(ii), the sender is not obliged to pay the order to the extent the amount received by the beneficiary is greater than the amount intended by the sender. In that case, the receiving bank is entitled to recover from the beneficiary the excess amount received to the extent the law governing mistake and restitution allows recovery.

(4) This subsection applies if the sender of an erroneous payment order described in subsection (1) is not obliged to pay all or part of the order, and the sender receives notification from the receiving bank that the order was accepted by the bank or that the sender's account was debited with respect to the order. The sender has a duty to exercise ordinary care, on the basis of information available to the customer, to discover the error with respect to the order and to advise the bank of the relevant facts within a reasonable time not to exceed 90 days after the bank's notification was received by the sender. If the bank proves that the sender failed to perform that duty, the sender is obliged to reimburse the bank for the loss the bank proves it incurred as a result of the failure, but the liability of the sender may not exceed the amount of the sender's order.

(5) This section applies to amendments to payment orders to the same extent it applies to payment orders.

§ 4A—206. Transmission of Payment Order Through Funds Transfer or Other Communication System.

If a payment order addressed to a receiving bank is transmitted to a funds transfer system or other third-party communication system for transmittal to the bank, the system is considered to be an agent of the sender for the purpose of transmitting the payment order to the bank. If there is a discrepancy between the terms of the payment order transmitted to the system and the terms of the payment order transmitted by the system to the bank, the terms of the payment order of the sender are those received by the bank. This section applies to amendments to payment orders to the same extent it applies to payment orders. This section does not apply to a funds transfer system of the Federal Reserve Banks.

§ 4A—207. Acceptance of Payment Order.

(1) Subject to subsection (4), a receiving bank other than the beneficiary's bank accepts a payment order when it executes the order.

(2) Subject to subsections (3) and (4), a beneficiary's bank accepts a payment order at the earliest of the following times:

(a) the time the bank (i) pays the beneficiary as stated in subsection (1) or (2) of Section 4A—405, or (ii) notifies the beneficiary of receipt of the order or that the account of the beneficiary has been credited with respect to the order unless the notice indicates that the bank is rejecting the order or that funds with respect to the order may not be withdrawn or used until receipt of payment from the sender of the order,

(b) the time the bank receives payment of the entire amount of the sender's order pursuant to subsection (1)(a) or (b) of Section 4A—403, or

(c) the opening of the next funds transfer business day of the bank following the payment date of the order if, at that time, the amount of the sender's order is fully covered by a withdrawable credit balance in an authorized account of the sender or the bank has otherwise received full payment from the sender, unless the order was rejected before that time or is rejected within (i) one hour after that time, or (ii) one hour after the opening of the next business day of the sender following the payment date if that time is later. If notice of rejection is received by the sender after the payment date and the authorized account of the sender does not bear interest, the bank is obliged to pay interest to the sender on the amount of the order for the number of days elapsing after the payment date to the day the sender receives notice, counting the day notice is received as an elapsed day.

(3) Acceptance of a payment order cannot occur before the order is received by the receiving bank. No acceptance occurs under subsection (2)(b) or (c) if the beneficiary of the payment order does not have an account with the receiving bank, the account has been closed, or the receiving bank is not permitted by law to receive credits for the beneficiary's account.

(4) A payment order issued to the originator's bank cannot be accepted until (i) the payment date if the bank is the beneficiary's bank, or (ii) the execution date if the bank is not the beneficiary's bank. If the originator's bank executes the originator's payment order before the execution date or pays the beneficiary of the originator's payment order before the payment date and the payment order is subsequently cancelled pursuant to subsection (2) of Section 4A—209, the bank may recover from the beneficiary any payment received to the extent allowed by the law governing mistake and restitution.

§ 4A—208. Rejection of Payment Order.

(1) A payment order is rejected by the receiving bank by a notice of rejection transmitted to the sender by an oral, written, or electronic communication. A notice of rejection need not use any particular words and is sufficient if it indicates that the receiving bank is rejecting the order or will not execute, pay or otherwise act to carry out the order. Rejection is effective when the notice

is given if transmission is by a means that is commercially reasonable. If notice of rejection is given by a means that is not commercially reasonable, rejection is effective when the notice is received. If an agreement of the sender and receiving bank establishes the means to be used to reject a payment order, (i) any means complying with the agreement is commercially reasonable and (ii) any means not complying is not commercially reasonable unless no significant delay in receipt of the notice resulted from the use of the non-complying means.

(2) This subsection applies if a receiving bank other than the beneficiary's bank fails to execute a payment order notwithstanding that on the execution date an authorized account of the sender has a withdrawable credit balance sufficient to cover the order. If the sender does not receive notice of rejection of the order on the execution date and the authorized account of the sender does not bear interest, the bank is obliged to pay interest to the sender on the amount of the order for the number of days elapsing after the execution date to the day the sender receives notice or learns that the order was not executed, counting that day as an elapsed day.

(3) In the case of suspension of payments by a receiving bank, all unaccepted payment orders issued to it are rejected by operation of law at the time the bank suspends payments.

(4) Acceptance of a payment order precludes a later rejection of the order. Rejection of a payment order precludes a later acceptance of the order.

§ 4A—209. **Cancellation and Amendment of Payment Order.**

(1) A cancellation or amendment of a payment order by the sender may be transmitted to the receiving bank by an oral, written, or electronic communication. If a security procedure is in effect between the sender and the receiving bank, a communication cancelling or amending a payment order is not effective unless the communication is verified pursuant to the security procedure or the bank agrees to the cancellation or amendment.

(2) Subject to subsection (1), a communication by the sender cancelling or amending a payment order is effective if notice of the communication is received at a time and in a manner affording the receiving bank a reasonable opportunity to act on the communication before the bank accepts the payment order.

(3) Cancellation or amendment of a payment order accepted by the receiving bank is effective only if the bank agrees or a funds transfer system rule allows cancellation or amendment without agreement of the bank.

   (a) With respect to a payment order accepted by a receiving bank other than the beneficiary's bank, cancellation or amendment is not effective unless the receiving bank is able to cancel or make a conforming amendment to the payment order issued by the bank.

   (b) With respect to a payment order accepted by the beneficiary's bank, cancellation or amendment is not effective unless the payment order was issued in execution of an unauthorized payment order, or because of a mistake by a sender in the funds transfer which resulted in the issuance of a payment order (i) that is a duplicate of a payment order previously issued by the sender, (ii) that orders payment to a beneficiary not intended by the sender, or (iii) that orders payment in an amount greater than the amount intended by the sender. If the payment order is cancelled or amended, the beneficiary's bank is entitled to recover from the beneficiary any amount paid to the beneficiary to the extent the law governing mistake and restitution allows recovery.

(4) An unaccepted payment order is cancelled by operation of law at the close of the fifth funds transfer business day of the receiving bank after the execution date or payment date of the order.

(5) A cancelled payment order cannot be accepted. If an accepted payment order is cancelled, the acceptance is nullified and no person has any right or obligation based on the acceptance. The effect of amendment of a payment order is to treat the order as having been issued in the amended form. If amendment occurs after acceptance, the payment order is treated as having been accepted in the amended form when the unamended payment order was accepted.

(6) Unless otherwise provided in an agreement of the parties or in a funds transfer system rule, if the receiving bank agrees to cancellation or amendment by the sender under subsection (3) or is bound by a funds transfer system rule allowing cancellation or amendment without the bank's agreement, the sender is obliged to compensate the bank for any loss and expenses, including reasonable attorney's fees, incurred by the bank as a result of the cancellation or amendment or attempted cancellation or amendment.

(7) A payment order is not revoked by death or legal incapacity of the sender unless the receiving bank has knowledge of the death or of an adjudication of incapacity by a court of competent jurisdiction and has reasonable opportunity to act before acceptance of the order.

(8) A funds transfer system rule is not effective to the extent it conflicts with subsection (3)(b).

§ 4A—210. **Liability and Duty of Receiving Bank Regarding Unaccepted Payment Order.**

If a receiving bank fails to accept a payment order that it is obliged by contract to accept, the bank may be held liable for breach of the contract as provided in the contract and in this Article, but does not otherwise have any duty to accept a payment order and, before acceptance, to take any action, or refrain from taking action, with respect to the order except as provided in this Article or by contract. Liability based on acceptance arises only when acceptance occurs as stated in Section 4A—207 and liability is limited to that provided in this Article. A receiving bank is not the agent of the sender or beneficiary of the payment order that it accepts, or of any other party to the funds transfer, and the bank owes no duty to any party to the funds transfer except as provided in this Article or by contract.

Part 3 Execution of Sender's Payment Order by Receiving Bank

§ 4A—301. Execution and Execution Date.

(1) A payment order received by a receiving bank is "executed" by the bank when it issues a payment order intended to carry out the payment order received by the bank. A payment order received by the beneficiary's bank can be accepted by the beneficiary's bank but it cannot be executed.

(2) "Execution date" of a payment order received by a receiving bank means the day on which the receiving bank may properly issue a payment order in execution of the sender's order. The execution date can be determined by instruction of the sender but cannot be earlier than the day the order is received and, unless otherwise determined, is the day the order is received. If the sender's instruction states a payment date, the execution date is the payment date or an earlier date on which execution is reasonably necessary to allow payment to the beneficiary on the payment date.

§ 4A—302. Manner of Execution of Payment Order.

(1) This subsection is subject to subsections (2) through (4). If a receiving bank accepts a payment order under subsection (1) of Section 4A—207, the bank has the following obligations in executing the order.

(a) The receiving bank is obliged to issue, on the execution date, a payment order complying with the sender's order and to follow the sender's instructions concerning (i) any intermediary bank or funds transfer system to be used in carrying out the funds transfer, or (ii) the means by which payment orders are to be transmitted in the funds transfer. If the originator's bank issues a payment order to an intermediary bank, the originator's bank is obliged to instruct the intermediary bank according to the instruction of the originator. Any intermediary bank in the funds transfer is similarly bound by an instruction given to it by the sender of the payment order that it accepts.

(b) If the sender's instruction states that the funds transfer is to be carried out telephonically or by wire transfer or otherwise indicates that the funds transfer is to be carried out by the most expeditious means, the receiving bank is obliged to transmit its payment order by the most expeditious available means, and to instruct any intermediary bank accordingly. If a sender's instruction states a payment date, the receiving bank is obliged to transmit its payment order at a time and by means reasonably necessary to allow payment to the beneficiary on the payment date or as soon thereafter as is feasible.

(2) Unless otherwise instructed, a receiving bank executing a payment order may (i) use any funds transfer system if use of that system is commercially reasonable, and (ii) issue a payment order to the beneficiary's bank or to an intermediary bank through which a payment order conforming to the sender's order can expeditiously be issued to the beneficiary's bank if the receiving bank exercises ordinary care in the selection of the intermediary bank. A receiving bank is not required to follow an instruction of the sender designating a funds transfer system to be used in carrying out the funds transfer if the receiving bank, in good faith, determines that it is not feasible to follow the instruction or that following the instruction would unduly delay completion of the funds transfer.

(3) Unless subsection (1)(b) applies or the receiving bank is otherwise instructed, the bank may execute a payment order by transmitting its payment order by first class mail or by any commercially reasonable means. If the receiving bank is instructed to execute the sender's order by transmitting its payment order by a particular means, the receiving bank may issue its payment order by the means stated or by any commercially reasonable means as expeditious as the means stated.

(4) Unless otherwise instructed, a receiving bank may obtain payment of its charges for services and expenses in connection with the execution of the sender's order by issuing a payment order in an amount equal to the amount of the sender's order less the amount of the charges.

§ 4A—303. Erroneous Execution of Payment Order.

(1) A receiving bank that (i) executes the payment order of the sender by issuing a payment order in an amount greater than the amount of the sender's order, or (ii) issues a payment order in execution of the sender's order and then issues a duplicate order, is entitled to payment under subsection (3) of Section 4A—402 only of the amount of the sender's order if that subsection is otherwise satisfied. The bank is entitled to recover from the beneficiary of the erroneous order the excess payment received to the extent allowed by the law governing mistake and restitution.

(2) A receiving bank that executes the payment order of the sender by issuing a payment order in an amount less than the amount of the sender's order is entitled to payment under subsection (3) of Section 4A—402 of the amount of the sender's order if (i) that subsection is otherwise satisfied and (ii) the bank corrects its mistake by issuing an additional payment order for the benefit of the beneficiary of the sender's order. If the error is not corrected, the issuer of the erroneous order is entitled to receive or retain payment from the sender of the order that it accepted only to the extent of the amount of the erroneous order.

(3) If a receiving bank executes the payment order of the sender by issuing a payment order to a beneficiary different from the beneficiary of the sender's order and the funds transfer is completed on the basis of that error, the sender of the payment order that was erroneously executed and all previous senders in the funds transfer are not obliged to pay the payment orders that they issued. The issuer of the erroneous order is entitled to recover from the beneficiary of the order the payment received to the extent allowed by the law governing mistake and restitution.

§ 4A—304. Duty of Sender to Report Erroneously Executed Payment Order.

If the sender of a payment order that is erroneously executed as stated in Section 4A—303 receives notification from the receiving bank that the order was executed or that the sender's account was debited with respect to the order, the sender has a duty to exercise ordinary care to determine, on the basis of information available to the sender, that the order was erroneously executed and to advise the bank of the relevant facts within a reasonable time not to exceed 90 days after the notification from the bank was received by the sender. If the sender fails to perform that duty, the bank is not obliged to pay interest on any amount that is refundable to the sender under subsection (4) of Section 4A—402 for the period before the bank learns of the execution error. The bank is not entitled to any recovery from the sender on account of a failure by the sender to perform the duty stated in this section.

§ 4A—305. Misdescription of Beneficiary.

(1) Subject to subsection (2), if, in a payment order received by the beneficiary's bank, the name, bank account number, or other identification of the beneficiary refers to a nonexistent or unidentifiable person or account, no person has rights as a beneficiary of the order and acceptance of the order cannot occur.

(2) This subsection applies if a payment order received by the beneficiary's bank identifies the beneficiary both by name and by an identifying or bank account number and the name and number identify different persons.

(a) Except as otherwise provided in subsection (3), the beneficiary's bank, unless it has otherwise agreed, may treat the person identified by number as the beneficiary of the order if the bank does not know that the name and number refer to different persons. If the beneficiary's bank pays the person identified by number, it has no duty to determine whether the name and number refer to the same person.

(b) If the beneficiary's bank pays the person identified by name or if it knows that the name and number identify different persons, no person has rights as beneficiary except the person paid by the beneficiary's bank if that person is the beneficiary intended by the originator of the funds transfer. If no person has rights as beneficiary, acceptance of the order cannot occur.

(3) This subsection applies to a funds transfer in which a payment order described in subsection (2)(a) is accepted and the beneficiary's bank pays the person identified by number. If the originator's payment order described the beneficiary inconsistently by name and number, the originator is obliged to pay the order unless (i) the originator proves that the person identified by number is not the beneficiary intended by the originator, and (ii) the originator's bank fails to prove that, before acceptance of the originator's order, it informed the originator that payment of payment orders issued by the originator might be made by the beneficiary's bank on the basis of an identifying or bank account number even if it identifies a person different from the named beneficiary. Proof by the originator's bank may be made by any admissible evidence, but in any event the bank satisfies the burden of proof if it proves that the required information was contained in a writing signed by the originator before the payment order was accepted.

(4) In a case governed by subsection (2)(a), if the beneficiary's bank rightfully pays the person identified by number and that person is not the beneficiary intended by the originator, there is a right to recover from that person the amount paid to the extent allowed by the law governing mistake and restitution. If the originator is obliged to pay its payment order as stated in subsection (3), the originator has the right to recover. If the originator is not obliged to pay its payment order, the originator's bank has the right to recover.

§ 4A—306. Liability for Late or Improper Execution or Failure to Execute Payment Order.

(1) If a funds transfer is completed but execution of a payment order by the receiving bank in breach of Section 4A—302 results in delay in payment to the beneficiary, the bank is obliged to pay interest to either the originator or the beneficiary of the funds transfer for the period of delay caused by the noncomplying execution. Except

as provided in subsection (3), additional damages are not recoverable.

(2) If execution of a payment order by a receiving bank in breach of Section 4A—302 results in (i) noncompletion of the funds transfer, (ii) failure to use an intermediary bank designated by the originator, or (iii) issuance of a payment order that does not comply with the terms of the payment order of the originator, the bank is obliged to compensate the originator for its expenses in the funds transfer and for incidental expenses and interest losses (to the extent not covered by subsection (1)) resulting from the improper execution. Except as provided in subsection (3), additional damages are not recoverable.

(3) In addition to the amounts payable under subsections (1) and (2), damages, including consequential damages, are recoverable to the extent provided in an express written agreement of the receiving bank.

(4) If a receiving bank fails to execute a payment order it was obliged to execute by express written contract, the sender is entitled to damages, including consequential damages, for breach of the contract to the extent stated in the contract. If the contract does not provide for damages, the receiving bank is obliged to compensate the sender only for its expenses in the transaction and for incidental expenses and interest losses resulting from the failure to execute.

(5) Reasonable attorney's fees are recoverable if demand for compensation under subsection (1) or (2) is made and refused before an action is brought on the claim. If a claim is made for breach of an agreement under subsection (4) and the agreement does not provide for damages, reasonable attorney's fees are recoverable if demand for compensation under subsection (4) is made and refused before an action is brought on the claim.

(6) The liability of a receiving bank under subsections (1) and (2) may not be reduced by agreement.

Part 4 Payment

§ 4A—401. Payment Date.

"Payment date" of a payment order means the day on which the amount of the order is payable to the beneficiary by the beneficiary's bank. The payment date can be determined by instruction of the sender but cannot be earlier than the day the order is received by the beneficiary's bank and, unless otherwise determined, is the day the order is received by the beneficiary's bank.

§ 4A—402. Obligation of Sender to Pay Receiving Bank.

(1) This section is subject to Section 4A—205.

(2) With respect to a payment order issued to the beneficiary's bank, acceptance of the order by the bank obliges the sender to pay the bank the amount of the order, but payment is not due until the payment date of the order.

(3) This subsection is subject to subsection (5) and to Section 4A—303. With respect to a payment order issued to a receiving bank other than the beneficiary's bank, acceptance of the order by the receiving bank obliges the sender to pay the bank the amount of the order, but this obligation is excused if the funds transfer is not completed by acceptance by the beneficiary's bank of a payment order instructing payment to the beneficiary of the sender's order. Payment by the sender is not due until the execution date of the sender's order.

(4) If the sender of a payment order pays the order and the sender is not obliged to pay all or part of the amount paid, the bank receiving payment is obliged to refund payment to the extent the sender is not obliged to pay the bank. Except as provided in Section 4A—204 and Section 4A—304, interest is payable on the refundable amount from the date of payment.

(5) This subsection applies if a funds transfer is not completed as stated in subsection (3) and an intermediary bank is obliged to refund payment as stated in subsection (4), but is unable to do so because not permitted by applicable law or because the bank suspends payments. Any sender in the funds transfer that executed a payment order in compliance with an instruction, as stated in subsection (1)(a) of Section 4A—302, to route the funds transfer through that intermediary bank is entitled to retain or enforce payment from the sender of the payment order that it accepted. The first sender in the funds transfer that issued an instruction requiring routing through that intermediary bank is subrogated to the right of the bank that paid the intermediary bank to refund as stated in subsection (4).

§ 4A—403. Payment by Sender to Receiving Bank.

(1) Payment of the sender's obligation under Section 4A—402 to pay the receiving bank occurs at the earliest of the following times:

(a) If the sender is a bank, payment occurs when the receiving bank receives final settlement of the obligation through a Federal Reserve Bank or through a funds transfer system.

(b) If the sender is a bank and (i) the sender credited an account of the receiving bank with the sender, or (ii) caused an account of the receiving bank in another bank to be credited, payment occurs when the credit is withdrawn or, if not withdrawn, at midnight of the day on which the credit is withdrawable and the receiving bank learns of that fact.

(c) If the receiving bank debits an account of the sender with the receiving bank, payment occurs when the debit is made to the extent the debit is covered by a withdrawable credit balance in the account.

(2) If the sender and receiving bank are members of a funds transfer system that nets obligations multilaterally among participants, the receiving bank receives final settlement when settlement is complete in accordance with the rules of the system. The obligation of the sender to pay the amount of a payment order transmitted through the funds transfer system may be satisfied, to the extent permitted by the rules of the system, by setting off and applying against the sender's obligation the right of the sender to receive payment from the receiving bank of the amount of any other payment order transmitted to the sender by the receiving bank through the funds transfer system. The aggregate balance of obligations owed by each sender to each receiving bank in the funds transfer system may be satisfied, to the extent permitted by the rules of the system, by setting off and applying against that balance the aggregate balance of obligations owed to the sender by other members of the system. The aggregate balance shall be determined after the right of setoff stated in the second sentence of this subsection has been exercised.

(3) If two banks transmit payment orders to each other under an agreement that settlement of the obligations of each bank to the other under Section 4A—402 will be made at the end of the day or other period, the total amount owed with respect to all orders transmitted by one bank shall be set off against the total amount owed with respect to all orders transmitted by the other bank. To the extent of the setoff, each bank has made payment to the other.

(4) In any case not covered by subsection (1), the time when payment of the sender's obligation under subsection (2) or subsection (3) of Section 4A—402 occurs is governed by applicable principles of law that determine when an obligation is satisfied.

§ 4A—404. Obligation of Beneficiary's Bank to Pay and Give Notice to Beneficiary.

(1) Subject to subsection (5) of Section 4A—209 and subsections (4) and (5) of Section 4A—405, if the beneficiary's bank accepts a payment order, the bank is obliged to pay the amount of the order to the beneficiary of the order. Payment is due on the payment date of the order, but if acceptance occurs on the payment date after the close of the funds transfer business day of the bank, payment is due on the next funds transfer business day. If the bank refuses to pay after demand by the beneficiary and receipt of notice of special circumstances that will give rise to consequential damages as a result of nonpayment, the beneficiary may recover damages resulting from the refusal to pay to the extent the bank had notice of such damages, unless the bank proves that it did not pay because of a reasonable doubt concerning the right of the beneficiary to payment.

(2) If a payment order instructs payment to an account of the beneficiary, the beneficiary's bank is obliged to give notice to the beneficiary of receipt of the order before midnight of the next funds transfer business day following the payment date. If the payment order does not instruct payment to an account of the beneficiary, the bank is required to give such notice to the beneficiary only if notice is required by the order. Notice may be given by first class mail or any commercially reasonable means. If the bank fails to give notice as required by this subsection, the bank is obliged to pay interest to the beneficiary on the amount of the payment order from the day notice should have been given until the day the beneficiary learned of receipt of the payment order by the bank. No other damages are recoverable. Reasonable attorney's fees are also recoverable if demand for interest is made and refused before an action is brought on the claim.

(3) The right of a beneficiary to receive payment and damages as stated in subsection (1) may not be varied by agreement or a funds transfer system rule. The right of a beneficiary to be given notice as stated in subsection (2) may be varied by agreement of the beneficiary or by a funds transfer system rule if the beneficiary is given notice of the rule before initiation of the funds transfer.

§ 4A—405. Payment by Beneficiary's Bank to Beneficiary.

(1) If the beneficiary's bank credits an account of the beneficiary of a payment order, payment of the bank's obligation under subsection (1) of Section 4A—405 occurs when and to the extent (i) the beneficiary is given notice of the right to withdraw the credit, (ii) the bank lawfully applies the credit to a debt of the beneficiary, or (iii) funds with respect to the order are otherwise made available to the beneficiary by the bank.

(2) If the beneficiary's bank does not credit an account of the beneficiary of a payment order, payment of the bank's obligation under subsection (1) of Section 4A—404 is governed by applicable principles of law that determine when an obligation is satisfied.

(3) Except as stated in subsections (4) and (5), if a beneficiary's bank pays the beneficiary of a payment order under a condition to payment or agreement of the beneficiary giving the bank the right to recover payment from the beneficiary if the bank does not receive payment of the order, the condition to payment or agreement is not enforceable.

(4) A funds transfer system rule may provide that payments made to beneficiaries of funds transfers made through the system are provisional until receipt of payment by the beneficiary's bank of the payment order it

accepted. A beneficiary's bank that makes a payment that is provisional under the rule is entitled to refund from the beneficiary if (i) the beneficiary's bank does not receive payment of the payment order that it accepted, (ii) both the beneficiary and the originator of the funds transfer were given notice of the provisional nature of the payment, and (iii) the beneficiary agreed to be bound by the rule. If the beneficiary is obliged to refund payment to the beneficiary's bank, acceptance of the payment order by the beneficiary's bank is nullified and no payment by the originator of the funds transfer to the beneficiary occurs under Section 4A—406.

(5) This subsection applies if a payment order to a beneficiary's bank is received over a funds transfer system that (i) nets obligations multilaterally among participants, and (ii) has in effect a loss-sharing agreement among participants for the purpose of providing funds necessary to complete settlement of the obligations of one or more participants that are unable to meet their settlement obligations. If the beneficiary's bank accepts the order and the system fails to complete settlement pursuant to its rules, the acceptance by the bank is nullified, the bank is entitled to recover payment from the beneficiary, and no payment by the originator of the funds transfer occurs under Section 4A—406.

§ 4A—406. **Payment by Originator to Beneficiary; Discharge of Underlying Obligation.**

(1) Subject to subsection (5) of Section 4A—209 and subsections (4) and (5) of Section 4A—405, the originator of a funds transfer pays the beneficiary of the originator's payment order (i) at the time a payment order for the benefit of the beneficiary is accepted by the beneficiary's bank in the funds transfer and (ii) in an amount equal to the amount of the order accepted by the beneficiary's bank but not more than the amount of the originator's order.

(2) If payment under subsection (1) is made to satisfy an obligation, the obligation is discharged to the same extent discharge would result from payment to the beneficiary of the same amount in money, unless (i) the payment under subsection (1) was made by a means prohibited by the contract of the beneficiary with respect to the obligation, (ii) the beneficiary notified the originator of the beneficiary's refusal of the payment within a reasonable time after receiving notice of receipt of the order by the beneficiary's bank, (iii) funds with respect to the order were not withdrawn by the beneficiary or applied to a debt of the beneficiary, and (iv) the beneficiary would suffer a loss that could reasonably have been avoided if payment had been made by a means complying with the contract. If payment by the originator does not result in discharge under this section, the originator is subrogated to the rights of the beneficiary to receive payment from the beneficiary's bank pursuant to subsection (1) of Section 4A—404.

(3) For the purpose of determining whether discharge of an obligation occurs under subsection (2), if the beneficiary's bank accepts a payment order in an amount equal to the amount of the originator's payment order less charges of one or more intermediary banks in the funds transfer, payment to the beneficiary is in the amount of the originator's order.

(4) Rights of the originator or of the beneficiary of a funds transfer under this section may be varied only by agreement of the originator and the beneficiary.

Part 5 Miscellaneous Provisions

§ 4A—501. **Variation by Agreement and Effect of Funds Transfer System Rule.**

(1) Unless the contrary is stated in this Article, rights and obligations under this Article of a party to a funds transfer may be varied by agreement of the affected party.

(2) "Funds transfer system rule" means a rule of (i) an association of banks governing transmission of payment orders by means of a funds transfer system of the association or rights and obligations with respect to those orders, or (ii) an association of banks to the extent the rule governs rights and obligations between banks that are parties to a funds transfer in which a Federal Reserve Bank, acting as an intermediary bank, sends a payment order to the beneficiary's bank. Unless the contrary is stated in this Article, a funds transfer system rule governing rights and obligations between participating banks utilizing the system may be effective even if the rule conflicts with this Article and indirectly affects another party to the funds transfer who does not consent to the rule. A funds transfer system rule may also govern rights and obligations of parties other than participating banks utilizing the system to the extent stated in subsection (3) of Section 4A—404, subsection (4) of Section 4A—405, and subsection (3) of Section 4A—507.

§ 4A—502. **Creditor Process Served on Receiving Bank; Set-off by Beneficiary's Bank.**

(1) As used in this section, "creditor process" means levy, attachment, garnishment, notice of lien, sequestration, or similar process issued by or on behalf of a creditor or other claimant with respect to an account.

(2) If a receiving bank accepts a payment order and debits the account of the sender, the resulting reduction in the account balance is effective notwithstanding service of creditor process with respect to the account, unless the creditor process is served at a time and in a manner affording the bank a reasonable opportunity to act on it before the bank accepts the payment order.

(3) This subsection applies if a beneficiary's bank has received a payment order for payment to the beneficiary's account in the bank.

> (a) The bank may credit the beneficiary's account and the amount credited may be set off against an obligation owed by the beneficiary to the bank or may be applied to satisfy creditor process served on the bank with respect to the account.
>
> (b) The bank may credit the beneficiary's account and may allow withdrawal of the amount credited unless creditor process with respect to the account is served at a time and in a manner affording the bank a reasonable opportunity to act to prevent withdrawal.
>
> (c) If creditor process with respect to the account has been served, the bank may not reject the payment order except for a reason unrelated to the service of process.

(4) The proper bank to receive creditor process with respect to a payment by the originator to the beneficiary pursuant to a funds transfer is the beneficiary's bank. Any other bank served with such creditor process is not obliged to act with respect to the process.

§ 4A—503. Injunction or Restraining Order With Respect to Funds Transfer.

For proper cause and in compliance with applicable law, a court may restrain (i) a person from issuing a payment order to initiate a funds transfer, (ii) an originator's bank from executing the payment order of the originator, or (iii) the beneficiary's bank from releasing funds to the beneficiary or the beneficiary from withdrawing the funds. A court may not otherwise restrain a person from issuing a payment order, paying or receiving payment of a payment order, or otherwise acting with respect to a funds transfer.

§ 4A—504. Order in Which Items and Payment Orders May Be Charged to an Account; Order of Withdrawals From an Account.

(1) If a receiving bank has received more than one payment order of the sender or one or more payment orders and other items that are payable from the sender's account, the bank may charge the sender's account with respect to the various orders and items in any sequence convenient to the bank.

(2) In determining whether a credit to an account has been withdrawn by the holder of the account or applied to a debt of the holder of the account, credits first made to the account are first withdrawn or applied.

§ 4A—505. Preclusion of Objection to Debit of Customer's Account.

If a receiving bank has received payment from its customer with respect to a payment order issued in the name of the customer as sender and accepted by the bank, and the customer received notification reasonably identifying the order, the customer is precluded from asserting that the bank is not entitled to retain the payment if the customer failed to notify the bank of the customer's objection to the payment within one year after the notification was received by the customer.

§ 4A—506. Rate of Interest.

(1) If, pursuant to this Article, a receiving bank is obliged to pay interest with respect to a payment order issued to the bank, the amount payable may be determined (i) by agreement of the sender and receiving bank, or (ii) if the payment order is transmitted through a funds transfer system, by a funds transfer system rule.

(2) If the amount of interest is not determined by an agreement or rule as stated in subsection (1), the amount is calculated by multiplying the amount on which interest is payable by the applicable Federal Funds rate and then multiplying the product by the number of days for which interest is payable. The applicable Federal Funds rate is the average of the Federal Funds rates published by the Federal Reserve Bank of New York for each of the days for which interest is payable divided by 360. The Federal Funds rate for any day on which a published rate is not available is the same as the published rate for the next preceding day for which there is a published rate. If a receiving bank that accepted a payment order is required to refund payment to the sender of the order because the funds transfer was not completed, the rate of interest payable on the refundable amount is reduced by a percentage equal to the reserve requirement on deposits of the receiving bank if the failure to complete the funds transfer was not due to any fault by the receiving bank.

§ 4A—507. Choice of Law.

(1) The following rules apply unless the affected parties otherwise agree or subsection (3) applies:

> (a) The rights and obligations between the sender of a payment order and the receiving bank are governed by the law of the jurisdiction in which the receiving bank is located.
>
> (b) The rights and obligations between the beneficiary's bank and the beneficiary are governed by the law of the jurisdiction in which the beneficiary's bank is located.
>
> (c) The issue of (i) when payment is made pursuant to a funds transfer by the originator to the beneficiary, and (ii) whether payment discharges an obligation owed to the beneficiary, is governed by the law of the jurisdiction in which the beneficiary's bank is located.

(2) If the parties described in each of the subparagraphs of subsection (1) have made an agreement selecting the law of a particular jurisdiction to govern rights and obligations between each other, the law of that jurisdiction governs, whether or not the payment order or the funds transfer bears a reasonable relation to that jurisdiction.

(3) A funds transfer system rule may select the law of a particular jurisdiction to govern (i) rights and obligations between participating banks with respect to payment orders transmitted or processed through the system, or (ii) the rights and obligations of some or all parties to a funds transfer any part of which is carried out by means of the system. A choice of law made pursuant to clause (i) is binding on participating banks. A choice of law made pursuant to clause (ii) is binding on the originator or other sender or a receiving bank having notice of the participation of the system in the funds transfer when the originator or other sender or receiving bank issued or accepted a payment order. The beneficiary of a funds transfer is bound by such choice of law if, at the time the funds transfer is initiated, the beneficiary has notice of the participation of the system in the funds transfer. The law of a jurisdiction selected pursuant to this subsection may govern whether or not that law bears a reasonable relation to the matter in issue.

(4) In the event of inconsistency between an agreement under subsection (2) and a choice of law rule under subsection (3), the agreement under subsection (2) prevails.

(5) If a funds transfer is made by use of more than one funds transfer system and there is inconsistency between choice of law rules of the systems, the matter in issue is governed by the law of the selected jurisdiction which has the most significant relationship to the matter in issue.

Article 5
LETTERS OF CREDIT

§ 5—101. Short Title.

This Article shall be known and may be cited as Uniform Commercial Code—Letters of Credit.

§ 5—102. Scope.

(1) This Article applies

(a) to a credit issued by a bank if the credit requires a documentary draft or a documentary demand for payment; and

(b) to a credit issued by a person other than a bank if the credit requires that the draft or demand for payment be accompanied by a document of title; and

(c) to a credit issued by a bank or other person if the credit is not within subparagraphs (a) or (b) but conspicuously states that it is a letter of credit or is conspicuously so entitled.

(2) Unless the engagement meets the requirements of subsection (1), this Article does not apply to engagements to make advances or to honor drafts or demands for payment, to authorities to pay or purchase, to guarantees or to general agreements.

(3) This Article deals with some but not all of the rules and concepts of letters of credit as such rules or concepts have developed prior to this act or may hereafter develop. The fact that this Article states a rule does not by itself require, imply or negate application of the same or a converse rule to a situation not provided for or to a person not specified by this Article.

§ 5—103. Definitions.

(1) In this Article unless the context otherwise requires

(a) "Credit" or "letter of credit" means an engagement by a bank or other person made at the request of a customer and of a kind within the scope of this Article (Section 5—102) that the issuer will honor drafts or other demands for payment upon compliance with the conditions specified in the credit. A credit may be either revocable or irrevocable. The engagement may be either an agreement to honor or a statement that the bank or other person is authorized to honor.

(b) A "documentary draft" or a "documentary demand for payment" is one honor of which is conditioned upon the presentation of a document or documents. "Document" means any paper including document of title, security, invoice, certificate, notice of default and the like.

(c) An "issuer" is a bank or other person issuing a credit.

(d) A "beneficiary" of a credit is a person who is entitled under its terms to draw or demand payment.

(e) An "advising bank" is a bank which gives notification of the issuance of a credit by another bank.

(f) A "confirming bank" is a bank which engages either that it will itself honor a credit already issued by another bank or that such a credit will be honored by the issuer or a third bank.

(g) A "customer" is a buyer or other person who causes an issuer to issue a credit. The term also includes a bank which procures issuance or confirmation on behalf of that bank's customer.

(2) Other definitions applying to this Article and the sections in which they appear are:

"Notation of Credit". Section 5—108.
"Presenter". Section 5—112(3).

(3) Definitions in other Articles applying to this Article and the sections in which they appear are:

"Accept" or "Acceptance". Section 3—410.
"Contract for sale". Section 2—106.
"Draft". Section 3—104.
"Holder in due course". Section 3—302.
"Midnight deadline". Section 4—104.
"Security". Section 8—102.

(4) In addition, Article 1 contains general definitions and principles of construction and interpretation applicable throughout this Article.

§ 5—104. **Formal Requirements; Signing.**

(1) Except as otherwise required in subsection (1)(c) of Section 5—102 on scope, no particular form of phrasing is required for a credit. A credit must be in writing and signed by the issuer and a confirmation must be in writing and signed by the confirming bank. A modification of the terms of a credit or confirmation must be signed by the issuer or confirming bank.

(2) A telegram may be a sufficient signed writing if it identifies its sender by an authorized authentication. The authentication may be in code and the authorized naming of the issuer in an advice of credit is a sufficient signing.

§ 5—105. **Consideration.**

No consideration is necessary to establish a credit or to enlarge or otherwise modify its terms.

§ 5—106. **Time and Effect of Establishment of Credit.**

(1) Unless otherwise agreed a credit is established

(a) as regards the customer as soon as a letter of credit is sent to him or the letter of credit or an authorized written advice of its issuance is sent to the beneficiary; and

(b) as regards the beneficiary when he receives a letter of credit or an authorized written advice of its issuance.

(2) Unless otherwise agreed once an irrevocable credit is established as regards the customer it can be modified or revoked only with the consent of the customer and once it is established as regards the beneficiary it can be modified or revoked only with his consent.

(3) Unless otherwise agreed after a revocable credit is established it may be modified or revoked by the issuer without notice to or consent from the customer or beneficiary.

(4) Notwithstanding any modification or revocation of a revocable credit any person authorized to honor or negotiate under the terms of the original credit is entitled to reimbursement for or honor of any draft or demand for payment duly honored or negotiated before receipt of notice of the modification or revocation and the issuer in turn is entitled to reimbursement from its customer.

§ 5—107. **Advice of Credit; Confirmation; Error in Statement of Terms.**

(1) Unless otherwise specified an advising bank by advising a credit issued by another bank does not assume any obligation to honor drafts drawn or demands for payment made under the credit but it does assume obligation for the accuracy of its own statement.

(2) A confirming bank by confirming a credit becomes directly obligated on the credit to the extent of its confirmation as though it were its issuer and acquires the rights of an issuer.

(3) Even though an advising bank incorrectly advises the terms of a credit it has been authorized to advise the credit is established as against the issuer to the extent of its original terms.

(4) Unless otherwise specified the customer bears as against the issuer all risks of transmission and reasonable translation or interpretation of any message relating to a credit.

§ 5—108. **"Notation Credit"; Exhaustion of Credit.**

(1) A credit which specifies that any person purchasing or paying drafts drawn or demands for payment made under it must note the amount of the draft or demand on the letter or advice of credit is a "notation credit".

(2) Under a notation credit

(a) a person paying the beneficiary or purchasing a draft or demand for payment from him acquires a right to honor only if the appropriate notation is made and by transferring or forwarding for honor the documents under the credit such a person warrants to the issuer that the notation has been made; and

(b) unless the credit or a signed statement that an appropriate notation has been made accompanies the draft or demand for payment the issuer may delay honor until evidence of notation has been procured which is satisfactory to it but its obligation and that of its customer continue for a reasonable time not exceeding thirty days to obtain such evidence.

(3) If the credit is not a notation credit

(a) the issuer may honor complying drafts or demands for payment presented to it in the order in which they are presented and is discharged pro tanto by honor of any such draft or demand;

(b) as between competing good faith purchasers of complying drafts or demands the person first purchasing his priority over a subsequent purchaser even though the later purchased draft or demand has been first honored.

§ 5—109. **Issuer's Obligation to Its Customer.**

(1) An issuer's obligation to its customer includes good faith and observance of any general banking usage but unless otherwise agreed does not include liability or responsibility

(a) for performance of the underlying contract for sale or other transaction between the customer and the beneficiary; or

(b) for any act or omission of any person other than itself or its own branch or for loss or destruction of a draft, demand or document in transit or in the possession of others; or

(c) based on knowledge or lack of knowledge of any usage of any particular trade.

(2) An issuer must examine documents with care so as to ascertain that on their face they appear to comply with the terms of the credit but unless otherwise agreed assumes no liability or responsibility for the genuineness, falsification or effect of any document which appears on such examination to be regular on its face.

(3) A non-bank issuer is not bound by any banking usage of which it has no knowledge.

§ 5—110. **Availability of Credit in Portions; Presenter's Reservation of Lien or Claim.**

(1) Unless otherwise specified a credit may be used in portions in the discretion of the beneficiary.

(2) Unless otherwise specified a person by presenting a documentary draft or demand for payment under a credit relinquishes upon its honor all claims to the documents and a person by transferring such draft or demand or causing such presentment authorizes such relinquishment. An explicit reservation of claim makes the draft or demand noncomplying.

§ 5—111. **Warranties on Transfer and Presentment.**

(1) Unless otherwise agreed the beneficiary by transferring or presenting a documentary draft or demand for payment warrants to all interested parties that the necessary conditions of the credit have been complied with. This is in addition to any warranties arising under Articles 3, 4, 7 and 8.

(2) Unless otherwise agreed a negotiating, advising, confirming, collecting or issuing bank presenting or transferring a draft or demand for payment under a credit warrants only the matters warranted by a collecting bank under Article 4 and any such bank transferring a document warrants only the matters warranted by an intermediary under Articles 7 and 8.

§ 5—112. **Time Allowed for Honor or Rejection; Withholding Honor or Rejection by Consent; "Presenter".**

(1) A bank to which a documentary draft or demand for payment is presented under a credit may without dishonor of the draft, demand or credit

(a) defer honor until the close of the third banking day following receipt of the documents; and

(b) further defer honor if the presenter has expressly or impliedly consented thereto.

Failure to honor within the time here specified constitutes dishonor of the draft or demand and of the credit [except as otherwise provided in subsection (4) of Section 5—114 on conditional payment].

Note: *The bracketed language in the last sentence of subsection (1) should be included only if the optional provisions of Section 5—114(4) and (5) are included.*

(2) Upon dishonor the bank may unless otherwise instructed fulfill its duty to return the draft or demand and the documents by holding them at the disposal of the presenter and sending him an advice to that effect.

(3) "Presenter" means any person presenting a draft or demand for payment for honor under a credit even though that person is a confirming bank or other correspondent which is acting under an issuer's authorization.

§ 5—113. **Indemnities.**

(1) A bank seeking to obtain (whether for itself or another) honor, negotiation or reimbursement under a credit may give an indemnity to induce such honor, negotiation or reimbursement.

(2) An indemnity agreement inducing honor, negotiation or reimbursement

(a) unless otherwise explicitly agreed applies to defects in the documents but not in the goods; and

(b) unless a longer time is explicitly agreed expires at the end of ten business days following receipt of the documents by the ultimate customer unless notice of objection is sent before such expiration date. The ultimate customer may send notice of objection to the person from whom he received the documents and any bank receiving such notice is under a duty to send notice to its transferor before its midnight deadline.

§ 5—114. **Issuer's Duty and Privilege to Honor; Right to Reimbursement.**

(1) An issuer must honor a draft or demand for payment which complies with the terms of the relevant credit

regardless of whether the goods or documents conform to the underlying contract for sale or other contract between the customer and the beneficiary. The issuer is not excused from honor of such a draft or demand by reason of an additional general term that all documents must be satisfactory to the issuer, but an issuer may require that specified documents must be satisfactory to it.

(2) Unless otherwise agreed when documents appear on their face to comply with the terms of a credit but a required document does not in fact conform to the warranties made on negotiation or transfer of a document of title (Section 7—507) or of a certificated security (Section 8—306) or is forged or fraudulent or there is fraud in the transaction:

(a) the issuer must honor the draft or demand for payment if honor is demanded by a negotiating bank or other holder of the draft or demand which has taken the draft or demand under the credit and under circumstances which would make it a holder in due course (Section 3—302) and in an appropriate case would make it a person to whom a document of title has been duly negotiated (Section 7—502) or a bona fide purchaser of a certificated security (Section 8—302); and

(b) in all other cases as against its customer, an issuer acting in good faith may honor the draft or demand for payment despite notification from the customer of fraud, forgery or other defect not apparent on the face of the documents but a court of appropriate jurisdiction may enjoin such honor.

(3) Unless otherwise agreed an issuer which has duly honored a draft or demand for payment is entitled to immediate reimbursement of any payment made under the credit and to be put in effectively available funds not later than the day before maturity of any acceptance made under the credit.

[(4) When a credit provides for payment by the issuer on receipt of notice that the required documents are in the possession of a correspondent or other agent of the issuer

(a) any payment made on receipt of such notice is conditional; and

(b) the issuer may reject documents which do not comply with the credit if it does so within three banking days following its receipt of the documents; and

(c) in the event of such rejection, the issuer is entitled by charge back or otherwise to return of the payment made.]

[(5) In the case covered by subsection (4) failure to reject documents within the time specified in sub-paragraph (b) constitutes acceptance of the documents and makes the payment final in favor of the beneficiary.]

Note: *Subsections (4) and (5) are bracketed as optional. If they are included the bracketed language in the last sentence of Section 5—112(1) should also be included.*

§ 5—115. **Remedy for Improper Dishonor or Anticipatory Repudiation.**

(1) When an issuer wrongfully dishonors a draft or demand for payment presented under a credit the person entitled to honor has with respect to any documents the rights of a person in the position of a seller (Section 2—707) and may recover from the issuer the face amount of the draft or demand together with incidental damages under Section 2—710 on seller's incidental damages and interest but less any amount realized by resale or other use or disposition of the subject matter of the transaction. In the event no resale or other utilization is made the documents, goods or other subject matter involved in the transaction must be turned over to the issuer on payment of judgment.

(2) When an issuer wrongfully cancels or otherwise repudiates a credit before presentment of a draft or demand for payment drawn under it the beneficiary has the rights of a seller after anticipatory repudiation by the buyer under Section 2—610 if he learns of the repudiation in time reasonably to avoid procurement of the required documents. Otherwise the beneficiary has an immediate right of action for wrongful dishonor.

§ 5—116. **Transfer and Assignment.**

(1) The right to draw under a credit can be transferred or assigned only when the credit is expressly designated as transferable or assignable.

(2) Even through the credit specifically states that it is nontransferable or nonassignable the beneficiary may before performance of the conditions of the credit assign his right to proceeds. Such an assignment is an assignment of an account under Article 9 on Secured Transactions and is governed by that Article except that

(a) the assignment is ineffective until the letter of credit or advice of credit is delivered to the assignee which delivery constitutes perfection of the security interest under Article 9; and

(b) the issuer may honor drafts or demands for payment drawn under the credit until it receives a notification of the assignment signed by the beneficiary which reasonably identifies the credit involved in the assignment and contains a request to pay the assignee; and

(c) after what reasonably appears to be such a notification has been received the issuer may without dishonor refuse to accept or pay even to a person otherwise entitled to honor until the letter of credit or advice of credit is exhibited to the issuer.

(3) Except where the beneficiary has effectively assigned his right to draw or his right to proceeds, nothing in this section limits his right to transfer or negotiate drafts or demands drawn under the credit.

§ 5—117. Insolvency of Bank Holding Funds for Documentary Credit.

(1) Where an issuer or an advising or confirming bank or a bank which has for a customer procured issuance of a credit by another bank becomes insolvent before final payment under the credit and the credit is one to which this Article is made applicable by paragraphs (a) or (b) of Section 5—102(1) on scope, the receipt or allocation of funds or collateral to secure or meet obligations under the credit shall have the following results:

(a) to the extent of any funds or collateral turned over after or before the insolvency as indemnity against or specifically for the purpose of payment of drafts or demands for payment drawn under the designated credit, the drafts or demands are entitled to payment in preference over depositors or other general creditors of the issuer or bank; and

(b) on expiration of the credit or surrender of the beneficiary's rights under it unused any person who has given such funds or collateral is similarly entitled to return thereof; and

(c) a charge to a general or current account with a bank if specifically consented to for the purpose of indemnity against or payment of drafts or demands for payment drawn under the designated credit falls under the same rules as if the funds had been drawn out in cash and then turned over with specific instructions.

(2) After honor or reimbursement under this section the customer or other person for whose account the insolvent bank has acted is entitled to receive the documents involved.

Article 6
BULK TRANSFERS

§ 6—101. Short Title.

This Article shall be known and may be cited as Uniform Commercial Code—Bulk Transfers.

§ 6—102. "Bulk Transfers"; Transfers of Equipment; Enterprises Subject to This Article; Bulk Transfers Subject to This Article.

(1) A "bulk transfer" is any transfer in bulk and not in the ordinary course of the transferor's business of a major part of the materials, supplies, merchandise or other inventory (Section 9—109) of an enterprise subject to this Article.

(2) A transfer of a substantial part of the equipment (Section 9—109) of such an enterprise is a bulk transfer if it is made in connection with a bulk transfer of inventory, but not otherwise.

(3) The enterprises subject to this Article are all those whose principal business is the sale of merchandise from stock, including those who manufacture what they sell.

(4) Except as limited by the following section all bulk transfers of goods located within this state are subject to this Article.

§ 6—103. Transfers Excepted From This Article.

The following transfers are not subject to this Article:

(1) Those made to give security for the performance of an obligation;

(2) General assignments for the benefit of all the creditors of the transferor, and subsequent transfers by the assignee thereunder;

(3) Transfers in settlement or realization of a lien or other security interests;

(4) Sales by executors, administrators, receivers, trustees in bankruptcy, or any public officer under judicial process;

(5) Sales made in the course of judicial or administrative proceedings for the dissolution or reorganization of a corporation and of which notice is sent to the creditors of the corporation pursuant to order of the court or administrative agency;

(6) Transfers to a person maintaining a known place of business in this State who becomes bound to pay the debts of the transferor in full and gives public notice of that fact, and who is solvent after becoming so bound;

(7) A transfer to a new business enterprise organized to take over and continue the business, if public notice of the transaction is given and the new enterprise assumes the debts of the transferor and he receives nothing from the transaction except an interest in the new enterprise junior to the claims of creditors;

(8) Transfers of property which is exempt from execution.

Public notice under subsection (6) or subsection (7) may be given by publishing once a week for two consecutive weeks in a newspaper of general circulation where the transferor had its principal place of business in this state an advertisement including the names and addresses of the transferor and transferee and the effective date of the transfer.

§ 6—104. Schedule of Property, List of Creditors.

(1) Except as provided with respect to auction sales (Section 6—108), a bulk transfer subject to this Article is ineffective against any creditor of the transferor unless:

(a) The transferee requires the transferor to furnish a list of his existing creditors prepared as stated in this section; and

(b) The parties prepare a schedule of the property transferred sufficient to identify it; and

(c) The transferee preserves the list and schedule for six months next following the transfer and permits inspection of either or both and copying therefrom at all reasonable hours by any creditor of the transferor, or files the list and schedule in (a public office to be here identified).

(2) The list of creditors must be signed and sworn to or affirmed by the transferor or his agent. It must contain the names and business addresses of all creditors of the transferor, with the amounts when known, and also the names of all persons who are known to the transferor to assert claims against him even though such claims are disputed. If the transferor is the obligor of an outstanding issue of bonds, debentures or the like as to which there is an indenture trustee, the list of creditors need include only the name and address of the indenture trustee and the aggregate outstanding principal amount of the issue.

(3) Responsibility for the completeness and accuracy of the list of creditors rests on the transferor, and the transfer is not rendered ineffective by errors or omissions therein unless the transferee is shown to have had knowledge.

§ 6—105. **Notice to Creditors.**

In addition to the requirements of the preceding section, any bulk transfer subject to this Article except one made by auction sale (Section 6—108) is ineffective against any creditor of the transferor unless at least ten days before he takes possession of the goods or pays for them, whichever happens first, the transferee gives notice of the transfer in the manner and to the persons hereafter provided (Section 6—107).

[§ 6—106. **Application of the Proceeds.**

In addition to the requirements of the two preceding sections:
(1) Upon every bulk transfer subject to this Article for which new consideration becomes payable except those made by sale at auction it is the duty of the transferee to assure that such consideration is applied so far as necessary to pay those debts of the transferor which are either shown on the list furnished by the transferor (Section 6—104) or filed in writing in the place stated in the notice (Section 6—107) within thirty days after the mailing of such notice. This duty of the transferee runs to all the holders of such debts, and may be enforced by any of them for the benefit of all.

(2) If any of said debts are in dispute the necessary sum may be withheld from distribution until the dispute is settled or adjudicated.

(3) If the consideration payable is not enough to pay all of the said debts in full distribution shall be made pro rata.]

Note: *This section is bracketed to indicate division of opinion as to whether or not it is a wise provision, and to suggest that this is a point on which State enactments may differ without serious damage to the principle of uniformity. In any State where this section is omitted, the following parts of sections, also bracketed in the text, should also be omitted, namely:*
Section 6—107(2)(e).
6—108(3)(c).
6—109(2).
In any State where this section is enacted, these other provisions should be also.

Optional Subsection (4)

[(4) The transferee may within ten days after he takes possession of the goods pay the consideration into the (specify court) in the county where the transferor had its principal place of business in this state and thereafter may discharge his duty under this section by giving notice by registered or certified mail to all the persons to whom the duty runs that the consideration has been paid into that court and that they should file their claims there. On motion of any interested party, the court may order the distribution of the consideration to the persons entitled to it.]

Note: *Optional subsection (4) is recommended for those states which do not have a general statute providing for payment of money into court.*

§ 6—107. **The Notice.**

(1) The notice to creditors (Section 6—105) shall state:

(a) that a bulk transfer is about to be made; and

(b) the names and business addresses of the transferor and transferee, and all other business names and addresses used by the transferor within three years last past so far as known to the transferee; and

(c) whether or not all the debts of the transferor are to be paid in full as they fall due as a result of the transaction, and if so, the address to which creditors should send their bills.

(2) If the debts of the transferor are not to be paid in full as they fall due or if the transferee is in doubt on that point then the notice shall state further:

(a) the location and general description of the property to be transferred and the estimated total of the transferor's debts;

(b) the address where the schedule of property and list of creditors (Section 6—104) may be inspected;

(c) whether the transfer is to pay existing debts and if so the amount of such debts and to whom owing;

(d) whether the transfer is for new consideration and if so the amount of such consideration and the time and place of payment; [and]

[(e) if for new consideration the time and place where creditors of the transferor are to file their claims.]

(3) The notice in any case shall be delivered personally or sent by registered or certified mail to all the persons shown on the list of creditors furnished by the transferor (Section 6—104) and to all other persons who are known to the transferee to hold or assert claims against the transferor.

§ 6—108. **Auction Sales; "Auctioneer".**

(1) A bulk transfer is subject to this Article even though it is by sale at auction, but only in the manner and with the results stated in this section.

(2) The transferor shall furnish a list of his creditors and assist in the preparation of a schedule of the property to be sold, both prepared as before stated (Section 6—104).

(3) The person or persons other than the transferor who direct, control or are responsible for the auction are collectively called the "auctioneer". The auctioneer shall:

(a) receive and retain the list of creditors and prepare and retain the schedule of property for the period stated in this Article (Section 6—104);

(b) give notice of the auction personally or by registered or certified mail at least ten days before it occurs to all persons shown on the list of creditors and to all other persons who are known to him to hold or assert claims against the transferor; [and]

[(c) assure that the net proceeds of the auction are applied as provided in this Article (Section 6—106).]

(4) Failure of the auctioneer to perform any of these duties does not affect the validity of the sale or the title of the purchasers, but if the auctioneer knows that the auction constitutes a bulk transfer such failure renders the auctioneer liable to the creditors of the transferor as a class for the sums owing to them from the transferor up to but not exceeding the net proceeds of the auction. If the auctioneer consists of several persons their liability is joint and several.

§ 6—109. **What Creditors Protected; [Credit for Payment to Particular Creditors].**

(1) The creditors of the transferor mentioned in this Article are those holding claims based on transactions or events occurring before the bulk transfer, but creditors who become such after notice to creditors is given (Sections 6—105 and 6—107) are not entitled to notice.

[(2) Against the aggregate obligation imposed by the provisions of this Article concerning the application of the proceeds (Section 6—106 and subsection (3)(c) of 6—108) the transferee or auctioneer is entitled to credit for sums paid to particular creditors of the transferor, not exceeding the sums believed in good faith at the time of the payment to be properly payable to such creditors.]

§ 6—110. **Subsequent Transfers.**

When the title of a transferee to property is subject to a defect by reason of his noncompliance with the requirements of this Article, then:

(1) a purchaser of any of such property from such transferee who pays no value or who takes with notice of such noncompliance takes subject to such defect, but

(2) a purchaser for value in good faith and without such notice takes free of such defect.

§ 6—111. **Limitation of Actions and Levies.**

No action under this Article shall be brought nor levy made more than six months after the date on which the transferee took possession of the goods unless the transfer has been concealed. If the transfer has been concealed, actions may be brought or levies made within six months after its discovery.

Note to Article 6: *Section 6—106 is bracketed to indicate division of opinion as to whether or not it is a wise provision, and to suggest that this is a point on which State enactments may differ without serious damage to the principle of uniformity.*

In any State where Section 6—106 is not enacted, the following parts of sections, also bracketed in the text, should also be omitted, namely:
Sec. 6—107(2)(e).
  6—108(3)(c).
  6—109(2).
In any State where Section 6—106 is enacted, these other provisions should be also.

Article 6
Alternative B*

§ 6—101. **Short Title.**

This Article shall be known and may be cited as Uniform Commercial Code—Bulk Sales.

§ 6—102. **Definitions and Index of Definitions.**

(1) In this Article, unless the context otherwise requires:

(a) "Assets" means the inventory that is the subject of a bulk sale and any tangible and intangible per-

---

* Approved in substance by the National Conference of Commissioners on Uniform State Laws and The American Law Institute. Subject to editorial revision. States have the choice of adopting this alternative to the existing Article 6 or repealing Article 6 entirely (Alternative A).

sonal property used or held for use primarily in, or arising from, the seller's business and sold in connection with that inventory, but the term does not include:

(i) fixtures (Section 9—313(1)(a)) other than readily removable factory and office machines;

(ii) the lessee's interest in a lease of real property; or

(iii) property to the extent it is generally exempt under nonbankruptcy law.

(b) "Auctioneer" means a person whom the seller engages to direct, conduct, control, or be responsible for a sale by auction.

(c) "Bulk sale" means:

(i) in the case of a sale by auction or a sale or series of sales conducted by a liquidator on the seller's behalf, a sale or series of sales not in the ordinary course of the seller's business of more than half of the seller's inventory, as measured by value on the date of the bulk-sale agreement, if on that date the auctioneer or liquidator has notice, or after reasonable inquiry would have had notice, that the seller will not continue to operate the same or a similar kind of business after the sale or series of sales; and

(ii) in all other cases, a sale not in the ordinary course of the seller's business of more than half the seller's inventory, as measured by value on the date of the bulk-sale agreement, if on that date the buyer has notice, or after reasonable inquiry would have had notice, that the seller will not continue to operate the same or a similar kind of business after the sale.

(d) "Claim" means a right to payment from the seller, whether or not the right is reduced to judgment, liquidated, fixed, matured, disputed, secured, legal, or equitable. The term includes costs of collection and attorney's fees only to the extent that the laws of this state permit the holder of the claim to recover them in an action against the obligor.

(e) "Claimant" means a person holding a claim incurred in the seller's business other than:

(i) an unsecured and unmatured claim for employment compensation and benefits, including commissions and vacation, severance, and sick-leave pay;

(ii) a claim for injury to an individual or to property, or for breach of warranty, unless:

(A) a right of action for the claim has accrued;

(B) the claim has been asserted against the seller; and

(C) the seller knows the identity of the person asserting the claim and the basis upon which the person has asserted it; and

(States to Select One Alternative)

Alternative A

[(iii) a claim for taxes owing to a governmental unit.]

Alternative B

[(iii) a claim for taxes owing to a governmental unit if:

(A) a statute governing the enforcement of the claim permits or requires notice of the bulk sale to be given to the governmental unit in a manner other than by compliance with the requirements of this Article; and

(B) notice is given in accordance with the statute.]

(f) "Creditor" means a claimant or other person holding a claim.

(g)(i) "Date of the bulk sale" means:

(A) if the sale is by auction or is conducted by a liquidator on the seller's behalf, the date on which more than ten percent of the net proceeds is paid to or for the benefit of the seller; and

(B) in all other cases, the later of the date on which:

(I) more than ten percent of the net contract price is paid to or for the benefit of the seller; or

(II) more than ten percent of the assets, as measured by value, are transferred to the buyer.

(ii) For the purposes of this subsection:

(A) Delivery of a negotiable instrument (Section 3—104(1)) to or for the benefit of the seller in exchange for assets constitutes payment of the contract price pro tanto;

(B) To the extent that the contract price is deposited in an escrow, the contract price is paid to or for the benefit of the seller when the seller acquires the unconditional right to receive the deposit or when the deposit is delivered to the seller or for the benefit of the seller, whichever is earlier; and

(C) An asset is transferred when a person holding an unsecured claim can no longer obtain through judicial proceedings rights to the asset that are superior to those of the buyer arising as a result of the bulk sale. A person holding an unsecured claim can obtain those superior rights to a tangible asset at least until the buyer has an unconditional right, under the bulk-sale agreement, to possess the asset, and a person holding an unsecured claim can obtain those superior rights to an intangible asset at least until the buyer has an unconditional right, under the bulk-sale agreement, to use the asset.

(h) "Date of the bulk-sale agreement" means:

(i) in the case of a sale by auction or conducted by a liquidator (subsection (d)(i)), the date on which the seller engages the auctioneer or liquidator; and

(ii) in all other cases, the date on which a bulk-sale agreement becomes enforceable between the buyer and the seller.

(i) "Debt" means liability on a claim.

(j) "Liquidator" means a person who is regularly engaged in the business of disposing of assets for businesses contemplating liquidation or dissolution.

(k) "Net contract price" means the new consideration the buyer is obligated to pay for the assets less

(i) the amount of any proceeds of the sale of an asset, to the extent the proceeds are applied in partial or total satisfaction of a debt secured by the asset; and

(ii) the amount of any debt to the extent it is secured by a security interest or lien that is enforceable against the asset before and after it has been sold to a buyer.

(l) "Net proceeds" means the new consideration received for assets sold at a sale by auction or a sale conducted by a liquidator on the seller's behalf less:

(i) commissions and reasonable expenses of the sale;

(ii) the amount of any proceeds of the sale of an asset, to the extent the proceeds are applied in partial or total satisfaction of a debt secured by the asset; and

(iii) the amount of any debt to the extent it is secured by a security interest or lien that is enforceable against the asset before and after it has been sold to a buyer.

(m) A sale is "in the ordinary course of the seller's business" if the sale comports with usual or customary practices in the kind of business in which the seller is engaged or with the seller's own usual or customary practices.

(n) "United States" includes its territories and possessions and the Commonwealth of Puerto Rico.

(o) "Value" means fair market value.

(p) "Verified" means signed and sworn to or affirmed.

(2) The following definitions in other Articles apply to this Article:

(a)	"Buyer."	Section 2—103(1)(a).
(b)	"Equipment."	Section 9—109(2).
(c)	"Good faith."	Section 1—201(19).
(d)	"Inventory."	Section 9—109(4).
(e)	"Sale."	Section 2—103(1).
(f)	"Seller."	Section 2—103(1)(d).

(3) In addition, Article 1 contains general definitions and principles of construction and interpretation applicable throughout this Article.

§ 6—103. **Applicability of This Article.**

(1) Except as otherwise provided in subsection (3), this Article applies to a bulk sale if:

(a) the seller's principal business is the sale of inventory from stock; and

(b) on the date of the bulk-sale agreement the seller is located in this state or, if the seller is located in a jurisdiction that is not a part of the United States, the seller's major executive office in the United States is in this state.

(2) A seller is deemed to be located at his [or her] place of business. If a seller has more than one place of business, the seller is deemed located at his [or her] chief executive office.

(3) This Article does not apply to:

(a) a transfer made to secure payment or performance of an obligation;

(b) a transfer of collateral to a secured party pursuant to Section 9—503;

(c) a sale of collateral pursuant to Section 9—504;

(d) retention of collateral pursuant to Section 9—505;

(e) a sale of an asset encumbered by a security interest or lien if (i) all the proceeds of the sale are applied in partial or total satisfaction of the debt secured by the security interest or lien or (ii) the security interest or lien is enforceable against the asset after it has been sold to the buyer and the net contract price is zero;

(f) a general assignment for the benefit of creditors or to a subsequent transfer by the assignee;

(g) a sale by an executor, administrator, receiver, trustee in bankruptcy, or any public officer under judicial process;

(h) a sale made in the course of judicial or administrative proceedings for the dissolution or reorganization of an organization;

(i) a sale to a buyer whose principal place of business is in the United States and who:

(i) not earlier than 21 days before the date of the bulk sale, (A) obtains from the seller a verified and dated list of claimants of which the seller has notice three days before the seller sends or delivers the list to the buyer or (B) conducts a reasonable inquiry to discover the claimants;

(ii) assumes in full the debts owed to claimants of which the buyer has knowledge on the date the buyer receives the list of claimants from the seller or on the date the buyer completes the reasonable inquiry, as the case may be;

(iii) is not insolvent after the assumption; and

(iv) gives written notice of the assumption not later than 30 days after the date of the bulk sale by sending or delivering a notice to the claimants identified in subparagraph (ii) or by filing a notice in the office of the [Secretary of State];

(j) a sale to a buyer whose principal place of business is in the United States and who:

(i) assumes in full the debts that were incurred in the seller's business before the date of the bulk sale;

(ii) is not insolvent after the assumption; and

(iii) gives written notice of the assumption not later than 30 days after the date of the bulk sale by sending or delivering a notice to each creditor whose debt is assumed or by filing a notice in the office of the [Secretary of State];

(k) a sale to a new organization that is organized to take over and continue the business of the seller and that has its principal place of business in the United States if:

(i) the buyer assumes in full the debts that were incurred in the seller's business before the date of the bulk sale;

(ii) the seller receives nothing from the sale except an interest in the new organization that is subordinate to the claims against the organization arising from the assumption; and

(iii) the buyer gives written notice of the assumption not later than 30 days after the date of the bulk sale by sending or delivering a notice to each creditor whose debt is assumed or by filing a notice in the office of the [Secretary of State];

(l) a sale of assets having:

(i) a value, net of liens and security interests, of less than $10,000; or

(ii) a value of more than $25,000,000 on the date of the bulk-sale agreement; or

(m) a sale required by, and made pursuant to, statute.

(4) The notice under subsection (3)(i)(iv) must state: (i) that a sale that may constitute a bulk sale has been or will be made; (ii) the date or prospective date of the bulk sale; (iii) the individual, partnership, or corporate names and the addresses of the seller and buyer; (iv) the address to which inquiries about the sale may be made, if different from the seller's address; and (v) that the buyer has assumed or will assume in full the debts owed to claimants of which the buyer has knowledge on the date the buyer receives the list of claimants from the seller or completes a reasonable inquiry to discover the claimants.

(5) The notice under subsections (3)(j)(iii) and (3)(k)(iii) must state: (i) that a sale that may constitute a bulk sale has been or will be made; (ii) the date or prospective date of the bulk sale; (iii) the individual, partnership, or corporate names and the addresses of the seller and buyer; (iv) the address to which inquiries about the sale may be made, if different from the seller's address; and (v) that the buyer has assumed or will assume the debts that were incurred in the seller's business before the date of the bulk sale.

(6) For purposes of subsection (3)(l), the value of assets is presumed to be equal to the price the buyer agrees to pay for the assets. However, in a sale by auction or a sale conducted by a liquidator on the seller's behalf, the value of assets is presumed to be the amount the auctioneer or liquidator reasonably estimates the assets will bring at auction or upon liquidation.

§ 6—104. Obligations of Buyer.

(1) In a bulk sale as defined in Section 6—102(1)(c)(ii) the buyer shall:

(a) obtain from the seller a list of all business names and addresses used by the seller within three years before the date the list is sent or delivered to the buyer;

(b) unless excused under subsection (2), obtain from the seller a verified and dated list of claimants of which the seller has notice three days before the seller sends or delivers the list to the buyer and including, to the extent known by the seller, the address of and the amount claimed by each claimant;

(c) obtain from the seller or prepare a schedule of distribution (Section 6—106(1));

(d) give notice of the bulk sale in accordance with Section 6—105;

(e) unless excused under Section 6—106(4), distribute the net contract price in accordance with the undertakings of the buyer in the schedule of distribution; and

(f) unless excused under subsection (2), make available the list of claimants (subsection (1)(b)) by:

(i) promptly sending or delivering a copy of the list without charge to any claimant whose written request is received by the buyer no later than six months after the date of the bulk sale;

(ii) permitting any claimant to inspect and copy the list at any reasonable hour upon request received by the buyer no later than six months after the date of the bulk sale; or

(iii) filing a copy of the list in the office of the [Secretary of State] no later than the time for giving a notice of the bulk sale (Section 6—105(5)). A list filed in accordance with this subparagraph must state the individual, partnership, or corporate name and a mailing address of the seller.

(2) A buyer who gives notice in accordance with Section 6—105(2) is excused from complying with the requirements of subsections (1)(b) and (1)(f).

§ 6—105. **Notice to Claimants.**

(1) Except as otherwise provided in subsection (2), to comply with Section 6—104(1)(d) the buyer shall send or deliver a written notice of the bulk sale to each claimant on the list of claimants (Section 6—104(1)(b)) and to any other claimant of which the buyer has knowledge at the time the notice of the bulk sale is sent or delivered.

(2) A buyer may comply with Section 6—104(1)(d) by filing a written notice of the bulk sale in the office of the [Secretary of State] if:

(a) on the date of the bulk-sale agreement the seller has 200 or more claimants, exclusive of claimants holding secured or matured claims for employment compensation and benefits, including commissions and vacation, severance, and sick-leave pay; or

(b) the buyer has received a verified statement from the seller stating that, as of the date of the bulk-sale agreement, the number of claimants, exclusive of claimants holding secured or matured claims for employment compensation and benefits, including commissions and vacation, severance, and sick-leave pay, is 200 or more.

(3) The written notice of the bulk sale must be accompanied by a copy of the schedule of distribution (Section 6—106(1)) and state at least:

(a) that the seller and buyer have entered into an agreement for a sale that may constitute a bulk sale under the laws of the State of _____;

(b) the date of the agreement;

(c) the date on or after which more than ten percent of the assets were or will be transferred;

(d) the date on or after which more than ten percent of the net contract price was or will be paid, if the date is not stated in the schedule of distribution;

(e) the name and a mailing address of the seller;

(f) any other business name and address listed by the seller pursuant to Section 6—104(1)(a);

(g) the name of the buyer and an address of the buyer from which information concerning the sale can be obtained;

(h) a statement indicating the type of assets or describing the assets item by item;

(i) the manner in which the buyer will make available the list of claimants (Section 6—104(1)(f)), if applicable; and

(j) if the sale is in total or partial satisfaction of an antecedent debt owed by the seller, the amount of the debt to be satisfied and the name of the person to whom it is owed.

(4) For purposes of subsections (3)(e) and (3)(g), the name of a person is the person's individual, partnership, or corporate name.

(5) The buyer shall give notice of the bulk sale not less than 45 days before the date of the bulk sale and, if the buyer gives notice in accordance with subsection (1), not more than 30 days after obtaining the list of claimants.

(6) A written notice substantially complying with the requirements of subsection (3) is effective even though it contains minor errors that are not seriously misleading.

(7) A form substantially as follows is sufficient to comply with subsection (3):

Notice of Sale

(1) _____, whose address is _____, is described in this notice as the "seller."

(2) _____, whose address is _____, is described in this notice as the "buyer."

(3) The seller has disclosed to the buyer that within the past three years the seller has used other business names, operated at other addresses, or both, as follows: _____.

(4) The seller and the buyer have entered into an agreement dated _____, for a sale that may constitute a bulk sale under the laws of the state of __

(5) The date on or after which more than ten percent of the assets that are the subject of the sale were or will be transferred is _____, and [if not stated in the schedule of distribution] the date on or after which more than ten percent of the net contract price was or will be paid is _____.

(6) The following assets are the subject of the sale: _____.

(7) [If applicable] The buyer will make available to claimants of the seller a list of the seller's claimants in the following manner: _____.

(8) [If applicable] The sale is to satisfy $_____ of an antecedent debt owed by the seller to _____.

(9) A copy of the schedule of distribution of the net contract price accompanies this notice.

[*End of Notice*]

§ 6—106. Schedule of Distribution.

(1) The seller and buyer shall agree on how the net contract price is to be distributed and set forth their agreement in a written schedule of distribution.

(2) The schedule of distribution may provide for distribution to any person at any time, including distribution of the entire net contract price to the seller.

(3) The buyer's undertakings in the schedule of distribution run only to the seller. However, a buyer who fails to distribute the net contract price in accordance with the buyer's undertakings in the schedule of distribution is liable to a creditor only as provided in Section 6—107(1).

(4) If the buyer undertakes in the schedule of distribution to distribute any part of the net contract price to a person other than the seller, and, after the buyer has given notice in accordance with Section 6—105, some or all of the anticipated net contract price is or becomes unavailable for distribution as a consequence of the buyer's or seller's having complied with an order of court, legal process, statute, or rule of law, the buyer is excused from any obligation arising under this Article or under any contract with the seller to distribute the net contract price in accordance with the buyer's undertakings in the schedule if the buyer:

(a) distributes the net contract price remaining available in accordance with any priorities for payment stated in the schedule of distribution and, to the extent that the price is insufficient to pay all the debts having a given priority, distributes the price pro rata among those debts shown in the schedule as having the same priority;

(b) distributes the net contract price remaining available in accordance with an order of court;

(c) commences a proceeding for interpleader in a court of competent jurisdiction and is discharged from the proceeding; or

(d) reaches a new agreement with the seller for the distribution of the net contract price remaining available, sets forth the new agreement in an amended schedule of distribution, gives notice of the amended schedule, and distributes the net contract price remaining available in accordance with the buyer's undertakings in the amended schedule.

(5) The notice under subsection (4)(d) must identify the buyer and the seller, state the filing number, if any, of the original notice, set forth the amended schedule, and be given in accordance with subsection (1) or (2) of Section 6—105, whichever is applicable, at least 14 days before the buyer distributes any part of the net contract price remaining available.

(6) If the seller undertakes in the schedule of distribution to distribute any part of the net contract price, and, after the buyer has given notice in accordance with Section 6—105, some or all of the anticipated net contract price is or becomes unavailable for distribution as a consequence of the buyer's or seller's having complied with an order of court, legal process, statute, or rule of law, the seller and any person in control of the seller are excused from any obligation arising under this Article or under any agreement with the buyer to distribute the net contract price in accordance with the seller's undertakings in the schedule if the seller:

(a) distributes the net contract price remaining available in accordance with any priorities for payment stated in the schedule of distribution and, to the extent that the price is insufficient to pay all the debts having a given priority, distributes the price pro rata among those debts shown in the schedule as having the same priority;

(b) distributes the net contract price remaining available in accordance with an order of court;

(c) commences a proceeding for interpleader in a court of competent jurisdiction and is discharged from the proceeding; or

(d) prepares a written amended schedule of distribution of the net contract price remaining available for distribution, gives notice of the amended schedule, and distributes the net contract price remaining available in accordance with the amended schedule.

(7) The notice under subsection (6)(d) must identify the buyer and the seller, state the filing number, if any, of the original notice, set forth the amended schedule, and be given in accordance with subsection (1) or (2) of Section 6—105, whichever is applicable, at least 14 days before the seller distributes any part of the net contract price remaining available.

§ 6—107. Liability for Noncompliance.

(1) Except as provided in subsection (3), and subject to the limitation in subsection (4):

(a) a buyer who fails to comply with the requirements of Section 6—104(1)(e) with respect to a creditor is liable to the creditor for damages in the amount of the claim, reduced by any amount that the creditor would not have realized if the buyer had complied; and

(b) a buyer who fails to comply with the requirements of any other subsection of Section 6—104 with respect to a claimant is liable to the claimant for damages in the amount of the claim, reduced by any amount that the claimant would not have realized if the buyer had complied.

(2) In an action under subsection (1), the creditor has the burden of establishing the validity and amount of the claim, and the buyer has the burden of establishing the amount that the creditor would not have realized if the buyer had complied.

(3) A buyer who:

(a) made a good faith effort to comply with the requirements of Section 6—104(1) or to exclude the sale from the application of this Article under Section 6—103(3); or

(b) on the date of the bulk-sale agreement held a good faith belief that this Article does not apply to the particular sale

is not liable to creditors for failure to comply with the requirements of Section 6—104. The buyer has the burden of establishing the good faith effort or belief.

(4) In a single bulk sale the cumulative liability of the buyer for failure to comply with the requirements of Section 6—104(1) may not exceed an amount equal to:

(a) if the assets consist only of inventory and equipment, twice the net contract price, less the amount of any part of the net contract price paid to or applied for the benefit of the seller or a creditor; or

(b) if the assets include property other than inventory and equipment, twice the net value of the inventory and equipment less the amount of the portion of any part of the net contract price paid to or applied for the benefit of the seller or a creditor which is allocable to the inventory and equipment.

(5) For the purposes of subsection (4)(b), the "net value" of an asset is the value of the asset less (i) the amount of any proceeds of the sale of an asset, to the extent the proceeds are applied in partial or total satisfaction of a debt secured by the asset and (ii) the amount of any debt to the extent it is secured by a security interest or lien that is enforceable against the asset before and after it has been sold to a buyer. The portion of a part of the net contract price paid to or applied for the benefit of the seller or a creditor that is "allocable to the inventory and equipment" is the portion that bears the same ratio to that part of the net contract price as the net value of the inventory and equipment bears to the net value of all the assets.

(6) A payment made by the buyer to a person to whom the buyer is, or believes he [or she] is, liable under subsection (1) reduces pro tanto the buyer's cumulative liability under subsection (4).

(7) No action may be brought under subsection (1)(b) by or on behalf of a claimant whose claim is unliquidated or contingent.

(8) A buyer's failure to comply with the requirements of Section 6—104(1) does not (i) impair the buyer's rights in or title to the assets, (ii) render the sale ineffective, void, or voidable, (iii) entitle a creditor to more than a single satisfaction of his [or her] claim, or (iv) create liability other than as provided in this Article.

(9) Payment of the buyer's liability under subsection (1) discharges pro tanto the seller's debt to the creditor.

(10) Unless otherwise agreed, a buyer has an immediate right of reimbursement from the seller for any amount paid to a creditor in partial or total satisfaction of the buyer's liability under subsection (1).

(11) If the seller is an organization, a person who is in direct or indirect control of the seller, and who knowingly, intentionally, and without legal justification fails, or causes the seller to fail, to distribute the net contract price in accordance with the schedule of distribution is liable to any creditor to whom the seller undertook to make payment under the schedule for damages caused by the failure.

§ 6—108. Bulk Sales by Auction; Bulk Sales Conducted by Liquidator.

(1) Sections 6—104, 6—105, 6—106, and 6—107 apply to a bulk sale by auction and a bulk sale conducted by a liquidator on the seller's behalf with the following modifications:

(a) "buyer" refers to auctioneer or liquidator, as the case may be;

(b) "net contract price" refers to net proceeds of the auction or net proceeds of the sale, as the case may be;

(c) the written notice required under Section 6—105(3) must be accompanied by a copy of the schedule of distribution (Section 6—106(1)) and state at least:

(i) that the seller and the auctioneer or liquidator have entered into an agreement for auction or liquidation services that may constitute an agreement to make a bulk sale under the laws of the State of ———;

(ii) the date of the agreement;

(iii) the date on or after which the auction began or will begin or the date on or after which the liquidator began or will begin to sell assets on the seller's behalf;

(iv) the date on or after which more than ten percent of the net proceeds of the sale were or will be paid, if the date is not stated in the schedule of distribution;

(v) the name and a mailing address of the seller;

(vi) any other business name and address listed by the seller pursuant to Section 6—104(1)(a);

(vii) the name of the auctioneer or liquidator and an address of the auctioneer or liquidator from which information concerning the sale can be obtained;

(viii) a statement indicating the type of assets or describing the assets item by item;

(ix) the manner in which the auctioneer or liquidator will make available the list of claimants (Section 6—104(1)(f)), if applicable; and

(x) if the sale is in total or partial satisfaction of an antecedent debt owed by the seller, the amount of the debt to be satisfied and the name of the person to whom it is owed; and

(d) in a single bulk sale the cumulative liability of the auctioneer or liquidator for failure to comply with the requirements of this section may not exceed the amount of the net proceeds of the sale allocable to inventory and equipment sold less the amount of the portion of any part of the net proceeds paid to or applied for the benefit of a creditor which is allocable to the inventory and equipment.

(2) A payment made by the auctioneer or liquidator to a person to whom the auctioneer or liquidator is, or believes he [or she] is, liable under this section reduces pro tanto the auctioneer's or liquidator's cumulative liability under subsection (1)(d).

(3) A form substantially as follows is sufficient to comply with subsection (1)(c):

Notice of Sale

(1) ———, whose address is ———, is described in this notice as the "seller."

(2) ———, whose address is ———, is described in this notice as the "auctioneer" or "liquidator."

(3) The seller has disclosed to the auctioneer or liquidator that within the past three years the seller has used other business names, operated at other addresses, or both, as follows: ———.

(4) The seller and the auctioneer or liquidator have entered into an agreement dated ——— for auction or liquidation services that may constitute an agreement to make a bulk sale under the laws of the State of ———.

(5) The date on or after which the auction began or will begin or the date on or after which the liquidator began or will begin to sell assets on the seller's behalf is ———, and [if not stated in the schedule of distribution] the date on or after which more than ten percent of the net proceeds of the sale were or will be paid is ———.

(6) The following assets are the subject of the sale: _____.

(7) [If applicable] The auctioneer or liquidator will make available to claimants of the seller a list of the seller's claimants in the following manner: ———.

(8) [If applicable] The sale is to satisfy $——— of an antecedent debt owed by the seller to ———.

(9) A copy of the schedule of distribution of the net proceeds accompanies this notice.

[*End of Notice*]

(4) A person who buys at a bulk sale by auction or conducted by a liquidator need not comply with the requirements of Section 6—104(1) and is not liable for the failure of an auctioneer or liquidator to comply with the requirements of this section.

§ 6—109. What Constitutes Filing; Duties of Filing Officer; Information from Filing Officer.

(1) Presentation of a notice or list of claimants for filing and tender of the filing fee or acceptance of the notice or list by the filing officer constitutes filing under this Article.

(2) The filing officer shall:

(a) mark each notice or list with a file number and with the date and hour of filing;

(b) hold the notice or list or a copy for public inspection;

(c) index the notice or list according to each name given for the seller and for the buyer; and

(d) note in the index the file number and the addresses of the seller and buyer given in the notice or list.

(3) If the person filing a notice or list furnishes the filing officer with a copy, the filing officer upon request shall

note upon the copy the file number and date and hour of the filing of the original and send or deliver the copy to the person.

(4) The fee for filing and indexing and for stamping a copy furnished by the person filing to show the date and place of filing is $_____ for the first page and $_____ for each additional page. The fee for indexing beyond the first two is $_____.

(5) Upon request of any person, the filing officer shall issue a certificate showing whether any notice or list with respect to a particular seller or buyer is on file on the date and hour stated in the certificate. If a notice or list is on file, the certificate must give the date and hour of filing of each notice or list and the name and address of each seller, buyer, auctioneer, or liquidator. The fee for the certificate is $_____ if the request for the certificate is in the standard form prescribed by the [Secretary of State] and otherwise is $_____. Upon request of any person, the filing officer shall furnish a copy of any filed notice or list for a fee of $_____.

(6) The filing officer shall keep each notice or list for two years after it is filed.

§ 6—110. Limitation of Actions.

(1) Except as provided in subsection (2), an action under this Article against a buyer, auctioneer, or liquidator must be commenced within one year after the date of the bulk sale.

(2) If the buyer, auctioneer, or liquidator conceals the fact that the sale has occurred, the limitation is tolled and an action under this Article may be commenced within the earlier of (i) one year after the person bringing the action discovers that the sale has occurred or (ii) one year after the person bringing the action should have discovered that the sale has occurred, but no later than two years after the date of the bulk sale. Complete noncompliance with the requirements of this Article does not of itself constitute concealment.

(3) An action under Section 6—107(11) must be commenced within one year after the alleged violation occurs.

Article 7
Warehouse Receipts, Bills of Lading and Other Documents of Title

Part 1 General

§ 7—101. Short Title.

This Article shall be known and may be cited as Uniform Commercial Code—Documents of Title.

§ 7—102. Definitions and Index of Definitions.

(1) In this Article, unless the context otherwise requires:

(a) "Bailee" means the person who by a warehouse receipt, bill of lading or other document of title acknowledges possession of goods and contracts to deliver them.

(b) "Consignee" means the person named in a bill to whom or to whose order the bill promises delivery.

(c) "Consignor" means the person named in a bill as the person from whom the goods have been received for shipment.

(d) "Delivery order" means a written order to deliver goods directed to a warehouseman, carrier or other person who in the ordinary course of business issues warehouse receipts or bills of lading.

(e) "Document" means document of title as defined in the general definitions in Article 1 (Section 1—201).

(f) "Goods" means all things which are treated as movable for the purposes of a contract of storage or transportation.

(g) "Issuer" means a bailee who issues a document except that in relation to an unaccepted delivery order it means the person who orders the possessor of goods to deliver. Issuer includes any person for whom an agent or employee purports to act in issuing a document if the agent or employee has real or apparent authority to issue documents, notwithstanding that the issuer received no goods or that the goods were misdescribed or that in any other respect the agent or employee violated his instructions.

(h) "Warehouseman" is a person engaged in the business of storing goods for hire.

(2) Other definitions applying to this Article or to specified Parts thereof, and the sections in which they appear are:
"Duly negotiate". Section 7—501.
"Person entitled under the document". Section 7—403(4).

(3) Definitions in other Articles applying to this Article and the sections in which they appear are:
"Contract for sale". Section 2—106.
"Overseas". Section 2—323.
"Receipt" of goods. Section 2—103.

(4) In addition Article 1 contains general definitions and principles of construction and interpretation applicable throughout this Article.

§ 7—103. Relation of Article to Treaty, Statute, Tariff, Classification or Regulation.

To the extent that any treaty or statute of the United States, regulatory statute of this State or tariff, classification or regulation filed or issued pursuant thereto is

§ 7—104. Negotiable and Nonnegotiable Warehouse Receipt, Bill of Lading or Other Document of Title.

(1) A warehouse receipt, bill of lading or other document of title is negotiable

(a) if by its terms the goods are to be delivered to bearer or to the order of a named person; or

(b) where recognized in overseas trade, if it runs to a named person or assigns.

(2) Any other document is nonnegotiable. A bill of lading in which it is stated that the goods are consigned to a named person is not made negotiable by a provision that the goods are to be delivered only against a written order signed by the same or another named person.

§ 7—105. Construction Against Negative Implication.

The omission from either Part 2 or Part 3 of this Article of a provision corresponding to a provision made in the other Part does not imply that a corresponding rule of law is not applicable.

Part 2 Warehouse Receipts: Special Provisions

§ 7—201. Who May Issue a Warehouse Receipt; Storage Under Government Bond.

(1) A warehouse receipt may be issued by any warehouseman.

(2) Where goods including distilled spirits and agricultural commodities are stored under a statute requiring a bond against withdrawal or a license for the issuance of receipts in the nature of warehouse receipts, a receipt issued for the goods has like effect as a warehouse receipt even though issued by a person who is the owner of the goods and is not a warehouseman.

§ 7—202. Form of Warehouse Receipt; Essential Terms; Optional Terms.

(1) A warehouse receipt need not be in any particular form.

(2) Unless a warehouse receipt embodies within its written or printed terms each of the following, the warehouseman is liable for damages caused by the omission to a person injured thereby:

(a) the location of the warehouse where the goods are stored;

(b) the date of issue of the receipt;

(c) the consecutive number of the receipt;

(d) a statement whether the goods received will be delivered to the bearer, to a specified person, or to a specified person or his order;

(e) the rate of storage and handling charges, except that where goods are stored under a field warehousing arrangement a statement of that fact is sufficient on a nonnegotiable receipt;

(f) a description of the goods or of the packages containing them;

(g) the signature of the warehouseman, which may be made by his authorized agent;

(h) if the receipt is issued for goods of which the warehouseman is owner, either solely or jointly or in common with others, the fact of such ownership; and

(i) a statement of the amount of advances made and of liabilities incurred for which the warehouseman claims a lien or security interest (Section 7—209). If the precise amount of such advances made or of such liabilities incurred is, at the time of the issue of the receipt, unknown to the warehouseman or to his agent who issues it, a statement of the fact that advances have been made or liabilities incurred and the purpose thereof is sufficient.

(3) A warehouseman may insert in his receipt any other terms which are not contrary to the provisions of this Act and do not impair his obligation of delivery (Section 7—403) or his duty of care (Section 7—204). Any contrary provisions shall be ineffective.

§ 7—203. Liability for Nonreceipt or Misdescription.

A party to or purchaser for value in good faith of a document of title other than a bill of lading relying in either case upon the description therein of the goods may recover from the issuer damages caused by the nonreceipt or misdescription of the goods, except to the extent that the document conspicuously indicates that the issuer does not know whether any part or all of the goods in fact were received or conform to the description, as where the description is in terms of marks or labels or kind, quantity or condition, or the receipt or description is qualified by "contents, condition and quality unknown", "said to contain" or the like, if such indication be true, or the party or purchaser otherwise has notice.

§ 7—204. Duty of Care; Contractual Limitation of Warehouseman's Liability.

(1) A warehouseman is liable for damages for loss of or injury to the goods caused by his failure to exercise such care in regard to them as a reasonably careful man would exercise under like circumstances but unless otherwise agreed he is not liable for damages which could not have been avoided by the exercise of such care.

(2) Damages may be limited by a term in the warehouse receipt or storage agreement limiting the amount of li-

ability in case of loss or damage, and setting forth a specific liability per article or item, or value per unit of weight, beyond which the warehouseman shall not be liable; provided, however, that such liability may on written request of the bailor at the time of signing such storage agreement or within a reasonable time after receipt of the warehouse receipt be increased on part or all of the goods thereunder, in which event increased rates may be charged based on such increased valuation, but that no such increase shall be permitted contrary to a lawful limitation of liability contained in the warehouseman's tariff, if any. No such limitation is effective with respect to the warehouseman's liability for conversion to his own use.

(3) Reasonable provisions as to the time and manner of presenting claims and instituting actions based on the bailment may be included in the warehouse receipt or tariff.

(4) This section does not impair or repeal . . .

Note: *Insert in subsection (4) a reference to any statute which imposes a higher responsibility upon the warehouseman or invalidates contractual limitations which would be permissible under this Article.*

§ 7—205. **Title Under Warehouse Receipt Defeated in Certain Cases.**

A buyer in the ordinary course of business of fungible goods sold and delivered by a warehouseman who is also in the business of buying and selling such goods takes free of any claim under a warehouse receipt even though it has been duly negotiated.

§ 7—206. **Termination of Storage at Warehouseman's Option.**

(1) A warehouseman may on notifying the person on whose account the goods are held and any other person known to claim an interest in the goods require payment of any charges and removal of the goods from the warehouse at the termination of the period of storage fixed by the document, or, if no period is fixed, within a stated period not less than thirty days after the notification. If the goods are not removed before the date specified in the notification, the warehouseman may sell them in accordance with the provisions of the section on enforcement of a warehouseman's lien (Section 7—210).

(2) If a warehouseman in good faith believes that the goods are about to deteriorate or decline in value to less than the amount of his lien within the time prescribed in subsection (1) for notification, advertisement and sale, the warehouseman may specify in the notification any reasonable shorter time for removal of the goods and in case the goods are not removed, may sell them at public sale held not less than one week after a single advertisement or posting.

(3) If as a result of a quality or condition of the goods of which the warehouseman had no notice at the time of deposit the goods are a hazard to other property or to the warehouse or to persons, the warehouseman may sell the goods at public or private sale without advertisement on reasonable notification to all persons known to claim an interest in the goods. If the warehouseman after a reasonable effort is unable to sell the goods he may dispose of them in any lawful manner and shall incur no liability by reason of such disposition.

(4) The warehouseman must deliver the goods to any person entitled to them under this Article upon due demand made at any time prior to sale or other disposition under this section.

(5) The warehouseman may satisfy his lien from the proceeds of any sale or disposition under this section but must hold the balance for delivery on the demand of any person to whom he would have been bound to deliver the goods.

§ 7—207. **Goods Must Be Kept Separate; Fungible Goods.**

(1) Unless the warehouse receipt otherwise provides, a warehouseman must keep separate the goods covered by each receipt so as to permit at all times identification and delivery of those goods except that different lots of fungible goods may be commingled.

(2) Fungible goods so commingled are owned in common by the persons entitled thereto and the warehouseman is severally liable to each owner for that owner's share. Where because of overissue a mass of fungible goods is insufficient to meet all the receipts which the warehouseman has issued against it, the persons entitled include all holders to whom overissued receipts have been duly negotiated.

§ 7—208. **Altered Warehouse Receipts.**

Where a blank in a negotiable warehouse receipt has been filled in without authority, a purchaser for value and without notice of the want of authority may treat the insertion as authorized. Any other unauthorized alteration leaves any receipt enforceable against the issuer according to its original tenor.

§ 7—209. **Lien of Warehouseman.**

(1) A warehouseman has a lien against the bailor on the goods covered by a warehouse receipt or on the proceeds thereof in his possession for charges for storage or transportation (including demurrage and terminal charges), insurance, labor, or charges present or future in relation to the goods, and for expenses necessary for preservation of the goods or reasonably incurred in their sale pursuant to law. If the person on whose account the goods are held is liable for like charges or expenses

in relation to other goods whenever deposited and it is stated in the receipt that a lien is claimed for charges and expenses in relation to other goods, the warehouseman also has a lien against him for such charges and expenses whether or not the other goods have been delivered by the warehouseman. But against a person to whom a negotiable warehouse receipt is duly negotiated a warehouseman's lien is limited to charges in an amount or at a rate specified on the receipt or if no charges are so specified then to a reasonable charge for storage of the goods covered by the receipt subsequent to the date of the receipt.

(2) The warehouseman may also reserve a security interest against the bailor for a maximum amount specified on the receipt for charges other than those specified in subsection (1), such as for money advanced and interest. Such a security interest is governed by the Article on Secured Transactions (Article 9).

(3) (a) A warehouseman's lien for charges and expenses under subsection (1) or a security interest under subsection (2) is also effective against any person who so entrusted the bailor with possession of the goods that a pledge of them by him to a good faith purchaser for value would have been valid but is not effective against a person as to whom the document confers no right in the goods covered by it under Section 7—503.

(b) A warehouseman's lien on household goods for charges and expenses in relation to the goods under subsection (1) is also effective against all persons if the depositor was the legal possessor of the goods at the time of deposit. "Household goods" means furniture, furnishings and personal effects used by the depositor in a dwelling.

(4) A warehouseman loses his lien on any goods which he voluntarily delivers or which he unjustifiably refuses to deliver.

§ 7—210. **Enforcement of Warehouseman's Lien.**

(1) Except as provided in subsection (2), a warehouseman's lien may be enforced by public or private sale of the goods in bloc or in parcels, at any time or place and on any terms which are commercially reasonable, after notifying all persons known to claim an interest in the goods. Such notification must include a statement of the amount due, the nature of the proposed sale and the time and place of any public sale. The fact that a better price could have been obtained by a sale at a different time or in a different method from that selected by the warehouseman is not of itself sufficient to establish that the sale was not made in a commercially reasonable manner. If the warehouseman either sells the goods in the usual manner in any recognized market therefor, or if he sells at the price current in such market at the time of his sale, or if he has otherwise sold in conformity with commercially reasonable practices among dealers in the type of goods sold, he has sold in a commercially reasonable manner. A sale of more goods than apparently necessary to be offered to ensure satisfaction of the obligation is not commercially reasonable except in cases covered by the preceding sentence.

(2) A warehouseman's lien on goods other than goods stored by a merchant in the course of his business may be enforced only as follows:

(a) All persons known to claim an interest in the goods must be notified.

(b) The notification must be delivered in person or sent by registered or certified letter to the last known address of any person to be notified.

(c) The notification must include an itemized statement of the claim, a description of the goods subject to the lien, a demand for payment within a specified time not less than ten days after receipt of the notification, and a conspicuous statement that unless the claim is paid within the time the goods will be advertised for sale and sold by auction at a specified time and place.

(d) The sale must conform to the terms of the notification.

(e) The sale must be held at the nearest suitable place to that where the goods are held or stored.

(f) After the expiration of the time given in the notification, an advertisement of the sale must be published once a week for two weeks consecutively in a newspaper of general circulation where the sale is to be held. The advertisement must include a description of the goods, the name of the person on whose account they are being held, and the time and place of the sale. The sale must take place at least fifteen days after the first publication. If there is no newspaper of general circulation where the sale is to be held, the advertisement must be posted at least ten days before the sale in not less than six conspicuous places in the neighborhood of the proposed sale.

(3) Before any sale pursuant to this section any person claiming a right in the goods may pay the amount necessary to satisfy the lien and the reasonable expenses incurred under this section. In that event the goods must not be sold, but must be retained by the warehouseman subject to the terms of the receipt and this Article.

(4) The warehouseman may buy at any public sale pursuant to this section.

(5) A purchaser in good faith of goods sold to enforce a warehouseman's lien takes the goods free of any rights of persons against whom the lien was valid, despite non-

compliance by the warehouseman with the requirements of this section.

(6) The warehouseman may satisfy his lien from the proceeds of any sale pursuant to this section but must hold the balance, if any, for delivery on demand to any person to whom he would have been bound to deliver the goods.

(7) The rights provided by this section shall be in addition to all other rights allowed by law to a creditor against his debtor.

(8) Where a lien is on goods stored by a merchant in the course of his business the lien may be enforced in accordance with either subsection (1) or (2).

(9) The warehouseman is liable for damages caused by failure to comply with the requirements for sale under this section and in case of willful violation is liable for conversion.

Part 3 Bills of Lading: Special Provisions

§ 7—301. Liability for Nonreceipt or Misdescription; "Said to Contain"; "Shipper's Load and Count"; Improper Handling.

(1) A consignee of a nonnegotiable bill who has given value in good faith or a holder to whom a negotiable bill has been duly negotiated relying in either case upon the description therein of the goods, or upon the date therein shown, may recover from the issuer damages caused by the misdating of the bill or the nonreceipt or misdescription of the goods, except to the extent that the document indicates that the issuer does not know whether any part of all of the goods in fact were received or conform to the description, as where the description is in terms of marks or labels or kind, quantity, or condition or the receipt or description is qualified by "contents or condition of contents of packages unknown", "said to contain", "shipper's weight, load and count" or the like, if such indication be true.

(2) When goods are loaded by an issuer who is a common carrier, the issuer must count the packages of goods if package freight and ascertain the kind and quantity if bulk freight. In such cases "shipper's weight, load and count" or other words indicating that the description was made by the shipper are ineffective except as to freight concealed by packages.

(3) When bulk freight is loaded by a shipper who makes available to the issuer adequate facilities for weighing such freight, an issuer who is a common carrier must ascertain the kind and quantity within a reasonable time after receiving the written request of the shipper to do so. In such cases "shipper's weight" or other words of like purport are ineffective.

(4) The issuer may by inserting in the bill the words "shipper's weight, load and count" or other words of like purport indicate that the goods were loaded by the shipper; and if such statement be true the issuer shall not be liable for damages caused by the improper loading. But their omission does not imply liability for such damages.

(5) The shipper shall be deemed to have guaranteed to the issuer the accuracy at the time of shipment of the description, marks, labels, number, kind, quantity, condition and weight, as furnished by him; and the shipper shall indemnify the issuer against damage caused by inaccuracies in such particulars. The right of the issuer to such indemnity shall in no way limit his responsibility and liability under the contract of carriage to any person other than the shipper.

§ 7—302. Through Bills of Lading and Similar Documents.

(1) The issuer of a through bill of lading or other document embodying an undertaking to be performed in part by persons acting as its agents or by connecting carriers is liable to anyone entitled to recover on the document for any breach by such other persons or by a connecting carrier of its obligation under the document but to the extent that the bill covers an undertaking to be performed overseas or in territory not contiguous to the continental United States or an undertaking including matters other than transportation this liability may be varied by agreement of the parties.

(2) Where goods covered by a through bill of lading or other document embodying an undertaking to be performed in part by persons other than the issuer are received by any such person, he is subject with respect to his own performance while the goods are in his possession to the obligation of the issuer. His obligation is discharged by delivery of the goods to another such person pursuant to the document, and does not include liability for breach by any other such persons or by the issuer.

(3) The issuer of such through bill of lading or other document shall be entitled to recover from the connecting carrier or such other person in possession of the goods when the breach of the obligation under the document occurred, the amount it may be required to pay to anyone entitled to recover on the document therefor, as may be evidenced by any receipt, judgment, or transcript thereof, and the amount of any expense reasonably incurred by it in defending any action brought by anyone entitled to recover on the document therefor.

§ 7—303. Diversion; Reconsignment; Change of Instructions.

(1) Unless the bill of lading otherwise provides, the carrier may deliver the goods to a person or destination

other than that stated in the bill or may otherwise dispose of the goods on instructions from

(a) the holder of a negotiable bill; or

(b) the consignor on a nonnegotiable bill notwithstanding contrary instructions from the consignee; or

(c) the consignee on a nonnegotiable bill in the absence of contrary instructions from the consignor, if the goods have arrived at the billed destination or if the consignee is in possession of the bill; or

(d) the consignee on a nonnegotiable bill if he is entitled as against the consignor to dispose of them.

(2) Unless such instructions are noted on a negotiable bill of lading, a person to whom the bill is duly negotiated can hold the bailee according to the original terms.

§ 7—304. Bills of Lading in a Set.

(1) Except where customary in overseas transportation, a bill of lading must not be issued in a set of parts. The issuer is liable for damages caused by violation of this subsection.

(2) Where a bill of lading is lawfully drawn in a set of parts, each of which is numbered and expressed to be valid only if the goods have not been delivered against any other part, the whole of the parts constitute one bill.

(3) Where a bill of lading is lawfully issued in a set of parts and different parts are negotiated to different persons, the title of the holder to whom the first due negotiation is made prevails as to both the document and the goods even though any later holder may have received the goods from the carrier in good faith and discharged the carrier's obligation by surrender of his part.

(4) Any person who negotiates or transfers a single part of a bill of lading drawn in a set is liable to holders of that part as if it were the whole set.

(5) The bailee is obliged to deliver in accordance with Part 4 of this Article against the first presented part of a bill of lading lawfully drawn in a set. Such delivery discharges the bailee's obligation on the whole bill.

§ 7—305. Destination Bills.

(1) Instead of issuing a bill of lading to the consignor at the place of shipment a carrier may at the request of the consignor procure the bill to be issued at destination or at any other place designated in the request.

(2) Upon request of anyone entitled as against the carrier to control the goods while in transit and on surrender of any outstanding bill of lading or other receipt covering such goods, the issuer may procure a substitute bill to be issued at any place designated in the request.

§ 7—306. Altered Bills of Lading.

An unauthorized alteration or filling in of a blank in a bill of lading leaves the bill enforceable according to its original tenor.

§ 7—307. Lien of Carrier.

(1) A carrier has a lien on the goods covered by a bill of lading for charges subsequent to the date of its receipt of the goods for storage or transportation (including demurrage and terminal charges) and for expenses necessary for preservation of the goods incident to their transportation or reasonably incurred in their sale pursuant to law. But against a purchaser for value of a negotiable bill of lading a carrier's lien is limited to charges stated in the bill or the applicable tariffs, or if no charges are stated then to a reasonable charge.

(2) A lien for charges and expenses under subsection (1) on goods which the carrier was required by law to receive for transportation is effective against the consignor or any person entitled to the goods unless the carrier had notice that the consignor lacked authority to subject the goods to such charges and expenses. Any other lien under subsection (1) is effective against the consignor and any person who permitted the bailor to have control or possession of the goods unless the carrier had notice that the bailor lacked such authority.

(3) A carrier loses his lien on any goods which he voluntarily delivers or which he unjustifiably refuses to deliver.

§ 7—308. Enforcement of Carrier's Lien.

(1) A carrier's lien may be enforced by public or private sale of the goods, in bloc or in parcels, at any time or place and on any terms which are commercially reasonable, after notifying all persons known to claim an interest in the goods. Such notification must include a statement of the amount due, the nature of the proposed sale and the time and place of any public sale. The fact that a better price could have been obtained by a sale at a different time or in a different method from that selected by the carrier is not of itself sufficient to establish that the sale was not made in a commercially reasonable manner. If the carrier either sells the goods in the usual manner in any recognized market therefor or if he sells at the price current in such market at the time of his sale or if he has otherwise sold in conformity with commercially reasonable practices among dealers in the type of goods sold he has sold in a commercially reasonable manner. A sale of more goods than apparently necessary to be offered to ensure satisfaction of the obligation is not commercially reasonable except in cases covered by the preceding sentence.

(2) Before any sale pursuant to this section any person claiming a right in the goods may pay the amount nec-

essary to satisfy the lien and the reasonable expenses incurred under this section. In that event the goods must not be sold, but must be retained by the carrier subject to the terms of the bill and this Article.

(3) The carrier may buy at any public sale pursuant to this section.

(4) A purchaser in good faith of goods sold to enforce a carrier's lien takes the goods free of any rights of persons against whom the lien was valid, despite noncompliance by the carrier with the requirements of this section.

(5) The carrier may satisfy his lien from the proceeds of any sale pursuant to this section but must hold the balance, if any, for delivery on demand to any person to whom he would have been bound to deliver the goods.

(6) The rights provided by this section shall be in addition to all other rights allowed by law to a creditor against his debtor.

(7) A carrier's lien may be enforced in accordance with either subsection (1) or the procedure set forth in subsection (2) of Section 7—210.

(8) The carrier is liable for damages caused by failure to comply with the requirements for sale under this section and in case of willful violation is liable for conversion.

§ 7—309. **Duty of Care; Contractual Limitation of Carrier's Liability.**

(1) A carrier who issues a bill of lading whether negotiable or nonnegotiable must exercise the degree of care in relation to the goods which a reasonably careful man would exercise under like circumstances. This subsection does not repeal or change any law or rule of law which imposes liability upon a common carrier for damages not caused by its negligence.

(2) Damages may be limited by a provision that the carrier's liability shall not exceed a value stated in the document if the carrier's rates are dependent upon value and the consignor by the carrier's tariff is afforded an opportunity to declare a higher value or a value as lawfully provided in the tariff, or where no tariff is filed he is otherwise advised of such opportunity; but no such limitation is effective with respect to the carrier's liability for conversion to its own use.

(3) Reasonable provisions as to the time and manner of presenting claims and instituting actions based on the shipment may be included in a bill of lading or tariff.

Part 4 Warehouse Receipts and Bills of Lading: General Obligations

§ 7—401. **Irregularities in Issue of Receipt or Bill or Conduct of Issuer.**

The obligations imposed by this Article on an issuer apply to a document of title regardless of the fact that

(a) the document may not comply with the requirements of this Article or of any other law or regulation regarding its issue, form or content; or

(b) the issuer may have violated laws regulating the conduct of his business; or

(c) the goods covered by the document were owned by the bailee at the time the document was issued; or

(d) the person issuing the document does not come within the definition of warehouseman if it purports to be a warehouse receipt.

§ 7—402. **Duplicate Receipt or Bill; Overissue.**

Neither a duplicate nor any other document of title purporting to cover goods already represented by an outstanding document of the same issuer confers any right in the goods, except as provided in the case of bills in a set, overissue of documents for fungible goods and substitutes for lost, stolen or destroyed documents. But the issuer is liable for damages caused by his overissue or failure to identify a duplicate document as such by conspicuous notation on its face.

§ 7—403. **Obligation of Warehouseman or Carrier to Deliver; Excuse.**

(1) The bailee must deliver the goods to a person entitled under the document who complies with subsections (2) and (3), unless and to the extent that the bailee establishes any of the following:

(a) delivery of the goods to a person whose receipt was rightful as against the claimant;

(b) damage to or delay, loss or destruction of the goods for which the bailee is not liable [, but the burden of establishing negligence in such cases is on the person entitled under the document];

Note: *The brackets in (1)(b) indicate that State enactments may differ on this point without serious damage to the principle of uniformity.*

(c) previous sale or other disposition of the goods in lawful enforcement of a lien or on warehouseman's lawful termination of storage;

(d) the exercise by a seller of his right to stop delivery pursuant to the provisions of the Article on Sales (Section 2—705);

(e) a diversion, reconsignment or other disposition pursuant to the provisions of this Article (Section 7—303) or tariff regulating such right;

(f) release, satisfaction or any other fact affording a personal defense against the claimant;

(g) any other lawful excuse.

(2) A person claiming goods covered by a document of title must satisfy the bailee's lien where the bailee so

requests or where the bailee is prohibited by law from delivering the goods until the charges are paid.

(3) Unless the person claiming is one against whom the document confers no right under Sec. 7—503(1), he must surrender for cancellation or notation of partial deliveries any outstanding negotiable document covering the goods, and the bailee must cancel the document or conspicuously note the partial delivery thereon or be liable to any person to whom the document is duly negotiated.

(4) "Person entitled under the document" means holder in the case of a negotiable document, or the person to whom delivery is to be made by the terms of or pursuant to written instructions under a nonnegotiable document.

§ 7—404. **No Liability for Good Faith Delivery Pursuant to Receipt or Bill.**

A bailee who in good faith including observance of reasonable commercial standards has received goods and delivered or otherwise disposed of them according to the terms of the document of title or pursuant to this Article is not liable therefor. This rule applies even though the person from whom he received the goods had no authority to procure the document or to dispose of the goods and even though the person to whom he delivered the goods had no authority to receive them.

Part 5 Warehouse Receipts and Bills of Lading: Negotiation and Transfer

§ 7—501. **Form of Negotiation and Requirements of "Due Negotiation".**

(1) A negotiable document of title running to the order of a named person is negotiated by his indorsement and delivery. After his indorsement in blank or to bearer any person can negotiate it by delivery alone.

(2) (a) A negotiable document of title is also negotiated by delivery alone when by its original terms it runs to bearer.

(b) When a document running to the order of a named person is delivered to him the effect is the same as if the document had been negotiated.

(3) Negotiation of a negotiable document of title after it has been indorsed to a specified person requires indorsement by the special indorsee as well as delivery.

(4) A negotiable document of title is "duly negotiated" when it is negotiated in the manner stated in this section to a holder who purchases it in good faith without notice of any defense against or claim to it on the part of any person and for value, unless it is established that the negotiation is not in the regular course of business or financing or involves receiving the document in settlement or payment of a money obligation.

(5) Indorsement of a nonnegotiable document neither makes it negotiable nor adds to the transferee's rights.

(6) The naming in a negotiable bill of a person to be notified of the arrival of the goods does not limit the negotiability of the bill nor constitute notice to a purchaser thereof of any interest of such person in the goods.

§ 7—502. **Rights Acquired by Due Negotiation.**

(1) Subject to the following section and to the provisions of Section 7—205 on fungible goods, a holder to whom a negotiable document of title has been duly negotiated acquires thereby:

(a) title to the document;

(b) title to the goods;

(c) all rights accruing under the law of agency or estoppel, including rights to goods delivered to the bailee after the document was issued; and

(d) the direct obligation of the issuer to hold or deliver the goods according to the terms of the document free of any defense or claim by him except those arising under the terms of the document or under this Article. In the case of a delivery order the bailee's obligation accrues only upon acceptance and the obligation acquired by the holder is that the issuer and any indorser will procure the acceptance of the bailee.

(2) Subject to the following section, title and rights so acquired are not defeated by any stoppage of the goods represented by the document or by surrender of such goods by the bailee, and are not impaired even though the negotiation or any prior negotiation constituted a breach of duty or even though any person has been deprived of possession of the document by misrepresentation, fraud, accident, mistake, duress, loss, theft or conversion, or even though a previous sale or other transfer of the goods or document has been made to a third person.

§ 7—503. **Document of Title to Goods Defeated in Certain Cases.**

(1) A document of title confers no right in goods against a person who before issuance of the document had a legal interest or a perfected security interest in them and who neither

(a) delivered or entrusted them or any document of title covering them to the bailor or his nominee with actual or apparent authority to ship, store or sell or with power to obtain delivery under this Article (Section 7—403) or with power of disposition under this Act (Sections 2—403 and 9—307) or other statute or rule of law; nor

(b) acquiesced in the procurement by the bailor or his nominee of any document of title.

(2) Title to goods based upon an unaccepted delivery order is subject to the rights of anyone to whom a negotiable warehouse receipt or bill of lading covering the goods has been duly negotiated. Such a title may be defeated under the next section to the same extent as the rights of the issuer or a transferee from the issuer.

(3) Title to goods based upon a bill of lading issued to a freight forwarder is subject to the rights of anyone to whom a bill issued by the freight forwarder is duly negotiated; but delivery by the carrier in accordance with Part 4 of this Article pursuant to its own bill of lading discharges the carrier's obligation to deliver.

§ 7—504. Rights Acquired in the Absence of Due Negotiation; Effect of Diversion; Seller's Stoppage of Delivery.

(1) A transferee of a document, whether negotiable or nonnegotiable, to whom the document has been delivered but not duly negotiated, acquires the title and rights which his transferor had or had actual authority to convey.

(2) In the case of a nonnegotiable document, until but not after the bailee receives notification of the transfer, the rights of the transferee may be defeated

(a) by those creditors of the transferor who could treat the sale as void under Section 2—402; or

(b) by a buyer from the transferor in ordinary course of business if the bailee has delivered the goods to the buyer or received notification of his rights; or

(c) as against the bailee by good faith dealings of the bailee with the transferor.

(3) A diversion or other change of shipping instructions by the consignor in a nonnegotiable bill of lading which causes the bailee not to deliver to the consignee defeats the consignee's title to the goods if they have been delivered to a buyer in ordinary course of business and in any event defeats the consignee's rights against the bailee.

(4) Delivery pursuant to a nonnegotiable document may be stopped by a seller under Section 2—705, and subject to the requirement of due notification there provided. A bailee honoring the seller's instructions is entitled to be indemnified by the seller against any resulting loss or expense.

§ 7—505. Indorser Not a Guarantor for Other Parties.

The indorsement of a document of title issued by a bailee does not make the indorser liable for any default by the bailee or by previous indorsers.

§ 7—506. Delivery Without Indorsement: Right to Compel Indorsement.

The transferee of a negotiable document of title has a specifically enforceable right to have his transferor supply any necessary indorsement but the transfer becomes a negotiation only as of the time the indorsement is supplied.

§ 7—507. Warranties on Negotiation or Transfer of Receipt or Bill.

Where a person negotiates or transfers a document of title for value otherwise than as a mere intermediary under the next following section, then unless otherwise agreed he warrants to his immediate purchaser only in addition to any warranty made in selling the goods

(a) that the document is genuine; and

(b) that he has no knowledge of any fact which would impair its validity or worth; and

(c) that his negotiation or transfer is rightful and fully effective with respect to the title to the document and the goods it represents.

§ 7—508. Warranties of Collecting Bank as to Documents.

A collecting bank or other intermediary known to be entrusted with documents on behalf of another or with collection of a draft or other claim against delivery of documents warrants by such delivery of the documents only its own good faith and authority. This rule applies even though the intermediary has purchased or made advances against the claim or draft to be collected.

§ 7—509. Receipt or Bill: When Adequate Compliance With Commercial Contract.

The question whether a document is adequate to fulfill the obligations of a contract for sale or the conditions of a credit is governed by the Articles on Sales (Article 2) and on Letters of Credit (Article 5).

Part 6 Warehouse Receipts and Bills of Lading: Miscellaneous Provisions

§ 7—601. Lost and Missing Documents.

(1) If a document has been lost, stolen or destroyed, a court may order delivery of the goods or issuance of a substitute document and the bailee may without liability to any person comply with such order. If the document was negotiable the claimant must post security approved by the court to indemnify any person who may suffer loss as a result of non-surrender of the document. If the document was not negotiable, such security may be required at the discretion of the court. The court may also in its discretion order payment of the bailee's reasonable costs and counsel fees.

(2) A bailee who without court order delivers goods to a person claiming under a missing negotiable document is liable to any person injured thereby, and if the delivery

is not in good faith becomes liable for conversion. Delivery in good faith is not conversion if made in accordance with a filed classification or tariff or, where no classification or tariff is filed, if the claimant posts security with the bailee in an amount at least double the value of the goods at the time of posting to indemnify any person injured by the delivery who files a notice of claim within one year after the delivery.

§ 7—602. **Attachment of Goods Covered by a Negotiable Document.**

Except where the document was originally issued upon delivery of the goods by a person who had no power to dispose of them, no lien attaches by virtue of any judicial process to goods in the possession of a bailee for which a negotiable document of title is outstanding unless the document be first surrendered to the bailee or its negotiation enjoined, and the bailee shall not be compelled to deliver the goods pursuant to process until the document is surrendered to him or impounded by the court. One who purchases the document for value without notice of the process or injunction takes free of the lien imposed by judicial process.

§ 7—603. **Conflicting Claims; Interpleader.**

If more than one person claims title or possession of the goods, the bailee is excused from delivery until he has had a reasonable time to ascertain the validity of the adverse claims or to bring an action to compel all claimants to interplead and may compel such interpleader, either in defending an action for nondelivery of the goods, or by original action, whichever is appropriate.

Article 8
INVESTMENT SECURITIES

Part 1 Short Title and General Matters

§ 8—101. **Short Title.**

This Article shall be known and may be cited as Uniform Commercial Code—Investment Securities.

§ 8—102. **Definitions and Index of Definitions.**

(1) In this Article, unless the context otherwise requires:

(a) A "certificated security" is a share, participation, or other interest in property of or an enterprise of the issuer or an obligation of the issuer which is

(i) represented by an instrument issued in bearer or registered form;

(ii) of a type commonly dealt in on securities exchanges or markets or commonly recognized in any area in which it is issued or dealt in as a medium for investment; and

(iii) either one of a class or series or by its terms divisible into a class or series of shares, participations, interests, or obligations.

(b) An "uncertificated security" is a share, participation, or other interest in property or an enterprise of the issuer or an obligation of the issuer which is

(i) not represented by an instrument and the transfer of which is registered upon books maintained for that purpose by or on behalf of the issuer;

(ii) of a type commonly dealt in on securities exchanges or markets; and

(iii) either one of a class or series or by its terms divisible into a class or series of shares, participations, interests, or obligations.

(c) A "security" is either a certificated or an uncertificated security. If a security is certificated, the terms "security" and "certificated security" may mean either the intangible interest, the instrument representing that interest, or both, as the context requires. A writing that is a certificated security is governed by this Article and not by Article 3, even though it also meets the requirements of that Article. This Article does not apply to money. If a certificated security has been retained by or surrendered to the issuer or its transfer agent for reasons other than registration of transfer, other temporary purpose, payment, exchange, or acquisition by the issuer, that security shall be treated as an uncertificated security for purposes of this Article.

(d) A certificated security is in "registered form" if

(i) it specifies a person entitled to the security or the rights it represents; and

(ii) its transfer may be registered upon books maintained for that purpose by or on behalf of the issuer, or the security so states.

(e) A certificated security is in "bearer form" if it runs to bearer according to its terms and not by reason of any indorsement.

(2) A "subsequent purchaser" is a person who takes other than by original issue.

(3) A "clearing corporation" is a corporation registered as a "clearing agency" under the federal securities laws or a corporation:

(a) at least 90 percent of whose capital stock is held by or for one or more organizations, none of which, other than a national securities exchange or association, holds in excess of 20 percent of the capital stock of the corporation, and each of which is

(i) subject to supervision or regulation pursuant to the provisions of federal or state banking laws or state insurance laws,

(ii) a broker or dealer or investment company registered under the federal securities laws, or

(iii) a national securities exchange or association registered under the federal securities laws; and

(b) any remaining capital stock of which is held by individuals who have purchased it at or prior to the time of their taking office as directors of the corporation and who have purchased only so much of the capital stock as is necessary to permit them to qualify as directors.

(4) A "custodian bank" is a bank or trust company that is supervised and examined by state or federal authority having supervision over banks and is acting as custodian for a clearing corporation.

(5) Other definitions applying to this Article or to specified Parts thereof and the sections in which they appear are:

"Adverse claim". Section 8—302.
"Bona fide purchaser". Section 8—302.
"Broker". Section 8—303.
"Debtor". Section 9—105.
"Financial intermediary". Section 8—313.
"Guarantee of the signature". Section 8—402.
"Initial transaction statement". Section 8—408.
"Instruction". Section 8—308.
"Intermediary bank". Section 4—105.
"Issuer". Section 8—201.
"Overissue". Section 8—104.
"Secured Party". Section 9—105.
"Security Agreement". Section 9—105.

(6) In addition, Article 1 contains general definitions and principles of construction and interpretation applicable throughout this Article.

Amended in 1962, 1973 and 1977.

§ 8—103. Issuer's Lien.

A lien upon a security in favor of an issuer thereof is valid against a purchaser only if:

(a) the security is certificated and the right of the issuer to the lien is noted conspicuously thereon; or

(b) the security is uncertificated and a notation of the right of the issuer to the lien is contained in the initial transaction statement sent to the purchaser or, if his interest is transferred to him other than by registration of transfer, pledge, or release, the initial transaction statement sent to the registered owner or the registered pledgee.

Amended in 1977.

§ 8—104. Effect of Overissue; "Overissue".

(1) The provisions of this Article which validate a security or compel its issue or reissue do not apply to the extent that validation, issue, or reissue would result in overissue; but if:

(a) an identical security which does not constitute an overissue is reasonably available for purchase, the person entitled to issue or validation may compel the issuer to purchase the security for him and either to deliver a certificated security or to register the transfer of an uncertificated security to him, against surrender of any certificated security he holds; or

(b) a security is not so available for purchase, the person entitled to issue or validation may recover from the issuer the price he or the last purchaser for value paid for it with interest from the date of his demand.

(2) "Overissue" means the issue of securities in excess of the amount the issuer has corporate power to issue.

Amended in 1977.

§ 8—105. Certificated Securities Negotiable; Statements and Instructions Not Negotiable; Presumptions.

(1) Certificated securities governed by this Article are negotiable instruments.

(2) Statements (Section 8—408), notices, or the like, sent by the issuer of uncertificated securities and instructions (Section 8—308) are neither negotiable instruments nor certificated securities.

(3) In any action on a security:

(a) unless specifically denied in the pleadings, each signature on a certificated security, in a necessary indorsement, on an initial transaction statement, or on an instruction, is admitted;

(b) if the effectiveness of a signature is put in issue, the burden of establishing it is on the party claiming under the signature, but the signature is presumed to be genuine or authorized;

(c) if signatures on a certificated security are admitted or established, production of the security entitles a holder to recover on it unless the defendant establishes a defense or a defect going to the validity of the security;

(d) if signatures on an initial transaction statement are admitted or established, the facts stated in the statement are presumed to be true as of the time of its issuance; and

(e) after it is shown that a defense or defect exists, the plaintiff has the burden of establishing that he or some person under whom he claims is a person against whom the defense or defect is ineffective (Section 8—202).

Amended in 1977.

§ 8—106. Applicability.

The law (including the conflict of laws rules) of the jurisdiction of organization of the issuer governs the validity of a security, the effectiveness of registration by the issuer, and the rights and duties of the issuer with respect to:

    (a) registration of transfer of a certificated security;

    (b) registration of transfer, pledge, or release of an uncertificated security; and

    (c) sending of statements of uncertificated securities.

Amended in 1977.

§ 8—107. Securities Transferable; Action for Price.

(1) Unless otherwise agreed and subject to any applicable law or regulation respecting short sales, a person obligated to transfer securities may transfer any certificated security of the specified issue in bearer form or registered in the name of the transferee, or indorsed to him or in blank, or he may transfer an equivalent uncertificated security to the transferee or a person designated by the transferee.

(2) If the buyer fails to pay the price as it comes due under a contract of sale, the seller may recover the price of:

    (a) certificated securities accepted by the buyer;

    (b) uncertificated securities that have been transferred to the buyer or a person designated by the buyer; and

    (c) other securities if efforts at their resale would be unduly burdensome or if there is no readily available market for their resale.

Amended in 1977.

§ 8—108. Registration of Pledge and Release of Uncertificated Securities.

A security interest in an uncertificated security may be evidenced by the registration of pledge to the secured party or a person designated by him. There can be no more than one registered pledge of an uncertificated security at any time. The registered owner of an uncertificated security is the person in whose name the security is registered, even if the security is subject to a registered pledge. The rights of a registered pledgee of an uncertificated security under this Article are terminated by the registration of release.

Added in 1977.

Part 2 Issue—Issuer

§ 8—201. "Issuer".

(1) With respect to obligations on or defenses to a security, "issuer" includes a person who:

    (a) places or authorizes the placing of his name on a certificated security (otherwise than as authenticating trustee, registrar, transfer agent, or the like) to evidence that it represents a share, participation, or other interest in his property or in an enterprise, or to evidence his duty to perform an obligation represented by the certificated security;

    (b) creates shares, participations, or other interests in his property or in an enterprise or undertakes obligations, which shares, participations, interests, or obligations are uncertificated securities;

    (c) directly or indirectly creates fractional interests in his rights or property, which fractional interests are represented by certificated securities; or

    (d) becomes responsible for or in place of any other person described as an issuer in this section.

(2) With respect to obligations on or defenses to a security, a guarantor is an issuer to the extent of his guaranty, whether or not his obligation is noted on a certificated security or on statements of uncertificated securities sent pursuant to Section 8—408.

(3) With respect to registration of transfer, pledge, or release (Part 4 of this Article), "issuer" means a person on whose behalf transfer books are maintained.

Amended in 1977.

§ 8—202. Issuer's Responsibility and Defenses; Notice of Defect or Defense.

(1) Even against a purchaser for value and without notice, the terms of a security include:

    (a) if the security is certificated, those stated on the security;

    (b) if the security is uncertificated, those contained in the initial transaction statement sent to such purchaser or, if his interest is transferred to him other than by registration of transfer, pledge, or release, the initial transaction statement sent to the registered owner or registered pledgee; and

    (c) those made part of the security by reference, on the certificated security or in the initial transaction statement, to another instrument, indenture, or document or to a constitution, statute, ordinance, rule, regulation, order or the like, to the extent that the terms referred to do not conflict with the terms stated on the certificated security or contained in the statement. A reference under this paragraph does not of itself charge a purchaser for value with notice of a defect going to the validity of the security, even though the certificated security or statement expressly states that a person accepting it admits notice.

(2) A certificated security in the hands of a purchaser for value or an uncertificated security as to which an initial transaction statement has been sent to a purchaser for value, other than a security issued by a government

or governmental agency or unit, even though issued with a defect going to its validity, is valid with respect to the purchaser if he is without notice of the particular defect unless the defect involves a violation of constitutional provisions, in which case the security is valid with respect to a subsequent purchaser for value and without notice of the defect. This subsection applies to an issuer that is a government or governmental agency or unit only if either there has been substantial compliance with the legal requirements governing the issue or the issuer has received a substantial consideration for the issue as a whole or for the particular security and a stated purpose of the issue is one for which the issuer has power to borrow money or issue the security.

(3) Except as provided in the case of certain unauthorized signatures (Section 8—205), lack of genuineness of a certificated security or an initial transaction statement is a complete defense, even against a purchaser for value and without notice.

(4) All other defenses of the issuer of a certificated or uncertificated security, including nondelivery and conditional delivery of a certificated security, are ineffective against a purchaser for value who has taken without notice of the particular defense.

(5) Nothing in this section shall be construed to affect the right of a party to a "when, as and if issued" or a "when distributed" contract to cancel the contract in the event of a material change in the character of the security that is the subject of the contract or in the plan or arrangement pursuant to which the security is to be issued or distributed.

Amended in 1977.

§ 8—203. **Staleness as Notice of Defects or Defenses.**

(1) After an act or event creating a right to immediate performance of the principal obligation represented by a certificated security or that sets a date on or after which the security is to be presented or surrendered for redemption or exchange, a purchaser is charged with notice of any defect in its issue or defense of the issuer if:

(a) the act or event is one requiring the payment of money, the delivery of certificated securities, the registration of transfer of uncertificated securities, or any of these on presentation or surrender of the certificated security, the funds or securities are available on the date set for payment or exchange, and he takes the security more than one year after that date; and

(b) the act or event is not covered by paragraph (a) and he takes the security more than 2 years after the date set for surrender or presentation or the date on which performance became due.

(2) A call that has been revoked is not within subsection (1).

Amended in 1977.

§ 8—204. **Effect of Issuer's Restrictions on Transfer.**

A restriction on transfer of a security imposed by the issuer, even if otherwise lawful, is ineffective against any person without actual knowledge of it unless:

(a) the security is certificated and the restriction is noted conspicuously thereon; or

(b) the security is uncertificated and a notation of the restriction is contained in the initial transaction statement sent to the person or, if his interest is transferred to him other than by registration of transfer, pledge, or release, the initial transaction statement sent to the registered owner or the registered pledgee.

Amended in 1977.

§ 8—205. **Effect of Unauthorized Signature on Certificated Security or Initial Transaction Statement.**

An unauthorized signature placed on a certificated security prior to or in the course of issue or placed on an initial transaction statement is ineffective, but the signature is effective in favor of a purchaser for value of the certificated security or a purchaser for value of an uncertificated security to whom the initial transaction statement has been sent, if the purchaser is without notice of the lack of authority and the signing has been done by:

(a) an authenticating trustee, registrar, transfer agent, or other person entrusted by the issuer with the signing of the security, of similar securities, or of initial transaction statements or the immediate preparation for signing of any of them; or

(b) an employee of the issuer, or of any of the foregoing, entrusted with responsible handling of the security or initial transaction statement.

Amended in 1977.

§ 8—206. **Completion or Alteration of Certificated Security or Initial Transaction Statement.**

(1) If a certificated security contains the signatures necessary to its issue or transfer but is incomplete in any other respect:

(a) any person may complete it by filling in the blanks as authorized; and

(b) even though the blanks are incorrectly filled in, the security as completed is enforceable by a purchaser who took it for value and without notice of the incorrectness.

(2) A complete certificated security that has been improperly altered, even though fraudulently, remains enforceable, but only according to its original terms.

(3) If an initial transaction statement contains the signatures necessary to its validity, but is incomplete in any other respect:

(a) any person may complete it by filling in the blanks as authorized; and

(b) even though the blanks are incorrectly filled in, the statement as completed is effective in favor of the person to whom it is sent if he purchased the security referred to therein for value and without notice of the incorrectness.

(4) A complete initial transaction statement that has been improperly altered, even though fraudulently, is effective in favor of a purchaser to whom it has been sent, but only according to its original terms.

Amended in 1977.

§ 8—207. Rights and Duties of Issuer With Respect to Registered Owners and Registered Pledgees.

(1) Prior to due presentment for registration of transfer of a certificated security in registered form, the issuer or indenture trustee may treat the registered owner as the person exclusively entitled to vote, to receive notifications, and otherwise to exercise all the rights and powers of an owner.

(2) Subject to the provisions of subsections (3), (4), and (6), the issuer or indenture trustee may treat the registered owner of an uncertificated security as the person exclusively entitled to vote, to receive notifications, and otherwise to exercise all the rights and powers of an owner.

(3) The registered owner of an uncertificated security that is subject to a registered pledge is not entitled to registration of transfer prior to the due presentment to the issuer of a release instruction. The exercise of conversion rights with respect to a convertible uncertificated security is a transfer within the meaning of this section.

(4) Upon due presentment of a transfer instruction from the registered pledgee of an uncertificated security, the issuer shall:

(a) register the transfer of the security to the new owner free of pledge, if the instruction specifies a new owner (who may be the registered pledgee) and does not specify a pledgee;

(b) register the transfer of the security to the new owner subject to the interest of the existing pledgee, if the instruction specifies a new owner and the existing pledgee; or

(c) register the release of the security from the existing pledge and register the pledge of the security to the other pledgee, if the instruction specifies the existing owner and another pledgee.

(5) Continuity of perfection of a security interest is not broken by registration of transfer under subsection (4)(b) or by registration of release and pledge under subsection (4)(c), if the security interest is assigned.

(6) If an uncertificated security is subject to a registered pledge:

(a) any uncertificated securities issued in exchange for or distributed with respect to the pledged security shall be registered subject to the pledge;

(b) any certificated securities issued in exchange for or distributed with respect to the pledged security shall be delivered to the registered pledgee; and

(c) any money paid in exchange for or in redemption of part or all of the security shall be paid to the registered pledgee.

(7) Nothing in this Article shall be construed to affect the liability of the registered owner of a security for calls, assessments, or the like.

Amended in 1977.

§ 8—208. Effect of Signature of Authenticating Trustee, Registrar, or Transfer Agent.

(1) A person placing his signature upon a certificated security or an initial transaction statement as authenticating trustee, registrar, transfer agent, or the like, warrants to a purchaser for value of the certificated security or a purchaser for value of an uncertificated security to whom the initial transaction statement has been sent, if the purchaser is without notice of the particular defect, that:

(a) the certificated security or initial transaction statement is genuine;

(b) his own participation in the issue or registration of the transfer, pledge, or release of the security is within his capacity and within the scope of the authority received by him from the issuer; and

(c) he has reasonable grounds to believe the security is in the form and within the amount the issuer is authorized to issue.

(2) Unless otherwise agreed, a person by so placing his signature does not assume responsibility for the validity of the security in other respects.

Amended in 1962 and 1977.

Part 3 Transfer

§ 8—301. Rights Acquired by Purchaser.

(1) Upon transfer of a security to a purchaser (Section 8—313), the purchaser acquires the rights in the security which his transferor had or had actual authority to convey unless the purchaser's rights are limited by Section 8—302(4).

(2) A transferee of a limited interest acquires rights only to the extent of the interest transferred. The creation or release of a security interest in a security is the transfer of a limited interest in that security.

Amended in 1977.

§ 8—302. "Bona Fide Purchaser"; "Adverse Claim"; Title Acquired by Bona Fide Purchaser.

(1) A "bona fide purchaser" is a purchaser for value in good faith and without notice of any adverse claim:

(a) who takes delivery of a certificated security in bearer form or in registered form, issued or indorsed to him or in blank;

(b) to whom the transfer, pledge, or release of an uncertificated security is registered on the books of the issuer; or

(c) to whom a security is transferred under the provisions of paragraph (c), (d)(i), or (g) of Section 8—313(1).

(2) "Adverse claim" includes a claim that a transfer was or would be wrongful or that a particular adverse person is the owner of or has an interest in the security.

(3) A bona fide purchaser in addition to acquiring the rights of a purchaser (Section 8—301) also acquires his interest in the security free of any adverse claim.

(4) Notwithstanding Section 8—301(1), the transferee of a particular certificated security who has been a party to any fraud or illegality affecting the security, or who as a prior holder of that certificated security had notice of an adverse claim, cannot improve his position by taking from a bona fide purchaser.

Amended in 1977.

§ 8—303. "Broker".

"Broker" means a person engaged for all or part of his time in the business of buying and selling securities, who in the transaction concerned acts for, buys a security from, or sells a security to, a customer. Nothing in this Article determines the capacity in which a person acts for purposes of any other statute or rule to which the person is subject.

§ 8—304. Notice to Purchaser of Adverse Claims.

(1) A purchaser (including a broker for the seller or buyer, but excluding an intermediary bank) of a certificated security is charged with notice of adverse claims if:

(a) the security, whether in bearer or registered form, has been indorsed "for collection" or "for surrender" or for some other purpose not involving transfer; or

(b) the security is in bearer form and has on it an unambiguous statement that it is the property of a person other than the transferor. The mere writing of a name on a security is not such a statement.

(2) A purchaser (including a broker for the seller or buyer, but excluding an intermediary bank) to whom the transfer, pledge, or release of an uncertificated security is registered is charged with notice of adverse claims as to which the issuer has a duty under Section 8—403(4) at the time of registration and which are noted in the initial transaction statement sent to the purchaser or, if his interest is transferred to him other than by registration of transfer, pledge, or release, the initial transaction statement sent to the registered owner or the registered pledgee.

(3) The fact that the purchaser (including a broker for the seller or buyer) of a certificated or uncertificated security has notice that the security is held for a third person or is registered in the name of or indorsed by a fiduciary does not create a duty of inquiry into the rightfulness of the transfer or constitute constructive notice of adverse claims. However, if the purchaser (excluding an intermediary bank) has knowledge that the proceeds are being used or that the transaction is for the individual benefit of the fiduciary or otherwise in breach of duty, the purchaser is charged with notice of adverse claims.

Amended in 1977.

§ 8—305. Staleness as Notice of Adverse Claims.

An act or event that creates a right to immediate performance of the principal obligation represented by a certificated security or sets a date on or after which a certificated security is to be presented or surrendered for redemption or exchange does not itself constitute any notice of adverse claims except in the case of a transfer:

(a) after one year from any date set for presentment or surrender for redemption or exchange; or

(b) after 6 months from any date set for payment of money against presentation or surrender of the security if funds are available for payment on that date.

Amended in 1977.

§ 8—306. Warranties on Presentment and Transfer of Certificated Securities; Warranties of Originators of Instructions.

(1) A person who presents a certificated security for registration of transfer or for payment or exchange warrants to the issuer that he is entitled to the registration, payment, or exchange. But, a purchaser for value and without notice of adverse claims who receives a new, reissued, or re-registered certificated security on regis-

tration of transfer or receives an initial transaction statement confirming the registration of transfer of an equivalent uncertificated security to him warrants only that he has no knowledge of any unauthorized signature (Section 8—311) in a necessary indorsement.

(2) A person by transferring a certificated security to a purchaser for value warrants only that:

(a) his transfer is effective and rightful;

(b) the security is genuine and has not been materially altered; and

(c) he knows of no fact which might impair the validity of the security.

(3) If a certificated security is delivered by an intermediary known to be entrusted with delivery of the security on behalf of another or with collection of a draft or other claim against delivery, the intermediary by delivery warrants only his own good faith and authority, even though he has purchased or made advances against the claim to be collected against the delivery.

(4) A pledgee or other holder for security who redelivers a certificated security received, or after payment and on order of the debtor delivers that security to a third person, makes only the warranties of an intermediary under subsection (3).

(5) A person who originates an instruction warrants to the issuer that:

(a) he is an appropriate person to originate the instruction; and

(b) at the time the instruction is presented to the issuer he will be entitled to the registration of transfer, pledge, or release.

(6) A person who originates an instruction warrants to any person specially guaranteeing his signature (subsection 8—312(3)) that:

(a) he is an appropriate person to originate the instruction; and

(b) at the time the instruction is presented to the issuer

(i) he will be entitled to the registration of transfer, pledge, or release; and

(ii) the transfer, pledge, or release requested in the instruction will be registered by the issuer free from all liens, security interests, restrictions, and claims other than those specified in the instruction.

(7) A person who originates an instruction warrants to a purchaser for value and to any person guaranteeing the instruction (Section 8—312(6)) that:

(a) he is an appropriate person to originate the instruction;

(b) the uncertificated security referred to therein is valid; and

(c) at the time the instruction is presented to the issuer

(i) the transferor will be entitled to the registration of transfer, pledge, or release;

(ii) the transfer, pledge, or release requested in the instruction will be registered by the issuer free from all liens, security interests, restrictions, and claims other than those specified in the instruction; and

(iii) the requested transfer, pledge, or release will be rightful.

(8) If a secured party is the registered pledgee or the registered owner of an uncertificated security, a person who originates an instruction of release or transfer to the debtor or, after payment and on order of the debtor, a transfer instruction to a third person, warrants to the debtor or the third person only that he is an appropriate person to originate the instruction and, at the time the instruction is presented to the issuer, the transferor will be entitled to the registration of release or transfer. If a transfer instruction to a third person who is a purchaser for value is originated on order of the debtor, the debtor makes to the purchaser the warranties of paragraphs (b), (c)(ii) and (c)(iii) of subsection (7).

(9) A person who transfers an uncertificated security to a purchaser for value and does not originate an instruction in connection with the transfer warrants only that:

(a) his transfer is effective and rightful; and

(b) the uncertificated security is valid.

(10) A broker gives to his customer and to the issuer and a purchaser the applicable warranties provided in this section and has the rights and privileges of a purchaser under this section. The warranties of and in favor of the broker, acting as an agent are in addition to applicable warranties given by and in favor of his customer.

Amended in 1962 and 1977.

§ 8—307. **Effect of Delivery Without Indorsement; Right to Compel Indorsement.**

If a certificated security in registered form has been delivered to a purchaser without a necessary indorsement he may become a bona fide purchaser only as of the time the indorsement is supplied; but against the transferor, the transfer is complete upon delivery and the purchaser has a specifically enforceable right to have any necessary indorsement supplied.

Amended in 1977.

§ 8—308. **Indorsements; Instructions.**

(1) An indorsement of a certificated security in registered form is made when an appropriate person signs on it or on a separate document an assignment or transfer of the security or a power to assign or transfer it or his signature is written without more upon the back of the security.

(2) An indorsement may be in blank or special. An indorsement in blank includes an indorsement to bearer. A special indorsement specifies to whom the security is to be transferred, or who has power to transfer it. A holder may convert a blank indorsement into a special indorsement.

(3) An indorsement purporting to be only of part of a certificated security representing units intended by the issuer to be separately transferable is effective to the extent of the indorsement.

(4) An "instruction" is an order to the issuer of an uncertificated security requesting that the transfer, pledge, or release from pledge of the uncertificated security specified therein be registered.

(5) An instruction originated by an appropriate person is:

   (a) a writing signed by an appropriate person; or

   (b) a communication to the issuer in any form agreed upon in a writing signed by the issuer and an appropriate person.

If an instruction has been originated by an appropriate person but is incomplete in any other respect, any person may complete it as authorized and the issuer may rely on it as completed even though it has been completed incorrectly.

(6) "An appropriate person" in subsection (1) means the person specified by the certificated security or by special indorsement to be entitled to the security.

(7) "An appropriate person" in subsection (5) means:

   (a) for an instruction to transfer or pledge an uncertificated security which is then not subject to a registered pledge, the registered owner; or

   (b) for an instruction to transfer or release an uncertificated security which is then subject to a registered pledge, the registered pledgee.

(8) In addition to the persons designated in subsections (6) and (7), "an appropriate person" in subsections (1) and (5) includes:

   (a) if the person designated is described as a fiduciary but is no longer serving in the described capacity, either that person or his successor;

   (b) if the persons designated are described as more than one person as fiduciaries and one or more are no longer serving in the described capacity, the remaining fiduciary or fiduciaries, whether or not a successor has been appointed or qualified;

   (c) if the person designated is an individual and is without capacity to act by virtue of death, incompetence, infancy, or otherwise, his executor, administrator, guardian, or like fiduciary;

   (d) if the persons designated are described as more than one person as tenants by the entirety or with right of survivorship and by reason of death all cannot sign, the survivor or survivors;

   (e) a person having power to sign under applicable law or controlling instrument; and

   (f) to the extent that the person designated or any of the foregoing persons may act through an agent, his authorized agent.

(9) Unless otherwise agreed, the indorser of a certificated security by his indorsement or the originator of an instruction by his origination assumes no obligation that the security will be honored by the issuer but only the obligations provided in Section 8—306.

(10) Whether the person signing is appropriate is determined as of the date of signing and an indorsement made by or an instruction originated by him does not become unauthorized for the purposes of this Article by virtue of any subsequent change of circumstances.

(11) Failure of a fiduciary to comply with a controlling instrument or with the law of the state having jurisdiction of the fiduciary relationship, including any law requiring the fiduciary to obtain court approval of the transfer, pledge, or release, does not render his indorsement or an instruction originated by him unauthorized for the purposes of this Article.

Amended in 1962 and 1977.

§ 8—309. **Effect of Indorsement Without Delivery.**

An indorsement of a certificated security, whether special or in blank, does not constitute a transfer until delivery of the certificated security on which it appears or, if the indorsement is on a separate document, until delivery of both the document and the certificated security.

Amended in 1977.

§ 8—310. **Indorsement of Certificated Security in Bearer Form.**

An indorsement of a certificated security in bearer form may give notice of adverse claims (Section 8—304) but does not otherwise affect any right to registration the holder possesses.

Amended in 1977.

§ 8—311. **Effect of Unauthorized Indorsement or Instruction.**

Unless the owner or pledgee has ratified an unauthorized indorsement or instruction or is otherwise precluded from asserting its ineffectiveness:

(a) he may assert its ineffectiveness against the issuer or any purchaser, other than a purchaser for value and without notice of adverse claims, who has in good faith received a new, reissued, or re-registered certificated security on registration of transfer or received an initial transaction statement confirming the registration of transfer, pledge, or release of an equivalent uncertificated security to him; and

(b) an issuer who registers the transfer of a certificated security upon the unauthorized indorsement or who registers the transfer, pledge, or release of an uncertificated security upon the unauthorized instruction is subject to liability for improper registration (Section 8—404).

Amended in 1977.

§ 8—312. **Effect of Guaranteeing Signature, Indorsement or Instruction.**

(1) Any person guaranteeing a signature of an indorser of a certificated security warrants that at the time of signing:

(a) the signature was genuine;

(b) the signer was an appropriate person to indorse (Section 8—308); and

(c) the signer had legal capacity to sign.

(2) Any person guaranteeing a signature of the originator of an instruction warrants that at the time of signing:

(a) the signature was genuine;

(b) the signer was an appropriate person to originate the instruction (Section 8—308) if the person specified in the instruction as the registered owner or registered pledgee of the uncertificated security was, in fact, the registered owner or registered pledgee of the security, as to which fact the signature guarantor makes no warranty;

(c) the signer had legal capacity to sign; and

(d) the taxpayer identification number, if any, appearing on the instruction as that of the registered owner or registered pledgee was the taxpayer identification number of the signer or of the owner or pledgee for whom the signer was acting.

(3) Any person specially guaranteeing the signature of the originator of an instruction makes not only the warranties of a signature guarantor (subsection (2)) but also warrants that at the time the instruction is presented to the issuer:

(a) the person specified in the instruction as the registered owner or registered pledgee of the uncertificated security will be the registered owner or registered pledgee; and

(b) the transfer, pledge, or release of the uncertificated security requested in the instruction will be registered by the issuer free from all liens, security interests, restrictions, and claims other than those specified in the instruction.

(4) The guarantor under subsections (1) and (2) or the special guarantor under subsection (3) does not otherwise warrant the rightfulness of the particular transfer, pledge, or release.

(5) Any person guaranteeing an indorsement of a certificated security makes not only the warranties of a signature guarantor under subsection (1) but also warrants the rightfulness of the particular transfer in all respects.

(6) Any person guaranteeing an instruction requesting the transfer, pledge, or release of an uncertificated security makes not only the warranties of a special signature guarantor under subsection (3) but also warrants the rightfulness of the particular transfer, pledge, or release in all respects.

(7) No issuer may require a special guarantee of signature (subsection (3)), a guarantee of indorsement (subsection (5)), or a guarantee of instruction (subsection (6)) as a condition to registration of transfer, pledge, or release.

(8) The foregoing warranties are made to any person taking or dealing with the security in reliance on the guarantee, and the guarantor is liable to the person for any loss resulting from breach of the warranties.

Amended in 1977.

§ 8—313. **When Transfer to Purchaser Occurs; Financial Intermediary as Bona Fide Purchaser; "Financial Intermediary".**

(1) Transfer of a security or a limited interest (including a security interest) therein to a purchaser occurs only:

(a) at the time he or a person designated by him acquires possession of a certificated security;

(b) at the time the transfer, pledge, or release of an uncertificated security is registered to him or a person designated by him;

(c) at the time his financial intermediary acquires possession of a certificated security specially indorsed to or issued in the name of the purchaser;

(d) at the time a financial intermediary, not a clearing corporation, sends him confirmation of the purchase and also by book entry or otherwise identifies as belonging to the purchaser

(i) a specific certificated security in the financial intermediary's possession;

(ii) a quantity of securities that constitute or are part of a fungible bulk of certificated securities in the financial intermediary's possession or of uncertificated securities registered in the name of the financial intermediary; or

    (iii) a quantity of securities that constitute or are part of a fungible bulk of securities shown on the account of the financial intermediary on the books of another financial intermediary;

(e) with respect to an identified certificated security to be delivered while still in the possession of a third person, not a financial intermediary, at the time that person acknowledges that he holds for the purchaser;

(f) with respect to a specific uncertificated security the pledge or transfer of which has been registered to a third person, not a financial intermediary, at the time that person acknowledges that he holds for the purchaser;

(g) at the time appropriate entries to the account of the purchaser or a person designated by him on the books of a clearing corporation are made under Section 8—320;

(h) with respect to the transfer of a security interest where the debtor has signed a security agreement containing a description of the security, at the time a written notification, which, in the case of the creation of the security interest, is signed by the debtor (which may be a copy of the security agreement) or which, in the case of the release or assignment of the security interest created pursuant to this paragraph, is signed by the secured party, is received by

    (i) a financial intermediary on whose books the interest of the transferor in the security appears;

    (ii) a third person, not a financial intermediary, in possession of the security, if it is certificated;

    (iii) a third person, not a financial intermediary, who is the registered owner of the security, if it is uncertificated and not subject to a registered pledge; or

    (iv) a third person, not a financial intermediary, who is the registered pledgee of the security, if it is uncertificated and subject to a registered pledge;

(i) with respect to the transfer of a security interest where the transferor has signed a security agreement containing a description of the security, at the time new value is given by the secured party; or

(j) with respect to the transfer of a security interest where the secured party is a financial intermediary and the security has already been transferred to the financial intermediary under paragraphs (a), (b), (c), (d), or (g), at the time the transferor has signed a security agreement containing a description of the security and value is given by the secured party.

(2) The purchaser is the owner of a security held for him by a financial intermediary, but cannot be a bona fide purchaser of a security so held except in the circumstances specified in paragraphs (c), (d)(i), and (g) of subsection (1). If a security so held is part of a fungible bulk, as in the circumstances specified in paragraphs (d)(ii) and (d)(iii) of subsection (1), the purchaser is the owner of a proportionate property interest in the fungible bulk.

(3) Notice of an adverse claim received by the financial intermediary or by the purchaser after the financial intermediary takes delivery of a certificated security as a holder for value or after the transfer, pledge, or release of an uncertificated security has been registered free of the claim to a financial intermediary who has given value is not effective either as to the financial intermediary or as to the purchaser. However, as between the financial intermediary and the purchaser the purchaser may demand transfer of an equivalent security as to which no notice of adverse claim has been received.

(4) A "financial intermediary" is a bank, broker, clearing corporation, or other person (or the nominee of any of them) which in the ordinary course of its business maintains security accounts for its customers and is acting in that capacity. A financial intermediary may have a security interest in securities held in account for its customer.

Amended in 1962 and 1977.

§ 8—314. Duty to Transfer, When Completed

(1) Unless otherwise agreed, if a sale of a security is made on an exchange or otherwise through brokers:

    (a) the selling customer fulfills his duty to transfer at the time he:

        (i) places a certificated security in the possession of the selling broker or a person designated by the broker;

        (ii) causes an uncertificated security to be registered in the name of the selling broker or a person designated by the broker;

        (iii) if requested, causes an acknowledgment to be made to the selling broker that a certificated or uncertificated security is held for the broker; or

        (iv) places in the possession of the selling broker or of a person designated by the broker a transfer instruction for an uncertificated security, providing the issuer does not refuse to register the requested transfer if the instruction is presented to the issuer for registration within 30 days thereafter; and

    (b) the selling broker, including a correspondent broker acting for a selling customer, fulfills his duty to transfer at the time he:

(i) places a certificated security in the possession of the buying broker or a person designated by the buying broker;

(ii) causes an uncertificated security to be registered in the name of the buying broker or a person designated by the buying broker;

(iii) places in the possession of the buying broker or of a person designated by the buying broker a transfer instruction for an uncertificated security, providing the issuer does not refuse to register the requested transfer if the instruction is presented to the issuer for registration within 30 days thereafter; or

(iv) effects clearance of the sale in accordance with the rules of the exchange on which the transaction took place.

(2) Except as provided in this section or unless otherwise agreed, a transferor's duty to transfer a security under a contract of purchase is not fulfilled until he:

(a) places a certificated security in form to be negotiated by the purchaser in the possession of the purchaser or of a person designated by the purchaser;

(b) causes an uncertificated security to be registered in the name of the purchaser or a person designated by the purchaser; or

(c) if the purchaser requests, causes an acknowledgment to be made to the purchaser that a certificated or uncertificated security is held for the purchaser.

(3) Unless made on an exchange, a sale to a broker purchasing for his own account is within subsection (2) and not within subsection (1).

Amended in 1977.

§ 8—315. Action Against Transferee Based Upon Wrongful Transfer

(1) Any person against whom the transfer of a security is wrongful for any reason, including his incapacity, as against anyone except a bona fide purchaser, may:

(a) reclaim possession of the certificated security wrongfully transferred;

(b) obtain possession of any new certificated security representing all or part of the same rights;

(c) compel the origination of an instruction to transfer to him or a person designated by him an uncertificated security constituting all or part of the same rights; or

(d) have damages.

(2) If the transfer is wrongful because of an unauthorized indorsement of a certificated security, the owner may also reclaim or obtain possession of the security or a new certificated security, even from a bona fide purchaser, if the ineffectiveness of the purported indorsement can be asserted against him under the provisions of this Article on unauthorized indorsements (Section 8—311).

(3) The right to obtain or reclaim possession of a certificated security or to compel the origination of a transfer instruction may be specifically enforced and the transfer of a certificated or uncertificated security enjoined and a certificated security impounded pending the litigation.

Amended in 1977.

§ 8—316. Purchaser's Right to Requisites for Registration of Transfer, Pledge, or Release on Books

Unless otherwise agreed, the transferor of a certificated security or the transferor, pledgor, or pledgee of an uncertificated security on due demand must supply his purchaser with any proof of his authority to transfer, pledge, or release or with any other requisite necessary to obtain registration of the transfer, pledge, or release of the security; but if the transfer, pledge, or release is not for value, a transferor, pledgor, or pledgee need not do so unless the purchaser furnishes the necessary expenses. Failure within a reasonable time to comply with a demand made gives the purchaser the right to reject or rescind the transfer, pledge, or release.

Amended in 1977.

§ 8—317. Creditors' Rights

(1) Subject to the exceptions in subsections (3) and (4), no attachment or levy upon a certificated security or any share or other interest represented thereby which is outstanding is valid until the security is actually seized by the officer making the attachment or levy, but a certificated security which has been surrendered to the issuer may be reached by a creditor by legal process at the issuer's chief executive office in the United States.

(2) An uncertificated security registered in the name of the debtor may not be reached by a creditor except by legal process at the issuer's chief executive office in the United States.

(3) The interest of a debtor in a certificated security that is in the possession of a secured party not a financial intermediary or in an uncertificated security registered in the name of a secured party not a financial intermediary (or in the name of a nominee of the secured party) may be reached by a creditor by legal process upon the secured party.

(4) The interest of a debtor in a certificated security that is in the possession of or registered in the name of a financial intermediary or in an uncertificated security registered in the name of a financial intermediary may

be reached by a creditor by legal process upon the financial intermediary on whose books the interest of the debtor appears.

(5) Unless otherwise provided by law, a creditor's lien upon the interest of a debtor in a security obtained pursuant to subsection (3) or (4) is not a restraint on the transfer of the security, free of the lien, to a third party for new value; but in the event of a transfer, the lien applies to the proceeds of the transfer in the hands of the secured party or financial intermediary, subject to any claims having priority.

(6) A creditor whose debtor is the owner of a security is entitled to aid from courts of appropriate jurisdiction, by injunction or otherwise, in reaching the security or in satisfying the claim by means allowed at law or in equity in regard to property that cannot readily be reached by ordinary legal process.

Amended in 1977.

§ 8—318. No Conversion by Good Faith Conduct

An agent or bailee who in good faith (including observance of reasonable commercial standards if he is in the business of buying, selling, or otherwise dealing with securities) has received certificated securities and sold, pledged, or delivered them or has sold or caused the transfer or pledge of uncertificated securities over which he had control according to the instructions of his principal, is not liable for conversion or for participation in breach of fiduciary duty although the principal had no right so to deal with the securities.

Amended in 1977.

§ 8—319. Statute of Frauds

A contract for the sale of securities is not enforceable by way of action or defense unless:

(a) there is some writing signed by the party against whom enforcement is sought or by his authorized agent or broker, sufficient to indicate that a contract has been made for sale of a stated quantity of described securities at a defined or stated price;

(b) delivery of a certificated security or transfer instruction has been accepted, or transfer of an uncertificated security has been registered and the transferee has failed to send written objection to the issuer within 10 days after receipt of the initial transaction statement confirming the registration, or payment has been made, but the contract is enforceable under this provision only to the extent of the delivery, registration, or payment;

(c) within a reasonable time a writing in confirmation of the sale or purchase and sufficient against the sender under paragraph (a) has been received by the party against whom enforcement is sought and he has failed to send written objection to its contents within 10 days after its receipt; or

(d) the party against whom enforcement is sought admits in his pleading, testimony, or otherwise in court that a contract was made for the sale of a stated quantity of described securities at a defined or stated price.

Amended in 1977.

§ 8—320. Transfer or Pledge Within Central Depository System

(1) In addition to other methods, a transfer, pledge, or release of a security or any interest therein may be effected by the making of appropriate entries on the books of a clearing corporation reducing the account of the transferor, pledgor, or pledgee and increasing the account of the transferee, pledgee, or pledgor by the amount of the obligation or the number of shares or rights transferred, pledged, or released, if the security is shown on the account of a transferor, pledgor, or pledgee on the books of the clearing corporation; is subject to the control of the clearing corporation; and

(a) if certificated,

(i) is in the custody of the clearing corporation, another clearing corporation, a custodian bank, or a nominee of any of them; and

(ii) is in bearer form or indorsed in blank by an appropriate person or registered in the name of the clearing corporation, a custodian bank, or a nominee of any of them; or

(b) if uncertificated, is registered in the name of the clearing corporation, another clearing corporation, a custodian bank, or a nominee of any of them.

(2) Under this section entries may be made with respect to like securities or interests therein as a part of a fungible bulk and may refer merely to a quantity of a particular security without reference to the name of the registered owner, certificate or bond number, or the like, and, in appropriate cases, may be on a net basis taking into account other transfers, pledges, or releases of the same security.

(3) A transfer under this section is effective (Section 8—313) and the purchaser acquires the rights of the transferor (Section 8—301). A pledge or release under this section is the transfer of a limited interest. If a pledge or the creation of a security interest is intended, the security interest is perfected at the time when both value is given by the pledgee and the appropriate entries are made (Section 8—321). A transferee or pledgee under this section may be a bona fide purchaser (Section 8—302).

(4) A transfer or pledge under this section is not a registration of transfer under Part 4.

(5) That entries made on the books of the clearing corporation as provided in subsection (1) are not appropriate does not affect the validity or effect of the entries or the liabilities or obligations of the clearing corporation to any person adversely affected thereby.

Added in 1962; amended in 1977.

§ 8—321. Enforceability, Attachment, Perfection and Termination of Security Interests

(1) A security interest in a security is enforceable and can attach only if it is transferred to the secured party or a person designated by him pursuant to a provision of Section 8—313(1).

(2) A security interest so transferred pursuant to agreement by a transferor who has rights in the security to a transferee who has given value is a perfected security interest, but a security interest that has been transferred solely under paragraph (i) of Section 8—313(1) becomes unperfected after 21 days unless, within that time, the requirements for transfer under any other provision of Section 8—313(1) are satisfied.

(3) A security interest in a security is subject to the provisions of Article 9, but:

(a) no filing is required to perfect the security interest; and

(b) no written security agreement signed by the debtor is necessary to make the security interest enforceable, except as provided in paragraph (h), (i), or (j) of Section 8—313(1). The secured party has the rights and duties provided under Section 9—207, to the extent they are applicable, whether or not the security is certificated, and, if certificated, whether or not it is in his possession.

(4) Unless otherwise agreed, a security interest in a security is terminated by transfer to the debtor or a person designated by him pursuant to a provision of Section 8—313(1). If a security is thus transferred, the security interest, if not terminated, becomes unperfected unless the security is certificated and is delivered to the debtor for the purpose of ultimate sale or exchange or presentation, collection, renewal, or registration of transfer. In that case, the security interest becomes unperfected after 21 days unless, within that time, the security (or securities for which it has been exchanged) is transferred to the secured party or a person designated by him pursuant to a provision of Section 8—313(1).

Added in 1977.

Part 4 Registration

§ 8—401. Duty of Issuer to Register Transfer, Pledge, or Release

(1) If a certificated security in registered form is presented to the issuer with a request to register transfer or an instruction is presented to the issuer with a request to register transfer, pledge, or release, the issuer shall register the transfer, pledge, or release as requested if:

(a) the security is indorsed or the instruction was originated by the appropriate person or persons (Section 8—308);

(b) reasonable assurance is given that those indorsements or instructions are genuine and effective (Section 8—402);

(c) the issuer has no duty as to adverse claims or has discharged the duty (Section 8—403);

(d) any applicable law relating to the collection of taxes has been complied with; and

(e) the transfer, pledge, or release is in fact rightful or is to a bona fide purchaser.

(2) If an issuer is under a duty to register a transfer, pledge, or release of a security, the issuer is also liable to the person presenting a certificated security or an instruction for registration or his principal for loss resulting from any unreasonable delay in registration or from failure or refusal to register the transfer, pledge, or release.

Amended in 1977.

§ 8—402. Assurance that Indorsements and Instructions Are Effective

(1) The issuer may require the following assurance that each necessary indorsement of a certificated security or each instruction (Section 8—308) is genuine and effective:

(a) in all cases, a guarantee of the signature (Section 8—312(1) or (2)) of the person indorsing a certificated security or originating an instruction including, in the case of an instruction, a warranty of the taxpayer identification number or, in the absence thereof, other reasonable assurance of identity;

(b) if the indorsement is made or the instruction is originated by an agent, appropriate assurance of authority to sign;

(c) if the indorsement is made or the instruction is originated by a fiduciary, appropriate evidence of appointment or incumbency;

(d) if there is more than one fiduciary, reasonable assurance that all who are required to sign have done so; and

(e) if the indorsement is made or the instruction is originated by a person not covered by any of the foregoing, assurance appropriate to the case corresponding as nearly as may be to the foregoing.

(2) A "guarantee of the signature" in subsection (1) means a guarantee signed by or on behalf of a person

reasonably believed by the issuer to be responsible. The issuer may adopt standards with respect to responsibility if they are not manifestly unreasonable.

(3) "Appropriate evidence of appointment or incumbency" in subsection (1) means:

(a) in the case of a fiduciary appointed or qualified by a court, a certificate issued by or under the direction or supervision of that court or an officer thereof and dated within 60 days before the date of presentation for transfer, pledge, or release; or

(b) in any other case, a copy of a document showing the appointment or a certificate issued by or on behalf of a person reasonably believed by the issuer to be responsible or, in the absence of that document or certificate, other evidence reasonably deemed by the issuer to be appropriate. The issuer may adopt standards with respect to the evidence if they are not manifestly unreasonable. The issuer is not charged with notice of the contents of any document obtained pursuant to this paragraph (b) except to the extent that the contents relate directly to the appointment or incumbency.

(4) The issuer may elect to require reasonable assurance beyond that specified in this section, but if it does so and, for a purpose other than that specified in subsection (3)(b), both requires and obtains a copy of a will, trust, indenture, articles of co-partnership, by-laws, or other controlling instrument, it is charged with notice of all matters contained therein affecting the transfer, pledge, or release.

Amended in 1977.

§ 8—403. Issuer's Duty as to Adverse Claims

(1) An issuer to whom a certificated security is presented for registration shall inquire into adverse claims if:

(a) a written notification of an adverse claim is received at a time and in a manner affording the issuer a reasonable opportunity to act on it prior to the issuance of a new, reissued, or re-registered certificated security, and the notification identifies the claimant, the registered owner, and the issue of which the security is a part, and provides an address for communications directed to the claimant; or

(b) the issuer is charged with notice of an adverse claim from a controlling instrument it has elected to require under Section 8—402(4).

(2) The issuer may discharge any duty of inquiry by any reasonable means, including notifying an adverse claimant by registered or certified mail at the address furnished by him or, if there be no such address, at his residence or regular place of business that the certificated security has been presented for registration of transfer by a named person, and that the transfer will be registered unless within 30 days from the date of mailing the notification, either:

(a) an appropriate restraining order, injunction, or other process issues from a court of competent jurisdiction; or

(b) there is filed with the issuer an indemnity bond, sufficient in the issuer's judgment to protect the issuer and any transfer agent, registrar, or other agent of the issuer involved from any loss it or they may suffer by complying with the adverse claim.

(3) Unless an issuer is charged with notice of an adverse claim from a controlling instrument which it has elected to require under Section 8—402(4) or receives notification of an adverse claim under subsection (1), if a certificated security presented for registration is indorsed by the appropriate person or persons the issuer is under no duty to inquire into adverse claims. In particular:

(a) an issuer registering a certificated security in the name of a person who is a fiduciary or who is described as a fiduciary is not bound to inquire into the existence, extent, or correct description of the fiduciary relationship; and thereafter the issuer may assume without inquiry that the newly registered owner continues to be the fiduciary until the issuer receives written notice that the fiduciary is no longer acting as such with respect to the particular security;

(b) an issuer registering transfer on an indorsement by a fiduciary is not bound to inquire whether the transfer is made in compliance with a controlling instrument or with the law of the state having jurisdiction of the fiduciary relationship, including any law requiring the fiduciary to obtain court approval of the transfer; and

(c) the issuer is not charged with notice of the contents of any court record or file or other recorded or unrecorded document even though the document is in its possession and even though the transfer is made on the indorsement of a fiduciary to the fiduciary himself or to his nominee.

(4) An issuer is under no duty as to adverse claims with respect to an uncertificated security except:

(a) claims embodied in a restraining order, injunction, or other legal process served upon the issuer if the process was served at a time and in a manner affording the issuer a reasonable opportunity to act on it in accordance with the requirements of subsection (5);

(b) claims of which the issuer has received a written notification from the registered owner or the registered pledgee if the notification was received at a time and in a manner affording the issuer a reasonable opportunity to act on it in accordance with the requirements of subsection (5);

(c) claims (including restrictions on transfer not imposed by the issuer) to which the registration of transfer to the present registered owner was subject and were so noted in the initial transaction statement sent to him; and

(d) claims as to which an issuer is charged with notice from a controlling instrument it has elected to require under Section 8—402(4).

(5) If the issuer of an uncertificated security is under a duty as to an adverse claim, he discharges that duty by:

(a) including a notation of the claim in any statements sent with respect to the security under Sections 8—408(3), (6), and (7); and

(b) refusing to register the transfer or pledge of the security unless the nature of the claim does not preclude transfer or pledge subject thereto.

(6) If the transfer or pledge of the security is registered subject to an adverse claim, a notation of the claim must be included in the initial transaction statement and all subsequent statements sent to the transferee and pledgee under Section 8—408.

(7) Notwithstanding subsections (4) and (5), if an uncertificated security was subject to a registered pledge at the time the issuer first came under a duty as to a particular adverse claim, the issuer has no duty as to that claim if transfer of the security is requested by the registered pledgee or an appropriate person acting for the registered pledgee unless:

(a) the claim was embodied in legal process which expressly provides otherwise;

(b) the claim was asserted in a written notification from the registered pledgee;

(c) the claim was one as to which the issuer was charged with notice from a controlling instrument it required under Section 8—402(4) in connection with the pledgee's request for transfer; or

(d) the transfer requested is to the registered owner.

Amended in 1977.

§ 8—404. Liability and Non-Liability for Registration

(1) Except as provided in any law relating to the collection of taxes, the issuer is not liable to the owner, pledgee, or any other person suffering loss as a result of the registration of a transfer, pledge, or release of a security if:

(a) there were on or with a certificated security the necessary indorsements or the issuer had received an instruction originated by an appropriate person (Section 8—308); and

(b) the issuer had no duty as to adverse claims or has discharged the duty (Section 8—403).

(2) If an issuer has registered a transfer of a certificated security to a person not entitled to it, the issuer on demand shall deliver a like security to the true owner unless:

(a) the registration was pursuant to subsection (1);

(b) the owner is precluded from asserting any claim for registering the transfer under Section 8—405(1); or

(c) the delivery would result in overissue, in which case the issuer's liability is governed by Section 8—104.

(3) If an issuer has improperly registered a transfer, pledge, or release of an uncertificated security, the issuer on demand from the injured party shall restore the records as to the injured party to the condition that would have obtained if the improper registration had not been made unless:

(a) the registration was pursuant to subsection (1); or

(b) the registration would result in overissue, in which case the issuer's liability is governed by Section 8—104.

Amended in 1977.

§ 8—405. Lost, Destroyed, and Stolen Certificated Securities

(1) If a certificated security has been lost, apparently destroyed, or wrongfully taken, and the owner fails to notify the issuer of that fact within a reasonable time after he has notice of it and the issuer registers a transfer of the security before receiving notification, the owner is precluded from asserting against the issuer any claim for registering the transfer under Section 8—404 or any claim to a new security under this section.

(2) If the owner of a certificated security claims that the security has been lost, destroyed, or wrongfully taken, the issuer shall issue a new certificated security or, at the option of the issuer, an equivalent uncertificated security in place of the original security if the owner:

(a) so requests before the issuer has notice that the security has been acquired by a bona fide purchaser;

(b) files with the issuer a sufficient indemnity bond; and

(c) satisfies any other reasonable requirements imposed by the issuer.

(3) If, after the issue of a new certificated or uncertificated security, a bona fide purchaser of the original cer-

tificated security presents it for registration of transfer, the issuer shall register the transfer unless registration would result in overissue, in which event the issuer's liability is governed by Section 8—104. In addition to any rights on the indemnity bond, the issuer may recover the new certificated security from the person to whom it was issued or any person taking under him except a bona fide purchaser or may cancel the uncertificated security unless a bona fide purchaser or any person taking under a bona fide purchaser is then the registered owner or registered pledgee thereof.

Amended in 1977.

§ 8—406. Duty of Authenticating Trustee, Transfer Agent, or Registrar

(1) If a person acts as authenticating trustee, transfer agent, registrar, or other agent for an issuer in the registration of transfers of its certificated securities or in the registration of transfers, pledges, and releases of its uncertificated securities, in the issue of new securities, or in the cancellation of surrendered securities:

>(a) he is under a duty to the issuer to exercise good faith and due diligence in performing his functions; and

>(b) with regard to the particular functions he performs, he has the same obligation to the holder or owner of a certificated security or to the owner or pledgee of an uncertificated security and has the same rights and privileges as the issuer has in regard to those functions.

(2) Notice to an authenticating trustee, transfer agent, registrar or other agent is notice to the issuer with respect to the functions performed by the agent.

Amended in 1977.

§ 8—407. Exchangeability of Securities

(1) No issuer is subject to the requirements of this section unless it regularly maintains a system for issuing the class of securities involved under which both certificated and uncertificated securities are regularly issued to the category of owners, which includes the person in whose name the new security is to be registered.

(2) Upon surrender of a certificated security with all necessary indorsements and presentation of a written request by the person surrendering the security, the issuer, if he has no duty as to adverse claims or has discharged the duty (Section 8—403), shall issue to the person or a person designated by him an equivalent uncertificated security subject to all liens, restrictions, and claims that were noted on the certificated security.

(3) Upon receipt of a transfer instruction originated by an appropriate person who so requests, the issuer of an uncertificated security shall cancel the uncertificated security and issue an equivalent certificated security on which must be noted conspicuously any liens and restrictions of the issuer and any adverse claims (as to which the issuer has a duty under Section 8—403(4)) to which the uncertificated security was subject. The certificated security shall be registered in the name of and delivered to:

>(a) the registered owner, if the uncertificated security was not subject to a registered pledge; or

>(b) the registered pledgee, if the uncertificated security was subject to a registered pledge.

Added in 1977.

§ 8—408. Statements of Uncertificated Securities

(1) Within 2 business days after the transfer of an uncertificated security has been registered, the issuer shall send to the new registered owner and, if the security has been transferred subject to a registered pledge, to the registered pledgee a written statement containing:

>(a) a description of the issue of which the uncertificated security is a part;

>(b) the number of shares or units transferred;

>(c) the name and address and any taxpayer identification number of the new registered owner and, if the security has been transferred subject to a registered pledge, the name and address and any taxpayer identification number of the registered pledgee;

>(d) a notation of any liens and restrictions of the issuer and any adverse claims (as to which the issuer has a duty under Section 8—403(4)) to which the uncertificated security is or may be subject at the time of registration or a statement that there are none of those liens, restrictions, or adverse claims; and

>(e) the date the transfer was registered.

(2) Within 2 business days after the pledge of an uncertificated security has been registered, the issuer shall send to the registered owner and the registered pledgee a written statement containing:

>(a) a description of the issue of which the uncertificated security is a part;

>(b) the number of shares or units pledged;

>(c) the name and address and any taxpayer identification number of the registered owner and the registered pledgee;

>(d) a notation of any liens and restrictions of the issuer and any adverse claims (as to which the issuer has a duty under Section 8—403(4)) to which the uncertificated security is or may be subject at the time of registration or a statement that there are

none of those liens, restrictions, or adverse claims; and

(e) the date the pledge was registered.

(3) Within 2 business days after the release from pledge of an uncertificated security has been registered, the issuer shall send to the registered owner and the pledgee whose interest was released a written statement containing:

(a) a description of the issue of which the uncertificated security is a part;

(b) the number of shares or units released from pledge;

(c) the name and address and any taxpayer identification number of the registered owner and the pledgee whose interest was released;

(d) a notation of any liens and restrictions of the issuer and any adverse claims (as to which the issuer has a duty under Section 8—403(4)) to which the uncertificated security is or may be subject at the time of registration or a statement that there are none of those liens, restrictions, or adverse claims; and

(e) the date the release was registered.

(4) An "initial transaction statement" is the statement sent to:

(a) the new registered owner and, if applicable, to the registered pledgee pursuant to subsection (1);

(b) the registered pledgee pursuant to subsection (2); or

(c) the registered owner pursuant to subsection (3).

Each initial transaction statement shall be signed by or on behalf of the issuer and must be identified as "Initial Transaction Statement".

(5) Within 2 business days after the transfer of an uncertificated security has been registered, the issuer shall send to the former registered owner and the former registered pledgee, if any, a written statement containing:

(a) a description of the issue of which the uncertificated security is a part;

(b) the number of shares or units transferred;

(c) the name and address and any taxpayer identification number of the former registered owner and of any former registered pledgee; and

(d) the date the transfer was registered.

(6) At periodic intervals no less frequent than annually and at any time upon the reasonable written request of the registered owner, the issuer shall send to the registered owner of each uncertificated security a dated written statement containing:

(a) a description of the issue of which the uncertificated security is a part;

(b) the name and address and any taxpayer identification number of the registered owner;

(c) the number of shares or units of the uncertificated security registered in the name of the registered owner on the date of the statement;

(d) the name and address and any taxpayer identification number of any registered pledgee and the number of shares or units subject to the pledge; and

(e) a notation of any liens and restrictions of the issuer and any adverse claims (as to which the issuer has a duty under Section 8—403(4)) to which the uncertificated security is or may be subject or a statement that there are none of those liens, restrictions, or adverse claims.

(7) At periodic intervals no less frequent than annually and at any time upon the reasonable written request of the registered pledgee, the issuer shall send to the registered pledgee of each uncertificated security a dated written statement containing:

(a) a description of the issue of which the uncertificated security is a part;

(b) the name and address and any taxpayer identification number of the registered owner;

(c) the name and address and any taxpayer identification number of the registered pledgee;

(d) the number of shares or units subject to the pledge; and

(e) a notation of any liens and restrictions of the issuer and any adverse claims (as to which the issuer has a duty under Section 8—403(4)) to which the uncertificated security is or may be subject or a statement that there are none of those liens, restrictions, or adverse claims.

(8) If the issuer sends the statements described in subsections (6) and (7) at periodic intervals no less frequent than quarterly, the issuer is not obliged to send additional statements upon request unless the owner or pledgee requesting them pays to the issuer the reasonable cost of furnishing them.

(9) Each statement sent pursuant to this section must bear a conspicuous legend reading substantially as follows: "This statement is merely a record of the rights of the addressee as of the time of its issuance. Delivery of this statement, of itself, confers no rights on the recipient. This statement is neither a negotiable instrument nor a security."

Added in 1977.

Article 9
SECURED TRANSACTIONS; SALES OF ACCOUNTS AND CHATTEL PAPER

Note: *The adoption of this Article should be accompanied by the repeal of existing statutes dealing with conditional sales, trust receipts, factor's liens where the factor is given a non-possessory lien, chattel mortgages, crop mortgages, mortgages on railroad equipment, assignment of accounts and generally statutes regulating security interests in personal property.*

Where the state has a retail installment selling act or small loan act, that legislation should be carefully examined to determine what changes in those acts are needed to conform them to this Article. This Article primarily sets out rules defining rights of a secured party against persons dealing with the debtor; it does not prescribe regulations and controls which may be necessary to curb abuses arising in the small loan business or in the financing of consumer purchases on credit. Accordingly there is no intention to repeal existing regulatory acts in those fields by enactment or re-enactment of Article 9. See Section 9—203(4) and the Note thereto.

Part 1 Short Title, Applicability and Definitions

§ 9—101. **Short Title.**

This Article shall be known and may be cited as Uniform Commercial Code—Secured Transactions.

§ 9—102. **Policy and Subject Matter of Article.**

(1) Except as otherwise provided in Section 9—104 on excluded transactions, this Article applies

  (a) to any transaction (regardless of its form) which is intended to create a security interest in personal property or fixtures including goods, documents, instruments, general intangibles, chattel paper or accounts; and also

  (b) to any sale of accounts or chattel paper.

(2) This Article applies to security interests created by contract including pledge, assignment, chattel mortgage, chattel trust, trust deed, factor's lien, equipment trust, conditional sale, trust receipt, other lien or title retention contract and lease or consignment intended as security. This Article does not apply to statutory liens except as provided in Section 9—310.

(3) The application of this Article to a security interest in a secured obligation is not affected by the fact that the obligation is itself secured by a transaction or interest to which this Article does not apply.

§ 9—103. **Perfection of Security Interest in Multiple State Transactions**

(1) Documents, instruments and ordinary goods.

  (a) This subsection applies to documents and instruments and to goods other than those covered by a certificate of title described in subsection (2), mobile goods described in subsection (3), and minerals described in subsection (5).

  (b) Except as otherwise provided in this subsection, perfection and the effect of perfection or non-perfection of a security interest in collateral are governed by the law of the jurisdiction where the collateral is when the last event occurs on which is based the assertion that the security interest is perfected or unperfected.

  (c) If the parties to a transaction creating a purchase money security interest in goods in one jurisdiction understand at the time that the security interest attaches that the goods will be kept in another jurisdiction, then the law of the other jurisdiction governs the perfection and the effect of perfection or non-perfection of the security interest from the time it attaches until thirty days after the debtor receives possession of the goods and thereafter if the goods are taken to the other jurisdiction before the end of the thirty-day period.

  (d) When collateral is brought into and kept in this state while subject to a security interest perfected under the law of the jurisdiction from which the collateral was removed, the security interest remains perfected, but if action is required by Part 3 of this Article to perfect the security interest,

   (i) if the action is not taken before the expiration of the period of perfection in the other jurisdiction or the end of four months after the collateral is brought into this state, whichever period first expires, the security interest becomes unperfected at the end of that period and is thereafter deemed to have been unperfected as against a person who became a purchaser after removal;

   (ii) if the action is taken before the expiration of the period specified in subparagraph (i), the security interest continues perfected thereafter;

   (iii) for the purpose of priority over a buyer of consumer goods (subsection (2) of Section 9—307), the period of the effectiveness of a filing in the jurisdiction from which the collateral is removed is governed by the rules with respect to perfection in subparagraphs (i) and (ii).

(2) Certificate of title.

  (a) This subsection applies to goods covered by a certificate of title issued under a statute of this state or of another jurisdiction under the law of which indication of a security interest on the certificate is required as a condition of perfection.

  (b) Except as otherwise provided in this subsection, perfection and the effect of perfection or non-perfection of the security interest are governed by the law (including the conflict of laws rules) of the jurisdiction issuing the certificate until four months after the goods are removed from that jurisdiction and thereafter until the goods are registered in another jurisdiction, but in any event not beyond surrender of the certificate. After the expiration of that period, the goods are not covered by the certificate of title within the meaning of this section.

(c) Except with respect to the rights of a buyer described in the next paragraph, a security interest, perfected in another jurisdiction otherwise than by notation on a certificate of title, in goods brought into this state and thereafter covered by a certificate of title issued by this state is subject to the rules stated in paragraph (d) of subsection (1).

(d) If goods are brought into this state while a security interest therein is perfected in any manner under the law of the jurisdiction from which the goods are removed and a certificate of title is issued by this state and the certificate does not show that the goods are subject to the security interest or that they may be subject to security interests not shown on the certificate, the security interest is subordinate to the rights of a buyer of the goods who is not in the business of selling goods of that kind to the extent that he gives value and receives delivery of the goods after issuance of the certificate and without knowledge of the security interest.

(3) Accounts, general intangibles and mobile goods.

(a) This subsection applies to accounts (other than an account described in subsection (5) on minerals) and general intangibles (other than uncertificated securities) and to goods which are mobile and which are of a type normally used in more than one jurisdiction, such as motor vehicles, trailers, rolling stock, airplanes, shipping containers, road building and construction machinery and commercial harvesting machinery and the like, if the goods are equipment or are inventory leased or held for lease by the debtor to others, and are not covered by a certificate of title described in subsection (2).

(b) The law (including the conflict of laws rules) of the jurisdiction in which the debtor is located governs the perfection and the effect of perfection or non-perfection of the security interest.

(c) If, however, the debtor is located in a jurisdiction which is not a part of the United States, and which does not provide for perfection of the security interest by filing or recording in that jurisdiction, the law of the jurisdiction in the United States in which the debtor has its major executive office in the United States governs the perfection and the effect of perfection or non-perfection of the security interest through filing. In the alternative, if the debtor is located in a jurisdiction which is not a part of the United States or Canada and the collateral is accounts or general intangibles for money due or to become due, the security interest may be perfected by notification to the account debtor. As used in this paragraph, "United States" includes its territories and possessions and the Commonwealth of Puerto Rico.

(d) A debtor shall be deemed located at his place of business if he has one, at his chief executive office if he has more than one place of business, otherwise at his residence. If, however, the debtor is a foreign air carrier under the Federal Aviation Act of 1958, as amended, it shall be deemed located at the designated office of the agent upon whom service of process may be made on behalf of the foreign air carrier.

(e) A security interest perfected under the law of the jurisdiction of the location of the debtor is perfected until the expiration of four months after a change of the debtor's location to another jurisdiction, or until perfection would have ceased by the law of the first jurisdiction, whichever period first expires. Unless perfected in the new jurisdiction before the end of that period, it becomes unperfected thereafter and is deemed to have been unperfected as against a person who became a purchaser after the change.

(4) Chattel paper.

The rules stated for goods in subsection (1) apply to a possessory security interest in chattel paper. The rules stated for accounts in subsection (3) apply to a nonpossessory security interest in chattel paper, but the security interest may not be perfected by notification to the account debtor.

(5) Minerals.

Perfection and the effect of perfection or non-perfection of a security interest which is created by a debtor who has an interest in minerals or the like (including oil and gas) before extraction and which attaches thereto as extracted, or which attaches to an account resulting from the sale thereof at the wellhead or minehead are governed by the law (including the conflict of laws rules) of the jurisdiction wherein the wellhead or minehead is located.

(6) Uncertificated securities.

The law (including the conflict of laws rules) of the jurisdiction of organization of the issuer governs the perfection and the effect of perfection or non-perfection of a security interest in uncertificated securities.

Amended in 1972 and 1977.

§ 9—104. Transactions Excluded From Article.

This Article does not apply

(a) to a security interest subject to any statute of the United States, to the extent that such statute governs the rights of parties to and third parties affected by transactions in particular types of property; or

(b) to a landlord's lien; or

(c) to a lien given by statute or other rule of law for services or materials except as provided in Section 9—310 on priority of such liens; or

(d) to a transfer of a claim for wages, salary or other compensation of an employee; or

(e) to a transfer by a government or governmental subdivision or agency; or

(f) to a sale of accounts or chattel paper as part of a sale of the business out of which they arose, or an assignment of accounts or chattel paper which is for the purpose of collection only, or a transfer of a right to payment under a contract to an assignee who is also to do the performance under the contract or a transfer of a single account to an assignee in whole or partial satisfaction of a preexisting indebtedness; or

(g) to a transfer of an interest in or claim in or under any policy of insurance, except as provided with respect to proceeds (Section 9—306) and priorities in proceeds (Section 9—312); or

(h) to a right represented by a judgment (other than a judgment taken on a right to payment which was collateral); or

(i) to any right of set-off; or

(j) except to the extent that provision is made for fixtures in Section 9—313, to the creation or transfer of an interest in or lien on real estate, including a lease or rents thereunder; or

(k) to a transfer in whole or in part of any claim arising out of tort; or

(*l*) to a transfer of an interest in any deposit account (subsection (1) of Section 9—105), except as provided with respect to proceeds (Section 9—306) and priorities in proceeds (Section 9—312).

Amended in 1972.

§ 9—105. Definitions and Index of Definitions

(1) In this Article unless the context otherwise requires:

(a) "Account debtor" means the person who is obligated on an account, chattel paper or general intangible;

(b) "Chattel paper" means a writing or writings which evidence both a monetary obligation and a security interest in or a lease of specific goods, but a charter or other contract involving the use or hire of a vessel is not chattel paper. When a transaction is evidenced both by such a security agreement or a lease and by an instrument or a series of instruments, the group of writings taken together constitutes chattel paper;

(c) "Collateral" means the property subject to a security interest, and includes accounts and chattel paper which have been sold;

(d) "Debtor" means the person who owes payment or other performance of the obligation secured, whether or not he owns or has rights in the collateral, and includes the seller of accounts or chattel paper. Where the debtor and the owner of the collateral are not the same person, the term "debtor" means the owner of the collateral in any provision of the Article dealing with the collateral, the obligor in any provision dealing with the obligation, and may include both where the context so requires;

(e) "Deposit account" means a demand, time, savings, passbook or like account maintained with a bank, savings and loan association, credit union or like organization, other than an account evidenced by a certificate of deposit;

(f) "Document" means document of title as defined in the general definitions of Article 1 (Section 1—201), and a receipt of the kind described in subsection (2) of Section 7—201;

(g) "Encumbrance" includes real estate mortgages and other liens on real estate and all other rights in real estate that are not ownership interests;

(h) "Goods" includes all things which are movable at the time the security interest attaches or which are fixtures (Section 9—313), but does not include money, documents, instruments, accounts, chattel paper, general intangibles, or minerals or the like (including oil and gas) before extraction. "Goods" also includes standing timber which is to be cut and removed under a conveyance or contract for sale, the unborn young of animals, and growing crops;

(i) "Instrument" means a negotiable instrument (defined in Section 3—104), or a certificated security (defined in Section 8—102) or any other writing which evidences a right to the payment of money and is not itself a security agreement or lease and is of a type which is in ordinary course of business transferred by delivery with any necessary indorsement or assignment;

(j) "Mortgage" means a consensual interest created by a real estate mortgage, a trust deed on real estate, or the like;

(k) An advance is made "pursuant to commitment" if the secured party has bound himself to make it, whether or not a subsequent event of default or other event not within his control has relieved or may relieve him from his obligation;

(*l*) "Security agreement" means an agreement which creates or provides for a security interest;

(m) "Secured party" means a lender, seller or other person in whose favor there is a security interest, including a person to whom accounts or chattel paper have been sold. When the holders of obligations issued under an indenture of trust, equipment trust agreement or the like are represented by a trustee or other person, the representative is the secured party;

(n) "Transmitting utility" means any person primarily engaged in the railroad, street railway or trolley bus business, the electric or electronics communications transmission business, the transmission of goods by pipeline, or the transmission or the production and transmission of electricity, steam, gas or water, or the provision of sewer service.

(2) Other definitions applying to this Article and the sections in which they appear are:
"Account". Section 9—106.
"Attach". Section 9—203.
"Construction mortgage". Section 9—313(1).
"Consumer goods". Section 9—109(1).
"Equipment". Section 9—109(2).
"Farm products". Section 9—109(3).
"Fixture". Section 9—313(1).
"Fixture filing". Section 9—313(1).
"General intangibles". Section 9—106.
"Inventory". Section 9—109(4).
"Lien creditor". Section 9—301(3).
"Proceeds". Section 9—306(1).
"Purchase money security interest". Section 9—107.
"United States". Section 9—103.

(3) The following definitions in other Articles apply to this Article:
"Check". Section 3—104.
"Contract for sale". Section 2—106.
"Holder in due course". Section 3—302.
"Note". Section 3—104.
"Sale". Section 2—106.

(4) In addition Article 1 contains general definitions and principles of construction and interpretation applicable throughout this Article.

Amended in 1966, 1972 and 1977.

§ 9—106. Definitions: "Account"; "General Intangibles".

"Account" means any right to payment for goods sold or leased or for services rendered which is not evidenced by an instrument or chattel paper, whether or not it has been earned by performance. "General intangibles" means any personal property (including things in action) other than goods, accounts, chattel paper, documents, instruments, and money. All rights to payment earned or unearned under a charter or other contract involving the use or hire of a vessel and all rights incident to the charter or contract are accounts.

§ 9—107. Definitions: "Purchase Money Security Interest".

A security interest is a "purchase money security interest" to the extent that it is

(a) taken or retained by the seller of the collateral to secure all or part of its price; or

(b) taken by a person who by making advances or incurring an obligation gives value to enable the debtor to acquire rights in or the use of collateral if such value is in fact so used.

§ 9—108. When After-Acquired Collateral Not Security for Antecedent Debt.

Where a secured party makes an advance, incurs an obligation, releases a perfected security interest, or otherwise gives new value which is to be secured in whole or in part by after-acquired property his security interest in the after-acquired collateral shall be deemed to be taken for new value and not as security for an antecedent debt if the debtor acquires his rights in such collateral either in the ordinary course of his business or under a contract of purchase made pursuant to the security agreement within a reasonable time after new value is given.

§ 9—109. Classification of Goods; "Consumer Goods"; "Equipment"; "Farm Products"; "Inventory".

Goods are

(1) "consumer goods" if they are used or bought for use primarily for personal, family or household purposes;

(2) "equipment" if they are used or bought for use primarily in business (including farming or a profession) or by a debtor who is a non-profit organization or a governmental subdivision or agency or if the goods are not included in the definitions of inventory, farm products or consumer goods;

(3) "farm products" if they are crops or livestock or supplies used or produced in farming operations or if they are products of crops or livestock in their unmanufactured states (such as ginned cotton, wool-clip, maple syrup, milk and eggs), and if they are in the possession of a debtor engaged in raising, fattening, grazing or other farming operations. If goods are farm products they are neither equipment nor inventory;

(4) "inventory" if they are held by a person who holds them for sale or lease or to be furnished under contracts of service or if he has so furnished them, or if they are raw materials, work in process or materials used or consumed in a business. Inventory of a person is not to be classified as his equipment.

§ 9—110. Sufficiency of Description.

For purposes of this Article any description of personal property or real estate is sufficient whether or not it is specific if it reasonably identifies what is described.

§ 9—111. Applicability of Bulk Transfer Laws.

The creation of a security interest is not a bulk transfer under Article 6 (see Section 6—103).

§ 9—112. Where Collateral Is Not Owned by Debtor.

Unless otherwise agreed, when a secured party knows that collateral is owned by a person who is not the debtor, the owner of the collateral is entitled to receive from the secured party any surplus under Section 9—502(2) or under Section 9—504(1), and is not liable for the debt or for any deficiency after resale, and he has the same right as the debtor

(a) to receive statements under Section 9—208;

(b) to receive notice of and to object to a secured party's proposal to retain the collateral in satisfaction of the indebtedness under Section 9—505;

(c) to redeem the collateral under Section 9—506;

(d) to obtain injunctive or other relief under Section 9—507(1); and

(e) to recover losses caused to him under Section 9—208(2).

§ 9—113. Security Interests Arising Under Article on Sales or Under Article on Leases.

A security interest arising solely under the Article on Sales (Article 2) or the Article on Leases (Article 2A) is subject to the provisions of this Article except that to the extent that and so long as the debtor does not have or does not lawfully obtain possession of the goods

(a) no security agreement is necessary to make the security interest enforceable; and

(b) no filing is required to perfect the security interest; and

(c) the rights of the secured party on default by the debtor are governed (i) by the Article on Sales (Article 2) in the case of a security interest arising solely under such Article or (ii) by the Article on Leases (Article 2A) in the case of a security interest arising solely under such Article.

§ 9—114. Consignment.

(1) A person who delivers goods under a consignment which is not a security interest and who would be required to file under this Article by paragraph (3)(c) of Section 2—326 has priority over a secured party who is or becomes a creditor of the consignee and who would have a perfected security interest in the goods if they were the property of the consignee, and also has priority with respect to identifiable cash proceeds received on or before delivery of the goods to a buyer, if

(a) the consignor complies with the filing provision of the Article on Sales with respect to consignments (paragraph (3)(c) of Section 2—326) before the consignee receives possession of the goods; and

(b) the consignor gives notification in writing to the holder of the security interest if the holder has filed a financing statement covering the same types of goods before the date of the filing made by the consignor; and

(c) the holder of the security interest receives the notification within five years before the consignee receives possession of the goods; and

(d) the notification states that the consignor expects to deliver goods on consignment to the consignee, describing the goods by item or type.

(2) In the case of a consignment which is not a security interest and in which the requirements of the preceding subsection have not been met, a person who delivers goods to another is subordinate to a person who would have a perfected security interest in the goods if they were the property of the debtor.

Part 2 Validity of Security Agreement and Rights of Parties Thereto

§ 9—201. General Validity of Security Agreement.

Except as otherwise provided by this Act a security agreement is effective according to its terms between the parties, against purchasers of the collateral and against creditors. Nothing in this Article validates any charge or practice illegal under any statute or regulation thereunder governing usury, small loans, retail installment sales, or the like, or extends the application of any such statute or regulation to any transaction not otherwise subject thereto.

§ 9—202. Title to Collateral Immaterial.

Each provision of this Article with regard to rights, obligations and remedies applies whether title to collateral is in the secured party or in the debtor.

§ 9—203. Attachment and Enforceability of Security Interest; Proceeds; Formal Requisites

(1) Subject to the provisions of Section 4—208 on the security interest of a collecting bank, Section 8—321 on

security interests in securities and Section 9—113 on a security interest arising under the Article on Sales, a security interest is not enforceable against the debtor or third parties with respect to the collateral and does not attach unless:

(a) the collateral is in the possession of the secured party pursuant to agreement, or the debtor has signed a security agreement which contains a description of the collateral and in addition, when the security interest covers crops growing or to be grown or timber to be cut, a description of the land concerned;

(b) value has been given; and

(c) the debtor has rights in the collateral.

(2) A security interest attaches when it becomes enforceable against the debtor with respect to the collateral. Attachment occurs as soon as all of the events specified in subsection (1) have taken place unless explicit agreement postpones the time of attaching.

(3) Unless otherwise agreed a security agreement gives the secured party the rights to proceeds provided by Section 9—306.

(4) A transaction, although subject to this Article, is also subject to ....*, and in the case of conflict between the provisions of this Article and any such statute, the provisions of such statute control. Failure to comply with any applicable statute has only the effect which is specified therein.

Amended in 1972 and 1977.

Note: At * in subsection (4) insert reference to any local statute regulating small loans, retail installment sales and the like.

The foregoing subsection (4) is designed to make it clear that certain transactions, although subject to this Article, must also comply with other applicable legislation.

This Article is designed to regulate all the "security" aspects of transactions within its scope. There is, however, much regulatory legislation, particularly in the consumer field, which supplements this Article and should not be repealed by its enactment. Examples are small loan acts, retail installment selling acts and the like. Such acts may provide for licensing and rate regulation and may prescribe particular forms of contract. Such provisions should remain in force despite the enactment of this Article. On the other hand if a retail installment selling act contains provisions on filing, rights on default, etc., such provisions should be repealed as inconsistent with this Article except that inconsistent provisions as to deficiencies, penalties, etc., in the Uniform Consumer Credit Code and other recent related legislation should remain because those statutes were drafted after the substantial enactment of the Article and with the intention of modifying certain provisions of this Article as to consumer credit.

§ 9—204. **After-Acquired Property; Future Advances.**

(1) Except as provided in subsection (2), a security agreement may provide that any or all obligations covered by the security agreement are to be secured by after-acquired collateral.

(2) No security interest attaches under an after-acquired property clause to consumer goods other than accessions (Section 9—314) when given as additional security unless the debtor acquires rights in them within ten days after the secured party gives value.

(3) Obligations covered by a security agreement may include future advances or other value whether or not the advances or value are given pursuant to commitment (subsection (1) of Section 9—105).

§ 9—205. **Use or Disposition of Collateral Without Accounting Permissible.**

A security interest is not invalid or fraudulent against creditors by reason of liberty in the debtor to use, commingle or dispose of all or part of the collateral (including returned or repossessed goods) or to collect or compromise accounts or chattel paper, or to accept the return of goods or make repossessions, or to use, commingle or dispose of proceeds, or by reason of the failure of the secured party to require the debtor to account for proceeds or replace collateral. This section does not relax the requirements of possession where perfection of a security interest depends upon possession of the collateral by the secured party or by a bailee.

§ 9—206. **Agreement Not to Assert Defenses Against Assignee; Modification of Sales Warranties Where Security Agreement Exists.**

(1) Subject to any statute or decision which establishes a different rule for buyers or lessees of consumer goods, an agreement by a buyer or lessee that he will not assert against an assignee any claim or defense which he may have against the seller or lessor is enforceable by an assignee who takes his assignment for value, in good faith and without notice of a claim or defense, except as to defenses of a type which may be asserted against a holder in due course of a negotiable instrument under the Article on Commercial Paper (Article 3). A buyer who as part of one transaction signs both a negotiable instrument and a security agreement makes such an agreement.

(2) When a seller retains a purchase money security interest in goods the Article on Sales (Article 2) governs the sale and any disclaimer, limitation or modification of the seller's warranties.

§ 9—207. **Rights and Duties When Collateral is in Secured Party's Possession.**

(1) A secured party must use reasonable care in the custody and preservation of collateral in his possession. In the case of an instrument or chattel paper reasonable care includes taking necessary steps to preserve rights against prior parties unless otherwise agreed.

(2) Unless otherwise agreed, when collateral is in the secured party's possession

(a) reasonable expenses (including the cost of any insurance and payment of taxes or other charges) incurred in the custody, preservation, use or operation of the collateral are chargeable to the debtor and are secured by the collateral;

(b) the risk of accidental loss or damage is on the debtor to the extent of any deficiency in any effective insurance coverage;

(c) the secured party may hold as additional security any increase or profits (except money) received from the collateral, but money so received, unless remitted to the debtor, shall be applied in reduction of the secured obligation;

(d) the secured party must keep the collateral identifiable but fungible collateral may be commingled;

(e) the secured party may repledge the collateral upon terms which do not impair the debtor's right to redeem it.

(3) A secured party is liable for any loss caused by his failure to meet any obligation imposed by the preceding subsections but does not lose his security interest.

(4) A secured party may use or operate the collateral for the purpose of preserving the collateral or its value or pursuant to the order of a court of appropriate jurisdiction or, except in the case of consumer goods, in the manner and to the extent provided in the security agreement.

§ 9—208. **Request for Statement of Account or List of Collateral.**

(1) A debtor may sign a statement indicating what he believes to be the aggregate amount of unpaid indebtedness as of a specified date and may send it to the secured party with a request that the statement be approved or corrected and returned to the debtor. When the security agreement or any other record kept by the secured party identifies the collateral a debtor may similarly request the secured party to approve or correct a list of the collateral.

(2) The secured party must comply with such a request within two weeks after receipt by sending a written correction or approval. If the secured party claims a security interest in all of a particular type of collateral owned by the debtor he may indicate that fact in his reply and need not approve or correct an itemized list of such collateral. If the secured party without reasonable excuse fails to comply he is liable for any loss caused to the debtor thereby; and if the debtor has properly included in his request a good faith statement of the obligation or a list of the collateral or both the secured party may claim a security interest only as shown in the statement against persons misled by his failure to comply. If he no longer has an interest in the obligation or collateral at the time the request is received he must disclose the name and address of any successor in interest known to him and he is liable for any loss caused to the debtor as a result of failure to disclose. A successor in interest is not subject to this section until a request is received by him.

(3) A debtor is entitled to such a statement once every six months without charge. The secured party may require payment of a charge not exceeding $10 for each additional statement furnished.

Part 3 Rights of Third Parties; Perfected and Unperfected Security Interests; Rules of Priority

§ 9—301. **Persons Who Take Priority Over Unperfected Security Interests; Rights of "Lien Creditor".**

(1) Except as otherwise provided in subsection (2), an unperfected security interest is subordinate to the rights of

(a) persons entitled to priority under Section 9—312;

(b) a person who becomes a lien creditor before the security interest is perfected;

(c) in the case of goods, instruments, documents, and chattel paper, a person who is not a secured party and who is a transferee in bulk or other buyer not in ordinary course of business or is a buyer of farm products in ordinary course of business, to the extent that he gives value and receives delivery of the collateral without knowledge of the security interest and before it is perfected;

(d) in the case of accounts and general intangibles, a person who is not a secured party and who is a transferee to the extent that he gives value without knowledge of the security interest and before it is perfected.

(2) If the secured party files with respect to a purchase money security interest before or within ten days after the debtor receives possession of the collateral, he takes priority over the rights of a transferee in bulk or of a lien creditor which arise between the time the security interest attaches and the time of filing.

(3) A "lien creditor" means a creditor who has acquired a lien on the property involved by attachment, levy or the like and includes an assignee for benefit of creditors from the time of assignment, and a trustee in bankruptcy from the date of the filing of the petition or a receiver in equity from the time of appointment.

(4) A person who becomes a lien creditor while a security interest is perfected takes subject to the security interest only to the extent that it secures advances made

before he becomes a lien creditor or within 45 days thereafter or made without knowledge of the lien or pursuant to a commitment entered into without knowledge of the lien.

§ 9—302. When Filing Is Required to Perfect Security Interest; Security Interests to Which Filing Provisions of This Article Do Not Apply

(1) A financing statement must be filed to perfect all security interests except the following:

(a) a security interest in collateral in possession of the secured party under Section 9—305;

(b) a security interest temporarily perfected in instruments or documents without delivery under Section 9—304 or in proceeds for a 10 day period under Section 9—306;

(c) a security interest created by an assignment of a beneficial interest in a trust or a decedent's estate;

(d) a purchase money security interest in consumer goods; but filing is required for a motor vehicle required to be registered; and fixture filing is required for priority over conflicting interests in fixtures to the extent provided in Section 9—313;

(e) an assignment of accounts which does not alone or in conjunction with other assignments to the same assignee transfer a significant part of the outstanding accounts of the assignor;

(f) a security interest of a collecting bank (Section 4—208) or in securities (Section 8—321) or arising under the Article on Sales (see Section 9—113) or covered in subsection (3) of this section;

(g) an assignment for the benefit of all the creditors of the transferor, and subsequent transfers by the assignee thereunder.

(2) If a secured party assigns a perfected security interest, no filing under this Article is required in order to continue the perfected status of the security interest against creditors of and transferees from the original debtor.

(3) The filing of a financing statement otherwise required by this Article is not necessary or effective to perfect a security interest in property subject to

(a) a statute or treaty of the United States which provides for a national or international registration or a national or international certificate of title or which specifies a place of filing different from that specified in this Article for filing of the security interest; or

(b) the following statutes of this state; [list any certificate of title statute covering automobiles, trailers, mobile homes, boats, farm tractors, or the like, and any central filing statute.]; but during any period in which collateral is inventory held for sale by a person who is in the business of selling goods of that kind, the filing provisions of this Article (Part 4) apply to a security interest in that collateral created by him as debtor; or

(c) a certificate of title statute of another jurisdiction under the law of which indication of a security interest on the certificate is required as a condition of perfection (subsection (2) of Section 9—103).

(4) Compliance with a statute or treaty described in subsection (3) is equivalent to the filing of a financing statement under this Article, and a security interest in property subject to the statute or treaty can be perfected only by compliance therewith except as provided in Section 9—103 on multiple state transactions. Duration and renewal of perfection of a security interest perfected by compliance with the statute or treaty are governed by the provisions of the statute or treaty; in other respects the security interest is subject to this Article.

Amended in 1972 and 1977.

§ 9—303. When Security Interest Is Perfected; Continuity of Perfection.

(1) A security interest is perfected when it has attached and when all of the applicable steps required for perfection have been taken. Such steps are specified in Sections 9—302, 9—304, 9—305 and 9—306. If such steps are taken before the security interest attaches, it is perfected at the time when it attaches.

(2) If a security interest is originally perfected in any way permitted under this Article and is subsequently perfected in some other way under this Article, without an intermediate period when it was unperfected, the security interest shall be deemed to be perfected continuously for the purposes of this Article.

§ 9—304. Perfection of Security Interest in Instruments, Documents, and Goods Covered by Documents; Perfection by Permissive Filing; Temporary Perfection Without Filing or Transfer of Possession

(1) A security interest in chattel paper or negotiable documents may be perfected by filing. A security interest in money or instruments (other than certificated securities or instruments which constitute part of chattel paper) can be perfected only by the secured party's taking possession, except as provided in subsections (4) and (5) of this section and subsections (2) and (3) of Section 9—306 on proceeds.

(2) During the period that goods are in the possession of the issuer of a negotiable document therefor, a security interest in the goods is perfected by perfecting a security interest in the document, and any security in-

terest in the goods otherwise perfected during such period is subject thereto.

(3) A security interest in goods in the possession of a bailee other than one who has issued a negotiable document therefor is perfected by issuance of a document in the name of the secured party or by the bailee's receipt of notification of the secured party's interest or by filing as to the goods.

(4) A security interest in instruments (other than certificated securities) or negotiable documents is perfected without filing or the taking of possession for a period of 21 days from the time it attaches to the extent that it arises for new value given under a written security agreement.

(5) A security interest remains perfected for a period of 21 days without filing where a secured party having a perfected security interest in an instrument (other than a certificated security), a negotiable document or goods in possession of a bailee other than one who has issued a negotiable document therefor

> (a) makes available to the debtor the goods or documents representing the goods for the purpose of ultimate sale or exchange or for the purpose of loading, unloading, storing, shipping, transshipping, manufacturing, processing or otherwise dealing with them in a manner preliminary to their sale or exchange, but priority between conflicting security interests in the goods is subject to subsection (3) of Section 9—312; or
>
> (b) delivers the instrument to the debtor for the purpose of ultimate sale or exchange or of presentation, collection, renewal or registration of transfer.

(6) After the 21 day period in subsections (4) and (5) perfection depends upon compliance with applicable provisions of this Article.

Amended in 1972 and 1977.

§ 9—305. When Possession by Secured Party Perfects Security Interest Without Filing

A security interest in letters of credit and advices of credit (subsection (2)(a) of Section 5—116), goods, instruments (other than certificated securities), money, negotiable documents, or chattel paper may be perfected by the secured party's taking possession of the collateral. If such collateral other than goods covered by a negotiable document is held by a bailee, the secured party is deemed to have possession from the time the bailee receives notification of the secured party's interest. A security interest is perfected by possession from the time possession is taken without a relation back and continues only so long as possession is retained, unless otherwise specified in this Article. The security interest may be otherwise perfected as provided in this Article before or after the period of possession by the secured party.

Amended in 1972 and 1977.

§ 9—306. "Proceeds"; Secured Party's Rights on Disposition of Collateral.

(1) "Proceeds" includes whatever is received upon the sale, exchange, collection or other disposition of collateral or proceeds. Insurance payable by reason of loss or damage to the collateral is proceeds, except to the extent that it is payable to a person other than a party to the security agreement. Money, checks, deposit accounts, and the like are "cash proceeds". All other proceeds are "noncash proceeds".

(2) Except where this Article otherwise provides, a security interest continues in collateral notwithstanding sale, exchange or other disposition thereof unless the disposition was authorized by the secured party in the security agreement or otherwise, and also continues in any identifiable proceeds including collections received by the debtor.

(3) The security interest in proceeds is a continuously perfected security interest if the interest in the original collateral was perfected but it ceases to be a perfected security interest and becomes unperfected ten days after receipt of the proceeds by the debtor unless

> (a) a filed financing statement covers the original collateral and the proceeds are collateral in which a security interest may be perfected by filing in the office or offices where the financing statement has been filed and, if the proceeds are acquired with cash proceeds, the description of collateral in the financing statement indicates the types of property constituting the proceeds; or
>
> (b) a filed financing statement covers the original collateral and the proceeds are identifiable cash proceeds; or
>
> (c) the security interest in the proceeds is perfected before the expiration of the ten day period.

Except as provided in this section, a security interest in proceeds can be perfected only by the methods or under the circumstances permitted in this Article for original collateral of the same type.

(4) In the event of insolvency proceedings instituted by or against a debtor, a secured party with a perfected security interest in proceeds has a perfected security interest only in the following proceeds:

> (a) in identifiable noncash proceeds and in separate deposit accounts containing only proceeds;
>
> (b) in identifiable cash proceeds in the form of money which is neither commingled with other money nor

deposited in a deposit account prior to the insolvency proceedings;

(c) in identifiable cash proceeds in the form of checks and the like which are not deposited in a deposit account prior to the insolvency proceedings; and

(d) in all cash and deposit accounts of the debtor in which proceeds have been commingled with other funds, but the perfected security interest under this paragraph (d) is

(i) subject to any right to set-off; and

(ii) limited to an amount not greater than the amount of any cash proceeds received by the debtor within ten days before the institution of the insolvency proceedings less the sum of (I) the payments to the secured party on account of cash proceeds received by the debtor during such period and (II) the cash proceeds received by the debtor during such period to which the secured party is entitled under paragraphs (a) through (c) of this subsection (4).

(5) If a sale of goods results in an account or chattel paper which is transferred by the seller to a secured party, and if the goods are returned to or are repossessed by the seller or the secured party, the following rules determine priorities:

(a) If the goods were collateral at the time of sale, for an indebtedness of the seller which is still unpaid, the original security interest attaches again to the goods and continues as a perfected security interest if it was perfected at the time when the goods were sold. If the security interest was originally perfected by a filing which is still effective, nothing further is required to continue the perfected status; in any other case, the secured party must take possession of the returned or repossessed goods or must file.

(b) An unpaid transferee of the chattel paper has a security interest in the goods against the transferor. Such security interest is prior to a security interest asserted under paragraph (a) to the extent that the transferee of the chattel paper was entitled to priority under Section 9—308.

(c) An unpaid transferee of the account has a security interest in the goods against the transferor. Such security interest is subordinate to a security interest asserted under paragraph (a).

(d) A security interest of an unpaid transferee asserted under paragraph (b) or (c) must be perfected for protection against creditors of the transferor and purchasers of the returned or repossessed goods.

§ 9—307. **Protection of Buyers of Goods.**

(1) A buyer in ordinary course of business (subsection (9) of Section 1—201) other than a person buying farm products from a person engaged in farming operations takes free of a security interest created by his seller even though the security interest is perfected and even though the buyer knows of its existence [subject to the Food Security Act of 1985 (7 U.S.C. Section 1631)].

(2) In the case of consumer goods, a buyer takes free of a security interest even though perfected if he buys without knowledge of the security interest, for value and for his own personal, family or household purposes unless prior to the purchase the secured party has filed a financing statement covering such goods.

(3) A buyer other than a buyer in ordinary course of business (subsection (1) of this section) takes free of a security interest to the extent that it secures future advances made after the secured party acquires knowledge of the purchase, or more than 45 days after the purchase, whichever first occurs, unless made pursuant to a commitment entered into without knowledge of the purchase and before the expiration of the 45 day period.

§ 9—308. **Purchase of Chattel Paper and Instruments.**

A purchaser of chattel paper or an instrument who gives new value and takes possession of it in the ordinary course of his business has priority over a security interest in the chattel paper or instrument

(a) which is perfected under Section 9—304 (permissive filing and temporary perfection) or under Section 9—306 (perfection as to proceeds) if he acts without knowledge that the specific paper or instrument is subject to a security interest; or

(b) which is claimed merely as proceeds of inventory subject to a security interest (Section 9—306) even though he knows that the specific paper or instrument is subject to the security interest.

§ 9—309. **Protection of Purchasers of Instruments, Documents and Securities**

Nothing in this Article limits the rights of a holder in due course of a negotiable instrument (Section 3—302) or a holder to whom a negotiable document of title has been duly negotiated (Section 7—501) or a bona fide purchaser of a security (Section 8—302) and the holders or purchasers take priority over an earlier security interest even though perfected. Filing under this Article does not constitute notice of the security interest to such holders or purchasers.

Amended in 1977.

§ 9—310. **Priority of Certain Liens Arising by Operation of Law.**

When a person in the ordinary course of his business furnishes services or materials with respect to goods subject to a security interest, a lien upon goods in the possession of such person given by statute or rule of law for such materials or services takes priority over a perfected security interest unless the lien is statutory and the statute expressly provides otherwise.

§ 9—311. **Alienability of Debtor's Rights: Judicial Process.**

The debtor's rights in collateral may be voluntarily or involuntarily transferred (by way of sale, creation of a security interest, attachment, levy, garnishment or other judicial process) notwithstanding a provision in the security agreement prohibiting any transfer or making the transfer constitute a default.

§ 9—312. **Priorities Among Conflicting Security Interests in the Same Collateral**

(1) The rules of priority stated in other sections of this Part and in the following sections shall govern when applicable: Section 4—208 with respect to the security interests of collecting banks in items being collected, accompanying documents and proceeds; Section 9—103 on security interests related to other jurisdictions; Section 9—114 on consignments.

(2) A perfected security interest in crops for new value given to enable the debtor to produce the crops during the production season and given not more than three months before the crops become growing crops by planting or otherwise takes priority over an earlier perfected security interest to the extent that such earlier interest secures obligations due more than six months before the crops become growing crops by planting or otherwise, even though the person giving new value had knowledge of the earlier security interest.

(3) A perfected purchase money security interest in inventory has priority over a conflicting security interest in the same inventory and also has priority in identifiable cash proceeds received on or before the delivery of the inventory to a buyer if

(a) the purchase money security interest is perfected at the time the debtor receives possession of the inventory; and

(b) the purchase money secured party gives notification in writing to the holder of the conflicting security interest if the holder had filed a financing statement covering the same types of inventory (i) before the date of the filing made by the purchase money secured party, or (ii) before the beginning of the 21 day period where the purchase money security interest is temporarily perfected without filing or possession (subsection (5) of Section 9—304); and

(c) the holder of the conflicting security interest receives the notification within five years before the debtor receives possession of the inventory; and

(d) the notification states that the person giving the notice has or expects to acquire a purchase money security interest in inventory of the debtor, describing such inventory by item or type.

(4) A purchase money security interest in collateral other than inventory has priority over a conflicting security interest in the same collateral or its proceeds if the purchase money security interest is perfected at the time the debtor receives possession of the collateral or within ten days thereafter.

(5) In all cases not governed by other rules stated in this section (including cases of purchase money security interests which do not qualify for the special priorities set forth in subsections (3) and (4) of this section), priority between conflicting security interests in the same collateral shall be determined according to the following rules:

(a) Conflicting security interests rank according to priority in time of filing or perfection. Priority dates from the time a filing is first made covering the collateral or the time the security interest is first perfected, whichever is earlier, provided that there is no period thereafter when there is neither filing nor perfection.

(b) So long as conflicting security interests are unperfected, the first to attach has priority.

(6) For the purposes of subsection (5) a date of filing or perfection as to collateral is also a date of filing or perfection as to proceeds.

(7) If future advances are made while a security interest is perfected by filing, the taking of possession, or under Section 8—321 on securities, the security interest has the same priority for the purposes of subsection (5) with respect to the future advances as it does with respect to the first advance. If a commitment is made before or while the security interest is so perfected, the security interest has the same priority with respect to advances made pursuant thereto. In other cases a perfected security interest has priority from the date the advance is made.

Amended in 1972 and 1977.

§ 9—313. **Priority of Security Interests in Fixtures.**

(1) In this section and in the provisions of Part 4 of this Article referring to fixture filing, unless the context otherwise requires

(a) goods are "fixtures" when they become so related to particular real estate that an interest in them arises under real estate law

(b) a "fixture filing" is the filing in the office where a mortgage on the real estate would be filed or recorded of a financing statement covering goods which are or are to become fixtures and conforming to the requirements of subsection (5) of Section 9—402

(c) a mortgage is a "construction mortgage" to the extent that it secures an obligation incurred for the construction of an improvement on land including the acquisition cost of the land, if the recorded writing so indicates.

(2) A security interest under this Article may be created in goods which are fixtures or may continue in goods which become fixtures, but no security interest exists under this Article in ordinary building materials incorporated into an improvement on land.

(3) This Article does not prevent creation of an encumbrance upon fixtures pursuant to real estate law.

(4) A perfected security interest in fixtures has priority over the conflicting interest of an encumbrancer or owner of the real estate where

(a) the security interest is a purchase money security interest, the interest of the encumbrancer or owner arises before the goods become fixtures, the security interest is perfected by a fixture filing before the goods become fixtures or within ten days thereafter, and the debtor has an interest of record in the real estate or is in possession of the real estate; or

(b) the security interest is perfected by a fixture filing before the interest of the encumbrancer or owner is of record, the security interest has priority over any conflicting interest of a predecessor in title of the encumbrancer or owner, and the debtor has an interest of record in the real estate or is in possession of the real estate; or

(c) the fixtures are readily removable factory or office machines or readily removable replacements of domestic appliances which are consumer goods, and before the goods become fixtures the security interest is perfected by any method permitted by this Article; or

(d) the conflicting interest is a lien on the real estate obtained by legal or equitable proceedings after the security interest was perfected by any method permitted by this Article.

(5) A security interest in fixtures, whether or not perfected, has priority over the conflicting interest of an encumbrancer or owner of the real estate where

(a) the encumbrancer or owner has consented in writing to the security interest or has disclaimed an interest in the goods as fixtures; or

(b) the debtor has a right to remove the goods as against the encumbrancer or owner. If the debtor's right terminates, the priority of the security interest continues for a reasonable time.

(6) Notwithstanding paragraph (a) of subsection (4) but otherwise subject to subsections (4) and (5), a security interest in fixtures is subordinate to a construction mortgage recorded before the goods become fixtures if the goods become fixtures before the completion of the construction. To the extent that it is given to refinance a construction mortgage, a mortgage has this priority to the same extent as the construction mortgage.

(7) In cases not within the preceding subsections, a security interest in fixtures is subordinate to the conflicting interest of an encumbrancer or owner of the related real estate who is not the debtor.

(8) When the secured party has priority over all owners and encumbrancers of the real estate, he may, on default, subject to the provisions of Part 5, remove his collateral from the real estate but he must reimburse any encumbrancer or owner of the real estate who is not the debtor and who has not otherwise agreed for the cost of repair of any physical injury, but not for any diminution in value of the real estate caused by the absence of the goods removed or by any necessity of replacing them. A person entitled to reimbursement may refuse permission to remove until the secured party gives adequate security for the performance of this obligation.

§ 9—314. Accessions.

(1) A security interest in goods which attaches before they are installed in or affixed to other goods takes priority as to the goods installed or affixed (called in this section "accessions") over the claims of all persons to the whole except as stated in subsection (3) and subject to Section 9—315(1).

(2) A security interest which attaches to goods after they become part of a whole is valid against all persons subsequently acquiring interests in the whole except as stated in subsection (3) but is invalid against any person with an interest in the whole at the time the security interest attaches to the goods who has not in writing consented to the security interest or disclaimed an interest in the goods as part of the whole.

(3) The security interests described in subsections (1) and (2) do not take priority over

(a) a subsequent purchaser for value of any interest in the whole; or

(b) a creditor with a lien on the whole subsequently obtained by judicial proceedings; or

(c) a creditor with a prior perfected security interest in the whole to the extent that he makes subsequent advances

if the subsequent purchase is made, the lien by judicial proceedings obtained or the subsequent advance under the prior perfected security interest is made or contracted for without knowledge of the security interest and before it is perfected. A purchaser of the whole at a foreclosure sale other than the holder of a perfected security interest purchasing at his own foreclosure sale is a subsequent purchaser within this section.

(4) When under subsections (1) or (2) and (3) a secured party has an interest in accessions which has priority over the claims of all persons who have interests in the whole, he may on default subject to the provisions of Part 5 remove his collateral from the whole but he must reimburse any encumbrancer or owner of the whole who is not the debtor and who has not otherwise agreed for the cost of repair of any physical injury but not for any diminution in value of the whole caused by the absence of the goods removed or by any necessity for replacing them. A person entitled to reimbursement may refuse permission to remove until the secured party gives adequate security for the performance of this obligation.

§ 9—315. Priority When Goods Are Commingled or Processed.

(1) If a security interest in goods was perfected and subsequently the goods or a part thereof have become part of a product or mass, the security interest continues in the product or mass if

(a) the goods are so manufactured, processed, assembled or commingled that their identity is lost in the product or mass; or

(b) a financing statement covering the original goods also covers the product into which the goods have been manufactured, processed or assembled.

In a case to which paragraph (b) applies, no separate security interest in that part of the original goods which has been manufactured, processed or assembled into the product may be claimed under Section 9—314.

(2) When under subsection (1) more than one security interest attaches to the product or mass, they rank equally according to the ratio that the cost of the goods to which each interest originally attached bears to the cost of the total product or mass.

§ 9—316. Priority Subject to Subordination.

Nothing in this Article prevents subordination by agreement by any person entitled to priority.

§ 9—317. Secured Party Not Obligated on Contract of Debtor.

The mere existence of a security interest or authority given to the debtor to dispose of or use collateral does not impose contract or tort liability upon the secured party for the debtor's acts or omissions.

§ 9—318. Defenses Against Assignee; Modification of Contract After Notification of Assignment; Term Prohibiting Assignment Ineffective; Identification and Proof of Assignment.

(1) Unless an account debtor has made an enforceable agreement not to assert defenses or claims arising out of a sale as provided in Section 9—206 the rights of an assignee are subject to

(a) all the terms of the contract between the account debtor and assignor and any defense or claim arising therefrom; and

(b) any other defense or claim of the account debtor against the assignor which accrues before the account debtor receives notification of the assignment.

(2) So far as the right to payment or a part thereof under an assigned contract has not been fully earned by performance, and notwithstanding notification of the assignment, any modification of or substitution for the contract made in good faith and in accordance with reasonable commercial standards is effective against an assignee unless the account debtor has otherwise agreed but the assignee acquires corresponding rights under the modified or substituted contract. The assignment may provide that such modification or substitution is a breach by the assignor.

(3) The account debtor is authorized to pay the assignor until the account debtor receives notification that the amount due or to become due has been assigned and that payment is to be made to the assignee. A notification which does not reasonably identify the rights assigned is ineffective. If requested by the account debtor, the assignee must seasonably furnish reasonable proof that the assignment has been made and unless he does so the account debtor may pay the assignor.

(4) A term in any contract between an account debtor and an assignor is ineffective if it prohibits assignment of an account or prohibits creation of a security interest in a general intangible for money due or to become due or requires the account debtor's consent to such assignment or security interest.

Part 4 Filing

§ 9—401. Place of Filing; Erroneous Filing; Removal of Collateral.

First Alternative Subsection (1)

(1) The proper place to file in order to perfect a security interest is as follows:

(a) when the collateral is timber to be cut or is minerals or the like (including oil and gas) or accounts subject to subsection (5) of Section 9—103, or when the financing statement is filed as a fixture filing

(Section 9—313) and the collateral is goods which are or are to become fixtures, then in the office where a mortgage on the real estate would be filed or recorded;

(b) in all other cases, in the office of the [Secretary of State].

Second Alternative Subsection (1)

(1) The proper place to file in order to perfect a security interest is as follows:

(a) when the collateral is equipment used in farming operations, or farm products, or accounts or general intangibles arising from or relating to the sale of farm products by a farmer, or consumer goods, then in the office of the .... in the county of the debtor's residence or if the debtor is not a resident of this state then in the office of the .... in the county where the goods are kept, and in addition when the collateral is crops growing or to be grown in the office of the .... in the county where the land is located;

(b) when the collateral is timber to be cut or is minerals or the like (including oil and gas) or accounts subject to subsection (5) of Section 9—103, or when the financing statement is filed as a fixture filing (Section 9—313) and the collateral is goods which are or are to become fixtures, then in the office where a mortgage on the real estate would be filed or recorded;

(c) in all other cases, in the office of the [Secretary of State].

Third Alternative Subsection (1)

(1) The proper place to file in order to perfect a security interest is as follows:

(a) when the collateral is equipment used in farming operations, or farm products, or accounts or general intangibles arising from or relating to the sale of farm products by a farmer, or consumer goods, then in the office of the .... in the county of the debtor's residence or if the debtor is not a resident of this state then in the office of the .... in the county where the goods are kept, and in addition when the collateral is crops growing or to be grown in the office of the .... in the county where the land is located;

(b) when the collateral is timber to be cut or is minerals or the like (including oil and gas) or accounts subject to subsection (5) of Section 9—103, or when the financing statement is filed as a fixture filing (Section 9—313) and the collateral is goods which are or are to become fixtures, then in the office where a mortgage on the real estate would be filed or recorded;

(c) in all other cases, in the office of the [Secretary of State] and in addition, if the debtor has a place of business in only one county of this state, also in the office of .... of such county, or, if the debtor has no place of business in this state, but resides in the state, also in the office of .... of the county which he resides.

Note: *One of the three alternatives should be selected as subsection (1).*

(2) A filing which is made in good faith in an improper place or not in all of the places required by this section is nevertheless effective with regard to any collateral as to which the filing complied with the requirements of this Article and is also effective with regard to collateral covered by the financing statement against any person who has knowledge of the contents of such financing statement.

(3) A filing which is made in the proper place in this state continues effective even though the debtor's residence or place of business or the location of the collateral or its use, whichever controlled the original filing, is thereafter changed.

Alternative Subsection (3)

[(3) A filing which is made in the proper county continues effective for four months after a change to another county of the debtor's residence or place of business or the location of the collateral, whichever controlled the original filing. It becomes ineffective thereafter unless a copy of the financing statement signed by the secured party is filed in the new county within said period. The security interest may also be perfected in the new county after the expiration of the four-month period; in such case perfection dates from the time of perfection in the new county. A change in the use of the collateral does not impair the effectiveness of the original filing.]

(4) The rules stated in Section 9—103 determine whether filing is necessary in this state.

(5) Notwithstanding the preceding subsections, and subject to subsection (3) of Section 9—302, the proper place to file in order to perfect a security interest in collateral, including fixtures, of a transmitting utility is the office of the [Secretary of State]. This filing constitutes a fixture filing (Section 9—313) as to the collateral described therein which is or is to become fixtures.

(6) For the purposes of this section, the residence of an organization is its place of business if it has one or its chief executive office if it has more than one place of business.

Note: *Subsection (6) should be used only if the state chooses the Second or Third Alternative Subsection (1).*

§ 9—402. Formal Requisites of Financing Statement; Amendments; Mortgage as Financing Statement.

(1) A financing statement is sufficient if it gives the names of the debtor and the secured party, is signed by the debtor, gives an address of the secured party from which information concerning the security interest may be obtained, gives a mailing address of the debtor and contains a statement indicating the types, or describing the items, of collateral. A financing statement may be filed before a security agreement is made or a security interest otherwise attaches. When the financing statement covers crops growing or to be grown, the statement must also contain a description of the real estate concerned. When the financing statement covers timber to be cut or covers minerals or the like (including oil and gas) or accounts subject to subsection (5) of Section 9—103, or when the financing statement is filed as a fixture filing (Section 9—313) and the collateral is goods which are or are to become fixtures, the statement must also comply with subsection (5). A copy of the security agreement is sufficient as a financing statement if it contains the above information and is signed by the debtor. A carbon, photographic or other reproduction of a security agreement or a financing statement is sufficient as a financing statement if the security agreement so provides or if the original has been filed in this state.

(2) A financing statement which otherwise complies with subsection (1) is sufficient when it is signed by the secured party instead of the debtor if it is filed to perfect a security interest in

(a) collateral already subject to a security interest in another jurisdiction when it is brought into this state, or when the debtor's location is changed to this state. Such a financing statement must state that the collateral was brought into this state or that the debtor's location was changed to this state under such circumstances; or

(b) proceeds under Section 9—306 if the security interest in the original collateral was perfected. Such a financing statement must describe the original collateral; or

(c) collateral as to which the filing has lapsed; or

(d) collateral acquired after a change of name, identity or corporate structure of the debtor (subsection (7)).

(3) A form substantially as follows is sufficient to comply with subsection (1):

Name of debtor (or assignor) ....
Address ....
Name of secured party (or assignee) ....
Address ....
1. This financing statement covers the following types (or items) of property:

(Describe) ....
2. (If collateral is crops) The above described crops are growing or are to be grown on:
(Describe Real Estate) ....
3. (If applicable) The above goods are to become fixtures on *
*Where appropriate substitute either "The above timber is standing on . . . ." or "The above minerals or the like (including oil and gas) or accounts will be financed at the wellhead or minehead of the well or mine located on . . . ."
(Describe Real Estate) ....
and this financing statement is to be filed [for record] in the real estate records. (If the debtor does not have an interest of record) The name of a record owner is ....
4. (If products of collateral are claimed) Products of the collateral are also covered.

(use ....
whichever   Signature of Debtor (or Assignor)

is   ....
applicable) Signature of Secured Party
                    (or Assignee)

(4) A financing statement may be amended by filing a writing signed by both the debtor and the secured party. An amendment does not extend the period of effectiveness of a financing statement. If any amendment adds collateral, it is effective as to the added collateral only from the filing date of the amendment. In this Article, unless the context otherwise requires, the term "financing statement" means the original financing statement and any amendments.

(5) A financing statement covering timber to be cut or covering minerals or the like (including oil and gas) or accounts subject to subsection (5) of Section 9—103, or a financing statement filed as a fixture filing (Section 9—313) where the debtor is not a transmitting utility, must show that it covers this type of collateral, must recite that it is to be filed [for record] in the real estate records, and the financing statement must contain a description of the real estate [sufficient if it were contained in a mortgage of the real estate to give constructive notice of the mortgage under the law of this state]. If the debtor does not have an interest of record in the real estate, the financing statement must show the name of a record owner.

(6) A mortgage is effective as a financing statement filed as a fixture filing from the date of its recording if

(a) the goods are described in the mortgage by item or type; and

(b) the goods are or are to become fixtures related to the real estate described in the mortgage; and

(c) the mortgage complies with the requirements for a financing statement in this section other than a recital that it is to be filed in the real estate records; and

(d) the mortgage is duly recorded.

No fee with reference to the financing statement is required other than the regular recording and satisfaction fees with respect to the mortgage.

(7) A financing statement sufficiently shows the name of the debtor if it gives the individual, partnership or corporate name of the debtor, whether or not it adds other trade names or names of partners. Where the debtor so changes his name or in the case of an organization its name, identity or corporate structure that a filed financing statement becomes seriously misleading, the filing is not effective to perfect a security interest in collateral acquired by the debtor more than four months after the change, unless a new appropriate financing statement is filed before the expiration of that time. A filed financing statement remains effective with respect to collateral transferred by the debtor even though the secured party knows of or consents to the transfer.

(8) A financing statement substantially complying with the requirements of this section is effective even though it contains minor errors which are not seriously misleading.

Note: *Language in brackets is optional.*

Note: *Where the state has any special recording system for real estate other than the usual grantor-grantee index (as, for instance, a tract system or a title registration or Torrens system) local adaptations of subsection (5) and Section 9—403(7) may be necessary. See Mass.Gen.Laws Chapter 106, Section 9—409.*

§ 9—403. What Constitutes Filing; Duration of Filing; Effect of Lapsed Filing; Duties of Filing Officer.

(1) Presentation for filing of a financing statement and tender of the filing fee or acceptance of the statement by the filing officer constitutes filing under this Article.

2) Except as provided in subsection (6) a filed financing statement is effective for a period of five years from the date of filing. The effectiveness of a filed financing statement lapses on the expiration of the five year period unless a continuation statement is filed prior to the lapse. If a security interest perfected by filing exists at the time insolvency proceedings are commenced by or against the debtor, the security interest remains perfected until termination of the insolvency proceedings and thereafter for a period of sixty days or until expiration of the five year period, whichever occurs later. Upon lapse the security interest becomes unperfected, unless it is perfected without filing. If the security interest becomes unperfected upon lapse, it is deemed to have been unperfected as against a person who became a purchaser or lien creditor before lapse.

(3) A continuation statement may be filed by the secured party within six months prior to the expiration of the five year period specified in subsection (2). Any such continuation statement must be signed by the secured party, identify the original statement by file number and state that the original statement is still effective. A continuation statement signed by a person other than the secured party of record must be accompanied by a separate written statement of assignment signed by the secured party of record and complying with subsection (2) of Section 9—405, including payment of the required fee. Upon timely filing of the continuation statement, the effectiveness of the original statement is continued for five years after the last date to which the filing was effective whereupon it lapses in the same manner as provided in subsection (2) unless another continuation statement is filed prior to such lapse. Succeeding continuation statements may be filed in the same manner to continue the effectiveness of the original statement. Unless a statute on disposition of public records provides otherwise, the filing officer may remove a lapsed statement from the files and destroy it immediately if he has retained a microfilm or other photographic record, or in other cases after one year after the lapse. The filing officer shall so arrange matters by physical annexation of financing statements to continuation statements or other related filings, or by other means, that if he physically destroys the financing statements of a period more than five years past, those which have been continued by a continuation statement or which are still effective under subsection (6) shall be retained.

(4) Except as provided in subsection (7) a filing officer shall mark each statement with a file number and with the date and hour of filing and shall hold the statement or a microfilm or other photographic copy thereof for public inspection. In addition the filing officer shall index the statement according to the name of the debtor and shall note in the index the file number and the address of the debtor given in the statement.

(5) The uniform fee for filing and indexing and for stamping a copy furnished by the secured party to show the date and place of filing for an original financing statement or for a continuation statement shall be $........ if the statement is in the standard form prescribed by the [Secretary of State] and otherwise shall be $........, plus in each case, if the financing statement is subject to subsection (5) of Section 9—402, $........ The uniform fee for each name more than one required to be indexed shall be $........ The secured party may at his option show a trade name for any person and an extra uniform indexing fee of $........ shall be paid with respect thereto.

(6) If the debtor is a transmitting utility (subsection (5) of Section 9—401) and a filed financing statement so states, it is effective until a termination statement is filed. A real estate mortgage which is effective as a fixture filing under subsection (6) of Section 9—402 remains effective as a fixture filing until the mortgage is released or satisfied of record or its effectiveness otherwise terminates as to the real estate.

(7) When a financing statement covers timber to be cut or covers minerals or the like (including oil and gas) or accounts subject to subsection (5) of Section 9—103, or is filed as a fixture filing, [it shall be filed for record and] the filing officer shall index it under the names of the debtor and any owner of record shown on the financing statement in the same fashion as if they were the mortgagors in a mortgage of the real estate described, and, to the extent that the law of this state provides for indexing of mortgages under the name of the mortgagee, under the name of the secured party as if he were the mortgagee thereunder, or where indexing is by description in the same fashion as if the financing statement were a mortgage of the real estate described.

Note: *In states in which writings will not appear in the real estate records and indices unless actually recorded the bracketed language in subsection (7) should be used.*

§ 9—404. **Termination Statement.**

(1) If a financing statement covering consumer goods is filed on or after . . . ., then within one month or within ten days following written demand by the debtor after there is no outstanding secured obligation and no commitment to make advances, incur obligations or otherwise give value, the secured party must file with each filing officer with whom the financing statement was filed, a termination statement to the effect that he no longer claims a security interest under the financing statement, which shall be identified by file number. In other cases whenever there is no outstanding secured obligation and no commitment to make advances, incur obligations or otherwise give value, the secured party must on written demand by the debtor send the debtor, for each filing officer with whom the financing statement was filed, a termination statement to the effect that he no longer claims a security interest under the financing statement, which shall be identified by file number. A termination statement signed by a person other than the secured party of record must be accompanied by a separate written statement of assignment signed by the secured party of record complying with subsection (2) of Section 9—405, including payment of the required fee. If the affected secured party fails to file such a termination statement as required by this subsection, or to send such a termination statement within ten days after proper demand therefor, he shall be liable to the debtor for one hundred dollars, and in addition for any loss caused to the debtor by such failure.

(2) On presentation to the filing officer of such a termination statement he must note it in the index. If he has received the termination statement in duplicate, he shall return one copy of the termination statement to the secured party stamped to show the time of receipt thereof. If the filing officer has a microfilm or other photographic record of the financing statement, and of any related continuation statement, statement of assignment and statement of release, he may remove the originals from the files at any time after receipt of the termination statement, or if he has no such record, he may remove them from the files at any time after one year after receipt of the termination statement.

(3) If the termination statement is in the standard form prescribed by the [Secretary of State], the uniform fee for filing and indexing the termination statement shall be $. . . . ., and otherwise shall be $. . . . ., plus in each case an additional fee of $. . . . . for each name more than one against which the termination statement is required to be indexed.

Note: *The date to be inserted should be the effective date of the revised Article 9.*

§ 9—405. **Assignment of Security Interest; Duties of Filing Officer; Fees.**

(1) A financing statement may disclose an assignment of a security interest in the collateral described in the financing statement by indication in the financing statement of the name and address of the assignee or by an assignment itself or a copy thereof on the face or back of the statement. On presentation to the filing officer of such a financing statement the filing officer shall mark the same as provided in Section 9—403(4). The uniform fee for filing, indexing and furnishing filing data for a financing statement so indicating an assignment shall be $. . . . . if the statement is in the standard form prescribed by the [Secretary of State] and otherwise shall be $. . . . ., plus in each case an additional fee of $. . . . . for each name more than one against which the financing statement is required to be indexed.

(2) A secured party may assign of record all or part of his rights under a financing statement by the filing in the place where the original financing statement was filed of a separate written statement of assignment signed by the secured party of record and setting forth the name of the secured party of record and the debtor, the file number and the date of filing of the financing statement and the name and address of the assignee and containing a description of the collateral assigned. A copy of the assignment is sufficient as a separate statement if it complies with the preceding sentence. On presentation to the filing officer of such a separate statement, the filing

officer shall mark such separate statement with the date and hour of the filing. He shall note the assignment on the index of the financing statement, or in the case of a fixture filing, or a filing covering timber to be cut, or covering minerals or the like (including oil and gas) or accounts subject to subsection (5) of Section 9—103, he shall index the assignment under the name of the assignor as grantor and, to the extent that the law of this state provides for indexing the assignment of a mortgage under the name of the assignee, he shall index the assignment of the financing statement under the name of the assignee. The uniform fee for filing, indexing and furnishing filing data about such a separate statement of assignment shall be $...... if the statement is in the standard form prescribed by the [Secretary of State] and otherwise shall be $......, plus in each case an additional fee of $...... for each name more than one against which the statement of assignment is required to be indexed. Notwithstanding the provisions of this subsection, an assignment of record of a security interest in a fixture contained in a mortgage effective as a fixture filing (subsection (6) of Section 9—402) may be made only by an assignment of the mortgage in the manner provided by the law of this state other than this Act.

(3) After the disclosure or filing of an assignment under this section, the assignee is the secured party of record.

§ 9—406. **Release of Collateral; Duties of Filing Officer; Fees.**

A secured party of record may by his signed statement release all or a part of any collateral described in a filed financing statement. The statement of release is sufficient if it contains a description of the collateral being released, the name and address of the debtor, the name and address of the secured party, and the file number of the financing statement. A statement of release signed by a person other than the secured party of record must be accompanied by a separate written statement of assignment signed by the secured party of record and complying with subsection (2) of Section 9—405, including payment of the required fee. Upon presentation of such a statement of release to the filing officer he shall mark the statement with the hour and date of filing and shall note the same upon the margin of the index of the filing of the financing statement. The uniform fee for filing and noting such a statement of release shall be $...... if the statement is in the standard form prescribed by the [Secretary of State] and otherwise shall be $......, plus in each case an additional fee of $...... for each name more than one against which the statement of release is required to be indexed. Amended in 1972.

§ 9—407. **Information From Filing Officer.**

[(1) If the person filing any financing statement, termination statement, statement of assignment, or statement of release, furnishes the filing officer a copy thereof, the filing officer shall upon request note upon the copy the file number and date and hour of the filing of the original and deliver or send the copy to such person.]

[(2) Upon request of any person, the filing officer shall issue his certificate showing whether there is on file on the date and hour stated therein, any presently effective financing statement naming a particular debtor and any statement of assignment thereof and if there is, giving the date and hour of filing of each such statement and the names and addresses of each secured party therein. The uniform fee for such a certificate shall be $...... if the request for the certificate is in the standard form prescribed by the [Secretary of State] and otherwise shall be $....... Upon request the filing officer shall furnish a copy of any filed financing statement or statement of assignment for a uniform fee of $...... per page.]

Note: *This section is proposed as an optional provision to require filing officers to furnish certificates. Local law and practices should be consulted with regard to the advisability of adoption.*

§ 9—408. **Financing Statements Covering Consigned or Leased Goods.**

A consignor or lessor of goods may file a financing statement using the terms "consignor," "consignee," "lessor," "lessee" or the like instead of the terms specified in Section 9—402. The provisions of this Part shall apply as appropriate to such a financing statement but its filing shall not of itself be a factor in determining whether or not the consignment or lease is intended as security (Section 1—201(37)). However, if it is determined for other reasons that the consignment or lease is so intended, a security interest of the consignor or lessor which attaches to the consigned or leased goods is perfected by such filing.

Part 5 Default

§ 9—501. **Default; Procedure When Security Agreement Covers Both Real and Personal Property.**

(1) When a debtor is in default under a security agreement, a secured party has the rights and remedies provided in this Part and except as limited by subsection (3) those provided in the security agreement. He may reduce his claim to judgment, foreclose or otherwise enforce the security interest by any available judicial procedure. If the collateral is documents the secured party may proceed either as to the documents or as to the goods covered thereby. A secured party in possession has the rights, remedies and duties provided in Section 9—207. The rights and remedies referred to in this subsection are cumulative.

(2) After default, the debtor has the rights and remedies provided in this Part, those provided in the security agreement and those provided in Section 9—207.

(3) To the extent that they give rights to the debtor and impose duties on the secured party, the rules stated in the subsections referred to below may not be waived or varied except as provided with respect to compulsory disposition of collateral (subsection (3) of Section 9—504 and Section 9—505) and with respect to redemption of collateral (Section 9—506) but the parties may by agreement determine the standards by which the fulfillment of these rights and duties is to be measured if such standards are not manifestly unreasonable:

    (a) subsection (2) of Section 9—502 and subsection (2) of Section 9—504 insofar as they require accounting for surplus proceeds of collateral;

    (b) subsection (3) of Section 9—504 and subsection (1) of Section 9—505 which deal with disposition of collateral;

    (c) subsection (2) of Section 9—505 which deals with acceptance of collateral as discharge of obligation;

    (d) Section 9—506 which deals with redemption of collateral; and

    (e) subsection (1) of Section 9—507 which deals with the secured party's liability for failure to comply with this Part.

(4) If the security agreement covers both real and personal property, the secured party may proceed under this Part as to the personal property or he may proceed as to both the real and the personal property in accordance with his rights and remedies in respect of the real property in which case the provisions of this Part do not apply.

(5) When a secured party has reduced his claim to judgment the lien of any levy which may be made upon his collateral by virtue of any execution based upon the judgment shall relate back to the date of the perfection of the security interest in such collateral. A judicial sale, pursuant to such execution, is a foreclosure of the security interest by judicial procedure within the meaning of this section, and the secured party may purchase at the sale and thereafter hold the collateral free of any other requirements of this Article.

§ 9—502. Collection Rights of Secured Party.

(1) When so agreed and in any event on default the secured party is entitled to notify an account debtor or the obligor on an instrument to make payment to him whether or not the assignor was theretofore making collections on the collateral, and also to take control of any proceeds to which he is entitled under Section 9—306.

(2) A secured party who by agreement is entitled to charge back uncollected collateral or otherwise to full or limited recourse against the debtor and who undertakes to collect from the account debtors or obligors must proceed in a commercially reasonable manner and may deduct his reasonable expenses of realization from the collections. If the security agreement secures an indebtedness, the secured party must account to the debtor for any surplus, and unless otherwise agreed, the debtor is liable for any deficiency. But, if the underlying transaction was a sale of accounts or chattel paper, the debtor is entitled to any surplus or is liable for any deficiency only if the security agreement so provides.

§ 9—503. Secured Party's Right to Take Possession After Default.

Unless otherwise agreed a secured party has on default the right to take possession of the collateral. In taking possession a secured party may proceed without judicial process if this can be done without breach of the peace or may proceed by action. If the security agreement so provides the secured party may require the debtor to assemble the collateral and make it available to the secured party at a place to be designated by the secured party which is reasonably convenient to both parties. Without removal a secured party may render equipment unusable, and may dispose of collateral on the debtor's premises under Section 9—504.

§ 9—504. Secured Party's Right to Dispose of Collateral After Default; Effect of Disposition.

(1) A secured party after default may sell, lease or otherwise dispose of any or all of the collateral in its then condition or following any commercially reasonable preparation or processing. Any sale of goods is subject to the Article on Sales (Article 2). The proceeds of disposition shall be applied in the order following to

    (a) the reasonable expenses of retaking, holding, preparing for sale or lease, selling, leasing and the like and, to the extent provided for in the agreement and not prohibited by law, the reasonable attorneys' fees and legal expenses incurred by the secured party;

    (b) the satisfaction of indebtedness secured by the security interest under which the disposition is made;

    (c) the satisfaction of indebtedness secured by any subordinate security interest in the collateral if written notification of demand therefor is received before distribution of the proceeds is completed. If requested by the secured party, the holder of a subordinate security interest must seasonably furnish reasonable proof of his interest, and unless he does so, the secured party need not comply with his demand.

(2) If the security interest secures an indebtedness, the secured party must account to the debtor for any surplus, and, unless otherwise agreed, the debtor is liable

for any deficiency. But if the underlying transaction was a sale of accounts or chattel paper, the debtor is entitled to any surplus or is liable for any deficiency only if the security agreement so provides.

(3) Disposition of the collateral may be by public or private proceedings and may be made by way of one or more contracts. Sale or other disposition may be as a unit or in parcels and at any time and place and on any terms but every aspect of the disposition including the method, manner, time, place and terms must be commercially reasonable. Unless collateral is perishable or threatens to decline speedily in value or is of a type customarily sold on a recognized market, reasonable notification of the time and place of any public sale or reasonable notification of the time after which any private sale or other intended disposition is to be made shall be sent by the secured party to the debtor, if he has not signed after default a statement renouncing or modifying his right to notification of sale. In the case of consumer goods no other notification need be sent. In other cases notification shall be sent to any other secured party from whom the secured party has received (before sending his notification to the debtor or before the debtor's renunciation of his rights) written notice of a claim of an interest in the collateral. The secured party may buy at any public sale and if the collateral is of a type customarily sold in a recognized market or is of a type which is the subject of widely distributed standard price quotations he may buy at private sale.

(4) When collateral is disposed of by a secured party after default, the disposition transfers to a purchaser for value all of the debtor's rights therein, discharges the security interest under which it is made and any security interest or lien subordinate thereto. The purchaser takes free of all such rights and interests even though the secured party fails to comply with the requirements of this Part or of any judicial proceedings

    (a) in the case of a public sale, if the purchaser has no knowledge of any defects in the sale and if he does not buy in collusion with the secured party, other bidders or the person conducting the sale; or

    (b) in any other case, if the purchaser acts in good faith.

(5) A person who is liable to a secured party under a guaranty, indorsement, repurchase agreement or the like and who receives a transfer of collateral from the secured party or is subrogated to his rights has thereafter the rights and duties of the secured party. Such a transfer of collateral is not a sale or disposition of the collateral under this Article.

§ 9—505. Compulsory Disposition of Collateral; Acceptance of the Collateral as Discharge of Obligation.

(1) If the debtor has paid sixty per cent of the cash price in the case of a purchase money security interest in consumer goods or sixty per cent of the loan in the case of another security interest in consumer goods, and has not signed after default a statement renouncing or modifying his rights under this Part a secured party who has taken possession of collateral must dispose of it under Section 9—504 and if he fails to do so within ninety days after he takes possession the debtor at his option may recover in conversion or under Section 9—507(1) on secured party's liability.

(2) In any other case involving consumer goods or any other collateral a secured party in possession may, after default, propose to retain the collateral in satisfaction of the obligation. Written notice of such proposal shall be sent to the debtor if he has not signed after default a statement renouncing or modifying his rights under this subsection. In the case of consumer goods no other notice need be given. In other cases notice shall be sent to any other secured party from whom the secured party has received (before sending his notice to the debtor or before the debtor's renunciation of his rights) written notice of a claim of an interest in the collateral. If the secured party receives objection in writing from a person entitled to receive notification within twenty-one days after the notice was sent, the secured party must dispose of the collateral under Section 9—504. In the absence of such written objection the secured party may retain the collateral in satisfaction of the debtor's obligation. Amended in 1972.

§ 9—506. Debtor's Right to Redeem Collateral.

At any time before the secured party has disposed of collateral or entered into a contract for its disposition under Section 9—504 or before the obligation has been discharged under Section 9—505(2) the debtor or any other secured party may unless otherwise agreed in writing after default redeem the collateral by tendering fulfillment of all obligations secured by the collateral as well as the expenses reasonably incurred by the secured party in retaking, holding and preparing the collateral for disposition, in arranging for the sale, and to the extent provided in the agreement and not prohibited by law, his reasonable attorneys' fees and legal expenses.

§ 9—507. Secured Party's Liability for Failure to Comply With This Part.

(1) If it is established that the secured party is not proceeding in accordance with the provisions of this Part disposition may be ordered or restrained on appropriate terms and conditions. If the disposition has occurred the debtor or any person entitled to notification or whose

security interest has been made known to the secured party prior to the disposition has a right to recover from the secured party any loss caused by a failure to comply with the provisions of this Part. If the collateral is consumer goods, the debtor has a right to recover in any event an amount not less than the credit service charge plus ten per cent of the principal amount of the debt or the time price differential plus 10 per cent of the cash price.

(2) The fact that a better price could have been obtained by a sale at a different time or in a different method from that selected by the secured party is not of itself sufficient to establish that the sale was not made in a commercially reasonable manner. If the secured party either sells the collateral in the usual manner in any recognized market therefor or if he sells at the price current in such market at the time of his sale or if he has otherwise sold in conformity with reasonable commercial practices among dealers in the type of property sold he has sold in a commercially reasonable manner. The principles stated in the two preceding sentences with respect to sales also apply as may be appropriate to other types of disposition. A disposition which has been approved in any judicial proceeding or by any bona fide creditors' committee or representative of creditors shall conclusively be deemed to be commercially reasonable, but this sentence does not indicate that any such approval must be obtained in any case nor does it indicate that any disposition not so approved is not commercially reasonable.

Article 10
EFFECTIVE DATE AND REPEALER

§ 10—101. **Effective Date.**

This Act shall become effective at midnight on December 31st following its enactment. It applies to transactions entered into and events occurring after that date.

§ 10—102. **Specific Repealer; Provision for Transition.**

(1) The following acts and all other acts and parts of acts inconsistent herewith are hereby repealed:
(Here should follow the acts to be specifically repealed including the following:
- Uniform Negotiable Instruments Act
- Uniform Warehouse Receipts Act
- Uniform Sales Act
- Uniform Bills of Lading Act
- Uniform Stock Transfer Act
- Uniform Conditional Sales Act
- Uniform Trust Receipts Act

Also any acts regulating:
- Bank collections
- Bulk sales
- Chattel mortgages
- Conditional sales
- Factor's lien acts
- Farm storage of grain and similar acts
- Assignment of accounts receivable)

(2) Transactions validly entered into before the effective date specified in Section 10—101 and the rights, duties and interests flowing from them remain valid thereafter and may be terminated, completed, consummated or enforced as required or permitted by any statute or other law amended or repealed by this Act as though such repeal or amendment had not occurred.

Note: *Subsection (1) should be separately prepared for each state. The foregoing is a list of statutes to be checked.*

§ 10—103. **General Repealer.**

Except as provided in the following section, all acts and parts of acts inconsistent with this Act are hereby repealed.

§ 10—104. **Laws Not Repealed.**

(1) The Article on Documents of Title (Article 7) does not repeal or modify any laws prescribing the form or contents of documents of title or the services or facilities to be afforded by bailees, or otherwise regulating bailees' businesses in respects not specifically dealt with herein; but the fact that such laws are violated does not affect the status of a document of title which otherwise complies with the definition of a document of title (Section 1—201).

[(2) This Act does not repeal . . . .*, cited as the Uniform Act for the Simplification of Fiduciary Security Transfers, and if in any respect there is any inconsistency between that Act and the Article of this Act on investment securities (Article 8) the provisions of the former Act shall control.]

Note: *At * in subsection (2) insert the statutory reference to the Uniform Act for the Simplification of Fiduciary Security Transfers if such Act has previously been enacted. If it has not been enacted, omit subsection (2).*

Article 11
(REPORTERS' DRAFT)
EFFECTIVE DATE AND TRANSITION PROVISIONS

This material has been numbered Article 11 to distinguish it from Article 10, the transition provision of the 1962 Code, which may still remain in effect in some states to cover transition problems from pre-Code law to the original Uniform Commercial Code. Adaptation may be necessary in particular states. The terms "[old

Dispossession by landlord, 338–9
Unlawful detainer, 335
Wrongful abandonment by tenant, 339–40
Wrongful eviction by landlord, 339
Sublease, 337
Repair of leased property, 344
Obligation of landlord, 341
Obligation of tenant, 344
Reversions, 314
Riparian rights, 318
Space rights, 318
Support, lateral, 318
Survivorship, right of, 310
Tangible, 282
Tenancy by the entireties, 311
Tenancy in common, 310
Title insurance, 325
Tort liability, 344
Landlord responsibility, 341–3
Tenant liability, 344
Treasure trove, 289
Trade fixtures, 291–2
Trademark law, 286–7
Trust deed, 681, 684
Uniform gifts to minors, 284
Waste, 336
Water, 319
Wild animals, 290
Wills, 326–7
Zoning, 319, 322

R

REMEDIES
See Contracts

S

SALES
Auction, 106
Bailments, 352
Contract, performance of the
In general, 352, 380
Buyer's performance,
Payment, 376
Payment and inspection, 379
Payment under installment contract, 377–9
Cure, right to, 383–4
Seller's performance, 380
Duty to ship, 380
Mercantile shipping terms, 374–7
Shipment with reservation, 387
Tender of delivery,
In general, 381
Effect of imperfect tender, 381–2
Effect of valid tender, 381
In possession of seller, 386
Substitution, 385
Under installment contract, 383
Without movement of goods held by bailee, 386
Uncertainty of performance, 385
Fungible goods, 355
Gift, 352
Installment contracts, 386
Nature of,
In general, 352
Auction sales, 353–5, 367
Bailments, 352
Bulk sales, 353
Conditional sale, 355
Contract for labor or services, 356
Contract to sell, 352
Definition, 352
Fungible goods, 355
Gift, 352
Option to buy, 352
Sales between merchants, 355–6
Option to buy, 352
Remedies,
Buyer, 391–5
Seller, 388–91
Restaurant cases, 406
Secondhand goods, 406
Self-service stores, 406
Shipment with reservation, 387
Shipping terms, 374–7
Transfer of title and risk of loss, 357–8
Automobiles, 367
Consignment, 367
Delivery requiring movement of goods, 363
Collect on delivery contracts, 365
Destination contracts, 365
Shipment contracts, 363–4
Delivery without movement of goods, 368
With document of title, 368
Without document of title, 368
Effect of breach of contract, 353
Buyer's breach, 388–91
Seller's breach, 391–5
Identification or designation, 360
In general, 360
Rights of buyer, 361
Rights of seller, 362
When identification occurs, 360
Sale by nonowner, 362
In general, 362–3
Resale by fraudulent buyer, 363
Sale on approval, 366
Sale or return, 366
Syndicate, 456
SECURED TRANSACTIONS
See under UCC
STARE DECISIS, 11–2
STATUTE OF FRAUDS
See Contracts
STATUTE OF LIMITATIONS, 214–5

T

TAXATION, 70
TITLE
See Sales, Transfer of title and risk of loss; Commercial paper, Documents of title
TORTS IN BUSINESS
See also Negligence
Assault and battery, 51
Conversion, 52
Defamation, 47–9
False imprisonment, 51
Fraud, 46
Intentional infliction of mental distress, 49
Interference with contract, 52
Invasion of privacy, 50
Malpractice, 46
Negligence, 44–5
Nuisance, 51
Strict liability, see Product liability
Tort defined, 44
Trespass, 52
Unfair competition, 53
TORTS, PARENTAL LIABILITY FOR, 131–2

TRADEMARK LAW, 286-7
TRUST
Defined, 771-2
Express trusts, 772
    Beneficiary, 778
    Form, 776
    Remedies, 778-9
    Termination, 779
    Trustee's duties, 777-8
    Trustee's powers, 777
    Types of trusts, 773-6
    Validity requirements, 772
Implied trusts, 779
    Constructive trusts, 779-80
    Resulting trusts, 779
TRUST DEED
Defined, 681, 684
Foreclosure, 684-5
Form, 682-3
Impairment, 684
Property transfer, 684

U

UNIFORM COMMERCIAL CODE
    See also Appendix B, text of, 11
History, 12
Purpose of, 12
Scope of, 12
Remedies of buyer under,
    Cancel contract, 392
    Cover, 394
    Damages, 395
    Deduction of damages from price, 394
    Obtain identified goods from insolvent seller, 391
    Replevin the goods, 392
    Revoke acceptance, 393
    Specific performance, 392
Remedies of seller under,
    Cancel the contract, 389
    Identify goods to contract on buyer's breach, 389
    Reclaim the goods, 389
    Recover damages, 390
    Recover price of the goods, 391
    Resell the goods, 389
    Stop delivery, 388-9
    Withhold delivery of goods, 388
Secured transactions under,
    In general, 678-9, 689-90
    After-acquired property, 701
    Attachment, 694
    Creation of security interest, 678-9, 689-90
    Default of debtor, 704
        Basic remedies on, 704
        Secured party's right to take possession, 704-5
    Future advances, 703
    Perfection of security interest, 695-6
        By attachment, 696-7
        By filing financing statement, 697-9
        By possession, 697
    Possession, 690
    Priorities, 699-700
        Between nonperfected interests, 701
        Between perfected interests, 700
        Between perfected and unperfected interests, 700
        Purchase money security interests, 701-2
    Repossession, 704,
        Sale of collateral, 705-6
    Security agreement, 691-3
UNINCORPORATED ASSOCIATION, 458
UNLIQUIDATED DEBT, 119-20
UNSOUND MIND, 132-3
USURY, 138-9

Code]" and "[new Code]" and "[old U.C.C.]" and "[new U.C.C.]" are used herein, and should be suitably changed in each state.

Note: *This draft was prepared by the Reporters and has not been passed upon by the Review Committee, the Permanent Editorial Board, the American Law Institute, or the National Conference of Commissioners on Uniform State Laws. It is submitted as a working draft which may be adapted as appropriate in each state.*

§ 11—101. **Effective Date.**

This Act shall become effective at 12:01 A.M. on , 19

§ 11—102. **Preservation of Old Transition Provision.**

The provisions of [here insert reference to the original transition provision in the particular state] shall continue to apply to [the new U.C.C.] and for this purpose the [old U.C.C. and new U.C.C.] shall be considered one continuous statute.

§ 11—103. **Transition to [New Code]—General Rule.**

Transactions validly entered into after [effective date of old U.C.C.] and before [effective date of new U.C.C.], and which were subject to the provisions of [old U.C.C.] and which would be subject to this Act as amended if they had been entered into after the effective date of [new U.C.C.] and the rights, duties and interests flowing from such transactions remain valid after the latter date and may be terminated, completed, consummated or enforced as required or permitted by the [new U.C.C.]. Security interests arising out of such transactions which are perfected when [new U.C.C.] becomes effective shall remain perfected until they lapse as provided in [new U.C.C.], and may be continued as permitted by [new U.C.C.], except as stated in Section 11—105.

§ 11—104. **Transition Provision on Change of Requirement of Filing.**

A security interest for the perfection of which filing or the taking of possession was required under [old U.C.C.] and which attached prior to the effective date of [new U.C.C.] but was not perfected shall be deemed perfected on the effective date of [new U.C.C.] if [new U.C.C.] permits perfection without filing or authorizes filing in the office or offices where a prior ineffective filing was made.

§ 11—105. **Transition Provision on Change of Place of Filing.**

(1) A financing statement or continuation statement filed prior to [effective date of new U.C.C.] which shall not have lapsed prior to [the effective date of new U.C.C.] shall remain effective for the period provided in the [old Code], but not less than five years after the filing.

(2) With respect to any collateral acquired by the debtor subsequent to the effective date of [new U.C.C.], any effective financing statement or continuation statement described in this section shall apply only if the filing or filings are in the office or offices that would be appropriate to perfect the security interests in the new collateral under [new U.C.C.].

(3) The effectiveness of any financing statement or continuation statement filed prior to [effective date of new U.C.C.] may be continued by a continuation statement as permitted by [new U.C.C.], except that if [new U.C.C.] requires a filing in an office where there was no previous financing statement, a new financing statement conforming to Section 11—106 shall be filed in that office.

(4) If the record of a mortgage of real estate would have been effective as a fixture filing of goods described therein if [new U.C.C.] had been in effect on the date of recording the mortgage, the mortgage shall be deemed effective as a fixture filing as to such goods under subsection (6) of Section 9—402 of the [new U.C.C.] on the effective date of [new U.C.C.].

§ 11—106. **Required Refilings.**

(1) If a security interest is perfected or has priority when this Act takes effect as to all persons or as to certain persons without any filing or recording, and if the filing of a financing statement would be required for the perfection or priority of the security interest against those persons under [new U.C.C.], the perfection and priority rights of the security interest continue until 3 years after the effective date of [new U.C.C.]. The perfection will then lapse unless a financing statement is filed as provided in subsection (4) or unless the security interest is perfected otherwise than by filing.

(2) If a security interest is perfected when [new U.C.C.] takes effect under a law other than [U.C.C.] which requires no further filing, refiling or recording to continue its perfection, perfection continues until and will lapse 3 years after [new U.C.C.] takes effect, unless a financing statement is filed as provided in subsection (4) or unless the security interest is perfected otherwise than by filing, or unless under subsection (3) of Section 9—302 the other law continues to govern filing.

(3) If a security interest is perfected by a filing, refiling or recording under a law repealed by this Act which required further filing, refiling or recording to continue its perfection, perfection continues and will lapse on the date provided by the law so repealed for such further filing, refiling or recording unless a financing statement is filed as provided in subsection (4) or unless the security interest is perfected otherwise than by filing.

(4) A financing statement may be filed within six months before the perfection of a security interest would otherwise lapse. Any such financing statement may be signed

by either the debtor or the secured party. It must identify the security agreement, statement or notice (however denominated in any statute or other law repealed or modified by this Act), state the office where and the date when the last filing, refiling or recording, if any, was made with respect thereto, and the filing number, if any, or book and page, if any, of recording and further state that the security agreement, statement or notice, however denominated, in another filing office under the [U.C.C.] or under any statute or other law repealed or modified by this Act is still effective. Section 9—401 and Section 9—103 determine the proper place to file such a financing statement. Except as specified in this subsection, the provisions of Section 9—403(3) for continuation statements apply to such a financing statement.

§ 11—107. **Transition Provisions as to Priorities.**

Except as otherwise provided in [Article 11], [old U.C.C.] shall apply to any questions of priority if the positions of the parties were fixed prior to the effective date of [new U.C.C.]. In other cases questions of priority shall be determined by [new U.C.C.].

§ 11—108. **Presumption that Rule of Law Continues Unchanged.**

Unless a change in law has clearly been made, the provisions of [new U.C.C.] shall be deemed declaratory of the meaning of the [old U.C.C.].

1987 OFFICIAL TEXT—UCC

The preceding articles and sections constitute the 1987 official text of the Uniform Commercial Code. As of January 1, 1987, the following states had adopted most of the proposed amendments of 1972, which was the year of the most recent major changes.

1972 Amendments

States	Effective Date	States	Effective Date
Alabama	2/01/82	Nebraska	7/19/80
Alaska	7/01/83	Nevada	7/01/75
Arizona	1/01/76	New Hampshire	8/21/79
Arkansas	1/01/74	New Jersey	12/01/81
California	1/01/76	New Mexico	6/14/85
Colorado	1/01/78	New York	7/02/78
Connecticut	10/01/76	North Carolina	7/01/76
Delaware	1/01/84	North Dakota	1/01/74
Florida	1/01/80	Ohio	1/01/79
Georgia	7/01/78	Oklahoma	10/19/81
Hawaii	7/01/79	Oregon	1/01/74
Idaho	7/01/79	Pennsylvania	5/25/83
Illinois	7/01/73	Rhode Island	1/01/80
Indiana	1/01/86	South Dakota	7/01/83
Iowa	1/01/75	Tennessee	1/01/86
Kansas	1/01/76	Texas	1/01/74
Kentucky	7/01/87	Utah	7/01/77
Maine	1/01/78	Virginia	7/01/74
Maryland	1/01/81	Washington	7/01/82
Massachusetts	1/01/80	West Virginia	7/01/75
Michigan	1/01/79	Wisconsin	7/01/74
Minnesota	1/01/77	Wyoming	9/01/83
Mississippi	4/01/78		
Montana	10/01/83	District of Columbia	3/16/82

Appendix C

Spanish Equivalents for Important Legal Terms in English

Abandoned property: bienes abandonados
Acceptance: aceptación; consentimiento; acuerdo
Acceptor: aceptante
Accession: toma de posesión; aumento; accesión
Accommodation indorser: avalista de favor
Accommodation party: firmante de favor
Accord: acuerdo; convenio; arreglo
Accord and satisfaction; transacción ejecutada
Act of state doctrine: doctrina de acto de gobierno
Administrative law: derecho administrativo
Administrative process: procedimiento o metódo administrativo
Administrator (-trix): administrador (-a)
Adverse possession: posesión de hecho susceptible de proscripción adquisitiva
Affirmative action: acción afirmativa
Affirmative defense: defensa afirmativa

After-acquired property: bienes adquiridos con posterioridad a un hecho dado
Agency: mandato; agencia
Agent: mandatorio; agente; representante
Agreement: convenio; acuerdo; contrato
Alien corporation: empresa extranjera
Allonge: hojas adicionales de endosos
Answer: contestación de la demanda; alegato
Anticipatory breach, or anticipatory repudiation: anuncio previo de las partes de su imposibilidad de cumplir con el contrato
Appeal: apelación; recurso de apelación
Appellate jurisdiction: jurisdicción de apelaciones
Appraisal right: derecho de valuación
Arbitration: arbitraje
Arson: incendio intencional
Articles of partnership: contrato social
Artisian's lien: derecho de retención que ejerce al artesano

Assault: asalto; ataque; agresión
Assignment of rights: transmisión; transferencia; cesión
Assumption of risk: no resarcimiento por exposición voluntaria al peligro
Attachment: auto judicial que autoriza el embargo; embargo

Bailee: depositario
Bailment: depósito; constitución en depósito
Bailor: depositante
Bankruptcy trustee: síndico de la quiebra
Battery: agresión; física
Bearer: portador; tenedor
Bearer instrument: documento al portador
Bequest or legacy: legado (de bienes muebles)
Bilateral contract: contrato bilateral
Bill of lading: conocimiento de embarque; carta de porte
Bill of Rights: declaración de derechos
Binder: póliza de seguro provisoria; recibo de pago a cuenta del precio

Blank indorsement: endoso en blanco
Blue Sky laws: leyes reguladoras del comercio bursátil
Bond: título de crédito; garantía; caución
Bond indenture: contrato de emisión de bonos; contrato del empréstito
Breach of contract: incumplimiento de contrato
Brief: escrito; resumen; informe
Burglary; violación de domicilio
Business judgment rule: regla de juicio comercial
Business tort: agravio comercial

Case law: ley de casos; derecho casuístico
Cashier's check: cheque de caja
Causation in fact: causalidad en realidad
Cease-and-desist order: orden para cesar y desistir
Certificate of deposit: certificado de depósito
Certified check: cheque certificado
Charitable trust: fideicomiso para fines benéficos
Chattel: bien mueble
Check: cheque
Chose in action: derecho inmaterial; derecho de acción
Civil law: derecho civil
Close corporation: sociedad de un solo accionista o de un grupo restringido de accionistas
Closed shop: taller agremiado (emplea solamente a miembros de un gremio)
Closing argument: argumento al final
Codicil: codicilo
Collateral: guarantía; bien objeto de la guarantía real
Comity: cortesía; cortesía entre naciones
Commercial paper: instrumentos negociables; documentos a valores commerciales
Common law: derecho consuetudinario; derecho común; ley común
Common stock: acción ordinaria
Comparative negligence: negligencia comparada

Compensatory damages: daños y perjuicios reales o compensatorios
Concurrent conditions: condiciones concurrentes
Concurrent estates: condominio
Concurrent jurisdiction: competencia concurrente de varios tribunales para entender en una misma causa
Concurring opinion: opinión concurrente
Condition: condición
Condition precedent: condición suspensiva
Condition subsequent: condición resolutoria
Confiscation: confiscación
Confusion: confusión; fusión
Conglomerate merger: fusión de firmas que operan en distintos mercados
Consent decree: acuerdo entre las partes aprobado por un tribunal
Consequential damages: daños y perjuicios indirectos
Consideration: consideración; motivo; contraprestación
Consolidation: consolidación
Constructive delivery: entrega simbólica
Constructive trust: fideicomiso creado por aplicación de la ley
Consumer-protection law: ley para proteger el consumidor
Contract: contrato
Contracts under seal: contrato formal o sellado
Contributory negligence: negligencia de la parte actora
Conversion: usurpación; conversión de valores
Copyright: derecho de autor
Corporation: sociedad anómina; corporación; persona juridica
Co-sureties: cogarantes
Counterclaim, or cross-complaint: reconvención; contrademanda
Counteroffer: contraoferta
Course of dealing: curso de transacciones
Course of performance: curso de cumplimiento
Covenant: pacto; garantía; contrato

Covenant not to sue: pacto or contrato a no demandar
Covenant of quiet enjoyment: garantía del uso y goce pacífico del inmueble
Creditors' composition agreement: concordato preventivo
Crime: crimen; delito; contravención
Criminal law: derecho penal
Cross-examination: contrainterrogatorio
Cure: cura; cuidado; derecho de remediar un vicio contractual
Customs receipts: recibos de derechos aduaneros

Damages: daños; indemnización por daños y perjuicios
Debit card: tarjeta de débito
Debtor: deudor
Debt securities: seguridades de deuda
Deceptive advertising: publicidad engañosa
Deed: escritura; título; acta translativa de domino
Defamation: difamación
Delegation of duties: delegación de obligaciones
Demand deposit: depósito a la vista
Depositions: declaración de un testigo fuera del tribunal
Derivative suit: acción judicial entablada por un accionista en nombre de la sociedad
Devise: legado; deposición testamentaria (bienes inmuebles)
Directed verdict: veredicto según orden del juez y sin participación activa del jurado
Direct examination: interrogatorio directo; primer interrogatorio
Disaffirmance: repudiación; renuncia; anulación
Discharge: descargo; liberación; cumplimiento
Disclosed principal: mandante revelado
Discovery: descubrimiento; producción de la prueba
Dissenting opinion: opinión disidente
Dissolution: disolución; terminación

Diversity of citizenship: competencia de los tribunales federales para entender en causas cuyas partes intervinientes son cuidadanos de distintos estados
Divestiture: extinción premature de derechos reales
Dividend: dividendo
Docket: orden del día; lista de causas pendientes
Domestic corporation: sociedad local
Draft: orden de pago; letrade cambio
Drawee: girado; beneficiario
Drawer: librador
Duress: coacción; violencia

Easement: servidumbre
Embezzlement: desfalco; malversación
Eminent domain: poder de expropiación
Employment discrimination: discriminación en el empleo
Entrepreneur: empresario
Environmental law: ley ambiental
Equal dignity rule: regla de dignidad egual
Equity security: tipo de participación en una sociedad
Estate: propiedad; patrimonio; derecho
Estop: impedir; prevenir
Ethical issue: cuestión ética
Exclusive jurisdiction: competencia exclusiva
Exculpatory clause: cláusula eximente
Executed contract: contrato ejecutado
Execution: ejecución; cumplimiento
Executor (-trix): albacea
Executory contract: contrato aún no completamente consumado
Executory interest: derecho futuro
Express contract: contrato expreso
Expropriation: expropiación

Federal question: caso federal
Fee simple: pleno dominio; dominio absoluto
Fee simple absolute: dominio absoluto
Fee simple defeasible: dominio sujeta a una condición resolutoria
Felony: crimen; delito grave
Fictitious payee: beneficiario ficticio
Fiduciary: fiduciaro
Firm offer: oferta en firme
Fixture: inmueble por destino, incorporación a anexación
Floating lien: gravamen continuado
Foreign corporation: sociedad extranjera; U.S. sociedad constituída en otro estado
Forgery: falso; falsificación
Formal contract: contrato formal
Franchise: privilegio; franquicia; concesión
Franchisee: persona que recibe una concesión
Franchisor: persona que vende una concesión
Fraud: fraude; dolo; engaño
Future estate: bien futuro

Garnishment: embargo de derechos
General partner: socio comanditario
General warranty deed: escritura translativa de domino con garantía de título
Gift: donación
Gift *causa mortis:* donación por causa de muerte
Gift *inter vivos:* donación entre vivos
Good faith: buena fe
Good-faith purchaser: comprador de buena fe

Holder: tenedor por contraprestación
Holder in due course: tenedor legítimo
Holographic will: testamento ológrafico
Homestead exemption laws: leyes que exceptúan las casas de familia de ejecución por duedas generales
Horizontal merger: fusión horizontal

Identification: identificación
Implied-in-fact contract: contrato implícito en realidad
Implied warranty: guarantía implícita
Implied warranty of merchantability: garantía implícita de vendibilidad
Impossibility of performance: imposibilidad de cumplir un contrato
Imposter: imposter
Incidental beneficiary: beneficiario incidental; beneficiario secundario
Incidental damages: daños incidentales
Indictment: auto de acusación; acusación
Indorsee: endorsatario
Indorsement: endoso
Indorser: endosante
Informal contract: contrato no formal; contrato verbal
Information: acusación hecha por el ministerio público
Injunction: mandamiento; orden de no innovar
Innkeeper's lien: derecho de retención que ejerce el posadero
Installment contract: contrato de pago en cuotas
Insurable interest: interés asegurable
Intended beneficiary: beneficiario destinado
Intentional tort: agravio; cuasi-delito intenciónal
International law: derecho internaciónal
Interrogatories: preguntas escritas sometidas por una parte a la otra o a un testigo
***Inter vivos* trust:** fideicomiso entre vivos
Intestacy laws: leyes de la condición de morir intestado
Intestate: intestado
Investment company: compañia de inversiones
Issue: emisión

Joint tenancy: derechos conjuntos en un bien inmueble
Joint tenancy with right of survivorship: derechos conjuntos en un bien inmueble en favor del beneficiario sobreviviente
Judgment n.o.v.: juicio no obstante veredicto

Judgment rate of interest: interés de juicio
Judicial process: acto de procedimiento; proceso jurídico
Judicial review: revisión judicial
Jurisdiction: jurisdicción

Larceny: robo; hurto
Law: derecho; ley; jurisprudencia
Lease: contrato de locación; contrato de alquiler
Leasehold estate: bienes forales
Legal rate of interest: interés legal
Legatee: legatario
Less-than-freehold estate: menos de derecho de dominio absoluto
Letter of credit: carta de crédito
Levy: embargo; comiso
Libel: libelo; difamación escrita
Life estate: usufructo
Limited partner: comanditario
Limited partnership: sociedad en comandita
Liquidation: liquidación; realización
Lost property: objetos perdidos

Majority opinion: opinión de la mayoría
Maker: persona que realiza u ordena; librador
Mechanic's lien: gravamen de constructor
Mediation: mediación; intervención
Merger: fusión
Mirror-image rule: fallo de reflejo
Misdemeanor: infracción; contravención
Mislaid property: bienes extraviados
Mitigation of damages: reducción de daños
Moral hazard: riesgo moral
Mortgage: hypoteca
Motion to dismiss, or demurrer: excepción parentoria
Municipal law: derecho municipal
Mutual fund: fondo mutual

Negotiable instrument: instrumento negociable
Negotiation: negociación
Nominal damages: daños y perjuicios nominales
Novation: novación
Nuncupative will: testamento nuncupativo

Objective theory of contracts: teoria objetiva de contratos
Offer: oferta
Offeree: persona que recibe una oferta
Offeror: oferente
Order paper: instrumento o documento a la orden
Original jurisdiction: jurisdicción de primera instancia
Output contract: contrato de producción

Parol evidence rule: regla relativa a la prueba oral
Partially disclosed principal: mandante revelado en parte
Partnership: sociedad colectiva; asociación; asociación de participación
Past consideration: causa o contraprestación anterior
Patent: patente; privilegio
Pattern or practice: muestra o práctica
Payee: beneficiario de un pago
Penalty: pena; penalidad
Per capita: por cabeza
Perfection: perfeción
Performance: cumplimiento; ejecución
Personal defenses: excepciones personales
Personal property: bienes muebles
Per stirpes: por estirpe
Plea bargaining: regateo por un alegato
Pleadings: alegatos
Pledge: prenda
Police powers: poderes de policia y de prevención del crimen
Policy: póliza
Positive law: derecho positivo; ley positiva
Possibility of reverter: posibilidad de reversión
Precedent: precedente
Preemptive right: derecho de prelación
Preferred stock: acciones preferidas

Premium: recompensa; prima
Presentment warranty: garantía de presentación
Price discrimination: discriminación en los precios
Principal: mandante; principal
Privity: nexo jurídico
Privity of contract: relación contractual
Probable cause: causa probable
Probate: verificación; verificación del testamento
Probate court: tribunal de sucesiones y tutelas
Proceeds: resultados; ingresos
Profit: beneficio; utilidad; lucro
Promise: promesa
Promisee: beneficiario de una promesa
Promisor: promtente
Promissory estoppel: impedimento promisorio
Promissory note: pagaré; nota de pago
Promoter: promotor; fundador
Proximate cause: causa inmediata o próxima
Proxy: apoderado; poder
Punitive, or exemplary, damages: daños y perjuicios punitivos o ejemplares

Qualified indorsement: endoso con reservas
Quasi-contract: contrato tácito o implícito
Quit-claim deed: acto de transferencia de una propiedad por finiquito, pero sin ninguna garantía sobre la validez del título transferido

Ratification: ratificación
Real defenses: defensas legitimas o legales
Real property: bienes inmuebles
Reasonable doubt: duda razonable
Rebuttal: refutación
Recognizance: promesa; compromiso; reconocimiento
Recording statutes: leyes estatales sobre registros oficiales
Redress: reparación
Reformation: rectificación; reforma; corrección

Rejoinder: dúplica; contrarréplica
Release: liberación; renuncia a un derecho
Remainder: substitución; reversión
Remedy: recurso; remedio; reparación
Replevin: acción reivindicatoria; reivindicación
Reply: réplica
Requirements contract: contrato de suministro
Rescission: rescisión
Res judicata: cosa juzgada; res judicata
Respondeat superior: responsabilidad del mandante o del maestro
Restitution: restitución
Restrictive indorsement: endoso restrictivo
Resulting trust: fideicomiso implícito
Reversion: reversión; sustitución
Revocation: revocación; derogación
Right of contribution: derecho de contribución
Right of reimbursement: derecho de reembolso
Right of subrogation: derecho de subrogación
Right-to-work law: ley de libertad de trabajo
Robbery: robo
Rule 10b-5: Regla 10b-5

Sale: venta; contrato de compreventa
Sale on approval: venta a ensayo; venta sujeta a la aprobación del comprador
Sale or return: venta con derecho de devolución
Sales contract: contrato de compraventa; boleto de compraventa
Satisfaction: satisfacción; pago
Scienter: a sabiendas
S corporation: S corporación
Secured party: acreedor garantizado
Secured transaction: transacción garantizada
Securities: volares; titulos; seguridades

Security agreement: convenio de seguridad
Security interest: interés en un bien dado en garantía que permite a quien lo detenta venderlo en caso de incumplimiento
Service mark: marca de identificación de servicios
Signature: firma; rúbrica
Slander: difamación oral; calumnia
Sovereign immunity: immunidad soberana
Special indorsement: endoso especial; endoso a la orden de una person en particular
Specific performance: ejecución precisa, según los términos del contrato
Spendthrift trust: fideicomiso para pródigos
Stale check: cheque vencido
Stare decisis: acatar las decisiones, observar los precedentes
State exemption laws: leyes que exceptúan los estados
Statutory law: derecho estatutario; derecho legislado; derecho escrito
Stock: acciones
Stock split: fraccionamiento de acciones
Stock warrant: certificado para la compra de acciones
Stop-payment order: orden de suspensión del pago de un cheque dada por el librador del mismo
Strict liability: responsabilidad uncondicional
Summary judgment: fallo sumario

Tangible property: bienes corpóreos
Tenancy at will: inguilino por tiempo indeterminado (según la voluntad del propietario)
Tenancy by sufferance: posesión por tolerancia
Tenancy by the entirety: locación conyugal conjunta
Tenancy for years: inguilino por un término fijo
Tenancy in common: specie de copropiedad indivisa
Tender: oferta de pago; oferta de ejecución

Testamentary trust: fideicomiso testamentario
Testator (-trix): testador (-a)
Third-party-beneficiary contract: contrato para el beneficio del tercero-beneficiario
Tort: agravio; cuasi-delito
Totten trust: fideicomiso creado por un depósito bancario
Trade acceptance: letra de cambio aceptada
Trademark: marca registrada
Trade name: nombre comercial; razón social
Traveler's check: cheque del viajero
Trespass to land: ingreso no authorizado a las tierras de otro
Trespass to personalty: violación de los derechos posesorios de un tercero con respecto a bienes muebles
Trust: fideicomiso; trust

Ultra vires: ultra vires; fuera de la facultad (de una sociedad anónima)
Unanimous opinion: opinión unámine
Unconscionable contract or clause: contrato leonino; cláusula leonino
Underwriter: subscriptor; asegurador
Unenforceable contract: contrato que no se puede hacer cumplir
Unilateral contract: contrato unilateral
Union shop: taller agremiado; empresa en la que todos los empleados son miembros del gremio o sindicato
Usage of trade: uso comercial
Usury: usura

Valid contract: contrato válido
Venue: lugar; sede del proceso
Vertical merger: fusión vertical de empresas
Voidable contract: contrato anulable
Void contract: contrato nulo; contrato inválido, sin fuerza legal
Voir dire: examen preliminar de un testigo a jurado por el tribunal para determinar su competencia

Voting trust: fideicomiso para ejercer el derecho de voto
Waiver: renuncia; abandono
Warranty of habitability: garantía de habitabilidad
Warranty of possession: garantía de posesión
Watered stock: acciones diluídos; capital inflado
White-collar crime: crimen administrativo
Writ of attachment: mandamiento de ejecución; mandamiento de embargo
Writ of certiorari: auto de avocación; auto de certiorari
Writ of execution: auto ejecutivo; mandamiento de ejecutión
Writ of mandamus: auto de mandamus; mandamiento; orden judicial

Table of Cases

Principal cases are in italic type. Summarized and cited cases are in roman type. References are to page numbers.

A. Alport & Son, Inc. V. Hotel Evans, Inc., 576
Ackerman v. Maddux, 108
Adams v. Barcomb, 128
Adams v. Cohen, 173
Adams v. Southern California First Nat. Bank, 704
Agaliotis v. Agaliotis, 588
Akwell Corp. v. Eiger, 518
Alafoss v. Premium Corp. of America, Inc., 404
Allen v. Houserman, 304
All-State Industries of North Carolina, Inc. v. F.T.C., 428
Allstate Ins. Co. v. Kleveno, 727
Almeida v. Trushin, 293
American Future Systems, Inc., United States v., 432
American Restaurant Supply Co. v. Wilson, 691
American Textile Mfrs. Institute, Inc. v. Donovan, 84
Amex-Protein Development Corp., In re, 691
AMF, Inc. v. McDonald's Corp., 393
Anderson v. Associated Grocers, Inc., 417
Arbet v. Gussarson, 416
Arcanum Nat. Bank v. Hessler, 607
Asdourian v. Araj, 144
Ashe v. Swenson, 56
Atkins v. Johnson, 136
Atlas Roofing Company, Inc., v. Occupational Safety and Health Review Commission, 36
At & T Technologies, Inc. v. Communications Workers of America, 24
Automotive Spares Corp. v. Archer Bearings Co., 172
Avner v. Longridge Estates, 419

Baldrige, Commonwealth ex rel. v. Philadelphia Electric Co., 522
Baltimore, City of v. De Luca-Davis Const. Co., 224
Bankamerica Corp. v. United States, 74
Bank of America Nat. Trust and Sav. Ass'n v. Morse, 516

Bank of Viola v. Nestrick, 576
Barker v. Lull Engineering Co., Inc., 421
Barnette v. McNulty, 776
Barton v. Scott Hudgens Realty & Mortg., Inc., 577
Basic Inc. v. Levinson, 556
Bayer v. Bayer, 492, 495
Beaver v. Harris' Estate, 155
Beck & Pauli Lith Co v. Colorado Milling & Elevator Co, 205
Beneficial Finance Co. of Norman v. Marshall, 635
Bergum v. Weber, 170
Berns Const. Co. v. Highley, 680
Bertolet v. Burke, 624
Beverly Glen Music, Inc. v. Warner Communications, Inc., 223
Bevles Co., Inc. v. Teamsters Local, 36
Birmingham Trust Nat. Bank v. Central Bank & Trust Co., 639
Birt v. St. Mary Mercy Hospital of Gary, Inc., 539
Black and Decker Mfg. Co. v. Sears, Roebuck and Co., 284
Blatty v. New York Times Co., 67
Block & Kleaver, Inc., People v., 427
Board of Home Missions and Church Extension of Methodist Episcopal Church v. Manley, 122
Boston Firefightes Union, Local 718 v. Boston Chapter NAACP, 23
Bovy v. Graham, Cohen & Wampold, 495
B. P. Oil Corp. v. Mabe, 458
Bravo v. Buelow, 222
Brewer, United States v., 64
Bricks Unlimited, Inc. v. Agee, 621
Broadway Management Corp. v. Briggs, 579
Brogan Cadillac-Oldsmobile Corp. v. Central Jersey Bank and Trust Co., 614
Brown v. Board of Education of Topeka, Shawnee County, Kan., 5

TC-1

Brown v. Coastal Truckways, Inc., 121
Brown University v. Laudati, 583, 603
Buckman v. Goldblatt, 472
Bukacek v. Pell City Farms, Inc., 509
Bunny Bread v. Shipman, 267
Burbank, City of v. Lockheed Air Terminal Inc., 35
Burchett v. Allied Concord Financial Corporation, 620
Burnett, In re, 697
Burrow v. Miller, 317

Cabaniss v. Cabaniss, 776
Calada Materials Co. v. Collins, 464
Callahan v. C. & S. Bank of Houston County, 588
Callaizakis v. Astor Development Co., 419
Callarama v. Associates Discount Corp. of Del., 443
Campbell v. Yokel, 172
Cannaday v. Cossey, 151
Cannon v. Texas Gulf Sulphur Co., 556
Carlill v. Carbolic Smoke Ball Co., 111
Carroll v. Exxon Co., 443
Casanova Guns, Inc. v. Connally, 506
Casarez v. Garcia, 589
Castle Cars, Inc. v. United States Fire Insurance Co., 724
Caudle v. Sherrard Motor Co., 359
Cervitor Kitchens, Inc. v. Chapman, 383
Chaiken v. Employment Sec. Commission, 465
Chancellor, Inc. v. Hamilton Appliance Co., Inc., 121
Chan Siew Lai, State ex rel. v. Powell, 643
Chapman v. Miller, 436
Chase Manhattan Bank v. Equibank, 659
Chase Resorts, Inc. v. Johns-Manville Corp., 402
Chicago Roller Skate Mfg. Co. v. Sokol Mfg. Co., 391
Ciambrone, United States v., 54
Cicci v. Lincoln Nat. Bank & Trust Co. of Cent. New York, 643
Cintrone v. Hertz Truck Leasing and Rental Service, 407
Ciofalo v. Vic Tanney Gyms, Inc., 145
Cirar v. Bank of Hartshorne, 644
Citizens Nat. Bank of Englewood v. Fort Lee Sav. & Loan Ass'n, 641
City Bank of Honolulu v. Tenn, 642
City of *(see name of city)*
C & J Fertilizer, Inc. v. Allied Mut. Ins. Co., 713
Clark v. Sumner, 339
Coblentz v. Riskin, 262
Cody v. Scott, 32
Collins v. Uniroyal, Inc., 409
Collister v. Nationwide Life Ins. Co., 717
Columbus Watch Co. v. Hodenpyl, 769
Commercial Bank & Trust Co. v. Middle Georgia Livestock Sales, 617
Common Cause v. Nuclear Regulatory Commission, 34
Commonwealth Capital Inv. Corp. v. McElmurry, 491

Commonwealth ex rel. v. ____(see opposing party and relator)
Conard, In re, 745
Connecticut Printers, Inc. v. Gus Kroesen, Inc., 121
Connor v. Great Western Sav. & Loan Ass'n, 419
Containerfreight Corp. v. United States, 31
Conte v. Dwan Lincoln-Mercury, Inc., 393
Cooper v. Saunders-Hunt, 460
Costanzo v. Lawrence, 485, 486
Cote v. Wadel, 36
Courtaulds North America, Inc. v. North Carolina Nat. Bank, 659
Cramblit, People v., 57
Crestview Cemetery Ass'n v. Dieden, 190
Crockford's Club Ltd. v. Si-Ahmed, 140
Cunningham, Matter of Estate of, 761
Cushing v. Thomson, 113
Custom Built Homes Co. v. Kansas State Commission of Revenue and Taxation, 358, 375
Cutler v. Bowen, 465

Daly v. General Motors Corp., 420
Daniell v. Ford Motor Co., Inc., 405
Danje Fbrics Div. of Kingspoint Intern. Corp. v. Morgan Guar. Trust Co., 595, 598
David Crystal, Inc. v. Cunard S. S. Co., 670
Davis v. Heath Development Co., 535
De Joseph v. Zambelli, 152, 153
de la Fuente v. Home Sav. Ass'n, 618
Delaney v. Fidelity Lease Limited, 467
DeWitt v. American Family Mut. Ins. Co., 724
Diamond v. Chakrabarty, 284
Directors of Willoughby Walk Co-op. Apartments, Inc., Petition of, 525
Dirks v. S.E.C., 557
Dodge v. Ford Motor Co., 548
Doherty v. Mutual Warehouse Co., 547
Dolitsky v. Dollar Savings Bank, 288
Donahue v. Rodd Electrotype Co. of New England, Inc., 510
Douglas v. Citizens Bank of Jonesboro, 640
Duffy, Matter of, 743
Duris Enterprises v. Moore, 466
Dutcher v. Owens, 312
D & W Cent. Station Alarm Co., Inc. v. Yep, 162

East Girard Sav. Ass'n v. Citizens Nat. Bank and Trust Co. of Baytown, 656
Eder v. Yvette B. Gervey Interiors, Inc., 121
Edwards v. Aguillard, 8
Edwards v. State Farm Mut. Auto. Ins. Co., 729
Edwards Feed Mill, Inc. v. Johnson, 478, 485, 486
Eickholt, Matter of Estate of, 763
Eldon's Super Fresh Stores, Inc. v. Merrill Lynch, Pierce, Fenner & Smith, Inc., 612

Elephant Lumber Co. v. Johnson, 143
Empire Bldg. Corp. v. Orput & Associates, Inc., 292
Epstein v. Giannattasio, 356
Erznoznik v. City of Jacksonville, 8
Escott v. BarChris Const. Corp., 554
Estate of (see name of party)
Ethyl Corp. v. E.P.A., 77
Exchange Bank & Trust Co. v. Arkansas Grain Co., 662

Fain v. Brooklyn College of City University of New York, 36
Fairfield Credit Corp. v. Donnelly, 445
Farris v. Glen Alden Corp., 517
F.C.C. v. ITT World Communications, Inc., 36
Feingold v. Davis, 486
Fiege v. Boehm, 115
First State Bank at Gallup v. Clark, 573, 592
FJS Electronics, Inc. v. Fidelity Bank, 644
Flambeau Products Corp. v. Honeywell Information Systems, Inc., 121
Fletcher v. Greiner, 88
Floyd v. Morristown European Motors, Inc., 258
Flynn v. Reaves, 488
Foley v. Interactive Data Corp., 91
Ford Motor Credit Co. v. Swarens, 218
Fortugno v. Hudson Manure Co., 499
Fotomat Corp. of Florida v. Chanda, 162
Foxx v. Williams, 223
Franco's Estate, In re, 760
Franklin v. McLean, 762
Fraydun Enterprises v. Ettinger, 337
Freedman v. Rector, Wardens & Vestrymen of St. Mathias Parish, 688
Frick v. Howard, 511
Frostifresh Corp. v. Reynoso, 430
Frosty Land Foods Intern., Inc. v. Refrigerated Transport Co., Inc., 670
Froysland v. Leef Bros., Inc., 401
F.T.C. v. Colgate-Palmolive Co., 425
Fultz v. First National Bank in Graham, 591

Gantman v. Paul, 366
Gardner v. Downtown Porsche Audi, 160
Gardner v. Nizer, 286
Garfinkel v. Lehman Floor Covering Co., 393
Garrett v. Coast and Southern Federal Sav. and Loan Ass'n, 220
Gastonia Personnel Corp. v. Rogers, 129
Gauldin v. Corn, 471
General Automotive Mfg. Co. v. Singer, 253
General Inv. Corp. v. Di Angelini, 609
Gentry's Estate, Matter of, 759
Georgia Timberlands, Inc. v. Southern Airways Co., 406
Gibson v. Hagberg, 705

Gilbert v. Old Ben Coal Corp., 82
Gillham v. Admiral Corp., 420
Gillilan v. Federated Guar. Life Ins. Co., 717
Gillispie v. Great Atlantic & Pacific Tea Co., 406
Gipson v. Davis Realty Co., 269
Girouard v. United States, 7
Givens v. Dougherty, 180
Gizzi v. Texaco, Inc., 243
Glassman v. Federal Deposit Ins. Corp., 617
Gleason v. Hillcrest Golf Course, 67
Globe American Cas. Co. v. Lyons, 730
Glock v. Howard & Wilson Colony Co., 687
Goldman v. Trans-United Industries, Inc., 526
Goncalves v. Regent Intern, Hotels, Ltd., 297
Gray v. American Exp. Co., 579
Gray v. Zurich Ins. Co., 191
Graybar Elec. Co. v. Shook, 385
Green v. Superior Court of City and County of San Francisco, 343
Greenberg v. A. & D Motor Sales, Inc., 594
Greene v. Cotton, 632
Griffin v. Ellinger, 580
Grimshaw v. Ford Motor Co., 421
Guess v. Gulf Ins. Co., 729
Guillory v. Courville, 273
Gump's Estate, 779

Hall v. Westmoreland, Hall and Bryan, 579
Hallowell v. Turner, 634
Hamer v. Sidway, 116
Hane v. Exten, 627
Hanks v. McNeil Coal Corporation, 132
Harris v. Great Atlantic & Pacific Tea Co., Inc., 401
Havalunch, Inc. v. Mazza, 49
Hawaii Jewelers Ass'n v. Fine Arts Gallery, Inc., 354
Hayes v. Hettinga, 384
Heath v. Alabama, 59
Heath v. Credit Bureau of Sheridan, Inc., 435
Heckman v. Federal Press Co., 416
Henningsen v. Bloomfield Motors, Inc., 410
Hob's Refrigeration & Air Conditioning, Inc. v. Poche, 406
Hodel v. Indiana, 80
Hodge v. Evans Financial Corp., 176, 180
Holiday Mfg. Co. v. B.A.S.F. Systems, Inc., 386, 387
Holland, Matter of, 740
Holley v. Mt. Zion Terrace Apartments, Inc., 345
Homa-Goff Interiors, Inc. v. Cowden, 337
Home Sav. Bank v. General Finance Corp., 662
Horn's Crane Service v. Prior, 490
Huber Glass Co. v. First Nat. Bank of Kenosha, 645
Hudson View Properties v. Weiss, 337
Humphrey's Ex'r v. United States, 28
Hustler Magazine v. Falwell, 50

Hutchinson Homes, Inc. v. Guerdon Industries, Inc., 411

Illinois Val. Acceptance Corp. v. Woodward, 619
In re (see name of party)
Instituto Nacional v. Continental Illinois Nat. Bank and Trust Co. of Chicago, 659, 660
International Ass'n of Machinists v. Southard, 67
International Paper Co., State ex rel. Reidy v., 520
Intraworld Industries, Inc. v. Girard Trust Bank, 655
Irwin v. West End Development Co., 552
Ivancic v. Olmstead, 318

Jackson v. Goodman, 264
Jacobs v. Jones, 210
Jamaica Tobacco & Sales Corp. v. Ortner, 600
Jebeles v. Costellos, 493
Jefferson v. Jones, 405
Jewett v. Manufacturers Hanover Trust Co., 642
J. Gordon Neely Enterprises, Inc. v. American Nat. Bank of Huntsville, 614
Johns-Manville Corp., In re, 747
Johnson v. B.& N., Inc., 303
Johnson v. School Dist. No. 12, Wallowa County, 207
Johnson v. Sears, Roebuck & Co., 419
Johnson v. Vincent Brass & Aluminum Co., 353
Jones v. Jones, 495
Jones v. Star Credit Corp., 101
Jonson, In re, 753
Joseph Forest Products, Inc. v. Pratt, 715
Joyner v. Alban Group, Inc., 538
Judd v. Citibank, 647
Justine Realty Co. v. American Can Co., 340

Kaiser Steel Corp. v. Westinghouse Elec. Corp., 417
Kaminoff v. Spiegel, 340
Kassel v. Consolidated Freightways Corp. of Delaware, 36
Kassouf v. Lee Bros., Inc., 412
Kates Millinery, Ltd. v. Benay-Albee Corp., 402
Kaufman v. Kaufman's Adm'r, 770
Kemp Motor Sales, Inc. v. Statham, 611
Kennedy v. Custom Ice Equipment Co., Inc., 416
Kennedy v. Reece, 211
Kersten v. Young, 301
Kesner v. Liberty Bank & Trust Co., 505
Kimberly-Clark Corp. v. Lake Erie Warehouse, Div. of Lake Erie Rolling Mill, Inc., 671
Kimbrell's Furniture Co., Inc. v. Sig Friedman, 696
King v. Stoddard, 497
Kleeb's Estate, In re, 765
Klomann v. Sol K. Graff and Sons, 589
Koonce v. Mims, 759
Kopp v. Kopp, 312
Koreska v. United Cargo Corp., 666

Kosloff v. Castle, 688
Kreigler v. Eichler Homes, Inc., 419
Kroulee Corp. v. A. Klein & Co., Inc., 120
K. & S. Intern., Inc. v. Howard, 632

Laborde v. Regents of University of California, 88
Lamson v. Commercial Credit Corp., 587
Landex, Inc. v. State ex rel. List, 540
Landmark at Plaza Park, Ltd., Matter of, 750
Lane v. C. A. Swanson & Sons, 403
Lane & Pyron, Inc. v. Gibbs, 140
Larsen v. Claridge, 499
LaRue v. Groezinger, 196
Lavin v. Ehrlich, 481
Lawless v. Temple, 662
Layne-Atlantic Co. v. Koppers Co., Inc., 408
Lazzara v. Howard A. Esser, Inc., 714
Leonard v. Counts, 780
Libby v. Perry, 458
Liles, Estate of, 762
Lincoln v. Fairfield-Nobel Co., 509
Lindstrom v. Minnesota Liquid Fertilizer Company, 235
Lingenfelter's Estate, In re, 760
Lockwood's Estate, In re, 760
Logoluso v. Logoluso, 500
Long v. Jones, 183
Lopez v. Puzina, 586, 605
Lopez v. Southern California Rapid Transit Dist., 301
Lorenzo, People v., 66
Low v. Pew, 352, 741
Lucas v. Whittaker Corp., 177, 180
Lucy v. Zehmer, 102
Lupertino v. Carbahal, 685

Mackey v. National Football League, 72
MacPherson v. Buick Motor Co., 399
Majors v. Kalo Laboratories, Inc., 408
Markham v. Colonial Mortg. Service Co., Associates, Inc., 434
Martin v. American Express, Inc., 440
Martin v. Heard, 314
Martin v. Ryder Truck Rental, Inc., 419
Marvin v. Connelly, 362
Mary M. v. City of Los Angeles, 269
Matter of (see name of party)
Matthews v. Aluminum Acceptance Corp., 615
Matthews v. Campbell Soup Co., 415
Mattox v. Cotton States Mut. Ins. Co., 730
McCarty v. E. J. Korvette, Inc., 409
McCook County Nat. Bank v. Compton, 611
McDonald v. Emporia-Lyon County Joint Bd. of Zoning Appeals, 319
McFadden, In re, 695, 696
McGee v. United States, 36
McIntosh v. McIntosh, 157

TABLE OF CASES

McKenzie & Mouk, Inc. v. Hall, 716
McKinnon and Mooney v. Fireman's Fund Indemnity Co., 257
McKisson v. Sales Affiliates, Inc., 415
McLaughlin v. United States, 8
McLean v. Paddock, 577
McNeill v. Maryland Ins. Guaranty Ass'n, 729
Measure Control Devices, Inc., In re, 741
Medak v. Hekimian, 219
Medical Committee for Human Rights v. Securities and Exchange Commission, 553
Meinhard-Commercial Corp. v. Hargo Woolen Mills, 357
Menke v. Board of Ed., Independent School Dist. of West Burlington, 662
Mesnick v. Caton, 326
Metts v. Central Standard Life Ins. Co. of Ill., 718
Mexican Produce Co. v. Sea-Land Service, Inc., 375
Mid-Eastern Electronics, Inc. v. First Nat. Bank of Southern Maryland, 700
Midgley v. S. S. Kresge Co., 416
Miles v. Perpetual Sav. & Loan Co., 252
Miller v. Underwriters at Lloyd's London, England, 714
Millstone v. O'Hanlon Reports, Inc., 435
Miron v. Yonkers Raceway, Inc., 110
Mirto v. News-Journal Co., 231
Mitchell, United States v., 8
Mix v. Ingersoll Candy Co., 406
Modell v. Kiamesha Concord, Inc., 298
Morgan v. Cincinnati Ins. Co., 726
Morris v. Morris, 762
Moses v. Newman, 385
Moulton Cavity & Mold, Inc. v. Lyn-Flex Industries, Inc., 383
Mourning v. Family Publications Service, Inc., 436
Mullenax v. National Reserve Life Ins. Co., 721
Muller's Estate, In re, 769
Mutual Sav. Life Ins. Co. v. Noah, 721
My Pie Intern., Inc. v. Debould, Inc., 242
Myrick v. Finance America Credit Corp., 436

Nader v. General Motors Corp., 67
National Cash Register Co. v. Firestone & Co., Inc., 702
National Crane Corp. v. Ohio Steel Tube Co., 399
National Ropes, Inc. v. National Diving Service, Inc., 377
National Shawmut Bank of Boston v. Jones, 704
National Surety Corp. v. Midland Bank, 656
Nationwide Acceptance Corporation v. Henne, 615
Nelson v. Hall, 46
Nelson's Estate, Matter of, 764
Neri v. Retail Marine Corp., 390
Nevada State Bank v. Fischer, 629, 639
New England Auto Inv. Co. v. Andrews, 366

New York Credit Men's Adjustment Bureau, Inc. v. Adler, 743
Nichols v. Arthur Murray, Inc., 244
Nicolosi, In re, 696
Ninth St. East, Limited v. Harrison, 374
Nixon, United States v., 35
Nobility Homes of Texas, Inc. v. Shivers, 401
Norman v. World Wide Distributors, Inc., 609
North Cherokee Village Membership v. Murphy, 320
Northern California Psychiatric Soc. v. City of Berkeley, 11
Northern Corp. v. Chugach Elec. Ass'n, 213
Northern Pipeline Const. Co. v. Marathon Pipe Line Co., 735
Northwest Airlines, Inc. v. Globe Indem. Co., 711
Northwestern Mut. Life Ins. Co. v. Wiemer, 778
Nu Dimensions Figure Salons v. Becerra, 428

Oesterle, Matter of, 742
Ohralik v. Ohio State Bar Ass'n, 67
Okamoto, In re, 737
O'Keefe v. Lee Calan Imports, Inc., 104
O.K. Moving & Storage Co., Inc. v. Eglin Nat. Bank, 592
Olivet v. Frischling, 483
Oregon State Highway Commission v. Delong Corp., 219
Overland Bond & Inv. Corp. v. Howard, 406

Pacific Nat. Bank v. Hernreich, 617
Palmer & Ray Dental Supply of Abilene, Inc. v. First Nat. Bank of Abilene, 590, 592
Palo Alto Tenants' Union v. Morgan, 8
Paramount Finance Co. v. United States, 702
Parker v. Arthur Murray, Inc., 213
Parking Management, Inc. v. Gilder, 302
Paschall's Inc. v. Dozier, 100
Patterson v. Bogan, 481
Paul v. First Nat. Bank of Cincinnati, 290
Pazol v. Citizens Nat. Bank of Sandy Springs, 607
Peairs v. Florida Pub. Co., 231
Pena v. Salinas, 720
Penthouse Intern., Ltd. v. Barnes, 189
People v. ——(see opposing party)
Perez v. Van Groningen & Sons, Inc., 267
Perry, In re, 742
Perry v. West, 570
Pestana v. Karinol Corp., 364
Petition of (see name of party)
Pettaway v. Commercial Automotive Service, Inc., 217
Philadelphia Electric Co., Commonwealth ex rel. Baldrige v., 522
Philipp Lithographing Co. v. Babich, 497
Pierce v. Austin, 317
Pitrolo v. Community Bank & Trust, N.A., 582

Polaroid Corp. v. Eastman Kodak Co., 42
Poole v. Marion Buick Co., 393
Powell, State ex rel. Chan Siew Lai v., 643
Powell, United States v., 68
Pratt v. Winnebago Industries, Inc., 413
Price v. Shell Oil Co., 414, 418
Principe v. McDonald's Corp., 72
Prudential Ins. Co. of America v. Marquette Nat. Bank of Minneapolis, 652, 656
Pullins v. Credit Exchange of Dallas, Inc., 442

Quaintance Associates, Inc. v. PLM, Inc., 121

Raffles v. Wichelhaus, 154
Ramos v. Wheel Sports Center, 360
Randono, People v., 68
Ransom v. Penn Mutual Life Insurance Company, 170
Ray v. Farmers State Bank of Hart, 615
Reading Trust Co. v. Hutchison (unpublished case), 620
Reed, Matter of, 737
Reidy, State ex rel. v. International Paper Co., 520
Republic-Odin Appliance Corp. v. Consumers Plumbing & Heating Supply Co., 378
Reynolds, In re, 753
Rheinberg-Kellerei GMBH v. Vineyard Wine Co., Inc., 365
Richardson v. J. C. Flood Co., 98
Robertson v. Levy, 506
Rodman v. State Farm Mut. Auto. Ins. Co., 713
Roe v. Wade, 7
Rubin v. Yellow Cab Co., 271
Russell v. Transamerica Ins. Co., 369
Russell v. United States, 14
Russello v. United States, 65
Rutyna v. Collection Accounts Terminal, Inc., 443

Saigh ex rel. Anheuser-Busch, Inc. v. Busch, 527, 532
Salter v. Vanotti, 610
Salvaty v. Falcon Cable Television, 316
Satterwhite, In re, 752
Saylor v. Saylor, 193
Schaeffer v. United Bank & Trust Co. of Maryland, 616
Schaneman v. Schaneman, 159
Schenectady Trust Co. v. Sciocchetti's Estate, 628
Scherer v. Hyland, 600
Schipper v. Levitt & Sons, Inc., 419
Scholl v. Tallman, 120
Schomer v. Smidt, 47
Schulze & Burch Biscuit Co. v. American Protection Ins. Co., 725
Scott v. Breeland, 14
Sea Air Support, Inc. v. Herrmann, 621
Seale v. Bates, 197
Seattle-First Nat. Bank v. Marshall, 461
Secor v. Pioneer Foundry Co., 721

Securities and Exchange Commission v. Glenn W. Turner Enterprises, Inc., 553
Securities and Exchange Commission v. Texas Gulf Sulphur Co., 556
Securities and Exchange Com'n v. Howey Co., 552
Shackett v. Schwartz, 342
Shaffer v. Brooklyn Park Garden Apts., 656
Shamrock Hilton Hotel v. Caranas, 305
Sheeskin v. Giant Food, Inc., 406
Sherman v. Kitsmiller, 106
Sherman County Bank v. Kallhoff, 702
Simon v. United States, 325
Singer Co. v. Stoda, 670
Smith v. Citation Mfg. Co., Inc., 536
Smith v. Dunlap, 533
Smith v. Gentilotti, 578
Smith v. Sharpenstein, 411
Smithtown General Hospital, People v., 489
Snug Harbor Realty Co. v. First Nat. Bank of Toms River, N.J., 594, 598
Soupcoff, In re Estate of, 283
South Carolina Ins. Co. v. Collins, 719
South Dakota v. Dole, 8
Spaziani, Matter of Estate of, 552
Spindulys v. Los Angeles Olympic Organizing Committee, 18
Sprague v. Frank J. Sanders Lincoln Mercury, Inc., 421
Sprecher v. Adamson Companies, 319
Spur Industries, Inc. v. Del E. Webb Development Co., 321
Squires v. Balbach Co., 543
S.S.I. Investors Ltd. v. Korea Tungsten Min. Co., Ltd., 106
Stack v. Hanover Ins. Co., 714
Stanton v. Stanton, 8
Starr v. Freeport Dodge, Inc., 173
Starr v. International Realty, Ltd., 483
State by Abrams v. General Motors Corp., 162
State ex rel. v. ____(see opposing party and relator)
Sterling Acceptance Co. v. Grimes, 703
Stone v. Martin, 526
Strother v. Morrison Cafeteria, 84
Stuart v. Overland Medical Center, 460
Summers v. Dooley, 476
Sundance v. Municipal Court (People), 8
Surety Development Corp. v. Grevas, 205
Sykee v. Roulo, 233
Sylvester v. Beck, 255

Tarolli Lumber Co., Inc. v. Andreassi, 273
Taylor v. Armiger Body Shop, 237
Tellez v. Tellez, 179
Teresi v. State, 322
Tesoro Petroleum Corp. v. Schmidt, 580
Teston v. Teston, 334
Texaco, Inc. v. Pennzoil, Co., 53

TABLE OF CASES

Texas Hydraulic & Equipment Co. v. Associates Discount Corp., 287
Thompson Crane & Trucking Co. v. Eyman, 156
Thomson v. Call, 142
Thorstenson v. Mobridge Iron Works Co., 394
Total Automation, Inc. v. Illinois Nat. Bank & Trust Co. of Rockford, 521
Totten v. Gruzen, 419
Trammell v. Elliott, 774
Travelers Indem. Co., State v., 395
Tudor v. Southern Trust Co., 768
Turpin, Matter of, 741
Tusso v. Security Nat. Bank, 643
Twin Lakes Mfg. Co. v. Coffey, 409

Union Sav. Ass'n v. Home Owners Aid, Inc., 504
United Bank Ltd. v. Cambridge Sporting Goods Corp., 661
United Paperworkers Intern. Union, AFL-CIO v. Misco, Inc., 25
United States v. ———(see opposing party)
United States Finance Co. v. Jones, 611
United States Trust Co. v. Bohart, 777
United Steelworkers of America, AFL-CIO-CLC v. Weber, 91

Van Alen v. Dominick & Dominick, Inc., 556
Vandermark v. Ford Motor Co., 410
Van Steinberg v. Pacific Southwest Airlines, 300
Vargas v. Esquire, 103
Veale v. Rose, 482
Vick v. Patterson, 135
Vidal v. Transcontinental & Western Air, 377
Vidal Sassoon, Inc. v. Bristol-Myers Co., 426

Waldrop v. Siebert, 332
Walker Bank & Trust Co. v. Harlan, 439
Wal-Noon Corp. v. Hill, 168

Warner-Lambert Co. v. F.T.C., 424
Waronek, United States v., 68
Warpool v. Floyd, 766
Washington Capitols Basketball Ball Club, Inc. v. Barry, 146
Watertown Federal Sav. & Loan Ass'n. v. Spanks, 604
Watkins v. Sheriff of Clark County, 590, 619
Weatherall Aluminum Products Co. v. Scott, 429
Weinberger v. Wiesenfeld, 8
Weingart v. Directoire Restaurant, Inc., 237
Wellenkamp v. Bank of America, 684
Weller v. American Tel. & Tel. Co., 551
Wesley United Methodist Church v. Harvard College, 773
Wheatley v. Halvorson, Inc., 456
White, In re, 750
White v. Orange County, 268
Whitfield v. Century 21 Real Estate Corp., 244
Wickham v. Southland Corp., 244
Williams v. Montana Nat. Bank of Bozeman, 604, 615
Willis v. Sharp., 769
Wilson v. Scampoli, 384
Winkie, Inc. v. Heritage Bank of Whitefish Bay, 645
Witmer v. Blair, 777
Wright's Estate, In re, 775

Yarbro v. Neil B. McGinnis Equipment Co., 178
Yee, In re, 753
Youse v. Employers Fire Ins. Co., Boston, Mass., 725
Yunghans v. O'Toole, 311

Zabner v. Howard Johnson's, Inc., 406
Zabriskie Chevrolet, Inc. v. Smith, 382, 384
Zaretsky v. E. F. Hutton & Co., Inc., 556
Zauderer v. Office of Disciplinary Counsel of Supreme Court of Ohio, 40
Zee v. Assam, 250
Zemelman v. Boston Ins. Co., 487

Glossary

Abandonment Knowingly giving up one's right to property.

Abatement of Legacy If the estate is not enough to meet the testator's wishes, residuary legacy is to be disregarded first, then the general, and then the specific legacy.

Acceptance Communication of assent with terms of an offer by the person to whom the offer was made.

Acceptance (Negotiable Instrument) A draft accepted by drawee for future payment.

Acceptance Financing Acceptance created to finance commercial activities.

Accession Something added to property either naturally or artificially.

Accommodation Endorser A party who endorses an instrument for the purpose of providing a guarantee.

Accommodation Party One who signs an instrument as a co-maker or guarantor, without receiving value therefor.

Accommodation Shipment The shipment of nonconforming goods to a buyer with notice that it is for accommodation of the buyer.

Accord and Satisfaction Payment of money or value in exchange for cancellation of the debt.

Account Party (Letter of Credit) Is the bank's customer who requests the issuance of an L/C.

Account Stated An agreement between parties who have had previous transactions, fixing the amount due from one to the other and stating the liability of the debtor.

Accounting Detailed statement of debt and credit between the parties arising out of the fiduciary relationship.

Accounting (Partnership) Each partner has a right to an accounting of profits and losses at the time of dissolution of a partnership.

Accounting Action An equity action asking for judicial determination of the rights of parties in a shared asset.

Accretion The adding on or adhering of something to real property.

Acquisition To obtain possession of something.

Act of God An act resulting exclusively from natural causes and not brought on by any human interference.

Ademption (Estate) If a specific devise is not in the estate when the decedent dies.

Adequate Protection (bankruptcy) Sufficient protection of creditor's interest in the collateral in debtor's possession.

Adhesion Contract A contract usually on a standard form and presented on a "take it or leave it" basis so that there is no true equality in bargaining power between the parties.

Administration (Probate) The process of settling the property affairs of a deceased person.

Administrative Agency A government body responsible for control and supervision of a particular activity or area of public interest.

Administrator/Administratrix A personal representative appointed by the probate court.

Admissions Pretrial discovery device by which one party asks another to admit or deny any important fact at issue.

Adverse Claim Claim of ownership of an instrument by a third party.

GLOSSARY

Adverse Possession A method of acquiring title to land by doing certain acts over an uninterrupted period of time as defined by state statute.

Advising Bank (Letter of Credit) Is the bank which, at the request of the issuing bank, notifies the beneficiary.

Affirmation A person's indication that what one said or did was true.

Affirmative Action Positive steps taken in order to correct conditions resulting from past discrimination.

After-Acquired Property Additional property acquired after the creditor's security interest has attached.

Age Discrimination in Employment Act A federal law that prohibits the unfair treatment of employees on the basis of age.

Agency Relation in which one party is authorized to act for another.

Agency (Partnership) Every partner is an agent of the partnership.

Agency by Estoppel Occurs when principal causes a third person to believe reasonably that another is his agent.

Agency Coupled with an Interest An irrevocable agency agreement made for the agent's or third party's benefit.

Agency Rules (Administrative Law) Standards or directives by governmental agencies made in accordance with procedures authorized by Congress or as set down in the Administrative Procedure Act.

Agent One who by mutual consent acts for another.

Agent as Bailee An agent may sue the third party for any damage to principal's property in agent's possession since the agent would be liable to account to the principal.

Alien One not a citizen of the country in which he resides.

ALJ Administrative Law Judge is the presiding officer at an administrative hearing.

Alluvium Deposits of sedimentary material which has accumulated gradually along the bank of a stream.

Ambiguity An expression with more than one possible meaning.

Ambulatory (Will) Is the status of a will before the testator dies.

Amendment An addition to or deletion from an existing law.

Amicus Curiae One who gives information to the court on some matter of law which is in doubt. Contrary to law, the judge may set it aside.

Animus Testandi Testamentary intent; testator's intent to make the will.

Answer Pleading filed by a defendant in response to plaintiff's complaint.

Antecedent Prior in point of time.

Antenuptial Agreement A contract entered into by two people who intend to marry each other and which sets forth the property rights of each in the event of divorce or death.

Anticipatory Breach A breach of contract committed before the time of required performance, usually by repudiation.

Antitrust Laws Laws designed to protect commerce from unfair trade practices and monopolies.

APA The Administrative Procedure Act designed to give uniformity to the rule-making and adjudicative proceedings of federal administrative agencies.

Apparent Authority When it is reasonably apparent to a third person that the agent has authority to act.

Apparent Authority (Partnership) There must be at least a partnership necessity for a partner's act to bind the partnership.

Appeal To go to a higher court asking for a review and reversal of a lower court decision.

Apurtenant Easement An easement that relates to adjoining land.

Arbiter One who decides a controversy according to law.

Arbitration Submission of controversies, by agreement of the parties thereto, for determination by persons they have chosen.

Arbitration Clause A clause in a contract providing for arbitration of disputes arising under the contract.

Arquendo For the purpose of argument.

Arrival Draft Draft payable upon arrival of the shipment.

Arson The willful and malicious burning of a building or property.

Articles of Incorporation The written instrument governing and declaring the purposes and scope of a corporation.

Assault The attempt or threat to inflict bodily injury

upon another with the apparent ability to do so.

Assignment Transfer of one's contractual rights to a third party.

Assumption of Risk A tort defense where the plaintiff had knowledge of a dangerous situation but voluntarily exposed himself to the hazard created by the defendant.

Assurances Guarantees or promises that make one confident that the assured thing will occur.

Attachment Enforceability of a security interest.

Attempt An overt act, beyond mere preparation, moving directly towards the actual commission of a crime.

Attestation Witnessing the will.

Attorney-in-Fact An agent given authority by another to act in that person's place or name.

Auction A sale of property to the highest bidder.

Authority The permission or power delegated to another.

Authority Delegation Unless a principal has authorized an agent to delegate authority, the right to do so is limited.

Authorized Stock Number of shares that the corporation is authorized to issue.

Automobile Statutes State laws that hold owners of vehicles liable for harms caused by anyone driving with the owners' consent.

Avulsion An abrupt change in the course of a stream boundary resulting in loss of land by one owner and increase by the other.

Back-to-Back Letters of Credit Where one credit is used as a collateral for the issuance of another.

Bad Check A check that is dishonored on presentation because of insufficient funds or a closed or nonexistent bank account.

Bailee One to whom bailment property is delivered.

Bailee's Lien The right of a bailee to hold goods until paid for work or services.

Bailment Transfer of possession of property to another for a particular purpose.

Bailor Person who delivers personal property to another for purpose of a bailment.

Bait and Switch Advertising of one price or product with the intention of inducing responding customers to buy a different product or at a different price.

Balloon Payment An installment payment substantially greater than the other installments (usually a final payment).

Bank Draft A draft drawn by one bank upon another bank.

Banker's Acceptance A draft accepted for payment by the drawee bank.

Bankruptcy Federal law designed to provide debtors relief from unsurmountable financial problems resulting from debts.

Bankruptcy Fraud Fraudulent use of bankruptcy laws, such as filing false claims or hiding assets to defraud creditors.

Battery The harmful or offensive use of any force upon the person of another.

Bearer Anyone possessing an instrument payable to "bearer" or to "cash."

Bearer Instrument Is payable to the bearer and is negotiated by delivery alone.

Beneficiary The person for whose benefit a trust exists.

Beneficiary (Insurance) A person who is to receive the proceeds of a life insurance policy.

Beneficiary (Letter of Credit) Is the addressee whose demand for payment is to be honored under the L/C.

Bequest A testamentary gift of personal property.

Bilateral Consideration A promise as consideration for a promise.

Bilateral Contract Mutual promises between the parties to a contract.

Bill of Exchange A draft used primarily in foreign trade to facilitate payment for export/import goods.

Bill of Lading Document issued by a carrier evidencing receipt of goods for shipment.

Binder A temporary insurance agreement.

Blank Endorsement An endorsement with signature only, not specifying any particular endorsee, thereby creating a bearer instrument.

Blind Trust A trust providing for management solely by the trustee with no instructions or interference by the trustor.

Blue Laws Any state or local law that for religious or moral purposes restricts activities on Sunday. Some early such laws in Connecticut were printed on blue paper.

Blue Pencil Rule The practice of some courts when

ruling on a divisible contract not to compete in a business to edit out any unreasonable part and then enforce the amended agreement.

Blue Sky Laws State laws to prevent securities fraud, regulating both public and private securities offerings.

Boilerplate Standard or formal language used in legal documents.

Bona Fide Occupational Qualification (BFOQ) Statute provision that permits discrimination based on religion, sex or national origin if it is reasonably necessary to the normal operation of a particular business.

Bonds Certificates of indebtedness for money borrowed.

Book Value Shareholder's equity (assets minus liabilities) divided by the number of outstanding shares.

Boycott As a means of protest, the refusal to work for, or to buy, use or handle the products of another.

Bribery The giving of something of value to influence the performance of an official duty.

Bulk Sale A transfer in bulk, not in the ordinary course of seller's business.

Bunkhouse Rule (Agency) Where agent or employee lives at place of work, going and coming to work is in the scope of employment.

Burglary The unlawful entry into a building with the intent to commit a crime.

Business Trust A trust created and operated to hold and manage properties for the benefit of investors who contribute money or other assets to the trust.

By Return Mail Acceptance must be by the next outgoing mail or at least during the same day in which the offer was received.

Bylaws (Corporation) Rules governing the day to day operation of a corporation.

C. & F. Cost and freight.

Cancellation Intentionally marking or destroying the instrument or its face or endorsement so as to void it.

Capacity Mental ability to make a rational decision.

Capital Contributions (Partnership) Money or other property of value contributed as capital to the partnership.

Case Brief An outline of a reported law case which includes the facts, issue, court decision, and reason.

Cash Surrender Value Value of life insurance policy based on premiums thus far paid.

Cashier's Check A draft drawn by a bank on itself.

Causa Mortis In anticipation of approaching death.

Caveat Emptor Let the buyer beware, a common law rule that buyers and renters contracted at their own risk.

Center of Gravity Theory In conflicts of laws the law of the jurisdiction with the most significant contacts regarding the subject matter of the conflict is followed.

Certificate A written or printed statement testifying to a fact, qualification, or promise.

Certificate of Deposit A receipt for money, issued by a bank.

Certification by Drawee Bank Certification of the availability of funds to cover the check.

Certified Check A check drawn by a bank depositor, and guaranteed by the bank to be backed with sufficient funds.

Certiorari An order from a higher to a lower court, commanding the latter to certify and return to the former the record of a certain case for review.

Cestui Que **Trust** When the duration of a trust is measured by the life of the beneficiary.

Charge-Back Cancellation of credit given to a customer's account due to nonpayment of a deposited check.

Charging Order A court order to satisfy a partner's personal debt by dissolving the partnership to reach the partner's interest.

Charitable Trust Is established to advance public welfare or public good.

Check A draft drawn on a bank for payment on demand.

Checkroom A room in which hat, coats and baggage may be left until called for.

Churning Excessive trading by a broker on a customer's account to improperly gain commission.

C.I.F. Cost, insurance, freight.

Circuit Judicial divisions of a state or the United States.

Circumstantial Evidence Indirect evidence, or secondary facts from which a primary fact may be inferred.

Citation As used here, it refers to the book, volume, and page where one can find the reported Court decision of a case.

Civil Rights Act of 1964 A federal law to amend statutes passed after the Civil War and to upgrade the rights of minorities.

Class Voting (Corporation) Where there are different classes of stock, each class votes as a separate unit.

Clayton Act   Antitrust Act amending the Sherman Act and adding further restrictions to control monopolies.

Clean Air Act   Federal law that classifies air pollution but places enforcement responsibility upon the individual states.

Clean Water Act (CWA)   Federal law intended to clean up water pollution.

Clearance   Collection of funds on a check from payor bank.

Close Connectedness   A close relationship in which the parties may be presumed to have special knowledge of each other.

Close Corporation   A corporation owned by a small number of people.

Closed Shop   A business subject to collective bargaining and that requires all workers to be union members as a condition of their employment.

C.O.D.   Collect on Delivery.

Code of Ethics   System of morals for a particular group or profession.

Codicil   A document that modifies the terms of a will.

Coinsurance   For full recovery of a loss, the property must be insured for a minimum percentage of its market value.

Collateral   Something of value pledged to secure the payment of a debt.

Collateral Heirs   Decedent's relatives based on common ancestry, such as brothers, sisters, and their children.

Collateral Impairment   Decreasing the value of a collateral.

Collision Coverage   Indemnifies policyholder for damage to his vehicle.

Co-Maker   One who assumes liability equal to the maker, signing the instrument in the same place as the maker.

Commencement (Insurance)   The time at which the insurance coverage takes effect.

Commerce Clause   Article I, Section 8, [3] of the U.S. Constitution which gives Congress the power to regulate interstate and foreign commerce.

Commercial Frustration   When an implied condition in a contract does not occur or cease to exist without fault of either party and "frustrates" a party's intentions.

Commercial Letter of Credit   An L/C used to assure payment for merchandise delivered.

Commerical Paper   Paper representing value that can be transferred.

Common Area (Real Property)   Portions of the premises used in common by all tenants.

Common Carrier   One in the business of transporting goods or persons for hire.

Common Stock   The ordinary stock of the corporation, usually with voting rights and pro-rata dividend rights.

Communicate   To make known.

Community Property   All property, real and personal, acquired by the efforts and earnings of a husband and wife during marriage.

Comparative Advertisement   Promotes one's product by comparing it with that of the competitor.

Comparative Negligence   The allocation of responsibility for damages between the parties based upon their proportionate fault.

Compensation   Pay for work done.

Compensatory Damages   Proven losses directly resulting from the breach of contract.

Competent   The capacity to understand and to act reasonably.

Complaint   The first pleading by a plaintiff setting out the facts on which the claim is based.

Composition of Debts (Bankruptcy)   Reduction of the amount of debt.

Compounding a Felony   The crime of a victim's refusal to prosecute a felon in return for a bribe or other favor.

Computer Crimes   Modern unlawful computer activity such as the theft of computer programs and the manipulation of computers for private gain.

Condemnation   A proceeding by which the government takes real property for public use under the eminent domain power.

Condition   Something attached to or made a part of an agreement.

Condition Concurrent   Mutual conditions precedent where the parties are to perform at the same time.

Condition Precedent   An act or event that must occur before the duty to perform a promise arises.

Condition Subsequent   A future event which ends the duty of the other party to perform the contract.

Conditional Delivery   A condition must occur before title is transferred.

Conditional Sale Seller reserves title until buyer pays the total price at which title passes to buyer.

Condominium A system of separate ownership of real property in individual units of multiunit projects.

Confirmation (Bankruptcy) The reorganization plan must be confirmed by the court before being placed in effect.

Confirming Bank (Letter of Credit) Is the bank which promises to honor an L/C written by its issuing bank.

Conflict of Laws Where the laws are different in two jurisdictions and the court must decide which to follow.

Confusion of Goods Property of more than one owner becomes intermingled so that it cannot be identified except as part of the mass.

Consent To approve something proposed or requested.

Consideration Something of value given in return for a performance or a promise of performance by another.

Consignment Entrusting of goods to consignee to sell for consignor.

Consolidation (Corporation) Joining of two or more corporations to become a newly formed corporation.

Conspiracy A combination of two or more persons to commit a criminal act or to commit a lawful act by unlawful means.

Constitution The original and fundamental principles of law by which a system of government is created.

Contract Voluntary agreement between two or more persons to do or not to do something.

Contract Interference Inducing a party to break a contract or interfering with a prospective contractual advantage.

Constructive Bailment A bailment imposed by law requiring a person in possession of property to deliver it to another.

Constructive Eviction Some act or omission by the landlord that makes the premises uninhabitable.

Constructive Fraud An act or situation creating an inference of fraud.

Constructive Notice Notice implied by law.

Constructive Trust Is created to redress a wrong or to prevent unjust enrichment.

Consumer Defenses Defenses that a consumer may use against the seller who demands payment.

Contempt of Court An act or omission that interferes with the orderly administration of justice or impairs the dignity of the court or respect for its authority.

Contingency Fee A charge made by an attorney depending upon the successful outcome of the case and often agreed to be a percentage of the recovery.

Contingent Beneficiary (Insurance) Receives the policy proceeds if the primary beneficiary predeceases the insured.

Contract to Sell Concerns the sale of future goods, i.e., goods presently not existing.

Contributory Negligence Conduct on part of the plaintiff which contributes to or causes plaintiff's injury, and may be used as a defense by the defendant.

Conversion Deprivation of another's personal property without authorization or justification.

Convict One who has been determined by a court to be guilty of the crime charged.

Cooperative (Business Organization) A group of individuals organized to gain some commercial advantage for their members.

Cooperative (Real Estate) A business entity that holds title to premises and grants rights to occupancy of specific units.

Copyright A protection giving artists and writers exclusive rights to their works.

Core Proceedings Matters that may be determined by a Bankruptcy Court.

Corporate Personality A corporation is a "person" created pursuant to statute, and has many, but not all, of the legal rights of a natural person.

Corporate Veil Corporate shield which may be pierced to make the corporate owner(s) personally liable.

Corporation A business organization created pursuant to statute, owned by one or more shareholders.

Corpus The assets in a trust.

Corpus Delecti Objective proof that a crime has been committed.

Counsel The terms of counsel, counselor, attorney, and lawyer are used interchangeably to refer to a person representing another in legal matters.

Counterfeit Something made in imitation of something else with an intent to defraud by passing the false copy as genuine.

Counteroffer Counterproposal by the offeree with different terms than were in the original offer.

Course of Dealing Previous conduct between the parties to a transaction which fairly establishes a common basis of understanding between them.

Course of Performance Performance according to the common practices and customs of such commercial transactions.

Covenant A promise to do or not to do something.

Covenant Not to Compete A clause in a contract by which one party agrees not to conduct business or professional activities similar to those of another party.

Coverage Purchase by buyer of substitute goods where goods shipped are defective.

Cramdown (Bankruptcy) Court confirmation of a reorganization plan that has been rejected by a class of creditors.

Creation The act of bringing something into existence.

Credit Advertising Offers money loans to the consumer for the purchase of certain goods.

Credit Card Misuse The use of another's credit card without the cardholder's or issuer's consent.

Creditor One to whom money is owed by the debtor.

Creditor Beneficiary A creditor beneficiary is a third party who has an obligation settled by agreement between the contracting parties.

Crime An act which the government has defined as contrary to the public good.

Crime (Partnership) A partnership may be liable for crimes committed in its business by one or more of the partners.

Criminal Negligence Injury or death caused by one's recklessness without regard of the consequences or with indifference to the safety and rights of others.

Cross Examination Questioning of a witness by a party or lawyer other than the one who called the witness.

Cumulative Voting (Corporation) Each share has as many votes as there are vacancies at the board of directors.

Custodian One who has immediate care or charge of something or someone.

Customary Authority Authority customary in a particular community for the type of activity involved.

***Cy Pres* Doctrine (Trust)** Allows the court to designate another purpose most similar to the original one which can no longer be attained.

Damages Money awarded to a party injured by the wrongful act or failure to act of another party.

***De facto* Corporation** Not in substantial compliance with the law, but where a good faith effort has been made to organize under the law, and business has been transacted as a corporation.

***De jure* Corporation** Established in compliance with applicable laws.

De Minimus Non Curat Lex The law does not concern itself with trifling matters.

Debentures Unsecured bonds.

Debt The obligation of one person to pay or compensate another.

Debtor One who owes a debt.

Debtor in Possession The debtor managing and operating a business under a plan for reorganization.

Deceit To be deceived one must reasonably rely upon an intentional misrepresentation and be injured as a result.

Deceptive Advertising Contains statements of facts that are false, less than the truth, or merely unproven.

Deed of Trust A conveyance of title of property to a trustee, as security for the payment of a debt.

Defamation The publication of anything injurious to the reputation of another.

Default Failure to keep a promise to pay or to do some other act required by a contract.

Default Judgment Judgment entered against a defendant due to failure to answer plaintiff's complaint or appear for trial.

Defeasance Provision voiding the mortgage upon complete repayment of the debt.

Defendant One who is sued by another.

Delegable Duty A duty that an obligor is able to transfer to another.

Delegated Powers (Administrative Law) Authority conferred by one (Congress) on another (Agency) to act for its (Congress) benefit.

Delivery A voluntary transfer of title from one person to another.

Depositary Bank Bank which payee deposits the check.

Deposition A statement by a witness under oath, taken in question and answer form as it would be in court, with the other party permitted to be present and cross-examine.

Derivative Action (Corporation) Action taken on behalf of the corporation.

Destination Contract Title and risk of loss pass to buyer upon tender of delivery at destination.

Detriment A disadvantage.

Devise Real property granted by will.

Directors (Corporation) Persons elected by the owners (shareholders) of a corporation to manage the corporation on behalf of the shareholders.

Disability The state of not being fully able to function, whether physical or mental.

Disaffirm To refuse to honor a contract.

Discharge Release of a debtor from his debts.

Disclaimer An express or implied denial of certain things in issue.

Disclosed Principal A disclosed principal is one named in the agency contract or of whom the third party has notice.

Disclosure Statement Shows the total finance charge translated into A.P.R. (annual percentage rate).

Discretionary Trust Allows the trustee to manage the trust in a way he sees fit.

Dishonor (Negotiable Instrument) Failure or refusal to accept or pay commercial paper.

Dissent To disagree with the majority.

Dissolution (Corporation) A corporation terminates upon its dissolution and winding up.

Dissolution (Partnership) The termination and "winding up" of the partnership.

Dissolution Notice (Partnership) Necessary to prevent continuing liability by one partner for the acts of another partner.

Distribution (Partnership) Paying out of partnership assets upon dissolution.

Distribution in Kind Distribution in property other than money.

Dividends Distribution of profit paid to shareholders by a corporation.

Divisible Contract An agreement that can be divided up into separate independent provisions.

Document of Title Documentary evidence of ownership of certain goods.

Documentary Bill of Exchange Bill of Exchange accompanied by documents relating to the shipment.

Documentary Collection A draft accompanied by a title document which is to be surrendered to drawee upon payment.

Documentary Draft Draft to be presented with documentation evidencing fulfillment of the conditions.

Donee Beneficiary A person not a party to a contract but for whom the agreement confers a benefit as a gift.

Door-to-Door Sale (Home Solicited Sale) A sale concluded in the consumer's home.

D/P Documents Against Payment.

Double Jeopardy Guarantee by the Fifth Amendment of the U.S. Constitution that a person cannot be prosecuted or punished more than once for the same offense.

Dower and Curtesy The right of husband or wife to a life estate upon the death of a spouse.

Draft An order by a party, the drawer, to another party, the drawee, to pay a third party, the payee.

Drawee Party to whom payment order is directed.

Dual Agency A dual agency exists when an agent represents both parties to a transaction.

Due-on-Sale Clause Provision rendering the entire debt due and payable upon the sale of the property by debtor.

Due Process Course of legal proceedings established under the U.S. Constitution, state and federal laws to protect individual rights and liberties.

Duly Negotiated Document Document negotiated to a holder who purchases it in good faith without notice of any defenses.

Durable Power of Attorney A power of attorney designed to survive the insanity or physical incapacity of the principal.

Duress Unlawful threats or action by one person that compels another to do what otherwise would not have been done.

Duty Performance The performance of duty, doing what one is legally bound to do, is not contract consideration.

Duty to Ship Obligation of seller to deliver goods to carrier.

Dynamic Relating to or tending toward change.

Easement A right of one to make beneficial use of the land of another.

Easement in Gross Easement not tied to adjoining land, but one granted to an individual.

Easement of Necessity An easement necessary for the continued use of the land.

Economic Compulsion The threat of irreparable loss or financial ruin as a form of economic duress.

EFT Act Electronic Funds Transfer Act.

Election Rule (Agency) A rule that requires a third party to decide whether to sue the agent or the undisclosed principal.

Eligible Acceptance Acceptances which may be discounted in the open market.

Emancipation A parent's giving up authority and control over a minor child.

Embezzlement The fraudulent appropriation to one's own use of property lawfully in his possession.

Eminent Domain The right of the government to take private property for public use.

Employee One who accepts a job for wages and works under the control of the employer.

Endangered Species Act An Act authorizing the Secretary of the Interior to list wildlife threatened with extinction and providing for the protection of such endangered species.

Endorsee The recipient of a transfer made by an endorsement.

Endorser A person who transfers his right to an instrument by signing his name, usually on the back of it.

Endorser's Warranties An endorser gives certain guarantees to the transferee(s).

Endowment Insurance Provides for payment to the policyholder when he reaches a certain age or upon his death if it occurs earlier.

Entity Something that exists independently.

Entrapment A defense that may excuse a defendant from criminal liability for crimes induced by certain types of governmental persuasion or trickery.

Environment One's surroundings.

Environmental Control Act An act of Congress intended to control the pollution and degradation of the environment.

Environmental Impact Statement (EIS) Required by NEPA to be prepared before any federal action is taken that might affect the quality of the human environment.

Environmental Pesticide Control Act An Act requiring registration and labeling of dangerous pesticides.

Environmental Protection Agency (EPA) A federal agency created to coordinate governmental action for the protection of the environment and control of pollution.

Equal Dignities Express authority given to an agent must be written if a contract the agent is making for the principal is required to be in writing.

Equal Employment Opportunity Act A federal law that prohibits discrimination in employment on the basis of race, color, sex, religion, or national origin.

Equal Employment Opportunity Commission (EEOC) An agency created to implement the equal opportunity policy.

Equal Pay Act A federal law providing that sex cannot be used as a reason for unequal pay for the same work.

Equity, Court of Established as a separate court and body of law in Common Law England to administer justice according to the principles of fairness when no common law remedy existed.

Escheat An estate belongs to the state if there is no will and no heir to inherit.

Estate The assets and liabilities that a person owns and owes.

Estate (Probate) The properties of a deceased person.

Estate (Real Estate) Interest, right, or ownership in land.

Estate for Years A lease for a definite period of time.

Esteem Favorable opinion.

Estoppel A legal doctrine prohibiting a person from denying his own previous acts or deeds to the detriment of another person.

Ethics Standard of conduct and moral judgment.

Eviction The expulsion of the tenant from all or some of the leased premises.

Evidence The means by which an alleged fact, the truth of which is at issue in a trial, is established or disproved.

Ex-Dividend Date Determines which shareholder is entitled to the dividend declared.

Ex Ship Title to goods passes to buyer upon their leaving the ship.

Exculpatory Clause A clause in a contract which excuses a party from liability for negligent acts.

Executed Contract An agreement that is fully performed.

Execution Signing the will.

Executive Order An order issued by the executive head of a government, such as the President, and which has the force of law.

Executor/Executrix A personal representative appointed by a will.

Executory Contract An agreement in which some performance remains to be done.

Exemption (Bankruptcy) Property specified by the Bankruptcy Code and/or state statutes that is exempt from seizure by the bankruptcy trustee.

Exhaustion of Remedies A requirement that certain administrative or non-federal judicial remedies be pursued by a litigant before a state or federal court will hear the case.

Expert Witness A witness who through study, education, experience, and observation has a special knowledge of the subject about which he is to testify.

Expertise Specialized knowledge or skill.

Express To put into words.

Express Authority Authority expressly given by words or in writing.

Express Warranty A warranty made by words or conduct.

Extension of Debts (Bankruptcy) Allowing the debtor a longer time to repay.

Extortion Also known as blackmail, is the illegal taking of money by anyone who uses threats or fear in order to obtain the money.

Fair Labor Standards Act (FLSA) A labor law that sets pay and work standards.

False Imprisonment The unjustified restraint and detention of a person.

False Pretenses Obtaining property by misrepresentation with intent to take title to such property.

Fair Comment (Libel) A defense in a libel suit that statements were not with malice but were intended to state the facts as the writer honestly understood them to be.

Fair Use Permitted use of copyrighted material by others for limited purposes.

F.A.S. Free alongside ship.

Federal District Courts Courts of original jurisdiction over all offenses against the federal laws of the United States.

Federal Trade Commission (FTC) A federal agency created to protect consumers against unfair competition and fraudulent trade practices.

Federal Unemployment Tax Act (FUTA) An act that provides for state unemployment compensation systems for eligible persons.

Fee Simple A freehold estate in land with the right of absolute inheritance.

Felony A serious crime, usually punishable by more than a year in prison.

Fictitious Name A business name different from the owner's real name.

Fiduciary Legal duty requiring one to act for the benefit of another.

Fiduciary Duty Duty owed by a person in a position of trust.

Final Order (Administrative Agency) Despite the name, a final order from an agency is appealable, but an appeal before its issuance is premature.

Finance Charge Consists of interest and other costs of borrowing money.

Financing Statement Statutory filing with a government agency to perfect security interest.

Findings Findings of fact are the factual determination made based on the evidence presented, and findings of law are the applications of rules of law to the facts found.

Fire Insurance Protects policyholder against losses resulting from fire.

Fixtures Personal property attached to land in such a way as to be considered part of the real estate.

Flexibility The quality of being adaptable and adjustable to change.

"Flooring" Where inventory is used to secure a business loan.

F.O.B. Free on board.

Foreclosure Sale of mortgaged property on default by mortgagor in satisfaction of the mortgage debt.

Forgery Making or altering of a writing with an intent to defraud.

Formal Will Must be written or typewritten, signed and witnessed.

Franchise An arrangement for licensing use of trademarks, copyrights or proprietary processes to persons who wish to use them in a business.

Franchise Disclosure Acts State laws requiring franchisors to register with the state and to furnish disclosure facts to prospective franchisees.

Franchisee One who receives from another (franchisor) the right to market products within a certain location or area.

Franchisor One granting to another (franchisee) the right to market products, use trade marks and methods in the sale of goods or services.

Fraud An intentional deception resulting in loss or injury to another.

Fraud in the Inception/Execution A misrepresentation causing a party to sign an instrument without knowledge or opportunity to learn of its essential terms.

Fraud in the Inducement Fraud where the defrauded party knows what he is signing, but his consent has been induced by misrepresentation as to the benefit he will receive.

Fraudulent Conveyance (Bankruptcy) Fraudulent transfer of property made within one year prior to filing a bankruptcy petition.

Freedom of Information Act A federal act that establishes a general policy of full agency disclosure unless information is clearly exempted.

Frolic and Detour (Agency) Acts for personal pleasure outside the scope of one's employment.

Fungible Goods Any unit of such goods is identical with every other like unit.

Future Draft Draft payable at a certain future time.

Gambling Wagering value against an uncertain event in the hope of gaining something of value.

Garnishment Seizure by court order of money owed by a third party (such as an employer) to a debtor.

General Agent An agent authorized by the principal to do all necessary acts concerning the trade or business involved.

Generic Related to a general group or class of related things not protected by a trademark.

Gift A voluntary transfer of property to another made without consideration.

Going and Coming Rule (Agency) Going to and from work and meals is generally considered outside the scope of one's employment.

Good Conduct Behavior which does not discredit one or cause disrepute.

Good Faith Honesty in fact and a sincere intention to fulfill one's obligations.

Good Samaritan One who unselfishly helps others.

Goods All types of property except real estate and some legal documents.

Good Will An intangible business asset that reflects the value of good will relationship with customers and suppliers, and the standing of the business in its community.

Grace Period (Insurance) A time period after a premium is due, within which the premium may still be paid to prevent lapse of the policy.

Grant Deed and Quitclaim Deed Documents evidencing title to real property.

Group Insurance Insurance provided at a reduced rate for people associated with the same organization.

Guarantee Has the same meaning as "warrantee."

Guarantor One who guarantees payment in the event the primary obligator defaults.

H.D.C. Holder in due course.

Habitability The condition of residential or other premises being reasonably fit for occupation.

Hearing A proceeding wherein evidence is taken for the purpose of determining an issue of fact and reaching a decision based on such evidence.

Hearsay Evidence Any statement other than that by a witness who is testifying at a hearing.

Heir One who inherits or is entitled to inherit.

Hidden Defect A defect not readily apparent upon a reasonable inspection.

Holder A person possessing an instrument made payable or endorsed to him or his order or in blank, or made to bearer.

Holographic Will Written entirely by the hand of the testator. Need not be witnessed.

Home Solicited Sale (Door-to-Door Sale) A sale concluded in the consumer's home.

Homestead Original federal homestead law grants of land from the government to private individuals.

Honorary Trust Designates a thing or an animal as beneficiary.

Hostile Fire (Insurance) Unintended fire.

"Hot Cargo" (Labor Law) The unfair labor practice of refusing to handle goods produced by a nonunion company.

Hypothecate To use a property as a collateral for a loan.

Identification of Goods Exact designation of the particular goods involved in the sale.

Ignorance of the Law The fact that the defendant thought his illegal act was lawful does not excuse him from being punished for the crime.

Illegally Obtained Evidence Evidence obtained by illegal police activities that usually makes such evidence inadmissible.

Illegality (Promissory Note) The status of being prohibited by law or of being against public policy, such as a promissory note for a gambling debt.

Illusory Offer A promise so indefinite that it cannot be enforced.

Immunity Freedom from prosecution granted to a witness to compel answers to questions otherwise exempted by the privilege against self incrimination.

Impairment Impairment of certain rights of an obligor resulting in discharge from his liability.

Implied Indicated but not explicitly written or stated.

Implied Agency An agency agreement implied from the actions of the parties.

Implied Authority Authority implied from the words or acts of the principal.

Implied Warranty A warranty created by operation of law.

Impossibility A defense to breach of contract when performance is impossible.

In Banc The full court, all of the judges on an appeals court, considering a particular case.

In Pari Delicto Equally at fault.

In Propria Persona Appearing in court in person without being represented by an attorney.

Inadequate Consideration The actual value of consideration is usually immaterial as the parties make that decision.

Incapacity Legal inability to contract, such as that of a minor or insane person.

Incidental Authority Right to do acts necessary to carry out an assignment.

Incidental Beneficiary A third party who is only remotely or incidentally benefited by a contract.

Income Tax Evasion The crime of failing to file an income tax return or of filing a return that is false and fraudulent.

Incontestability (Insurance) Prohibits insurer to contest the policy for misstatements in the insured's application, after the insurance has been in force for a certain length of time.

Indemnify To provide compensation for or to repair loss or damage suffered.

Indemnification (Partnership) Reimbursement for expense or loss by one partner for the benefit of the partnership.

Independent Contractor One who contracts to do work using his own methods without employer control.

Infancy That period of youth wherein there is no criminal responsibility.

Infraction A petty offense usually not classified as a crime.

Internal Revenue Service Federal agency primarily concerned with the administration of federal tax laws.

Infirmity Irregularity that impairs.

Infringement A violation or encroachment upon the rights of another.

Inherently Dangerous Dangerous from the nature of the work itself.

Injunction A court order requiring a party either to stop or to continue doing a particular act or activity.

Insanity In criminal law, by whatever test used, it is that degree of mental disorder that relieves one of criminal responsibility for his or her actions.

Insider Information Information not available to the public at large.

Insider Trading Trading of corporate stock by a corporate officer or other insider who profits by his access to information not available to the public.

Insolvency A financial condition in which one is unable to meet obligations as they mature or where one's liabilities exceed assets.

Installment Contracts Contracts permitting delivery of goods in more than one shipment.

Installment Contract Payments Partial payments made on account of a debt due.

Installment Sales Contracts by which goods are bought now but paid for over a period of time by a number of installments.

Insubordination The act of not submitting to authority or of being disobedient.

Insurable Interest Interest in property or in a person held by purchaser of an insurance policy.

Insurable Interest in Property Interest in property which may be insured against loss or damage.

Insurance An agreement by an insurer to give to the insured money or some other benefit in the event of destruction, loss or injury to a specified person or thing in which the insured has a legal interest.

Insurance Policy The written contract of insurance between the insurer and the insured policyholder.

Intended Beneficiary A person who is intended to receive a benefit or advantage from a contract.

Intent A state of mind wherein the person knows and desires the consequences of his words and actions.

Intention of the Parties A mutual determination to do a specified thing or to act in a particular manner.

Inter Vivos Between living persons.

Interference To come in between, intervene or intermeddle for some purpose.

Interrogatories Discovery tool in which written questions are asked by one party and served on the adversary, who must then answer by written replies made under oath.

Intestate The state of having no valid will.

Intoxication A state of drunkenness or some similar condition caused by use of drugs other than alcohol.

Invasion of Privacy Wrongful intrusion into another's private activities by an individual or the government.

Involuntary Bankruptcy Bankruptcy initiated by the bankrupt's creditors.

Irrevocable Agency An agency which can only be terminated under the terms of the original contract or with the consent of an agent.

Issued Stock Number of shares that the corporation actually has issued.

Issuer (Letter of Credit) Is the bank, or the nonbank enterprise, which issues the L/C.

Joint Stock Comapny An unincorporated business organization whose owners are issued shares of stock to evidence their ownership.

Joint Tenants Ownership by two or more persons where on the death of one, his or her interest passes to the survivor or survivors.

Joint Venture A partnership for a special or limited purpose.

Judgment The determination by a court of matters submitted to it.

Judgment Notwithstanding the Verdict (N.O.V. = *Non Obstante Veredicto***)** A judge may set aside a jury verdict that is believed to have no reasonable support in fact or is in conflict with the law.

Judicial Interpretation The explanation by a court of the meaning of a contract.

Judicial Review The review by a court of law of some act, or failure to act, by a government official or entity.

Jurisdiction The power to hear and decide a lawsuit.

Jury A group of people, cross section of the community, summoned and sworn to decide facts at issue in a trial.

Justice The quality of being righteous, impartial and fair.

Kidnapping Forceable abduction of a person.

Kin or kindred Relationship by blood; relatives.

Kiting Wrongfully taking advantage of the float of a deposited check.

Knowledge Acquaintance with the facts or truth.

Lack of Delivery (Negotiable Instrument) When an executed or endorsed instrument is not actually delivered to payee or endorsee.

Land The earth and the things of a permanent nature found there or affixed thereto.

Land Contract A real estate installment sale contract in which title to the property remains in the vendor to secure payment by the vendee.

Lanham Act Federal law providing for federal registration and protection of trademarks.

Landrum-Giffin Act An Act intended to clean up internal union affairs and eliminate corruption.

Lapse (Insurance) Termination for failure to pay a premium when due or within a grace period.

Larceny The taking of personal property by a person not entitled to its possession and with the intent to deprive the owner of such property.

Latent Defect A defect not discoverable even by the use of ordinary and reasonable care.

Lateral Support An owner of property has the right to have his land, in its natural condition, supported and held in place by the adjoining land.

Law The body of rules of conduct expected to be followed in an organized society.

Lease A contract whereby the owner of real property (lessor) gives up possession of the property to another (lessee).

Leasehold The estate in real property of a lessee, created by a lease.

Legal Brief A written argument based on legal points and authorities submitted by a lawyer seeking a favorable ruling from the court.

Legal Duty That which the law requires to be done by a person.

Legacy Gift of money made by will.

Legalese A term referring to technical, formal legal language.

Legislation The exercise of sovereign power to make laws.

Legitimate Portion (Estate) Portion of estate exclusively reserved for a decedent's immediate family.

Letter of Credit A promise by its issuer to honor a demand for payment upon the fulfillment of certain conditions.

Liability Insurance Protects policyholder against liability for injuring a third party's person or property.

Libel False and malicious publication printed for the purpose of defamation.

License A right granted which gives one permission to do something that could not legally be done without such permit.

License (Real Estate) A license of real property is the right to use the land of another with the permission of the owner.

Life Estate An estate whose duration is measured by the life of the person holding it or that of some other person.

Life Insurance Requires insurer to pay beneficiary upon death of the insured.

Limited Liability Limitation placed on the amount of money that one can lose in a lawsuit.

Limited Partner A partner who does not participate in management of the partnership and is not personally responsible for partnership losses beyond his agreed investment in the business.

Limited Partnership A partnership organized pursuant to statute, with provision for limiting the liability of some of the partners.

Limited Payment Life Insurance Premiums are paid only for a specified length of time.

Lineal Ascendants Parents of the decedent.

Lineal Descendants Children of the decedent.

Liquidated Damages An amount agreed in the contract by the parties as a reasonable estimate of damages owing to one in event of breach by the other.

Liquidated Debt When both parties agree as to the amount owed the debt is liquidated.

Liquidation Procedure for converting debtors assets to cash, paying creditors, and discharging the debtor.

Litigant A party involved in a lawsuit.

Living Trust More properly called an *inter vivos* trust; a trust created during the lifetime of the trustor. It may continue beyond the trustor's lifetime.

Lobbyists Those who are in the business of persuading legislators to pass laws that are favorable and to defeat those that are unfavorable to the lobbyists' clients.

Long-Arm Statues Laws that allow local courts to obtain jurisdiction over nonresident defendants when the cause of action occurred locally and affects local plaintiffs.

Lost Property Property involuntarily parted with by the owner through neglect, carelessness, or inadvertance.

Loyalty In agency, faithfulness to one's principal.

Lunch Hour Rule (Agency) Taking lunch is reasonably incidental to employment.

Mail Box Rule Rule that acceptance of an offer is binding at the time it is mailed.

Mail Fraud Using the mail or wire services to further a plan to defraud others.

Maintenance (Real Property) The upkeep and preservation of property.

Maker/Drawer Maker of a note or drawer of a draft is the party that executes the instrument.

Malpractice A professional person's negligent performance of duties.

Malum in Se Naturally evil, as judged by civilized standards.

Malum Prohibitum Wrong because it is prohibited by statute.

Management Powers (Partnership) Each partner has an equal vote in management of the partnership.

Marine Protection Act An Act that prohibits ocean dumping of certain hazardous wastes.

Market Value Share price determined by the stock market.

Marshalling of Assets (Partnership) Application of partnership assets to satisfy partnership obligations, and personal assets to satisfy personal obligations, before using personal assets for partnership obligations.

Material (Evidence) Evidence that is important or necessary to prove or disprove a certain fact.

Material Alteration Fraudulent alteration of the essential terms of an instrument.

Material Fact A fact that is of legal consequence or other importance.

Mechanical Utility Something useful done as if by a machine.

Mediation A method of settling disputes outside of a court setting.

Mental Incapacity A mental condition under which a party to a contract does not understand the nature of the act or the extent of the property involved.

Mental Suffering Compensible injury resulting from mental pain, as opposed to mere physical pain, including deep grief distress, anxiety, and fright.

Merchant Under the UCC a merchant is a person who deals in the goods under contract or by his occupation holds himself out as having knowledge or skill peculiar to such goods.

Merchantability Reasonable fitness of goods for use for the purpose for which such goods are sold.

Merger (Corporation) Joining of two or more corporations to become one of the original corporation.

Mineral Any naturally occurring substance that is neither animal nor vegetable.

Ministerial Requiring little or no judgment or discretion.

Minor One who is not of legal age.

Minor's Driver's License Most states have laws making parents liable for damages caused by minor drivers if the parents signed the driver's license application.

Misdemeanor A criminal offense less serious than a felony.

Mislaid Property Property placed somewhere by its owner and then forgotten.

Mistake of Fact A mistake of fact due to ignorance or a misconception could excuse a defendant from criminal liability.

Mistake of Law One's ignorance of the legal consequences of an act.

Mitigation of Damages The requirement that the injured party act reasonably to avoid or limit losses.

Modification A change in the form or terms of a contract.

Moot Controversy without legal significance.

Moral Obligation A voluntary meritorious or moral act is usually treated as a gift and is not consideration.

Mortgage A pledge of real property whereby title of the property remains with the debtor.

Mortgage Agreement and Trust Deed Documents evidencing lender's interest in borrower's real property.

Motion An application to a court requesting an order or rule in favor of the applicant.

Mutual Insurance Company An insurance company whose policyholders are simultaneously the insurers.

Mutual Mistake Error on the part of both parties regarding the same fact.

National Energy Act (NEA) Federal law intended to reduce reliance upon imported gas and oil.

National Environmental Policy Act (NEPA) An Act of Congress intended to help control pollution.

National Labor Relations Act Labor law, known as the Wagner Act, intended to support unionization and collective bargaining.

National Labor Relations Board (NLRB) An independent agency created by Congress to oversee relationships between unions and employers.

Necessities Food, clothing, shelter, medical care and other things reasonably necessary to maintain a person's status in life.

Needs Contract The same as a requirements contract and enforceable if made in good faith.

Negligence Failure to exercise the care expected of an ordinary reasonable person under similar circumstances.

Negotiable Instrument A commercial paper than can be assigned as well as negotiated.

Negotiation Credit Allows a third party, who purchases the beneficiary's draft, to receive payment under the L/C.

No Arrival, No Sale Title and risk pass to buyer upon arrival of goods.

No-fault Insurance Covers injuries sustained by policyholder regardless of who was at fault.

No-par Stock Stock without a designated par value.

Noise Control Act A law requiring controls to be set in order to have an environment free from excessive noise.

Nominal Damages A nominal sum awarded in recognition that a legal injury was sustained, though slight.

Nonpayment (Negotiable Instrument) Failure to pay before close of business on the day of presentment.

Nonprofit Corporation May make a profit, but cannot distribute it to its members; a charitable corporation.

Nonowner A bailee, a thief, or a finder is a nonowner without title to the goods.

Nonrecourse Endorsement An endorsement limiting the liability of the endorser.

Norris-LaGuardia Act A 1932 law passed by Congress to protect labor movements.

Notice Information concerning a fact actually communicated to a person or derived by him from a proper source.

Notice of Dishonor (Negotiable Instrument) Notice to be given to any secondary parties who are to be made liable for payment of an instrument.

Novation The substitution of a party for one of the original parties to a contract with the consent of the other party.

Nuclear Regulatory Commission (NRC) Formerly the Atomic Energy Commission, the federal agency responsible for civilian nuclear regulation.

Nuclear Waste Policy Act An Act requiring the federal government to develop a site for nuclear waste disposal.

Nuisance A wrong arising from an unreasonable or unlawful use of property to the discomfort, annoyance, inconvenience, or damage of another.

Nuncupative Will An oral will.

Obedience Compliance with a known law, prescribed rule, direction, order, command, or prohibition.

Objective Uninfluenced by emotion or personal prejudice.

Occupational Safety and Health Act (OSHA) A federal law for the purpose of protecting employees from being injured or getting ill during the course of their employment.

Offer A proposal to enter into a contract.

Officers (Corporation) Persons appointed by the directors to conduct the actual day to day business of the corporation.

Open Account Seller allows buyer to purchase goods on unsecured credit.

Open Price When no price is stated in a contract for the sale of goods, the market price will be used.

Operation of Law The determination of rights and duties through the automatic effects of the law and not by agreement or acts of the parties.

Option A contract wherein the seller agrees that the buyer has the right to buy property at a fixed price within a stated period of time.

Order Instrument Is payable to a certain party and is negotiated by an endorsement and delivery.

Ostensible Authority When a principal causes a third person to believe the agent can act, the authority is ostensible.

Overdraft Takes place when a bank pays its customer's check without funds available in the account.

Overdue Instrument Instrument that has passed its maturity date.

Par Value The minimum price at which a share of stock is supposedly sold by the corporation.

Parental Liability Responsibility of parents for torts committed by their minor children.

Parol Evidence A witness's testimony.

Parol Evidence Rule A rule that disallows any evidence offered to a show a prior or contemporaneous understanding of the parties that contradicts or modifies a written contract.

Partially Disclosed Principal A principal is partially disclosed if the third party has knowledge of the existence but not his identity.

Partition A judicial separation of the respective land interests of joint owners.

Patent A document giving an inventor exclusive right to the use of his invention.

Partners' Liability Each partner has personal and unlimited liability for all business obligations of the partnership that cannot be satisfied by the partnership's assets.

Partner's Right on Dissolution Upon dissolution, partners are empowered to do the things necessary to wind up the affairs of the partnership.

Partnership An undertaking in which two or more persons do business for profit.

Party to be Charged The party sought to be bound by the contract, usually the defendant.

Past Consideration Acts already completed cannot be consideration for a new promise.

Payee Party to whom a money instrument is payable.

Paying Bank (Letter of Credit) Is the bank which pays on an L/C on behalf of the issuing bank.

Payment Delivery of money in fulfillment of an obligation.

Payment and Inspection Shipping terms govern relative time of payment for and inspection of goods.

Payor Bank Drawer's bank that pays drawer's check.

Pendente Lite Pending litigation.

Per Capita Equal division by head-count among heirs of the same degree of relationship.

Per Curiam These latin words used in court languge mean "by the court," referring to an opinion given by the court as a whole as opposed to an opinion written by an individual judge. Sometimes the term also denotes an opinion rendered by the presiding judge or chief justice.

***Per Se* Violations** The act itself is a violation without actual proof of injury.

Per Stirpes By right of representation; through deceased parents.

Percolating Water The water under the earth's surface.

Perfect Tender versus Substantial Performance Tender of delivery meeting 100 percent of the contract requirements, as opposed to tender meeting most, but not all, of the contract terms.

Perfection Validation of a security interest as against third parties.

Performance The fulfillment of an obligation.

Periodic Tenancy A tenancy for a particular period, such as week, month, or year.

Perjury The crime of making false statements under oath.

Personal Deviation (Agency) The turning aside from a course or a duty for personal reasons.

Personal Property Moveable things.

Personal Representative The person responsible for administration and distribution of a decedents estate.

Plaintiff The one who initially brings a lawsuit.

Pledge A deposit of personal property as security for a debt.

Police Power Limits imposed on private rights and property by the government under its inherent power to maintain health, safety, and public welfare.

Possession Control of property.

Pour-Over Trust When by testamentary disposition decedent's assets are to be added to an existing living trust.

Power Given as a Security Another term that means the same as irrevocable agency or agency coupled with an interest.

Power of Attorney The document giving the attorney-in-fact the power and authority to act.

Practicable Capable of being done, effected, or performed.

Preferred Stock Stock having a preference over the common stock, usually as to dividends. It may be cumulative or noncumulative, participating or non participating, convertible or nonconvertible, callable or noncallable.

Pregnancy Discrimination Act An Act that adds pregnancy to the list of categories protected from discrimination.

Preincorporation Stock Subscription Agreement to purchase shares after the corporation is formed.

Premium (Insurance) The consideration paid by insured to the insurer for insurance.

Prerequisite Something required beforehand.

Prerogative An exclusive right or priviledge.

Prescriptive Easement An easement acquired through the uninterrupted use of another's land for the prescribed statutory period of time.

Presentment (Negotiable Instrument) Demand for payment due on commercial paper.

Preservation of American Antiquities An Act giving the President the right to make executive orders to preserve certain objects of historic or scientific interest.

Presumption of Innocence The principal that a person is innocent of a crime until proven guilty.

Pretrial Conference Conference held after pleadings filed and before trial to bring the parties together to outline discovery procedures and define the issues to be tried.

Price Fixing A combination or conspiracy formed for the purpose of fixing the price on a commodity in interstate commerce.

***Prima Facie* Case** A case sufficient on its face, supported by at least a minimum of evidence and free from obvious defects.

Principal One who has permitted or directed another to act for his benefit and subject to his direction or control.

Prior Payment (Negotiable Instrument) Paying an instrument prior to its maturity date, in which event the instrument should be cancelled.

Priority The right to a precedence or preference in claims.

Privacy Act Law designed to protect the privacy of individuals from disclosure of certain personal information contained in government files.

Private Trust Has private individual(s) as beneficiary(ies).

Privilege Benefits or exemptions from burdens available to some people because of the office they hold.

Privity A contractual or other legal relationship between two or more parties.

Probate Court procedure for carrying out the terms of a will, or for distributing the estate of an intestate person.

Product Promotion Stirring up interest in an enterprise.

Professional Corporation A corporation for the practice of a profession such as law or medicine.

Promissory Estoppel When a person acts to his detriment in reliance upon a reasonable promise a court may estop the promisor from denying the existence of the contract.

Promissory Note A promise by a party, the maker, to pay another party, the payee.

Promoters (Corporation) Persons who plan and arrange for the formation of a new corporation.

Proof of Claim (Bankruptcy) A creditor's written statement describing his claim.

Proof of Loss (Insurance) The formal written statement of a claimant under an insurance policy.

Property Things that may be owned and/or possessed.

Property Insurance Protects policyholder against loss, destruction, or damage of his property.

Protest (Negotiable Instrument) Formal declaration or certification of dishonor.

Proximate Clause A cause that produces an event without which an injury would not have occurred.

Proxy Authorization or a person authorized to act for another person.

Proxy Director's Meeting (Corporation) Is usually not allowed.

Public Policy The general attitude of the public toward good conduct and behavior required of the community members.

Publication (Will) Making the witness aware that he is witnessing the testator signing a will.

Puffing Statements of opinions made by a seller; not made as representations of fact.

Punitive Damages Compensation in excess of actual damages as a form of punishment to the wrongdoer.

Purchase Money Loan funds to purchase property used as collateral for the loan.

Quasi Contract A contract created by the law for reason of justice.

Quid Pro Quo Something for something.

Quiet Enjoyment (Real Property) The right of unimpaired use and enjoyment of the leased property.

Quitclaim Deed A deed wherein the grantor grants to the grantee all of the rights, if any, that the grantor has in the deeded land.

Quorum Director's Meeting (Corporation) The majority of the number of directors.

Quorum Shareholder's Meeting (Corporation) Minimum number of shareholders, usually a simple majority, who must be present to make decisions of a shareholders' meeting valid.

Racial Discrimination The unequal treatment of persons because of racial ancestry.

Ratification Approval of something already done.

Rational Based on reason.

Reacquisition (Negotiable Instrument) Return of an instrument to a prior party who may cancel unnecessary endorsements on the paper.

Reaffirmation A formal agreement by the bankrupt debtor to pay a debt that has been discharged.

Real Property Land and things imbedded in it or permanently attached to it.

Rebuttal Time given to a party who made the first closing argument to rebut any claims made in his opponent's closing argument.

Receiver A person appointed to take charge of assets under a court decree.

Receiving Stolen Property Receiving property that the receiver knows or reasonably should have known was stolen by another person.

Record A precise history of a suit from its commencement to its completion.

Recordation Constructive notice of land transfers through the recording of deeds with proper local authorities.

Red Clause Letter of Credit Allows the beneficiary to receive an advance toward delivery of the goods.

Red Herring (Corporation) Notice of a forthcoming stock issue which has not yet been approved by the Securities and Exchange Commission.

Referral Sales For a purportedly reduced purchase price, commission, or bonus, buyer is required to find other buyers for the product.

Reformation An equitable remedy consisting of rewriting the contract in cases where the writing does not express what was actually agreed upon.

Regulatory License A license required for one to engage in a business or profession and granted only when set standards of expertise have been demonstrated.

Rehabilitation Act A federal law that attempts to assist the handicapped to obtain employment, training, and access to facilities.

Remibursement or Indemnification (Agency) If an innocent agent is required to pay damages, he is entitled to be repaid by the principal.

Reimbursement Agreement (Letter of Credit) Is the contract in which the account party promises to repay the issuer for payments made to the beneficiary.

Rejection An act or statement by the offeree conveying that the offer is not accepted.

Release The act or writing whereby some claim, right, or interest is given up to the person against whom it could have been enforced.

Relevant (Evidence) Evidence that tends to prove or disprove a fact in issue.

Remainder That part of an estate left upon the termination of a preceding estate.

Rent The consideration paid for a lease.

Renunciation Surrender of the instrument, or a written release cancelling it.

Reorganization A procedure under the Bankruptcy Code for the relief of business organizations with financial difficulties.

Reorganization Plan The plan finally agreed upon for the restructuring of a debtor's liabilities under a reorganization.

Repentance To feel sorrow or regret for what has been done or left undone by oneself.

Replevin Legal action to physically recover property wrongfully held by another.

Report Requirements Obligation to give accounts and information at regular intervals.

Repossession Taking possession of a collateral from debtor.

Repudiation An act or declaration by a contracting party indicating definitely that he or she will not perform, or further perform, the contract.

Requirements Contract A good faith contract to purchase all goods that a buyer may require is enforceable under the UCC.

Rescind To cancel a contract.

Res Ipsa Loquitor An evidence rule where negligence by the wrongdoer can be inferred from the mere fact that the accident happened. "The thing speaks for itself."

Rescission The cancellation of a contract and the return of the parties to their original position.

Reservation A clause in a conveyance which creates a lesser estate to be retained by the grantor.

Residuary Bequest Property remaining after the general and specific bequests.

Resource Conservation and Recovery Act (RCRA) An Act to control use of chemical products and hazardous waste.

Respondeat Superior Let the superior reply, meaning that an employer is liable for the torts of an agent committed in the scope of the employment.

Respondeat Superior **(Corporation)** Let the master answer; makes the corporation liable for tort committed by an officer within the scope of employment.

Restitution Contract remedy usually limited to the value of the performance by the injured party.

Restrictive Convenants Promises in an agreement that restrict the use of real property.

Restrictive Endorsement An endorsement specifying use or conditions which are required to receive payment for the instruments.

Resulting Trust Is created by circumstances indicating trustor's implied intention to have the property ultimately returned to him.

Retained Earnings Portions of corporate profits reinvested in the business instead of distributed to shareholders.

Retaliatory Eviction Eviction as retaliation against the tenant for reporting illegal or substandard conditions.

Revenue License A license issued for the primary purpose of raising tax money.

Revocation Cancellation; annulling by recalling or withdrawing.

Revoke Acceptance in a Sale Buyer may withdraw acceptance where goods are subsequently discovered to be defective.

Revolving Letter of Credit Is an L/C covering the payment of a series of shipments.

RICO The Racketeer Influenced and Corrupt Organization Act was passed by Congress to aid prosecutors in apprehending and convicting persons involved in organized crime, and includes a provision for criminal forfeiture of any money or property acquired in violation of the act.

Rider (Insurance) A separate document to change term(s) of a policy.

Right-to-Work Law State laws that provide for an open shop, a business that employs workers without regard to whether or not they are members of a labor union.

Riparian Rights Rights that result from ownership of land on the banks of waterways.

Ripeness Doctrine of the court, in accordance with a policy of self-restraint, that cases will not be decided before it is necessary to decide them.

Robbery The taking of property from the person of another by violence or by causing fear.

Robinson-Patman Act A section of the Clayton Act which prohibits price discrimination between purchasers of like goods when it might tend to create a monopoly.

Rule of Reason Rule made by the U.S. Supreme Court that antitrust laws applied only to "unreasonable" restraints of trade.

Safe-Deposit Box A strong metal container for storing valuables, usually in a bank vault.

Sale Passing of title from seller to buyer for a price.

Sale on Approval Sale becomes final upon buyer's approval of the goods.

Sale or Return An executed sale, but buyer has the option to cancel it by returning the goods.

Sanctions Punishments for violations of accepted rules of social conduct.

Satisfaction Something that gratifies fully the wants, wishes, likes, or desires of a person.

Scope of the Employment An act done in the course of the agency and by virtue of the authority as agent.

Scrupulous Good Faith and Candor Conscientiously honest, sincere, frank, fair and upright.

Secured Credit Credit extended with security of collateral.

Securities Stock certificates, bonds, or other evidence of a secured indebtedness creating a right in the holder to participate in profits or distribution of assets.

Securities and Exchange Commission The Federal agency charged with the regulation of security transactions. Also called SEC.

Security Deposit A money deposit paid in advance to a landlord to cover possible damage or breakage during the tenancy.

Security Interest The right of a secured creditor to the protection afforded by the security.

Security Interest in a Sale Right of party in possession of goods to retain or sell them to recover his loss.

Self-Defense The right to protect one's person, family, and to a lesser extent, one's property, from harm by an aggressor.

Seller's Delivery Transfer of goods by seller to buyer.

Seller's Repossession Seller's recovery of goods delivered to buyer.

Seller's Right to Cure The right of a seller to make a proper delivery of goods after having first tendered a defective delivery.

Severalty (Ownership) Ownership of property by one individual.

Servant One who works for and is under the control of a master.

Servitude Working for a creditor to repay debt.

Sexual Harassment An employee policy or acceptance of the practice of exposing employees to the physical or verbal sexual advances or abuse by superiors or other co-workers.

Shareholders The owners of a corporation; also called "stockholders."

Shareholders' Equity Shareholders' net worth in the corporation.

Sherman Antitrust Act Federal law intended to prevent unreasonable restraint of trade and monopolies in interstate or foreign commerce.

Shipment Contract Title and risk of loss pass to buyer upon seller's delivery of the goods to the carrier.

Shipment with Reservation Shipment of goods in which seller has reserved a security interest to guarantee payment by buyer.

Short-Swing Profit Profit made within six months by an insider.

Sight Draft Draft payable upon presentation.

Signature Card Contains the agency's agreement between the customer and the customer's bank.

Silent Partner Does not take part in management of the partnership, but is jointly liable with the other general partners for all partnership debts.

Sine Qua Non An indispensable condition.

Slander Spoken words that tend to damage the reputation of another.

Small Claims Court A court of limited money jurisdiction where the parties usually represent themselves.

Sole Proprietorship A business owned by one person.

Solicitation Commanding, encouraging, or requesting another person to commit a crime with the intent that the crime be committed.

Special Agent An agent authorized to do a specific act or to take care of limited business transactions.

Special Endorsement Specifies to whom or to whose order the instrument is payable.

Specific Performance A court order to a party guilty of breach of contract to perform or complete performance of the obligation.

Specifications A particular and detailed account or description of a thing.

Speculative Damages Theoretical, not actual damages.

Spendthrift Trust Prohibit the beneficiary to borrow or assign his interest in the trust.

Standby L/C Ensures payment to the beneficiary upon a default by the account party.

Stare Decisis A common law rule to stand by cases already decided and to follow the decisions as precedents in similar future cases.

Statute An act of a legislature passed under its constitutional authority.

Statute of Frauds Statutory requirement that certain types of contracts be in writing to be enforceable.

Statute of Limitations The statutory time beyond which an action may not be brought.

Stay Placing court actions, orders, or remedies on "hold."

Stipulation An agreement made by the parties in a lawsuit or by their attorneys, relating to the business before the court.

Stock The shares of ownership of a corporation.

Stock Dividend Shares of stock issued to shareholders in place of cash dividends.

Stock Insurance Company An insurance company owned as a corporation by shareholders.

Stock Split Division of stock shares into more units. The total value of the new shares remains basically the same as the old.

Stop Payment Customer's instruction to his bank to refuse payment on a check written by him.

Straight Credit Allows the named beneficiary only to draw the draft(s) for payment.

Straight Life Insurance Premiums are paid throughout entire life of insured.

Straight Voting (Corporation) One share one vote for each business matter.

Strict Liability Liability without proof of negligence.

Strike A combined effort by a group to exert pressure on a person or entity to yield to certain demands.

Subjective Determined by the feeling or attitude of the person thinking rather than the quality of the thing considered.

Sublease The transfer by a tenant to another of some, but not all, of the tenancy rights.

Subpoena A court order to compel the appearance of a witness at a trial, punishable as contempt of court for failure to comply.

Subrogation (Banking Procedures) To recover loss incurred by its failing to honor a stop-payment order, a bank may assert the rights of certain other parties.

Subsequent Conduct The way one acts after an agreement was made.

Substantial Compliance Performance of the essential terms of a contract so that the purpose has been accomplished even though unimportant omissions or technical defects may exist.

Substitution Commercially reasonable alternate performance.

Succession The process by which property rights of a deceased person are transferred by will or through the state law of descent.

Summons A document notifying a defendant that he or she has been sued.

Sunshine Act Law that requires government agencies and departments to permit the public to attend their meetings.

Superfund A fund created by Congress to help pay for cleanup costs of hazardous materials.

Supervisory Control Actual management and direction.

Supremacy Clause Article VI, Section [2] of the U.S. Constitution that makes federal acts the supreme law of the country.

Surety One who undertakes to pay money or perform other acts in the event that his principal fails to do so.

Surface Mining Act An Act to control strip mining and to protect prime farmlands.

Surviving Corporation The corporation that remains after a merger.

Sycophant A person who seeks favor by flattering people of wealth and influence.

Symbolic Delivery Delivery of a token with intent to pass title.

Syndicate Two or more investors joined in a partnership or corporation to finance a business project.

Taft-Hartley Act An Act that contains provisions to protect employers from unfair labor practices by unions.

Tangible Property Recognizable property that can be touched.

Tax Sale A sale of land for the nonpayment of taxes.

Taxing Power The power of the government to raise and collect taxes.

Tenancy The right of the lessee (tenant) to occupy the premises of the lessor (landlord).

Tenancy at Sufferance A tenancy that exists when a tenant continues to occupy premises after termination of the lease.

Tenancy at Will A tenancy that may be terminated by either party at any time.

Tenants in Common Ownership by two or more persons, each with a possessory interest that can be partitioned, sold, willed, or encumbered.

Tenants by the Entirety Ownership of property by husband and wife together without possibility of transfer by one of the spouses to a third party.

Tender An unconditional offer to perform coupled with the ability to do so.

Tender of Delivery The offer of delivery of goods, with present ability of seller to deliver them.

Tender of Payment Offer to pay the full amount due.

Tenor or Usance Point in time when drawee is required to pay a bill of exchange.

Tentative Trust (Totten Trust) Customer trust account at a bank.

Tenure The period of holding a job.

Term insurance Provides for insurance only for a certain time period.

Terms Conditions of a contract that limit or define its scope.

Testamentary Capacity The capacity to make a legally valid will.

Testamentary Intent Actual and genuine intent to make a certain will.

Testamentary Trust A trust created by a will or other testamentary document to take effect only after the death of the trustor.

Testate The state of having a valid will.

Testator A man who makes or has made a testament or will, or who dies leaving a will.

Testatrix A woman who makes a will.

Theft The intentional and unlawful taking of property that belongs to another.

Third Party Someone other than the parties directly involved in the contract.

Third Party (Agency) In agency, the party an agent deals with when representing the interests of the principal.

Timber Wood suitable for building, whether cut or in the form of trees.

Time of the Essence A term used in contracts that fixes time of performance as an essential requirement.

Title Document Document evidencing ownership of a property.

Tort A private or civil wrong or injury not based on contract but resulting from the breach of a legal duty that one owes to another.

Tort (Partnership) All partners are jointly and severally liable for tort committed in the scope of the partnership business.

Totten Trust See Tentative Trust.

Toxic Substances Control Act (TSCA) An act that attempts to control and prevent hazardous exposure to toxic (poisonous) substances.

Trade Acceptance A draft accepted for payment by the drawee other than a bank, such as a company.

Trade Fixtures Articles put by a tenant on leased premises for the conduct of business.

Trade Libel Defamation against business.

Trade Secret A list, plan, process, tool, or mechanism known only to its owner and those employees to whom disclosure is necessary.

Trademark Any word, name, symbol, or device used by a manufacturer or merchant to identify certain goods.

Treasure Trove Hidden property whose owner is unknown and to which the finder usually has the best legal claim.

Treasury Stock Share repurchased by the corporation.

Trespass The wrongful interference with or disturbance of the possession of property of another.

Trust A legal device for the management or distribution of property by a trustee for the benefit of one or more other persons.

Trust Endorsement Makes endorsee agent or trustee of the endorser.

Trustee The manager and legal owner of property held for the benefit of another.

Trustee in Bankruptcy The court-appointed administrator of the bankrupt's property.

Trustor The originator of the trust, also called the settlor.

UCC The Uniform Commercial Code, a code of laws governing business transactions and designed to bring uniformity among state laws on these topics.

U.S. Code, Title 42 The original Civil Rights Act, sections 1981–1986 of which allow federal lawsuits as remedies in cases of racial discrimination.

***Ultra Vires* (Corporation)** Behavior on the part of a corporation that is not authorized by its articles or bylaws.

Unauthorized Completion Completing the blanks on an instrument without permission of the party who executed it.

Uncertainty of Performance Grounds for demand by either party for assurance that performance will be forthcoming.

Unconscionable A contract that is unreasonably unfair to one of the parties is unconscionable and unenforceable.

Underlying Transaction A transaction, such as a sale, for which a money instrument, such as a check, is written.

Undisclosed Principal A principal is undisclosed when the third party has no notice of the agency.

Undue Influence If one party unduly influences the other into an agreement they have not dealt on equal terms and the contract is voidable.

Unenforceable Something that cannot be enforced under the law.

Unfair Competition Representations that tend to mislead or deceive the public and conduct that is contrary to honest commercial practice.

Unilateral Contract A contract established by a promise by one party and the performance by the other.

Unilateral Mistake A mistake on the part of only one of the parties.

Unincorporated Association A nonprofit organization such as a social, fraternal or political club.

Uninsured Motorist Coverage Indemnifies policyholder for loss caused by an uninsured motorist.

Unlawful Detainer When a tenant remains after a lease has ended or been terminated.

Unliquidated Debt When the amount owed is in dispute the debt is unliquidated.

Unsecured Credit Credit extended without security of collateral.

Usage and Custom Frequent or established use or practice.

Usage of Trade A practice widely accepted and relied upon in many transactions in a particular trade or industry.

Usury An illegal excessive rate of interest.

Value The price a willing buyer would pay a willing seller in a voluntary sale where both have knowledge of the relevant facts.

Verbatim Word for word.

Verbosity Using or containing more words than necessary.

Void Having no legal force.

Voidable Capable of being annulled later.

Voidable Preference (Bankruptcy) Voidable payment by a bankrupt person to a creditor so as to prejudice the other creditors.

Voidable Transfers (Bankruptcy) The trustee may void and recover fraudulent transfers made by the bankrupt.

Voluntary Bankruptcy Bankruptcy proceeding initiated by the debtor.

Voting Agreement (Corporation) Agreement to vote in a certain way.

Voting Trust Holding voting rights of a group of shareholders to concentrate voting power.

Waiver A voluntary and intentional giving up or surrender of some known right.

Warehouse Receipt Document issued by a warehouseman evidencing receipt of goods for storage.

Warehouseman One engaged in the storing of goods of others for compensation.

Warranty of Authority Every agent guarantees to third parties that he is authorized by the principal to do what is being done.

Warranty Deed A deed that guarantees that the grantor has good title to the land being deeded.

Warranty in Sale A promise by a seller regarding the goods sold.

Wash Sale on Securities Simultaneously buying and selling the same security to influence the market.

West Reporter System Volumes printed by West Publishing Company wherein all reported court decisions can be found.

Will A written expression of a person providing for the disposal of property after his or her death.

Will Contest An attack in the probate court on the validity of a will.

Winding Up (Corporation) Liquidating the operation when a corporation is dissolved.

Winding Up (Partnership) Liquidating the operation when a partnership is dissolved.

Without Reserve (Auction) Once an auctioneer calls for a bid the article must be sold unless there is no bid within a reasonable time.

Without Recourse Endorsement An endorsement transferring the instrument but limiting the liability of the endorser.

Workers' Compensation Acts Laws that establish liability of an employer for injuries or sicknesses of an employee arising out of and during the worker's employment.

Wrongful Discharge (Labor Law) Some states hold that firing an employee without reasonable cause, for a reason against public policy, or by breach of good faith, is a wrongful discharge.

Zoning Legislative action to control or limit the use of private land.

Index

A

ACCESSION, 287
ADMINISTRATIVE AGENCIES
    In general, 26–7
    Exhaustion of remedies, 32
    Judicial review, 31–4
    Powers, 27
    Procedure, 29–31
AGENCY
    Agent,
        Authority of, 229–31
        Defined, 230, 250
        Distinguished from independent contractor, 230
        Liability to third persons,
            In general, 262, 266, 272
            Tort liability, 266, 272
    Authority of agent to bind principal,
        In general, 251, 262
        Actual authority, express or implied, 262–3
        Apparent or ostensible authority, 264
        Equal dignities, 264
    Automobiles, liability statutes, 272
    Creation of,
        In general, 234
        By agreement, 235
        By estoppel, 235–6
        By implication, 236–7
        By operation of law, 238
        By ratification, 237
    Delegation of authority, 265
    Distinguished from independent contractor, 230
    Distinguished from servant, 230, 233
    Dual agency, 254
    Duties of agent to principal,
        In general, 250
        After termination, 254–5
        Care, 251
        Fiduciary, 250–2
        Good conduct, 251
        Loyalty, 253–4
        Not to attempt the impossible or impracticable, 252
        To keep and render accounts, 252
        To obey, 253
        To perform, 252
    Duties of principal to agent,
        Good conduct, 256
        Not to interfere with agent's work, 256
        Not to terminate, 258
        To compensate, 258
        To give agent information, 256
        To indemnify, 257
        To keep and render accounts, 256
    Franchises, 241
    Independent contractor,
        Defined, 230
        Distinguished from agent and servant, 230, 233
    Liability of employer for torts of, 266
    Liability to third persons,
        Contract in the name of agent, 265, 272
        Disclosed agency, 265
        Undisclosed agency, 265
        Incompetency of principal, 274
        Wrongful receipt of money, 274
    Liability to third persons for intentional torts, 266, 270
        Fraud, 271
        Maintain order or protect property, 271
    Liability to third persons in contract,
        In general, 262
        Authority of agent, 262
    Liability to third persons in tort,
        Acts for personal convenience, 267
        Respondeat superior, 266–7
        Special errand or dual purpose, 269
        Torts in scope of employment,
            In general, 266, 272
        Torts not in scope of employment, 266, 272
            Going and coming rule, 269
            Exceptions, 269
                Bunkhouse rule, 269
                Employer provides travel, 269
                Special errand, 269
                Traveling sales people, 269
    Respondeat superior, 266–7
    Scope or course of employment, 266–7
    Termination of,
        In general, 238
        By acts of parties,
            Expiration of contract, 238

Mutual agreement, 238
Option of a party, 239
Renunciation by agent, 238
Revocation by principal, 238
By operation of law,
  Bankruptcy, 239
  Change in business conditions, 240
  Death of principal or agent, 239
  Impossibility, 240
  Insanity of principal or agent, 239
  War, 240
Duty after termination, 254–5
Irrevocable agencies,
  Agency coupled with interest, 240
Third persons,
  Liability to agent, 275–6
    Exceptions, 275–6
      Agent as assignee, 276
      Agent intends to be bound, 276
      Injury to principal's property, 276
      Torts, 275
      Undisclosed principal, 275–6
  Liability to principal in contract, 262
  Liability to principal in tort, 266
Undisclosed principal, 265, 272–3

AIR RIGHTS
Clean Air Act, 76–7

ANTITRUST LAWS
Clayton Act, 74
Defined, 4
Federal Trade Commission Act, 74–5
Robinson-Patman Act, 75
Sherman Antitrust Act, 71–2

ARBITRATION
In general, 23–5

ASSIGNMENT
See Contracts, Third parties

AUTOMOBILE STATUTES
Agent,
  Liability under statute, 272

B

BAILEE
Defined, 292
Duty of, 294
Duty to return goods, 295
  Exception, 295
Liability of, 294, 302
Lien, 295
  In general, 295
  Statutory, 295
  Unpaid seller, 295

BAILMENT
Basic elements, 292
Contract of, 294
Distinguished from,
  Lease, 294
  Pledge, 293
  Sale, 293
Elements of, 292
Liability,
  Degrees, 294
Liens, 295
Special,
  Check room, 303
  Common carrier, 298–301
    Liability of, 298–301
    Limitation of liability, 298–9
    Passengers, 300
    Termination of strict liability, 299
  Constructive, 304
  Contents of container, 304
  Hotel keeper, 297–8
  Lessee of personal property, 301
  Parking lot, 302–3
  Safe deposit box, 304
  Warehouseman, 301
Termination of, 296
  Acts of parties, 296
  Destruction of bailed property, 296
  Operation of law, 296
  Performance, 296
Types of,
  Benefit of both parties, 294
  Sole benefit to bailee, 294
  Sole benefit to bailor, 294
Warranty, implied, 294

BAILOR
Defined, 292
Liability of, 301
Sole benefit to, 294

BAIT AND SWITCH, 426

BANKER'S ACCEPTANCE, 661
Defined, 661
Eligible acceptances, 665
Form, 662
Liabilities, 662

BANKRUPTCY
Adequate protection, 739
Automatic stay, 739–40
  Relief from, 739–40
Bad faith, 742, 752
Bankruptcy courts, 734–5
Bankruptcy Reform Act, 735
Chapter 7 liquidation, 736
Chapter 11 reorganization, 747
  Discharge, 750
  Petition, 747
  Plan confirmation, 749–50
  Proceeding, 749
Chapter 12, family farmer, 753
  Petition, 754
  Proceeding, 754
Chapter 13 debt adjustment, 751
  Discharge, 753
  Plan confirmation, 751–3
Creditors' meeting, 740
Debtors',
  Discharge, 744
  Duties, 740
Discharge, 744
  Denial, 744–5
  Exceptions, 744–5
  Reaffirmation of debt, 746
Distribution of proceeds, 743–4
Exemptions, 741
Fraudulent transfers, 742
Involuntary, 737
Legislative policies, 734–5
Petition, 736–7
Provable claims, 743
Reaffirmation of discharged debt, 746
Trustee, 740
  Duties, 740–1
  Powers, 740–1
Voidable preferences, 742
Voidable transfers, 742
Voluntary, 736

BUSINESS STRUCTURES, 452
Forms of, 453

BUSINESS TRUST, 457

C

COMMERCIAL PAPER
Adverse claim, 621
Bailee, rights and obligations of, 669–71
Banking procedures, 636
  Collection of checks, 637–8
  Customer's duty, 644–5

Electronic banking, 646–7
Overdraft, 642
Payor bank and customer, 641
Recovery rights of payor bank, 645–6
Stop payment, 642–4
Subrogation by payor bank, 645–6
Consumer protection, 618
Defined, 564
Discharge of parties, 631–6
Impairment, 634–5
Reacquisition, 635
Documents of title, 564, 665
Bill of lading, 666
Defined, 666
Duly and unduly negotiated, 668–9
Liability, 669–72
Transferability, 667
Warehouse receipt, 667
Execution by agent, 579–80
Holder in due course,
Defenses and adverse claims, 613–21
Requirements of, 606
Good faith, 607–9
Overdue or dishonored instrument, 610
Value, 606–7
Who may become, 606, 611–3
Imposter provisions, 593–5
Money instruments, classification, 564
Bank draft, 568
Bill of exchange, 571–3
Cashier's check, 568–9
Certificates of deposit, 565
Certified check, 569
Check, 566
Draft, 566
Promissory note, 565
Negotiability requirements, 573–9
Parties to money instruments, 581–8
Accommodation party, 582
Bearer, 581
Co-maker, 583
Endorser-endorsee, 585–8
Guarantor, 583
Holder, 581
Liabilities, 598
Warranties, 603
Personal defenses,
Duress, relative, 620
Failure of consideration, 618

Fraud in the inducement, 620
Illegality as to public policy, 621
Incapacity, circumstancial, 621
Lack of delivery, 619
Payment or cancellation, 619
Unauthorized completion, 619–20
Presentment
In general, 624–6
Defined, 624
Notice of dishonor, 626–30
Protest, 630
Real defenses,
Duress, absolute, 616
Forgery, 614
Fraud in the inception, 615–6
Illegality as to law, 616–7
Incapacity, legal, 616
Material alteration, 614–5
Title documents, 564
Transfer of commercial paper, 598–9
Assignment, 605
Bank endorsement, 592–3
Blank endorsement, 589–91
Endorsements in general, 588
Nonrecourse endorsement, 592, 604–5
Restrictive endorsement, 591–2
Special endorsement, 588–9
COMMON CARRIER
Bailment by, 298–301
Defined, 298
Regulation of, 298–9
Carmack Amendment, 299
Strict liability of, 298–301
Exceptions, 298–9
Passengers, 300–1
Termination of, 299
CONFLICT OF LAWS
See Contracts
CONSUMER LAW
Advertising, 424
Bait and switch, 426–8
Of credit, 433
Of products, 424–6
Balloon payment, 440–1
Credit cards, 439–40
Credit disclosure, truth in lending regulation, 436–8
Collection practices, 442–4
Defenses, 444
Direction of, 424
Equal Credit Opportunity Act, 432–4

Fair Credit Billing Act, 441–2
Fair Credit Reporting Act of 1970, 434–5
Other federal legislation, 445–7
Sales practices,
Door-to-door, 428
Referral sales and leases, 430
State legislation, 447
CONTRACTS
See also Sales
Acceptance,
By act, 112–3
Defined, 103–110
Knowledge of, 103
Rejection after, 114
Silence, 112
Time of, 113
Unqualified, 111
Accord and satisfaction, 120–1
Account stated, 208–9
Adhesion, 161–2
Alteration, 209
Anticipatory breach, 210
Arbitration, 23–5
Assignment, see Third parties.
Auction, 106
Bilateral, 100
Capacity of parties, 128
Aliens, 133–4
Convicts, 134
Insane persons, 132–3
Intoxicated persons, 132
Minors, see Minors
Corporations, see Corporations
Certainty of offer, 105
Classification,
Bilateral, 100
Executed, 100, 123
Executory, 100
Express, 98
Implied, 98–9
Quasi-contract, 99
Unconscionable, 100
Unenforceable, 100
Unilateral, 100
Void, 100
Voidable, 100
Conditions,
Defined, 168
Concurrent, 169
Precedent, 168
Subsequent, 169
Conflict of laws, 191–2
Consent, 101, 150
Consideration,
Act as, 115

CONTRACTS

Adequacy of, 117
Bound to perform, 118
Charitable subscription, 122
Defined, 114
Executed transaction, 123
Guarantee for another's debt, 124
Illusory offer, 117
Liquidated debt, 119
Moral obligation, 118
Necessity for, 114
Paid in full, 120
Part payment with additional advantage, 121
Past consideration, 118
Promise as, 116–7
Promissory estoppel, 121–2
UCC, promise under, 123
Unliquidated debt, 119–20
Construction, see Interpretation
Contract to sell, 353
Covenant, 170
　Not to compete, 145–6
Customs and usage, see Interpretation
Damages, see Remedies
Debt,
　Liquidated, 119
　Unliquidated, 119–120
Defined, 98
Destination contract, 365
Discharge, see Termination
Disclaimer, 160
Duress, 156
Elements of, 98
Equitable relief, see Remedies
For labor or services, 356
Fraud and misrepresentation
　Concealment, 154
　Defined, 150
　Elements, 150
　Execution, 152
　Inception, 152
　Inducement, 152
　Innocent misrepresentation, 151
　Sales talk, 150
　Silence as, 152
　Stipulation, 153
Illegality,
　In general, 134–6
　Agreement interfering with public duty, 142
　Agreement not to prosecute for a crime, 141
　Agreement to commit a crime, 136

Agreement to commit a tort, 136–7
Discrimination contracts, 87
Failure to obtain license required by law, 142
Promise not to compete, 145–6
Stipulation against liability for negligence, 144–5
Gambling, 140
Lobbying, 142
Lottery, 140
Public policy, 139
Repentance, 137–8
Sunday laws, 137
Suppression of justice, 141
Usury, 138–9
Impossibility,
　In general, 210–1
　Act of enemy, 212
　Act of God, 212
　Commercial frustration, 212–3
　Death or disability, 213
　Destruction of subject matter, 212
　Extraordinary difficulty or expense, 212–3
　Operation of law, 214
　Strikes, 212
　Under the UCC, 214
Insane persons, see Capacity
Insurance contracts, 190–1
Intent, 101
Interest recoverable as damage, 220
Interpretation,
　In general, 188
　Insurance contracts, 190–1
　Intention of parties, 188
　Parol evidence rule, 180–1
　Party causing uncertainty, 190
　Subsequent conduct, 190
　Usage and custom, 189
　Whole, 188–9
　Written and printed terms, 189
Intoxicated persons, 132
Liquidated damages, 119
Liquidated debt, 119–120
Manifestation of intent, 101
Merchants, 111
Minors,
　Capacity to contract, 128
　Contracts cannot avoid, 129–30
　Contracts for necessities, 129–30

Emancipation, 131
Misrepresentation of age, 131
Parental liability, 131–2
Ratification, 130–1
Restitution of avoidance, 128–9
Right to avoid, 128
Mistake,
　As to value, 154
　As to subject matter, 154
　Failure to read contract, 156
　Of law, 156
　Unilateral, 154–5
Nature of, 98
"Needs", 117
Negligence in, 44–45
Offer,
　Advertisement, 104
　Certainty, 105
　Counteroffer, 109–10
　Defined, 103
　Duration, 107–8
　Estimate, 105
　Illegal or impossible, 108
　Illusory, 117
　Jest, 104
　Knowledge, 103
　Lapse, 107–8
　Preliminary negotiations, 105
　Quotation of prices, 104
　Rejection and counteroffer, 110
　Revocation of, 108–9
　Under the UCC, 107
Operation of law,
　In general, 214
　Bankruptcy, 214
　Insolvency, 214
　Statute of limitations, 214–5
Paid in full, 120–1
Parental liability, 131–2
Parol evidence rule,
　In general, 180–1
　Exceptions,
　　Ambiguity, 181
　　Condition precedent, 182
　　Consideration, 184
　　Later oral changes, 183–4
　　Mistake, fraud, undue influence, illegality, lack of capacity, 182
　　Subsequent change, 183–4
　　UCC, 184
Performance,
　Payment, 204
　Satisfaction, 206–7
　Substantial, 205
　Tender as, 204

I-4   INDEX

Time, 204–5
Promise not to compete, 145–6
Promoters of corporations' contracts, 512
Quasi-contracts, 92
Reality of consent, 150
Remedies,
    Damages,
        Attorney's fees as, 216–7
        Compensatory, 215–6
        Duty to mitigate, 220
        Emotional, 217
        Liquidated, 219
        Proximate, 215, 218
        Punitive, 219
        Speculative, 218
    Equitable relief,
        Injunction, 222–3
        Recission, 223
        Reformation, 224
        Specific performance, 221
Revocation of offer, 108–9
Shipment contracts, 363–4
Specific performance, 221
Statute of Frauds,
    Contract not to be performed within a year, 175–7
    Leading benefit, 177–8
    Memorandum or note, requirements of, 171–2
    Modification of written contract, 179
    Nature and effect, 171
    Promise made in consideration of marriage, 179
    Promise to pay debt of another, 177–8
    Sale of goods in general, 172
        Effect of delivery, 173
        Effect of partial payment, 173
        Merchants, 172
        Sales of personal property, 172
        Sale of securities, 154
        Specially manufactured, 172
    Sale of land, 175
    Sale of timber, minerals, 174
    Services, 175–7
    Under the UCC, 172
Statute of limitations, 214–5
Stipulation against negligence, 144–5
Sunday laws, 137
Termination of,
    Act of parties,

Accord and Satisfaction, 208
Account stated, 208
Alterations, 209
Anticipatory breach, 210
Condition in contract, 207
Material alteration of existing contract, 209
Mutual release, 208
Novation, 208
Prevention or waiver, 209
Substitution of new agreement, 208
Impossibility, 210–3
Operation of law, 214
Performance, 204–5
Third parties,
    Assignments,
        In general, 195
        Contracts not assignable, 198–9
        Contracts ordinarily assignable, 195
        Effect of assignment, 199
        Effect on liability, 199
        Priorities among successive assignees, 201
        Ratification, 197
        Under UCC, 198–9
    Third party beneficiaries,
        In general, 192–3
        Creditor contract, 193–4
        Donee, 193
        Incidental or remote, 194
        Recission, 194
Types of contracts, 98–100
Unconscionable, 100–1, 159
Undue influence, 158–9
Unenforceable, 100
Unilateral, 100, 112, 115
Unliquidated debt, 119–20
Unsound mind,
    Capacity to contract, 132–3
Usury, 138–9
Void, 100
Voidable, 100
COOPERATIVE, 456
COPYRIGHT, 285–6
CORPORATIONS
    In general, 455
Articles of incorporation, 514–5
Bonds, 546
Bylaws, 515
Classification of,
    By estoppel, 508
    Close, 506–7, 510
    De facto, 508
    De jure, 507–8

Domestic, 509–10
Foreign, 509–10
Nonprofit, 509
Private, 509
Professional, 510
Public, 509
Corporate veil, 506
Directors, 532–7
    As fiduciaries, 536
    Compensation of, 534
    Election of, 532
    Liability of, 536–7
    Meetings of, 535–6
    Powers of, 534–5
    Qualifications of, 534
    Removal of, 534
Dissolution of,
    Involuntary, 515–6
    Voluntary, 515
Dividends,
    In general, 547
    Declaration of, 547–8
    Person entitled to, 548–9
    Sources of, 547
    Stock dividend, 549
Formation of, 514
Legal entity, 504–7
Merger or consolidation, 516–9
    Rights of dissenting shareholders, 518–9, 527–8
Nature of, 504
Officers, 537
    Appointment, 537
    As fiduciaries, 538
    Compensation of, 537
    Liability of, 538
    Powers of, 537–8
    Qualifications of, 537
    Removal of, 537
Personality, 504–5
Powers of, 520
    Express, 520–1
    Implied, 521
    Ultra vires, 521–2
Preincorporation stock subscriptions, 512–4
Promoters, 511
    Contracts of promoters, 512
    Duties of disclosure, 511
Proxies, 524, 535
Retained earnings, 546–7
Securities,
    Antifraud provisions, 555
    Defined, 552
    Government regulatory policies, 552

Industry regulation, 559
Insider, 556
Negotiability, 550
Other enactments, 557–8
Penalties, 557
Restriction, 551–2
SEC, 553
Securities Act of 1933, 553–5
Securities Exchange Act of 1934, 555–7
Short swing, 556
State legislation, 558–9
Shareholders,
   Actions and, 527
   Bylaws and resolutions and, 526
   Election and removal of directors, 526
   Equity, 541
   Inspection of books, 526
   Liabilities of, 528
   Meetings of, 523
   Preemptive, 551
   Rights of, 523
   Voting rights, agreements, and trusts, 523–4
Stock
   In general, 540–1
   Blue sky laws, 558
   Book value, 545
   Capital stock, 541
   Certificate of, 544
   Classification of,
      Common, 542
      Preferred, 542–5
   Consideration for issuance of, 546
   Issuance of, 540–1
   Liability for, 546
   Market value, 545
   No par value, 541
   Par value, 541
   Split, 549–50
   Transfer of shares, 545, 550
Winding up, 519
COURTS
Counsel, 4
Court systems, 13, 18–23
Federal, 13–7
Sanctions, 26
State, 17–8
CRIMES IN BUSINESS
Arson, 61
Assault and battery, 61
Bad checks, 62
Bribery, 62
Computer crimes, 64

Conspiracy, 65
Counterfeiting, 62
Credit cards, 62
Criminal procedure, 55–7
Defenses, 57
Defined, 54
Embezzlement, 60
Extortion, 62
Felonies/misdemeanors, 54
Forgery, 62
Fraud, 63
Income tax evasion, 63
Larceny, 60
Obtaining property false pretenses, 60
Organized crime, 64
Political crimes, 63
Receiving stolen property, 61
Robbery and burglary, 61
Solicitation, 65
Theft, 60
White-collar crime, 60

D

DAMAGES
See Contracts, Remedies
DEEDS
   In general, 323
Abstract of title, 324
Delivery, 324
Elements, 323–4
Form and requirements,
   In general, 323–4
   Consideration, 323
   Covenants of title, 324
   Description of land conveyed, 323
   Exceptions or reservations, 324
   Execution, 324
   Names of parties, 323
   Quantity of estate conveyed, 323–4
   Words of conveyance, 323
Grant, 323
Quitclaim, 324
Title insurance, 325
Trust, of, 681, 684
Warranty, 324

E

EMPLOYMENT REGULATION
Employment discrimination, 87–90

Affirmative action programs, 91
Age discrimination, 90
Civil Rights Act, 87
Equal Pay Act, 87
Rehabilitation Act, 91
Title VII, 87
Employment protection, 81
Safety Act, 84–5
Unemployment compensation, 86
Workmens compensation, 83
Labor law, 81–3
Fair Labor Standards Act, 82
Landrum-Griffin Act, 83
NLRB, 82
Norris-LaGuardia Act, 81
Taft-Hartley Act, 82–3
Wagner Act, 81
ENVIRONMENTAL PROTECTION
Air, 76
Antiquities, 80
Endangered species, 79
Energy, 77
Mining, 79
Marine, 78
National Environmental Policy Act, 76
Noise, 79
Nuclear, 78
Pesticides, 79
Pollution, 75–6
Toxic substances, 77
Water, 77
ESTATES
Estate planning, 758
Intestate succession,
   Distribution per capita, 767–8
   Distribution per stirpes, 767
   Heirs, 765–7
Probate, 768
   Admission of a will, 768
   Priorities of liabilities, 770–1
   Representation, 768
Testate distribution, 763
   Abatement, 763
   Ademption, 763
   Disinheritance, 763–4
Will,
   Contesting a will, 764
   Defined, 758
   Execution, 760–1
   Holographic, 761
   Modification, 762
   Nuncupative, 762
   Revocation, 762
   Testamentary capacity, 759

Testamentary intent, 760
ETHICS IN BUSINESS
Codes of ethics, 40
Ethical issues, 42–4
Ethics defined, 38

F

FAIR-TRADE LAWS
    In general, 46–54, 71–4
FEDERAL TRADE COMMISSION ACT
See also Consumer law
    In general, 74–5
FRANCHISES, 241, 457
    Control, 242
    Disclosure, 242
    Lanham Act, 242–5
FRAUD
See Contracts, Fraud and misrepresentation

G

GIFTS
Causa mortis, 283
Defined, 282
Engagement rings, 283
Inter vivos, 282
    Promise to give, 115
Uniform gift to minors, 284

I

ILLEGALITY
See Contracts
INSANE PERSONS
See Contracts, Capacity
INSURANCE
Agents and brokers, 714–5
Automobile insurance, 728
    Collision coverage, 728–9
    Comprehensive, 729
    No fault, 730
    Liability coverage, 729–30
    Uninsured motorist, 728
Defined, 710
Insurance company, 710
Insurance contract, 710
    Binder, 711
    Commencement, 716–7
    Interpretation, 711–4
    Modification, 714
    Termination, 718
Life insurance, 719

Beneficiary, 720
Cash surrender value, 723
Incontestability, 722
Insurable interest, 720–2
Types, 719–20
Premium, 715–6
Property insurance, 724
    Coinsurance, 728
    Coverage, extent of, 727–8
    Fire insurance, 725
    Insurable interest, 724–5
Regulatory authority, 710
INTEREST
See Contracts, Interest recoverable as damages
INTOXICATED PERSON
See Contracts, Capacity

J

JOINT STOCK COMPANY, 457
JOINT VENTURE
    In general, 455–6
Distinguished from partnership, 455–6

L

LABOR LAW, 81–92
Discrimination, 87–92
ERISA, 86
Fair Labor Standards Act, 82
Landrum-Griffin Act, 83
NLRB, 82
Norris-LaGuardia Act, 81
OSHA, 84
Taft-Hartley Act, 82–3
Unemployment, 86
Wagner Act, 81–2
Workers' compensation, 83–4
Wrongful discharge, 90–1
LANDLORD AND TENANT
    In general, 332
Assignment, 337–8
Condemnation, 336
Eviction, 338–40
    Breach of covenant, 338
    Constructive eviction, 338–9
    Retaliatory, 339
    Wrongful eviction by landlord, 338–9
Lease covenants,
    Cleaning and repair, 336
    Rent, 336
    Restrictive, 336–7

Security deposit, 336
    Refund, 336
Use of premises, 336
    Quiet enjoyment, 338–9
Leasehold tenancies, 332
    Assignment, 337–8
    Creation of, 332
    Writing, necessity of, 332
Leases, period of, 332
    Definite term, 332
    Holdover tenant, 334
    Periodic tenancy, 332
    Tenancy at sufferance, 334
    Tenancy at will, 333
    Tenancy for years, 332
Rent, duty to pay, 336
    Eviction, 338–40
    Rent control, 140–1
Repair of leased property,
    Obligation of landlord, 341–4
    Obligation of tenant, 344
    Rights of landlord on nonpayment, 339–40
    Sublease, 337–8
Sublease, 337–8
Termination of lease, 334–5
    Breach of covenant, 335
    Destruction of premises, 334–5
    Terms of lease, 334
Tort liability,
    Landlord liability, 344
    Tenant liability, 344
Unlawful detainer, 335
Waste, 336
LAW
Case brief, 4
Case law, 11
Defined, 4
Function, 4
Justice, 7
Uniform Commercial Code, 12
United States, 10, 13–7
U.S. Constitution, 10
West Reporter System, 6
LETTER OF CREDIT, 650
Account party, 653
Advising bank, 653–4
Confirming bank, 654
Contractual bases, 654–5
Defined, 650
Documentary draft, 658
Form, 656
Governing law, 655
Issuer, 653
Liabilities, 657–8
Negotiability, 650
Paying bank, 654

Payment, 659–60
Reimbursement, 660
Remedies, 660
Types, 656–7

M

MINORS
See Contracts
MISTAKE
See Contracts
MORTGAGES
Collateral impairment, 680
Defeasance, 679
Defined, 679
Foreclosure, 680
Form, 679
Lien theory, 679
Mortgagee,
    Defined, 679
    Rights and duties of, 680
    Transfer of interest, 680
Mortgagor,
    Defined, 679
    Rights and duties of, 680
    Transfer of interest, 680
Property subject to, 680
Redemption, 680
Title theory, 679

N

NEGLIGENCE
Assumption of risk, 45
Contributory and comparative, 45
Defined, 44–5
Product liability, 398
Tort in business, 46–54

O

OFFER
See Contracts
OWNERSHIP
Community property, 311
Condominium, 312–3
Cooperative, 313
Co-owners, 310
    Partnerships, 471
Fee simple, 314
Joint tenancy, 310–1
Life estates, 314–5
Partition, 310
Remainders, 314–5
Tenancy by the entireties, 311–2
Tenancy in common, 310
Waste, 336

P

PAROL EVIDENCE RULE
See Contracts
PARTNERSHIPS
Agreement to form partnership, 459–63
Charging order, 472
Cooperatives, 456
Creation of, 459–63
Defined, 454, 460
Dissolution, 492–7
    Act of parties, 493
        In violation of agreement, 493
        Without violation of agreement, 493
            Agreement, 493
            By will, 493
            Termination of term, 493
    Bankruptcy, 494
    Continuing business, 495
    Death, 473, 494
    Decree of court, 494
    Distribution of property upon, 499–500
    Effect of, 494–5
        Liability of continuing partners, 491
        Powers of partners, 494
        Rights of partners, 479–81, 494
            Application of property, 499–500
            Wind up, to, 497–500
        Supervening illegality, 493
    Notice, 495
    Rules of distribution, 497
    War, 493
Determining the existence of, 464–5
Distinguished from corporation, 459
Elements of, 459
Estoppel, 464
Fictitious name, 465
Joint venture, 455–6
Limited partnership, defined, 466–70
Partner,
    Duties of,
        Accountability, 481
        Fiduciary, 481
        Full time and energy, 482
        Good faith and loyalty, 482
        Information, 480
        Obedience, 482
        Reasonable care, 482
    Individual, powers of,
        Acts not within apparent authority, 478
        Agency authority, 477
        Customary powers, 477
        Unauthorized acts, 478
    Liability of, 484–92
        Contract, 484–6
        Criminal, 489
        Extent, 489–91
        Incoming partner, 491
        Outgoing partner, 491
        Partner's admission, 479
        Tort, 487–9
        Tort of copartner, for, 487–9
    Powers of,
        Management of business, 471
    Rights of,
        Accounting, 479
        Contribution, to, 479, 499
        Dissolution, on, 492–7
        Information, 480
        Inspection of books, 479
        Participation in management, 476
        Possession, 472, 480
        Reimbursement, 479
        Return of capital, 479
        Share in profits, 479
    Property,
        In general, 470–1
    Assignability, 472
    Capital, 471
    Charging order, 472
    Crops, 471
    Disposition upon death of partner, 473
    Execution, 472
    Good will, 471
    Rights of partners, 472
    Title to,
        Personal property, 471
        Real property, 471
    Trading,
        Partner,
            Authority of, 477
    Unincorporated association, 458
PATENT LAW, 284–5

PLEDGE
Distinguished from bailment, 293–4
Nature of, 293–4
Security device as, 293–4

PLEDGEE
Duty of, 293–4
Rights of, 293–4

PRECEDENT
Discussed, 11–2

PRODUCT LIABILITY
Bases of a claim, 398
Breach of warranty,
  In general, 400
  Assumption of risk as defense, 412
  Contributory negligence as defense, 412
  Exclusion, modification, and disclaimer, 408
    Automobile warranties, 410
    Exclusion by inspection, 409
    Family use of goods, 410
    Merchantability warranty, 411
    Other ways of excluding implied warranties, 411
    Particular purpose warranty, 411
    Title warranty, 410
    Trade usage warranty, 409
    Warranties of description, 409
  Express warranties,
    By affirmation of promise, 401
    Federal protection for buyers, 413
    Warranty by description, 403
    Warranty by sample or model, 403
  Implied by law,
    Restaurant cases, 406
    Secondhand goods, 406
    Self-service stores, 406
    Warranty of merchantability, 405
    Warranty of fitness for particular purpose, 408
    Warranty of title, 404
  Notice of defect, 411
  Statute of limitations, 412
Injury, 398
Negligence, 399
Privity, 400
Statutory duty, 400
Strict liability in tort,
  In general, 414
  All involved in marketing process are liable, 417
    Lessor or bailor, 418–9
    Secondhand dealers, 418
    Seller of real estate, 419
    Suppliers of parts, 418
    Wholesaler, 417
  Assumption of risk in, 420
  Contributory negligence in, 420
  Damages in, 420–1
  Dangerous or defective product, 415–7
  Intentional torts, 421
  Services, 419
Violation of statutory duty, 400

PROPERTY
Abandonment, 289
Accession, 287
Accretion, 327
Adverse possession, 326
Alluvium, 327
Avulsion, 327
Buried, 289
Community property, 311
Condominiums, 312–3
Confusion, title by, 287
Cooperative, 313
Co-ownership, 310
Copyrights, 285–6
Deeds, 323–4
  Grant deed, 323
  Quitclaim deed, 324
Descent and distribution, 327
Dower, 315
Easements,
  Appurtenant, 316
  Creation of, 315
  Defined, 315
  Extinction of, 316
  Implied, 317
  In gross, 316
  Necessity, by, 317
  Prescription, 316
Eminent domain, 322
Escheat, 290, 322
Fee simple, 314
Finder, 288–9
Fixtures, 290–2
Freehold estates, 314
Gifts, 282–4
Homestead, 322
Intangible, 282
Joint tenancy, 310
Land contract, 685
  Default, 687–9
  Defined, 685
  Form, 685–7
  Transfer, 687
  Vendor/Vendee, 685
Landlord and tenant,
  Condemnation, 335
  Eviction, 339
  Lease, period of,
    Definite term, 332
    Holdover tenant, 334
    Periodic tenancy, 332
    Tenancy at sufferance, 333
    Tenancy at will, 333
    Termination, 334–5
Lanham Act, 286–7
Leasehold estate, 332
  Assignment, 337
  Creation of, 332
  Writing, necessity of, 332
Licenses, 317
Life estates,
  Conventional, 314
  Creation of, 314
  Curtesy, 315
  Dower, 315
  Life tenant, 314
Lost, 288
Mortgages, 679
Natural rights,
  Lateral support, 318–9
  Riparian, 318
  Space rights, 318
  Unpolluted air, 321
Nuisances, 321
Partition, 310–1
Patent law, 284–5
Personal,
  Defined, 282
Police power, 322
Probate, 326–7
Real,
  Defined, 313
  Sale of, 323
Recordation, 324
Remainders, 314
Rent,
  Duty to pay, 336
  Duty to pay affected by,
    Assignment, 337
    Condemnation, 335
    Destruction of premises, 334–5
    Eviction,
      Breach of covenant, 335
      Constructive eviction, 338–40